W9-BAF-245

Frommer's®

Canada

Here's what the critics say about Frommer's:

"Amazingly easy to use. Very portable, very complete."
—*Booklist*

♦

"The only mainstream guide to list specific prices. The Walter Cronkite of guidebooks—with all that implies."
—*Travel & Leisure*

♦

"Complete, concise, and filled with useful information."
—*New York Daily News*

♦

"Hotel information is close to encyclopedic."
—*Des Moines Sunday Register*

♦

"The best series for travelers who want one easy-to-use guidebook."
—*U.S. Air Magazine*

Other Great Guides for Your Trip:

Frommer's Toronto

Frommer's Montréal & Québec City

Frommer's Irreverent Guide to Vancouver

Frommer's Nova Scotia, New Brunswick & Prince Edward Island

Frommer's British Columbia & the Canadian Rockies

Frommer's®

11th
Edition

Canada

by
Shawn Blore
Wayne Curtis
Hilary Davidson
Herbert Bailey Livesey
Bill McRae

IDG Books Worldwide, Inc.
An International Data Group Company
Foster City, CA • Chicago, IL • Indianapolis, IN • New York, NY

IDG BOOKS WORLDWIDE, INC.

An International Data Group Company
919 E. Hillsdale Blvd.
Suite 400
Foster City, CA 94404

Find us online at **www.frommers.com**

Copyright © 2000 by IDG Books Worldwide, Inc.
Maps copyright © 2000 by IDG Books Worldwide, Inc.

ISBN 0-02-863627-9
ISSN 1044-2251

Editor: Ron Boudreau
Production Editor: Christina Van Camp
Photo Editor: Richard Fox
Design by Michele Laseau
Staff Cartographers: John Decamillis and Roberta Stockwell
Page creation by: Marie Kristine Parial-Leonardo, Julie Trippetti, and David Faust

SPECIAL SALES

For general information on IDG Books Worldwide's books in the U.S., please call our Consumer Customer Service department at 1-800-762-2974. For reseller information, including discounts, bulk sales, customized editions, and premium sales, please call our Reseller Customer Service department at 1-800-434-3422.

Manufactured in the United States of America

5 4 3 2 1

Contents

4   New Brunswick   92

by Wayne Curtis

5   Prince Edward Island   129

by Wayne Curtis

6   Newfoundland & Labrador   153

by Wayne Curtis

14   Alberta & the Rockies   523

by Bill McRae

15   Vancouver   612

by Shawn Blore

List of Maps

ABOUT THE AUTHORS

A native of California and resident by turns of Ottawa, Amsterdam, Moscow, and (for the past half-decade) Vancouver, **Shawn Blore** is an award-winning magazine writer and the best-selling author of *Vancouver: Secrets of the City*. He's also the author of *Frommer's Vancouver & Victoria*.

Wayne Curtis is a freelance writer whose articles about travel and the natural world have appeared in publications ranging from the *New York Times* to *House Beautiful* to Discovery Channel Online. He's also the author of *Frommer's Vermont, New Hampshire & Maine; Frommer's Nova Scotia, New Brunswick & Prince Edward Island;* and *Maine: Off the Beaten Path (Globe Pequot)*. He lives in coastal Maine, just a few hundred yards from the Canadian border.

Hilary Davidson divides her time between her hometown of Toronto and New York City. She's a restaurant critic for *Toronto Life* and has worked for *Harper's,* the *Globe and Mail, Chatelaine, Profit,* and *Equinox*. She's also the author of *Frommer's Toronto*. Her recent travels have taken her to Northern Ireland, Spain, and Thailand, though her most exciting trips have been of the aquatic variety—since learning to scuba dive she has explored shipwrecks in Eastern Ontario and swum with reef sharks in The Bahamas. She can be reached at hilary.davidson@usa.net.

Herbert Bailey Livesey has written about travel and food for many publications, including *Travel & Leisure, Food & Wine,* and *Playboy*. He's the author or coauthor of several guidebooks, including *Frommer's Montréal & Québec City, Frommer's Europe from $60 a Day,* and *Frommer's New England*.

Bill McRae was born and raised in rural eastern Montana, though he spent the better years of his youth attending university in Great Britain, France, and Canada. He has previously written about Montana and Utah for Moon Publications and about the Pacific Northwest and Seattle for Lonely Planet. Other publications he has written for include *National Geographic* and *Microsoft Expedia*. Bill is also coauthor of *Frommer's British Columbia & the Canadian Rockies*. He makes his home in Portland, Oregon.

AN INVITATION TO THE READER

In researching this book, we discovered many wonderful places—hotels, restaurants, shops, and more. We're sure you'll find others. Please tell us about them, so we can share the information with your fellow travelers in upcoming editions. If you were disappointed with a recommendation, we'd love to know that, too. Please write to:

Frommer's Canada, 11th Edition
IDG Travel
1633 Broadway
New York, NY 10019

AN ADDITIONAL NOTE

Please be advised that travel information is subject to change at any time—and this is especially true of prices. We therefore suggest that you write or call ahead for confirmation when making your travel plans. The authors, editors, and publisher cannot be held responsible for the experiences of readers while traveling. Your safety is important to us, however, so we encourage you to stay alert and be aware of your surroundings. Keep a close eye on cameras, purses, and wallets, all favorite targets of thieves and pickpockets.

WHAT THE SYMBOLS MEAN

✪ Frommer's Favorites

Our favorite places and experiences—outstanding for quality, value, or both.

The following abbreviations are used for credit cards:

AE	American Express	EURO	Eurocard
CB	Carte Blanche	JCB	Japan Credit Bank
DC	Diners Club	MC	MasterCard
DISC	Discover	V	Visa
ER	EnRoute		

FIND FROMMER'S ONLINE

www.frommers.com offers up-to-the-minute listings on almost 200 cities around the globe—including the latest bargains and candid, personal articles updated daily by Arthur Frommer himself. No other Web site offers such comprehensive and timely coverage of the world of travel.

The Best of Canada

Planning a trip to such a vast and diverse country can present you with a bewildering array of choices. We've scoured all of Canada in search of the best places and experiences, and in this chapter we share our very personal and opinionated choices. We hope they'll give you some ideas and get you started.

1 The Best Travel Experiences

- **Exploring the Cabot Trail** (Nova Scotia): This wildly scenic driving loop around Cape Breton Highlands National Park delivers a surplus of dramatic coastal scenery. Take a few days to explore the area. You can hike along blustery headlands, search for whales on a tour boat, and dabble around a cove or two in a sea kayak. See chapter 3.
- **Hiking Gros Morne National Park** (Newfoundland): When the earth's land masses broke apart and shifted 500 million years ago, a piece of the mantle, the very shell of the planet, was thrust upward to form tableland mountains of rock here. Spend a week or more trekking along the coastal trails, venturing to scenic waterfalls, and strolling alongside landlocked fjords. See chapter 6.
- **Watching the World Go By in a Québec City Cafe** (Québec): On a sunny summer Saturday, sit outside at Le Marie-Clarisse restaurant in the Quartier Petit-Champlain at the foot of the Breakneck Stairs. From there you can watch the goings-on in one of the oldest European communities in the New World while enjoying the best seafood in town or just sipping coffee. A folksinger may do a half-hour set, then be followed by a classical guitarist. See chapter 8.
- **Houseboating on the Trent-Severn Waterway** (Ontario): The Trent-Severn Waterway will take you 387km (240 miles) via 44 locks from Trenton to Georgian Bay on Lake Huron. Enjoy drawing into the locks or being drawn up or let down by the lock master. You can cruise aboard a fully equipped houseboat that usually sleeps up to six; weekly rentals on the canal system in summer average C$1,000 (US$667). Call **Big Rideau Boats** at ☎ 613/828-0138 or **Houseboat Holidays** at ☎ 613/382-2842. See chapter 9.

- **Seeing the Polar Bears in Churchill** (Manitoba): In October or November, travel by train or plane to Churchill and the shores of Hudson Bay to view hundreds of magnificent polar bear, who migrate to the bay's icy shores and even lope into Churchill itself. In the evening, you can glimpse the famous aurora borealis (northern lights). Either take **VIA Rail**'s *Hudson Bay* train (☎ **800/ 561-3949**), a 2-night/1-day trip from Winnipeg, or fly in on **Canadian Airlines** (☎ **800/426-7000** in the U.S. or 800/665-1177 in Canada; www.cdnair.ca). See chapter 13.

- **Horseback Riding in the Rockies** (Alberta): Rent a cabin on a rural guest ranch and get back in the saddle again. Spend a day fishing, then return to the lodge for a country dance or barbecue. Ride a horse to a backcountry chalet in the rugged mountain wilderness. Forget the crowded park highways and commercialized resort towns and just relax. **Brewster's Kananaskis Guest Ranch** (☎ **800/691-5085** or 403/673-3737) in Kananaskis Village, near Banff, Alberta, offers a variety of guided horseback trips, from C$125 to C$140 (US$83 to US$93) per day, including food, lodging, and the horse you ride in on. See chapter 14.

- **Sailing the Great Bear Rain Forest** (British Columbia): About halfway up BC's west coast is an isolated region of mountains, fjords, bays, rivers, and inlets. It's one of the last places where grizzly bear are still found in large numbers, plus salmon, killer whales, otters, and porpoises. You need a boat to get there, so why not take the gorgeous 100-year-old schooner *Maple Leaf*? **Maple Leaf Adventures** (☎ **888/599-5323** or 250/715-0906; fax 250/715-0912) runs a number of trips to the area, from 4 days to 2 weeks, all including gourmet meals and comfortable accommodation aboard the *Maple Leaf*. See chapter 16.

- **Dogsledding Through Baffin Island** (Nunavut): Spectacular fjords, knife-edged mountains draped with glaciers, and friendly craft-oriented Inuit villages make this rarely visited island—the world's fifth largest—a great off-the-beaten-path destination. Arrange a dogsled tour to the floe edge, where the protected harbor ice meets the open sea and where seals, polar bears, and bowhead whales converge. A weeklong dogsledding trip with **NorthWinds** (☎ **819/979-0551**) costs C$2,300 (US$1,534). See chapter 17.

2 The Best Family Vacations

- **Parrsboro** (Nova Scotia): On the Bay of Fundy, Parrsboro is a fossil- and mineral-collector's mecca. You needn't be an expert—a fine accessible museum and helpful local guides will get you started. Kids will remember finding a chunk of amethyst; you'll remember the incredible scenery. See chapter 3.

- **Fundy National Park and Vicinity** (New Brunswick): You'll find swimming, hiking, and kayaking at this extraordinary national park. And don't overlook biking in the hills east of the park or rappelling and rock climbing at Cape Enrage. See chapter 4.

- **Prince Edward Island's Beaches:** The red-sand beaches will turn white swim trunks a bit pinkish, but it's hard to beat a day or two splashing around these tepid waters while admiring pastoral island landscapes. See chapter 5.

- **Club Tremblant** (Laurentian Mountains; ☎ **800/567-8341** in the U.S. and Canada, or 819/425-2731): This resort faces Mont-Tremblant, eastern Canada's highest peak, with a ski village at the base and gondolas and chairlifts to carry you to the top. Ten lakes and connecting rivers around the mountain offer boating, swimming, and windsurfing. There are indoor and outdoor pools, plus biking and hiking trails. A day-care program for kids lets parents take a break. Most lodgings are one- to three-bedroom suites. See chapter 7.

- **Ottawa** (Ontario): In this family-friendly city, you and your kids can watch soldiers strut their stuff and red-coated Mounties polish their equestrian and musical skills. Canoeing or skating on the canal is lots of fun, and Ottawa boasts a host of live museums to explore —like the National Aviation Museum, the National Museum of Civilization, and the National Museum of Science and Technology. See chapter 9.

- **The Muskoka Lakes** (Ontario): This region is filled with resorts that welcome families. Kids can swim, canoe, bike, fish, and more. Since most resorts offer children's programs, parents can enjoy a rest as well. See chapter 12.

- **Whistler/Blackcomb Ski Resorts** (British Columbia): Whistler and Blackcomb's twin ski resorts offer lots of family-oriented activities. You'll find everything from downhill and cross-country skiing, snowboarding, snowshoeing, and snowmobiling lessons in winter to horseback riding, mountain biking, golfing, in-line skating, paragliding, heli-skiing, swimming, kayaking, and rafting summer trips designed for families with schoolage children. See chapter 16.

- **The Klondike Gold Rush Route** (Yukon): Follow in a latter-day Klondike Stampede by traveling from Skagway, Alaska, up over White Pass to the Yukon's capital, Whitehorse. Canoe through the once-daunting Miles Canyon on the mighty Yukon River. Drive to Dawson City and visit the gold fields, walk the boardwalks of the old town center, listen to recitations of Robert Service poetry, and attend an old-fashioned musical revue. Inexpensive public campgrounds abound in the Yukon, making this one of the more affordable family vacations in western Canada. See chapter 17.

3 The Best Nature & Wildlife Viewing

- **Whales at Digby Neck** (Nova Scotia): For a chance to see fin, minke, or humpback whales, choose from a dozen whale-watching outfitters located along this narrow peninsula of remote fishing villages. Right, sperm, blue, and pilot whales, along with the infrequent orcas, have also been seen over the years. Getting to the tip of the peninsula is half the fun—it requires two ferries. See chapter 3.

- **Birds and Caribou on the Avalon Peninsula** (Newfoundland): In one busy day you can see a herd of caribou, the largest puffin colony in North America, and an extraordinary gannet colony visible from the mainland cliffs. See chapter 6.

- **Whales at Baie Ste-Catherine** (Québec): At Baie Ste-Catherine, about a 2-hour drive northeast of Québec City, and along the northern shore to the resort area of La Malbaie, hundreds of resident beluga and minke whales are joined by several additional species of their migratory cousins, including humpbacks and blues. Mid-June to early October, you can spot the graceful giants from land, but whale-watching cruises depart from Baie Ste-Catherine for closer looks. See chapter 8.

- **Pelicans in Prince Albert National Park** (Saskatchewan): On Lavallee Lake roosts the second-largest pelican colony in North America. Bison, moose, elk, caribou, black bear, and red fox also roam free in this million acres of wilderness. See chapter 13.

- **Wood Buffalo at Elk Island National Park** (east of Edmonton, Alberta): Before homesteaders put the plow to the northern Canadian prairies, bison, elk, deer, moose, beaver, and dozens of other animals roamed the land. This small and easily accessible national park preserves the original prairie-lake ecosystem and large numbers of wildlife, including two species of bison and a genetically pure herd of prairie elk. See chapter 14.

- **Bald Eagles Outside Vancouver and Victoria** (British Columbia): Two of the best places to see bald eagles are outside BC's two largest cities. Just north of Victoria, as many as 1,500 eagles have been counted in Goldstream Provincial Park during January. Even larger numbers—up to 3,700, a North American record—gather for the winter on the banks of the Squamish River an hour's drive north of Vancouver. You can see them from the riverbank or, more interesting, can drift down the river on a raft and eagle-spot along the way. November to February, the **Canadian Outback Adventure Company** (☎ 604/921-7250) runs daylong raft trips. See chapters 15 and 16.
- **Orcas off Vancouver Island** (British Columbia): The waters surrounding Vancouver Island teem with orcas (killer whales), as well as harbor seals, sea lions, bald eagles, and harbour and Dahl's porpoises. At the island's southern tip, **Victoria Marine Adventures** (☎ 250/995-2211) is one of many companies offering whale-watching tours in Zodiacs and covered boats. In Telegraph Cove at the island's wilder northern end, **Stubbs Island Charters Ltd.** (☎ 250/928-3185) can bring you up close to the orca pods inhabiting the waters of Johnstone Straight. See chapter 16.
- **Rare Seabirds, Beluga Whales, and Narwhals near Bylot Island** (Nunavut): Spend a week in August rounding Bylot Island (soon to be redesignated North Baffin National Park) on sea kayaks. Off the northern tip of Baffin Island, Bylot's soaring mountain peaks choked with ancient glaciers don't look hospitable, but during the short summer season they're the nesting grounds of rare gulls, puffins, and other seabirds. In addition, you may come kayak-to-tusk with a narwhal, the unicorn-like cousin of the whale and walrus that sports a twisted horn in its forehead. And watch for the noses of creamy white Beluga whales as they gather to breathe holes in the ice. **Polar Sea Adventures** (☎ 867/899-8870) offers guided sea kayak tours to Bylot Island. See chapter 17.

4 The Best Views

- **Cape Enrage** (New Brunswick): Just east of Fundy National Park, you'll find surprisingly harsh coastal terrain of high rocky cliffs pounded by the sea. Route 915 offers a wonderful detour off the beaten path. See chapter 4.
- **Signal Hill** (Newfoundland): Signal Hill marks the entrance to St. John's harbor. Never mind the history that was made here; it's uncommonly scenic, with views of a coast that hasn't changed in 500 years. The North Head Trail is one of Newfoundland's most dramatic, and it's entirely in city limits. See chapter 6.
- **Bonavista Peninsula** (Newfoundland): The peninsula's northernmost tip offers a superb vantage point for spotting icebergs, even into midsummer. You'll also see puffins, whales, and one of the most scenic lighthouses in eastern Canada. See chapter 6.
- **Terrasse Dufferin in Québec City** (Québec): This boardwalk promenade with benches and green-and-white–roofed gazebos runs along the cusp of the bluff rearing up behind the original colonial settlement. At its back is the landmark Château Frontenac, and out front is the long silvery sweep of the St. Lawrence, where ferries glide back and forth and cruise ships and Great Lakes freighters and tankers put in at the port. To the east is the trailing edge of the Adirondacks, and downriver you can see the last of the Laurentian Mountains. See chapter 8.

- **Niagara Falls** (Ontario): This is still a wonder of nature despite its commercial exploitation. You can experience the falls from the decks of the *Maid of the Mist*, which takes you into the roaring maelstrom, or look down from the cockpit of a helicopter. The least scary view is from the Skylon Tower. See chapter 10.
- **Agawa Canyon** (Ontario): To see the northern Ontario wilderness that inspired the Group of Seven, take the Agawa Canyon Train Tour on a 184km (114-mile) trip from the Soo to Hearst through the Agawa Canyon, where you can spend a few hours exploring scenic waterfalls and vistas. The train snakes through a vista of deep ravines and lakes, hugging the hillsides and crossing gorges on skeletal trestle bridges. See chapter 12.
- **Takakkaw Falls in Yoho National Park** (British Columbia): One of Canada's highest falls, Takakkaw Falls plunges more than 1,200 feet into a glacier-carved valley. Hike up to the base of the falls, hear the roar of crashing water, and stand in clouds of mist. See chapter 14.
- **Moraine Lake in Banff National Park** (Alberta): Ten snow-clad peaks towering more than 10,000 feet rear up dramatically behind this eerily green tiny lake. Rent a canoe and paddle to the mountains' base. See chapter 14.
- **Vancouver as Seen from Mount Seymour** (British Columbia): This small ski area overlooks Vancouver, the Burrard Inlet, the Straight of Georgia, and Vancouver Island. On a clear day, the entire city and the coastal islands spread out below. You can see a similar view from Grouse Mountain, easily accessible by a tram. See chapter 15.

5 The Most Dramatic Drives

- **Cape Breton's Cabot Trail** (Nova Scotia): This 280km (174-mile) loop through the uplands of Cape Breton Highlands National Park is a world-class excursion. You'll see Acadian fishing ports, pristine valleys, and some of the most picturesque coastline anywhere. See chapter 3.
- **Viking Trail** (Newfoundland): Travelers looking to leave the crowds behind needn't look any further. This beautiful drive to Newfoundland's northern tip is wild and solitary, with views of curious geology and a wind-raked coast. And you'll end up at one of the world's great historic sites—L'Anse aux Meadows. See chapter 6.
- **Icefields Parkway** (Highway 93 through Banff and Jasper national parks, Alberta): This is one of the world's grandest mountain drives. Cruising along it is like a trip back to the ice ages. The parkway climbs past glacier-notched peaks to the Columbia Icefields, a sprawling cap of snow, ice, and glacier at the very crest of the Rockies. See chapter 14.
- **Highway 99** (British Columbia): The Sea to Sky Highway from Vancouver to Lillooet takes you from a dramatic seacoast past glaciers, pine forests, and a waterfall that cascades from a mountaintop and through Whistler's majestic glacial mountains. The next leg of the 4-hour drive winds up a series of switchbacks to the thickly forested Cayoosh Creek valley and on to the craggy mountains surrounding the Fraser River gold-rush town of Lillooet. See chapter 16.
- **Dempster Highway** (from Dawson City to Inuvik, Northwest Territories): Canada's most northerly highway, the Dempster is a year-round gravel road across the top of the world. From Dawson City, the road winds over the Continental Divide three times, crosses the Arctic Circle, and fords the Peel and Mackenzie rivers by ferry before reaching Inuvik, a native community on the mighty Mackenzie River delta. See chapter 17.

6 The Best Walks & Rambles

- **Halifax's Waterfront** (Nova Scotia): Take your time strolling along Halifax's working waterfront. You can visit museums, board a historic ship or two, enjoy a snack, and take an inexpensive ferry ride across the harbor and back. Come evening, there's fiddle and guitar playing at the pubs. See chapter 3.
- **Cape Breton Highlands National Park** (Nova Scotia): You'll find bog and woodland walks aplenty at Cape Breton, but the best trails follow rugged cliffs along the open ocean. The Skyline Trail is among the most dramatic pathways in the province. See chapter 3.
- **Green Gardens Trail** (Gros Morne, Newfoundland): This demanding hike at Gros Morne National Park takes you on a 16km (9.9-mile) loop, much of which follows coastal meadows atop fractured cliffs. It's demanding but worth every step of the way. See chapter 6.
- **Old Montréal** (Québec): Wander the cobblestone streets, where you'll find some remains—above and below the streets—of what founder Paul de Chomedey, sieur de Maisonneuve, christened Ville-Marie in 1642. Aboveground, buildings have been restored into homes, stores, restaurants, and nightclubs. Horse-drawn carriages clop and creak along the streets, past the heart of the district, place Jacques-Cartier, which is lined with cafes. Below ground, a tunnel leads from the new Museum of Archaeology to the old Custom House. See chapter 7.
- **Lake Superior Provincial Park** (Ontario): Follow any trail in this park to a rewarding vista. The 16km (9.9-mile) Peat Mountain Trail leads to a panoramic view close to 500 feet above the surrounding lakes and forests. The moderate Orphan Lake Trail offers views over the Orphan Lake and Lake Superior, plus a pebble beach and Baldhead River falls. The 26km (16-mile) Toawab Trail takes you through the Agawa Valley to the 81-foot Agawa Falls. See chapter 12.
- **Johnston Canyon** (Banff National Park, Alberta): Just 24km (15 miles) west of Banff, Johnson Creek cuts a deep, very narrow canyon through limestone cliffs. The trail winds through tunnels, passes waterfalls, edges by shaded rock faces, and crosses the chasm on footbridges before reaching a series of iridescent pools, formed by springs that bubble up through highly colored rock. See chapter 14.
- **Plain of Six Glaciers Trail** (Lake Louise, Alberta): From Chateau Lake Louise, a lakeside trail rambles along the edge of emerald-green Lake Louise, then climbs up to the base of Victoria Glacier. At a rustic teahouse you can order a cup of tea and a scone—each made over a wood-burning stove—and gaze up at the rumpled face of the glacier. See chapter 14.
- **Long Beach** (Vancouver Island, British Columbia): Part of Pacific Rim National Park, Long Beach is more than 16km (10 miles) long and hundreds of meters wide and is flanked by awe-inspiring rain forests of cedar, fir and Sitka Spruce. Beyond the roaring surf you'll see soaring eagles, basking sea lions, and occasionally even migrating gray whales. See chapter 16.

7 The Best Biking Routes

- **Nova Scotia's South Shore:** Not in a hurry to get anywhere? Peddling the peninsulas and coasting along placid inlets is a great tonic for a weary soul. You'll pass through graceful villages like Shelburne, Lunenburg, and Chester and rediscover a quiet way of life. See chapter 3.
- **Prince Edward Island:** This island province sometimes seems like it was created specifically for bike touring. The villages are reasonably spaced, the hills are

virtually nonexistent, the coastal roads are picturesque in the extreme, and a new islandwide bike path offers detours through marshes and quiet woodlands. See chapter 5.

- **Old Port Route** (Montréal): The city has 239km (148 miles) of biking paths, and the Métro permits bicycles in the last car of its trains. One popular route is from the Old Port west along the side of the Lachine Canal. A little under 11km (6.8 miles) one way, it's tranquil, vehicle-free, and mostly flat. You can rent bikes at the Old Port. See chapter 7.
- **Ile d'Orléans** (Québec): You can enjoy a day or two of biking around this bucolic island 15 minutes downriver from Québec City. A main road runs around the island, never far from the water's edge. You can stop at a pick-your-own orchard or strawberry field or in a tiny village with 18th- and 19th-century houses and churches. Two roads cut across the island at the southern end, and a third does the same a little beyond midpoint. You can rent bikes on the island. See chapter 8.
- **Niagara Region** (Ontario): The flatlands here make for terrific biking terrain. A bike path runs along the Niagara Parkway, which follows the Niagara River. You'll bike past fruit farms, vineyards, and gardens with picnicking spots. See chapter 10.
- **Highways 1 and 93 Through Banff and Jasper National Parks** (Alberta): This well-maintained wide highway winds through some of the world's most dramatic mountain scenery. Take the Bow Valley Parkway, between Banff and Lake Louise, and Highway 93A between Athabasca Falls and Jasper for slightly quieter peddling. Best of all, there are seven hostels (either rustic or fancy) at some of the most beautiful sights along the route, so you don't have to weigh yourself down with camping gear. See chapter 14.
- **Seawall** (Vancouver, British Columbia): Vancouver's Seawall surrounds the Stanley Park shoreline on the Burrard Inlet and English Bay. Built just above the high-tide mark, it offers nonstop breathtaking views, no hills, and no cars. See chapter 15.

8 The Best Culinary Experiences

- **Fresh Lobster** (Nova Scotia & New Brunswick): Wherever you see the wooden lobster traps piled on a wharf, you'll know a fresh lobster meal isn't far away. The most productive lobster fisheries are around Shediac, New Brunswick, and all along Nova Scotia's Atlantic coast. Sunny days are ideal for cracking open a crustacean while sitting at a wharfside picnic table, preferably with a locally brewed beer close at hand. See chapters 3 and 4.
- **Newfoundland Berries:** The unforgivingly rocky and boggy soil of this blustery island resists most crops but produces some of the most delicious berries you can imagine. Look for roadside stands in midsummer or pick your own blueberries, strawberries, partridgeberries, or bakeapples. Many restaurants add berries (on cheesecake, in custard) when they're in season. See chapter 6.
- **Dining at the Best in Montréal** (Québec): Montréal boasts one of the hottest dining scenes in Canada. The current favorite is **Toqué!** (☎ **514/499-2084**), the kind of restaurant that raises the gastronomic expectations of an entire city. The silky greeting-to-tab performance of the kitchen and waitstaff is a pleasure to observe, and the postnouvelle presentations are visually winning and completely filling. No restaurant in eastern Canada surpasses this contemporary French gem. See chapter 7.

- **Sampling Smoked Meat in Montréal** (Québec): Somewhere between pastrami and corned beef, this deli delight appears to have had its origins with the immigrations of eastern Europeans during the late 19th century. Meat eaters are ravenous at the sight and aroma of it, and *the* place to inhale smoked meat is **Chez Schwartz** on The Main (☎ **514/842-4813**). Elegant it's not; immensely satisfying it is. See chapter 7.

- **Eating Ethnic in Toronto** (Ontario): If you explore the city's neighborhoods, you'll find ethnic dining spots in Little Italy, Little Portugal, and Greek sections of the Danforth. Order spaghettini with seafood, garlic, capers, white wine, and a touch of anchovies at **Trattoria Giancarlo** (☎ **416/533-9619**); poached fillet of cod at **Chiado** (☎ **416/538-1910**); or imaginatively updated Greek at **Pan on the Danforth** (☎ **416/466-8158**). Each is at the heart of its ethnic neighborhood. See chapter 10.

- **Feasting on Danish Specialties** (Saskatchewan): Enjoy seven superlative dishes, from *frikadeller* (Danish meat patties served with red cabbage and potato salad) to *aeggekage* (a Danish omelet served with home-baked bread) at the warmly inviting **Bistro Dansk**, Saskatoon (☎ **204/775-5662**). See chapter 13.

- **Going Organic in Calgary** (Alberta): You'll walk through a quiet tree-filled park on an island in the Bow River to reach the bustling **River Cafe** (☎ **403/261-7670**). An immense wood-fired oven and grill produces soft, chewy flat breads and smoky grilled meats and vegetables, all organically grown and freshly harvested. On warm summer evenings, picnickers loll in the grassy shade, nibbling this and that from the cafe's picnic-like menu. See chapter 14.

- **Dining at a Hotel in Lake Louise** (Alberta): At its cozy dining room in an old log lodge, the **Post Hotel** (☎ **403/522-3989**) serves up the kind of sophisticated yet robust cuisine that perfectly fits the backdrop of glaciered peaks, deep forest, and glassy streams. Both the wine list and the cooking are French and hearty, with the chef focusing on the best of local ingredients—lamb, salmon, and Alberta beef. After spending time out on the trail, a meal here will top off a quintessential day in the Rockies. See chapter 14.

- **Enjoying Dim Sum in Vancouver's Chinatown** (British Columbia): With its burgeoning Chinese population, Vancouver's Chinatown has more than half a dozen dim-sum parlors where you can try steamed or baked barbecued-pork buns, dumplings filled with fresh prawns and vegetables, or steamed rice-flour crêpes filled with spicy beef. One favorite is the **Floata Seafood Restaurant** (☎ **604/602-0368**). See chapter 15.

- **Eating Local in Lotus Land** (British Columbia): Self-sufficiency is the new watchword on the West Coast, with top chefs sourcing all their ingredients locally. On Vancouver Island, the **Sooke Harbour House** (☎ **250/642-3421**) offers lamb from nearby Saltspring Island, seasoned with herbs from the chef's own garden. In Vancouver, the **Raincity Grill** (☎ **604/685-7337**) makes a specialty of fresh-caught seafood, while the vast selection of BC wines by the glass makes dinner an extended road trip through the West Coast wine country, with no need for a designated driver. See chapters 15 and 16.

9 The Best Festivals & Special Events

- **International Busker Festival** (Halifax, Nova Scotia): In early August, the 10-day International Busker Festival brings together talented street performers from around the world, performing in their natural habitat. Best of all, it's free. See chapter 3.

- **Newfoundland and Labrador Folk Festival** (St. John's, Newfoundland): How did such a remote island develop such a deep talent pool? That's one of the questions you'll ponder while tapping your feet at this 3-day festival, which is laden with local talent. It's cheap, folksy, and fun. See chapter 6.
- **International Jazz Festival** (Montréal, Québec): Ten days every summer glorify America's truest art form with this immensely successful jazz festival, in operation since 1979. Big stars always appear, but their concerts cost money. No problem: Hundreds of free concerts are held, most often in the streets and plazas of midtown. See chapter 7.
- **Winter Carnival** (Québec City, Québec): Think Mardi Gras in New Orleans, without the nudity (well, maybe a little). Ice sculptures, parades, a canoe race across the frozen St. Lawrence, and an impressive castle of ice are among the principal features. The general jollity is fueled by a nasty drink called Caribou, whiskey sloshed with red wine. See chapter 8.
- **Toronto International Film Festival** (Ontario): Second only to Cannes, this film festival draws Hollywood's leading luminaries to town for 10 days in early September; more than 250 films are on show. See chapter 10.
- **Stratford Festival** (Ontario): This world-famous festival of superb repertory theater, launched by Tyrone Guthrie in 1953, has featured major players like Sir Alec Guinness, Christopher Plummer, Dame Maggie Smith, and Sir Peter Ustinov. Productions, which run from May to October or early November on three stages, range from classic to contemporary. You can also participate in informal discussions with company members. See chapter 11.
- **Northern Trappers' Festival** (The Pas, Manitoba): This festival celebrates the traditions of the frontier pioneers each February with world-championship dogsled races, ice fishing, beer fests, bannock baking, moose calling, and more. See chapter 13.
- **Calgary Stampede** (Alberta): In all North America, there's nothing quite like the Calgary Stampede. Of course it's the world's largest rodeo, but it's also a series of concerts, an art show, an open-air casino, a carnival, a street dance—you name it, it's undoubtedly going on somewhere. In July, all of Calgary is converted into a party and everyone's invited. See chapter 14.
- **Symphony of Fire** (Vancouver, British Columbia): This 4-night fireworks extravaganza takes place over English Bay. Three of the world's leading manufacturers are invited to represent their countries in competition against one another, setting their best displays to music. On the fourth night, all three companies launch their finales. Last year more than 500,000 people showed up each night. The best seats are at the "Bard on the Beach" Shakespeare festival across False Creek. See chapter 15.
- **Kamloops Cattle Drive** (southern British Columbia): This rollicking 6-day trail ride draws about 1,000 people annually. A parade of wagons, horses, and cows sets off from a different location every July, driving the cattle along a predetermined route through the High Country's sagebrush mesas to a triumphant finish (and huge party) in Kamloops. Beginners are welcome, and horses (and even space on wagons) can be rented. See chapter 16.

10 The Best Luxury Hotels & Resorts

- **Keltic Lodge** (Cape Breton Island, Nova Scotia; ☎ **800/565-0444** or 902/285-2880): It's got grand natural drama in the sea-pounded cliffs that surround it, plus a generous measure of high culture. (Jackets on men at dinner, please!)

The adjacent golf course is stupendous, and some of the national park's best hikes are close at hand. See chapter 3.

- **Kingsbrae Arms** (St. Andrews, New Brunswick; ☎ 506/529-1897): This new deluxe inn manages the trick of being opulent and comfortable at the same time. The shingled manse is lavishly appointed, beautifully landscaped, and well situated for exploring charming St. Andrews. See chapter 4.
- **Dalvay-by-the-Sea** (Grand Tracadie, Prince Edward Island; ☎ 902/672-2048). This intimate resort (just 30 rooms and cottages) is on a quiet stretch of beach. The Tudor mansion was built by a business partner of John D. Rockefeller, and the woodwork alone is enough to keep you entertained for your stay. Bring your bike. See chapter 5.
- **Loews Hôtel Vogue** (Montréal, Québec; ☎ 800/465-6654 or 514/285-5555): What was just an anonymous mid-rise office building has turned into the king of the hill of Montréal hotels. The Vogue targeted international executives on the go, and little was left to chance. Even the standard rooms come with fax machines, four phones, computer ports, bathroom TVs, and whirlpool bathtubs. Tins of caviar are tucked into the minibars. People with cell phones at the ready fill the lobby espresso bar and adjacent dining room. Even after two changes in management, the Vogue remains steady on its course. See chapter 7.
- **Langdon Hall** (Cambridge, Ontario; ☎ 800/268-1898 or 519/740-2100): This quintessential English country house, built in 1902 for the granddaughter of John Jacob Astor, is now a small hotel where you can enjoy 200 acres of lawns, gardens, and woodlands. The guest rooms feature the finest amenities, fabrics, and furnishings. Facilities include a full spa, a pool, a tennis court, a croquet lawn, and an exercise room. The airy dining room overlooking the lily pond offers fine continental cuisine. See chapter 11.
- **Manitowaning Lodge Golf & Tennis Resort** (Manitowaning, Ontario; ☎ 705/859-3136): This resort on Manitoulin Island is an idyllic island retreat. A lodge and cottages are set on 11 acres of beautiful gardens. The lodge, with its huge hand-hewn beams, a mask of the Spirit of Manitowaning, and images of the Native-American protective spirit, provides a serene setting to restore the spirit. See chapter 12.
- **Chateau Lake Louise** (Banff National Park, Alberta; ☎ 800/441-1414 or 403/522-3511): First of all, there's the view. Across a tiny gem-green lake rise massive cliffs shrouded in glacial ice. And then there's the hotel. Part hunting lodge, part European palace, the Chateau is its own community, with sumptuous boutiques, sports rental facilities, seven dining areas, two bars, magnificent lobby areas, and beautifully furnished guest rooms. See chapter 14.
- **Hotel Macdonald** (Edmonton, Alberta; ☎ 800/441-1414 or 403/424-5181): When the Canadian Pacific bought and refurbished this landmark hotel in the 1980s, all the charming period details were preserved, while all the inner workings were modernized and brought up to snuff. The result is a regally elegant but friendly small hotel. From the kilted bellman to the gargoyles on the walls, this is a real class act. See chapter 14.
- **Wickaninnish Inn** (Tofino, British Columbia; ☎ 800/333-4604 in North America, or 250/725-3300): No matter which room you book in this beautiful new lodge, you'll wake to a magnificent view of the untamed Pacific. The inn is on a rocky promontory, surrounded by an old-growth spruce and cedar rain forest and the sprawling sands of Long Beach. In summer, try golfing, fishing, or whale watching. In winter, shelter by the fire in the Pointe restaurant and watch the wild Pacific storms roll in. See chapter 16.

11 The Best Bed & Breakfasts

- **The Manse** (Mahone Bay, Nova Scotia; ☎ 902/624-1121): There's not a bad room in this four-room B&B, built in 1870 on a low hill in the picturesque village of Mahone Bay. Spend the day browsing local shops, then retreat in the evening to the casual luxury of this top-rated lodge. See chapter 3.
- **Shipwright Inn** (Charlottetown, Prince Edward Island; ☎ 902/368-1905): This in-town seven-room B&B is within easy walking distance of all the city's attractions yet has a settled and pastoral feel. It's informed by a Victorian sensibility without being over-the-top about it. See chapter 5.
- **At Wit's Inn** (St. John's, Newfoundland; ☎ 877/739-7420 or 709/739-742): The centrally located B&B is bright, cheerful, and whimsical. Opened in 1999 by a restaurateur from Toronto, the inn preserves the best of the historical elements in this century-old home while graciously updating it for modern tastes. See chapter 6.
- **Les Passants du Sans Soucy** (Montréal, Québec; ☎ 514/842-2634): One of the first B&Bs in Old Montréal has a lot more going for it than that enviable distinction. Indeed, it almost qualifies as a boutique hotel, but with much lower prices. Housed in a renovated 1723 building, it makes the most of its stone walls and exposed dark ceiling beams, using them to contain brass or wrought-iron beds and cushy sofas. A fireplace is the focal point of the common room. Breakfast includes café au lait and pain au chocolat. See chapter 7.
- **Clifton Manor Inn** (Bayfield, Ontario; ☎ 519/565-2282): You'll find romance at this elegant house, built in 1895 for the reve (bailiff or governor) of Bayfield. All the bathrooms have candles and bubble bath, and one has a deep tub for two. Four comfortable rooms are each named after an artist or a composer. All the rooms have cozy touches like mohair throws, sheepskin rugs, wingback chairs, and fresh flowers. Breakfast consists of omelets or crêpes, plus fresh fruit often plucked from the trees in the garden. See chapter 11.
- **Beild House** (Collingwood, Ontario; ☎ 705/444-1522): On Fridays, you can sit down to a splendid five-course dinner before retiring to the bed that belonged to the duke and duchess of Windsor. A sumptuous breakfast will follow the next morning. This handsome 1909 house contains 17 rooms, 7 with private bathroom. See chapter 12.
- **Abigail's Hotel** (Victoria, British Columbia; ☎ 800/561-6565 or 250/388-5363): Abigail's began as a 1920s luxury apartment house, then was converted to an elegant boutique hotel. The rooms are bright and beautiful, with fresh flowers and Mission-style beds with goose-down comforters. Some boast soaker tubs and double-sided fireplaces, so you can relax in the tub by the firelight and later slip on a robe and lounge on the sofa by the fire's other side. A gourmet breakfast is served in the dining room, and in the evening cider and sherry are poured in the comfy library. See chapter 16.
- **Oceanwood Country Inn** (Mayne Island, British Columbia; ☎ 250/539-5074): Overlooking Navy Channel in the Gulf Islands off the coast of BC and Washington State, the Oceanwood offers top-notch lodgings and fine dining in one of the most scenic locations on the West Coast. The array of accommodations ranges from very affordable cozy garden rooms to luxury suites fronting hot-tub decks and 100-mile views. The friendly professional service and relaxed formality complete the package. See chapter 16.
- **Pearson's Arctic Home Stay** (Baffin Island, Nunavut; ☎ 867/979-6408): Staying at this lovely private home overlooking Frobisher Bay is like staying at a

museum of Inuit arts and crafts. The innkeeper is the town's former mayor and currently the island's public coroner, so you also get a real insight into life and death on Baffin Island. See chapter 17.

12 The Best Camping & Wilderness Lodges

- **Green Provincial Park** (Tyne Valley, Prince Edward Island; ☎ 902/831-2370): Can't afford your own well-maintained estates? This provincial campground makes a decent substitute. Set on a quiet inlet, the 219-acre park is built around an extravagant gingerbread mansion that's open to the public. See chapter 5.
- **Gros Morne National Park** (Newfoundland): Backpackers will find wild, spectacular campsites in coastal meadows along the remarkable Green Gardens Trail. Car campers should head to Trout River Pond, at the foot of one of Gros Morne's dramatic landlocked fjords. See chapter 6.
- **Sir Sam's Inn** (Eagle Lake, Ontario; ☎ 705/754-2188): You'll have to search a bit for this remote stone-and-timber lodge, built in 1917 in the woods above Eagle Lake for politician/militarist Sir Sam Hughes. You can stay in the inn or in new chalets or lakefront suites. At this friendly yet sophisticated place, you can play tennis, swim, sail, windsurf, water-ski, canoe, or mountain bike. See chapter 12.
- **Arowhon Pines** (Algonquin Park, Ontario; ☎ 705/633-5661 in summer, 416/483-4393 in winter): Located 8 miles off the highway down a dirt road, this is one of the most entrancing places anywhere. You can enjoy peace, seclusion, and natural beauty, plus comfortable accommodations and fresh good food. There are no TVs or phones—just the call of the loons, the gentle lapping of the water, the croaking of the frogs, and the splash of canoe paddles cutting the surface of the lake. See chapter 12.
- **Tunnel Mountain** (Banff, Alberta; ☎ 403/762-1500): If you find Banff too expensive and too crowded, these campgrounds—three within 5km (3.1 miles) of town—are a great antidote. There are showers and real toilets, and most sites have full hookups. And you'll pay just one-tenth of what hotel dwellers are paying for equally good access to the Rockies. See chapter 14.
- **Emerald Lake Lodge** (Yoho National Park, Alberta; ☎ 250/343-6321): This historic log lodge sits on the edge of a glacial lake just below the rim of the Continental Divide. Rent a cabin that sleeps four and come here in winter, when the snowbound lodge is a center for cross-country ski expeditions. See chapter 14.
- **Mulvehill Creek Wilderness Inn & B&B** (British Columbia; ☎ 877/837-8649): The only lodging on string-bean Arrow Lake, south of Revelstoke National Park, this superlative inn is steps from a 300-foot waterfall and a 100-mile-long lake with incredible fishing. Best of all, the guest rooms are simple and elegant, the common rooms are colorful and comfortable, the hens and organic garden provide much of the breakfast, and the pool offers a great place to relax. The wilderness was never so close and yet so commodious. See chapter 14.
- **Clayoquot Wilderness Resort** (British Columbia; ☎ 888/333-5405 in North America, or 250/725-2688): Recently designated a World Heritage Site, Clayoquot Sound boasts fjords and rain forests best discovered by sea kayak. The preferred route leaves Tofino and travels for 2 or 3 days to the bubbling Hot Springs Cove. For a bit of comfort, try staying at this resort, floating in splendid isolation on Quoit Bay. From here you can set out on fishing or whale-watching expeditions and go horseback riding or mountain biking. See chapter 16.

Planning a Trip to Canada

2

by Bill McRae

This chapter can save you money, time, and headaches. Here's where you'll find travel know-how, such as when to visit, what documents you'll need, and where to get more information. These basics can make the difference between a smooth ride and a bumpy one.

1 Visitor Information

TOURIST OFFICES

The various provincial offices below dispense visitor information. Canadian consulates do not.

- **Nova Scotia Dept. of Tourism,** P.O. Box 130, Halifax, NS B3J 2M7 (☎ **800/565-0000**).
- Tourism New Brunswick, P.O. Box 12345, Fredericton, NB E3B 5C3 (☎ **800/561-0123**).
- **Tourism Prince Edward Island,** West Royalty Industrial Park, Charlottetown, PEI C1E 1B0 (☎ **800/463-4734**).
- **Newfoundland and Labrador Dept. of Tourism,** Culture and Recreation, P.O. Box 8700, St. John's, NF A1B 4J6 (☎ **800/ 563-6353** or 709/729-2806).
- **Tourisme Québec,** C.P. 979, Montréal, PQ H3C 2W3 (☎ **800/ 363-7777**).
- **Ontario Travel,** Queen's Park, Toronto, ON M7A 2E5 (☎ **800/ 668-2746**).
- **Travel Manitoba,** 155 Carlton St., Winnipeg, MB RC3 3H8 (☎ **800/665-0040**).
- **Tourism Saskatchewan,** 500-1900 Albert St., Regina, SK S4P 4L9 (☎ **800/667-7191**).
- **Alberta Economic Development and Tourism,** Commerce Place, 10155 102nd St., Edmonton, AB T5J 4L6 (☎ **800/ 661-8888**).
- **Tourism British Columbia,** Parliament Building, Victoria, BC V8V 1X4 (☎ **800/663-6000** or 250/387-1642).
- **Tourism Yukon,** P.O. Box 2703, Whitehorse, YK Y1A 2C6 (☎ **403/667-5340**).
- **Northwest Territories Economic Development and Tourism,** P.O. Box 1320, Yellowknife, NWT X1A 2L9 (☎ **800/ 661-0788**).
- **Nunavut Tourism,** P.O. Box 1450, Iqaluit, NT X0A 0H0, (☎ **800/491-7910**).

Canada

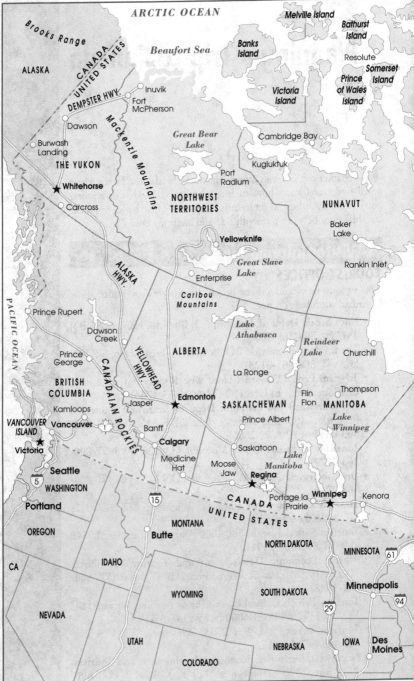

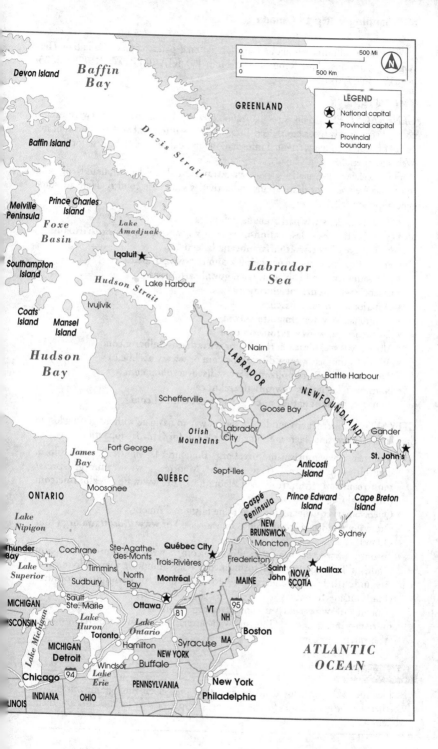

For general information about Canada's national parks, contact **Canadian Heritage,** Publications Unit, Room 10H2, Hull, PQ K1A 0M5 (☎ **819/994-6625;** fax 819/953-8770).

THE INTERNET

GENERAL SITES   Major sites like Yahoo (**www.yahoo.com**), Excite (**www.excite. com**), Lycos (**www.lycos.com**), and Infoseek (**www.infoseek.com**) contain subcategories on travel, country/regional information, and culture—search these for links to Web sites specializing in Canada.

The excellent all-Canada site at **www.travelcanada.ca** has thousands of links to official Web sites for destinations and activities across the country. Here are some general provincial sites:

- Parks Canada: **www.parkscanada.pch.gc.ca**
- Nova Scotia: **www.destination-ns.com** or **www.explore.gov.ns.ca/virtualns**
- New Brunswick: **www.tourismnbcanada.com**
- Prince Edward Island: **www.peiplay.com** or **www.gov.pe.ca**
- Newfoundland and Labrador: **www.gov.nf.ca/tourism**
- Québec: **www.tourisme.gouv.qc.ca**
- Ontario: **www.travelinx.com**
- Manitoba: **www.travelmanitoba.com**
- Saskatchewan: **www.sasktourism.com**
- Alberta: **www.explorealberta.com** or **www.discoveralberta.com**
- British Columbia: **wwww.discoverbc.com** or **www.travel.bc.ca**
- Yukon: **www.touryukon.com** or **www.discoveryukon.com**
- Northwest Territories: **www.nwttravel.nt.ca**
- Nunavut: **www.nunatour.nt.ca** or **www.arctic-travel.com**

CITY SITES   Internet city guides are a good way to navigate without getting lost in the virtual countryside. Here are some to check out for Canada's top cities:

- Montréal: **www.tourism-montreal.org** (Bonjour à la Montréal), **www.cglbrd. com/cities/qc/montreal** (Gay Canada: Montréal), **www.cam.org/~vpress/ montreal.html** (Montréal: A Celebration), or **www.montrealonline.com** (Montréal Online)
- Québec: **www.quebecregion.com** (Une Histoire d'Amour)
- Ottawa: **www.ottawakiosk.com** (Ottawa Kiosk) or **www.tourottawa.org** (Tour Ottawa)
- Toronto: **www.toronto.com** (Toronto.com), **www.tourism-toronto.com** (Tourism Toronto), **www.gaytoronto.com** (Gay Toronto), **www.rickym.com/ cityguide** (Ricky McMountain Toronto City Guide), or **www.outsidetoronto. com** (Outside Toronto)
- Vancouver: **www.tourism-vancouver.org** (Discover Vancouver), **www. tourism-vancouver.org** (Tourism Vancouver), or **www.vancouverwow.com** (Vancouverwow.com)

<hr>

Site-seeing

Besides the Web pages listed here, you'll find sites given throughout this guide, whether they be general sites for the provinces or specific sites for the cities and their attractions.

• Victoria: **www.city.victoria.bc.ca** (City of Victoria), **victoriabc.com** (Victoria BC), **www.greatervictoria.com/tourist.htm** (Greater Victoria), or **www. whistler.net** (Whistler Resort Guide)

2 Entry Requirements & Customs

ENTRY REQUIREMENTS

Entry requirements for entering Canada have tightened in recent years. All visitors to Canada must be able to provide proof of citizenship. For U.S. citizens and permanent U.S. residents, a passport is not required, though it is the easiest and most convenient method of proving citizenship. If you don't have a passport, you'll need to carry other forms of proof of citizenship, such as a certificate of naturalization, a certificate of citizenship, a certificate of birth abroad with a photo ID, a birth certificate with photo ID, a voter's registration card with photo ID or social security card. Some form of photo ID is usually a good idea. Although officers at border control are allowed to ask for these forms of identity, in most cases a U.S. driver's license is all that is asked for. Permanent U.S. residents who aren't U.S. citizens must have their Alien Registration Cards (green cards). If you plan to drive into Canada, be sure to bring your car's registration papers.

Citizens of most European countries and of former British colonies and certain other countries (Israel, Korea, and Japan for instance) do not need visas but must carry passports. Entry visas are required for citizens of more than 130 countries. Entry visas must be applied for and received from the Canadian embassy in your home country. For more information on entry requirements to Canada, see the Web site at **http://cicnet.ci.gc.ca/english/visit/index-visit.html**.

An important point: Any person under 18 requires a letter from a parent or guardian granting him or her permission to travel to Canada. The letter must state the traveler's name and the duration of the trip. It's essential that teenagers carry proof of identity; otherwise, their letter is useless at the border.

CUSTOMS

WHAT YOU CAN BRING IN   Customs regulations are very generous in most respects but get pretty complicated when it comes to firearms, plants, meats, and pets. Fishing tackle poses no problems, but the bearer must possess a nonresident license for the province or territory where he or she plans to use it. You can bring in free of duty up to 50 cigars, 200 cigarettes, and 2 pounds of tobacco, providing you're over 18. You're also allowed 40 ounces of liquor or wine. Dogs, cats, and most pets can enter Canada with their owners, though you should have proof of rabies vaccinations within the last 36 months.

For more details concerning customs regulations, write to **Customs and Revenue Agency,** Connaught Building, Sussex Drive, Ottawa, ON, K1A 0L5 (www.ccra-adrc. gc.ca/).

WHAT YOU CAN BRING HOME For U.S. Citizens   Contact the **U.S. Customs Service,** 1301 Constitution Ave. (P.O. Box 7407), Washington, DC 20044 (☎ 202/927-6724), and request the free pamphlet *Know Before You Go.* It's also available on the Web at **www.customs.ustreas.gov/travel/kbygo.htm**.

For U.K. Citizens   Contact **HM Customs & Excise,** Passenger Enquiry Point, 2nd Floor, Wayfarer House, Great South West Road, Feltham, Middlesex TW14 8NP (☎ 020/8910-3744), or consult their Web site at **www.open.gov.uk**.

For Australian Citizens   Contact the **Australian Customs Services,** G.P.O. Box 8, Sydney, NSW 2001 (☎ **02/9213-2000**), for its *Know Before You Go* brochure.

For New Zealand Citizens   Contact **New Zealand Customs,** 50 Anzac Ave., P.O. Box 29, Auckland (☎ **09/359-6655**), for its *New Zealand Customs Guide for Travellers, Notice no. 4.*

3 Money

CURRENCY

Canadians use dollars and cents, but with a very pleasing balance: The **Canadian dollar** is worth around 65¢ in U.S. money, give or take a couple of points' daily variation. So your American money gets you roughly 50% more the moment you exchange it for local currency. And since the price of many goods is roughly on a par with that in the United States, the difference is real, not imaginary. (Before you get too excited, however, remember that sales taxes are astronomical.) You can bring in or take out any amount, but if you're importing or exporting sums of $5,000 or more, you must file a report of the transaction with U.S. Customs. Most tourist places in Canada will take U.S. cash, but for the best rate you should change your funds into Canadian currency.

Note that Canada has no $1 bills. The lowest paper denomination is $5. Single bucks come in brass coins bearing the picture of a loon—hence their nickname "loonies." There's also a two-toned $2 coin.

If you do spend American money at Canadian establishments, you should understand how the conversion is done. Often by the cash register there'll be a sign reading U.S. CURRENCY __%, with some percentage in the blank. This percentage, say 25%, is the "premium"—it means that for every U.S. greenback you hand over, the cashier will see it as $1.25 in Canadian dollars. Thus, for an $8 tab you need pay only $6 in U.S. bills. However, 25% is a bad exchange rate, so shop around to get the best rate. In fact, best of all, exchange your money at a bank.

TRAVELER'S CHECKS

These days traveler's checks seem less necessary than they once were because most larger cities have 24-hour ATMs allowing you to withdraw cash as needed. Some banks, however, impose a fee every time you use a card at an ATM in a different city or bank. If you plan to withdraw money every day, you might be better off with traveler's checks—provided you don't mind showing ID every time you want to cash a check. When you cash U.S. dollar traveler's checks at banks, most will charge you a $5 fee per transaction (not per check). Hotels, restaurants, and shops don't charge fees as a rule, but their exchange rate may be somewhat lower than the current figure.

You can get traveler's checks at almost any bank. **American Express** offers them in denominations of $10, $20, $50, $100, $500, and $1,000 and impose a service charge of 1% to 4%. You can get American Express traveler's checks over the phone by calling ☎ **800/221-7282**; by using this number, AmEx gold and platinum cardholders are exempt from the 1% fee. AAA members can obtain checks without a fee at most AAA offices.

Visa offers traveler's checks at Citibank locations nationwide, as well as several other banks. The service charge ranges from 1.5% to 2%; checks come in denominations of $20, $50, $100, $500, and $1,000. **MasterCard** also offers traveler's checks. Call ☎ **800/223-9920** for a location near you.

Be sure to keep a record of the **serial numbers** of your traveler's checks (separately from the checks, of course) so you're ensured a refund if they're lost or stolen.

The Canadian Dollar & the U.S. Dollar

The prices cited in this guide are given first in Canadian dollars, then in U.S. dollars; amounts over $5 have been rounded to the nearest dollar. Note that the Canadian dollar is worth about 50% less than the American dollar but buys nearly as much. As we go to press, $1 U.S. is worth about $1.50 Canadian, and that was the equivalency used to figure the prices in this guide.

ATMS

The best rate of exchange is usually through use of an ATM with a bank card. Not only is it convenient not to have to carry cash and checks, but you'll get the best commercial rate. It's always wise to bring in sufficient Canadian cash to pay for an initial cab or bus and a meal.

ATMs are linked to a national network that most likely includes your bank at home. Both the **Cirrus** (☎ **800/424-7787;** www.mastercard.com/atm) and the **Plus** (☎ **800/843-7587;** www.visa.com/atms) networks have automated ATM locators listing the banks in Canada that'll accept your card. Or just search out any machine with your network's symbol emblazoned on it. You can also get a cash advance through Visa or MasterCard (contact the issuing bank to enable this feature and get a PIN); but note that the credit-card company will begin charging you interest immediately, and many have begun assessing a fee every time. American Express card cash advances are usually available only from AMEX offices.

CREDIT CARDS

Credit cards are invaluable when traveling—a safe way to carry money and a convenient record of all your expenses. You can also withdraw cash advances from your cards at any bank (though you'll start paying hefty interest the moment you receive the cash and won't receive frequent-flyer miles on an airline credit card). At most banks, you don't even need to go to a teller; you can get a cash advance at an ATM with your PIN.

Almost every credit-card company has an emergency toll-free number you can call if your wallet or purse is stolen. They may be able to wire you a cash advance off your credit card immediately, and in many places, they can deliver an emergency card in a day or two. The issuing bank's number is usually on the back of the credit card (though that doesn't help you much if the card was stolen). A toll-free information directory at ☎ 800/555-1212 will provide the number for you. Citicorp Visa's U.S. emergency number is ☎ **800/336-8472. American Express** cardholders and traveler's check holders should call ☎ **800/221-7282,** and **MasterCard** holders should call ☎ **800/307-7309.**

WIRE SERVICES

If you find yourself out of money, a wire service can help you tap willing friends and family for funds. Through **MoneyGram,** 6200 S. Quebec St., P.O. Box 5118, Englewood, CO 80155 (☎ **800/945-2264**), you can get money sent to you in less than 10 minutes. Cash and Visa or MasterCard are the only acceptable forms of payment. MoneyGram's fee is $20 for the first $200 and $30 for up to $400, with a sliding scale for larger sums. A similar service is offered by **Western Union** (☎ **800/325-6000**), which accepts cash and Visa, MasterCard, or Discover. You can arrange for the service over the phone or at a Western Union office. A sliding scale begins at $15 for sums paid for by cash ($33 when paid by credit card) for the first $100.

4 When to Go

THE WEATHER

In southern and central Canada, the weather is the same as that in the northern United States. As you head north, the climate becomes Arctic, meaning long and extremely cold winters, brief and surprisingly warm summers (with lots of flies), and magical springs.

As a general rule, **spring** runs mid-March to mid-May, **summer** mid-May to mid-September, **fall** mid-September to mid-November, and **winter** mid-November to mid-March. Pick the season best suited to your tastes and temperament, and remember that your car should be winterized through March and that snow sometimes falls as late as April (in 1995 a foot of snow blanketed Prince Edward Island in May). September and October bring autumn foliage and great opportunities for photographers.

Evenings tend to be cool everywhere, particularly on or near water. In late spring and early summer, you'll need a supply of insect repellent if you're planning bush travel or camping.

With the huge size of some provinces and territories, you naturally get considerable climate variations inside their borders. Québec, for instance, sprawls all the way from the temperate south to the Arctic, and the weather varies accordingly. British Columbia shows the slightest changes: It rarely goes above the 70s in summer or drops below the 30s in winter.

HOLIDAYS

National holidays are celebrated throughout the country, meaning that all government facilities close down, as well as banks, but some department stores and a scattering of smaller shops stay open. If the holiday falls on a weekend, the following Monday is observed.

Canadian holidays include New Year's Day, Good Friday, Easter Monday, Victoria Day (in mid- to late May, the weekend before U.S. Memorial Day), Canada Day (July 1), Labour Day, Thanksgiving (in mid-Oct), Remembrance Day (Nov 11), Christmas Day, and Boxing Day (Dec 26).

In addition, you may run into **provincial holidays,** festivals, and special events. You'll find the best of these listed in chapter 1, as well as in each regional or city chapter.

5 The Outdoor Adventure Planner

SPORTS A TO Z

See the individual chapters for specific details on how and where to enjoy the activities below.

BIKING   Most of Canada's highways are wide and well maintained, and thus well suited for long-distance bicycle touring. Most resort areas have ample supplies of rentals, so you don't have to worry about transporting your own (it's a good idea to call ahead and reserve a bike). You'll need to be in good shape to embark on a long bike trip and be able to deal with minor bike repairs.

While most hiking trails are closed to mountain bikes, other trails are developed specifically for backcountry biking. Ask at national-park and national-forest info centers for a map of mountain-bike trails.

Probably the most rewarding biking anywhere is in Banff and Jasper national parks. The Icefields Parkway, running between the parks, is an eye-popping route past soaring peaks and glaciers and is wide and well graded.

CANOEING & KAYAKING   Much of Canada was first explored by canoe, as low-lying lakes and slow rivers form vast waterway systems across the central and northern regions. Canoes are still excellent for exploring the backcountry. Several-day canoe/camping trips through wilderness waterways make popular summer and early-fall expeditions for small groups; you'll see lots of wildlife (especially mosquitoes) and keep as gentle a pace as you like. Generally speaking, the longer the trip, the more experience you should have with a canoe and with wilderness conditions (weather, wildlife, and chance of injury). Lake-filled Manitoba is a good place to plan a canoe trip.

DOGSLEDDING   Just imagine taking a traditional dogsled out into the Arctic ice floes and snowy tundra. Outfitters in the North run several-day trips to see the aurora borealis in early spring, and in late spring they offer trips to the floe edge, where wildlife viewing is great (this is your best chance to see a polar bear). You'll get a turn at driving the dog team and will sleep in comfort in special room-sized tents heated with small stoves (no igloos!). Outfitters will usually provide all the gear necessary for the weather, though you should be prepared to get a little cold. Outfitters on Baffin Island provide dogsled trips ranging from part-day to a week out on the tundra amid dramatic mountain and fjord scenery; February to May is the best time.

FISHING   Angling is another sport enjoyed across the entire country. The famed salmon fisheries along the Atlantic and Pacific coasts face highly restricted catch limits in most areas, and outright bans on fishing in others. However, not all salmon species on all rivers are threatened, and rules governing fishing change quickly; so check locally with fishing outfitters to find out if a season will open while you're visiting. Other species aren't so heavily restricted and probably make a better focus for a fishing-oriented vacation. Trout are found throughout Canada, some reaching great size in the thousands of lakes in the north country; northern pike and walleye are also wary fish that grow to massive size in the North. The Arctic char, a cousin of the salmon, is an anadromous fish running in the mighty rivers that feed into the Arctic Ocean; char fishing is often combined with other backcountry adventures by Arctic outfitters.

Fishing in Canada is regulated either by local government or by tribes, and appropriate licenses are necessary. Angling for some fish is regulated by season; in some areas, catch-and-release fishing is enforced. Be sure to check with local authorities before casting your line.

Perhaps Canada's most famous fishing hole is Great Slave Lake. This deep and massive lake is home to enormous lake trout and northern pike; the latter can reach lengths over 6 feet. You'll want to plan a trip with an outfitter, because weather conditions change rapidly and maneuvering small craft can be dangerous.

HIKING   Almost every national and provincial park in Canada is webbed with hiking trails, ranging from easy interpretive nature hikes to long-distance trails into the backcountry. Late summer and early fall are good times to plan a walking holiday, since spring comes late to much of Canada—trails in the high country may be snow-bound until July.

Most parks have developed free hiking and trail information, as well as details on accessible trails for people with mobility concerns. Before setting out, be sure to request this info and buy a good map. If you're taking a long trip, evaluate your fitness and equipment before you leave; once in the backcountry, there's no way out except on foot, so make sure your boots fit and you understand the risks you're undertaking.

Though there are great trails and magnificent scenery across Canada, for many people the Canadian Rockies, with their abundance of parks and developed trail systems, provide the country's finest hiking.

HORSEBACK RIDING   Holidays on horseback have a long pedigree in western Canada, and most outfitters and guest ranches offer a variety of options. Easiest are short rides that take a morning or an afternoon; you'll be given an easygoing horse and sufficient instruction to make you feel comfortable no matter what your previous riding ability. Longer pack trips take riders off into the backcountry on a several-day guided expedition, with lodging in tents or at rustic camps. These trips are best for those who don't mind "roughing it": You'll probably go a day or two without showers or flush toilets and end up saddle sore and sunburned. While these trips are generally open to riders with varying degrees of experience, it's a good idea to spend some time on horseback before heading out: You get very sore if you haven't been in a saddle for a while. The Canadian Rockies in Alberta are filled with guest ranches offering a wide range of horseback activities.

SEA KAYAKING   Though it may seem like a newer sport, sea kayaking is an ancient activity: The Inuit have used hide-covered kayaks for centuries. New lightweight kayaks make it possible to transport these crafts to remote areas and explore previously inaccessible areas along sheltered coasts; kayaks are especially good for wildlife viewing. Most coastal towns in British Columbia will have both kayak rentals and instruction, as well as guided trips. Handling a kayak isn't as easy as it looks, and you'll want to have plenty of experience in sheltered coves before heading out onto the surf. Be sure to know the tide schedule and weather forecast before setting out, as well as what the coastal rock formations are. You'll need to be comfortable on the water and ready to get wet, as well as be a strong swimmer. One of the best places in the world to practice sea kayaking is in the sheltered bays, islands, and inlets along the coast of British Columbia.

SKIING   It's no wonder that Canada, a mountainous country with heavy snowfall, is one of the world's top ski destinations. If you've never skied before, you've got a basic choice between the speed and thrills of downhill skiing and the more Zen-like pleasure of cross-country skiing. Both sports are open to all ages, though downhill skiing is less forgiving of older bones and joints and carries a higher price tag: A day on the slopes, with rental gear and lift ticket, can easily top C$90 (US$60).

For **downhill skiing,** the Canadian Rockies and Whistler-Blackcomb resort near Vancouver are the primary destinations. The 1988 Winter Olympics were held at Nakiska, just outside Banff National Park, and the park itself is home to three other ski areas, including Lake Louise, the country's largest. If you're just learning to ski or are skiing with the family, then the easier slopes at Banff Mount Norquay are made to order. Readers of *Condé Nast Traveler* repeatedly award Whistler-Blackcomb the title of Best Ski Resort in North America. At all these ski areas, instruction, rentals, and day care are available, and world-class lodging is available at Banff, Lake Louise and Whistler. The slopes are usually open November to May.

The dry, heavy snows of eastern Canada make this the best destination for a **cross-country skiing** vacation. The Laurentians, north of Québec, are a range of low mountains with many ski trails and small resort towns with rural French-Canadian charm. The best skiing is January to March.

WHITE-WATER RAFTING   Charging down a mountain river in a rubber raft is one of the most popular adventures for many people visiting Canada's western mountains. Trips range from daylong excursions that demand little of a participant other than sitting tight to long-distance trips through remote backcountry where all members of the crew are expected to hoist a paddle through the rapids. Risk doesn't correspond to length of trip: Individual rapids and water conditions can make even a short trip a real adventure. On long trips, you'll be camping in tents and spending evenings by a campfire. Even on short trips, plan on getting wet; it's not unusual to get thrown out of a raft, so you should be comfortable in water and a good swimmer if you're floating an adventurous river (outfitters will always provide life jackets).

Jasper National Park is a major center for short yet thrilling white-water trips. For a weeklong white-water adventure in a wilderness setting, contact an outfitter about trips through Nahanni National Park.

SHOULD YOU USE AN OUTFITTER OR PLAN YOUR OWN TRIP?

A basic consideration for most people who embark on an adventure vacation is time versus money. If you have time on your hands and have basic skills in dealing with sports and the outdoors, then planning your own trip can be fun. On the other hand, making one phone call and writing one check makes a lot more sense if you don't have a lot of time and lack the background to safely get you where you want to go.

TRANSPORTATION & EQUIPMENT   In general, the more remote the destination, the more you should consider an outfitter. In many parts of Canada, simply getting to the area where your trip begins requires a great deal of planning. Frequently, outfitters will have their own airplanes or boats or work in conjunction with someone who does. These transportation costs are usually included in the price of an excursion and are usually cheaper than the same flight or boat trip on a chartered basis.

The same rule applies to equipment rental. Getting your raft or canoe to an out-of-the-way lake can be an adventure in itself. But hire an outfitter and they'll take care of the hassle.

Another option is to use an outfitter to "package" your trip. Some outfitters offer their services to organize air charters and provide equipment for a fee but leave you to mastermind the trip.

SAFETY   Much of Canada is remote and given to weather extremes. What might be considered a casual camping trip or boating excursion in more populated or temperate areas can become life-threatening in the Canadian backcountry—which often starts right at the edge of town. Almost all outfitters are certified as first-aid providers, and most carry two-way radios in case there's a need to call for help. Local outfitters also know the particular hazards of the areas where they lead trips. In some areas, like the Arctic, where hazards range from freakish weather to ice-floe movements and polar bears, outfitters are nearly mandatory.

OTHER PEOPLE   Most outfitters will lead groups on excursions only after signing up a minimum number of participants. This is usually a financial consideration for the outfitter, but for participants this can be both good and bad news. Traveling with the right people can add to the trip's enjoyment, but the wrong companions can lead to exasperation and disappointment. If you're sensitive to other peoples' idiosyncrasies, ask the potential outfitter specific questions regarding who else is going on the trip.

SELECTING AN OUTFITTER

An outfitter will be responsible for your safety and your enjoyment of the trip, so make certain you choose one wisely. All outfitters should be licensed or accredited by the province and should be happy to provide you with proof. This means they're bonded, carry the necessary insurance, and have the money and organizational wherewithal to register with the province. This rules out fly-by-night operations and college students who've decided to set up business for the summer. If you're just starting to plan an excursion, ask the provincial tourist authority for its complete list of licensed outfitters.

Often a number of outfitters offer similar trips. When you've narrowed down your choice, call and talk to those outfitters. Ask questions and try to get a sense of who these people are; you'll be spending a lot of time with them, so make sure you feel comfortable. If you have special interests, like bird or wildlife watching, be sure to mention them. A good outfitter will also take your interests into account when planning a trip.

If there's a wide disparity in prices between outfitters for the same trip, find out what makes the difference. Some companies economize on food. If you don't mind having cold cuts for each meal of your weeklong canoe expedition, then perhaps the least expensive outfitter is okay. However, if you prefer a cooked meal, alcoholic beverages, or a choice of entrees, then be prepared to pay more. On a long trip, it might be worth it to you.

Ask how many years an outfitter has been in business and how long your particular escort has guided this trip. While a start-up outfitting service can be perfectly fine, you should know what level of experience you're buying. If you have questions, especially for longer or more dangerous trips, ask for referrals.

OUTFITTERS & ADVENTURE-TRAVEL OPERATORS

Most outfitters offer trips in specific geographic areas only, though some larger outfitters package trips across the country. In the chapters that follow, we'll recommend lots of local operators and tell you about the outings they run. We've found a few, though, that operate in more than one region of Canada.

Nahanni and Whitewolf River Adventures, P.O. Box 4869, Whitehorse, YT Y1A 4N6 (☎ **800/297-6927** or 867/668-3180; fax 867/668-3056; www.nahanni.com; e-mail nahanni@yknet.yk.ca), offers whitewater and naturalist float trips in rivers across western and northern Canada, with the Nahanni River a specialty.

Canusa Cycle Tours, Box 35104, Sarcee RPO, Calgary, AB T3E 7C7 (☎ **800/ 938-7986** or 403/254-8361; www.tcel.com/~canusa; e-mail canusa@tcel.com), offers guided cycle tours along some of Canada's most scenic highways.

Ecosummer Expeditions, 5640 Hollybridge Way, Unit 130, Vancouver, BC V7C 4N3 Canada, or P.O. Box 8014-240, 936 Peace Portal Drive, Blaine, WA 98230 U.S.A. (☎ **800/465-8884** or 604/214-7484; fax 604/214-7485; www.ecosummer. com; e-mail trips@ecosummer.com), offers a wide variety of adventures in British Columbia, the Yukon, Nunavut, and the Northwest Territories. Activities include sea kayaking, whitewater rafting, dogsledding, photography expeditions, and more. Ecosummer offers kayaking trips to remote Ellesmere Island in the Canadian Arctic and trips to destinations in South and Central America, as well as Greenland.

WHAT TO PACK

Be sure that it's clearly established between you and your outfitter what you're responsible for bringing along. If you need to bring a sleeping bag, find out what weight of

A Warning

All outfitters should be licensed by their province, and local tourist offices can provide listings of outfitters licensed to operate in the areas you intend to visit.

bag is suggested for the conditions you'll encounter. If you have any special dietary requirements, bring them along.

While it's fun and relatively easy to amass the equipment for a backcountry expedition, none of it will do you any good if you don't know how to use it. Even though compasses aren't particularly accurate in the North, bring one along and know how to use it. If you're trekking on your own, bring along a first-aid kit.

For all summer trips in Canada, make sure to bring along insect repellent, as mosquitoes are particularly numerous and hungry in the North. If you know you're heading into bad mosquito country, consider buying specialized hats with mosquito netting attached. Sunglasses are a must, even above the Arctic Circle. The farther north you go in summer, the longer the sun stays up; the low angle of the sun can be particularly annoying. In winter, the glare off snow can cause sun blindness. For the same reasons, sunscreen is a surprising necessity.

Summer weather is changeable in Canada. If you're planning outdoor activities, be sure to bring along wet-weather gear, even in high summer. The more exposure you'll have to the elements, the more you should consider bringing high-end Gortex and artificial-fleece outerwear. The proper gear can make the difference between a miserable time and a great adventure.

If you're traveling in Canada in winter, you'll want to have the best winter coat, gloves, and boots you can afford. A coat with a hood is especially important, as Arctic winds can blow for days at a time.

6 Getting There

BY PLANE

THE MAJOR AIRLINES   Canada is served by almost all the international air carriers. The major international airports in the east are in Halifax, Toronto, and Montréal; in the west they're in Winnipeg, Edmonton, Calgary, and Vancouver.

As this book goes to press, the Canadian government has given Air Canada tentative permission to buy and merge with Canadian Air. According to current plans, Canadian Air will continue to operate as a separate airline and service to most Canadian Air destinations will continue, so in theory travelers shouldn't notice great changes in service. **Air Canada** (☎ 800/776-3000; www.aircanada.ca) has by far the most flights between the United States and Canada (including 18 daily from New York to Toronto), but most major U.S. and Canadian carriers fly daily between major cities in Canada and the United States as well, including **America West** (☎ 800/292-9378; www.americawest.com), **American Airlines** (☎ 800/433-7300; www.americanair.com), **Canadian Airlines** (☎ 800/426-7000; www.cdnair.ca), **Continental** (☎ 800/525-0280; www.flycontinental.com), **Delta** (☎ 800/221-1212; www.delta-air.com), **Northwest** (☎ 800/447-4747; www.nwa.com), **United** (☎ 800/241-6522; www.ual.com), and **US Airways** (☎ 800/428-4322; www.usairways.com).

International airlines with non-stop service to Canada include **British Air** (☎ 800/247-9297; www.british-airways.com), **Air France** (☎ 800/237-2747; www.airfrance.fr), **Lufthansa** (800/645-3880; www.lufthansa.com), **SAS** (☎ 800/221-2350; www.sas.se), and **KLM** (800/347-7747; www.klm-logistik.de). Additionally, **Canadian Air** and **Air Canada** have international flights to/from Mexico, most cities in northern Europe, and to many centers in Asia. **Canada 3000** (☎ 888/CAN3000; www.Canada3000.com), one of Canada's new discount airlines, also offers flights to/from Europe at considerable discount. Flights between Canada, Australia, and New Zealand usually connect through Honolulu or Los Angeles.

Flying for Less: Tips for Getting the Best Airfares

- **Take advantage of APEX fares.** Advance-purchase booking or APEX fares are often the key to getting the lowest fare. You generally must be willing to make your plans and buy your tickets as far ahead as possible: The **21-day APEX** is seconded only by the **14-day APEX,** with a stay of 7 to 30 days. Since the number of seats allocated to APEX fares is sometimes less than 25% of plane capacity, the early bird gets the low-cost seat. There's often a surcharge for flying on a weekend, and cancellation and refund policies can be strict.

- **Watch for sales.** You'll almost never see them during July and August or the Thanksgiving or Christmas seasons, but at other times you can get great deals. If you already hold a ticket when a sale breaks, it may even pay to exchange it, which usually incurs a $50 to $75 charge.

- **Ask if you can secure a cheaper fare by staying an extra day or flying mid-week.** If your schedule is flexible, you can definitely save money this way. Many airlines won't volunteer this information.

- **Be aware that consolidators (a.k.a. bucket shops) are good places to find low fares.** They buy seats in bulk from airlines and sell them to the public at prices below even the airlines' discounted rates. Their small boxed ads usually run in the Sunday travel section. **Council Travel** (☎ **800/226-8624;** www.counciltravel.com) and **STA Travel** (☎ **800/781-4040;** www.sta.travel.com) cater especially to young travelers, but their bargain prices are available to all ages. **Travel Bargains** (☎ **800/AIR-FARE;** www.1800airfare.com) was once owned by TWA but now offers the deepest discounts on many other airlines, with a 4-day advance purchase. Other consolidators are **1-800-FLY-CHEAP** (www.1800flycheap.com); **TFI Tours International** (☎ **800/745-8000** or 212/736-1140), a clearinghouse for unused seats; and "rebators" like **Travel Avenue** (☎ **800/333-3335** or 312/876-1116) and the **Smart Traveller** (☎ **800/448-3338** in the U.S. or 305/448-3338; www.smarttraveller@juno.com), which rebate part of their commissions to you.

- **Book a seat on a charter flight.** Most charter operators advertise and sell their seats through travel agents. Before deciding to take a charter, however, check the ticket restrictions: You may be asked to buy a tour package, pay in advance, be amenable if the departure day is changed, pay a service charge, fly on an airline you're not familiar with (unusual), and pay harsh penalties if you cancel (but be understanding if the charter doesn't fill up and is canceled up to 10 days before departure). Summer charters fill up more quickly than others and are almost sure to fly, but if you decide on a charter, seriously consider cancellation and baggage insurance.

- **Search for deals on the Web.** It's possible to get some great deals on airfare, hotels, and car rentals via the Internet. See below for details on getting the most from the Web.

INTERNET DEALS   Not only can you buy your tickets directly through any airline's individual Web site—in fact, some airlines offer over-the-Internet discounted fares not available anywhere else—but the number of virtual travel agents on the Web has also exploded in recent years.

On Wednesdays, the sites of **Air Canada** (www.aircanada.ca) and **Canadian Airlines** (www.cdnair.ca) offer highly discounted flights to Canada for the following weekend. You need to reserve the flight on Wednesday or Thursday to fly on Friday (after 7pm only) or Saturday (all day) and return on Monday or Tuesday (all day). For Air Canada, you need to register with the Web Specials page; then they'll e-mail you every Wednesday about available discounts. There's no need to register for the Canadian Airlines site, where every Wednesday morning they post their specials.

A good general place to start is the **Frommer's** site (www.frommers.com), home of *Arthur Frommer's Budget Travel* magazine and daily newsletter as well as up-to-the-minute listings on almost 200 cities around the globe. The better-respected virtual travel agents are **Travelocity** (www.travelocity.com), which also advertises last-minute deals; **Microsoft Expedia** (www.expedia.com), which will e-mail you weekly with the best fares for a chosen destination; and **Yahoo's Flifo Global** (travel.yahoo.com/travel), whose "Fare Beater" compares airlines to find the best going rate. For most, just enter your dates and cities and the computer looks for the lowest fares. **Preview Travel**'s (www.reservations.com) "Best Fare Finder" will search the Apollo computer reservations system for the three lowest fares for any route on any day of the year. Great last-minute deals are often available directly from many airlines through a free service called **E-Savers.** Each week, the airline e-mails you a list of discounted flights from the city or cities of your choice to any of a number of destinations. Usually, these are weekend getaway deals, leaving the upcoming Thursday to Saturday and returning the following Monday to Wednesday. Sign up at any airline's Web site (see above).

If the thought of all that surfing and comparison shopping gives you a headache, head right for **Smarter Living** (www.smarterliving.com). Sign up for their newsletter service and every week you'll get a customized e-mail summarizing the discount fares available from your departure city. Smarter Living tracks more than 15 airlines, so it's a worthwhile time-saver.

You can now even "bid" for tickets at auction at **Priceline** (priceline.com): You type in the price you want to pay, then wait to see if any airline is willing to fly you for that rate. Of course, you might always overbid; your best bet is to shop around by other means for the cheapest ticket, then post a bid, say, 10% lower than that at priceline.com to see if they can do any better.

BY CAR

Hopping across the border by car is no problem, since the U.S. freeway system leads directly into Canada at 13 points. Once across the border, you can link up with the Trans-Canada Highway, which runs from St. John's, Newfoundland, to Victoria, British Columbia—a total of 5,000 miles. Be sure to bring your car's registration papers.

BY BUS

Greyhound Canada (☎ 800/878-1290; www.greyhound.ca) operates the major intercity bus system in Canada, with frequent cross-border links to cities in the U.S. northern tier. You can use Greyhound's reservation system to make arrangements on smaller local carriers (like Voyageur and SMT) as well.

BY TRAIN

Amtrak serves the East Coast with four main routes into Canada. The *Adirondack,* starting at New York City's Pennsylvania Station, is a day train that travels daily via Albany and upstate New York to Montréal. The *Montrealer* travels nightly from New York City's Penn Station through Vermont to Montréal. Round-trip coach fares are

US$102 to US$300. The *Maple Leaf* links New York City and Toronto via Albany, Buffalo, and Niagara Falls, departing daily from Penn Station. Round-trip coach fares are US$104 to US$130. From Chicago, the *International* carries passengers to Toronto via Port Huron, Michigan, for a round-trip coach fare of US$104 to US$130. On the West Coast, the *Mt. Baker* runs between Seattle and Vancouver, British Columbia. Round-trip fare is US$36.

From Buffalo's Exchange Street Station you can make the trip to Toronto on the Toronto/Hamilton/Buffalo Railway (THB), a two-car Budd train. In Toronto, you can make connections to Montréal, Ottawa, and so on.

Connecting services are available from other major cities along the border in addition to these direct routes. Call **Amtrak** at ☎ **800/USA-RAIL** for details. Remember that the prices don't include meals; you can buy meals on the train or carry your own food.

BY FERRY

Ocean ferries operate from Maine to Nova Scotia and New Brunswick and from Seattle and Port Angeles, Washington, to Victoria and Vancouver, British Columbia. For details, see the relevant chapters.

7 Package Tours & Escorted Tours

Tour packages divide into two main categories: tours that take care of all the details and tours that simply give you a package price on the big ticket items and leave you free to find your own way. Independent tours give you much more flexibility but require more effort on your part. Those who prefer not to drive and don't relish the notion of getting from train or bus stations to hotels on their own might prefer an escorted tour. But if you're the kind of traveler who doesn't like to be herded around in a group and wants to be able to linger at various sights at your leisure, a bus tour will drive you to distraction. The samples below will give you an idea of your choices.

INDEPENDENT PACKAGES

Air Canada offers an array of package deals specially tailored to trim the costs of your vacation. Collectively, these packages come under the title "Air Canada's Canada." This term covers a whole series of travel bargains ranging from city packages to fly/drive tours, escorted tours, motor-home travel, ski holidays, and Arctic adventures. For details, pick up the brochure from an Air Canada office, have it sent to you by calling ☎ **800/776-3000,** or visit their Web site at **www.aircanada.ca.**

Canadian Airlines operates an array of package tours in conjunction with World of Vacations, including a number of fly/rail packages. Contact **World of Vacations,** 3507 Frontage Rd., Suite 100, Tampa, FL 33607 (☎ **800/237-0190;** www.worldofvacations.com).

FULLY ESCORTED TOURS

Collette Tours offers a wide variety of trips by bus, including several in the Rockies and several in the Atlantic Provinces. A 10-day tour of Newfoundland includes the seldom-visited northern peninsula and the Viking site at L'Anse aux Meadows, as well as a visit to Labrador. Shorter trips explore the Toronto/Niagara area, and some combine Québec with New England or the Yukon with Alaska. An escorted train tour goes from Vancouver to Banff aboard the *Rocky Mountaineer.* Ask for its *USA and Canada* brochure by contacting **Collette Tours,** 162 Middle St., Pawtucket, RI 02860 (☎ **800/340-5158;** www.collettetours.com).

If your destination is the Canadian Rockies, contact **Brewster Transportation** (☎ **800/661-1152;** www.brewster.ca) for tours in the west. Some packages include stays at guest ranches, hikes across glaciers, and whitewater raft trips.

8 Getting Around

Canada is a land of immense distances, so transportation from point A to point B forms a prime item in your travel budget as well as your timetable.

BY PLANE

Canada has two major transcontinental airlines: **Air Canada** (☎ **800/776-3000;** www.aircanada.ca) and **Canadian Airlines** (☎ **800/426-7000;** www.cdnair.ca), which at press time are in the process of merging. However, according to announced plans, both airlines will remain operating as separate entities with little change to current coverage and service. Together with their regional partner companies, they handle most of the country's air transport. There are also numerous small local outfits, but these will concern you only when you get into their particular territories.

Within Canada, Air Canada operates daily service between 18 major cities, and its schedules dovetail with a string of allied connector carriers like Air Nova, Air Ontario, and NWT Air to serve scores of smaller Canadian towns. Fares vary widely with the day of the week and the availability of seats.

BY CAR

Canada has scores of rental-car companies, including **Hertz** (☎ 800/654-3131; www.hertz.com), **Avis** (☎ 800/331-1212; www.avis.com), **Dollar** (☎ 800/800-4000; www.dollarcar.com), **Thrifty** (☎ 800/367-2277; www.thrifty.com), and **Budget** (☎ 800/527-0700; www.budgetrentacar.com). Nevertheless, rental vehicles tend to get tight during the tourist season, from around mid-May to summer. It's a good idea to reserve a car as soon as you decide on your vacation.

The biggest and most thoroughly Canadian car-rental outfit is **Tilden Interrent,** with 400 locations coast to coast and affiliates in the United States and throughout the world. To book a Tilden car or get additional information while in the States, contact **National Car Rental** (☎ **800/CAR-RENT**). In Canada, contact the local stations listed in this book or **Tilden Interrent headquarters** at 250 Bloor St. E., Suite 1300, Toronto, ON M4W 1E6 (☎ **800/387-4747**).

Tilden rentals offer a Roadside Assistance Program. In case of an accident, a breakdown, a dead battery, a flat tire, a dry gas tank, getting stuck, or locking yourself out of your car, you can call ☎ **800/268-9711,** available 24 hours, and get an immediate response for roadside help anywhere in Canada.

Members of the **American Automobile Association (AAA)** should remember to take their membership cards since the Canadian Automobile Association (CAA) extends privileges to them in Canada.

Sample Distances Between Major Cities

Montréal to Vancouver, 4,910km (3,041 miles); Vancouver to Halifax, 6,295km (3,897 miles); Toronto to Victoria, 4,700km (2,911 miles); Winnipeg to St. John's, 5,100km (3,159 miles); Calgary to Montréal, 3,710km (2,299 miles); St. John's to Vancouver, 7,625km (4,723 miles); Ottawa to Victoria, 4,810km (2,979 miles).

The *Rocky Mountaineer:*
One of the World's Great Train Trips

It's billed as the "Most Spectacular Train Trip in the World," and it may very well be. Operated by the privately owned Great Canadian Railtour Company, this sleek blue-and-white train winds past foaming waterfalls, ancient glaciers, towering snowcapped peaks, and roaring mountain streams. The *Rocky Mountaineer* gives you the option of traveling east from Vancouver, traveling west from Jasper or Calgary, or taking a round-trip. The journey entails 2 days on the train and 1 night in a hotel and lets you see the Rocky Mountains as you never would behind the wheel of a car.

The train operates late May to October, entirely in daylight hours. For information and bookings, contact the **Great Canadian Railtour Company,** Suite 104, 340 Brooksbank Ave., North Vancouver, BC V7J 2C1 (☎ **800/665-7245;** www.rockymountaineer.com).

GASOLINE   As in the United States, the trend in Canada is toward self-service stations, and in some areas you may have difficulty finding the full-service kind. Though Canada (specifically Alberta) is a major oil producer, gasoline isn't particularly cheap. Gas sells by the liter and pumps at around C55¢ to C60¢ (US35¢ to US40¢) per liter, or C$2.20 to C$2.40 (US$1.45 to US$1.60) per gallon; prices vary slightly from region to region. Filling the tank of a medium-sized car will cost you roughly C$30 (US$20).

DRIVING RULES   Wearing seat belts is compulsory (and enforced) in all provinces, for all passengers. Throughout the country, pedestrians have the right-of-way and crosswalks are sacrosanct. The speed limit on the autoroutes (limited-access highways) is 100km per hour (62 m.p.h.). Right turns cannot be made at red lights unless a sign or green arrow makes an exception.

BY TRAIN

Most of Canada's passenger rail traffic is carried by the government-owned **VIA Rail** (☎ **800/561-3949;** www.viarail.ca). You can traverse the continent very comfortably in sleeping cars, parlor coaches, bedrooms, and roomettes. Virtually all Canada's major cities (save Calgary) are connected by rail, though service is less frequent than it used to be. Some luxury trains, like *The Canadian,* boast dome cars with panoramic picture windows, hot showers, and elegant dining cars.

You can also buy a **Canrailpass,** C$589 (US$393) in high season and C$379 (US$253) in low season, giving you 12 days of unlimited travel in one 30-day period throughout the VIA national network. Seniors 60 and over and students receive a 10% discount on all fares. Fares for children up to 11 are half the adult rate.

Fast Facts: Canada

American Express   See the city chapters that follow for the locations of individual American Express offices. To report lost or stolen traveler's checks, call ☎ **800/221-7282.**

Electricity   Canada uses the same electrical current as does the United States, 110 to 115 volts, 60 cycles.

Embassies & Consulates All embassies are in Ottawa, the national capital; the **U.S. embassy** is at 100 Wellington St., Ottawa, ON K1P 5T1 (☎ 613/238-4470). For the other embassies in Ottawa, see "Fast Facts" in chapter 9.

You'll find **U.S. consulates** in the following locations: Nova Scotia—Cogswell Tower, Suite 910, Scotia Square, Halifax, NS B3J 3K1 (☎ 902/429-2480); Québec—2 place Terrasse-Dufferin (P.O. Box 939), Québec City, PQ G1R 4T9 (☎ 418/692-2095), and Complexe Desjardins, South Tower, Ground Floor, Montréal, PQ H5B 1E5 (☎ 514/398-9695); Ontario—360 University Ave., Toronto, ON M5G 1S4 (☎ 416/595-1700); Alberta—Room 1050, 615 Macleod Trail SE, Calgary, AB T2G 4T8 (☎ 403/266-8962); British Columbia—1095 W. Pender St., Vancouver, BC V6E 2Y4 (☎ 604/685-4311).

There's a **British consulate general** at 777 Bay St., Toronto (☎ 416/593-1267), and an **Australian consulate general** at 175 Bloor St. E., Toronto (☎ 416/323-1155).

Emergencies In life-threatening situations, call ☎ 911.

Liquor Laws Laws regarding beer, wine, and liquor vary from province to province. In some provinces all beer, wine, and spirits are sold only in government liquor stores, which keep very restricted hours. Only Alberta and Québec have liquor laws that resemble those in the United States. The minimum drinking age is 19.

Mail At press time, it costs C46¢ (US30¢) to send a first-class letter or postcard within Canada and C55¢ (US37¢) to send a first-class letter or postcard from Canada to the United States. First-class airmail service to other countries is C95¢ (US65¢) for the first 20 grams. Rates go up frequently. Delivery time is unaccountably slow between Canada and the States: Expect a letter from Calgary to take a week to reach Seattle.

Taxes In January 1991, the Canadian government imposed the **goods and service tax (GST),** a 7% federal tax on virtually all goods and services. Some hotels and shops include the GST in their prices; others add it on separately. When included, the tax accounts for the odd hotel rates, such as C$66.04 per day, that you might find on your final bill. The GST is also the reason you pay C50¢ (US33¢) for a newspaper at a vending machine, but C54¢ (US36¢) over a shop counter: The machines haven't been geared for the new price.

Thanks to a government provision designed to encourage tourism, you can **reclaim the GST** portion of your hotel bills and the price of goods you've purchased in Canada—in due course. The minimum GST rebate is C$7 (US$4.65, the tax on C$100/US$67) and the claim must be filed within a year of purchase. You must submit all your original receipts (which will be returned) with an application form. Receipts from several trips during the same year may be submitted together. Claims of less than C$500 (US$334) can be made at certain designated duty-free shops at international airports and border crossings. Or you can mail the forms to **Revenue Canada,** Customs and Excise, Visitors' Rebate Program, Ottawa, ON K1A 1J5. You can get the forms in some of the larger hotels, in some duty-free shops, or by phone at ☎ 613/991-3346 outside Canada or **800/66-VISIT** in Canada.

The rebate doesn't apply to car rentals or restaurant meals. And the GST isn't levied on airline tickets to Canada bought in the United States.

Time Six time zones are observed in Canada. In winter, when it's 7:30pm Newfoundland standard time, it's 6pm Atlantic standard time (Labrador, Prince Edward Island, New Brunswick, and Nova Scotia); 5pm eastern standard time

(Québec and most of Ontario); 4pm central standard time (western Ontario, Manitoba, and most of Saskatchewan); 3pm mountain standard time (northwestern Saskatchewan, Alberta, eastern British Columbia, and the Northwest Territories); and 2pm Pacific standard time (the Yukon and most of British Columbia).

Each year, on the first Sunday in April, daylight saving time comes into effect in most of Canada and clocks are advanced by 1 hour. On the last Sunday in October, Canada reverts to standard time. During these summer months, all of Saskatchewan observes the same time zone as Alberta.

Nova Scotia 3

by Wayne Curtis

Nova Scotia proves cagey when you try to characterize it. It generally feels more cultured than wild . . . but then at Cape Breton Highlands National Park you stumble on blustery, boggy uplands that seem a good home for Druids and trolls. It's full of rolling hills and cultivated farms, especially near the Northumberland Straits on the northern shore . . . but it also boasts Halifax's vibrant and edgy arts-and-entertainment scene. The province has earned its name—*Nova Scotia* is Latin for "New Scotland"—with Highland games and kilts and a touch of a brogue here and there . . . but then you find enclaves of rich Acadian culture along the coast between Digby and Yarmouth. The place resists characterization at every turn.

This picturesque and historic province is ideal for travelers who are quick to hit the remote control when parked on the couch back home. You'll find an extravagant variety of landscapes and low-key attractions, and the scene seems to change kaleidoscopically as you travel along the winding roads: from dense forests to bucolic farmlands, from ragged coast to melancholy bogs, from old villages to dynamic downtowns. (About the only terrain it doesn't offer is towering mountain peaks.)

Nova Scotia is twice blessed: It's compact enough that you needn't spend all your time in a car. Yet it has fewer than a million residents (and one in three are in and around Halifax), making it unpopulated enough to provide empty places when you're seeking solitude. Even along the more populated shoreline it's possible to find a sense of remoteness, of being surrounded by big space and a profound history.

1 Exploring the Province

You'd do well spending some time poring over a Nova Scotia map and this guide before leaving home. The hardest chore will be to narrow your options before setting off. Numerous loops and circuits are available, made more complicated by ferry links to the United States, New Brunswick, Prince Edward Island, and Newfoundland. Figuring out where to go and how to get there is the hardest part.

VISITOR INFORMATION

Be sure to get a free copy of the 350-plus–page official tourism guide, ***Nova Scotia: Complete Guide for Doers and Dreamers,*** the province's best effort to put travel-book writers like me out of business. This well-organized, colorful guide lists all the hotels, campgrounds, and attractions in the province, with brief descriptions and current prices. (Restaurants are given only limited coverage.)

The guide is available starting each March by phone (☎ **800/565-0000** in North America or 902/425-5781 elsewhere), mail (P.O. Box 130, Halifax, NS B3J 2M7), fax (902/453-8401), and e-mail (nsvisit@fox.nstn.ns.ca). If you wait until you arrive before obtaining a copy, ask for one at the numerous visitor info centers, where you can also request the excellent free road map.

The provincial government administers about a dozen official **Visitor Information Centres** throughout the province, as well as in Portland, Maine, and Wood Islands, Prince Edward Island. These mostly seasonal centers are amply stocked with brochures and tended by knowledgeable staffers. In addition, virtually every town of any note has a local tourist center filled with brochures covering the entire province, staffed with locals who know the area.

For general questions about travel in the province, call **Nova Scotia's information hot line** at ☎ **800/565-0000** (North America) or 902/425-5781 (elsewhere). And you can find a tour of "Virtual Nova Scotia," presented by Nova Scotia Economic Development and Tourism, at **explore.gov.ns.ca**.

GETTING THERE

BY CAR & FERRY   Most travelers reach Nova Scotia overland by car from New Brunswick. Plan on a 4-plus–hour drive from the U.S. border at Calais, Maine, to Amherst (at the New Brunswick–Nova Scotia border). Using ferries can significantly reduce your time behind the wheel. Daily seasonal ferries connect both Portland and Bar Harbor, Maine, to Yarmouth, Nova Scotia, at the peninsula's southwest end.

The **Portland–Yarmouth ferry** trip is about 11 hours and costs around US$80 adults, US$40 children, and US$98 vehicles. Cabins are available for an extra fare, from about US$32 for a day cabin to US$165 for an overnight suite. Reservations are essential. Call **Prince of Fundy Cruises** at ☎ **800/341-7540** or 207/775-5616. On the Web, head to **www.princeoffundy.com**.

Bay Ferries (☎ **888/249-7245**) operates the Bar Harbor–Yarmouth ferry. The Cat (short for catamaran) claims to be North America's fastest ferry and cuts the crossing time from 6 to 2¾ hours, zipping along at up to 50 miles per hour. Some passengers complain the experience is a bit dull once the initial thrill fades, more like lingering in an airport lounge than taking a boat trip. There's an open deck on the rear, but I've received complaints that those trying to enjoy the fresh air find it mingled with exhaust fumes. Summer rates are US$46 adults, US$41 seniors, US$23 children 5 to 12, and US$60 autos. Off-season and family rates are available. Reservations are vital during summer.

To shorten the slog around the Bay of Fundy, a 3-hour ferry links **Saint John, New Brunswick,** and **Digby, Nova Scotia.** It sails year-round, with as many as three crossings daily in summer. Summer fares are C$25 (US$17) adults, C$13 (US$9) children, and C$55 (US$37) vehicles. It's also operated by **Bay Ferries** (☎ **888/249-7245**). You can find schedules and more details at **www.nfl-bay.com**.

BY PLANE   Halifax is the air hub of the Atlantic Provinces. **Air Canada** (☎ **800/776-3000;** www.aironada.ca) provides direct service from New York and Boston, and **Air Nova,** its commuter partner (☎ **800/776-3000** in the U.S. or 800/565-3940 in the Maritimes), serves Sydney and Yarmouth, plus about a dozen other Atlantic Canada destinations. Halifax, Sydney, and Yarmouth are also served by **Canadian Airlines International** (☎ **800/426-7000** in the U.S., 800/665-1177 in the Maritime

Nova Scotia, Prince Edward Island & Cape Breton Island

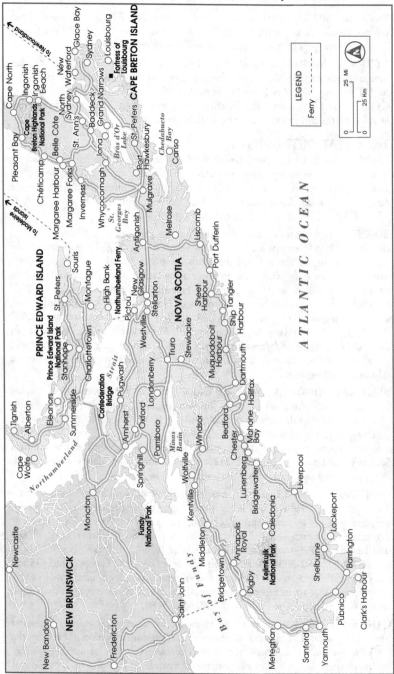

Provinces, 902/427-5500 locally, and 709/576-0274 in Newfoundland; www.cdnair.ca). *Note:* At press time, both Air Canada and Canadian Airlines were considering mergers with one another as well as with outside airlines.

BY TRAIN   Via Rail (☎ **800/561-3949** in the U.S. or 800/561-3952 in the Maritimes; www.viarail.ca) offers train service 6 days a week between Halifax and Montréal. The entire trip takes 18 to 21 hours, depending on direction. The fare is about C$185 (US$123) each way, with discounts for those buying at least a week in advance. Sleeping berths and private cabins are available at extra cost.

THE GREAT OUTDOORS

Nova Scotia's official *Complete Guide for Doers and Dreamers* has a very helpful "Outdoors" section listing camping outfitters, bike shops, whale-watching tour operators, and the like. A free brochure listing adventure outfitters is published by the **Adventure Tourism Association,** 1099 Marginal Rd., Suite 201, Halifax, NS B3H 4P7 (☎ **902/423-4480**). Write or call for a copy.

BIKING   Nova Scotia's low hills (the highest peak is just 532m/1,745 ft.) and gentle, largely empty roads make for wonderful cycling. Cape Breton is the most challenging of destinations; the south coast and Bay of Fundy regions yield wonderful ocean views while making fewer demands on cyclists. A number of bike outfitters can aid in your trip planning. **Freewheeling Adventures** at ☎ **902/ 857-3600** offers guided bike tours throughout Nova Scotia, Prince Edward Island, and Newfoundland. Prices range from C$350 (US$233) for a 2-day tour to C$2,600 (US$1,734) for a 10-day tour. Walter Sienko's *Nova Scotia & the Maritimes by Bike: 21 Tours Geared for Discovery* is helpful in planning a bike excursion. For an Internet introduction to cycling in Nova Scotia and beyond, check out **www. atl-canadacycling.com**.

BIRD WATCHING   More than 400 bird species have been spotted here, ranging from exotic birds blown off course in storms to majestic bald eagles, of which some 250 nesting pairs reside in Nova Scotia, mostly on Cape Breton Island. Many whale-watching tours also offer specialized sea bird–spotting tours, including trips to puffin colonies. Experienced birders will enjoy checking regularly with the **Nova Scotia Bird Society**'s info line at ☎ **902/852-2428,** which features up-to-date recorded details about intriguing sightings around the province.

CAMPING   With backcountry options rather limited, Nova Scotia's forte is drive-in camping. The 20 provincial parks with campgrounds are uniformly clean, friendly, well managed, and reasonably priced, offering some 1,500 campsites among them. For a brochure and a map listing all sites, write to the **Nova Scotia Department of Natural Resources, Parks and Recreation Division,** R.R. #1, Belmont, NS B0M 1C0, or call ☎ **902/662-3030.** Another helpful free guide is the Campground Owners Association of Nova Scotia's *Campers Guide,* which includes a directory of private campgrounds that are members of the association. Ask for it at the visitor information centers or contact the association at ☎ **902/423-4480.**

CANOEING   Nova Scotia offers an abundance of accessible canoeing on inland lakes and ponds. The premier destination is **Kejimkujik National Park** in the southern interior, with 44 backcountry sites accessible by canoe. A number of other fine canoe trails allow paddlers and portagers to venture off for hours or days. General info is available from **Canoe Nova Scotia,** 5516 Spring Garden Rd., Halifax, NS B3J 3G6 (☎ **902/425-5450**). Tour maps outlining 22 canoe trips in Annapolis County are available for C$16 (US$11) from **Canoe Annapolis County,** P.O. Box 100, Annapolis Royal, NS B0S 1A0 (☎ **902/532-2334**).

FISHING   Saltwater fishing tours are easily arranged on charter boats berthed at many of the province's harbors. Inquire locally at the visitor information centers, or consult the "Boat Tours & Charters" section of the *Doers & Dreamers* guide. No fishing license is needed for those on charters. For saltwater regulations, contact the **Department of Fisheries and Oceans** at ☎ **902/426-5952.**

Committed freshwater anglers come to Nova Scotia in pursuit of the dwindling Atlantic salmon, which requires a license separate from that for other freshwater fish. **Salmon licenses** must be obtained from a provincial Natural Resources office, provincial campground, or licensed outfitter. Other freshwater species popular with anglers are brown trout, shad, smallmouth bass, rainbow trout, and speckled trout. For a copy of the current fishing regulations, contact the **Department of Natural Resources License Section** at ☎ **902/424-6608.**

GOLF   More than 50 golf courses are located throughout Nova Scotia. Among the most memorable are the **Cape Breton Highland Links** (☎ **902/285-2600**) in Ingonish, which features a dramatic oceanside setting, and the **Bell Bay Golf Club** (☎ **800/565-3077**) near Baddeck, which is also wonderfully scenic and was voted "Best New Canadian Golf Course" by *Golf Digest* in 1998. For one-stop shoppers, **Golf Nova Scotia** at ☎ **877/204-4653** (www.golfnovascotia.com) represents 18 well-regarded properties and can arrange customized golfing packages at its member courses. A handy directory of Nova Scotia's golf courses (with phone numbers) is published in the "Outdoors" section of the *Complete Guide for Doers and Dreamers.*

HIKING & WALKING   Serious hikers make tracks for ✪ **Cape Breton Highlands National Park,** home to the most dramatic terrain in the province. But you're certainly not limited to here. Trails are found throughout Nova Scotia, though in many cases they're a matter of local knowledge. (Ask at the visitor information centers.) An ambitious and exceptionally attractive 30km (19-mile) hiking loop is under construction on the Fundy Coast near **Parrsboro;** for more information, see "Parrsboro," below. Published hiking guides are widely available at local bookstores. Especially helpful are the back-pocket–sized guides published by **Nimbus Publishing of Halifax** (☎ **800/646-2879** or 902/455-4286).

SAILING   Any area with so much convoluted coastline is clearly inviting to sailors and gunkholers. Tours and charters are available almost everywhere there's a decent-sized harbor. Those with the inclination and skills to venture out on their own can rent 16-foot Wayfarers, or one of several slightly larger boats, by the hour and maneuver among beautiful islands at **Sail Mahone Bay** (☎ **902/624-8864**) on the south shore near Lunenburg. Rentals are C$50 (US$33) for 3 hours, C$90 (US$60) for 8 hours, and C$100 (US$67) for 24 hours; a charter with a skipper is C$26 (US$17) per hour. The province's premier sailing experience is an excursion aboard the *Bluenose II,* virtually an icon for Atlantic Canada. See "Lunenburg," below.

SEA KAYAKING   Nova Scotia is increasingly attracting the attention of kayakers worldwide. Kayakers traveling on their own should be especially cautious on the Bay of Fundy side, since the massive tides create strong currents that overmatch even the fittest of paddlers. Nearly 40 kayak outfitters (and growing) do business in Nova Scotia, offering everything from 1-hour introductory paddles to intensive weeklong trips; consult the directory in *Doers and Dreamers.* Among the more respected outfitters is **Coastal Adventures,** P.O. Box 77, Tangier, NS B0J 3H0 (☎ **902/772-2774**). The company is headed up by veteran kayaker Scott Cunningham, who leads trips throughout the Maritimes and Newfoundland. For kayaking on the eastern side of Cape Breton, check with **Island Seafari,** 20 Paddys Lane, Louisbourg, NS B0A 1M0 (☎ **902/733-2309**).

WHALE WATCHING   If you're on the coast, it's likely you're not far from a whale-watching operation. Around two dozen outfits offer trips in search of finback, humpback, pilot, and minke whales, among others. The richest waters for whale watching are found on the **Fundy Coast,** where the endangered right whale is often seen feeding in summer. ✪ **Digby Neck** has the highest concentration of whale-watching excursions, but you'll find them in many other coves and harbors. Just ask the staff at visitor information centers to direct you to the whales.

2 Minas Basin & Cobequid Bay

If you're not content except off the beaten track, a detour along the **Minas Basin** and **Cobequid Bay** will be one of the highlights of your trip. With the exception of Truro, this region is rural and quiet and full of hidden surprises. You can turn down a dirt road, shut off your car's engine, and hear not much other than the wind and maybe a blackbird or two. And you can trek along spectacular hiking trails or picnic alone on a stretch of remote misty coast, literally watching the tides roll in.

There's also a rich history here, but it tends to be subtle. Don't look for the quaint seaside villages or surf-washed rocky coast for which Nova Scotia is famous; you'll have to wait until Yarmouth and the South Shore. The natural drama here is pegged to the region's profound remoteness and the powerful but silent tides, among the world's highest.

PARRSBORO

Samuel de Champlain stumbled on amethyst while exploring Partridge Island in 1604, and he brought the gemstones back to France to be cut, polished, and made part of the French crown jewels. A few centuries later and a few miles away near ✪ **Parrsboro,** another momentous discovery was made. In 1986, two scientists uncovered one of the world's largest caches of dinosaur fossils—some 100,000 pieces of bones dating back 200 million years, the cusp between the Jurassic and Triassic periods. The trove included skulls, teeth, and bones that belonged to dinosaurs, lizards, sharks, and crocodiles. These finds have gone a long way in expanding our understanding of prehistoric animals.

Parrsboro's richness in gems and fossils stems from a confluence of two factors: First, it's at the seam where two continents collided back in the days of primeval ooze. (Evidence: The fossils found here are the same as those you'll find in parts of Africa.) And second, the region's shores are exposed to the world's highest tides, meaning that constant erosion reveals new geological treasures.

The town is terminally somnolent and has only a handful of tourist amenities, but that only adds to its appeal.

ESSENTIALS

GETTING THERE   You can get to Parrsboro via Route 2 from either Springhill (46km/29 miles) or Truro (90km/56 miles).

VISITOR INFORMATION   The **Parrsboro Tourist Info Centre** (☎ 902/254-3266) faces the bandstand and small park in the village center. Summer, it's open daily 8:30am to 8:30pm.

ROCKHOUNDING

If you're an experienced rock hound, you know the drill. If you're a novice, you'll want guidance. Start with a trip to the **Fundy Geological Museum** (below) to get up to speed on the region's unique geology. Then sign up for a guided mineral- or fossil-collecting tour with either the museum or Eldon George.

Another option is to explore with **Dinatours** (☎ 902/254-3700), an outfit that maintains a headquarters and gift shop in a converted lobster boat at the causeway near the museum. Sonja Prell and Randy Corcoran offer various guided collecting tours both by foot and by boat around the Minas Basin. Costs range from C$40 (US$27) adult (C$20/US$13 children under 16) for a 6-hour boat trip to the mineral-rich Five Islands to C$20 (US$13) for a 2½-hour interpretive walking tour. (Some minimums apply on boat tours.)

Fundy Geological Museum. 6 Two Island Rd. ☎ **902/254-3814.** www.fundygeo museum.com. Admission C$3.50 (US$2.35) adults, C$1.75 (US$1.15) children (6–17), C$2.75 (US$1.85) seniors, C$9 (US$6) families. Summer daily 9:30am–5:30pm (closed Mon in winter).

Operated by the Cumberland Geological Society, this modern museum (built in 1993) does a fine job of putting the region's complex geology into context. It starts with displays and a video presentation to help you brush up on various epochs and eras (does Jurassic come before or after Triassic?). Then you can view various minerals and fossils on display and learn what to look for when you head out on your own. Kids seem especially fascinated by the dioramas featuring dinosaurs. There's more than enough to engage curious adults, but it's displayed in a fashion that makes it accessible to most children. Field trips are regularly made to mineral- and fossil-rich areas; ask at the front desk for a schedule.

Parrsboro Rock and Mineral Shop & Museum. 39 Whitehall Rd. ☎ **902/254-2981.** Free admission to shop; donations requested for museum. May–Christmas Eve Mon–Sat 9am–dusk, Sun by chance. From town, bear right at the war memorial and follow the road toward Ottawa House. Look for the shop on your left with the dinosaur in front.

Eldon George is a celebrity in rock-collecting circles for his extraordinary finds—including the world's smallest dinosaur footprints (they're about the size of a penny, from dinosaurs as big as sparrows). His shop sells prospecting gear along with raw and polished stones. You can see the famed tiny footprints, huge amethyst geodes, and other wondrous geological displays at the small museum. George himself is often here, and he's congenial and accessible. He and his son also lead guided 1- to 3-hour tours to collecting areas, starting at C$20 (US$13) per person (under 12 free).

HIKING

Just 3km (1.9 miles) southwest of town is **Partridge Island,** connected to the mainland by a pebbly causeway. You can park along the beach, and then hike out to the high tree-studded island, which offers trails for exploring. You'll get great views of Minas Basin and the stupendous tides. Watch the ground from time to time to ensure that you don't trip over amethyst or other rare stones like Champlain did.

Cape Chignecto Provincial Park (about 45km/28 miles west of Parrsboro on Route 209) has been developed over the past couple of years as one of Nova Scotia's premier hiking destinations, giving even the national park at Cape Breton a run for its money. This is by far the largest provincial park (10,500 acres) and is wild and remote, with the highest coastal cliffs on mainland Nova Scotia—as much as 600 feet above tide-raked Advocate Bay and the Bay of Fundy. A hiking trail circuit of about 30km (19 miles) runs along the cliffs and through the rugged backcountry. You can camp at some 40 sites spread among five locations. Day hikes to secluded beaches are also an option. Camping is C$14 (US$9) per night plus the C$2 (US$1.35) day-use fee; advance reservations are strongly recommended. For details, stop by the park's visitor center on Route 209 in Advocate Harbour or call ☎ **902/392-2085.**

WHERE TO STAY

Gillespie House Inn. 358 Main St., Parrsboro, NS B0M 1S0. ☎ **902/254-3196.** 5 units, none with bathroom. C$50–C$75 (US$33–US$50) double. Rates include continental breakfast. AE, MC, V. Closed Nov–Apr.

This handsome 1890s Victorian farmhouse sits on a shady rise—an easy walk from the village center—and was originally home to prominent shipbuilders and merchants. Innkeepers Lori Lynch and David Beattie offer a pleasant, homey atmosphere with five guest rooms sharing two bathrooms (plans call for creating two rooms with private bathrooms by summer 2000). Room no. 3 is the largest and brightest; room no. 5 has wonderful maple wainscoting. The public spaces are limited, though there are a small TV room and a first-floor sauna and hot tub. Ask about packages like the yoga and hiking weekends.

Maple Inn. 2358 Western Ave. (P.O. Box 457), Parrsboro, NS B0M 1S0. ☎ **902/254-3735.** 9 units, 6 with bathroom. C$65 (US$43) double without bathroom, C$75–C$85 (US$50–US$57) double with bathroom; C$115 (US$77) suite. Rates include full breakfast. AE, MC, V.

These two century-old homes were joined and served as the town hospital for 30 years but have been made over in a glossy country Victorian style with dried flowers and period furniture. The inn may be considered a bit overly renovated by those who prize historic authenticity, though it's comfortable and cheerful, and many of the guest rooms are spacious. The third-floor suite is perfect for families, with its king canopied bed and spare room with two twin beds (plus the only in-room TV). The three rooms with shared bathrooms offer especially good value; of these, cozy room no. 4 has a sitting area in the bay window.

Riverview Cottages. Rte. 2 (P.O. Box 71), Parrsboro, NS B0M 1S0. ☎ **902/254-2388.** 19 units. C$38–C$65 (US$25–US$43) double. No credit cards. Closed Nov 15–Apr 30.

This tidy assortment of simple rustic cottages is a mile from the village in a grassy riverside setting dotted with Adirondack chairs. Some of the cabins have been updated (I prefer the older, more rustic ones), 10 have kitchenettes, and a dozen have wood stoves. All guests have access to the free rowboats and canoes.

WHERE TO DINE

Stowaway Restaurant. 69 Main St. ☎ **902/254-3371.** Main courses C$6–C$13 (US$4–US$9). AE, ER, MC, V. Daily 9am–10pm (to 11pm July–Aug). CANADIAN.

The down-home Stowaway is a family-style restaurant, which is to say the food is good but not fancy, fresh but not elaborate. They do all their baking on the premises, and all meals are home-cooked—the fish in the fish-and-chips is local flounder. The pies are tasty, and a meal here is usually light on the wallet.

TRURO

Truro is the region's commercial hub, with an old-fashioned downtown surrounded by a sprawling mass of strip malls and shopping plazas. The town (pop. 12,000) has served as a traveler's crossroads since 1858, when the rail line between Montréal and Halifax first passed through. (Passenger rail service is still available.) With a convenient location just off the Trans-Canada Highway and a profusion of motels and chain restaurants, Truro still serves the traveler well. It is, however, best regarded as an intermediate stop rather than a destination.

ESSENTIALS

GETTING THERE   Truro is on Route 102, just south of the junction with Route 104 (the Trans-Canada Highway). Truro is served by **Via Rail** (☎ 800/361-8010;

www.viarail.ca), which connects Moncton to Halifax. The train station is at 104 Esplanade St., next to the downtown Esplanade Mall.

VISITOR INFORMATION   The **Truro Information Centre and Tourist Bureau** (☎ **902/893-2922**) is in a glass-walled pavilion downtown at Victoria Square (at the corner of Prince and Willow streets). Mid-May to early November, it's open daily 8am to 8pm.

EXPERIENCING THE TIDAL BORE

Let it be said: The **tidal bore** has to be one of Nova Scotia's more overrated attractions. It's quite interesting in theory—a bore is a low wave around a meter in height that rolls upstream ahead of the incoming tide, marking the moment the flows of rivers and brooks change direction. Bores are found in England, India, Brazil, and China but in North America are seen only around the Bay of Fundy, including some rivers in New Brunswick. The bore tends to be especially pronounced around Cobequid Bay, where the tides are greatly amplified (up to 50 ft.) thanks to its funnel-like shape.

I'm told the tidal bore can be truly impressive at times, but this hasn't been my experience. As seen from the shore, it's a curious geographic quirk and nothing more, offering little to inspire awe or wonder. If you happen to be in the area when the bore is due, by all means swing by and have a look. But I wouldn't rearrange travel plans to view it.

In Truro, you're directed to **Tidal Bore Park** along the Salmon River, located on a grassy slope next to a motel and restaurant (take Exit 14 off Route 102). Be forewarned: The site isn't all that charming. A busy highway runs along one side of the viewing area, and power lines clutter the horizon. However, you get a good view of the bore steadfastly chugging up the muddy river. Ask at the visitor center for tide times, check the local paper, or call **Dial-a-Tide** at ☎ **902/426-5494.**

A more heart-thumping way to experience the bore is to incorporate some outdoor adventure into the experience. Several **rafting outfitters** are based south of Truro on the Shubenacadie, Nova Scotia's largest river. Here you can spend 2 to 4 hours charting the bore's progress aboard motorized Zodiacs (rafts) that follow the wave's progress upstream. You'll typically don rain suits and prowl around the mouth of the river, then follow the bore upstream, crashing through the wave time and again. It's often about 3 feet high, but when the winds and moon work together the wave can crest at 8 feet high.

Tidal Bore Rafting (☎ **888/244-9283** or 902/752-0899) offers half-day adventures on the Shubenacadie that include a riverside lunch. **Shubenacadie Tidal Bore Park Rafting** (☎ **800/565-7238**) has 2- and 4-hour trips; as many as 75 adventurers at a time follow the bore in a herd of noisy Zodiacs. Other options include trips with **Shubenacadie River Adventure Tours** in South Maitland (☎ **888/ 878-8687** or 902/471-6595) and **Shubenacadie River Runners Ltd.** in Maitland (☎ **800/ 856-5061** or 902/261-2770). Plan on paying C$40 to C$65 (US$27 to US$43) per person, depending on the tour length. Times, of course, vary according to the tide.

WHERE TO STAY & DINE

Truro is at a major fork on the Trans-Canada Highway: You can continue on the Trans-Canada toward Cape Breton or veer south toward Halifax (about an hour away). Because of its key location, the town is home to about a dozen serviceable motels and B&Bs. Among the chains are **Comfort Inn,** 12 Meadow Dr. (☎ **800/228-5150** or 902/893-0330), and **Best Western Glengarry,** 150 Willow St. (☎ **800/567-4276** or 902/893-4311). The rooms are typically C$70 to C$90

(US$47 to US$60) and often book up early in summer; plan to call in advance for reservations if you're likely to arrive later in the day.

Palliser Motel & Restaurant. Tidal Bore Rd. (Rte. 102/Exit 14), Truro, NS B2N 5G6. ☎ **902/893-8951.** Fax 902/895-8475. E-mail palliser@auracom.com. 42 units. TV. C$47 (US$31) double. Rates include buffet breakfast. Discounts off-season. AE, DC, ER, MC, V.

This vintage 1950s motel is arrayed in a horseshoe pattern around a well-tended lawn sloping down toward the Palliser Restaurant and the tidal bore viewing area. The guest rooms are basic, as are the meals at the restaurant (fried scallops, fried haddock, lobster rolls). The Palliser has the most character of any Truro motel, but I don't foresee circumstances under which anyone would be compelled to spend more than a night. The tidal bore is floodlit at night for after-dark viewing.

WOLFVILLE

The trim Victorian village of **Wolfville** (pop. 3,500) has a distinctly New England feel to it, in both its handsome architecture and its layout—a small commercial downtown just 6 blocks long is surrounded by shady neighborhoods of elegant homes. And it's not hard to trace that sensibility to its source. The area was largely populated in the wake of the American Revolution by transplanted New Englanders, who forced off the Acadian settlers who had earlier done so much to tame the wilds.

The town has emerged in recent years as a popular destination for weekending Halifax residents, who come to relax at the many fine inns, wander the leafy streets, and explore the countryside. Also a consistent draw is the **Atlantic Theatre Festival** (☎ **800/337-6661** or 902/542-4242), which has attracted plaudits in the few years it has been presenting shows (including classics like *Tartuffe* and *Uncle Vanya*). Performances are staged throughout summer in a comfortable 500-seat theater. Reservations are encouraged; ticket prices are C$21 to C$38 (US$14 to US$25).

EXPLORING WOLFVILLE

The town's mainstay is handsome **Acadia University,** which has nearly as many full-time students as there are residents of Wolfville. The university's presence gives the small village an edgier, more youthful air. Don't miss the university's **Art Gallery at the Beveridge Arts Center** (☎ **902/585-1373**), which showcases both contemporary and historic Nova Scotian art.

Strolling the village is the activity of choice. The towering elms and maples shading the extravagant Victorian architecture provide the dappled light and rustling sounds for an ideal stroll. A good place to start is the **Wolfville Tourist Bureau** at Willow Park (☎ **902/542-7000**) on the north edge of the downtown. If you'd prefer to cover more ground, you can rent a mountain or touring bike at **Valley Stove and Cycle,** 232 Main St. (☎ **902/542-7280**).

One of the more intriguing sights in town occurs each summer day at dusk, in an unprepossessing park surrounded by a parking lot a block off Main Street. At **Robie Swift Park,** a lone chimney (dating from a long-gone dairy plant) rises straight up like a stumpy finger pointed at the heavens. Around sunset, between 25 and 100 chimney swifts flit about and then descend into the chimney for the night. Alas, the swifts have been declining in number in recent years, ever since predatory merlins starting nesting nearby and found the swifts easy targets. But you'll learn a lot by browsing the informational plaques posted here—you can read interesting tidbits such as this: No one knew where swifts migrated in winter until 1943, when explorers in the Peruvian jungle found natives wearing necklaces adorned with small aluminum rings. These, it turned out, were tracking bands placed on swifts by North American ornithologists.

At **Blomidon Provincial Park** (☎ 902/582-7319), 25km (16 miles) north of Route 101 (Exit 11), some 13.7km (8½ miles) of trail at the park take walkers through forests and along the coast. Among the most dramatic trails is the 6km (3.7-mile) **Jodrey Trail,** which follows towering cliffs that offer broad views over the Minas Basin.

Grand-Pré National Historic Site. Rte. 1, Grand-Pré. ☎ **902/542-3631.** Admission C$2.50 (US$1.65) adults, C$2 (US$1.35) seniors, C$1.10 (US75¢) children 6–16, C$7 (US$4.65) families. Daily 9am–6pm. Closed Nov to mid-May.

Long before roving New Englanders arrived in this region, hardworking Acadians had vastly altered the landscape. They did this in large part by constructing a series of dikes outfitted with ingenious log valves, allowing farmers to convert the saltwater marshes to productive farmland. At Grand-Pré, a short drive east of Wolfville and just off Route 1, you can learn about these dikes along with the tragic history of the Acadians, who populated the Minas Basin between 1680 and their expulsion in 1755.

More a memorial park than a living history exhibit, Grand-Pré ("great meadow") offers superbly tended grounds that are excellent for idling or enjoying a picnic lunch. Among the handful of buildings on the grounds is a graceful **stone church,** built in 1922 on the presumed site of the original church. Evangeline Bellefontaine, the revered (albeit fictional) heroine of Longfellow's epic poem, was said to be born here; look in the garden for the statue of the tragic heroine, created in 1920 by Canadian sculptor Philippe Hébert—the image has been reproduced widely since.

WHERE TO STAY

Gingerbread House Inn. 8 Robie Tufts Dr. (P.O. Box 819), Wolfville, NS B0P 1X0. ☎ **888/ 542-1458** or 902/542-1458. Fax 902/542-4718. www.gingerbreadhouse.ns.ca. E-mail hedly@gingerbreadhouse.ns.ca. 10 units. TV. C$69–C$79 (US$46–US$53) double; C$109–C$145 (US$73–US$97) suite. Rates include full breakfast. Ask about theater packages. MC, V.

The ornate Gingerbread House Inn was first the carriage house for the building now housing Victoria's Historic Inn (below). A former owner went woodshop wild, adding all manner of swirly accoutrements and giving the place a convincingly authentic air. The guest rooms are a modern interpretation of the gingerbread style and generally comfortable, though the two rooms in back are dark and small. The floral Carriage House Suite is the most spacious, with luxe touches like a propane fireplace and two-person Jacuzzi. The budget choice is the lovely Terrace Room, which is minuscule but has a lovely private deck on the second floor under a gracefully arching tree. The breakfasts tend toward the elaborate and are served by candlelight.

✪ **Tattingstone Inn.** 434 Main St. (P.O. Box 98), Wolfville, NS B0P 1X0. ☎ **800/ 565-7696** or 902/542-7696. Fax 902/542-4427. E-mail tattingstone@ns.sympatico.ca. 10 units. A/C TV TEL. C$89–C$138 (US$59–US$92) double; C$168 (US$112) suite. AE, MC, V.

"We sell romance and relaxation," says innkeeper Betsy Harwood. And that pretty well sums it up. This handsome Italianate-Georgian mansion from 1874 overlooks the village's main artery and is furnished with a mix of reproductions and antiques, as well as traditional and modern art. The attitude isn't over-the-top Victorian as you might guess by looking at the manse, and children over 12 are welcome. The Carriage House rooms tend to be smaller but are still pleasant and showcase fine examples of modern Canadian art. The spacious dining room is rather refined and boasts white tablecloths and Doric columns. Ask for a seat on the enclosed porch, which captures the lambent early-evening light. Dinner is served daily in summer 5:30 to 9:30pm, with entrees at

C$16 to C$26 (US$11 to US$17). House specialties are rack of lamb and chicken with pear-and-ginger sauce; the latter uses pears grown on the property. Facilities include a heated outdoor pool, a steam room, and a tennis court.

Victoria's Historic Inn. 416 Main St., Wolfville, NS B0P 1X0. ☎ **800/556-5744** or 902/542-5744. Fax 902/542-7794. 15 units. A/C TV TEL. C$95–C$175 (US$63–US$117) double. Rates include full breakfast. AE, ER, MC, V.

The sturdy Queen Anne–style Victoria's was built by apple mogul William Chase in 1893 and is architecturally elaborate, featuring bold pediments and massed pavilions. Inside, the effect is a bit as if you'd wandered into one of those stereoscopic views of a Victorian parlor. While the nearby Tattingstone Inn (above) resists theme decor, Victoria's embraces it. There's dense mahogany and cherry woodwork throughout, along with exceptionally intricate ceilings. The deluxe Chase Suite features a large sitting room with a gas fireplace and an oak mantle. The less-expensive third-floor rooms are smaller and somewhat less historic in flavor.

WHERE TO DINE

Al's Homestyle Deli. 314 Main St. ☎ **902/542-5908.** No reservations. All selections C$2–C$4 (US$1.35–US$2.65). V. Mon–Thurs 9am–6:30pm, Fri–Sun 9am–9pm. DELI.

Randy and Linda Davidson now operate the place, but Al Waddell's popular recipes for sausages live on: choose from Polish, German, hot Italian, and honey garlic. Buy some links to cook later or order up a quick road meal. You won't find a better cheap lunch: A sausage on a bun with a cup of soup will run you less than C$5.

Chez la Vigne. 117 Front St. ☎ **902/542-5077.** Reservations suggested. Lunch C$6–C$11 (US$4.30–US$8); dinner C$13–C$25 (US$9–US$17). AE, ER, MC, V. Daily 11am–10pm (to 9pm in winter). INTERNATIONAL.

Chez la Vigne is on a quiet side street a few steps off Main Street. The place is informal and comfortable, and the chef maintains the welcome philosophy that everyone should be able to afford a good meal. Dishes range from the country simple (paella for two) to the rather more complex (rabbit stuffed with herbs and rice). The quality varies but more often than not is very good.

3 Annapolis Royal: Nova Scotia's Most Historic Town

Annapolis Royal is arguably Nova Scotia's most historic town—it even bills itself as "Canada's birthplace," with justification. The nation's first permanent settlement was established at Port Royal, across the river from the present-day Annapolis Royal, in 1605 by a group of doughty settlers who included Samuel de Champlain. (Champlain called the beautiful Annapolis Basin "one of the finest harbours that [I've] seen on all these coasts.") The strategic importance of this well-protected harbor was proven in the tumultuous later years, when a series of forts was constructed on the low hills overlooking the water.

Annapolis Royal is truly a treat to visit. Because the region was largely overlooked by later economic growth (trade and fishing moved to the Atlantic side of the peninsula), it requires little in the way of imagination to see Annapolis Royal as it once was. (The current population is just 700.) The original settlement was rebuilt on the presumed site. Fort Anne overlooks the upper reaches of the basin, much as it did when abandoned in 1854. And the village itself maintains much of its original historic charm, with narrow streets and historic buildings fronting the now-placid waterfront. For anyone curious about Canada's early history, Annapolis Royal is one of Nova Scotia's don't-miss destinations.

ESSENTIALS

GETTING THERE   Annapolis is at Exit 22 of Route 101, 206km (128 miles) from Halifax and 133km (82 miles) from Yarmouth.

VISITOR INFORMATION   The **Annapolis District Tourist Bureau** (☎ 902/ 532-5454) is 1.2km (0.7 miles) north of the town center (follow Prince Albert Road and look for the Annapolis Royal Tidal Generating Station). Summer hours are daily 8am to 8pm (9am to 5pm in spring and fall).

EXPLORING THE TOWN

Start by seeking out the tourist bureau (above) at the **Annapolis Royal Tidal Generating Station** (☎ 902/532-5454), where the extreme tides have been harnessed to produce electricity. The dam is opened when the tide flows in, then closed before it flows out. Water is then released through turbines to generate electricity. It's North America's only tidal generator and the world's largest straight-flow turbine. Learn about the generator at the free exhibit upstairs from the visitor center. Informative displays, models, and a video will explain the whole endeavor of producing electricity from the tides.

Before leaving the center, request a copy of the free *Footprints with Footnotes* walking-tour brochure. The annotated map provides architectural and historic context for a stroll around the downtown and waterfront. Take a moment to note that as you walk down lower St. George Street, you're walking down the oldest town street in Canada.

❂ **Fort Anne National Historic Site.** Entrance on St. George St. ☎ **902/532-2321.** Admission to grounds free; museum C$2.75 (US$1.85) adults, C$2.25 (US$1.50) seniors, C$1.35 (US90¢) children, C$7 (US$4.65) families. May 15–Oct 15 daily 9am–6pm; offseason by appointment only (grounds open year-round).

What you'll likely remember most from a visit here are the impressive grassy earthworks that cover some 35 acres of high ground overlooking the confluence of the Annapolis River and Allains Creek. The first fort here was built by the French around 1643, and since then dozens of buildings and fortifications have occupied this site. You can visit the 1708 gunpowder magazine (the oldest building of any Canadian National Historic Site), then peruse the museum in the 1797 British field officer's quarters. The model of the site as it appeared in 1710 is particularly intriguing. If you find all the history a bit tedious, ask a guide if you can borrow a croquet set and practice your technique on the lush rolling lawns. A good strategy for visiting is to come during the day to tour the museum and get a feel for the lay of the land, then return for sunset, long after the bus tours have departed, to walk the Perimeter Trail with its river and valley vistas.

❂ **Historic Gardens.** 441 St. George St. ☎ **902/532-7018.** Admission C$5 (US$3.35) adults, C$3.50 (US$2.35) seniors/students, C$11 (US$7) families. Mid-May to mid-Oct daily 8am–dusk.

You don't need to be a flower nut to enjoy an hour or two at these exceptional gardens. Created in 1981, the 10-acre grounds are uncommonly beautiful, with a mix of formal and informal gardens from varied epochs. Set on a gentle hill, the gardens overlook a beautiful salt marsh (now diked and farmed) and include a geometric Victorian garden, a knot garden, a rock garden, and a colorful perennial border garden. Rose fanciers should allow plenty of time—some 2,000 rose bushes track the history of rose cultivation from the earliest days through the Victorian era to the present. A garden cafe (see below) offers an enticing spot for lunch.

⭕ **Port Royal National Historic Site.** 10km (6.2 miles) south of Rte. 1, Granville Ferry (turn left shortly after passing the tidal generating station). ☎ **902/532-2321.** Admission C$2.75 (US$1.85) adults, C$2.25 (US$1.50) seniors, C$1.35 (US90¢) children, C$8 (US$5) families. May 15–Oct 15 daily 9am–6pm.

Canada's first permanent settlement, Port Royal was located on an attractive point with sweeping views of the Annapolis Basin. Those settlers who survived the dreadful winter of 1604 on an island in the St. Croix River (along the current Maine–New Brunswick border) moved to this better-protected location and lived here for 8 years in a high style that approached decadent given the harsh surroundings. Many of the handsome French-style farmhouse buildings were designed by Samuel de Champlain to re-create the comfort they might've enjoyed at home. Though the original settlement was abandoned and eventually destroyed, this 1939 re-creation is convincing in all the details. You'll find a handful of costumed interpreters engaged in traditional handicrafts like woodworking, and they're happy to fill you in on life in the colony during those difficult early years, an "age of innocence" when the French first forged an alliance with local natives.

WHERE TO STAY

Garrison House Inn. 350 St. George St., Annapolis Royal, NS B0S 1A0. ☎ **902/532-5750.** Fax 902/532-5501. www.come.to/garrison. E-mail garhed@ns.sympatico.ca. 7 units. C$65–C$95 (US$43–US$63) double. Rates include full breakfast. AE, MC, V. Street parking. Open May–Oct; call in advance for weekends the rest of the year.

The Garrison House Inn sits across from Fort Anne in the town center and has bedded and fed guests since it opened to accommodate fort officers in 1854. Flowers make the inn welcoming, and the guest rooms are nicely appointed with antiques, some worn, some pristine. There's no air-conditioning, but fans are provided; the top floor can still get a bit stuffy on warm days. Room no. 2 is appealing, with wide pine floors, a braided rug, and a settee, but it faces the street and at times can be a bit noisy; room no. 7 is tucked in the back away from the St. George Street hubbub and has two skylights to let in a wonderfully dappled light. The inn's restaurant is recommended below.

The Moorings. P.O. Box 118, Granville Ferry, NS B0S 1K0. ☎ **902/532-2146.** E-mail tileston@tartannet.ns.ca. 3 units, 1 with bathroom. C$49 (US$33) double without bathroom, C$52 (US$35) double with bathroom. Rates include full breakfast. MC, V. Closed Oct 31–Apr 30.

Across the river from Annapolis Royal is the personable and appealing Moorings, a B&B with great views of the town and Fort Anne across the water. This spot is much less "historic" than Annapolis's high-Victorian inns but is comfortably decorated with brushed walls and an attractive mix of antique furniture and modern art. Guests have run of the two downstairs parlors, one of which has a TV. One guest room has a private bathroom, but it was actually my least favorite. The two others face the water and are brighter and more cheerful. The yellow room is flooded with afternoon light and has a half-bathroom in the room; showers are in the shared bathroom in the hall.

Queen Anne Inn. 494 St. George St., Annapolis Royal, NS B0S 1A0. ☎ **902/532-7850.** Fax 902/532-2078. www.queenanneinn.ns.ca. E-mail queenanne@queenanneinn.ns.ca. 10 units. C$85–C$130 (US$57–US$87) double. Rates include full breakfast. MC, V.

This Second Empire mansion (1865) looks like the city hall of a small city. You won't miss it driving into town. Like Hillsdale House across the street, the Queen Anne (built for the sister of the Hillsdale's owner) has benefited from a preservation-minded owner, who has restored the Victorian detailing to its former luster. This includes the zebra-striped dining-room floor (alternating planks of oak and maple) and the grand central staircase. The guest rooms are quite elegant, furnished appropriate to the Victorian era. With their towering elms, the parklike grounds are shady and inviting.

WHERE TO DINE

Fat Pheasant. 200 St. George St. ☎ **902/532-5315.** Reservations suggested on weekends and Mon. Main courses C$4.50–C$10 (US$3–US$7) at lunch, C$13–C$20 (US$9–US$13) at dinner. V. Daily 11:30am–9pm (usually to 10pm in summer). ECLECTIC.

The Fat Pheasant offers creative dining on two levels in what used to be the town post office. The decor is a blend of modern and traditional, with eggplant walls, oak antiques, and an unobtrusive pheasant theme. The menu is likewise creative, and the chef manages to surprise even with run-of-the-mill items. Lunches feature a selection of pastas, sandwiches, and omelets. At dinner, you might start with an appetizer of fried camembert with cranberry chutney or roasted onion and garlic soup. Main courses include lamb chops with mint-citrus glaze, spicy creole pork (with a "cooling" Greek salad), and seafood pasta.

Garrison House. In the Garrison House Inn, 350 St. George St. ☎ **902/532-5750.** Reservations recommended in summer. Main courses C$12–C$17 (US$8–US$11). AE, MC, V. Daily 5:30–8:30pm. ECLECTIC.

Garrison House is the most intimate and attractive of the village's restaurants. Each of the three cozy dining rooms in this historic home across from Fort Anne has a different feel—perhaps colonial colors, perhaps black Windsor chairs and modern piscine art. My favorite is the one with the green floors and the humpback whale. The menu is also tricky to categorize, with starters like Acadian seafood chowder and carrot vichyssoise with coconut, and entrees ranging from jambalaya to scallops in Vietnamese curry to a simple pasta with garden vegetables. There are also individual-serving pizzas.

✪ **Newman's.** 218 St. George St. ☎ **902/532-5502.** Reservations recommended. Main courses C$7–C$25 (US$4.65–US$17). V. July–Aug daily 11:30am–9pm; June and Sept Tues–Sun 11:30am–9pm; May and Oct Tues–Sun 11:30am–2:30pm and 5:30–8:30pm. SEAFOOD.

Newman's is an informal spot in an out-of-place pink Spanish Revival building on the historic waterfront. But don't let that confuse you. Inside, you'll find some of the most carefully prepared food in Nova Scotia, with an eye to fresh produce and meats. The place has been run by the same folks for 20 years, and they haven't let standards slip. It's hard to nail down a specialty—the kitchen does so much so well. The seafood is especially delectable (grilled Atlantic salmon with tarragon sauce, halibut sautéed with sliced almonds), as are the generous old-fashioned desserts (bananas with chocolate and whipped cream, homemade strawberry shortcake). An unexpected bonus: The wine list is surprisingly creative.

4 Kejimkujik National Park

About 46km (28 miles) southeast of Annapolis Royal is a popular national park a world apart from coastal Nova Scotia. **Kejimkujik National Park,** founded in 1968, is in the heart of south-central Nova Scotia, and it is to lakes and bogs what the south coast is to fishing villages and fog. Bear and moose are the full-time residents; park visitors are the transients. The park, largely scooped and shaped during the last glacial epoch, is about 20% water, which makes it especially popular with canoeists. A handful of trails also weave through the park, but hiking is limited; the longest hike can be done in 2 hours. Bird-watchers are also drawn to the park in search of the

205 species that have been seen here and at the Seaside Adjunct of the park, a 22-square-kilometer coastal holding west of Liverpool. Among the more commonly seen birds are pileated woodpeckers and loons, and at night you can listen for the raspy call of the barred owl.

ESSENTIALS

GETTING THERE Kejimkujik National Park is about midway on Kejimkujik Scenic Drive (Route 8), which extends 115km (71 miles) between Annapolis Royal and Liverpool. The village of Maitland Bridge (pop. 130) is near the park's entrance. Plan on about 2 hours' drive from Halifax.

VISITOR INFORMATION The **visitor center** (☎ 902/682-2772) features slide programs and exhibits about the park's natural history. It's open daily: June 18 to September 5 8:30am to 9pm, September 6 to October 10 to 6pm, and October 11 to June 17 to 4:30pm.

FEES Mid-May to late October, daily fees are C$3.25 (US$2.15) adults, C$2.50 (US$1.65) seniors, C$1.75 (US$1.15) children 6 to 16, and C$8 (US$5) families; 4-day passes are available in all categories for the price of 3 days.

EXPLORING THE PARK

The park's 381 square kilometers of forest, lake, and bog are peaceful and remote. Part of what makes the terrain so appealing is the lack of access by car. One short forked park road from Route 8 gets you partway into the park, but then you need to continue by foot or canoe. A stop at the visitor center is well worthwhile, both for the exhibits on the region's natural history and for a **preliminary walk** on one of the three short trails. The Beech Grove loop (2.2km/1.4 miles) takes you around a glacial hill called a drumlin. The park has a taped walking tour available for use; ask at the information center.

Canoeing is the optimal means of voyaging in the park. Bring your own or rent a canoe at **Jake's Landing** for C$4 (US$2.65) per hour or C$20 (US$13) per day. (The same rate applies to rentals of bikes, paddleboats, kayaks, and rowboats.) Canoeists can cobble together wilderness excursions from one lake to the other, some involving slight portaging. Multiday trips are easily arranged to backcountry campsites and are the best way to get to know the park. Canoe route maps are provided at the visitor center. Rangers also lead short guided canoe trips for novices.

The park also has 15 **walking trails,** ranging from short easy strolls to, well, longer easy strolls. (There's no elevation gain to speak of in the park.) The 6km (3.7-mile) **Hemlocks and Hardwoods Trail** loops through stately groves of 300-year-old hemlocks; the 3km (1.9-mile) **Merrymakedge Beach Trail** skirts a lakeshore to end at a beach. A free map available at the visitor center has trails described on the reverse.

CAMPING

Backcountry camping is the park's chief draw. The canoe-in and hike-in sites are assigned individually, which means you needn't worry about noisy neighbors. Backcountry rangers keep the sites in top shape, and each site is stocked with firewood for the night, with the wood included in the campsite fee. Most sites can handle a maximum of six campers. Naturally, there's high demand for the best sites; you're better off here midweek, when fewer weekenders are down from Halifax. You can also reserve backcountry sites up to 60 days in advance for an extra C$4.25 (US$2.85); call the **visitor center** at ☎ 902/682-2772. The backcountry camping fee is C$16 (US$11) per night.

The park's drive-in campground at **Jeremys Bay** offers 329 sites, some quite close to the water's edge. Campground rates are C$14 (US$9) per night. (During the shoulder seasons in spring and fall, campsites are C$10/US$6.) Starting early each May, you can make reservations at the drive-in campground for an extra C$7 (US$4.65) by calling ☎ **800/414-6765.**

5 From Digby to Yarmouth: A Taste of the Other Nova Scotia

This 113km (70-mile) stretch of coast is bracketed by two towns that serve as gateways to Nova Scotia. Whereas the South Shore—the stretch between Yarmouth and Halifax—serves to confirm popular conceptions of Nova Scotia (small fishing villages, shingled homes), the Digby-to-Yarmouth route seems determined to confound them. Look for Acadian enclaves, fishing villages with more corrugated steel than weathered shingle, miles of sandy beaches, and spruce-topped basalt cliffs that seem transplanted from Labrador.

DIGBY

The unassuming port town of **Digby** (pop. 2,300) is on the water at Digby Gap—where the Annapolis River finally forces an egress through the North Mountain coastal range. At the south end of the broad expanse of the Annapolis Basin, it's home to the world's largest inshore scallop fleet, which drags the ocean bottom for tasty and succulent Digby scallops. Ferries to Saint John, New Brunswick, sail year-round from a dock a few miles west of downtown.

The town is named after Adm. Sir Robert Digby, who arrived from New England in 1783. He led a group of loyalists who found relations with their neighbors somewhat strained following the unfortunate outcome of the War of Independence. Today Digby is an active community where life centers around fishing boats, wood-frame houses, and no-frills seafood restaurants. It's certainly worth a brief stop when you're heading to or from the ferry.

ESSENTIALS

GETTING THERE   Digby is Nova Scotia's gateway for those arriving from Saint John, New Brunswick, via ferry. The ferry terminal is on Route 303 west of Digby. If you're arriving by ferry and want to visit the town before pushing on, watch for signs directing you downtown from the bypass; otherwise, you'll end up on Route 101 before you know it. From other parts of Nova Scotia, Digby is accessible via Exit 26 off Route 101.

VISITOR INFORMATION   The province maintains a **Visitor Information Center** on Route 303 (☎ **902/245-2201**), on your right shortly after you disembark from the Saint John ferry. There's also the municipal **Visitor Information Centre** on the harbor at 110 Montague Row (☎ **902/245-5714**). Mid-June to mid-October, it's open daily 9am to 8:30pm.

EXPLORING DIGBY

Water Street runs along the water (of course), with its views of the scallop fleet from various points. A narrow grassy promenade extends from the visitor center to the small downtown; parking is usually plentiful.

Near the visitor center is the **Admiral Digby Museum,** 95 Montague Row (☎ **902/245-6322**). The Georgian home dates from the mid–19th century; inside

Whale Watching at Digby Neck

The thin strand of **Digby Neck** extends southwest about 75km (46 miles) from the town of Digby. You might guess from its appearance on a map that it's a low scrubby sandspit. You'd be wrong. In fact, it's a long bony finger of high ridges, spongy bogs, dense forest, and expansive ocean views. The last two knuckles of this narrow peninsula are islands, both of which are connected via 10-minute ferries across straits swept with currents as strong as 9 knots.

In the Bay of Fundy just offshore, ocean currents mingle and the vigorous tides cause upwelling, bringing a rich assortment of plankton to the surface. That makes it an all-you-can-eat buffet for cetaceans, which feed on these minuscule bits of plant and animal. As the fishing industry has declined, the number of fishers offering whale-watching tours has boomed. As of late 1999, there were 11 whale-watching outfitters on Digby Neck and the islands, up from just 3 in the mid-1990s. Most are down-home operations on converted lobster boats—don't expect the gleaming whale-watch ships with comfy seats and full-service cafeterias you find in larger cities or on the New England coast.

Declining inshore herring stocks means tours need to head farther out into the bay than in years past, but you'll almost always have sightings of fin, minke, or humpback whales. Right, sperm, blue, and pilot whales, along with the infrequent orcas, have also been seen over the years. Plan on spending around C$35 to C$45 (US$23 to US$) for a 3- to 4-hour cruise. **Mariner Cruises** in Westport on Brier Island (☎ **800/239-2189** or 902/839-2346) sails aboard the 45-foot *Chad and Sisters Two,* with a heated cabin. Whale- and bird-watching tours are offered. **Pirate's Cove Whale Cruises** in Tiverton (☎ **888/480-0004** or 902/839-2242) has been leading offshore cruises since 1990; three tours are offered daily aboard the 34-foot M/V *Todd.* **Petite Passage Whale Watch** (☎ **902/834-2226**) sails out of East Ferry aboard a 37-foot, 20-passenger boat with a partially covered deck.

For a saltier adventure, **Ocean Explorations** (☎ **902/839-2417**) offers tours on rigid-hulled inflatable Zodiacs. The largest boat holds up to a dozen passengers and moves with tremendous speed and dampness through the fast currents and frequent chop around the islands and the open bay. You're provided with survival suits for warmth and safety.

you'll find a wide selection of artifacts, from documentary photos of a Mi'kmaq porpoise hunt in the 1930s to ship models and early Victorian fashions. Also on display are 2 of the 100 toy stuffed dogs made of old coats by local craftsperson Alma Melanson. June to August, it's open Tuesday to Sunday 9am to 5pm; September to mid-October, hours are Monday to Friday 9am to 5pm; open by appointment the rest of the year. Admission is by donation.

You can learn about the scallop industry at the **Lady Vanessa** fisheries exhibit, 34 Water St. (☎ **902/245-4555**). Set in a 98-foot scallop dragger, it features videos and exhibits about the prized local catch. Summer, it's open daily 10am to 5pm; admission is C$1.75 (US$1.15).

WHERE TO STAY

Digby is an entryway for those arriving and departing by ferry and so has a number of basic motels. Two within walking distance of the promenade and downtown are the cottage-style efficiency units of **Seawinds Motel,** 90 Montague Row (☎ 902/ 245-2573), which offers good sea views at C$65 to C$75 (US$43 to US$50) double; and the more basic **Siesta Motel,** across the street at 81 Montague Row (☎ 902/ 245-2568), at C$50 to C$65 (US$33 to US$43) double.

✪ **The Pines.** Shore Rd., P.O. Box 70, Digby, NS B0V 1A0. ☎ **800/667-4637** or 902/245-2511. Fax 902/245-6133. www.gov.ns.ca/resorts. 84 units, 30 cottages. TV TEL. C$135–C$280 (US$90–US$187) double; C$280 (US$187) and up cottage. AE, DC, DISC, ER, MC, V. Closed mid-Oct to mid-May.

The Pines, built in 1929 in a Norman château style on 300 acres with marvelous Annapolis Basin views, represents an era when old money headed to fashionable resorts for an entire summer. The inn is owned/operated by the province of Nova Scotia and should silence those who believe that government can't do anything right. The imposing stucco-and-stone building is surrounded by the eponymous pines, which rustle softly in the wind. Throughout, the emphasis is more on comfort than on historical verisimilitude, though the gracious lobby features old-world touches like Corinthian capitals, floral couches, and parquet floors. The guest rooms vary slightly as to size and views (ask for a water-view room), and all now have ceiling fans, though air-conditioning is on the way. The cottages are one- to three-bedroom and most feature wood fireplaces.

Dining: The Annapolis Dining Room is open for all three meals, and the cuisine might best be described as Nova Scotian with a French flair. Look for entrees (C$14 to C$27/US$9 to US$18) like roasted pork tenderloin with apples and cider sauce or poached char infused with green Chinese tea. Dinner reservations are advised.

Amenities: Concierge, babysitting, dry cleaning/laundry, VCR rentals, afternoon tea, turndown service, courtesy car to ferry, tour desk; pool and fitness center, hiking trails, shuffleboard, bike rentals, two night-lit tennis courts, 18-hole golf course, sauna, children's center, shopping arcade.

WHERE TO DINE

A meal at **The Pines** (above) offers a grand setting. Otherwise, the handful of downtown seafood restaurants are more or less interchangeable, serving up heaps of the local specialty: fried scallops. Of these, the spot with the best harbor view is the **Fundy Restaurant,** 34 Water St. (☎ 902/245-4950); ask for a seat in the solarium. It's open daily 11am to 8pm. If you'd like your scallops with a more exotic tang, head to the **Kaywin Restaurant,** 51 Water St. (☎ 902/245-5543), an above-average Chinese-Canadian restaurant serving scallops stir-fried with vegetables, as well as the more common fried variant. It's open Monday to Saturday 11am to 10pm.

YARMOUTH

The constant lament of **Yarmouth** restaurateurs and shopkeepers is this: The summer tourists who steadily stream off the incoming ferries rarely linger long enough to appreciate the city before they mash the accelerator and speed off to more popular places along the coast. There might be a reason for that: Yarmouth may be a pleasant burg offering some noteworthy historic architecture from the golden age of seafaring, but the town is not terribly unique and thus not high on my list of places I'd choose to spend a few days. It's too big (pop. 7,800) to be charming yet too small to generate urban buzz and vitality. It has more of the flavor of a handy pit stop than a destination.

By all means plan to dawdle a few hours while awaiting the ferry (Portland-bound passengers could enjoyably spend the night here before their early-morning departure) or to while away an afternoon looping around the coast. Take the time to follow the self-guided walking tour, enjoy a meal, or wander around the newly renovated waterfront, where efforts to coax it back from decrepitude have started to take root.

ESSENTIALS

GETTING THERE   About 300km (186 miles) from Halifax, Yarmouth is where two of the province's principal highways—Route 101 and Route 103—converge. It's the gateway for two daily ferries (seasonal) connecting to Maine. **Air Nova** serves Yarmouth with infrequent flights; call ☎ 888/247-2262 or 902/742-2450. The airport is a few minutes' drive east of town on Starrs Road.

VISITOR INFORMATION   The **Yarmouth Visitor Centre** is at 228 Main St. (☎ 902/742-6639 or 902/742-5033), just up the hill from the ferry in a modern shingled building you can't miss. Both the provincial and the municipal tourist offices are here. May to October, they're open daily 8am to 7pm.

EXPLORING THE TOWN

The tourist office and the local historical society publish a very informative **walking-tour brochure** covering downtown Yarmouth. It's well worth requesting at the visitor center (above). The guide offers general tips on what to look for in local architectural styles (how *do* you tell the difference between Georgian and classic revival?), as well as brief histories of significant buildings. The whole tour is 4km (2½ miles) long.

The most scenic side trip—and an ideal excursion by bike or car—is to ۞ **Cape Forchu** and the Yarmouth Light. Head west on Main Street (Route 1) for 2.2km (1.4 miles) from the visitor center, then turn left at the horse statue. The road winds picturesquely out to the cape, past seawalls and working lobster wharves, meadows and old homes. When the road finally ends, you'll be at the red-and-white–striped concrete lighthouse marking the harbor's entrance. (This modern lighthouse dates to the early 1960s, when it replaced a much older octagonal light that succumbed to wind and time.) In the visitor center in the keeper's house is a tiny photographic exhibit on the cape's history. Leave enough time to ramble around the dramatic rock-and-grass bluffs—part of Leif Ericson Picnic Park—surrounding the lighthouse. Don't miss the short trail out to the point below the light. Bright-red picnic tables and benches are scattered about; bring lunch or dinner if the weather is right.

The two-story **Firefighters Museum of Nova Scotia,** 451 Main St. (☎ 902/742-5525), will appeal mostly to confirmed fire buffs, historians, and impressionable kids. The museum is home to a broadly varied collection of early fire-fighting equipment, with hand-drawn pumpers as the centerpiece. Also showcased are uniforms, badges, helmets, and pennants. Look for the photos of notable Nova Scotian fires ("Hot Shots"). Admission is C$2 (US$1.35) adults and C$4 (US$2.65) families. July and August, it's open Monday to Saturday 9am to 9pm and Sunday 10am to 5pm; the rest of the year, it's open only limited hours Monday to Saturday.

The **Yarmouth County Museum,** 22 Collins St. (☎ 902/742-5539), consists of the museum itself (with displays of seafaring artifacts, Victorian furniture, paintings, costumes, and examples of early decorative arts) and the **Pelton-Fuller House** next door. The Queen Anne–style house (ca. 1895) was the summer home of Primrose and Alfred Fuller, who, a Nova Scotia native, was best known as the founder of the famed Fuller Brush Co. The home was donated to the museum in 1996 and is richly furnished with antiques, much as it was left. Admission to the museum and house is C$4 (US$2.65) adults (C$2.50/US$1.65 museum or house only), C$2 (US$1.35) students, C$1 (US65¢) children, and C$8 (US$5) families. It's open June to mid-October, Monday to Saturday 9am to 5pm and Sunday 2 to 5pm; mid-October to May, hours are Tuesday to Sunday 2 to 5pm. The house is open summers only.

WHERE TO STAY

Yarmouth is home to a number of chain motels. Among them are the **Best Western Mermaid Motel,** 545 Main St. (☎ **800/772-2774** or 902/742-7821), costing C$90 to C$100 (US$60 to US$67) double; **Comfort Inn,** 96 Starrs Rd. (☎ **902/ 742-1119**), C$70 to C$100 (US$47 to US$67) double; and the **Rodd Grand Hotel,** 417 Main St. (☎ **902/742-2446**), C$80 to C$115 (US$53 to US$77) double.

Churchill Mansion Inn. Rte. 1 (15km/9 miles west of Yarmouth), Yarmouth, NS B5A 4A5. ☎ **902/649-2818.** 10 units. C$40–C$60 (US$27–US$40) double. DISC, MC, V. Closed Nov to mid-May.

From 1891 to 1920, the Churchill Mansion was occupied just 6 weeks a year, when Aaron Flint Churchill, a Yarmouth native who amassed a shipping fortune in Atlanta, Georgia, returned to Nova Scotia to summer. This extravagant mansion with its garish furnishings, on a low bluff overlooking the highway and a lake, was converted to an inn in 1981 by Bob Benson, who's likely to be found on a ladder or with a hammer in hand when you arrive ("It never ends," he sighs). The home is furnished with flea-market antiques and a spooky portrait of Churchill in the hall. The mansion boasts some original carpeting, lamps, and woodwork, though it can be a little threadbare, flaky, or water-stained in other spots. This is a fine place for those who like quirky history and don't mind a little mustiness and for kids with lively imaginations.

Harbour's Edge B&B. 12 Vancouver St., Yarmouth NS B5A 2N8. ☎ **902/742-2387.** Fax 902/742-4471. E-mail harboursedge@klis.com. 3 units, 1 with private hall bathroom. C$86–C$98 (US$57–US$65) double. Rates include full breakfast. MC, V. Head toward Cape Forchu (above); watch for the inn shortly after turning at the horse statue.

This exceptionally attractive early Victorian home (1864) sits on 2 leafy acres and 250 feet of harbor frontage. You can lounge on the lawn while watching herons and king-fishers below, making it hard to believe you're right in town and only a few minutes from the ferry terminal. The Harbour's Edge opened in 1997 after 3 years of intensive restoration (it had been abandoned for 5 years). All the high-ceilinged guest rooms have handsome spruce floors and are lightly furnished, which serves to highlight the architectural integrity of the design. The very attractive Audrey Kenney Room is the largest. The Ellen Brown Room is my favorite—it has fine oak furniture and a great harbor view, though the private bathroom is down the hall.

Lakelawn Motel. 641 Main St., Yarmouth, NS B5A 1K2. ☎ **902/742-3588.** E-mail mackie@auracom.com. 31 units. TV. C$49–C$64 (US$33–US$43) double. AE, DC, DISC, ER, MC, V. Closed Nov–Apr.

The well-kept Lakelawn offers basic motel rooms done up in colors that were fashionable some years ago, like harvest orange and brown plaid. It's been a downtown Yarmouth mainstay since the 1950s, when the centerpiece Victorian house (where the office is located) was moved back from the road to make room for the motel wings. Looking for something a bit cozier? The house also has four B&B guest rooms upstairs, each furnished simply with antiques.

WHERE TO DINE

Harris Quick-N-Tasty. Rte. 1, Dayton. ☎ **902/742-3467.** Sandwiches C$2.95–C$12 (US$1.95–US$8); main courses C$7–C$18 (US$4.65–US$12). AE, DC, MC, V. Daily 11am–9pm (to 8pm in winter). Located just east of Yarmouth on the north side of Rte. 1. SEAFOOD.

The name about says it all. This vintage 1960s restaurant has no pretensions (it's the kind of place that still lists cocktails on the menu) and is hugely popular with locals. The Harrises sold the place a few years ago, but current owner Paul Surette is committed to preserving the place as is. The restaurant is adorned with that sort of paneling that was rather au courant about 30 years back, and the meals are likewise old-fashioned and generous. The emphasis is on seafood, and you can order your fish either fried or broiled. The "Scarlet O'Harris" lobster club sandwich is notable, as is the seafood casserole.

Queen Molly's Brewpub. 96 Water St. ☎ **902/742-6008.** Reservations not needed. Sandwiches C$6–C$9 (US$4–US$6); main courses C$11–C$15 (US$7–US$10). AE, DC, MC, V. Daily 11am–11pm (shorter hours off-season). BREWPUB.

Yarmouth's first (and Nova Scotia's fourth) brewpub opened in 1997 on the newly revitalized waterfront. It occupies a mid-1800s warehouse, and you can see the wear and tear of the decades on the battered floor and stout beams and rafters. The place has been nicely spruced up, and the menu features creative pub fare, with additions including Acadian and Cajun specialties, like rappie pie and jambalaya. The steaks are quite good, as is the beer, especially the best bitter. In summer, there's outdoor seating on a deck with a view of the harbor across the parking lot.

6   The South Shore: Quintessential Nova Scotia

The Atlantic coast between Yarmouth and Halifax is that quaint maritime Nova Scotia you see on laminated place mats, postcards, and calendars. It's all lighthouses and weathered shingled buildings perched at the rocky edge of the sea, as if tenuously trespassing on the good graces of the sea. If your heart is set on exploring this fabled landscape, be sure to leave enough time to poke in all the nooks and crannies along this stretch of the coast.

As rustic and beautiful as this area is, you may find it a bit stultifying to visit *every* quaint village along the coast—about 350km (217 miles) of twisting road along the water's edge. A more sane strategy would be to sit down with a map and target two or three villages, then stitch together selected coastal drives near the chosen villages with speedier links on Route 103, which runs straight and fast a short distance inland.

SHELBURNE

Shelburne comes with an unimpeachable pedigree. Settled in 1783 by United Empire Loyalists fleeing New England after the unfortunate outcome of the late war, the town swelled with newcomers and by 1784 was believed to have a population of 10,000—larger than Montréal, Halifax, or Québec. With the decline of boat building and fishing in the 20th century, the town edged into that dim economic twilight familiar to other seaside villages (it now has a population of about 3,000), and the waterfront began to deteriorate, despite valiant preservation efforts.

A Fog Alert

When driving along the south shore, allow extra time because of fog. When the cool waters of the Arctic currents mix with the warm summer air over land, the results are predictable and soupy. The fog certainly adds atmosphere, but it can also slow driving to a crawl.

And then Hollywood came calling. In 1992, the producers of *Mary Silliman's War* found the waterfront a reasonable facsimile of circa-1776 Fairfield, Connecticut. The crew spruced up the town a bit and buried power lines along the waterfront. Two years later, director Roland Joffe arrived to film the spectacularly miscast *Scarlet Letter*, starring Demi Moore, Gary Oldman, and Robert Duvall. The film crew buried more power lines, built some 15 "historic" structures near the waterfront (most demolished after filming), dumped tons of rubble to create dirt lanes (since removed), and generally made the place look like 17th-century Boston.

When the crew departed, it left behind three buildings and an impressive shingled steeple you can see from all over town. Among the "new old" buildings is the waterfront cooperage across from the Cooper's Inn. The original structure, clad in asphalt shingles, was generally considered an eyesore and torn down, replaced by the faux–17th-century building. Today barrel makers painstakingly make and sell traditional handcrafted wooden barrels in what amounts to a souvenir of a notable Hollywood flop.

ESSENTIALS

GETTING THERE Shelburne is 223km (144 miles) southwest of Halifax on Route 3. It's a short hop from Route 103 via either Exit 25 (southbound) or Exit 26 (northbound). It's 123km (76 miles) from Yarmouth; take Route 103 and Route 3.

VISITOR INFORMATION The **Shelburne Tourist Bureau** (☎ 902/875-4547) is in a tidy waterfront building at the corner of King and Dock streets. It's open daily mid-May to October, 9am to 8pm during peak season and 10am to 6pm off-season.

EXPLORING SHELBURNE

The central **historic district** runs along the waterfront, where you can see legitimately old buildings, Hollywood fakes (above), and spectacular views of the harbor from small grassy parks. (Note that some of the remaining *Scarlet Letter* buildings weren't meant to last and may have been demolished by the time you arrive.) A block inland from the water is Shelburne's more commercial stretch, where you can find services like banks, shops, and a wonderful bakery (see "Where to Dine" below).

The **Shelburne Historic Complex,** Dock Street (☎ 902/875-3219), is an association of three local museums within steps of one another. The most engaging is the **Dory Shop,** on the waterfront. On the first floor you can admire examples of the simple elegant craft (said to be invented in Shelburne) and see videos about the late Sidney Mahaney, a master builder who worked in this shop from the time he was 17 until he was 96. Then you head upstairs, where all the banging is going on, to meet Sidney's son and grandson, still building the classic boats using traditional methods. "The dory is a simple boat, but there are a lot of things to think about," says the grandson with considerable understatement. While you're there, ask about the difference between a Shelburne dory and a Lunenburg dory.

The **Shelburne County Museum** features a potpourri of locally significant artifacts from the town's Loyalist past. Most intriguing is the 1740 fire pumper; it was made in London and imported here in 1783. If you keep track of such things, it's said to be the "oldest fire pumper in Canada." Behind the museum is the austerely handsome **Ross-Thomson House** (1784–85). The first floor contains a general store as it might've looked in 1784, with bolts of cloth and cast-iron teakettles. Upstairs is a militia room with displays of antique and reproduction weaponry.

Admission to all three museums is C$4 (US$2.65) adults; children under 16 are free. Individual museums cost C$2 (US$1.35) adults. June to mid-October, they're open daily 9:30am to 5:30pm (Dory Shop closes at the end of Sept).

WHERE TO STAY & DINE

✪ **Cooper's Inn.** 36 Dock St., Shelburne, NS B0T 1W0. ☎ **800/688-2011** or 902/
875-4656. E-mail coopers@ns.sympatico.ca. 10 units. C$80–C$110 (US$53–US$73)
double; C$155 (US$103) suite. Rates include full breakfast. AE, ER, MC, V.

Facing the harbor in the Dock Street historic area, the Cooper's Inn was built by Loyalist merchant George Gracie in 1785. Subsequent additions and updating have been
historically sympathetic. The downstairs sitting and dining rooms set the mood nicely,
with worn wood floors, muted wall colors, classical music in the background, and even
a book of Leonard Cohen poems on the table. The guest rooms in the main building
mostly feature painted wood floors (they're carpeted in the cooper-shop annex) and
are decorated in a comfortable country style. The third-floor suite was designed by a
talented architect and features wonderful detailing, two sleeping alcoves, and harbor
views. The George Gracie Room features a four-poster bed and water view; the small
Roderick Morrison Room has a clawfoot tub perfect for a late-evening soak. The two
small dining rooms serve the best meals in town (entrees at C$14 to C$24/US$9 to
US$16), with sophisticated dishes like Atlantic salmon with citrus sauce, beef tender-
loin with port-and-salsa sauce, and scallops sautéed in pine-nut butter; lobster is usually served in one form or another. Dinner is served daily 6 to 9pm, and reservations
are strongly recommended.

WHERE TO DINE

Shelburne Pastry. 151 Water St. ☎ **902/875-1168.** Sandwiches C$3.50–C$4.25
(US$2.35–US$2.85); main courses C$7–C$10 (US$4.65–US$7). V. Mon–Sat 9:30am–7pm.
BAKERY/CAFE.

When a family of German chefs opened this shop in 1995, the idea was to sell fancy
pastries. But everyone who stopped by during the restoration of the Water Street
building asked whether they would be selling bread. So they added bread. And
today it's among the best you'll taste in the province—especially the delectable Nova
Scotian oatmeal brown bread. The simple cafe also offers great pastries (try the
pinwheels), as well as sandwiches served on their own bread and filling meals from a
limited menu that includes German bratwurst and chicken cordon bleu. Everything
is made from scratch, and everything (except the marked-down day-old goods) is
just-baked fresh.

LUNENBURG

Lunenburg is one of Nova Scotia's most historic and appealing villages, a fact recognized in 1995 when UNESCO declared the old downtown a **World Heritage Site.**
The town was settled in 1753, primarily by German, Swiss, and French colonists, and
laid out on the "model town" plan then in vogue (Savannah, Georgia, and Philadelphia, Pennsylvania, were also set out along these lines), which meant seven north-
south streets intersected by nine east-west streets. Such a plan worked quite well in the
coastal plains. Lunenburg, however, is on a harbor flanked by steep hills, and imple-
menters of the model town plan saw no reason to bend around these. As a result, some
of the streets can be exhausting to walk.

About 70% of the downtown buildings date from the 18th and 19th centuries, and
many of these are possessed of a distinctive style and painted in bright colors. Looming
over all is the architecturally unique **Lunenburg Academy,** with its exaggerated
mansard roof, pointy towers, and extravagant use of ornamental brackets. It sets the
tone for the town the way the Citadel does for Halifax. The first two floors are still
used as a public school (the top floor was deemed a fire hazard some years ago), and
the building is open to the public only on special occasions.

ESSENTIALS

GETTING THERE Lunenburg is 103km (64 miles) southwest of Halifax on Route 3. It's 133km (82 miles) from Shelburne.

VISITOR INFORMATION The **Lunenburg Tourist Bureau** (☎ 902/634-8100) is at the top of Blockhouse Hill Road, open daily in summer 9am to 8pm. It's not in an obvious place, but the brown "?" signs posted around town will lead you there. The staff is especially good at helping you find a place to spend the night if you've arrived without reservations. You can also call up local info on the Web at **www.lunco.com**.

EXPLORING LUNENBURG

Leave plenty of time to explore Lunenburg by foot. The excellent **walking tour brochure** outlining the town's architectural heritage went out of print in 1999, but plans called for a newer, expanded version to be available again in 2000. Ask for one at the tourist office (above).

When strolling, note the architectural influence of later European settlers—especially Germans. Many of the homes feature a distinctive architectural element known as the "Lunenburg bump"—a five-sided dormer and bay window combo installed directly over an extended front door. Other homes feature the more common Scottish dormer. Also look for the double or triple roofs on some projecting dormers, which serve absolutely no function other than to give the home the vague appearance of a wedding cake.

Well worth visiting is **St. John's Anglican Church** at Duke and Cumberland streets. The original structure was rendered in simple New England meetinghouse style, built in 1754 of oak timbers shipped from Boston. Between 1840 and 1880, the church went through a number of additions and was overlaid with ornamentation and shingles to create a fine example of the "carpenter Gothic" style. It's open to the public.

Eric Croft, a knowledgeable Lunenburg native in possession of a sizeable store of good stories, leads 1½-hour **walking tours** (☎ 902/634-3848) that include lore about local architecture and legends. Tours depart daily at 10am, 2pm, and 9pm from Bluenose Drive (across from the parking lot for the Atlantic Fisheries Museum); the cost is C$8 (US$5).

Several boat tours operate from the waterfront, most tied up near the Fisheries Museum. **Lunenburg Whale Watching Tours** (☎ 902/527-7175) sails in pursuit of several species of whales, along with seals and seabirds, on 3-hour excursions. There are four departures daily, with reservations recommended. The *Harbour Star* (☎ 902/634-3535) takes you on a mellow 45-minute tour of Lunenburg's inner harbor (no swells!) in a converted fishing boat. The same folks also offer 1½-hour sailing trips on the *Eastern Star*, a 48-foot wooden ketch, with several sailings daily.

Blue Rocks is a picturesque tiny harbor a short drive from Lunenburg. It's every bit as scenic as Peggy's Cove, but without the tour buses. Head out of town on Pelham Street and keep driving east. Look for signs indicating either THE POINT or THE LANE and steer in that direction; the winding roadway gets narrower as the homes get more humble. Eventually, you'll reach the tip, where it's just fishing shacks and rocks, with views of spruce- and heath-covered islands offshore. The rocks are said to glow in a blue hue in certain light, hence the name.

✪ **Fisheries Museum of the Atlantic.** On the waterfront. ☎ 902/634-4794. Admission C$7 (US$4.65) adults, C$6 (US$4) seniors, C$2 (US$1.35) children, C$17 ($11) families. June to mid-Oct daily 9:30am–5:30pm; late Oct to May Mon–Fri 8:30am–4:30pm.

The Dauntless *Bluenose*

Take a Canadian dime out of your pocket and have a close look. That graceful schooner on one side? That's the ***Bluenose,*** Canada's most-recognized and most-storied ship.

The *Bluenose* was built in Lunenburg in 1921 as a fishing schooner. But it wasn't just any schooner. It was an exceptionally *fast* schooner. U.S. and Canadian fishing fleets had raced informally for years. Starting in 1920, the *Halifax Herald* sponsored the International Fisherman's Trophy, which was captured that first year by Americans sailing out of Massachusetts. Peeved, the Nova Scotians set about taking it back. And did they ever. The *Bluenose* retained the trophy for 18 years running, despite the best efforts of Americans to recapture it. The race was shelved as World War II loomed; in the years after the war, fishing schooners were displaced by long-haul, steel-hulled fishing ships, and the schooners sailed into the footnotes of history. The *Bluenose* was sold in 1942 to labor as a freighter in the West Indies. Four years later it foundered and sank off Haiti.

What made the *Bluenose* so unbeatable? A number of theories exist. Some said it was because of last-minute hull design changes. Some said it was frost "setting" the timbers as the ship was being built. Still others claim it was blessed with an unusually talented captain and crew.

The replica *Bluenose II* was built in 1963 from the same plans as the original, in the same shipyard, and even by some of the same workers. It's been owned by the province since 1971 and sails throughout Canada and beyond as Nova Scotia's seafaring ambassador. When it's in port in Lunenburg, you can sign up for 2-hour harbor sailings (C$20/US$13 adults, C$10/US$7 children 12 and under). Call the ***Bluenose II* Preservation Trust** at ☎ **800/763-1963** or 902/634-1963.

The sprawling Fisheries Museum, professionally designed and curated, manages to take a topic some might consider a little dull and make it fun and exciting. On the first floor you'll find aquarium exhibits, including a touch-tank where kids can play with starfish and hermit crabs. Look also for the massive 15-pound lobster, estimated to be 25 to 30 years old. Detailed dioramas depict the whys and wherefores of fishing from dories, colonial schooners, and other historic vessels. You'll also learn a whole bunch about the *Bluenose,* a replica of which ties up in Lunenburg when it's not touring elsewhere (see the box above). Outside, you can tour two other ships—a trawler and a salt-bank schooner—and visit a working boat shop.

WHERE TO STAY

Blue Rocks Road B&B. 579 Blue Rocks Rd., Lunenburg, NS B0J 2C0. ☎ **800/818-3426** or 902/634-8033. E-mail nika@tallships.ca. 3 units, 1 with bathroom. C$55–C$75 (US$37–US$50) double. Rates include full breakfast. V. Closed mid-Oct to mid-May.

Outdoorsy folks who like a place where they can put their feet up will be happy with Merrill and Al Heubach in their cozy 1879 home, a short drive (or pleasant 20-min. walk) from downtown Lunenburg. It's on the way to scenic Blue Rocks, and from an outbuilding behind the house Al runs the **Lunenburg Bicycle Barn** (☎ **902/ 634-3426**), a complete bike shop/rental operation. The handsomely painted floors and pleasant veranda with a view across the marsh to the water beyond make the place instantly relaxing. You'll share the first-floor living areas with the owners, who are very tidy and knowledgeable about the area. The morning coffee is organic and strong.

Boscawen Inn. 150 Cumberland St., Lunenburg, NS B0J 2C0. ☎ **800/354-5009** or 902/634-3325. Fax 902/634-9293. E-mail boscawen@ns.sympatico.ca. 20 units, 1 with private hall bathroom. C$50–C$120 (US$33–US$80) double. Rates include full breakfast. AE, ER, MC, V. Pets allowed with prior permission.

This imposing 1888 mansion occupies a prime hillside a block from the heart of town. It's almost worth it just to get access to the main-floor deck and its harbor views. Most of the guest rooms are in the main building, which had a wing added in 1945. The decor is Victorian but not aggressively so. Even if you prefer Shaker, you'll still do okay here because it has been appointed with measured taste. Some rooms, including two spacious suites, are in the 1905 MacLachlan House, just below the main house. A few things to know: Room no. 6 lacks a shower but has a nice tub. Third-floor guests need to navigate steep steps. Two rooms have TVs, and room phones are available on request. Breakfast is buffet style, with both hot and cold dishes. The restaurant, more banally modern than one might expect in this historic mansion, serves reliable and sometimes imaginative dinners in season 5:30 to 9pm. Entrees (C$13 to C$18/US$9 to US$12) emphasize seafood and may include a mixed seafood platter, Digby scallops, and Cornish game hen.

Hillcroft Guest House. 53 Montague St. (P.O. Box 1665), Lunenburg, NS B0J 2C0. ☎ **902/634-8031.** 3 units, none with bathroom. C$65 (US$43) double. Rates include continental breakfast. MC, V. Closed Dec to mid-Apr.

This enjoyable spot bills itself as a "guest house" rather than an inn, and that's appropriate. The guest rooms share a single bathroom, and the rooms, tucked under slanting eaves, are decidedly small. But they're furnished with a light touch, and the effect is more cozy than claustrophobic. There are also a guest parlor downstairs and an intimate backyard with luridly painted Adirondack chairs for relaxing. The innkeepers are personable and welcoming, and the first-floor restaurant is among the best in town (see below).

Lennox Inn. 69 Fox St. (P.O. Box 254). Lunenburg, NS B0J 2C0. ☎ **902/634-4043.** 6 units, 4 with bathroom. C$60–C$80 (US$40–US$53) double. Rates include full breakfast. MC, V. Open year-round; by appointment only mid-Oct to Apr.

In 1991, this strikingly handsome but simple 1791 house in a quiet residential area was slated for demolition. Robert Cram didn't want to see it go, so he bought it and spent several years restoring it, filling it with antiques and period reproductions. It's more rustic than opulent, but this fine inn should be high on the list for anyone fond of authentically historic houses. In fact, it claims, quite plausibly, to be the oldest unchanged inn in Canada. Three of the four spacious second-floor guest rooms have the original plaster, and all four have the original fireplaces (nonworking). Two rooms are planned for the third floor in 2000, one with the original wide-plank walls. A simple country breakfast is served in the former tavern; be sure to note the ingenious old bar.

WHERE TO DINE

Hillcroft Cafe. In the Hillcroft Guest House, 53 Montague St. ☎ **902/634-8031.** Reservations recommended. Main courses C$10–C$17 (US$7–US$11). MC, V. Daily 5:30–9pm. Closed Nov to mid-Apr. MIXED INTERNATIONAL.

This cozy cafe, on the Hillcroft Guest House's first floor, is run by globe-trotters Rafel Albo and Peter Fleischmann. It's adorned with the gleanings of their trips, lending the place a fun atmosphere and a sort of parlor-game amusement. ("I bet that's from Bali," you can guess while awaiting dinner. "Or maybe Thailand.") The menu is equally eclectic, with starters like baba ghannouj, hummus, Greek salad, and the local favorite, clam chowder. Dinner entrees include Thai chicken with green beans and baby corn in coconut curry, roasted lamb with a mild cheese and green-peppercorn sauce, and penne with local scallops and mussels in Mediterranean sauce. The desserts feature fresh Italian ices, along with apple crisp and shortbread-crust cheesecake.

Magnolia's Grill. 128 Montague St. ☎ **902/634-3287.** Main courses C$5–C$12 (US$3.35–US$8). AE, MC, V. Daily 11:30am–10pm. Closed Nov–Mar. SEAFOOD/ECLECTIC.

This is a bright, cheerful, funky storefront with a checkerboard linoleum floor, lively rock playing in the background, and walls adorned with old Elvis and Beatles iconography. It also serves some of the most delectable food in town. Look for barbecue pork sandwiches, chicken tostadas, and sesame-ginger shrimp stir-fry—or whatever else the kitchen feels like scrawling on the chalkboard. The restaurant is especially famed for its fishcakes (served with homemade rhubarb chutney) and Mrs. Zinck's Chocolate Sloppy for dessert. Come at off-peak hours or expect a wait. There's also a deli for takeout.

Old Fish Factory Restaurant. At the Fisheries Museum, 68 Bluenose Dr. ☎ **902/ 634-3333.** Reservations recommended (ask for a window seat). Lunch C$7–C$12 (US$4.65–US$8); dinner C$14–C$30 (US$9–US$20). AE, DC, DISC, ER, MC, V. Daily 11am–9pm (to 9:30pm July–Aug). Closed mid-Oct to early May. SEAFOOD.

The Old Fish Factory Restaurant is located in a huge old fish processing plant it shares with the Fisheries Museum. This popular large restaurant can swallow whole bus tours at once; come early and angle for a window seat or a spot on the patio. The specialty is seafood, which tends to involve medleys of varied fish. At lunch you might order a seafood sandwich (made with crab, scallops, and lobster). At dinner, lobster is served four ways, along with bouillabaisse, snow crab, and curried mango seafood pasta. There are steak, lamb, and chicken for more terrestrial tastes.

MAHONE BAY

Mahone Bay, first settled in 1754 by European Protestants, is postcard-perfect Nova Scotia. It's tidy and trim with an eclectic Main Street that snakes along the bay and is lined with inviting shops. This is a town that's remarkably well cared for by its 1,100 residents, a growing number of whom live here and commute to work in Halifax. Architecture buffs will find a range of styles to keep them ogling. The **visitor information center,** 165 Edgewater St., near the three church steeples (☎ 902/624-6151), is open daily in summer 9am to 7:30pm.

EXPLORING THE TOWN

The **Mahone Bay Settlers Museum,** 578 Main St. (☎ 902/624-6263), provides historic context for your explorations (closed Mon). A good selection of historic decorative arts is on display. Before leaving, be sure to request a copy of *Three Walking Tours of Mahone Bay,* a handy brochure outlining easy historic walks around the compact downtown.

Thanks to the looping waterside routes nearby, Mahone Bay is a popular destination for bikers. And the deep protected harbor offers superb sea kayaking. If you'd like to give kayaking a go, stop by **Mahone Bay Kayak Adventures,** 618 Main St. (☎ 902/624-6632), offering everything from half-day introductory classes to a 5-day coastal tour. Among the more popular adventures is the daylong introductory tour, in which paddlers explore the complex shoreline nearby and learn about kayaking in the process. The price is C$85 (US$57) per person, including lunch. Rentals are also available, starting at C$30 (US$20) a half day for a single kayak.

Another appealing means of exploring the harbor and islands beyond is aboard the *Spirit*, a 36-passenger sailing ship built in 1998 using traditional means and materials (☎ 902/624-8443). During the peak summer sailing season, four sailings daily are offered from the Mahone Bay town wharf. Cruises are C$20 (US$13) adults and C$10 (US$7) children 6 to 12; children under 6 are free.

Mahone Bay serves as a magnet to all manner of creative and crafty types, and Main Street has become a **shopping** mecca for those who treasure handmade goods. Shops are typically open late spring until Christmas, when Haligonians travel the 55 minutes here for holiday shopping.

WHERE TO STAY

✪ **The Manse.** Orchard St. (P.O. Box 475), Mahone Bay, NS B0J 2E0. ☎ **902/624-1121.** Fax 902/624-1182. 4 units. C$85–C$105 (US$57–US$70) double. Rates include full breakfast. MC, V.

This is one of my favorite places in Nova Scotia. Innkeepers Rose and Allan O'Brien have made a cozy retreat of their 1870 home, tucked on a side street that's at once removed from and close to the activity in Mahone Bay. I'd be happy in any of the four guest rooms, two of which are in the old barn. All are bright and uncluttered, with old pine floors and tasteful furniture that's both modern and classic. If it's available, I'd opt for the Loft, the former hayloft on the second floor of the barn. With its whitewashed barn-board walls, large sitting area, small balcony, queen-sized bed, and CD player, it's hard to imagine not enjoying a few days hidden away here. (Caveat: The room can get a bit hot and stuffy in late afternoon but almost always cools off by evening.) TVs are available on request. The rest of the house is equally attractive, and a morning spent with a cup of coffee in one of the oversized Adirondack chairs on the front deck is a morning well spent indeed.

WHERE TO DINE

Innlet Cafe. Edgewater St. ☎ **902/624-6363.** Reservations suggested for dinner. Main courses C$12–C$21 (US$9–US$15). MC, V. Daily 11:30am–8:30pm. SEAFOOD/GRILL.

Jack and Katherine Sorensen have been serving up great meals here for 2 decades, and they've styled a menu that's brought back legions of devoted customers. Everything is good; the seafood is especially delicious. The menu is all over the place (oven-braised lamb shank to scallop stir-fry), but the smart money hones in on the unadorned seafood. Notable are the "smoked and garlicked mackerel" and the mixed seafood grill. The best seats are on the stone patio, which has a view of the harbor and the famous three-steepled townscape of Mahone Bay.

✪ **Mimi's Ocean Grill.** 662 Main St. ☎ **902/624-1342.** Main courses C$6–C$9 (US$4–US$6) at lunch, C$12–C$18 (US$8–US$12) at dinner. AE, MC, V. Summer daily noon–9pm; limited hours off-season. Closed Jan–Mar. ECLECTIC.

Under an overarching tree in a historic colonial-style home painted Cherokee red, Mimi's offers some of the region's most wonderful cooking amid a relaxed atmosphere. The whimsical wall paintings put you immediately at ease (this is no period piece with stiff chairs and stiff service), and the servers are jovial without overdoing it. The menu changes every 6 weeks or so to reflect available ingredients. For lunch you might opt for the shrimp-and-lobster roll or mussel linguine with pesto cream. For dinner, how about the famous bayou haddock (with a spicy cornmeal crust), salmon napoleon, or grilled steak with wild mushroom butter?

CHESTER

Chester is a short drive off Route 103 and has the feel of an old-money summer colony, perhaps somewhere along the New England coast circa 1920. It was first settled in 1759 by immigrants from New England and Great Britain, and today it has a population of 1,250. The village is noted for its regal homes and quiet streets and the picturesque islands offshore. The atmosphere is untrammeled and lazy—the way life used to be in summer resorts around the world. Change may be on the horizon, however: Actors and authors have discovered the place and are snapping up waterfront homes in town and on the islands as private retreats.

The **Chester Visitor Information Center** is in the old train station on Route 3 on the south side of town (☎ **902/275-4616**). Summer, it's open daily 10am to 5pm.

EXPLORING THE TOWN

Like so many other towns in Nova Scotia, Chester is best seen out of your car windows. But unlike other towns, where the center of gravity seems to be in the commercial district, here the focus is on the graceful, shady residential areas radiating out from the Lilliputian village.

Some creative shops are beginning to find a receptive audience in and around Chester, and right now there's good browsing for new goods and antiques both downtown and in the outlying areas. Among them are **Fiasco,** 54 Queen St. (☎ **902/ 275-2173**), which has an appealing selection of funky and fun home accessories and clothing, and **Christal Design,** 33 Queen St. (☎ **902/275-4580**), where you can shop for jewelry, watchbands, and belts made of fish leather.

For an even slower pace, plan an excursion out to the **Tancook Islands,** a pair of lost-in-time islands with a couple hundred year-round residents. The islands, accessible via a short ferry ride, are good for walking the lanes and trails. On Big Tancook is a small cafe but little else to cater to travelers. Several ferry trips are scheduled daily 6am to 6pm. The ferry ties up on the island, however, so don't count on a last trip back to the mainland. Tickets are C$5 (US$3.35) round-trip (children under 12 ride free).

WHERE TO STAY

✪ **Haddon Hall.** 67 Haddon Hill Rd., Chester NS B0J 1J0. ☎ **902/275-3577.** Fax 902/275-5159. 10 units. A/C TV TEL. C$150–C$400 (US$100–US$267) double. Rates include continental breakfast. MC, V.

If there's no fog, Haddon Hall offers the best view of any inn in Atlantic Canada, bar none. Perched atop an open hill with panoramic views of island-studded Mahone Bay, this distinctive inn dates from 1905 and was built in what might be called "heroic Arts and Crafts" style. You'll recognize the bungalow form of the main house, but it's rendered in an outsized manner. Three stylish guest rooms are in this house; the remaining seven are in cottages around the property. Four rooms have wood fireplaces, three have Jacuzzis, and two have kitchenettes. The styling is eclectic—wood stoves and twig furniture in the rustic log cabins, spare continental lines in the main house—but everything is united by understated good taste. April to mid-October, the dining room serves dinner 5:30 to 8:30pm. Make reservations early and ask for a table on the front porch with its sweeping vistas. The creative menu may include grilled lamb and papaya or vegetable strudel with basil and feta. Prix-fixe dinners are C$45, plus tax and gratuity. The inn has a tennis court and an outdoor pool and can arrange for boat tours. Ask about using the free guest bikes or visiting the inn-owned island for picnics or tours.

Mecklenburgh Inn. 78 Queen St., Chester, NS B0J 1J0. ☎ **902/275-4638.** E-mail frnthrbr@atcon.com. 4 units, none with bathroom. C$55–C$75 (US$37–US$50) double. Rates include full breakfast. AE, V. Closed Nov–June.

The wonderfully funky and appealing Mecklenburgh (ca. 1890) is on a low hill in a residential neighborhood. On the first and second floors the inn is dominated by broad porches where you can sit and rock and watch the town wander by (the post office is next door). Innkeeper Suzi Fraser has been running the place with casual bonhomie for over 10 years, and she's a great breakfast cook to boot. The guest rooms are modern Victorian and generally quite bright. What's the catch? The four rooms share two hall bathrooms, but because guests often end up feeling like family, it's usually not much of a bother. Children over 10 are welcome.

7 Halifax: More Than a Natural Harbor

During a stop at the sprawling Nova Scotia visitor center near Amherst, I heard an elderly couple ask an eager young staffer why they should bother to visit **Halifax.** "It's just a city, isn't it?" they asked.

"Well," the staffer responded brightly, "it's on the second-largest natural harbor in the world, after Sydney, Australia!" And then she seemed at a loss for words.

Oh, dear. I hope that's not the best the tourism folks can come up with. In fact, Halifax is a fun, vibrant, exciting city that's loaded with history but not staid, modern but not slick, big enough to get lost in but not big enough to be intimidating. Should you bother to visit? By all means.

This unusually pleasing harborside setting, now home to a city of some 115,000 (about three times as many in the greater metro area), first attracted Europeans in 1749, when Col. Edward Cornwallis established a military outpost here. (The site was named after George Montagu Dunk, second earl of Halifax. Residents tend to agree it was a great stroke of luck the city avoided the name Dunk, Nova Scotia.) Halifax plodded along as a colonial backwater for the better part of a century; one historian wrote it was generally regarded as "a rather degenerate little seaport town."

But Halifax's natural advantages—including that well-protected harbor and its location near major fishing grounds and shipping lanes—eventually allowed it to emerge as a major port and military base. In recent years, the city has grown aggressively (it annexed adjacent suburbs in 1969) and carved out a niche as the vital commercial/financial hub of the Maritimes. The city is also home to a number of colleges and universities, which gives it a youthful, edgy air. Skateboards and bicycles often seem to be the vehicles of choice. In addition to the many attractions, downtown Halifax is home to a number of fine restaurants and hotels.

ESSENTIALS

GETTING THERE   From New Brunswick and the west, the most direct route is via Route 102 from Truro; allow about 2 to 2½ hours from the provincial border at Amherst.

Halifax International Airport is 35km (22 miles) north of downtown Halifax in Elmsdale. (Take Route 102 to Exit 6.) Nova Scotia's notorious fogs make it advisable to call before heading out to the airport to reconfirm flight times. More than 100 daily departures serve Atlantic Canada's largest city. Airlines serving Halifax include **Air Canada, Air Nova, Canadian Airlines International, Air Atlantic,** and **Icelandair.** (See "Getting There" in chapter 2 for phone numbers.)

Airbus (☎ **902/873-2091**) offers frequent shuttles to and from the airport to major downtown hotels daily 6:30am to 11:15pm. The rate is C$12 (US$8) one way or C$20 (US$13) round-trip. **Via Rail** (☎ **800/361-8010;** www.viarail.ca) offers train service 6 days a week between Halifax and Montréal. The entire trip takes 18 to 21 hours, depending on the direction. Stops include Moncton and Campbellton (and bus connections to Québec). Halifax's **CN Station,** at Barrington and Cornwallis streets, is within walking distance of downtown attractions.

VISITOR INFORMATION   The huge **Halifax International Visitor Centre** is downtown at 1595 Barrington St., at the corner of Barrington and Sackville (☎ **800/ 565-0000** or 902/490-5946). Summer, it's open daily 8:30am to 7pm (to 6pm in winter); it's staffed with friendly folks who'll point you in the right direction or help you make room reservations. If you're on the waterfront, there's a helpful provincial center at **Red Store Visitor Information Centre** (☎ **902/424-4248**) at Historic Properties. The second week in May to the end of October, it's open daily 8:30am to 8pm; November to the first week of May, hours are Wednesday to Sunday 8:30am to 4:30pm.

GETTING AROUND   Parking in Halifax can be problematic. Long-term metered spaces are in high demand downtown, and many of the parking lots and garages fill up fast. If you're headed downtown for a brief visit, you can usually find a 2-hour meter. But if you're looking to spend a day, I'd suggest venturing out early to ensure a spot at a parking lot. Your best bet is along Lower Water Street, south of the Maritime Museum of the Atlantic, where you can park all day for around C$6 (US$4).

Metro Transit operates buses throughout the city. Route and timetable information is available at the information centers or by phone at ☎ 902/490-6600. Bus fare is C$1.65 (US$1.10) adults and C$1.15 (US75¢) seniors/children. Monday to Saturday in summer, a free **bright yellow bus named Fred** (☎ **902/423-6658**) cruises a loop through downtown, passing each stop about every 20 minutes. Stops include the Maritime Museum, the Grand Parade, and Barrington Place Shops. Request a schedule and map at the visitor center.

EVENTS   The annual **Nova Scotia International Tattoo** (☎ **902/451-1221**) features military and marching bands totaling some 2,000-plus military and civilian performers. This rousing event takes place over the course of a week in early July and is held indoors at the Halifax Metro Center. Tickets are C$12 to C$26 (US$8 to US$17). In early August, expect to see a profusion of street performers, from avantgarde fire-eaters to comic jugglers. They descend on Halifax each year for the 10-day ✪ **International Busker Festival** (☎ **902/429-3910**). Performances take place along the waterfront walkway all day long and are often remarkable. It's free, with donations requested.

EXPLORING HALIFAX

Halifax is fairly compact and easily covered on foot or by mass transportation. The major landmark is the **Citadel**—the stone fortress looming over downtown from its grassy perch. From the ramparts, you can look into the windows of the 10th floor of downtown skyscrapers. The Citadel is only 9 blocks from the waterfront—albeit 9 sometimes steep blocks—and you can easily roam both areas in 1 day.

A lively neighborhood worth seeking out runs along **Spring Garden Road,** between the Public Gardens and the library (at Grafton Street). You'll find intriguing boutiques, bars, and restaurants along these 6 blocks, set amid a mildly Bohemian street scene. If you have strong legs and a stout constitution, you can start on the waterfront, stroll up and over the Citadel to descend to the Public Gardens, and then return via Spring Garden to downtown, perhaps enjoying a meal or two along the way.

THE WATERFRONT

Halifax's rehabilitated ✪ **waterfront** is at its most inviting and vibrant between Sackville Landing (at the foot of Sackville Street) and the Sheraton Hotel, near Purdy

Cogswell St.

Rainnie Dr.

Trollope St.

Ahern Ave.

Market St.

7

Scotia
Square
Duke St.

Metro
Centre

George St.

Grand
Parade

Brunswick St.

Market St.

Grafton St.

Argyle St.

Prince St.

Sackville St.

Neptune Theatre

Blowers St.

Barrington St.

Granville St.

Hollis St.

Bedford Row

Upper Water St.

Ferry to
Dartmouth
Cable
Wharf

H.M.C.S.
Sackville

WANDERERS
GROUNDS

GARRISON
GROUNDS

Summer St.

Bell Rd.

PUBLIC
GARDENS

Spring Garden Rd.

Lower Water St.

College St.

VICTORIA
PARK

Brenton St.

Dresden Row

Birmingham St.

University Ave.

Morris St.

South Park St.

Queen St.

LEGEND

Ferry — — — —
Information ⓘ

South St.

CORNWALLIS
PARK

Tobin St.

Tower Rd.

Fenwick St.

ATTRACTIONS
Art Gallery of Nova Scotia ⑭
Barrington Place ⑪
Halifax Citadel National
    Historic Park ⑤
Historic Properties ⑨
Maritime Museum
    of the Atlantic ⑮
Nova Scotia Museum
    of National History ①
Old Burying Ground ㉒
Old City Hall ⑫
Old Town Clock ⑥
Pier 21 ㉖
Point Pleasant Park ㉗
Province House ⑯
St. Paul's Church ⑰

ACCOMMODATIONS
Cambridge Suites ⑲
Delta Halifax ⑦
Halliburton House Inn ㉓
Halifax Heritage House Hostel ㉕
Lord Nelson Hotel & Suites ②
Maranova Suites ⑧
Prince George Hotel ⑱
Waverly Inn ㉔

DINING
Cheapside Café ⑭
deMaurizio ㉑
Il Mercato ③
Joe's Fish Smack ④
Maple ⑬
Satisfaction Feast ⑳
Sweet Basil Bistro ⑩

Wharf. (You could keep walking, but north of here the waterfront lapses into an agglomeration of charmless modern towers with sidewalk-level vents assailing passersby with unusual odors.) On sunny summer afternoons, the waterfront is bustling with tourists enjoying the harbor, businessfolks playing hooky while sneaking an ice-cream cone, and baggy-panted skateboarders striving to stay out of trouble. Plan on about 2 to 3 hours to tour and gawk from end to end.

In addition to the attractions below, the waterfront walkway is studded with small diversions, intriguing shops, takeout food emporia, and minor monuments. The waterfront's **shopping** core is in and around the 3-block **Historic Properties,** near the Sheraton. These stout buildings of wood and stone are Canada's oldest surviving warehouses and were once the center of the city's booming shipping industry. Today, the historic architecture is stern enough to provide ballast for the somewhat-precious boutiques and restaurants they now house.

A number of boat tours depart from the Halifax waterfront. You can browse the offerings on **Cable Wharf,** near the foot of George Street, where many tour boats are based. On-the-water adventures range from 1-hour harbor tours (about C$12/US$8) to 5-hour deep-sea fishing trips (about C$40/US$27). **Murphy's on the Water** (☎ 902/420-1015) runs the most extensive tour operation, with three boats and a choice of tours, ranging from a cocktail sailing cruise to whale watching to tours of historic Nab's Island, near the mouth of the harbor (see below).

✪ **Maritime Museum of the Atlantic.** 1675 Lower Water St. ☎ **902/424-7490.** June–Oct 15 admission (includes admission to CSS *Acadia,* below) C$4.50 (US$3) adults, C$1 (US65¢) children, C$10 (US$7) families. Free Oct 16–May 31. June to mid-Oct Mon–Sat 9:30am–5:30pm (to 8pm Tues), Sun 1–5:30pm; mid-Oct to May closed Mon and to 5pm Wed–Sun.

Everything from birchbark canoes to the *Titanic* is the subject of this standout museum, which opened at this prime waterfront location in 1982. You're greeted by a 10-foot lighthouse lens from 1906; then you proceed through a parade of shipbuilding and seagoing eras. Visit the deckhouse of a coastal steamer (ca. 1940). Learn the colorful history of Samuel Cunard, a Nova Scotia native (born 1787) who founded the Cunard Steam Ship Co. to carry the royal mail and along the way established an ocean dynasty. Learn about the tragic 1917 Halifax Explosion, when two warships collided in Halifax harbor not far from the museum, detonating tons of TNT. More than 1,700 people died, and windows were shattered 100km (62 miles) away. And if you didn't hear about this during the frenzy surrounding the film, you'll also learn that 150 victims of the *Titanic* disaster are buried in Halifax (out of 1,503 dead), where rescue efforts were centered—see "Gardens & Open Spaces," below. Perhaps the most poignant exhibit is the lone deck chair from the *Titanic,* a metaphor made real. Also memorable are the Age of Steam exhibit and Queen Victoria's barge.

The museum is obviously of interest to those with an inquisitiveness about life at sea. But all Nova Scotia visitors owe themselves a stop here to better understand the underpinnings of the province's rich maritime history. The exhibits are involving and well executed, and you'll be astounded at how fast 2 hours can fly by.

CSS *Acadia.* 1675 Lower Water St. ☎ **902/424-7490.** Free admission with museum ticket or C$1 (US65¢) to be applied to museum admission. June 2 to mid-Oct Mon–Sat 9:30am–5:30pm, Sun 1–5pm.

In front and part of the Maritime Museum (above) is the unusually handsome 1913 *Acadia* ("our largest artifact"), but you can view it independently if you wish. The *Acadia* was used by the Canadian government to chart the ocean floor for 56 years, until her 1969 retirement. Much of the ship is open for self-guided tours, including

the captain's quarters, upper decks, wheelhouse, and oak-paneled cha
want to see more of the ship, ask about the guided half-hour tours (k
offering access to the engine room and more

Nearby is the **HMCS** *Sackville* (☎ **902/429-5600**), a blue-and-white corvette (a speedy warship smaller than a destroyer) tied up at a wood-planked wharf behind a small visitor center. A short multimedia presentation provides some background. The ship, outfitted as it was in 1944, is maintained as a memorial to the Canadians who served in World War II. Admission is free, and hours are Monday to Saturday 10am to 5pm and Sunday 1 to 5pm.

Pier 21. 1055 Marginal Rd. (on the waterfront behind the Westin Hotel). ☎ **902/ 425-7770.** C$6 (US$4) adults, C$2.75 (US$1.85) children 14 and under. Late May to Oct daily 9am–8pm (last ticket sold at 6:30pm); Nov to mid-May daily 9am–5pm.

Between 1928 and 1971, more than 1 million immigrants arrived in Canada by disembarking at Pier 21, Canada's version of New York's Ellis Island. In 1999, the pier was restored and reopened, filled with engaging interpretive exhibits that aid you in vividly imagining the confusion and anxiety of the immigration experience. The pier is divided roughly into three sections, recapturing the boarding of the ship amid the cacophony of many languages, the crossing of the Atlantic (a 26-min. multimedia show enacts the voyage in a shiplike theater), and the dispersal of the recent arrivals throughout Canada via passenger train.

THE CITADEL & DOWNTOWN

Downtown Halifax cascades 9 blocks down a slope between the imposing stone Citadel and the waterfront. There's no fast-and-ready tour route; don't hesitate to follow your own desultory course, alternately ducking down quiet streets and striding along busy arteries. A good spot to regain your bearings periodically is the **Grand Parade,** where military recruits once practiced their drilling. It's a lovely urban landscape—a broad terrace carved into the hill, presided over on either end by St. Paul's (below) and City Hall.

✪ **Halifax Citadel National Historic Site.** Citadel Hill. ☎ **902/426-5080.** Mid-May to late Oct admission C$6 (US$4) adults, C$4.50 (US$3) seniors, C$3 (US$2) youths 6–16, C$15 (US$10) families. Free the rest of the year. Mid-June to Aug daily 9am–6pm; Sept to mid-June daily 9am–5pm. Limited parking C$2.75 (US$1.85).

Even if the stalwart stone fort weren't here, it would be worth the uphill trek for the astounding views alone. The panoramic sweep across downtown and the harbor finishes up with vistas out toward the broad Atlantic beyond. At any rate, an ascent makes it obvious why this spot was chosen for the harbor's most formidable defenses: There's simply no sneaking up on the place. Four forts have occupied the summit since Col. Edward Cornwallis was posted to the colony in 1749. The Citadel has been restored to look much as it did in 1856, when the fourth fort was built out of concern over bellicose Americans. The fort has never been attacked.

The site is impressive to say the least: Sturdy granite walls topped by grassy embankments form a rough star; in the sprawling gravel-and-cobblestone courtyard you'll find costumed interpreters in kilts and bearskin hats marching in unison, playing bagpipes, and firing the noon cannon. The former barracks and other chambers are home to exhibits about life at the fort. If you still have questions, stop a soldier, bagpiper, or washerwoman and ask.

Art Gallery of Nova Scotia. 1741 Hollis St. (at Cheapside). ☎ **902/424-7542.** Admission C$5 (US$3.35) adults, C$2 (US$1.35) students, C$8 (US$5) families. Tues–Fri 10am–6pm, Sat and Sun noon–5pm.

, a pair of sandstone buildings between the waterfront and the Grand Parade, this is arguably the premier gallery in the Maritimes, with a focus on local and regional art. You'll also find a selection of other works by Canadian, British, and European artists, with a well-chosen selection of folk and Inuit art. In 1998, the gallery expanded to include the Provincial Building next door, where the entire house (it's tiny) of Nova Scotian folk artist Maud Lewis has been reassembled and is on display. You can cover the museum in 60 to 90 minutes; consider a lunch break in the attractive Cheapside Cafe (below).

Province House. Hollis St. (near Prince St.). ☎ **902/424-4661.** Free admission. July–Aug Mon–Fri 9am–5pm, Sat–Sun and holidays 10am–4pm; the rest of the year Mon–Fri 9am–4pm.

Canada's oldest seat of government, Province House has been home to the Nova Scotian legislature since 1819. This Georgian building is a superb example of the rigorously symmetrical Palladian style. And like a jewel box, its dour stone exterior hides gems of ornamental detailing and artwork inside; note especially the fine plasterwork, rare for a Canadian building of this era. If the legislature is in session, you can obtain a visitor's pass and sit up in the gallery and watch the business of the province take place.

Nova Scotia Museum of Natural History. 1747 Summer St. ☎ **902/424-7353.** C$3.50 (US$2.35) adults, C$3 (US$2) seniors, C$1 (US65¢) children, C$8 (US$5) families. June to mid-Oct Mon–Sat 9:30am–5:30pm (to 8pm Wed), Sun 1–5:30pm; late Oct to May Tues–Sat 9:30am–5pm (to 8pm Wed), Sun 1–5pm.

On the far side of the Citadel from downtown, this midsize modern museum offers a good introduction to the flora and fauna of Nova Scotia. Galleries include geology, botany, mammals, and birds, plus exhibits of archaeology and Mi'kmaq culture.

St. Paul's Church. 1749 Argyle St. (on the Grand Parade near Barrington St.). ☎ **902/429-2240.** Daily 9am–4:30pm; Sun services 8, 9:15, and 11am. Free guided tours Tues–Sat in summer.

Forming one end of the Grand Parade, St. Paul's was the first Anglican cathedral established outside of England and is Canada's oldest Protestant place of worship. Part of the 1750 building was fabricated in Boston and erected in Halifax with the help of a royal endowment from King George II. A classic white Georgian building, St. Paul's has fine stained-glass windows. A piece of flying debris from the 1917 explosion (see the entry for the Maritime Museum of the Atlantic, above) is lodged in the wall over the doors to the nave.

GARDENS & OPEN SPACES

When the *Titanic* went down April 15, 1912, nearly 2,000 people died. Halifax ship captains were recruited to help retrieve the corpses (you'll learn about this grim episode at the Maritime Museum, above). Some 121 victims, mostly crew members, were buried at the quiet **Fairview Lawn Cemetery,** Chisholm Avenue off Connaught Avenue, a short drive north of downtown Halifax (☎ **902/490-4883**), open daylight hours year-round. Some of the simple graves have names, others just numbers. Number 227 was J. Dawson, a young crew member who worked in the boiler room. Many teenage girls have convinced themselves this is Jack Dawson, the fictional character played by Leonardo DiCaprio in the hit movie, and still leave the occasional flower or other token. Interpretive signs highlight some of the stories that survived the tragedy. You'll find a brochure with driving directions to this and two other *Titanic* cemeteries at the Maritime Museum and visitor information centers.

The ✪ **Public Gardens,** at Spring Garden Road and South Park Street, took seed in 1753, when it was founded as a private garden. It was acquired by the Nova Scotia Horticultural Society in 1836 and assumed its present look in 1875, making it a Victorian masterpiece, more rare and evocative than any mansard-roofed mansion. You'll find wonderful examples of many of the 19th century's dominant trends in outdoor landscaping, from the "natural" winding walks and ornate fountains to the duck ponds and fussy Victorian bandstand. (Stop by 2pm on Sun in summer for a free concert.) There are lots of leafy trees, lush lawns, cranky ducks who've long since lost their fear of humans, and tiny ponds. The overseers have been commendably stingy with memorial statues and plaques. You'll usually find dowagers feeding pigeons and smartly uniformed guards slowly walking the grounds. Admission is free, and the gardens are open spring to late fall daily 8am to dusk.

Point Pleasant Park, Point Pleasant Drive, at the south end of Halifax, is one of Canada's finer urban parks, and there's no better place for a walk along the water on a balmy day. This 186-acre park occupies a wooded peninsular point and served for years as one of the linchpins in the city's military defense. You'll find the ruins of early forts and a nicely preserved martello tower. Halifax has a 999-year lease from Great Britain for the park, for which it pays 1 shilling—about 10¢—per year. You'll also find a lovely gravel carriage road around the point, a small swimming beach, miles of walking trails, and groves of graceful fir trees. The park is about 2km (1.2 miles) south of the Public Gardens; head south on South Park Street near the Public Gardens and continue on Young Street. Admission is free, and it's open daily during daylight hours.

A SIDE TRIP TO PEGGY'S COVE

About 43km (27 miles) southwest of Halifax is the picturesque fishing village of **Peggy's Cove** (pop. 120). The village offers a postcard-perfect tableau: an octagonal lighthouse (surely one of the world's most photographed), tiny fishing shacks, and graceful fishing boats bobbing in the postage-stamp–size harbor. The bonsai-like perfection hasn't gone unnoticed by the big tour operators, however, so it's a rare summer day when you're not sharing the experience with a few hundred of your personal bus-tour friends. The village is home to a handful of B&Bs and boutiques (Wood n' Wool, The Christmas Shoppe), but scenic values draw the day-trippers with cameras and lots of film.

WHERE TO STAY
EXPENSIVE

Cambridge Suites. 1583 Brunswick St., Halifax NS B3J 3P5. ☎ **888/417-8483** or 902/420-0555. Fax 902/420-9379. www.centennialhotels.com/cambridge. E-mail reservations@hfx.cambridgesuites.ns.ca. 200 units. A/C MINIBAR TV TEL. C$139–C$240 suite (US$93–US$160). Children under 18 free with parents. AE, CB, DC, ER, MC, V. Valet parking C$11 (US$7).

The attractive modern Cambridge Suites is nicely located near the foot of the Citadel and well positioned for exploring Halifax. It's perfect for families—40 of the units are two-room suites featuring kitchenettes with microwaves, two phones, coffeemakers, and hair dryers. Expect a comfortable, inoffensive decor and above-average service.

Dining: Dofsky's Grill is open for all three meals, which are palatable if not exciting. Look for pasta, blackened haddock, burgers, and jerked chicken (C$8 to C$19/US$5 to US$13).

Amenities: Concierge, room service, self-service laundry, babysitting, dry cleaning, rooftop sundeck with barbecue grill, safe-deposit boxes; fitness center with whirlpool, sauna, weights, exercise bikes.

Delta Halifax. 1990 Barrington St., Halifax, NS B3J 1P2. ☎ **800/268-1133** or 902/425-6700. Fax 902/425-6214. 300 units. A/C MINIBAR TV TEL. C$139–C$189 (US$93–US$126) double. AE, ER, JCB, MC, V. Valet parking C$13 (US$9).

The Delta Halifax (formerly the Hotel Halifax, more formerly the Chateau Halifax) is a slickly modern (built in 1972) downtown hotel that offers premium service. It's just a block off the waterfront, to which it's connected via skyway, but navigating it involves an annoying labyrinth of parking garages and charmless concrete structures. The lobby is streetside; you take elevators up above a six-floor parking garage to reach your room. The hotel is frequented largely by businesspeople during the week. The rooms are in two classes—300 or 500 square feet—and are furnished simply and unexceptionably, with irons, coffeemakers, hair dryers, and bathrobes. Ask for a room in the "resort wing" near the pool, which feels a bit farther away from the chatter of downtown and the press of business. A number of rooms have balconies and many have harbor views; make inquiries when you book.

Dining: The Crown Bistrot offers informal continental cuisine, including pan-fried halibut with macadamia nuts and seared sea scallops with basmati rice. The summer-time lobster-and-steak buffet costs C$25 (US$17). The Sam Slick Lounge next door is "cigar friendly."

Amenities: Concierge, limited room service, voice mail, safe-deposit boxes, com-plimentary coffee, shopping arcade, car-rental desk, dry cleaning/laundry, babysitting, fitness facility with indoor pool, sundeck, sauna, whirlpool.

Halliburton House Inn. 5184 Morris St., Halifax, NS B3J 1B3. ☎ **902/420-0658.** Fax 902/423-2324. www.halliburton.ns.ca. E-mail innkeeper@halliburton.ns.ca. 28 units. A/C TV TEL. C$115–C$165 (US$77–US$110) double. Rates include continental breakfast and parking (limited). AE, ER, MC, V.

Well appointed and well run, the Halliburton is an elegant country inn placed at the heart of downtown. Named after former resident Sir Brenton Halliburton (Nova Scotia's first chief justice), it's spread among three town house–style buildings con-nected via gardens and sundecks in the rear but not internally. The main building was constructed in 1809 and converted to an inn in 1995, when it was modernized without any loss of its charm. All the guest rooms are subtly furnished with fine antiques, but few are so rare you'd fret about damaging them. They're rich and mas-culine in tone and light on frilly stuff. Among my favorites is room no. 113, which is relatively small but has a lovely working fireplace and unique skylighted bathroom. Room nos. 102 and 109 are suites with wet bars and fireplaces. Halliburton is the inn of choice among business travelers, but it's also a romantic spot for couples.

Dining: The intimate dining room, which serves from 5:30pm nightly, is dusky and wonderful, with an inventive small menu. The chef has a predilection for local game and Atlantic seafood. Look for bison medallions, grilled red deer, and grilled fresh char. The fresh seafood is always reliable. Entrees are C$18 to C$27 (US$12 to US$18). Afternoon refreshments are set out in the sitting room.

Amenities: Room service, VCRs on request, babysitting, dry cleaning, conference rooms.

Lord Nelson Hotel and Suites. 1515 South Park St., Halifax, NS B3J 2L2. ☎ **800/ 565-2020** or 902/423-6331. Fax 902/423-7148. 280 units. A/C TV TEL. C$149–C$179 (US$99–US$119) double peak season, C$99–C$139 (US$66–US$93) double off-season. Parking C$6 (US$3.85). AE, DC, DISC, ER, MC, V.

Built in 1928, the Lord Nelson was for years the city's preeminent hotel but gradually sank in esteem and ended up as a flophouse. In 1998, it received a top-to-bottom ren-ovation and is now back near the top of the heap as one of the city's better hotels. For starters, it has location: It is right across from the lovely Public Gardens and abuts lively Spring Garden Road. The standard guest rooms come with Georgian reproduc-tions and hair dryers and coffeemakers; some 40 have kitchenettes, and more than 100 have fax machines. Business-class rooms feature desk chairs, robes, bottled water, and free local calls. Rooms facing the street or the gardens are C$15 to C$20 (US$10 to US$13) extra—the others face into the bleak courtyard filled with service equipment.

Dining: The Victoria Arms is a convincingly cozy English-style pub off the handsome coffered lobby. It serves pub fare like steak-and-kidney pie, fish-and-chips, and liver with bacon and onions, along with a daily roast (turkey on Mon, roast beef on Wed). Pub sandwiches are C$7 to C$9 (US$4.65 to US$6) and entrees C$7 to C$15 (US$4.65 to US$10).

Amenities: Concierge, limited room service, free newspaper, washer/dryer, babysitting, dry cleaning/laundry, safe-deposit boxes, midsized fitness room with basic equipment and sauna.

✪ **Prince George Hotel.** 1725 Market St., Halifax, NS B3J 3N9. ☎ **800/565-1567** or 902/425-1986. Fax 902/429-6048. www.princegeorgehotel.com. E-mail reservations@ princegeorgehotel.com. 206 units. A/C MINIBAR TV TEL. C$160–C$220 double (US$107–US$147); C$250 (US$167) suite. AE, CB, DC, DISC, MC, V. Valet parking C$11 (US$7).

This contemporary large downtown hotel features all the underpinnings of elegance, like highly polished wainscoting, plush carpeting, and the discreet use of marble. Expect comfortably appointed guest rooms, most with balconies and all with a selection of complimentary tea and coffee, irons and boards, coffeemakers, and hair dryers. The Prince George is popular among business travelers, but the cordial staff makes individual travelers feel very much at home. It's nicely situated near the Citadel and restaurants and is linked to much of the rest of downtown via underground passageways.

Dining: Georgio's features contemporary bistro styling, with a menu to match. Dinners include burgers and pizza (most under C$10/US$7), along with more upscale offerings like bouillabaisse, striploin with Asian spices, and scallop stir-fry (C$13 to C$18/US$9 to US$12).

Amenities: Concierge, limited room service, business center, safe-deposit boxes, in-room massages, babysitting, dry cleaning/laundry; health club with indoor pool, sauna, whirlpool.

MODERATE

Maranova Suites. 65 King St., Dartmouth, NS B2Y 4C2. ☎ **888/798-5558** or 902/ 463-9520. Fax 902/463-2631. E-mail maranova@istar.ca. 35 units. A/C TV TEL. C$65–C$110 (US$43–US$73) double. AE, DC, MC, V. Underground parking available.

Across the harbor from Halifax and a 2-minute walk to frequent ferry service to downtown, the Maranova Suites is one of the better options for travelers on a ginger-ale budget. Housed in a modern concrete building, it features large and tidy but basic guest rooms, with sitting areas, kitchenettes, and balconies. Some have wonderful harbor views—ask when you book. Facilities include a coin-operated laundry and dry cleaning; access to Dartmouth Sportplex can be arranged.

Waverly Inn. 1266 Barrington St., Halifax, NS B3J 1Y5. ☎ **800/565-9346** or 902/ 423-9346. Fax 902/425-0167. www.waverlyinn.com. E-mail welcome@waverlyinn.com. 32 units. A/C TV TEL. June–Oct C$82–C$155 (US$55–US$103) double; Nov–May C$75–C$139 (US$50–US$93) double. Rates include continental breakfast and parking. DC, ER, MC, V.

The 1866 Waverly Inn has been adorned in high Victorian style. Flamboyant playwright Oscar Wilde was a guest in 1882, and one suspects he had a hand in the decorating scheme. You'll find walnut trim, red upholstered furniture, and portraits of sourpuss Victorians at every turn. The guest-room headboards are especially elaborate—some look like props from Gothic horror movies (guests of delicate constitution might suffer from a fitful slumber). Room no. 130 has a unique Chinese wedding bed and a Jacuzzi (nine rooms have private Jacuzzis). There's a common deck on which to enjoy sunny afternoons; a hospitality room stocks complimentary snacks and beverages.

INEXPENSIVE

The **Halifax Heritage House Hostel,** 1253 Barrington St. (☎ **902/422-3863**), is within walking distance of downtown attractions. You'll usually share rooms with other travelers (several private and family rooms are available); there are lockers in each room, shared bathrooms, and a fully equipped shared kitchen. Rates are C$19 (US$13) per person in a dorm or C$40 (US$27) double for a private room.

A short way from downtown but convenient to bus lines are university dorm rooms open to travelers throughout midsummer, when school isn't in session. **Dalhousie University** (☎ **902/494-8840**) has two-bedroom units in a 33-story tower on Fenwick Street. Rates are C$34 to C$51 (US$23 to US$34) per day (parking C$4/US$2.65 extra), which includes access to the athletic facility. **Saint Mary's University** (☎ **888/345-5555** or 902/420-5486, or 902/420-5591 after 4:30pm) has 600 dorm rooms and apartments spread about its campus, between Dalhousie University and Point Pleasant. The rooms are very basic, and some border on bleak. Rates are C$32 (US$21) double, with free parking. The campus is a 10-minute bike ride from downtown and is convenient to Point Pleasant Park.

WHERE TO DINE
EXPENSIVE

✪ **daMaurizio.** In The Brewery, 1496 Lower Water St. ☎ **902/423-0859.** Reservations highly recommended. Main courses C$20–C$23 (US$13–US$15). AE, ER, MC, V. Mon–Sat 5:30–10pm. ITALIAN.

Halifax's best restaurant does everything right. The vast space of a cleverly adapted former brewery has been divided into a complex of hives with columns and exposed brick that add to the atmosphere and heighten the anticipation of the meal. The decor shuns decorative doodads for clean lines and simple class. The same can be said of the menu. You could start with an appetizer of squid quick-cooked with olive oil, tomato, and chiles or grilled polenta with wild mushrooms. You won't be disappointed if you order from the pasta appetizers, like the open raviolo with lobster and shrimp. The main courses tax even the most decisive of diners: There are veal scaloppine in puff pastry with goose liver pâté, rack of lamb with roasted garlic, and veal chops with fresh sage. The kitchen doesn't try to dazzle with creativity but relies instead on the best ingredients and a close eye on perfect preparation.

Maple. 1813 Granville St. ☎ **902/425-9100.** Reservations recommended. Main courses C$9–C$15 (US$6–US$10) at lunch, C$20–C$30 (US$13–US$20) at dinner. AE, DC, ER, MC, V. Mon–Fri 11am–2pm; Mon–Sat 5:30–11pm. PROGRESSIVE CANADIAN.

Chef/proprietor/TV cooking show host Michael Smith is the Emeril Lagasse of eastern Canada. He began his crusade for an authentic Canadian cuisine while chef at the well-regarded Inn at Bay Fortune on Prince Edward Island and has brought his campaign to the mainland with the late 1999 opening of this splashy trilevel restaurant with an open kitchen on the middle level. Smith caters to a hip and discerning audience of foodies who appreciate his mission, making it "approachable, friendly, and enjoyable." (Those familiar with Canoe in Toronto may find echoes here.) Maple didn't open early enough for me to review it by press time, but Smith was anticipating offerings like saffron oyster broth with chive essence and oyster fritters, potato-crusted monkfish with an onion-and-leek tart, and roast boar with sage-walnut ravioli.

MODERATE

Cheapside Café. Inside the Art Gallery of Nova Scotia, 1723 Hollis St. ☎ **902/425-4494.** Sandwiches C$7–C$9 (US$4.65–US$6); main courses to C$11 (US$7). MC, V. Sat–Mon and holidays noon–5pm, Tues–Fri 10am–6pm. CREATIVE SANDWICHES.

The cheerful Cheapside Café is tucked inside the Provincial Building, one of two structures housing the Art Gallery of Nova Scotia. A whole groaning board of sandwiches and other delectables (named after artists) is offered during the day, such as chicken breast with avocado-and-mango chutney, roast beef with fried onions, and smoked salmon with an egg pancake and asparagus. Other fare includes fish cakes, quiche, and poached salmon with sun-dried–tomato chutney. For kids, there are peanut butter and jelly and egg salad with carrot sticks. The desserts are delicious, especially the Cheapside Café Torte.

✪ Il Mercato. 5475 Spring Garden Rd. ☎ **902/422-2866.** Reservations not accepted. Main courses C$9–C$15 (US$6–US$10). AE, DC, MC, V. Mon–Sat 11am–11pm. NORTHERN ITALIAN.

Light-colored Tuscan sponged walls and big rustic terra-cotta floor tiles set an appropriate mood at this popular spot amid the clamor of Spring Garden. Come early or late or expect to wait a bit, but it's worth the effort. You'll find a great selection of meals at prices around bargain level. Start by selecting antipastos from the deli counter in front (you point and the waitstaff will bring them to your table). Pastas run C$9 to C$12 (US$6 to US$8); every main course is less than C$15 (US$10). The foccacias are superb and come with a pleasing salad, and the ravioli with roast chicken and wild mushrooms is sublime. Non-Italian entrees include a seafood medley and grilled striploin with wild mushroom sauce. For dessert, head to the counter and ogle the luscious offerings, then point and sit, awaiting a fine finale.

Sweet Basil Bistro. 1866 Upper Water St. ☎ **902/425-2133.** Reservations recommended. Sandwiches C$8–C$13 (US$5–US$9); main courses C$13–C$19 (US$9–US$13). AE, DC, ER, MC, V. Daily 11:30am–11pm. UPMARKET PASTA.

If hunger overtakes you while you're snooping around the waterfront's shopping district, this should be your destination. It has the casual feel of a favorite trattoria, but the menu transcends the limited regional offerings that implies. Pastas are well represented (especially good is the squash ravioli with Parmesan-and-hazelnut sauce), but you'll also find seared scallops with five-spice broth and Asian vegetables, crusted lamb chops with demi-glace, and a selection of stir-fries ("Have it wimpy or volcano!" says the menu). The best name? Slash 'n Burn, a spicy salmon fillet with mango-basil sauce.

INEXPENSIVE

✪ Joe's Fish Smack. 1520 Queen St. ☎ **902/423-8435.** Main courses C$7–C$13 (US$4.65–US$8). AE, MC, V. Mon–Sat 11am–10pm, Sun 1–8pm. CASUAL/SEAFOOD.

Joe's trademark fish-and-chips are outstanding—haddock lightly coated with a beer batter and served with fries and a coleslaw that's among the province's zestiest. There are also chowder and a selection of fish (catfish, tuna, rainbow trout, shark, and more) you can have broiled, pan-fried, baked, poached, or Cajun style. For the weekend brunch you'll need to arrive with an appetite: The meal includes fish cakes, eggs, hash browns, baked beans, and toast. Joe's opened in spring 1999 and quickly attracted a devoted crowd with its excellent value for your money.

Satisfaction Feast. 1581 Grafton St. ☎ **902/422-3540.** Main courses C$5–C$12 (US$3.35–US$8). AE, DC, MC, V. Mon–Sat 10:30am–10pm (to 9pm Mon–Thurs in winter), Sun 11am–10pm. VEGETARIAN.

Along the newly cool stretch of Grafton Street, Satisfaction Feast is Halifax's original vegetarian restaurant and was recently voted one of Canada's top 10 veggie restaurants by the *Globe and Mail.* It's funky and fun, with a certain spare grace inside and a canopy and sidewalk tables for summer lounging. Main courses include lasagna, bean burritos, pesto pasta, veggie burgers, and a macrobiotic rice casserole. There are also "neatloaf" and tofu-and-rice "peace burgers" for those who like their food with cute names. The vegan fruit crisp is the dessert to hold out for. Satisfaction Feast also does a brisk business in takeout—consider a hummus-and-pita picnic atop nearby Citadel Hill.

HALIFAX AFTER DARK

THE PERFORMING ARTS   **Shakespeare by the Sea** (☎ 888/759-1516 or 902/ 422-0295) stages a line of Bardic and non-Bardic productions July to September at several alfresco venues. Most are held at Point Pleasant Park, where the ruins of old forts and buildings are used as the stage settings for delightful performances, with the audience sprawled on the grass, many enjoying picnic dinners. Most shows ask for a donation of C$5 (US$3.35). The more elaborate productions (past shows have included *King Lear* at the Citadel and *Titus Andronicus* at the park's Martello Tower) have limited seating, with tickets at C$25 to C$27 (US$17 to US$18).

The **Neptune Theatre,** 1593 Argyle St. (☎ 902/429-7070), benefited from a C$13.5 million (US$9 million) renovation and now also includes an intimate 200-seat studio theater. Top-notch dramatic productions are offered throughout the year. (The main season runs Oct to May, with a summer season filling in the gap with eclectic performances.) Mainstage tickets are C$20 to C$35 (US$13 to US$23).

THE CLUB & BAR SCENE   In the evening there's usually lively Maritime music and good beer at the **Lower Deck** (☎ 902/425-1501), one of the popular restaurants in the Historic Properties compound on the waterfront. There's music nightly at 9:30pm and late afternoons on Saturdays. Also recommended for live Celtic music and the occasional open mike night is **O'Bryne's Irish Pub,** 1565 Argyle St. (☎ 902/ 422-0187).

The young and the restless tend to congregate in pubs, nightclubs, and street corners along two axes that converge at the public library: **Grafton Street** and **Spring Garden Road.** If you're thirsty, wander the neighborhoods around here, and you're likely to find a spot that could serve as a temporary home for the evening. A number of popular clubs offer live music around town. Check *The Coast,* Halifax's free weekly newspaper (widely available).

8 The Eastern Shore: Rugged Coastline from Halifax to Cape Breton Island

Heading from Halifax toward Cape Breton Island (or vice versa), you have to choose from two basic routes. If you're burning to get to your destination, take the main roads of Route 102 connecting to Route 104 (Trans-Canada Highway). If you're in no particular hurry and are most content venturing down narrow lanes, destination unknown, by all means allow a couple of days to wind along the eastern shore, mostly along Route 7. Along the way you'll be rewarded with glimpses of a rugged coastline that's wilder and more remote than the coast south of Halifax. Communities here tend to be farther apart and less genteel, and those you come on have fewer services and fewer tourists. This region is perfect for those drawn to the outdoors and seeking coastal solitude.

ESSENTIALS

GETTING THERE   Routes 107 and 7 run along or near the coast from Dartmouth to Stillwater (near Sherbrooke). A patchwork of other routes—including 211, 316, 16, and 344—continues onward along the coast to the causeway to Cape Breton. (It's all pretty obvious on a map.) An excursion along the entire coastal route—from Dartmouth to Cape Breton Island with a detour to Canso—is 422km (262 miles).

VISITOR INFORMATION   Several tourist centers are staffed along the route. You'll find the best-stocked and most-helpful centers at **Sheet Harbor,** next to the waterfall (☎ 902/885-2595); **Sherbrooke Village,** at the museum (☎ 902/522-2400); and **Canso,** 1297 Union St. (☎ 902/366-2170).

EXPLORING THE EASTERN SEASHORE

This section assumes travel northeastward from Halifax toward Cape Breton. If you're traveling the opposite direction, hold this guide upside down (just kidding).

Between Halifax and Sheet Harbor, the route plays hide-and-seek with the coast, touching the water periodically before veering inland. The most scenic areas are around wild and open **Ship Harbor,** as well as **Spry Harbor,** noted for its attractive older homes and islands looming offshore.

Northeast of Spry Harbor, watch for signs to **Taylor Head Provincial Park** (no phone). A 3-mile washboard dirt road offers access to several attractive hiking trails, or you can continue to the end. Short trails through a scrubby wood lead to a long and beautiful fine-grained sand beach with views of evergreen-clad islands. Hearty bathers splash around on weekends, but weekdays it's often empty and wild. Admission is free.

Continuing on Route 211 beyond historic Sherbrooke Village (below), you'll drive through a wonderful landscape of lakes, ocean inlets, and upland bogs and soon come to the scenic **County Harbor Ferry.** The 12-car cable ferry crosses each direction every half an hour; it's a picturesque crossing of a broad river encased by rounded and wooded bluffs. The fare is C$1.75 (US$1.15) per car, including driver and passengers. The ferry isn't always running, so it's wise to check at the Canso or Sherbrooke visitor centers before detouring down this way.

Farther along (you'll be on Route 316 after the ferry), you'll come to **Tor Bay Provincial Park,** 4km (2½ miles) off the main road but well worth the detour on a sunny day. The park features three crescent-shaped beaches backed by grassy dunes and small ponds that are slowly being taken over by bog and spruce forest. The short boardwalk loop is especially picturesque.

Way out on the eastern tip of Nova Scotia's mainland is the end-of-the-world town of **Canso** (pop. 1,200). It's a rough-edged fishing and oil-shipping town, often windswept and foggy. The chief attraction here is the **Grassy Island National Historic Site** (☎ 902/366-3136). First stop by the small interpretive center on the waterfront and ask about the boat schedule. A park-run boat will take you out to the island, which once housed a bustling community of fishermen and traders from New England. (The interpretive center features artifacts recovered from the island.) A trail links several historic sites on this island, which tends to be a bit melancholy whether foggy or not. The boat serves the island May to mid-August daily 10am to 6pm. Fares are C$2.50 (US$1.65) adults, C$2 (US$1.35) seniors, and C$1.25 (US85¢) children 6 to 16.

Fisherman's Life Museum. Rte. 7, Jeddore Oyster Ponds. ☎ **902/889-2053.** Free admission but donations encouraged. June to mid-Sept Mon–Sat 9:30am–5:30pm, Sun 1–5:30pm.

In this museum you'll get a glimpse of life on the eastern shore a century ago. The humble white-shingle-and-green-trim cottage was built by James Myers in the 1850s; early in the 20th century it became the property of his youngest son, Ervin. Ervin and his wife raised a dozen daughters here ("This was quite a popular spot among the young men in the area," reports the laconic guide), and the home and grounds have been restored to look as they might have around 1900 or 1920. A walk through the house and barn and down to the fishing dock won't take much more than 20 minutes or so.

✪ **Sherbrooke Village.** Rte. 7, Sherbrooke. ☎ **902/522-2400.** Admission C$6 (US$4) adults, C$5 (US$3.35) seniors, C$3 (US$2) children, C$18 (US$12) families. Daily 9:30am–5:30pm. Closed mid-Oct to June 1.

About half of the town of Sherbrooke composes Sherbrooke Village, a historic section surrounded by low fences, water, and fields. (It's managed as part of the Nova Scotia Museum.) You'll have to pay admission to wander around, but the price is well worth it. This is Nova Scotia's largest restored village: Some 25 buildings have been restored and opened, from a convincing general store to the operating blacksmith shop and post office. Look also for the temperance hall, courthouse, printery, boat-building shop, drugstore, and schoolhouse. The village is unique in several respects. Almost all the buildings are on their original sites (only two have been moved); many homes are still occupied by locals, and private homes are interspersed with the buildings open to visitors. The church is still used for Sunday services, and you can dine at the old Sherbrooke Hotel (try the fishcakes and oven-baked beans).

WHERE TO STAY & DINE

Other than a handful of motels and B&Bs, few accommodations are available on the eastern shore.

Liscomb Lodge. Rte. 7, Liscomb Mills, NS B0J 2A0. ☎ **800/665-6343** or 902/779-2307. Fax 902/779-2700. 65 units. TV TEL. C$115–C$125 (US$77–US$83) double; C$150 (US$100) suite. Inquire about packages. AE, DISC, MC, V. Pets allowed in chalets.

This modern complex, owned/operated by the province, consists of a central lodge and a series of smaller cottages and outbuildings. It's in a remote part of the coast, adjacent to hiking trails and a popular boating area at the mouth of the Liscomb River. The lodge bills itself as "the nature lover's resort," and indeed it offers good access to both forest and water. But it's not exactly rustic, with well-tended lawns, bland modern architecture, shuffleboard, a marina, and even an oversized outdoor chessboard. The guest rooms are modern and motel-like; the cottages and chalets have multiple bedrooms and are well suited to families. The dining room is open to the public and serves resort fare; especially popular is the salmon cooked on a cedar plank. Some packages include meals, which is recommended given the dearth of other options nearby. There are also an indoor pool and fitness center, a tennis court, room service, and a gift shop.

✪ **Seawind Landing Country Inn.** 1 Wharf Rd., Charlos Cove, NS B0H 1T0. ☎ **800/ 563-4667.** Fax 902/525-2108. www.seawind.ns.ca. E-mail jcolvin@auracom.com. 13 units. C$70–C$105 (US$47–US$70) double. MC, V.

What to do when your boat-building business plummets as the fisheries decline? How about opening an inn? That's what Lorraine and Jim Colvin did, and their 20-acre oceanfront compound is delightful. Half the guest rooms are in the 130-year-old main house, which has been tastefully modernized and updated. The others are in a more recent outbuilding—what you lose in historic charm, you make up in brightness, ocean views, and double Jacuzzis. The innkeepers are especially knowledgeable about local artists (much of the work on display was produced nearby), and they've compiled an unusually literate and helpful guide to the region for you to peruse. The property has three private sand beaches, and coastal boat tours and picnic lunches can be arranged. Full or continental breakfasts are available, and the inn serves dinner nightly (guests only) with local products prepared in a country-French style. Entrees are C$13 to C$25 (US$9 to US$17).

9 Pictou: A Taste of Scotland in Canada

Pictou was established as part of a development scheme hatched by speculators from Philadelphia in 1760. Under the terms of their land grant, they needed to place some 250 settlers at the harbor. That was a problem. Few Philadelphians wanted to live there. So in 1773 the company sent a ship called the *Hector* to Scotland to drum up some impoverished souls who might be more amenable to starting life over in North America. This worked out rather better, and the ship returned with some 200 passengers, mostly Gaelic-speaking Highlanders. The voyage was brutal and full of storms, and the passengers were threatened with starvation. But they eventually arrived at Pictou and disembarked wearing Tartans and playing bagpipes.

The anniversary of the settlers' arrival is celebrated mid-August each year with the **Hector Festival** (☎ **800/353-5338**), when you might spot members of the clans wearing kilts and dining out in high style in memory of their ancestors. Pictou is Scottish enough you might find yourself a bit wary that locals will try to slip some haggis into your meal while you're not paying attention.

ESSENTIALS

GETTING THERE   Pictou is on Route 106, just north of Exit 22 off Route 104 (the south branch of the Trans-Canada Highway). The Prince Edward Island ferry is several kilometers north of town at the coast near Caribou (see chapter 5 for details on the ferry).

VISITOR INFORMATION   The **Tourist Information Centre** (☎ **902/485-6213**) is just off the rotary at the junction of Route 106 and Route 6. Mid-May to mid-October, it's open daily 8:30am to 7:30pm.

EXPLORING PICTOU

Pictou is a pleasant and historic harborside town with an abundance of interesting architecture. There's a surfeit of dour sandstone buildings adorned with five-sided dormers, and at times you might think you've wandered down an Edinburgh side street. **Water Street** is especially attractive, and it offers an above-average selection of boutiques, casual restaurants, and pubs. Look for the headquarters and factory outlet of **Grohmann Knives,** 116 Water St. (☎ **902/486-4224**). At Grohmann's, in a 1950s-mod building with a large knife piercing one corner, you'll find a good selection of quality knives (each with a lifetime guarantee) at marked-down prices. It's open daily; free factory tours are offered 9am to 3pm.

Pictou's one downside is the unsightly and noisome paper mill across the harbor. Even when it's obscured in the fog, you can often tell it's there by the sulfurous smell.

Hector Heritage Quay. 33 Caladh Ave. ☎ **902/485-4371.** Admission C$4 (US$2.65) adults, C$3 (US$2) seniors/teens, C$1 (US65¢) children 6–12, C$12 (US$8) families. Mid-May to mid-Oct daily 9am–9pm (to 6pm in shoulder seasons).

Learn about the hardships endured on the 1773 voyage of the unseaworthy *Hector*—which brought Scottish settlers to the region—at this modern small museum on the waterfront in downtown Pictou. You'll pass by intriguing exhibits en route to the museum's centerpiece: a full-sized replica of the 110-foot *Hector* under construction at the water's edge. (It's expected to be launched by fall 2000.) Stop by the blacksmith and carpentry shops to get a picture of life in the colonies in the early days.

WHERE TO STAY

Auberge Walker Inn. 34 Coleraine St. (P.O. Box 629), Pictou, NS B0K 1H0. ☎ **800/ 370-5553** or 902/485-1433. Fax 902/85-1222. E-mail walkerinn@ns.sympatico.ca. 11 units. TV. C$65–C$82 (US$43–US$55) double; C$149 (US$99) suite. AE, MC, V. Parking on street, at rear of building, and in lot 1 block away.

This handsome downtown inn is in a brick town house–style building (1865) overlooking one of Pictou's more active intersections. The innkeepers have done a commendable job giving the place a comfortable feel while retaining its historic sensibility. Some rooms (like no. 10 on the third floor) have nice harbor views. A new-in-1999 first-floor suite has a small kitchen, a Jacuzzi, and a dark bedroom in back. All rooms have bathrooms, but the conversions have come at some sacrifice. (The upstairs rooms have showers only, and one reader wrote that his was so small he couldn't bend over to wash his legs.) On the upside: The inn is perfectly situated to enjoy Pictou's restaurants and attractions.

✪ **Custom House Inn.** 38 Depot St., Pictou, NS B0K 1H0. ☎ **902/485-4546.** Fax 902/485-2546. E-mail customhouseinn@ns.sympatico.ca. 8 units. A/C TV TEL. Summer C$79–C$139 (US$53–US$93) double; off-season C$79–C$109 (US$53–US$73) double. AE, DC, ER, MC, V.

This hulking brick-and-sandstone building with heroic arches and dentils was built in 1872 and thoroughly renovated in 1997. The former office building is now home to some of the more spacious and dramatic guest rooms in the province, each with high ceilings (13½ feet on the first floor), lustrous maple floors, and a certain Spartan grace. The innkeepers have been reserved in their decorating, letting the architectural space speak for itself. Three rooms have kitchenettes with refrigerators; all have whirlpool tubs. Many are also adorned with the moody and notable nautical paintings of local painter Dave Macintosh. Among the best rooms is no. 2F, a bright corner room with kitchenette and water views. In the basement is the Old Stone Pub, a wonderfully renovated space with an informal menu (lots of seafood and pasta), 16 beers on tap, and live Celtic music some evenings.

Pictou Lodge Resort. Shore Rd. (P.O. Box 1539), Pictou, NS B0K 1H0. ☎ **800/495-6343** or 902/485-4322. Fax 902/485-4945. E-mail pictou.lodge@north.nsis.com. 65 units. TV TEL. C$94–C$225 (US$63–US$150) double. AE, DC, DISC, MC, V. Closed mid-Oct to May. Follow Shore Rd. from downtown toward the PEI ferry; watch for signs.

The original rustic log lodge and a handful of log outbuildings have gone through a number of owners—including the Canadian National Railway—since entrepreneurs built the compound on a grassy bluff overlooking a pristine beach early in the 20th century. It is now owned by Maritime Inns and Resorts (which has four other properties) and has been modestly upgraded and improved. The older log rooms, most with kitchenettes, have considerably more character, but some still regard them as a bit dowdy. The newer rooms, alas, have the bland sameness of modern motel rooms everywhere. The lodge is about 10 minutes' drive from downtown but has a wonderfully remote feel. Lunch and dinner are served in the Adirondack-style lodge, with its soaring spaces hammered together with time-burnished logs. Dinner entrees might be termed "creative traditional" and feature wild blueberry chicken, seafood linguine, and cedar-planked salmon at C$15 to C$26 (US$10 to US$17). Facilities include an out-door heated pool, recreational boats and bikes, 500m of private beach, a playground, nature trails, and a games room.

WHERE TO DINE

Fougere's. 91 Water St. ☎ **902/485-1575.** Reservations suggested. Main courses C$6–C$14 (US$4–US$9) at lunch, C$14–C$30 (US$9–US$20) at dinner. AE, MC, V. Summer daily 11am–9pm; off-season call first. UPSCALE TRADITIONAL.

Fougere's is in a simply furnished, bright dining room that's as appealing as it is tidy. This local institution was run for years by Ben Fougere; in 1998, it was taken over by Stefan and Giovanna Sieber, who've impressed regular diners with their broadly appealing menu and their deftness in the kitchen. The couple moved to Nova Scotia after 12 years in Switzerland, and some Swiss dishes appear from time to time. But the menu is mostly anchored by traditional and locally popular dishes, like surf and turf, seafood casserole, and smoked haddock. Nonseafood dishes include T-bone steak, roast turkey dinner, and jaegerschnitzel.

Piper's Landing. Rte. 376, Lyons Brook. ☎ **902/485-1200.** Reservations recommended. Main courses C$5–C$11 (US$3.35–US$7) at lunch, C$13–C$23 (US$9–US$15) at dinner. AE, MC, V. Mon–Sat 11:30am–2:30pm and 4–9pm, Sun 11am–9pm. From the Pictou Rotary take Rt. 376 toward Lyons Brook; it's 3km (1.9 miles) on your left. UPSCALE TRADITIONAL.

This contemporary, attractive dining room on a residential road outside Pictou remains a local favorite and your best bet in Antigonish for a sophisticated meal, despite sometimes-frustrating service. The interior is sparely decorated and under-stated. Likewise, the menu looks simple—main courses include grilled beef tender-loin, pork schnitzel, and a filling seafood platter—but you'll be impressed by the flair in preparation. The wine list, alas, is small and tired.

10 Cape Breton Island

The isolated and craggy island of **Cape Breton**—Nova Scotia's northernmost land-mass—should be high on your list of don't-miss destinations, especially if you have an adventurous bent. The island's chief draw is **Cape Breton Highlands National Park,** far north on the island's western lobe. But there's also the historic fort at Louisbourg and scenic Bras d'Or Lake, the inland saltwater lake that nearly cleaves the island in two. Above all, there are the picturesque drives. It's hard to find a road that's not a scenic route in Cape Breton. By turns the vistas are wild and dramatic, then settled and pastoral.

When traveling on the island, be alert to the cultural richness. Just as southern Nova Scotia was largely settled by English Loyalists fleeing the United States after they lost the War of Independence, Cape Breton was principally settled by Highland Scots whose families had come out on the wrong side of rebellions against the Crown. You can still see that heritage in the accents of elders in some of the more remote villages and in the great popularity of British-style folk music.

You'll often hear references to the ✪ **Cabot Trail.** This is the official designation for the 300km (186-mile) roadway around the northwest part of the island, which encompasses the national park. It's named after John Cabot, whom many believe first set foot on North American soil near Cape North. (Many don't believe that, however, especially those in Newfoundland.)

Note: I've divided Cape Breton into two sections: Cape Breton Island and Cape Breton Highlands National Park. Jump ahead to the next section for information on adventures in the park itself.

ESSENTIALS

GETTING THERE   Cape Breton is connected to the mainland via the Canso Causeway, 271km (168 miles) from the New Brunswick border at Amherst or 282km (175 miles) from Halifax.

VISITOR INFORMATION   Nine tourist centers dot the island. The best stocked (and a much recommended first stop) is the bustling **Port Hastings Info Centre** (☎ 902/625-4201), on your right just after crossing the Canso Causeway. Mid-May to mid-October, it's open daily 8am to 8:30pm.

MABOU & VICINITY

Mabou (pop. 400) is on a deep protected inlet along the island's picturesque west shore. Scenic drives and bike rides are a dime a dozen hereabouts; few roads fail to yield up opportunities to break out the camera or just lean against your vehicle and enjoy the panorama. The residents are strongly oriented toward music in their activities, unusually so even for musical Cape Breton Island. Evening entertainment tends to revolve around fiddle playing, square dancing, or a traditional gathering of musicians and storytellers called a *ceilidh* (pronounced *kay*-lee). To find out where things are going on, stop by The Mull (below) and scope out the bulletin board.

In a handsome valley between Mabou and Inverness is the distinctive post-and-beam **Glenora Distillery** (☎ 800/839-0491 or 902/258-2662). This modern distillery began producing single-malt whisky in 1990 in charred oak barrels. This includes scotch, which can't technically be called such because it isn't made in Scotland. Production runs take place later in the fall, but half-hour tours of the facility are offered during summer at C$5 (US$3.35) daily 9am to 5pm; closed November to mid-June. The product has been aged for 10 years, making it eligible for sampling in 2000. Swing by and be among the first to savor this new contribution to local highland lore. The distillery has an adjoining restaurant and nine-room hotel; traditional music is often scheduled for weekends or evenings in the contemporary pub.

WHERE TO STAY

✪ **Duncreigan Country Inn.** Rte. 19, Mabou, NS B0E 1X0. ☎ **800/840-2207** or 902/945-2207. Fax 902/945-2206. E-mail duncreigan@auracom.com. 8 units. TV TEL. C$90–C$140 (US$60–US$93) double. Rates include continental breakfast. AE, MC, V.

The Duncreigan occupies a quiet wooded bluff across the bridge from the village. Modern and airy (it was built in 1991), the inn manages to meld contemporary and traditional in a most appealing way. The guest rooms are in the main lodge and an outbuilding (connected via boardwalk), and the landscaping is beginning to mature quite nicely. The rooms are wonderful, many decorated in soothing burgundy tones, and all have radios and ceiling fans. Many are furnished with Nova Scotian antiques, with headboards creatively designed by a local artisan to match the furnishings. Room no. 2 has a superb water view, though my favorite is no. 5, with its wood-burning stove, whirlpool, and deck overlooking the estuary. There's no charge to use the inn's bikes or canoe. Mid-June to mid-October, dinners are served nightly (except Mon), and entrees might include seafood with basil cream, lemon-peppered pork tenderloin, or scallops with pesto. The prix-fixe three-course dinner ranges from C$23 to C$30 (US$15 to US$20); reservations are requested.

Cape Breton Island

WHERE TO DINE

The Mull. Rte. 19 (north of the village), Mabou. ☎ **902/945-2244.** Reservations accepted for parties of 6 or more. Sandwiches C$4–C$7 (US$2.65–US$4.65); main courses C$12–C$16 (US$8–US$11). AE, MC, V. Daily 11am–9pm (closes an hour or 2 earlier off-season). CAFE.

The Mull is a country deli that serves simple, well-prepared food. Lunches tend toward items like seafood chowder, fish-and-chips, and deli-style sandwiches. After 5pm, the dinner menu kicks in, with entrees like grilled halibut, T-bone steak, and scallops in light wine sauce. Don't expect to be wowed by fancy; do expect a satisfying and filling meal.

MARGAREE VALLEY

West of Baddeck and south of Chéticamp, the **Margaree Valley** region loosely consists of the area from the village of Margaree Valley near the headwaters of the

Margaree River down the river to Margaree Harbor on Cape Breton's west coast. Seven small communities are clustered in along the valley floor, and it's a world apart from the rugged drama of the surf-battered coast; it's vaguely reminiscent of the farm country of upstate New York. The Cabot Trail gently rises and falls on the shoulders of the rounded hills flanking the valley, offering views of the farmed floodplains and glimpses of the river.

The **Margaree River** has been accorded celebrity status in fishing circles—it's widely regarded as one of North America's most productive Atlantic salmon rivers, and salmon have continued to return to spawn here in recent years, which isn't the case in many other waterways of Atlantic Canada. The river has been open to fly-fishing only since the 1880s and in 1991 was designated a Canadian Heritage River. It was a revered spot among a slew of noted anglers, including baseball legend Ted Williams and fly-fishing demigod Lee Wulff, who once wrote of the river, "The Margaree was my first love among salmon rivers."

Learn about the river's heritage at the **Margaree Salmon Museum** in Northeast Margaree (☎ **902/248-2848**). The handsome building features a brief video about the salmon's life cycle, and exhibits include antique rods (like one impressive 18-footer), examples of poaching equipment, and hundreds of hand-tied salmon flies (why a salmon will strike a fly remains a subject of lore and heated conjecture—unlike trout, they don't eat insects when in freshwater). Museum docents can help you find a guide to try your hand on the water. (Mid-June to mid-July and Sept and early Oct are the best times.) Mid-June to mid-October, the museum is open daily 9am to 5pm. Admission is C$1 (US65¢) adults and C25¢ (US15¢) children.

WHERE TO STAY

✪ **Normaway Inn.** P.O. Box 121, Margaree Valley, NS B0E 2C0. ☎ **800/565-9463** or 902/564-5433. Fax 902/248-2600. www.normaway.com. E-mail normaway@atcon.com. 29 units. C$85–C$109 (US$57–US$73) double in lodge; C$99–C$139 (US$66–US$93) cottage. MC, V. Closed late Oct to May 31. Pets allowed in cottages only.

From the moment you turn down the drive lined with tall Scotch pines, you'll feel you're in another world—a sort of 1920s Bertie Wooster world, elegant and rustic at the same time. The lodge was built in 1928 on some 500 acres and has been run by the MacDonald family since the 1940s. You might imagine running into tweedy gentlemen anglers, but it's not a true fishing resort. It appeals to both families and honeymooners and is spread out enough to accommodate all. Nine of the rooms are in the main lodge and have a timeless quality; the cottages are spread around the property an easy walk from the main lodge and have hardwood floors and an almost Scandinavian quality. The older cottages were built in the 1940s and are a bit smaller. Eight cottages have Jacuzzis, and all but two have wood stoves.

The country farm–style dining room is known for its Atlantic salmon and its lamb, which is raised for the inn about 10 miles away. The menu changes nightly but includes dishes like roast duck with peach-and-brandy sauce and pan-fried trout with red onion/orange relish. Dinners are C$30 (US$20) for three courses and C$35 (US$23) for four. A limited number of nonguests (about half a dozen or fewer each night) can dine by advance reservation. The inn's strong card is evening entertainment, with events from films to live performances, including Acadian music, storytelling, and local fiddling. The famous weekly square dance, held in the inn's barn, attracts up to 350 people, about evenly split between locals and tourists (C$6/US$4). The inn has one tennis court and additional acreage along the river a short drive away that includes five salmon pools.

CHÉTICAMP

The Acadian town of **Chéticamp** (pop. 1,000) is the western gateway to Cape Breton Highlands National Park and the center for French-speaking culture on Cape Breton. The change is striking as you drive northward from Margaree Harbour—the family names suddenly go from MacDonald to Doucet and the whole culture and cuisine change.

The town itself consists of an assortment of restaurants, boutiques, and tourist establishments spread along Main Street, which closely hugs the harbor. A winding boardwalk follows the harbor's edge through much of town and offers a good spot to stretch your legs and get your bearings. (That's Chéticamp Island just across the water; the tall coastal hills of the national park are visible up the coast.) Chéticamp is a good stop for provisioning, topping off the gas tank, and finding shelter.

Chéticamp is noted worldwide for its hooked rugs, a craft perfected by early Acadian settlers. Those curious about the craft should allow time for two stops. **Les Trois Pignons, the Elizabeth LeFort Gallery and Museum,** Main Street, at the north end of town (☎ **902/224-2612**), displays 20 of the 300 fine tapestries created by Dr. LeFort, along with rugs made by local craftspeople. It's open daily: July and August 8am to 6pm and September, October, May, and June 9am to 5pm. Admission is C$3.50 (US$2.35) adults and C$3 (US$2) seniors; children 12 and under are free. In the 1930s, artisans formed the **Cooperative Artisanale de Chéticamp,** 774 Main St. (☎ **902/224-2170**), open June 2 to mid-October. A selection of hooked rugs—from the size of drink coaster on up—are sold here, along with other trinkets and souvenirs. There's often a weaver or other craftsperson at work in the shop. A small museum downstairs (free) chronicles the life and times of the early Acadian settlers and their descendents.

Page ahead to the next section for more details on national park activities.

WHERE TO STAY

A handful of motels service the thousands of travelers who pass through each summer. **Laurie's Motor Inn,** Main Street (☎ **800/959-4253** or 902/224-2400), has more than 50 motel rooms in three buildings right in town, with rates at C$72 to C$125 (US$48 to US$83) double. **Parkview Motel,** Route 19 north of town (☎ **902/ 224-3232**), is near the park entrance and peacefully away from the hubbub of town, with rooms at around C$80 (US$53) double.

Pilot Whale Lodge. Rte. 19, Chéticamp, NS B0E 1H0. ☎ **902/224-2592.** Fax 902/ 224-1540. www.pilotwhale.com. E-mail chalets@pilotwhale.com. 6 cottages. TV. C$119 (US$79) double. Extra person C$10 (US$7); children 6 and under free. AE, MC, V. Closed Nov to mid-May.

These spare cottages have a bit of an antiseptic air but contain two bedrooms and full housekeeping facilities, including microwaves, gas barbecues, coffeemakers, decks, and wood stoves. The best feature, though, is the grand view north toward the coastal mountains. (Cottages 1, 2, 4, and 5 have the best vistas.) In 1999, the lodge added apartments to the walkout basements beneath two of the cottages (C$80/US$53 double), which impinges slightly on the privacy of those both upstairs and down.

WHERE TO DINE

La Boulangerie Aucoin (☎ **902/224-3220**) has been a staple of Chéticamp life since 1959. Located just off the Cabot Trail between town and the national park (look for the signs), the bakery is constantly restocking its shelves with fresh-baked goods; ask what's still warm when you order at the counter. Among the options are croissants, scones, bread, and berry pies.

Harbour Restaurant and Bar. 15299 Cabot Trail (Main St.). ☎ **902/224-2042.** Reservations recommended in peak season. Light fare C$5-$8 (US$3.35–US$5); dinner main courses C$13–C$17 (US$9–US$11). A, MC, V. Daily 11am–11pm. Closed late-Oct to early-May. SEAFOOD.

The Harbour is Chéticamp's sleekest restaurant, in an easy-to-pass-by building on the waterfront. The water views are excellent, and the food is well above average for the region. The light-fare menu consists of pub favorites (hamburgers, club sandwiches, fish-and-chips), along with an Acadian specialty or two. The dinner menu favors seafood, with options like an East Coast casserole (scallops, lobster, shrimp, and haddock in cheese sauce), broiled salmon, and farm-raised Margaree trout, served charbroiled and finished with tarragon butter.

INGONISH

The area includes a number of similarly named towns (Ingonish Centre, Ingonish Ferry, South Ingonish Harbor) with a combined population of about 1,300. Like Chéticamp on the peninsula's east side, **Ingonish** serves as a gateway to the national park and is home to a park visitor center and a handful of motels and restaurants. Oddly, there's really no critical mass here—the services are spread along a lengthy stretch of the Cabot Trail, and there's never any sense of arrival. You pass a liquor store, some shops, a bank, a post office, and a handful of cottages. Then you're suddenly in the park.

Highlights in the area are a **sandy beach,** good for chilly splashing around (near Keltic Lodge), and a number of short **hiking trails** (see "Cape Breton Highlands National Park," below). The **Highland Links** golf course (☎ 800/441-1118) is one of the best in Nova Scotia, if not in all Atlantic Canada. South of Ingonish the Cabot Trail climbs and descends the hairy 1,000-foot-high promontory of **Cape Smokey,** which explodes into panoramic views from the top. At the height of land there's a provincial park where you can cool your engine and admire the views. An 11km (6.8-mile) hiking trail leads to the tip of the cape along the high bluffs, studded with unforgettable viewpoints along the way.

WHERE TO STAY

Cape Breton Highlands Bungalows. Cabot Trail, Ingonish, NS B0C 1L0. ☎ 888/469-4816 or 902/285-2000. 25 units. TV. C$69 (US$46) double. MC, V. Closed early-Oct to June 1.

This attractive cluster of vintage cottages boasts a Cape Breton rarity: It's on the shore of a freshwater lake rather than the ocean. But the ocean, at Ingonish Beach, is a short walk or paddle away. The green-trimmed white cottages (one- and two-bedroom) were built in the 1940s and are pleasantly rustic, all but one with kitchenettes. The larger ones are perfect for families, who make up much of the clientele. Nos. 1 to 10 are in an open grassy area, some with views across the lake to the Keltic Lodge. The rest are tucked in a grove of birches and hardwoods; nos. 11 and 12 are nicely sited at the edge of the lake.

✪ **Keltic Lodge.** Middle Head Peninsula, Ingonish Beach, NS B0C 1L0. ☎ 800/565-0444 or 902/285-2880. Fax 902/285-2859. www.gov.ns.ca/resorts. 72 inn units, 26 cottage units. TV TEL. C$268–C$283 (US$179–US$189) double. Rates include breakfast and dinner. AE, DC, DISC, ER, MC, V. Closed Oct–Dec and Apr–May (main lodge closed in winter).

To reach the Keltic Lodge, you pass through a grove of white birches, cross an isthmus atop angular cliffs, and then arrive at the stunning, vaguely Tudor resort. The views are extraordinary. Owned/operated by the province, the Keltic is comfortable without being slick, nicely worn without being threadbare. Some of the guest rooms are painted in that soothing mint green popular in the 1940s; most are furnished rather plainly with run-of-the-mill motel furniture. (You might expect more for the price.) The cottages are set amid birches and have four bedrooms; you can rent one bedroom and share a common living room with other guests. Be aware that some of the rooms are at the more modern Inn at the Keltic a couple hundred meters away, which has better views but a more sterile character. A reader wrote to lament the inadequate soundproofing in the modern annex and recommended an upstairs room here to avoid hearing heavy footfalls.

Dining: The management keeps up appearances in the main dining room: no jeans, shorts, or sweat clothes allowed. The food here is among the best on the island; the excellent C$40 (US$27) fixed-price dinner menu (included in room rates) offers several selections, with prime rib and lemon-pepper salmon fillet among the favorites. A less formal option is the new-in-1999 Atlantic Restaurant, a 3-minute walk away, housed in a new timber-frame building that's airy and bright and filled with coastal views. The Atlantic is reasonably priced (dinner entrees C$6 to C$16/US$3.65 to US$11) and specializes in lighter fare like grilled salmon and pasta.

Amenities: Heated oceanside pool, game room, laundry, guest safe, great hiking trail; tennis courts and beach nearby; adjacent Highland Links 18-hole golf course (under separate management; ask about packages).

BADDECK

Though **Baddeck** (pronounced Bah-*deck*) is at a distance from the national park, it's often considered the de facto "capital" of the Cabot Trail. The town offers the widest selection of accommodations along the loop, an assortment of restaurants, and a handful of useful services like grocery stores and Laundromats. Baddeck is also famed as the summer home of revered inventor Alexander Graham Bell, who's memorialized at a national historic site. What's more, the town is compact and easy to reconnoiter by foot, is scenically located on the shores of Bras d'Or Lake, and is within striking distance of the excellent Fortress at Louisbourg. This is the best base for those with limited vacation time and those who plan to drive the Cabot Trail in a day (figure 6 to 8 hours). If, however, your intention is to spend a few days exploring the hiking trails, bold headlands, and remote coves of the national park (which I'd recommend!), you're better off finding a base farther north.

The **Baddeck Welcome Center** is south of the village at the intersection of Route 105 and Route 205 (☎ **902/295-1911**). In season, it's open daily 8:30am to 8:30pm.

Exploring the Town

Baddeck is much like a modern New England village, centered around a small commercial boulevard, **Chebucto Street,** just off the lake. Ask for a free **walking tour brochure** at the welcome center (above). A complete tour of the village's architectural highlights won't take much more than 15 or 20 minutes.

Government Wharf (head down Jones Street from the Yellow Cello restaurant) is home to three boat tours, which offer the best way to experience Bras d'Or Lake. **Amoeba Sailing Tours** (☎ **902/295-2481**) offers a mellow cruise on a 50-foot sailboat, from which you'll likely spot bald eagles and other birds and watch Baddeck's fine lakeshore drift past. Four sailings daily are offered in peak season; the cost is C$15 (US$10) per person. **Fan-A-Sea** (☎ **902/295-1900**) runs charter fishing trips from Baddeck, and with some luck you may land cod, haddock, or trout. Bait and rods are supplied; the rate is C$35 (US$23) per person per hour. **Loch Bhreagh Boat Tours** (☎ **902/295-2016**) offers motorboat tours that pass Alexander Graham Bell's palatial former estate and other attractions at this end of the lake.

About 200 yards offshore from the downtown wharf is **Kidston Island,** owned by the town. It has a wonderful sand beach with lifeguards and an old lighthouse to explore. The Lion's Club offers frequent pontoon boat shuttles 10am to 6pm (noon to 6pm on weekends) across St. Patrick's Channel; the crossing is free, but donations are encouraged.

Alexander Graham Bell National Historic Site. Chebucto St., Baddeck. ☎ 902/295-2069. Admission C$4.25 (US$2.85) adults, C$3.25 (US$2.15) seniors, C$2.25 (US$1.50) students, C$11 (US$7) families. June daily 9am–6pm; July–Aug daily 8:30am–7:30pm; Sept to mid-Oct daily 8:30am–6pm; mid-Oct to May daily 9am–5pm.

Each summer for much of his life, noted inventor Alexander Graham Bell fled the heat of Washington, D.C., for a hillside retreat high above Bras d'Or Lake. The mansion, which is still owned and occupied by the Bell family, is visible across the harbor from various spots around town. But to learn more about Bell's career and restless mind, you should visit this modern exhibit center, perched on a grassy hillside at the north edge of the village. You'll find extensive exhibits about Bell's invention of the telephone at age 29, as well as considerable information about Bell's less-lauded contraptions, like his ingenious kites, hydrofoils, and airplanes.

WHERE TO STAY

If the places below lack vacancies, try the **Auberge Gisele,** 387 Shore Rd. (☎ 800/304-0466 or 902/295-2849), a modern 63-room hotel that's popular with bus tours, or the **Cabot Trail Motel,** Route 105, 1.5km/0.9 mile west of Baddeck (☎ 902/295-2580), with 40 rooms overlooking the lake and a heated outdoor pool. Doubles run C$85 to C$100 (US$57 to US$67) at both.

✪ **Duffus House Inn.** Water St. (P.O. Box 427), Baddeck, NS B0E 1B0. ☎ 902/295-2172. 7 units. C$95–C$125 (US$63–US$83) double; C$135–C$150 (US$90–US$100) suite. Rates include continental breakfast. V. Closed mid-Oct to mid-May.

A visit to the Duffus House is like a visit to the house of the grandmother everyone wishes they had. These two adjacent buildings (from 1820 and 1885) overlook the channel and are cozy and tastefully furnished with a mix of antiques. The Duffus House is far enough from Baddeck's downtown to keep the commotion at arm's length, yet you can still walk everywhere in a few minutes. (The inn also has its own dock, where you can swim or just sit peacefully.) The several cozy common areas are comfortably furnished and offer great places to chat with other guests, as does the intimate garden. The inn is run with considerable good cheer by innkeepers John and Judy Langley.

Inverary Resort. Shore Rd. (P.O. Box 190), Baddeck, NS B0E 1B0. ☎ 800/565-5660 or 902/295-3500. Fax 902/295-3527. www.inveraryresort.com. E-mail inverary@atcon.com. 144 units. AC TV TEL. C$95–C$150 (US$63–US$100) double; C$195 (US$130) suite. AE, DC, MC, V. Closed Dec–May.

This is a good choice for families with active kids. The sprawling Inverary Resort, on 12 lakeside acres within walking distance of town, has a slew of activities to keep kids busy, from fishing to paddleboats to nightly bonfires on the beach. The resort began in the late 19th century as the ostentatious home of "Millionaire MacNeil," a local boy who made good in Boston. It's been a resort for more than 50 years and has been added to steadily over the decades. The guest rooms vary in size and style but all are quite comfortable, even the snug motel-style units in the cottages; many are appointed with colonial revival reproductions.

Dining: The Lakeside Cafe overlooks the resort's small marina and serves informal fare like penne with pesto and vegetable lasagne (C$11 to C$17). The more formal

Flora's, in the main lodge, has more upscale fare served in a sun-porch setting. Look for mixed grill, broiled halibut, and chicken breast with apple-and-onion compote (C$16 to C$20/US$10 to US$13).

Amenities: Room service, safe, indoor pool, hot tub, sauna, three tennis courts, volleyball court, boat tours, boat rentals (canoes, kayaks, paddleboats, surf bikes, Zodiacs), marina, playground, shuffleboard.

Telegraph House. Chebucto St. (P.O. Box 8), Baddeck, NS B0E 1B0. ☎ **902/295-1100.** Fax 902/295-1136. 43 units, 39 with bathroom. TV. C$65–C$72 (US$43–US$48) double without bathroom, C85–C$92 (US$57–US$61) double with bathroom. AE, MC, V.

This 1861 hotel on Baddeck's bustling main street offers guest rooms divided among the original inn and two motel units on a rise behind it. This is where Alexander Graham Bell stayed when he first visited Baddeck. And not all that much has changed in the main inn—the rooms are still small and decorated eclectically with both antiques and plain old furniture. Four rooms on the top floor share two bathrooms, an arrangement that works well with families. I prefer the larger if unexciting motel rooms in back; ask for room nos. 22 to 32, which have small sitting decks outside their front doors with glimpses of the lake. The dining room serves traditional favorites for lunch and dinner, like shepherd's pie, ham plate, meat loaf, roast turkey, and fish cakes.

WHERE TO DINE

Baddeck Lobster Suppers. Ross St. ☎ **902/295-3307.** Reservations accepted for groups of 10 or more. Lobster dinner around C$25 (US$17); lunch items C$3–C$7 (US$2–US$4.65). Kids' menu available. MC, V. Daily 11:30am–1:30pm and 4–9pm. Closed Nov–June 1. SEAFOOD.

Save your burgeoning appetite for an over-the-top seafood feast at this cavernous no-frills restaurant. It has the charm of a Legion Hall, but the crowds contentedly and noisily chowing down provide the real atmosphere. The lobster dinner—which virtually everyone orders—includes one steamed crustacean, plus all you-can-eat mussels, chowder, biscuits, dessert, and drinks. Not in the mood for lobster? There's also planked salmon (C$21/US$14).

Yellow Cello. 525 Chebucto St. ☎ **902/295-2303.** Reservations suggested in peak season. Main courses C$5–C$9 (US$3.35–US$6). MC, V. In season daily 8am–11pm. PUB FARE.

If you don't set your culinary expectations too high, this is a convivial spot to while away an afternoon or evening. Angle for a seat outdoors under the awning facing Chebucto Street. The menu will be familiar to those who watch a lot of sports on TV: pizza, nachos, chili, lasagna, sandwiches, and the like.

LOUISBOURG

In the early 18th century, **Louisbourg,** on Cape Breton's remote and windswept easternmost coast, was home to an ambitious French fortress and settlement. Despite its brief prosperity and durable construction of rock, it virtually disappeared after the British finally forced the French out (for the second time) in 1760. Through the miracle of archaeology and historic reconstruction, much of the imposing settlement has been re-created, and today Louisbourg is among Canada's most ambitious national historic parks. It's an attraction everyone coming to Cape Breton Island should make an effort to visit.

EXPLORING THE VILLAGE

The hamlet of Louisbourg—which you'll pass through en route to the historic park—is pleasantly low-key, still scouting for ways to rebound from one devastating economic loss after another, including the cessation of the railway, the decline in boat building, and the loss of the fisheries. Louisbourg is now striving to gear its economy more toward tourism, and you can see the progress year by year.

A short **boardwalk** with interpretive signs fronts the town's tiny waterfront. (You'll get a glimpse of the national historic site across the water.) Nearby is a faux-Elizabethan theater, the **Louisbourg Playhouse** (☎ 902/733-2996). This was originally built near the old town by Disney for filming the movie *Squanto*. After the production wrapped up, Disney donated it to the village, which dismantled it and moved it to a side street near the harbor. Various performances and concerts are staged here throughout summer.

Leave enough time for the detour a couple of miles out to **Lighthouse Point,** the site of the first Canadian lighthouse. (The current lighthouse is a replacement.) The rocky coastline is dramatic and undeveloped, and it's a perfect spot for a picnic to just idle away a late afternoon. The road, which is partly gravel, departs from the main road near the visitor information center.

✪ **Fortress of Louisbourg National Historic Park.** Louisbourg. ☎ **902/733-2280.** Admission June–Sept C$11 (US$7) adults, C$8 (US$5) seniors, C$6 (US$3.65) children, C$28 (US$18) families. Discounts May and Oct. July and Aug daily 9am–7pm; May, June, Sept, and Oct daily 9:30am–5pm. Costumed interpreters limited in off-season. Closed Nov–Apr.

The historic French village of Louisbourg has had three lives. The first was early in the 18th century, when the French colonized this area aggressively in a bid to stake their claim in the New World. With the help of creative engineers and strong backs, they built an imposing stone fortress. Imposing but not impregnable, as the British proved when they captured the fort following a 1745 siege. The fortress had a second, if short, life after it was returned to the French following negotiations in Europe. War soon broke out again, though, and it was recaptured by the British in 1758. This time they blew it up for good measure.

The final resurrection came in the 1960s, when the Canadian government decided to rebuild one-fourth of the stone-walled town—virtually creating a settlement out of a handful of grass hummocks and some scattered documents about what once was. (The project also served as an economic lifeline for recently unemployed miners.) The historic park was built to re-create life as it looked in 1744, when this was an important French military capital and seaport.

You arrive after walking through an interpretive center and boarding a bus for the short ride to the site. (Keeping cars at a distance does much to enhance the historic flavor.) You'll wander through the impressive gatehouse—perhaps being challenged by a costumed guard on the lookout for English spies—and then begin wandering the narrow lanes and poking around the faux-historic buildings, some of which contain informative exhibits, others of which are restored and furnished with convincingly worn reproductions. Chickens, geese, and other barnyard animals peck and cluck. Vendors sell freshly baked bread out of wood-fired ovens. Allow at least 4 hours to explore. It's an extraordinary destination, as picturesque as it is historic.

WHERE TO STAY

Cranberry Cove. 12 Wolfe St., Louisbourg, NS B0A 1M0. ☎ **902/733-2171.** Fax 902/733-249. www.auracom.com/~crancove. E-mail crancove@auracom.com. 7 units. TEL. C$85–C$145 (US$57–US$97) double. Rates include continental breakfast. AE, MC, V. Closed mid-Oct to early May.

You won't miss this attractive inn when en route to the fortress—it's a three-story Victorian farmhouse painted a boisterous cranberry red. Inside it's decorated in a light

Victorian motif. The upstairs rooms are carpeted and furnished around themes—Anne's Hideaway is the smallest but has a nice old tub and butterfly collection; Isle Royale is done up in Cape Breton tartan. My favorite room is also the quirkiest: Field and Stream, with a twig headboard and a mounted deer head and pheasant. Dinner is served 5 to 8:30pm in the handsome first-floor dining room, which has a polished wood floor and cherry-wood tables and chairs. Entrees, at C$12 to C$19 (US$8 to US$13), range from charbroiled Atlantic salmon steak with yogurt dressing to cranberry-marinated breast of chicken.

Louisbourg Harbor Inn. 9 Warren St. (P.O. Box 110), Louisbourg, NS B0A 1M0. ☎ **888/888-8466** or 902/733-3222. E-mail louisbourg@sprint.ca. 8 units. C$95–C$140 (US$63–US$93) double. Rates include continental breakfast. MC, V. Closed mid-Oct to June 1.

This century-old golden-yellow clapboard home is conveniently located in the village, a block off the main street and overlooking fishing wharves, the blue waters of the harbor, and the Fortress of Louisbourg across the way. The inn's lustrous pine floors have been nicely restored, and all the guest rooms are tidy and attractive, with some fussier than others. The best rooms are on the third floor, requiring a bit of a trek; room no. 6 is bright and cheerful, and no. 7 is spacious and boasts an in-room Jacuzzi and a pair of rockers from which to monitor the happenings at the fish pier. A nice touch: All rooms facing the harbor have Jacuzzis. Room nos. 1 and 3 also have private balconies. Dinner is occasionally available by advance reservations to guests, and a three-course meal (entree choices typically include steak, lobster, or crab) runs C$20 to C$30 (US$13 to US$20), depending on what's being offered.

11 Cape Breton Highlands National Park

✪ **Cape Breton Highlands National Park** is one of the two crown-jewel national parks in Atlantic Canada (Gros Morne in Newfoundland is the other). Covering some 950 square kilometers (365 square miles) and stretching across a rugged peninsula from the Atlantic to the Gulf of St. Lawrence, the park is famous for its starkly beautiful terrain. It also features one of the most dramatic coastal drives east of Big Sur, California.

The mountains of Cape Breton are probably unlike those you're familiar with elsewhere. The heart of the park is fundamentally a huge plateau. In the vast interior, you'll find a flat and melancholy landscape of wind-stunted evergreens, bogs, and barrens. This is the **taiga,** a name that refers to the zone between tundra and the northernmost forest. In this largely untracked area (which is also Nova Scotia's largest remaining wilderness), you might find 150-year-old trees that are only knee-high.

But it's the park's edges that capture the attention. On the western side of the peninsula, the tableland has eroded into the sea, creating a dramatic landscape of ravines and rust-colored ragged cliffs pounded by the ocean. The ✪ **Cabot Trail,** a paved road built in 1939, winds dramatically along the flanks of the mountains, offering extraordinary vistas at every turn. On the park's other coastal flank—the eastern, Atlantic side—the terrain is less dramatic, with a coastal plain interposed between mountains and sea. But the lush green hills still offer an exceptionally picturesque backdrop.

Note: This section focuses only on the park proper, which offers no lodging or services other than camping. You'll find limited lodging and restaurants in the handful of villages ringing the park. See "Cape Breton Island," above.

ESSENTIALS

GETTING THERE   Access to the park is via the Cabot Trail, one of several tourist routes well marked by provincial authorities. The entire loop is 300km (186 miles).

The distance from the park entrance at Chéticamp to the park entrance at Ingonish is 106km (66 miles). Though you can do the loop in either direction, I encourage you to drive in a clockwise direction solely because the Chéticamp visitor center offers a far more detailed introduction to the park.

VISITOR INFORMATION Visitor centers are at both Chéticamp and Ingonish and are open in summer daily 8am to 7pm. The Chéticamp center has more extensive info about the park, including a 10-minute slide presentation, natural history exhibits, a large-scale relief map, and a good bookstore specializing in natural and cultural history. The park's main phone number is ☎ **902/224-2306.** In winter, call ☎ **902/ 285-2691.**

FEES You can buy entrance permits at one of the information centers or at toll houses at the two main park entrances. Permits are required for any activity along the route, even stopping to admire the view. Daily fees are C$3.50 (US$2.35) adults, C$2.50 (US$1.65) seniors, C$1.50 (US$1) children 6 to 16, and C$8 (US$5) families; 4-day passes are C$11 (US$7) adults, C$8 (US$5) seniors, C$4.50 (US$3) children, and C$24 (US$16) families.

CAMPING

The park has five drive-in campgrounds. The largest are at **Chéticamp** (on the west side) and **Broad Cove** (on the east), both of which have the commendable policy of never turning campers away. Even if all regular sites are full, they'll find a place for you to pitch a tent or park an RV at an overflow area. All the national-park campgrounds are well run and well maintained. Chéticamp and Broad Cove offer three-way hookups for RVs. Rates are C$15 (US$10) for an unserviced site, C$17 (US$11) for electric only, and C$21 (US$14) for a fully serviced site. It costs C$2 (US$1.35) more for a site with a fire pit (otherwise you must build fires at picnic areas in the campground). Camp more than 4 days and you get 25% off the daily rate. Remember that you're also required to buy a day-use permit when camping at Cape Breton.

Cape Breton also has two backcountry campsites. ✪ **Fishing Cove** is especially attractive, set on a pristine cove an 8km (5-mile) hike from the Cabot Trail. Watch for pilot whales at sunset from the cliffs. **Lake of Islands** is 13km (8 miles) from the trailhead on a remote lake in the interior; it's accessible by mountain bike. Fees are C$15 (US$10) per night; make arrangements at one of the visitor centers.

A SCENIC DRIVE

Cape Breton Highlands National Park offers basically one drive, and with few lapses it's scenic along the entire route. The most breathtaking stretch is the 44km (27-mile) jaunt from **Chéticamp to Pleasant Bay** along the western coast. Double the time you figure you'll need to drive this route, because you'll want to spend time at the pullouts admiring the views and perusing informational signboards. If it's foggy, save yourself the entrance fee and gas money. Without the views, there's little reason to travel, and you'd be well advised to wait until the fog lifts. Until then, you could hike in the foggy forest or across the upland bogs or explore some of the nearby villages in the atmospheric mist.

You'll want to be very confident in your car's brakes before setting out on the Cabot Trail. The road rises and falls with considerable drama, and when cresting some ridges you might feel mildly afflicted with vertigo. Especially stressful on the brakes (when traveling the Cabot Trail clockwise) are the descents to Pleasant Bay, into the Aspy Valley, and off Cape Smokey.

HIKING

The park has 27 hiking trails departing from the Cabot Trail. Many excursions are quite short and have the feel of a casual stroll rather than a vigorous tromp, but those determined to be challenged will find suitable destinations. All trails are listed with brief descriptions on the reverse side of the map you'll receive when you pay your entry fee.

The ✪ **Skyline Trail** offers all the altitude with none of the climbing. You ascend the tableland from Chéticamp by car, then follow a 7km (4.3-mile) hiking loop out along dramatic bluffs and through wind-stunted spruce and fir. A spur trail descends to a high, exposed point overlooking the surf; it's capped with blueberry bushes. Moose are often spotted along this trail. Downside: It's a very popular trek and often is crowded.

Farther along the Cabot Trail, the half-mile–long **Bog Trail** offers a glimpse of the tableland's unique bogs from a dry boardwalk. **Lone Shieling** is an easy half-mile loop through a verdant hardwood forest in a lush valley that includes 350-year-old sugar maples. A re-creation of a hut of a Scottish crofter (shepherd) is a feature along this trail.

On the eastern shore, a superb hike is out to **Middle Head,** beyond the Keltic Lodge resort. This dramatic and rocky peninsula thrusts well out into the Atlantic. The trail is wide and relatively flat; you'll cross open meadows with wonderful views north and south. The tip is grassy and open and offers a fine spot to scan for whales or watch the waves crash in following a storm. Allow an hour or two for a relaxed excursion out and back.

BIKING

The 292km (181-mile) **Cabot Trail loop** is the ironman tour for bike trekkers, both arduous and rewarding. The route twists up ravines and plummets back down toward the coast. One breathtaking vista after another unfolds, and the plunging, brake-smoking descent from Mt. MacKenzie to Pleasant Bay will be one you're not likely to forget. Campgrounds and motels are well spaced for a 3- or 4-day excursion. As for disadvantages, the road is uniformly narrow and almost universally without shoulders, and bikers often get the sense that motor-home drivers don't always know where the far side of their rig is located. This can be a bit harrowing.

If you're not inclined to pedal the whole loop, pick and choose. Especially scenic stretches for fit bikers include Chéticamp to Pleasant Bay and back and the climb and descent from Lone Shieling eastward into the Aspy Valley.

Mountain bikes are allowed on just four trails in the park—check with the visitor center when you arrive for details. **Island Eco Adventures,** 16 Chebucto St., Baddeck (☎ **902/295-3303;** e-mail island@atcon.com), rents hybrid bikes outfitted with racks, panniers, and toolkits for self-guided tours around the Cabot Trail. The rate is C$45 (US$30) per day (negotiable for longer trips), which includes a toll-free number for roadside assistance. Mountain bikes without gear may be rented for C$30 (US$20) per day. The longest backcountry trail is the 13km (8-mile) route into the Lake of Islands, which doesn't appear on all maps. Ask at one of the two park visitor centers.

4 New Brunswick

by Wayne Curtis

New Brunswick seems to be the Rodney Dangerfield of Atlantic Canada—it don't get no respect. Among many Canadians, it has a reputation more for pulp mills, industrial forests, cargo ports, and oil refineries (the huge Irving Oil conglomerate is based here) than for quaint villages and charming byways. And many visitors tend to view New Brunswick as a place they need to drive through (preferably really fast) en route from Québec or Maine to the rest of Atlantic Canada.

Granted, there's a grain of truth behind the province's reputation. But rest assured, New Brunswick boasts pockets of wilderness and scenic beauty unrivaled in eastern Canada. You'll find sandy beaches on warm ocean waters that hold their own to anything on Prince Edward Island and surf-pounded rocky headlands that could be in the farthest reaches of Newfoundland. The province's appeal tends to be more hidden than that of other locales. But with a little bit of homework—and by making inquiries at the innovative Day Adventure Centres the province has established—you can enjoy a memorable trip through an exquisite landscape.

Culturally, New Brunswick is Canada in microcosm, split between Anglophone and Francophone populations (about one-third of the residents speak French). Its heritage is both proudly Acadian and proudly pro-British—in fact, New Brunswick is sometimes called the "Loyalist Province" since so many Loyalists fleeing the United States settled here after the American Revolution. But the cultural divide is less contentious here than in Québec. Interestingly, French-speaking New Brunswick residents share few cultural roots with French-speaking Québecois. (New Brunswick's French ancestors came mostly from central and western France; Québecois trace their ancestry to Brittany and Normandy.) Acadians celebrate the Feast of the Assumption as their national holiday. In Québec, it's the day of St-Jean-Baptiste. With its unusually harmonious détente between two cultures, New Brunswick likes to offer itself as a model for Québec. Québec, in turn, tends to ignore New Brunswick.

1 Exploring the Province

Visitors drawn to rugged beauty should focus on the Fundy Coast with its stupendous tides, rocky cliffs, and boreal landscape. (The south coast actually feels more remote and northerly than the more densely settled northeast coast.) Those interested in Acadian history or sandy

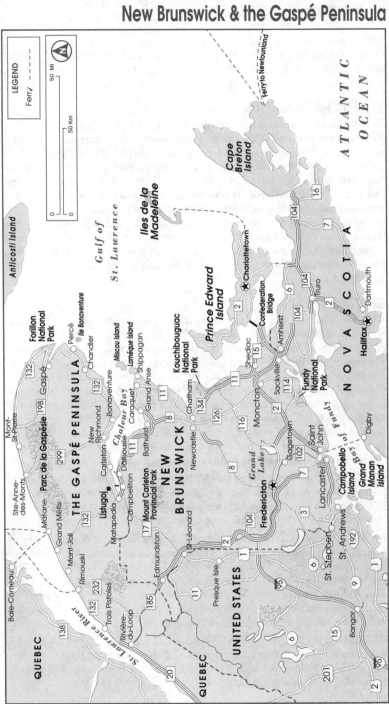

LEGEND

Ferry - - - -

50 Mi

50 Km

Anticosti Island

QUEBEC

Baie-Comeau

St. Lawrence River

138

Rivière-du-Loup

Trois Pistoles

232

132

Rimouski

Mont-Joli

Grand Métis

Ste-Anne-des-Monts

299

Mont-St-Pierre

Forillon National Park

Ile Bonaventure

Percé

Gaspé

Chandler

132

198

132

THE GASPÉ PENINSULA

Matane

Parc de la Gaspésie

Bonaventure

New Richmond

Carleton

Chaleur Bay

Caraquet

Grand Anse

Shippagan

Lamèque Island

Miscou Island

Dalhousie

132

Campbellton

Listuguj

Matapedia

17

Mount Carleton Provincial Park

Bathurst

11

8

Kouchibouguac National Park

185

Edmundston

St-Léonard

104

Fredericton

2

NEW BRUNSWICK

Newcastle

Chatham

134

126

8

Grand Lake

116

Gagetown

102

Moncton

114

Sackville

2

Shediac

15

Amherst

Confederation Bridge

Prince Edward Island

2

Charlottetown

104

104

Ile de la Madeleine

Gulf of St. Lawrence

Cape Breton Island

16

104

7

6

104

Truro

2

NOVA SCOTIA

Dartmouth

Halifax

11

Digby

Fundy National Park

Bay of Fundy

Saint John

Lancaster

7

3

6

St. Stephen

St. Andrews

192

Campobello Island

Grand Manan Island

9

15

11

Bangor

201

95

2

Presque Isle

11

UNITED STATES

1

2

95

6

QUEBEC

20

ATLANTIC OCEAN

Ferry to Newfoundland

beaches should veer toward the Gulf of St. Lawrence. Those interested in hurrying through the province to get to Prince Edward Island or Nova Scotia should at least detour through Fundy National Park and visit Cape Enrage and Hopewell Rocks, which number among eastern Canada's more dramatic attractions.

VISITOR INFORMATION

New Brunswick publishes several free annual directories and guides that are helpful in planning a trip to the province, including *Welcome to New Brunswick,* with listings of attractions, accommodations, and campgrounds, and the *Travel Planner,* which includes a catalog of multiday and daylong adventure packages. Write to **Tourism New Brunswick,** P.O. Box 12345, Fredericton, NB E7M 5C3, or call ☎ **800/ 561-0123** (from Canada and the continental United States). On the Web, head to **www.tourismnbcanada.com** and **www.eastmarket.com/nb.htm**.

The province staffs five **visitor info centers;** most cities and larger towns also have their own municipal centers. A complete listing of phone numbers for these centers is in the *Travel Planner* guide, or you can look for "?" direction signs on the highway. Phone numbers and addresses for the appropriate visitor centers are provided in each section of this chapter.

GETTING THERE

BY CAR   The Trans-Canada Highway bisects the province, entering from Québec at St-Jacques. It follows the Saint John River Valley before veering through Moncton and exiting into Nova Scotia at Aulac. The entire distance is about 550km (341 miles). The fastest route from New England to southwestern New Brunswick is taking the Maine turnpike to Bangor, then heading east on Route 9 to connect to Route 1 into Calais, just across the river from St. Stephen, New Brunswick. A more scenic variation is driving to Campobello Island across the bridge from Lubec, Maine (see "Around Passamaquoddy Bay," below), then taking a ferry to Deer Island, driving the length of the island, and boarding a second ferry to the mainland. Those headed to Fredericton or Moncton will speed their trip somewhat by following US I-95 to Houlton, then connecting with the Trans-Canada after crossing the border.

BY FERRY   Bay Ferries (☎ **888/249-7245**) operates a 3-hour ferry linking Saint John and Digby, Nova Scotia. The ferry sails year-round, with as many as three cross-ings daily each way in summer. Summer fares are C$25 (US$17) adults, C$13 (US$9) children, and C$55 (US$37) vehicles. Reservations are advised.

BY AIR   The province's main **airports** are at Fredericton (the provincial capital), Saint John, and Moncton, all served by major rental-car companies. Most flights into these airports are on **Air Canada** (☎ **800/776-3000** in the U.S., 800/565-3940 in the Maritimes, or 800/563-5151 in Newfoundland; www.aircanada.ca) and **Cana-dian Airlines International** (☎ **800/426-7000** in the U.S. or 800/665-1177 in Canada; www.cdnair.ca). At press time, a merger between Air Canada and Canadian Airlines was being discussed but not yet consummated.

BY TRAIN   Via Rail (☎ **800/561-3949** in the U.S. or 800/561-3952 in the Mar-itimes; www.viarail.ca) offers train service through the province (en route from Mon-tréal to Halifax) 6 days per week. The train follows a northerly route, with stops in Campbellton, Miramichi, and Moncton.

THE GREAT OUTDOORS

The province has put together a well-conceived campaign—called **"The New Tide of Adventure"**—to encourage visitors of all budgets to explore its outdoor attractions. The province has funded **Day Adventure Centers** (well marked from most major roads) where you can stop in, peruse the local adventure options, and then sign up on the spot. The *Travel Planner* also outlines dozens of multiday and day adventures, ranging from a C$10 (US$7) guided hike at Fundy National Park to C$389 (US$259) biking packages that include inn accommodations and gourmet dinners. For details on the program, call ☎ **800/561-1112.**

BACKPACKING Among the best destinations for a backcountry tromp are **Mount Carleton Provincial Park** and **Fundy National Park,** both of which maintain backcountry sites. See the appropriate sections below for details.

BICYCLING The islands and peninsulas of **Passamaquoddy Bay** lend themselves to cruising in the slow lane—especially Campobello, which also has good dirt roads for mountain biking. **Grand Manan** holds appeal for cyclists, though the main road (Route 776) has narrow shoulders and fast cars. The best coastal biking is **east of Fundy National Park**—especially the backroads to Cape Enrage. Along the Acadian Coast, **Kouchibouguac National Park** has limited but unusually nice biking trails through mixed terrain (rentals available). A handy guide is Kent Thompson's *Biking to Blissville,* covering 35 rides in the Maritimes and costing C$15 (US$10). Contact Goose Lane Editions, 469 King St., Fredericton, NB E3B 1E5 (☎ **506/450-4251**).

BIRD WATCHING **Grand Manan** is among the province's most noted destinations for birders, located smack on the Atlantic flyway. (Ur-birder John James Audubon lodged here when studying local bird life more than 150 years ago.) Over the course of a year, as many as 275 species are observed on the island; September is typically best for sightings. It's not hard to swap information with other birders: On the ferry, look for excitable folks with binoculars and Tilley hats dashing from port to starboard and back. Boat tours from Grand Manan will bring you to Machias Seal Island, with its colonies of puffins, arctic terns, and razorbills. On **Campobello Island,** the varied terrain also attracts a good mix of birds, including sharp-shinned hawk, common eider, and black guillemot. Ask for a checklist and map at the visitor center. Shorebird enthusiasts flock to **Shepody Bay National Wildlife Area,** which maintains preserves in the mudflats between Alma (near Fundy National Park) and Hopewell Cape. Also offering excellent birding is the marsh that surrounds Sackville, near the Nova Scotia border.

CANOEING New Brunswick has 3,600km (2,232 miles) of inland waterways, plus lakes and protected bays. Canoeists can find everything from glass-smooth waters to daunting rapids. Novices often enjoy the 3-hour **Voyager Canoe Marine Adventure** (☎ **506/876-2443**) in Kouchibouguac National Park, costing C$25 (US$17) adults and C$15 (US$10) youths 6 to 16. More experienced canoeists looking for a longer expedition should head to the **St. Croix River** on the U.S. border, where you can embark on a multiday paddle trip and get lost in the woods, spiritually if not in fact.

FISHING The **Miramichi River** has long attracted anglers both famous and obscure, lured by the wily Atlantic salmon. This ranks among the best salmon rivers in the world, though diminished runs have plagued this river in recent years as they have all rivers in the Maritimes. Salmon must be caught on flies, and nonresidents need to hire a guide to go after salmon. For other freshwater species, like bass, and for saltwater angling, the restrictions are less onerous. Get up-to-date on the rules and regulations by requesting copies of two brochures, *Sport Fishing Summary* and *Atlantic Salmon Angling,* available from **Fish and Wildlife,** P.O. Box 6000, Fredericton, NB E3B 5H1 (☎ **506/453-2440**).

HIKING The province's highest point is in the center of the woodlands region at **Mount Carleton Provincial Park.** Several demanding hikes in the park yield glorious views. There's also superb hiking at **Fundy National Park,** with a mix of coastal and woodland hikes on well-marked trails. **Grand Manan** is a good destination for independent-minded hikers who enjoy the challenge of finding the trail as much as the hike itself. An excellent resource is the C$15 (US$10) *A Hiking Guide to New Brunswick,* published by Goose Lane Editions and available in bookstores around the province or directly from the publisher at 469 King St., Fredericton, NB E3B 1E5 (☎ 506/450-4251).

SEA KAYAKING　The huge tides that make kayaking so fascinating along the Bay of Fundy also make it exceptionally dangerous—even the strongest kayakers are no match for a fierce ebb tide if they're in the wrong place. Fortunately, the number of skilled sea-kayaking guides has boomed in recent years. Among the most extraordinary places to explore is **Hopewell Rocks,** which stand like Brancusi statues on the ocean floor at low tide but offer sea caves and narrow channels to explore at high tide. **Baymount Outdoor Adventures** (☎ 506/734-2660) offers 90-minute sea kayak tours of Hopewell Rocks for C$35 (US$23) adults and C$30 (US$20) youth. Other kayak outfitters along the Fundy Coast are the **Outdoor Adventure Company** (☎ 800/365-3855 or 506/755-2007) in St. George and **Fresh Air Adventure** (☎ 800/545-0020 or 506/887-2249) in Alma.

SWIMMING　Parts of New Brunswick offer wonderful ocean swimming. The best beaches are along the **Acadian Coast,** especially near Shediac and in Kouchibouguac National Park. The water is much warmer and the terrain more forgiving along the Gulf of St. Lawrence than in the Bay of Fundy.

WHALE WATCHING　The **Bay of Fundy** is rich with plankton and therefore rich with whales. You can spot some 15 types of whales in the bay, like finback, minke, humpback, the infrequent orca, and the endangered right whale. Whale-watching expeditions sail throughout summer from Campobello Island, Deer Island, Grand Manan, St. Andrews, and St. George. Any visitor center can point you in the right direction; the province's travel guide also lists many of the tours, which typically cost around C$40 or C$50 (US$27 or US$33) for 2 to 4 hours of whale watching.

2　Around Passamaquoddy Bay: Campobello Island & More

The **Passamaquoddy Bay** region is often the first point of entry for those arriving overland from the United States. The deeply indented bay is wracked with massive tides that produce currents powerful enough to stymie even doughty fishing boats. It's a place of lasting fogs, spruce-clad islands, bald eagles, and widely scattered development. It's also home to a grand old summer colony and a peninsula boasting two five-star inns and a rambling early-1900s resort.

Mid-May to mid-October, those entering overland through St. Stephen should allow time for a stop at the **Provincial Visitor Information Centre,** in the old train station on Milltown Boulevard (☎ 506/466-7390), open daily 10am to 6pm. It's about a mile from Canadian customs; turn right after crossing the border (following the signs for St. Andrews and Saint John) and watch for the center at the light where the road turns left.

CAMPOBELLO ISLAND: FDR'S RETREAT

Campobello is a compact island (about 16km/9.9 miles long and 5km/3.1 miles wide) at the mouth of Passamaquoddy Bay. You'll find it's easier to get here from the

United States than from Canada because of the graceful modern bridge connecting it to the Maine town of Lubec. To arrive from the Canadian mainland without driving through the United States requires two ferries, one of which operates only in summer.

Campobello has been home to both humble fishers and wealthy families over the years, and they have coexisted quite nicely. (Locals approved when summer folks built golf courses in the early 1900s, since it gave them a place to graze their sheep.) Today, the island is a mix of elegant summer homes and less interesting tract homes of a more recent vintage.

ESSENTIALS

GETTING THERE   Campobello Island is accessible year-round from the United States. From Route 1 in Whiting, Maine, take Route 189 to Lubec, where a bridge links it with Campobello. In summer there's another option. From the Canadian mainland, take the free ferry to Deer Island, drive the length of the island, and board the small seasonal ferry to Campobello. The ferry is operated by **East Coast Ferries** (☎ 506/747-2159) and runs late June to early September. The fare is C$13 (US$9) for car/driver and C$2 (US$1.35) for each extra passenger, with a maximum of C$18 (US$12) per car.

VISITOR INFORMATION   The **Campobello Welcome Center,** 44 Route 774, Welshpool, NB E5E 1A3 (☎ 506/752-7043), will be on the right just after you cross the bridge from Lubec. Mid-May to mid-October, it's open daily 9am to 7pm (limited hours after Labour Day).

EXPLORING THE ISLAND

The island offers excellent shoreline **walks** at both **Roosevelt Campobello International Park** (below) and **Herring Cove Provincial Park** (☎ 506/752-7010). The landscapes are extraordinarily diverse. On some trails you'll enjoy a Currier and Ives tableau of white houses and church spires across the channel in Lubec and Eastport; 10 minutes later, you'll be walking along a wild rocky coast pummeled by surging waves. Herring Cove has a mile-long beach perfect for a slow stroll in the fog. Camping and golf are offered at the provincial park.

Roosevelt Campobello International Park. Rte. 774. ☎ **506/752-2922.** Free admission. Daily 10am–6pm. Closed mid-Oct to late May.

Like a number of other affluent Americans, the family of Franklin Delano Roosevelt made an annual trek to the prosperous summer colony at Campobello Island. The island lured folks from the sultry cities with a promise of cool air and a salubrious effect on the circulatory system. ("The extensive forests of balsamic firs seem to affect the atmosphere of this region, causing a quiet of the nervous system and inviting sleep," read an 1890 real-estate brochure.) The future U.S. president came to this island every summer between 1883, the year after he was born, and 1921, when he was suddenly stricken with polio. Franklin and his siblings (then, in time, his wife and children) spent those summers exploring the coves and sailing around the bay, and he always recalled his time here fondly. (It was his "beloved island," he said, coining a phrase that gets no rest in local brochures.)

You'll learn much about Roosevelt and his early life at the visitor center, where you can watch a brief film, and during a self-guided tour of the elaborate mansion, covered in cranberry-colored shingles. For a "cottage" this huge, it's surprisingly comfortable and intimate. The park is truly an international park—run by a commission with representatives from both the States and Canada, making it like none other in the world.

Leave some time to explore farther afield in the 2,800-acre park, which offers scenic coastline and 14km (8.7 miles) of walking trails. Maps and walk suggestions are available at the visitor center.

WHERE TO STAY

Lupine Lodge. Welshpool Rd., Campobello, NB E0G 3H0. ☎ **506/752-2555.** 11 units. C$50–C$125 (US$33–US$83) double. MC, V. Closed mid-Oct to mid-June. Pets C$15 (US$10) extra.

This handsome compound of log buildings not far from the Roosevelt cottage was built in 1915 by family cousins. A busy road runs between the lodge and the water, but the buildings are on a slight rise and will make you feel removed from the traffic. The guest rooms are in two long lodges adjacent to the main building and restaurant; those with bay views cost a bit more but are worth it—they're slightly bigger and better furnished in a log-rustic style. All guests have access to a deck overlooking the bay. All meals are served in the attractive restaurant, boasting log walls, a stone fireplace, bay views, and mounted moosehead and swordfish. Dinner entrees include salmon, T-bone steak, turkey, and steamed lobster, at C$10 to C$16 (US$7 to US$11).

Owen House. 11 Welshpool St., Welshpool, Campobello, NB E5E 1G3. ☎ **506/752-2977.** 9 units, 6 with bathroom. C$78 (US$52) double without bathroom, C$103–C$118 (US$69–US$79) double with bathroom. Rates include full breakfast. V. Closed mid-Oct to late May. No children under 6 in Aug.

This three-story clapboard captain's house from 1835 sits on 10 tree-filled acres at the edge of the bay. The first-floor common rooms are nicely decorated in a busy Victorian manner, with Persian and braided carpets and mahogany furniture. The guest rooms are a mixed lot, with an eclectic mélange of antique and modern furniture that sometimes blends nicely. Likewise, some rooms are bright and filled with the smell of salty air (no. 1 is the largest, with waterfront views on two sides); others, like no. 5, are tucked under stairs and rather dark. The third-floor rooms share a bathroom but have excellent views. The filling breakfast is served family style.

ST. ANDREWS

The lovely village of **St. Andrews**—or St. Andrews by-the-Sea, as the chamber of commerce likes to call it—traces its roots back to the days of the Loyalists. After the American Revolution, New Englanders who supported the British in the struggle were made to feel unwelcome. They decamped first to Castine, Maine, which they presumed was safely on British soil. It wasn't; the St. Croix River was later determined to be the border between Canada and the United States. Uprooted again, the Loyalists dismantled their houses, loaded the pieces aboard ships, and rebuilt them on the welcoming peninsula of St. Andrews. Some of these houses still stand today.

This historic community emerged as a fashionable summer resort in the late 19th century, when many of Canada's affluent nabobs built homes here and gathered annually for an active social season. In 1889, the Tudor-style **Algonquin Hotel** was built on a low rise overlooking the town, and it quickly became the social hub and defining landmark.

St. Andrews is beautifully sited at the tip of a long wedge-shaped peninsula. Because it's off the beaten track, the village hasn't been spoiled much by modern development, and walking the wide shady streets—especially those around the Algonquin—will make you feel as if you've stepped back into a more genteel era. Some 250 homes around the village are more than a century old. A number of appealing boutiques and shops are spread along Water Street, which stretches for some distance along the town's shoreline.

ESSENTIALS

GETTING THERE   St. Andrews is at the apex of Route 127, which dips southward from Route 1 between St. Stephen and St. George. The turnoff is well marked from either direction. **SMT** bus lines (☎ **800/567-5151** or 506/859-5060) offers one bus daily between St. Andrews with Saint John; the one-way fare is about C$15 (US$10).

VISITOR INFORMATION   St. Andrews has two info centers. At the western intersection of Routes 1 and 27 is the seasonal **St. Andrews Tourist Bureau** (☎ **506/ 466-4858**), staffed by local volunteers. A second facility, the **Welcome Centre,** 46 Reed Ave., on your left as you enter the village (☎ **506/529-3000**), is in a handsome 1914 home. May and September, it's open daily 9am to 6pm (to 8pm July and Aug). The rest of the year, contact the **Chamber of Commerce,** in the same building (☎ **800/563-7397** or 506/529-3555; e-mail stachmb@nbnet.nb.ca).

EXPLORING ST. ANDREWS

The chamber of commerce produces two brochures, the *Town Map and Directory* and the *St. Andrews by-the-Sea Historic Guide,* both of which are free at the two visitor centers above. Also look for *A Guide to Historic St. Andrews,* produced by the St. Andrews Civic Trust. With these in hand, you'll be able to launch an informed exploration.

The village's compact, handsome downtown flanks lengthy commercial **Water Street,** paralleling the bay. You'll find low, understated, commercial architecture, much of it from the early 1900s, encompassing a gamut of styles. Allow an hour or so for browsing in boutiques and art galleries. There's also a mix of restaurants and inns.

Two blocks inland on King Street, you'll get a dose of local history at the **Ross Memorial Museum,** 188 Montague St. (☎ **506/529-5124**). This home was built in 1824; in 1945, it was left to the town by Rev. Henry Phipps Ross and Sarah Juliette Ross, complete with their eclectic and intriguing collection of period furniture, carpets, and paintings. Late June to mid-October, it's open Tuesday to Saturday 10am to 4:30pm (also Mon in July and Aug). Admission is by donation.

St. Andrews is an excellent spot to launch an exploration of the bay, which is very much alive, biologically speaking. You'll look for whales, porpoises, seals, and bald eagles, no matter which trip you select. **Quoddy Link Marine** (☎ **506/529-2600**) offers whale-watch tours on a 50-foot power catamaran, including use of binoculars and seafood snacks. Whale-watch and sunset tours are offered aboard the *Seafox* (☎ **506/636-0130**), a 40-foot Cape Islander boat with viewing from two decks. Two-hour tours in search of wildlife aboard 24-foot rigid-hull Zodiacs are offered by **Fundy Tide Runners** (☎ **506/529-4481**); passengers wear floatation suits as they zip around the bay. **Seascape Kayak Tours** (☎ **506/529-4866**) offers an up-close-and-personal view of the bay on full- and half-day tours, with lunch provided on full-day trips and snacks on the 2½-hour tours. No kayaking experience is needed.

Kingsbrae Horticultural Gardens. 220 King St. ☎ **506/529-3335.** Admission C$6 (US$4) adults; C$4 (US$2.65) children/students/seniors; under 6 free. Admission fees are taxed. Daily 9am–dusk. Closed mid-Oct to mid-May.

This 27-acre public garden opened in 1998 on the former grounds of a long-gone estate. The designers incorporated the existing high hedges and trees and have ambitiously planted open space around the mature plants. The entire project is very promising, and, as the plantings take root and mature it's certain to become a noted stop for garden lovers. Eventually, the grounds will include 800 varieties of trees and 900 perennials. Among the notable features are a day-lily collection, an extensive rose garden, and a small maze.

⭘ **Ministers Island Historic Site/Covenhoven.** Rte. 127 (northeast of St. Andrews), Chamcook. ☎ **506/529-5081** (recorded tour schedule). C$5 (US$3.35) adults, C$2.50 (US$1.65) youths 13–18; under 12 free. Closed mid-Oct to May 31.

This rugged 500-plus–acre island is linked to the mainland by a sandbar at low tide, and the 2-hour tours are scheduled around the tides. (Call for upcoming times.) You'll meet your tour guide on the mainland side, then drive your car out convoy style across the ocean floor to the magical island estate created in 1890 by Sir William Van Horne, president of the Canadian Pacific Railway and the person behind the extension of the rail line to St. Andrews. He then built a sandstone mansion called Covenhoven, with some 50 rooms (including 17 bedrooms), a circular bathhouse (where he indulged his passion for landscape painting), and one of Canada's largest and most impressive barns. The estate also features heated greenhouses, which produced grapes and mushrooms, along with peaches that weighed up to 2 pounds each. When Van Horne was home in Montréal, he had fresh dairy products and vegetables shipped daily (by rail, of course) so he could enjoy fresh produce year-round.

WHERE TO STAY

Those traveling on a budget should head for the trim and tidy **Picket Fence Motel,** 102 Reed Ave. (☎ **506/529-8985**), near the Algonquin golf course and within walking distance of the village center. Doubles are C$55 to C$65 (US$37 to US$43) in peak season.

The Algonquin. 184 Adolphus St., St. Andrews, NB E0G 2X0. ☎ **800/441-1414** or 506/529-8823. Fax 506/529-7162. 250 units. MINIBAR TV TEL. May–Oct C$99–C$239 (US$66–US$159) double. Meal package C$45 (US$30) per person. Other packages available. Nov–Apr (limited operations with 51 units) C$85–C$145 (US$57–US$97), with continental breakfast. AE, CB, DC, DISC, ER, MC, V. Pets accepted first floor only. Free valet parking.

The Algonquin's distinguished pedigree dates back to 1889, when it opened to wealthy vacationers seeking respite from city heat. The original was destroyed by fire in 1914, but the surviving annexes were rebuilt in sumptuous Tudor style; in 1993, an architecturally sympathetic addition was built across the road, linked by a gatehouse-inspired bridge. The red-tile–roofed resort commands your attention through its sheer size and aristocratic bearing. The inn is several long blocks from the water's edge, but it perches on the brow of a hill and affords panoramic bay views from the second-floor roof garden and many rooms. The guest rooms have been recently redecorated and are comfortable and tasteful; all have coffeemakers and hair dryers. One caveat: The hotel happily markets itself to bus tours and conferences, and if your timing is unfortunate you might feel a bit overwhelmed and small.

Dining: The main dining room is one of the more enjoyable spots in town—it's often bustling (great for people watching), and the kitchen produces some surprisingly creative meals. Informal dining options are The Library (off the main lobby) and the downstairs lounge.

Amenities: Safe-deposit boxes, baby-sitting, dry cleaning/laundry, daily children's programs; 18-hole golf course that's among the region's best; two outdoor tennis courts, outdoor heated pool, bike rentals, beauty salon, gift shop, game room, squash court, fitness center, locker room, saunas, indoor whirlpool; shuttle to the Saint John airport (charge).

⭘ **Kingsbrae Arms.** 219 King St., St. Andrews, NB E0G 2X0. ☎ **506/529-1897.** Fax 506/529-1197. www.kingsbrae.com. E-mail kingbrae@nb.aibn.com. 8 units. A/C TV TEL. Off-season midweek C$325–C$475 (US$217–US$317) double, with breakfast; weekends, holidays, and peak season C$475–C$625 (US$317–US$417), with breakfast and dinner. 2-night minimum; 3 nights July and Aug weekends. 5% room-service charge extra. MC, V. Pets allowed with advance permission.

The grand shingled Kingsbrae Arms, a member of the upscale Relais & Châteaux network, is a five-star inn informed by an upscale European elegance. Atop King Street, it occupies an 1897 manor house built by prosperous jade merchants, where the furnishings—from the gracefully worn leather chesterfield to the Delft-tiled fireplace—seem to have stories to tell. A heated pool sits amid rose gardens at the foot of a lawn, and immediately next door is the 27-acre Kingsbrae Horticultural Gardens (some guest rooms have wonderful views of the gardens; others, a panoramic sweep of the bay). Guests will feel pampered here, with the 325-thread-count sheets, plush robes, VCRs, hair dryers, and complete guest-services suite stocked with complimentary snacks and refreshments. Five rooms have Jacuzzis; all have gas fireplaces. Children 10 and older are welcome.

Dining: Guests enjoy a four-course meal around a stately table in the dining room during peak season. (The dining room isn't open to the public.) One meal is offered nightly, and the cuisine is new Canadian. Entrees might include beef tenderloin with buttered noodles or frenched rack of lamb with garlic polenta. Afternoon tea is served in the living room.

Amenities: Baby-sitting, dry cleaning/laundry, heated pool; use of the Algonquin's facilities (extra charge) a short stroll away.

Salty Towers. 340 Water St., St. Andrews, NB E5B 2R3. ☎ **506/529-4585.** E-mail steeljm@ nbnet.nb.ca. 17 units, 5 with bathroom. C$45 (US$30) double without bathroom, C$65 (US$43) double with bathroom. V.

Behind the facade of this somewhat-staid Queen Anne home lurks the soul of a wild eccentric. Salty Towers is equal parts early-1900s home, 1940s boarding house, and 1960s commune. Overseen with great affability by artist/naturalist Jamie Steel, this is a world of wondrous clutter—from the early European landscapes with overly wrought gilt frames to exuberant modern pieces. Think Addams family meets Timothy Leary. The guest rooms lack the visual chaos of the public spaces and are nicely done, with eclectic antiques and old magazines. (Especially nice is room no. 2, with hand-sponged walls and a sitting area surrounded by windows.) The top floor is largely given over to single rooms, bargains at C$30 (US$20) with shared bathroom. Guests have full run of the large if sometimes confused kitchen. Don't be surprised to find musicians strumming on the porch, artists lounging in the living room, and others of uncertain provenance swapping jokes around the stove. If that sounds pretty good to you, this is your place.

✪ **Windsor House.** 132 Water St., St. Andrews, NB E0G 2X0. ☎ **888/890-9463** or 506/529-3330. Fax 506/529-4063. 6 units. TV TEL. Summer C$225–C$300 (US$150–US$200) double; off-season C$150–C$250 (US$100–US$167) double. AE, DC, ER, MC, V. Restaurant closed Jan–Apr.

In the middle of the village, the lovely Windsor offers a quiet retreat amid lustrous antiques in a top-rate restoration. The three-story home was built in 1798 by a ship captain and has served almost every purpose (a stagecoach stop, an oil-company office, a family home) before reopening as a luxury inn in 1999. New owners Jay Remer and Greg Cohane spent more than 2 years and C$2 million (US$1.3 million) renovating the place, and their attention to detail shows. The guest rooms are furnished with antiques (no reproductions) far above what one normally expects at an inn; Remer spent 5 years at Sotheby's in New York and knows what he's looking for. All the rooms are superbly appointed, most with detailed etchings of animals adorning the walls. The best two are a pair of third-floor suites, with peaceful sitting areas, clawfoot tubs and glass shower stalls, exposed beams, Asian carpets, handsome armoires, and limited bay views. The basement features an appealing terra-cotta–floored billiard room; the first-floor pub is perfect for an early-evening libation or after-dinner drink. The restaurant is covered below.

WHERE TO DINE

The Gables. 143 Water St. ☎ **506/529-3440.** Main courses C$3.95–C$7 (US$2.65–US$4.65) at breakfast, C$8–C$18 (US$5–US$12) at lunch and dinner. MC, V. Daily 8am–11pm. Closed Nov–Apr 15. SEAFOOD/PUB FARE.

This informal eatery is in a trim home with prominent gables fronting Water Street, but you enter down a narrow alley where sky and water views suddenly blossom through a soaring window from an outside deck. Inside, expect a lively spot with a casual maritime decor; outside there's a plastic–porch-furniture informality. Breakfast is served during peak season, with homemade baked goods and rosemary potatoes. Lunch and dinner options include burgers, steaks, and seafood entrees like breaded haddock and a lobster clubhouse (chopped lobster salad with cheese, cucumber, lettuce, and tomato). Margaritas and sangria are available by the pitcher. The view tends to outclass the menu, but those ordering simpler fare will be satisfied.

✪ **Windsor House.** In the Windsor House hotel, 132 Water St. ☎ **506/529-3330.** Reservations recommended. Lunch C$9–C$12 (US$6–US$8); 3-course dinner C$55 (US$37); 5-course dinner C$75 (US$50). AE, DC, ER, MC, V. Daily 11:30am–2pm and 6–9pm. Closed Mon–Tues spring and fall; closed Jan–Apr. FRENCH/CONTINENTAL.

You're seated in one of two intimate dining rooms on the first floor of this historic home. The setting is formal, so dress with a bit more starch than you would elsewhere in town; the service is excellent. Lunches are somewhat less formal and very delectable and include spinach and wild mushroom crêpes and smoked salmon with brie soufflé and pear chutney. At dinner, you'll choose a three-course or a five-course meal—you can mix and match the minor courses (two appetizers) or maybe save room for two desserts. Appetizers include a country pâté with toasted pumpkin seeds and a seafood chowder with lobster, shrimp, and scallops. Main courses include dishes like rack of lamb, seafood baked in phyllo, and breast of chicken topped with lobster sauce and truffles. The desserts range from the traditional custard with caramel sauce to lime mousse and rum butter cream sandwiched in a coconut biscuit.

3 Grand Manan Island

Geologically rugged, profoundly peaceable, and indisputably remote, this handsome island of 2,800 residents is a 90-minute ferry ride from Blacks Harbour, southeast of St. George. For adventurous travelers, **Grand Manan** is a much-prized destination and a highlight of their vacation. Yet the island remains a mystifying puzzle for others who fail to be smitten by its rough-edged charm. "Either this is your kind of place or it isn't," said one island resident. "There's no in between." The only way to find out is to visit.

Grand Manan is a special favorite among serious birders and enthusiasts of novelist Willa Cather. Hiking the island's noted trails, don't be surprised to come across knots of very quiet people peering intently through binoculars. These are the birders. Nearly 300 species of birds either nest here or stop by the island during their long migrations, and it's a good place to add to one's life list, with birds ranging from bald eagles to puffins (you'll need to sign up for a boat tour for the latter).

Willa Cather kept a cottage here and wrote many of her most beloved books while living on the island. Her fans are as easy to spot as the birders, say locals. In fact, islanders are still talking about a Willa Cather conference some summers ago, when 40 participants wrapped themselves in sheets and danced around a bonfire during the summer solstice. "Cather people, they're a wild breed," one innkeeper intoned gravely to me.

ESSENTIALS

GETTING THERE   Grand Manan is connected to Blacks Harbour on the mainland via frequent ferry service in summer. **Coastal Transport ferries** (☎ 506/662-3724), each capable of hauling 60 cars, depart from the mainland and the island every 2 hours between 7:30am and 5:30pm during July and August; a ferry makes three to four trips the rest of the year. The round-trip fare is C$9 (US$6) per passenger (C$4.40/US$2.95 ages 5 to 12) or C$26 (US$17) per car. Boarding the ferry on the mainland is free; you buy tickets when leaving the island.

No reservations are accepted (though you can buy an advance ticket for the first trip each day off the island); get in line early to secure a spot. A good strategy for departing from Blacks Harbour is to bring a picnic lunch, arrive an hour or two early, put your car in line, and head to the grassy waterfront park adjacent to the wharf. It's an attractive spot; there's even an island to explore at low tide.

VISITOR INFORMATION   The island's **Visitor Information Centre,** P.O. Box 193, Grand Manan, NB E0G 2M0 (☎ 506/662-3442), is beneath the Grand Manan Museum (below) in the town of Grand Harbor. Summer, it's open daily 10am to 5pm. If the center is closed, ask around at island stores or inns for one of the free island maps published by the **Grand Manan Tourism Association,** which includes a listing of key island phone numbers.

EXPLORING THE ISLAND

Start your explorations before you arrive. As you come abreast of the island aboard the ferry, head to the starboard side. You'll soon see **Seven Day's Work** in the rocky cliffs of Whale's Cove, where seven layers of hardened lava and sill (intrusive igneous rock) have come together in a sort of geological Dagwood sandwich.

You can begin to open the Japanese puzzle box that is local geology at the **Grand Manan Museum** (☎ 506/662-3524) in Grand Harbor, one of three villages on the island's eastern shore. The basement geology exhibit offers pointers about what to look for as you roam the island. Birders will enjoy the Allan Moses collection upstairs, featuring 230 stuffed and mounted birds in glass cases. The museum also has an impressive lighthouse lens from the Gannet Rock Lighthouse and a collection of stuff that has washed ashore from the frequent shipwrecks. Mid-June to October, the museum is open Monday to Saturday 10:30am to 4:30pm and Sunday 1 to 5pm. Admission is C$2 (US$1.35) adults and C$1 (US65¢) seniors/students; children under 12 are free.

Numerous **hiking trails** lace the island, offering a popular diversion in summer. You can find trails just about everywhere, but most are a matter of local knowledge. Don't hesitate to ask at your inn or the tourist center or to ask anyone you might meet on the street. *A Hiking Guide to New Brunswick* (☎ 506/450-4251) lists 12 hikes with maps; this handy book is often sold on the ferry. The most accessible clusters of trails are at the island's northern and southern tips. Head north up Whistle Road to Whistle Beach for the Northwestern Coastal Trail and the Seven Day's Work Trail, both of which track along the rocky shore. Near the low lighthouse and towering radio antennae at Southwest Head (follow Route 776 to the end), trails radiate out along cliffs topped with scrappy forest; the views are remarkable when the fog's not in.

WHALE WATCHING & BOAT TOURS

A fine way to experience island ecology is to mosey offshore. Several outfitters offer complete nature tours, providing a nice sampling of the world above and beneath the sea. **Island Coast Boat Tours** (☎ 506/662-8181) sets out for 4- to 5-hour expeditions in search of whales and birds. On an excursion you might see minke, finback, or humpback whales, along with exotic birds like puffins and phalaropes. The cost is C$44 (US$29) adults, C$40 (US$27) seniors, and C$22 (US$15) children. **SeaView Adventures** (☎ 800/586-1922 in Canada or 506/662-3211) offers 3½-hour educational tours with a unique twist: Divers provide a live underwater video feed to an onboard monitor. Prices are C$41 (US$27) adults, C$38 (US$25) seniors, and C$24 (US$16) children. **Sea Watch Tours** (☎ 506/662-8552) runs 5-hour excursions with whales guaranteed aboard a 42-foot vessel with canopy. The rate is C$44 (US$29) adults and C$10 to C$34 (US$7 to US$23) per child, depending on age.

WHERE TO STAY

Anchorage Provincial Park (☎ 506/662-7022) has 100 campsites scattered about forest and field. A small beach and a hiking trail are on the property, and it's well situated for exploring the southern part of the island. The park is very popular midsummer; call before you board the ferry to ask about campsite availability.

Compass Rose Inn. North Head, Grand Manan, NB E0G 2M0. ☎ **506/662-8570** or 514/ 458-2607 (Nov–Apr). 7 units. C$79–C$89 (US$53–US$59) double. Rates include full breakfast. MC, V. Closed Nov–Apr.

The Compass Rose Inn occupies two small but historic homes overlooking the waterfront. All guest rooms have a water view and are tastefully decorated in a light country style. Among the best rooms: Calico, a corner room with a couch and pine floors and great windows to watch the ferry come and go. Breakfast, lunch, and dinner are served in a cheerful dining room overlooking the harbor. Seafood is the specialty. Dishes include coquilles St-Jacques, sautéed scallops with rosemary, and pork tenderloin with wild blueberry chutney. Entrees run C$13 to C$19 (US$9 to US$13).

✪ **Inn at Whale Cove Cottages.** Whistle Rd. (P.O. Box 233), North Head, Grand Manan, NB E0G 2M0. ☎ **506/662-3181.** 3 units, 45 cottages. C$85 (US$57) double, with full breakfast; C$500–C$600 (US$334–US$400) per week cottage. MC, V. Closed Nov–Apr. Pets accepted.

The Inn at Whale Cove is a delightful family-run compound in a grassy meadow overlooking a picturesque cove. The original building is a cozy 1816 farmhouse that has been restored with a nice selection of simple country antiques. The guest rooms are comfortable (Sally's Attic has a small deck and a large view); the living room has a couple years' worth of good reading and a welcoming fireplace. The cottages, scattered about the property, vary from one to four bedrooms. The 10-acre grounds are wonderful to explore, especially the path down to the quiet coveside beach. Innkeeper Laura Buckley received her culinary training in Toronto and demonstrates a deft touch with local ingredients. The menu might include bouillabaisse, seafood risotto, salmon in phyllo, or pork tenderloin with green-peppercorn sauce. Dinner is served 6 to 8:30pm, and entrees are C$11 to C$20 (US$7 to US$13). On Saturday, a full dinner is served with one seating at 7pm.

WHERE TO DINE

The options for dining out aren't exactly extravagant on Grand Manan. The inns listed in "Where to Stay" offer appetizing meals and decent value.

In the mood for a dare? Try walking into the **North Head Bakery,** Route 776, on the left when you're heading south from the ferry (☎ 506/662-8862), and walking out without buying anything. *It can't be done.* This superb bakery has used traditional baking methods and whole grains since it opened in 1990. Breads made daily include a crusty seven-grain Saint John Valley bread and a delightful egg-and-butter bread.

And don't overlook the chocolate-chip cookies. For a ready-made picnic, detour to **Cove Cuisine,** at the Inn at Whale Cove Cottages, Whistle Road, which forks off Route 776 near the bakery (☎ **506/662-3181**). Laura Buckley offers a limited but tasty selection of "new traditional" fixin's, like hummus, tabouli, and curried chicken salad to go.

4 Saint John: New Brunswick's Largest City

Centered around a sizable commercial harbor, **Saint John** is New Brunswick's largest city and the center of much of the province's industry. Spread over a low hill, the downtown boasts wonderfully elaborate Victorian flourishes on the rows of commercial buildings. (Be sure to look high along the cornices to appreciate the intricate brickwork.) A handful of impressive mansions lord over side streets, their interiors a forest of intricate wood carving—appropriate for the timber barons who built them.

There's a certain industrial grittiness to Saint John—some find it raw and unappealing, others find in it a certain ragged raffishness. It all depends on your outlook. Just don't expect a tidy garden city with lots of neat homes; it's got a surfeit of brick architecture in various states of repair, and throughout the downtown you'll get glimpses of industry like large shipping terminals, oil-storage facilities, and paper mills (the sort that was so popular with the Ashcan artists). A 1978 book on New Brunswick put it diplomatically: "Saint John's heavy industries ensure that the city is not famed for beauty, but the setting is magnificent."

Don't let this put you off—make the effort to detour from the highway to downtown. And it does take some effort: The traffic engineers have been very mischievous here. When you finally arrive, you'll discover an intriguing place to stroll around for an afternoon while awaiting the ferry to Digby, to grab a delicious bite to eat, or to break up village hopping with an urban overnight. The streets are often bustling with everyone from skateboarders sporting nose rings to impeccably coiffed dowagers shopping at the public market.

A final note: Saint John is always spelled out, never abbreviated St. John. That's to better keep mail aimed for St. John's in Newfoundland from ending up here, and vice versa. Locals will be quick to correct you if you err.

ESSENTIALS

GETTING THERE   Saint John is on Route 1. It's 107km (66 miles) from the U.S. border at St. Stephens and 424km (263 miles) from Halifax, Nova Scotia.

Year-round **ferry service** connects Saint John to Digby, Nova Scotia (see "Exploring the Province," at the beginning of this chapter). Saint John's airport has regular flights to Toronto, Halifax, and other Canadian points; contact **Air Canada** (☎ **800/776-3000** in the U.S., 800/565-3940 in the Maritimes, or 506/632-1500; www.aircanada.ca) or **Canadian Airlines** (☎ **800/426-7000** in the U.S. or 800/665-1177 in Canada; www.cdnair.ca) for details. Since September 1999, the airport has levied a C$10 (US$7) fee to all departing passengers to finance improvements.

VISITOR INFORMATION   Saint John has three visitor centers. Arriving from the west, look for a contemporary triangular building just off Route 1 (☎ **506/658-2940**), where you'll find a trove of information and brochures mid-May to mid-October. A smaller seasonal center is inside the observation building overlooking the Reversing Falls on Route 100 (☎ **506/658-2937**).

If you've already made your way downtown, look for the **City Centre Tourist Information Centre** inside Market Square, a downtown shopping mall just off the waterfront (☎ **888/364-4444** or 506/658-2855). Find the info center by entering the square at street level at the corner of St. Patrick and Water streets. The center is open daily: mid-June to mid-September 9am to 8pm and the rest of the year 9:30am to 6pm.

EXPLORING SAINT JOHN

If the weather's cooperative, start by wandering around downtown near the water-front. The Visitor and Convention Bureau has published three **walking tour brochures** that offer plenty of history and architectural trivia. Saint John is noted for the odd and interesting gargoyles and sculpted heads adorning the brick-and-stone 19th-century buildings downtown. If you have time for only one self-guided tour, I'd opt for "Prince William's Walk," an hour-long tour of the impressive commercial buildings. Request the free tour brochures at the Market Square info center.

If the weather's disagreeable, head indoors. Over the past decade, Saint John has been busy linking up its downtown malls and shops with an elaborate network of underground and overhead pedestrian walkways, dubbed **"The Inside Connection."** It's not just for shopping—two major hotels, the provincial museum, the city library, the city market, the sports arena, and the aquatic center are all part of the network.

✪ **Old City Market.** 47 Charlotte St. ☎ **506/658-2820.** Free admission. Mon–Thurs 7:30am–6pm, Fri 7:30am–7pm, Sat 7:30am–5pm.

Hungry travelers venture here at their peril! This bustling, bright marketplace is crammed with vendors hawking meat, fresh seafood (beautiful fish!), cheeses, flowers, baked goods, and bountiful fresh produce. You can even sample dulse, a snack of dried seaweed from the Bay of Fundy. (One traveler has compared the experience to licking a wharf.) The market was built in 1876 and has been a center of commerce for the city ever since. Note the construction of the roof—local lore says it resembles an inverted ship because it was made by boat builders who didn't know how to build anything else. And watch for the enduring traces of tradition: The handsome iron gates at either end have been in place since 1880, and the loud bell is rung daily by the Deputy Market Clerk, who signals the market's opening and closing. A number of vendors offer meals to go, and there's a bright seating area in an enclosed terrace on the market's south side.

Loyalist House. 120 Union St. ☎ **506/652-3590.** Admission C$3 (US$2) adults, C$1 (US65¢) children, C$7 (US$4.65) families. July–Aug daily 10am–5pm; May–June Mon–Fri 10am–5pm; Sept–Apr by appointment only.

This is a mandatory destination for serious antiques buffs. This stately Georgian was built in 1817 for the Merritt family, who were wealthy Loyalists from Rye, New York. Inside is an extraordinary collection of furniture dating from before 1833, most pieces of which were original to the house and have never left. Especially notable are the extensive holdings of Duncan Phyfe Sheraton furniture and a rare piano-organ combination. Other unusual detailing includes the doors steamed and bent to fit into the curved sweep of the stairway and the carvings on the wooden chair rails. Tours last 30 to 45 minutes, depending on the number of questions you muster.

✪ **New Brunswick Museum.** Market Sq. ☎ **506/643-2360.** Admission C$6 (US$4) adults, C$4.75 (US$3.15) seniors, C$3.25 (US$2.15) students/youth 4–18, C$13 (US$9) families. Mon–Fri 9am–9pm, Sat 10am–6pm, Sun noon–5pm.

The New Brunswick Museum opened in modern new quarters downtown in 1996, and it's an excellent stop for anyone the least curious about the province's natural or cultural history. The collections, displayed on three open floors, offer a nice mix of tra-ditional artifacts and quirky objects. (Among the more memorable items is a frightful-looking "permanent wave" machine from a 1930s beauty parlor.) The exhaustive exhibits include the complete interior of Sullivan's Bar (where longshoremen used to

Saint John

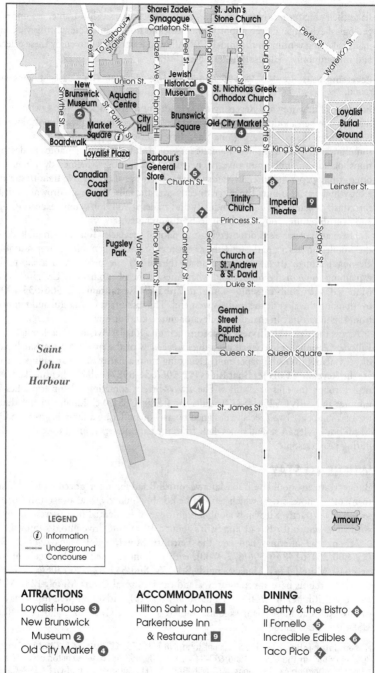

LEGEND
🛈 Information
⚬⚬⚬ Underground Concourse

ATTRACTIONS
Loyalist House ❸
New Brunswick
   Museum ❷
Old City Market ❹

ACCOMMODATIONS
Hilton Saint John ❶
Parkerhouse Inn
   & Restaurant ❾

DINING
Beatty & the Bistro ❽
Il Fornello ❺
Incredible Edibles ❻
Taco Pico ❼

slake their thirst a few blocks away), a massive section of a ship frame, a wonderful geological exhibit, and even a sporty white Bricklin from a failed New Brunswick auto manufacturing venture in the mid-1970s. Allow at least 2 hours to enjoy these eclectic and uncommonly well-displayed exhibits.

Reversing Falls. Rte. 100. ☎ **506/658-2937.** Free admission. Open daylight hours year-round.

Just west of downtown is Reversing Falls, in an impressive rocky gorge. Owing to the massive tide hereabouts, rapids, low waterfalls, and large slurping whirlpools flow one way through the gorge during one tide, then reverse during the opposite tide. It's a sometimes dramatic sight in a dramatic location, but few publicity photos or descriptions include one important caveat: The gorge is all but overwhelmed by a huge and often stinky paper mill literally yards upriver. There are also an active train trestle and a busy highway spanning the gorge directly over the falls, which are drowned out by the constant clang and hum of industry and trade. If you don't come expecting wild and brutish nature, you're less likely to be disappointed.

There are several ways of observing this natural spectacle. You can scramble down the wooden steps to a park along the river's edge. You can scramble up atop a rooftop viewing platform (free). And in a small theater off the platform is a short film explaining some of the history and wherefores of the phenomenon (C$1.50/US$1). More sedentary souls can enjoy a meal in **The Falls Restaurant** (☎ **506/635-1999**) overlooking the river at the bridge's west end. The restaurant is peaceful and removed from the urban fray in that chirpy elevator-music kind of way.

Across the river is **Fallsview Park** (turn left on Douglas Avenue, then left again on Fallsview Avenue). Here you'll get a duck's-eye view of the river from this small park directly across from the paper mill. Departing from a narrow cove at Fallsview Park are the **Reversing Falls Jet Boat Rides** (☎ **506/634-8987**), which offer fun, fast boat trips through the falls at all tides. The always-breezy, sometimes-damp trip takes 20 minutes and costs C$25 (US$17) adults and C$20 (US$13) children, which includes use of a raincoat. Two specially designed boats—one offering a more heart-pounding "thrill ride"—depart several times daily from the park. Reservations are recommended during peak season.

WHERE TO STAY

Budget travelers should head to **Manawagonish Road** for lower-priced motels. Unlike many other motel strips, which tend to be notably unlovely, Manawagonish Road is reasonably attractive. It winds along a high ridge of residential homes west of town, with views out to the Bay of Fundy. It's about a 10-minute drive into downtown.

Among the offerings here are the **Fairport Motel,** 1360 Manawagonish Rd. (☎ **800/251-6158** or 506/672-9700), with its home-cooked–meals restaurant; the **Seacoast Motel,** 1441 Manawagonish Rd. (☎ **800/541-0277** or 506/635-8700), where the rooms have sweeping views; and the **Balmoral Court Motel,** 1284 Man-awagonish Rd. (☎ **888/463-3779** or 506/672-3019), with clean, well-lit rooms and cabins. Rates at most Manawagonish motels are about C$60 to C$70 (US$40 to US$47) in peak season.

Hilton Saint John. 1 Market Sq., Saint John, NB E2L 4Z6. ☎ **800/561-8282** in Canada, 800/445-8667 in the U.S., or 506/693-8484. Fax 509/657-6610. www.hilton.nb.ca. E-mail hiltonnb@nbnet.nb.ca. 197 units. A/C MINIBAR TV TEL. Summer to mid-Oct C$99–C$139 (US$66–US$93) double; off-season C$89–C$109 (US$59–US$93) double. AE, DC, DISC, MC, V. Free parking weekends, otherwise C$13 (US$9). Pets allowed.

This 12-story waterfront hotel was built in 1984 and offers the amenities you'd expect from an upscale chain hotel, including coffeemakers and hair dryers in each room. It boasts the best location in Saint John, overlooking the harbor yet just steps from the rest of downtown by street or indoor walkway. The windows in all rooms open—a nice touch when the breeze is coming from the sea, but not when it's blowing in from the paper mill to the west. The Hilton is connected to the convention center and attracts major events; ask whether anything's scheduled before you book if you don't want to be overwhelmed by conventioneers.

Dining: The Brigantine Lounge offers light meals daily 11:30am to 1am. For more refined fare, head to Turn of the Tide, which serves three meals daily in an understated classical harborside setting. Entrees include creatively prepared steaks, pheasant, and salmon at C$18 to C$29 (US$12 to US$19).

Amenities: Concierge, 24-hour room service, laundry, baby-sitting, safe-deposit boxes; small indoor pool, fitness room, Jacuzzi, sauna, game room, business center.

Homeport Historic Bed & Breakfast. 80 Douglas Ave., Saint John, NB E2K 1E4. ☎ **888/ 678-7678** or 506/672-7255. www.homeport.nb.ca. E-mail stay@homeport.nb.ca. 5 units. A/C TV TEL. C$79–C$125 (US$53–US$93) double. Rates include full breakfast. AE, MC, V.

This architecturally impressive Italianate home sits atop a rocky ridge on the north side of Route 1, overlooking downtown and the harbor. Built around 1858, it opened to guests in 1997 and is one of Saint John's more gracious options for overnighting. (It's the only place in the city to be awarded five stars from Canada Select.) The guest rooms are furnished eclectically with pieces gleaned from area auctions and shops; all have individually controlled heat and three have clawfoot tubs. Ask for the spacious Veranda Room—it boasts fine harbor views and gets superb afternoon sun (I'm also partial to the pink-tiled bathroom). The Harbour Master Suite has a small separate sitting room, ideal for those traveling with a child. "Come-hungry" breakfasts are served family style around a long antique table in the formal dining room.

Parkerhouse Inn & Restaurant. 71 Sydney St., Saint John, NB E2L 2L5. ☎ **888/457-2520** or 506/652-5054. Fax 506/636-8076. 9 units. TV TEL. C$79–C$99 (US$53–US$66) double. AE, DC, ER, MC, V.

The Parkerhouse is a grand 1890 mansion designed in high Victorian style by a wealthy timber merchant. The attention to architectural detail is above and beyond the usual, from the beveled leaded glass in the front doorway to the exquisite carved staircase of regal mahogany. Much of the downstairs is given over to a restaurant, and a bright sitting area fronts the street. The guest rooms are decorated in a light Victorian country style, all with robes and hair dryers, several with gas fireplaces. Among the best rooms are no. 5, with a sitting room, wood floors, a pine armoire, and wonderful morning light, and no. 3, with maple floors, a bay window, old-fashioned shutters, and a handsome birdseye mahogany bed (alas, the bathroom is small). Children over 10 are welcome.

One of Saint John's better restaurants, 71 Sydney Street, is on the ground floor. Angle for a seat in the Victorian solarium with its mosaic floor, though the two other dining rooms are cozy and romantic. There's also an outside deck for dining in clement weather. Dinner is served Monday to Saturday 5 to 8:30pm (or to 9:30pm on "busy nights"), with entrees like herb-crusted lamb, striploin with garlic, and roasted Atlantic salmon (C$18 to C$23/US$12 to US$15). Reservations are encouraged.

WHERE TO DINE

For lunch, don't overlook the **Old City Market,** mentioned above. With a little snooping you can turn up tasty light meals and fresh juices in the market, then enjoy your finds in the alley atrium. For dinner, check out **71 Sydney Street,** the wonderful restaurant at the Parkerhouse Inn (above).

Beatty and the Beastro. 60 Charlotte St. (on King's Sq.). ☎ **506/652-3888.** Reservations recommended on weekends and when shows are slated at the Imperial Theatre. Main courses C$6–C$9 (US$4–US$6) at lunch, C$17–C$20 (US$11–US$13) at dinner. AE, DC, ER, MC, V. Mon–Fri 11:30am–3pm; Mon–Sat 5:30–9pm (to 10pm Fri–Sat). BISTRO/CONTINENTAL.

The small but attractive interior of this large-windowed place fronting King's Square features a mild European-modern look. The service is cordial and efficient, and the meals are among the best in the city, always good, sometimes excellent. Lunch includes soups, salads, omelets, and elaborate sandwiches. At dinner, the restaurant is noted for its lamb, the preparation of which varies nightly according to the chef's desire. When dessert time rolls around, be aware that both the butterscotch pie and the lemon chess pie have large local followings.

Incredible Edibles. 42 Princess St. ☎ **506/633-7554.** Reservations recommended on weekends. Main courses C$8–C$12 (US$5–US$8) at lunch, C$11–C$24 (US$7–US$16) at dinner. Daily 11am–11pm. ECLECTIC.

This is another fine Saint John restaurant with a regrettably cutesy name. On the first floor of the Brodie Building a block off King Street, this relaxed, casual spot has three dining rooms (two no-smoking), high tin ceilings, mix-and-match seating, and little sand-and-rock Zen gardens on each table to while away the time. The menu is appealingly eclectic. Lunch ranges from omelets to pizza and pad thai. At dinner, there are roasted salmon, prime rib with Yorkshire pudding, and a pineapple curry with prawns and a heap of mussels. Among the more popular dishes is pasta with a white clam sauce. The service is friendly and the food consistently good.

Taco Pico. 96 Germain St. ☎ **506/633-8492.** Reservations suggested on weekends. Main courses C$8–C$17 (US$5–US$11). AE, MC, V. Mon–Sat 10am–10pm. LATINO.

This worker-owned cooperative is owned/run by a group of Guatemalans and their friends. It's bright, festive, and just a short stroll off King Street. The restaurant has developed a devoted local following since it opened in 1994 and features a menu that's a notch above the usually dreary Canadian adaptations of Mexican or Latin American fare. Among the most reliably popular dishes are *pepian* (a spicy beef stew with chayote), garlic shrimp, and shrimp taco with potatoes, peppers, and cheese. There's also a good selection of fresh juices.

5 Fredericton

New Brunswick's provincial capital, **Fredericton** is a compact historic city of brick and concrete that unfolds along the banks of the wide St. John River. The handsome buildings, broad streets, and wide sidewalks make the place feel more like a big tidy village than a small city. Keep an eye out for the two icons that mark Fredericton: the stately elm trees that have resisted Dutch elm disease and still shade the occasional park and byway and the Union Jack that you'll occasionally see fluttering from various buildings, attesting to long-standing ties with the Loyalists who shaped the city.

Travelers can view the city as divided into three zones: the malls and motels atop the hills and near the link to the Trans-Canada Highway; the impressive Georgian-style University of New Brunswick on the hillside just south of downtown; and the downtown proper, with its casual blend of modern and historic buildings. Most visitors focus on downtown. The main artery—where you'll find the majority of the attractions and many restaurants—is Queen Street, paralleling the river between 1 and 2 blocks inland. An ill-considered limited-access four-lane bypass separates much of downtown from the river, but you can still reach the water's edge via the Green or by crossing a pedestrian bridge at the foot of Carleton Street.

Fredericton

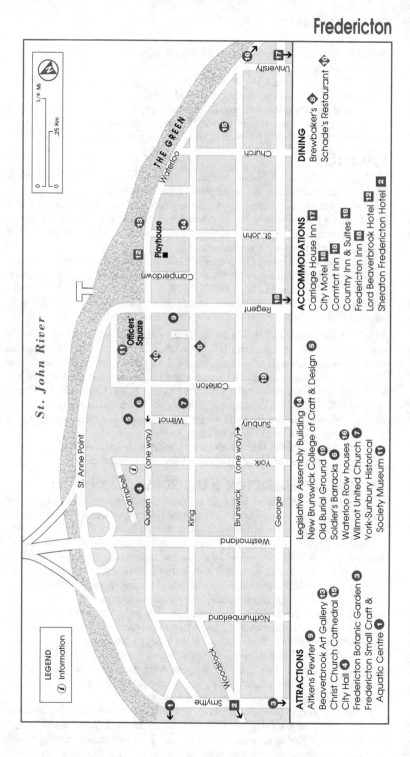

LEGEND
(i) Information

ATTRACTIONS
Aitkens Pewter 9
Beaverbrook Art Gallery 13
Christ Church Cathedral 15
City Hall 4
Fredericton Botanic Garden 3
Fredericton Small Craft &
Aquatic Centre 1
Legislative Assembly Building 14
New Brunswick College of Craft & Design 5
Old Burial Ground 10
Soldier's Barracks 6
Waterloo Row houses 16
Wilmot United Church 7
York-Sunbury Historical
Society Museum 11

ACCOMMODATIONS
Carriage House Inn 17
City Motel 18
Comfort Inn 13
Country Inn & Suites 18
Fredericton Inn 18
Lord Beaverbrook Hotel 12
Sheraton Fredericton Hotel 2

DINING
Brewbaker's 8
Schade's Restaurant 10

Fredericton, with a population of 79,000, is appealing in an understated way. There's really no must-see attraction, but the collective impact of strolling the streets and visiting several spots adds up to a full sense of history and place. Fredericton's subtle charms won't be everyone's cup of tea. My advice: If eastern Canada's allure for you is the shimmering sea, deep woods, and wide open spaces, you won't miss much by bypassing Fredericton. If your passions include history—especially the history of British settlement in North America—then it's well worth the detour.

ESSENTIALS

GETTING THERE   A major relocation and widening of the Trans-Canada Highway near Fredericton was being planned for 2000, which is likely to result in some inconveniences and confusion until the feeder roadways and signage is sorted out. Look for signs directing you to downtown. From the west, follow Woodstock Road, which tracks along the river to downtown. From Saint John, look for Route 7 to Regent Street, then turn right down the hill.

The **Fredericton Airport** (☎ **506/444-6100**) is 10 minutes southeast of downtown on Route 102 and served by cab and rental-car companies. For flight information, contact **Air Canada** (☎ **800/776-3000** in the U.S., 800/565-3940 in the Maritimes, or 506/632-1500; www.aircanada.ca) or **Canadian Airlines** (☎ **800/426-7000** in the U.S. or 800/665-1177 in Canada; www.cdnair.ca).

VISITOR INFORMATION   Fredericton was in the throes of rethinking its visitor centers in late 1999. A new center is likely to open near the relocated Trans-Canada in 2000, and officials were considering moving the longtime downtown center out of city hall to an as-yet-undetermined location. But Fredericton caters well to travelers, so the new centers are certain to be well marked; check first at **City Hall,** 397 Queen St., or call ☎ **506/460-2129** for more information. When you find a visitor center, request a **Visitor Parking Pass,** allowing visitors from outside the province to park free at city lots and meters in town for up to 3 days.

You can request travel info in advance by visiting the city's Web site at **www.city.fredericton.nb.ca** or e-mailing tourism@city.fredericton.nb.ca.

EXPLORING FREDERICTON & ENVIRONS

The free *Fredericton Visitor Guide,* available at the information centers and many hotels around town, contains a well-written and informative walking tour of downtown. It's worth tracking down before launching an exploration of the city.

Officer's Square, on Queen Street between Carleton and Regent, is now a handsome city park. In 1785, the park was the center of military activity and used for drills, first as part of the British garrison and later (until 1914) by the Canadian Army. Today, the only soldiers are local actors who put on a show for tourists. Look also for music and dramatic events staged at the square in the warmer months. The handsome colonnaded stone building facing the parade grounds is the former officer's quarters, now the York-Sunbury Historical Society Museum (below).

Two blocks upriver of Officer's Square is the **Soldier's Barracks,** housed in a similarly grand stone building. Check your watch against the sundial high on the end of the barracks, a replica of the original timepiece. A small exhibit shows the life of the enlisted man in the 18th century. Along the ground floor, local craftspeople sell their wares from small shops carved out of former barracks.

July and August, an entertaining and enlightening way to learn about the city's history is to sign up for a walking tour with the **Calithumpians** of Fredericton's Outdoor Summer Theatre. Costumed guides offer free tours daily, pointing out highlights with anecdotes and dramatic tales. Recommended is the evening "Haunted Hike" tour, running 3 nights each week; it's about 2 hours and costs C$12 (US$8) adults and C$8 (US$5) children; call ☎ **506/457-1975** for details.

Beaverbrook Art Gallery. 703 Queen St. ☎ **506/458-8545.** Admission C$3 (US$2) adults, C$2 (US$1.35) seniors, C$1 (US65¢) students; children under 6 free. June–Sept Mon–Fri 9am–6pm, Sat–Sun 10am–5pm; Oct–May Tues–Fri 9am–5pm, Sat 10am–5pm, Sun noon–5pm.

This surprisingly fine modern museum overlooks the waterfront and is home to an impressive collection of British paintings, including works by Reynolds, Gainsborough, Constable, and Turner. Antiques buffs gravitate to the rooms with period furnishings and early decorative arts. Most everyone finds themselves drawn to Salvador Dali's massive *Santiago El Grande* and studies for an ill-fated portrait of Winston Churchill. A new curator has brought in more controversial modern art exhibits in the past few years; stop by to find out what's currently on display.

Legislative Assembly Building. Queen St. (across from the Beaverbrook Art Gallery). ☎ **506/453-2527.** Free admission. Summer daily 8:45am–7pm; off-season Mon–Fri 9am–4pm.

The Legislative Assembly Building, begun in 1880, boasts an exterior designed in the bulbous extravagant Second Empire style. But that's just the prelude. Inside, it's even more dressed up and fancy. Entering takes a bit of courage if the doors are closed; they're heavy and intimidating, with slits of beveled glass for peering out. (They're a bit reminiscent of the gates of Oz.) Beyond, it's creaky and wooden and comfortable, in contrast to the cold, unyielding stone of many seats of power. In the small rotunda, look for the razor-sharp prints from John James Audubon's elephant folio, on display in a special case.

The assembly chamber nearly takes the breath away, especially when viewed from the heights of the visitor gallery on the upper floors. (You ascend via a graceful wood spiral stairway housed in its own rotunda.) The chamber is ornate and draperied in the fussy Victorian way, which is quite a feat given the vast scale of the room. Note all the regal trappings, including the portrait of the young Queen Elizabeth. This place just feels like a setting for high drama, whether or not it actually delivers when the chamber is in session.

York-Sunbury Historical Society Museum. Off Queen St. near Regent St. ☎ **506/455-6041.** Admission C$2 (US$1.35) adults, C$1 (US65¢) students, C$4 (US$2.65) families. Summer daily 10am–5pm; spring and fall Tues–Sat noon–5pm.

This well-done small museum lures you with the promise of a stuffed 42-pound frog. It was said to belong to Fred Coleman, who in the late 19th century fed it a nasty concoction of June bugs, cornmeal, buttermilk, and whiskey to give it Rubenesque proportions. After it perished at the hands of some miscreants, the famous frog was displayed at the Burke House Hotel until 1959, when it traveled with little ceremony to the museum. It's displayed on the top floor to ensure that you wander through all the exhibits looking for it—a clever trick on the part of the curator.

Actually, the frog is a disappointment. (Not to mention suspect—it looks like it's made of bad papier-mâché.) But the rest of the museum is nicely done. Displays feature the usual artifacts of Life Gone By, but several exhibits rise well above the clutter, including a fine display on Loyalist settlers. Kids will love the claustrophobic re-creation of a German World War II trench on the second floor—and likely will end up talking more about that on the way home than Fred's portly frog.

✪ Kings Landing Historical Settlement. Exit 259 off the Trans-Canada Highway (Rte. 2 west). ☎ **506/363-4999** or 506/363-4959 for recorded info. www.kingslanding. nb.ca. Admission C$10 (US$7) adults, C$8 (US$5) seniors, C$7 (US$4.85) students over

16, C$6 (US$3.65) children 6–16, C$25 (US$17) families. June to mid-Oct daily 10am–5pm.

Kings Landing, on the bank of the St. John River, is 34km (21 miles) and about 150 years from Fredericton. The authentic re-creation brings to life New Brunswick from 1790 to 1910, with 10 historic houses and 9 other buildings relocated here and saved from destruction by the flooding during the Mactaquac hydro project. The aroma of freshly baked bread mixes with the smell of horses and livestock, and the sound of the blacksmith's hammer alternates with that of the church bell. More than 160 costumed "early settlers" chat about their lives. You could easily spend a day exploring the 150 acres, but if you haven't that much time, focus on the **Hagerman House** (with furniture by Victorian cabinetmaker John Warren Moore), **Ingraham House** (with fine New Brunswick furniture and a formal English garden), **Morehouse House** (where you'll see a clock Benedict Arnold left behind), and **Victorian Perley House.** The **Ross Sash and Door Factory** will demonstrate the work and times of an early-1900s manufacturing plant.

Afterward, hitch a ride on the **sloven wagon** or relax at the **Kings Head Inn,** which served up grub and grog to hardy travelers along the St. John River a century or more ago. Today it serves lemonade, chicken pie, and corn chowder, along with other traditional dishes. Lunch is C$8 to C$13 (US$5 to US$9) and dinner is C$13 to C$19 (US$9 to US$13).

OUTDOOR PURSUITS

Fredericton recently expanded its trail system for walkers and bikers. The system's centerpiece is **The Green,** a 5km (3.1-mile) pathway following the river from the Sheraton hotel to near the Princess Margaret Bridge. It's a lovely walk, and you'll pass the Old Government House, downtown, and the open parklands near Waterloo Row. Connecting with The Green is a well-used pedestrian bridge crossing an abandoned railroad trestle just east of downtown. From this vantage point you'll get wonderful views of downtown and the river valley. If you continue onward, the **Nashwaak/Marysville Trail** follows an abandoned rail bed along the attractive Nashwaak River; after about 4km (2½ miles) you can cross the Nashwaak at Bridge Street and loop back to the pedestrian rail-bridge via the **Gibson Trail.**

A number of other trails link up to this expanding network, which comprised about 60km (37 miles) as of late 1999. A trail-guide brochure is available free at the information centers, or you can contact the **New Brunswick Trails Council** at ☎ **506/459-1931.**

You can rent bikes by the hour or day at the **Fredericton Lighthouse** at the Regent Street Wharf (☎ **506/459-2515**), or at **Radical Edge,** 386 Queen St. (☎ **506/459-3478**).

WHERE TO STAY

A handful of motels and chain hotels are in the bustling mall zone on the hill above town, mostly along Regent and Prospect streets. Allow about 10 minutes to drive downtown from here. Among the classiest of the bunch is the **Fredericton Inn,** 1315 Regent St. (☎ **800/561-8777** or 506/455-1430), between two malls. It's a soothing-music-and-floral-carpeting kind of place that does a brisk business with conventions. But with its indoor pool and classically appointed rooms, it's a comfortable spot for vacation travelers as well. Peak-season rates are C$73 to C$129 (US$49 to US$86) double and up to C$169 (US$113) for suites.

Also near the malls are the **Comfort Inn,** 255 Prospect St. (☎ **506/453-0800**), at C$78 to C$105 (US$52 to US$70) double; **City Motel,** 1216 Regent St. (☎ **800/**

268-2858 or 506/459-9900), at C$70 to C$90 (US$47 to US$60) double; and the **Country Inn and Suites,** 455 Prospect St. (☎ **506/459-0035**), at C$93 to C$106 (US$62 to US$71) double.

Carriage House Inn. 230 University Ave., Fredericton, NB E3B 4H7. ☎ **800/267-6068** or 506/452-9924. Fax 506/458-0799. E-mail chinn@nbnet.nb.ca. 11 units, 2 with hall bathrooms. TEL. C$75–C$85 (US$50–US$57) double. Rates include full breakfast. AE, DC, MC, V. "Small, well-trained pets" allowed.

Fredericton's premier B&B is a short stroll from the riverfront pathway in a quiet residential neighborhood. This imposing three-story Victorian manse was built by a former mayor in 1875, and inside it's a bit somber in that heavy Victorian way, with dark wood trim and deep colors—the place feels solid enough to resist glaciers. The guest rooms are eclectically furnished and comfortable without being opulent. A friendly rottweiler named Bailey is on the premises. Delicious and elaborate breakfasts are served in a sunny room in the rear of the house. Dinner (around C$25/US$17 per person) is available with 48-hour notice; ask about the menu when you book.

Lord Beaverbrook Hotel. 659 Queen St., Fredericton, NB E3B 5A6. ☎ **800/561-7666** (Canada and New England only) or 506/455-3371. Fax 506/455-1441. E-mail lbhotel@ nbnet.nb.ca. 165 units. A/C TV TEL. C$95–C$139 (US$63–US$93) double; to C$450 (US$300) suite. AE, DC, ER, MC, V.

This hulking 1947 waterfront hotel is severe in that early deco kind of way, a look that may at first suggest that it houses the Ministry of Dourness. Inside, the mood lightens considerably, with composite stone floors, Georgian pilasters, and chandeliers. The downstairs indoor pool/recreation area is whimsical, a sort of tiki-room grotto kids adore. The guest rooms are nicely appointed with traditional reproduction furniture in dark wood. Standard rooms can be somewhat dim, and most of the windows don't open (ask for a room with opening windows when you book). The suites are spacious, and many have excellent river views. The hotel, which was part of the troubled Keddy chain, went into receivership in 1999, but at my last inspection it appeared not to be suffering in the least from the turmoil and was still tidy and well managed.

Dining/Diversions: The Terrace Room is the main dining area, with an indoor gazebo and a seasonal outdoor deck overlooking the river. Main courses (C$11 to C$17/US$7 to US$11) range from Oriental shrimp stir-fry to chicken fettuccine Alfredo. The more intimate Governor's Room has higher aspirations, with dinner entrees like duck breast with raspberry and Grand Mariner coulis or shrimp Provencal at C$17 to C$26 (US$11 to US$17). The River Room lounge is the spot for a beer and a snack.

Amenities: Baby-sitting, dry cleaning/laundry, safe-deposit boxes, conference rooms, business center, free airport shuttle; small indoor pool, Jacuzzi, limited fitness equipment.

Sheraton Fredericton Hotel. 225 Woodstock Rd., Fredericton, NB E3B 2H8. ☎ **800/ 325-3535** or 506/457-7000. Fax 506/457-4000. www.sheraton.com. 223 units. A/C MINIBAR TV TEL. C$92–C$145 double. AE, CB, DC, MC, V.

This modern resort hotel, built in 1992, occupies a prime location along the river about 10 minutes' walk from downtown via the riverfront pathway. Much of summer life revolves around the outdoor pool on the deck overlooking the river, and on Sunday the lobby is surrendered to an over-the-top breakfast buffet. Though decidedly up-to-date, the interior is done with classical styling and is comfortable and well appointed. All the guest rooms include irons and hair dryers.

Dining/Diversions: The lounge is popular on many nights, especially weekends. Across the lobby is Bruno's Seafood Cafe, which offers a good alternative to the restaurants downtown. Look also for seasonal and regional specialties, including fiddleheads in early summer. Main courses are C$7 to C$23 (US$4.65 to US$15).

Amenities: Fitness room, indoor and outdoor pools, gift shop, complete conference facilities.

WHERE TO DINE

Brewbakers. 546 King St. ☎ **506/459-0067.** Reservations recommended on weekends. Main courses C$7–C$9 (US$4.85–US$6) at lunch, C$13–C$22 (US$9–US$15) at dinner. AE, CB, DC, ER, MC, V. Daily 11am–11pm (to midnight Fri–Sat). PASTA/PUB FARE.

Brewbakers is a convivial pub/cafe/restaurant on three levels in a cleverly adapted downtown building. It's informal, creatively cluttered with artifacts and artworks, and it does booming business during lunch hours and early evenings. The cafe section is more quiet, as is the mezzanine dining room above. The third floor bustles, with an open kitchen and folks lined up for the popular build-your-own pasta buffet. And pasta is the main attraction, served with the usual array of sauces. Also good are the personal pizzas, roasted chicken, grilled striploin, and herb-crusted tenderloin. The lunch buffet is one of the better deals in town—bring a large appetite. For a meal on the go, the cafe offers a creative selection of boxed lunches.

Schade's Restaurant. 536 Queen St. ☎ **506/450-3340.** Reservations recommended. Main courses C$4–C$8 (US$2.65–US$5) at lunch, C$10–C$18 (US$7–US$12) at dinner. AE, DC, MC, V. Tues–Fri 11:30am–2pm and 5–9pm, Sat 5–9pm. GERMAN.

This German-owned/run restaurant features traditional meals from the mid-continent, including a variety of schnitzels (schnitzel specials change daily), beef stroganoff, and beef with broccoli, mushrooms, and spaetzle. The decor at this relaxed storefront restaurant isn't overly fussy (note the attractive tin ceiling), making it an appealing spot for a casual meal over a tall glass of beer. More rarified German specialties (like sauerbraten and schweinehaxe) are offered with advance notice for groups of four or more.

6 Fundy National Park: Accessing the Wild Coast

The Fundy Coast between Saint John and Alma is for the most part wild, remote, and unpopulated. It's plumbed by few roads other than the new Fundy drive (see the "Saint John" section, above), making it difficult to explore unless you have a boat. The best access to the wild coast is through ✪ **Fundy National Park,** a gem that's hugely popular with travelers with an outdoor bent. Families often settle in for a week or so, filling their days with activities in and around the park that include hiking, sea kayaking, biking, and splashing around a seaside pool. Nearby are lovely drives and an innovative adventure center at Cape Enrage. If a muffling fog moves in to smother the coast, head inland for a hike to a waterfall or through lush forest. If it's a day of brilliant sunshine, venture along the rocky shores by foot or boat.

ESSENTIALS

GETTING THERE   Route 114 runs through the center of Fundy National Park. If you're coming from the west, follow the prominent national-park signs just east of Sussex. If you're coming from Prince Edward Island or Nova Scotia, head southward on Route 114 from Moncton.

VISITOR INFORMATION   The park's main **Visitor Centre** is just inside the Alma (eastern) entrance to the park (☎ **506/887-6000**). During peak season, the stone building is open daily 8am to 10pm (limited hours off-season). You can watch a video presentation, peruse a handful of exhibits on wildlife and tides, and shop at the nicely stocked nature bookstore. At the park's western entrance is the smaller

Wolfe Lake Information Centre (☎ **506/432-6026**), open daily 10am to 6pm in summer but weekdays only in spring.

FEES   Mid-May to mid-October, the entrance fee is C$3.50 (US$2.35) adults, C$2.75 (US$1.85) seniors, C$1.75 (US$1.15) children 6 to 16, and C$7 (US$4.65) families. Four-day passes are available for the price of 3 days.

EXPLORING THE PARK

Most national-park activities are centered around the **Alma (east) side** of the park, where the entrance has a cultivated and manicured air, as if part of a landed estate. Here you'll find stone walls, well-tended lawns, and attractive landscaping, along with a golf course, an amphitheater, lawn bowling, and tennis. Also in this area is a **heated saltwater pool,** set near the bay with a sweeping ocean view and open late June to August. A lifeguard is on duty, and it's popular with families. The cost is C$2 (US$1.35) adults, C$1.50 (US$1) children, and C$5 (US$3.35) families.

Sea **kayaking tours** are a way to get a good close look at the ocean landscape and the tides. **Fresh Air Adventure** (☎ **800/545-0020** or 506/887-2249) in Alma offers tours from 2 hours to several days. The half-day tours explore marsh and coastline (C$50/US$33 including lunch); the full-day adventure includes a hot meal and 6 hours of exploring the wild shores (C$90/US$60).

The park maintains 104km (64 miles) of **hiking and walking trails,** from a 20-minute loop to a 4-hour trek, passing through varied terrain. The trails are arranged so that several can be linked into a 50km (31-mile) backpacker's loop, dubbed the **Fundy Circuit,** which typically requires 3 nights in the backcountry. Preregistration is required for the overnight trek, so ask at the visitor center.

Among the most accessible hikes is the **Caribou Plain Trail,** a 3.4km (2.1-mile) loop that provides a wonderful introduction to the local terrain. You'll hike along a beaver pond, on a boardwalk across a raised peat bog, and through lovely temperate forest. Read the interpretive signs to learn about deadly "flarks," which lurk in bogs and can kill a moose. The **Third Vault Falls Trail** is a 7.4km (4.6-mile) in-and-back hike that takes you to the park's highest waterfall, about 45 feet high. The trail is largely a flat stroll through leafy woodlands until you begin a steady descent into a mossy gorge. You round a corner and there you are, suddenly facing the cataract.

All the park's trails are covered in the pullout trail guide you'll find in *Salt & Fir,* the booklet you'll receive when you pay your entry fee.

CAMPING   The national park maintains four drive-in campgrounds and 15 back-country sites. The two main campgrounds are near the Alma entrance. **Headquarters Campground** is within walking distance of Alma, the saltwater pool, and numerous other attractions. Since it overlooks the bay, it tends to be cool and subject to fogs. **Chignecto Campground** is higher on the hillside, sunnier and warmer. You can hike down to Alma on an attractive trail in 1 to 2 hours. Both campgrounds have hookups for RVs, flush toilets, and showers, and you can reserve sites in advance by calling ☎ **800/213-7275** or 506/887-6000.

The **Point Wolfe** and **Wolfe Lake** campgrounds lack RV hookups and are slightly more primitive (Wolfe Lake lacks showers), but they're the preferred destinations for campers seeking a quieter camping experience. Rates at all campgrounds are C$12 to C$19 (US$8 to US$13), depending on services required; Wolfe Lake has pit toilets only and is C$10 (US$7) per night.

Backcountry sites are scattered throughout the park, with only one directly on the coast (at the confluence of the coast and Goose River). Ask at the visitor centers for more details or to reserve a site (mandatory). Backcountry camping fees are C$3 (US$2) per person per night.

Seeking Adventure on Cape Enrage

Cape Enrage is a blustery and bold cape jutting impertinently into Chignecto Bay. It's also home to a wonderful adventure center that could be a model for similar centers worldwide.

✪ **Cape Enrage Adventures** (☎ **506/856-6081,** or 506/887-2273 after May 15; fax 506/856-3480; monctonlife.com/cape_enrage/index.htm) traces its roots back to 1993, when a group of Harrison Trimble High School students in Moncton decided to do something about the decay of the cape's historic lighthouse, which had been abandoned in 1988. They put together a plan to restore the lighthouse and keeper's quarters and establish an adventure center. It worked. Today, with the help of experts in kayaking, rock climbing, rappelling, and other rugged sports, a couple dozen high-school students staff and run this program throughout summer. The program closes in late August, when the student-managers head back to school.

Part of what makes the program so notable is its flexibility. **Day adventures** are scheduled throughout summer, and you can pick and choose, as if from a menu. These include rappelling workshops, rock-climbing lessons, kayak trips, and canoeing excursions. Prices are C$45 (US$30) per person for a 2-hour rock climbing or rappelling workshop and C$50 (US$33) for a half-day canoe or kayak trip. (Note to parents: This is an ideal spot to drop off restless teens while you indulge in scenic drives or a trip to Hopewell Rocks.)

As if running the center didn't keep the students busy enough, they also operate a restaurant (open to the public), **The Keeper's Lunchroom.** Light but tasty meals include a notable fish chowder made with fresh haddock from a recipe provided by a local fisherman's wife, served with hot biscuits. A few other selections are offered—like grilled cheese and cheesecake—but the smart money gets the chowder.

A SIDE TRIP TO HOPEWELL ROCKS

There's no better place to witness the extraordinary power of the Fundy tides than at **Hopewell Rocks** (☎ 506/734-3429), about 40km (25 miles) northeast of Fundy National Park on Route 114. Think of it as a natural sculpture garden. At low tide (the best time to visit), eroded columns as high as 15 meters (50 ft.) tower above the ocean floor. They're sometimes called the "flowerpots," on account of the trees and plants that still flourish on their narrowing summits.

You park at the new visitor center and restaurant and wander down to the shore. Signboards fill you in on the natural history. If you're here at the bottom half of the tide, you can descend the steel staircase to the sea floor and admire these wondrous freestanding rock sculptures, chiseled by waves and tides. The site can be crowded, but that's understandable. If your schedule allows it, come early in the day when the sun is fresh over Nova Scotia across the bay, the dew is still on the ground, and most travelers are still sacked out in bed. The park charges an entry fee of C$4.25 (US$2.85) adults, C$2.25 (US$1.50) children 4 to 18, and C$10 (US$7) families.

If you arrive at the top half of the tide, consider a sea kayak tour around the islands and caves. **Baymount Outdoor Adventures** (☎ 506/734-2660) runs 90-minute tours daily for C$35 (US$23) adults and C$30 (US$20) youths. (Caving tours at nearby caverns are also offered; ask if interested.)

WHERE TO STAY

Fundy Park Chalets. Rte. 114 (P.O. Box 72), Alma, NB E0A 1B0. ☎ **506/887-2808.** 29 cabins. TV. C$50–C$73 (US$33–US$49) double; discounts in spring and fall MC, V. Closed Oct to mid-May.

These storybook-like cabins are set amid birch and pines just inside the park's eastern entrance and will have immediate appeal to fans of classic motor courts. The steeply gabled white clapboard cabins have interiors that'll bring to mind a national-park vacation circa 1950—painted wood floors, pine paneling, metal shower stalls, and small kitchenettes. Two beds are in the main rooms, separated by a hospital-style track curtain that pulls around one bed. What the cabins lack in privacy they more than make up for in convenience and an unironic retro charm. The golf course, playground, tennis courts, lawn bowling, and saltwater pool are all within walking distance.

WHERE TO DINE

Seawinds Dining Room. Rte. 114 (near park headquarters), Alma, NB E0A 1B0. ☎ **506/887-2098.** Reservations recommended. Sandwiches C$3–C$7 (US$2–US$4.65); main courses C$9–C$16 (US$6–US$11). MC, V. June–Sept daily 8am–9:30pm. PUB FARE/CANADIAN.

Seawinds overlooks the park golf course and serves as a de facto clubhouse for hungry duffers. The handsome open dining room is decorated in rich forest green and mahogany hues, and it has hardwood floors, a flagstone fireplace, and wrought-iron chandeliers. The menu offers enough variations to please most anyone. Lunches include a variety of hamburgers, fish-and-chips, and bacon-and-cheese dogs. Dinner is somewhat more refined, with main courses like grilled trout, roast beef, and fried clams.

7 Moncton: A Rival to Saint John

Moncton, a city of some 113,500 residents, has been butting heads with Saint John in recent years as it strives to overtake the older port city as the province's economic powerhouse. As such, it's more notable as a regional commercial center than as a vacation destination. Travelers who detour off the Trans-Canada will find a mix of the antique and the modern. Brick buildings with elaborate facades and cornices exist cheek by jowl with boxy office towers of a less ornamental era. Moncton's low, unobtrusive skyline is dominated by an unfortunate concrete tower that houses a cluster of microwave antennae—it looks like a project designed by a former Soviet bureaucrat in a bad mood but serves as a good landmark to keep yourself oriented.

The residents are also a mix of old and new. Moncton makes the plausible claim that it's at the crossroads of the Maritimes, and it hasn't been bashful about using its geographic advantage to promote itself as a business hub. Much of the hotel/restaurant trade caters to people-in-suits, at least on weekdays. But walk along Main Street in the evening or on weekends, and you're likely to spot spiked hair, grunge flannel, skateboards, and other youthful fashion statements from current and lapsed eras. There's life here.

Moncton offers a good stopover if you're traveling with kids. Magnetic Hill and Crystal Palace both offer entertaining (albeit somewhat pricey) ways to fill an afternoon. The latter is especially appealing for younger kids on rainy days.

ESSENTIALS

GETTING THERE Moncton is at the crossroads of several major routes through New Brunswick, including Route 2 (the Trans-Canada Highway) and Route 15.

Moncton's airport is about 10 minutes from downtown on Route 132 (head northeast on Main Street from Moncton and keep driving). The city is served by daily flights on **Air Canada** (☎ **800/776-3000** in the U.S. or 800/565-3940 in the Maritimes; www.aircanada.ca) and **Canadian Airlines International** (☎ **800/ 426-7000** in the U.S. or 800/665-1177 in Canada; www.cdnair.ca). **Via Rail's** (☎ **800/561-3949** in the U.S. or 800/561-3952 in the Maritimes; www.viarail.ca) line from Montréal to Halifax stops in Moncton 6 days a week. The rail station is downtown on Main Street, next to Highfield Square.

VISITOR INFORMATION   Moncton's primary **visitor center** is at Magnetic Hill, Exit 488 off the Trans-Canada Highway (☎ **506/853-3540**). It's in the wharf village section and isn't particularly convenient—you're required to walk from the parking lot through the faux village of shops and boutiques to reach the center. It's open daily: summer 8am to 8pm and off-season 9am to 5pm. Another visitor center is downtown at 655 Main St., in the lobby of modern **City Hall** (☎ **506/853-3590**). Summer, it's open daily 8am to 8pm.

EXPLORING MONCTON

You can easily cover Moncton's downtown on foot—once you find parking, which can be vexing. (Look for the paid lots a block or so north and south of Main Street.) **Downtown Moncton Inc.** (☎ **506/857-2991**) publishes a nicely designed **"Historic Walking Tour"** brochure that touches on some of the more significant buildings; ask for it at either visitor center.

Moncton's **Tidal Bore** is a low wave that rolls up the Petitcodiac River at the leading edge of the turning tide. Sadly, the bore has been living up to its name since a dam and causeway were constructed upstream in 1968. Silt has built up in the chocolaty-brown river below the causeway, which has reduced the height and drama of the bore. The wave, when it comes up around the bend of the river, is rather tiny. (Think of the Stonehenge scene in *Spinal Tap*.) It's more dramatic in winter and fall, but in summer it's not all that impressive.

The bore rolls in twice daily on the tides (at Bore Park it's illuminated at night with banks of floodlights). Check the arrival time in the brochure produced by the tourism authority, or swing by Bore Park on Main Street (across from the Hollins Lincoln-Mercury dealership) and note the time of the next bore on the digital clock. The park has bleachers to sit on and railings to lean against while awaiting the ripple.

A simple way to get a good sense of Moncton's past is to spend 45 minutes or so roaming through the **Moncton Museum,** 20 Mountain Rd., at King Street (☎ **506/ 856-4383**). This handsome museum opened in 1973 (note the clever reuse of the old City Hall facade) and displays various artifacts of city life on two floors, including early hotel dishware, fashions, and intriguing grainy photos of downtown in the early days. Admission is by donation. July and August, it's open Monday to Saturday 9:30am to 4:30pm and Sunday 1 to 5pm; call for an appointment the rest of the year.

On Moncton's northwest outskirts, **Magnetic Hill,** Trans-Canada Highway Exit 488 (☎ **800/217-8111**), began as a simple quirk of geography. Cars that stopped at the bottom of a short stretch of downhill started to roll back uphill! Or at least what appeared to be uphill. It's a nifty illusion—not to pull back the curtain, but it works because the slope is on the side of a far larger hill, which tilts the whole countryside and effectively skews one's perspective. Starting in the 1930s, locals capitalized on the phenomenon by opening canteens and gift shops nearby. By the 1950s, the hill boasted the largest souvenir shop in the Maritimes.

This mysterious stretch of country road was preserved for posterity when a bypass was built around it, and today you can still experience the mystery. The atmosphere is a bit more glossy than a half-century ago, however. You enter a well-marked drive with magnet-themed road signs and streetlights, pay a C$2 (US$1.35) toll at a gatehouse, and wind around a comically twisting road to wait your turn before being directed to the hill.

Young kids often find the "uphill roll" entertaining—for about 3 yards. Then their attention is riveted by the two amusement complexes that have sprouted in the fields on either side of the road. Attractions within a few hundred yards of the hill include **Wharf Village** (a quaint collection of boutiques and snack bars designed to look like a seaside village), a minigolf course, a sizable zoo, video arcades, go-cart racing, batting cages, a driving range, a kiddie train, and bumper boats. But the chief attraction is the **Magic Mountain Water Park,** which features wave pools and numerous slides, including the towering Kamikaze Slide, where daredevils can reach speeds of 64kmph (40 m.p.h.). The water park is open daily 10am to 8pm in peak season (to 6pm in shoulder season). Other attractions open at varied hours; call for details. Admission for Magnetic Hill is C$2 (US$1.35) per car; rates for the other attractions vary.

Despite—or perhaps because of—the unrepentant cheesiness, Magnetic Hill is actually a great destination for families weary of beaches, hikes, and the dreary natural world. Just be aware that nothing's cheap after you fork over C$2 (US$1.35) to roll up the hill; an afternoon here can put a serious hurt on your wallet.

The indoor amusement park at **Crystal Palace,** Champlain Place Mall (Trans-Canada Highway Exit 504-A West), Dieppe (☎ 506/859-4386), can shorten an otherwise endless rainy day. The enclosed park includes a four-screen cinema, shooting arcades, numerous games (from old-fashioned SkeeBall to cutting-edge video games), a medium-sized roller coaster, a carousel, a swing ride, laser tag, bumper cars, mini-airplane and mini-semitruck rides, minigolf, batting cages, and a virtual-reality ride. In summer, outdoor activities include go-carts and bumper boats. The park will particularly appeal to kids under 12, though teens will likely find video games to occupy them. To really wear the kids down, you can stay virtually inside the park by booking a room at the adjoining Best Western. Crystal Palace is open Monday to Thursday noon to 8pm, Friday noon to 9pm, Saturday 10am to 9pm, and Sunday 10am to 8pm. Admission is free; the rides are one to four tickets each (C$1/US65¢ per ticket, 10 for C$9/US$6); unlimited ride passes are also available for C$22 (US$14), which doesn't include go-carts.

WHERE TO STAY

Several chain hotels have set up shop near Magnetic Hill (Trans-Canada Highway Exit 488). These include **Comfort Inn,** 2495 Mountain Rd. (☎ 800/228-5150 or 506/ 384-3175); **Country Inn & Suites,** 2475 Mountain Rd. (☎ 800/456-4000 or 506/ 852-7000); and **Holiday Inn Express,** 2515 Mountain Rd. (☎ 506/384-1050). Rooms range from C$85 to C$180 (US$57 to US$120).

Delta Beauséjour. 750 Main St., Moncton, NB E1C 1E6. ☎ 800/268-1133 or 506/ 854-4344. Fax 506/858-0957. 310 units. AC MINIBAR TV TEL. C$89–C$159 (US$59–US$106) double summer and weekends; higher midweek in off-season. AE, DC, ER, MC, V.

The downtown Delta Beauséjour, from 1972, is boxy, bland, and concrete, and the entrance courtyard is sterile and off-putting in a Cold War Berlin sort of way. But inside, the decor is inviting in a spare International Modern manner. The property is well maintained, and its guest rooms and public areas were recently renovated. The third-floor indoor pool offers year-round swimming. (There's also a pleasant outdoor deck overlooking the distant marshes of the Petitcodiac River.) The hotel is a favorite among business travelers, but in summer and on weekends, leisure travelers largely have it to themselves.

Dining/Diversions: In addition to the elegant Windjammer (below), the hotel has a basic cafe/snack bar, a piano bar/lounge, and a rustic restaurant serving all meals.

Amenities: 24-hour room service, baby-sitting, dry cleaning/laundry, safe-deposit boxes, turndown service, indoor pool, health club, conference rooms, business center, washer/dryer, beauty salon, shopping arcade.

Victoria Bed & Breakfast. 71 Park St., Moncton, NB E1C 2B2. ☎ **506/389-8296.** 3 units, 1 with bathroom across the hall. A/C TV TEL. C$85 (US$57) double. Rates include breakfast. MC, V.

This vaguely Craftsman-style 1910 home in a reasonably quiet neighborhood across from a church offers mid-sized guest rooms that feature stucco walls, lustrous maple floors, TVs with VCRs, and a relaxed country styling. Room no. 1 is the best: It faces Park Street, is brighter and slightly larger than the other two, and is decorated in soothing dark tones. Guests often linger in the attractive downstairs common room, playing "Chopsticks" and more on the baby grand piano. For multinight stays, ask about the corporate suites in a separate building around the corner.

WHERE TO DINE

Boomerang's Steakhouse. 130 Westmoreland St. ☎ **506/857-8325.** Call-ahead seating in lieu of reservations. Hamburgers and grilled sandwiches C$7–C$9 (US$4.65–US$6); dinners C$12–C$18 (US$8–US$12). AE, DC, DISC, ER, MC, V. Sun–Wed 4–10pm, Thurs–Sat 4–11:30pm. STEAKHOUSE.

Boomerang's is likely to remind you of the Aussie-themed Outback Steakhouse chain, right down to the oversized knives. But this is the only Boomerang's, so the service is rather more personal and the Aussie-whimsical decor done with a lighter hand. It's a handsome spot with three dining rooms, all quite dim with slatted dividers, drawn shades, and ceiling fans, creating the impression that it's blazingly hot outside. (That's a real trick in Feb in New Brunswick.) The menu features the usual stuff from the barbie, including grilled chicken breasts and ribs. The steak selection is grand, from an 8-ounce bacon-wrapped tenderloin to a 14-ounce porterhouse. The burgers are also excellent.

✪ **The Windjammer.** In the Delta Beauséjour, 750 Main St. ☎ **506/854-4344.** Reservations recommended. Main courses C$23–C$35 (US$15–US$23). AE, DC, ER, MC, V. Tues–Sun 5:30–11pm. CONTINENTAL.

Off the lobby of Moncton's best hotel is The Windjammer, an intimate dining room serving the city's best meals. With its heavy wood and nautical theme, it resembles the private officer's mess of an exclusive ship. The menu is ambitious, and the dining room has garnered an excellent reputation for its seafood dishes, including an appetizer of scallops with truffle jus, and an entree of pan-fried salmon marinated in molasses and ginger. The chef also serves up treats for carnivores, including tournedos of caribou with jus and blueberries, served with wild-mushroom fricasse.

8 Kouchibouguac National Park

Much is made of the fact that the sprawling **Kouchibouguac National Park** has all sorts of ecosystems worth studying, from sandy barrier islands to ancient peat bogs. But that's a little bit like saying Disney World has nice lakes. It causes one's eyes to glaze over and entirely misses the point. In fact, this artfully designed national park is a wonderful destination for relaxing biking, hiking, and beach-going. If you can, plan to spend a couple of days here doing a whole lot of nothing. The varied ecosystems (which, incidentally, are spectacular) are just an added attraction.

A Weather Warning

Be aware that Kouchibouguac is a fair-weather destination. If the weather is blustery and rainy, there's little to do here except take damp and melancholy strolls on the beach. It's best to save a visit for more cooperative days.

ESSENTIALS

GETTING THERE   Kouchibouguac National Park is between Moncton and Miramichi. The exit for the park off Route 11 is well marked.

VISITOR INFORMATION   The park is open mid-May to mid-October. The **Visitors Centre** (☎ 506/876-2443) is just off Route 134, a short drive past the park entrance. It's open daily 8am to 8pm in peak season, with shorter hours off-season. There are a slide show to introduce you to the park's attractions and a small collection of field guides to peruse.

FEES   A daily pass is C$3.50 (US$2.35) adults, C$1.75 (US$1.15) children 6 to 16, C$2.75 (US$1.85) seniors, and C$7 (US$4.65) families. Four-day passes are also available. A map of the park costs C$1 (US65¢) at the information center. You should have permits for everyone in your car when you enter the park. There are no formal checkpoints, only occasional roadblocks during the summer to ensure compliance.

EXPLORING THE PARK

Kouchibouguac is, above all, a place for bikers and families. (By the way, the ungainly name is a Mi'kmaq Indian word meaning "River of the Long Tides." It's pronounced "*Koosh*-uh-*boog*-oo-*whack*." If you don't get it right, don't worry. Few do.) The park is laced with well-groomed bike trails made of finely crushed cinders that traverse forest and field and meander along rivers and lagoons. Where bikes aren't permitted (such as on boardwalks and beaches), there are usually clusters of bike racks for locking them up while you continue on foot. If you camp here and bring a bike, there's no need to ever use your car.

Families can easily divide their days to keep kids entertained. Mornings might be spent at the broad sandy beach and afternoons biking along the lagoon, crossing a springy bog on a boardwalk, or poking around in a paddleboat. Though the park is ideal for campers, day-trippers also find it worthwhile. *A tip:* Plan to remain here until sunset. The trails tend to empty out, and the dunes, bogs, and boreal forest take on a rich, almost iridescent hue as the sun sinks over the spruce.

The **hiking and biking trails** are as short and undemanding as they are appealing. The one hiking trail that requires slightly more fortitude is the **Kouchibouguac River Trail,** running for some 13km (8 miles) along the banks of the river. The **Bog Trail** is just 1.8km (1.1 miles) each way, but it opens the door to a wonderfully alien world. The 4,500-year-old bog is a classic domed bog, made of peat from decaying shrubs and other plants. At the bog's edge is a wooden tower ascended by a spiral staircase that affords a panoramic view of this eerie habitat.

The boardwalk crosses to the thickest, middle part of the bog. Where the boardwalk stops, you can feel the bouncy surface—you're actually standing on a mat of thick vegetation that's floating atop water. Look for the pitcher plant, a carnivorous species that lures flies into its bell-shaped leaves, where downward-pointed hairs prevent them from fleeing. Eventually, the plant's enzymes digest the insect, providing nutrients for growth in this hostile environment.

Callanders Beach and **Cedar Trail** are at the end of a short dirt road. There are an open field with picnic tables, a small protected beach on the lagoon (with fine views of dunes across the way), and a 1km (0.6-mile) hiking trail on a boardwalk that passes through a cedar forest, past a salt marsh, and through a mixed forest. This is a good alternative for those who'd prefer to avoid the larger crowds at Kellys Beach (below).

BEACHES

The park features some 15km (9.3 miles) of sandy beaches, mostly along barrier islands of sandy dunes, delicate grasses and flowers, and nesting plovers and sand-pipers. ✪ **Kellys** is the principal beach, and it's one of the best-designed and best-executed recreation areas I've come across in Eastern Canada. At the forest's edge, a short walk from the main parking area, you'll find showers, changing rooms, a snack bar, and some interpretive exhibits. From here, you walk some 540m (600 yd.) across a winding boardwalk that's plenty fascinating on its own. It crosses a salt marsh, lagoons, and some of the best-preserved dunes in the province.

The long sandy beach features comfortably warm water, with waves that are usually quite mellow—they lap rather than roar, unless a storm's offshore. A roped-off section of about 90m (100 yd.) is overseen by lifeguards; elsewhere you're on your own. For very young children who still equate waves with certain death, there's supervised swimming on a sandy stretch of the quiet lagoon.

Ryans—a cluster of buildings between the campground and Kellys Beach—is the place for renting bikes, kayaks, paddleboats, and canoes. Bikes rent for C$4.60 (US$3.05) per hour. Most of the water-sports equipment (including canoes and pedal boats) rent for about C$7 (US$4.65) per hour, with double kayaks at C$12 (US$8) per hour. You can rent canoes for longer excursions—C$30 (US$20) for a day or C$42 (US$28) for 2 days. Ryans is on the lagoon, so you can explore up toward the dunes or upstream on the winding river.

WHERE TO STAY & DINE

Kouchibouguac is at heart a camper's park, best enjoyed by those who plan to spend at least a night here. **South Kouchibouguac,** the main campground, is centrally located and very nicely laid out with 311 sites (C$16/US$11 per night), most rather large and private. The 46 sites with electricity are nearer the river and somewhat more open. The newest sites (1 to 35) lack grassy areas for pitching tents, and campers have to pitch tents on gravel pads. It's best to bring a good sleeping pad or ask for another site. Reservations are accepted for about half of the campsites; call ☎ **800/414-6765** starting in late April. The remaining sites are doled out first come, first served.

Across the river on Kouchibouguac Lagoon is the more remote, semiprimitive **Côte-à-Fabien.** It lacks showers and some sites require a short walk, but it's more appealing for tenters. The cost is C$14 (US$9) per night. The park also maintains three back-country sites, which cost C$10 (US$7) per night for two, including firewood.

Habitant Motel and Restaurant. Rte. 134 (RR#1, Box 2, Site 30), Richibucto, NB E0A 2M0. ☎ **888/442-7222** or 506/523-4421. Fax 506/523-9155. E-mail habitant@nbnet. nb.ca. 29 units. A/C TV TEL. C$90 (US$60) double. AE, CB, DC, DISC, ER, MC, V. "Small, well-trained pets" allowed.

About 15km (9.3 miles) from the park entrance, Habitant is the best choice for overnighting if you're exploring Kouchibouguac by day. It's a mansard-roofed Tudor-style complex—let's just say "architecturally mystifying"—with a restaurant and small campground on the premises. The guest rooms are decorated in a contemporary motel style. The motel features a distinctive indoor pool, along with a fitness center and sauna. The restaurant next door serves all meals and is informal, comfortable, and reasonably priced. Seafood dinners are the specialty, including a heaping "fisherman's feast" for C$23 (US$15). (Most main courses are C$8 to C$15/US$5 to

US$10.) One nice touch: There's a self-serve wine cellar, where wines are sold at liquor-store prices, many under C$20 (US$13).

9 The Acadian Peninsula

The **Acadian Peninsula** is that bulge on the northeast corner of New Brunswick, forming one of the arms of the Baie des Chaleurs (Québec's Gaspé Peninsula forms the other—see chapter 8). It's a land of tidy if generally nondescript houses, miles of shoreline (much of it beaches), modern concrete harbors filled with commercial fishing boats, and residents proud of their Acadian heritage. (You'll see everywhere the *stella maris* flag—the French tricolor with a single gold star in the field of blue.)

On a map it looks like much of the coastline would be wild and remote. It's not. Although a number of picturesque farmhouses dot the route and you'll come on brilliant meadows of hawkweed and lupine, the coast is more defined by manufactured housing that's been erected on squarish lots between the sea and fast two-lane highways. Other than the superb Acadian Village historical museum near Caraquet, there are few organized attractions here. It's more a place to unwind while walking on a beach or sitting along harbors while watching fishing boats come and go.

To remind yourself of where you are, every once in a while turn your back on the beach and look over the homes and cultivated fields. You'll see the sharp spires of the boreal forest—spruce and cedar and tamarack—poised as if ready to resume their march to the water's edge if the inhabitants lower their vigilance for just a moment or two.

ESSENTIALS

GETTING THERE   Route 11 is the main highway serving the Acadian Peninsula.

VISITOR INFORMATION   Each of the areas mentioned below maintains a visitor center. **Caraquet Tourism Information** is at 51 bd. St-Pierre Est in the Callefour de la Mer (☎ 506/726-2676). This office offers convenient access to other activities in the harbor (below), and there's plenty of parking. Shippagan dispenses information from a wooden lighthouse near the Marine Centre.

CARAQUET

The historic beach town of **Caraquet**—widely regarded as the spiritual capital of Acadian New Brunswick—just keeps on going and going, geographically speaking. It's spread thinly along a commercial boulevard parallel to the beach. Caraquet once claimed the honorific "longest village in the world" when it ran to some 22km (14 miles) long. As a result of its length, Caraquet lacks a well-defined downtown or any sort of urban center of gravity; there's one stoplight, and that's where boulevard St-Pierre Est changes to boulevard St-Pierre Ouest. (Most establishments mentioned below are somewhere along this boulevard.)

A good place to start a tour is the **Callefour de la Mer,** 51 bd. St-Pierre Est, a modern complex overlooking the man-made harbor. It has a spare Scandinavian feel to it, and here you'll find the tourist office (see above), a seafood restaurant, a snack bar, a children's playground, and two short strolls that lead to picnic tables on jetties with fine harbor views.

While you're here you can consider your options for viewing the bay. Two-hour boat tours aboard the *Ile Caramer* (☎ 506/727-0813) cost C$15 (US$10) adults or C$7 (US$4.65) children 12 and under. With **Sea of Adventure** (☎ 506/727-2727), an exhilarating and fun 3-hour whale-watch tour aboard a high-speed zodiac costs C$50 (US$33) adults or C$30 (US$20) children 12 and under. You can also rent a kayak from **Tours Kayaket** (☎ 506/727-6309) for C$12 (US$8) per hour

(C$24/US$16 for a double kayak) and putter around inside the sea wall or venture out into the bay if conditions are agreeable.

✪ **Village Historique Acadien.** Rte. 11 (9.7km/6 miles west of Caraquet). ☎ **506/726-2600.** Admission C$10 (US$7) adults, C$8 (US$5) seniors, C$5 (US$3.35) youths 6–16, C$25 (US$17) families; under 6 free. Mid-June to Aug, daily 10am–6pm (to 5pm Sept–Oct).

New Brunswick sometimes seems awash in Acadian museums and historic villages. If you're interested in visiting just one such site, this is the place to hold out for. Some 45 buildings—most of which were dismantled and transported here from other villages on the peninsula—depict life as it was lived in an Acadian settlement between 1770 and 1890. The buildings are set throughout 458 acres of woodland, marsh, and field. You'll learn all about the exodus and settlement of the Acadians from costumed guides, who are also adept at skills ranging from letterpress printing to blacksmithing. Plan on spending at least 2 to 3 hours exploring the village.

In June 2000 the village will open a major addition: Some 26 buildings (all but one are replicas) will be devoted to continuing the saga, showing Acadian life from 1890 to 1939, with a special focus on industry. Among the buildings will be a traditional hotel, which will house students enrolled in multiday workshops in traditional Acadian arts and crafts.

WHERE TO STAY

Hotel Paulin. 143 bd. St-Pierre Ouest. ☎ **506/727-9981.** Fax 506/727-3300. 8 units. A/C TV TEL. C$65–C$85 (US$43–US$57) double. MC, V. Closed Nov–May.

This attractive Victorian hotel (1891) has been operated by the Paulin family for the past three generations. It's a three-story red clapboard building with a green-shingled mansard roof, just off the main boulevard and overlooking the bay. (Some of the charm has been compromised by encroaching buildings nearby.) The lobby puts you immediately in mind of summer relaxation, with royal-blue wainscoting, canary-yellow walls, and stuffed furniture upholstered in white with blue piping. The guest rooms were extensively renovated in 1999; six were combined into three suites, and all rooms now have bathrooms. (The original suite has the only ocean view.) Expect rooms comfortably but sparely furnished with antiques. In the handsome restaurant, specialties include delectable crab mousse and brown-sugar pie.

WHERE TO DINE

Caraquet is a good place for seafood, naturally. My preference is still with the **Hotel Paulin**'s restaurant for its charm, but the several inexpensive-to-moderate spots along the main drag all serve fresh seafood nicely if simply prepared.

For a delicious and sophisticated snack, head to **Les Blancs d'Arcadia,** 340A bd. St-Pierre Est (☎ **506/727-5952**), en route to Bas Caraquet on Route 145 (watch for the goat sign on the right shortly after you pass the road to St-Simon). This handsome compound of yellow farm buildings is hard against the forest just east of town. The specialties are cheese and yogurt from the milk of a Swiss breed of goats called Saanen. The goats are raised indoors year-round; you can learn about the goats and the cheese- and yogurt-making process on a tour that includes tastings. The 90-minute tour is C$6 (US$4); reservations are appreciated. There's also a small shop to buy fresh cheeses and milk. I recommend both the peppercorn and the garlic soft cheeses.

GRANDE-ANSE

Grande-Anse is a wide-spot-in-the-road village of low modern homes near bluffs overlooking the bay. The town is lorded over by the stern, stone **Saint Jude church.**

The best view of the village, and a good spot for a picnic, is along the bluffs just below the church. (Look for the sign indicating QUAI 50 yards west of the church.) Here you'll find a small man-made harbor with a fleet of fishing boats, a tiny sand beach, and some grassy bluffs where you can park overlooking the bay.

Pope Museum. 184 Acadie St., Grande-Anse. ☎ **506/732-3003.** Admission C$5 (US$3.35) adults, C$2.50 (US$1.65) children, C$3.50 (US$2.35) seniors, C$10 (US$7) families. Daily 10am–6pm (tickets sold to 5pm). Closed Sept to mid-June.

Deep vermilion hues and liturgical strains piped into all the rooms mark the modern Pope Museum, founded in 1985—the year after the Pope visited Moncton. The devout will enjoy the portrait gallery featuring portraits of all 264 popes. But all will be fascinated by the intricate model of the Vatican, which occupies much of the central hall (the top of the dome stands about 6 ft. high). Other models of houses of worship include a smaller Florence Duomo, Bourges Cathedral, Cheops pyramid, and Great El Hakim Mosque. Head upstairs for displays of various Roman Catholic artifacts and contemporary religious accoutrements, including vestments and chalices. Most descriptions are bilingual, but a handful are in French only.

10 Mt. Carleton Provincial Park

New Brunswick isn't all sandy beaches and rushing tides. There's the vast interior, a sprawling land marred by few roads and filled with rolling hills, dense forest, and tenacious blackflies (at least in early summer). This isn't wilderness—most of the land is employed as a vast timber plantation to feed the province's voracious paper and lumber mills. But in 1969, New Brunswick carved out some of the choicest land and set it aside as wilderness park. **Mt. Carleton Provincial Park** contains 7,052 acres of azure lakes, pure streams, thick boreal forest, and gently rounded mountains, the largest of which are ledgy and afford excellent views. When visiting, look for moose, black bear, coyotes, bobcat, and more than 100 species of birds. And, of course, blackflies.

ESSENTIALS
GETTING THERE Mt. Carleton Provincial Park is 43km (27 miles) east of Saint-Quentin on Route 180. Be aware that Saint-Quentin is the nearest community for supplies; there are no convenient general stores just outside the park gates. The park is also accessible from Bathurst to the east, but it's a 115km (71-mile) drive on a road that's mostly paved but gravel in spots. There are no services along the road and many logging trucks.

VISITOR INFORMATION The park's gates are open daily 7am to 10pm in summer (8am to 8pm in spring and fall). A **small interpretive center** at the entrance gate (☎ **506/235-0793**) offers background on the park's natural and cultural history. The park is open but unstaffed mid-October to May.

FEES The day-use fee is C$4 (US$2.65) per car from spring to fall.

EXPLORING THE PARK
The park boasts 10 **hiking trails** that total 68km (42 miles). The helpful park staff at the gatehouse will be happy to direct you to a hike that suits your experience and mood. The park's premier hike is to the summit of **Mt. Carleton,** the province's highest point at 820m (2,697 ft.). Although that elevation isn't going to impress those who've hiked in the Canadian Rockies, height is relative here, and the views seem endless. The summit is marked by a craggy comb of rocks affording a 360-degree view of the lower mountains and the sprawling lakes. The trailhead is about a 25-minute

drive from the gatehouse; allow about 4 hours for a round-trip hike of about 10km (6.2 miles).

Overlooking Nictau Lake is **Mt. Sagamook,** at an altitude of 777m (2,555 ft.). It's a steep and demanding hike of about 3km (1.9 miles) to the summit, where you're rewarded with spectacular views of the northern park. And for the truly gung-ho, there's the ridge walk connecting Sagamook and Carleton via **Mt. Head.** The views from high above are unforgettable; you'll need to set up a shuttle with two cars to do the whole ridge in a day.

If you've got a mountain bike, bring it. The gravel roads are perfect for exploring. Motor vehicles have been banned from two of the roads, which take you deep into the woods past clear lakes and rushing streams.

CAMPING

Armstrong Brook is the principal destination for visiting campers, with 88 sites split between the forest near Lake Nictau's shore (no lakeside sites) and an open grassy field. Campers can avail themselves of hot showers and a bathhouse for washing up. A path leads to the lake's edge; there's a spit of small flat pebbles that's wonderful for swimming and sunbathing. Camping fees are C$11 (US$7) weekdays and C$14 (US$9) weekends.

Four backcountry sites are high on the slopes of Mt. Carleton (preregistration required). The sites, which require a 4km (2½-mile) hike, offer views into a rugged valley and a great sense of remoteness. Water is available but should be treated (beavers are nearby). No fires are permitted, so bring a stove. The fee is C$5 (US$3.35) per night.

Two other remote campsites on the shores of Lake Nictau are accessible by either canoe or a moderate walk. Register in advance; the fee is C$9 (US$6) per night.

Prince Edward Island 5

by Wayne Curtis

Prince Edward Island (also called **PEI**) might not be the world's leading manufacturer of relaxation and repose, but it's certainly a major distribution center. Visitors soon suspect there's something about the richly colored landscape of azure seas and henna-tinged cliffs capped with lush farm fields that triggers an obscure relaxation hormone, resulting in a pleasant ennui. It's hard to conceive that verdant PEI and boggy, blustery Newfoundland share a region, never mind the same gulf.

The north coast is lined with red-sand beaches washed with the warmish waters of the Gulf of St. Lawrence. Swimming here isn't quite like taking a tepid dip in North Carolina, but the water is quite a bit warmer than that in Maine or New Hampshire. Away from the beaches are low rolling hills blanketed in trees and crops, especially potatoes, for which the island is justly famous. Small farms make up the island's backbone—one-quarter of it is dedicated to agriculture, with that land cultivated by more than 2,300 individual farms.

The island was first explored in 1534 by Jacques Cartier, who discovered the Mi'kmaq living here. Over the next 2 centuries, dominion over the island bounced between Great Britain and France (who called it Isle St-Jean). Great Britain was awarded the island in 1763 as part of the Treaty of Paris; just over a century later, the first Canadian Confederation was held at Charlottetown and resulted in the creation of Canada in 1867 (PEI didn't join the confederation until 1873). The island was named for Edward Augustus (1767 to 1820), son of George III of England.

The island is compact and its roads are unusually well marked. It's difficult to become disoriented and confused. But do try. I can think of few joys in life as simple and pleasurable as getting lost on some of PEI's backroads.

One final note: PEI, somewhat remarkably, managed to retain its bucolic flavor of a century ago, and pockets of kitsch and sprawl are still happily few. But the handwriting is on the wall, especially in the central part of the island. The handwriting reads COTTAGE LOTS FOR SALE. Such signs have been springing up in greater number in alfalfa and potato fields, and in coming years more and more of the island is certain to be claimed by subdivisions and shopping plazas. The sooner you can visit the better.

1 Exploring the Island

VISITOR INFORMATION

Tourism PEI publishes a comprehensive free guide to island attractions and lodgings that's well worth picking up. The *Visitors Guide* is available at all information centers on the island (see below), or you can get one in advance by calling ☎ 888/ 734-7529 or 902/368-4444. You can also request it by fax (902/629-2428), e-mail (tourpei@gov.pe.ca), or mail (P.O. Box 940, Charlottetown, PEI C1A 7M5). The official Web site is **www.peiplay.com.** Another good starting point for trip planning is **www.peionline.com.**

GETTING THERE

BY CAR f you're coming from the west by car, you'll arrive via the Confederation Bridge, which opened with great fanfare in 1997. Sometimes you'll hear it referred to as the "fixed link," a reference to the guarantee Canada made in 1873 to provide a permanent link from the mainland. The dramatic 13km (8-mile) bridge is open 24 hours and takes about 10 to 12 minutes to cross. Unless you're high up in a van, a truck, or an RV, the views are mostly obstructed by the concrete Jersey barriers forming the guardrails along the sides.

The bridge toll is C$36 (US$24) round-trip. No fare is paid when you travel to the island; the entire toll is collected when you leave. Credit cards are accepted. Call ☎ 888/437-6565 for details.

BY FERRY For those arriving from Cape Breton Island or other points east, **Northumberland Ferries Limited** (☎ 888/249-7245 or 902/566-3838) provides seasonal service between Caribou, Nova Scotia (just north of Pictou), and Woods Island, PEI. Ferries with a 250-car capacity run May to mid-December. June to mid-October, ferries depart each port about every 90 minutes, with the last departing at 8pm. The crossing takes about 75 minutes.

No reservations are accepted; it's best to arrive at least an hour before departure to boost your odds of securing a berth on the next boat. Early-morning ferries tend to be less crowded. Fares are C$47 (US$31) for a car and all its passengers, and major credit cards are honored. As with the bridge, you pay the fare on exiting the island; the ferry to the island is free.

BY PLANE The island's main airport is a few miles north of Charlottetown. Commuter flights to Halifax are just half an hour; direct flights from Toronto are offered summers only. For details, contact **Air Canada** (☎ 800/776-3000 in the U.S., 800/ 565-3940 in Eastern Canada; www.aircanada.ca) or **Canadian Airlines** (☎ 800/ 426-7000 in the U.S., 800/665-1177 in Eastern Canada, or 902/427-5500; www. cdnair.ca). *Note:* At press time, both Air Canada and Canadian Airlines were considering mergers with one another as well as with outside airlines.

THE GREAT OUTDOORS

BICYCLING The main off-road bike trail is the **Confederation Trail,** which eventually will cover some 350km (217 miles) from Tignish to Souris along the path of the ill-fated provincial railway. At present, about half the trail has been completed, mostly in Prince and Kings counties; Queens County is still largely under development. The path is covered mostly in rolled stone dust, which makes for good travel with a mountain bike or hybrid. Services are slowly being developed by groups along the route, with bike rentals and inns cropping up; ask at the local tourist bureaus for updated info on completed segments. An excellent place to base for exploring the trail is the

Prince Edward Island

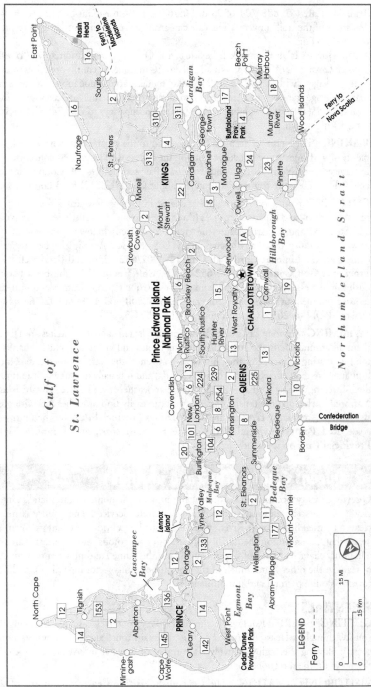

131

Trailside Cafe (☎ 888/704-6595 or 902/676-3130) in Mount Stewart, where several spurs of the trail converge. The cafe can arrange for return shuttles if you'd prefer one-way cycling.

MacQueen's Island Tours & Bike Shop, 430 Queen St. in Charlottetown (☎ 800/969-2822 or 902/368-2453; e-mail biketour@macqueens.com), organizes bicycle tour packages, with prices including bike rentals, accommodations, route cards, maps, luggage transfers, and emergency road repair service. Tour packages range from C$899 (US$600) for a 5-night package (double occupancy) to C$1,749 (US$1,167) for a 10-night tour.

FISHING   For a taste of deep-sea fishing, head to the north coast, where you'll find plenty of outfitters happy to take you out on the big swells. The greatest concentrations of services are at North Rustico and Covehead Bay; see the "Queens County" section, below. Rates are quite reasonable, generally about C$20 (US$13) for 3 hours or so.

GOLF   PEI's reputation for its golf has soared in the past few years, in part because of a slew of new and expanded courses (three in 1999 alone: Countryview, Dundarave, and St. Felix) and in part because the greens fees haven't followed the same sharply upward trajectory that has afflicted many U.S. courses. Among the best-regarded courses are the **Links at Crowbush Cove** (☎ 902/652-2356) and **Brudenell River Provincial Golf Course** (☎ 902/652-2342). **Golf Island PEI** publishes a booklet outlining the essentials of the 16 island courses. Request a copy from island info centers or from the provincial tourist info number (☎ 800/463-4734 or 902/368-4444), or write P.O. Box 2653, Charlottetown, PEI C1A 8C3.

SWIMMING   Among PEI's chief attractions are its red-sand ✪ **beaches.** You'll find them all around the island, tucked in among dunes and crumbling cliffs. Thanks to the moderating influence of the Gulf of St. Lawrence, the water temperature is more humane here than elsewhere in Atlantic Canada, and it usually doesn't result in unbridled shrieking among bathers. The most popular beaches are at **Prince Edward Island National Park** along the north coast, but you can easily find other beaches with great swimming. Among my favorites are **Cedar Dunes Provincial Park** on the southwest coast, **Red Point Provincial Park** on the northeast coast, and **Panmure Island Provincial Park** on the southeast coast.

2 Queens County: The Land of Anne

Queens County occupies the center of the province, is home to the island's largest city, and hosts the greatest concentration of traveler services. The county is neatly cleaved by the Hillsborough River, which is spanned by a bridge at Charlottetown. Be aware that Cavendish on the north shore has built a vigorous tourist industry around a fictional character, Anne of Green Gables, and this Anne Land may not be your cup of tea. On the other hand, much of the rest of the county—not including Charlottetown—is quite pastoral and untrammeled.

ESSENTIALS

GETTING THERE   Route 2 is the fastest way to travel east-west through the county, though it lacks charm. Route 6 is the main route along the county's north coast; following the highway involves a number of turns at intersections, so keep a sharp eye on the directional signs.

VISITOR INFORMATION   The **Cavendish Visitors Centre,** just north of the intersection of Routes 13 and 6 (☎ 902/963-2391 summer or 902/566-7050 off-season), is open June to mid-September daily 8am to 10pm.

The Birth of Anne Shirley

All visitors to Prince Edward Island owe it to themselves to read **Anne of Green Gables** at some point. Not that you won't enjoy your stay here without doing this. But you may feel a bit out of touch, unable to understand the inside references that seep into many aspects of PEI culture, much the way sand gets into everything at the beach. (Even some gas stations in Cavendish sell Anne dolls.) In fact, Anne has become so omnipresent and popular on the island that in 1994 a licensing authority was created to control the crushing glacier of Anne-related products.

Some background: *Anne of Green Gables* was written by Lucy Maud Montgomery in 1908. It's a fictional account of Anne Shirley, a precocious 11-year-old redheaded orphan who's mistakenly sent from Nova Scotia to the PEI farm of the taciturn Matthew and Marilla Cuthbert. (The mistake? The Cuthberts had requested a *boy* orphan to help with farm chores.) Anne's vivid imagination and outsized vocabulary get her into a series of pickles, from which she generally emerges beloved by everyone who encounters her. It's a bright, bittersweet story, and it went on to huge popular success, spawning a number of sequels as well as a number of TV series, most starring Megan Follows.

The story has proven especially enduring in Japan, where it's taught in schools and where the cheeky heroine seems to have boundless appeal. As a result, plane-loads of Japanese make the summer pilgrimage to PEI to walk where Anne walked, stroll past the oddly familiar landmarks, and even get married in Anne settings. At any rate, this enduring fascination explains why you'll often see billboards and brochures hereabouts printed with Japanese translations.

CAVENDISH: ANNE'S HOMETOWN

Cavendish is the home of the fictional character Anne Shirley, known to the world as Anne of Green Gables. If you mentally screen out the tourist traps constructed over the past couple of decades, you'll find a bucolic mix of woodlands and fields, rolling hills and sandy dunes—a fine setting for a series of pastoral novels.

However, the tremendous and enduring popularity of the novels and the subsequent TV series has attracted droves of curious tourists, who in turn have attracted droves of entrepreneurs who've constructed new buildings and attractions. The bucolic character of the area has thus become somewhat compromised.

SEEING EVERYTHING ANNE

Green Gables. Rte. 6, Cavendish (just west of the intersection with Rte. 13). ☎ **902/ 672-6350.** Admission C$2.50 (US$1.65) adults, C$2 (US$1.35) seniors, C$1.25 (US85¢) children, C$6 (US$4) families. June 21–Aug 27 daily 9am–8pm; Aug 28–Oct and May–June 20 daily 9am–5pm; Nov–Dec Wed–Sun noon–4pm; Mar–Apr Wed–Sun 9am–5pm; Jan–Feb by appointment.

The best place to start an Anne tour is at Green Gables itself. The house is operated by Parks Canada, which also operates a helpful visitor's center on the site. You can watch a 7-minute video presentation about author Lucy Maud Montgomery, view a handful of exhibits, and then head out to explore the farm and trails. The farmhouse dates to the mid–19th century and belonged to cousins of Montgomery's grandfather. It was the inspiration for the Cuthbert farm and has been furnished according to descriptions in the books.

Cavendish Cemetery. At the intersection of Rte. 13 and Rte. 6, Cavendish. Daily 24 hours.

This historic cemetery was founded in 1835, but is best known now as the final resting spot for author Lucy Maud Montgomery. It's not hard to find her gravesite: Follow the pavement blocks from the arched entryway, which is across from the Anne Shirley Motel. Montgomery's grave is the one planted with flowers.

Avonlea. Rte. 6 (across from the Rainbow Valley amusement park), Cavendish. ☎ **902/ 963-3050.** C$5 (US$3.35) adults, C$4 (US$2.65) seniors, C$3 (US$2) youth 6–16, C$12 (US$8) families.

This development of faux-historic buildings was opened in summer 1999 with the idea of creating the sort of a village center you'd imagine when reading the Anne novels. It's on a large lot amid amusement parks and motels, and the new buildings have been constructed with an eye to historical accuracy. Several Anne-related build-ings and artifacts are on the site, including the schoolhouse in which Montgomery taught (moved here from Belmont) and a Presbyterian church Montgomery occasion-ally attended (moved from Long River). There are also a variety show, hayrides, staff in period dress, a restaurant, several stores (including an art gallery and a music shop), and a spot for ice cream and candy.

Anne of Green Gables Museum at Silver Bush. Rte. 20, Park Corner. ☎ **902/ 436-7329.** C$2.35 (US$1.55) adults, C75¢ (US50¢) children under 16. June–Oct daily 9am–5pm (to 7pm July–Aug).

About 20km (13 miles) west of Cavendish near the intersection of Route 6 and Route 20 is the Anne of Green Gables Museum at Silver Bush. It's in the home of Mont-gomery's aunt and uncle; the author was married here in 1911. For the best view of the "Lake of Shining Waters," take the wagon ride.

Lucy Maud Montgomery Heritage Museum. Rte. 20, Park Corner. ☎ **902/886-2807.** C$2.50 (US$1.65) adults; children under 12 free. July–Aug daily 9am–7pm; June and Sept daily 9am–5pm.

This museum supposedly occupies the 1879 home of Montgomery's grandfather (its lineage is a bit unclear). Attractions include antiques from the family, along with arti-facts mentioned in her books. Three times weekly, special daylong events are held (costing C$80/US$53), which include readings, picnics by the lake, and the creation of flower-adorned straw hats.

Anne of Green Gables—The Musical ™. Confederation Arts Centre, Charlottetown. ☎ **800/ 565-0278** or 902/566-1267. Tickets C$20–C$36 (US$13–US$24).

This sprightly professional musical has been playing for years at the downtown arts center, bringing to the stage many of Montgomery's stories and characters. Perfor-mance times vary year to year, so check with the theater.

WHERE TO STAY

Cottage courts are to Cavendish what 19th-century inns are to Vermont—they're everywhere and they vary tremendously as to quality. Be aware that many of the

Can't Get Enough of Anne?

If you're a die-hard fan of the *Anne of Green Gables* TV series and its sequels and are looking for familiar landmarks, you may be in the wrong province. Much of the series was filmed in Rockton, Ontario, at the **Westfield Heritage Village,** a living history museum with 30 historic buildings. For details on what you can see at West-field, check on the Web at **http://worldchat.com/public/westfield**.

cottage courts and motels are more interested in high volume and rapid turnover than personal attention to guests. A number also believe that hanging a straw hat or two on a door allows them to boast of "country charm" when they have anything but.

Cavendish Beach Cottages. Gulf Shore Dr., Cavendish (mailing address: 166 York Lane, Charlottetown, PEI C1A 7W5). ☎ **902/963-2025.** 13 units. TV. C$116–C$160 (US$77–US$107) double. MC, V. Closed early Oct to late May.

Location, location, location. This compound of 13 cottages is on a grassy rise within the national park, just past the gatehouse into the park. The pine-paneled cottages are available in one-, two-, or three-bedroom configurations, and all feature ocean views, kitchenettes with microwaves, and outdoor propane barbecue grills. The cottages are a 2-minute walk from the beach. There's also easy access to Gulf Shore Drive, where you'll find some of the island's premier biking.

Green Gables Bungalow Court. Rte. 6 (Hunter River RR#2), Cavendish, PEI C0A 1N0. ☎ **800/965-3334** or 902/892-3542. 40 cottages. TV. C$80–C$115 (US$53–US$77) for up to 4. MC, V. Closed mid-Sept to June.

Next to the Green Gables house, this pleasant cluster of one- and two-bedroom cottages began as a government make-work project promoting tourism in the 1940s. As a result, they're sturdily built and nicely arrayed among lawn and pines. All have kitchens with refrigerators and coffeemakers, and many have outdoor gas grills. The linoleum floors and Spartan furnishings take on a certain retro charm after a few hours of settling in. Some cabins were trimmed out with cheap sheet paneling, and others have the original pine paneling; ask for one with the latter. The beach is about 1km (0.6 miles) away, and there's a small heated outdoor pool on the premises.

WHERE TO DINE

Cavendish itself offers limited opportunities for creative dining, though it's well stocked with restaurants offering hamburgers, fried clams, and the like. Both places below require a 10- to 15-minute drive from Cavendish proper, but they're worth it. See also the box on lobster suppers, page 137.

Café on the Clyde. Intersection of Rte. 224 and Rte. 258 (6.5km/4 miles south of Rte. 6 on Rte. 13), New Glasgow. ☎ **902/964-4304.** Main courses C$2–C$8 (US$1.35–US$5) at breakfast and lunch, C$9–C$16 (US$6–US$11) at dinner. AE, DC, JCB, MC, V. July–Aug daily 8am–9pm; June and Sept limited hours. LIGHT FARE.

This cafe is part of the noted Prince Edward Island Preserve Co., itself a worthwhile stop for the delicious homemade preserves. Light meals are served in the bright and modern dining room just off the preserve showroom. In this popular and often-crowded spot, you can order from a menu that has a small but appealing selection; the smoked fish platter and lobster chowder are just the ticket on a drizzly afternoon.

✪ **Herb Garden.** Rte. 224 between New Glasgow and St. Ann's (2km/1.2 miles west of Rte. 6), Hunter River. ☎ **902/621-0765.** Reservations recommended. Main courses C$16–C$19 (US$10–US$13). MC, V. July–Aug daily 5–10pm; Sept–June usually Sat–Sun (call ahead for exact hours). REGIONAL/GERMAN.

Off the road in a quiet landscape of gardens and forest, the Herb Garden is attractive in a sparely decorated, knotty-pine kind of way. The restaurant is justly famous for its wholesome middle-European–inspired cooking. Organically grown ingredients are used (much of it from the five gardens on the property), and all baking is done on the premises. The island-raised lamb is especially good, and other perennials include Wiener schnitzel and scallops in wine sauce. The desserts are outstanding, like cheesecake and homemade ice cream. Everything is prepared in small batches, so come early for a better selection—favorites tend to run out before the evening is over.

FROM NORTH & SOUTH RUSTICO TO BRACKLEY BEACH

A few miles east of Cavendish are the **Rusticos,** of which there are five: North Rustico, South Rustico, Rusticoville, Rustico Harbor, and Anglo Rustico. The region was settled by Acadians in 1790, and many residents are descendants of the original settlers. North and South Rustico are both attractive villages that have fewer tourist traps and are more amenable to exploring by foot or bike than Cavendish. Though out of the hubbub, they still provide easy access to the national park and Anne Land, with beaches virtually at your doorstep.

North Rustico clusters around a scenic harbor with views out toward Rustico Bay. Plan to park and walk around, perusing the deep-sea fishing opportunities (see below) and peeking in the shops. The village curves around Rustico Bay to end at **North Rustico Harbor,** a sandspit with fishing wharves, summer cottages, and a couple of informal restaurants.

In **South Rustico,** turn off Route 6 and ascend the low hill overlooking the bay. Here you'll find a handsome cluster of buildings that were home to some of the more prosperous Acadian settlers. Among the structures is the sandstone **Farmer's Bank of Rustico,** established with the help of a visionary local cleric in 1864 to help farmers get ahead of the hand-to-mouth cycle. Renovations have been ongoing for several years; it should be open for tours starting in 2000. Next door are handsome **St. Augustine's Parish Church** (1838) and a cemetery beyond. If the church's door is open, head in for a look at this graceful structure.

Brackley Beach is the gateway to the eastern section of the national park and has the fewest services of all. It's a quiet area with no village center to speak of that will be best appreciated by those who prefer their beach vacations unadulterated.

DEEP-SEA FISHING

PEI's north shore is home to the greatest concentration of deep-sea fishing boats. For about C$20 (US$13) per person, you'll get 3 hours out on the seas in search of mackerel, cod, and flounder. Don't worry about lack of experience: Equipment is supplied, and crew members are very helpful (most will even clean and fillet your catch for you).

In North Rustico, about half a dozen captains offer fishing trips. Among them are **Aiden Doiron's Deep Sea Fishing** (☎ 902/963-2442), **Bob's Deep-Sea Fishing** (☎ 902/963-2666), **Bearded Skipper's Deep-Sea Fishing** (☎ 902/963-2334), and **Court Brothers Deep Sea Fishing** (☎ 902/963-2322). A 20-minute drive east of North Rustico, at Covehead Harbor (within the national park), try **Richard's Deep-Sea Fishing** (☎ 902/672-2376) or **Salty Seas Deep-Sea Fishing** (☎ 902/672-3246).

WHERE TO STAY

Barachois Inn. Church Rd., South Rustico (mailing address: P.O. Box 1022, Charlottetown, PEI C1A 7M4). ☎ **902/963-2194.** E-mail barachoisinn@pei.sympatico.ca. 4 units, 1 with private bathroom down the hall. C$125–C$145 (US$83–US$97) double. Rates include full breakfast. MC, V. Closed Nov–Mar.

This proud Victorian was built in 1870 and is a soothing retreat for the roadweary. It is topped with a lovely mansard roof adorned with pedimented dormers and boasts a fine garden and historic furnishings throughout. Innkeepers Judy and Gary MacDonald bought the place as derelict property in 1982 and have done an outstanding job bringing it back from the brink, adding modern art to soften the staid Victorian architecture. It's furnished with high-quality period antiques; the two third-floor guest rooms are a bit cozier than the spacious second-floor suites, but you'll feel far away from the world when tucked under the slanted eaves.

A PEI Tradition: Come to a Lobster Supper

The north shore of Prince Edward Island is home to the famous **lobster suppers,** which are a good bet if you have a craving for one of the succulent local crustaceans. These suppers took root years ago as events held in church basements, in which parishioners would bring a covered hot dish to share and the church would provide a lobster. Everyone would contribute some money, and the church netted a few dollars. Outsiders discovered these good deals, the fame of the dinners spread, and today several places offer the bountiful lobster dinners, though few are raising money for charity these days.

Expect a large and impersonal dining experience (Fisherman's Wharf can accommodate 500 diners at a time), especially if you have the misfortune to pull up after a couple of tour buses have unloaded. Lobster is naturally the main feature, though you'll usually find roast beef, ham, or other alternatives. These are typically accompanied by an all-you-can-eat buffet with a button-bursting selection of rolls, salads, chowders, mussels, desserts, and more. The cost? Figure on C$20 to C$30 (US$13 to C$20) per person, depending on the options.

St. Ann's Church Lobster Suppers (☎ 902/621-0635) remains a charitable organization, as it was 3 decades ago when it was the first and only lobster supper on PEI. Located in a modern church hall in the small town of St. Ann, just off Route 224 between Routes 6 and 13, St. Ann's has a full liquor license, and the home-cooked food is served to your table (no buffet lines). Lobster dinners are served Monday to Saturday 4 to 9pm. As befits a church, it's closed on Sunday.

Fisherman's Wharf Lobster Suppers (☎ 902/963-2669) in North Rustico boasts a 60-foot salad bar to go with the lobster; it's open daily noon to 9pm. And near the PEI Preserve Company in New Glasgow is **New Glasgow Lobster Suppers,** on Route 258 just off Route 13 (☎ 902/964-2870), open daily 4:30 to 8:30pm. Meals include unlimited mussels and chowder.

Shaw's Hotel. Rte. 15, Brackley Beach, PEI C1E 1Z3. ☎ **902/672-2022.** Fax 902/672-3000. E-mail shaws@auracom.com. 15 units, 20 cottages. C$195–C$255 (US$130–US$150) double, with breakfast and dinner; C$225–C$350 (US$150–US$233) cottage. AE, ER, MC, V. Closed Oct–May. Pets allowed in cottages only.

Shaw's is a delightfully old-fashioned compound down a tree-lined dirt road along a marsh-edged inlet. It has been in the same family since 1860, and even with its regimen of modernization—new in 1999 were a sundeck, a bar, and a dining-room addition that accommodates 40 more people—the place still has the feel of a farm-stay vacation in the 19th century, where ripply and worn carpeting in the halls adds to the charm. (One caveat: A new subdivision across the river is starting to encroach on the pastoral environment.) The hotel's centerpiece is the Victorian farmhouse with its lipstick-red mansard roof. The upstairs guest rooms are "boarding-house style" (read: small). The cottages vary in size and vintage; none is terribly lavish, but all have TVs and most have the essentials (some with kitchenettes, some just with cube refrigerators).

Dining: The spare but handsome main dining room serves breakfast and dinner daily. The dinner menu changes frequently, but typical entrees (C$17 to C$23/US$11 to US$15) are filet mignon au poivre, poached halibut with béarnaise, and penne with smoked salmon in vodka-cream sauce. The Lobster Trap Lounge, in a nearby outbuilding, is open to 1am daily and offers more casual fare like chicken pot pie, nachos, and steamed island mussels.

Amenities: Baby-sitting, laundry, secretarial services; outfitter based on the grounds renting canoes, kayaks, bikes; beach 0.5km (0.3 mile) away.

WHERE TO DINE

Cafe St. Jean. Where Rte. 6 crosses the Wheatley River on Oyster Bed Bridge, at the southern tip of Rustico Bay. ☎ **902/963-3133.** Reservations recommended. Main courses C$7–C$9 (US$4.65–US$6) at lunch, C$12–C$25 (US$8–US$17) at dinner. Daily 11:30am–9:30pm. Closed Oct to mid-June. ECLECTIC.

Cafe St. Jean emphasizes local and Celtic music, with original tunes in the background, live music on the deck some evenings, and even CDs and tapes for sale at the register. Don't worry—this isn't a ploy to compensate for the food quality. The kitchen often scales culinary heights and produces zesty originals, but meals can be inconsistent at times. The menu should appeal to most taste buds, offering Cajun salmon with creole sauce, shrimp with peppercorns, chateaubriand, fish-and-chips, and excellent cafe salads.

3 Prince Edward Island National Park

Prince Edward Island National Park encompasses a 40km (25-mile) swath of red-sand beaches, wind-sculpted dunes topped with marran grass, vast salt marshes, and placid inlets. The park is along the island's sandy north-central coast, which is broached in several spots by broad inlets that connect to harbors. As a result, you can't drive along the entire park's length in one shot. The coastal road is disrupted by inlets, requiring backtracking to drive the entire length. And, actually, there's little point in trying to tour the whole length. It's a better use of your time to pick one spot, settle in, and enjoy your surroundings.

The national park also oversees the Green Gables house and grounds; see "Cavendish," above.

ESSENTIALS

GETTING THERE   From Charlottetown, Route 15 offers the most direct route to the eastern segments of the park. To head to the Cavendish area, take Route 2 to Hunter River, then head north on Route 13.

VISITOR INFORMATION   Two visitor centers provide information on park destinations and activities between June and October. The **Cavendish Visitors Centre** is near the intersection of Routes 6 and 13 (☎ 902/963-2391 or 902/963-7830); summer, it's open daily 9am to 10pm (it closes earlier during the shoulder seasons). The **Brackley Visitors Centre** is at the intersection of Routes 6 and 15 (☎ 902/672-7474); July and August, it's open daily 9am to 9pm (to 4:30pm in June, Sept, and Oct). In the off-season, contact the **park administration office** (☎ 902/672-6350) near the Dalvay Hotel.

FEES   June to September, you must stop at one of the toll houses to pay entry fees. Daily rates in 1999 were C$3 (US$2) adults, C$2 (US$1.35) seniors, C$1.50 (US$1) children 6 to 16, and C$7 (US$4.65) families. Ask about multiday passes if you plan to visit for more than 3 days.

EXPLORING THE PARK

Hiking is limited here compared to what you'll find at Atlantic Canada's other national parks, but there are a handful of pleasant strolls. And, of course, the beach is perfect for long walks.

The park maintains eight trails for a total of 20km (12 miles). Among the most appealing is the **Homestead Trail,** departing from the Cavendish campground. The trail offers a 5.5km (3.4-mile) loop and an 8km (5-mile) loop, skirting wheat fields, woodlands, and estuaries, with frequent views of the distinctively lumpy dunes at the west end of the park. Mountain bikes are allowed on this trail, and it's a busy destination on sunny days.

Biking along the shoreline roads in the park is sublime. The traffic is light, and it's easy to make frequent stops to explore beaches, woodlands, or the marshy edges of inlets. The two shoreline drives within the national park—between Dalvay and Rustico Island and from Cavendish to North Rustico Harbor—are especially beautiful on a clear evening as sunset edges into twilight. Snack bars are at Brackley Beach and Covehead Bay.

BEACHES

PEI National Park is nearly synonymous with its beaches. The park is home to two kinds of sandy strands: popular and sometimes crowded beaches with changing rooms, lifeguards, snack bars, and other amenities; and all the other beaches. Where you go depends on your temperament. If it's not a day at the beach without the aroma of other people's coconut tanning oil, head to Brackley Beach or Cavendish Beach. The latter is within walking distance of the Green Gables house and many other amusements (see "Cavendish," above) and makes a good destination for families.

If you'd just as soon be left alone with the waves, sun, and sand, you'll need to head a bit farther afield or just keep walking down the beaches until you leave the crowds behind. I won't reveal the best spots here for fear of crowding. But suffice it to say, they're out there.

WHERE TO STAY & DINE

The park offers three campgrounds. Reservations aren't accepted, so plan to arrive early in the day for the best selection of sites. Campground fees start at C$17 (US$11) per night (slightly less at Rustico Island), with serviced sites C$23 (US$15). For more details, contact the **Cavendish Visitors Centre** at ☎ **902/963-2391** or 902/963-7830.

The most popular (and first to fill) campground is **Cavendish,** just off Route 6 west of Green Gables. It has more than 300 sites spread among piney forest and open sandy bluffs; the sites at the edge of the dunes overlooking the beach are the most popular. However, the sites aren't especially private or scenic. A limited number of two-way hookups are available for RVs, and the campground has free showers, kitchen shelters, and evening programs.

The **Stanhope** campground lies just across the park road from lovely Stanhope Beach, on the eastern segment of the park (enter through Brackley Beach). **Rustico Island** is down a dead-end sandspit, with a number of sites overlooking a placid cove and the rolling countryside beyond. It lacks hookups for RVs, which might explain why sites are usually available here after the other campgrounds fill up.

Also see the listings for Cavendish and North and South Rustico, above.

✪ **Dalvay-by-the-Sea.** Off Rte. 6, Grand Tracadie (mailing address: P.O. Box 8, Little York, PEI C0A 1P0). ☎ **902/672-2048.** Fax (summer only) 902/672-2741. www. aco.ca/dalvay. E-mail dalvay@isn.net. 26 units; 8 cottages. Mid-June to mid-Sept C$190–C$300 (US$127–US$200) double, with breakfast and dinner ($20 less in shoulder seasons); C$300 (US$200) cottage. National-park entrance fees also charged. 2-night minimum in summer. AE, DC, ER, MC, V. Closed mid-Oct to early June.

This imposing Tudor mansion was built in 1895 by Alexander MacDonald, a partner of John D. Rockefeller. The place is unusually large for a private home but rather intimate for a luxury inn. You get glimpses of the ocean across the road from the upper floors, but the landscaping largely focuses on a beautiful freshwater pond out front. You'll be taken aback by the extraordinary cedar woodwork in the main entryway and the grand stone fireplace. The guest rooms are elegantly appointed and wonderfully solid and quiet; in the evening you'll hear mostly the roar of the sea.

Dining: The Dalvay added a pavilion-style dining room to the main inn in 1999. Not to worry—it has been built in a classic style that blends nicely with the original architecture. The result has been to add some much-needed seats, along with improved views of the gardens and pond. The well-regarded kitchen features dishes like tea-smoked Atlantic salmon with artichoke salad and crème fraiche. For dessert, try the sticky date pudding with toffee sauce, featured in *Gourmet* magazine. For those not on the meal plan, entrees run C$20 to C$25 (US$13 to US$17). Afternoon tea is served daily 2 to 4pm.

Amenities: One of the park's better beaches across the road, tennis, croquet, lawn bowling, horseshoes, canoeing, bike rentals, two-hole fairway, nearby nature trails.

4 Charlottetown

It's not hard to figure out why early settlers put the province's political and cultural capital where they did: It's on a point of land between two rivers and within a large protected harbor. For ship captains plying the seas, this quiet harbor with ample anchorage and wharf space must've been a welcome sight. Of course, travelers rarely arrive by water these days (unless a cruise ship is in port), but the city's harborside location translates into a lovely setting for one of Atlantic Canada's most graceful and relaxed cities.

Named after Queen Charlotte, consort of King George III, **Charlottetown** is home to some 40,000 people—nearly one of every three islanders. Within Canada, the city is famous for hosting the 1864 conference that 3 years later led to the creation of the independent Dominion of Canada. For this reason, you're never far from the word *confederation*, which graces buildings, malls, and bridges. (In a historic twist, PEI itself actually declined to join the new confederation until 1873.)

Today, the downtown has a brisk and busy feel, with a pleasing mix of modern and Victorian commercial buildings, as well as government and cultural centers. Outside the business core, you'll find leafy streets and large elegant homes dating from various eras, with the most dramatic from the late 19th century. Charlottetown is also blessed with a number of pocket parks, which provide a quiet respite amid the gentle clamor. Charlottetown's only charmless place? The outlying suburbs off Route 2, where you'll find traffic and strip malls of the sort that seem to be proliferating throughout North America.

Charlottetown is centrally located and serves admirably as a base for exploring the rest of the island (only the far-western coast is a bit distant for relaxed day-tripping). You can tour Green Gables, relax on a north-shore beach, or tee off at Brudenell Provincial Park within 45 minutes of leaving Charlottetown. The capital has the island's best selection of inns and hotels, plus a fine assortment of restaurants which ensure that you can dine out every night for a week and still be pleasantly surprised. As for scheduling time for exploring the city itself, I'd suggest saving it for a rainy day. And you don't really need much more than a day to take in all the highlights.

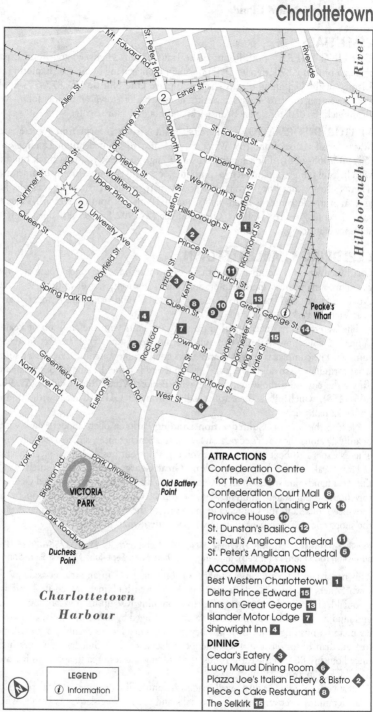

Charlottetown

ATTRACTIONS
Confederation Centre
  for the Arts **9**
Confederation Court Mall **8**
Confederation Landing Park **14**
Province House **10**
St. Dunstan's Basilica **12**
St. Paul's Anglican Cathedral **11**
St. Peter's Anglican Cathedral **5**

ACCOMMMODATIONS
Best Western Charlottetown **1**
Delta Prince Edward **15**
Inns on Great George **13**
Islander Motor Lodge **7**
Shipwright Inn **4**

DINING
Cedar's Eatery **3**
Lucy Maud Dining Room **6**
Piazza Joe's Italian Eatery & Bistro **2**
Piece a Cake Restaurant **8**
The Selkirk **15**

LEGEND
i Information

ESSENTIALS

GETTING THERE   Both Route 1 (the Trans-Canada Highway) and Route 2 pass through or near Charlottetown. For information on arriving by air, see "Exploring the Island," at the beginning of this chapter. **Square One Shuttle** (☎ 877/675-3830) runs seven-person vans 4 days a week among Charlottetown and Saint John, New Brunswick; Fredericton, New Brunswick; and Halifax, Nova Scotia.

VISITOR INFORMATION   The city's main **Visitor Information Centre** is on Water Street, across from 169 Water St. and next to Confederation Landing Park (☎ 902/368-4444). Look for the brown "?" sign to direct you to a brick building with helpful staffers, an interactive computer kiosk, and an ample supply of brochures. There's also a vacancy board to let you know where rooms are currently available. July and August, the center is open daily 8am to 10pm (to 5pm off-season). There's a second center at **City Hall** on Queen Street (☎ 902/566-5548), open daily in summer 8am to 5pm.

EXPLORING CHARLOTTETOWN

Charlottetown is a compact city that's easy to reconnoiter once you park your car. Three main areas merit exploration: the waterfront, the downtown area near Province House and the Confederation Court Mall, and parks and residential areas near Victoria Park.

The waterfront has been spruced up in recent years with the addition of **Peake's Wharf,** a collection of touristy boutiques and restaurants that attracts hordes in summer. The complex is attractive and offers good people watching, but it has a somewhat-formulaic "festival marketplace" feel to it and is rather lacking in local character. To see the city from the water, sign up with **Peake's Wharf Boat Cruises** (☎ 902/566-4458), which offers three tours daily starting at C$12 (US$8), with children under 12 half price.

Next to the wharf is **Confederation Landing Park,** an open, modern park with a boardwalk along the water's edge, lush lawns, and benches nicely situated for indolence. There's also a 220-boat marina, where you can scope out freshly arrived pleasure craft.

From Peake's Wharf, you can stroll up **Great George Street.** This is surely one of the most handsome streets in all of Canada, with leafy trees, perfectly scaled Georgian row houses, and stately churches. At the top of Great George Street, stop by the Province House and the Confederation Centre of the Arts (below), and then explore the shops and restaurants of downtown Charlottetown.

Province House National Historic Site. 165 Richmond St. ☎ 902/566-7626. Free admission (donations requested). July–Aug daily 9am–6pm; Sept–June Mon–Fri 9am–5pm.

This neoclassical downtown landmark was built in 1847 in an area set aside by the town fathers for colonial administration and church buildings. When it served as a colonial legislature, the imposing sandstone building rose up from vacant lots of dust and mud; today, as the provincial legislature, it's ringed by handsome trees, an inviting lawn, and a bustling downtown just beyond. Province House occupies a special spot in Canadian history as the place where the details of the Confederation were hammered out in 1864; in the early 1980s, the building was restored to appear as it would have looked in 1864.

Start your tour by viewing a well-made 17-minute film documenting the process of confederation. Afterward, wander the halls and see the Legislative Assembly, where legislators have been meeting since 1847. It's surprisingly tiny but perhaps appropriate given that PEI's legislature has just 27 members, making it the smallest in Canada. Especially impressive is the second-floor Confederation Chamber, where a staffer is usually on hand to explain what took place and to answer that persistent question. Why did PEI wait 9 years to join Canada?

Confederation Centre Art Galley and Museum. Queen and Grafton sts. ☎ **902/ 628-6142.** C$4 (US$2.65) adults, C$3 (US$2) seniors, C$2 (US$1.35) students, C$10 (US$7) families. Summer daily 9am–7pm; off-season Tues–Sat 11am–5pm, Sun 1–5pm.

Part of the Confederation Centre of the Arts (which includes three theaters), this is the largest art gallery in Atlantic Canada. The center is housed in a bland and boxy modern complex of glass and rough sandstone; about the best I can say of it is that it doesn't detract too much from the stylishly classical Province House next door. (Canadian writer Will Ferguson has referred to the building as "one of the greatest unprosecuted crimes of urban planning in Canadian history.") Inside, however, the gallery is spacious and nicely arranged on two levels, and it features displays from the permanent collection as well as imaginatively curated changing exhibits.

It's also worth checking the schedule at the **Confederation Centre of the Arts** (☎ **800/565-0278** or 902/566-1267), which bustles with the performing arts throughout the year, with special shows slated for summer. The musical *Anne of Green Gables,* a perennial favorite, is performed here each summer, as are revivals and new shows.

WHERE TO STAY

Two motels are within easy walking distance of downtown attractions. The **Islander Motor Lodge,** 146–148 Pownal St. (☎ **902/892-1217**), has 50 units a few minutes' walk from Province House, beginning at C$103 (US$69) double. **Best Western Charlottetown,** 238 Grafton St. (☎ **800/528-1234** or 902/566-2979), has 173 units in two buildings a couple blocks east of the Confederation Court Mall. Rooms are C$179 to C$239 (US$119 to US$159) double, and suites are C$179 to C$259 (US$119 to US$173).

Delta Prince Edward. 18 Queen St., Charlottetown, PEI C1A 8B9. ☎ **902/566-2222.** Fax 902/566-2282. 211 units. A/C MINIBAR TV TEL. Peak season C$159–C$319 (US$106–US$213) double; call for off-season rates. AE, DC, DISC, ER, MC, V. Valet parking C$8 (US$5). Pets allowed.

A boxy, 10-story modern hotel overlooking the harbor, the Prince Edward is part of the Canadian Pacific chain and has all the things expected by business travelers, including coffeemakers, hair dryers, irons and ironing boards, free exercise bikes delivered to your room, and even cordless phones (about half the rooms are cordless). You enter the hotel through a two-story atrium (home to a well-regarded restaurant), then head up to the guest rooms. The better rooms are furnished with reproduction Georgian-style furniture; others have those oak and beige-laminate furnishings that are virtually invisible. The higher rooms have the better views; there's a premium for water views, but the city views are actually nicer (and you can usually glimpse the water anyway). The Selkirk (below) may be the city's best restaurant, with upscale service and presentation to complement the fine menu. Summers only, a more informal restaurant serves tasty lunches for C$6 to C$12 (US$4 to US$8) on a patio near the harbor. The hotel features an indoor pool and fitness room, a sauna, an outdoor hot tub, afternoon tea, safe-deposit boxes, turndown service, a concierge, room service (to 2am), a shopping arcade, a beauty salon, a business center, and conference rooms. Baby-sitting, dry cleaning, and laundry service are available.

Inns on Great George. 589 Great George St., Charlottetown, PEI C1A 4K3. ☎ **800/ 361-1118** or 902/892-0606. Fax 902/628-2079. www.innsongreatgeorge.com. E-mail innsongg@atcon.com. 40 units, 35 with bathroom. A/C TV TEL. C$145–C$225 (US$97–US$150) double. Rates include continental breakfast. AE, DC, ER, MC, V. Free parking.

The Inns on Great George opened in 1997 and has established itself as one of the classiest Charlottetown hostelries. The inn encompasses six striking buildings on and near historic Great George Street. Twenty-four rooms are in the 1846 Pavilion Hotel; others are in smaller town houses and homes nearby. All have been thoroughly updated and refurbished with antiques, down duvets, hair dryers, and early black-and-white prints; all but two are carpeted. The more expensive rooms have fireplaces and Jacuzzis, but many of the others have clawfoot tubs, perfect for soaking in after a day of roaming the city. Room no. 403 has buttery pine floors, a wonderful tub, and lots of light. Room no. 308 has a Shaker-style canopied bed, a two-person Jacuzzi, and a gas fireplace. The inn features a small fitness room. It also has safe-deposit boxes, offers limited room service from an affiliated restaurant, and can arrange for baby-sitting, dry cleaning, and laundry.

✪ **Shipwright Inn.** 51 Fitzroy St., Charlottetown, PEI C1A 1R4. ☎ **902/368-1905.** Fax 902/628-1905. www.isn.net/shipwrightinn. E-mail shipwright@isn.net. 7 units. A/C TV TEL. C$125–C$250 (US$83–US$167) double. Rates include continental breakfast. AE, DC, ER, MC, V. Free parking.

This understated Victorian was built by a shipbuilder and expertly renovated and refurbished. It's decorated with period furniture and with a deft touch—don't expect over-the-top Victoriana here. All the guest rooms have lovely wood floors (some with original ship-planking floors), and three are in a recent addition built with a number of nice touches. Amenities include hair dryers and down duvets in all rooms, and about half the rooms have Jacuzzis, gas fireplaces, or both. Among the best are the Ward Room, a suite with a private deck, and the Purser's State Room, which shares a lovely deck with another room. The inn is right in the city but has a settled, pastoral farmhouse feel to it.

WHERE TO DINE

A locally popular spot for inexpensive meals is **Cedar's Eatery,** 81 University between Fitzroy and Kent (☎ **902/892-7377**). Lebanese dishes are the specialty, like *yabrak* (stuffed vine leaves) and *kibbee* (ground beef with crushed wheat and spices). There are also sandwiches and burgers. Specials start at C$4.95 (US$3.30), both lunch and dinner. It's open Monday to Saturday 11am to midnight and Sun 11am to 11pm.

Lucy Maud Dining Room. 4 Sydney St. ☎ **902/894-6868.** Reservations recommended for lunch and dinner June–Sept. Main courses C$11–C$13 (US$7–US$9) at lunch, C$18–C$26 (US$12–US$17) at dinner. Tues–Fri 11:30am–1:30pm; Tues–Sat 5:30–9pm. Closed during school holidays. REGIONAL.

The Lucy Maud Dining Room is in the Culinary Institute of Canada's campus. The building itself is a bit institutional and charmless, and the 80-seat dining room has the feel of a hotel restaurant. But plenty of nice touches offset the lack of personality, like custom china and a beautiful view of the bay and Victoria Park from oversized windows. Best of all, you get to sample some of the best of island cuisine, prepared and served by Institute students eager to please. The lunch and dinner menus change each semester, but typical dinner entrees include duck breast with sour cherry sauce and venison loin with blueberry peppercorn sauce (the kitchen is noted for its venison). Salmon is always on the menu, and you'll often find curried seafood chowder with fresh tarragon, a local favorite.

Piazza Joe's Italian Eatery and Bistro. 189 Kent St. ☎ **902/894-4291.** Reservations not accepted. Main courses C$9–C$16 (US$6–US$11); individual pizzas C$8 (US$5) and up. AE, MC, V. Mon–Wed 11am–11pm, Thurs–Sat 11am–midnight, Sun 10am–11pm. PIZZA/ITALIAN.

Plazza Joe's, in a handsome historic building a long block from the Confederation Mall, has gone a bit overboard with the Tuscan-style washed tones and fake ivy climbing fake trellises. But it works in a comic-book kind of way. The place is pleasantly casual and can be loud on weekends, but it offers friendly service, a long menu, and lots of fun mixed drinks. (It's the best spot for a late-night meal.) The wood-fired pizza is consistently quite good; take your chances on the rest of the selections, like five-vegetable lasagna and veal ala limone. There's also a bistro menu, with items like burgers, chicken wings, fish-and-chips, and "nasty nachos."

✪ **Piece a Cake Restaurant.** 119 Grafton St. (upstairs in the Confederation Court Mall). ☎ **902/894-4585.** Reservations recommended. Main courses C$7–C$14 (US$4.65–US$9) at lunch, C$12–C$20 (US$8–US$13) at dinner. AE, DC, ER, MC, V. Daily 11am–11pm. Closed Sun Oct–May. ECLECTIC.

This very modern, very handsome restaurant occupies the second floor of a building that's part of the Confederation Court Mall. The hardwood floors, high ceilings, rich custard-colored walls, and window frames suspended whimsically from the ceiling lend an airy grace to the spot. It's the kind of place where friends who don't see each other very often like to get together and relax over a lively meal. The menu is wonderfully far-ranging, so I can't imagine someone not finding something appealing— lunches range from a teriyaki salmon wrap to Thai scallop salad to Tuscan grilled-chicken sandwiches. Dinners are similarly eclectic and include a range of adventurous pastas. (A personal favorite is "penne on fire," with charred onions, grilled zucchini, toasted pecans, and tangerine relish.) Other dinner options include Thai seafood medley, blackened salmon, and pecan-crusted pork loin. Only the unimaginative wine list is bit of a disappointment.

The Selkirk. In the Delta Prince Edward, 18 Queen St. ☎ **902/566-2222.** Reservations recommended. Main courses C$6–C$9 (US$4–US$6) at breakfast, C$6–C$13 (US$4–US$9) at lunch, C$20–C$28 (US$13–US$19) at dinner. AE, DC, DISC, ER, MC, V. Daily 6:30am–2pm and 5–11pm. NEW CANADIAN.

Charlottetown's most stylish restaurant is smack in the middle of the lobby of the high-end Prince Edward Hotel. Yet it has a more informal character than many upscale hotel restaurants, with an eclectic mix of chairs and a piano player providing the live soundtrack. The menu is also more ambitious and creative than you'll find elsewhere. The signature appetizer is lobster and prawns with a three-melon salsa, or you might opt for pheasant confit. Main courses could include sashimi of salmon, oysters, and scallops with a sauce of lime, ginger, and garlic; or Maritime jambalaya with lobster, mussels, shrimp, scallops, and salmon. Carnivores aren't ignored, with a selection that includes duck breast with raspberry/green peppercorn vinaigrette and beef tenderloin with shiitake ragout. A downside: The lobby location can get clamorous at times, especially when conferees are milling about.

5 Kings County: An Escape from Anne Land

After a visit to Charlottetown and the island's central towns, **Kings County** comes as a bit of a surprise. It's far more tranquil and uncluttered than Queens County (Anne's reach is much diminished here), and the landscapes feature woodlots alternating with corn, grain, and potato fields. Though much is made of the county's two great commercial centers on the coast—Souris and Montague—it's good to keep in mind that each of these has a population of around 1,500. In some parts of North America, that wouldn't even rate a dot on the map.

ESSENTIALS

GETTING THERE Several main roads—including Highways 1, 2, 3, and 4—connect eastern PEI with Charlottetown and western points. The ferry to Nova Scotia sails from Woods Island on the south coast. See "Exploring the Island," at the beginning of this chapter, for more information.

VISITOR INFORMATION A large **provincial information center** is in Pooles Corner at the intersections of Route 3 and Route 4, north of Montague (☎ **902/838-0670**). The center, open June to mid-October, also contains well-presented exhibits about local commerce and history, including how to identify local architectural styles. Another helpful **visitor center** (☎ **902/838-4778**), open daily in summer, is at the old railway depot in Montague on the river.

MONTAGUE

Montague is the region's main commercial hub, but it's a hub in low gear. It's compact and attractive, with a handsome business district on a pair of flanking hills sloping down to a bridge across the Montague River. (A century and a half ago, the town was called Montague Bridge.) Shipbuilding was the economic mainstay in the 19th century; today dairy and tobacco are the leading industries.

Exploring the Outdoors

Cruise Manada (☎ **800/986-3444** or 902/838-3444) offers seal- and bird-watching tours daily during peak season aboard restored fishing boats; the cost is C$17 (US$11) adults, C$15 (US$10) seniors/students, and C$9 (US$6) children under 12. Trips depart from the marina on the Montague River, just below the visitor center in the old railway depot. Reservations are advised.

Southeast of Montague (en route to Murray River) is the **Buffaloland Provincial Park** (☎ **902/652-2356**), where you'll spot a small herd of buffalo. These were a gift to PEI from the province of Alberta and now number about 25. Walk down the 100-yard fenced-in corridor into the paddock and ascend the wooden platform for the best view of the shaggy beasts. Often they're hunkered down at the far end of the meadow, but they sometimes wander near. The park is right off Route 4; watch for signs.

Brudenell River Provincial Park (☎ **902/652-8966**) is one of the province's more active and better-bred parks, a great spot to work up an athletic glow on a sunny afternoon. On its 1,500 riverfront acres you'll find two well-regarded golf courses, a golf academy, a full-blown resort (below), tennis, lawn bowling, a wildflower garden, a playground, a campground, and nature trails. Kids' programs, like Frisbee golf, shoreline scavenger hunts, and crafts workshops, are scheduled daily in summer. You can also rent canoes, kayaks, and jet skis from private operators located in the park. The park is open daily 9am to 9pm; admission is free. Head north of Montague on Route 4, then east on Route 3 to the park signs.

Where to Stay

Brudenell River Resort. Rte. 3 (P.O. Box 67), Cardigan, PEI C0A 1G0. ☎ **800/565-7633** or 902/652-2332. Fax 902/652-2886. www.rodd-hotels.ca/. 51 units, 82 cabins. TV TEL. Peak season C$134–C$225 (US$89–US$150) double, C$95–C$124 (US$63–US$83) basic cabin, C$154–C$325 (US$103–US$217) deluxe cabin; off-season C$92–C$150 (US$61–US$100) double, C$68–C$89 (US$45–US$59) basic cabin, C$104–C$275 (US$69–US$183) deluxe cabin. AE, DC, ER, MC, V. Closed mid-Oct to mid-May. C$10 (US$7) per pet per night.

Built in 1991, this sleek Frank Lloyd Wright–esque resort is especially popular with golfers—it's set amid two excellent golf courses (one new in 1999). You choose among three types of rooms. The hotel proper has 51 lovely guest rooms, each with a balcony or a terrace. The new-in-1999 upmarket Echelon Gold Cottages have two bedrooms, cathedral ceilings, fireplaces, and large-screen TVs. The more basic Countryside Cabins are the best bet for those on a budget; just beware that the detailing isn't of the highest quality, and the units are clustered together a bit oddly, like pavilions left over from some forgotten world exposition.

Dining: The Gordon Dining Room overlooks the golf course. It's a bit cavernous, but the high-backed chairs carve out a sense of intimacy. Breakfast and dinner are served; you'll enjoy creative country-club cuisine, with entrees (C$14 to C$19/US$9 to US$13) like charbroiled steak, sole in puff pastry, and pasta primavera.

Amenities: Dry cleaning, baby-sitting; two golf courses (one host to a Golf Academy offering extensive lessons), two pools (indoor and out), river swimming, Jacuzzi, sauna, two night-lit tennis courts, health club, jogging and hiking trails, children's center.

Rodd Marina Inn & Suites. 1150 Sackville St. (P.O. Box 1540), Montague, PEI C0A 1R0. ☎ **800/865-7633** or 902/838-4075. Fax 902/838-4180. 52 units. A/C TV TEL. C$99–C$124 (US$66–US$83). Rates include continental breakfast. AE, MC, V.

The Marina Inn was built in 1999 and has the casually modern feel of the sort of midsized chain hotel you'd expect to find on a strip at the edge of a midsized town. With this difference: It boasts a great location tucked off Montague's main street, right along the Montague River (boat tours available) and smack on a spur of the Confederation Trail. The guest rooms are mostly standard sized and come with the usual amenities, like coffeemakers and hair dryers; I'd request a room on the river side for the view. A dozen "studio-suites" (their term) offer small sitting areas along with microwaves, refrigerators, and Jacuzzis. There are also a sundeck, a breakfast room, and a small exercise room.

WHERE TO DINE

Windows on the Water. 106 Sackville St. (at Main St.). ☎ **902/838-2080.** Reservations encouraged. Main courses C$8–C$9 (US$5–US$6) at lunch, C$11–C$20 (US$7–US$13) at dinner. MC, V. Daily 11:30am–10pm. SEAFOOD.

If you haven't yet dined on PEI mussels, this is the place to let loose. The blue mussels are steamed in a root mirepoix, with sesame, ginger, and garlic. It's a winner. Main courses include sole stuffed with crab and scallop and topped with hollandaise, and the chef's peppered steak (filet mignon with sweet peppers, red onion, and mushrooms in peppercorn sauce). Lunches are lighter, with choices like grilled chicken and mandarin salad, as well as homemade fish cakes. The appealing open dining room features pressback chairs and a lively buzz, but if the weather's agreeable, angle for a seat under the canopy on the deck.

SOURIS & NORTHEAST PRINCE EDWARD ISLAND

Some 44km (27 miles) northeast of Montague is **Souris,** an active fishing town attractively set on a gentle hill overlooking the harbor. Souris (pronounced *Soo-ree*) is French for "mouse"—so named because early settlers were beset by voracious field mice that destroyed their crops. The town is the launching point for an excursion to the Magdalen Islands, and it makes a good base for exploring northeastern PEI, which more urban residents considered the island's outback—remote and sparsely populated. You'll also find it somewhat less agricultural and more forested, especially away from the coast, than the rest of the island.

EXPLORING THE AREA

Several good beaches ring this wedge-shaped peninsula that points like an accusing finger toward Nova Scotia's Cape Breton Island. **Red Point Provincial Park** (☎ 902/ 357-2463) is 13km (8 miles) northeast of Souris. It offers a handsome beach and supervised swimming, along with a campground that's popular with families. Another inviting and often-empty beach is a short distance northeast at **Basin Head,** which features a "singing sands" beach that allegedly sings (actually, it's more like a squeak) when you walk on it. The dunes here are especially appealing.

At the island's far-eastern tip is the aptly named **East Point Lighthouse** (☎ 902/ 357-2106). You can simply enjoy the dramatic setting or take a tour of the building. Ask for your East Point ribbon while you're here. If you make it to the North Cape Lighthouse on the western shore, you'll receive a Traveller's Award documenting that you've traveled PEI tip to tip. Admission to the lighthouse is C$2.50 (US$1.65) adults and C$1 (US65¢) children (closed Sept to mid-June).

WHERE TO STAY

✪ **Inn at Bay Fortune.** Rte. 310 (off Rte. 2), Bay Fortune, PEI C0A 2B0. ☎ **902/ 687-3745,** or 860/296-1348 off-season. Fax 902/687-3540. www.innatbayfortune.com. E-mail innatbayft@auracom.com. 18 units. TEL. Summer C$125–C$250 (US$83– US$167) double; fall C$105–C$230 (US$70–US$153) double. Rates include full breakfast. DC, ER, MC, V. Closed mid-Oct to late-May.

This exceptionally attractive shingled compound on 46 acres was built by playwright Elmer Harris in 1910 as a summer home, and it quickly became a nucleus for a colony of artists, actors, and writers. (Most recently it was owned by Canadian actress Colleen Dewhurst, who sold it to current innkeeper David Wilmer in 1988.) Wilmer pulled out the stops in renovating, bringing it back from the brink of decay. In 1998 he added a wing with six new rooms (two with Jacuzzis), including the wonderful North Tower Room 4, with a high ceiling and a balcony overlooking the lodge and bay beyond. My favorite room remains South Tower Room 4, which requires a schlep up a narrow staircase, but once you're in this high lair it feels a world removed. The newer rooms are larger than the older ones, but all are quite cozy, with a mix of antiques and custom-made furniture. Eight rooms have wood-burning fireplaces, and six have propane fireplaces. The inn is home to one of PEI's best restaurants (see below).

WHERE TO DINE

✪ **Inn at Bay Fortune.** Rte. 310 (off Rte. 2). ☎ **902/687-3745.** Reservations strongly recommended. Main courses C$21–C$26 (US$14–US$17). DC, ER, MC, V. Daily 5–9pm. Closed mid-Oct to late May. CREATIVE CONTEMPORARY.

To fully appreciate a meal at the Inn at Bay Fortune, arrive early enough to wander the gardens behind the inn. The herbs and edible flowers are a short walk from the kitchen; a little farther beyond is the 3-acre vegetable garden. This is a good introduction because the inn puts an emphasis on local products. Chef Jeff McCourt worked with founding chef Michael Smith (now at Maple in Halifax) to develop the inn's local cuisine and the vaunted openness—how many restaurants feature a KITCHEN—WELCOME sign inviting diners to stop in for a visit?

6 Prince County: PEI in the Rough

Prince County encompasses the western end of PEI and offers a varied mix of lush agricultural land, rugged coastline, and unpopulated sandy beaches. This is Prince Edward Island with calluses. With a few exceptions, the region is a bit more ragged around the edges in a working-farm, working-waterfront kind of way. It typically lacks the pristine-village charm of Kings County or much of Queens County.

Within this unrefined landscape, however, you'll find pockets of considerable charm, such as the village of Victoria on the south coast at the county line, and in Tyne Valley near the north coast, which is reminiscent of a Cotswold hamlet.

ESSENTIALS

GETTING THERE   Route 2 is the main highway connecting Prince County with the rest of the island. Feeder roads typically lead to and from Route 2. The Confederation Bridge from the mainland connects to Prince County at Borden Point, southeast of Summerside.

VISITOR INFORMATION   The best source of travel info for the county is **Gateway Village,** an assortment of modern buildings built to look like old buildings at the end of the Confederation Bridge (☎ **902/437-8750**). It's open daily: June to late August daily 8am to 10pm, early June and September 9am to 9pm, October to May 9am to 6pm.

VICTORIA

Tiny **Victoria**—a short detour off Route 1 between the Confederation Bridge and Charlottetown—is an unusually scenic village that's attracted a number of artists, boutique owners, and craftspeople. It's perfect for strolling—parking is near the wharf and off the streets, keeping the narrow lanes free for foot traffic. Wander the short shady lanes while admiring the architecture, much of which is in that elemental farmhouse style, clad in clapboard or shingle and constructed with sharply creased gables. (Some elaborate Victorians break the mold.) What makes the place so singular is that the village, first settled in 1767, has utterly escaped the creeping sprawl that has plagued so many otherwise-attractive places. The entire village consists of 4 square blocks, which are surrounded by potato fields and the Northumberland Strait. It's not hard to imagine that the village looked much the same a century ago.

EXPLORING VICTORIA

The **Victoria Seaport Museum** is in a shingled, square lighthouse near the town parking lot. (You can't miss it.) You'll find a rustic local history museum with the usual assortment of artifacts from the past century or so. Summer, it's open Tuesday to Sunday noon to 5pm; admission is by donation.

In the middle of town is the well-regarded **Victoria Playhouse** (☎ **800/925-2025** or 902/658-2025). Built in 1913 as a community hall, the building has a unique raked stage (it drops 7 inches over 21 feet) to create the illusion of space, four beautiful stained-glass lamps, and a proscenium arch (also unusual for a community hall). Plays staged here in summer attract folks out from Charlottetown for the night. It's hard to say what's more enjoyable: the high quality of the acting or the wonderful big-night-out air of a professional play in a small town where nothing else is going on. There's also a Monday-night concert series, with everything from traditional folk to Latin jazz. Tickets are C$16 (US$11) adults and C$14 (US$9) seniors/students; discounts are given at matinees.

WHERE TO STAY

Orient Hotel. Main St. (mailing address: P.O. Box 162, Charlottetown, PEI C1A 7K4). ☎ **800/565-6743** or 902/658-2503. Fax 902/658-2078. E-mail orient@pei.sympatico.ca. 6 units. C$85–C$135 (US$57–US$90) double. Rates include full breakfast. AE, MC, V. Closed mid-Oct to mid-May.

The circa-1900 Orient, with yellow shingles and maroon trim, has been a Victoria mainstay for years—a 1926 guide notes that it had 20 rooms at C$2.50 (US$1.65) (back then a trip to the bath required a walk to the carriage house). The inn has been modernized in recent years but retains much of its antique charm (try to ignore the lobby's velour furniture and the industrial carpeting). It's at the edge of the village overlooking potato fields with purple blooms in late summer. The guest rooms are painted in warm pastels and furnished eclectically with flea-market antiques. Mrs. Proffit's Tea Shop on the first floor serves lunch and afternoon tea daily noon to 5pm and has a growing reputation for its scones. The light lunches include tea sandwiches, lobster rolls, soups, and salads at C$2.95 to C$10 (US$1.95 to US$6).

WHERE TO DINE

Landmark Cafe. Main St. ☎ **902/658-2286.** Reservations recommended. Sandwiches around C$6 (US$3.65); main courses C$11–C$16 (US$7–US$11). MC, V. Daily 11am–9:30pm. Closed mid-Sept to mid-June. CAFE.

Across from the Victoria Playhouse, the Landmark Cafe occupies a cozy storefront teeming with shelves filled with crockery, pots, jars, and more, some of which are for sale. But the effect is more funky than Ye Olde Quainte, and the limited menu is very inviting. The steamed mussels and vine leaves with feta cheese are a favorite of regulars. Other offerings include salads, lasagna, meat pie, and tarragon-steamed salmon.

TYNE VALLEY

The village of **Tyne Valley** is just off Malpeque Bay and is one of the most attractive and pastoral areas of western PEI. There's little to do but much to admire. The village of gingerbread homes is surrounded by verdant barley and potato fields. Azure inlets encroach here and there; these are the arms of the bay, which is famous for its succulent Malpeque oysters. A former 19th-century shipbuilding center, Tyne Valley now attracts artisans and others in search of a quiet lifestyle. A handful of good restaurants, inns, and shops cater to visitors.

EXPLORING TYNE VALLEY

Just north of the village on Route 12 is the lovely ✪ **Green Provincial Park** (☎ **902/831-2370**). Once the site of an active shipyard, the 219-acre park is now a lush riverside destination with lush lawns and trees, and it has the feel of an early-1900s estate. Which, in fact, it was. In the heart of the park is the extravagant gingerbread mansion (1865) once owned by James Yeo, a merchant, shipbuilder, and landowner who in his time was the island's wealthiest and most powerful man.

Managed by the Prince Edward Island Museum and Heritage Foundation, the historic **Yeo House and the Green Park Shipbuilding Museum** (☎ **902/831-2206**) are now the park's centerpieces. Exhibits in two buildings provide a good view of the prosperous life of a shipbuilder and the golden age of PEI shipbuilding. Summer, the museum and house are open daily 10am to 5pm. Admission is C$3 (US$2) plus tax for adults; children under 12 are free.

WHERE TO STAY & DINE

Caernarvon in Bayside. Rte. 12, Bayside, PEI (mailing address: Richmond RR1, C0B 1Y0). ☎ **800/514-9170** or 902/854-3418. www.cottagelink.com/caernarvon. 1 unit, 4 cottages. C$100 (US$67) double, with breakfast; C$120 (US$80) cottage per night (3-night minimum), C$665 (US$444) cottage per week (up to 4 people). AE, MC, V.

The sense of quiet and the views over Malpeque Bay across the road are the lure at this attractive 5-acre cottage compound a few minutes' drive from Tyne Valley. Owners

Rusty and Graham Capper have furnished their circa-1990 knotty-pine cottages simply but comfortably. Each has two bedrooms and a sleeping loft, an outdoor gas barbecue, a cathedral ceiling, and a porch with a bay view. This is a good choice if you're looking to get away, but note that it is also popular with families (there's a playground out back) so may not be the best option for a romantic getaway. In the main house the Cappers offer an attractive three-bedroom suite that may be rented by one couple, a family, or friends traveling together and is priced accordingly.

✪ **Doctor's Inn.** Rte. 167 (P.O. Box 92), Tyne Valley, PEI C0B 2C0. ☎ **902/831-3057.** www.peisland.com/doctorsinn. 2 units, neither with bathroom. C$60 double. Rates include breakfast. MC, V. "Well-mannered" pets allowed.

Staying at the Doctor's Inn is a bit like visiting relatives you didn't know you had. Upstairs in this handsome in-town farmhouse are just two guest rooms sharing a bath. (You could rent both for less than the cost of a room at some other inns.) There are an upstairs sitting area and the extensive organic gardens out back to peruse. It's a pleasant retreat, and innkeepers Jean and Paul Offer do a fine job of making you feel relaxed and at home. The Offers serve up one of Atlantic Canada's most memorable dining experiences, catering to a maximum of six people on any night at a single sitting. You first gather for appetizers and wine in the sitting room, then move to the large oval dining-room table. The extraordinary salads feature produce from the Offer's famous garden (they grow more than two dozen kinds of lettuce), and you'll have a choice of entrees, which are cooked on the wood stove in an old-fashioned kitchen. Look for scallops, arctic char, salmon, veal, or whatever else the Offers can get fresh. The desserts are freshly baked and wonderful. Reservations are requested at least 24 hours in advance; dinner is served at 7pm. A four-course meal with wine is C$40 (US$27) per person.

WESTERN PRINCE COUNTY

PEI's far-western coast—from West Point to North Cape—is well suited to a driving tour or exploring more leisurely by bike. You'll find vast agricultural lands and open ocean views and a more rugged beauty than elsewhere on the island. What you won't find are many tourist services—or even many of the usual services. Even general stores are infrequent, and it's surprisingly hard to find fresh fish or produce, especially given the number of fishmongers and vegetable stands elsewhere in the province. On the other hand, relatively few travelers make it to this far end of the island, lending it a sometimes-eerie, sometime-exquisite remoteness.

EXPLORING WESTERN PRINCE COUNTY

At the southwest tip of the island is **Cedar Dunes Provincial Park** (☎ 902/859-8785). Set on 100 oceanside acres, the park features extensive beaches (with lifeguard) and views across the strait to New Brunswick and down to the Confederation Bridge. You'll get a good illustration of the shifting sand here: The changing room has been all but engulfed in sand over the past few years.

Edging the beach is the distinctive black-and-white **West Point Lighthouse Museum.** Open summers, it features displays about lighthouse history and local lore, including rooms with some of the original furnishings. This is also the headquarters of the PEI Lighthouse Society, so it's a good stop for info about other island lights. If you're not afraid of heights, scramble up the narrow stairs to the beacon at the top, where you'll be rewarded with sweeping ocean views. Admission is C$2.50 (US$1.65) adults, C$1.50 (US$1) children, and C$7 (US$4.65) families. The lighthouse also houses an inn and restaurant (see below).

North Cape is a blustery, dramatic point where the seas swirl around from north and west, mixing off the point. You can take pictures of the lighthouse (1866), walk along the low crumbling cliffs, and then visit the small **Interpretive Centre and Aquarium** (☎ **902/882-2991**) for more details about local marine life and history. (Above the center is the Wind & Reef Restaurant, which offers seafood with a view of the sea.) Admission to the center is C$2 (US$1.35) adults and C$1 (US65¢) seniors/children; it's open late May to mid-October.

And all those strange towering devices next to the center? That's the **Atlantic Wind Test Site,** where an array of traditional and state-of-the-art windmills is being refined to better harness the winds. You can admire the eerie sound they make in the cape's persistent breeze, but the site itself is closed to the public. Guides at the center can answer any questions you might have.

WHERE TO STAY & DINE

West Point Lighthouse. RR#2, West Point, PEI C0B 1V0. ☎ **800/764-6854** or 902/ 859-3605. Fax 902/859-3117. 9 units. Sept 9–30 and June 1–19 C$85–C$130 (US$57–US$87) double; June 20–Sept 8 C$70–C$115 (US$47–US$77) double. AE, MC, V. Closed Oct–May.

Two of the guest rooms at the West Point Lighthouse are actually in the lighthouse itself—something quite unique. One room, Keepers Quarters, faces landward and has a low ceiling; if you can, hold out for the Tower Room, with a 13-foot ceiling, an extravagant canopied bed, and unrivaled views. (Book well in advance.) The other rooms are in a newer addition and are the size of cozy motel units, but they're nicely decorated with quilts. The best of these is corner room no. 9, with a wonderful breeze and great views. The first-floor restaurant is a popular destination for day-trippers who venture here for the beach and seafood. Breakfast is under C$5 (US$3.35), lunch is mostly under C$10 (US$7), and dinners range from C$10 to C$26 (US$7 to US$17). Expect traditional dinner entrees like fisherman's platter, seafood fettuccine, chicken breast, and steak and scallops.

Newfoundland & Labrador   6

by Wayne Curtis

Newfoundland and **Labrador** might be the Eastern seaboard's last best place. (These two distinct geographic areas are administered as one province, so sometimes the phrase "Newfoundland and Labrador" refers to a single place, sometimes to two places.) Wild, windswept, and isolated, the province often reveals a powerful paradox. Although the landscape is rocky and raw—at times it looks as if the glaciers had receded only a year or two ago—the residents often display a genuine warmth that makes visitors feel right at home. Tourists only recently starting arriving here in any number, and longtime residents more than not like to chat, offer advice, and hear your impressions of their home. Travelers who are normally reluctant to ask questions of locals for fear of embarrassment usually drop their hesitance after an encounter or two.

An excursion to The Rock—as the island of Newfoundland is commonly called—is magical in many ways. Not only in the extraordinary northern landscape and the gracious people but also in the rich history that catches many first-timers off guard. This is where European civilization made landfall in the New World—by both the Vikings and later the fishermen and settlers in the wake of John Cabot's arrival in 1497—and you'll find traces of that rich legacy at almost every turn. Other parts of North America might claim an equally historic lineage, but there are few places in the New World where you feel as if not a whole lot has transpired since the first settlers sailed into the harbor some centuries ago. History isn't buried here; it's right on the surface.

1 Exploring the Province

A couple of weeks is enough for a bare-bones tour of the whole island, though you'll be frustrated by all that gets left out. You're better off selecting a few regions and focusing on those.

VISITOR INFORMATION

Visitor centers aren't as numerous or well organized in Newfoundland as they are in Nova Scotia or on Prince Edward Island, where almost every small community has a place to load up on brochures and ask questions. In Newfoundland, you're better off stocking up on maps and information in St. John's or just after you disembark from the ferries, where excellent centers are maintained.

A Timely Note

Note that Newfoundland keeps its own clock, and "Newfoundland time" is *half an hour* ahead of Atlantic time.

The *Newfoundland and Labrador Travel Guide,* published by the province's department of tourism, is hefty and helpful, with listings of all attractions and accommodations. Request a free copy before arriving by calling ☎ 800/563-6353 or 709/729-2830. You can also request it by fax (709/729-1965), e-mail (info@tourism.gov.nf.ca), or mail (P.O. Box 8730, St. John's, NF A1B 4K2).

GETTING THERE By Plane Air transportation to Newfoundland is typically through Gander or St. John's. Airlines serving the island include **Air Canada** (☎ 800/422-6232 in Canada, 800/776-3000 in the United States; www.aircanada.ca), **Canadian Airlines** (☎ 800/426-7000; www.cdnair.ca), **Air Labrador** (☎ 800/563-3042 within Newfoundland, or 709/896-3387), and **Interprovincial Airlines** (☎ 800/563-2800 within Newfoundland, 709/576-1666 elsewhere).

By Ferry Marine Atlantic (☎ 800/341-7981; www.marine-atlantic.ca) operates year-round ferry service from North Sydney, Nova Scotia, to Port aux Basques, with as many as three sailings each way daily during summer. The crossing is about 5 hours; one-way fares are C$20 (US$13) adults or C$62 (US$41) cars. A summer-only ferry also connects North Sydney with Argentia on the southwest tip of the Avalon Peninsula. This crossing is offered three times weekly and takes 14 to 15 hours. The one-way fare is C$55 (US$37) adults or C$124 (US$83) cars. On both ferries, children 5 to 12 are half price (children under 5 free). Reserved reclining seats, sleeping berths, and private cabins are available.

Seasonal ferries also connect Lewisporte, Newfoundland, with Goose Bay, Labrador. The trip is about 38 hours, and fares are C$97 (US$65) adults or C$160 (US$107) cars. Call ☎ 800/563-6353 for information or reservations.

For all ferries, advance reservations are strongly advised during the peak travel season.

GETTING AROUND

Newfoundland has no rail service, but several bus lines connect the major ports and cities. **DRL Coachlines** (☎ 709/738-8090) has one bus daily from Port aux Basques to St. John's. The trip takes 13 hours, and one-way fare is C$90 (US$60).

To explore the countryside, you'll need a car. Major rental companies with fleets in Newfoundland include **Avis** (☎ 800/879-2847), **Budget** (☎ 800/268-8900), **Hertz** (☎ 800/263-0600), **Thrifty** (☎ 800/367-2277), **Tilden** (☎ 800/387-4747), **Enterprise** (☎ 800/325-8007), and **Rent-A-Wreck** (☎ 800/337-0116).

THE GREAT OUTDOORS

BIKING Bike touring in Newfoundland is for the hearty. It's not that the hills are necessarily brutal (though many are) but that the weather can be downright demoralizing. Expect more than a handful of blustery days, complete with horizontal rains that seem to swirl around from every direction. The happiest bike tourists seem to be those who allow themselves frequent stays in motels or inns, where they can find hot showers and places to dry their gear. **Aspenwood Hike and Bike Tours,** P.O. Box 622, Springdale, NF A1C 5K8 (☎ 709/673-4255), arranges mountain-biking trips in and around central Newfoundland; **Freewheeling Adventures,** RR#1, Hubbards, NS B0J 1T0 (☎ 902/857-3600), runs van-supported trips based out of hotels and B&Bs.

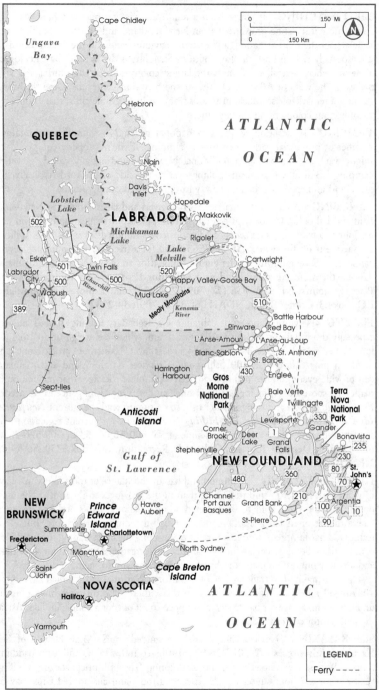

BIRD WATCHING   If you're from a temperate climate, bird watching won't get much more interesting or exotic than in Newfoundland and Labrador. Seabirds typically attract the most attention, and eastern Newfoundland and the Avalon Peninsula are especially rich in bird life. Just south of St. John's is the **Witless Bay Ecological Reserve,** where several islands host the largest colony of breeding puffins and kittiwakes in the western Atlantic. On the southern Avalon Peninsula, **Cape St. Mary's** features a remarkable sea stack, just yards from easily accessible cliffs, that's home to a cacophonous colony of northern gannets.

CAMPING   In addition to the two national parks, Newfoundland maintains a number of provincial parks open for car camping. If you're properly equipped, you might want to take part in a traditional Newfoundland activity called "gravel-pit camping." Basically, that means pulling over to the side of the road (typically in a gravel pit) and spending the night away from organized campgrounds.

CANOEING   A glance at a map shows that rivers and lakes abound in Newfoundland and Labrador. Canoe trips can range from placid puttering around a pond near St. John's to world-class descents of Labrador rivers hundreds of miles long. Call the **Department of Tourism** at ☎ **800/563-6353** for a free brochure outlining several canoe trips. Several outfitters offer guided canoe trips on the island and the mainland. Among them are **Newfoundland and Labrador Ecotour Adventures,** 8 Virginia Place, St. John's, NF A1A 3G6 (☎ **709/579-8055**), and **X-plore Newfoundland,** P.O. Box 63, Corner Brook, NF A2H 6C3 (☎ **709/634-2237**).

FISHING   Newfoundland and Labrador are legendary among serious anglers, especially those stalking the cagey Atlantic salmon, which can weigh up to 18kg (40 lb.). Other prized species include landlocked salmon, lake trout, brook trout, and northern pike. More than 100 fishing-guide services on the island and mainland can provide everything from simple advice to complete packages that include bush-plane transportation, lodging, and personal guides. One fishing license is needed for Atlantic salmon and one for other fish, so be sure to read the current *Newfoundland & Labrador Hunting and Fishing Guide* closely for current regulations. It's available at most visitor centers; by phone at ☎ **800/563-6353** or 709/576-2830; or by mail at **Dept. of Tourism, Culture & Recreation,** P.O. Box 8730, St. John's, NF A1B 4K2.

HIKING & WALKING   Newfoundland has an abundance of trails, but you'll have to work a bit harder to find them here than in the provinces to the south. The most obvious hiking trails tend to be centered around national parks and historic sites, where they're often fairly short—good for a half-day's hike, rarely more. But Newfoundland has hundreds of miles of trails, many along the coast leading to abandoned communities. Some places are finally realizing the recreational potential for these trails and are now publishing maps and brochures directing you to them.

The best-maintained trails are at ✪ **Gros Morne National Park,** which has around 100km (62 miles) of trails. In addition to these, there's also off-track hiking on the dramatic Long Range for backpackers equipped to set out for a couple of days. Ask at the park visitor center for details.

SEA KAYAKING   Novices should stick to guided tours. Mike Henley of **Sea Kayaking Adventures** (☎ **709/726-9283**) is based in St. John's and leads paddling tours at Witless Bay, Cape Broyle, and Conception Bay, with prices starting at C$35 (US$23) for a 2-hour sunset paddle. Extended tours and customized trips may be arranged. At **Terra Nova National Park,** 2-hour sea kayak tours leave from the Marine Interpretation Centre and explore protected Newman's Cove (see the "Terra Nova National Park" section).

2 Southwestern Newfoundland: Your Introduction to The Rock

For most travelers arriving by ferry, this region is their introduction to The Rock. And it's like starting the symphony without a prelude, jumping right to the crescendo. There's instant drama in the brawny, verdant Long Range Mountains running parallel to the Trans-Canada Highway en route to Corner Brook, and there are towering seaside cliffs on the Port au Port Peninsula and intriguing coastal villages that await exploration. You might also be surprised that winds can blow with such intensity hereabouts yet not attract any comment from the locals.

ESSENTIALS

GETTING THERE   Southwestern Newfoundland is commonly reached via ferry from Nova Scotia. See "Exploring the Province," above, for ferry information. The Trans-Canada Highway (Route 1) links the major communities of southwestern Canada. Port aux Basques is 905km (561 miles) from St. John's via the Trans-Canada Highway.

VISITOR INFORMATION   In Port aux Basques, the **Provincial Interpretation and Information Centre** is on the Trans-Canada Highway about 2 miles from the ferry terminal (☎ 709/695-2262). Mid-May to late October, it's open daily 6am to 11pm. The **Corner Brook Tourist Chalet** is just off the Trans-Canada Highway at the intersection of West Valley Road and Confederation Drive, near the Best Western Mamateek (☎ 709/639-9792). It's open daily in summer.

PORT AUX BASQUES

Port aux Basques is a major gateway for travelers arriving in Newfoundland, with ferries connecting to Nova Scotia year-round. It's a good way station for those arriving late on a ferry or departing early in the morning. Otherwise, you can easily see it in a couple of hours when either coming or going.

The **Gulf Museum,** 118 Main St. (☎ 709/695-3408), across from the Town Hall, contains a quirky assortment of artifacts related to local history. The museum's centerpiece is a 1628 Portuguese astrolabe recovered from local waters in 1981. Also intriguing is a display about the *Caribou,* a ferry torpedoed by a German U-boat in 1942 with a loss of 137 lives. The museum is open daily 9am to 7pm; admission is C$2 (US$1.35) adults, C$1 (US65¢) children, and C$5 (US$3.35) families.

On the way out of town, you'll pass the **Port aux Basques Railway Heritage Center,** Route 1 (☎ 709/956-2170), dedicated to the memory of the Newfie Bullet, the much-maligned, much-reminisced-about passenger train that ran between Port aux Basques and St. John's from 1898 to 1969. (The highway across the island opened in 1966, dooming the train.) The train required 27 hours to make the trip (at an average speed of 48km/30 m.p.h.), and during a tour of several restored rail cars you'll learn how the train made the run through deep snows of winter, how the passengers slept at night (very cozily, it turns out), and how the train workers occupied themselves in the mail car and caboose. The 15-minute tours cost C$2 (US$1.35) adults, C$1 (US65¢) children, and C$5 (US$3.35) families.

Departing from the Railway Heritage Center is the **T'Railway,** a coast-to-coast pathway being converted from the old train line. It's used by pedestrians, bikers, and ATVers, and in this stretch it runs several miles through marsh and along the ocean to Cheeseman Provincial Park, which boasts a lagoon and a sandy beach that's home to a population of endangered piping plovers. It's a good spot to get your mountain bike limbered up for further adventures.

WHERE TO STAY

About half a dozen hotels and B&Bs offer no-frills shelter here. The two largest are the **Hotel Port aux Basques,** Route 1 (☎ 709/695-2171), and **St. Christopher's Hotel,** Caribou Road (☎ 800/563-4779). Both might be described as "budget modern," with clean basic rooms in architecturally undistinguished buildings. I'd give St. Christopher's the edge since it's on a high bluff with views of the town and the harbor. Both have around 50 rooms and charge around C$60 (US$40) double.

WHERE TO DINE

Dining opportunities are limited. Both hotels above have dining rooms, serving basic, filling meals. A 10-minute walk from the ferry terminal on the boardwalk is the family-style **Harbour Restaurant,** 121 Caribou Rd. (☎ 709/695-3238), serving budget-oriented meals (entrees C$5 to C$14/US$3.30 to US$9, with most under C$10/US$7). Expect fried fish, fried chicken, fish cakes, sandwiches, and the like. Most tables have good views of the harbor.

CORNER BROOK

With a population of about 35,000, **Corner Brook** is Newfoundland's second-largest city. Like St. John's, it's also dramatically sited—in this case, on the banks of the glimmering Humber River, which winds down through verdant mountains from beyond Deer Lake, then turns the corner to flow into Humber Arm. The hills on the south shore of the Humber are nearly as tall as the those in Gros Morne National Park, making a great backdrop for the town, which has gradually expanded up the shoulders of the hills.

Corner Brook is a young city with a long history. The area was first explored and charted in 1767 by Capt. James Cook, who spent 23 days mapping the islands at the mouth of the bay. But it wasn't until early in the 20th century that the city started to take its present shape. Copper mines and the railroad brought in workers; in the early 1920s the paper mill, which still dominates downtown, was constructed. By 1945, it was the largest paper mill in the world.

The **Corner Brook Museum and Archive,** 2 West St. (☎ 709/634-2518), is housed in a solid 1920s-era building that once was home to customs offices, the court, and the post and telegraph offices. A visit here offers a quick way to learn just how young the city really is (grainy black-and-white photos show empty hills surrounding the paper mill as late as the 1920s) and how civilized it has become. An assortment of locally significant artifacts (a prominent doctor's desk, ship models) rounds out the collection. The museum is open daily 10am to 8pm; admission is C$2 (US$1.35) adults and C$1 (US65¢) youths.

WHERE TO STAY

Corner Brook is home to several convenient chain motels. Among others, you'll find the **Best Western Mamateek Inn,** 64 Maple Valley Rd., near the tourist info booth (☎ 800/563-8600 or 709/639-8901), and the **Holiday Inn,** 47 West St. (☎ 709/634-5381), which is within walking distance of the city's best restaurant (see below). Rooms start at C$89 (US$59) double at both places.

Glynmill Inn. 1 Cobb Lane (near West St.), Corner Brook, NF A2H 6E6. ☎ 800/563-4400 in Canada or 709/634-5181. Fax 709/634-5106. 81 units. A/C TV TEL. C$94 (US$63) double; C$113–C$165 (US$75–US$110) suite. AE, DC, ER, MC, V.

This in-town Tudor inn is set in a quiet parklike setting an easy stroll from West Street's services and shops. Built in 1924 (and extensively renovated in 1994), the four-story hotel has a surfeit of charm and lovely detailing. The guest rooms are tastefully decorated with Colonial reproductions; the popular Tudor Suite has a

Newfoundland

private Jacuzzi. You'll get far more character here than at the chain motels and for about the same price. The inn's two dining rooms are quite popular among locals, with steaks the big draw; dinner entrees run C$12 to C$21 (US$8 to US$14).

WHERE TO DINE

✪ **Thirteen West.** 13 West St. ☎ **709/634-1300.** Reservations recommended on weekends. Main courses C$8–C$14 (US$5–US$9) at lunch, C$16–C$27 (US$10–US$18) at dinner. AE, DC, ER, MC, V. Mon–Fri 11:30am–2:30pm and 5:30–9:30pm (to 10:30pm Fri), Sat 5:30–10:30pm, Sun 5:30–9:30pm. GLOBAL.

Western Newfoundland's best restaurant can easily compete with the better restaurants of St. John's in both the quality of the food and the casual but professional attitude. Tucked along shady West Street in an unobtrusive building (there's a patio fronting the street for the rare balmy night), the kitchen does an outstanding job preparing top-notch meals, and the staff knows how to make good service seem easy. At lunch look for offerings like grilled chicken-breast wrap and baked scallop crêpes with bacon and leeks. In the evening, you'll find a menu with items like grilled salmon with dill pesto, grilled chicken breast with curry rub, and a steak-and-shrimp combo with Asian spices.

DEER LAKE

Deer Lake is an unassuming crossroads town near the head of the Humber River where travelers coming from the south either continue on the Trans-Canada Highway toward St. John's or veer northwest to Gros Morne National Park, some 71km (44 miles) distant. Deer Lake is the gateway for those coming by air directly to western Newfoundland. There's little to detain you here; it's a good spot to buy gas, peruse the brochures at the provincial info center, then push on.

Lucky is the traveler who arrives here during the short **strawberry season** (mid- to late July some years or early Aug in others). If you're here at the right time, do yourself a favor and stop at one of the several seasonal roadside stands for a pint or two. They're plump, cheap, and sinfully sweet and flavorful—nothing at all like the tasteless commercial berries that have lately invaded grocery stores in the United States and elsewhere.

3 Gros Morne National Park: One of Canada's Treasures

"Gros Morne" translates roughly from the French as "big gloomy," and if you arrive on a day when ghostly bits of fog blow across the road and scud clouds hover in the glacial valleys, you'll get a pretty good idea how this area got its name. Even on brilliantly sunny days there's something about the stark mountains, lonely fjords cut off from the ocean, and miles of tangled spruce forest that can trigger a mild melancholy.

✪ **Gros Morne National Park** is one of Canada's true treasures, and few who visit here fail to come away awed. The park is divided into two sections, north and south, riven by the multi-armed Bonne Bay (locally pronounced like "Bombay"). Alas, a ferry connecting the two areas hasn't operated for years, so exploring both sections by car requires backtracking. The park's visitor center and most tourist services are in the village of Rocky Harbour in the north section. But you'd be shortchanging yourself to miss a detour through the dramatic southern section, a place that looks like it had a rough birth, geologically speaking.

If you'd prefer to let someone else do the planning for you, contact **Gros Morne Adventure Guides** (☎ **709/458-2722**), which organizes guided sea-kayaking and hiking excursions around the park.

ESSENTIALS

GETTING THERE   From the Trans-Canada Highway in Deer Lake, turn west on Route 430 (the Viking Trail). This runs through the northern section of the park. For the southern section, turn left (south) on Route 431 in Wiltondale.

VISITOR INFORMATION   The main national park **visitor center** is just south of Rocky Harbour on Route 430 (☎ **709/458-2066**), open daily 9am to 10pm. The center features exhibits on park geology and wildlife; there's also a short film about the park that's picturesque but not terribly informative. The interactive media kiosks are exceptionally well done; you can view video clips depicting highlights of all hiking trails and other attractions simply by touching a video screen. The center is also the place to stock up on field guides, as well as to request backcountry camping permits.

Across the bay just outside Woody Point on Route 431 en route to Trout River is the brand-new-in-2000 **Discovery Centre** (☎ **709/458-2417**). At press time no phone number, admission price, or other information was available, but the new building promises to be an enlightening stop, with plans calling for interactive exhibits, a fossil room, and a multimedia theater to help make sense of the Gros Morne landscape.

FEES   All visitors must obtain a permit for any activity in the park. Daily fees are C$3.25 (US$2.15) adults, C$2.50 (US$1.65) seniors, C$1.75 (US$1.15) children 6 to 18, and C$7 (US$4.35) families. Four-day passes are available for the price of 3 days.

GROS MORNE'S SOUTHERN SECTION

The road through the southern section dead-ends at Trout River and seems to discourage unadventurous visitors who like loops and through-routes. That's too bad, because the south contains some of the park's most dramatic terrain. Granted, you can glimpse the rust-colored Tablelands from north of Bonne Bay near Rocky Harbour, thereby saving the 50km (31-mile) detour. But without actually walking through the desolate landscape, you miss much of the impact. The south also contains several lost-in-time fishing villages that predate the park's 1973 creation and a new Discovery Centre (above) with exhibits about the park's natural history.

The region's scenic centerpiece is **Trout River Pond,** a landlocked fjord some 15km (9.3 miles) long. You can hike along the north shore to get a great view of the Narrows, where cliffs nearly pinch the pond in two. For a more relaxed view, sign up for a boat tour and be surrounded with breathtaking panoramic views. ✪ **Tableland Boat Tours** (☎ 709/451-2101) offers excursions aboard a 40-passenger tour boat. Two-and-a-half-hour trips are offered daily at 10am, 1pm, and 4pm in July and August (1pm only in June and Sept). The cost is C$25 (US$17) adults and C$9 (US$6) children 6 to 16. Tickets are sold at a gift shop between the village of Trout River and the pond; watch for the signs.

For a hike offering a superb panorama encompassing ocean and mountains, watch for the **Lookout Trail** just outside of Woody Point en route to Trout River. This steep trail is about 5km (3.1 miles) round-trip. The **Tablelands Trail** departs from barren Trout River gulch and follows an old gravel road up to Winterhouse Brook Canyon. You can bushwhack along the rocky river a bit farther upstream or turn back. It's about 2km (1.2 miles) each way, depending on how adventurous you feel. This is a good trail to get a feel for the unique ecology of the Tablelands. Look for the signboards explaining the geology at the trailhead and at the roadside pull-off on your left before reaching the trailhead.

Experienced hikers looking for a challenge should seek out the ✪ **Green Gardens Trail.** There are two trailheads to this loop; I recommend the second one (closer to Trout River). You'll start by trekking through a rolling infertile landscape, then the plunge begins as you descend down, down, down wooden steps and a steep trail toward the sea. The landscape grows more lush by the moment, and soon you'll be walking through extraordinary coastal meadows on crumbling bluffs high above the surf.

The trail follows the shore northward for about 4km or 5km (2.5 miles or 3.1 miles), and it's one of the most picturesque coastal trails I've hiked anywhere. In July, the irises and a whole symphony of other wildflowers bloom wildly. The entire loop is about 16km (9.9 miles) and is rugged and very hilly; allow about 5 or 6 hours. An abbreviated version involves walking clockwise on the loop to the shore's edge, then retracing your steps uphill. That's about 9km (5.6 miles).

WHERE TO STAY

The two **drive-in campsites** in the southern section—**Trout River Pond** and **Lomond**—offer showers and nearby hiking trails. Of the two, Trout River Pond is more dramatic, located on a plateau overlooking the pond; a short stroll brings you to the pond's edge with wonderful views up the fjord. Lomond is near the site of an old lumber town and is popular with anglers. Camping is C$15 (US$10) per site.

Victorian Manor. Main St. (P.O. Box 165), Woody Point, NF A0K 1P0. ☎ **709/453-2485.** www.grosmorne.com/victorianmanor. 10 units, 6 with bathroom; 1 guest house. C$50–C$70 (US$33–US$47) double; C$125 (US$83) guest house. Rates include continental breakfast. AE, MC, V.

Journey to the Center of the Earth

If you see folks walking around the Tablelands looking twitchy and excited, they're probably amateur geologists. The Tablelands are one of the world's great geological celebrities and a popular destination among pilgrims who love the study of rock.

To the uninitiated, the Tablelands area—south of Woody Point and the south arm of Bonne Bay—will seem rather bleak and barren. From a distance, the muscular hills rise up all rounded and rust colored, devoid of trees or even that pale-green furze that seems to blanket all other hills. Up close, you discover just how barren they are—little plant life seems to have established a toehold.

There's a reason for that. Some 570 million years ago, this rock was part of the earth's mantle, that part of the earth just under the crust. Riding on continental plates, two land masses collided forcefully hereabouts, and a piece of the mantle was driven up and over the crust, rather than being forced under, as is usually the case. Years of erosion followed, and what's left is a rare glimpse of the earth's skeleton. The rock is so laced with magnesium that few plants can live here, giving it a barrenness that seems more appropriate for a desert landscape in the American southwest than the rainy mountains of Newfoundland.

This 1920 home is one of the most impressive in the village, but that doesn't mean it's extravagant. It's more solid than flamboyant, set in a residential neighborhood near the town center and a few minutes' walk to the harbor. The attractive guest house has its own whirlpool. If that's booked, ask for one of the efficiencies, which cost about the same as the rooms but afford much greater convenience, especially considering the slim dining choices in town.

WHERE TO DINE

Seaside Restaurant. Main St., Trout River. ☎ **709/451-3461.** Main courses C$9–C$19 (US$6–US$13). MC, V. Daily noon–9pm. Closed Oct–June. SEAFOOD.

The Seaside has been a Trout River institution for years, and it's clearly a notch above the tired fare you often find in tiny coastal villages. The restaurant is nicely polished without being swank and features magnificent harbor views. The pan-fried cod is superb, as are a number of other seafood dishes, like shrimp and lobster. Sandwiches and burgers are at hand for those who don't care for seafood. The desserts are quite good, such as the partridgeberry parfait, but the service can be slow when the place fills up.

GROS MORNE'S NORTHERN SECTION

Gros Morne's northern section flanks Route 430 for some 75km (47 miles) between Wiltondale and St. Paul's. The road winds through the abrupt forested hills south of Rocky Harbour; beyond these, the road levels out, following a broad coastal plain covered mostly with bog and tuckamore. East of the plain rises the extraordinarily dramatic monoliths of the Long Range. This section contains the park's visitor center as well as the one must-see attraction: **Western Brook Pond.**

The hardscrabble fishing village of **Rocky Harbour** is home to the greatest concentration of motels, B&Bs, Laundromats, and so on. One caveat: Rocky Harbour and the surrounding area lack a well-lit, well-stocked grocery store of the sort you'd expect near a national park of international importance. What you'll find are modest-sized grocery stores—the sorts of places where you'll want to check the dates on bread and milk very carefully.

If you have time for only one activity in Gros Morne—and heaven forbid that's the case—make it the boat trip up ☼ **Western Brook Pond.** The trip begins a 20-minute drive north of Rocky Harbour. Park at the Western Brook Pond trailhead, and then set off on an easy 45-minute hike across the northern coastal plain, with interpretive signs explaining the wildlife and bog ecology you'll see along the way. (Keep an eye out for moose.) Always ahead, the mighty monoliths of the Long Range rise high above, inviting and mystical, more like a 19th-century scene from the Rockies than the Atlantic seaboard.

You'll soon arrive at the pond's edge, where there's a small collection of outbuildings near a wharf. Once aboard one of the vessels (there are two), you'll set off into the maw of the mountains, winding between the sheer rock faces that define this landlocked fjord. The spiel on the boat is recorded, but even that unfortunate bit of cheese fails to detract from the grandeur of the scene. You'll learn about the glacial geology and the remarkable quality of the water, among the purest in the world. Bring lots of film and a wide-angle lens. The trip lasts about 2½ hours and costs C\$30 (US\$20) adults and C\$14 (US\$9) students 6 to 16 (must be accompanied by an adult); children under 6 are free when with their parents. For reservations, contact the **Ocean View Motel** in Rocky Harbour at ☎ **709/458-2730.**

Even if you're not planning on signing up for the **Western Brook Pond** boat tour (reconsider!), you owe yourself a walk up to the pond's wharf and possibly beyond. The 45-minute one-way trek from the parking lot north of Sally's Cove follows well-trod trail and boardwalk through bog and boreal forest. When you arrive at the wharf, the view to the mouth of the fjord will take your breath away. A very well-executed outdoor exhibit explains how glaciers shaped the landscape in front of you.

Two spur trails continue on either side of the pond for a short distance. The **Snug Harbour Trail,** following the northern shore to a primitive campsite (registration required), is especially appealing. After crossing a seasonal bridge at the pond outlet, you'll pass through scrubby woods before emerging on a long and wonderful sand-and-pebble beach; this is a great destination for a relaxed afternoon picnic and requisite nap. The hike all the way to Snug Harbour is about 8km (5 miles) one-way.

WHERE TO STAY

The northern section has three campgrounds open to car campers. The main campground is **Berry Hill,** just north of Rocky Harbour. There are 146 drive-in sites, plus 6 walk-in sites on the shores of the pond itself. It's just a 10-minute drive from the visitor center, where evening activities and presentations are held. **Shallow Bay** has 50 campsites and is near the park's northern border and an appealing 4km (2½-mile) sand beach. Both campgrounds have showers and flush toilets.

Rocky Harbour has more tourist services than any other village in or around the park, but it still has trouble handling the influx of travelers in July and August. Two or three bus tours can pretty well fill up the town. One B&B owner told me she turned away 20 people seeking a room one night in July. It's an unwise traveler who arrives without a reservation.

The largest motel in town is the **Ocean View Motel** (☎ 709/458-2730), on the harbor. It has 44 basic rooms (some have small balconies with bay views), but everything feels a bit chintzy here, from the carpeting to the walls to the furnishings. The motel is popular with bus tours, and it often fills up early in the day. Rooms are C$65 to C$70 (US$43 to US$47) double in season.

Gros Morne Cabins. P.O. Box 151, Rocky Harbour, NF A0K 4N0. ☎ **709/458-2020** or 709/458-2369. 22 cabins. TV. C$75 (US$50) 1-bedroom cabin for 2; C$99 (US$66) 2-bedroom cabin for 2. Extra person C$5 (US$3.35). Off-season rates available. AE, DC, MC, V. Pets allowed.

My favorite thing about the Gros Morne Cabins? Pulling up and seeing the long lines of freshly laundered sheets billowing in the sea breeze, like a Christo installation. The trim and tidy log cabins are clustered tightly along a grassy rise overlooking Rocky Harbour, and all have outstanding views toward the Lobster Cove Head Lighthouse. Inside they're new and clean, more antiseptically modern than quaintly worn. Each cabin is equipped with a kitchenette, and gas barbecues are scattered about the property. The complex also includes Endicott's Store and a Laundromat. There's a pizza place across the street for relaxed sunset dining at your own picnic table.

Wildflower Inn. Main St. N., Rocky Harbour, NF A0K 4N0. ☎ **888/811-7378** or 709/458-3000. 7 units, 3 with bathroom. C$49–C$64 (US$33–US$43) double. Rates include continental breakfast. MC, V.

This circa-1930s home near the village center was modernized and updated before its opening as a B&B in 1997, giving it a casual country look inside. The guest rooms are tastefully appointed if a bit small, though two new rooms have private bathrooms and are a bit larger. The neighborhood isn't especially scenic (there's an auto-repair shop across the way), but the house is very peaceful, the innkeepers are exceptionally friendly, and this is a great choice for those seeking reasonably priced lodging with a comfortable, homey feel.

WHERE TO DINE

Fisherman's Landing. Main St., Rocky Harbour. ☎ **709/458-2060.** Sandwiches C$3.50–C$8 (US$2.35–US$5); main courses C$7–C$15 (US$4.65–US$10). MC, V. Summer daily 6am–11pm; limited hours off-season. SEAFOOD.

With its industrial carpeting and generic chain-restaurant chairs and tables, Fisherman's Landing is lacking in homespun character. But it does offer efficient service and dependable meals, with specialties like fish-and-chips, cod tongues, and squid rings. For breakfast, there's the traditional Newfie fisherman's breakfast of a mug of tea, served with homemade bread and molasses. Meals are quite reasonably priced, and you can get in and out faster than at most other joints. There's also a glimpse of the harbor from a few tables, provided that not too many RVs park out front.

4 The Great Northern Peninsula: Way Off the Beaten Path

The **Great Northern Peninsula** looks on a map like a stout cudgel threatening the shores of Labrador. If Newfoundland can even be said to have a beaten track, rest assured that the peninsula is well off it. It's not as mountainous or starkly dramatic as Gros Morne, but the road unspools for kilometer after kilometer through tuckamore and evergreen forest, along restless coast and the base of geologically striking hills. There are few services and even fewer organized diversions. But it has early history in spades, a handful of fishing villages clustering along the rocky coast, and some of the most unspoiled terrain anywhere. The road is in good repair, with the chief hazard being the stray moose or caribou. In spring, the infrequent polar bear might wander through a village, often hungry after a long trip south on ice floes.

ESSENTIALS

GETTING THERE   Route 430, also called the Viking Trail, runs from Deer Lake (at the Trans-Canada Highway) to St. Anthony, a 433km (268-mile) jaunt. Scheduled flights on **Air Labrador** (☎ **800/563-3042** within Newfoundland, 709/896-3387 elsewhere) and **Interprovincial Airlines** (☎ **800/563-2800** within Newfoundland, 709/576-1666 elsewhere) stop at St. Anthony, where rental cars are available. The airport is on Route 430 about 30km (19 miles) west of St. Anthony.

VISITOR INFORMATION   For information about the Great Northern Peninsula and the ✪ **Viking Trail,** contact the **Viking Trail Tourism Association,** P.O. Box 430, St. Anthony, NF A0K 4S0 (☎ **709/454-8888**). A visitor center is in **St. Anthony** on West Street at the corner of Marvel Road (☎ **709/454-4010**).

PORT AU CHOIX

A visit to **Port au Choix** (pronounced port-a-*shwaw*) requires a 13km (8-mile) detour off the Viking Trail, out to a knobby peninsula that's home to a sizable fishing fleet. The windswept lands overlooking the sea are low, predominantly flat, and lush with grasses. Simple homes speckle the landscape; most are of recent vintage.

Port au Choix National Historic Site. Point Riche Rd., Port au Choix. ☎ **709/861-3522.** Admission C$2.50 (US$1.65) adults, C$2 (US$1.35) seniors, C$1.50 (US$1) children 6–16, C$6 (US$4) families. Mid-June to mid-Sept daily 9am–8pm.

Back in 1967, a local businessman began digging the foundation for a new movie theater in town. He came on some bones. A lot of bones. In fact, what he stumbled on turned out to be a remarkable burying ground for what are now called the Maritime Archaic Indians. This group of hunters populated parts of Atlantic Canada starting 7,500 years ago, far predating the Inuit, who arrived only around 4,000 years ago. These early natives relied chiefly on the sea, and among the artifacts recovered here are slate spears and antler harpoon tips, which featured an ingenious toggle that extended after being thrust into flesh. One of the enduring historical mysteries is the disappearance of the Maritime Archaic Indians from the province about 3,500 years ago—to this day no one can explain their sudden departure.

   You'll learn about this fascinating historic episode at the modern visitor center. From here, staffers will be able to direct you to various nearby sites, including the **original burial ground,** now surrounded by village homes. You can also visit the nearby **lighthouse,** scenically located on a blustery point thrusting into the Gulf of St. Lawrence.

L'ANSE AUX MEADOWS

Newfoundland's northernmost tip is not only exceptionally remote and dramatic but also one of the most historically significant spots in the world. A Viking encampment dating from A.D. 1,000 was discovered here in 1960, and it has been thoroughly documented by archaeologists in the decades since. An unusually well-conceived and well-managed national historic site (below) probes this earliest chapter in European expansion, and an afternoon spent at **L'Anse aux Meadows** goads the imagination.

✪ **L'Anse aux Meadows National Historic Site.** Rte. 436, L'Anse aux Meadows. ☎ **709/623-2608.** Admission C$5 (US$3.35) adults, C$4.25 (US$2.85) seniors, C$2.75 (US$1.85) children 6–16, C$10 (US$7) families. Peak season daily 9am–8pm; shoulder season daily 9:30am–4:30pm. Closed mid-Oct to early June.

In the late 1950s, a pair of determined archaeologists named Helge Ingstad and Anne Stine Ingstad pored over 13th-century Norse sagas searching for clues about where the Vikings might've landed on the shores of North America. With just a few scraps of description, the Ingstads began cruising the coastlines of Newfoundland and Labrador, asking locals about unusual hummocks and mounds.

They struck gold at L'Anse aux Meadows. In a remote cove noted for its low grassy hills, they found the remains of an ancient Norse encampment that included three large halls and a forge where nails were made from locally mined pig iron. As many as 100 people lived here for a time, including some women (spindle whorls and bone knitting needles seem to attest to that). The Vikings abandoned the settlement after a few years to return to Greenland and Denmark, thus ending the first European experiment in the colonization of North America. It's telling that no graves have ever been discovered here.

Start your visit by viewing the recovered artifacts in the visitor center and watching the half-hour video about the site's discovery. Then I suggest signing up for one of the free guided tours of the site. The guides offer considerably more info than the simple markers around the grounds. Near the original encampment are several re-created sod-and-timber buildings, depicting how life was lived 1,000 years ago. These are tended by costumed interpreters who have a wonderful knack of staying in character without making you feel like a dork when you ask them questions.

WHERE TO STAY

✪ **Tickle Inn at Cape Onion.** RR#1, Cape Onion, NF A0K 4J0. ☎ **709/452-4321** (June–Sept) or 709/739-5503 (Oct–May). E-mail adams.tickle@nf.sympatico.ca. 4 units, none with bathroom. C$50–C$65 (US$33–US$43) double. Rates include deluxe continental breakfast. MC, V. Closed Oct–May. About a 40-min. drive from L'Anse aux Meadows.

If you're seeking that end-of-the-world flavor, you'll be more than content here. On a remote cove at the end of a road near Newfoundland's northernmost point (you can see Labrador across the straits), the Tickle Inn occupies a solid fisherman's home built around 1890 by the great-grandfather of current innkeeper David Adams. (He's a retired school counselor from St. John's.) After lapsing into decrepitude, it was expertly restored in 1990 and has recaptured much of the charm of a Victorian outport home. The guest rooms are small but comfortable and share two washrooms. Before dinner, guests often gather in the parlor and enjoy snacks and complimentary cocktails. One of the highlights of a stay here is exploring the small but superb network of hiking trails maintained by Adams, which ascend open bluffs to beautiful views of the Labrador Straits. Meals are served family-style at 7:30pm each evening. (Your only other option for a meal is to drive a considerable distance to the nearest restaurant.) The food is excellent, featuring local cuisine. You might have Cape Onion soup with a touch of Newman's port or Polaris paella with squid, scallops, and shrimp. Time your visit for berry season and you can expect such delights as northern berry flan for dessert.

5 Terra Nova National Park

Terra Nova National Park is an exceedingly pleasant spot with lots of boreal forest and quiet ocean landscapes along inlets, along with a surplus of low rolling hills. Within its boundaries, forest and shoreline are preserved for wildlife and recreation, and they make for excellent exploration. Activities and facilities here have mostly been designed with families in mind. There's always something going on, from playing with starfish at the interpretation center to games and movies at the main campground. The park has a junior naturalist program, many of the hikes are just the right length for younger kids, and there's a fine (and relatively warm) swimming area at Sandy Pond.

If your goal is to put some distance between yourself and the noisy masses, plan to head into the backcountry. A number of campsites are accessible by foot, canoe, or ferry. Out here, you'll be able to scout for bald eagles and shooting stars in silence.

ESSENTIALS

GETTING THERE   Terra Nova is on the Trans-Canada Highway, about 240km (149 miles) from St. John's and 630km (391 miles) from Port aux Basques.

VISITOR INFORMATION   Try the modern **Marine Interpretation Centre** at the Saltons Day-Use Area (☎ **709/533-2801**), about 5km (3.1 miles) north of the Newman Sound Campground. June to mid-October, it's open daily 9am to 9pm (limited hours after Labour Day).

FEES   A park entry fee is required of all visitors, even those just overnighting at a park campground. Fees are C$3.25 (US$2.15) adults, C$2.50 (US$1.65) seniors, C$1.75 (US$1.15) children 6 to 16, and C$7 (US$4.35) families. Four-day passes are available in all categories for the price of 3 days. Fees may be paid at the Marine Interpretation Centre.

EXPLORING THE PARK

Begin with a visit to the spiffy **Marine Interpretation Centre** (above). It's on a scenic part of the sound, encased in verdant hills, and from here the sound looks suspiciously like a lake. Oceangoing sailboats tied up at the wharf will suggest otherwise, however. The center has a handful of exhibits focusing on local marine life, many geared toward kids. There's a touch tank where you can reach in and scoop up starfish and other aquatic denizens, as well as displays on life underwater. Especially nifty is an underwater video monitor, where you can check out the action under the adjacent wharf with a joystick and zoom controls. There's also a Wet Lab, where you can conduct your own experiments under the guidance of a park naturalist. The center is free with your paid park admission. You'll also find a snack bar and gift shop.

The park has 80km (50 miles) of maintained **hiking trails.** Many of these are fairly easy treks of an hour or so through undemanding woodlands. The booklet you'll receive when you pay your entrance fee describes the various treks. Among the more popular is the 4.5km (2.8-mile) **Coastal Trail,** running between Newman Sound Campground and the Marine Interpretation Centre. You'll get great views of the sound, and en route you'll pass the wonderfully named Pissing Mare Falls. The most demanding is the **Outport Trail,** a 50km (31-mile) loop currently under development that winds in and around the south shore of Newman Sound past abandoned settlements. It's possible to overnight at two backcountry sites. The whole trip typically takes 3 days, with the going often slowed by bogs and rough, wet trail sections.

The park also lends itself quite nicely to **sea kayaking.** If you've brought your own boat, ask for route suggestions at the information center. (Overnight trips to Minchin and South Broad coves are good options, as are day trips to Swale Island.) If you're a paddling novice, sign up with **Terra Nova Adventure Tours** (☎ **709/256-8687**), at the Marine Interpretation Centre. The crew leads guided tours of the sound three times daily, when you're likely to spot eagles and maybe even a whale. The tours last 2 to 3 hours and cost C$45 (US$30) adults and C$35 (US$23) youths. Reservations aren't required but are often helpful.

For a more passive view from the water, consider a tour with **Ocean Watch Tours** (☎ 709/533-6024), which sails in a converted fishing boat four times daily from the wharf at the Marine Interpretation Centre. You're all but certain to see bald eagles and old outports and, with some luck, whales and icebergs. Two-hour tours are C$25 (US$17) and 3-hour tours C$30 (US$20).

WHERE TO STAY & DINE

Campgrounds are the only option within the park itself. Terra Nova's main campground is at **Newman Sound,** with 417 campsites (mostly of the gravel-pad variety) set in and around spruce forest and sheep laurel clearings. The lengthy amenities list includes free showers, limited electrical hookups, a grocery store and snack bar, evening programs, a Laundromat, and hiking trails. Be aware that the campgrounds can be quite noisy and bustling in peak season. Camping fees are C$12 to C$17 (US$8 to US$11).

At the north end of the park, the town of Eastport is 16km (9.9 miles) from the Trans-Canada Highway on Route 310 and offers several places to overnight. Try **Laurel Cottage Bed & Breakfast,** 41 Bank Rd., Eastport, NF A0G 1Z0 (☎ 888/677-3138 or 709/677-3138), with three bedrooms (C$52 to C$65/US$35 to US$43 double) in a 1926 bungalow tucked off the main road with ocean views. Right on a sandy beach are **Seaview Cottages,** 325 Beach Rd., Eastport, NF A0G 1Z0 (☎ 709/677-2271), with 23 basic cottages (C$45 to C$55/US$30 to US$37 double) and a small indoor heated pool.

At the southern edge of the park you'll find the following.

Terra Nova Park Lodge. Rte. 1, Port Blandford, NF A0C 2G0. ☎ **709/543-2525.** Fax 709/543-2201. www.terranovagolf.com. E-mail info@terranovagolf.com. 82 units. A/C TV TEL. C$94–C$102 (US$63–US$68) double; C$124–C$199 (US$83–US$133) suite. AE, DC, DISC, MC, V.

This modern three-story resort is a short drive off Route 1 about 2km (1.2 miles) south of the park's southern entrance. Most notably, it's adjacent to the 6,500-yard Twin River Golf Course, one of Atlantic Canada's more scenic and better regarded links. The hotel isn't lavish and lacks a certain personality. It feels rather inexpensively built (pray you don't have heavy-footed children staying overhead) and features bland cookie-cutter rooms. On the other hand, it's clean, comfortable, and well located for a golfing holiday or exploring the park. It's a popular spot with families, since kids can roam the grounds, splash around the pool, and congregate at the downstairs video games.

Dining: The Clode Sound Dining Room is open daily for all meals. It offers standard resort fare with an emphasis on chicken and beef with some seafood; dinners include fried cod, filet mignon, pork chops and applesauce, and surf and turf. Dinner entrees are C$10 to C$21 (US$7 to US$14). Mulligan's Pub is downstairs.

Amenities: Free laundry; pro shop, driving range, minigolf, gift shop; heated outdoor pool, fitness room, sauna, Jacuzzi, two tennis courts, game room.

6 The Bonavista Peninsula: Into Newfoundland's Past

The ✪ **Bonavista Peninsula** juts northeast into the sea from just south of Terra Nova National Park. It's a worthy side trip for travelers fascinated by the island's past. You'll find a historic village, a wonderfully curated historic site, and one of the province's most intriguing lighthouses. It's also a good spot for scouting for whales, puffins, and icebergs.

Along the south shore of the peninsula is **Trinity,** an impeccably maintained old village. (It's the only village in Newfoundland where the historic society has say over what can and can't be built.) Some longtime visitors grouse that it's becoming overly popular and a bit dandified with too many B&Bs and traffic restrictions. That might be. But there's still a palpable sense of history to this profoundly historic spot. And anyway, it's the region's only destination to find good shelter and a decent meal.

From Trinity it's about 40km (25 miles) out to the tip of the peninsula. Somewhere along the route, which isn't always picturesque, you'll wonder whether it's worth it. Yes, it is. Keep going. Plan to spend at least a couple of hours exploring the dramatic ocean-carved point and the fine fishing village of **Bonavista** with its three excellent historic properties.

ESSENTIALS

GETTING THERE You can reach the Bonavista Peninsula from the Trans-Canada Highway via—depending on the direction you're coming from—Route 233, Route 230, or Route 230A. Route 230 runs all the way to the tip of the cape; Route 235 forms a partial loop back and offers some splendid water views along the way. The round-trip from Clarenville to the tip is about 240km (149 miles).

VISITOR INFORMATION The **Southern Bonavista Bay Tourist Chalet** is on Route 230 just west of the intersection with Route 235 (☎ **709/545-2130**). Summer hours are daily 8:30am to 8:30pm.

TRINITY

The tiny coastal hamlet of **Trinity,** with a year-round population of just 200, once had more residents than St. John's. For more than 3 centuries, from its first visit by Portuguese fishermen in the 1500s until well into the 19th century, Trinity benefited from a long and steady tenure as a hub for traders, primarily from England, who supplied the booming fishing economy of Trinity Bay and eastern Newfoundland.

Technological advances (including the railroad) doomed Trinity's merchant class, and the town lapsed into an extended economic slumber. But even today, you can see lingering traces of the town's former affluence, from the attractive flourishes in much of the architecture to the rows of white picket fences all around the village (no rustic quiggly fences for Trinity). In recent years the provincial government and concerned individuals have taken a keen interest in preserving Trinity, and it's clearly benefiting from a revival in which many homes have been preserved and a good number made into B&Bs. Several buildings are open to the public as provincial historic sites, and two others as local historical museums. Most are open mid-June to early October, then shuttered the remainder of the year. Allow about 3 hours to wander about and explore.

Days on which the popular historic pageant are held (see below) bring a flood tide of visitors to Trinity, making parking and rooms scarce and meals sometimes difficult to obtain. If you opt not to see the pageant, try to plan a visit here on one of the off days, when a great quiet settles on the village.

Start your adventure into history at the **Trinity Interpretation Center** in the Tibbs House (☎ **709/464-2042**), open daily 10am to 5:30pm. It's a bit tricky to find, since signs don't seem a priority. Follow the one-way road around the village and continue straight past the parish hall. Look on the left for the pale-green home with the prominent gable. Here you can pick up a walking-tour map and get oriented with a handful of history exhibits. Several ticket options exist: If you want to visit just one or two places, individual tickets are C$2 (US$1.35) or C$2.50 (US$1.65). For a full day, the better bet is the C$6 (US$3.65) ticket, admitting you to six buildings. Most maintain the same hours as the interpretation center.

A minute's walk away is the **Lester-Garland Premises,** where you can learn about the traders and their times. This handsome Georgian-style brick building is a convincing 1997 replica of one of the earlier structures, built in 1819. The original was occupied until 1847, when it was abandoned and began to deteriorate. It was torn down (much to the horror of local historians) in the 1960s, but parts of the building hardware, including some doors and windows, were salvaged and warehoused until the rebuilding. Next door is the **Ryan Building,** where a succession of the town's most prominent merchants kept shop. The grassy lots between these buildings and the water were once filled with warehouses, none of which has survived. The new Rising Tide Theatre (below) approximates one of the warehouses; a good imagination is helpful in envisioning the others.

A short walk away, just past the parish house, is the **Hiscock House,** a handsome home where Emma Hiscock raised her children and kept a shop after the untimely death of her husband in a boating accident at age 39. The home has been restored to appear as it might have been in 1910, and helpful guides fill in the details. The **Trinity Museum** on Church Road (☎ **709/464-3720**) contains a selection of everyday artifacts you might have seen in Trinity a century or more ago; the nearby **Green Family Forge Blacksmith Museum** will leave you well informed about one of the essential local industries.

An entertaining way to learn about the village's history is through the **Trinity Pageant** (☎ **888/464-1100** or 709/464-3232). On Wednesdays, Saturdays, and Sundays at 2pm, actors lead a peripatetic audience through the streets, acting out episodes from Trinity's past. Tickets are C$6 (US$4), with children under 12 free. In the evenings, the innovative **Rising Tide Theatre** (same phone as the pageant) offers a number of performances in summer, most depicting island episodes or themes. In the past, the cast staged their shows at impromptu venues around town. In 2000, they opened a 255-seat theater in a newly constructed building architecturally styled after a historic waterfront warehouse. The performances are top rate and well worth the C$12 to C$20 (US$8 to US$13).

WHERE TO STAY

All properties below are in the heart of Trinity's historic area. Reservations are essential during the peak summer season, especially on days when the pageant is scheduled. Those who come unprepared risk a drive to Clarenville to secure a room.

✪ **Campbell House.** High St., Trinity, Trinity Bay, NF A0C 2S0. ☎ **877/464-7700** or 709/464-3377. www.campbellhouse.nf.ca. 4 units. TEL. C$95 (US$63) double; C$225 (US$150) 2-bedroom suite (up to 4 people). Rates include full breakfast. AE, DC, ER, MC, V. Closed mid-Oct to late May.

This handsome 1840 home and two nearby cottages are set amid lovely gardens on a twisting lane overlooking Fisher Cove. Two rooms are on the second floor of the main house, and these have a nice historic flair, even to the point that they'll require some stooping under beams if you're over 5 feet 10 inches. Two guest rooms are in the lovely pine-paneled Gover House just beyond the gardens, and they feature an adjacent waterfront deck and a full kitchen on the first floor. Innkeeper Tineke Gow recently added a third property on Fisher Cove—the Kelly House, from the 1940s. The cottages are rented to just one party at a time, who can use one, two, or three bedrooms (priced accordingly).

Hangashore Bed & Breakfast. 1 Ash's Lane, Trinity, Trinity Bay, NF A0C 2S0. ☎ **709/ 464-3807,** or 709/754-7324 off-season. 3 units, none with bathroom. C$55–C$75 (US$37– US$50) double. Rates include full breakfast. AE, MC, V. Closed Nov–May. Pets allowed.

The Hangashore is owned by the same folks who run the always-cordial Monkstown Manor in St. John's. This is a place for travelers who are happy to trade space for conviviality. The guest rooms in this 1860 home are cozy (read: tiny), just as they would have been in 1860. But they're utterly uncluttered in a modern Scandinavian sort of way and painted with bold, welcoming colors. There's a parlor with a TV and phone downstairs, and relaxed breakfasts are served around a pine picnic-style table in a cheerful room.

Village Inn. Taverner's Path (P.O. Box 10), Trinity, Trinity Bay, NF A0C 2S0. ☎ **709/ 464-3269.** Fax 709/464-3700. www.oceancontact.com. E-mail beamish@nf.sympatico.ca. 8 units. C$52–C$72 (US$35–US$48) double. MC, V. Open by advance arrangement Nov–Apr. "Small, well-behaved pets" allowed.

The guest rooms in this handsome old inn, on what passes for a busy street in Trinity (busy with pedestrians, that is), have a pleasantly lived-in feel, with eclectic but leaning-toward-Victorian furniture; the small dining room feels as if it hasn't changed a whit in 75 years. Innkeepers Christine and Peter Beamish do a fine job of making guests feel at home; they also run **Ocean Contact,** a whale-watch operation that uses a 26-foot rigid-hull inflatable. Ask about tour availability when you book your room. For details on the inn's restaurant, see below.

WHERE TO DINE

Eriksen Premises. West St. ☎ **709/464-3698.** Reservations advisable in peak season. Main courses C$4.95–C$7 (US$3.30–US$4.65) at lunch, C$10–C$19 (US$7–US$13) at dinner. MC, V. Daily 8am–9:30pm. Closed Nov to mid-May. TRADITIONAL.

Despite some inelegant touches (like butter served in those pesky plastic tubs with the peel-off tops), this is Trinity's best restaurant, and it offers good value. The restaurant shares the first floor of a B&B with a gift shop and provides a homey feel with oak floors, a beadboard ceiling, and Victorian accents. (There's also dining on an outside deck, which is especially inviting at lunchtime.) The meals are mostly traditional: cod tongue, broiled halibut, scallops, liver and onion, and chicken. The service and the food quality are consistently a notch above the expected. The desserts—especially the cheesecake with fresh berry toppings—are especially good.

Village Inn. Taverner's Path. ☎ **709/464-3269.** Main courses C$7–C$17 (US$4.65– US$11). MC, V. Daily 8am–9pm. TRADITIONAL/VEGETARIAN.

The pleasantly old-fashioned dining room at the Village Inn has a good local reputation for its vegetarian meals (something of a rarity in Newfoundland), with options including a lentil shepherd's pie and rice-and-nut casserole. But those looking for comfort food are also well served, with options like meat loaf, fried cod, liver and onions, and a ham plate. This is country cooking at its finest; everything is made from scratch, from soups to dessert.

BONAVISTA

Bonavista is a 45-minute drive from Trinity and is a strongly recommended day trip for those spending a night or two in the area.

The ✪ **Ryan Premises National Historic Site** (☎ 709/468-1600) opened in 1997 with Queen Elizabeth herself presiding over the ceremonies. Located in downtown Bonavista, the new site is an exceedingly photogenic compound of white clapboard buildings at the harbor's edge. For more than a century, this was the town's most prominent salt-fish complex, where fishermen sold their catch and bought all the sundry goods needed to keep an outport functioning. Michael Ryan opened for business here in 1857; his heirs kept the business going until 1978. (One elderly resident recalled that you could "get everything from a baby's fart to a clap of thunder" from the Ryans.) The complex today features an art gallery, a local history museum, a gift shop, a handcrafted furniture store, and what may be the most rare and extraordinary of all—a truly fascinating exhibit on the role of the codfish industry in Newfoundland's history. An hour or two here will greatly abet you in making sense of the rest of your visit to the island. Mid-June to mid-October, the property is open daily 10am to 6pm. Admission is C$3 (US$2) adults, C$2.25 (US$1.50) seniors, C$1.50 (US$1) youths, and C$7 (US$4.35) families.

On the far side of the harbor, across from a field of magnificent irises, is the beautiful **Mockbeggar Property** (☎ 709/729-2460). Named after an English seaport that shared characteristics with Bonavista, the home was occupied by prominent Newfoundland politician F. Gordon Bradley. It has been restored to how it appeared when Bradley moved here in 1940 and features much of the original furniture. With a few telltale exceptions (note the wonderful 1940s-era carpet in the formal dining room), it shows a strong Victorian influence. The house is managed as a provincial historic site, and admission is C$2.50 (US$1.65) adults, with children under 12 free (also includes admission to the Cape Bonavista Lighthouse, below). Summer, it's open daily 10am to 5:30pm.

Slated to open at Bonavista's harbor in 2000 is a replica of the *Mathew* (☎ 709/468-1493), the ship John Cabot sailed when he first landed in Newfoundland in 1497. This compact ship is an exact replica, based on plans of the original (don't confuse this ship with the other *Mathew* replica, which crossed the Atlantic and sailed around Newfoundland in 1997). It's designed as a floating museum and will look roughly as it did 500 years ago. An interpretive center and occasional performances staged wharfside will provide context for your tour aboard the ship. Because it's an exact replica, the ship doesn't have an engine or any modern safety devices, and thus isn't allowed to leave the dock for passenger cruises. It'll stay tied up along the dock in summer and be stored in an architecturally striking white-clapboard boat house in the off-season. Mid-June to early September, the ship is open daily 10am to 6pm. The costs of tours at press time were C$2 (US$1.35) adults and C$1 (US65¢) children/seniors, with rates subject to change.

The extraordinary ✪ **Cape Bonavista Lighthouse** is 6km (3.7 miles) north of town on a rugged point. This 1843 lighthouse is fundamentally a stone tower around which a red-and-white wood-frame house has been built. The keepers' quarters (the light keeper and his assistant both lived here) have been restored to the year 1870. You can clamber up the narrow stairs to the light itself and inspect the ingenious clockwork mechanism that kept six lanterns revolving all night long between 1895 and 1962. (With some help—it took 15 minutes to wind the counterweight by hand, a job that had to be performed every 2 hours.) This light served mariners until 3 decades ago, when its role was usurped by an inelegant steel tower and beacon. Summer, it's open daily 10:30am to 5:30pm; admission is C$2.50 (US$1.65) adults, with children under 12 free (also includes admission to Mockbeggar Property, above).

Below the lighthouse on a rocky promontory cleft from the mainland is a lively **puffin colony.** Dozens of these stumpy, colorful birds hop around the grassy knob and take flight into the sea winds. They're easily seen from just below the lighthouse; bring binoculars for a clearer view. Red-footed common murres dive for fish below, and whales are often sighted just offshore. This is the only place I've ever had whales and puffins in sight through my binoculars at the same time. And there was a beautiful iceberg just off to my left.

7 St. John's: Bright Lights, Big City

St. John's is a world apart from the rest of Newfoundland. The island's small outports and long roads through spruce and bog are imbued with a deep melancholy. St. John's, on the other hand, is vibrant and bustling. Coming into the city after traveling the hinterlands is like stepping from Kansas into Oz—the landscape seems to suddenly burst with color and life.

This attractive port city of just over 100,000 residents crowds the steep hills around a deep harbor. Like Halifax, Nova Scotia, and Saint John, New Brunswick, St. John's serves as a magnet for youth culture in the province, and the clubs and restaurants tend to have a more cosmopolitan feel and a sharper edge. St. John's harbor is impressive, protected from the open seas by stony hills and accessible only through a pinched gap called The Narrows, a rocky defile of the sort you'd expect to see Hercules astraddle. The Narrows is at the north end of the harbor and hidden from view from much of downtown, so first-timers may think they've stumbled on a small lake—albeit one with tankers and other oceangoing ships.

This is very much a working harbor, the hub of much of the province's commerce, so don't expect quaint. Across the way are charmless oil-tank farms, along with offloading facilities for tankers. A major containership wharf occupies the head of the harbor. Along the water's edge on Harbour Street downtown, you'll usually find hulking ships tied up; pedestrians are welcome to stroll and gawk, but wholesale commerce is the focus here, not boutiques.

ESSENTIALS

GETTING THERE   St. John's is 131km (81 miles) from the ferry at Argentia, 905km (561 miles) from Port aux Basques. The **St. John's International Airport** offers flights to Halifax, Montréal, Ottawa, Toronto, and London, England. See page 154 for ferry and airline information. The airport is 6km (3.7 miles) from downtown; taxis from the airport to downtown hotels are about C$12 (US$8) for one traveler and C$2 (US$1.35) for each extra traveler.

VISITOR INFORMATION   In summer, you can get visitor info at the **Tourist Information Rail Car** on Harbour Drive (☎ 709/576-8514), along the waterfront. Summer hours are daily 9am to 5pm. Off-season, look for information at **City Hall** on New Gower Street (☎ 709/576-8106). The e-mail address is tourism@city.st-johns.nf.ca.

GETTING AROUND   **Metrobus** serves much of the city, costing C$1.50 (US$1) for a single trip. Route information is available at the visitor center or by phone at ☎ 709/722-9400. Taxis are plentiful around St. John's, and they charge an initial fee of C$2 (US$1.35) plus C$2 (US$1.35) each additional mile. One of the larger and more dependable outfits in the city is **Bugden Taxi** at ☎ 709/726-4400.

EVENTS   The annual ✪ **Newfoundland and Labrador Folk Festival** will celebrate its 25th year in 2001. The 3-day festival is held over a weekend in early August and includes performers from all over the province, who gather to play at Bannerman Park in downtown St. John's. (Bring a lawn chair.) Even after all these years, tickets are still very affordable (in 1999 it cost just C$5/US$3.35 for an afternoon slate of performers, C$7/US$4.65 for the evening). For details, contact St. John's tourism office at ☎ 709/576-8514.

EXPLORING ST. JOHN'S

The city produces a free 40-page pocket-sized brochure, *Exploring the City of Legends: Your Guide to Walking Tours and Auto Tours of St. John's.* It's a good resource for launching your visit. Ask for it at the Tourist Information Rail Car (above).

DOWNTOWN

Newfoundland Museum. 285 Duckworth St. ☎ **709/729-2329.** C$3 (US$2) adults, C$2.50 (US$1.65) seniors/students; under 18 free. Summer daily 9:30am–4:45pm; closed Mon off-season.

This compact downtown museum offers a good introduction to the island's natural and cultural history. On the first floor you'll learn about the flora and fauna and find out that the moose wasn't native to Newfoundland but was introduced (twice, actually, once unsuccessfully). The second floor concentrates on the various native cultures, from Beothuk through Inuit (look for the delicate carvings of bear heads). The more sparsely exhibited third floor suggests how 19th-century life was lived in Newfoundland's outports. Allow about an hour for a leisurely tour.

✪ **Signal Hill.** Atop Signal Hill at the entrance to St. John's harbor. ☎ **709/772-5367.** Free admission to grounds; admission to interpretive center C$2.50 (US$1.65) adults, C$2 (US$1.35) seniors, C$1.50 (US$1) children 6–16, C$6 (US$4) families. Open daylight hours.

You'll come for the history but stay for the views. Signal Hill is St. John's most worthy attraction. The rugged barren hill is the city's preeminent landmark, rising up over the entrance to the harbor and topped by a craggy castle with a flag fluttering high overhead (that's the signal of the name). The layers of history here are rich and complex—flags have flown atop this hill since 1704, and over the centuries a succession of military fortifications occupied these strategic slopes, as did three different hospitals. The "castle" (Cabot Tower) dates from 1897, built in honor of Queen Victoria's Diamond Jubilee and the 400th anniversary of John Cabot's arrival in the new world. The hill also secured a spot in history in 1901, when Nobel laureate Guglielmo Marconi received the first wireless transatlantic broadcast—three short dots indicating the letter *S* in Morse code, sent from Cornwall, England—on an antennae raised 400 feet on a kite in powerful winds.

A good place to start a tour is at the interpretive center, where you'll get a good briefing about the hill's history. Wednesday and Thursday at 7pm and Saturday and Sunday at 3 and 7pm, military drills and cannon firings take place in the field next to the center. From here, you can follow serpentine trails up the hill to the Cabot Tower, where you'll be rewarded with breathtaking views of the Narrows and the open ocean beyond. You can see Cape Spear in the distance to the south. Look for icebergs in the early summer and whales anytime. Interpretive placards, scattered about the summit, feature engaging photos from various epochs.

FARTHER AFIELD

Quidi Vidi (pronounced "kitty vitty") is a tiny harbor village that sets new standards for the definition of *quaint.* The village is tucked in a rocky defile behind Signal Hill, where a narrow ocean inlet provides access to the sea. It's photogenic in the extreme, a wonderful spot to investigate by foot or bike (it's rather more difficult by car). The village consists mostly of compact homes, including the oldest home in St. John's, with very few shops. Visit here while you can—in late 1999, development plans had been approved following rancorous local debate calling for the addition of modern housing in the area, which many fear will start to erode the timeless quality of the place. To get to Quidi Vidi, follow Signal Hill Road to Quidi Vidi Road; turn right onto Forest Road.

St. John's

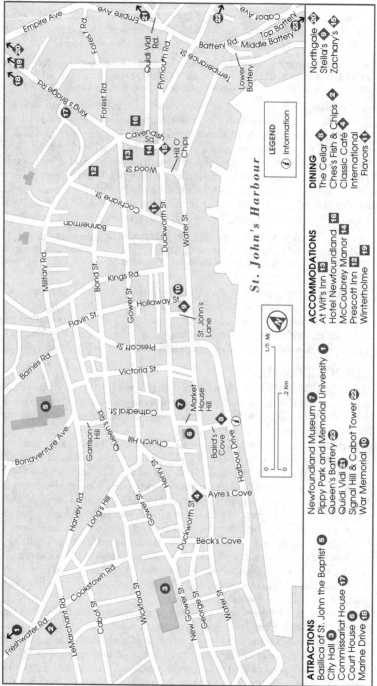

St. John's Harbour

LEGEND
ⓘ Information

ATTRACTIONS
Basilica of St. John the Baptist ⑤
City Hall ③
Commissariat House ⑰
Court House ⑥
Marine Drive ⑱
Newfoundland Museum ⑦
Pippy Park and Memorial University ①
Queen's Battery ㉓
Quidi Vidi ㉑
Signal Hill & Cabot Tower ㉒
War Memorial ⑩

ACCOMMODATIONS
At Wit's Inn ⑬
Hotel Newfoundland ⑯
McCoubrey Manor ⑭
Prescott Inn ⑫
Winterholme ⑲

DINING
The Cellar ⑧
Ches's Fish & Chips ②
Classic Café ④
International Flavors ⑪
Northgale ㉖
Stella's ⑨
Zachary's ⑮

From here you can easily connect to **Quidi Vidi Lake,** where St. John's Regatta is held the first Wednesday in August, as it has been since 1826. Look for the trail leading to the lake from near the entrance to Quidi Vidi, or ask locally.

Memorial University Botanical Garden at Oxen Pond. Mt. Scio Rd. ☎ **709/ 737-8590.** Admission C$2 (US$1.35) adults, C$1 (US65¢) seniors/children 5–17. May–Nov daily 10am–5pm. Drive on Thorburn Rd. past Avalon Mall, turn right on Mt. Scio Rd.

An abundant selection of northern plants makes this garden well worth seeking out (it's over a wooded ridge on the city's western edge, behind Pippy Park). The main plots are arranged in gracious "theme gardens," including a cottage garden, a rock garden, and a peat garden. Among the most interesting is the Newfoundland Heritage Garden, with examples of 70 types of perennials traditionally found in island gardens. The floral displays aren't as ostentatious or exuberant as you'll find in other public gardens in Atlantic Canada (the gardens of Halifax and Annapolis Royal come to mind), but they'll be of great interest to amateur horticulturists curious about boreal plants. Behind the gardens are winding hiking trails leading down to marshy Oxen Pond.

Fluvarium. Pippy Park, off Allandale Rd. ☎ **709/754-3474.** Admission C$4 (US$2.65) adults, C$3.25 (US$2.15) seniors/students, C$2.25 (US$1.50) children. Summer daily 10am–6pm; limited hours and days off-season. Guided tours on the half hour; feeding time 4pm.

This low octagonal structure at the edge of Long Pond (near the University) actually descends three stories into the earth. The second level features exhibits on river ecology, including life in the riffles (that's where trout spawn) and in shallow pools, which are rich with nutrients. On the lowest level you'll find yourself looking up into a deep pool alongside the building. Watch for brown trout swimming lazily by.

OUTDOOR PURSUITS

Pippy Park (☎ 709/737-3655) is on the city's hilly western side adjacent to the university and contains 3,350 acres of developed recreation land and quiet trails. The popular park is home to the city campground and Fluvarium (above), as well as miniature golf, picnic sites, and playgrounds.

One highly recommended hike is the ✪ **North Head Trail,** running from Signal Hill to an improbable cluster of small buildings between rock face and water called The Battery. You should be reasonably fit and unafraid of heights; allow about 2 hours, assuming departure and return from near the Hotel Newfoundland. On foot, follow Duckworth Street between the hotel and Devon House, then bear right on Battery Road. Stay on the main branch (a few smaller branches may confuse you) as it narrows and then rises and falls while skirting a rock face to the Outer Battery. The former fishermen's homes at the Battery are literally inches from the road and not much farther from the water, and most have drop-dead views of the Narrows and the city skyline. There's a whimsical, storybook character to the place, and the real estate is now much sought after by city residents. When homes come on the market, they're snatched up quickly, and usually at a premium.

At the end of the Battery you'll cross right over someone's front porch (it's okay), and then the North Head Trail begins in earnest. It runs along the Narrows, past old gun emplacements, up and down heroic sets of steps, and along some narrow ledges (chains are bolted to rock as handrails for a little extra security in one spot). The trail then ascends an open headland before looping back and starting the final ascent up Signal Hill. After some time exploring here and soaking up the view, you can walk on the paved road back down Signal Hill to Duckworth Street.

WHERE TO STAY
EXPENSIVE

✪ **Hotel Newfoundland.** Cavendish Square (P.O. Box 5637), St. John's, NF A1C 5W8.
☎ **800/441-1414** or 709/726-4980. Fax 709/726-2025. 301 units. A/C MINIBAR
TV TEL. Weekends C$110–C$190 (US$73–US$127) double; midweek C$129–C$252
(US$86–US$168) double. AE, DC, DISC, MC, V. Pets C$20 (US$13).

The 1982 Newfoundland was built in a starkly modern style but boasts a refined sensibility and attention to detail reminiscent of a lost era. What I like most about the hotel is how the designers and architects hid their best surprises. The lobby has one of the city's best views of the Narrows, but you have to wander around to find it. It's a wonderful effect used nicely throughout. (This helps compensate for the somewhat-generic conference-hotel feel of much of the decor.) The guest rooms themselves are standard sized and nothing remarkable, though all have ironing boards, coffeemakers, and bathrobes. About half have harbor views.

Dining/Diversions: The rather-formal Cabot Club ranks among the best restaurants in the city and is known for tableside Caesar salads for two, caribou soup, and entrees like traditional pan-fried cod and halibut with saffron-truffle butter. Dinner entrees run C$23 to C$40 (US$15 to US$27). The colorful Mediterranean-inspired Bonavista Cafe, new in 1999, is lighter on the wallet, with lunch offerings like burgers and generous sandwiches (C$6 to C$9/US$4 to US$6) and dinners like Greek lamb chops, vegetable fettuccine, and poached salmon (C$10 to C$19/US$7 to US$13). The Narrows lounge is the spot for a nightcap.

Amenities: Concierge, 24-hour room service, safe-deposit boxes, baby-sitting, dry cleaning/laundry; indoor pool, fitness room (with computerized golf-course simulator), Jacuzzi, sauna, business center, beauty salon, art gallery.

Winterholme. 79 Rennies Mill Rd., St. John's, NF A1C 3R1. ☎ **800/599-7829** or 709/739-7979. Fax 709/753-9411. E-mail winterholme@nf.sympatico.ca. 11 units. TV TEL. C$99–C$179 (US$66–US$119). AE, DC, ER, MC, V.

This handsome Victorian mansion was built in 1905 for C$120,000 (US$80,000) when C$120,000 was more than chump change. It's as architecturally distinctive a place as you'll find in Newfoundland, with prominent turrets, bowfront windows, bold pediments, elaborate molded plaster ceilings, and woodwork extravagant enough to stop you in your tracks. (The oak woodwork was actually carved in England and shipped here for installation.) Room no. 7 is one of the most lavish I've seen; the former billiards room features a fireplace and two-person Jacuzzi, along with a plasterwork ceiling and a supple leather wing chair. Room no. 1 is oval and occupies one of the turrets; it also has a Jacuzzi. The attic rooms are less extraordinary but still appealing with their odd angles and nice touches. The mansion is a 10-minute walk from downtown.

MODERATE

✪ **At Wit's Inn.** 3 Gower St., St. John's, NF A1C 1M9. ☎ **877/739-7420** or 709/739-7420. Fax 709/576-3641. E-mail sleepongower@roadrunner.nf.net. 4 units. TV. C$79–C$99 (US$53–US$66) double. Rates include full breakfast. AE, MC, V.

Forgive the innkeepers their pun. This lovely century-old home was wonderfully restored and opened as an inn in 1999 by a former Toronto restaurateur. It'll appeal to anyone who loathes the "kountry klutter" found in places striving too hard for a personality. Decorated with a sure eye to bold color and simple style, this is a welcoming urban oasis around the corner from the Hotel Newfoundland. The guest rooms aren't all that spacious but aren't all that small, and each is nicely furnished with down duvets and VCRs. (The largest room is on the top floor, requiring a bit of a hike.) The beautifully refinished floors and elaborately carved banister are notable, as are many of the old fixtures (like the servant's intercom) that have been left in place. A full breakfast is served in the dining room, wine and cheese are offered in the late afternoon, and there's a butler's pantry for snacking in between times.

McCoubrey Manor. 8 Ordnance St., St. John's, NF A1C 3K7. ☎ **888/753-7577** or 709/722-7577. Fax 709/579-7577. www.wordplay.com/mccoubrey. E-mail mccmanor@nfld.com. 6 units. TV TEL. C$89–C$149 (US$59–US$99) double; C$109 (US$73) apt. for 2 (extra person C$10/US$7). Rates include continental breakfast. AE, DC, MC, V.

McCoubrey Manor offers the convenient location of the Newfoundland (across the street), but with Victorian charm and a more casual B&B atmosphere. The pair of adjoining 1904 town houses is decorated in what might be called a "contemporary Victorian" style that's quite inviting. The upstairs rooms have private double Jacuzzis; room no. 1 is the brightest and faces the street. Room no. 2 has a sunken Jacuzzi, a mantled oak fireplace, and lustrous trim of British Columbia fir. Around the corner are two spacious two-bedroom apartments with full kitchens. What they lack in elegance they make up for in space; families take note. There's also a washer and dryer for guests (C$10/US$7 extra). Kids older than toddler age are welcome.

Prescott Inn. 19 Military Rd. (P.O. Box 204), St. John's, NF A1C 2C3. ☎ **709/753-7733.** Fax 709/753-6036. E-mail jpeters@nfld.com. 16 units, 9 with bathroom; 7 units at The Battery with kitchen and bathroom. TV TEL. C$50–C$105 (US$33–US$70) double. Rates include full breakfast. AE, DC, MC, V. Pets allowed.

The Prescott is composed of an unusually attractive grouping of wood-frame town houses painted a vibrant lavender-blue. Some of the historical detailing has been restored inside, but mostly the homes have been modernized. Some guest rooms have carpeting; others have hardwood floors. All are furnished with eclectic antiques that rise above flea-market quality but aren't quite collectibles. The lower-priced rooms share bathrooms and are among the city's better bargains. All guests are welcome to relax on the shared balcony that runs along the back of the building. Room no. 3 might be the best of the bunch, and it's the only one with a private Jacuzzi. If you're looking for great views, ask about the suites scattered about several cottages at The Battery, a small village hugging rocky cliffs on the harbor and within city limits.

WHERE TO DINE

A locally popular spot is **Ches's Fish and Chips,** 8 Freshwater Rd. (☎ 709/722-4083), which has been serving up pleasingly unhealthy portions of fish-and-chips at this location since 1958. There are also chicken wings and burgers. It's open Sunday to Thursday 9am to 2am (to 3am Fri and Sat). Ches's will also deliver, so call ☎ **709/726-3434.**

EXPENSIVE

The Cellar. Baird's Cove (near the waterfront, just downhill from the Supreme Court building). ☎ **709/579-8900.** Reservations suggested. Main courses C$8–C$15 (US$5–US$10) at lunch, C$15–C$29 (US$10–US$19) at dinner. AE, DC, DISC, ER, MC, V. Mon–Fri 11:30am–2:30pm and 5:30–9:30pm (to 10:30pm Fri), Sat 5:30–10:30pm, Sun 5:30–9:30pm. ECLECTIC.

The classy interior is a surprise here—the restaurant is on a nondescript street and through a nondescript entrance. It's intimate and warm, not unlike an upper-crust gentleman's club. The kitchen has been turning out fine meals for some time now, developing a reputation for creativity and consistency. The menu is constantly in play, but look for reliable standbys like the delicious gravlax and the homemade bread and pastas. Fish is prepared especially well, with some cuts paired with innovative flavors like ginger-and pear butter. Lunches are the better bargain, with tasty offerings like baked brie in phyllo with red currant/pineapple chutney, or scallop crêpes with bacon, leeks, and Swiss cheese.

✪ **Northgale.** 8 Kenna's Hill. ☎ **709/753-2425.** Reservations suggested. Main courses C$9–C$18 (US$6–US$12) at lunch, C$18–C$29 (US$12–US$19) at dinner. AE, ER, MC, V. Mon–Fri 11:30am–2pm; daily 5:30–10pm. Drive north on King's Bridge Rd. to Kenna's Hill. HAUTE NEWFOUNDLAND.

The Northgale was known for years as the Stone House before undergoing a recent ownership and name change. Longtime fans fretted, but most were ultimately pleased that the creative menu and even some of attentive waitstaff have remained unchanged, and the restaurant continues to serve up some of the best meals in Newfoundland. The focus is on local fare, with dishes like wild game and seafood prominent on the menu. You might start with cod au gratin or onion soup with cognac and camembert croutons, but leave room for the generous main courses, like lamb with garlic sauce, grilled salmon with dill sauce, or Labrador partridge with partridgeberries. Caribou and moose appear as specialties from time to time, when high-quality meat is available. The setting is wonderful, in an 1834 stone house with walls 3 feet thick. Quidi Vidi Lake is a short walk away, offering a perfect spot for a postprandial stroll.

MODERATE

Classic Café. 364 Duckworth. ☎ **709/722-4083.** Reservations not needed. Main courses, breakfast, and lunch C$4–C$11 (US$2.65–US$7); dinner C$8–C$17 (US$5–US$11). DC, ER, MC, V. Daily 24 hours. CANADIAN.

This come-as-you-are spot is appropriately named—it's truly classic St. John's, and everyone seems to drop in at one time or another. There's a more sedate dining room upstairs in this 1894 hillside home, but the real action is in the crowded street-level bistro. Breakfast is served 24 hours a day—but don't expect a limp croissant and tea. Macho breakfasts (for example, a sirloin with eggs, toast, home fries, and baked beans) appeal to a mixed group, from burly longshoremen to hung-over musicians. Non-breakfast entrees in the evening are equally generous and often surprisingly good.

Stella's. 106 Water St. ☎ **709/753-9625.** Reservations suggested. Main courses C$4–C$9 (US$2.65–US$6) at lunch, C$11–C$14 (US$7–US$9) at dinner. MC, V. Tues–Fri noon–3pm, Wed 6–9pm, Thurs–Fri 6–10pm, Sat noon–10pm. NATURAL/WHOLE FOODS.

This is *the* destination for those pining away for an oversized plate of fresh greens after too much time in the canned-vegetable hinterlands. The cozy restaurant on Water Street is often hectic and the service can be strained, but the food is consistently impressive. Among your choices are pan-fried cod, chicken burrito, curried scallops, Thai veggie stir-fry, and Oriental almond tofu. There's no soda but a good selection of wonderful homemade concoctions, including a partridgeberry milk shake and "bogwater" (a mix of carrot, ginger, and celery juices).

Zachary's. 71 Duckworth (across from the Hotel Newfoundland). ☎ **709/579-8050.** Reservations suggested. Main courses C$3.30–C$8 (US$2.20–US$5) at breakfast, C$6–C$9 (US$3.65–US$6) at lunch, C$9–C$20 (US$6–US$13) at dinner. AE, ER, MC, V. Daily 8am–10pm. TRADITIONAL.

This informal spot with wood-slat booths offers a slew of Newfoundland favorites, like fish cakes, fried bologna, and toutons—and that's just for breakfast. Dinners emphasize seafood—entrees include grilled salmon, seafood fettuccine, and pan-fried cod—but you'll also find steaks and chicken. The desserts are all homemade; especially tempting are the cheesecake, carrot cake, and date squares. You'll find more inventive spots for dinner, but you probably won't do better for reliable quality if you're on a tight budget. The breakfasts are outstanding and served all day.

INEXPENSIVE

International Flavors. 124 Duckworth St. ☎ **709/738-4636.** Reservations not needed. Dinner plates C$7 (US$4.60). V. Mon–Sat 11am–5:30pm (often later). INDIAN.

This is my favorite cheap meal in St. John's. This storefront restaurant has just five tables, and all the dinners are priced at C$7 (US$4.60), which includes a decent mound of food. You'll usually have a choice of four or so dishes. Smart money gets the basic curry. Also recommended is the very satisfying mango milk shake.

ST. JOHN'S AFTER DARK

The nightlife in St. John's is extraordinarily vibrant, and you'd be doing yourself an injustice if you didn't spend at least one evening on a pub crawl.

The first stop for a little local music and cordial imbibing should be **George Street,** running for several blocks near New Gower and Water streets, close to City Hall. Every St. John's resident confidently asserts that George Street is home to more bars per square foot than anywhere else on the planet. I've been unable to track down a global authority that verifies pubs-per-square-foot, but a walk down the street did little to rebut their claims.

George Street is packed with energetic pubs and lounges, some fueled by beer, others by testosterone, still more by lively Celtic fiddling. The best strategy for selecting a pub is a slow ramble around 10pm or later, vectoring in to spots with appealing music wafting from the door. At places with live music, cover charges are universally very nominal, rarely topping C$5 (US$3.35).

If you're looking for good local folk music, arrive early to get seats at the **Blarney Stone,** George Street near Queen Street (☎ 709/754-1798), which puts on few airs and features wonderful Newfoundland and Irish folk music. **Trapper John's,** 2 George St. (☎ **709/579-9630**), is also known for outstanding provincial folk music, but it tries a bit harder for that Ye Olde Newfoundland character. This is a traditional "screeching in" spot for visitors (this involves cheap Newfoundland rum and some amount of embarrassment). For blues, there's the lively **Fat Cat,** 5 George St. (☎ 709/722-6409). For a more upscale spot with lower decibel levels, try **Christian's Bar,** 23 George St. (☎ **709/753-9100**), which offers the nonalcoholic option of specialty coffees.

If George Street's beery atmosphere reminds you of those nights in college you'd just as soon forget, a few blocks away are two pubs tucked down tiny alleys known for their genial public-house atmospheres. The **Duke of Duckworth,** 325 Duckworth St. (☎ **709/739-6344**), specializes in draft beers and pub lunches. And **The Ship Inn,** 265 Duckworth St. (☎ 709/753-3870), is a St. John's mainstay, featuring a variety of local musical acts that seem to complement rather than overwhelm the pub's cozy atmosphere.

8 The Southern Avalon Peninsula

The ✪ **Avalon Peninsula**—or just "The Avalon," as it's commonly called—is home to some of Newfoundland's most memorable and dramatic scenery, including high coastal cliffs and endless bogs. More good news: It's also relatively compact and manageable, and you can view it on long day trips from St. John's or in a couple of days of scenic poking around. It's a good destination for anyone short on time yet wanting to get a taste of the wild. The area is especially notable for its bird colonies, as well as its herd of wild caribou. The bad news? It's thrust out in the sea where cold and warm currents collide, resulting in legendary fogs and blustery moist weather. Bring a rain suit and come prepared for bone-numbing dampness.

ESSENTIALS

GETTING THERE   Several well-marked, well-maintained highways follow the coast of the southern Avalon Peninsula; few roads cross the damp and spongy interior. A map is essential.

VISITOR INFORMATION   Your best bet is to stop in one of the **St. John's tourist bureaus** (above) or at the well-marked **tourist bureau** just up the hill from the Argentia ferry before you begin your travels. Witless Bay has a **tourist booth** at the edge of the cobblestone beach and is stocked with a handful of brochures. It's open irregularly.

✪ THE WITLESS BAY ECOLOGICAL RESERVE

The Witless Bay area, about 35km (22 miles) south of St. John's, makes an easy day trip from the city or can serve as a launching point for an exploration of the Avalon Peninsula. The main attraction is the **Witless Bay Ecological Reserve** (☎ 709/729-2424), comprising four islands and the waters around them a short boat ride offshore. Literally millions of seabirds nest and fish here, and it's a spectacle even if you're not a bird-watcher.

On the islands you'll find the **largest puffin colony in the western Atlantic Ocean,** with some 60,000 puffins burrowing into the grassy slopes above the cliffs and awkwardly launching themselves from the high rocks. The tour boats are able to edge right along the shores, about 20 or 25 feet away, allowing puffin watching on even foggy days. Also on the islands is North America's **second-largest murre colony.**

Although the islands are publicly owned and managed, access is via **privately operated tour boats,** several of which you'll find headquartered along Route 10 in Bay Bulls and Bauline East. It's worth shopping around since prices can vary considerably. Bay Bulls is the closest town to St. John's and home to three of the more popular tours: **Mullowney's** (☎ 877/783-3467), **O'Brien's** (☎ 877/639-4253), and **Gatherall's** (☎ 800/419-4253). The 2½-hour tours from here are C$32 to C$39 (US$21 to US$26) adults.

Captain Murphy's Seabird & Whale Tours (☎ 709/334-2002) is based in Witless Bay, a bit farther south, and offers several trips daily; tours last 2 to 2½ hours and cost C$30 (US$20) adults, C$20 (US$13) teens, and C$15 (US$10) children. Budget travelers would do well to continue farther south to Bauline East, where the 30-foot *Molly Bawn* (☎ 709/334-2621) offers 1¼-hour tours in search of puffins, whales, and icebergs. Tours depart every 1½ hours during peak season; the cost is C$15 (US$10) adults and C$10 (US$7) children under 12. A quieter and more intimate way to explore the area is to sign up for a 3-hour tour with **Bay Bulls Sea Kayaking Tours** (☎ 709/334-3394). You'll kayak along the bay's shores, visit sea caves and small beaches, and possibly spot puffins and whales visiting the bay. The price is C$45 (US$30) per person.

FERRYLAND

Historic **Ferryland** is among the most picturesque of the Avalon villages, set at the foot of rocky hills on a harbor protected by a series of abrupt islands at its mouth.

Ferryland was among the first permanent settlements in Newfoundland. In 1621, the **Colony of Avalon** was established here by Sir George Calvert, First Baron of Baltimore (he was also behind the settlement of Baltimore, Maryland). Calvert sunk the equivalent of C$4 million (US$2.65 million) into the colony, which featured luxe touches like cobblestone roads, slate roofs, and fine ceramics and glassware from Europe. So up-to-date was the colony that privies featured drains leading to the shore just below the high-tide mark, making them the first flush toilets in North America (or so the locals insist). The colony was later sacked by the Dutch and then the French during ongoing squabbles over territory and eventually was abandoned.

Recent excavations have revealed much about life here nearly 4 centuries ago. Visit the modern **Colony of Avalon Interpretation Centre** (☎ 877/326-5669 or 709/432-3200), an archaeological museum offering numerous glass-topped drawers filled with engrossing artifacts, and then ask for a tour of the six **archaeological sites** currently being excavated (the tour is included in the cost of admission). Other interpretive exhibits include a reproduction of a 17th-century kitchen and three gardens of the sort you might've overseen had you been alive 400 years ago. After your tour, take a walk to the lighthouse at the point (about 1 hour round-trip), where you can scan for whales and icebergs. Ask for directions at the museum. The site is open daily: May 22 to June 20 and September 7 to October 22, 10am to 5pm; June 21 to September 6, 9am to 7pm. Admission is C$3 (US$2) adults, C$2.50 (US$1.65) seniors, C$2 (US$1.35) students, and C$6 (US$4) families.

WHERE TO STAY

The Downs Inn. Rte. 10, Ferryland, NF A0A 2H0. ☎ **709/432-2808.** Fax 709/432-2659. E-mail acostello@nf.sympatico.ca. 4 units, 2 with bathroom. C$55 (US$37) double. V.

This attractive building overlooking the harbor served as a convent between 1914 and 1986, when it was converted to an inn. The furnishings reflect its heritage as an institution rather than a historic building—there are dated carpeting and old linoleum, and the furniture is uninspired. (Much of the religious statuary was left in place—a nice touch.) Ask for one of the two front rooms so you can watch for whales from your windows. The front parlor has been converted to a tearoom, where you can order a nice pot of tea and a light snack, like carrot cake, rhubarb tart, or a sandwich. Innkeeper Aidan Costello also operates **Southern Shore Eco Adventures** and can create custom tour packages for kayaking, hiking, or whale watching.

THE AVALON WILDERNESS RESERVE

Where there's bog, there's caribou. Or at least that's true in the southern part of the peninsula, which is home to the island's **largest caribou herd,** numbering some 13,000. You'll see signs warning you to watch for caribou along the roadway; the landscape hereabout is so misty and primeval, though, that you might feel you should also watch for druids in robes with tall walking staffs.

The caribou roam freely throughout the 1,700 km² reserve, so it's largely a matter of happenstance to find them. Your best bet is to scan the high upland barrens along Route 10 between Trepassey and Peter's River (an area that's actually out of the reserve). You'll commonly see caribou here. For more, check with the **Provincial Parks Division** in St. John's at ☎ 709/729-2421.

On Route 90 between St. Catherines and Hollyrood is the **Salmonier Nature Park** (☎ 709/729-6974), where you're certain to see caribou—along with other wildlife—if you can't find the herd on the reserve. This intriguing and well-designed park is fundamentally a 2.5km (1.6-mile) nature trail, almost entirely on a boardwalk, which tracks through bog and forest and along streams and ponds. Along the route are more than a dozen unobtrusive pens, in which you can observe orphaned or injured wildlife. (It's the only such facility in the province.) Among the animals represented are arctic fox, snowy owl, moose, bald eagle, mink, otter, beaver, and lynx. It's 11km (6.8 miles) south of the Trans-Canada Highway; admission is free. Gates are open in summer daily 10am to 5pm, and all visitors must depart by 6pm. Closed mid-October to June 1.

CAPE ST. MARY'S

The Cape St. Mary's Ecological Reserve ranks high on my list of favorite places on Newfoundland. Granted, it's off the beaten track—some 100km (62 miles) from the Trans-Canada Highway—but it's worth every kilometer of it.

The ○ **Cape St. Mary's Ecological Reserve,** off Route 100, 5km (3.1 miles) east of St. Bride's (☎ **709/729-2424**), is home to some 5,500 pairs of northern gannets—big, noisy, graceful white birds with cappuccino-colored heads and black wing tips. While they can been seen wintering off the coast of Florida and elsewhere to the south, they're seldom seen in such cacophonous number as here. Most are nesting literally on top of one another on a compact 100m (300-ft.) sea stack. At any given moment hundreds are flying above, around, and below you, which is all the more impressive given their nearly 2m (6-ft.) wingspan.

You needn't take a boat ride to see this colony. Start at the visitor center, which offers a quick and intriguing introduction to the indigenous bird life. Then walk 15 minutes along a grassy clifftop pathway—through harebell, iris, and dandelion—until you arrive at an unfenced cliff just a couple dozen yards from the sea stack (it's close enough that it's impressive even in a dense fog). Also nesting on and around the island are 10,000 pairs of murre, 10,000 kittiwakes, and 100 razorbills. Note that the viewing area isn't fenced, and peering down at the surging surf and hundreds of birds on the wing *below* is not recommended for acrophobes.

Admission to the interpretive center is C$3 (US$2) adults, C$1 (US65¢) children, and C$7 (US$4.65) families. Guided tours, offered twice daily, are C$5 (US$3.35) (includes admission to the center). May to October, it's open Monday, Wednesday, and Friday 9am to 7:30pm; Tuesday, Thursday, and Saturday 8am to 7pm; and Sunday 9am to 7pm.

WHERE TO STAY

Bird Island Resort. Rte. 100, St. Bride's, NF A0B 2Z0. ☎ **709/337-2450.** Fax 709/337-2903. 20 units. TV. C$49–C$69 (US$33–US$46) double. AE, ER, MC, V.

This modern, unaffected motel is behind Manning's food market, where you'll stop to ask for a room. It's the preferred spot in town and it offers some unexpected amenities, like a laundry room, tiny fitness room with a universal, and minigolf course (all rooms come with clubs and balls). The guest rooms vary in size. The double efficiency units feature a separate sitting room, and several of the rooms have kitchenettes, which come in handy given the dearth of restaurants in town. The rooms that get snapped up first are nos. 1 to 5, and with good reason: They all have kitchenettes (some have two bedrooms) and all face the ocean, with great views (assuming that the fog hasn't moved in).

9 The Labrador Coast: Wilderness Adventure & More

Labrador may be far removed and remote, but it has long played an outsized role in the collective conscious of the region. For several centuries this deeply indented coastline was noted for its robust fisheries, and itinerant fleets plied the waters both inshore and offshore, harvesting what the sea had to offer. The empty, melancholy landscape of rolling hills along the coasts and inland serves much the same function the American West frontier played in the United States—it's both a land of opportunity stemming from the natural resources (primarily mining these days) and a place where outdoorspeople have historically tested their mettle in a harsh environment, stalking big game and big salmon.

Although the region is sparsely settled, people have been part of the landscape for centuries. The Innu (Indian) culture in Labrador goes back 8,000 years; the Inuit (Eskimo) culture, 4,000 years. The Vikings sighted Labrador in 986 but didn't come ashore until 1010. Traces of the Vikings remain in the shape of "fairy holes"—deep cylindrical holes in the rocks, angled away from the sea, where they were thought to have tied up their boats. The 16th century brought Basque whalers, as many as 2,000 of them, and they returned to Europe with 20,000 barrels of whale oil in what might be one of the globe's first oil booms. It has been said the whale oil of Newfoundland and Labrador was as valuable to the Europeans as the gold of South America. Vestiges of a whaling station remain on Saddle Island, off the coast of Red Bay on the Labrador Straits. Next came the British and French fishermen, fur traders, and merchants, who first came here in summers to fish, hunt, and trade, and then established permanent settlements in the 1700s. Many of the Europeans married Innu and Inuit women, but conflicts between Inuit whalers and the European settlers along the south coast prompted the Inuit communities to move to the far north, where they remain today.

Only about 30,000 people live in Labrador: 13,000 in western Labrador, 8,000 in Happy Valley–Goose Bay, with the remaining residents spread along the coast. Approximately four-fifths of those born here remain here, with strong ties to family and neighbors. These close-knit communities typically welcome visitors warmly.

Many visitors come here for the sportfishing of brook trout, Atlantic salmon, arctic char, lake trout, whitefish, and northern pike. Others come for wilderness adventure, hiking, and camping under the undulating northern lights. Still others are simply curious about a remote part of the world.

THE LABRADOR STRAITS

The **Labrador Straits** are the easiest part of Labrador to explore from Newfoundland. The southeast corner of Labrador is served by ferries shuttling between St. Barbe, Newfoundland, and Blanc Sablon, Québec. (Blanc Sablon is on the Québec-Labrador border.) From Blanc Sablon, you can travel on the one and only road, running 80km (50 miles) northward and dead-ending at Red Bay. (Plans call for extending this road in the future, but it may be another decade.)

Ferries are timed so you can cross over in the morning, drive to Red Bay, and still be back for the later ferry to Newfoundland. Such a hasty trip isn't recommended, however. Better to spend a night, when you'll have a chance to meet the people, who offer the most compelling reason to visit.

The **MS *Northern Princess*** (☎ 709/931-2309 or 418/461-2056) runs May to ice season, usually sometime in early January. The crossing takes about 1¾ hours, and reservations are encouraged in summer (half the ferry can be reserved; the other half is first come, first served). One-way fares are C$9 (US$6) adults, C$4.75 (US$3.15) children, and C$19 (US$12) cars.

The terrain along the Labrador Straits is rugged, and the colors are muted except for a vibrant stretch of green along the Pinware River. The few small houses are clustered close together; during winter, it's nice to have neighbors so nearby. The homes are often brightened up with "yard art"—replicas of windmills, wells, and churches. In summer, icebergs float by the coast, and whales breach and spout offshore. The landscape is covered with cotton grass, clover, partridgeberries, bakeapples, fireweed, buttercups, and bog laurel. The fog rolls in frequently; it'll either stay a while or roll right back out. The capelin come and go as well—the tiny migrating fish crash-land on the shore by the thousands during a week in late June or early July. Locals crowd the beach to scoop up the fish and take them home for an easy supper.

The **Visitor Information Centre** (☎ 709/931-2013) in the small restored **St. Andrews Church** in L'Anse au Clair, the first town after the ferry, is open June to September. The tourist association has developed several footpaths and trails in the area, so be sure to ask about them; also ask about the "fairy holes." If you come in mid-August, plan to attend the annual **Bakeapple Festival,** celebrating the berry that stars in the desserts of Newfoundland and Labrador.

EXPLORING THE LABRADOR STRAITS

Drive the "slow road" connecting the villages of the Labrador Straits. Traveling southwest to northeast, here are some highlights you'll find along the way.

In L'Anse au Clair, **Moore's Handicrafts,** 8 Country Rd., just off Route 510 (☎ 709/931-2022), sells handmade summer and winter coats, traditional cassocks, moccasins, knitted items, handmade jewelry, and other crafts, as well as homemade jams. They also do traditional embroidery on Labrador cassocks and coats, and if you stop on the way north and choose your design, they'll finish it by the time you return to the ferry—even the same day. Prices are quite reasonable. The shop is open daily in season 8am to 10pm.

A 3.3km (2-mile) drive from the main road, the 1858 **Point Amour Lighthouse** (☎ 709/927-5825), at the western entrance to the Strait of Belle Isle, is the tallest lighthouse in the Atlantic provinces and the second tallest in all of Canada. The walls of the slightly tapered circular tower are 6½ feet thick at the base, and you'll have to climb 122 steps for the view. The dioptric lens was imported from Europe for the princely sum of C$10,000 (US$6,670). The lighthouse, which kept watch for submarines during World War II, is still in use and was maintained by a resident light keeper right up until 1995. June to mid-October, it's open daily 10am to 5:30pm; admission is C$2.50 (US$1.65), with children under 12 free.

After you pass the fishing settlements of **L'Anse au Loup** ("Wolf's Cove") and **West St. Modeste,** the road follows the scenic Pinware River, where the trees become noticeably taller. Along this stretch of road, you'll see glacial erratics—those odd boulders deposited by the melting ice cap. **Pinware Provincial Park,** 43km (27 miles) from L'Anse au Clair, has a picnic area, hiking trails, and 15 campsites. The 50-mile-long Pinware River is known for salmon fishing.

The highway ends in Red Bay. The **Red Bay National Historic Site Visitor Centre** (☎ 709/920-2197) showcases artifacts from the late 1500s, when Basque whalers came in number to hunt the right and bowhead whales. Starting in 1977, excavations turned up whaling implements, pottery, glassware, and even partially preserved seamen's clothing. From here you can also arrange tours of **Saddle Island,** the home of Basque whaling stations in the 16th century. Transportation to archaeological sites on the island is available in summer Monday to Saturday 9am to 4pm. You can also opt to view Saddle Island from the observation level on the third floor. Admission is C$5 (US$3.35) adults, C$3.75 (US$2.50) seniors, C$2.75 (US$1.85) children 6 to 16, and C$10 (US$7) families. Midsummer, the site is open daily 9am to 6:30pm; early summer and fall, it's open daily 10am to 6pm. Closed mid-October to mid-June.

WHERE TO STAY

Grenfell Louie A. Hall. 3 Willow Ave. (P.O. Box 137), Forteau, Labrador A0K 2P0. ☎ **709/ 931-2916.** 5 units, none with bathroom. C$45 (US$30) double. V.

History buffs love the Grenfell Hall—it was built in 1946 by the International Grenfell Association as a nursing station, and there's plenty of reading material about the coast's early days. The guest rooms are furnished with basic contemporary-country furniture, and there's a common room with a TV, VCR, and fireplace. The innkeepers can arrange to transport you to or from the ferry. (If you're just curious about the place, you're invited to stop in for C$3/US$2 per person or C$5/US$3.35 per couple.) Meals are available by advance arrangement and usually feature seafood (typically cod or salmon) along with homemade bread, preserves, and dessert; the cost is C$15 to C$20 (US$10 to US$13) for the three-course meal.

Northern Light Inn. L'Anse au Clair, Labrador A0K 3K0. ☎ **800/563-3188** (from Atlantic Canada) or 709/931-2332. Fax 709/931-2708. 59 units. TV TEL. C$70 (US$47) double; C$120 (US$80) suite. AE, DC, ER, MC, V.

The largest and most modern hotel in the region (it added 28 rooms in 1998), the Northern Light Inn offers well-maintained guest rooms, a gift shop, a friendly staff, and a dining room. The restaurant, open daily 8am to 11pm, serves soups, sandwiches, baskets of scallops, fried chicken, and pizza from C$2 to C$9 (US$1.35 to US$6). In the adjacent Basque Dining Room, seafood is the specialty, with prices at C$2 to C$5 (US$1.35 to US$3.35) for appetizers and C$11 to C$14 (US$7 to US$9) for main courses. The coffee shop doubles as a lounge in the evening.

LABRADOR WEST

The most affluent and industrialized part of Labrador, **Labrador West** lies on the Québec border and is home to the twin towns of **Wabush** and **Labrador City,** 7km (4.3 miles) apart. The two towns share many attractions, activities, and services. This region offers top-notch cross-country skiing and has hosted two World Cup events. Labrador West is also home to the largest open-pit iron ore mine in North America, which produces almost half of Canada's ore. Exhibits on local history are shown at the **Height of Land Heritage Centre,** 1750 Bartlett Dr. (☎ **709/944-2284**), in the city's first bank and post office; it's open daily and is free.

Labrador City or Wabush make good bases for hiking, canoeing, and birding trips. Ask for directions to **Crystal Falls,** where a half-mile hike takes you to the falls and a view over the city. Labrador City is the terminus of the **Québec North Shore and Labrador Railway** (the QNS&L), which departs from Sept-Iles, Québec, and is the only passenger train service in the entire province of Newfoundland and Labrador. The 8- to 10-hour trip covers 420km (260 miles), across 19 bridges; through 11 tunnels; along riverbanks; through forests; past rapids, mountains, and waterfalls; and finally through subarctic vegetation. In summer, a highlight is the **vintage dome car** (1958) with sofa seats that was once part of the Wabash Cannonball (☎ **418/968-7805** in Québec; 709/944-8205 in Newfoundland and Labrador).

For more details about activities in the area, contact **Labrador West Tourism Development Corporation** at ☎ **709/282-3337.**

Montréal & the Resorts of the Laurentides & Estrie

by Herbert Bailey Livesey

The duality of Canadian life has been called the "Twin Solitudes." One Canada, English and Calvinist, is portrayed as staid, smug, and work obsessed. The other, French and Catholic, is more creative, light-hearted, and inclined to see pleasure as the result of labor. Or so go the stereotypes. These two peoples live side by side throughout Québec and in the nine provinces of English Canada, but the blending occurs with particular intensity in Québec province's largest city, **Montréal.** French speakers (Francophones) constitute 66% of the city's population, and most of the rest are English speakers (Anglophones).

Over the past decade, there has been an impression of decline in Montréal. A bleak mood has prevailed in many quarters, driven by lingering recession and uncertainty over the future. There's some truth in the perception. After all, it's still possible that Québec will choose to fling itself into independence, an event that would lead to increased Anglo flight, loss of federal subsidies, and even the possibility of outright civil war.

The defining dialectic of life here is language, the thorny issue that might yet tear the country apart. Many Québecois believe a separate state is the only way to maintain their culture in the face of the Anglophone ocean enveloping them. Québec's role in the Canadian federation is the most volatile issue in Canadian politics. Would a politically independent Québec continue to share a common currency, a central bank, and a tariff-free relationship with the rest of Canada? Would the North American Free Trade Agreement (NAFTA) be extended to an independent Québec? Would the Atlantic provinces, cut off from the rest of Canada, apply to the United States for statehood? Would the Crees of northern Québec or Anglophone parts of Montréal be allowed to remain in Canada?

There are reasons for the intransigence of the Québecois—about 240 years' worth. After what they call the "Conquest" of 1759, their English rulers made a few concessions to French-Canadian pride, including allowing them a version of jurisprudence. But a kind of linguistic exclusionism prevailed, with Scottish and English bankers and merchants denying French-Canadians access to upper levels of business and government. Intentionally or thoughtlessly, Anglophones lowered an opaque ceiling on Francophone advancement. Resentment festered for years, and in the 1960s the Québecois began to assert greater pride in their roots. This fueled a burgeoning nationalism, punctuated by a series of violent extremist acts. By 1976, mainstream sentiments of the French-speaking minority in the province resulted in the election of the separatist Parti Québecois. Its leader, René Lévesque, promoted a referendum on sovereignty in 1980, but the measure was defeated.

Federalists later attempted to smooth Francophone fur with a formal recognition of the province as a "distinct society." That effort failed too, leading with glacial certainty to the sovereignty referendum of October 30, 1995. That vote went in favor of the pro-unity camp, but by a margin of barely 1%. For the moment, the separatist movement appears to be losing support, but the popular provincial premier promises yet another vote when he feels conditions are more favorable, ensuring heated debate and ideological posturing for years to come.

None of this fractious history should deter you, however. The Québecois are exceedingly gracious hosts. Many American city dwellers see Montréal as an urban near-paradise. The subway is modern and swift and the streets are clean and safe. There are rarely more than 60 homicides a year, compared to the hundreds in U.S. cities of comparable size. Montréal's best restaurants are the equal of their south-of-the-border compatriots yet are as much as 30% to 40% cheaper. And the government gives visitors back most of the taxes it collects. Most Montréalers grow up speaking both French and English, switching from one to the other as the situation dictates. This is especially true for telephone operators, store clerks, waiters, and hotel staff. It's less true in country villages and in Québec City, but there's virtually no problem that can't be solved with a few French words, some expressive gestures, and a little goodwill.

1 Essentials

ARRIVING

BY PLANE **Dorval International Airport,** 22km (14 miles) west of the city, is served by most of the world's major airlines. (Mirabel Airport, farther from the city, now accepts only air freight and some charter flights.) The major car-rental agencies have desks at the airport.

Most visitors fly into Dorval from other parts of North America on **Air Canada** (☎ 514/393-3333 or 800/776-3000 outside Canada; www.aircanada.ca), **American** (☎ 800/433-7300; www.americanair.com), **Canadian Airlines** (☎ 800/426-7000; www.cdnair.ca), **Continental** (☎ 800/231-0856; www.flycontinental.com), **Delta** (☎ 514/337-5520 or 800/221-1212; www.delta-air.com), **Northwest** (☎ 800/441-1818; www.nwa.com), or **US Airways** (☎ 800/428-4322; www.usairways.com). In the United States, Air Canada flies out of New York (Newark and LaGuardia), Miami, Tampa, Chicago, Los Angeles, and San Francisco. Other carriers that serve Dorval include **Air France** (☎ 800/847-1106; www.airfrance.ca), **British Airways** (☎ 800/247-9297; www.british-airways.com), and **Swissair** (☎ 800/879-9154; www.swissair.com). Regional airlines like Air Atlantic, American Eagle, and Inter-Canadian also serve the city.

BY CAR Interstate 87 runs due north from New York City to link up with Canada's Autoroute 15, and the entire 400-mile journey is on expressways. From Boston, I-93 north joins I-89 just south of Concord, New Hampshire. At White River Junction you have a choice of either continuing on I-89 to Lake Champlain, crossing the lake by roads and bridges to join I-87 and Canada Autoroute 15 north, or picking up I-91 at White River Junction to go due north toward Sherbrooke, Québec. At the border, I-91 becomes Canada Route 55 and joins Canada Route 10 west through Estrie to Montréal. The Trans-Canada Highway runs right through the city, connecting both ends of the country.

From Boston to Montréal is about 510km (316 miles), from Toronto 540km (335 miles), from Ottawa 190km (118 miles). Once you're in Montréal, Québec City is an easy 3-hour drive away.

BY TRAIN   Montréal is a major terminus on Canada's **VIA Rail** network (☎ 800/561-3949 in the U.S. or 514/989-2626 in Canada; www.viarail.ca), and its **Gare Centrale** is at 935 rue de la Gauchetière ouest (☎ 514/871-1331). Some of the comfortable trains have dining cars, sleeping cars, and cellular phones. There's scheduled service to and from Québec City via Trois-Rivières and to and from Ottawa, Toronto, Winnipeg, and points west.

Amtrak (☎ 800/872-7245; www.amtrak.com) runs one train a day to Montréal from Washington and New York, with intermediate stops. The *Adirondack* takes about 10½ hours from New York if all goes well, but delays aren't unusual. Passengers from Chicago can get to Montréal most directly by taking Amtrak to Toronto, then switching to VIA Rail.

Seniors 62 and older are eligible for a 15% **discount** on some Amtrak trains on the U.S. segment of the trip. VIA Rail also has a senior discount. Don't forget to bring along proof of citizenship (a passport or birth certificate) for passing through Customs.

BY BUS   Montréal's main terminal is the **Terminus Voyageur,** 505 bd. de Maisonneuve est (☎ 514/842-2281). The **Voyageur** company operates buses between here and all parts of Québec, with frequent runs through the Estrie region to Sherbrooke, to the various villages in the Laurentians, and to Québec City. Morning, noon, early-afternoon, and midnight buses cover the distance between Toronto and Montréal in under 7 hours. From Boston or New York there's daily bus service to Montréal on **Greyhound** (☎ 800/231-2222 or 514/843-8495; www.greyhound.ca). The trip from Boston takes about 8 hours; from New York City, with five departures daily, it takes 9 hours.

VISITOR INFORMATION

TOURIST OFFICES   Québec tourism authorities produce volumes of detailed and highly useful publications, and they're easy to obtain by mail, by phone, or in person. To contact **Tourisme Québec,** write C.P. 979, Montréal, PQ H3C 2W3, or call ☎ 800/363-7777, operator 806 (within the Montréal area, call ☎ 514/873-2015).

The main info center is the large and efficient **Infotouriste,** 1001 rue du Square-Dorchester, between Peel and Metcalfe streets in the hotel/business district (☎ 800/363-7777 from anywhere in Canada and the U.S., or 514/873-2015; Métro: Peel or Bonaventure). The office is open daily: June to early September 8:30am to 7:30pm and mid-September to May 9am to 6pm. Its bilingual staff can help with questions about the entire province, as well as Montréal itself.

The city has its own convenient **information bureau** in Old Montréal at 174 rue Notre-Dame, at the corner of place Jacques-Cartier (☎ 514/871-1595; Métro: Place-d'Armes). Easter to mid-October, it's open daily 9am to 7pm; mid-October to Easter, hours are Thursday to Sunday 9am to 5pm.

WEB SITES   Among many Montréal Web sites, these are among the most productive starting points: **www.tourisme-montreal.org**, **www.quebec-region.cuq.qc.ca**, **www.quebecweb.com/tourisme**, and **www.tourisme.gouv.qc.ca**.

CITY LAYOUT

The city borders the **St. Lawrence River.** As far as its citizens are concerned, that's south, looking toward the United States, though the river runs more nearly north and south, not east and west. For that reason, it has been observed that Montréal is the

Finding an Address

Boulevard St-Laurent is the dividing point between east and west (*est* and *ouest*). There's no equivalent division for north and south (*nord* and *sud*)—the numbers start at the river and climb from there. For instance, when you're driving along boulevard St-Laurent and passing no. 500, that's Vieux-Montréal, near rue Notre-Dame; no. 1100 is near boulevard René-Lévesque, no. 1500 near boulevard de Maisonneuve, and no. 3400 near rue Sherbrooke. Even numbers are on the west side of north-south streets and the south side of east-west streets; odd numbers are on the east and north sides, respectively.

only city where the sun rises in the south. Don't fight it: Face the river. That's south. Turn around. That's north.

When examining a map of the city, note that such prominent thoroughfares as Ste-Catherine and René-Lévesque are said to run "east" and "west," the dividing line being boulevard St-Laurent, which runs "north" and "south." To ease the confusion, the directions given in this chapter conform to local tradition.

In downtown Montréal, the principal east-west streets are boulevard **René-Lévesque, rue Ste-Catherine, boulevard de Maisonneuve,** and **rue Sherbrooke.** Prominent north-south arteries are **rue Crescent, rue McGill, rue St-Denis,** and **boulevard St-Laurent,** dividing east and west Montréal (most of the downtown area of interest to tourists and businesspeople lies to the west). In Plateau Mont-Royal, northeast of downtown, major streets are **avenue du Mont-Royal** and **avenue Laurier.** In Vieux-Montréal (Old Montréal), **rue St-Jacques, rue Notre-Dame,** and s are the major streets, along with **rue de la Commune,** hugging the park that borders the St. Lawrence River.

In earlier days, Montréal was split geographically between those who spoke English, centered in the city's western regions, and those who spoke French, concentrated to the east. Things still do sound more French as you walk east. While boulevard St-Laurent is the official east-west divider, the spiritual split comes farther west, roughly at avenue de Bleury/avenue de Parc.

Good **street plans** are found inside the free tourist guide supplied by the Greater Montréal Convention & Tourism Bureau and distributed widely throughout the city. The bureau also provides a free foldout city map.

Neighborhoods in Brief

DOWNTOWN   This area contributes the most striking elements to the dramatic Montréal skyline and contains the main rail station, as well as most of the city's luxury hotels, principal museums, corporate headquarters, and large department stores. Loosely bounded by rue Sherbrooke to the north, boulevard René-Lévesque to the south, boulevard St-Laurent to the east, and rue Drummond to the west, downtown incorporates the former "Golden Square Mile," an Anglophone district once characterized by mansions erected by the Scottish and English merchants and industrialists who dominated the city's political and social life well into this century. Many of those homes were torn down when skyscrapers began to rise here after World War II, but some remain, often converted to institutional use. At the area's northern edge is the urban campus of prestigious McGill University, which retains its Anglophone identity.

THE UNDERGROUND CITY   During Montréal's long winters, people escape down escalators and stairways into *la ville souterraine*—a parallel subterranean universe. In a controlled eternal-spring climate, it's possible to arrive at the rail station, check into a hotel, lunch at any of hundreds of fast-food counters and full-service restaurants, see a movie, attend a concert, conduct business, go shopping, and even take a swim—all without opening an umbrella or donning an overcoat. This "city" evolved when major downtown building developments (Place Ville-Marie, Place Bonaventure, Complexe Desjardins, Palais des Congrès, Place des Arts) put their below-street-level areas to profitable use, leasing space for shops and other purposes. Over time, in fits and starts and with no master plan, these spaces became connected with Métro stations and with one another through mazes of corridors, tunnels, and plazas. There are now more than 1,600 shops and about 30 cinemas down there. Without the convenience of a logical street grid, the area can be confusing to navigate. There are plenty of signs, but make careful note of landmarks at key corners—and expect to get lost anyway.

RUE CRESCENT   One of Montréal's major dining-and-nightlife districts lies in the western shadow of the massed phalanxes of downtown skyscrapers. It holds hundreds of restaurants, bars, and clubs of all styles between rue Sherbrooke and boulevard René-Lévesque, centering on rue Crescent and spilling over onto neighboring streets. From east to west, the Anglophone origins of the quarter are evident in the surviving street names: Stanley, Drummond, de la Montagne (changed from "Mountain"), Crescent, Bishop, and MacKay. The party atmosphere never quite fades, building to crescendos as weekends approach, especially in warm weather, when its largely 20- and 30-something denizens spill out into sidewalk cafes and onto balconies.

VIEUX-MONTRÉAL   The city was born in "Old Montréal" in 1642, down by the river at Pointe-à-Callière, and today activity centers around place Jacques-Cartier, especially in summer, when cafe tables line narrow terraces and sun worshipers, flower sellers, artists, street performers, and locals and tourists congregate. The area is larger than it might seem at first—bounded on the north by rue St-Antoine, once Montréal's "Wall Street" and still home to some banks; on the south by the recently developed Vieux-Port (Old Port), a linear park bordering rue de la Commune that gives access to the river and provides breathing room for cyclists, in-line skaters, and picnickers; on the east by rue Berri; and on the west by rue McGill. Several small but intriguing museums are housed in historic buildings, and the district's architectural heritage has been substantially preserved. Its restored 18th- and 19th-century structures have been adapted as shops, studios, cafes, bars, offices, and apartments.

THE LATIN QUARTER   Rue St-Denis, from rue Ste-Catherine est to avenue du Mont-Royal, running from downtown to Plateau Mont-Royal, is the central artery of Montréal's Latin Quarter, thick with cafes, bistros, offbeat shops, and lively nightspots. It is to Montréal what boulevard St-Germain is to Paris. At the southern end of rue St-Denis, near the campus of the Université du Québec à Montréal, the avenue is student oriented, with alternative rock cranked up in the inexpensive bars and clubs. Farther north, above rue Sherbrooke, a raffish quality persists along the facing rows of three- and four-story row houses, but the average age of residents and visitors rises past 30. The prices are higher too, and some of the city's better restaurants are located here.

PLATEAU MONT-ROYAL   Northeast of downtown, this may be the part of the city where Montréalers feel most at home—away from the nonstop pace of downtown and the tourist crowds of Vieux-Montréal. Bounded by boulevard St-Joseph to the

Greater Montréal

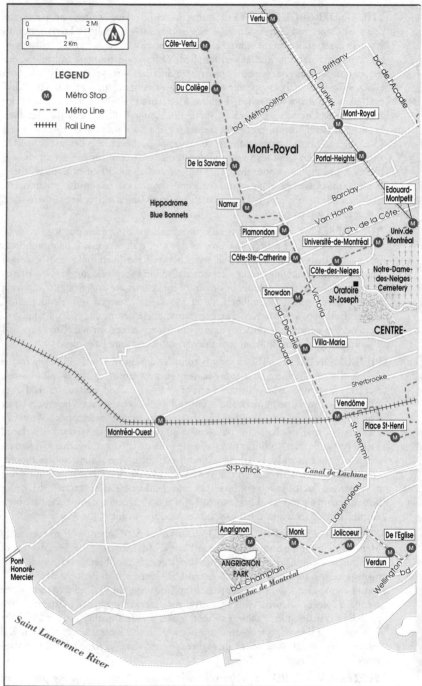

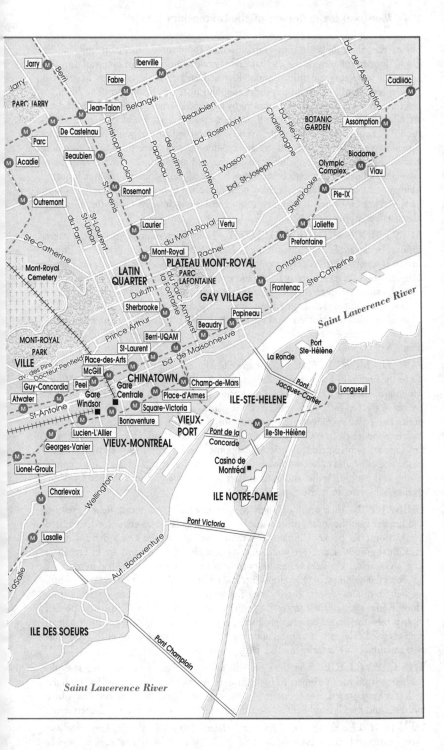

Jarry ⓜ · Berri · Jarry · Iberville ⓜ · Fabre ⓜ · Cadillac ⓜ · bd. de l'Assomption

PARC JARRY · Jean-Talon ⓜ · Belanger · Beaubien · bd. de Rosemont

De CasteInau ⓜ · Christophe-Colon · Papineau · de Lorimer · Frontenac · bd. Pie-IX · Charlemagne · BOTANIC GARDEN · Assomption ⓜ

ⓜ Parc · Beaubien ⓜ · Masson · Biodome

ⓜ Acadie · St-Laurent · bd. St-Joseph · Olympic Complex · Viau ⓜ

Rosemont ⓜ · Sherbrooke · Pie-IX ⓜ

ⓜ Outremont · du Parc · St-Urbain · St-Denis · Ste-Catherine

Laurier ⓜ · du Mont-Royal · Vertu · Joliette ⓜ

Mont-Royal Cemetery · Mont-Royal ⓜ · Rachel · Ontario · Prefontaine ⓜ

LATIN QUARTER · PLATEAU MONT-ROYAL · Ste-Catherine

Duluth · PARC LAFONTAINE · du Parc · la fontaine · Amherst · GAY VILLAGE · Frontenac ⓜ

Sherbrooke ⓜ · Saint Lawerence River

MONT-ROYAL PARK · Prince Arthur · Beaudry ⓜ · Papineau ⓜ

Berri-UQAM ⓜ · bd. de Maisonneuve

VILLE · av. des Pins · St-Laurent ⓜ · Port Ste-Hélène

Docteur-Penfield · Place-des-Arts ⓜ · La Ronde

McGill ⓜ · CHINATOWN · Champ-de-Mars ⓜ · Pont Jacques-Cartier · Longueuil ⓜ

Guy-Concordia ⓜ · Peel ⓜ · Gare Centrale · ILE-STE-HELENE

Atwater ⓜ · Gare Windsor · Place-d'Armes ⓜ

ⓜ St-Antoine · ⓜ Square-Victoria · VIEUX-PORT

Bonaventure ⓜ · Ile-Ste-Hélène

ⓜ Lucien-L'Allier · VIEUX-MONTRÉAL · Pont de la Concorde

Georges-Vanier ⓜ · Casino de Montréal

ⓜ Lionel-Groulx · ILE NOTRE-DAME

ⓜ Charlevoix · Wellington · Pont Victoria

ⓜ Lasalle · Aut. Bonaventure

Lasalle · ILE DES SOEURS · Pont Champlain

Saint Lawerence River

north, rue Sherbrooke to the south, avenue Papineau to the east, and rue St-Dominique to the west, it has a vibrant ethnicity that fluctuates in tone and direction with each new surge in immigration. Rue St-Denis runs the district's length, but parallel boulevard St-Laurent has the more polyglot flavor. Known as "The Main," it was once the boulevard first encountered by foreigners arriving at the waterfront. New arrivals still come here to start their lives again, creating a patchwork of colors and cultures. Without its people and their diverse interests, St-Laurent would be just another paper-strewn urban eyesore. But its ground-floor windows are filled with glistening golden chickens, collages of shoes and pastries and aluminum cookware, curtains of sausages, and daring garments by designers on the edge of Montréal's fashion industry. Many warehouses and tenements have been converted to house this panoply of shops, bars, and low-cost eateries, and their often-garish signs draw eyes from the still-dilapidated upper stories.

RUES PRINCE-ARTHUR & DULUTH   These two essentially pedestrian streets connect boulevard St-Laurent with rue St-Denis, 8 blocks east. The livelier rue Prince-Arthur is lined with ethnic restaurants, primarily Greek and Portuguese, plus a sprinkling of newcomers. Mimes, jugglers, and street musicians try to cajole passersby into parting with their spare change. Four blocks north, rue Duluth is fairly quiet in the blocks near boulevard St-Laurent but more engaging near rue St-Denis. The mix of cuisines is much like that on rue Prince-Arthur. Tourists are evident in greater numbers on rue Prince-Arthur, many attracted by menus promising lobster dinners for less than C$12 (US$8) at some times of year.

PARC DU MONT-ROYAL   Not many cities have a mountain at their core. Okay, it's really a tall hill, not a true mountain. Still, Montréal is named for it—the "Royal Mountain"—and it's a notable urban pleasure to drive, walk, or take a horse-drawn *calèche* to the top for a view of the city, the island, and the St. Lawrence, especially at dusk. The park, encompassing the mountain, was designed by American landscape architect Frederick Law Olmsted, who also created New York's Central Park. On its far slope are two cemeteries—one Anglophone, one Francophone—silent reminders of the linguistic and cultural division that persists in the city. With its skating ponds, hiking and running trails, and even a short ski run, the park is well used by Montréalers, who refer to it affectionately as "the mountain."

CHINATOWN   Just north of Vieux-Montréal, south of boulevard René-Lévesque, and centered on the intersection of rues Clark and de la Gauchetière (pedestrianized here), Montréal's pocket Chinatown is mostly restaurants and a tiny park, with the occasional grocery, laundry, church, and small business. Most signs are in French or English as well as Chinese. Community spirit is strong, because it has had to resist the bulldozers of commercial redevelopment, and Chinatown's inhabitants remain faithful to their traditions despite encroaching modernism. In recent years, investors from Hong Kong, wary of their uncertain future as part of mainland China, have poured money into the neighborhood, producing signs that its shrinkage has been halted, even reversed. The area is colorful and deserves a look, though some of the best Chinese restaurants are actually in other parts of the city.

THE GAY VILLAGE   The city's gay and lesbian enclave runs east along rue Ste-Catherine from rue St-Hubert to rue Papineau. A small but vibrant district, it's filled with clothing stores, small eateries, a bar/club complex in a former post-office building, and the Gay and Lesbian Community Centre, at 1301 rue Ste-Catherine est.

ILE STE-HÉLÈNE   Ile Ste-Hélène (St. Helen's Island) in the St. Lawrence was altered extensively to become the site of Expo '67, Montréal's very successful world's fair. In the 4 years before Expo opened, construction crews reshaped the island and doubled its surface area with landfill, then went on to create beside it a new island, Ile Notre-Dame. Much of the earth needed to do this was dredged from the river bottom, and 15 million tons of rock from the excavation of the Métro and the Décaric Expressway were carried in by truck. The city built bridges and 83 pavilions and, when Expo closed, preserved the site and a few of the exhibition buildings. Parts were used for Olympic Games events in 1976, and today the island is home to Montréal's popular new casino and an amusement park, La Ronde.

2 Getting Around

For a city of more than a million inhabitants, Montréal is easy to negotiate. The Métro is fast and efficient, but of course walking is the best way to get to know this vigorous multidimensional city.

BY METRO OR BUS

For speed and economy, nothing beats Montréal's **Métro** (subway) system. Clean, relatively quiet trains whisk you through an expanding network of underground tunnels, with 65 stations at present and more scheduled to open. A single ride is C$1.90 (US$1.25) and a strip of six tickets is C$8 (US$5). Depending on how you use the system, you can save money with a *carte touristique* (tourist card), offering unlimited rides for 1 day (C$5/US$3.35) or 3 days (C$12/US$8).

Buy tickets at the booth in any station, then slip one into the slot in the turnstile to enter. Take a transfer (*correspondence*) from the machine just inside the turnstiles of every station; it allows transfers from a train to a bus at any other Métro station for no extra fare. Remember to take the transfer ticket at the station where you first enter the system. (When starting a trip by bus and intending to continue on the Métro, ask the bus driver for a transfer.) You can make most connections from one Métro line to another at the Berri–UQAM (Université de Québec à Montréal), Jean-Talon, and Snowdon stations. The Métro runs Sunday to Thursday about 5:30am to 12:30am (Fri and Sat to 1am).

Buses cost the same as Métro trains, and Métro tickets are good on buses too. Exact change is required to pay bus fares in cash. Though they run throughout the city, buses don't run as frequently or as swiftly as the Métro.

Call ☎ **514/288-6287** for information about the Métro and city buses.

BY TAXI

Plenty of taxis are run by several companies. Cabs come in a variety of colors and styles, so their principal distinguishing feature is the plastic sign on the roof. At night, it's illuminated when the cab is available. Fares aren't too expensive, with an initial charge of C$2.25 (US$1.50), C$1.10 (US75¢) per kilometer, and C40¢ (US25¢) per minute of waiting. A short ride from one point to another downtown usually costs about C$5 (US$3.35). Tip about 10% to 15%. Members of hotel and restaurant staffs can call cabs, many of which are dispatched by radio. They line up outside most large hotels or can be hailed on the street.

BY CAR

You won't need a car to explore the city, but you might like one to explore the environs or head elsewhere in Canada. Remember, you'll save money by arranging your rental before leaving home.

Major car-rental companies in Montréal include **Avis,** 1225 rue Metcalfe (☎ **800/879-2847** or 514/866-7906; Métro: Peel); **Budget,** Gare Centrale (☎ **800/ 268-8900** or 514/866-7675; Métro: Bonaventure); **Hertz,** 1475 rue Aylmer

Downtown Montréal

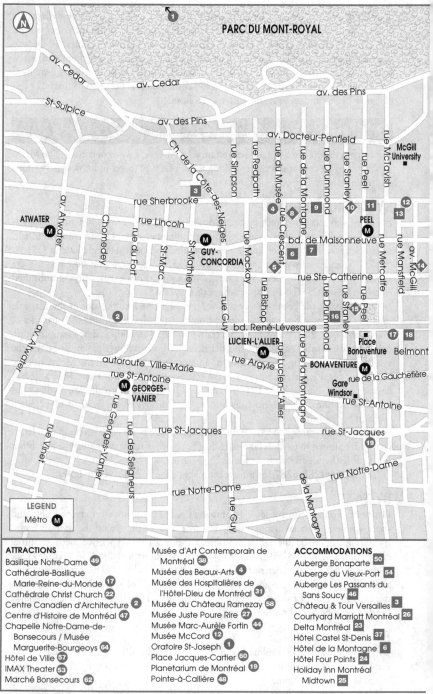

PARC DU MONT-ROYAL

McGill University

ATWATER

GUY-CONCORDIA

PEEL

LUCIEN-L'ALLIER

BONAVENTURE

Place Bonaventure   Belmont

Gare Windsor

GEORGES-VANIER

LEGEND
Métro Ⓜ

ATTRACTIONS
Basilique Notre-Dame 49
Cathédrale-Basilique
  Marie-Reine-du-Monde 17
Cathédrale Christ Church 22
Centre Canadien d'Architecture 2
Centre d'Histoire de Montréal 47
Chapelle Notre-Dame-de-
  Bonsecours / Musée
  Marguerite-Bourgeoys 64
Hôtel de Ville 57
IMAX Theater 53
Marché Bonsecours 62

Musée d'Art Contemporain de
  Montréal 38
Musée des Beaux-Arts 4
Musée des Hospitalières de
  l'Hôtel-Dieu de Montréal 31
Musée du Château Ramezay 58
Musée Juste Poure Rire 27
Musée Marc-Aurèle Fortin 44
Musée McCord 12
Oratoire St-Joseph 1
Place Jacques-Cartier 60
Planetarium de Montréal 19
Pointe-à-Callière 48

ACCOMMODATIONS
Auberge Bonaparte 50
Auberge du Vieux-Port 54
Auberge Les Passants du
  Sans Soucy 46
Château & Tour Versailles 3
Courtyard Marriott Montréal 26
Delta Montréal 23
Hôtel Castel St-Denis 37
Hôtel de la Montagne 6
Hôtel Four Points 24
Holiday Inn Montréal
  Midtown 25

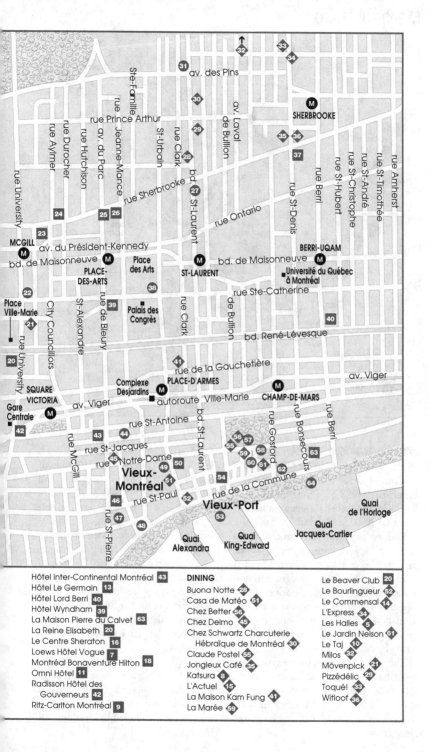

Hôtel Inter-Continental Montréal **43**
Hôtel Le Germain **13**
Hôtel Lord Berri **40**
Hôtel Wyndham **39**
La Maison Pierre du Calvet **63**
La Reine Elisabeth **20**
Le Centre Sheraton **16**
Loews Hôtel Vogue **7**
Montréal Bonaventure Hilton **18**
Omni Hôtel **11**
Radisson Hôtel des
  Gouverneurs **42**
Ritz-Carlton Montréal **9**

DINING
Buona Notte **28**
Casa de Matéo **51**
Chez Better **56**
Chez Delmo **45**
Chez Schwartz Charcuterie
  Hébraïque de Montréal **30**
Claude Postel **55**
Jongleux Café **35**
Katsura **8**
L'Actuel **15**
La Maison Kam Fung **41**
La Marée **59**

Le Beaver Club **20**
Le Bourlingueur **52**
Le Commensal **14**
L'Express **34**
Les Halles **5**
Le Jardin Nelson **61**
Le Taj **10**
Milos **32**
Mövenpick **21**
Pizzédélic **29**
Toqué! **33**
Witloof **36**

197

Montréal Métro

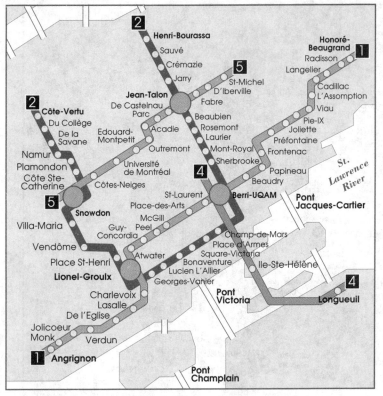

(☎ **800/263-0600** or 514/842-8537; Métro: McGill); **Thrifty,** 1076 rue de la Montagne (☎ **800/367-2277** or 514/989-7100; Métro: Lucien-l'Allier); **National/ Tilden,** 1200 rue Stanley (☎ **800/227-7368** or 514/878-2771; Metro: Peel); and **Enterprise,** 4028 Ste-Catherine ouest (☎ **800/736-8222** or 514/931-3722; Metro: Peel). Gas in Québec is somewhat more expensive than that in the States, and it'll cost about C$20 (US$13) to fill the tank of a small car with unleaded gasoline.

Parking can be difficult on downtown's heavily trafficked streets. There are plenty of metered spaces, with varying hourly rates. Look around before walking off without paying. Meters are set well back from the curb so they won't be buried by plowed snow in winter. Check for signs noting restrictions, usually showing a red circle with a diagonal slash (*"Livraison Seulement,"* for example, means "Delivery Only"). Most downtown shopping complexes have underground parking lots, as do the big downtown hotels. Some of the hotels don't charge extra to take cars in and out of their garages during the day, which can save money for those who plan to do a lot of sightseeing by car.

The limited-access expressways in Québec are called *autoroutes,* and distances and speed limits are given in kilometers (km). Some highway signs are in French only, though Montréal's autoroutes and bridges often bear dual-language signs. Seat-belt use is required by law, and turning right on a red light is prohibited in Montréal and throughout the province of Québec, except where specifically allowed by an additional green arrow.

The 24-hour hotline for emergency service provided by the **Canadian Automobile Association (CAA),** affiliated with the AAA, is ☎ **514/861-7575** in Montréal. For information on **road conditions** in and around Montréal, call ☎ **514/636-3026;** outside Montréal, call ☎ **514/636-3248.**

Fast Facts: Montréal

American Express   Offices of the **American Express Travel Service** are at 1141 bd. de Maisonneuve ouest near rue Stanley (☎ 514/284-3300; Métro: Peel) and in **La Baie (The Bay)** department store, 585 rue Ste-Catherine ouest (☎ **514/ 281-4777;** Métro: McGill). For lost or stolen cards, call ☎ **800/268-9824.**

Area Code   The area code for Montréal is **514.**

Currency Exchange   There are currency-exchange offices near most locations where they're likely to be needed: at the airports, in the train station, in and near Infotouriste at Dorchester Square, and near Notre-Dame cathedral at 86 rue Notre-Dame. The **Bank of America Canada,** 1230 rue Peel (Métro: Peel) offers foreign-exchange services Monday to Friday 8:30am to 5:30pm and Saturday 9am to 5pm.

Doctors/Dentists   The front desks at hotels can contact a doctor quickly. If it's not an emergency, call your country's consulate and ask for a recommendation (see "Embassies/Consulates," below). Consulates don't guarantee or certify local doctors, but they maintain lists of physicians with good reputations. Even if the consulate is closed, a duty officer should be available to help. For dental information, call the hotline at ☎ **514/288-8888** or the 24-hour dental clinic at ☎ **514/342-4444.** In an emergency, dial ☎ **911.**

Drugstores   Open 24 hours, the branch of **Pharmaprix** at 5122 Côte-des-Neiges, at chemin Queen Mary (☎ **514/738-8464;** Métro: Côte-des-Neiges), is fairly convenient.

Embassies/Consulates   All embassies are in Ottawa, the national capital. In Montréal, the **U.S. consulate general** is at 1155 rue St-Alexandre (☎ **514/ 398-9695;** Métro: Square-Victoria), and the **U.K. consulate general** is at 1155 rue University, Suite 901 (☎ **514/866-5863;** Métro: McGill).

Emergencies   Dial ☎ **911** for the police, firefighters, or an ambulance.

Hospitals   Hotel staffs and consulates can offer advice and information. Hospitals with emergency rooms are the **Hôpital Général de Montréal** (☎ **514/ 937-6011**) and the **Hôpital Royal Victoria** (☎ **514/842-1231**). The **Hôpital de Montréal pour Enfants** (☎ **514/934-4400**) is a children's hospital with a poison center. Other prominent hospitals are the **Hôtel-Dieu** (☎ **514/ 843-2611**) and the **Hôpital Notre-Dame** (☎ **514/281-6000**).

Internet Access   At the **CyberGround NetCafé,** 3672 bd. St-Laurent, north of rue Prince-Arthur (☎ **514/842-1726;** Métro: Sherbrooke), you can send e-mail and check on your messages. It's open Monday to Friday 10am to midnight and Saturday and Sunday 11am to midnight. Also see "Montréal After Dark."

Liquor Laws   All hard liquor and spirits in Québec are sold through official government stores operated by the Québec Société des Alcools (look for maroon signs with the acronym SAQ). You can buy wine and beer in grocery stores and convenience stores, called *dépanneurs.* The legal drinking age is 18.

Newspapers/Magazines   Montréal's prime English-language newspaper is the *Montréal Gazette.* (To familiarize yourself with events in the city and province before your arrival, log on to the paper's Web site, **www.montrealgazette.com.**) Most large newsstands and those in the larger hotels also carry the *Wall Street Journal,* the *New York Times, USA Today,* and the *International Herald Tribune.* So do the several branches of the **Maison de la Presse Internationale,** two of which are at 550 and 728 rue Ste-Catherine ouest (Métro: Peel). In Plateau Mont-Royal, a similar operation called **Multimags,** 3550 av. St-Laurent (Métro: Sherbrooke), sells hundreds of foreign newspapers and magazines. For information about current happenings in Montréal, pick up the Friday or Saturday edition of the *Gazette* or the free bimonthly booklet called *Montréal Scope,* available in some shops and many hotel lobbies.

Pets   You can bring dogs and cats into Québec, but Canadian Customs at the frontier will want to see a rabies vaccination certificate less than 3 years old signed by a licensed veterinarian. If a pet is less than 3 months old and obviously healthy, the certificate isn't likely to be required. Check with U.S. Customs about bringing your pet back into the States. Most hotels in Montréal don't accept pets, so inquire about their policy before booking a room.

Police   Dial ☎ **911** for the police. There are three types of officers: municipal police in Montréal, Québec City, and other towns; Sûreté de Québec officers, who are comparable to state police or highway patrol in the States; and RCMP (Royal Canadian Mounted Police), who are similar to U.S. Marshals or the FBI and handle cases involving infraction of federal laws. RCMP officers speak English and French. Other officers aren't required to know English, though many do.

Post Office   The **main post office** is at 1250 rue University, near Ste-Catherine (☎ **514/395-4909;** Métro: McGill), open Monday to Friday 8am to 6pm. A convenient post office in Old Montréal is at 155 rue St-Jacques, at rue St-François-Xavier (Métro: Square-Victoria). At this writing, it costs C46¢ (US31¢) to send a first-class letter or postcard within Canada and C55¢ (US37¢) to send a first-class letter or postcard from Canada to the States. First-class airmail service to other countries costs C95¢ (US63¢) for the first 20 grams (about two-thirds of an ounce). These prices are increased by the astonishing imposition of a *sales tax,* another C8¢ (US5¢) for a first-class stamp!

Smoking   It's true that French-speaking Québecers smoke more than other Canadians, despite heavy taxes on tobacco, and the province hasn't yet really clamped down on smoking in public places. Few restaurants have set aside no-smoking sections, and the establishment of cigar lounges is a peaking fad. When asked, hosts will attempt to seat you away from smokers.

Taxes   Most goods and services in Canada are taxed 7% by the federal government. On top of that, the province of Québec adds 7.5% tax on goods and services, including those provided by hotels. In Québec, the federal tax appears on the bill as the TPS (elsewhere in Canada, it's called the GST), and the provincial tax is known as the TVQ. Tourists may receive a rebate on both the federal and the provincial tax on items they've bought but not used in Québec, as well as on lodging. To take advantage of this, request the necessary forms at duty-free shops and hotels and submit them, with the original receipts, within a year of the purchase. Contact the Canadian consulate or Québec tourism office for up-to-the-minute details about taxes and rebates.

Telephones   The phone system, operated by Bell Canada, closely resembles the U.S. model. All operators (dial ☎ **0**—zero—to get one) speak French and English. Pay phones in Québec require C25¢ (US18¢) for a 3-minute local call. Directory information calls (dial ☎ **411**) are free. Both local and long-distance calls usually cost more from hotels—sometimes a lot more, so check. Directories (*annuaires des téléphones*) come in white pages (residential) and yellow pages (commercial).

Time   Montréal, Québec City, and the Laurentians are all in the Eastern time zone. Daylight saving time is observed as in the States, moving clocks ahead an hour in the spring and back an hour in the fall.

3 Accommodations

Montréal hoteliers make everyone welcome, partly because they offer more rooms than can be filled with certainty throughout the year. That competition and the robust value of the U.S. dollar in relation to its Canadian counterpart make this city the place to splurge or at least step up in class. Except in B&Bs, you can usually count on discounts and package deals, especially on weekends, when business guests have gone home.

Nearly all hotel staff members, from front-desk personnel to the porters, are reassuringly bilingual. The busiest times are July and August, especially during the frequent summer festivals, during annual holiday periods (Canadian or American), and when Montréal and Québec City hold their winter carnivals. At those times, reserve well in advance, especially if special rates or packages are desired. Most other times, expect to find plenty of available rooms.

Note: The rates below don't include the 7% federal (TPS) or 7.5% provincial (TVQ) taxes. All rooms have private bathrooms unless otherwise noted. In the two top categories, hair dryers, cable color TVs, and in-room movies are to be expected, as are restaurants, bars, meeting rooms, and parking garages.

DOWNTOWN

See the "Downtown Montréal" map (p. 196) to locate hotels in this section.

VERY EXPENSIVE

✪ **Loews Hôtel Vogue.** 1425 rue de la Montagne (between bd. de Maisonneuve and rue Ste-Catherine), Montréal, PQ H3G 1Z3. ☎ **800/465-6654** or 514/285-5555. Fax 514/849-8903. www.loewshotels.com/vogue.html. E-mail loewsvogue@loewshotels. com. 142 units. A/C MINIBAR TV TEL. C$169–C$399 (US$113–US$266) double; from C$375 (US$250) suite. Children under 16 stay free in parents' room. Weekend rates available. AE, DC, ER, MC, V. Valet parking C$15 (US$10). Métro: Peel.

The Vogue created quite a stir when it opened in late 1990 after the stunning conversion of an undistinguished office building. Not a few observers felt it instantly displaced the Ritz-Carlton at the apex of the local hotel pantheon. Confidence resonates from every staff member, and the lobby and well-appointed guest rooms exude

Reserving Rooms on the Web

Useful Web sites for exploring possibilities and making reservations are **www.tourism-montreal.org**, **www.celestia.all-hotels.com**, and **www.destination quebec.com**.

Looking for a B&B?

Choose the embrace of a B&B and expect to get to know a Montréaler or two and to pay relatively little for the privilege. B&B owners are among the most knowledgeable and outgoing guides. For information about downtown B&Bs, contact **Relais Montréal Hospitalité,** 3977 av. Laval, Montréal, PQ H2W 2H9 (☎ **800/363-9635** or 514/287-9635; fax 514/287-1007), or the **Bed & Breakfast Downtown Network,** 3458 av. Laval (at rue Sherbrooke), Montréal, PQ H2X 3C8 (☎ **800/267-5180** or 514/289-9749). For B&Bs in Plateau Mont-Royal, try the **Hébergement Touristique du Plateau Mont-Royal,** 1301 rue Rachel est, Montréal, PQ H2J 2K1 (☎ **800/597-0597** or 514/597-0166; fax 514/597-0496), operated by the people who manage the popular Auberge de la Fontaine. It's wise to ask all pertinent questions up front: Are children welcome? Is smoking allowed? Do all guests share the bathroom? Deposits are usually required, with the balance payable on arrival.

the luxury you'd expect. Though some may find the hotel chilly in look and tone, that feeling is difficult to reconcile with the feather pillows and duvets on the oversized beds, fresh flowers, cherry-wood furniture, and marble bathrooms with Jacuzzis, TVs, and plush robes. Other pluses are fax machines, modem access, safes, and in-room movies.

Dining/Diversions: The Société Café serves all meals, with outside tables in summer. The lobby bar, L'Opéra, has piano music Thursday to Saturday and an outdoor terrace in summer.

Amenities: Concierge, 24-hour room service, dry cleaning/laundry, baby-sitting, secretarial services, express checkout, small exercise room.

Montréal Bonaventure Hilton. 1 place Bonaventure (at rue Mansfield), Montréal, PQ H5A 1E4. ☎ **800/445-8667** in the U.S., 800/267-2575 in Canada, or 514/878-2332. Fax 514/878-3881. www.hilton.com. E-mail yulbh_po@hilton.com. 395 units. A/C MINIBAR TV TEL. C$130–C$299 (US$87–US$199) double. Children stay free in parents' room. Weekend packages available. AE, CB, DC, ER, MC, V. Self-parking C$14 (US$9); valet parking C$19 (US$13). Métro: Bonaventure.

The Hilton's main entrance is at rues de la Gauchetière and Mansfield, but the lobby is on the 17th floor. It has elevator access to Central Station and the Underground City. From aloft, the hotel looks as if it has a square hole in its top—that's the 2½-acre roof garden, with strolling pheasants, paddling ducks, and a heated pool. The guest rooms have color TVs in the bedrooms and black-and-white sets in the compact bathrooms, as well as views of the city or the garden. There are no-smoking rooms and an executive floor. All rooms, public and private, underwent renovation a few years ago.

Dining: Le Castillon is a French restaurant, and La Bourgade is less expensive. Both have summer dining terraces.

Amenities: Concierge, 24-hour room service, baby-sitting, year-round heated outdoor pool, fitness center with sauna, business center.

✪ **Omni Hôtel.** 1050 Sherbrooke ouest, Montréal, PQ H3A 2R6. ☎ **800/228-3000** or 514/284-1110. Fax 514/845-3025. www.omnihotels.com. E-mail dumaberg@microtec.net. 329 units. A/C MINIBAR TV TEL. C$149–C$259 (US$99–US$173) double; from C$370 (US$247) suite. Rates include breakfast. Children under 18 stay free in parents' room. Weekend rates and special packages available. AE, CB, DC, ER, MC, V. Self-parking C$11 (US$7); valet parking C$19 (US$13). Métro: Peel.

This once was Le Quatre Saisons and the Westin Mont-Royal, but in whatever guise it was a worthy competitor to the Ritz-Carlton. It still is, especially after an ongoing

C$5.5 million (US$3.65 million) renovation by the new owners. The austere lobby, lined with marble, is softened by statuary, plants, and flowers. The guest rooms are large, but make sure you're assigned one of the already-refurbished ones. They're offered in escalating categories of luxury, from standard to premium. Robes are ready for your use, and security is enhanced by in-room safes. On-demand movies can be chosen from a library of more than 60 titles. There are 12 no-smoking floors.

Dining/Diversions: Zen, an upscale Chinese restaurant, offers lunch and dinner daily, as does the light-filled Opus II, which has featured a form of world cuisine through frequent chef changes. Buffet breakfasts and lunches are served in the lobby bar, L'Apèro, which features piano music in the evenings.

Amenities: Concierge, 24-hour room service, in-room massage, twice-daily maid service, car and limo rentals, secretarial services; impressive health club with heated outdoor pool, aerobics classes, weight machines, whirlpool, sauna, and workout gear or swimsuits on request; car-rental desk; boutiques.

✪ **Ritz-Carlton Montréal.** 1228 Sherbrooke ouest (at rue Drummond), Montréal, PQ H3G 1H6. ☎ **800/363-0366** in Canada and the U.S., or 514/842-4212. Fax 514/842-2268. www.ritzcarlton.com. E-mail ritz@citenet.net. 229 units. A/C MINIBAR TV TEL. C$160–C$275 (US$107–US$183) double; from C$395 (US$263) suite. Children under 14 stay free in parents' room. Packages available. AE, CB, DC, ER, MC, V. Self-parking or valet parking C$15 (US$10), with in/out privileges. Pets accepted. Métro: Peel.

In 1912, the Ritz-Carlton opened to the carriage trade, and that clientele has remained faithful. Over the years, their Pierce-Arrows gave way to Rolls-Royces and Lamborghinis, and a few of these (or at least a Cadillac limo or custom-built Lincoln) are always parked in readiness near the front door. Males used to be required to wear jackets in public rooms after 5pm, but management has eased up on that requirement. The bathrooms come with robes, makeup mirrors, hair dryers, and speakers carrying TV sound. Fax machines are available on request, the phones have dataports, and the rooms have safes and irons with boards, and even umbrellas. A recent period of perceptible decline prompted a C$10 million (US$7 million) renovation, completed in 1999. Upgrading was largely devoted to soft goods—drapes, upholstery, and carpeting.

Dining/Diversions: The Café de Paris is favored for its high tea and weekday power breakfasts. Meals are served on the terrace in summer, next to a duck pond. An adjacent room spreads a lunch buffet. There's piano music in the Ritz Bar and Le Grand Prix, with dancing nightly in the latter.

Services: Concierge, 24-hour room service, same-day dry cleaning/laundry, twice-daily maid service, baby-sitting, express checkout, secretarial services; modest fitness room, barbershop, newsstand, gift shop.

EXPENSIVE

Delta Montréal. 450 Sherbrooke ouest (at rue Aylmer), Montréal, PQ H3A 2T4. ☎ **800/268-1133** or 514/286-1986. Fax 514/284-4342. www.deltamontreal.com. E-mail reservation@deltamontreal.com. 459 units. A/C MINIBAR TV TEL. C$149–C$290 (US$99–US$193) double; from C$310 (US$207) suite. Children under 19 stay free in parents' room. Weekend packages available. AE, DC, DISC, ER, MC, V. Parking C$12 (US$8). Métro: Place-des-Arts.

This well-maintained unit of the Canadian chain, with its expansive business center and better-than-average health club, is targeted to businesspeople. However, its supervised children's crafts-and-games center and outdoor pool (open in summer) make it clear families are welcome too. The guest rooms have angular dimensions, escaping the boxiness of many contemporary hotels, and most have small balconies; all have coffeemakers and voice mail. For an extra C$30 (US$20), upgrade to the Signature executive floor. Enter the 23-story tower from avenue du Président-Kennedy.

Dining: Le Bouquet Bistro is open most of the day, with a popular lunch buffet, while the adjacent dining room is more formal, with an international menu. Drinks, light meals, and a weekday lunch buffet are offered by the casual Le Cordial.

Amenities: Concierge, room service, dry cleaning/laundry, courtesy airport transport, indoor and outdoor pools; health club with aerobics instructor, indoor lap pool, two squash courts, whirlpool, sauna, massage; business center with rental computers and translation service.

✪ **Hôtel Le Germain.** 2050 rue Mansfield (at the west end of av. du Président-Kennedy), Montréal, PQ H3A 1Y9. ☎ **514/849-2050.** Fax 514/849-1437. www. hotelgermain.com. 100 units. A/C MINIBAR TV TEL. C$210–C$550 (US$140–US$367) double. Rates include breakfast. AE, CB, DC, ER, MC, V. Valet parking C$12 (US$8). Métro: Peel.

This latest meritorious undertaking by the eponymous owner of two equally desirable boutique hotels in Québec City and suburban Ste-Foy brings a fresh panache to Montréal. She has converted a small office tower with her sturdy sense of style, one that magically contrives to combine an Oriental minimalism with all the Western comforts an international executive might expect. These include handy modem ports, irons and boards, CD players, big wicker chairs with fat cushions, and beds that'll cure insomnia, piled with pillows and comforters. The location is near every downtown sightseeing and shopping destination. When checking out, allow half an hour for the attendant to bring your car around.

Dining: Self-serve breakfasts are set out on the mezzanine, with perfect croissants, a machine that makes excellent café au lait, and newspapers in French and English. The owner plans to introduce short lunch and dinner menus here, next to the bar, featuring Asian soups, salads, sandwiches, and light main courses.

Amenities: Room service, dry cleaning/laundry, express checkout.

Hôtel Wyndham. 4 Complexe Desjardins, Montréal, PQ H5B 1E5. ☎ **800/361-8234** or 514/285-1450. Fax 514/285-1243. www.wyndham-mtl.com. E-mail infoAwyndham-mtl.com. 600 units. A/C MINIBAR TV TEL. C$99–C$210 (US$66–US$140) double; from C$380 (US$253) suite. Children under 18 stay free in parents' room. Packages available. AE, DC, ER, MC, V. Self-parking C$9 (US$6); valet parking C$15 (US$10). Métro: Place-des-Arts.

This used to be Le Meridien and then the Complexe Desjardins, but nothing much besides the name has changed. It's still an integral part of the striking Complexe Desjardins, across from the Place des Arts and the Montréal Museum of Contemporary Art. The guest rooms, decorated in restful tones, are comfortable enough, with voice mail and modem access; however, the bathrooms are on the skimpy side (with hair dryers). Glass-enclosed elevators glide up to rooms and down to the lower levels of the complex, which contain a shopping plaza and an indoor pool cantilevered over garden terraces. Chinatown is a block away, and Vieux-Montréal, the downtown district, and the ethnic neighborhoods along The Main are within easy walking distance. This is usually the official headquarters of the annual jazz festival. No-smoking floors are available.

Dining/Diversions: Café Fleuri provides all meals, while Le Club, with a French menu, serves only lunch and dinner. Le Bar overlooks the Complexe Desjardins and has piano music nightly.

Amenities: Concierge, 24-hour room service, dry cleaning/laundry, express checkout; indoor pool, exercise room with whirlpool and sauna, business center.

La Reine Elisabeth (Queen Elizabeth). 900 bd. René-Lévesque ouest (at rue Mansfield), Montréal, PQ H3B 4A5. ☎ **800-441-1414** or 514/861-3511. Fax 514/954-2258. www. cphotels.ca. 1,080 units. A/C MINIBAR TV TEL. C$99–C$215 (US$66–US$143) double;

concierge-level rates about C$60 (US$40) higher; from C$325 (US$217) suite. Children 18 and under stay free in parents' room. Various discounts, weekend, and excursion packages available. AE, CB, DC, DISC, ER, MC, V. Valet parking C$12 (US$8). Métro: Bonaventure.

Montréal's largest hotel opened in 1958. Its 21 floors sit atop Gare Centrale, with place Ville-Marie, place Bonaventure, and the Métro accessible by underground arcades. That desirable location makes it a prime choice for heads of state and celebrities, even though other hotels offer higher standards of personal pampering. Those who can afford it close the gap by staying on the Entree Gold 19th floor, with a private concierge and check-in and a lounge serving complimentary breakfasts and cocktail-hour canapés to go with the honor bar. The less exalted rooms on floors 4 through 17 are entirely satisfactory and come with most of the expected comforts and gadgets (including On Command in-room movies, hair dryers, coffeemakers, and voice mail). No-smoking floors are available.

Dining/Diversions: Le Beaver Club (see "Dining") features a combo for dancing on Saturday. Several other more casual bistro/bars serve meals in a variety of settings.

Amenities: Concierge, 24-hour room service, dry cleaning/laundry, baby-sitting; well-equipped health club with indoor pool and Jacuzzi, steam room, and instructors; business center, beauty salon, shopping arcade.

Le Centre Sheraton. 1201 bd. René-Lévesque ouest (between rues Drummond and Stanley), Montréal, PQ H3B 2L7. ☎ **800/325-3535** or 514/878-2000. Fax 514/878-3958. www.sheraton.com. 865 units. A/C TV TEL. C$117–C$225 (US$78–US$150) double; from C$280 (US$187) suite. Children under 17 stay free in parents' room. Weekend rates available. AE, DC, DISC, ER, MC, V. Self-parking C$9 (US$6) with in/out privileges; valet parking C$10 (US$7). Métro: Bonaventure or Peel.

Le Centre Sheraton rises near Gare Centrale, a few steps off Dorchester Square and within a short walk of the rue Crescent dining/nightlife district. A high glass wall transforms the lobby atrium into an immense greenhouse, big enough to shelter royal palms and a luxuriance of tropical plants. The staff is efficient, and the guest rooms are comfortably corporate in style. That figures, since earnest people in suits make up most of the clientele. They gravitate to the executive Towers section, which bestows complimentary breakfast, newspapers of choice, and an expansive private lounge with great views and free evening hors d'oeuvres. Half the rooms have minibars and all have robes, coffeemakers, and in-room movies. Seventeen of the 35 floors are reserved for nonsmokers.

Dining/Diversions: The Boulevard restaurant serves all meals; the Musette serves breakfast and lunch only. Jazz is performed Tuesday to Saturday in the Impromptu Bar, and there's a separate sports bar.

Amenities: Concierge in Towers, 24-hour room service, same-day dry cleaning/laundry, baby-sitting, secretarial services, express checkout, business center, airport transport; indoor pool; fitness center with pool, whirlpool, and sauna.

Radisson Hôtel des Gouverneurs. 777 rue University (at rue St-Antoine), Montréal, PQ H3C 3Z7. ☎ **800/361-8155** or 514/879-1370. Fax 514/879-1761. www.radisson.com/montrealca. E-mail hotel@radissonmontreal.com. 550 units. A/C TV TEL. C$135–C$225 (US$90–US$150) double. AE, DC, DISC, ER, MC, V. Parking nearby. Métro: Square Victoria.

Adjacent to the Bourse (stock exchange) and within walking distance of Gare Centrale, downtown offices, and Vieux-Montréal, this hotel well serves both businesspeople and families. There are an indoor pool and in-room movies for the kids, a fitness center with Nautilus machines and a sauna for their parents, and a special floor for execs with minibars in the rooms. All the guest rooms—in the usual Radisson style—have hair dryers, modem ports, voice mail, and irons and ironing boards.

ⓘ Family-Friendly Hotels

Delta Montréal *(see p. 203)* The Activity Centre for supervised play and crafts making is a big draw for small kids, along with the pool and (for bigger kids) an electronic-games room.

Holiday Inn Montréal Midtown *(see p. 207)* Two kids under 19 stay free with their parents, kids under 12 eat free, and everyone gets to enjoy free in-room movies and the big pool. There are special packages for families.

Hotel Wyndham *(see p. 204)* The glass-enclosed elevators scooting up and down through the heart of the complex are fun for kids, as are the indoor pool and the subterranean levels of the Underground City. Children stay free with their parents.

YMCA It has three family rooms, a cafeteria that serves three meals a day, and a big indoor pool that guests may use.

Dining/Diversions: Twenty-eight floors up is the city's only revolving restaurant, Tour de Ville, fun for a drink at sunset even if you eat elsewhere, though you might be tempted to stay for the "theme" buffets (Tues to Sat) or dancing to live music (Wed to Sat). Down below are a bistro bar and a connection with the Underground City and the Métro.

MODERATE

Château & Tour Versailles. 1659 rue Sherbrooke ouest (at rue St-Mathieu), Montréal, PQ H3H 1E3. ☎ **800/361-3664** in the U.S., 800/361-7199 in Canada, or 514/933-3611. Fax 514/933-6967. www.tourversailles.com. E-mail sales@tourversailles.com. 70 units in town houses, 107 units in tower. A/C MINIBAR TV TEL. C$119–C$169 (US$79–US$113) double. Children under 17 stay free in parents' room. Special weekend rates Nov–May. AE, CB, DC, ER, MC, V. Valet parking C$13 (US$8). Métro: Guy.

This has long been a local favorite, if overpraised. It began as a European-style pension in 1958, but the owners have since expanded into four adjacent pre–World War I town houses and added a modern tower across the street. I'd choose the former over the motel-ish *tour*, even though it has no elevator and the furnishings verge on dowdy. The guest rooms are good-sized and comfortable enough, with hair dryers and coffeemakers. A few antiques grace the public rooms. The service remains more personal than that in the big downtown hotels, and breakfast and afternoon tea are served in a small dining room with a fireplace. There are two no-smoking floors and a French restaurant in the tower. Price and location keep both popular, so reserve well in advance.

Courtyard Marriott Montréal. 410 rue Sherbrooke ouest (at av. du Parc), Montréal, PQ H3A 1B3. ☎ **800/449-6654** or 514/844-8851. Fax 514/844-0912. E-mail info@courtyard montreal.com. 180 units. A/C TV TEL. C$94–C$199 (US$63–US$133) double. AE, DC, DISC, ER, MC, V. Parking C$10 (US$7). Métro: Place-des-Arts.

Formerly La Citadelle, this recent acquisition of the Marriott subdivision fits the chain's profile of service to businesspeople at moderate cost. While this mid-rise slab can hardly be described as grand, needed renovations have perked it up. The guest rooms now provide hair dryers, coffeemakers, and phones with voice mail, and the junior suites provide space for longer stays, some with extra fax and modem lines. The compact fitness center has Nautilus machines, a sauna, and a steam room. The restaurant sets out a buffet breakfast each morning. Add in the self-service Laundromat and indoor pool, and most of these facilities and services are also desirable for families on tight budgets.

Holiday Inn Montréal Midtown. 420 rue Sherbrooke ouest (at av. du Parc), Montréal, PQ H3A 1B4. ☎ **800/465-4329** in the U.S., 800/387-3042 in Canada, or 514/842-6111. Fax 514/842-9381. www.hospitalitequebec.com. E-mail himidtown@hospitalitequebec.com. 485 units. A/C TV TEL. C$119–C$180 (US$79–US$120) double. Children 19 and under stay free in parents' room. Summer and family packages available. AE, CB, DC, DISC, ER, MC, V. Parking C$14 (US$9). Métro: Place-des-Arts.

Not to be confused with the Holiday Inn in the Quartier Chinois (Chinatown), this midlevel entry stands among the similar hotels clustered around the intersection of rues Sherbrooke and Durocher (which include the two above). Like them, it's among the city's best values in its class, especially for economizing families. Self-operated washers and dryers, for example, are provided for guests' use, rare in the city. No-smoking and executive floors are available. A large heated indoor pool is attended by a lifeguard, and the adjoining fitness center has weights, exercise bikes, whirlpool, and sauna.

✪ Hôtel de la Montagne. 1430 rue de la Montagne (north of rue Ste-Catherine), Montréal, PQ H3G 1Z5. ☎ **800/361-6262** or 514/288-5656. Fax 514/288-9658. www.intermatch.qc.ca/hoteldelamontagne. 138 units. A/C TV TEL. C$145–C$155 (US$97–US$103) double. AE, CB, DC, DISC, ER, MC, V. Parking C$12 (US$8). Métro: Peel.

Two white lions stand sentinel at the front door, along with a doorman in a pith helmet. The fauna fixation continues in a crowded lobby with a pair of 6-foot carved elephants, two gold-colored crocodiles, and a nude female figure boasting stained-glass butterfly wings atop a fountain. On the mezzanine is the main dining room, Le Lutétia. Light meals are available beside the pool on the roof, 20 stories up, and there's dancing under the stars. Off the lobby, a cabaret lounge featuring a piano player and jazz duos (Mon to Sat) leads into Thursday's, a bar/restaurant with a spangly disco and a terrace on rue Crescent. After all that, the relatively serene guest rooms seem downright bland. A stay here is a genuine bargain, especially in contrast to the superexpensive Loews Vogue across the street.

Hôtel Four Points. 475 rue Sherbrooke ouest (at rue Aylmer), Montréal, PQ H3A 2L9. ☎ **514/842-3961** or 800/325-3535. Fax 514/842-0945. 195 units. A/C TV TEL. C$99–C$144 (US$66–US$96) double; from C$154 (US$103) suite. Children under 17 stay free in parents' room. Packages available. AE, CD, DC, ER, MC, V. Parking C$12 (US$8). Metro: Place-des-Arts.

A new division of the Starwood hotel colossus (which also incorporates Westin and Sheraton), this mid-priced business hotel is a refurbished Howard Johnson. It provides a modest exercise room with aerobic devices, as well as roomy suites for businesspeople (and families) on longer stays, with fax machines, copiers, and a computer on call. The guest rooms come with hair dryers, Nintendo play stations, unstocked fridges, coffeemakers, and irons and ironing boards; the newspaper of your choice is made available. The towels are unaccountably skimpy, though, and bathroom lighting is often dim. The Bistro le Monde sets out an appetizing buffet breakfast and has economical lunch and dinner table d'hôte menus at C$10 (US$7) and C$19 (US$13). A door next to the reception desk leads into the Presse Café, part of a local chain.

INEXPENSIVE

Hôtel Castel St-Denis. 2099 rue St-Denis, Montréal, PQ H2X 3K8. ☎ **514/842-9719.** Fax 514/843-8492. 18 units. A/C TV. C$55 (US$37) double. Extra person C$10 (US$7). MC, V. No parking available. Métro: Berri–UQAM or Sherbrooke.

Among the budget choices in the Latin Quarter, the Castel St-Denis is one of the most desirable. It's a little south of rue Sherbrooke, among the cafes of the lower reaches of the street, and two long blocks from the Terminus Voyageur. Most of the guest rooms are fairly quiet, and all are tidy and simply decorated, if hardly chic. The bilingual owner is a good source for guidance about nearby restaurants and attractions. His Web site should be online by the time you buy this book, so do a search.

Hôtel Lord Berri. 1199 rue Berri (between bd. René-Lévesque and rue Ste-Catherine), Montréal, PQ H2L 4C6. ☎ **888/363-0363** or 514/845-9236. Fax 514/849-9855. www.lord berri.com. E-mail info@lordberri.com. 154 units. A/C TV TEL. C$75–C$82 (US$50–US$55) double. Extra person C$7 (US$4.65). AE, CB, DC, DISC, ER, MC, V. Outdoor parking C$10 (US$7). Métro: Berri-UQAM.

After a stint as a Days Inn, this economy hotel has returned to its old name, along with some needed upgrading of the furniture and wallpaper. The resulting decor is still as interesting as a bus schedule, and this remains a place primarily for people who plan to do nothing but sleep here; you do get in-room movies though. The Latin Quarter location a 5-minute walk from Vieux-Montréal helps make up for the hotel's limitations. Several floors are set aside for nonsmokers.

VIEUX-MONTRÉAL (OLD MONTRÉAL)
VERY EXPENSIVE

✪ **Hôtel Inter-Continental Montréal.** 360 rue St-Antoine ouest (at rue Bleury), Montréal, PQ H2Y 3X4. ☎ **800/361-3600** or 514/987-9900. Fax 514/847-8550. www. montreal.interconti.com. E-mail montreal@interconti.com. 357 units. A/C MINIBAR TV TEL. C$180–C$305 (US$120–US$203) double; from C$350 (US$233) suite. Packages available. AE, CB, DC, DISC, ER, MC, V. Valet parking C$19 (US$13). Small pets accepted. Métro: Square Victoria.

A few minutes' walk from Notre-Dame and Vieux-Montréal's restaurants and nightspots, this striking luxury hotel opened in 1991 and instantly became one of the top three properties in town. Its new tower houses the sleek reception area and guest rooms, while the restored annex, the Nordheimer building (ca. 1888), contains some of the restaurants and bars. (Take a look at the early–19th-century vaults down below.) The rooms are quiet and well lit, with photos and lithographs by local artists. The turret suites are fun, offering round bedrooms and wraparound windows. All rooms have coffeemakers, two or three phones, and in-room movies; robes and hair dryers are supplied. Four floors are reserved for nonsmokers, and there are executive floors with a lounge.

Dining/Diversions: Les Continents serves all meals and Sunday brunch. Le Cristallin, the piano bar, offers a light menu and has music nightly. In the Nordheimer building is the congenial Chez Plume bistro, popular for lunch and after work.

Amenities: Concierge, 24-hour room service, same-day laundry/valet Monday to Friday, complimentary newspaper, nightly turndown, express checkout; health club with enclosed rooftop lap pool, sauna/steam rooms, massage, weight room; business center.

EXPENSIVE

✪ **Auberge du Vieux-Port.** 97 rue de la Commune est (near St-Gabriel), Montréal, PQ H2Y 1J1. ☎ **888/660-7678** or 514/876-0081. Fax 514/876-8923. www. aubergeduvieuxport.com. E-mail avp@dsuper.net. 27 units. A/C MINIBAR TV TEL. C$130–C$265 (US$87–US$177) double. Extra person C$15 (US$10). Rates include full breakfast. AE, DC, DISC, ER, MC, V. Valet parking C$12 (US$8). Métro: Place-d'Armes.

Expanding on their own fine example, the owners of Sans Soucy (below) produced this larger, more luxurious inn in an 1882 building, adding a romantic cellar restaurant. Though it's gone through four managers in a year, that doesn't seem to have affected the performance. Polished hardwood floors, massive beams, and the original windows shape the hideaway no-smoking guest rooms, 15 of which face the waterfront. Some have whirlpool bathtubs; all have hair dryers and phones with dataports.

Dining: Drinks and sandwiches are served on the roof terrace, with unobstructed views of the Old Port, a particular treat when fireworks are scheduled at La Ronde. Les Ramparts restaurant sticks to traditional French fare in fixed-price meals carefully prepared and adroitly served; at one end of the room is an excavated fragment of the colonial fortification.

Amenities: Room service (7:30am to 10pm).

La Maison Pierre du Calvet. 405 rue Bonsecours (at rue St-Paul), Montréal, PQ H27 1Z5. ☎ **514/282-1725.** Fax 514/282-0456. www.pierreducalvet.ca. E-mail calvet@pierredu calvet.ca. 9 units. A/C TEL. C$165–C$225 (US$110–US$150) double; C$450 (US$300) suite. Extra person C$35 (US$23). Rates include full breakfast. AE, MC, V. Métro: Place-d'Armes.

This house was already 50 years old when Ben Franklin came here in 1775 during his attempt to enlist Canada in the revolt against the British. After a recent stint as a themed restaurant, Les Filles du Roi, the same owners made it into an inn that transports you to an elegant *manoir* beside the Loire. The beamed public rooms are furnished with antiques, like carpets on the ancient stone floors, leather sofas, gilt-framed portraits, a marquetry-topped reception desk, ship models, and a gloriously romantic dining room. The guest rooms are no less opulent, some with fireplaces and heavily carved four-poster canopied beds. TVs would only spoil the ambiance. The food and service don't always live up to the setting, but Vieux-Montréal has plenty of places to eat. A 50% deposit is required.

MODERATE

Auberge Bonaparte. 447 rue St-François-Xavier (north of rue St-Paul), Montréal, PQ H2Y 1Z5. ☎ **514/844-1448.** Fax 514/844-0272. E-mail bonaparte@securenet.net. 31 units. A/C TV TEL. C$135–C$185 (US$90–US$123) double; C$325 (US$217) suite. Extra person C$10 (US$7). Rates about 20% lower Oct–Apr. Rates include full breakfast. AE, MC, V. Metro: Place-d'Armes or Square Victoria.

The restaurant of the same name on the ground floor has long been one of Old Montréal's favorites. Romantic and faded in a Left Bank way, it has undergone massive renovation. While they were at it, the owners undertook to transform the overhead floors into this modish urban inn that opened in 1999. Even the smallest rooms are spacious, and they contain a variety of combinations of furniture—king beds alone, queens with doubles, or doubles with singles—that are useful for families. Of the eight units on each floor, four have whirlpool bathtubs with separate showers; hair dryers are available. Spring for the handsome top-floor suite and you'll get superb views of Notre-Dame, gardens, and cobblestone streets. Room service is available around the clock, including the possibility of a full dinner at 3am. The inn's Web site should be up by the time you buy this book, so do a search.

✪ Auberge Les Passants du Sans Soucy. 171 rue St-Paul ouest (8 blocks from place Jacques-Cartier), Montréal, PQ H2Y 1Z5. ☎ **514/842-2634.** Fax 514/842-2912. 9 units. A/C TV TEL. C$105–C$140 (US$70–US$93) double; C$175 (US$117) suite. Extra person C$10 (US$7). Rates include full breakfast. AE, DC, ER, MC, V. Parking C$12 (US$8). Métro: Place-d'Armes.

This delightful B&B occupies a 1723 house on even older foundations craftily converted by the bilingual owners. (Its seemingly misspelled name is a play on the name of one of them, Daniel Soucy.) Exposed brick, beams, and a marble floor form the entry area, which leads to a sitting area and a breakfast nook with a skylight. The guest rooms are upstairs, each with mortared stone walls, a buffed wood floor, a clock radio, fresh flowers, lace curtains, and a wrought-iron or brass bed. They're in the process of adding gas fireplaces to three rooms. The substantial breakfasts spin on from chocolate croissants and café au lait.

4 Dining

Montréal brims with more than 4,000 restaurants. Until only a few years ago, they were overwhelmingly French. There were a few *temples de cuisine* that delivered (or pretended to) haute gastronomy, scores of accomplished bistros that employed humbler ingredients and less grand settings, and folksy places that served the hearty fare of the days of the colonial era—game, maple sugar, and root vegetables. Everything else was French. Yes, some places offered Asian and Mediterranean cooking, but they didn't enjoy the same favor they did in other North American cities. Québec was French, and that was that.

While waves of food crazes washed over Los Angeles, Chicago, Toronto, and New York in the 1980s, introducing Cajun, Tex-Mex, Southwestern, and the fusion cuisines known as Franco-Asian, Pacific Rim, and Cal-Ital, Montréalers were resolute. Now that has changed dramatically. The early-1990s recession, from which Canada has been slow to recover, put many restaurateurs out of business and forced others to streamline their operations. Immigration continued to grow, and with it came the introduction of more foreign cuisines. Montréalers, secure in their image as epicures, began sampling the exotic edibles emerging in new storefront eateries all around—Thai, Indian, Moroccan, Vietnamese, Portuguese, Turkish, Mexican, Créole, Szechuan, Japanese. Innovation and the intermingling of styles, ingredients, and techniques were inevitable. The city is now as cosmopolitan in its tastes and offerings as any on the Continent.

Picking through this forest of tempting choices can be both gratifying and bewildering. Besides the places suggested below, there are many worthy choices, concentrated along **rues Crescent, St-Denis,** and **St-Laurent.** Nearly all have menus posted outside, prompting the local pastime of stopping every few yards for a little mouthwatering reading and comparison shopping before deciding on a place for dinner.

It's a good idea to reserve at one of the city's top restaurants. Unlike in larger American and European cities, however, a few hours or a day in advance is usually sufficient. Dress codes are all but nonexistent, except in a handful of luxury restaurants, but you should still dress well for the better places. And since parking is at a premium in most restaurant districts, take the Métro or a taxi to the restaurant (most are within 1 or 2 blocks of a Métro station), or ask if valet parking is available when making a reservation.

Québecers are the heaviest smokers in Canada, despite the high cost, but even in addicted Montréal, no-smoking areas in restaurants are increasingly available, if far from common. Larger restaurants are the most likely to have set aside blocks of tables out of the nicotine slipstream.

Take Advantage of the Table d'Hôte

The city's table d'hôte (fixed-price) meals are eye-openers. You can enjoy entire two- to four-course meals, often with a beverage, for little more than the price of an à la carte main course alone. Even the best restaurants offer them, so the table d'hôte represents considerable savings and the chance to sample some excellent restaurants at reasonable prices.

Note: The prices below don't include the 7% federal tax and 7.5% provincial tax that are added to a restaurant bill. Food purchased in a market or grocery store isn't taxed.

DOWNTOWN

See the "Downtown Montréal" map (p.196) to locate the restaurants in this section.

VERY EXPENSIVE

✪ **Le Beaver Club.** In Le Reine Elisabeth hotel, 900 René-Lévesque ouest (at rue Mansfield). ☎ **514/861-3511.** Reservations recommended. Jackets required. Main courses C$26–C$32 (US$17–US$21); table d'hôte menu C$17–C$21 (US$11–US$14) at lunch, C$36–C$42 (US$24–US$28) at dinner. AE, CB, DISC, MC, V. Mon–Fri noon–3pm and 6–11pm, Sat 6–11pm. Métro: Bonaventure. FRENCH.

The restaurant takes its name from an organization of socially prominent explorers and trappers established in 1785, which is why you dine under the glassy stares of a polar bear, musk-ox, and bison. Stained-glass and carved-wood panels depict their wilderness adventures and undergird the clubby tone of the dining room. It has been a magnet for the city's power brokers for decades (though, with 225 seats to fill, it's hardly exclusive). Lunch is the time for the gentlest prices. The menu changes twice a year, but if you can eat only one meal here, lean toward the roast beef. The determined dieter will appreciate the nutritional information provided for each lunch dish. On Saturdays, a trio begins playing at 7:30pm for dancing.

✪ **Les Halles.** 1450 rue Crescent (between rue Ste-Catherine and bd. de Maisonneuve). ☎ **514/844-2328.** Reservations recommended. Main courses C$12–C$25 (US$8–US$17) at lunch, C$25–C$34 (US$17–US$23) at dinner; table d'hôte menu C$25 (US$17) at lunch, C$34 (US$23) or C$46 (US$31) at dinner. AE, CB, DC, DISC, ER, MC, V. Tues–Fri 11:45am–2:30pm, Mon–Sat 6–10pm. Closed Dec 23–Jan 19. Métro: Guy-Concordia or Peel. FRENCH.

Les Halles continues to thrive as one of the city's most accomplished French restaurants, despite being squeezed into the most frenetic block of rue Crescent, right up against the Hard Rock Cafe. It's unquestionably pricey, so consider having lunch here instead of dinner. Despite the prices, this isn't a dignified "event" place—the tables are close, the service is correct but chummy, and animated conversations often start up between strangers. Alberta beef, Québec lamb, and such game dishes as red deer and guinea hen are stars on the menu, but so is the seafood, including snowy halibut and walleye, simply prepared. The ingredients are rarely exotic, yet the kitchen dresses them in unexpected ways. Main courses and desserts come in such hefty portions you don't really need appetizers, but the table d'hôte lunch is a good deal. The wine cellar has more than 10,000 bottles of 400 wines.

EXPENSIVE

Katsura. 2170 rue de la Montagne (between bd. de Maisonneuve and rue Sherbrooke). ☎ **514/849-1172.** Reservations recommended. Main courses C$11–C$27 (US$7–US$18); table d'hôte menu C$8–C$15 (US$5–US$10) at lunch, C$27–C$37 (US$18–US$25) at dinner. AE, DC, ER, MC, V. Mon–Fri 11:30am–2:30pm and 5:30–10pm (Fri to 10:30pm); Sat 5:30–10:30pm; Sun 5:30–9:30pm. Métro: Peel or Guy-Concordia. JAPANESE.

A tuxedoed maître d' greets you at the door and leads you to one of the large convivial tables in the front room, to the smaller areas in back, or to the three-sided marble sushi bar in the middle (which serves as a refuge for those who arrive without a reservation). Katsura has been around long enough to claim credit for introducing sushi to Montréal. While no longer a novelty, sushi and sashimi are still prepared with close attention by the three chefs behind the bar. Part of the pleasure of dining here is watching them at work—precise, measured, deliberate. Depending on your choices, this can be a relatively economical meal. Sample a lot of their creations, though, and the bill shoots into a much costlier category.

MODERATE

L'Actuel. 1194 rue Peel (on square Dorchester). ☎ **514/866-1537.** Main courses C$14–C$33 (US$9–US$22). AE, MC, V. Mon–Wed 11:30am–3pm and 7–10pm; Thurs–Fri 11:30am–3pm and 7–11pm; Sat 7–11pm. BELGIAN.

Dine one flight up, where the most desirable of a sea of tables overlook the square. It's a Belgian restaurant, so mussels are the house specialty—in big portions in more than a dozen variations, provençale to curried, brought to the table in the cast-iron pot in which they were cooked. Double-fried potatoes are the delectable accompaniment, and complimentary second helpings are customary. A sturdy Muscadet goes well with mussels, and there are two good ones on the list. If mollusks aren't to your liking, options include club steaks and tournedos in 18 sauces and preparations and spicy steak tartare. The daily lunch specials are always easy on the wallet. Though the place is popular, there's almost always a free table, even on Saturday night.

✪ Le Taj. 2077 rue Stanley (near rue Sherbrooke). ☎ **514/845-9015.** Main courses C$9–C$17 (US$6–US$11); lunch buffet C$9 (US$6). AE, DC, ER, MC, V. Sun–Fri 11:30am–2:30pm; daily 5–10:30pm. Métro: Peel. NORTHERN INDIAN.

A large relief temple sculpture occupies pride of place in this dramatic cream-and-apricot setting. In the corner glassed cubicle, a chef works diligently over a pair of tandoor ovens. His specialty is the mughlai repertoire of the north of the Indian subcontinent. Seasonings of the dishes he sends forth tend more toward the tangy than the incendiary, but say you want your food spicy and you'll get it. (Watch out for the innocent-looking green coriander sauce.) Whatever the level of heat, the dishes are perfumed with turmeric, saffron, ginger, sumin, mango powder, and garam masala. For a rare treat, order the marinated lamb chops roasted in the tandoor; they arrive sizzling and nested on braised vegetables. Vegetarians have a choice of eight dishes, the chickpea-based *channa masala* among the most complex. Main courses are huge, served in a boggling array of bowls, saucers, cups, and dishes, all with *nan,* the pillowy flat bread, and basmati rice. Evenings are quiet and lunchtimes busy but not hectic.

INEXPENSIVE

La Maison Kam Fung. 1008 rue Clark (near rue de la Gauchetièrie est). ☎ **514/878-2888.** Main courses C$7–C$13 (US$4.65–US$9). AE, DC, ER, MC, V. Daily 7am–3pm and 5–10:30pm. Métro: Place-d'Armes. SZECHUAN/CANTONESE.

Weekends are the event days, when Chinese families who moved into the suburbs return for their comfort food. While regular meals are served in the evening, the morning to mid-afternoon hours are reserved for dim sum. That's the time to go. Here's the drill: Go to the second floor, obtain a ticket from the young woman at the podium, and wait. Once summoned to a table, be alert to the carts being trundled out of the kitchen. They're stacked with covered baskets and pots, most of which contain dumplings of one kind or another, such as balls of curried shrimp or glistening envelopes of pork nubbins or scallops, plus items like fish purée slathered on wedges of sweet pepper and, for the venturesome, steamed chicken feet and squid. Resist the desire to gather up the first five items that appear. Much more is on the way.

Le Commensal. 1204 av. McGill College (at rue Ste-Catherine). ☎ **514/871-1480.** Reservations not accepted. Dishes priced by weight: C$1.75 (US$1.15) per 100g (about 3.5 oz.). AE, MC, V. Daily 7am–midnight. Métro: McGill. VEGETARIAN.

⊕ Family-Friendly Restaurants

Pizzédélic *(see p. 218)* Pizza never fails to please the younger set, and this place caters to any taste, with toppings that stretch the imagination.

McDonald's For something familiar, but with a twist, this McDonald's, only a block from Notre-Dame at the corner of rues Notre-Dame and St-Laurent, deserves a mention. In a house that was once the home of Antoine Lamet de la Mothe Cadillac, the founder of Detroit and a governor of Louisiana, it offers the usual menu, along with pizzas and the Québec favorite, *poutine* (french fries doused with gravy and cheese nuggets).

Mövenpick *(see below)* This new something-for-everyone emporium has a dozen stations selling omelets, pizzas, burgers, and just about anything a young-ster might crave, in a Disneyland setting with a romper room, games, and no fear about making too much of a mess.

Le Commensal serves vegetarian fare buffet style. Most of the dishes are so artfully conceived, with close attention to aroma, color, and texture, that even avowed meat eaters won't feel deprived. The only likely complaint is that those dishes that are sup-posed to be hot are too often lukewarm. Patrons circle the table helping themselves, then pay the cashier by weight. The second-floor location affords a view, which com-pensates for the utilitarian decor. There's no tipping.

Le Commensal has been expanding, with roadside branches starting to open out in the suburbs. One of the most convenient in-town locations is at 1720 rue St-Denis, at rue Sherbrooke (☎ 514/845-2627), with the same hours as above.

Mövenpick. At the corner of rues University and Cathcart. ☎ **514/861-8181.** Most items under C$15 (US$10). MC, V. Daily 7am–2am. Métro: McGill or Bonaventure. INTERNATIONAL.

The central gimmick of this new outpost of the Swiss chain, long a successful presence in Toronto, is its theme-park simulation of a European market. Placed at intervals around the 30,000-square-foot space are more than a dozen food stations where you line up for pizzas, crêpes, sushi, coffee, pastas, omelets, waffles, salads, rôtisserie birds, grilled meats, baked goods, and seafood, including freshly opened oysters. Faux grapevines, fake flowers, and an ersatz tree are meant to evoke a Mediterranean set-ting. The food, much of it prepared to order, ranges from satisfactory to pretty good. Eat a course at a time or load a tray with a complete meal and take it to the nearby tables. Children are welcome in the designated romper room, the bistro has table ser-vice, and two bars serve wine, beer, and spirits. Almost everything is available for takeout.

VIEUX-MONTRÉAL
VERY EXPENSIVE

Claude Postel. 443 rue St-Vincent (near Notre-Dame). ☎ **514/875-5067.** Reservations recommended. Main courses C$24–C$34 (US$16–US$23); table d'hôte menu C$13–C$21 (US$9–US$14) at lunch, C$24–C$32 (US$16–US$21) at dinner. AE, CB, DC, ER, MC, V. Mon–Fri 11:30am–3pm and 5:30–10pm, Sat–Sun 5:30–10pm. Métro: Place-d'Armes or Champ-de-Mars. FRENCH.

One of Vieux-Montréal's best-known restaurants is named for its chef/owner, who once shook the skillets at Bonaparte, a few blocks away. The animated Mr. Postel moves diligently through his dining room, greeting regulars and newcomers with equal warmth and (when encouraged) suggesting off-menu items and possible wines. While the crowd is composed largely of businesspeople and government employees, tourists fill up the two rooms and the dining terrace between June and Labour Day. They come for dishes like lobster bits and scallops on a bed of linguini-shaped zucchini strips steamed in lobster bouillon.

Postel has a take-out shop nearby at 75 rue Notre-Dame (☎ 514/844-8750), with most of the makings of a satisfying picnic, including baguettes, cheeses, sandwiches, and quiches.

✪ **La Marée.** 404 place Jacques-Cartier (near Notre-Dame). ☎ **514/861-8126.** Reservations required. Main courses C$24–C$30 (US$16–US$20); table d'hôte menu C$14–C$17 (US$9–US$11) at lunch. AE, CB, DC, DISC, ER, MC, V. Mon–Fri noon–3pm; daily 5:30–11:30pm. Métro: Champ-de-Mars. FRENCH.

Despite the T-shirted masses who fill the May-to-October terrace of this 1807 house on the west side of the plaza, dining of a high order takes place behind these stone walls. Begin with the setting: fireplaces, paintings of fish and game, delicately figured wallpaper, and furnishings recall the eras of Louis XIV and Louis XIII. Candlelight enhances the romantic mood in the evening, while power lunches prevail at midday. Known especially for its refined treatment of seafood, the kitchen is lauded for such fabrications as trout stuffed with salmon and lobster mousse and lobster with tomato and fresh basil and white-wine sauce. Natural flavors are allowed to prevail, and presentations aren't so flashy they bring conversation to a halt. In cooler weather, chateaubriand tops the list. The service is disciplined and professional.

EXPENSIVE

Chez Delmo. 211 rue Notre-Dame (near rue St-François-Xavier). ☎ **514/849-4061.** Reservations recommended. Main courses C$20–C$24 (US$13–US$16). AE, MC, V. Mon 11:30am–3pm; Tues–Fri 11:30am–3pm and 5:30–10pm; Sat 5:30–10:30pm. Métro: Square Victoria. SEAFOOD.

This venerable fish house has resisted change for decades. But that's a good thing: It's a deeply atmospheric retreat evoking a time nearly lost, when the freshest available fruits of the sea were quickly broiled, baked, or sautéed and presented with wisps of saucing and not a fennel brush or oven-dried tomato in sight. You enter a dim room with twin facing bars and their stools, just the place for single diners after a light lunch of opened-to-order clams or oysters. Other diners are funneled into the larger, relatively characterless back room where full meals are served. Salmon from the Maritime Provinces and real Dover sole are often featured, substantial in portion and lacking in flash, the better to lubricate the insider talk of deal makers from nearby law offices and the stock exchange.

MODERATE

✪ **Casa de Matéo.** 440 rue St-François-Xavier (near St-Paul). ☎ **514/844-4154.** Reservations suggested Fri–Sat nights. Main courses C$14–C$18 (US$9–US$12); daily lunch specials C$10 (US$7). AE, CB, DC, ER, MC, V. Mon–Fri 11:30am–10pm; Sat–Sun 11am–11pm. Métro: Place-d'Armes. MEXICAN.

Stepping into Casa de Matéo feels like wandering into a party, especially on Friday and Saturday evenings, when mariachis come to kick the fiesta up a notch. Get in the mood with a birdbath-sized frozen margarita, which arrives with chips and salsa at the center horseshoe bar, encased with rough terra-cotta tiles. The cheerful staff from Mexico, Guatemala, and other Latin American countries lend authenticity, and most of them are delighted to be addressed in even a few words of Spanish. You can skip an appetizer because of the generous servings. But that would mean missing the *plato Mexicano,* a sampler of all the starters—it's a meal in itself, so you may want to stop there. But *that* would mean missing the *pescado Veracruzano:* whole red snapper quickly marinated and fried and served with a nest of crisp vegetables. The usual burritos and enchiladas are easy to forget.

Chez Better. 160 rue Notre-Dame (near place Jacques-Cartier). ☎ **514/861-2617.** Main courses C$8–C$14 (US$5–US$9); table d'hôte menu C$14 (US$9). AE, DC, ER, MC, V. Daily 11am–10pm. Métro: Champ-de-Mars. GERMAN.

They aren't making a half-hearted boast with the name. This and the other five outposts of this local chain are named for the founder, a Canadian born in Germany. Presumably he grew homesick for tastes of his native land and opened his first restaurant to assuage that hunger. Think variations of knackwurst, chipolata, kasseler, and sauerkraut, plus 100 brands of beer. Forget grease and oozing globules of fat, though, for these are lighthearted sausages, brightly seasoned with herbs, curry, hot pepper, and even truffle shavings. A special lunch sampler of bratwurst, cevapcici, and diable comes with fries and kraut and costs only C$8 (US$5)—a terrific deal. While sausage plates are the stars, there are also mixed grills, chicken schnitzels, grilled smoked pork chops, salads, and mussels nine ways. The service can be disjointed but rarely to the point of irritation.

Two other convenient branches are at 4382 bd. St-Laurent (☎ **514/845-4554**) and 1430 rue Stanley (☎ **514/848-9859**), open the same hours as above.

✪ **Le Bourlingueur.** 363 rue St-François-Xavier (near rue St-Paul). ☎ **514/845-3646.** Reservations suggested on weekends. Table d'hôte menu C$10–C$16 (US$7–US$11). MC, V. Daily 11:30am–9pm; Sat–Sun 5–9pm. Métro: Place-d'Armes. FRENCH.

While it doesn't look especially promising on first approach, this place is a real find. The star designation is for the almost-unbelievably low prices they charge for 8 to 10 four-course meals daily. The chalkboard menu changes with market availability, making it possible to dine here twice a day for a week without repeating anything except the indifferent salad. Roast pork with apples and *choucroute garnie* are likely to show up, but the specialty of the house is seafood—watch for the cold lobster with herb mayonnaise. Well short of chic, it doesn't make the most of its stone walls and old beams, choosing somewhat-jarring white chairs and maroon tablecloths. The crowd is diverse—you'll be dining with the widest possible range of ages, genders, and occupations. They now have a no-smoking section.

INEXPENSIVE

Le Jardin Nelson. 407 place Jacques-Cartier (at rue de la Commune). ☎ **514/861-5731.** Reservations accepted only by phone. Main courses C$6–C$10 (US$3.85–US$7). AE, MC, V. May–Labour Day daily 11:30am–3am; Labour Day–Nov daily 11:30am–midnight (later on weekends); Dec–Apr weekends 11:30am–5pm. Métro: Place-d'Armes. LIGHT FARE.

Near the foot of the hill, a passage leads into the garden court in back of a stone building from 1812. It's more a place to spend a pleasant hour or two than for anything like serious dining, with jazz Friday to Sunday and classical chamber groups Monday to Thursday during lunch and dinner (weekends in the good months). A crab apple tree shades the garden, a horticultural counterpoint to the music. The food takes second place, with the kitchen doling out crêpes with both sweet and savory fillings, as well as soups, omelets, individual pizzas, salads, and sandwiches. There's a people-watching porch in front.

PLATEAU MONT-ROYAL
VERY EXPENSIVE

○ **Milos.** 5357 av. du Parc (between rues St-Viateur and Fairmont). ☎ **514/272-3522.** Reservations recommended. Main courses C$23–C$29 (US$15–US$19); table d'hôte menu C$30 (US$20). AE, MC, V. Mon–Fri noon–3pm and 5–11pm, Sat 5–11pm, Sun 5–10pm. Métro: Outremont, then a 12-block walk. GREEK/SEAFOOD.

Avenue du Parc used to be a virtual Little Mykonos, hip-to-hip with Hellenic fish houses. The top dog remains and still holds to a standard higher than those its rivals are ever likely to achieve. It's what a *taberna* at a picturesque Aegean fishing port would look like if it had the necessary drachmas: white plaster walls, bleached wooden floors, amphorae, blue tiles, stations for salad prep and cooking, and refrigerated cases for the finny main events. The freshest available fish are the reason Milos prevails. Show the slightest interest and you'll be taken on a tour of the iced Icelandic char, yellowfin tuna, Nova Scotia lobsters, Florida pompano, Mediterranean loup-de-mer, and cephalopods (priced by the pound). You can pick your own meal or leave it to the chefs (they'll even cook a veal chop if you insist). Order the excellent Greek salad as a starter. The main course will be along soon, brushed with olive oil and charcoal-grilled. Expect to part with about C$140 (US$93) for two with tax, wine, and tip—well worth it.

✪ **Toqué!** 3842 rue St-Denis (at rue Roy). ☎ **514/499-2084.** Reservations essential at least a day ahead. *Ménu dégustation* C$67 (US$45); main courses C$22–C$29 (US$15–US$19). AE, DC, ER, MC, V. Daily 6–11pm (from 5:30 in summer). Closed Dec 24–Jan 6. Métro: Sherbrooke. CONTEMPORARY FRENCH.

This restaurant is the sort that can single-handedly raise the gastronomic expectations of an entire city. A meal here is virtually obligatory for anyone who admires superb food dazzlingly presented. The chef/owners have created a place as postmodernist in its cuisine as in its decor, which includes a wall down the middle to separate smokers from nonsmokers. Success has forced the owners to forego the open kitchen that used to be in front—they needed the space for tables. "Post-nouvelle" might be an apt description of the creations, with sufficient portions and intensely flavorful combinations of ingredients. Asian influences are evident these days, but experimentation is kept on a tether. They use only top ingredients, some rarely seen on a plate—foie gras with milkweed buds, for example. The menu is never set in stone. Consider one recent dish: sautéed scallops with flageolet bean salsa laced with cumin, coriander, and jalapeño, the light heat countered with salsify and cinnamon-touched plantain chips. The duck, veal, quail, and venison are memorable, and the salmon and Arctic char are often the most desirable fish. An exciting selection of mostly French cheeses can precede dessert. The restaurant fills up later than most, with prosperous-looking suits and women who sparkle at throat and wrist—there's no stated dress code, yet you'll want to look your best. The service is efficient and not a whit self-important. Allow 2 hours for dinner.

EXPENSIVE

○ **Jongleux Café.** 3434 av. St-Denis (north of rue Sherbrooke). ☎ **514/841-8080.** Main courses C$18–C$24 (US$12–US$16); table d'hôte menu C$17–C$28 (US$11–US$19). AE, CB, DC, ER, MC, V. Mon–Fri 11:30am–2:30pm and 6–11pm, Sat 6–11pm. Métro: Sherbrooke. CONTEMPORARY FUSION.

Montréal's best new restaurant doesn't look like it from the sidewalk of this raffish district. Things perk up inside, though, its two levels calm beneath Milanese-style wire lighting. The young co-owner and her exceptionally cheerful waitstaff are women who make people welcome and proceed to demonstrate their mastery of their craft. Her partner disingenuously claims merely to be updating traditional bistro cooking, an assertion belied by his remarkable paella of snails and crisp-fried sweetbreads and by the salmon tournedos in a tapenade crust accompanied by saffron-touched chickpea raviolis. It may require a small leap of faith to order the braised pig cheeks, but that rich silken flesh is a revelation, draped with delicate Camembert-flavored pasta envelopes. Unsalted butter, unusual in Québec, comes with the excellent chewy bread; wines by the glass cost C$6 to C$8 (US$4 to US$5). The proprietors will be looking for larger quarters for a wider audience before this book hits the shelves.

MODERATE

Buona Notte. 3518 rue St-Laurent (near rue Sherbrooke). ☎ 514/848-0644. Reservations recommended. Main courses C$9–C$15 (US$6–US$10); table d'hôte menu C$19–C$29 (US$13–US$19). AE, DC, MC, V. Mon–Wed 11:30am–midnight; Thurs–Sat 11:30am–1am; Sun 5pm–midnight. Métro: St-Laurent. CONTEMPORARY ITALIAN.

With its high ceiling masked by electric fans and heating ducts, Buona Notte could easily be in New York's SoHo. A principal component of the remaining decor are plates painted by celebrity diners, among them Ben Kingsley, Danny DeVito, Winona Ryder, and Nicolas Cage; they're boxed (the plates, that is) and arrayed along the walls. Funk and hip-hop thump over the stereo, and the waitresses look ready to depart on the next fashion shoot. They're in black (with splashes of carefree gray) as are most of their customers, cell phones at the ready. The front opens up in warm weather. Although the food inevitably takes second place to preening, it's surprisingly worthwhile. Pastas prevail, tumbled with crunchy vegetables or silky walnut sauce or any of 10 or more combinations. The kitchen exhibits less reliance on meat than the norm and makes an imaginative risotto with two cheeses and two sauces. The service is stretched thin as the weekend and dinner hour approach, and the noise level cranks up after 7pm. The active bar in back features single-malt scotches; it stays open to 2am Sunday to Wednesday and to 3am Thursday to Saturday.

✪ L'Express. 3927 rue St-Denis (at rue Roy). ☎ 514/845-5333. Reservations recommended. Main courses C$11–C$17 (US$7–US$11). AE, CB, DC, ER, MC, V. Mon–Fri 8am–3am; Sat 10am–3am; Sun 10am–2am. Métro: Sherbrooke. FRENCH BISTRO.

No obvious sign announces this restaurant, only its name discreetly spelled out in white tiles embedded in the sidewalk. There's no need to call attention to itself, since *tout* Montréal knows exactly where it is. While there are no table d'hôte menus, the food is fairly priced for such an eternally busy place and costs the same at midnight as at noon. Substantial starters that include bone marrow with coarse salt and potted chicken pâté may suggest one of the lighter main courses, like the ravioli *maison,* round pasta pockets flavored, more than stuffed, with a mix of beef, pork, and veal. Larger appetites might step up to full-flavored duck breast with chewy chanterelles in a sauce with the scent of deep woods. Or you can simply stop by for a *croque monsieur* (grilled-cheese sandwich) or a bagel with smoked salmon and cream cheese. While reservations are usually necessary for tables, single diners can often find a seat at the zinc-topped bar, where meals are also served. Breakfast is served 8 to 11:30am.

Witloof. 3619 rue St-Denis (at rue Sherbrooke). ☎ 514/281-0100. Reservations recommended. Main courses C$15–C$19 (US$10–US$13); early-bird table d'hôte menu C$9–C$15 (US$6–US$10); regular table d'hôte menu C$11–C$21 (US$7–US$14). AE, CB, DC, DISC, ER, MC, V. Mon–Wed 11:30am–11pm; Thurs–Fri 11:30am–midnight; Sat 5pm–midnight; Sun 5–11pm. Métro: Sherbrooke. BELGIAN.

Its name is Flemish for "endive," and when Witloof sticks to the Belgian dishes in which it specializes, it's one of the most gratifying restaurants in town. The place contrives to be both casual and elegant, as exemplified by snowy linen tablecloths covered with butcher paper. Steaming casseroles of mussels with tents of *frites* on the side are deservedly the most popular on the menu, but the classic Belgian stew, *waterzooi*, is a close second. Because it's always busy, the kitchen can fall behind on orders, but the convivial atmosphere dissuades grousing. Several Belgian beers are available, including Blanche de Bruges. The restaurant has a large selection of desserts, from crème caramel to praline crêpes. Many diners take advantage of the early-bird table d'hôtes to soak up the late-afternoon sun on the terrace.

INEXPENSIVE

✪ **Chez Schwartz Charcuterie Hébraïque de Montréal.** 3895 bd. St-Laurent (north of rue Prince-Arthur). ☎ **514/842-4813.** Most items C$5–C$12 (US$3.35–US$8). No credit cards. Sun–Thurs 9am–1am; Fri 9am–2am; Sat 9am–3am. Métro: St-Laurent. DELI.

The imposition of French-first laws turned this old-line delicatessen into this linguistic mouthful, but it's still known simply as Schwartz's to its ardent fans. They're convinced this is the only place on the continent to indulge in the guilty treat of smoked meat. Housed in a long, narrow space, it has a lunch counter and a collection of simple tables and chairs crammed together. Any empty seat is up for grabs. Few mind this, for they're soon delivered plates described as small (meaning large) or large (meaning humongous) heaped with slices of the trademark delicacy, along with piles of rye bread. Most people also order sides of french fries and one or two mammoth garlicky pickles. There are a handful of alternative edibles, but tofu and leafy green vegetables aren't among them. Schwartz's has no liquor license.

Pizzédélic. 3509 bd. St-Laurent (near rue Sherbrooke). ☎ **514/282-6784.** Pizzas and pastas C$7–C$14 (US$4.85–US$9); table d'hôte menu C$7 (US$4.65) at lunch. MC, V. Sun and Wed–Thurs 11:30am–1am; Tues 11:30am–2am; Fri–Sat 11:30am–3am. Métro: St-Laurent. ITALIAN.

Pizza here runs the gamut from traditional to as imaginative as anyone might conceive, with toppings from feta cheese to escargots to artichokes to pesto. All arrive on thin, not-quite-crispy crusts. The difference over ordinary pizzerias is the use of fresh, not canned, ingredients, as in the antipasto plate of grilled vegetables and calamari strips. Pastas and meat dishes are also available. The front opens in warm weather, and there's a terrace in back.

It's a growing chain, with units all over town, but two convenient ones are at 1329 Ste-Catherine (☎ **514/526-6011**) and 370 av. Laurier ouest (☎ **514/948-6290**), with generally the same hours as above.

PICNICKING

When planning a picnic or a meal to eat back in your hotel, consider a stop at the **Faubourg Ste-Catherine,** on rue Ste-Catherine ouest between rues Guy and St-Mathieu. It's a market/fast-food complex that sells a substantial variety of prepared take-out foods like sushi and sandwiches, as well as breads, fruits, pastries, and ice cream. You'll find similar bounty at **Les Halles de la Gare,** an accumulation of food stalls, delis, and cafes beneath the Queen Elizabeth hotel and adjacent to the main concourse of the rail station. Among them is an SAQ wine store. Downtown, the new **Marché Mövenpick,** at the corners of rues Cathcart and University and rue Mansfield and boulevard René-Lévesque, sells just about everything for takeout, including sushi, panini, fruits, baked goods, cheeses, pizzas, and grills.

Better still, make the short excursion by Métro (the Lionel-Grouix stop) to the **Marché Atwater,** the public market at 3025 St-Ambroise. The long shed is bordered by stalls of gleaming produce and flowers, the two-story center section given to wine purveyors, food counters, bakeries, and cheese stores. The best representatives of the last two are **La Fromagerie** (☎ 514/932-4653), whose attendants know every detail of production of the 450 to 550 North American and European cheeses on offer, and the **Boulangerie Première Moison** (☎ 514/932 0328), which fills its space with the tantalizing aromas of baskets of breads and cases of pastries. From either location, it isn't far by taxi to Parc du Mont-Royal, a wonderful place to enjoy a picnic.

In Vieux-Montréal, pick up supplies at the new food market in the historic **Marché Bonsecours** (☎ 514/872-4560) on rue de la Commune and take them to the linear park of the Vieux-Port, only steps away.

5 Seeing the Sights

A superb Métro system, a fairly logical street grid, wide boulevards, and the vehicle-free Underground City all aid in the swift, largely uncomplicated movement of people from one place to another. The difficulty lies in making choices to fit your available time. After all, the possibilities include hiking up imposing Mont-Royal in the middle of the city, biking along the redeveloped waterfront or out beside the Lachine Canal, visiting museums or historic homes, and taking in a professional hockey, football, or baseball game. With riverboat rides, the fascinating Biodôme, and a sprawling amusement park, Montréal also assures kids of a good time.

A number of the following sights opened or expanded in 1992 to coincide with Montréal's 350th birthday. Efforts to enhance cultural opportunities have continued since then, as with the Biosphère, which opened in 1995 on Ile Ste-Hélène.

DOWNTOWN

See the "Downtown Montréal" map (p. 196) to locate sights in this section.

✪ **Musée des Beaux-Arts.** 1379–1380 rue Sherbrooke ouest (at rue Crescent). ☎ **514/285-2000.** www.mmfa.qc.ca. Permanent collection free, temporary exhibits C$12 (US$8) adults, C$6 (US$4) seniors/students, C$3 (US$2) children 12 and under. AE, MC, V. Half price Wed 5:30–9pm. Tues and Thurs–Sun 11am–6pm, Wed 11am–9pm. Métro: Peel or Guy-Corcordia.

The Museum of Fine Arts, Montréal's most prominent museum, opened in 1912 on the north side of rue Sherbrooke; the neoclassical pavilion was Canada's first building designed specifically for the visual arts. Eventually the collection outgrew the building, and curators were forced to make painful decisions about which few items could be placed on view at any one time. The resulting exhibits often seemed sketchy and incomplete. That problem was solved in late 1991 with the completion of the stunning annex, the Jean-Noël Desmarais Pavilion, across the street. Designed by Montréal architect Moshe Safdie, who first gained international notice with his Habitat housing complex at Expo '67, the pavilion tripled exhibit space, adding two substreet floors and underground galleries connecting the new building with the old.

For the best look at the results, enter the new annex, take the elevator to the top, and work your way down. The permanent collection is largely devoted to international

The Montréal Museums Pass

The Montréal Museums Pass, allowing entry to 19 of the city's museums, is available year-round. The 1-day pass is C$15 (US$10) per adult and the 3-day pass is C$28 (US$19). When planning visits, note in the listings below which museums have restaurants, a few of which are pretty good. For information, call ☎ **800/ 363-7777** or 514/845-6873.

contemporary art and Canadian art created after 1960, as well as to European paintings, sculpture, and decorative arts from the Middle Ages to the 19th century. On the upper floors are many of the collection's gems. On the fourth floor alone are paintings by Hogarth, Reynolds, Brueghel, El Greco, and van Dyck. (For an extra bonus, be sure to walk to the sculpture court for a splendid panoramic view.) On subsequent levels, view examples of more recent artists, like Renoir, Monet, Picasso, Cézanne, and Rodin. On the subterranean floors are works by 20th-century modernists, including the Abstract Expressionists and those who followed.

From the lowest level of the new pavilion, follow the understreet corridor past primitive artworks from Oceana and Africa, and then take the elevator into the old building, with its displays of pre-Columbian ceramics, Inuit carvings, and Amerindian crafts. The rest of that building is used primarily for temporary exhibits, though 1999's high-profile "Monet at Giverny" exhibition was in the pavilion. The major show in 2000 is expected to be "From Renoir to Picasso," with 81 paintings from Cézanne, Matisse, Modigliani, their contemporaries, and the headliners of the title. Montréal is one of only two North American stops on the tour.

Adjoining the new pavilion, the museum store offers an impressive selection of quality books, games, and folk art. There's a cafe as well.

Musée Juste Poure Rire. 2111 bd. St-Laurent (north of rue Sherbrooke). ☎ **514/845-4000.** www.hahaha.com. Admission C$8 (US$5). Tues–Sun 11am–6pm (to 9pm Wed). Métro: St-Laurent. Bus: 55.

The Just for Laughs comedy festival that inspired this Latin Quarter enterprise is still going strong, but what the future holds for its misbegotten offspring is far less certain. It opened with high hopes and great fanfare, offering rooms to show videos and historic film clips, a 250-seat cabaret theater, a humor hall of fame, and a cafe. But despite the official hours above, it closes without warning much of the time, and its exhibits and calendar are subject to frequent change and cancellations. Until it achieves a more certain direction, my suggestion is to skip it, but if you insist, ask about its current status before making the trip.

Musée McCord. 690 rue Sherbrooke ouest (at rue Victoria). ☎ **514/398-7100.** www.musee-mccord.qc.ca. Admission C$7 (US$4.65) adults, C$5 (US$3.35) seniors, C$4 (US$2.65) students, C$1.50 (US$1) ages 7–11, C$14 (US$9) families; free for children under 7. Free admission Sat–Sun 10am–noon. Tues–Fri 10am–6pm, Sat–Sun 10am–5pm (summer daily from 9am). Métro: McGill. Bus: 24.

Associated with McGill University, the McCord Museum of Canadian History showcases the eclectic—and not infrequently eccentric—collections of scores of 19th- and 20th-century benefactors. Objects from its holdings of 29,000 costumes, artifacts, and 750,000 historical photographs are rotated in and out of storage, so it isn't possible to be specific about what you'll see. In general, expect furniture, clothing, china, silver, paintings, photos, and folk art revealing rural and urban life as it was lived by English-speaking immigrants of the past 3 centuries. An atrium connects the original 1905 building with a wing added during extensive renovations in 1992. Beyond it are galleries for temporary exhibits. The First Nations room displays portions of the extensive collection of ethnology and archaeology, including jewelry and meticulous beadwork. The exhibits are intelligently mounted, with texts in English and French, though the upstairs rooms are of narrower interest.

Cathédrale-Basilique Marie-Reine-du-Monde. Bd. René-Lévesque (at rue Mansfield). ☎ **514/866-1661.** Free admission; donations accepted. Mon–Fri 7am–7:30pm, Sat 7:30am–8:30pm, Sun 8:30am–7:30pm. Métro: Bonaventure.

No one who has seen both will confuse Montréal's Mary Queen of the World Cathedral with Rome's St. Peter's Basilica, but a scaled-down homage was the intention of its guiding force. Bishop Ignace Bourget was moved to act in the middle of the 19th century, after the first Catholic cathedral burned to the ground in 1852. Construction lasted from 1875 to 1894, delayed by his desire to place it not in Francophone east Montréal but in the heart of the Protestant Anglophone west. The resulting structure covers less than a quarter of the area of its Roman inspiration, and no curving arcades embrace a sweeping plaza in front. The stairs to the entrance are only a few yards away from the boulevard. Most impressive is the 252-foot-high dome, about half the size of the original. A local touch is provided by the statues standing on the roofline, representing patron saints of the region. The interior is less rewarding visually than the outside. A planned restoration is expected to cost at least C$7.5 million (US$5 million).

Centre Canadien d'Architecture (CCA). 1920 rue Baile (at rue du Fort). ☎ **514/ 939-7026.** www.cca.qc.ca. Admission C$6 (US$4) adults, C$4 (US$2.65) seniors/students; free for children under 12. June–Sept Tues–Sun 11am–6pm (Thurs to 9pm); Oct–May Wed–Fri 11am–6pm (Thurs to 9pm), Sat–Sun 11am–5pm. Guided tours available on request. Métro: Atwater or Guy-Concordia.

The understated but handsome Canadian Center of Architecture occupies a city block, with lawns joining a contemporary building with the 1875 Shaughnessy House. The CCA doubles as a study center and a museum with changing exhibits devoted to the art of architecture and its history, including architects' sketchbooks, elevation drawings, and photography. The collection is international in scope and encompasses architecture, urban planning, and landscape design. Texts are in French and English. Since opening in 1989 the museum has received raves from scholars, critics, and architecture buffs, but it's only fair to note that the ordinary visitor is likely to find it somewhat less than enthralling. The bookstore has a special section on Canadian architecture, with emphasis on Montréal and Québec City. The sculpture garden across the Ville-Marie autoroute is part of the CCA, designed by artist/architect Melvin Charney.

Cathédrale Christ Church. 1444 Union Ave. (at rues Ste-Catherine and University). ☎ **514/843-6577** (office) or 514/288-6421 (recorded info). www.montreal.anglica. org/cathedral. Free admission; donations accepted. Daily 8am–6pm; services Sun 8am, 10am, and 4pm. Métro: McGill.

This Anglican cathedral, reflected in the postmodernist Maison des Coopérants office tower, stands in glorious Gothic contrast to the city's glassy downtown skyscrapers. Sometimes called the "floating cathedral" because of the many tiers of malls and corridors of the Underground City beneath it, the building was completed in 1859. The original steeple, too heavy for the structure, was replaced by a lighter aluminum version in 1940. Christ Church Cathedral hosts concerts throughout the year, notably June to August on Wednesdays at 12:30pm.

Musée d'Art Contemporain de Montréal. 185 rue Ste-Catherine ouest. ☎ **514/ 847-6226.** Admission C$6 (US$4) adults, C$4 (US$2.65) seniors, C$3 (US$2) students, C$12 (US$8) families; free for children under 12. Free to all Wed 6–9pm. Tues–Sun 11am–6pm (Wed to 9pm). Métro: Place-des-Arts.

Montréal's Museum of Contemporary Art, the only such repository in Canada devoted to contemporary art, moved into this new facility at Place des Arts in 1992 after years in an isolated riverfront building. "Contemporary" is defined here as art produced since 1939. About 60% of the permanent collection of 5,000 works is from Québec and other Canadian artists; the rest includes examples of international artists like Jean Dubuffet, Max Ernst, Jean Arp, Larry Poons, and Antoni Tàpies, as well as photographers Robert Mapplethorpe, Ansel Adams, and Montréaler Michel Campeau. A few larger pieces are on the ground floor, but most are one flight up, with space for temporary exhibits to the right and selections from the permanent collection to the left. No single style prevails, so expect to see minimalist installations small and large; video displays; evocations of Pop, Op, and Abstract Expressionism; and accumulations of objects simply piled on the floor. That the works often arouse strong opinions signifies a museum doing something right. The museum's restaurant, La Rotonde, features a menu of Provençal food and has a summer dining terrace.

VIEUX-MONTRÉAL

Across from the Hôtel de Ville (below) is the focus of summer activity in Vieux-Montréal: **place Jacques-Cartier,** between rues Notre-Dame and de la Commune. The most active of the old city's plazas has two recently repaved streets bracketing a center promenade that slopes down to the port past venerable stone buildings from the 1700s. Its outdoor cafes, its street performers, its flower sellers, and the horse-drawn carriages that gather at its base recall the Montréal of a century ago. Montréalers insist they'd never go to a place so thronged by tourists—which begs the question of why so many of them congregate here. They take the sun and sip sangria on the bordering terraces on warm days, enjoying the unfolding pageant just as much as visitors do. For more details about this quarter, log on to **www.vieux.montreal.qc.ca**.

✪ **Basilique Notre-Dame.** 110 rue Notre-Dame ouest (on Place d'Armes). ☎ **514/842-2925.** Basilica C$2 (US$1.35) adults, "for praying" free. Basilica June 24–Labour Day daily 7am–8pm; rest of the year daily 7am–6pm; tours mid-May to mid-Oct Mon–Fri 9am–4pm (to 4:30pm in summer). Museum Sat–Sun 9:30am–4pm. Métro: Place-d'Armes.

Big enough to hold 4,000 worshipers and breathtaking in the richness of its interior furnishings, this magnificent structure was designed in 1824 by Irish-American Protestant architect James O'Donnell. So profoundly was he moved by the experience, he converted to Catholicism after the basilica was completed. The impact is understandable. None of the hundreds of churches on the island of Montréal approaches this interior in its wealth of exquisite detail, most of it carved from rare woods delicately gilded and painted. O'Donnell, one of the proponents of the Gothic Revival style in the early 19th century, is the only person honored by burial in the crypt.

The main altar was carved from linden wood, the work of Victor Bourgeau. Behind it is the Chapelle Sacré-Coeur (Sacred Heart Chapel), much of it destroyed by a deranged arsonist in 1978 but rebuilt and rededicated in 1982. It's such a popular place for weddings that couples have to book it 18 months in advance. The altar was cast in bronze by Charles Daudelin of Montréal, with 32 panels representing birth, life, and death. A 10-bell carillon resides in the east tower, while the west tower contains a single massive bell. Nicknamed "Le Gros Bourdon" and tolled only on special occasions, it weighs more than 12 tons and has a low, resonant rumble that vibrates right up through the feet.

Guided tours in English leave at various times during tourist season, but usually on the hour and half hour.

✪ **Pointe-à-Callière (Montréal Museum of Archaeology and History).** 350 place Royale (at rue Commune). ☎ **514/872-9150.** www.musee-pointe-a-calliere.qc.ca. Admission C$9 (US$6) adults, C$6 (US$4) seniors, C$6 (US$3.65) students, C$3 (US$2) children 6–12, C$17 (US$11) families; free for children under 6. AE, MC, V. June 25–Labour Day Tues–Fri 10am–6pm, Sat–Sun 11am–6pm; rest of the year Tues–Fri 10am–5pm, Sat–Sun 11am–5pm. Métro: Place-d'Armes.

A first visit to Montréal might best begin here. Built on the site where the original colony began in 1642 (Pointe-à-Callière), the modern Museum of Archaeology and History engages you in rare, beguiling ways. The striking new building echoes the triangular Royal Insurance building (1861) that stood there for many years. Go first to the 16-minute multimedia show in an auditorium that stands above exposed ruins of the earlier city. Images pop up, drop down, and slide out on rolling screens accompanied by music and a playful bilingual narration that keeps the history slick and utterly painless, with enough quick cuts and changes to keep even the youngest viewers from fidgeting.

Pointe-à-Callière was the point where the St-Pierre River merged with the St. Lawrence. Evidence of the many layers of occupation at this spot—from Amerindians to French trappers to Scottish merchants—were unearthed during archaeological digs that persisted here for more than a decade. They're on view in display cases set among ancient building foundations and burial grounds below street level. The bottom shelves of the cabinets are for items dating to before 1600, and there are other shelves for consecutive centuries. Wind your way on the self-guided tour through the subterranean complex until reaching the former Custom House, where there are more exhibits and a well-stocked gift shop. Allow at least an hour for a visit.

New expansion has incorporated the restored Youville Pumping Station (1915), across from the main building, as an interpretation center. The main building contains L'Arrivage cafe and affords a fine view of Old Montréal and the Old Port.

Vieux-Port. Stretching along the waterfront from rue McGill to rue Berri. Interpretation center at 333 rue de la Commune ouest (at rue McGill). ☎ **514/496-7678.** www. oldportofmontreal.com. Port and interpretation center free. Tram rides C$3.50 (US$2.35) adults, C$2.50 (US$1.65) seniors/students, C$1.50 (US$1) children under 13. Charges vary for other attractions. Interpretation center mid-May to early Sept daily 10am–9pm; hours for specific attractions vary. Métro: Champ-de-Mars, Place-d'Armes, or Square-Victoria.

Montréal's Old Port, once a dreary commercial wharf area, was transformed in 1992 into an appealing 1.2-mile-long, 133-acre promenade and park with public spaces, exhibition halls, family activities, bike paths, and a permanent flea market. Cyclists, in-line skaters, joggers, strollers, lovers, and sunbathers all make use of the park in good weather. There's a large-scale wraparound IMAX theater as well (see "Especially for Kids"). A variety of harbor cruises leave from here. To get an idea of all there is to see and do, hop aboard the small Balade tram that travels throughout the port. At the far eastern end of the port is a clock tower built in 1922, with 192 steps leading past the exposed clockworks to observation decks at three levels (admission free). Most cruises, entertainment, and special events take place mid-May to October. Information booths with bilingual attendants assist visitors during that period. Quadricycles, bicycles, and in-line skates are available for rent.

Hôtel de Ville. 275 rue Notre-Dame (at rue Gosford). ☎ **514/872-3355.** Free admission. Daily 8:30am–4:30pm. Métro: Champ-de-Mars.

The City Hall, finished in 1878, is relatively young by Vieux-Montréal standards. The French Second Empire design makes it look as though it was imported stone by stone from the mother country. Balconies, turrets, and mansard roofs detail the exterior, seen to particular advantage when illuminated at night. It was from the balcony above the awning that an ill-mannered Charles de Gaulle proclaimed, "Vive le Québec Libre!" in 1967, thereby pleasing his immediate audience but straining relations with the Canadian government for years. Fifteen-minute guided tours are given on weekdays May to October. The Hall of Honour is made of green marble from Italy and houses art deco lamps from Paris and a bronze-and-glass chandelier, also from France, that weighs a metric ton. In the display cabinet to the left by the elevator are gifts from mayors of other cities from around the world. Council Chamber meetings, on the first floor, are open to the public. The chamber has a hand-carved ceiling and five stained-glass windows representing religion, the port, industry and commerce, finance, and transportation. The mayor's office is on the fourth floor; infrequently scheduled guided tours are given.

Centre d'Histoire de Montréal. 335 place d'Youville (at rue St-Pierre). ☎ **514/872-3207.** www.ville.montreal.qc.ca/chm/chm.htm. Admission C$4.50 (US$3) adults, C$3 (US$2) seniors/students/children 6–17; free for children under 6. Late Jan to early May and early Sept to mid-Dec Tues–Sun 10am–5pm; early May to mid-June daily 9am–5pm; late June to early Sept daily 10am–5pm. Closed mid-Dec to mid-Jan. Métro: Square-Victoria.

Built in 1903 as Montréal's Central Fire Station, this red-brick–and–sandstone building is now the Montréal History Center, tracing the development of the city from its first occupants, the Amerindians, to the European settlers who arrived in 1642, to the present day. Throughout its 14 rooms, carefully conceived presentations chart the contributions of the city fathers and mothers and subsequent generations. The developments of the railroad, Métro, and related infrastructure are recalled, as is that of domestic and public architecture, in imaginative exhibits, videos, and slide shows. On the second floor, reached by a spiral staircase, are memorabilia from the early 20th century. Labels are in French, so ask at the front desk for a visitor's guide in English. One or two rooms are given over to temporary exhibits.

Note that the museum is to be closed for renovations until the fall of 2000.

Chapelle Notre-Dame-de-Bonsecours/Musée Marguerite-Bourgeoys. 400 rue St-Paul (at the foot of rue Bonsecours). ☎ **514/845-9991.** Chapel free; admission to museum and archaeological site C$5 (US$3.35) adults; C$3 (US$2) seniors/students, C$2 (US$1.35) ages 6–12; free for children under 6. May–Oct Tues–Sun 10am–5pm; Nov–Jan 15 and Mar 15–Apr 30 Tues–Sun 11am–3:30pm. Closed Jan 16–Mar 14. Métro: Champ-de-Mars.

Just east of the Marché Bonsecours (below), the Notre-Dame-de-Bonsecours Chapel is called the Sailors' Church because of the special attachment to it felt by fishermen and other mariners. That devotion is manifest in the many ship models hanging inside, their votive offerings. A revered 16th-century 6-inch-high carving of the Madonna is once again on display. The first church building, the project of an energetic teacher named Marguerite Bourgeoys, was built in 1678. She arrived with Sieur de Maisonneuve to undertake the education of Montréal's children in the latter half of the 17th century. Later on, she and several sister teachers founded a nuns' order called the Congregation of Notre-Dame, Canada's first. The pioneering Bourgeoys was recognized as a saint in 1982. You get an excellent view of the harbor and the old quarter from the church's tower.

The present church, from 1773, incorporates a museum and a restored 18th-century crypt, an archaeological site that has unearthed ruins and materials from the earliest days of the colony. Mandatory guided tours are limited to seven people; tours in English are Thursday to Sunday at 2pm.

Marché Bonsecours. 350 rue St-Paul (at the foot of rue St-Claude). ☎ **514/872-4560.** Free admission. Daily 9am–5pm. Métro: Champ-de-Mars.

The Bonsecours Market, an imposing neoclassical building with a long facade, a colonnaded portico, and a silvery dome, was built in the mid-1800s and first used as Montréal's City Hall, then for many years after 1878 as the central market. Restored in 1964, it housed city government offices and in 1992 became the information/ exhibition center for the celebration of the city's 350th birthday. It continues to be used as an exhibit space, and room has been made for shopping stalls and a sidewalk cafe. The architecture alone makes a brief visit worthwhile.

Musée du Château Ramezay. 280 rue Notre-Dame (east of Place Jacques-Cartier). ☎ **514/861-3708.** Admission C$6 (US$4) adults, C$5 (US$3.35) seniors, C$4 (US$2.65) students, C$12 (US$8) families; free for children under 6. June–Sept daily 10am–6pm; Oct–May Tues–Sun 10am–4:30pm. Métro: Champ-de-Mars.

Claude de Ramezay, the colony's 11th governor, built his home here in 1705. The château was the residence of the royal French governors for almost 4 decades, but in 1745 de Ramezay's heirs sold it to a trading company that rebuilt it, utilizing portions of the original. Fifteen years later, it was taken over by the British conquerors. In 1775 an army of American revolutionaries invaded and held Montréal, using the château as their headquarters. Benjamin Franklin, sent to persuade Québecers to rise with the American colonists against British rule, stayed here for a time but failed to persuade the city's people to join his cause. After the American interlude, the house was used as a courthouse, a government office building, a teachers' college, and headquarters for Laval University before being converted into a museum in 1895. Filling the main floor are old coins and prints, portraits, furnishings, tools, a loom, Amerindian artifacts, and other memorabilia related to the socioeconomic activities of the 18th century and first half of the 19th century. In the cellar are the vaults of the original house. Descriptive placards are in both French and English.

Musée Marc-Aurèle Fortin. 118 rue St-Pierre (at rue d'Youville). ☎ **514/845-6108.** Admission C$4 (US$2.65) adults, C$2 (US$1.35) seniors/students; free for children under 12. Tues–Sun 11am–5pm. Métro: Square-Victoria.

This is Montréal's only museum dedicated to the work of a single French-Canadian artist. Landscape watercolorist Marc-Aurèle Fortin (1888 to 1970) interpreted the beauty of the Québec countryside, especially the Laurentians and Charlevoix. His work is on the ground floor, while temporary exhibits—varied in style but typically representative rather than nonobjective or abstract—usually feature the work of other Québec painters.

ELSEWHERE IN THE CITY

○ **Biodôme de Montréal.** 4777 av. Pierre-de-Coubertin (next to the Olympic Stadium). ☎ **514/868-3000.** www.montreal.qc.ca/biodome. Admission C$10 (US$6) adults, C$7 (US$4.65) seniors/students over 17, C$4.75 (US$3.15) children 6–17; free for children under 6. AE, MC, V. Daily 9am–5pm (to 7pm in summer). Métro: Viau.

Near Montréal's Jardin Botanique is the engrossing Biodôme, possibly the only museum of its kind. Built as the velodrome for the 1976 Olympics, it has been refitted to house replications of four ecosystems—a Laurentian forest, the St. Lawrence marine system, a tropical rain forest, and a replication of a polar environment—with appropriate temperatures, flora, fauna, and changing seasons. All four re-creations are allowed a measure of freedom to grow and shift, so the exhibits are never static. With 6,200 creatures of 210 species and 4,000 trees and plants, the Biodôme incorporates exhibits gathered from the old aquarium and the modest zoos at the Angrignon and LaFontaine parks. Among these are specimens of certain threatened and endangered species, like the macaw, marmoset, and tamarin, while the Polar World has puffins and four kinds of penguins. You'll also find a game room for kids called Naturalia, a shop, a restaurant, and a cafeteria.

Stade Olympique. 4141 av. Pierre-de-Coubertin (at bd. Pie-IX). ☎ **514/252-8687.** www.rio.gouv.qc.ca. Funicular ride, C$9 (US$6) adults, C$6 (US$3.65) students/children. Guided tours of the stadium are available. Public swim periods are daily, with low admission fee. Cable car mid-June to early Sept, Mon noon–6pm, Tues–Thurs 10am–9pm, Fri–Sat 10am–11pm; early Sept to mid-Jan and mid-Feb to mid-June, Mon–Sun noon–6pm. Closed mid-Jan to mid-Feb. Métro: Pie-IX or Viau (choose Viau for the guided tour).

Centerpiece of the 1976 Olympic Games, Montréal's controversial Olympic Stadium and its associated facilities provide considerable opportunities for active and passive diversion. It incorporates a natatorium with six pools, including one of competition dimensions with an adjustable bottom and a 50-foot-deep version for scuba diving. The stadium seats 60,000 to 80,000 spectators, who come here to see the Expos, the CFL Montréal Alouettes, rock concerts, and trade shows. Its 65-ton retractable Kevlar roof is winched into place by 125 tons of steel cables attached to a 626-foot inclined tower looming over the arena like an egret bobbing for fish in a bowl. When everything functions correctly, it takes about 45 minutes to raise or lower the roof. However, it often malfunctions, and high winds have torn large rents in the fabric. This is only one reason that what was first known as the "Big O" was scorned as the "Big Owe" after cost overruns led to heavy tax increases. The idea to construct a fixed Teflon roof has been put on the back burner while proposals to build a new downtown stadium and raze this one are chewed over.

The tower, leaning at a 45° angle, also does duty as an observation deck, with a funicular that whisks 90 passengers to the top in 95 seconds. On a clear day, you get a 35-mile view over Montréal and into the neighboring Laurentides. A free shuttle bus links the Olympic Park and the Botanical Garden.

La Biosphère. 160 chemin Tour-de-l'Isle (Ile Ste-Hélène). ☎ **514/283-5000.** Admission C$7 adults (US$4.35), C$5 (US$3.35) seniors/students, C$4 (US$2.65) children 7–17, C$16 (US$11) families; free for children under 7. June 24–Labour Day daily 10am–6pm; Sept–May Tues–Sun 10am–5pm. Métro: Ile Ste-Hélène, then a short walk or the shuttle bus.

Not to be confused with the Biodôme at Olympic Park (above), this facility is in the geodesic dome designed by Buckminster Fuller to serve as the American Pavilion for Expo '67. A fire destroyed the sphere's acrylic skin in 1976, and it served no purpose other than as a harbor landmark until 1995. The motivation behind the Biosphère is unabashedly environmental, with four exhibit areas, a water theater, and an amphitheater all devoted to promoting awareness of the St. Lawrence–Great Lakes ecosystem. Multimedia shows and hands-on displays invite your active participation. In the highest point of the so-called Visions Hall is an observation level with an unobstructed river view. Connections Hall offers a "Call to Action" presentation employing six giant screens and three stages. There's a preaching-to-the-choir quality to all this that slips over into zealous philosophizing, but the displays and exhibits are put together thoughtfully and will divert and enlighten most visitors, at least for a while. Just don't make a special trip.

Musée David M. Stewart. Vieux Fort, Ile Ste-Hélène. ☎ **514/861-6701.** www. stewart-museum.org. Admission May–Oct C$10 (US$7) adults, C$7 (US$4.65) seniors/ students, C$20 (US$13) families; free for children under 7; Nov–Apr C$6 (US$4) adults, C$4 (US$2.65) seniors/students, C$12 (US$8) families. Late May to Aug daily 10am–6pm; Sept to late-May Wed–Mon 10am–5pm. Métro: Ile Ste-Hélène, then a 15-min. walk. By car: Take the Jacques-Cartier Bridge to the "Parc des Iles" exit, then follow the signs to Vieux Fort.

After the War of 1812, the British prepared for a possible American invasion by building this moated fortress, completed in 1824, which now houses the David M. Stewart Museum. The duke of Wellington ordered its construction as another link in the chain of defenses along the St. Lawrence, but it was never involved in armed conflict. The British garrison left in 1870, after confederation of the former Canadian colonies. Today the low stone barracks and blockhouses contain the museum's display of maps and scientific instruments that helped Europeans explore the New World, as well as military and naval artifacts, weaponry, uniforms, housewares, and related paraphernalia from the time of Jacques Cartier (1535) through the end of the colonial period. Useful labels are in both French and English.

Late June to late August, the fort comes to life with reenactments of military parades and retreats by La Compagnie Franche de la Marine and the 78th Fraser Highlanders, at 11am, 3pm, and 4:30pm. The presence of the French unit is an unhistorical sop to Francophone sensibilities, since New France had become English Canada almost 65 years before the fort was erected. If you absolutely must be photographed in stocks, they're provided on the parade grounds.

PLATEAU MONT-ROYAL

Musée des Hospitalières de l'Hôtel-Dieu de Montréal. 201 av. des Pins ouest. ☎ **514/ 849-2919.** Admission C$5 (US$3.35) adults, C$3 (US$2) seniors/students 12 and over. Mid-June to mid-Oct Tues–Fri 10am–5pm, Sat–Sun 1–5pm; mid-Oct to mid-June Wed–Sun 1–5pm. Métro: Sherbrooke. Bus: 144.

Opened in 1992 to coincide with the city's 350th birthday, this unusual museum, in the former chaplain's residence of Hôtel-Dieu Hospital, traces the history of Montréal from 1659 to the present and focuses on the evolution of health care spanning 3 centuries, including an exhibit of medical instruments. It bows to missionary nurse Jeanne Mance, who arrived in 1642 and founded of Montréal's first hospital, the only woman among the first settlers who left France with Sieur de Maisonneuve. The museum's three floors are filled with memorabilia, including paintings, books, reliquaries, furnishings, and a reconstruction of a nun's cell. Its architectural high point is a marvelous "floating" oak staircase brought to the New World in 1634 from the Maison-Dieu hospital in La Flèche, France. The original Hôtel-Dieu was built in 1645 near the site of the present Notre-Dame Basilica, in Vieux-Montréal; this building was erected in 1861. Guided tours are Sunday at 2pm.

Oratoire St-Joseph. 3800 chemin Queen-Mary (on the north slope of Mont-Royal). ☎ **514/733-8211.** www.saint-joseph.org. Free admission, but donations are requested. Daily 6am–9:30pm; museum daily 10am–5pm. The 56-bell carillon plays Wed–Fri noon–3pm, Sat–Sun noon–2:30pm. Métro: Côtes-des-Neiges.

This huge basilica with a giant copper dome was built by Québec's Catholics to honor St. Joseph, Canada's patron saint. Its imposing dimensions are seen by some as inspiring, by others as forbidding. It came into being through the efforts of Brother André, a lay brother in the Holy Cross order who enjoyed a reputation as a healer. By the time he had built a small wooden chapel in 1904 near the site of the basilica, he was said to have effected hundreds of cures. Those celebrated powers attracted supplicants from great distances, and Brother André performed his work until his death in 1937. His dream of building this shrine to his patron saint became a reality only in 1967; he's buried here and was beatified by the Pope in 1982. The basilica is largely Italian Renaissance, its dome recalling the shape of the Brunelleschi's at the Duomo in Florence but of much greater size and less grace. Inside is a museum where a central exhibit is Brother André's heart. Outside, a Way of the Cross lined with sculptures was the setting of scenes for the Canadian film *Jesus of Montréal.* Brother André's wooden chapel, with his tiny bedroom, is on the grounds and open to the public. Pilgrims, some ill, come to seek intercession from St. Joseph and Brother André and often climb the middle set of 100 steps on their knees. At 862 feet (263m), the shrine is the highest point in Montréal. A cafeteria and snack bar are on the premises. Guided

90-minute tours are offered in several languages at 10am and 2pm daily in summer and on weekends in September and October (donation only).

PARKS & GARDENS

✪ **Jardin Botanique.** 4101 rue Sherbrooke est (opposite the Olympic Stadium). ☎ **514/872-1400.** www.ville.montreal.qc.ca.jardin. For the outside gardens, greenhouses, and Insectarium, May–Oct C$10 (US$6) adults, C$7 (US$4.65) seniors/students, C$4.75 (US$3.15) children 6–17; Nov–Apr C$7 (US$4.50) adults, C$5 (US$3.50) seniors/students, C$3.50 (US$2.35) children 6–17. Ticket for the Botanical Garden, Insectarium, and Biodôme, good for 30 days, C$15 (US$10) adults, C$11 (US$8) seniors, C$8 (US$5) children 6–17. Daily 9am–5pm (to 7pm in summer). Métro: Pie-IX; walk up the hill to the gardens, or from mid-May to mid-Sept take the shuttle bus from Olympic Park (Métro: Viau).

The 180-acre Botanical Garden was begun in 1931 and has grown to include 21,000 varieties of plants in 31 specialized segments, ensuring something beautiful and fragrant for you year-round. Ten large conservatory greenhouses shelter tropical and desert plants, and bonsai and penjings, from the Canadian winter. One greenhouse, the Wizard of Oz, is especially fun for kids. Roses bloom here from mid-June to the first frost, May is the month for lilacs, and June is for the flowering hawthorn trees. Inaugurated in 1991, the 6-acre Chinese Garden, a joint project of Montréal and Shanghai, is the largest of its kind ever built outside Asia, with pavilions, inner courtyards, ponds, and myriad plants indigenous to China. The serene Japanese Garden fills 15 acres and contains a cultural pavilion with an art gallery, a tearoom where the ancient tea ceremony is performed, and a Zen garden. The grounds are also home to the Insectarium, displaying some of the world's most beautiful insects, not to mention some of its sinister ones (see "Especially for Kids"). Birders should bring along binoculars on summer visits to spot some of the more than 130 species that spend at least part of the year in the garden. In summer, an outdoor aviary is filled with Québec's most beautiful butterflies. Year-round, a free shuttle bus links the Botanical Garden and nearby Olympic Park; a small train runs regularly through the gardens and is worth the small fee charged.

Parc du Mont-Royal. ☎ **514/844-4928** (general info) or 514/872-6559 (special events). Daily 6am–midnight. Métro: Mont-Royal. Bus: 11; debark at Lac des Castors.

Montréal is named for the 761-foot (232m) hill that rises at its heart—the "Royal Mountain." Joggers, cyclists, dog walkers, skaters, and others use it throughout the year. On Sundays, hundreds congregate around the statue of George-Etienne Cartier to listen and sometimes dance to improvised music. In summer, Lac des Castors (Beaver Lake) is surrounded by sunbathers and picnickers (no swimming allowed). In winter, cross-country skiers follow the miles of paths, snowshoers tramp along other trails laid out for their use, and there's a tow for the short downhill run above the lake; the lake fills with whirling ice skaters of various levels of aptitude. The refurbished Chalet Lookout near the crest of the hill provides both a sweeping view of the city from its terrace and an opportunity for a snack. Up the hill behind the chalet is the spot where, tradition has it, Sieur de Maisonneuve erected his wooden cross in 1642. Today the cross is a 100-foot-high steel structure visible from all over the city, illuminated at night. Park security is provided by mounted police. There are three cemeteries on the northern slope of the mountain—Catholic, Protestant, and Jewish.

Parc Lafontaine. Rue Sherbrooke and av. Parc Lafontaine. ☎ **514/872-2644.** Free admission; small fee for use of tennis courts. Park daily 24 hours; tennis courts summer daily 9am–10pm. Métro: Sherbrooke.

This European-style park near downtown is one of the city's oldest. Illustrating the dual identities of the populace, half the park is landscaped in the formal French manner and half in the more casual English style. Among its several bodies of water is a lake used for paddleboating in summer and ice skating in winter. Snowshoeing and cross-country trails curl through the trees. An open amphitheater, the Théâtre de Verdure, is the setting for free outdoor theater and movies in summer. Joggers, bikers, picnickers, and tennis buffs (there are 14 outdoor courts) share the space.

ESPECIALLY FOR KIDS

IMAX Theater. Vieux-Port at Quai King Edward (end of bd. St-Laurent). ☎ **800/349-4629** or 514/496-4629 (info and tickets). www.svpm.ca/imax. Admission C$13 (US$8) adults, C$11 (US$7) seniors/students 13–17, C$9 (US$6) children 4–12, C$38 (US$25) families (4 people). MC, V. Tues–Sun year-round. Call for current schedule of shows in English. Métro: Place-d'Armes.

The images and special effects are larger than life, sometimes in 3-D and always visually dazzling, thrown on a seven-story screen. Recent films made the most of charging elephants, racing Indy cars, and cameras swooping low over Alaskan wildlife and glaciers. Running time is usually under an hour. Arrive for shows at least 10 minutes before starting time, earlier on weekends and evenings.

La Ronde Amusement Park. Parc des Iles, Ile Ste-Hélène. ☎ **800/797-4537** or 514/872-4537. Unlimited all-day pass C$24 (US$16) for those 12 and over, C$13 (US$8) for those under 12, C$12 (US$8) grounds admission only. Reserved seating for fireworks, from C$26 (US$17), including all rides. Late May to mid-June daily 10am–9pm; late June to Labour Day daily 10:30am–11pm. Parking C$8 (US$5). Métro: Papineau, then bus 169; Ile Ste-Hélène, then bus 167.

Montréal's ambitious amusement park fills the northern reaches of the Ile Ste-Hélène with more than 30 rides, an international circus, a medieval village, roller coasters, and places to eat and drink. Thrill seekers like the rides called Le Boomerang, Le Monstre, and Le Cobra, a stand-up roller coaster that incorporates a 360° loop and reaches speeds in excess of 60 m.p.h. A big attraction is the International Fireworks Competition, held on Saturdays in June and Sundays in July (postponed in bad weather). The pyromusical displays are launched at 10pm and last at least 30 minutes. (Many Montréalers choose to watch them from the Jacques Cartier Bridge, which is closed to traffic then. Take along a Walkman to listen to the accompanying music.) The park's future is uncertain, because it has been losing money for several years and Montréal has been chosen as the site for a new C$900 million (US$600 million) indoor theme park called Destination: Technodome (tentatively sited at the west end of the Vieux-Port, not far from Habitat '67).

Planetarium de Montréal. 1000 rue St-Jacques (at rue Peel). ☎ **514/872-4530.** www.planetarium.montreal.qc.ca. Admission C$6 (US$4) adults, C$4.50 (US$3) seniors/students, C$3 (US$2) children 6–17. Schedule of shows changes frequently; call ahead. Métro: Bonaventure (Cathédrale exit).

A window on the night sky with mythical monsters and magical heroes, Montréal's planetarium is right downtown, only 2 blocks south of Windsor Station. Changing shows under the 65-foot (20m) dome dazzle and inform kids at the same time. Shows change with the seasons, exploring time and space travel and collisions of celestial bodies. The special Christmas show (Dec to early Jan), "Star of the Magi," is based on recent investigations of historians and astronomers into the mysterious light that guided the Magi. Shows in English alternate with those in French. The future location of the Planetarium, if not its existence, is in doubt: It stands on desirable acreage that's being eyed by developers for a new baseball stadium and possibly two new hotels.

6 Outdoor Activities & Spectator Sports

OUTDOOR ACTIVITIES

BICYCLING   Cycling is hugely popular here, and the city enjoys a network of 174 miles of cycling paths, with another 60 to be completed by 2000. Heavily used routes are the nearly flat 11km (6.8-mile) *piste cyclable* (bicycle path) along the Lachine Canal that leads from the Old Port to Lac St-Louis, the 16km (9.9-mile) path west from the St-Lambert Lock to the city of Côte Ste-Catherine, and Angrignon Park with its 4-mile biking path and inviting picnic areas (take the Métro, which accepts bikes in the last two doors of the last car, to Angrignon station). You can rent bikes at the Vieux-Port (at the end of boulevard St-Laurent) for around C$7 (US$4.65) per hour or C$20 to C$22 (US$13 to US$15) per day. **Velo Aventure** on Quai King Edward is a principal source (see also "In-line Skating," below). Another place to rent bikes, along with the popular four-wheel "Q Cycles," is at the place Jacques-Cartier entrance to the Vieux-Port. The Q Cycles, for use in the Old Port only, cost C$4.25 (US$2.85) per half an hour for adults and C$3.50 (US$2.35) per half an hour for children.

A useful booklet, *Pédaler Montréal,* is available at the Infotourist office on Square Dominion. For additional info, log on to **www.velo.qc.ca**.

CROSS-COUNTRY SKIING   Parc Mont-Royal has a 2.1km (1.3-mile) cross-country course called the *parcours de la croix.* The Botanical Garden has an ecology trail used by cross-country skiers. The problem for either is that you have to supply your own equipment. Just an hour from the city, in the Laurentides, are almost 20 ski centers, all offering cross-country as well as downhill skiing.

HIKING   The most popular—and obvious—hike is to the top of Mont-Royal. Start downtown on rue Peel, which leads north to a stairway, which in turn leads to an 800m (½ mile) path of switchbacks called Le Serpent. Or opt for the 200 steps leading up to the Chalet Lookout, with the reward of a panoramic view of the city. Figure about 1¼ miles one-way.

IN-LINE SKATING   You can rent in-line skates and all the requisite protective gear from **Velo Adventure** on Quai King Edward in the Vieux-Port (☎ **514/ 847-0666**). The cost is C$9 (US$6) for the first hour and C$4 (US$2.65) for each extra hour, up to a maximum of C$30 (US$20) for an 8-hour day. Protective gear is included and a deposit is required. Lessons on skates are available for C$25 (US$17) for 2 hours.

JOGGING   There are many possibilities for running. One is to follow rue Peel north to Le Serpent switchback path on Mont-Royal, continuing uphill on it for 800m (½ mile) until it peters out. Turn right and continue 2km (1.2 miles) to the monument of George-Etienne Cartier, one of Canada's fathers of confederation. From here, either take a bus back downtown or run back down the same route or along avenue du Parc and avenue des Pins (turn right when you get to it). It's also fun to jog along the Lachine Canal.

SWIMMING   The St. Lawrence is too polluted for swimming. Bordering the river, though, is the artificial **Plage de l'Ile Notre-Dame** (☎ **514/872-6093;** Métro: Ile Ste-Hélène), the former Regatta Lake from Expo '67. The water is drawn from the Lachine Rapids and treated by a mostly natural filtration system of sand, aquatic plants, and ultraviolet light (and a bit of chlorine) to make it safe for swimming.

Those who prefer a pool but are staying in a hotel that doesn't have one can head to the **Parc Olympique,** 4141 Pierre-de-Coubertin (☎ **514/252-4622;** Métro: Viau), which has six pools, open Monday to Friday about 9:30am to 9pm and

Saturday and Sunday 1 to 4pm. Call ahead to confirm swim schedules, which are affected by competitions and holidays. The **City of Montréal Department of Sports and Leisure** can provide info about other city pools, indoor or outdoor (☎ 514/872-6211). Admission to the pools varies from free to about C$5 (US$3.35), with C$2.50 (US$1.65) for children; the exception is the artificial Plage de l'Ile Notre-Dame, which is C$7 (US$4.65) for adults/seniors/students and C$2.50 (US$1.65) for children 6 to 17.

SPECTATOR SPORTS

Montréalers are as devoted to ice hockey as other Canadians, with plenty of enthusiasm left over for baseball, football, and soccer. There are several prominent annual sporting events of other kinds, such as the Molson Grand Prix in June, The Player's Ltd. International men's tennis championship in late July, and the Montréal Marathon in September.

BASEBALL   April to September, the **Montréal Expos,** part of the National League, continue to play at the Stade Olympique (Olympic Stadium), 4549 av. Pierre-de-Coubertin (☎ 514/790-1245; Métro: Pie-IX), though there's talk about building a new stadium downtown. Tickets are C$7 (US$4.65) for general admission, C$13 (US$9) for the terrace, and C$23 (US$15) for box seats, and you can order them by phone, with a credit card.

FOOTBALL   Canadian professional football returned to Montréal after a 3-year experiment with U.S. teams. The team that briefly was the Baltimore Colts is now in its second incarnation as the **Montréal Alouettes.** June to September, the CFL team plays at the Stade Olympique (Olympic Stadium), 4549 av. Pierre-de-Coubertin (☎ 514/254-2400; Métro: Pie-IX).

HARNESS RACING   Popularly known as Blue Bonnets Racetrack, the **Hippodrome de Montréal,** 7440 bd. Décarie, in Jean-Talon (☎ 514/739-2741; Métro: Namur, then the shuttle bus), is the host facility for international harness-racing events, including the Coupe des Elevers (Breeders Cup). Restaurants, bars, a snack bar, and pari-mutuel betting can make for a satisfying evening or Sunday-afternoon outing. There are no races on Tuesday and Thursday. General admission is free, but you'll pay C$5 (US$3.35) for the VIP section. Monday, Wednesday, Friday, and Saturday races begin at 7:30pm; Sunday races begin at 1:30pm.

HOCKEY   The NHL's **Montréal Canadiens** play at the Centre Molson, 1260 rue de la Gauchetière (☎ 514/932-2582; Métro: Bonaventure), replacing the beloved old Forum. They've won 24 Stanley Cup championships since 1929. The season runs October to April, with play-offs continuing to mid-June. Tickets are about C$16 to C$95 (US$11 to US$63).

7 Shopping

You'll find much to delight you in Montréal. The thriving fashion industry, from couture to ready-to-wear, boasts a history reaching back to the earliest trade in furs and leather. Beyond that, it's unlikely that any reasonable consumer needs—and even outlandish fantasies—can't be met here. There are more than 1,500 shops in the Underground City alone, and many more than that at street level and above.

Try **rue Sherbrooke** for fashion, art, and luxury items, including furs and jewelry. **Rue Crescent** has a number of scattered upscale boutiques, while funkier **boulevard St-Laurent** covers everything from budget practicalities to off-the-wall handmade clothing. Look along **rue Laurier** between St-Laurent and de l'Epée for

Getting Your Tax Refund

Save your sales receipts from any store in Montréal or the rest of Québec and ask shopkeepers for tax-refund forms. After returning home, mail the originals (not copies) to the specified address with the completed form. Refunds usually take a few months but are in the currency of your home country. A small service fee is charged. For faster refunds, follow the same procedure but hand in the receipts and form at a duty-free shop designated in the government pamphlet *Goods and Services Tax Refund for Visitors,* available at tourist offices and in many stores and hotels.

home-accessories shops and young Québecois designers. **Rue St-Paul** in Vieux-Montréal has a growing number of art galleries. More than 30 antiques stores line **rue Notre-Dame** between Guy and Atwater. **Rue Ste-Catherine** near Christ Church Cathedral has most of the major department stores and myriad satellite shops, while **rue Peel** is known for men's fashions and some crafts. Some of the best shops in Montréal are in its museums, tops among them being **Pointe-à-Callière** in Vieux-Montréal and the **Musée des Beaux-Arts** and the **Musée McCord** on rue Sherbrooke in the center of the city.

Usual **shopping hours** are Monday to Saturday 9:30 or 10am to 5:30 or 6pm, with many stores remaining open to 8 or 9pm Thursdays. In tourist areas and the larger downtown malls, many shops and department stores are open Sunday noon to 5pm.

SHOPPING A TO Z

The best places to find antiques and collectibles is in the more than 30 storefronts along **rue Notre-Dame** between rues Guy and Atwater. Or visit **Antiques Puces Libres,** 4240 rue St-Denis, near rue Rachel (☎ **514/842-5931;** Métro: Mont-Royal). Three fascinatingly cluttered floors are packed with pine and oak furniture, lamps, clocks, vases, and more, most of it 19th- and early–20th-century French-Canadian art nouveau.

ARTS & CRAFTS The ongoing development of the Bonsecours Market has altered the focus from nonprofit exhibition space to shops and food stalls, including the **Boutique Canadiana Worn Doorstep,** 350 rue St-Paul est, Vieux-Montréal (☎ **514/ 397-0666;** Métro: Champ-de-Mars), which concentrates on crafts, children's storybooks, maps, small furniture, and packaged foods, all with a Canadian connection. A choice collection of craft items is displayed in a gallery setting at the **Guilde Canadienne des Métiers d'Art Québec,** 2025 rue Peel, at boulevard de Maisonneuve (☎ **514/849-6091;** Métro: Peel). Among the objects are blown glass, paintings on silk, pewter, tapestries, and ceramics. The stock is particularly strong in avant-garde jewelry and Inuit sculpture. **L'Empreinte,** 272 rue St-Paul est, a block off place Jacques-Cartier in Vieux-Montréal (☎ **514/861-4427;** Métro: Champ de Mars), is a craftspersons' collective. The ceramics, textiles, glassware, and other items on sale often occupy that vaguely defined territory between art and craft. The quality is uneven.

BOOKS Chapters, 1171 rue Ste-Catherine ouest, at rue Stanley (☎ **514/ 849-8825;** Métro: Peel), is the flagship of a chain with many branches. Thousands of titles are available in both French and English. Prowl the rows of shelves of **Paragraphe,** 2220 av. McGill College, south of rue Sherbrooke (☎ **514/845-5811;** Métro: McGill), and then take your purchases to the adjoining Second Cup cafe, popular with students from the McGill campus, a block away. The store hosts frequent autograph parties, author readings, and occasional musical performances. Travelers' needs are served by the stock of **Ulysse,** 4176 rue St-Denis (☎ 514/843-9447; Métro: Sherbrooke), and 560 av. du Président-Kennedy, at rue Alymer (☎ 514/843-7222; Métro: Place-des-Arts). Featured are guidebooks, many in English, along with accessories, including maps, day packs, money pouches, electrical adapters, and coffeemakers. For gay and lesbian books, try **L'Androgyne,** 3636 rue St-Laurent (☎ 514/842-4765; Métro: St-Laurent).

DEPARTMENT STORES   Montréal's major shopping emporia are along a 12-block strip of **rue Ste-Catherine** (except for Holt Renfrew), from rue Guy eastward to Carré Phillips at rue Aylmer. Most of the stores below have branches elsewhere.

Since 1925, **Eaton,** 677 rue Ste-Catherine ouest, at rue University (☎ 514/284-8411; Métro: McGill), has offered a conventional range of middle-of-the-road branded fashions and home furnishings. Its sales staff is uncommonly helpful. The future of Montréal's largest store is in doubt, however, since its parent company is up for sale. The beautiful **Henry Birks et Fils,** 1240 Carré Phillips, at rue Union (☎ 514/397-2511; Métro: McGill), with dark-wood display cases, stone pillars, and marble floors, is a living part of Montréal's Victorian heritage. Products displayed go beyond jewelry to encompass pens and desk accessories, watches, leather goods, glassware, and china. **Holt Renfrew,** 1300 rue Sherbrooke ouest, at rue Montagne (☎ 514/842-5111; Métro: Guy or Peel), is a showcase for international style for men and women offering such prestigious names as Giorgio Armani, Prada, Gucci, and Chanel. The marquee outside reads only HOLTS.

No retailer has an older or more celebrated name than that of the Hudson's Bay Company, a name shortened in recent years to The Bay, then transformed into **La Baie,** 585 rue Ste-Catherine ouest, near rue Aylmer (☎ 514/281-4422; Métro: McGill). Its main store emphasizes clothing but also offers crystal, china, and Inuit carvings. Its Canadiana Boutique features historical souvenir items and wool merchandise, including their famous Hudson's Bay blankets. This is the first foray out of its home area for Québec City's **La Maison Simons,** 977 rue Ste-Catherine ouest, at rue Mansfield (☎ 514/282-1840; Métro: McGill), a long-established family-owned department store. Attention has been captured by the imaginative displays of fashions filling the refurbished building that once housed the old Simpson's store. Opened in 1866, **Ogilvy,** 1307 rue Ste-Catherine ouest, at rue Montagne (☎ 514/842-7711; Métro: Guy or Peel), has been at this location since 1912. Besides having a reputation for quality merchandise, the store is known for its eagerly awaited Christmas windows. Once thought of as hidebound with tradition, it now contains a collection of high-profile international boutiques like Guy Laroche, Escada, Anne Klein, Aquascutum, and Rodier Paris.

FASHION   For Men   One of the many links in a popular Canadian chain, **America,** 1101 Ste-Catherine ouest, at rue Stanley (☎ 514/289-9609; Métro: Peel), carries casual and dressy clothes, including suits, jackets, and slacks. A women's section is upstairs. At **Brisson & Brisson,** 1472 rue Sherbrooke ouest, near rue Mackay (☎ 514/937-7456; Métro: Guy), apparel of the nipped-and-trim British and European cuts fills three floors, from makers as diverse as Burberry, Brioni, and Valentino. Hugo and Boss styles prevail at **Club Monsieur,** 1407 rue Crescent, near boulevard de Maisonneuve (☎ 514/843-5476; Métro: Guy), for those with the fit frames to carry them and with the required discretionary income. **L'Uomo,** 1452 rue Peel, near rue Ste-Catherine (☎ 514/844-1008; Métro: Peel) carries largely Italian menswear by forward-thinking designers like Valentino, Cerruti, Versace, Armani, and Ermenegildo Zegna.

For Women   Sonia Kozma designs the fashions at **Ambre,** 201 rue St-Paul ouest, Place Jacques-Cartier (☎ **514/982-0325;** Métro: Square-Victoria), including suits, cocktail dresses, and dinner and casual wear made of linen, rayon, and cotton. Browse at **Artefact,** 4117 rue St-Denis, near rue Rachel (☎ **514/842-2780;** Métro: Mont-Royal), to find articles of clothing and paintings by up-and-coming Québecois designers and artists. The hyper-chic designer wear from Italy at **Giorgio Femme,** 1455 rue Peel, near boulevard de Maisonneuve (☎ **514/282-0294;** Métro: Peel), isn't for everyone, but the fresh ideas here are bound to be seen on the streets not long after, if in modified form. Eye-catching creations of Québecois and other Canadian designers are featured at **Kyoze,** Centre Mondial du Commerce, 393 rue St-Jacques ouest, second floor (☎ **514/847-7572;** Métro: Square-Victoria), including jewelry and accessories.

For Men & Women   **Club Monaco,** 1455 rue Peel, north of rue Ste-Catherine (☎ **514/499-0959;** Métro: Peel), is an expanding Canadian-owned international chain appreciated for its minimalist monochromatic garments along with silver jewelry, eyewear, and cosmetics. Think Prada but affordable. **Les Cuirs Danier,** 730 rue Ste-Catherine ouest, near avenue McGill College (☎ **514/392-0936;** Métro: McGill), is a coast-to-coast national chain with quality leather garments, belts, bags, and such mostly for women, but men aren't ignored. There's another branch in Place Ville Marie. A diverse selection of designers and manufacturers, mostly Italian, makes choices difficult at **Felix Brown,** 1233 rue Ste-Catherine ouest, at rue Drummond (☎ **514/287-5523;** Métro: Peel). Among them are Bruno Magli, Moschino, Casadel, and Vicini. The British origins of **Marks & Spencer,** at Place Montréal Trust, 1500 av. McGill College, at rue Ste-Catherine (☎ **514/499-8558;** Métro: McGill), grow less obvious as the mother chain continues to spread over several continents, but the clothing still represents a favorable price-to-value ratio. At **Polo/Ralph Lauren,** 1290 rue Sherbrooke, near rue de la Montagne (☎ **514/ 288-3988;** Métro: Peel), the international designer has set up shop in a town house in the poshest part of the city, near the Ritz-Carlton. Apparel for the well-heeled family, plus house accessories.

8 Montréal After Dark

Montréal's reputation for effervescent nightlife goes back to the 1920s—to the U.S. experiment with Prohibition, to be exact. Canadian distillers and brewers made fortunes, not much of it legal, and Americans streamed into Montréal for temporary relief from alcohol deprivation. That the city already enjoyed a sophisticated and slightly naughty reputation as the Paris of North America added to the allure. Nightclubbing and barhopping remain popular, with much later hours than those of archrival Toronto, still in thrall to Calvinist notions of propriety and early bedtimes.

Montréalers' nocturnal pursuits are often as cultural as they are social. The city boasts its own outstanding symphony, French- and English-speaking theater companies, and the incomparable Cirque du Soleil (Circus of the Sun). It's also on the standard concert circuit that includes Chicago, Boston, and New York, so internationally known entertainers, rock bands, orchestra conductors and classical virtuosos, and ballet and modern-dance companies pass through frequently.

For details of current performances or special events, pick up a free copy of *Montréal Scope,* a weekly ads-and-events booklet, at any large hotel reception desk or the free weekly newspapers *Mirror* (in English) or *Voir* (in French). Place des Arts puts out a monthly calendar of events, the *Calendrier des Spectacles,* describing concerts

Special Events

In summer, the city becomes even livelier than usual with several enticing events: the **Festival de Théâtre des Amériques** (late May to early June), the **Benson & Hedges International Fireworks Competition** (June to July), the renowned ✪ **Festival International de Jazz** (early July), and the **Juste Pour Rire/Just for Laughs Festival** (late July). And every year, late September to early October, the **Festival International de Nouvelle Danse** attracts modern-dance troupes and choreographers from around the world.

---

and performances to be held in the various halls of the performing-arts complex. Pick one up in most large hotels or near the box offices in Place des Arts. Montréal's newspapers, the French *La Presse* and the English *Gazette,* carry listings of films, clubs, and performances in their Friday and Saturday editions. For extensive listings of largely mainstream cultural and entertainment events, log on to **www.montreal gazette.com**; a similar service is provided by the alternative newspaper, *Hour,* at **www.afterhour.com.** Also try the Place des Arts page, **www.infoarts.net,** and the official site of Tourisme Montréal, **www.tourism-montreal.org.**

Concentrations of pubs and discos underscore the city's linguistic dichotomy too. While there's a great deal of crossover mingling, the parallel blocks of **rue Crescent, rue Bishop,** and **rue de la Montagne** north of rue Ste-Catherine have a pronounced Anglophone character, while Francophones dominate the **Latin Quarter,** with college-age patrons most evident along the lower reaches of **rue St-Denis** and their yuppie elders gravitating to the nightspots of the more uptown blocks of the same street. **Vieux-Montréal,** especially along **rue St-Paul,** has a more universal quality, where many of the bars and clubs feature live jazz, blues, and folk music. In the **Plateau Mont-Royal** area, **boulevard St-Laurent,** parallel to St-Denis and known locally as "The Main," has become a miles-long haven of hip restaurants and clubs, roughly from rue Laurier to rue Sherbrooke. St-Laurent is a good place to wind up in the wee hours, because there's always some place with the welcome mat still out.

THE PERFORMING ARTS

THEATER The **Festival de Théâtre des Amériques** (☎ 514/842-0704), held in odd-numbered years from late May to early June, presents innovative dramatic and musical stage productions that are international in scope, not simply North American, as the name suggests. There have been works from Vietnam and China, as well as from Canada, the United States, and Mexico. The plays are performed in the original languages, as a rule, with simultaneous translations in French and/or English, when appropriate.

A former stock-exchange building (1903) is home to Montréal's principal English-language theater, the **Centaur Theatre,** 453 rue St-François-Xavier, near rue Notre-Dame (☎ 514/288-3161; Métro: Place-d'Armes). A mix of classics, foreign adaptations, and works by Canadian playwrights is presented, with past productions including *Anthony and Cleopatra, The Visitor, The Substance of Fire, Waiting for Godot, The Search for Signs of Intelligent Life in the Universe, Dancing at Lughnasa,* and *Cabaret.* Off-season, the theater is rented to other groups, both French- and English-speaking. Performances are October to June, Tuesday to Saturday at 8pm and Sunday at 7pm, with Saturday (and most Sun) matinees at 2pm. Tickets run C$12 to C$34 (US$8 to US$23).

Montréal's Yiddish Theatre, founded in 1937, is housed in the **Saidye Bronfman Centre for the Arts,** 5170 Côte-Ste-Catherine, near boulevard Décarie (☎ 514/739-2301 for information, or 514/739-4816 for tickets; Métro: Côte-Ste-Catherine; Bus: 129 ouest), not far from St. Joseph's Oratory. It stages plays in both Yiddish and English, usually running 3 to 4 weeks in June and October. At other times, the 300-seat theater hosts dance and music recitals, a bilingual puppet festival, occasional lectures, and three English-language plays. There's also an art gallery on the premises, with exhibits that change almost monthly. Across the street, in the Edifice Cummings House, is a small Holocaust museum and the Jewish Public Library. The center takes its name from philanthropist Saidye Bronfman, widow of Samuel Bronfman, founder of the Seagram Company; she died in 1995 at age 98. The box office is usually open Monday to Thursday 11am to 8pm and Sunday noon to 7pm (call ahead). Performances are Tuesday to Thursday at 8pm and Sunday at 1:30 and 7pm. Tickets run C$15 to C$45 (US$10 to US$30).

DANCE   Frequent appearances by notable dancers and troupes from other parts of Canada and the world—among them Paul Taylor, the Feld Ballet, and Le Ballet National du Canada—augment the accomplished native company. During summer, the prestigious ✪ **Les Grands Ballets Canadiens** often performs at the outdoor Théâtre de Verdure in Parc Lafontaine. In winter, it's scheduled at various venues, but especially in the several halls at Place des Arts, 200 bd. de Maisonneuve ouest (☎ 514/849-8681; Métro: Place-des-Arts). The company has developed a following far beyond national borders over more than 35 years, performing both a classical and a modern repertoire. In the process, it has brought prominence to many gifted Canadian choreographers and composers. It tours internationally and was the first Canadian ballet company to be invited to the People's Republic of China. The troupe's production of *The Nutcracker* the last couple of weeks in December is always a big event. The box office is open Monday to Saturday noon to 8pm. Performances are held late October to early May at 8pm. Tickets run C$12 to C$40 (US$8 to US$27). The fall season is kicked off by the always-provocative **Festival International de Nouvelle Danse,** in late September and early October.

CLASSICAL MUSIC & OPERA   Founded in 1980, the outstanding L'Opéra de Montréal appears at the Salle Wilfrid-Pelletier, Place des Arts, 260 bd. de Maisonneuve ouest (☎ 514/985-2222 for information, or 514/985-2258 for tickets; Métro: Place-des-Arts). It mounts six productions a year in Montréal, with artists from Québec and abroad participating in such productions as *La Traviata, Don Carlo, Carmen, Salome, La Bohème, Otello,* and *Mefistofele.* Video translations are provided from the original languages into French and English. The box office is open Monday to Friday 9am to 5pm. Performances are September to June, usually at 8pm, at Place des Arts and occasionally at other venues. Tickets run C$32 to C$99 (US$21 to US$66).

The world-famous ✪ **Orchestre Symphonique de Montréal (OSM)** plays at the Salle Wilfrid-Pelletier, Place des Arts, 260 bd. de Maisonneuve ouest (☎ 514/842-9951; Métro: Place-des-Arts), and the Notre-Dame Basilica, 110 rue Notre-Dame ouest, as well as around the world. It's led by Swiss conductor Charles Dutoit (and Zubin Mehta before him). In the well-balanced repertoire are works from Elgar to Rabaud to Saint-Saëns, in addition to Beethoven and Mozart. The box office is open Monday to Saturday noon to 8pm. Performances are usually at 8pm, during a full season that runs September to May, supplemented by Mozart concerts at Notre-Dame in June and July and free performances at three parks in the metropolitan region. Tickets run C$15 to C$55 (US$10 to US$37). The **Orchestre Métropolitain de Montréal** has a regular season at the Maisonneuve Theatre, Place des Arts, 260 bd. de Maisonneuve ouest (☎ 514/598-0870; Métro: Place-des-Arts), but also performs in the St-Jean-Baptiste Church and tours regionally. Most musicians are in their mid-30s or younger. The box office is open Monday to Saturday noon to 8pm. Performances are held mid-October to early April, usually at 8pm. Outdoor concerts are given in Parc Lafontaine in August. Tickets run C$13 to C$40 (US$9 to US$27).

CONCERT HALLS & AUDITORIUMS Montréal has a score of venues, so check the papers to see who's playing where during your stay. Big-name rock bands and pop stars usually play at the **Centre Molson,** 1260 rue de la Gauchetière ouest (☎ 514/989-2841 ticket office; Métro: Atwater), also the new home of the Montréal Canadiens hockey team. If a concert is scheduled, printed flyers, posters, and radio and TV ads make certain everyone knows. Up to 20,000 can be seated. The box office is open Monday to Friday 10am to 6pm (to 9pm on days of events).

A broad range of Canadian and international performers, usually of a modest celebrity unlikely to fill the larger Centre Molson, use the **Spectrum de Montréal,** 318 rue Ste-Catherine ouest (☎ 514/861-5851; Métro: Place-des-Arts). Rock acts on the order of Marilyn Manson and Phish are among the higher-profile acts, and the space also hosts part of the city's annual jazz festival. Seats are on a first-come, first-served basis. The box office is open Monday to Saturday 10am to 9pm and Sunday noon to 5pm. Performances are at 8:30 or 9pm.

Founded in 1963 and in its striking present home in the heart of Montréal since 1992, ✪ **Place des Arts,** 260 bd. de Maisonneuve ouest (☎ 514/285-4200 for information, 514/842-2112 for tickets, or 514/285-4275 for guided-tour reservations; Métro: Place-des-Arts), mounts performances of musical concerts, opera, dance, and theater in five halls: the **Salle Wilfrid-Pelletier** (2,982 seats), where the Orchestre Symphonique de Montréal often performs; the **Maisonneuve Théâtre** (1,460 seats), where the Orchestre Métropolitan de Montréal and the McGill Chamber Orchestra perform; the **Jean-Duceppe Théâtre** (755 seats); the **Cinquième Salle** (350 seats); and the small **Studio-Théâtre du Maurier Ltée** (138 seats). Traveling productions of Broadway classics like *Smokey Joe's Cafe* and *Bring in da Noise, Bring in da Funk* have limited runs at the center. Noontime performances are often scheduled. The box office is open Monday to Saturday noon to 8pm, and performances are usually at 8pm.

In a landmark 1899 building on the McGill University campus, **Pollack Concert Hall,** 555 rue Sherbrooke ouest (☎ 514/398-4547; Métro: McGill), is in nearly constant use, especially during the university year. Among the attractions are concerts and recitals by professionals, students, or soloists from McGill's music faculty. Recordings of some of the more memorable concerts are available on the university's own label, McGill Records. Concerts are also given in the campus's smaller **Redpath Hall,** 3461 rue McTavish (☎ 514/398-4547). Performances are at 8pm and usually are free. Nestled in Parc Lafontaine in Plateau Mont-Royal, the **Théâtre de Verdure** (☎ 514/872-2644; Métro: Sherbrooke) presents free music and dance concerts and theater, often with well-known artists and performers. Sometimes they show outdoor movies. Many in the audience pack picnics. Performances are held June to August; call for days and times. The recently refurbished **Théâtre St-Denis,** 1594 rue St-Denis (☎ 514/849-4211; Métro: Berri–UQAM), in the heart of the Latin Quarter, hosts a variety of shows, including pop singers and groups and comedians, as well as segments of the Juste Pour Rire (Just for Laughs) Festival in summer. It's actually two theaters, one seating more than 2,000, the other almost 1,000. The box office is open daily noon to 9pm. Performances are usually at 8pm.

A Circus Extraordinaire

Through the exposure generated by its frequent tours across North America, Europe, and Australia, the hip ✪ **Cirque du Soleil,** 8400 av. 2e, St-Michel (☎ **800/361-4595** or 514/790-1245; www.cirquedusoleil.com), is enjoying an ever-multiplying following. One reason, curiously, is the absence of animals in the troupe, which means no one need be troubled by the possibility of mistreated lions and elephants. What is experienced during a Cirque du Soleil performance is nothing less than magical, a celebration of pure skill and theater, with plenty of acrobats, clowns, trapeze artists, tightrope walkers, and contortionists.

Since 1984, more than 15 million people, in some 120 cities, have seen the Cirque in action. The troupe is so much in demand it's difficult to track from year to year how long it'll alight here in its hometown, though most recently it stayed mid-April to mid-June. Check ahead for its current plans. Its all-new production, "Dralion," is presented in the trademark yellow-and-blue Big Top erected on the grounds of the Cirque du Soleil Studio in the St-Michel district. Last time out, performances were scheduled Tuesday and Wednesday at 8pm, Thursday and Friday at 5:30 and 9:30pm, Saturday at 4 and 8pm, and Sunday at 1 and 5pm. Tickets run C$25 to C$50 (US$17 to US$33) adults and C$18 to C$35 (US$12 to US$23) children.

COMEDY & MUSIC CLUBS

COMEDY   The 1980s explosion in comedy venues has cooled, but Montréal still has a couple of laugh spots, mostly because it's home to the **Juste Pour Rire/Just for Laughs Festival** every summer (☎ **514/845-2322**). Those who have so far eluded the comedy-club experience should know that profanity, scatological references, and assorted ethnic slurs are common fodder for performers.

Mostly local talent is showcased at the **Comedy Nest,** in the Nouvel Hotel, 1740 bd. René-Lévesque, at rue Guy (☎ **514/932-6378;** Métro: Guy-Concordia), but among the comics who've stopped here on their way up were Howie Mandel, Norm MacDonald, and rubber-faced Jim Carrey. Shows are held Wednesday to Sunday at 8:30pm, with added shows Friday and Saturday at 11:30pm. The cover is C$12 (US$8) and the dinner-and-show package is C$24 (US$16) Wednesday, Thursday, and Sunday or C$29 (US$19) Friday and Saturday; dinner starts at 6:30pm. There's a full card of comedy at the long-running **Comedyworks,** 1238 rue Bishop, at rue Ste-Catherine (☎ **514/398-9661;** Métro: Guy-Concordia), up the stairs from Jimbo's Pub on a jumping block of rue Bishop south of rue Ste-Catherine. Monday is open-mike night, and Tuesday and Wednesday improv groups usually work the audience. Headliners of greater or lesser magnitude—usually from Montréal, Toronto, New York, or Boston—take the stage Thursday to Sunday. No food is served, just drinks. Reservations are recommended, especially on Friday, when early arrival may be necessary to secure a seat. Shows are daily at 8:30pm and also at 11:15pm Fridays and Saturdays. Cover goes up to C$12 (US$8), plus a one-drink minimum.

FOLK, ROCK & POP   Scores of bars, cafes, theaters, clubs, and even churches present live music occasionally, even if only at Sunday brunch. The performers, local or touring, traffic in every idiom, from metal to funk and reggae to grunge and unvarnished Vegas. In most cases acts play a venue only for a night or two. Here are a few selections that focus their energies on the music.

When anyone over 25 shows up inside the bleak **Café Campus,** 57 rue Prince-Arthur est, near boulevard St-Laurent (☎ **514/844-1010;** Métro: Sherbrooke), it's probably a parent of one of the musicians. Alternative rock prevails, but metal and retro-rock bands also make appearances. Followers of the scene may be familiar with such groups as Skyjuice, Come, and Cosmic Surgery, all of whom have hit the stage. Dance parties are often scheduled Wednesdays. The cover is usually C$4 to C$12 (US$2.65 to US$8). **Club Soda,** 5240 av. du Parc, near rue Bernard (☎ **514/270-7848;** Métro: Place-des-Arts, then bus no. 80 north), is one of the city's larger venues for attractions below the megastar level, and performers are given a stage before a hall seating several hundred. Three bars lubricate audience enthusiasm. Musical choices include folk, rock, blues, country, Afro-Cuban, heavy metal, you name it. Acts for the annual jazz and comedy festivals are booked here too. The cover is C$5 (US$3.35) and up.

Over a club called Bowser & Blue, the casual **Déjà Vu,** 1224 rue Bishop, near rue Ste-Catherine (☎ **514/866-0512;** Métro: Guy-Concordia), puts on live music nightly. The management has eclectic tastes, hiring bands specializing in old-time rock, country, blues, whatever. It's a loose, fun, relatively inexpensive place (no cover), with three floors and two small dance floors. The Irish have been one of the largest immigrant groups in Montréal since the 1840s famine, and their musical tradition thrives at **Hurley's Irish Pub,** 1225 rue Crescent, south of rue Ste-Catherine (☎ **514/861-4111;** Métro: Peel or Guy-Concordia). Celtic instrumentalists and dancers perform nightly, often both on the ground floor and upstairs, usually starting at 9:30pm. There's no cover.

Perhaps the best known of Montréal's *boîtes-à-chansons,* **Le Pierrot/Les Deux Pierrots,** 114 and 104 rue St-Paul est, west of place Jacques-Cartier (☎ **514/861-1270;** Métro: Place-d'Armes), is an intimate French-style club. The singer interacts animatedly with the crowd, often bilingually, and encourages them to join in the lyrics. Le Pierrot is open year-round (daily early June to late Sept, Thurs to Sun the other months), with music into the wee hours. Its sister club next door, the larger Les Deux Pierrots, features live bands playing rock Friday and Saturday, half in French and half in English. The terrace joining the two clubs is open Friday and Saturday in summer. Le Pierrot is open only May to September. The cover for Le Pierrot is C$3 (US$2) on Friday and Saturday; the cover for Aux Deux Pierrots is C$5 (US$3.35).

JAZZ & BLUES   Every summer, the respected and heavily attended **Festival International de Jazz** (☎ **800/361-4595** or 514/871-1881; www.montrealjazzfest.com) sustains interest in the most original American art form. During the 10 days of the event, more than 2,000 musicians perform on 16 stages for an average total audience of a million. Scores of events are scheduled, indoors and out, many of them free. "Jazz" is broadly interpreted, including everything from Dixieland to reggae, world beat, and unclassifiable experimental. Artists who've performed at the Festival have included Thelonious Monk, Pat Metheny, John McLaughlin, Dave Brubeck, and BB King. Piano legend Oscar Peterson grew up here and often returns to perform.

Pick up a copy of *Mirror* or *Hour,* distributed free everywhere, or buy the Saturday edition of the *Gazette* for the entertainment section. These publications have full listings of the bands and stars appearing during the week. Downtown, where there isn't much other after-dark action, the longtime stalwart **Biddle's,** 2060 rue Aylmer, south of rue Sherbrooke (☎ **514/842-8656;** Métro: McGill), is a club/restaurant with hanging plants and faux art nouveau glass. It fills up early with lovers of barbecued ribs and jazz. The live music starts around 5:30pm (at 7pm Sun and Mon) and continues until closing. Charlie Biddle plays bass Tuesday to Friday when he doesn't have a gig elsewhere. He and his stand-ins favor jazz of the swinging mainstream variety, with occasional digressions into more esoteric forms. There's no cover, but there is a minimum on Friday and Saturday, as well as a mandatory paid coat check.

A Montréal tradition since 1976, **۞ L'Air du Temps,** 191 rue St-Paul ouest, at rue St-François-Xavier (**☎ 514/842-2003;** Métro: Place-d'Armes), is an ardent jazz emporium of the old school—a little seedy and beat up, with no gimmicks or frippery to distract from the music. The main room and an upper floor in back can hold more than 135, and the bar stools and tables fill up quickly. Get there by 9:30pm to secure a seat. The bands go on at 10:30pm or so. L'Air du Temps doesn't serve food, just a wide variety of drinks, but several good mid-priced restaurants are nearby. The club, the most likely jazz club to get semi-name acts, doesn't take reservations. The cover is C$5 to C$25 (US$3.35 to US$17). Blues gets a wide hearing in this musical city, as demonstrated at **Les Beaux Esprits,** 2073 rue St-Denis, at rue Sherbrooke (**☎ 515/844-0882;** Métro: Sherbrooke), in the thumping heart of the youthful Latin Quarter. Simple and unpretentious, the place attracts avid fans of the music, mostly of university age. Local musicians perform nightly, usually from 10:30pm on. There's no cover.

DANCE CLUBS

Montréal's dance clubs change in tenor and popularity in mere eye blinks, and new ones sprout like toadstools after a heavy rain and wither as quickly. For the latest fever spots, quiz concierges, guides, waiters—all those who look as if they might follow the scene. Here are a few that appear more likely to survive the whims of night owls and landlords. At some, you'll encounter steroid abusers with funny haircuts guarding the doors. Usually, they'll let you inside: The admittance game isn't the strict "hipper than thou" criteria found in some New York and Los Angeles clubs.

An infectious, sensual tropical beat issues from **Batalou,** 4372 bd. St-Laurent, at rue Marie-Anne (**☎ 514/845-5447;** Métro: Mont-Royal), a club-with-a-difference on The Main. Although most of the patrons revel in their ancestral origins in the Caribbean and Africa, the sources of the live and recorded music, an ecumenical welcome is extended to all comers. Admittedly, the hip-waggling expertise of the dancers might be intimidating to the uninitiated. Things get going about 10pm every night but Monday, and the C$7 (US$4.65) cover on Friday and Saturday includes one beer or glass of wine. On the scene for over a decade, the multilevel disco/rock club **Les Foufounes Electriques,** 87 Ste-Catherine est, near rue St-Denis (**☎ 514/844-5539;** Métro: Berri–UQAM), has mellowed somewhat from its outlaw days, though you can't tell from a list of the live bands—Over Kill, Last Breath, Martyr. An occasional one-hit wonder puts in an appearance (Vanilla Ice, anyone?). With three dance floors and a couple of beer gardens in back, there's plenty to keep you busy. Look for the rocket ship over the door. The cover is C$10 (US$7) and up.

Housed in a handsome opera house from the 1890s, the monster **Metropolis,** 59 rue Ste-Catherine est, near boulevard St-Laurent (**☎ 514/844-3500;** Métro: Berri-UQAM), can accommodate 2,200 gyrating bodies. The sound system and the light show are state-of-the-art, and there are six bars on three levels. Recent attractions have included Tito Puente, Steve Winwood, Bjork, and Ben Harper. The neighborhood is scruffy but not especially worrisome and not far from the Université du Québec. The cover is C$10 (US$7) and up. **Salsathèque,** 1220 rue Peel, at rue Ste-Catherine (**☎ 514/875-0016;** Métro: Peel), has been on the scene for years, so it's obviously doing something right. The big upstairs room is all glittery, bouncing, mirrored light, the better to get the dancers moving to mambo, merengue, and other hot tropical beats. It rarely kicks into high before midnight. The house band comes on at 11pm or so, and they bring in other acts. The main source of entertainment, though, is the patrons themselves, a highly proficient lot on the dance floor. The cover on Friday and Saturday is C$5 (US$3.35).

A jovial racially mixed crowd ankles over to the **Wax Lounge,** 3481 bd. St-Laurent, second floor, north of rue Sherbrooke (☎ **514/282-0919;** Metro: Sherbrooke), after dinner at one of the half-dozen scene restaurants clustered around this busy south end of The Main. The rope policy is more in the interest of crowd control than restrictiveness. When the live band (usually soul/rock with rap undertones) takes a break, the DJ pumps the house music up through the soles of your shoes. The cover is C$5 (US$3.35) Monday to Thursday and C$7 (US$4.65) Friday and Saturday.

BARS & CAFES

An abundance of restaurants, bars, and cafes masses along the streets near the **downtown commercial district,** from rue Stanley to rue Guy between rue Ste-Catherine and boulevard de Maisonneuve. **Rue Crescent,** in particular, hums with activity from late afternoon until far into the evening, especially after 10pm on a cool summer weekend night, when the street swarms with people careening from club to bar to restaurant. **Boulevard St-Laurent,** another nightlife hub, abounds in bars and clubs, most with a distinctive European—particularly French—personality, as opposed to the Anglo flavor of the rue Crescent area. Increasingly active **rue St-Paul,** west of place Jacques-Cartier in Vieux-Montréal, falls somewhere in the middle on the Anglophone-Francophone spectrum. It's also a little more likely to get rowdy on late weekend nights.

In all cases, bars tend to open around 11:30am and go late. Many of them have *heures joyeuses* (happy hours) from as early as 3pm to as late as 9pm, but usually a shorter period within those hours. At those times, two-for-one rather than discount drinks are the rule. Last call for orders is 3am, but patrons are often allowed to dawdle over those drinks until 4am.

DOWNTOWN & RUE CRESCENT   Memorable. Breathtaking. The view, that is, from Montréal's only revolving bar/restaurant, **Le Tour de Ville,** in the Radisson Hôtel des Gouverneurs, 777 rue University (☎ **514/879-1370;** Métro: Square-Victoria). The best time to go is when the sun is setting and the city lights are beginning to blink on. In the bar (open at 6pm) one floor down from the restaurant, the same wonderful vistas are augmented by a dance floor, with a band Thursday to Saturday 9pm to 1 or 2am. The food in the restaurant is okay and not too expensive. Within sight of the Hôtel de la Montagne's trademark lobby fountain with its nude bronze sprite sporting stained-glass wings, the appealing **Lutétia Bar,** 1430 rue de la Montagne, north of rue Ste-Catherine (☎ **514/288-5656;** Métro: Guy-Concordia), draws a standing-room-only crowd of youngish to middle-aged professionals after 5:30pm. Later on, there's often music by jazz duos. In summer, the hotel opens the terrace bar on the roof by the pool.

A mature, prosperous crowd seeks out the quiet **Ritz Bar,** in the Ritz-Carlton Kempinski Hôtel, 1228 rue Sherbrooke ouest, at rue Drummond (☎ **514/ 842-4212;** Métro: Peel), adjacent to its semilegendary Café de Paris. Anyone can take advantage of the tranquil room, but the atmosphere is rather formal, so men should wear a jacket. Piano music dances softly around conversation at cocktail hour Monday to Friday 5 to 8pm and at dinner 5 to 11pm September to mid-May. Trilevel upstairs/downstairs bar/cafes are rue Crescent landmarks: One reason is the sidewalk terrace (open in summer, enclosed in winter), a vantage for checking out the pedestrian traffic. One of these houses the **Sir Winston Churchill Pub,** 1459 rue Crescent, near rue Ste-Catherine (☎ **514/288-0623;** Métro: Guy-Concordia). Inside and down the stairs, the pub, with English ales on tap, attempts to imitate a British public house, with marginal success. Dishy waitresses in miniskirts bring food, but the burgers and such have to look up to reach mediocrity. A mixed crowd of questing young professionals mills around a total of 17 bars and two dance floors. During the 5-to-8pm happy hour, drinks are two-for-one. **Winnie's,** on the second floor, is a restaurant with a terrace of its own and a new cigar lounge.

Thursday's, in the Hôtel de la Montagne at 1441–1449 rue Crescent, near rue Ste-Catherine (☎ 514/288-5656; Métro: Guy-Concordia), is a prime watering hole of the young professional set (those ever alert to the possibilities of companionship). The pubby bar spills out onto the terrace that hangs over the street, and a glittery disco is in back. The place presumably takes its name from the Montréal custom of prowling nightspots on Thursday evening in search of the perfect date for Friday.

PLATEAU MONT-ROYAL   Wear anything better than a tank top and jeans or the January equivalent thereof and feel overdressed at **Bleu et Noir,** 812 rue Rachel est, near rue St-Hubert (☎ 514/524-4809; Metro: Mont-Royal). Grungy and beery it is, with a battered sheet-metal bar, a pool table, and a beat-up fireplace, as well as a crowd of neighborhood regulars from 3pm to dinnertime and a clog of students from then until the third wee hour. A DJ works the turntables most nights, with live bands appearing many Sundays, when there's a C$5 to C$7 (US$3.35 to US$4.65) cover. Remnants of 1950s Modern, much of it mismatched, fill the space around the small dance floor at **Blizzarts,** 3956a bd. St-Laurent, near rue Duluth (☎ 514/843-4860; Metro: Mont-Royal). Heavy-beat dance music is designed to get the 20-ish crowd up and moving. Next to the DJ booth is a full bar with an espresso machine.

At the **CyberGround NetCafé,** 3672 bd. St-Laurent, north of rue Prince-Arthur (☎ 514/842-1726; Metro: Sherbrooke), you can keep in touch, word-process, play games, or just cruise the Net on any of half a dozen 'puters, on 21-inch monitors. Time at the keyboard is just C$4 (US$2.65) per half hour. There's no booze, just coffee and soft drinks. Newer than most of the St-Laurent places, the bright little boîte called **Laïka,** 4040 bd. St-Laurent, near rue Duluth (☎ 514/842-8088; Metro: Mont-Royal), has an open front in summer and fresh flowers on the bar and some of the tables. Pretty tasty sandwiches, tapas, and meze are served, and Sunday brunch is popular. The DJ spins house and funk and the mirrored ball 8pm to 3am. Most patrons fit the 18-to-35 demographic.

A wall plaque dated 1983 honors **Le Bar Felix,** 980 rue Rachel est, west of avenue du Parc Lafontaine (☎ 514/596-3981; Metro: Mont-Royal), for "Distinction in Architecture." It must be stolen or the color scheme wasn't orange and black at the time. This is a friendly no-pretense joint with an open front, a pool table, a disco ball, and a DJ booth. Music is live Wednesday to Saturday—retro, alternative, hip-hop, francophone. Two-for-one drinks are the policy much of the time. The after-curtain crowd from the Théâtre St-Denis gathers at **Le Continental Bistro Américain,** 4169 rue St-Denis, at rue Rachel (☎ 514/845-6842; Métro: Mont-Royal), for drinks or late meals, which range far enough afield to be called "international." A guy with a cigarette dangling from his lips sits at the upright piano when the mood strikes, sometimes joined by a guitarist or two. Their music is often submerged beneath the crackling buzz of conversation. Designer Jacques Sabourin fashioned the revivalist deco decor, including the bar, which doubles as a display counter.

The ✪ **Shed Café,** 3515 bd. St-Laurent, north of rue Sherbrooke (☎ 514/842-0220; Métro: Sherbrooke), used to look as if the ceiling were caving in. Now, transformed into a Gothic dungeon, it's not a whit less frenetically popular. There are local beers on tap, as well as good fries and oversize portions of cake. The crowd skews young, but with enough diversity to make an hour or two interesting.

QUARTIER GAI (GAY VILLAGE)   The drag cabaret **L'Entre-Peau,** 1115 rue Ste Catherine, near rue Amherst (☎ 514/525-7566; Métro: Beaudry), has prospered for over 10 years, drawing an increasingly straight audience to cheer on up to 20 female impersonators got up as the usual suspects, plus some unexpected figures. The name of the club, I'm told, means "between the skins," which couldn't be more apt. The owner/star boasts a personal wardrobe of more than 200 dresses, 100 wigs, and more shoes than Imelda. The cover runs C$5 (US$3.35) and up. **Sisters,** 1333 rue Ste-Catherine est, near rue St-Hubert (☎ 514/522-4717; Métro: Berri–UQAM), comes and goes, so to speak, but this dance club above the Saloon restaurant is thriving once again. Lesbians constitute most of the celebrants and contribute the high energy level. Men straight or gay, although admitted, are likely to find more congenial surroundings elsewhere.

Thought by many to be the city's best gay club, the ✪ **Sky Complex,** 1474 rue Ste-Catherine est, near rue Amherst (☎ 514/529-6969; Métro: Beaudry), continues to thrive. In the open-fronted ground-floor pub, a couple of go-go boys in Calvins and waffle stomper boots dance continuously on platforms between the two bars. The spiffy decor and thumping (usually house) music in the upstairs disco contribute to the popularity. Up to six drag performers constitute a cabaret show 2 or 3 nights a week. There's an outdoor terrace in summer. A leather bar called **Sky Jack** with a separate entrance is around the corner on rue Alexandre-de-Sève. **Unity,** 1900 rue Montcalm, at rue Ste-Catherine (☎ 514/523-4429; Métro: Beaudry), is easily the Village's biggest nightclub, with several rooms, dance floors, a top-floor terrasse (popular for viewing the fireworks from La Ronde in summer), and five bars on different levels. There's plenty of room for dancing to house and techno music and a modest light show. On the third floor are drag shows, in French mostly. Nothing too raunchy, except for Thursdays, designated "Sex Nights." Women are welcomed Fridays. Happy hours are 4 to 10pm Friday to Sunday, with two-for-one drinks. The cover is C$2 (US$1.35) most nights.

QUARTIER LATIN (LATIN QUARTER)   Central to the burgeoning rep of **Jello Bar,** 151 rue Ontario est, near rue Beaudry (☎ 514/285-2601; Métro: Beaudry), a goofy 1950s throwback, is its card of more than 30 martinis. Most of those, like wine coolers, are flavored excuses for people who don't really like liquor, but the classic gin and vodka versions are stalwarts to be savored. Live music helps fuel the rollicking good mood.

Aided by Guinness "on draught," **Le Ste-Elisabeth,** 1412 rue Ste-Elizabeth, north of rue Ste-Catherine (☎ 514/286-4302; Métro: Berri–UQAM), comes closer to resembling an Irish pub than most of the many efforts in town. Past the Queen Anne Victorian facade is a copper-topped bar near the fireplace with a couple of heavily used sofas, and beyond all that is a tree-shaded, vine-covered open courtyard, known as a *terrasse* in these parts. University and grad students predominate but don't overwhelm. Blues and jazz are on the stereo and in situ (Tues). At **Le St-Sulpice,** 1680 rue St-Denis, near rue St-Catherine (☎ 514/844-9458; Métro: Berri–UQAM), you'll find lines of waiting people six deep and a block long on any night of even slightly tolerable weather. They're very young, in shorts and T-shirts when it's warm, jeans and sweaters when it isn't. Lately, the mix has included a growing number of gays and lesbians. The club has a crowded terrace, a DJ most nights, live music on some, and dance floors and bars always. Beer is the favored quaff.

A CASINO

In 1993, the **Montréal Casino** (☎ 800/665-2274 or 514/392-2746), Québec's first, opened on Ile Notre-Dame in the former French Pavilion, left over from Expo '67. The casino has 116 gaming tables, including roulette, blackjack, and midi-baccarat, and nearly 3,000 slot machines on several floors (no craps tables, though). It can accommodate 8,000 people, most of whom come to try their luck, of course; but the three restaurants, especially Nuances, get good notices, and there are four bars, live shows, and two shops selling gifts and souvenirs. Gambling hours are daily 9am to 5am.

Patrons must be 18 or over, and no alcoholic beverages are served in the gambling areas. The originally strict dress code has been relaxed somewhat, but the following items of clothing are still prohibited: "cut-off sweaters and shirts, tank tops, jogging outfits, cut-off shorts and bike shorts, beachwear, work or motorcycle boots, and clothing associated with violence or with an organization known to be violent." Admission and parking are free. To get to the casino, take the Métro to the Ile Ste-Hélène stop, which is adjacent to Ile Notre-Dame, and walk or take the shuttle bus from there.

9 Resorts Near Montréal: The Laurentides & Estrie

For respite from urban stresses, Montréalers need drive only 30 minutes or so north or east to find themselves in the heart of either the **Laurentides** or **Estrie.** Lakes and mountains have invited development of year-round vacation retreats and ski centers in both areas. The pearl of the Laurentides is Mont-Tremblant (at 968m/3,175 ft. the highest peak in eastern Canada), but the region boasts 18 other ski centers with scores of trails at every difficulty level.

Bucolic Estrie, known as the Eastern Townships when it was a haven for English Loyalists and their descendants, is blessed with a trio of memorable country inns on Lake Massawippi and promotes four seasons of outdoor diversions. It contains fewer ski centers, and the hotels serving them are generally smaller and less extensive in their facilities; but the area's many lakes and gentler pastimes give it an edge for warm-weather vacations. Since the people of these regions rely heavily on tourism, knowledge of at least rudimentary English is widespread, even outside the hotels and ski resorts.

EXPLORING THE REGION

Most of the major resorts and ski centers of the Laurentides ("Laurentians" in English) are within sight of the limited-access Autoroute 15 and roughly parallel but slightly slower Route 117. Both roads follow scenic routes through tidy hamlets and villages, with humpbacked hills giving way to higher and higher mountains. In Estrie, the same observations hold for Autoroute 10, running east from Montréal to Sherbrooke, except the terrain rises and falls less dramatically. In this chapter, the suggestions for enjoying both regions are laid out as driving tours, beginning with the towns or other sites of interest closest to Montréal and ending with those most distant.

VISITOR INFORMATION

Québec tourism authorities produce volumes of detailed and highly useful publications, and they're easy to obtain by mail, by phone, or in person. To contact **Tourisme Québec,** write C.P. 979, Montréal, PQ H3C 2W3, or call ☎ **800/363-7777,** operator 806 (in the Montréal area, call ☎ **514/873-2015**). On the Web, check out **www.tourisme.gouv.qc.ca** and **www.laurentides.com.**

GETTING AROUND

Québec's limited-access expressways are called autoroutes, and speed limits are given in kilometers. Most highway signs are in French only, though Montréal's autoroutes and bridges often bear dual-language signs. Seat-belt use is required by law while driving or riding in a car, and turning right on a red light is prohibited throughout the province, except where specifically allowed by an additional green arrow.

For information on **road conditions** in and around Montréal, call ☎ **514/ 636-3026;** outside Montréal, call ☎ **514/636-3248.** To get from downtown Montréal to the Laurentian Autoroute 15, take ring Route 40 around the city; to Estrie, take the Pont (Bridge) Champlain east onto Autoroute 10.

THE GREAT OUTDOORS

There doesn't seem to be an outdoor sport or game yet conceived that doesn't enjoy at least one or two venues somewhere in the Laurentides or the Estrie.

BIKING   Both strenuous mountain biking and gentler forms of cycling are possible throughout the Laurentides, notably along the linear park, **P'tit Train du Nord,** a 200km (124-mile) cycling/snowmobiling trail that follows the roadbed of an old railroad. **Rentals** are available in most of the towns along the way and at a concession stand in Mont-Tremblant park (☎ **818/688-2281**), which has 100km (62 miles) of trails. **Magog,** in Estrie, has an 18.5km (11½-mile) bike path linking its Lake Mephremagog with Mont-Orford.

BIRD WATCHING   The lakes of Québec's mountain regions are home to an estimated 16,000 loons, a native waterfowl that gives its name to the dollar coin. These excellent divers and swimmers are unable to walk on land, which makes nesting a trial, and they're identified by a distinctive call that might be described as an extended mournful giggle.

CANOEING   June to September, **Escapade Nature** in Ste-Agathe-des-Monts (☎ **514/226-6521**) conducts canoe trips along the rivers Diable and Rouge from a few hours in duration to made-to-measure expeditions of up to a week. Canoes, equipment, and guides are part of the package.

CROSS-COUNTRY SKIING   Among the best cross-country trails in the Laurentides are at the **Hôtel l'Estérel** (☎ **514/228-2571**) and on the grounds of the monastery **Domaine du St-Bernard,** near Mont-Tremblant. In Estrie, 35km (22 miles) of courses run across **Lake Massawippi** and over the low surrounding hills. The bike path between **Lake Mephremagog** and **Mont-Orford** becomes a cross-country trail in winter. You can rent skis at the hotels featuring cross-country skiing (like the Estérel) and at the bike/ski shops in almost every village.

DOGSLEDDING   In Entrelacs, an hour north of Montréal, **A'Crocs d'Aventure** (☎ **450/228-4121**) introduces novices to the sport with 1-hour to whole-day guided outings. Guests at the **Hôtel l'Estérel** (☎ **514/228-2571**) have that opportunity too. For longer, more venturesome expeditions of up to 4 days, meals and lodging in heated tents provided, contact **Aventures à Traineau à Chiens de la Lièvre** (☎ **819/587-4990**). Expeditions are mid-December to mid-March. The outfitter is based in Lac St-Paul, north of Mont-Laurier, an excursion in itself. In Waterloo, near Exit 90 off Autoroute 10, **Safari Loowak** (☎ **514/539-0501**) schedules daily excursions by reservation.

DOWNHILL SKIING   Half a century ago the first ski schools, rope tows, and trails began to appear, and today there are more than 20 ski centers within a 40-mile radius of Montréal. These sprawling resorts and modest lodges and inns are packed each winter with skiers, some of them through April. Trails for advanced skiers typically have short pitches and challenging moguls, with broad, hard-packed avenues for beginners and the less experienced. In addition to the 19 ski centers scattered along Autoroute 15, there are four prominent centers in Estrie, near Autoroute 10; they're smaller and tend to be more family-oriented. Bromont, Orford, Owl's Head, and Sutton cooperate through their **Ski East Network** to offer a lift ticket acceptable at all four centers (☎ 819/820-2020). For information on **ski packages** in Estrie, call ☎ 800/355-5755.

GARDEN & VINEYARD TOURS   **Les Jardins de Rocailles,** 1319 rue Lavoie in Val-David (☎ 819/322-6193), is a small but delightful floral retreat with more than 250 varieties of flowers and shrubs; admission is C$3 (US$2) adults, with kids under 13 free. There's a cafe with a terrace from which to observe. All four of the vineyards in and around Dunham in Estrie conduct free tours. Three are along Route 202, west of the town: **L'Orpailleur** (☎ 514/295-2763), **Les Trois Clochers** (☎ 514/295-2034), and **Domaine** (☎ 514/295-2020). Outside of Magog, **Le Vignoble Le Cep d'Argent** (☎ 819/864-4441) offers tastings and a simple cafe.

GOLF   Courses in the Laurentides now number almost 30, most of them 18 holes and open to the public. Reservations are required and daily fees are C$25 to C$40 (US$17 to US$27). Most of the resort hotels covered in this chapter can make arrangements, but three have courses on their premises—**Gray Rocks** (☎ 819/425-2771) and the **Hôtel l'Estérel** (☎ 514/228-2571) feature 18-hole courses, and **Le Chantecler** (☎ 514/229-3555) makes do with a 9-hole course. In Estrie, there are 25 more courses open to the public, with greens fees at C$24 to C$36 (US$16 to US$24) for 18 holes.

SAILING & WINDSURFING   You can rent small sailboats and sailboards at the lakefront in Ste-Agathe-des-Monts, where there's also a **sailing school** (☎ 819/326-2282). The larger **lake resorts** in both the Laurentides and the Estrie rent or make available canoes, pedal boats, and sailing dinghies. Yamaska Park in Granby, for example, rents sailboards, kayaks, sailboats, and rowboats, as does the recreational park at Mont-Orford.

SCUBA DIVING   The many clear lakes of the Laurentides have visibility of up to 50 feet. Notable are **Lac Tremblant,** at the base of the mountain of the same name, and the several lakes in or near the Papineu-Labelle wildlife preserve, west of Tremblant and St-Jovite. Information, dive classes, and rental equipment are available through the **Centre de Plongée Lac-des-Ecorces** (☎ 819/585-3472), in the village of that name near the town of Mont-Laurier, 110km (68 miles) north of St-Jovite.

TENNIS   All the large resorts and many of the smaller auberges have courts, including **Manoir St-Sauveur** (☎ 514/227-1811), **Mont-Gabriel** (☎ 514/229-3547), **Hôtel l'Estérel** (☎ 514/228-2571), **Club Tremblant** (☎ 819/425-2731), and **Club Intrawest** (☎ 819/681-3535), all in the Laurentides; and **Manoir des Sables** (☎ 819/847-4747), **Auberge Lakeview** (☎ 514/243-6183), and **Manoir Hovey** (☎ 819/842-2421) in the Estrie.

WHITE-WATER RAFTING   Several companies offer rafting trips of 4 to 5 hours on the Rivière Rouge (Red River), which flows down to the Ottawa River. Access is via Route 158 west of Autoroute 15 (Exit 39) toward Lachute and on Route 148 past Calumet, turning north on chemin de la Rivière Rouge. Launching points are clearly marked. Passengers must weigh at least 40kg (88 lb.). Guides, rafts, safety helmets, and jackets are provided, as is an end-of-trip meal. Inquire ahead to determine details and make reservations. Two of the more prominent companies are **Aventure en Eau Vive** (☎ 819/242-6084) and **Nouveau Monde** (☎ 818/242-7238).

THE LAURENTIDES: MONT-TREMBLANT & MORE

Expect no spiked peaks or high ragged ridges. The rolling hills and rounded mountains of the **Laurentian Shield** are among the oldest in the world, worn down by wind and water over eons. They average between 300m and 520m (980 ft. and 1,700 ft.), with the highest being Mont-Tremblant at 968m (3,175 ft.). In the lower precincts, nearer Montréal, the terrain resembles a rumpled quilt, its folds and hollows cupping a multitude of lakes large and small. Farther north, the summits are higher and craggier, with patches of snow persisting well into spring, but these are still not the Alps or Rockies. They're welcoming and embracing rather than awe-inspiring.

The busiest times are July and August, the Christmas–New Year's period, and February and March. Other times of the year, reservations are easier to get, prices of virtually everything are lower, and crowds are less dense. May and September are often characterized by warm days, cool nights, and just enough people so the streets don't seem deserted. In May and June, the indigenous black flies and mosquitoes can seem as big and as ill-tempered as buzzards, so take along an effective repellent. Some of the resorts, inns, and lodges close for a couple of weeks in spring and fall. A handful are open only for a few winter months.

March and April is the season when the maple trees are tapped, and *cabanes à sucre* ("sugar shacks") open up everywhere, some selling only maple candies and syrup, others serving full meals featuring the principal product and even entertainment. July and August usher in glorious summer in the Laurentians. In mid-July, the region's annual **Fête de Vins (Wine Festival)** is held for 2 days in St-Jérôme, with the emphasis on gastronomy and wine tasting; a dozen area restaurants participate. An attractive event in late July to early August is the 4-day **Festival International du Blues Tremblant,** and during the last 2 weeks in September the leaves put on a stunning color show. Skiers can usually expect reliable snow from early December to mid-April.

Prices are difficult to pin down. The large resorts have so many various types of rooms, suites, cottages, meal plans, discounts, and packages that a travel agent may be needed to pick through the thicket of options. Remember that Montréalers fill the highways when they "go up north" on weekends, particularly in February and March, so plan ahead when making reservations. Pet owners, take note: Few Laurentian resorts accept animals.

ESSENTIALS

VISITOR INFORMATION   For an orientation to the entire region, stop at the red-roofed stone cottage **La Maison du Tourisme des Laurentides,** 14142 rue de la Chapelle (RR 1), St-Jérôme, PQ J7Z 5T4 (☎ 800/561-6673 or 450/436-8532), at Exit 39 off Autoroute 15. It offers racks of helpful brochures and a staff that can make free reservations for lodging throughout the Laurentides. It's open daily: mid-June to Labour Day 8:30am to 8:30pm and the rest of the year 9am to 5pm. For information on the Web, log on to **www.tourisme.gouv.qc.ca.**

A Driving Warning

Be aware that Québec's equivalent of the Highway Patrol maintains a strong presence along the stretch of Autoroute 15 between St-Faustin and Ste-Adèle. Remember that radar detectors are illegal in the province and subject to confiscation.

GETTING THERE   By Car   The fast and scenic **Autoroute des Laurentides** (Autoroute 15) goes straight from Montréal to the Laurentian mountains. Just follow the signs. The exit numbers are actually the distance in kilometers the village is from Montréal: One likely early stop is La Maison du Tourisme at Exit 39 in St-Jérôme, 39km (24 miles) from Montréal. This is a pretty drive, once you're out of the clutches of the tangle of expressways surrounding Montréal. The Autoroute des Laurentides gives a panoramic introduction to the area, from the rolling hills and forests of the lower Laurentians to the mountain drama of the upper Laurentians.

Those with the time to meander can exit at St-Jérôme and pick up the older, parallel Route 117, which plays tag with the autoroute all the way to Ste-Agathe-des-Monts, where the highway ends. Most of the region's more appealing towns are strung along or near Route 117. As you approach each town, you'll see signs directing you to the local tourist office, where attendants provide helpful tips on lodging, restaurants, and things to do. North of Ste-Agathe, the autoroute ends and **Route 117** becomes the region's major artery, continuing deep into Québec's north country and finally ending at the Ontario border, hundreds of miles from Montréal.

By Bus   **Limocar Laurentides** buses depart Montréal's Terminus Voyageur, 505 bd. de Maisonneuve est, stopping in the larger Laurentian towns, including Ste-Agathe, Ste-Adèle, and St-Jovite; call ☎ **514/842-2281** for schedules. An express bus can make the run to St-Jovite and Mont-Tremblant in less than 2 hours, while a local bus, making all stops, takes almost 3. From Montréal to Ste-Adèle takes about 1½ hours, 15 minutes more to Val-Morin and Val-David. Some of the major resorts provide their own bus service at an extra charge.

By Limousine   Taxis and limousines await arrivals at Dorval Airport in Montréal, where all domestic and international commercial flights arrive, and will take you to any Laurentian hideaway—for a price. While the fare for the 1-hour trip by limo from Dorval is steep, four or five people can share the cost and lessen the pain. Ask for the standard fare to your inn or lodge when calling to make reservations. The inn usually will take responsibility for seeing that a taxi or limo is indeed waiting at the airport and may even help to find other guests arriving at the same time to share the cost. If your destination is Tremblant or the Gray Rocks resort, a service called the **Mont-Tremblant Express** (☎ **800/471-1155** or 514/631-1155) makes the one-way trip from Dorval at C$65 (US$43) Monday to Thursday and C$63 (US$42) Friday to Sunday.

ST-HIPPOLYTE

A detour off Route 117 leads to **St-Hippolyte,** a residential village with a body of water known as the "Millionaire's Lake"—you'll understand after viewing the stately homes facing its shores and the seaplanes and sleek motorboats moored at their docks. Lac Achigan is also known for an inn long admired for its cuisine. It's close enough for a day trip from Montréal.

To get there, take Exit 39 off Autoroute 15 and pick up Route 117 north. After about 6km (3.7 miles), branch right on Route 333 north and continue another 16km (9.9 miles) to the village center. Turn right on boulevard du Lac Achigan, then right again before the lake, following the signs to the inn below.

Where to Stay & Dine

Auberge des Cèdres. 26 av. 305e, St-Hippolyte, PQ J8A 3P5. ☎ **877/563-2083** or 450/563-5050. Fax 450/563-1663. www.inter-actif.qc.ca/auberge-inn. 7 units. TV TEL. C$80–C$140 (US$53–US$93) double. AE, MC, V.

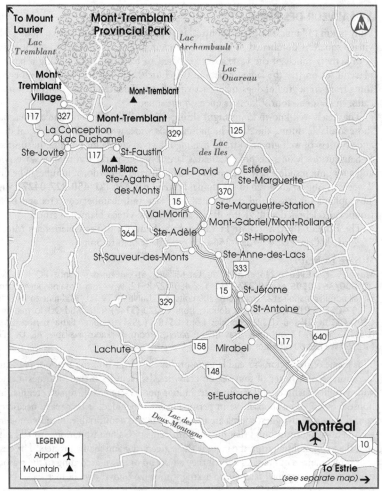

Built in 1906, the shambling lakeside house operated as an inn for many years, drifting into somnolence and then closing as the owners aged. Now it has been reawakened, the new proprietors installing a bar and a cigar/computer room and redecorating the guest rooms and public areas. The plans to install a lakeside terrace and convert a carriage house should've been realized by the time you get here. The original guest rooms are on the second and third floors of the main building, and most are on the small side, with closet space from little to none; however, six have lake views. The biggest room, up a narrow staircase, has a double whirlpool, sofa bed, and balcony. For the moment, the emphasis is on the dining room. The diffident young chef assembles dishes like twin salmon fillets dressed with creamy tarragon sauce and little sprays of seven steamed vegetables. His seasonings could be perked up and the bread improved, but this is a project in progress. And who can complain about the lake views from the dining room's long windows?

St-Sauveur-des-Monts

Only 60km (37 miles) north of Montréal is **St-Sauveur-des-Monts** (pop. 5,864). The village square is dominated by a handsome church, and the streets around it bustle with activity much of the year; so be prepared to have difficulty finding a parking place in season (try the large lot behind the church). Dining and snacking on everything from crêpes to hot dogs are big activities here, evidenced by the many beckoning cafes. In season, a tourist kiosk is open on the square.

The area is well-known for its **night skiing**—23 well-lit trails, only three fewer than those available during the day. The mountain is wide, with a 700-foot vertical drop and a variety of well-groomed trails, making it a good choice for families. In summer, St-Sauveur-des-Monts becomes Canada's largest **water park,** featuring a wave pool and a mountain slide where you go up in chair lifts and come down in tubes. The first 2 weeks in August are given to the annual **Festival des Arts** (☎ 450/227-0427), with an emphasis on music and dance, including jazz and chamber concerts and ballet troupes as celebrated as the Kirov Ballet and the José Greco Flamenco group.

The **Bureau Touristique de la Vallée de St-Sauveur,** in Les Galeries des Monts, 75 av. de la Gare (☎ 450/227-2564), is open daily 9am to 5pm.

Where to Stay

Manoir St-Sauveur. 246 chemin du Lac-Millette, St-Sauveur-des-Monts, PQ J0R 1R3. ☎ **800/361-0505** or 450/227-1811. Fax 450/227-8512. www.manoir-saint-sauveur.com. E-mail admin@manoir-st-sauveur.com. 200 units. A/C MINIBAR TV TEL. Mid-June to mid-Oct C$209–C$225 (US$139–US$150) double; from C$220 ($147) suite. Mid-Oct to mid-June C$99–C$138 (US$66–US$92) double; from C$180 (US$120) suite. Extra person C$10 (US$7); children 17 and under stay free in parents' room. Packages available. AE, DC, ER, MC, V. Take Exit 60 off Autorte. 15.

This is one of the region's several large resort hotels, with a monster outdoor pool and a comprehensive roster of four-season activities. Its facilities include a fitness center with weight machines and a sauna, an indoor pool, racquetball, squash, tennis, in-house movies, and a shop. A warm personality isn't included. It isn't really necessary, considering that the guest rooms are commodious and comfortable, blandly modern with light-wood furnishings that hint of 19th-century Gallic inspirations. You'll easily spot the main building from the road, with its green roof and many dormers. The desk staff is reluctant to quote rates, which they adjust up or down according to the season, demand, and occupancy rate—keep asking if they have anything cheaper.

Where to Dine

The adjoining restaurant is no more than ordinary, but the **Charcuterie St-Sauveur,** 90 rue de la Gare (☎ 450/227-2228), has an entrancing array of salads, quiches, pâtés, meats, cheeses, breads, cakes, and tarts—all the ingredients of a red-letter picnic. It's open Saturday to Thursday 7am to 6:30pm (to 9pm Fri).

L'Armorique. 231 rue Principale. ☎ **450/227-0080.** Main courses C$3–C$13 (US$2–US$8). DC, MC, V. Summer daily 8am–2am; rest of the year Tues–Sun 11am–10:30pm. CRÊPES/LIGHT FARE.

Occupying a well-preserved Victorian house in the middle of town, this crêperie is only one of a number of casual eateries on the streets radiating from the village square. Main-course fillings for the crêpes run from conventional eggs and cheese or smoked salmon to chicken with ratatouille and shrimp, mushrooms, and mussels with béchamel. Other possibilities are nine hearty salads and raclette, the fondue-like dish with all manner of things to dip. In summer, the front porch and a large side deck have vantages for watching the street scene.

MONT-GABRIEL

Mont-Gabriel is only 4km (2½ miles) from St-Sauveur-des-Monts. To get there, follow Autoroute 15 to Exit 64 and turn right at the stop sign. Though popular in summer, Mont-Gabriel comes into its own each winter when guests schuss down its 21 **trails and slopes** and then slide back up again on the seven T-bar lifts, the triple chair, or the quadruple chair lift. Eight trails are lit for night skiing. Cross-country trails girdle the mountain and range through the surrounding countryside.

Where to Stay & Dine

Mont-Gabriel Resort. 1699 chemin Montée Gabriel, PQ J8B 1A5. ☎ **450/229-3547,** 514/861-2852 in Montréal, or 800/668-5253 in Canada. Fax 450/229-7034. www. montgabriel.com. E-mail info@montgabriel.com. 126 units. A/C TV TEL. C$119 (US$79) double. Rates include full breakfast. MAP and other packages available. AE, DC, ER, MC, V. Take Exit 64 from Autorte. 15.

Perched way above highways and the valley and looking like the rambling log "cottages" of the early-1900s wealthy, this desirable hotel is only 20 miles from Montréal's Dorval Airport. The resort complex is set on a 1,200-acre forest estate and features golf and tennis programs in summer and ski packages in winter. The Tyrol section's spacious guest rooms are the most desirable, many with views of the hills; those in the Old Lodge are older and more rustic, but a C$7 million (US$4.7 million) renovation in 1998 upgraded most of these. Coffeemakers and hair dryers are standard. With the Club Package come three meals and unlimited access to all sports facilities, and prices include tax and service charge. Rates drop for stays of 2 to 5 nights.

Dining/Diversions: Meals are served in the resort's dining rooms and at poolside. Evenings, there's dancing in the main lodge.

Amenities: Summer activity programs for children; indoor pool, sauna, whirlpool, exercise room; outdoor heated pool (summer only); par-71 golf course, six tennis courts.

STE-ADÈLE

Route 117 swings directly into **Ste-Adèle** to become its main street, boulevard Ste-Adèle; or you can take Exit 67 off Autoroute 15 North. The village (pop. 7,800), only 67km (42 miles) north of Montréal, is a near-metropolis compared to the other Laurentian villages lining the upper reaches of Route 117. What makes it seem big are its services: police, doctors, ambulances, a shopping center, art galleries, and a large collection of places to stay and dine. As rue Morin mounts the hill to Lac Rond, Ste-Adèle's resort lake, you can easily see why the town is divided into a lower part (*en bas*) and an upper part (*en haut*).

The **Bureau Touristique de Ste-Adèle,** at 333 bd. Ste-Adèle (☎ **450/229-2921,** ext. 207), is open daily: July and August 9am to 7pm (to 5pm the rest of the year).

One of the main streets, **rue Valiquette,** is a busy one-way thoroughfare lined with cafes, galleries, and bakeries, but **Lac Rond** is the center of activities during the Ste-Adèle summer. Canoes, sailboats, and *pédalos* (pedal-powered watercraft), which you can rent at several docks, glide over the placid surface, while swimmers splash and play near shoreside beaches.

In winter, the surrounding green hills are swathed in white, and the **ski trails** descend to the shores of the frozen lake. You can rent downhill ski equipment and get lessons at Le Chantecler resort, which has 22 trails served by six chair lifts and two T-bars. Some of the trails end right by the main hotel. At the town's **Centre Municipal,** Côtes 40/80, 1400 rue Rolland (☎ **450/229-2921**), the trails are good for beginners: Three T-bar lifts carry skiers up the slopes for the run down five trails.

For 4 days in late May, the food festival **Les Arts Gourmands de Ste-Adèle** features author lectures, cooking demonstrations, workshops, and wine tastings. Call ☎ **450/ 229-3729** for details.

Where to Stay

Hôtel le Chantecler. 1474 chemin Chantecler, Ste-Adèle, PQ J8B 1A2. ☎ **800/363-2420** or 450/229-3555. Fax 450/229-5593. www.lechantecler.com. E-mail lechantecler@ sympatico.ca. 200 units. TV TEL. C$107 (US$71) double with breakfast, C$158–C$188 (US$105–US$125) double with breakfast/dinner; C$263–C$293 (US$175–US$195) suite. Children 17 and under stay free in parents' room. Many packages available. AE, DC, DISC, ER, MC, V. Take Exit 67 off Autorte. 15, turn left at the 4th traffic light onto rue Morin, then turn right at the top of the hill onto chemin Chantecler.

Sprawled across steep slopes cupping Lac à la Truite, this resort is composed of several stone buildings of varying heights, its roofs bristling with steeples and dormers. It offers 22 slopes for all levels of skiers, including a 622-foot vertical drop, plus a ski school. The guest rooms are decorated with pine furniture made locally; most have air-conditioning. Many of the suites have fireplaces, and most have whirlpool bathtubs. A bountiful buffet breakfast is served in the glass-enclosed dining room overlooking the active slopes and the lake with its small beach. Apart from the dings and dents that afflict heavily used family resorts, it's maintained reasonably well.

Dining/Diversions: The dining room with a terrace serves regional cuisine. You'll also find a piano bar, a disco (winter only), movies in the projection room, and a summer-stock theater.

Amenities: Baby-sitting, dry cleaning/laundry, video rental, express checkout; day camp, ski lockers, ski school, 22 runs on four mountains (including 13 night-lit runs), ski chalet (with cafeteria and bar), cross-country trails, ice skating, indoor sports complex (with pool, sauna, Jacuzzi, squash, racquetball, badminton, some fitness equipment), 18-hole and lit 9-hole golf courses, six lit tennis courts, windsurfing, canoeing, paddleboats, rowboats, mountain bikes.

Hôtel l'Eau à la Bouche. 3003 bd. Ste-Adèle (Rte. 117), Ste-Adèle, PQ J0R 1L0. ☎ **514/ 229-2991,** or 800/363-2582 from Montréal. Fax 514/229-7573. www.integra.fr/relais chateaux/eaubouche. E-mail eaubouch@ietc.ca. 25 units. A/C TV TEL. From C$165 (US$110) double; from C$280 (US$187) suite. Rates include breakfast. Packages available. AE, DC, ER, MC, V.

L'Eau à la Bouche started as a restaurant and the chef/owners later added the hotel. It's a member of the international Relais & Châteaux group of inns and small hotels, which emphasizes gastronomy rather than physical exertion. That it does here admirably (see "Where to Dine" for the recommendation of its restaurant). For those wanting more than some great meals, the hotel faces the Mont-Chantecler ski trails, is across from a golf course, and has a heated outdoor pool. Inside is a large living room with a brick fireplace and bar and sofas in conversation groups. The guest rooms have queen- or king-size beds, sitting areas, ceiling fans, and reproductions of Québec country furniture; six also have fireplaces and balconies or patios. The large bathrooms have hair dryers and robes. There's no elevator and no porters, but you can get help with your luggage if necessary.

Hôtel-Spa L'Excelsior. 3655 bd. Ste-Adèle (Rte. 117), Ste-Adèle, PQ J0R 1L0. ☎ **800/ 363-2483** or 514/229-7676. Fax 514/229-8310. www.spaexcelsior.com. E-mail hotel@ spawxcelsior.com. 52 units. A/C TV TEL. C$80–C$100 (US$53–US$67) double. Rates include breakfast. MAP available. AE, MC, V. Coming from Montréal, take Exit 67 off the autoroute.

L'Excelsior is more distinctive architecturally and larger than most roadside resorts in the Laurentians, and the management maintains high standards of housekeeping in the guest rooms (many with balconies, some reserved for nonsmokers). Also offered are indoor and outdoor pools and whirlpools, a tennis court, squash courts, an exercise room, a sauna, a whirlpool, and the Amadéus restaurant/bar. Elaborate spa treatments are available, including hydrotherapy, mineral and algae wraps, massages, and salt baths. A full-day package for one person is C$214 (US$143), including 4 to 5 hours of treatments, lodging for a night, and three meals.

Where to Dine

✪ **Hôtel l'Eau à la Bouche.** 3003 bd. Ste-Adèle (Rte. 117). ☎ **514/229-2991,** or 800/363-2582 from Montréal. Reservations recommended. Main courses C$34–C$42 (US$23–US$28); fixed-price lunch from C$16 (US$11); fixed-price 5-course dinners C$55–C$75 (US$37–US$50). AE, MC, V. Daily 6–9pm. CONTEMPORARY FRENCH.

Owners Anne Desjardins and Pierre Audette leave no doubt where their priorities lie. Their nearby hotel (above) is entirely satisfactory; but their restaurant is their love child, and it has the glow-in-the-dark reviews to prove it. False modesty isn't a factor— *l'eau à la bouche* means "mouth-watering," and the kitchen delivers. The faux Provençal interior employs heavy ceiling beams, white plaster walls, and pine paneling to set the mood. On one occasion, the pre-appetizer was a dollop of salmon tartare laced with flecks of ginger and sweet red pepper. It provided an interlude to appreciate the generous martinis that exceeded the skimpy Québec norm and to study the carefully assembled wine list. Native ingredients and ample portions are meshed with nouvelle presentations, and the menu changes by the week, even daily. Advantage is taken of seasonal products, as with the springtime starter of trout roe layered atop a lobster timbale with fiddleheads and baby asparagus heads; game dishes arrive in fall. The desserts are impressive, but the cheese plate—pungent nubbins of French and Québec varieties delivered with warm baguette slices—is special. The mostly young staff is both efficient and unintrusive. A meal here might well be the most memorable—and pricey—dining experience of a Laurentian visit.

STE-MARGUERITE & ESTÉREL

To get to **Ste-Marguerite** (pop. 2,000) or the even less populous **Estérel,** only 2 miles apart, follow Autoroute 15 north to Exit 69. Or if driving from Ste-Adèle, look for a street heading northeast named chemin Ste-Marguerite (Route 370). It becomes a narrow road that crosses the Laurentian Autoroute (at Exit 69), bridges the Rivière du Nord, and leads into an area of many lakes bordered by upscale vacation properties.

Ste-Marguerite and Estérel are 85km (53 miles) and 88km (55 miles) north of Montréal, respectively. In summer, information about the area is available from the **Pavillon du Parc,** 74 chemin Masson, Ste-Marguerite-du-Lac-Masson (☎ **514/ 228-3525**); year-round, go to the nearby **Bureau Touristique de Ste-Adèle** (see above).

Where to Stay & Dine

Hôtel l'Estérel. Bd. Fridolin-Simard (C.P. 38), Ville d'Estérel, PQ J0T 1E0. ☎ **514/228-2571,** or 888/378-3735 from Montréal. Fax 514/228-4977. www.esterel.com. E-mail info@ esterel.com. 135 units. A/C TV TEL. C$252–C$309 (US$168–US$206) double, including full breakfast and dinner and use of most facilities. Lower rates Dec–May. Discounts for stays of 3 or more nights. Packages available. AE, DC, ER, MC, V. Take the Limocar bus from Montréal into Ste-Adèle; the hotel picks up guests there.

One of the more prominent Laurentian resorts lies a few miles past Ste-Marguerite in the hamlet of Estérel. This year-round complex is capable of accommodating 300 guests on its 5,000-acre estate with three linked lakes. Occupying an expanse of otherwise-vacant lakeshore, l'Estérel offers conventionally furnished guest rooms, many with balconies. Those with a view of the lake are more expensive.

Dining: In the dining room, you're offered views along with the continental cuisine.

Amenities: Concierge, room service (7am to 10pm), dry cleaning/laundry, self-service Laundromat, kids' club. Rates include use of all indoor facilities and the tennis courts. For a special winter experience, inquire about the dogsled trips through the woods and over the frozen lake. There are 85km (53 miles) of cross-country ski trails, nearby downhill skiing, ice skating on a rink, and a heated indoor pool; in summer, an 18-hole golf course and school, tennis, nature trails, horseback riding, sailing, bicycle rental, parasailing, and waterskiing.

Where to Dine

✪ **Le Bistro à Champlain.** 75 chemin Masson, Ste-Marguerite. ☎ **450/228-4988.** Reservations recommended. Main courses C$18–C$33 (US$12–US$22); table d'hôte C$33 (US$22); *menu dégustation* C$68 (US$45). AE, MC, V. Summer Mon–Sat 6–10pm, Sun noon–10pm; rest of the year Wed–Sat 6–10pm. FRENCH.

On the shore of Lac Masson is one of the most honored restaurants in the Laurentians. Its 1864 building used to be a general store and retains the rough-hewn board walls, exposed beams, wood ceiling, and cash register. Gastronomy, not hardware, is now the motivation for patrons who routinely motor up from Montréal for dinner. The 35,000-bottle cellar is a big reason, and you can sample 20 of the stocked wines by the glass. (You can actually get a 2-oz. taste of the fabled Sauterne, Château d'Yquem.) Tours of the cellar are often conducted by the waiter/sommelier or his equally enthusiastic boss, a practicing radiologist. The food matches the wines, arriving both flavorful and attractively presented. There's a comfortably appointed cigar lounge with dozens of single-malt scotches available.

VAL-DAVID & VAL-MORIN

Follow Route 117 north to Exit 76 or 80, respectively, to reach Val-David or Val-Morin. To those who know it, the faintly bohemian enclave of **Val-David** (pop. 3,225), 80km (50 miles) north of Montréal, conjures up images of cabin hideaways set among hills rearing above ponds and lakes and laced with creeks tumbling through fragrant forests.

Val-David sits astride a 200km (124-mile) parkway called the **Parc Linéaire le P'Tit Train du Nord,** a former rail right-of-way. It's now a trail running from St-Jérôme to Mont-Laurier, heavily used for cycling in summer and cross-country skiing in winter. Have a picnic beside the North River in the **Parc des Amoureax,** 4km (2½ miles) from the main road through town. It has plenty of benches and some parking spaces on the approach to the park. Watch for the sign SITE PITTORESQUE and turn at chemin de la Rivière.

The **tourist office** is on the main street at 2501 rue de l'Eglise (☎ 888/322-7030 or 819/322-2900). It's open daily: June 20 to Labour Day 9am to 7pm and September 5 to June 19 10am to 4pm. Another possibility for assistance is **La Maison du Village,** a cultural center that mounts art exhibits in a two-story wooden building at 2495 rue de l'Eglise (☎ **819/322-2900,** ext. 237). Note that this far north into the Laurentians, the area code changes to 819.

Where to Stay & Dine

Hôtel Far Hills Inn. Val-Morin, PQ J0T 2S0. ☎ **800/567-6636** or 819/990-4409. Fax 819/322-1995. www.farhillsinn.com. 72 units. TEL. C$198 (US$132) double. Rates include breakfast and dinner. Children 11 and under stay for half price in parents' room. Packages available. AE, MC, V. Leave the autoroute at Exit 76, go through Val-Morin, and follow the signs up into the hills for almost 3 miles.

Well away from main roads, this stone-and-clapboard resort (opened before World War II) is set in the midst of gardens and birch trees. The main building has a spacious public room with picture windows and two sitting areas; a large outdoor pool is cut into the hillside below it. More than half of the guest rooms are air-conditioned and a third have TVs. The most desirable are the 24 in the recently redecorated Spruce Lodge. Much of the furniture and decor dates to major makeovers in the 1950s and late 1960s.

Dining/Diversions: The pine-paneled dining room with a beamed ceiling and picture windows is the setting for meals employing local produce when possible. The cuisine is French, with fusion overtones, widely acknowledged to be some of the best in these mountains. The wine list features French bottlings, with several available by the glass. When making reservations, ask for a table overlooking the grounds. Diners who aren't overnight guests can expect to pay about C$38 (US$25) for a five-course dinner. Patio brunches in summer are enjoyable, and the Panorama piano bar has live music some nights.

Amenities: Room service (daily 9am to 9pm), dry cleaning/laundry, newspaper, in-room massage, baby-sitting, secretarial services, express checkout; cross-country ski school and 62 miles of cross-country trails; motor-free lake and indoor and outdoor pools; sauna; tennis, squash, and racquetball courts; Ping-Pong; hiking and mountain climbing; canoeing, sailing, and paddleboating. Golf courses and horse trails nearby.

Where to Stay

Hôtel la Sapinière. 1244 chemin de la Sapinière, Val-David, PQ J0T 2N0. ☎ **800/ 567-6635** or 819/322-2020. Fax 819/322-6510. www.sapiniere.com. E-mail sapiniere@ polyinter.com. 70 units. A/C TV TEL. C$135 (US$90) double; C$145–C$155 (US$97–US$103) suite. Rates include full breakfast and dinner. AE, DC, ER, MC, V. Drive through downtown and pick up the sign to the inn on the right.

This sedate lakeside inn celebrated its 60th anniversary in 1996 with a thorough renovation and paint job. It's a tranquil lakeside retreat, upper-middle-class in tone, with a largely 40-plus clientele returning faithfully year after year, in large part to escape childish shrieks and orchestrated hyperactivity. Demanding diners, they're treated to a menu of five-course meals that's changed daily and embellished with wines from a 10,000-bottle cellar. The lake is private, with motorized boats banned. Shuffleboard and croquet are expectably popular with the guests, but there are two tennis courts and a pool on site, and golf and hiking and cross-country trails are available nearby. On Saturday nights, live music is offered in the bar for dancing. The guest rooms, comfortable but undistinguished, have hair dryers and coffeemakers.

Where to Dine

Le Grand Pa. 2481 rue de l'Eglise. ☎ **819/322-3104.** Pizzas and pastas C$6–C$16 (US$4–US$11); main courses C$17–C$25 (US$11–US$17). MC, V. Daily 11:30am–midnight. ITALIAN/CANADIAN.

In the middle of the town, an open deck reaches out to the sidewalk. It's crowded with white resin chairs and tables under big umbrellas, where locals dig into a dozen varieties of pizzas, baked in the brick oven inside. With their puffy crusts and fresh ingredients, in two sizes, they're the star attractions, often taken with pitchers of beer or sangria. Full meals are also available, and in summer they fire up a barbecue pit that sends out irresistible aromas. Friday and Saturday nights there's live music by small combos.

STE-AGATHE-DES-MONTS

With a population approaching 10,000, **Ste-Agathe-des-Monts,** 85km (53 miles) north of Montréal, is the largest town in the Laurentians and marks the end of Autoroute 15. Follow the Autoroute north to Exit 83 or 86.

Early settlers and vacationers flocked here in search of land fronting Lac des Sables, and entrepreneurs followed. Ste-Agathe's main street, **rue Principale,** is the closest to citification in these mountains, but it's only a touch of urbanity. Follow rue Principale from the highway through town and end up at the town dock on the lake. Watch out for four-way stops along the way.

The dock and surrounding **waterfront park** make Ste-Agathe a good place to pause for a few hours. One possibility is renting a bicycle from **Jacques Champoux Sports,** 74 rue St-Vincent, for the 3-mile ride around the lake. Lake cruises, beaches, and watercraft rentals seduce many visitors into lingering for days. For a night or two, the motels near town on Route 117 are sufficient, but for longer stays, consider a lakeside lodge.

The **Bureau Touristique de Ste-Agathe-des-Monts,** 190 rue Principale est (☎ **819/326-0457**), is open daily in summer 9am to 8:30pm (to 5pm the rest of the year).

Alouette Cruises (☎ **819/326-3656**) departs the dock at the foot of rue Principale. It's a 50-minute, 12-mile voyage on a boat equipped with a bar; the running commentary observes, among other things, that Ste-Agathe and the Lac des Sables are famous for waterskiing competitions and windsurfing. The cost is C$12 (US$8) adults, C$11 (US$7) seniors, and C$6 (US$3.65) children 5 to 15; children under 5 are free. There are regular departures mid-May to late October at 10:30am, 11:30am, 1:30pm, 2:30pm, and 3:30pm (also at 5 and 7pm late June to late Aug).

Where to Stay & Dine

Auberge La Sauvagine. 1592 Rte. 329 nord, Ste-Agathe, PQ J8C 2Z8. ☎ **888/787-7172** or 819/326-7673. Fax 819/326-9351. www.polyinter.com/sauvigine. 9 units, 7 with bathroom. C$75 (US$50) double without bathroom, C$130 (US$87) double with bathroom. Rates include breakfast. MC, V. The inn is 2km (1.2 miles) north of Ste-Agathe, on the road to St-Donat.

For something a little different, check this out—an 1890s auberge housed in a deconsecrated chapel. (An order of nuns added the chapel when they ran the property as a retirement home.) Antiques and near-antiques are scattered throughout, with an impressive armoire in the surprisingly elegant dining room. Chef/owner René Kissler gathered many culinary awards in his native Belgium and has started accumulating them here. If it's true that the best French cooking is Belgian, his *cuisine gastronomique* carries the flag proudly, from *amuse-bouche* to *les mignardises.* His table d'hôte menu is C$37 (US$24) and the *ménu dégustation* for two is C$48 (US$32) each. Only two of the guest rooms upstairs share a bathroom; five have TVs. A new outdoor pool has been added. June 15 to October 15, the restaurant is open daily 6 to 9pm for dinner; in winter it's open Wednesday to Sunday. If it's full, ask about the inn Kissler is planning to buy on a nearby lake.

Chez Girard. 18 rue Principale ouest, St-Agathe-des-Monts, PQ J8C 1A3. ☎ **819/326-0922.** www.polyinter.com/girard. 8 units. C$100–C$105 (US$67–US$70) double. Rates include breakfast. MAP available. AE, ER, MC, V. Restaurant closed Mon, inn closed Apr and Nov.

Head toward the town dock, and near the end of rue Principale, on the left, is a Québec-style house with a crimson roof. That's Chez Girard. In good weather, diners can sit on the terrace overlooking the lake. Game is a central interest of the kitchen in autumn, while the summer menu emphasizes lighter pasta and seafood dishes, such as fusilli with snails in pungent pesto sauce. Among dinner possibilities are tournedos of caribou with mushrooms and wild grain and tortellini with razor clams, langostinos, and scallops in goat-cheese sauce. The kitchen prides itself on using the freshest ingredients and on the absence of a deep fryer. Dinner table d'hôtes are C$19 to C$27 (US$12 to US$18), lunch (served only in summer) about 50% less. The auberge offers serviceable guest rooms and suites behind the restaurant. Most have fireplaces, whirlpool bathtubs, and TVs; suites have serving pantries stocked with breakfast fixings. Bikes are available, and guests have access to a private beach.

ST-JOVITE & MONT-TREMBLANT

Follow Route 117 about 37km (23 miles) north from Ste-Agathe to the **St-Jovite** exit. It's 122km (76 miles) north of Montréal. To get to **Mont-Tremblant,** turn right on Route 327, just before the church in St-Jovite. Most vacationers make their base at one of the resorts or lodges scattered along Route 327. Mont-Tremblant is 45km (28 miles) north of Ste-Agathe and 130km (81 miles) north of Montréal. At the intersection of Routes 327 and 117 between St-Jovite and Mont-Tremblant is a new **visitor information office,** open daily 9am to 5pm.

Mont-Tremblant, at 650m (2,135 ft.), is the highest peak in the Laurentians. In 1894 the provincial government set aside almost 1,000 square miles of wilderness as **Mont-Tremblant Park,** and the foresight of this early conservation effort has yielded outdoor enjoyment to skiers and four-season vacationers. The mountain's name comes from a legend of the area's first inhabitants: Amerindians named the peak after the god Manitou; when humans disturbed nature in any way, Manitou became enraged and made the great mountain tremble—*montagne tremblante.*

St-Jovite (pop. 4,118) is about 12km (7.4 miles) south of Mont-Tremblant, the commercial center for this most famous and popular of Laurentian districts. A pleasant community, it provides all the expected services. The main street, **rue Ouimet,** is lined with cafes and shops, including Le Coq Rouge, selling folk art and country antiques.

Tourist info, including maps of local ski trails, is available at the **Bureau Touristique de Mont-Tremblant,** rue du Couvent at Mont-Tremblant (☎ 819/425-2434), open daily in summer 9am to 9pm (the rest of the year to 5pm); and from the **Tourist Bureau of St-Jovite/Mont-Tremblant,** 305 chemin Brébeuf in St-Jovite (☎ 819/ 425-3300), open daily in summer 9am to 7pm (the rest of the year to 5pm).

Skiing, Water Sports & More

Water sports in summer are as popular as the ski slopes and trails in winter, because the base of Mont-Tremblant is surrounded by no fewer than 10 lakes: Lac Tremblant, a gorgeous stretch of water 10 miles long, and also Lac Ouimet, Lac Mercier, Lac Gelinas, Lac Desmarais, and five smaller bodies of water, not to mention rivers and streams. June to mid-October, **Grand Manitou Cruises,** chemin Principale, Mont-Tremblant (☎ 819/425-8681), offers a 75-minute narrated tour of Lac Tremblant, focusing on its history, nature, and legends.

Mont-Tremblant, with a vertical drop of 649m (2,131 ft.), draws the area's biggest downhill ski crowds. Founded in 1939 by Philadelphia millionaire Joe Ryan,

A Tremblant by Any Other Name

Here are a few words of clarification about the name *Tremblant,* a subject of confusion for first-timers. First, there's **Mont-Tremblant,** the mountain. On its slope is **Tremblant,** the growing resort village. At the moment its most important hotel is the **Château Mont-Tremblant,** with a new Westin on the way. At the base of the mountain is **Lac Tremblant,** and on the opposite shore is **Club Tremblant,** a resort with no connection to the Tremblant resort (though its guests ski the mountain). And finally there's the organic village of **Mont-Tremblant,** about 3 miles west, with its own market, post office, restaurants, and inns that have no specific affiliation with any of the above properties and geographical features.

Mont-Tremblant is one of North America's oldest ski areas and the first to create trails on both sides of a mountain. It was the second in the world to install a chair lift. There are higher mountains with longer runs and steeper pitches, but something about Mont-Tremblant compels people to return time and again.

Today Mont-Tremblant has the snowmaking capability to cover 1.3km² (328 acres), making skiing possible early November to late May, and keeping at least 30 of the total of 77 trails open at Christmastime (as opposed to nine in 1992). There are now 43 downhill runs and trails, including the recently opened Dynamite and Verige trails, with 245m (810-ft.) and 225m (745-ft.) drops, respectively, and the Edge, a peak with two gladed trails. The nine lifts are gondolas (one heated) and quad chairs, no T-bars. There's plenty of cross-country action on 90km (56 miles) of maintained trails. And in summer, you can choose from golf, tennis, horseback riding, boating, swimming, biking, and hiking—for starters.

Where to Stay

✪ **Club Tremblant.** Av. Cuttle, Mont-Tremblant, PQ J0T 1Z0. ☎ **800/567-8341** in the U.S. and Canada, or 819/425-2731. Fax 819/425-5617. www.clubtremblant.com. 100 suites. TV TEL. From C$121 (US$81) per person double. Rates include breakfast and dinner. Children 6–12 are charged C$40 (US$27). Rates lower for stays of 2 days or more. Packages available. AE, DC, ER, MC, V. Turn left off Montée Ryan, then right on Lac Tremblant North and follow the signs for under a mile.

Terraced into a hillside sloping steeply to Lac Tremblant, this attractive property consists of several lodges in muted alpine style. It's a concentration of private condos operated by one management, and the accommodations represent excellent value and provide that greatest of luxuries—space. Most of the units are suites of one to three bedrooms, for the price of a single room at many other area resorts. A typical suite has a fireplace; a balcony; a sitting room with cable TV and dining table; a full kitchen with fridge, cookware, and dishwasher; one or two bathrooms with Jacuzzis; and a clothes washer and dryer. Nearly all have views of the lake and Mont-Tremblant. This is a family resort, so expect childish yips and squeals in the dining rooms in peak months—July, August, February, and March. A drawback on the hottest days of summer is the lack of air-conditioning in the suites, but they'll deliver a portable fan on request.

Dining/Diversions: The dining room serves a largely French menu, with a five-course table d'hôte. A bar with a stone fireplace and picture windows is an inviting spot any evening, and there's usually piano music Thursday to Saturday.

Amenities: Day-care program for children 3 to 13, new spa with therapeutic baths and massages, indoor and outdoor pools, Jacuzzi, workout room (weight machine, Exercycles, rowing machines), four tennis courts; six nearby golf courses; 22-passenger shuttle bus between the lodge and the slopes in season.

Gray Rocks. 525 chemin Principal, Mont-Tremblant, PQ J0T 1Z0. ☎ **800/567-6767** or 819/425-2771. Fax 819/425-3474. www.grayrocks.com. E-mail info@grayrocks.com. 122 units, 56 condos. A/C TV TEL. C$198–C$320 (US$132–US$213) double, C$160–C$390 (US$107–US$260) condo (4–8 persons). Rates include breakfast and dinner in hotel, but not in condos. Discounts for children sharing parents' room. Meals optional in condos. Ski-school packages available. AE, DISC, MC, V.

The area's dowager resort has been under new management since 1993, and its ministrations are evident, not least in the 18-hole golf course that opened in 1998. The accommodations—rooms and condos—are in a huge rambling main lodge, in the cozier Le Château lodge, and in four-person cottages. The resort covers most of the recreational bases, including golf, tennis, a spa, horseback riding, and boating. There's not only a private airport for guests who fly in but also a seaplane base for joyrides over Lac Ouimet.

Dining/Diversions: The dining room serves three meals daily, and there's a bar with piano and other music for dancing.

Amenities: Same-day dry cleaning/laundry, self-service Laundromat, bicycle rental, baby-sitting, express checkout, business center; junior and adult tennis school, par-72 golf course, indoor pool and fitness center, playground with child-care attendants, 22 tennis courts, horseback riding, sailboat rentals, shuffleboard, croquet; skiing, lifts, ski school, access to 90km (56 miles) of cross-country skiing.

Villa Bellevue. 845 chemin Principale, Mont-Tremblant, PQ J0T 1Z0. ☎ **800/567-6763** or 819/425-2734. Fax 819/425-9360. 130 units. TV TEL. C$60–C$258 (US$40–US$172) double without meals, C$130–C$328 (US$87–US$219) double with breakfast and dinner. Children 17 and under stay free in parents' room. Condos for 4 to 8 people available. Weekly rates and ski weekend packages available. DC, ER, MC, V.

Run by the Dubois family for three generations, the bi-level shingled Bellevue sits at the edge of Lac Ouimet. The guest rooms look somewhat worn but have large windows; some have air-conditioning, and a few even have kitchenettes. Choices are between those in the lodge and deluxe units in a newer building. There's an indoor pool, augmented by sauna, steam baths, and weight room. In summer, staff members can take children off their parents' hands during the afternoon and evening at an extra charge. Cross-country skiing is nearby, and a shuttle bus carries you to and from the lifts.

Where to Dine

Though most Laurentian inns and resorts have their own dining facilities and often require you to use them, especially in winter, Mont-Tremblant and places in the vicinity have several decent independent dining options for casual lunches or the odd night out. Note that restaurants in the area open and close with irritating unpredictability, so call ahead. Those recommended below are among the more reliable.

Antipasto. 855 rue Ouimet, St-Jovite. ☎ **819/425-7580.** Main courses C$12–C$20 (US$8–US$13); "express" lunch C$6 (US$3.95). MC, V. Daily 11am–11pm. ITALIAN.

Antipasto is housed in an old train station moved to this site, so there are the expected railroad memorabilia on the walls; but the owners have resisted the temptation to play up the theme to excess. Captain's chairs are drawn up to big tables with green Formica tops. Almost everyone orders the César salad (their spelling), which is dense and strongly flavored—the half portion is more than enough as a first course. Individual pizzas emerge from the brick ovens in more than 50 versions, on a choice of regular or whole-wheat crust. Pastas are available in even greater variety, those with shellfish among the winners. The sauces are savory, if a bit thin. There are outdoor tables in summer.

Brunch Café. 816 rue Ouimet, St-Jovite. ☎ **819/425-8233.** Main courses C$8–C$16 (US$5–US$11); table d'hôte C$9–C$15 (US$6–US$10). MC, V. Apr–Oct daily 8am–10pm; Nov–Mar daily 8am–4pm. INTERNATIONAL.

While the menu lists many sandwiches, salads, pastas, and pizzas, a most satisfying choice is the sausages picked from a roster of six designer varieties, served with sauerkraut, mustard, and pan fries. They serve complementary *bières en fût* (beer on tap), plus an interesting selection of regional microbrews and imports. Food takes a while to arrive. The cafe is downtown, not far from Antipasto (above), under the same management. There are umbrellas over the tables facing the main street and close tables inside. Live music is offered most summer weekends.

Le Verre Bouteille. 888 rue Ouimet, St-Jovite. ☎ **819/425-8776.** Main courses C$9–C$19 (US$6–US$13); dinner table d'hôte C$13–C$24 (US$9–US$16). MC, V. Summer Mon–Tues 5:30–10pm, Wed–Sat noon–3pm and 5:30–10pm. Closed Sun–Tues in winter; closed 2 weeks in Nov and Apr. FRENCH BISTRO.

The married owners (he cooks, she handles the front) arrived here from France 5 years ago and made themselves a neighborhood bistro that would be at home in rural France. A dozen tables are around the fully stocked service bar, supplemented by a few more out on the porch facing the street. Madame and her minions are warmly welcoming, bringing competent renditions of standards like onion soup and game terrine and lamb ribs with rosemary and 10-ounce pepper steaks. Lunch specials are C$7 (US$4.65) or less, typically a soup or salad followed by pizza or mussels. Glasses of several wines cost only C$3.95 (US$2.65). No one leaves raving about the chef's creativity, but neither do they depart grumbling about the portions or prices. More likely they return again and again, for this has a loyal local clientele.

TREMBLANT: A RESORT VILLAGE

Tremblant is a growing resort village stretching from the mountain's skirts to the shores of 10-mile-long Lac Tremblant. It'll be a pretty nice place if they ever finish it, but this is the kind of enterprise that always has another "phase" to go. It has the prefabricated look of a theme park, but at least they used the Québecois architectural style of pitched or mansard roofs in bright colors, not ersatz Tyrolean or Bavarian Alpine flourishes. At recent count, there were several hotels and condo complexes; an 18-hole golf course (with another on the way); 14 shops, including a liquor store; and 15 eating places and bars. When the snow is deep, skiers here like to follow the sun around the mountain, making the run down slopes with an eastern exposure in the morning and taking the western-facing ones in the afternoon.

To get to the village, drive 4.8km (3 miles) north of St-Jovite on Route 117; then take Montée Ryan and follow the blue signs for about 9.7km (6 miles). The Limocar bus from Montréal stops at the entrance, and there's door-to-door shuttle service from Dorval Airport; call ☎ 800/471-1155 for reservations.

Where to Stay

You can make reservations for lodgings at the resort through the central number (☎ 800/567-6760) or by contacting the establishments directly. The general reception area is in a building labeled Les Cèdres, announced by a large brown sign with gold lettering reading RECEPTION—take the right turn just before the old church. The following are the more prominent hotels, all of which incorporate privately owned condos.

Château Mont-Tremblant. Mont-Tremblant, PQ J0T 1Z0. ☎ **800/441-1414.** Fax 819/ 681-7099. www.chateaumonttremblant.com. 316 units. A/C TV TEL. C$129–C$329 (US$86–US$219) double. AE, DC, ER, MC, V.

This 1996 luxury entry of the Canadian Pacific chain commands a crest above the village, as befits its stature among the Tremblant hostelries. It has a health club, a spa, and indoor and outdoor pools, as well as no-smoking floors.

Club Intrawest. Mont-Tremblant, PQ J0T 1Z0. ☎ **800/799-3258.** www.clubintrawest. com. 42 units. A/C TV TEL. C$197–C$495 (US$131–US$330). AE, DC, ER, MC, V.

Not on the main resort property but at the nearby intersection of chemin Principal and Montée Ryan, this luxury facility has the look of an exclusive golf club, validated by the 18-hole course around which it's positioned. The accommodations are generously proportioned and the appointments impressively tasteful. One- to three-bedroom suites (the highest price quoted above) have full kitchens, deep two-person whirlpool bathtubs, gas fireplaces, stereos, VCRs, and large TVs. There are also a small fitness center, a pool, and eight tennis courts, but no restaurant.

Les Suites Tremblant. Mont-Tremblant, PQ J0T 1Z0. ☎ **800/461-8711.** 569 units. TV TEL. C$116–C$147 (US$77–US$98) double; C$96–C$174 (US$64–US$116) 1-bedroom condo; C$228–C$287 (US$152–US$191) 2-bedroom condo. AE, DC, ER, MC, V.

A collection of several buildings scattered around the complex, each with slightly different profiles of decor and amenities, these are the choices for families, couples traveling together, or those who require economical accommodation. The most expensive two-bedroom unit, at C$287 (US$191), can accommodate up to six, bringing the cost down to less than C$48 (US$32) per person. The units also have kitchenettes, and many have fireplaces and/or washing machines.

Marriott Residence Inn. Mont-Tremblant, PQ J0T 1Z0. ☎ **888/272-4000.** 127 units. A/C TV TEL. C$125–C$145 (US$83–US$97) double; C$145–C$299 (US$97–US$199) suite. Rates include breakfast. Packages available. AE, DC, ER, MC, V.

Near the terminus of the lower chair lift running through the central part of the village, this midlevel hotel has its own restaurant, a heated outdoor pool, and indoor parking. The higher-priced suites have two bedrooms.

Where to Dine
In addition to the hotel bars and restaurants, there are many freestanding places at which to get a meal or a snack in the resort's pedestrian areas. That isn't to say they're very satisfying, for if there's a restaurant in the village that rises above flat mediocrity, it has yet to reveal itself. It wouldn't hurt the powers to consider luring a "fine dining" establishment to the resort in an attempt to elevate its gastronomical standards. Las Vegas did. In the meantime, my recommendation is to ski, sport about, have cocktails, and hear some music in the resort, but take serious meals off the premises.

That said, there are plenty of eating options for the exhausted or carless. Serving a variety of kinds of food implicit in their names are the **Pizzateria, Coco Pazzo, Crêperie Catherine, Aux Truffes, Le Savoie** (fondues), **Mexicali Rosa's,** and **Le Gascon.** The **Microbrasserie La Diable** pours craft beers to accompany live jazz on weekends, and **P'tit Caribou** brings in pop performers weekly. On the summit of the mountain is **Le Rendezvous** cafe, with a circular fireplace, and the 1,000-seat **Le Grand Manitou** restaurant complex, with a dining room called La Légende, plus a bistro and a cafeteria.

ESTRIE: ONE OF QUÉBEC'S BEST-KEPT SECRETS
Estrie serves, in part, as Québec's breadbasket. Known also as the Eastern Townships and Les Cantons de l'Est, it's a largely pastoral region marked by billowing hills and the 792m (2,600-ft.) peak of Mont-Orford, centerpiece of a provincial park and the region's premier downhill ski area. A short distance from Mont-Orford is Sherbrooke, the industrial/commercial capital of Estrie, and throughout the Mont-Orford–Sherbrooke area are serene glacial lakes attracting summer anglers, sailors, and swimmers. Estrie is one of Québec's best-kept secrets, because it's mostly Québecois who occupy rental houses to ski, fish, cycle, or launch their boats.

Once out of Montréal, drive east along arrow-straight Autoroute 10 past silos and fields, herds of cows, and wildflower-strewn meadows. Clumps of mountain rise with improbable suddenness from the rolling terrain that flattens as it approaches the St. Lawrence. Cresting the hill at km 100 is an especially beguiling view of countryside stretching toward New England, not far over the horizon.

Unlike the Laurentians, which virtually close down in "mud time," when spring warmth thaws the ground, Estrie kicks into gear as crews penetrate every "sugar bush" (stand of sugar maples) to tap the sap and "sugar off." Maple festivals result, and farms host "sugaring parties" at which guests partake of prodigious country meals capped by traditional maple-syrup desserts.

Autumn has its special attractions too. In addition to the glorious fall foliage (usually best in the weeks on either side of the third weekend in September), Estrie orchards sag under the weight of apples of every variety, and cider mills hum day and night to produce what has been described as Québec's "wine." You're invited to help with the harvest, paying a low price for the baskets of fruit you gather yourself. Cider mills open their doors for tours and tastings.

Although town names like Granby, Waterloo, and Sherbrooke are obviously English, vestiges of the time when Americans loyal to the Crown migrated here during and shortly after the Revolutionary War, the Estrie is now about 90% French-speaking. A few words of French and a little sign language are sometimes necessary outside hotels and other tourist facilities, since the area draws fewer Anglophone visitors than do the Laurentides.

For extended stays in the region, consider basing yourself in one of the several inns along the shores of Lac Massawippi, especially in and around **North Hatley,** and taking day trips from there.

ESSENTIALS

VISITOR INFORMATION   **La Maison du Tourisme** for the Estrie, at Exit 68 off Autoroute 10 (☎ **800/263-1068** or 450/375-8774; fax 450/375-3530), is open daily: 10am to 6pm in summer and 9am to 5pm the rest of the year. Or contact **Tourisme Estrie,** 25 rue Bocage, Sherbrooke, PQ J1L 2J4 (☎ **800/355-5755** or 819/820-2020; fax 819/566-4445); it has the same hours as the above.

The **telephone area codes** are 450 or 819, depending on the part of the region (towns with a 450 area code are closer to Montréal). Before June 1998, the 450 code was 514, which still appears on much tourist literature.

GETTING THERE   By Car   Leave Montréal by the Champlain Bridge, which funnels into Autoroute 10, heading toward Sherbrooke. People in a hurry can remain on Autoroute 10—and plenty of express buses do this too—but to get to know the countryside, turn off the autoroute at Exit 37 and go north the short distance to join Route 112 east.

By Bus   Local buses leave Montréal to follow Route 112 more than a dozen times a day, arriving in Sherbrooke, 160km (99 miles) away, 3¼ hours later. Express buses use Autoroute 10, making a stop in Magog and arriving in Sherbrooke in 2 hours and 10 minutes (2½ hours from Québec City). Call ☎ **450/842-2281** at the Terminus Voyageur in Montréal for information.

GRANBY

North of the Autoroute at Exit 68, the not-especially-beguiling city of **Granby** (pop. 45,200) does have a couple of surprises.

First is the **Granby Zoo,** 347 bd. David-Bouchard (☎ **450/372-9113**). Take Exit 68 or 74 off Autoroute 10 and follow the signs. Its 70 wooded acres harbor more than 1,000 mammals, exotic birds, reptiles, and amphibians of 225 species from around the world. Founded in 1953, the zoo has an educational program for children and presents shows every day in summer, including demonstrations of raptors. Among the newer exhibits are a nocturnal cave, a display of robotic whales, and the "Afrika" pavilion, notable for its group of gorillas. There are restaurants, picnic areas, gift shops,

Estrie

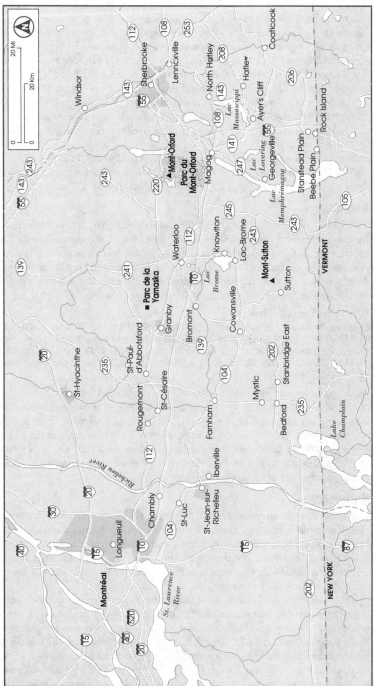

and free rides. Late May to June 11, the zoo is open Friday to Sunday; June 12 to Labour Day, it's open daily; and Labour Day to mid-October, it's open only weekends. Open times vary but are usually 10am to 6pm in high season, to 5pm in shoulder periods. Admission is C$14 (US$9) ages 13 and older, C$9 (US$6) seniors/children 5 to 12, and C$5 (US$3.35) children 2 to 4. Parking is C$4 (US$2.65). The visitor entrance is on boulevard David-Bouchard nord.

Granby also has **Parc de la Yamaska,** with swimming from the longest beach in the area, a 3km (1.9-mile) hiking trail, 40km (25 miles) of cross-country ski trails, and 22km (14 miles) of cycling trails along an old rail track between Granby and the towns of Bromont and Waterloo.

Tourisme Granby is at 650 rue Principale, Granby, PQ J2G 8L4 (☎ **800/ 567-7273** or 450/372-7273; fax 450/372-7782). In summer it's open daily 8am to 7pm; the rest of the year, hours are Monday to Friday 8:30am to 5pm.

BROMONT

Take Exit 78 off Autoroute 10 to reach **Bromont** (pop. 5,000), a popular destination for day and night skiing, mountain biking (rent bikes at the entrance to the town opposite the tourist office), golf, hiking, and horseback riding. Shoppers will find two of Canada's largest **factory outlets**—Versants de Bromont and Les Manufacturiers de Bromont—and the area's largest **flea market,** with 350 stalls set up in the local drive-in from 9am to 5pm the first Sunday in May to the last Sunday in October.

Where to Stay & Dine

Château Bromont. 90 rue Stanstead, Bromont, PQ J2L 1K6. ☎ **800/304-3433** or 450/534-3433. Fax 450/534-0514. www.chateau-bromont.qc.ca/chato2an.htm. E-mail chateau@chateau-bromont.qc.ca. 152 units. A/C MINIBAR TV TEL. C$160–C$190 (US$107–US$127) double. Rate includes breakfast. Spa, ski, and other packages available. AE, DC, DISC, ER, MC, V.

All the guest rooms at the château have rocking chairs and loft beds, and half have fireplaces; some no-smoking rooms are available. A landscaped terrace and two hot tubs look up at the mountain. The staff is young and bilingual. Les Quatre Canards restaurant serves lunch and dinner, and there are a bistro bar, L'Equestre, and the Château Terrasse Bar-BBQ. In addition to indoor and outdoor pools and Jacuzzis, a sauna, a small gym, and squash and racquetball courts, there's a European spa featuring mud and algae baths (use of the spa facilities costs extra).

KNOWLTON

Those who shop for amusement, not mere necessity, will want to make this a destination. **Knowlton** is compact, but its two main shopping streets (Lakeside Street and Knowlton Road) have a number of clothing and antiques stores that reveal a creeping chic influenced by refugees and day-trippers from Montréal. Ralph Lauren is here, and a shop that replaced a Liz Claiborne outlet sells outdoor gear and clothing and whimsically refers to itself as L.L. Brome.

Knowlton, at the southeast corner of **Lac Brome,** is part of the seven-village municipality known as Lac Brome (pop. 5,048). It's one of the region's last towns where a majority of residents have English as their mother tongue. The first settler here was Paul Holland Knowlton, a Loyalist from Vermont who arrived in 1815 and established a farm where the golf course is now. By 1834, he had added a sawmill, a blacksmith shop, a gristmill, and a store. He also founded the first high school. Another Knowlton resident, Reginald Aubrey Fessenden, invented a wireless radio in 1906, a year ahead of Marconi, and relayed a message from Brant Rock, Massachusetts, to ships in the Caribbean. Large mansions overlook the lake on either side of town.

There's a **Blue Grass Festival** in June, and the **Brome Fair** is held over Labour Day weekend.

The **tourist information office** is in the local museum, the **Musée Historique du Comté de Brome,** 130 Lakeside St. (Route 243) (☎ **450/243-6782**), which occupies five historic buildings, including the town's first school, established by Paul Holland Knowlton. Exhibits focus on the various aspects of town life, with re-creations of a schoolroom, bedroom, parlor, and kitchen. The Martin Annex (1921) is dominated by the 1917 Fokker single-seat biplane, the foremost German aircraft in World War I. Also on the premises are collections of old radios and 18th- to early–20th-century weapons. The museum sells books about the area. Admission is C$3 (US$2) adults, C$2 (US$1.35) seniors/students, and C$1.50 (US$1) ages 16 and under. Mid-May to mid-September, it's open Monday to Saturday 10am to 4:30pm and Sunday 11am to 4:30pm.

Where to Stay & Dine

Auberge Lakeview. 50 rue Victoria, Knowlton (Lac Brome), PQ J0E 1V0. ☎ **800/661-6183** or 514/243-6183. Fax 514/243-0602. www.quebecweb.com/lakeview. E-mail lakeview@ tele-page.com. 28 units. A/C TEL. C$93–C$135 (US$62–US$90) double. MAP available. AE, MC, V. A block south of the town hall.

The core structure of this Victorian inn dates from 1874, and that flavor has been sustained throughout the later extensions, the most important renovation taking place in 1986. Leather chairs are arranged around the fireplace in the lobby; stamped tin ceilings prevail; and Spencer's, the brass-and-mahogany pub that's a replica of the London original, is a place to settle in for an evening. The four-course table d'hôte dinner in Sheffield's dining room is only C$38 (US$25), prepared by a chef who trained in Provence. On weekends, there's dancing to live music. The guest rooms come in four categories—go for the best ones and get two robes, a sitting area, access to the veranda, and a heart-shaped Jacuzzi. Much of the furniture is locally crafted in Québecois country style. In the least expensive category, there are no TVs, but the rest have cable. A pool awaits outside, banked with flowers.

SUTTON

A pleasant outing from Knowlton, or anywhere in the vicinity, **Sutton** (pop. 3,209) is a town with a number of promising cafes and the best bookstore in the region, **The Book Nook,** at 14 rue Principale sud (☎ **450/538-2207**), open daily. Nearby **Mont-Sutton** is known in summer for its 54km (33 miles) of hiking trails linking up with the Appalachian Trail and in winter for its glade skiing. The surrounding country roads are popular with bikers. For more info, drop by the **Tourist Office of Sutton,** 11B rue Principale sud (☎ **450/538-8455**), opposite the bookstore.

MONT-ORFORD

Exit 115 north off the autoroute leads into one of Québec's most popular provincial parks. Mid-September to mid-October, the **Parc du Mont-Orford** blazes with autumn color, and visitors come in summer to try the 18-hole golf course and in winter for the more than 25 miles of ski trails and slopes, with a vertical drop of over 1,600 feet, or for the extensive network of cross-country ski and snowshoe trails.

Mont-Orford is a veteran ski area compared to Bromont (above) and has long provided slopes of choice for the moneyed families of Estrie and Montréal. It's composed of contiguous Mont-Giroux, Mont-Desrochers, and Mont-Orford itself, the highest peak. Children enjoy special treatment with "Kinderski," where 100 instructors conduct a ski/snowboard school and supervise a tube slide. Après-ski drinks, dinner, and entertainment are provided by the Slalom Pub. The other ski resorts in the area

(Bromont, Owl's Head, and Mont-Sutton) are more family oriented and less glitzy. These four ski centers have banded together to form **Ski East,** enabling skiers to buy all-inclusive 2- to 7-day tickets good at all four areas anytime. Prices range from C$64 to C$203 (US$43 to US$135) for ages 14 and older and C$35 to C$140 (US$23 to US$93) seniors/ages 6 to 13. Similarly economical lesson plans are available.

Orford has another claim to fame in the **Centre d'Arts Orford** (☎ 800/567-6155 or 819/843-3981), set on a 222-acre estate in the park and providing music classes for talented young musicians every summer. Early July to mid-August, a series of more than 30 classical and chamber music concerts is given in connection with **Festival Orford.** Prices usually are C$12 to C$25 (US$8 to US$17) for professional organizations but free for student performances. Concerts are held Thursday to Sunday. A complete lunch is served outside following the Saturday concert. Visual-arts exhibits at the center are open to the public, and walking trails connect it to a nearby campground.

For additional info, call ☎ 800/361-6548 or 819/843-6548 or log on to **www. mt-orford.com**.

Where to Stay

✪ **Manoir des Sables.** 90 av. des Jardins, Magog-Orford, PQ J1X 3W3. ☎ **800/ 567-3514** or 819/847-4747. Fax 819/847-3519. www.hotel.manoirdessables.com. E-mail hotel.manoirdessables@sympatico.ca. 117 units. A/C TV TEL. C$150–C$175 (US$100–US$117) double. Rates include breakfast. MAP available, ski, golf, and other packages available. Take Exit 118 from Autorte. 10 and follow Rte. 141 north to the hotel, on the right.

This attractive, thoroughly contemporary facility deserves to be considered the most complete resort hotel in the Estrie, serving business conferees, couples, families, golfers, skiers, skaters, fitness enthusiasts, tennis players, kayakers, and those who find solace in being wrapped in seaweed and oil, baked in saunas, massaged with water sprays, and kneaded by experts. Add indoor and outdoor pools, snowshoeing trails, snowmobiling, toboggan rides, tube slides, fishing in the hotel's lake, and Saturday-night horse-drawn sleigh rides. The guest rooms have all the big-city gadgets and niceties, since this began life as a Sheraton—coffeemakers and hair dryers are standard, and all have either one queen or two double beds and sitting areas. About half have fireplaces.

Down the road a bit, the same ownership group has initiated needed renovations of an older property, the **Chéribourg,** 2603 Route 141, Magog, PQ J1X 3W9 (☎ **800/567-6132** or 819/843-3308; fax 819/843-2639). Assuming that the work is completed, it should be a decent alternative to the Manoir des Sables.

MAGOG & LAC MEMPHRÉMAGOG

Magog came by its handle through the corruption of an Amerindian word. The Abenaki name *Memrobagak* ("Great Expanse of Water") somehow became *Memphré-magog,* which was eventually shortened to Magog (*May*-gog). The town is positioned at the northernmost end of **Lac Memphrémagog** (Mem-*phree*-may-gog), *not* on Lac Magog, which is about 13km (8 miles) north of Magog. The lake spills across the U.S.-Canadian border into Vermont. It has its own legendary sea creature, nicknamed Memphre, which supposedly surfaced for the first time in 1798. Other sightings have been claimed since then.

The helpful **Bureau d'Information Touristique Magog-Orford** is at 55 rue Cabana (via Route 112), Magog, PQ J1X 2C4 (☎ **800/267-2744** or 819/843-2744; fax 819/847-4036). It's open daily: in summer 8:30am to 7:30pm and in winter 10:30am to 6pm.

A Quintessential Québec Experience:
Fun at a Sugar Shack

For a don't-miss Québec experience near Orford, take Exit 106 off Autoroute 10, turn right, and then turn right again. In about 1km (0.6 mile), watch for the CAMPING NORMAND sign and make a left on rue Georges-Bonnallie. In about 5km (3.1 miles), turn into the parking lot at the sign for **La Sucrerie des Normand,** 426 rue Georges-Bonnallie, Easton (☎ **450/297-2659**). The long, angled, log-and-plank-sided building is a classic sugar shack, as that institution has evolved from the time when it was merely a place that processed the sap drained from maple trees.

Entering, you'll see the rendering room on the right. Here the sap gathered from taps in more than 13,000 maple trees is boiled in an evaporator trough, then cooked further on a stove. Temperatures must be precise (216°F), because if the emerging syrup is too cold it might ferment and explode in the can, and if it's too hot crystals may form. Then the syrup is filtered and poured into cans. One popular sales device is to set up a long, narrow tray of snow and pour a wriggly stream of syrup down the middle. This forms a sort of maple taffy, which is then rolled up on Popsicle sticks and eaten.

To the left is what happened when producers realized they drew audiences ripe for a wider experience. There are a full bar to one side and wooden tables next to a fireplace, and the walls are crowded with vintage radios, a sewing machine, apple corers, oxbows, snowshoes, and a moose head. Beyond that is a larger room with a dance floor and a stage for musicians, and finally a still-larger dining room with long plank tables.

The lady of the house speaks fluent English, though that's not really necessary. Costing all of C$18 (US$12) per person, including tips and taxes, meals are served February to April (reservations required). There's no menu: You sit down at a table, and she starts bringing food—crudités with a mustard/mayo dip, thick pea soup, fragrant bread, a plate with an omelet supported by sausage and ham slices, home fries, pork rinds, baked beans, coleslaw, a stack of pancakes, then samples of four maple desserts. At the ready are preserves, pickles, and all the maple syrup you can ingest. Few diners can finish it all. If you can't move afterward, they have four basic guest rooms for rent.

Sleigh rides can be arranged, and there's a campground. The basic products are available in several sizes and forms, primarily syrup and candy. Keep in mind that the best syrup is from the first run of sap and is clear and light in color. It gets darker as the weeks of the season proceed.

Sugar shacks usually use the words *"cabane à sucre"* or *"érablière."* While most restrict meal service to the sugaring-off season, some provide food through the summer for tourists. Small directional signs are often positioned at the roadside. The Web site **http://arcsq.qc.ca** lists the names and numbers of 90 Québec sugar shacks that serve meals (not all do).

Magog has a fully utilized waterfront, and in July each year the **Lac Memphrémagog International Swimming Marathon** creates a big splash. Participants start out in Newport, Vermont, at 6am and swim 39km (24 miles) to Magog, arriving around 3:30 or 4pm. To experience the lake without such soggy exertion, take a 1¾-hour **lake cruise** aboard the *Aventure I* or *Aventure II* (☎ **819/843-8068**). The cost is C$11 (US$7) adults and C$6 (US$4) children 11 and under; a daylong cruise is C$40 (US$27). The boats leave from Point Merry Park, the focal point for many of the town's outdoor activities.

A 19km (11½-mile) bike path links the lake with Mont-Orford. In winter it's transformed into a **cross-country ski trail,** and a 2.5km-long (1.6-miles) **skating rink** is created on the lakeshore. Snowmobiling trails crisscross the region. Other popular activities include golf, tennis, and horseback riding.

Drive west from Magog on Route 112 and watch for the first road on the left on the far side of the lake; take chemin Bolton est 19km (12 miles) south to the turnoff to the **Abbaye de St-Benoît-du-Lac,** Chemin Fisher (☎ **819/843-4080**). There's no mistaking the abbey, with its granite steeple thrusting above the lake, against the backdrop of Owl's Head Mountain. Peek into the tiny stone chapel to the left at the property's entrance, opposite the small cemetery. Though St-Benoît-du-Lac dates only from 1912, the site's serenity is timeless. Some 40 monks help keep the art of Gregorian chant alive in their liturgy, and you can attend the 45-minute service (times below) by walking to the rear of the abbey and down the stairs; follow the signs for the *oratoire* and sit in back to avoid a lot of otherwise-obligatory standing and sitting. A bleu cheese known as L'Ermite, among Québec's most famous, is produced here, along with a creamy version and Swiss and cheddar types. They're on sale in the little shop, which also sells chocolate from Oka, honey, nonalcoholic cider, and tapes of religious chants. Visitors during the last 2 weeks of September or the first 2 weeks of October may want to help pick apples in the orchard.

Admission to the abbey is free, but donations are accepted. It's open daily 6am to 8pm; mass with Gregorian chant is given at 11am and vespers with Gregorian chant at 5pm (7pm on Thurs). There are no vespers on Tuesday in July and August. The abbey receives 7,000 pilgrims a year, 60% between 16 and 25, and maintains separate **hostels** for men (☎ **819/843-4080**) and women (☎ **819/843-2340**). Make reservations in advance, figuring about C$35 (US$23) per person.

Where to Stay

There are at least a dozen B&Bs in Magog, three of the most convenient of which are along the blocks of rue Merry nord, immediately north of its intersection with rue Principale.

Auberge l'Etoile-sur-le-Lac. 1150 rue Principale ouest, Magog, PQ J1X 2B8. ☎ **819/843-6521,** or 800/567-2727 in Québec. Fax 819/843-5007. 26 units. A/C TV TEL. C$162–C$194 (US$108–US$129) double. Rates include breakfast and dinner. Golf, sailing, and other packages available. AE, CB, DC, DISC, ER, MC, V. Take Exit 115 from Autorte. 10 and follow Rte. 112 into Magog; the hotel is on the right soon after passing the Tourist Information Bureau.

Its name means "star on the lake," not exactly hyperbole given the unremarkable state of Magog lodgings. The primary virtues are its lakeside location (all the guest rooms overlook the lake and have patios or balconies) and ready access to Mont-Orford, 6km (3.7 miles) away. Upstairs are a rustic lounge and a glass-enclosed Jacuzzi overlooking the water. A dining room and bar occupy much of the ground floor, with terrace dining in summer. An outdoor pool is available, if not especially inviting, and bikes and ice skates are for rent. Another 22 rooms are being added.

GEORGEVILLE

Established in 1797 on the eastern shore of Lac Memphrémagog, the peaceful settlement of **Georgeville** was once a stop along the stagecoach route from Montréal to

Brome, then a 5-day trip. Development has been scant, and today the town has just enough buildings to shelter 845 residents, a general store, a little Anglican church, and a nine-hole golf course with lake views. It's also a summer home to actor Donald Sutherland.

The 22km (14-mile) drive along Route 247 south from Georgeville to Beebe Plain (below) is pleasant rather than stunning. Owl's Head is the name of the prominent mountain off to the right.

Where to Stay & Dine

Auberge Georgeville 1889. 71 chemin Channel (Rte. 247), Georgeville, PQ J0B 1T0. ☎ **888/843-8686** or 819/843-8683. Fax 819/843-5045. Reservations recommended. Table d'hôte dinner C$40 (US$27). AE, MC, V. Daily 6–10pm. Closed Oct 30–Dec 16 and Sun–Mon off-season. Take Rte. 247 10 miles south from Magog.

Built in 1889 to serve stagecoach traffic, this inn has long been known for the meals served in its three dining rooms. The new owners reinvigorated the place, buffing its culinary image while perking up the small guest rooms with antiques and Laura Ashley designs. The five-course table d'hôte menu varies according to the season and the chef/owner's whim, but at least 50% of his products are raised or gathered in Québec, like the organic greens and Lac Brome duck. He's especially proud of his head-grazing cellar, stocked primarily with top French and California labels. The fresh paint job retains the house's traditional pink-and-white scheme, and there's a fancy new sign out front, so the inn is hard to miss.

The 12 guest rooms, 8 with bathrooms, go for C$180 to C$190 (US$120 to US$127) double, while the new suite goes for C$195 (US$130). There are no phones or TVs, but button-busting breakfasts are included and MAP is available. Lunch is served only to houseguests, on request. They have free use of the inn's bikes.

LAKE MASSAWIPPI & NORTH HATLEY

Southeast of Magog, reachable by Route 141 or 108, east of Autoroute 55, is ✪ **Lake Massawippi,** easily the Estrie's most desirable resort area. The 12-mile-long lake is set among rolling hills and fertile farm country, and its scalloped shoreline was discovered in the early 1900s by people of wealth and power, many of whom were American Southerners trying to escape the sultry summers of Virginia and Georgia. (They came up by train and are said to have pulled down their window shades as long as they were in Yankee territory.) They built grand "cottages" on slopes in prime locations along the lakeshore, with enough bedrooms to house their extended families and friends for months at a time. Several of these have now been converted to inns. For a few days' escape from work or intensive travel, it's difficult to do better than Lake Massawippi.

In winter, the lands around the lake have 56km (35 miles) of cross-country ski trails, and a special 3- or 6-night package, called **Skiwippi,** allows you to spend brisk days skiing the exemplary Auberge Ripplecove, Manoir Hovey, and Auberge Hatley (below), reveling each night in the varied accommodations and accomplished kitchens of the three. In summer, there's a comparable golf version. For the less athletically inclined, a similar package (sans skis), called **A Moveable Feast,** is also available. Book the packages through any of the inns.

The jewel of Lake Massawippi, the town of **North Hatley** (pop. 704), only half an hour from the U.S. border and 138km (86 miles) from Montréal, has a river meandering through it. Old photos show flocks of people coursing along the one main village street. Apart from impressive lake sunsets, it offers a variety of lodgings and places to dine, shops, golf, a marina, and an unlabeled Laundromat between the general store and the post office. Horse lovers will want to know about **Equitation Jacques-Robidas,** 32 chemin McFarland (☎ **819/563-0166**). Guides lead trail rides through forest and meadow beside the Massawippi in summer, with rates at C$20 to C$25 (US$13 to US$17) per hour. Buggy and winter sleigh rides are possibilities, and they have packages that include longer rides, meals, and vineyard visits.

An English-language theater, the **Piggery,** on a country road outside town (☎ 819/ 842-2431), presents plays of an often-experimental nature in summer. For 10 Sundays mid-April to late June, **Le Festival du Lac Massawippi** (☎ 819/346-7379) brings classical music recitals to North Hatley at the Ste-Elisabeth Church on chemin Capelton.

Where to Stay & Dine

✪ **Auberge Hatley.** 325 rue Virgin (P.O. Box 330), North Hatley, PQ J0B 2C0. ☎ 819/ **842-2451.** Fax 819/842-2907. www.relaischateaux.fr/hatley. E-mail hatley@ relaischateaux. 25 units. A/C TV TEL. C$230–C$425 (US$153–US$283) double. Rates include breakfast, dinner, and gratuities. AE, MC, V. Take Exit 29 from Autorte. 55 and follow Rte. 108 east, watching for the signs.

This acclaimed gastronomic resort occupies a hillside above the lake, not far from the town center. Abundant antiques, many of them sizable Québecois country pieces, are joined by complementary reproductions. All the guest rooms have hair dryers, and more than half have Jacuzzis and/or fireplaces. There's a pool, and the staff advises on nearby activities. But owners Liliane and Robert Gagnon place their priority on the pleasures of the table. The dining room boasts a bank of windows overlooking the lake and tables set with Rosenthal china, thin-stemmed glasses, flowers, and candles. Updated classical French techniques are applied to such ingredients as salmon, bison, and wild boar. Most herbs and edible flowers and some vegetables come from the Gagnons' hydroponic farm; the ducks and pheasants, from their 100-acre game island. A particular treat is the meal-ending cheese selection, half French, half Québecois, served with the waiter's careful description and not a little ceremony. They've expanded their already-prodigious wine holdings, still providing a number of interesting wines by the glass and enough half bottles to satisfy lighter imbibers. Table d'hôte menus start at C$50 (US$33) and top out with the gastronomic spectacular at C$95 (US$63).

✪ **Manoir Hovey.** Chemin Hovey (P.O. Box 60), North Hatley, PQ J0B 2C0. ☎ 800/ **661-2421** or 819/842-2421. Fax 819/842-2248. www.manoirhovey.com. E-mail manhovey@manoirhovey.com. 40 units. A/C TV TEL. C$180–C$436 (US$120–US$291) double. Rates include full breakfast, dinner, tax, gratuities, and use of most recreational facilities. Packages available. AE, MC, V. Take Exit 29 off Autorte. 55 and follow Rte. 108 east, watching for the signs.

Named for Capt. Ebenezer Hovey, a Connecticut Yankee who came on the lake in 1793 and was the first white settler, this columned manor was built in 1899. It encompasses 20 acres and 1,600 feet of lakefront property and is one of eastern Canada's most complete resort inns, a member of the international Romantik Hotels group. The guest rooms are ranked in five price categories, the bottom two small but adequate, with few frills, and the top three desirable, even luxurious, with fireplaces, balconies, and whirlpool bathtubs; several are no-smoking. Coffeemakers, hair dryers, magnifying mirrors, and radios are standard. The richly appointed library lounge has floor-to-ceiling bookshelves, deep chairs and sofas, and a stone fireplace, with chess sets and daily newspapers laid out. A lighted tennis court, touring bikes, a heated outdoor pool, and two beaches add to the appeal. In winter, they push a heated cabin out onto the lake for ice fishing. The paneled dining room serves updated French cuisine, with a menu that changes seasonally and features fresh herbs, vegetables, and edible flowers from the kitchen garden. All are fragrant and full-bodied, in attractive presentations. Take brandy in the atmospheric pub, and work it all off the next morning in the small fitness room. Steve and Kathy Stafford are the gracious hosts.

Where to Dine

Le Moulin. 225 rue Mill. ☎ **819/842-2380.** Main courses C$9–C$19 (US$6–US$13); table d'hôte menu C$13 (US$9) at lunch, C$26 (US$17) at dinner. MC, V. May–Nov daily noon–2:30pm and 5:30–10pm. Closed Mon–Tues rest of the year and Mar. BELGIAN.

With its big beams, wavy floors, and plywood bar, this former grist mill has an utterly casual air, the better to dig into the Belgian house specialty, *moules et frites.* That's a pot of mussels with a choice of six sauces and a plate of fries on the side; they come in large or small servings, priced accordingly and an agreeable variation on the burger-and-fries standard lunch. Steak is another possibility, and the table d'hôte meals are more elaborate. There's a terrace. Closings during cold months are capricious.

Pilsen. 55 rue Principale. ☎ **819/842-2971.** Reservations recommended on weekends. Main courses C$7–C$21 (US$4.65–US$14). MC, V. Wed–Sun 11:30am–9pm (closed Wed late Oct to late May); bar open to 3am Fri–Sat. INTERNATIONAL.

All drives through North Hatley pass the Pilsen, a pub/restaurant in the center of town with a terrace in front and a narrow deck overhanging the river that feeds the lake. The place fills up quickly on warm days, the better to watch boats setting out or returning. Patrons snaffle up renditions of nachos and burgers, pastas, and lobster bisque. Vegetarian plates are available. There's an extensive choice of beers, including local micro-brews Massawippi Blonde and Townships Pale Ale. Park behind the restaurant.

Where to Stay & Dine in Ayer's Cliff

✪ **Auberge Ripplecove.** 700 rue Ripplecove (P.O. Box 26), Ayer's Cliff, PQ J0B 1C0. ☎ **819/838-4296.** Fax 819/838-5541. www.ripplecove.com. E-mail ripcove@ cabacom.com. 26 units. A/C TV TEL. C$232–C$472 (US$155–US$315) double or cottage for 2; C$310–C$400 suite (US$207–US$267). Rates include breakfast and dinner, gratuities, and most recreational facilities. AE, MC, V. Take Rte. 55 to Exit 21; follow Rte. 141 east, watching for the signs.

A warm welcome is extended by the staff of this handsome inn, and impeccable house-keeping standards are observed throughout. The core structure dates from 1945, but subsequent expansions have added rooms, suites, and cottages. About half have gas fireplaces, balconies, whirlpool tubs, and cable TVs, and the suites add kitchenettes and stocked minibars. An additional eight rooms and suites should be ready in 2000. The 12-acre property beside Lake Massawippi has a private beach, tennis courts, and a heated outdoor pool. Instruction and equipment are available for sailing, sail-boarding, waterskiing, canoeing, kayaking, and cross-country skiing. Golf courses and riding stables are a short drive away. The inn's award-winning lakeside restaurant fills up most nights in season with diners drawn to the kitchen's contemporary French creations, prettily garnished and interpreted by the young chef. Wapiti and caribou appear on the card. Smoking isn't permitted. The four table d'hôte dinners range from C$42 to C$85 (US$28 to US$57). The hull of a fishing dory has been recycled as a buffet table. Check out the lobby lounge and its ornate 14-foot-high breakfront built in 1880. Innkeeper Jeffrey Stafford is the brother of the owner of Manoir Hovey in North Hatley.

8 Québec City & the Gaspé Peninsula

by Herbert Bailey Livesey

Québec City is the soul of New France. It was Canada's first settlement and today is the capital of politically prickly Québec, a province larger than Alaska. With its splendid location above the St. Lawrence River and its virtually unblemished old town—a tumble of slate-roofed granite houses clustered around the august Château Frontenac—the city is a haunting evocation of the motherland, as romantic as any on the continent. Because of its history, beauty, and unique stature as the only walled city north of Mexico, Québec's historic district was named a UNESCO World Heritage site in 1985.

Québec City is almost solidly French in feeling, spirit, and language (about 95% of its population speaks the mother tongue). Perhaps because of that homogeneity and its status as the putative capital of a future independent nation, its citizens seem to suffer less over what might happen down the road. They're also aware that a critical part of their economy is based on tourism and are far less likely to show the hostility Americans can encounter in English Canada. There are far fewer bilingual residents here than in Montréal, but many of Québec City's 648,000 citizens speak some English, especially those who work in hotels, restaurants, and shops. This is also a college town, and thousands of young people study English as a second language.

You can spend almost all your visit in Vieux-Québec, the old walled city, since many hotels, restaurants, and visitor services are there. The original colony was built down by the St. Lawrence at the foot of Cap Diamant (Cape Diamond), and it was there that merchants, traders, and boatmen earned their livelihoods. But due to unfriendly fire in the 1700s, this Basse-Ville (Lower Town) became primarily a wharf/warehouse area, and residents moved to safer houses atop the steep cliffs. That trend is being reversed today, with several new auberges and many attractive bistros and shops revitalizing the area.

The Haute-Ville (Upper Town), the Québecois discovered, wasn't immune from cannon fire either, as British general James Wolfe was to prove. Nevertheless, the division into Upper and Lower Towns persisted for obvious topographical reasons. The Upper Town remains enclosed by fortification walls, and several ramplike streets and a cliffside funicular (*funiculaire*) connect it to the Lower Town. (A fatal 1996 accident closed the funicular for over 2 years, but it has been repaired and is running again.)

Strolling through old Québec is comparable to exploring similar quarters in northern Europe. Carriage wheels creak behind muscular horses, sunlight filters through leafy canopies to fall on drinkers and diners in sidewalk cafes, stone houses huddle close, and childish shrieks of laughter echo down cobblestoned streets. In addition, Québec offers a bewitching vista of river and mountains that the Dufferin promenade bestows. In winter, the city takes on a Dickensian quality, with lamp glow behind curtains of falling snow.

Once you've had a chance to explore the city, you may want to consider a trip to the Ile d'Orléans, an agricultural/resort island within sight of the Château Frontenac; a drive along the northern coast to the provincial park and ski center at Mont Ste-Anne; a visit to the resort villages of Charlevoix and the possibility of a whale-watching cruise; or a drive through the picturesque villages on the southern bank of the St. Lawrence.

1 Essentials

ARRIVING

BY PLANE   About 19km (12 miles) west of the city, the **Jean-Lesage International Airport** is small, despite its grand name. Buses from there to several large hotels in town are operated by **Autobus La Québecoise** (☎ 418/872-5525), the trip costing C$9 (US$6) one-way or C$17 (US$11) round-trip. Buses leave at variable times, depending on the season, but roughly every 1½ hours Monday to Friday 8:45am to 8:45pm and every 2 hours Saturday and Sunday 9am to 8:30pm. A taxi into town costs about C$28 (US$19).

BY CAR   From New York City and points south, follow I-87 to Autoroute 15 to Montréal, picking up Autoroute 20 to Québec City. Take 73 Nord across Pont Pierre-Laporte and exit onto boulevard Champlain immediately after crossing the bridge. This skirts the city at river level. Turn left at the Parc des Champs-de-Bataille (Battlefields Park) and right onto the Grande Allée. Alternatively, take Autoroute 40 from Montréal, which follows the north shore of the St. Lawrence. The trip takes about 2½ hours.

From Boston, take I-89 to I-93 to I-91 in Montpelier, Vermont, which connects with Autoroute 55 in Québec to link up with Autoroute 20. Or follow I-90 up the Atlantic coast, through Portland, Maine, to Route 201 west of Bangor, then Autoroute 173 to Lévis, where there's a car-ferry to Québec City, a 10-minute ride across the St. Lawrence. The ferry between Lévis and Québec City runs daily, every 30 minutes 6am to 3:45pm and every 60 minutes 3:45pm to 3:45am. It costs C$4.50 or C$4.75 (US$3 or US$3.15) for the car, C$1.50 or C$1.75 (US$1 or US$1.15) for passengers 12 to 65, C$1.10 or C$1.20 (US75¢ or US80¢) for passengers 5 to 11, and C$1.40 or C$1.60 (US95¢ or US$1.05) for passengers over 64; children under 5 are free.

BY TRAIN   The train station in Québec City, the **Gare du Palais,** 450 rue de la Gare-du-Palais (☎ 418/692-3940), is a handsome building, but the Lower Town location isn't central. Plan on a moderately strenuous uphill hike or a C$6 (US$4) cab ride to the Upper Town. That's C$6 per ride, incidentally, not per passenger, as an occasional cabby may pretend.

BY BUS   The bus station, the **Gare d'Autobus de la Vieille Capitale,** 320 rue Abraham-Martin (☎ 418/525-3000), is near the train station. It's an uphill climb or quick cab ride to Château Frontenac and the Upper Town. A taxi should cost about C$6 (US$4), the same as from the train station.

Québec City

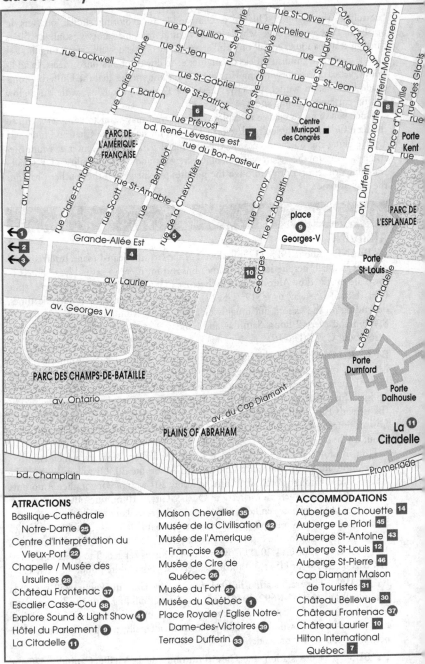

ATTRACTIONS

Basilique-Cathédrale Notre-Dame 25
Centre d'Interprétation du Vieux-Port 22
Chapelle / Musée des Ursulines 28
Château Frontenac 37
Escalier Casse-Cou 38
Explore Sound & Light Show 41
Hôtel du Parlement 9
La Citadelle 11

Maison Chevalier 35
Musée de la Civilisation 42
Musée de l'Amerique Française 24
Musée de Cire de Québec 26
Musée du Fort 27
Musée du Québec 1
Place Royale / Eglise Notre-Dame-des-Victoires 39
Terrasse Dufferin 33

ACCOMMODATIONS

Auberge La Chouette 14
Auberge Le Priori 45
Auberge St-Antoine 43
Auberge St-Louis 12
Auberge St-Pierre 46
Cap Diamant Maison de Touristes 31
Château Bellevue 30
Château Frontenac 37
Château Laurier 10
Hilton International Québec 7

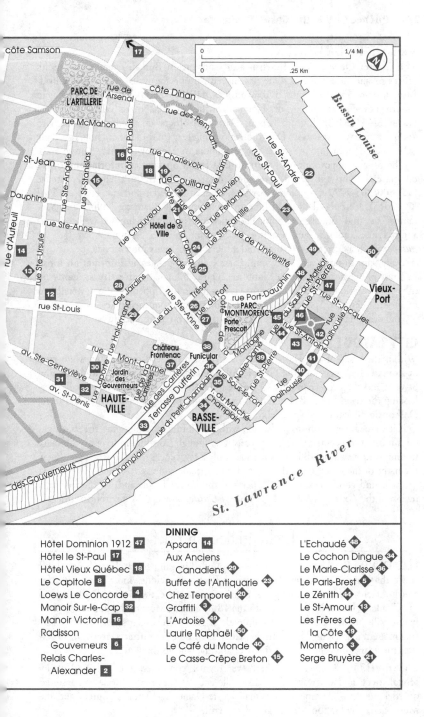

côte Samson

17

PARC DE L'ARTILLERIE
rue de l'Arsenal
côte Dinan

rue McMahon
rue des Remparts

rue du Palais
côte Dinan

St-Jean
rue Ste-Angèle
rue Ste-Stanislas
rue Charlevoix
16
18 **19**
rue Couillard
rue St-Flavien
rue Hamel
rue St-André
rue St-Paul
22

Dauphine
15
20
côte de la Fabrique
rue Ferland
rue Ste-Famille
rue de l'Université

rue d'Auteuil
rue Ste-Ursule
rue Ste-Anne
rue Chauveau
21
Hôtel de Ville
23

14
13
Buade
24
49
50

12
28
des Jardins
25
48
rue du Sault-au-Matelot
rue St-Pierre
47
Vieux-Port

rue St-Louis
rue Haldimand
Trésor
rue du Fort
rue Port-Dauphin
45
46

29
rue Ste-Anne
26
27
PARC MONTMORENCY
Porte Prescott
rue du Sault
rue St-Antoine
Dalhousie
rue St-Jacques

av. Ste-Geneviève
30
rue Mont-Carmel
Château Frontenac
38 Funicular
Montagne
Notre-Dame
44
42
43

31
32
Jardin des Gouverneurs
37
36
rue des Carrières
39
rue St-Pierre
41

av. St-Denis
HAUTE-VILLE
Terrasse Dufferin
35
40
Dalhousie

33
rue du Petit-Champlain
34
BASSE-VILLE

des Gouverneurs
bd. Champlain
T. du Marché-Champlain

St. Lawrence River

Bassin Louise

DINING

Hôtel Dominion 1912 **47**	Apsara **14**	L'Echaudé **48**
Hôtel le St-Paul **17**	Aux Anciens	Le Cochon Dingue **34**
Hôtel Vieux Québec **18**	Canadiens **29**	Le Marie-Clarisse **36**
Le Capitole **8**	Buffet de l'Antiquarie **23**	Le Paris-Brest **5**
Loews Le Concorde **4**	Chez Temporel **20**	Le Zénith **44**
Manoir Sur-le-Cap **32**	Graffiti **3**	Le St-Amour **13**
Manoir Victoria **16**	L'Ardoise **49**	Les Frères de
Radisson	Laurie Raphaël **50**	la Côte **19**
Gouverneurs **6**	Le Café du Monde **40**	Momento **3**
Relais Charles-	Le Casse-Crêpe Breton **15**	Serge Bruyère **21**
Alexander **2**		

VISITOR INFORMATION

The **Greater Québec Area Tourism and Convention Bureau** operates two useful offices in and near the city. One has moved outside the walls to 835 av. Wilfrid-Laurier, bordering the Plaines d'Abraham (☎ **418/649-2608**). The other office is in suburban Ste-Foy at 3300 av. des Hôtels, near the Québec and Pierre-Laporte bridges (☎ **418/651-2882**). June to Labour Day, both offices are open daily 8:30am to 7:45pm; the day after Labour Day to Thanksgiving Day (mid-October), hours are daily 8:30am to 5:15pm; and the rest of the year, hours are Monday to Friday 9am to 5pm.

The provincial government's tourism department operates an **information office** on place d'Armes, at 12 rue Ste-Anne, down the hill from Château Frontenac (☎ **800/363-7777** from other parts of Québec, Canada, and the U.S., or 514/873-2015). It's open daily: mid-June to September 1 8:30am to 7:30pm and September 2 to mid-June 9am to 5pm. The office offers many brochures as well as details about cruise and bus-tour operators, a souvenir shop, a 24-hour ATM (*guichet automatique*), a currency exchange, and a free lodging reservation service.

Daily 9am to noon and 1 to 5pm, Parks Canada operates an **information kiosk** in front of Château Frontenac. June to August, bilingual **university students** on motorbikes station themselves near the visitor sites in the Upper and the Lower Towns to answer questions. Spot them by the flags on the backs of their bikes.

For additional information, log on to **www.quebec-region.cuq.qc.ca**.

CITY LAYOUT

Within the walls of the **Haute-Ville** (Upper Town), the principal streets are **rues St-Louis** (which becomes the **Grande-Allée** outside the city walls), **Ste-Anne,** and **St-Jean** and the pedestrian-only ✪ **Terrasse Dufferin,** essentially a boardwalk overlooking the river. In the **Basse-Ville** (Lower Town), major streets are **rues St-Pierre, Dalhousie, St-Paul,** and (parallel to it) **St-André.**

If it were larger, the historic district, with its winding and plunging streets, might be confusing to negotiate. As compact as it is, though, you should have no difficulty finding your way around. Most streets are only a few blocks long, so when you know the name of the street, it's fairly easy to find a specific address.

You'll find good maps of the Upper and the Lower Towns and the metropolitan region in the *Greater Québec Area Tourist Guide,* provided by any tourist office.

Neighborhoods in Brief

HAUTE-VILLE   The Upper Town is surrounded by ramparts and stands on a bluff above the Fleuve St-Laurent (St. Lawrence River). It includes most of the sites for which the city is famous, among them Château Frontenac, the Terrasse Dufferin, and the Citadelle, begun by the French in the 18th century. Most of the buildings of the Haute-Ville are at least 100 years old, made of granite in similar styles, with few jarring modern intrusions. The Dufferin pedestrian promenade attracts crowds in all seasons for its magnificent views of the river and the land to the south.

BASSE-VILLE   At river level, the Lower Town is connected to the Haute-Ville by several streets and stairways. The Basse-Ville encompasses place Royale, the restored quartier du Petit-Champlain, the small Notre-Dame-des-Victoires church, and the Musée de la Civilisation, a highlight of any visit.

GRANDE-ALLÉE   This major artery runs from the St-Louis Gate in the fortified walls to avenue Taché. It passes the stately Parliament building and numerous terraced bars and restaurants, then later skirts the Musée du Québec and the Plains of Abraham. The city's large contemporary hotels are on or near the Grande-Allée.

2 Getting Around

Once you're within or near the walls of the Haute-Ville, virtually no place of interest, hotel, or restaurant is out of walking distance. In bad weather or when you're traversing between opposite ends of the Lower and Upper Towns, a taxi might be necessary, but in general, walking is the best way to explore.

BY BUS
Local buses run quite often and charge C$2.25 (US$1.50) in exact change; tickets purchased in a *dépanneur* (convenience store) cost C$1.70 (US$1.15). Bus no. 7 travels up and down rue St-Jean. No. 11 shuttles along Grande-Allée/rue St-Louis and, along with nos. 7 and 8, travels well into suburban Ste-Foy, for those who want to visit the shopping centers there. One-day bus passes are available for C$4.60 (US$3.05).

BY FUNICULAR
Though there are streets and stairs between the Upper Town and the Lower Town, there's also a funicular, which has long operated along an inclined 210-foot track between the Terrasse Dufferin and the quartier du Petit-Champlain. It was closed for a couple of years due to a fatal accident in 1996. Now that it's repaired (yet subject to occasional stoppages), the **upper station** is near the front of Château Frontenac and place d'Armes, while the **lower station** is actually inside the Maison Louis-Jolliet, on rue du Petit-Champlain.

BY TAXI
Taxis are everywhere, but they cluster in the largest packs near the big hotels and some of the larger squares of the Upper Town. In theory, you can hail one, but your best bet is to find one of their ranks, such as the one in place d'Armes or in front of the Hôtel de Ville (City Hall). Restaurant managers and hotel bell captains can also summon one for you. Fares are expensive, in part to compensate for the short distances of most rides. The starting rate is C$2.25 (US$1.50). To call a cab, try **Taxi Coop** (☎ 418/525-5191) or **Taxi Québec** (☎ 418/525-8123).

BY HORSE-DRAWN CARRIAGE
A romantic—and expensive—way to see the city is in a horse-drawn carriage, called a *calèche*. You can hire one at place d'Armes or on rue d'Auteuil, just within the city walls near the St-Louis Gate. A 30-minute tour with an English-speaking driver/guide is about C$50 (US$33). Carriages operate all summer, rain or shine.

BY CAR
You don't want to drive in Québec. On-street parking is very difficult in the cramped quarters of Vieux-Québec. If you find one of those rare spaces, be sure to check the signs for hours when parking is permissible. Where meters are in place, the charge is C25¢ (US15¢) per 15 minutes up to 120 minutes. Metered spots are free on Sundays, before 9am and after 6pm Monday to Wednesday and Saturday, and before 9am and after 9pm on Thursday and Friday.

Many of the smaller hotels have special arrangements with local garages, so their guests receive a C$3 or C$4 (US$2 or US$2.65) discount on the cost of a day's parking, usually C$10 (US$7) per day or more. Check with your hotel before parking in a lot or garage. If your hotel or auberge doesn't have access to a lot, plenty are available, clearly marked on the foldout city map available at tourist offices.

If you want to rent a car to explore the environs or travel elsewhere in Canada, try **Avis,** at the airport (☎ 800/879-2847 or 418/872-2861) and in the city (☎ 418/523-1075); **Budget,** at the airport (☎ 800/268-8900 or 418/872-9885) and in the city (☎ 418/692-3660); **Hertz Canada,** at the airport (☎ 800/654-3131 or 418/871-1571) and in the city (☎ 418/694-1224); **Thrifty,** at the airport (☎ 800/367-2277 or 418/877-2870) and in the city (☎ 418/683-1542); and **National/Tilden,** at the airport (☎ 418/871-1224) and in the city (☎ 418/692-1727). As the name says, **Discount,** 12 rue Ste-Anne in Vieux-Québec (☎ 418/692-1244), emphasizes economy. Remember, you'll save money by reserving a car before leaving home.

Fast Facts: Québec City

Area Code   The area code for Québec City is **418.**

American Express   There's no office right in town, but for lost traveler's checks, call ☎ **800/221-7282.** American Express keeps a customer service desk in two shopping centers in Ste-Foy, a bus or taxi ride away: **Les Galeries de la Capitale,** 5401 bd. des Galeries (☎ **418/627-2580**), and **Place Laurier,** 2740 bd. Laurier (☎ **418/658-8820**).

Consulate   The **U.S. Consulate** is near Château Frontenac, facing the Jardin des Gouverneurs at 2 place Terrasse-Dufferin (☎ **418/692-2095**).

Currency Exchange   Conveniently located near Château Frontenac, the bureau de change at 19 rue Ste-Anne and rue des Jardins is open Monday, Tuesday, and Friday 10am to 3pm and Wednesday and Thursday 10am to 6pm. On weekends, it's possible to change money in hotels and shops, but you'll get an equal or better rate at an ATM, such as the one at the corner of rues Ste-Anne and des Jardins.

Dentists   Call ☎ **418/653-5412** Monday 9am to 8pm, Tuesday and Wednesday 8am to 8pm, Thursday 8am to 6pm, and Friday 8am to 4pm. For weekend emergencies, call ☎ **418/656-6060.**

Doctors   For emergency treatment, call **Info-Santé** at ☎ **418/648-2626** 24 hours or the **Hôtel-Dieu de Québec Hospital** emergency room at ☎ **418/691-5042.**

Drugstores   **Caron and Bernier,** in the Upper Town at 38 côte du Palais (☎ **418/692-4252**), is open Monday to Friday 8:15am to 8pm and Saturday 9am to 3pm. In an emergency, it's necessary to travel to the suburbs to the **Pharmacie Brunet,** in Les Galeries Charlesbourg, 4266 Première Ave. (1er or First Avenue), in Charlesbourg (☎ **418/623-1571**), open 24 hours.

Emergencies   For the **police,** call ☎ **911.** For **Marine Search and Rescue** (the Canadian Coast Guard), call ☎ **800/648-3599** (Greater Québec area) 24 hours a day or ☎ **800/463-4393** (St. Lawrence River). For the **Poison Control Center,** call ☎ **800/463-5060** or 418/656-8090. For pet injuries or illnesses, call **Vet-Medic** at ☎ **418/647-2000,** 24 hours. (Incidentally, pet owners must pick up after their animals.)

Internet Access   You can check on your e-mail and send messages at **Brasserie Internet,** 855 Decarie, Ville St-Laurent (☎ **514/744-5345;** www.brasserie.ca), open Monday to Saturday 11am to 1am. Computer rental is C$3 (US$2) per half hour. A limited menu is available and the active bar serves a dozen imported beers.

Liquor Laws   All hard liquor in Québec is sold through official government stores operated by the Québec Société des Alcools. However, you can buy wine and beer in grocery stores and supermarkets. The legal drinking age in the province is 18.

Newspapers/Magazines   Québec City's English-language newspaper, the *Chronicle-Telegraph,* is the equivalent of a small-town paper, published each Wednesday. Major Canadian and American English-language newspapers and magazines are available in the newsstands of the large hotels and at vending machines around tourist corners in the old town. The leading French-language newspapers are *Le Soleil* and *Le Journal de Québec.*

Pets   Dogs and cats can be taken into Québec, but the Canadian Customs authorities at the frontier will want to see a rabies vaccination certificate less than 3 years old signed by a licensed veterinarian. If a pet is less than 3 months old and obviously healthy, the certificate isn't likely to be required. Check with U.S. Customs about bringing your pet back into the States. Most hotels in Québec City don't accept pets, so inquire about their policy before booking a room.

Police   For the **Québec City police,** call ☎ **911.** For the **Sûreté du Québec,** comparable to state police, call ☎ **418/461-2131.**

Post Office   The **main post office** (*bureau de poste*) is in the Lower Town, at 300 rue St-Paul near rue Abraham-Martin, not far from carré Parent (Parent Square) by the port (☎ **418/694-6176**). Hours are Monday to Friday 8am to 5:45pm. A convenient branch in the Upper Town, half a block down the hill from Château Frontenac, is at 3 rue Buade (☎ **418/694-6102**), with the same hours.

Smoking   It's true that French-speaking Québecers smoke more than other Canadians, despite heavy taxes on tobacco, and the province hasn't yet really clamped down on smoking in public places. Few restaurants have set aside no-smoking sections, and the establishment of cigar lounges is a peaking fad. When asked, hosts will attempt to seat you away from smokers.

Taxes   Most goods and services in Canada are taxed 7% by the federal government. The province of Québec adds an extra 7.5% tax on goods and services, including hotel stays. In Québec, the federal tax appears on the bill as the TPS (elsewhere in Canada, it's called the GST), and the provincial tax is known as the TVQ. You may receive a rebate on both the federal and the provincial tax on items you've bought but not used in Québec, as well as on lodging. To take advantage of this, request the necessary forms at duty-free shops and hotels and submit them, with the original receipts, within a year of the purchase. Contact the Canadian consulate or Québec tourism office for up-to-the-minute details about taxes and rebates.

Telephones   The phone system, operated by Bell Canada, closely resembles the U.S. model. All operators (dial ☎ **0**—zero—to get one) speak French and English. Pay phones in Québec require C25¢ (US17¢) for a 3-minute local call. Directory information calls (dial ☎ **411**) are free. Both local and long-distance calls usually cost more from hotels—sometimes a lot more, so check. Directories (*annuaires des téléphones*) come in white pages (residential) and yellow pages (commercial).

Time   Québec City is on the same time as New York, Boston, Montréal, and Toronto. It's an hour behind Halifax.

3 Accommodations

Staying in one of the small hotels or auberges within the walls of the Upper Town can be one of Québec's memorable experiences. That isn't a guarantee it'll be enjoyable. Standards of comfort, amenities, and prices fluctuate so wildly from one small hotel to another—even within a single place—that it's wise to shop around and examine rooms before registering. From rooms with private bathrooms, minibars, and cable TVs to walk-up budget accommodations with linoleum floors and toilets down the hall, Québec has a wide enough variety of lodgings to suit most tastes and wallets.

If cost is a prime consideration, note that prices drop significantly November to April, except around Christmas and Winter Carnival. On the other hand, if you prefer the conveniences of large chain hotels and Château Frontenac is fully booked, you'll need to go outside the walls to the newer part of town. The three high-rise hotels out there are within walking distance of the attractions in the Old City or are only a quick bus or taxi ride away. Though Québec City has far fewer first-class hotels than Montréal, there are still a sufficient number to provide for the crowds of businesspeople and well-heeled tourists who flock to the city year-round. And in recent years, a clutch of new small hotels and inns has greatly enhanced the lodging stock.

The city's inexpensive auberges are generally smaller places, often converted residences or carved out of several row houses. They offer fewer of the usual electronic gadgets—air-conditioning and TVs are far from standard—and may be several floors high, without elevators. Even with an advance reservation, always ask to see two or three rooms before making a choice in this price category. Unless otherwise noted, all rooms in the lodgings below have private bathrooms.

Note: See the "Québec City" map (p. 274) to locate most of the hotels in this section.

HAUTE-VILLE (UPPER TOWN)
VERY EXPENSIVE

✪ **Château Frontenac.** 1 rue des Carrières (at rue St-Louis), Québec, PQ G1R 4P5. ☎ **800/828-7447** or 418/692-3861. Fax 418/692-1751. www.cphotels.ca. E-mail agentres@lcf.cphotels.ca. 626 units. A/C MINIBAR TV TEL. Mid-May to mid-Oct C$209–C$409 (US$139–US$273) double, C$669–C$1,250 (US$446–US$834) suite; late Oct to early May C$129–C$329 (US$86–US$219) double, C$559–C$975 (US$373–US$650) suite. AE, CB, DC, DISC, ER, MC, V. Valet parking C$15 (US$10).

Québec's magical "castle" turned 100 years old in 1993, and in celebration the management added a new 66-room wing—since the hotel serves as the very symbol of the city, care was taken to replicate the original architectural style throughout. In the past, the hotel hosted Queen Elizabeth and Prince Philip, and during World War II, Churchill and Roosevelt had the entire place to themselves for a conference. The hotel was built in phases, following the landline, so the wide halls take crooked paths. The price of a guest room depends on its size, location, and view or lack of one, and on

Reserving on the Web

For more information about hotels in the city and nearby, log on to **www. destinationquebec.com.**

A Home Away from Home

Many owners of private homes make one to five rooms available for guests and provide breakfast, generally at C$50 to C$80 (US$33 to US$53) double. This kind of B&B doesn't have a sign out front, and the only way to reserve one is through one of the umbrella organizations with listings. One is **Bonjour Québec,** 3765 bd. de Monaco, Québec, PQ G1R 1N4 (☎ **418/527-1465**). Be aware that some hosts don't permit smoking or children or pets. They may have only one or two bathrooms to be shared by four or five rooms, or all their rooms may be on the fourth floor in a walk-up, or they may be located far from the center. As with the inexpensive lodgings listed below, TVs and air-conditioning aren't standard. A deposit is typically required, and minimum stays of 2 nights are common. Credit cards may not be accepted.

how recently it was renovated. In-room movies are available, and many rooms are no-smoking.

Dining/Diversions: The fare in the dining rooms has yet to measure up to the grandeur of the physical spaces, though the kitchen of Le Champlain is striving to improve. The casual Café de la Terrasse offers a buffet breakfast and dinner/dancing on Saturday nights. Two bars overlook the Terrasse Dufferin. Le Bistro is the lower-level snack bar.

Amenities: Concierge, room service (daily 6:30am to 11:30pm), dry cleaning/laundry, baby-sitting, limo service, massage, secretarial services, express checkout; indoor pool, large gym with specialized weight machines, kiddie pool, Jacuzzi; business center.

EXPENSIVE

Manoir Victoria. 44 côte du Palais (at rue St-Jean), Québec, PQ G1R 4H8. ☎ **800/463-6283** or 418/692-1030. Fax 418/692-3822. www.manoir-victoria.com. E-mail admin@manoir-victoria.com. 145 units. A/C TV TEL. Mid-May to mid-Oct C$109–C$199 (US$73–US$133) double, C$225–C$350 (US$150–US$233) suite; late Oct to early May C$89–C$159 (US$59–US$106) double, C$150–C$300 (US$100–US$200) suite. Extra person C$20–C$25 (US$13–US$17). MC, V. Children under 18 share parents' room free.

The sprawling lobby with gloomy wood paneling and chunky sofas isn't especially beguiling, but the location beside the St-Jean restaurant/bar scene is a plus for many. An additional extra is the indoor pool, rare in the city. The hotel sprawls all the way from the main entrance on côte de Palais to adjacent St-Jean, zigging around a couple of stores. A long staircase reaches the lobby, but elevators make the trip to most of the guest rooms. The rooms follow no pattern in furnishings or dimensions—with step-downs, split-levels, and triangular and L-shapes, sometimes all together—so by all means see two or three.

Dining: The Resto-Bistro St-James and La Table du Manoir Victoria are serviceable, the latter serving a number of traditional Québecois dishes. Guests get a 20% discount on meals.

Amenities: Dry cleaning, laundry/valet; indoor pool, fitness center with Nautilus machines and 10 exercycles.

MODERATE

Cap Diamant Maison de Touristes. 39 av. Ste-Geneviève (near rue de Brébeuf), Québec, PQ G1R 4B3. ☎ **418/694-0313.** www.hcapdiamant.qc.ca. E-mail hcapdiamant@oricom.ca. 12 units. A/C TV. Summer C$80–C$125 (US$53–US$83) double; winter C$65–C$85 (US$43–US$57) double. Rates include breakfast. Extra person C$15 (US$10). MC, V. Parking C$10 (US$7) in nearby lot.

Every room is different in this amiable guest house only 2½ blocks from the Jardin des Gouverneurs, its assortment of furniture including brass beds, Victorian memorabilia, and nonspecific retro pieces retrieved from attics. In back of the 1826 house are an enclosed porch and a garden. The Plains of Abraham are right behind it, leading up to the Citadelle. All guest rooms have small unstocked refrigerators and overlook the Old City rooftops. The stairs are very steep throughout, including the entrance, and there's no elevator. When reserving, ask about the just-renovated rooms next door.

Château Bellevue. 16 rue Laporte (at rue Ste-Genevieve), Québec, PQ G1R 4M9. ☎ **800/ 463-2617** or 418/692-2573. Fax 418/692-4876. www.vieux-quebec.com/bellevue. E-mail bellevueAvieux-quebec.com. 57 units. A/C TV TEL. Late Oct to Apr 30 C$79–C$119 (US$53–US$79) double; Winter Carnival and May to late Oct C$109–C$149 (US$73–US$99). Extra person C$10 (US$7). Rates include breakfast (except May to mid-Oct). Packages available Oct–May. AE, CB, DC, ER, MC, V. Free valet parking.

Occupying several row houses at the top of the Parc des Gouverneurs, this minihotel has a pleasant lobby with leather couches and chairs and a helpful staff, as well as some of the creature comforts lacking in smaller auberges nearby. While the guest rooms are small and often suffer from unfortunate decorating choices, they're quiet for the most part; a few higher-priced units overlook the park. The hotel's private parking is behind the building, a notable convenience in this congested part of town, though there are only a few spaces. A first-night deposit by check or credit card is required. If you're shopping for a room on the spot and find that this is full, be aware there are 10 other choices within a block in any direction.

Hôtel Vieux Québec. 1190 rue St-Jean (main entrance on rue de l'Hôtel-Dieu), Québec, PQ G1R 4J2. ☎ **800/361-7787** or 418/692-1850. Fax 418/692-5637. www.hvq.com. E-mail reserv@hvq.com. 41 units. A/C TV TEL. May to mid-Oct, Christmas week, and Winter Carnival C$119–C$149 (US$79–US$99) double; late Oct to Apr C$59–C$69 (US$39–US$46) double. Extra person C$10 (US$7). AE, DC, ER, MC, V. Parking C$6 (US$4).

This century-old brick hotel has been renovated with care. The guest rooms are equipped with sofas, two double beds, hair dryers, and modern bathrooms; most have kitchenettes. Ask for one of the 24 rooms recently redone with new carpeting and furniture; two of these are junior suites with Jacuzzis. The place is popular with families, skiers, and the groups of visiting high-school students who descend on the city in late spring. In addition to Les Frères de la Côte on the ground floor, there are many moderately priced restaurants and nightspots nearby.

Manoir Sur-le-Cap. 9 av. Ste-Geneviève (near rue LaPorte), Québec, PQ G1R 4A7. ☎ **418/ 694-1987.** Fax 418/667-4234. www.manoir-sur-le-cap.com. 14 units. TV. June–Oct C$95–C$125 (US$63–US$83) double, C$225 (US$150) condo; Nov–May C$70–C$105 (US$47–US$70) double, C$150 (US$100) condo. AE, MC, V.

All is freshly painted and shellacked at this overhauled-from-top-to-bottom inn on the south side of the Parc des Gouverneurs, opposite Château Frontenac. Many guest rooms have exposed stone or brick walls. Obviously the price is right, unless you require air-conditioning or a phone and don't want to climb possibly four floors of stairs. Upgrade to the "condo," in a separate building in back, and you'll get an apartment with a working fireplace, a phone, a VCR, and a kitchenette with microwave, coffeemaker, and basic crockery. When booking, request parking at one of the nearby lots. There's no smoking, but English is spoken.

INEXPENSIVE

Auberge La Chouette. 71 rue d'Auteuil (near rue St-Louis), Québec, PQ G1R 4C3. ☎ **418/ 694-0232.** 10 units. A/C TV TEL. May–Sept C$65–C$90 (US$43–US$60) double; Oct–Apr C$60–C$75 (US$40–US$50) double. AE, MC, V. Parking C$6 (US$4).

Across from Esplanade Park and near the Porte St-Louis, this auberge has a capable Asian restaurant, Apsara (see "Dining"), on the main floor. Despite its presence, the no-frills guest rooms on three floors reached by the spiral stairway (no elevator) are quiet. Examine your room first. The Citadelle and Winter Carnival and Québec Summer Festival activities are only minutes away.

Auberge St-Louis. 48 rue St-Louis (between rues Ste-Ursule and Parloir), Québec, PQ G1R 3Z3. ☎ **418/692-2424.** Fax 418/692-3797. 27 units, 14 with bathroom. A/C TV. May–Oct 15 C$49 (US$33) double without bathroom, C$82 (US$55) double with bathroom; Oct 16–Apr 30 C$49 (US$33) double without bathroom, C$65 (US$43) double with bathroom. Rates include breakfast. Extra person C$10 (US$7). MC, V. Nearby parking C$7 (US$4.75).

Guest rooms come in a variety of configurations, with occasional features that add some visual interest, like a carved fireplace mantel or a stained-glass window. But the reasons to stay here are the low prices and the good location near city hall. Some rooms have a sink and shower but no toilet, and some have a color or black-and-white TV.

ON OR NEAR THE GRANDE-ALLÉE
EXPENSIVE

Hilton International Québec. 3 place Québec, PQ G1K 7M9. ☎ **800/445-8667** or 418/647-2411. Fax 418/847-6488. www.hilton.com. 604 units. A/C MINIBAR TV TEL. C$149–C$265 (US$99–US$177) double; from C$355 (US$237) suite. Extra person C$20 (US$13). Children any age stay free in parents' room. Packages available. AE, CB, DC, DISC, ER, MC, V. Parking C$16 (US$11). Head east along the Grande-Allée, and just before the St-Louis Gate turn left on rue Dufferin, then left again as you pass the Parliament building; the hotel is 1 block ahead.

Superior on virtually every count to the other mid-rise contemporary hotels outside the old town (excluding Le Capitole, below), this Hilton is true to the breed, the clear choice for executives and leisure travelers who can't bear to live without their gadgets. The location—across from the city walls and near the Parliament—is excellent. It's also connected to the Place Québec complex of 75 shops, two cinemas, and the Convention Center. The public rooms are big and brassy, while the guest chambers are in need of freshening and have started getting it. Most have one or two large beds, plus in-room movies. The upper-floor views of the St. Lawrence, old Québec, and the Laurentian Mountains are grand. The staff is generally efficient and congenial. No-smoking rooms are available.

Dining/Diversions: The recently overhauled Le Caucus restaurant serves buffet-style as well as à la carte meals. Fridays and Saturdays are theme nights, with live entertainment.

⊕ Family-Friendly Hotels

Château Frontenac *(see p. 280)* Yes, you can sleep in a fairy-tale castle that's the symbol of a city, with an indoor pool just for kids and street performers just outside the door.

Hôtel Vieux Québec *(see p. 282)* Popular with families and school groups, it's in a good location for exploring the Upper or the Lower Town.

Radisson Gouverneurs *(see p. 284)* The rooftop pool here is a treat, with its indoor water route to the outside. Winter Carnival activities are a quick and easy walk away.

Amenities: Room service, dry cleaning/laundry, baby-sitting, car rental, airport shuttle; heated outdoor pool (summer only), health club with sauna and whirlpool; jogging track; business center.

✪ Le Capitole. 972 rue St-Jean (1 block west of Porte St-Jean), PQ G1R 1R5. ☎ **800/363-4040** or 418/694-4040. Fax 418/694-1916. www.lecapitole.com. E-mail admin@lecapitole.com. 40 units. A/C MINIBAR TV TEL. June to early Oct C$145–C$205 (US$97–US$137) double, C$215 (US$143) suite; mid-Oct to May C$99–C$175 (US$66–US$117) double, C$209 (US$139) suite. Packages available. AE, MC, V.

Le Capitole is as happily eccentric as the three business hotels below are conventional, and its entrance is squeezed almost to anonymity between a restaurant, a theater, and a shuttered cinema on place d'Youville. The guest rooms borrow from art deco and incorporate stars in the carpets and clouds on the ceiling. Most tubs have whirlpools and beds have down comforters. All rooms have VCRs and CD players, with 120 videos available free. Coffeemakers, hair dryers, and phones with dataports are standard.

Dining/Diversions: Ristorante Il Teatro is half continental and half show biz, with platinum records on the walls, boxed plates autographed by celebrities, and a busy sidewalk terrace. Down the central hall is the Théâtre Capitole, which presents live shows when it isn't hosting weddings and banquets.

Amenities: Concierge, room service, dry cleaning/laundry.

Loews Le Concorde. 1225 place Montcalm (at Grande-Allée), Québec, PQ G1R 4W6. ☎ **800/463-5256** or 418/647-2222. Fax 418/647-4710. www.loewshotels.com. 431 units. A/C MINIBAR TV TEL. May–Oct C$125–C$245 (US$83–US$163) double, Nov–Apr C$99–C$149 (US$66–US$99) double; from C$225 (US$150) suite. Extra person over 17 C$20 (US$13); children under 17 share parents' room free. Ski and weekend packages available. AE, DC, ER, MC, V. Parking garage C$14 (US$9).

From outside, this building is a visual insult to the skyline, blighting a neighborhood of late Victorian town houses. Once you enter, though, you may forget the affront, at least if you have business to do and can't be bothered with aesthetics. The standard guest rooms have marble bathrooms with hair dryers, prints of Québec City street scenes, in-room movies, and three phones. They bestow spectacular views of the river and the old city, even from the lower floors. There are seven no-smoking floors and seven business-class floors. Of all the hotels listed here, this is the farthest from the old town, about a 10-minute walk to the walls, then another 10 minutes to the center of the Haute-Ville.

Dining/Diversions: L'Astral is a revolving rooftop restaurant, with a bar and live piano music Tuesday to Sunday. Le Café serves light lunch or dinner, and La Place Montcalm offers buffet or à la carte breakfasts.

Amenities: Concierge, room service (daily 6am to midnight), dry cleaning/laundry; small fitness facility with sauna and some exercise equipment, outdoor heated pool (Apr to Nov; access to pool in a private club during other months).

Radisson Gouverneurs. 690 bd. René-Lévesque est, Québec, PQ G1R 5A8. ☎ **800/463-2820** or 418/647-1717 from eastern Canada and Ontario, 800/333-3333 from elsewhere. Fax 418/647-2146. 383 units. A/C TV TEL. C$140–C$195 (US$93–US$130) double; from C$225 (US$150) suite. Extra adult C$15 (US$10); children under 16 stay free in parents' room. AE, DC, DISC, ER, MC, V. Parking C$11 (US$7). Turn left off Grande-Allée, and then left again onto Dufferin, just before the St-Louis Gate in the city wall. Once past the Parliament building, take the first left. The hotel is 2 blocks ahead.

Part of Place Québec, a multiuse complex, the hotel is connected to the city's convention center. It's 1 block from the Hilton, 2 blocks from Porte Kent in the city wall, and not far from the Québec Parliament, a location likely to fit almost any businessperson's needs. It is, however, an uphill climb from the old city (like all the hotels and inns along or near the Grande-Allée). Some guest rooms have minibars; all have in-room movies, hair dryers, and coffeemakers. There are three no-smoking floors and two executive floors, with reception two levels up. The rooms are scheduled for renovation during 2000—ask for one on which work has been completed.

Dining: Le Café serves buffet and à la carte meals.

Amenities: Room service, dry cleaning/laundry, baby-sitting; indoor waterway leading to outdoor pool (open summer); fully equipped and staffed health club with exercycles, sauna, and whirlpool; business center.

MODERATE

Château Laurier. 695 Grande-Allée est (at rue Georges-V est), Québec, PQ G1R 2K4. ☎ **418/522-8108.** Fax 418/524-8768. www.vieux-quebec.com/laurier. E-mail laurier@ vieux-quebec.com. 113 units. A/C TV TEL. May to mid-Oct C$109–C$179 (US$73–US$119) double; late Oct to Apr C$79–C$129 (US$53–US$86) double. AE, DC, ER, MC, V. Parking C$10 (US$7).

Smack in the midst of the action and racket of the Grande-Allée, this old-timer has just lifted its rather dowdy countenance by taking over an adjoining building and adding 65 larger, jazzier guest rooms. Some of them have working fireplaces, Jacuzzis, and king beds and are clearly more desirable than the plainer and more cramped older rooms. A bar and bistro remain in front, down a few steps from the street. The lobby is being relocated to the rue Georges-V side, and the hotel is only 2 blocks west of the St-Louis Gate.

INEXPENSIVE

✪ **Relais Charles-Alexander.** 91 Grande-Allée est (at av. Galipeault), Québec, PQ G1R 2H5. ☎ **418/523-1220.** Fax 418/523-9556. www.quebecweb.com/rca. E-mail relais@ oricom.ca. 22 units, 14 with bathroom. A/C TV. C$75–C$95 (US$50–US$63) double. Rates include breakfast. AE, MC, V. Parking nearby C$6 (US$4).

On the ground floor of this charming brick-faced B&B is an art gallery, which also serves as the breakfast room. This stylish use of space extends to the guest rooms as well, which are crisply maintained and decorated with eclectic antique and wicker pieces and reproductions. The front rooms are larger, and most rooms have phones; they're quiet for the most part, since the inn is just outside the orbit of the sometimes-raucous Grande-Allée terrace bars. Yet the St-Louis Gate is less than a 10-minute walk away from the hubbub.

BASSE-VILLE (LOWER TOWN)
VERY EXPENSIVE

✪ **Auberge St-Antoine.** 10 rue St-Antoine (at rue Dalhousie), Québec, PQ G1K 4C9. ☎ **888/692-2211** or 418/692-2211. Fax 418/692-1177. www.saint-antoine.com/ info.html. E-mail info@saint-antoine.com. 31 units. A/C TV TEL. C$219–C$299 (US$146–US$199) double; C$299–C$479 (US$199–US$319) suite. Rates include breakfast. Extra person C$20 (US$13). Children under 12 stay free in parents' room. AE, DC, MC, V. Free parking. Follow rue Dalhousie around the Lower Town to rue St-Antoine; the hotel is next to the Musée de la Civilisation.

The centerpiece of this uncommonly attractive boutique hotel is the 1830 maritime warehouse that contains the lobby and meeting rooms, with the original dark beams and stone floor. Buffet breakfasts and afternoon wine and cheese are set out in the lobby, where guests relax in wing chairs next to the hooded fireplace. The owners' other occupation as interior designers is seen to great effect everywhere. Canny mixes of antique and reproduction furniture are in both the public and the private areas. The guest rooms, in an adjoining modern wing and a newly remodeled 1727 house, are spacious, with such extra decorative touches as custom-made iron bedsteads and tables. The big bathrooms have robes and hair dryers. Several rooms have private terraces, one of which has a three-hole putting green. Prices are highest for the 13 rooms with river views, but since a large parking lot intervenes, those without the view are a better deal. The eight new suites have kitchenettes, fax machines, and computer jacks.

EXPENSIVE

Auberge St-Pierre. 79 rue St-Pierre (behind the Musée de la Civilisation), Québec, PQ G1K 4A3. ☎ **888/268-1017** or 418/694-7981. Fax 418/694-0406. www.auberge.qc.ca. E-mail st-pierre@auberge.qc.ca. 32 units. A/C TV TEL. May 17–Oct 14 C$119–C$209 (US$79–US$139) double, C$169–C$199 (US$113–US$133) suite; Oct 15–May 16 C$119–C$179 (US$79–US$119) double, C$189–C$209 (US$126–US$139) suite. Rates include breakfast. AE, CB, DC, ER, MC, V. Parking nearby C$10 (US$7).

The paint has dried and the start-up bugs have been scoured since the doors opened in 1997, and this is yet another welcome entry in the lengthening roster of Basse-Ville auberges. The full breakfasts are special, cooked to order by the chef in the open kitchen. The commodious suites are a possible extra luxury on a longer visit, especially since they have modest kitchen facilities. The window air conditioners are somewhat underpowered for the extra space, if that's a consideration. Robes and hair dryers are provided. The early–19th-century building started out as a headquarters for a fire-insurance company.

✪ **Hôtel Dominion 1912.** 126 rue St-Pierre (at rue St-Paul), Québec, PQ G1K 4A8. ☎ **888/833-5253** or 418/692-2224. Fax 418/692-4403. www.hoteldominion.com. E-mail hotel.dominion@sympatico.ca. 40 units. A/C MINIBAR TV TEL. Oct 15–Apr 30 C$119–C$179 (US$79–US$119) double; May 1–Oct 14 C$139–C$239 (US$93–US$159) double. Rates include breakfast. AE, DC, ER, MC, V. Parking C$5–C$10 (US$3.35–US$7).

If there were space enough to recommend only one hotel, this would be it. The owners stripped the inside of the 1912 Dominion Fish & Fruit building down to the studs and pipes and started over. Even the least expensive rooms are large, the queen- or king-sized beds heaped with linen-covered pillows and feather duvets. Neutral colors extend to the spacious bathrooms and their robes. Hair dryers and coffeemakers are standard, and a fruit basket awaits. Continental breakfast is set out in the handsome lobby and can be taken out to the terrace in back. For lodgings this good, prices started out remarkably low, but as expected, they're now close to market norms. Even so, this remains one of the most desirable hotels in town. Go before the masses find it.

MODERATE

Auberge Le Priori. 15 rue Sault-au-Matelot (at rue St-Antoine), Québec, PQ G1K 3Y7. ☎ **800/351-3992** or 418/692-3992. Fax 418/692-0883. www.quebecweb.com/lepriori. E-mail priori@sympatico.ca. 26 units. TV TEL. May–Oct C$125–C$140 (US$83–US$93) double, C$160–C$290 (US$107–US$193) suite; Nov–Apr C$110–C$125 (C$73–C$83) double, C$145–C$250 (US$97–US$167) suite. Packages available. AE, DC, ER, MC, V. Parking C$8 (US$5).

A forerunner of the blossoming Lower Town hotel scene, Le Priori provides a playful postmodern ambiance behind the somber facade of a 1766 house. Hot French designer Phillipe Starck inspired the owners, who deployed versions of his conical stainless-steel sinks in the guest rooms and sensual multinozzle showers in the small bathrooms. The queen-size beds have black tubular frames and soft duvets. The dim lighting doesn't help readers, however, and in some rooms, a clawfoot tub sits beside the bed. The suites have sitting rooms with wood-burning fireplaces, kitchens, and bathrooms with Jacuzzis. The hotel houses the new Le Zénith restaurant (see "Dining"), an only-adequate replacement for the admirable Laurie Raphaël, which moved to larger quarters (see "Dining").

Hôtel le St-Paul. 229½ rue St-Paul (near rue Abraham-Martin), Québec, PQ G1K 3W3. ☎ **888/794-4414** or 418/694-4414. Fax 418/694-0889. www.quebecweb.com/ hotellest-paul. 26 units. A/C TV TEL. June–Oct C$110–C$225 (US$73–US$150) double; Nov–May C$90–C$170 (US$60–US$113) double. AE, DC, ER, MC, V.

This 1854 mid-Victorian near the rail station became the Basse Ville's latest addition to the hotel scene with its 1997 renovation. While it isn't quite up to the considerable standards of most of those mentioned above, neither is it as expensive, and staying here represents no deprivation. Half the guest rooms have king-sized beds, and the phones have dataports; some rooms have small fridges and/or whirlpool bathtubs. The ground-floor Péché Véniel restaurant is under separate management. Rue St-Paul's antique row is steps away.

4 Dining

Once you're within the ancient walls, walking along streets that look to have been transplanted intact from Brittany or Provence, you might imagine that one superb dining experience after another is in store. Alas, that isn't true. If that French tire company decided to cast its hotly contested stars on Québec restaurants, they might grudgingly part with three or four. The truth is that this gloriously scenic city has only one or two restaurants that even approach comparison with the best of Paris, Manhattan, or Montréal. While it's easy to eat well in the capital (even, in a few isolated cases, quite well), the dining highlight of your stay will lie elsewhere.

But that's not to imply you're in for barely edible meals served by sullen waiters. By sticking to any of the many competent bistros, the handful of Asian eateries, and one or two of the emerging *nuovo Italiano* trattorias, you'll do fine. Another step up, two or three ambitious enterprises tease the palate with hints of higher achievement. Even the blatantly touristy restaurants along rue St-Louis and around place d'Armes can produce decent meals.

Curiously, for a city standing beside a great waterway and a day's sail from some of the world's best fishing grounds, seafood isn't given much attention. Mussels and salmon are on most menus, but cherish any place that goes beyond those staples. Game is popular, however, and everything from venison, rabbit, and duck to more exotic quail, goose, caribou, and wapiti is available.

At the better places, and even some of those that might seem inexplicably popular, reservations are all but essential during traditional holidays and the festivals that pepper the social calendar. Other times, it's usually necessary to book ahead only for weekend evenings. Dress codes are required in only a few restaurants, but Québecers are a stylish lot. "Dressy casual" works almost everywhere. Remember that for the Québecois, *dîner* (dinner) is lunch and *souper* (supper) is dinner, though for the sake of consistency, I've used the word *dinner* in the common American sense. They tend to have that evening meal earlier than Montréalers, at 6 or 7pm rather than at 8pm. When figuring costs, add the 14½% in federal and provincial taxes.

Note: See the "Québec City" map (p. 274) to locate most of the restaurants in this section.

Dining on the Web

The useful Web site **www.otc.cuq.qc.ca** gives restaurant addresses and phone numbers and often their menus and prices, if often with less detail than you might hope. Another possibility is **www.restaurant.ca**.

HAUTE-VILLE (UPPER TOWN)
EXPENSIVE

Aux Anciens Canadiens. 34 rue St-Louis (at rue Haldimand). ☎ **418/692-1627.** Reservations recommended. Main courses C$13–C$19 (US$9–US$13), table d'hôte menu C$14 (US$9) at lunch, C$25–C$41 (US$17–US$27) at dinner. AE, CB, DC, ER, MC, V. Daily noon–midnight. QUÉBECOIS.

In the middle of the tourist swarms, this venerable restaurant is in what's probably the city's oldest (1677) house. Putting aside a reluctance to take up space pointing out restaurants readers will inevitably encounter on their own, let me assure you the food at this famous attraction is both well prepared and fairly priced. It is, in addition, one of the best places in La Belle Province to sample the cooking that has its roots in the earliest years of New France: Don't count on the ancient Québecois recipes tasting this good anywhere else. Caribou flesh and maple syrup figure in many of the dishes, including the meat pie, Lac Brome duck, tournedos, and a definitive rendering of luscious sugar pie. The servings are large enough to ward off winter for a week. The kitchen's greatest sin is oversalting, so always taste first. The servers are in costume, and there are carved wooden bas-reliefs of regional genre scenes.

Le St-Amour. 48 rue Ste-Ursule (near rue St-Louis). ☎ **418/694-0667.** Reservations recommended for dinner. Main courses C$21–C$29 (US$14–US$19); table d'hôte menu C$10–C$16 (US$7–US$10) at lunch, C$29–C$33 (US$19–US$22) at dinner; gastronomic dinner C$54 (US$36). AE, DC, ER, MC, V. June to early Oct daily 11:30am–2:30pm; daily 6–11pm; rest of the year closed for lunch Sat–Mon. CONTEMPORARY FRENCH.

At the most romantic restaurant in a city that knows seductive atmosphere, you pass a front room with lace curtains and potted greenery into a covered terrace lit by candles and flickering Victorian gas fixtures. The roof is retracted on warm nights, revealing a splash of stars. However, there has been a perceptible slip in the food and the service. The kitchen lacks the focused imagination it once had, perhaps because the chef has been at this post for 20 years, and the waitstaff is less attentive than the prices warrant. But if it has dipped from its award-winning stature of a few years ago, it remains a favorite for a hand-holding dinner *à deux*. The herb-crusted rack of lamb and saffron-touched pike fillet garnished with seafood niblets are good enough and not too distracting. The dessert menu selections are broken down into the categories "Chocolatey," "Fruity," "Warm," and "Cold."

Serge Bruyère. 1200 rue St-Jean (at côte de la Fabrique). ☎ **418/694-0618.** Reservations recommended for dinner. Main courses C$10–C$29 (US$7–US$19) at Chez Livernois, C$17–C$32 (US$11–C$21) at La Grand Table; table d'hôte menu C$10–C$16 (US$7–US$11) at lunch, C$19–C$35 (US$13–US$23) at dinner at Chez Livernois; gastronomic dinners C$75 and C$120 (US$50 and US$80) at La Grand Table. AE, DC, MC, V. Daily 8am–10:30pm. ECLECTIC.

The eponymous owner bought this wedge-shaped building in 1979 and set about creating a multilevel dining emporium that had something for everyone. Serge Bruyère, however, died young and tragically. His executive chef carries on along a similar path, serving all meals from informal breakfasts to lavish late dinners. At ground level is a casual **cafe** with a cold case displaying salads and pastries—just the place for a leisurely afternoon snack. Up a long staircase at the back is **Chez Livernois,** with three semi-circular windows looking down on the street. This bistro is best for lunches, concentrating on grills and pastas that come with rounds of crusty, chewy bread. Another flight up is the formal **La Grand Table,** offering a pricey menu both highly imaginative and immaculately presented. Gaps between the eight courses of the gastronomic extravaganza stretch on—and on—for an entire evening. Whether the showy creations justify the raves and the sedate pace of the meal is up to you. Dress well and arrive with a healthy credit card.

MODERATE

Les Frères de la Côte. 1190 rue St-Jean (near côte de la Fabrique). ☎ **418/692-5445.** Reservations recommended. Main courses C$10–C$18 (US$7–US$12); table d'hôte C$15–C$17 (US$10–US$11). AE, DC, ER, MC, V. Daily 11:30am–11pm. MEDITERRANEAN.

At the east end of the old town's liveliest nightlife strip, this supremely casual cafe/pizzeria is as loud as any dance club, all hard surfaces with patrons shouting over the booming stereo music. None of this discourages a single soul—even on a Monday night. Chefs in straw hats in the open kitchen in back crank out a dozen kinds of pizza—thin-crusted, with unusual toppings that work—and about as many pasta versions, which are less interesting. The bountiful platters of fish and meats, often in the form of brochettes, make appetizers unnecessary. Keep this spot in mind when kids are in tow—there's no way they could make enough noise to bother other customers. Outside tables are available in warm weather, and breakfast is served June 24 to September 5, 8 to 10am.

INEXPENSIVE

Apsara. 71 rue d'Auteuil (near the St-Louis Gate). ☎ **418/694-0232.** Main courses C$12–C$14 (US$8–US$9). AE, MC, V. Mon–Fri 11:30am–2pm; daily 5:30–11pm. SOUTH ASIAN.

This 1845 Victorian row house is home to one of the city's best Asian restaurants. The interior looks rather like the British consulate in Shanghai might, welcoming diners who come for a gastronomic tour arching from Vietnam to Cambodia to Thailand. Head straight for the last stop, since the Thai dishes are clearly masters over the mostly wan alternatives. The menu includes phad-Thai (fried rice with shrimp and beans), satays, mou sati (brochettes), and spicy roast beef. An enticing possibility is the seven-course sampler meal of all three cuisines for two at C$38 (US$25). House wines aren't expensive, but they aren't too good either. Opt for beer. The service swoops from adequate to appallingly inept.

Chez Temporel. 25 rue Couillard (near côte de la Fabrique). ☎ **418/694-1813.** Most items C$2–C$7 (US$1.35–US$4.55). V. Daily 7am–2am. LIGHT FARE.

This Latin Quarter cafe with tile floors and wooden tables attracts denizens of nearby Université Laval, who play chess, swap philosophical insights, and clack away at their

Take Advantage of the Table d'Hôte

As throughout the province, the best dining deals are the table d'hôte (fixed-price) meals. Most full-service restaurants offer them, if only at lunch. As a rule, they include at least soup or salad, a main course, and dessert. Some places add in an extra appetizer and/or a beverage, for the approximate à la carte price of the main course alone.

> ### ⓕ Family-Friendly Restaurants
>
> **Le Cochon Dingue** *(see p. 292)*   It's big so kids can let themselves go here (to a point). And eating in a place called "The Crazy Pig" is something to write home to grandma about.
>
> **Les Frères de la Côte** *(see p. 289)*   This pizza place is so loud even fussy kids won't bother the other customers. The 8-year-old can have her slice with nothing on it and the teenager can slouch over his pie with everything (except anchovies). And it won't cost the world.

laptops from breakfast until well past midnight. It could be a Left Bank hangout for Sorbonne students and their profs. Capture a table and you can hold it forever for just a cappuccino or two. Croissants, jam, butter, and a bowl of café au lait cost half as much as a hotel breakfast. Later in the day, drop by for a *croque-monsieur* (grilled-cheese sandwich), quiche, or plate of cheese with a beer or glass of wine. Just about everything is made on the premises. Only 20 people can be seated downstairs, with another 26 upstairs, where the light is filtered through stained-glass windows.

Le Casse-Crêpe Breton. 1136 rue St-Jean (near rue Garneau). ☎ **418/692-0438.** Most items C$3.50–C$6 (US$2.35–US$3.65). No credit cards. Daily 7:30am–1am. CRÊPES/LIGHT FARE.

Eat at the bar and watch the crêpes being made, or attempt to snag one of the 14 tables nearby or in the adjoining room. Often as not, you'll have to wait a while. The main-course crêpes come with two to five ingredients of your choice, usually a combo of ham, cheese, mushrooms, eggs, and pepperoni. The dessert versions are stuffed with jams or fruit and cream. Soups, salads, and sandwiches are as inexpensive as the crêpes. The name of the cafe is a play on the word *casse-croûte*, which means "break crust." When it gets busy, the service is glacial. Beer is served in bottles or on tap.

ON OR NEAR THE GRANDE-ALLÉE
EXPENSIVE

✪ **Le Paris-Brest.** 590 Grande-Allée est (at rue de la Chevrotière). ☎ **418/529-2243.** Reservations recommended. Main courses C$18–C$25 (US$12–US$16); table d'hôte menu C$9–C$14 (US$6–US$9) at lunch, C$18–C$25 (US$12–US$16) at dinner. AE, DC, ER, MC, V. Mon–Fri 11:30am–2:30pm; Mon–Sat 6–11:30pm; Sun 5:30–11:30pm. CONTEMPORARY FRENCH.

Named for a French dessert, this is easily one of the best restaurants within or outside the walls, tendering a polished performance from beginning to end. A recent expansion that resulted in a space partitioned into several rooms by floor-to-ceiling wine racks seems to have energized both the management and the kitchen. Within minutes after opening the doors, a happy noise ensues, drowning out the cell-phone users. This fashionable crowd comes in everything from bespoke suits to designer jeans—T-shirts, shorts, and children are out of place and would clash with a staff attired in black from throat to toe, the men more often sporting earrings than the women. The menu shuns hyperbole; the mere listing of ingredients is sufficiently intriguing. Sparkling appetizers are the caramelized apple/red onion tart and the thinly sliced game pâté shot with pistachios and dressed with confits. Game and seafood are featured, like pheasant strudel, orange roughy, and lobster ragout. But what they can do with simple pasta is impressive: the black squid-ink variety is tossed in a spicy tomato sauce with calamari and topped with leaves of crispy fried spinach, as pretty a visual and taste sensation as you can imagine. How odd that the bread is dry and wooly. Find the entrance around on rue de la Chevrotière, under 200 Grande-Allée. There's a small patio for outdoor dining, and free valet parking is available from 5:30pm.

MODERATE

Graffiti. 1191 av. Cartier (near the Grand-Allée). ☎ **418/529-4949.** Reservations recommended. Main courses C$19–C$27 (US$13–US$18); table d'hôte menu C$8–C$14 (US$5–US$9) at lunch, C$19–C$28 (US$13–US$19) at dinner. AE, CB, DC, ER, MC, V. Mon–Sat 5–11pm; Sun noon–10pm. CONTEMPORARY FRENCH/ITALIAN.

The 2 or 3 blocks north of rue Cartier off the Grand-Allée are just outside the perimeter of tourist Québec, far enough removed to avoid flashy banality, close enough to remain convenient. This ebullient place blends bistro with trattoria, often on the same plate. Emblematic are the pike with leeks and grilled almonds and the sautéed rabbit with puréed carrot, broccoli florets, and angel-hair pasta powerfully scented with tarragon. The choice seats are in the glassed-in terrace, the better to scope the street scene.

Momento. 1144 av. Cartier (near the Grande-Allée). ☎ **418/647-1313.** Reservations suggested at dinner. Main courses C$16–C$17 (US$10–US$11); table d'hôte menu C$11–C$16 (US$7–US$11) at lunch, C$13–C$22 (US$9–US$15) at dinner. AE, DC, MC, V. Mon–Fri 11:30am–11pm, Sat–Sun 5:30–10:30pm. CONTEMPORARY ITALIAN.

Considering its manic popularity elsewhere on the continent, updated Italian cooking was late arriving in Québec. The city had the usual parlors shoveling overcooked spaghetti with thin tomato sauce, but not the kind of spiffy neo-trattoria trafficking in light-but-lusty dishes meant for lives lived fast. This racy spot is helping to take up the slack, and though it lags somewhat in execution compared to its rival, Graffiti (above), it's a welcome antidote to prevailing Franco-Italian clichés of the city's tourist troughs. The pizza crusts are almost as thin as crêpes, and the all-veggie version is a winner, as are the not-too-sweet desserts.

BASSE-VILLE (LOWER TOWN)
EXPENSIVE

✪ **Laurie Raphaël.** 117 rue Dalhousie (at rue St-André). ☎ **418/692-4555.** Reservations recommended. Main courses C$24–C$32 (US$16–US$21); table d'hôte menu C$10–C$14 (US$6–US$9) at lunch, C$26–C$44 (US$17–US$29) at dinner. AE, DC, ER, MC, V. Mon–Fri noon–2pm and 6–10pm; Sat–Sun 6–10pm. CONTEMPORARY FRENCH.

In 1996, the owners moved from a cramped space in the Auberge Le Priori (above) to these larger, more glamorous quarters, a suitable arena for the city's most accomplished kitchen. An *amuse-gueule* arrives with the cocktail, which might be the special Kir Royale, sparkling wine laced with blackberry liqueur. The waiter happily explains every menu dish in as much detail as you care to absorb. An appetizer isn't really necessary, since the main course comes with soup or salad, but they're so good, a couple might wish to share one—like the little stack of lightly fried calamari rings with their garnish of edible nasturtium blossoms. Main courses run to caribou and salmon in unconventional guises, often with Asian touches. Coupled with an evident concern for "healthy" saucing and exotic combinations, the food closely resembles that associated with elevated California restaurants, as exemplified by towering presentations, held together with skewers and panache. If the service can be faulted, it is for its occasional forgetfulness. But that's quibbling, for this is a restaurant that's all but alone at the pinnacle of the local dining pantheon.

MODERATE

L'Ardoise. 71 rue St-Paul (near rue Navigateurs). ☎ **418/694-0213.** Reservations suggested at dinner. Main courses C$8–C$16 (US$6–US$11); table d'hôte menu C$11 (US$7) at lunch, C$23–C$28 (US$15–US$19) at dinner. AE, DC, MC, V. Mon–Fri 11am–10pm, Sat–Sun 9am–10pm. BISTRO FRENCH.

This is one of several bistros wrapping around the corner of rues St-Paul and Sault-au-Matelot. Most are inexpensive and cater more to locals than to tourists . . . so far. Mussels are staples at Québec restaurants, prepared in the Belgian manner, with bowls of frites on the side. Here they come with eight sauces, and, with dessert and coffee, cost only C$16 (US$11). That the chef cares about what he sends out of his kitchen is evident. His food is vibrant and flavorful, served at banquettes along the walls and at tables both inside and out on the sidewalk. Piaf and Aznavour clones warble laments on the stereo. This is a place to leaf through a book, sip a double espresso, and meet locals.

✪ **Le Café du Monde.** 57 rue Dalhousie (at côte de la Montagne). ☎ **418/692-4455.** Reservations recommended on weekends. Main courses C$9–C$17 (US$6–US$11); table d'hôte menu C$9–C$13 (US$6–US$9) at lunch, C$18–C$24 (US$12–US$16) at dinner. AE, DC, ER, MC, V. Mon–Fri 11:30am–11pm; Sat–Sun brunch 9:30am–11pm. FRENCH/INTERNATIONAL.

This convivial spot near the Musée de la Civilisation enjoys ever-increasing popularity. While it promotes the roster of world dishes promised in its name, the atmosphere is definitely Lyonnaise brasserie. That is seen in the culinary origins of its most-ordered items—pâtés, quiches, confit de canard, and several versions of mussels with frites—prepared in a kitchen overseen by a chef from Brittany. One of his extravaganzas is a five-course evening meal, called "Le Ciel, La Terre, La Mer" ("Sky, Earth, Sea")—think of it as a kind of upscale surf 'n' turf. Pastas and couscous are some of the non-French preparations. Imported beers are favored beverages, along with wines by the glass. The service is friendly but easily distracted. Waiters and customers sit down at the upright piano for impromptu performances.

✪ **L'Echaudé.** 73 rue Sault-au-Matelot (near rue St-Paul). ☎ **418/692-1299.** Main courses C$12–C$27 (US$8–US$18); table d'hôte menu C$9–C$16 (US$6–US$11) at lunch, C$23–C$36 (US$15–US$24) at dinner. AE, DC, ER, MC, V. Mon–Wed 11:30am–2:30pm and 5:30–10pm; Thurs–Fri 11:30am–2:30pm and 5:30–11pm; Sat 5:30–11pm; Sun 10am–2:30pm and 5:30–10pm. Closed 2 weeks in Jan. BISTRO FRENCH.

One of the necklace of restaurants rounding this Basse-Ville corner, L'Echaudé is the most polished, boasting sidewalk tables with butcher paper on top and a zinc-topped bar inside the door. The grilled meats and fishes and seafood stews blaze no new trails, but they're very satisfying and prove an excellent price-value ratio. The good-deal lunch main courses go from cheese omelet to steak tartare, wrapped around with appetizer, dessert, and coffee. Among many winners is the chilled pasta tossed in oil with a touch of lemon and a spray of dill, ringed with mussels and minced red pepper. They keep 24 brands of beer on ice and cellar 125 varieties of wine, a generous 10 of which are available by the glass. Aznavour on the stereo and wisps of Gitanes complete the Parisian ambiance.

Le Cochon Dingue. 46 bd. Champlain (at rue du Marché-Champlain). ☎ **418/692-2013.** Main courses C$10–C$15 (US$7–US$10); table d'hôte menu C$8–C$13 (US$5–US$9) at lunch, C$17–C$19 (US$11–US$13) at dinner. AE, CB, ER, MC, V. Mon–Fri 7am–11pm; Sat–Sun 8am–11pm. BISTRO/INTERNATIONAL.

This "Crazy Pig" faces the ferry dock in the Lower Town and has some sidewalk tables and several indoor dining rooms (some no-smoking) with rough fieldstone walls and black-and-white floor tiles. It's heavily used and shows it, as a result of its highly successful efforts to be a one-stop eatery with long hours. Choose from mussels, chicken-liver pâté, spring rolls, smoked salmon, half a dozen salads, onion soup, pastas, quiches, sandwiches, grilled meats, and more than 20 desserts. Good shoestring frites accompany most dishes. Check the daily specials board for items often seen on the standard card that are discounted for the day, and there's an offering for kids 10 and under for only C$4.95 (US$3.30). Maybe they're the audience for the mistakenly cutesy menu urging you to eat parts of the trademark anthropomorphic pig. Wine is sold by the glass, quarter liter, half liter, or bottle, at reasonable prices. The service is rushed but attentive. The same people own the nearby, smaller **Le Lapin Sauté**, 52 rue Petit-Champlain (☎ 418/692-5325), open Monday to Friday noon to 11pm and Saturday and Sunday noon to 9pm.

✪ **Le Marie-Clarisse.** 12 rue du Petit-Champlain (near rue Sous-le-Fort). ☎ **418/ 692-0857.** Main courses C$8–C$12 (US$5–US$8); table d'hôte menu C$10–C$15 (US$7–US$10) at lunch, C$17–C$20 (US$11–US$13) at dinner. AE, DC, ER, MC, V. Mon–Fri 11:30am–2:30pm; Mon–Sat 6–10pm, terrace 11:30am–10pm (daily Apr 15– Oct 31). BISTRO/SEAFOOD.

Nothing much beyond sustenance is expected of restaurants at the intersections of galloping tourism. That's why this ambitious cafe at the bottom of the Breakneck Stairs is such a happy surprise, serving what many consider the best seafood in town, chosen by a finicky owner who makes his selections personally at market. A more pleasant hour can't be passed anywhere else in Québec City, over a platter of shrimp or pâtés, out on the terrace on an August afternoon. In January, cocoon by the stone fireplace inside, indulging in bouillabaisse (a stew of mussels, scallops, tuna, talapia, and shrimp), with a plate of rice and veggies on the side and a boat of saffron mayo to slather on croutons. Try a Québec wine to wash it down, maybe the l'Orpailleur from Dunham in the Estrie. The two rooms are formed of stone and brick and rafters in place for more than 200 years.

Le Zénith. In the Auberge Le Priori, 17 rue du Sault-au-Matelot (at rue St-Antoine). ☎ **418/ 692-2962.** Main courses C$16–C$23 (US$11–US$15); table d'hôte menu C$10–C$13 (US$6–US$8) at lunch, C$26–C$44 (US$17–US$29) at dinner. AE, DC, ER, MC, V. Daily 7am–11pm. CONTEMPORARY FRENCH.

While this replacement for the departed Laurie Raphaël (above) doesn't come within hailing distance of the champ, it's a thoroughly pleasant spot for a bite and in which to pass an hour or so. There's a dining patio in back of the old stone house, and the interior is made more intimate when the windows are closed and logs are set to flame in the fireplace. The service is none too vigilant, but what arrives on the plate compensates, with creative takes on French recipes. Keep it in mind for breakfast too.

INEXPENSIVE

Buffet de l'Antiquarie. 95 rue St-Paul (near rue Sault-au-Matelot). ☎ **418/692-2661.** Most menu items under C$10 (US$7); table d'hôte C$6–C$12 (US$3.95–US$8). AE, MC, V. Daily 7am–11pm. QUÉBECOIS.

Another inhabitant of the rue St-Paul antiques row, this is the humblest bistro of the lot, with exposed brick and stone walls lending what there is of decor. It's the place to go when every other Lower Town cafe is closed, as for Sunday breakfast. And since it caters to home folks rather than tourists, reliable versions of native Québecois cooking are always available, including, but not limited to, pea soup, poutine, and feves au lard. Essentially a slightly upgraded luncheonette, it serves sandwiches, salads, and pastries at all hours, backed by full bar service.

5 Seeing the Sights

Wandering at random through the streets of Vieux-Québec is a singular pleasure. On the way, you can happen on an ancient convent, blocks of gabled houses with steep tin roofs, a battery of 18th-century cannons in a leafy park, or a bistro with a blazing fireplace on a chilly day. This is such a compact city it's hardly necessary to plan precise itineraries. Start at the Terrasse Dufferin and go off on a whim, down the Breakneck Stairs to the Quartier Petit-Champlain and place Royale, or up to the Citadelle and onto the Plains of Abraham, where Wolfe and Montcalm fought to the death in a 20-minute battle that changed the destiny of the continent.

Most of what there is to see is within the city walls, in the Lower Town. It's fairly easy walking. While the Upper Town is hilly, with sloping streets, it's nothing like San Francisco, and only people with physical limitations will experience difficulty. If rain or ice discourages exploration on foot, tour buses and horse-drawn calèches are options. Most attractions have discounted admission fees for families.

Note: See the "Québec City" map (p. 274) to locate the sights in this section.

BASSE-VILLE (LOWER TOWN)

The **Escalier Casse-Cou (Breakneck Stairs)** connects the **Terrasse Dufferin** at the top of the cliff with rue Sous-le-Fort at the base. The name will be self-explanatory as soon as you see the stairs. They lead from Haute-Ville to the **Quartier Petit-Champlain** in Basse-Ville. A stairway has existed here since the settlement began, but human beings weren't the only ones to use it. In 1698, the town council forbade citizens to take their animals up or down the stairway or face a fine.

A short walk from the bottom of the Breakneck Stairs, via rue Sous-le-Fort, is picturesque ✪ **place Royale,** Lower Town's literal and spiritual heart. In the 17th and 18th centuries, it was the town marketplace and the center of business and industry. Dominating the square is the **Eglise Notre-Dame-des-Victoires,** Québec's oldest stone church, built in 1688 and restored in 1763 and 1969. The paintings, altar, and large model boat suspended from the ceiling were votive offerings brought by early settlers to ensure safe voyages. The church usually is open during the day, unless a wedding is in progress.

An empty storefront on the square was refurbished in 1997 to become an **information center,** 215 rue du Marché-Finlay (☎ **418/643-6631**); June 5 to October 1, it's open daily 10am to 6pm. Note the ladders on some of the other roofs, a common Québec device for removing snow and fighting fires. Folk dances, impromptu concerts, and other festive gatherings are often held near the bust of Louis XIV in the square.

✪ **Musée de la Civilisation.** 85 rue Dalhousie (at rue St-Antoine). ☎ **418/643-2158.** Admission C$7 (US$4.65) adults, C$6 (US$4) seniors, C$4 (US$2.65) students over 17, C$2 (US$1.35) children 12–16; children under 12 free. Tues free to all (except summer). June 24–Labour Day daily 10am–7pm; day after Labour Day–June 23 Tues–Sun 10am–5pm.

Try to set aside at least 2 hours for a visit to this special museum, one of the most engrossing in all Canada. Designed by Boston-based, McGill University–trained Moshe Safdie and opened in 1988, the Museum of Civilization is an innovative presence in the historic Basse-Ville, near place Royale. A dramatic atrium lobby sets the tone with a massive sculpture rising like jagged icebergs from the watery floor, a representation of the mighty St. Lawrence at spring breakup. Through the glass wall in back you can see the 1752 Maison Estèbe, now restored to contain the museum shop; it stands above vaulted cellars you can view. In the galleries upstairs are five permanent exhibits, supplemented by up to six temporary shows on a variety of themes. The museum's mission has never been entirely clear, leading to some opaque metaphysical meanderings in its early years. Never mind. Using highly imaginative display techniques, hands-on devices, computers, holograms, videos, and even an ant farm, the curators have ensured that you'll be so enthralled by the experience you won't pause to question its intent. Notice, as an example of the museum's thoroughness, how a squeaky floorboard has been installed at the entrance to a dollhouse-size display of old Québec houses.

If time is short, definitely take in "Memoires" (Memories), a permanent exhibit that's a sprawling examination of Québec history, moving from the province's roots as a fur-trading colony to the present. Furnishings from frontier homes, tools of the trappers' trade, old farm implements, 19th-century religious garments, old campaign posters, and a re-created classroom from the past envelop you with a rich sense of Québec's daily life from generation to generation. A new permanent exhibit is "Encounter with the First Nations," examining the products and metaphysical visions of the aboriginal bands who inhabit Québec. For a year from its opening in May 2000, an important exhibit is devoted to illuminations of the civilizations that germinated and grew in what's now Syria. Exhibit texts are in French and English. There's a cafe on the ground floor.

Explore Sound & Light Show. 63 rue Dalhousie (at rue St-Antoine). ☎ **418/692-2063.** Admission C$6 (US$4.15) adults, C$5 (US$3.50) seniors, C$4 (US$2.65) ages 7–25. June 1–Sept 30 daily 10am–5pm.

This splashy 30-minute multimedia production chronicles the Age of Exploration through the impressions of Columbus, Vespucci, Verrazano, Cartier, and Champlain. The theater is shaped like an early sailing vessel, complete with rigging. Among the depictions are the difficulties of Champlain and his crew of 28 who came here in 1608. Twenty men died during the first winter, mainly of scurvy and dysentery (one was hanged for mutiny).

Maison Chevalier. 60 rue du Marché-Champlain (at rue Notre-Dame). ☎ **418/643-2158.** Free admission. May–June 22 and Sept 8–Oct 31 Tues–Sun 10am–6pm, June 23–Sept 7 daily 10am–6pm, Nov–Apr Sat–Sun 10am–5pm.

Built in 1752 for shipowner Jean-Baptiste Chevalier, the existing structure incorporated two buildings from 1675 and 1695. It was run as an inn throughout the 19th century, the Québec government restored the house in 1960, and it became a museum 5 years later. Inside, with its exposed wood beams, wide-board floors, and stone fireplaces, are changing exhibits on Québec history and civilization, especially in the 17th and 18th centuries. While exhibit texts are in French, guidebooks in English are available at the sometimes-unattended front desk.

Centre d'Interprétation du Vieux-Port. 100 rue St-Andre (at rue Rioux). ☎ **418/648-3300.** Admission May to Labor Day, C$3 (US$2) adults, C$2 (US$1.35) seniors, C$2 (US$1.35) children ages 6–16. May–Labour Day daily 10am–5pm; schedule varies the rest of the year (call for hours).

A unit of Parks Canada, the Old Port Interpretation Center reveals the Port of Québec as it was during its maritime zenith in the 19th century with four floors of exhibits. You can view the modern port and city from the top level, where reference maps identify landmarks. One of these is the Daishowa Pulp and Paper Mill (1927), which sells newsprint and cardboard to international markets, including the *New York Times*. Texts are in French and English, and most exhibits invite tactile interaction.

HAUTE-VILLE (UPPER TOWN)

✪ **La Citadelle.** Côte de la Citadelle (enter off rue St-Louis). ☎ **418/694-2815.** Admission C$ (US$3.65) adults, C$4 (US$2.65) seniors, C$2.75 (US$1.85) children 7–17; persons with disabilities/children under 7 free. Guided 55-min. tours daily: Apr to mid-May 10am–4pm; mid-May to June 9am–5pm; July to Labour Day 9am–6pm; Sept 9am–4pm; Oct 10am–3pm. Nov–Mar group reservations only. Changing of the guard (30 min.) June 24–Labour Day Wed–Sun at 10am, beating the retreat (20 min.) July and Aug Wed–Sat at 6pm. May be cancelled in the event of rain. Walk up the côte de la Citadelle from the St-Louis gate.

The Duke of Wellington had this partially star-shaped fortress built at the east end of the city walls in anticipation of renewed American attacks after the War of 1812. Some remnants of earlier French military structures were incorporated into the Citadel, including a 1750 magazine. Dug into the Plains of Abraham and never having exchanged fire with an invader, the fort continues its vigil from the tip of Cap Diamant, with a low profile that keeps it all but invisible until you're actually upon it. British construction of the fortress, now a national historic site, was begun in 1820 and took 30 years. As events unfolded, it proved to be an exercise in obsolescence. Since 1920, the Citadel has been home to Québec's Royal 22e Régiment, the only fully Francophone unit in Canada's armed forces. That makes it North America's largest fortified group of buildings still occupied by troops. As part of a guided tour only, you can visit the Citadel and its 25 buildings, including the regimental museum in the former powderhouse and prison, and watch the changing of the guard or beating the retreat.

Basilique-Cathédrale Notre-Dame. 20 rue Buade (at côte de la Fabrique). ☎ **418/694-0665.** Free admission to basilica and guided tours. "Act of Faith" sound-and-light show, C$8 (US$5) adults, C$7 (US$4.65) seniors, C$5 (US$3.35) students 12 and over with ID; children 11 and under free. Cathedral daily 8am–2:30pm. Guided tours May 1–Oct 31 daily 9am–2:30pm. "Act of Faith" multimedia sound-and-light show May 1–Thanksgiving (mid-Oct) Mon–Fri 3:30, 5, 6:30, and 8pm; Sat–Sun 6:30 and 8pm (and at 9pm in July and Aug).

Notre-Dame Basilica, the oldest Christian parish north of Mexico, has weathered a tumultuous history of bombardment, reconstruction, and restoration. Parts of the existing basilica date to the original 1647 structure, including the bell tower and portions of the walls, but most of today's exterior is from the reconstruction completed in 1771. The interior, a re-creation undertaken after a fire in 1922, is flamboyantly neo-Baroque, with shadows wavering by the fluttering light of votive candles. Paintings and ecclesiastical treasures still remain from the time of the French regime, including a chancel lamp given by Louis XIV. In summer, the basilica is the backdrop for the "Act of Faith" multimedia sound-and-light show dramatically recalling 5 centuries of Québec's history and that of this building itself. The basilica is connected to the group of old buildings that makes up Québec Seminary; to enter that complex, go to 7 rue de l'Université (about a block away).

Chapelle/Musée des Ursulines. 12 rue Donnacona (at rue des Jardins). ☎ **418/694-0694.** Museum C$4 (US$2.65) adults, C$3 (US$2) seniors, C$2.50 (US$1.65) students; chapel free. Museum Sept 1–Apr 30 Tues–Sun 1–4:30pm; May 1–Aug 31 Tues–Sat 10am–noon and 1–5pm. Chapel May–Oct same days and hours as museum.

The chapel is notable for the sculptures informing its pulpit and two retables, created by Pierre-Noel Levasseur between 1726 and 1736. Though the building dates only to 1902, much of the interior decoration is nearly 2 centuries older. The tomb of the founder of the Ursuline teaching order, Marie de l'Incarnation, is to the right of the entry. She arrived here in 1639 at age 40 and was declared blessed by Pope John Paul II in 1980. The museum displays accoutrements of the daily and spiritual life of the order. On the third floor are exhibits of vestments woven with gold thread, and a cape made of drapes from the bedroom of Anne of Austria and given to Marie de l'Incarnation when she left for New France in 1639 is on display. There are also musical instruments and Amerindian crafts, including the *flèche*, or arrow sash, still worn during Winter Carnival. Some of the docents are nuns of the still-active order. The Ursuline convent, built as a girls' school in 1642, is the oldest one in North America.

Château Frontenac. 1 rue des Carrières, at place d'Armes. ☎ **418/692-3861.** or 418/691-2166 for tour reservations. Guided 50-min. tours C$6 (US$4) adults, C$5 (US$3.35) seniors, C$3.50 (US$2.35) children 6–16. May 1–Oct 15 tours daily 10am–6pm; Oct 16–Apr 30 tours Sat–Sun 1–5pm. Departures on the hour.

Opened in 1893 to house railroad passengers and encourage tourism, the monster version of a Loire Valley palace is the city's emblem, its Eiffel Tower. You can see the hotel from almost every quarter, commanding its majestic position atop Cap Diamant. Visitors curious about the interior may wish to take one of the guided tours.

Musée de Cire de Québec. 22 rue Ste-Anne (at rue du Trésor). ☎ **418/692-2289.** Admission C$7 (US$4.65) adults, C$4 (US$2.65) seniors/students; children under 6 free. June–Labour Day daily 9am–10pm; rest of the year daily 10am–5pm.

Occupying a 17th-century house, this briefly diverting wax museum, renovated in 1994, skims across the pageant of Québec's history and heroes. Generals Wolfe and Montcalm are portrayed, of course, along with effigies of politicians, singers, Olympic gold medalists, and other newsmakers. Texts are in French and English.

Musée de l'Amerique Française. 9 rue de l'Université. ☎ **418/692-2843.** Admission C$3 (US$2) adults, C$2 (US$1.35) seniors/students over 17, C$1 (US65¢) children 12–16; children under 12 free. June 24–Sept 7 daily 10am–5:30pm; Sept 8–June 23 Tues–Sun 10am–5pm. Guided tours of exhibits and some buildings daily in summer, Sat and Sun rest of the year (call the number above for reservations).

Housed at the site of the historic Québec Seminary (1663), the Museum of French America focuses on the beginnings and the evolution of French culture and civilization in North America. Its extensive collections include paintings by European and Canadian artists, engravings and parchments from the early French regime, old and rare books, coins, early scientific instruments, and even mounted animals and an Egyptian mummy. The mix makes for an engrossing visit.

The museum is in three parts of the large complex. In the Guillaume-Couillard wing, adjacent to the Basilique-Cathédrale Notre-Dame, are the entrance hall and information desk. In the Jérôme-Demers wing, bordering the rue de l'Université down the hill, are the exhibition galleries. The third part is the beautiful François-Ranvoyze wing, with its trompe-l'oeil ornamentation, which served as a chapel for the seminary priests and students. Concerts are held in the chapel as well.

Musée du Fort. 10 rue Ste-Anne (at place d'Armes). ☎ **418/692-1759.** Admission C$6 (US$4) adults, C$5 (US$3.35) seniors, C$4 (US$2.65) students. Apr–June and Sept 16–Oct daily 10am–5pm; July–Sept 15 daily 10am–8pm, Dec 26–Jan 4 daily noon–4pm; Feb–Mar Thurs–Sun noon–4pm.

Not far from the UNESCO World Heritage monument, this commercial enterprise presents a sound-and-light show using a 400-square-foot model of the city and the surrounding region. The 30-minute production concerns itself primarily with the six sieges of Québec, including the famous battle on the Plains of Abraham. Commentary is in French or English. Military and history buffs are the ones most likely to enjoy a visit here.

NEAR THE GRANDE-ALLÉE

✪ **Musée du Québec.** 1 av. Wolfe-Montcalm (at av. George-VI). ☎ **418/643-2150.** Admission (excluding special exhibits) C$7 (US$4.65) adults, C$6 (US$4) seniors, C$2.75 (US$1.85) students, C$2 (US$1.35) ages 12–16; children under 12 free; Wed free for everyone. June 1–Sept 7 daily 10am–5:45pm (Wed to 9:45pm); Sept 8–May 31 Tues–Sun 11am–5:45pm (Wed to 8:45pm). Bus: 11.

In the southern reaches of the Parc des Champs de Bataille (below), just off the Grande-Allée and a half-hour walk or a short bus ride from the Haute-Ville, the Museum of Québec is an art museum that now occupies two buildings, one a former prison, linked by a soaring glass-roofed "Grand Hall" housing the reception area, a stylish cafe, and a shop. The 1933 building contains the permanent collection, North America's largest aggregation of Québec art, filling eight galleries with works from the beginning of the colony to the present. On the top floor are regional landscapes and other Québec themes, with some examples of North American and British painters. On the ground floor is a splendid assortment of African masks, carvings, musical instruments, and ceremonial staffs. Alas, most descriptive plaques are only in French. Traveling exhibits and musical events are often arranged. The new addition is the 1867 Baillairgé Prison, which in the 1970s was a youth hostel nicknamed the "Petite Bastille." One cell block has been left intact as an exhibit. Here four galleries house temporary shows, and the tower contains a provocative sculpture called *Le Plongeur* (The Diver) by Irish artist David Moore. Also in the building is the Battlefields Interpretation Centre (below) and a children's play-room stocked with toys and books. The surprisingly accomplished cafe/restaurant serves lunch Monday to Saturday, brunch Sunday, and dinner Wednesday and Saturday.

Parc des Champs-de-Bataille. Covering more than 260 acres on the Plains of Abraham. Battlefields Interpretation Centre in the Musée du Québec (above), av. Wolfe-Montcalm. ☎ **418/648-3638.** Free admission to park. Interpretation center, martello tower no. 1, astronomy tower, and bus tour in summer, C$2 (US$1.35) ages 18–64, C$1.50 (US$1) ages 13–17 and 65 and over; ages 12 and under free. Rates are expected to increase. May 18–Labour Day daily 10am–5:30pm; Sept 8–May 17 Tues–Sun 11am–5:30pm.

Covering more than 260 acres of grassy knolls, sunken gardens, monuments, fountains, and trees, Québec's Battlefields Park stretches over the Plains of Abraham, where Wolfe and Montcalm engaged in their swift but crucial battle in 1759. It's a favorite place for all Québecois when they want some sunshine, a jog, or a bike ride. Be sure to see **Jardin Jeanne d'Arc (Joan of Arc Garden),** just off avenue Laurier between Loews Le Concorde Hôtel and the Ministry of Justice. The statue was a gift from anonymous Americans, and it was here that "O Canada," the country's national anthem, was sung for the first time. Within the park are two **martello towers,** cylindrical stone defensive structures built between 1808 and 1812, when Québec feared an invasion from the United States.

The park contains almost 5,000 trees representing more than 80 species. Prominent among these are sugar maple, silver maple, Norway maple, American elm, and American ash. Frequent special activities, including theatrical and musical events, are presented during summer. Year-round, the **Interpretation Center** provides an in-depth look at the historical significance of the Plains of Abraham over the years. A new **Discovery Pavilion** at 835 av. Wilfrid-Laurier serves as a reception/information center and starting point for bus and walking tours of the park. In summer, a shuttle bus tours the park in 45 minutes with narration in French and English.

Hôtel du Parlement. Grande-Allée est (at av. Dufferin). ☎ **418/643-7239.** Free admission. Guided tours early Sept to June Mon–Fri 9am–4:30pm; June 24–Labour Day Mon–Fri 9am–4:30pm; year-round Sat–Sun 10am–4:30pm.

Since 1968, what the Québecois choose to call their "National Assembly" has occupied this imposing Second Empire château constructed in 1886. Twenty-two bronze statues of some of the most prominent figures in Québec's tumultuous history gaze out from the facade. You can tour the sumptuous chambers of the building with a guide for no charge, but tour times change without warning. Highlights are the Assembly Chamber and the Room of the Old Legislative Council, where parliamentary committees meet. Throughout, representations of the French fleur-de-lys and the initials "VR" (for Victoria Regina) remind you of Québec's dual heritage.

ESPECIALLY FOR KIDS

Québec is such a storybook town that children, especially those who have responded to Arthurian tales of fortresses and castles, often delight in simply walking around in it.

As soon as possible, head for the **Terrasse Dufferin,** which has those coin-operated telescopes kids like. In decent weather, there are always street entertainers, whether a Peruvian musical group or men who play saws or wineglasses. A few steps away at place d'Armes are **horse-drawn carriages,** and not far in the same direction is the **Musée de Cire Grévin (Wax Museum),** on place d'Armes at 22 rue Ste-Anne. Also at place d'Armes is the top of **Breakneck Stairs.** Halfway down, across the road, are giant **cannons** ranged along the battlements on rue des Ramparts. The gun carriages are impervious to the assaults of small humans, so kids can scramble over them at will.

At the bottom of the Breakneck, on the left, is a **glass-blowing workshop,** the Verrerie la Maïloche. In the front room, craftsmen give glass-blowing demonstrations, always intriguing and informative, especially for children who haven't seen it before. Also in the Lower Town, at 86 rue Dalhousie, the playful **Musée de la Civilisation** keeps kids occupied for hours in its exhibits, shop, and cafe. Military sites are usually a hit: The **Citadelle** has tours of the grounds and buildings and colorful **Changing of the Guard** and **Beating Retreat** ceremonies.

The **ferry** to Lévis across the St. Lawrence is inexpensive, convenient from the Lower Town, and exciting for kids. The crossing, over and back, takes less than an hour. To run off the kids' excess energy, head for the **Plains of Abraham,** also known as Battlefields Park. To get there, take rue St-Louis, just inside the St-Louis Gate or, more vigorously, the walkway along the Terrasse Dufferin and the promenade des Gouverneurs, with a long set of stairs. Acres of grassy lawn give children room to roam and provide the perfect spot for a family picnic.

Even better is the **Village des Sports,** 1860 bd. Valcartier in St-Gabriel-de-Valcartier (☎ 418/844-2200), about 20 minutes' drive north of downtown. In summer, it's a water park, with slides, a huge wave pool, and diving shows. In winter, those same facilities are put to use for snowrafting on inner tubes, ice slides, and skating.

6 Special Events & Festivals

Usually, Québec is courtly and dignified, but all that's cast aside when the symbolic snowman called Bonhomme (Good Fellow) presides over 10 days of merriment in early February during the annual ✪ **Carnaval d'Hiver (Winter Carnival).** More than a million revelers descend, eddying around the monumental ice palace and ice sculptures and attending a full schedule of concerts, dances, and parades. The mood is heightened by the availability of plastic trumpets and canes filled with a concoction called Caribou, the principal ingredients of which are cheap whisky and sweet red wine. Perhaps its presence explains the eagerness with which certain Québecers participate in the canoe race across the treacherous ice floes of the St. Lawrence. You must make hotel reservations far in advance. Scheduled events are free.

On June 24, **St-Jean Baptiste Day** honors St. John the Baptist, the patron saint of French Canadians. It's marked by more festivities and far more enthusiasm throughout Québec Province than national Dominion Day on July 1. It's their "national" holiday.

The largest cultural event in the French-speaking world, the **Festival d'Eté International (International Summer Festival)** has attracted artists from Africa, Asia, Europe, and North America since it began in 1967. The more than 250 events showcase theater, music, and dance, with 600 performers from 20 countries. One million people come to watch and listen. Jazz and folk combos perform free in an open-air theater next to City Hall; visiting dance and folklore troupes put on shows; and concerts, theatrical productions, and related events fill the days and evenings. It's held for about 10 days in mid-July. Call ☎ **418/651-2882** for details.

During the 5-day **Medievales de Québec (Québec Medieval Festival),** hundreds of actors, artists, entertainers, and other participants from Europe, Canada, and the United States converge on Québec City in period dress to re-create scenes from 5 centuries ago, playing knights, troubadours, and ladies-in-waiting. The highlights are parades, jousting tournaments, recitals of ancient music, and La Grande Chevauchée (Grand Cavalcade) featuring hundreds of costumed horseback riders. Fireworks are the one modern touch. It's held only in odd-numbered years for about a week in early to mid-August. Call ☎ **418/692-1993** for details.

7 Outdoor Activities & Spectator Sports

OUTDOOR ACTIVITIES

The waters and hills around Québec City provide countless opportunities for outdoor recreation—from swimming, rafting, and fishing to skiing, snowmobiling, and sleighing. There are two centers in particular to keep in mind for most winter and summer activities, both easy drives away. Thirty minutes from Québec City, off Route 175 north, is the provincial **Parc de la Jacques-Cartier** (☎ **418/848-3169**). Closer by 10 minutes or so is the **Parc Mont-Ste-Anne** (☎ **418/827-1871**), only 40km (25 miles) northeast of the city. Both are mentioned below.

Mid-November to late March, taxis participate in a **winter shuttle** program, picking up passengers at 16 hotels at 8:30am, taking them to Mont-Sainte-Anne and Station Stoneham, and returning them to Québec City at about 4:30pm. Round-trip fare is C\$18 (US\$12). Ask if your hotel participates when reserving a room.

BIKING   Given the Upper Town's hilly topography, biking isn't a particularly attractive option. But rented bicycles are available in the flatter Lower Town, near the lighthouse, at **Location Petit-Champlain,** 94 rue du Petit-Champlain (☎ **418/692-2817**); they cost about C\$6 (US\$4) per hour or C\$30 (US\$20) per day. The shop also rents strollers and is open daily 9am to 11pm. You can also rent bikes on relatively level ✪ **Ile d'Orléans,** across the bridge from the north shore at the gas station (☎ **418/828-9215**). For more vigorous mountain biking, the **Mont-Ste-Anne recreational center** (☎ **418/827-4561**) has 200km (124 miles) of trails.

CAMPING   There are almost 30 campgrounds in the greater Québec area, with as few as 20 campsites and as many as 368. All have showers and toilets. One of the largest is in the **Parc de Mont-Ste-Anne,** and it accepts credit cards. One of the smallest, but with a convenience store and snack bar, is **Camping La Loutre** on Lac Jacques-Cartier in the park of the same name (☎ **418/846-2201**). It's north of the city, off Route 175. The booklet available at the tourist offices provides details about all the sites.

CANOEING   The several lakes and rivers of the **Parc de la Jacques-Cartier** are fairly easy to reach yet in the midst of virtual wilderness. Canoes are available to rent in the park itself.

CROSS-COUNTRY SKIING   Greater Québec has 22 cross-country ski centers with 278 trails. In town, the **Parc des Champs-de-Bataille** (Battlefields Park) has 11km (6.8 miles) of groomed cross-country trails, a convenience for those who don't have cars or the time to get out of town. Those who do have transportation should consider the **Station Mont-Ste-Anne,** which has more than 225km (140 miles) of cross-country trails at all levels of difficulty; equipment is available for rent.

DOGSLEDDING   **Aventures Nord-Bec** (☎ **418/889-8001**) at 665 rue Ste-Aimé in St-Lambert-de-Lévis, about 20 minutes south of the city, offers dogsledding expeditions. While they aren't the equivalent of a 2-week mush across Alaska, there are choices of half-day to 5-day expeditions. You get a four-dog sled meant for two and take turns standing on the runners and sitting on the sled. Out on the trail it's a hushed world of snow and evergreens. With the half-day trip at C$69 (US$46) adults, C$59 (US$39) students, and C$20 (US$13) children 12 and under, it's expensive, especially for families, but the memory will stay with you. Also providing this experience are **Aventure Québec** (☎ **418/827-2227**) and **Nordic Aventure** (☎ **418/ 848-6781**).

DOWNHILL SKIING   Foremost among the five area downhill centers is the one at the **Parc Mont-Ste-Anne,** the largest ski area in eastern Canada, with 51 trails (many of them lit for night skiing) and 11 lifts. November 15 to March 30, a daily shuttle service operates between downtown hotels and alpine and cross-country ski centers. The cars or minivans are equipped to carry ski gear and cost about C$18 (US$12) round-trip per person. For details, call ☎ **418/525-4953** or 418/525-5191.

FISHING   May to early September, anglers can wet their lines in the river that flows through the **Parc de la Jacques-Cartier** and at the national wildlife reserve at **Cap-Tourmente** (☎ **418/827-3776**), on the St. Lawrence, not far from Mont-Ste-Anne. Permits are available at many sporting-goods stores.

GOLF   The **Parc Mont-Ste-Anne** has two 18-hole courses, plus practice ranges and putting greens. Reservations are required, and fees are C$28 to C$39 (US$19 to US$26). The only night-lit facility in Québec City is the nine-hole course at the **Club de Golf,** 1250 rue Gabin in Val-Bélair (☎ **418/845-2222**), about 15 minutes west of the city. Reservations are required; a round costs C$14 (US$9) on weekends. In all, there are two dozen courses in the area, most in the suburbs of Ste-Foy, Beauport, and Charlesbourg; all but three in the nearby suburbs are open to the public.

ICE SKATING   Outdoor rinks are at place d'Youville and the Parc de l'Esplanade inside the walls and at the Parc de Champs-de-Bataille, where rock climbing, camping, canoeing, and mountain biking are also possible. You can rent skates at **Vélo Passe-Sport Plein Air** (☎ **418/692-3643**) in the old town.

SWIMMING   Those who want to swim during their visit should plan to stay at one of the handful of hotels with pools. **Château Frontenac** has a new one, and the **Radisson Gouverneurs** has a heated outdoor pool you can enter from inside. Other possibilities are the **Hilton** and **Loews Le Concorde.**

   The **Village des Sports,** a two-season recreational center in St-Gabriel-de-Valcartier, 1860 bd. Valcartier (☎ **418/844-2200**), has an immense wave pool and water slides, as well as 38 trails for snowrafting. It's about 20 minutes west of the city.

TOBOGGANING A **toboggan run** is created every winter down the stairs at the south end of the Terrasse Dufferin and all the way to Château Frontenac. Tickets (only C$1/US65¢ per person) are sold at a temporary booth near the end of the run.

SPECTATOR SPORTS

The Nordiques, Québec's representatives in the misnamed National Hockey League, departed in 1995 for Denver, leaving the city without a team in any of the professional major leagues. For hardcore hockey fans, however, there's the new **Rafales,** the Québec team in the International Hockey League. They play at the **Colisée de Québec** (☎ **418/522-3000**).

Harness races take place at the **Hippodrome de Québec,** 2205 av. du Colisée, parc de l'Exposition (☎ **418/524-5283**). General admission is only C$1 (US65¢) but free with presentation of your parking ticket. Races take place year-round Thursday to Tuesday at 1:30pm or 7:30pm (times vary from season to season; call ahead). Fans have been coming to the Hippodrome for afternoons or evenings of harness racing since 1916. Le Cavallo clubhouse is open year-round.

8 Shopping

The compact size of the old town, upper and lower, makes it especially convenient for shopping. Deserving attention are several **art galleries** in the Upper Town featuring Inuit and folk art. **Antiques shops** proliferate along rue St-Paul in the Lower Town, the heaviest concentration running east from the parking lot opposite the Vieux-Port Interpretation Centre. Other **streets to browse** are rue St-Jean, both within and outside the city walls, and rue Garneau and côte de la Fabrique, which branch off the east end of St-Jean. There's a shopping concourse on the lower level of Château Frontenac.

The **Quartier du Petit-Champlain,** especially along rue du Petit-Champlain and rue Sous-le-Fort, offers many possibilities (clothing, souvenirs, gifts, household items, collectibles) and so far avoids the trashiness that often afflicts heavily touristed areas.

SHOPPING A TO Z

ARTS & CRAFTS Crafts, handmade sweaters, and Inuit art are among the desirable items that aren't seen everywhere else. An official igloo trademark identifies authentic Inuit (Eskimo) art, though the differences between the real thing and the manufactured variety become apparent with a little careful study. Inuit artworks, usually carvings in stone or bone, are best buys not because of low prices but because of their high quality. Expect to pay hundreds of dollars for even a relatively small piece.

For Inuit art in stone, bone, and tusk, check out **Aux Multiples,** 69 rue Ste-Anne (☎ 418/692-1230). Prices are high, C$100 to C$10,000 (US$67 to US$6,670) and more, but are competitive with goods of similar quality. The **Galerie d'Art du Petit-Champlain,** 88 rue du Petit-Champlain (☎ 418/692-5647), features the wood carvings of Roger Desjardins, who applies his skills to meticulous renderings of waterfowl. At the **Galerie d'Art Trois Colombes,** 46 rue St-Louis (☎ 418/694-1114), the weavings, carvings, snowshoes, and duck decoys are supplemented by handmade hats, coats, sweaters, and moccasins. Artists hang their prints and paintings of Québec scenes along **rue du Trésor** between rue Ste-Anne and rue Baude, a pedestrian lane mostly covered by awnings. Some of the artists, positioned near adjacent sidewalk cafes, draw portraits or caricatures.

BOOKS & RECORDS Most of Québec City's bookstores cater to the solidly French-speaking citizenry and students at the university, but a few shops carry some

English books for visitors. One is the **Librairie du Nouveau Monde,** 103 rue St-Pierre in Old Québec (☎ **418/694-9475**), which features titles dealing with Québec history and culture, including books in English. For travel books and accessories, visit the **Librairie Ulysses,** 4 bd. René-Lévesque, near avenue Cartier (☎ **418/529 5349**). The **Maison de la Presse Internationale,** 1050 rue St-Jean (☎ **418/694-1511**), stocks magazines, newspapers, and paperbacks from around the world. Two floors of recorded music, mostly CDs with some cassettes, constitute the stock of **Archambault,** 1095 rue St-Jean (☎ **418/694-2088**). The helpful staff goes to some lengths to find what you want.

FOOD   Not far from the 1916 train station is the **Marché du Vieux-Port,** a colorful farmers market with rows of booths heaped with fresh fruits and vegetables, relishes, jams, handicrafts, flowers, and honey from local hives. Above each booth hangs a sign with the name and phone number of the seller. A lot of them bear the initials "I.O.," meaning they come from the Ile d'Orléans, 10 miles outside the city. The market is enclosed, and the central part of it is heated. Billed as a "little sugar shack," **La Petite Cabane à Sucre,** 94 rue Petit Champlain, at the south end (☎ **418/692-5875**), sells ice cream, honey, maple syrup and candy, and related products, many in packaging suitable for gifts, including the tin log cabins that pour from their chimneys.

WINE   A supermarket-size **Société des Alcools** store is at 1059 av. Cartier, near rue Fraser (☎ **418/643-4334**), with thousands of bottles in stock. They recently expanded the selling area to incorporate a section of more than 120 kinds of imported beers.

9 Québec City After Dark

While Québec City can't pretend to match the volume of nighttime diversions in exuberant Montréal, there's more than enough to do. And apart from theatrical productions, almost always in French, a knowledge of the language is rarely necessary. Drop in at the tourism information office for a list of events.

Check the "Night Life" section of the *Greater Québec Area Tourist Guide* for suggestions. A weekly information leaflet called *L'Info-Spectacles,* listing headline attractions and the venues in which they're appearing, is found at concierge desks and in many bars and restaurants, as is the free tabloid-size *Voir,* which provides greater detail. Both are in French, but salient points aren't difficult to decipher.

THE PERFORMING ARTS

At the **Grand Théâtre de Québec,** 269 bd. René-Lévesque est, at avenue Turnbull (☎ **418/643-8131**), classical music concerts, opera, dance, and theatrical productions are performed in two halls, one housing Canada's largest stage. The **Québec Symphony Orchestra,** Canada's oldest, performs here September to May; the **Québec Opéra** mounts performances here in spring and fall, as does, more occasionally, the **Danse-Partout** dance company. Visiting conductors, orchestras, and dance companies often perform here when the resident companies are away. Québec's Conservatory of Music is underneath the theater. The box office is open Monday to Friday 10am to 6pm.

The 5,500-seat amphitheater **Agora,** 120 rue Dalhousie, at the Vieux-Port (☎ **418/692-4672**), is the scene of rock and occasional classical concerts and a variety of other shows in summer. Iron Maiden, Joe Cocker, and Johnny Winter have appeared recently. The city makes a dramatic backdrop. The box office, at 84 rue Dalhousie, is open daily 10am to 6pm. Rock concerts by name attractions on the order of Phil Collins are generally held at the **Colisée de Québec,** 250 bd. Wilfrid-Hamel, at ExpoCité (☎ **418/691-7211**), located in a park on the north side of the St-Charles River. The box office is open Monday to Friday: in summer 9am to 4pm and in winter 10am to 5pm.

At the edge of the Battlefields Park, the **Kiosque Edwin-Bélanger,** 390 av. de Bernières, near the Musée du Québec (☎ **418/648-4050**), is the site of a 10-week music season mid-June to late August. Performances are Wednesday to Sunday and range from operas, chorales, and classical recitals to jazz, pop, and blues. All are free. Mixes of live shows and attractions are offered on an irregular schedule in the historic 1,312-seat **Théâtre Capitole,** 972 rue St-Jean, near Porte St-Jean (☎ **800/261-9903** ticket office). Dramatic productions and comedic performances are in French, but they also host rock groups and occasional classical recitals.

Many of the city's churches host **sacred and secular music concerts,** as well as special Christmas festivities. Among them are the Cathedral of the Holy Trinity, the Eglise St-Jean-Baptiste, and the Chapelle Bon-Pasteur. **Outdoor performances** in summer are staged beside the City Hall in the Jardins de l'Hôtel-de-Ville, in the Pigeonnier at Parliament Hill, on the Grande-Allée, and at place d'Youville.

LIVE-MUSIC CLUBS

Most bars and clubs stay open until 2 or 3am, closing earlier if business doesn't warrant the extra hour or two. Cover charges and drink minimums are rare in the bars and clubs that provide live entertainment. There are three principal streets among which to choose for nightlife: the **Grande-Allée, rue St-Jean,** and the emerging **avenue Cartier.**

Above the Eldorado boutique, the unusual **Café des Arts,** 1000 rue St-Jean, at the corner of rue Auteuil (☎ **418/694-1499**), puts on theatrical pieces, poetry readings, dance, and jazz. It serves sandwiches and cheese plates and is licensed to sell wine and beer. The cover is usually C$5 to C$10 (US$3.35 to US$7). A musical institution in Québec since 1960, **Chez Son Père,** 24 rue St-Stanislas, a few steps uphill from rue St-Jean (☎ **418/692-5308**), is the place where French-Canadian folksingers often get their start. The stage is on the second floor, with a young, friendly crowd and the usual brick walls and sparse decor.

Visitors who are well into their mortgages will want to keep in mind the chummy pub/bistro **D'Orsay,** 65 rue Baude, opposite the Hôtel de Ville (☎ **418/694-1582**). Most of the crowd is on the far side of 35, and they start up conversations easily. There's a small dance floor with a DJ, and in summer a folksinger perches on a stool on the terrace. Full meals are served. Over the Pizzeria d'Youville, **Kashmir,** 1018 rue St-Jean, near rue St-Stanislas (☎ **418/694-1648**), the show bar that replaced Café Blues, puts on an eclectic variety of musical and artistic presentations, including rock, blues, and art exhibits, with the added attraction of dancing 3 or 4 nights a week. Scheduling is erratic. Pass the time before the evening's performances at the pool tables or poker machines.

At **Le d'Auteuil,** 35 rue d'Auteuil, near Porte Kent (☎ **418/692-2263**), university students and hip 20- and 30-somethings play pool in the bar until the bands start thumping upstairs. Live performers are booked almost every night. Sometimes, they're semifamiliar names, but more often they're local alternative bands or "homage" rock groups. Recent renovations gave the 1822 hall a splashy new look. Listening to jazz, usually of the mainstream or fusion variety, is a long-standing tradition in the agreeable **L'Emprise,** 57 rue Ste-Anne, at rue des Jardins (☎ **418/692-2480**). The bar, off the lobby of the once-elegant Hôtel Clarendon, has large windows and art deco touches. Seating is at tables and around the bar. It has a mellow atmosphere, with serious jazz fans who come to listen. Music is nightly from about 10:15pm.

At the **Palais Montcalm,** 995 place d'Youville, near Porte St Jean (☎ **418/ 670-9011** ticket office), the main performance space is the 1,100-seat Raoul-Jobin theater, with a mix of dance programs, classical music concerts, and plays. More intimate recitals and jazz groups are seen in the much smaller Café-Spectacle. Québecois and French singers alternate with jazz groups in the roomy **Théâtre du Petit-Champlain,** 78 rue du Petit-Champlain, near the funiculaire (☎ **418/692-2631**), with cabarets and revues. Have a drink on the patio before the show. The box office is open Monday to Friday 1 to 5pm or to 7pm the night of a show. Performances are usually Tuesday to Saturday.

BARS & CAFES

The strip of the **Grande-Allée** between place Montcalm and place George-V, near the St-Louis Gate, has been compared to boulevard St-Germain in Paris. That's a real stretch, but it's lined on both sides with cafes, giving it a passing resemblance. Many have terraces abutting the sidewalks, so cafe hopping is an active pursuit. Eating is definitely not the main event. Meeting and greeting and partying are, aided in some cases by glasses of beer so tall they require stands to hold them up. This leads to a beery frathouse atmosphere that can get sloppy and dumb as the evening wears on. But early on, it's fun to sit and sip and watch. The following bars are away from the Grande-Allée melee.

Roomy and sophisticated, the **Saint Alexandre Pub,** 1087 rue St-Jean, near rue St-Stanislas (☎ **418/694-0015**), is the best-looking bar in town. It's done in a British pub mode, with polished mahogany, exposed brick, and a working fireplace that's a particular comfort 8 months of the year. It claims to serve 40 single-malt scotches and more than 200 beers, 20 on tap, along with hearty food that complements the brews. Sometimes it presents jazz duos, usually Monday 7:30 to 11:30pm. Large front windows provide easy observation of the busy St-Jean street life.

A favorite with the after-work crowd since 1945, the **Aviatic Club,** Gare-du-Palais, near rue St-Paul, Lower Town (☎ **418/522-3555**), is in the front of the city's train station. The theme is aviation (odd, given the venue), signaled by two miniature planes hanging from the ceiling. Food is served, ranging from Thai to Tex-Mex in inspiration, along with local and imported beers. Behind the bar, the **Pavillon** (☎ **418/522-0133**), a casual Italian restaurant with pizza, pasta, and pool tables, is under the same ownership.

Spinning slowly in the Loews Le Concorde Hôtel above a city that twinkles like tangled necklaces, the restaurant/bar **L'Astral,** 1225 place Montcalm, at the Grande-Allée (☎ **418/647-2222**), unveils a breathtaking 360° panorama. Many people come for dinner. Make it for drinks and the view. **Le Pape-Georges,** 8 rue Cul-de-Sac, at boulevard Champlain, Lower Town (☎ **418/692-1320**), features jazz or a French singer from Thursday to Sunday at 10pm. Light fare (cheese plates, assorted cold meats, and smoked salmon) is served during the day.

DANCE CLUBS

The top disco in Québec City, the three-story **Chez Dagobert,** 600 Grande-Allée, near rue Turnbull (☎ **418/522-0393**), has an arena arrangement on the ground floor for live bands, with raised seating around the sides. Upper floors have a large dance floor, more bars, TV screens to keep track of sports events, and video games. Sound, whether live or recorded, is a decibel short of bedlam, and more than a few habitués use earplugs. Things don't start jamming until well after 11pm. The crowd divides into students and their more fashionably attired older brothers and sisters. A whole lot of eyeballing and approaching goes on. Challenging Chez Dagobert, the triple-tiered **Maurice,** 575 Grande-Allée est (☎ **418/640-0711**), occupies a converted mansion at the thumping heart of the Grande-Allée scene. The dance room rotates live Latin and blues bands, filling the gaps with house music. Theme nights are frequent, and the balconies, cigar lounge, and Le Charlotte bar can accommodate more than 1,000 post-Boomers. Happy hour has two-for-one drinks.

At **Le Bistro Plus,** 1063 rue St-Jean, near rue St-Stanislas (☎ **418/694-9252**), the dance floor in back, with a light show, is full of writhing young bodies—very young, in many cases. During the week, the music is recorded, with live groups on some weekends. It gets raucous and messy, especially after the 4-to-7pm happy hour, but it's congenial too, with a pool table and TVs tuned to sports. The pair of double-decked bars **Vogue/Sherlock Holmes,** 1170 d'Artgny, off the Grande-Allée (☎ **418/529-9973**), is far less frenetic than Chez Dagobert. There's a small disco upstairs in Vogue and the pubby eatery Sherlock below, with a pool table and dart board. Grad students and Gen-Xers in their first jobs make up most of the crowd.

GAY & LESBIAN CLUBS
The gay scene in Québec City is a small one, centered in the Upper Town just outside the city walls, on **rue St-Jean** between avenue Dufferin and rue St-Augustin and also along **rue St-Augustin** and nearby **rue d'Aiguillon,** which runs parallel to rue St-Jean. One popular bar/disco, frequented by both men and women (and by men who look like women), is **Le Ballon Rouge,** 811 rue St-Jean (☎ **418/647-9227**).

EVENING CRUISES
Dancing and dining await passengers on the MV *Louis Jolliet* (☎ **418/692-1159**), which offers a 2½-hour "Love Boat" evening cruise 8 to 10:30pm. Full dinners are available for C$18 to C$27 (US$12 to US$18) and a complete bar lubricates the evening. The fare is C$22 (US$15). Cruises depart from quai Chouinard at the port.

10 Day Trips from Québec City: Ile d'Orléans & More

You can combine the first four excursions below and complete them in a day. It'll be a breakfast-to-dark undertaking, especially if you take much time to explore each destination, but the farthest of the four destinations is only 25 miles from Québec City.

Bucolic **Ile d'Orléans,** with its maple groves, orchards, farms, and 18th- and 19th-century houses, is a mere 15 minutes away. The famous shrine of **Ste-Anne-de-Beaupré** and the **Mont Ste-Anne** ski area are only about half an hour from the city by car. With 2 or more days available, you can continue along the northern shore to **Charlevoix,** where inns and a new casino invite an overnight. Then take the ferry across the river—in summer and early fall you might sight a whale. At Rivière-du-Loup on the opposite shore, drive back toward Québec City.

While it's preferable to drive through this region, tour buses go to Montmorency Falls and the shrine of Ste-Anne-de-Beaupré and circle the Ile d'Orléans. For organized bus tours, contact **Visite Touristique de Québec** (☎ **418/563-9722**), which offers English-only tours; **Old Québec Tours** (☎ **418/624-0460**); **Maple Leaf Sightseeing Tours** (☎ **418/687-9226**); or **Gray Line** (☎ **418/622-7420**).

For more information, log on to **www.quebec-region.cuq.qc.ca.**

ILE D'ORLÉANS

The **Ile d'Orléans** is only a short 16km (9.9-mile) drive from Québec City. Follow rue Dufferin (in front of the Parliament building) to connect with Autoroute 440 east, in the direction of Ste-Anne-de-Beaupré. In about 15 minutes, you'll see the Ile d'Orléans bridge on the right. You can rent bikes at the gas station/grocery store, **Dépanneur Godbout,** right across the road from the bridge (☎ **418/828-9215**).

After arriving on the island, turn right on Route 368 east toward Ste-Pétronille. The **tourist information office** (☎ **418/828-9411**) is in the house on the right, and it has a useful guidebook (C$1/US65¢) for the island. June to August, it's open daily 9am to 7pm; September to May, hours are Monday to Friday 9am to 5pm. A good substitute for the Ile d'Orléans guide is the Greater Québec guide, which includes a short tour of Ile d'Orléans. You can rent or buy a driving-tour cassette at the tourist office, and cycling maps are available.

Until 1935, the only way to get to the island was by boat (in summer) or over the ice (in winter). The highway bridge since built has allowed the fertile fields of Ile d'Orléans to become Québec City's primary market garden. During harvest periods, fruits and vegetables are picked fresh on the farms and trucked into the city daily. In mid-July, hand-painted signs posted by the main road announce FRAISES: CUEILLIR VOUS-MÊME (Strawberries: pick 'em yourself). The same invitation is made during apple season, September and October. Farmers hand out baskets and quote the price, paid when the basket's full. Bring along a bag or box to carry away the bounty.

Three stone churches here date back to the days of the French regime, due in part to the island's long isolation from the mainland. There are only seven such churches left in all Québec. A firm resistance to development has kept many of its old houses intact as well. This could easily have become just another sprawling bedroom community, but it has remained a rural farming area. Island residents work to keep it that way. They even have plans to bury their telephone lines and to put in a bicycle lane to cut down on car traffic.

A coast-hugging road circles the island, 34km (21 miles) long and 8km (5 miles) wide, and another couple of roads bisect it. Farms and picturesque houses dot the east side of the island, and abundant apple orchards enliven the west side. There are six tiny villages on Ile d'Orléans, each with a church as its focal point. It's possible to do a quick circuit of the island in half a day, but you may be able to justify a full day by eating in a couple of restaurants, visiting a sugar shack, skipping stones from the beach, and staying the night in one of the waterside inns. If you're strapped for time, drive as far as St-Jean, then take Route du Mitan across the island, and return to the bridge, and Québec City, via Route 368 west.

STE-PÉTRONILLE

The first village you reach on my recommended counterclockwise tour is **Ste-Pétronille,** only 3km (1.9 miles) from the bridge. With 1,050 inhabitants, it's best known for its Victorian inn, La Goéliche (below), and it also claims the northernmost stand of red oaks in North America, dazzling in autumn. The houses were once the summer homes of wealthy English in the 1800s; the church dates from 1871. Even if you don't stay at the inn, drive down to the water's edge, where you'll find a small public area with benches. Strolling down the picturesque rue Laflamme is another pleasant way to while away an hour or two as well.

Where to Stay & Dine

La Goéliche. 22 av. du Quai, Ste-Pétronille, PQ G0A 4C0. ☎ **888/511-2248** or 418/828-2248. Fax 418/828-2745. www.oricom.ca/aubergelagoeliche. E-mail aubergelagoeliche@oricom.com. 20 units. MINIBAR TEL. C$108–C$127 (US$72–US$85) double; C$140 (US$93) suite. Rates include breakfast. AE, DC, DISC, ER, MC, V. Free parking.

On a rocky point of land at the southern tip of the island stands this country house with a wraparound porch and a pool. Actually, this is a virtual replica of the 1880 Victorian that was here until 1996, when it burned to the ground, leaving nothing but the staircase. This one was completed in record time and managed to retain the period flavor with tufted chairs, Tiffany-style lamps, and a few antiques. Only the two suites have TVs. The river slaps at the foundation of the glass-enclosed terrace dining room, which is a grand observation point for watching cruise ships and Great Lakes freighters steaming past. The dining room is well regarded, with updated French cooking that's easy on the butter and cream. A modified American plan is available.

St-Laurent

From Ste-Pétronille, continue on Route 368 east. After 6km (3.7 miles), you'll arrive at **St-Laurent,** once a boat-building center turning out 400 craft a year. To learn more about that heritage, visit **Le Parc Maritime de St-Laurent** (☎ 418/828-9672), an active boat yard from 1908 to 1967. Before the bridge was built, it provided islanders the means to get across the river to Québec City. The Maritime Park incorporates the old Godbout Boatworks and offers demonstrations of the craft. June 15 to Labour Day, it's open daily 10am to 5pm.

The town's church was erected in 1860, and there are a couple of picturesque roadside chapels as well. Good views of farmlands and the river are available from the St-Laurent golf course—follow the signs from the main road.

Where to Stay & Dine

Le Canard Huppé. 2198 chemin Royal, St-Laurent, PQ G0A 3Z0. ☎ **800/838-2292** or 418/828-2292. Fax 418/828-2292. www.canard-huppe.qc.ca. E-mail canard-huppe@mediom.qc.ca. 8 units. A/C. C$100–C$125 (US$67–US$83) double. Rates include full breakfast. AE, DC, ER, MC, V.

A roadside inn reminiscent of those found in the motherland, this tidy young place takes considerable pride in its kitchen. Local products and gentle saucings are its hallmarks. Consider this one item: Crimson ravioli stuffed with duck confit and smoked snails and drizzled with lobster butter. All meals are served: You can have breakfast and lunch in the inviting bistro/bar or out on the terrace under the linden tree, while dinner is in the main dining room, where the service meets professional standards. The guest rooms upstairs don't have TV or phones, but they're attractively decorated. Smoking is confined to the bathrooms, with the fan on.

Where to Dine

Le Moulin de St-Laurent. 754 chemin Royal. ☎ **888/629-3888** or 418/829-3888. Reservations recommended at dinner. Main courses C$11–C$23 (US$7–US$15); table d'hôte menu C$10–C$16 (US$7–US$11) at lunch, C$23–C$45 (US$15–US$30) at dinner. AE, CB, DC, ER, MC, V. Daily 10:30am–2pm and 6–9pm. Closed mid-Oct to May 1. COUNTRY FRENCH.

This former flour mill, in operation from 1720 to 1928, has been transformed into one of the island's most romantic restaurants. Rubble-stone walls and hand-wrought beams form the interior, with candlelight glinting off hanging copper and brass pots (be sure to wander upstairs to see the Québecois antiques). On a warm day, sit on the terrace beside the waterfall. Lunch can be light—an omelet or a plate of assorted pâtés or cheeses, perhaps. There are at least half a dozen main courses, only one of them fish, despite all that amply stocked water out there. On weekend evenings, a small combo plays. The owners also have a cottage for rent at the shore.

St-Jean

St-Jean, 6km (3.7 miles) from St-Laurent, was home to sea captains; the homes in the village appear more prosperous than others on the island. The yellow bricks in the

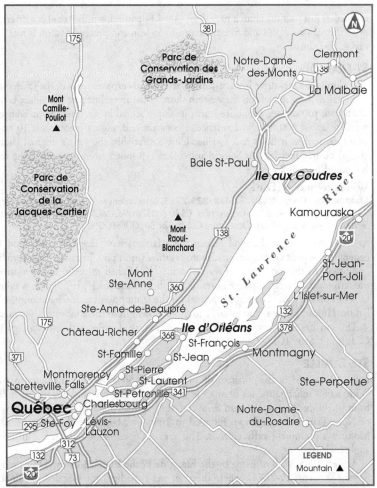

facades of several of the houses were ballast in boats that came over from Europe. The village church was built in 1732, and the walled cemetery is the final resting place of many fishermen and seafarers.

On the left as you enter the village is one of the largest and best-preserved houses on the island: the **Manoir Mauvide-Genest,** 1451 av. Royale (☎ **418/829-2630**). Completed in 1752, it's filled with period furnishings. A "beggar's bench" on view was so named because a homeless person who appeared at the door late in the day would be offered a bed for the evening (otherwise, he might cast a spell on the house). A small chapel was added in 1930, and Huron Indians made the altar. Admission is C$4 (US$2.65) adults, C$2.50 (US$1.65) seniors/students, and C$2 (US$1.35) children under 14. June to August, it's open daily 10:30am to 5:30pm (other times by appointment). In summer, the dining room is open daily 11am to 9pm, with the table d'hôte menu C$8 (US$5) at lunch and C$18 (US$12) at dinner. Next to the manor house is an active summer theater.

If you're pressed for time, pick up Route du Mitan, which crosses Ile d'Orléans from here to St-Famille on the west side of the island. Route du Mitan, not easy to spot, is on the left just past the church in St-Jean. A brief detour down that road is a diverting drive through farmland and forest. Return to St-Jean and proceed east on Route 368 east to St-François.

ST-FRANÇOIS

The 9km (5.6-mile) drive from St-Jean to **St-François** exposes vistas of the Laurentian Mountains off to the left on the western shore of the river. Just past the village center of St-Jean, you can see Mont Ste-Anne, its slopes scored by ski trails. At St-François, home to about 500, the St. Lawrence, a constant and mighty presence, is 10 times wider than when it flows past Québec City. Regrettably, the town's original church (1734) burned in 1988. At St-François, 24km (15 miles) from the bridge, the road becomes Route 368 west.

Where to Stay & Dine

Chaumonot. 425 av. Royale. ☎ **418/829-2735.** Reservations recommended. Main courses C$18–C$27 (US$12–US$18); table d'hôte C$30 (US$20). AE, MC, V. Daily 11am–3pm and 5–9pm (to 10pm July–Aug). Closed mid-Oct to Apr 30. QUÉBECOIS.

At this riverside inn, the food reflects what farmers have eaten on this island for generations—pork chops, lamb, salmon, *tourtière* (meat pie), pheasant pâté, tomato-and-onion relish, and plenty of warm bread. The kitchen mixes in a few relatively modern touches, such as quiche Lorraine and shrimp-and-duck pâté. Picture windows look out on the river. The place is named for the Jesuit priest Pierre Chaumonot, who led the Hurons to the island in 1651 to protect them from the attacking Algonquins.

The inn has eight ordinary but tidy guest rooms; doubles with breakfast go for C$129 to C$139 (US$86 to US$93).

STE-FAMILLE

Founded in 1661 at the northern tip of the island, **Ste-Famille** is the oldest parish. With 1,660 inhabitants, it's 8km (5 miles) from St-François and 19km (12 miles) from the bridge. Across the road from the triple-spired church (1743) is the convent of Notre-Dame Congregation, founded in 1685 by Marguerite Bourgeoys, one of Montréal's prominent early citizens. This area supports dairy and cattle farms and apple orchards.

Anglers might wish to swing by the **Etang de Pêche Richard-Boily,** 4739 chemin Royal (☎ **418/829-2874**), where they can wet their lines for speckled or rainbow trout in a stocked pond, daily 9am to sunset. It isn't *entirely* like fishing in a rain barrel. Poles and bait are supplied—no permit is required—and you pay only for what you catch, about C30¢ per inch; the fish run 9 to 12 inches. They'll clean, cut, and pack what you catch. Some island restaurants can even be persuaded to cook the fish for you. For more passive activity, buy a handful of fish pellets for C25¢, toss them in the water, and watch the ravenous trout jump. On the same property is a *cabane à sucre,* a traditional "sugar shack" where maple syrup is made. See demonstrations of the equipment and get debriefed on the process that turns the sap of a tree into syrup. Free tastes are offered, and several types of products are for sale in a shop on the premises.

Farther along, near the village church, you might wish to visit the **Boulangerie G. H. Blouin** (☎ **418/829-2590**), run by a family of bakers who have lived on the island for 300 years, and a little shop called **Le Mitan** (☎ **418/829-3206**) that stocks local crafts and books about the island. Alas, the popular restaurant L'Arte has closed after 40 years.

ST-PIERRE

By Ile d'Orléans standards, **St-Pierre** is a big town, with a population of about 2,000. Its central attraction is the island's oldest church (1717). Services are no longer held there; it now contains a large handicraft shop in the back, behind the altar, which is even older than the church (1695). The pottery, beeswax candles, dolls, scarves, woven rugs, and blankets aren't to every taste but are worth a look.

Thousands of migrating snow geese, Canada geese, and ducks stop by in spring, a spectacular sight when they launch themselves into the air in flapping hordes so thick they almost blot out the sun.

Where to Stay & Dine

Le Vieux Presbytère. 1247 av. Mgr. d'Esgly, St-Pierre, PQ G0A 4E0. ☎ **418/828-9723** or 888/828-9723. Fax 418/828-2189. www.presbytere.com. 6 units, 2 sharing a bathroom; 2 cottages. C$60–C$100 (US$40–US$67) double; C$60–C$70 (US$40–US$47) cottage. Rates include breakfast. Half board available. MC, V.

Down the street running past the front of the church, the former 1790 rectory has been converted into a homey auberge. Filled with antiques and other old pieces, its sitting and dining rooms and glassed sun porch coax strangers into conversation. For privacy, choose one of the cottages 100 feet from the main house; for more space and enough beds for a family of five, ask for room no. 1. A fireplace warms the dining room much of the year. The kitchen is fond of game, including ostrich, bison, and wapiti. Main courses run C$9 to C$26 (US$6 to US$17), with a table d'hôte of C$49 (US$33), which includes a bottle of wine.

MONTMORENCY FALLS & STE-ANNE-DE-BEAUPRÉ

Take Autoroute 40, north of Québec City, going east. At the end of the autoroute, where it intersects with Route 360, the falls come into view. A **tourist booth** (☎ **418/663-2877**) is beside the parking area at the falls, just after the turnoff from the highway. It's open daily: early June to early September 9am to 7pm and early September to mid-October 11am to 5pm. Admission to the falls is free.

Montmorency Falls is surrounded by a provincial park where you can stop to take in the view or have a picnic early May to late October. At 274 feet, the falls, named by Samuel de Champlain for his patron, the duc de Montmorency, are 100 feet higher than Niagara, a boast no visitor is spared. They are, however, far narrower. In winter, the plunging waters contribute to a particularly impressive sight: the freezing spray sent up by the falls builds a mountain of white ice at the base called the "Sugarloaf," which sometimes grows as high as 100 feet. On summer nights the falls are illuminated, and in the last 2 weeks of July is a fireworks festival. The yellow cast of the waterfall results from the high iron content of the river bed. The Manoir Montmorency, above the falls, opened in 1994, replacing an earlier structure that burned down. Lunch and dinner are served there daily, except Monday and Tuesday dinners January to March.

From Montmorency Falls, it's a 20-minute drive along Route 138 east to the little town of **Ste-Anne-de-Beaupré.** The highway goes right past the basilica, with an easy entrance into the large parking lot. An **information booth** at the southwestern side of the basilica, 10018 av. Royale (☎ **418/827-3781**), is open early May to mid-September daily 8:30am to 5pm. The basilica itself is open year-round, and admission is free. Masses are held daily but hours vary.

Legend has it that French mariners were sailing up the St. Lawrence River in the 1650s when they ran into a terrifying storm. They prayed to their patroness, St. Anne, to save them, and when they survived, they dedicated a wooden chapel to her on the north shore of the St. Lawrence, near the site of their perils. Not long afterward, a laborer on the chapel was said to have been cured of lumbago, the first of many documented miracles. Since that time, pilgrims have made their way here—more than a million a year—to pay their respects to St. Anne, the mother of the Virgin Mary and grandmother of Jesus.

Reactions to the resulting **religious complex** inevitably vary. To the faithful, this is a place of wonder, perhaps the most important pilgrimage site in North America. Others see it as a building that lacks the grandeur its great size is intended to impart, a raw and ponderous structure without the ennobling patina of age. The former group will want to schedule at least a couple of hours to absorb it all; the latter won't need more than 15 minutes to satisfy their curiosity.

The towering **basilica** is the most recent building raised on this spot in St. Anne's honor. After the sailors' first modest wooden chapel was swept away by a flood in the 1600s, another chapel was built on higher ground. Floods, fires, and the ravages of time dispatched later buildings, until a larger, presumably sturdier structure was erected in 1887. In 1926, it too lay in ruins, gutted by fire.

As a result of a lesson finally learned, the present basilica is constructed in stone, following an essentially neo-Romanesque scheme. Marble, granite, mosaics, stained glass, and hand-carved wood are employed with a generous hand throughout. The pews are of wood with hand-carved medallions at the ends, each portraying a different animal. Behind the main altar are eight side chapels and altars, each unique. The hundreds of crutches, canes, braces, and artificial limbs strapped to columns and stacked on the floor of the vestibule—left behind by those who no longer needed them—attest to the conviction that miracles routinely occur here.

Other attractions in Ste-Anne-de-Beaupré include the **Way of the Cross,** with life-size cast-iron figures, on the hillside opposite the basilica; the **Scala Santa Chapel** (1891); and the **Memorial Chapel** (1878), with a bell tower and altar from the late 17th and early 18th centuries, respectively. I suggest you skip the **Historial** museum, the **wax museum,** and the **Cyclorama,** a 360° painting of Jerusalem.

WHERE TO STAY & DINE

✪ **Auberge La Camarine.** 10947 bd. Ste-Anne, Beaupré, PQ G0A 1E0. ☎ **800/567-3939** or 418/827-5703. Fax 418/827-5430. www.total.net/~camarine/index. 31 units. TV TEL. C$99–C$129 (US$66–US$86) double. AE, DC, MC, V. Go just past the Promenades Ste-Anne outlet center, turning left off Rte. 138.

Why they named it after a bitter berry is uncertain, but this inn has a kitchen equaled by only a bare handful of restaurants in the entire province—and that includes Montréal. (Reservations are essential for dinner, daily 6 to 8:30pm.) The cuisine bears a resemblance to that variety of fusion cookery joining French, Italian, and Asian techniques and ingredients. Salmon tartar married with leaves of smoked sturgeon and crisply sautéed lettuce is illustrative. Further specifics are fruitless, for the menu changes frequently. The owners are justly proud of their wine cellar, which includes a wide selection of half bottles. The guest rooms blend antique and contemporary notions, and some have fireplaces, air-conditioning, and/or exercycles; two have Jacuzzis. The ski slopes of Mount Ste-Anne are a short drive away.

MONT STE-ANNE: SKIING & SUMMER SPORTS

Continue along Route 138 from Ste-Anne-de-Beaupré to **Mont Ste-Anne's** recreational area. The park entrance is easy to spot from the highway.

Like Montréal, Québec City has its Laurentian hideaways. But there are differences: The Laurentians sweep down quite close to the St. Lawrence at this point, so Québecois need drive only about 30 minutes to be in the woods. And since Québec City is much smaller than Montréal, the Québec resorts are more modest in size and fewer in number; however, their facilities and amenities are equal to those of resorts elsewhere in the Laurentian range.

The park's 78km² (30 sq. miles) surround a 2,625-foot-high peak. In summer, there are camping, golfing, in-line skating, hiking, jogging, paragliding, and a 150-mile network of mountain-biking trails (you can rent bikes at the park). Late June to early September, an eight-passenger gondola to the top of the mountain operates daily for the benefit of cyclists, weather permitting. In winter, the park is Québec's largest and busiest ski area. Twelve lifts, including the gondola and three quad chair lifts, transport downhill skiers to the starting points of 50 trails and slopes.

Condos are available for rent, and there are seven restaurants on the park grounds or in the vicinity. Golf, camping, and cycling packages are offered. For information and reservations, call ☎ **418/827-2002** or fax 418/827-6666.

CHARLEVOIX

Take Route 138 as far as Baie St-Paul, 87km (54 miles) from Québec City. Baie St-Paul has a **tourist office** at 4 rue Ambroise-Fafard (☎ **418/435-4160**). It's open daily: mid-June to Labour Day 9am to 9pm and September to early June 9am to 5pm.

The Laurentians move closer to the shore of the St. Lawrence as they approach what used to be called Murray Bay at the mouth of the Malbaie River. I say the entire length of Route 138 from Beaupré is fascinating, but the Route 362 detour from Baie St-Paul is scenic, with wooded hills slashed by narrow riverbeds and billowing meadows ending in harsh cliffs plunging down to the river. The air is scented by sea salt and rent by the shrieks of gulls.

From Baie St-Paul to Cap à l'Aigle, a few miles beyond La Malbaie, there are several good-to-memorable inns. Nearby Pointe-au-Pic has a casino, a smaller offshoot of the one in Montréal. The northern end of the region is marked by the confluence of the Saguenay River and the St. Lawrence. These waters attract six species of whales, many of which you can see from shore mid-June to late October, though whale-watching cruises are increasingly popular.

In 1988, **Charlevoix** was named a UNESCO World Biosphere Reserve. Though only 1 of 325 such regions throughout the world, it was the first one to include human settlement.

BAIE ST-PAUL

The first town of any size reached in Charlevoix via Route 138, **Baie St-Paul,** an attractive community of 6,000, holds onto a reputation as an artist's retreat that began in the early 1900s. More than a dozen boutiques and galleries and a couple of small museums show the work of local painters and artisans. Given the setting, it isn't surprising that many of the artists are landscapists.

One undertaking, opened in 1992, is **Le Centre d'Exposition,** 23 rue Ambroise-Fafard (☎ **418/435-3681**), a brick-and-glass museum with three floors of work primarily by regional artists, past and present. Inuit sculptures are included, and temporary one-person and group shows are mounted throughout the year. Admission is C$3 (US$2) adults and C$2 (US$1.35) seniors/students; children under 12 are free. It's open daily: June to August 9am to 7pm (to 5pm Sept to May).

Where to Stay & Dine

La Maison Otis. 23 rue St-Jean-Baptiste, Baie St-Paul, PQ G0A 1B0. ☎ **800-267-2254** or 418/435-2255. Fax 418/435-2464. www.quebecweb.com/maisonotis. 30 units. A/C TV TEL. Late June to late Oct and Christmas to mid-Apr C$204–C$274 (US$136–US$183) double; late Oct to Dec 23 and mid-Apr to late June C$175–C$265 (US$117–US$177) double. Rates include breakfast and dinner. AE, DC, ER, MC, V.

The prices may look steep at first, but big breakfasts and dinners are included (and required), so lunch is redundant. A wide range of facilities and amenities allows guests who reserve far enough in advance to customize their lodgings. Combinations of fireplaces, whirlpools, stereo systems, VCRs, four-poster beds, and suites that sleep four are available, distributed among three buildings. The housekeeping is meticulous. A long porch fronts the colorful main street, and a kidney-shaped indoor pool and sauna are on the premises, as is a jovial piano bar. The required meals are no sacrifice, served in a room with a stone fireplace. Excellent clam chowder, salmon tartare, and pheasant have been notable in the past.

ST-IRÉNÉE

From Baie St-Paul, take Route 362 toward La Malbaie. It roller-coasters over bluffs above the river, and in about 33km (20 miles) is **St-Irénée,** a cliff-top hamlet of fewer than 800 year-round residents. Apart from the setting, the best reason for dawdling here is the lengthy music and dance festival held every mid-June to late August: **Domaine Forget,** 398 chemin les Bains (☎ **888/336-7438,** ext. 800, or 418/452-3535, ext. 800, for tickets), offers concerts on Wednesday, Saturday, some Friday evenings, and Sunday 11am to 2pm. Ten more weekend concerts are spaced from September to late November. This performing-arts festival was initiated in 1977, with the purchase of a large hillside property overlooking the river. Stables and barns were converted into studios and rehearsal halls, and the surrounding lawns were used to stage the concerts and recitals. Their success prompted the construction of a new 600-seat hall. While the program emphasizes classical music with solo instrumentalists and chamber groups, it's peppered with appearances by jazz combos. During summer, tickets are C$21 to C$27 (US$14 to US$18), with children under 12 admitted free. The fall concerts cost C$12 to C$24 (US$8 to US$16).

POINTE-AU-PIC

From St-Irénée, the road starts to bend west after 6 miles (10km), as the mouth of the Malbaie River starts to form. **Pointe-au-Pic** is one of the trio of villages collectively known as La Malbaie, or Murray Bay, as it was known to the wealthy Anglophones who made this their resort of choice from the Gilded Age on through the 1950s. While inhabitants of the region wax poetic about their hills and trees and wildlife "where the sea meets the sky," they have something quite different to preen about now.

The **Casino de Charlevoix,** 183 av. Richelieu/Route 362 (☎ 800/665-2274 or 418/665-5300), is the second of Québec's gambling casinos (the first is in Montréal and the third opened in the Ottawa/Hull area in 1996). It's about as tasteful as such places get this side of Monte Carlo. Cherry-wood paneling and granite floors enclose the ranks of 303 slot machines and 15 tables, including blackjack, roulette wheels, stud poker, and minibaccarat (no craps). Only soft drinks are allowed at the machines and tables, so players have to go to an adjacent bar to mourn their losses. And there's a dress code, forbidding, among other items, tank tops, bustiers, and "clothing associated with organizations known to be violent." Running shoes and "neat" blue jeans are allowed, though the management can get picky on weekends, when it gets very crowded. Admission is free to persons 18 and over. June to September, the casino is open daily 10am to 4am; October to May, hours are Monday to Friday 11am to 1am and Saturday to Sunday 11am to 3am. Signs are frequent on Route 362 coming from the south and on Route 138 from the north.

Opened in 1975, the **Musée de Charlevoix,** 1 chemin du Havre, at the intersection with Route 362/boulevard Bellevue (☎ **418/665-4411**), moved to its present quarters in 1990. Folk art, sculptures, and paintings of variable quality by regional artists figure prominently in the permanent collection, supplemented by frequent temporary exhibits with diverse themes. Admission is C$4 (US$2.65) adults and C$3 (US$2) seniors/students; children under 12 are free. June 25 to September 4, the museum is open daily 10am to 6pm; September 5 to June 24, hours are Tuesday to Friday 10am to 5pm and Saturday to Sunday 1 to 5pm.

Where to Stay & Dine

✪ **Auberge des Falaises.** 18 chemin des Falaises, Pointe-au-Pic, PQ G0T 1M0. ☎ **800/386-3731** or 418/665-3731. Fax 418/665-6194. www.aubergedesfalaises. com. 48 units. TV TEL. C$98–C$154 (US$65–US$103). Rates include breakfast. MAP and other packages available. AE, DC, ER, MC, V.

"Falaise" means "bluff," and most guest rooms here enjoy engrossing views of the Charlevoix coast. They're of good size, with functional furniture and Laura Ashley prints. Most have whirlpool bathtubs and some have balconies. The highlights of a stay here (and the reason for the star) are the meals in a dining room that ranks among the province's best, starting with the graceful service. The food is memorable—your evening may began with silky chilled cucumber soup with flecks of crabmeat and a plate of zucchini blossoms that the chef, by some legerdemain, has stuffed with lobster mousse. You can finish with the plate of four cheeses and the frozen lime sorbet.

Manoir Richelieu. 181 rue Richelieu, Pointe-au-Pic, PQ G0T 1M0. ☎ **800/441-1414** or 418/665-3703. Fax 418/665-3093. www.quebecweb.com/manoir.richelieu. 372 units. A/C TV TEL. C$115–C$125 (US$77–US$83) double. Rates include breakfast. MAP, golf, and other packages available. AE, DC, ER, MC, V.

Since 1899, there has been a resort hotel here (the present version dates from 1929), long the aristocratic haven of swells summering in Murray Bay. The opening of the new casino across the drive-up circle has changed the makeup of visitors. To the mix of the elderly who've been coming here since they were youngsters and families who've discovered they can be together and still have time for themselves have been added those people who'll go anywhere for the pleasure of losing money. With the large numbers coursing through the halls, there's no denying that individuals get lost, and services sometimes fall short. The guest rooms are comfortable enough; many have good views of the river and shore. After a recent overhaul that required the closing of the hotel for months, the rate structure noted above is certain to be revised. Buffet lovers are bound to be pleased with the dozens of platters and trays set out for all three meals in the main dining room. There are sit-down menus too. Downstairs, the informal Winston Pub is an able alternative. Golf on the hillside course above the hotel provides the bonus of river views. A fitness center has weight machines and a sauna.

CAP À L'AIGLE

Route 362 rejoins Route 138 in La Malbaie, the largest town in the area, with almost 4,000 inhabitants. It serves as a provisioning center, with supermarkets, hardware stores, and gas stations. The **tourist office** is at 630 bd. de Comporté; mid-June to Labour Day, it's open daily 9am to 9pm (the rest of the year to 5pm). Continue through the town center and cross the bridge on the right, making a sharp right again on the other side. This is Route 138, with signs pointing to **Cap à l'Aigle.**

William Howard Taft spent many summers in Murray Bay, starting in 1892 and extending well past his one-term presidency. For much of that time, the only way to get here was by boat; the railroad didn't arrive until 1919. Given his legendary girth, it may be assumed that Taft knew something about the good life. Some of the other folks who made this their summer home, namely the Cabots of Boston, a Duke of Windsor, and Charlie Chaplin, could confirm that Taft loved the region.

Where to Stay & Dine

✪ **La Pinsonnière.** Cap à l'Aigle, PQ G0T 1B0. ☎ **418/665-4431.** Fax 418/665-7156. 27 units. A/C TV TEL. May–Oct 7 and Christmas–New Year's C$140–C$500 (US$93–US$334) double; Nov–Apr C$125–C$500 (US$83–US$334) double. MAP available but not required. Packages available. AE, DISC, MC, V.

In all Canada, this is one of only eight members in the prestigious Relais and Châteaux organization. As aficionados know, member properties offer limited size, guest rooms that often border on princely luxury, and an emphasis on food and wine. The rooms come in five categories, the priciest of which have Jacuzzis and gas fireplaces. A substantial renovation of six of the larger rooms and the public areas has just been completed. Packages include whale-watching cruises, dogsled runs, and skiing at Mont Grand-Fonds.

Dining: You'll know where the owners focus their laser-like attention when you're seated in the serene dining room beside the picture window. With drinks and menus comes the customary *amuse-guele*—say, a quail leg on a bed of slivered asparagus and fettuccine tossed with plump mussels, spiked with a spray of pungent tarragon and brightened with an edible pansy—immediately followed by soup. The main event might be a succulent veal chop with a nest of shaved carrots, fiddleheads, and purple potatoes. Wines are a particular point of pride here.

Amenities: Indoor pool, sauna, tennis, beach (very cold water), massages.

ST-SIMEON

Rejoin Route 138 and continue 33km (20 miles) to **St-Simeon.** If you've decided to cross to Rivère-du-Loup on the other side of the St. Lawrence, returning to Québec City along the south shore, the ferry departs from here. With discretionary time left, I recommend continuing on to Baie Ste-Catherine and Tadoussac, but if that isn't an option, it's only 150km (93 miles) back to the city the way you came on the north shore.

Once in St-Simeon, you'll see signs directing cars and trucks down to the ferry terminal. Boarding is on a first-come, first-served basis, and ferries leave on a carefully observed schedule, weather permitting, late March to early January. Departure times of the five daily sailings vary substantially from month to month, however, so to get a copy of the schedule contact **Clarke Transport Canada** at ☎ **418/862-9545.** For current fares, call ☎ **418/862-5094.** At last look, but always subject to change, one-way fares were C$10 (US$7) adults, C$9 (US$6) seniors, C$7 (US$4.55) children 5 to 11, and C$26 (US$17) cars. Arrive at least 30 minutes before departure, 1 hour ahead in summer. The boat is equipped with a luncheonette, lounges, and a newsstand. Voyages take 65 to 75 minutes.

Late June to September, you may enjoy a bonus. Those are the months the **whales** are most active; they're estimated at more than 500 in number when pelagic (migratory) species join the resident minke and beluga whales. They prefer the northern side of the Estuary, roughly from La Malbaie to Baie Ste-Catherine, at the mouth of the Saguenay River. Since that's the area the ferry steams through, sightings are an ever-present possibility, especially in summer.

BAIE STE-CATHERINE

To enhance your chances of seeing whales, continue northeast from St-Simeon on Route 138, arriving 33km (20 miles) later in ✪ **Baie Ste-Catherine,** near the estuary of the Saguenay River. A half-dozen companies offer cruises to see whales or the majestic Saguenay Fjord from here or from Tadoussac, on the opposite shore. The cruise companies use different sizes and types of craft, from powered inflatables called zodiacs that carry 10 to 25 passengers up to stately catamarans and cruisers that carry up to 500. The zodiacs don't provide food, drink, or narration, while the larger boats have snack bars and naturalists on board to describe the action. The small boats, though, are more maneuverable, darting about at each sighting to get closer to the rolling and breeching behemoths.

Zodiac passengers are issued life jackets and waterproof overalls, but expect to get wet anyway. It's cold out there too, so layers and even gloves are a good idea. People on the large boats sit at tables inside or ride the observation bowsprit, high above the waves. Big boats are the wimp's choice for whale watching. Mine too.

Most cruises last 2 to 3 hours. One of the most active companies offering trips is **Croisières AML,** with offices in Québec City (☎ **800/563-4643** all year, 418/692-1159 in season). June to mid-October, it offers up to four departures daily, costing C$32 (US$21) adults and C$20 (US$13) children 6 to 12. Excursions of comparable duration and with similar fares are provided on the catamaran maintained by **Croisières Dufour** (☎ **800/463-5250,** ext. 901).

From Baie Ste-Catherine, it's less than a half-hour drive back to St-Simeon and the ferry across to the opposite shore. Alternatively, you can continue north to the ferry, **Traverse Tadoussac** (☎ **418/235-4395**), at the mouth of the dramatic Saguenay River. Palisades rise sharply from both shores, the reason it's often referred to as a fjord. The ferry can board up to 400 passengers and 75 vehicles for the trip across to Tadoussac, which takes only 10 minutes. Departure times vary according to season and demand, but in summer figure every hour midnight to 6am, every 40 minutes 6:20am to 8am, every 20 minutes 8am to 8pm, and every 40 minutes 8:20pm to midnight.

TADOUSSAC

The oldest permanent European settlement north of Mexico, **Tadoussac** was established in 1600 at the point where the Saguenay and St. Lawrence Rivers meet. Missionaries followed and stayed until the mid–19th century. The hamlet might've vanished soon after, had a resort hotel not been built there in 1864. A steamship line brought vacationers downriver from Montréal and points farther west and deposited them here for stays that often lasted all summer. Apart from the hotel—the current building was erected in 1942—a few small support businesses, a post office, a marina, and more than a dozen small motels and B&Bs constitute the town. Its port is an important starting point for whale-watching and Saguenay cruises. Tadoussac is the southernmost point of the tourist region designated as Manicouagan.

Where to Stay & Dine

Hôtel Tadoussac. 165 rue Bord de l'Eau, Tadoussac, PQ G0T 2A0. ☎ **888/561-0718** or 418/235-4421. Fax 418/235-4607. www.familledufour.com/eng. 149 units. TV TEL. C$80–C$210 (US$53–US$140) double. Rates include breakfast. MAP, golf, and whale-watching cruise packages available. AE, DC, ER, MC, V. Closed Nov to early Apr.

From the opposite shore, the bright-red mansard roof of this sprawling hotel dominates the point of land sloping down to the river. The lawns have a petanque court and an outdoor pool, as well as groupings of chairs from which to watch the comings and goings of boats and zodiacs. The public spaces and guest rooms have a shambling, country cottage appearance—no pretense of luxe here. The maple furnishings and handwoven rugs and bedspreads are all made in Québec. Meals in the large dining room are better than you might expect, while falling well short of impressive. The fixed-price meals have a substantial number of choices in each course, from appetizer to dessert. Advance reservations must be made for dinner, with the earlier seating drawing older guests and most of the families with children. Tennis and golf are available.

11 The Gaspé Peninsula: A Great Escape

The southern bank of the St. Lawrence sweeps north and then eastward toward the Atlantic. At the river's mouth, the thumb of land called the **Gaspé Peninsula**—Gaspésie in French—pokes into the Gulf of St. Lawrence. The Gaspé is a primordial region heaped with aged, blunt hills covered with hundreds of square miles of woodlands. Over much of its northern perimeter, their slopes fall directly into the sea, then back away to define the edges of a coastal plain. Winter here is long and harsh, making the crystal days of summer all the more precious.

The fishing villages huddled around the coves cut from the coast are as sparsely populated as they've always been, with many of the young residents moving inland toward brighter lights (unemployment in the region is close to 30%). That leaves the crash of the surf, eagles and elk in the high grounds, and timber to be harvested gingerly by lumber companies, the principal industry.

All that makes it the perfect place for camping, hiking, biking, hunting, and fishing in near-legendary salmon streams. Almost every little town has a modest but clean motel and a restaurant to match. The purpose of a trip is a complete escape from the cities, and your destination is the tip of the thumb, the village of Percé and the famous rock for which it's named.

From Québec City, driving around the peninsula and back to the city takes about 5 days, assuming only an overnight stay when you get to Percé. The first half of the trip is the most scenic, while the underside of the peninsula is largely a flat coastal plain beside a regular shoreline. That southern shore is the route of the Via Rail trains, a thrice-weekly service recently restored between Montréal, Québec, and intermediate stops on the way to the town of Gaspé. The train, called the *Chaleur,* makes a stop at Lévis, opposite Québec City, and the ferry ride is complimentary for VIA Rail passengers. It leaves Lévis at 10:35pm on Monday, Thursday, and Saturday and arrives at Percé at 10:34am the next morning. Passengers in sleeping cars have the use of showers and a domed lounge car.

For more information about the Gaspé, log on to **www.gaspesie.qc.ca**.

Note: For a quick overview of the peninsula, see the "New Brunswick & the Gaspé Peninsula" map on p. 93.

FROM RIVIÉRE-DU-LOUP TO RIMOUSKI

Past **Riviére-du-Loup** along Route 132, the country slowly grows more typically Gaspésien. Bogs on the river side of the road yield bales of peat moss, shipped to gardeners throughout the continent. Past the town of Trois Pistoles (the name comes from a French coin, the pistole, not from firearms) are miles of low rolling hills and fenced fields for dairy cattle. Along the roadside, hand-painted signs advertise *pain de ménage* (homemade bread) and other baked goods for sale.

Rimouski (pop. 40,000) is the region's largest city. It has the look of a boomtown, with many new buildings, but travelers not there on business are likely to pass on through. Rimouski marks the start of the true Gaspé, free of the gravitational pull of Greater Québec. The number of the two-lane highway is 132, running all the way around the peninsula to join itself again at Mont Joli. Thus the confusing signs: 132 EST (east) and 132 OUEST (west).

THE JARDINS DE MÉTIS

Near Grand Métis is the former Reford estate, now the ✪ **Jardins de Métis** (☎ 418/775-2221)—easily the north shore's stellar attraction. The gardens were last owned by a woman with such a passion for gardening that even in Gaspé's relatively severe climate she was able to cultivate a horticultural wonderland of some 100,000 plants in 2,500 varieties. Full of fragrances and birdsong and tumbling water, the six sections are laid out in the informal English manner. Butterflies float and hummingbirds zip among the blossoms, all but oblivious to humans. The provincial government took over the gardens in 1962, and you can visit them June to August daily 8:30am to 6:30pm (Sept and Oct to 5pm). Admission is C$8 (US$5) adults, C$7 (US$4.65) seniors/students, and C$3.50 (US$2.35) ages 6 to 14; children under 6 are free. Elsie Reford's mansion now houses a museum of limited interest and a busy restaurant, open daily 9am to 5pm.

MATANE

The highway enters **Matane** and passes gas stations and a new shopping center whose traffic rivals the bustle in Rimouski. But the focal point is the Matane River, a thoroughfare for the annual migration of up to 3,000 spawning salmon. They begin their swim up the Matane in June through a specially designed dam that facilitates their passage, continuing to September. Near the lighthouse the town maintains a seasonal **information bureau** (☎ **418/562-1065**), open mid-June to early September daily 8am to 8pm.

It takes 5 nonstop driving hours to get to Percé from Matane, so plan to spend a full day getting there. There are frequent picnic grounds, a couple of large nature preserves, and ample opportunities to sit by the water and collect driftwood. While towns along the way are smaller and more spread out, you'll find many modest motels, called *gîtes*, and tourist cabins. Simple sustenance isn't a problem either, for there are many *casse-croûtes*, the roadside snack stands also known as *cantines*.

WHERE TO STAY

Riôtel. 250 av. du Phare est, Matane, PQ G4W 3N4. ☎ **800/463-7468** or 418/566-2651. Fax 418/562-7365. 96 units. www.riotel.qc.ca. A/C TV TEL. C$119–C$189 (US$79–US$126) double. Packages and Sept–May discounts available. AE, CB, DC, DISC, ER, MC, V. Free parking.

On the water near the harbor, the former Hôtel des Gouverneurs is now part of a small Gaspé chain. It hasn't changed much. Half of its guest rooms have ocean views, and some have minibars. The licensed dining room serves all meals, with dinner main courses running C$14 to C$24 (US$9 to US$16). A piano bar helps pass an evening, and on the premises are a heated pool, a sauna, an exercise room, and a lighted tennis court. You may be encouraged to eat at the beach restaurant next door. Don't.

STE-ANNE-DES-MONTS & THE PARC DE LA GASPÉSIE

Ste-Anne-des-Monts (pop. 6,000), another fishing town, has a seasonal **tourist booth** (☎ 418/763-5832) on Route 132, half a mile past the bridge, and also stores, garages, gas stations, and other necessary services.

Rising higher inland are the Chic-Choc mountains, the northernmost end of the Appalachian range. Most of them are contained by the **Parc de la Gaspésie** and adjoining preserves. Turn onto Route 299 in Ste-Anne-des-Monts and head for the Gîte du Mont-Albert, about 40km (25 miles) south. The road climbs into the mountains, some of which are naked rock at the summits. Back there, the rivers brim with baby salmon and speckled trout, and the forests and meadows sustain herds of moose, caribou, and deer.

WHERE TO STAY & DINE

Gîte du Mont-Albert. Parc de la Gaspésie, C.P. 1150, Ste-Anne-des-Monts, PQ G0E 2G0. ☎ **888/270-4483** or 418/763-2288. Fax 418/763-7803. www.sepaq.com. E-mail gitmalb@quebectel.com. 53 units. C$119–C$179 (US$79–US$119) double. AE, MC, V.

Reservations are essential for a meal or lodging at this remote lodge, operated as a training ground for people planning to enter the hospitality profession. The guest rooms in the main lodge or outlying cottages are summer-camp rustic, but the food served in the dining room is considerably more sophisticated than you might expect.

MONT ST-PIERRE: PERFECT FOR HANG GLIDING

Back on Route 132, turning right from Ste-Anne, you'll find the highway becoming a narrow band crowded up to water's edge by sheer rock walls. Offshore, seabirds perch on rocks, pecking at tidbits. High above the shore are many waterfalls that spill from the cliffs beside the highway.

Around a rocky point and down a slope, **Mont St-Pierre** is much like other Gaspésian villages except for the eye-catching striations in the rock of the mountain east of town. Such geological phenomena are quickly forgotten at the startling sight of hang gliders suddenly appearing overhead. The site is regarded as nearly perfect for the sport due to its favorable updrafts. In late July and early August, the town holds a 2-week **Fête du Vol-Libre** (Hang-Gliding Festival), when the sky is filled with birdmen and birdwomen in flight hundreds of feet above the town, looping and curving on the air currents until landing in the sports grounds behind city hall. For more information about the event, contact the **Corporation Vol Libre,** C.P. 82, Mont St-Pierre, Gaspésie (☎ **418/797-2222;** fax 418/797-5101).

THE PARC NATIONAL FORILLON

Soon the road winds up into the mountains, over a rise, down into the valley, and again up to the next. The settlements get smaller, but still there are roadside stands advertising fresh-baked homemade bread and fresh fish. At Petite-Rivière-au-Renard, Route 197 heads southwest toward Gaspé while Route 132 continues east to the tip of the peninsula. Shortly after that intersection is the reception center for the **Parc National Forillon** (☎ **418/368-5505**). Bilingual attendants on duty there can advise on park facilities, regulations, and activities. Route 132 continues along the edge of the park until it turns south at a lighthouse into the grounds.

Chosen because of its representative terrain, the park's 238km² (92 sq. miles) of headlands capture a surprising number of the features characteristic of eastern Canada. A rugged coastline, dense forests, and an abundance of wildlife attract hikers and campers from all over North America. On the northern shore are sheer rock cliffs carved by the sea from the mountains, and on the south is the broad Bay of Gaspé. The park has a full program of nature walks, trails for hiking and cycling, beaches, sea kayaking, picnic spots, and campgrounds. A daily pass to enter the park is C$4.50 (US$3) adults, C$3.25 (US$2.15) seniors, C$2 (US$1.35) students/children 6 to 16, and C$9 (US$6) families. Camping fees are C$17 to C$21 (US$11 to US$14). Of the 371 campsites at four designated campgrounds, 77 have electricity. Only four are open all year; most of the others are closed mid-October to late May.

Croisière Forillon (☎ **418/892-5629** in summer or 418/368-2448 in winter) operates "discovery" cruises from Cap des Rosiers harbor daily in the warm months. Its 95-passenger *Félix-Leclerc* steams around the rim of the headlands past colonies of seals and seabirds. Fares are C$16 (US$11) adults and C$10 (US$7) children. Whales are sometimes encountered, but cruises specifically intended to get close to those magnificent creatures are provided by **Croisières Baie de Gaspé** (☎ **418/892-5500**). The

Narval III, a powered inflatable, is the means of transport, with a capacity of 46 passengers. Its 2½-hour cruises leave from Grande-Grave Harbor, on the south shore of the park. Fares are C$32 (US$21) adults, C$27 (US$18) seniors/students, and C$10 (US$7) children. Reserve in advance, if possible.

GASPÉ

In 1534, Jacques Cartier stepped ashore in **Gaspé** to claim the land for the king of France, erecting a wooden cross to mark the spot. Today Gaspé is important economically because of its deep-water port and the three salmon rivers emptying into it. Otherwise unprepossessing, it doesn't offer much to detain travelers. The principal attraction is the **Gaspésie Museum**, at Jacques Cartier Point on Route 132 (☎ **418/368-5710**), which endeavors to tell the story of Cartier's landing (hours vary), and the granite dolmens out front are reminiscent of the explorer's native Brittany.

PERCÉ

As you wind through the hills and along the water toward **Percé,** the Pic de l'Aurore (Peak of the Dawn), dominating the town's northern reaches, will come into view. Over the hill from the Pic, you'll see Percé Rock and the bird sanctuary of Ile Bonaventure. The rock is Percé's most famous landmark, a narrow butte rising straight out of the water and pierced by a sea-level hole at its far end. It's especially striking in the sunlight of late afternoon.

The town of Percé (*"Pair-*see") isn't large, and except for a few quiet, well-groomed inland residential streets, it's confined to the main road winding along the shore. Little private museums, cafes, snack bars, gift shops, restaurants, and motels line the highway, and people in swimsuits or shorts and T-shirts give it all a beach-party ambiance. But perhaps because the only way to get here is by this fairly long drive, it has thus far avoided the honky-tonk aspect afflicting many beach communities closer to big cities.

An **information center** (☎ **418/782-5448**) is in town at 142 Rte. 132, open daily 8am to 8pm in summer (shorter hours off-season).

EXPLORING THE AREA

After checking into a motel, most people take a boat trip out to the **Rock** and to the humpbacked bird sanctuary, **Ile Bonaventure,** a provincial park. The island's lure is the quantity, rather than the diversity, of its tens of thousands of nesting birds. Among them are gannets, cormorants, puffins, black guillemots, kittiwakes, and razorbills. For a photographic exhibit of the island's history, visit the **Information Centre** (☎ **418/ 782-2721**) at the foot of the Percé wharf; June to Labour Day, it's open daily 10am to 6pm. Naturalists are on the island to answer questions. Transportation is provided to and from Percé wharf. Birders and hikers can get off at the dock, later picking up one of the ferries arriving two or three times an hour 8am to 5pm. Fares are C$13 (US$9) adults and C$5 (US$3.35) children under 12.

Two glass-bottomed **catamarans,** *Capitaine Duval I* and *III* (☎ **418/782-5401** or 418/782-5355), sail from the same wharf on whale-watching cruises. The cats have lounges, large windows, bar service, rest rooms, and a bilingual crew. Tours go to Percé Rock, Bonaventure Island, and even Forillon National Park. Fares are C$16 (US$11) adults and C$8 (US$5) children. For underwater explorations of the area, contact the **Club Nautique de Percé** (☎ **418/782-5403** in summer or 418/782-5222 in winter; fax 418/782-5624), which can lead you to a dozen or more dive sites. The water is about 50°F to 64°F (10°C to 18°C) June to August and about 57°F (14°C) until mid-October.

The **Parc de l'Ile-Bonaventure-et-du-Rocher-Percé Interpretation Centre,** on l'Irlande Road (☎ **418/782-2240**), focuses on the ecology of the Gulf of St. Lawrence and the natural features of Ile Bonaventure. A 10-minute film of the bird colonies is shown here, and there are saltwater aquariums. June to mid-October, it's open daily 9am to 5pm, with shorter hours the rest of the year.

More? Take a **picnic** up to the roadside rest just north of the Pic de l'Aurore, and then take in different views of Percé Rock. At low tide walk out to the fossil-filled rock on a sandbar, a temptation few visitors resist.

WHERE TO STAY & DINE

La Normandie. 221 Rte. 132 ouest, C.P. 129, Percé, PQ G0C 2L0. ☎ **800/463-0820** or 418/782-2112. Fax 418/782-2337. www.gaspesie.qc.ca/perce. E-mail hnormand@ quebectel.com. 45 units. A/C TV TEL. C$99–C$135 (US$66–US$90) double. Packages available. AE, CB, DC, ER, MC, V. Closed mid-Oct to Apr.

Slightly south of the center, this small hotel occupies a building more stylish than others in town, sheathed in weathered wood. All the guest rooms have small sitting areas, and those facing the water have decks. The Normandie's handsome dining room is respected as one of the peninsula's most ambitious, with unobstructed views of the Rock from every bentwood-and-wicker chair; the five-course table d'hôte dinners (C$23 to C$37/US$15 to US$25) are admirable. Almost always offered are lobster, salmon, scallops, and an especially good halibut steak poached with orange and white-wine sauce. There are an exercise room and a sauna.

WHERE TO DINE

✪ **L'Auberge du Gargantua.** Chemin des Falls. ☎ **418/782-2852.** Reservations recommended. Table d'hôte C$27–C$37 (US$18–US$25). V. Mid-May to mid-Oct daily 4–10pm. Drive south on Rte. 132 from town, watching for the sign L'AUBERGE DU GARGANTUA on the right. CANADIAN.

The owner doesn't sit at your table to take your order anymore—all those ups and downs are a chore when you're past 80. But dining at his log-cabin mountaintop restaurant is as much fun as ever. Check this procession of courses: A plate of hors d'oeuvres that includes a bowl of periwinkles (sea snails) extracted from their shells with pins. A big tureen of soup from which you serve yourself—repeatedly, if you wish. A choice of several fish and game main courses with copious portions of veggies from the garden out back. Sweets from the dessert buffet. All are served by the busy but infectiously cheerful staff, most of whom speak English.

Ottawa & Eastern Ontario

by Herbert Bailey Livesey

9

Ottawa may be the most underappreciated national capital east of Ulan Bator, even though on most counts it's an urban standard against which many medium-sized North American cities might well gauge themselves. Ottawa's downtown is striking, with more renovations to its 19th- and early–20th-century buildings every year and miles of tidy late-Victorian brick houses serving as shops, restaurants, and homes. The Gothic spires and towers of Parliament Hill look like the grand estate of an overachieving Scottish laird, with the voluptuous Gatineau Hills as a backdrop. In spring, carpets of tulips and daffodils embrace residences and ministries and cast visual fire against the deep greens of the city's scores of parks. Cutting a vibrant swath through Ottawa is the Rideau Canal, a magnet for houseboats and cabin cruisers and a scene out of a Dutch painting in winter, when the citizenry takes to the ice on sleighs and skates.

The reality of Ottawa is far from the dour Calvinist sobriety it's often depicted as. It's clean—men with pans and brooms let not a wad of paper linger in downtown gutters—and so far, the city hasn't been visited by choked streets. It possesses, in fact, an often-haunting romance in its lanes and parks and culs-de-sac. See for yourself with a walk down to Victoria Island, between the Portage and Chaudières bridges. Looking east from the island's tip, as the Ottawa River rushes by the bluffs where Parliament stands, you'll find that it won't take much imagination to summon a picture of those early days when fur traders and explorers were drawn westward and great logs rolled down these waterways to what was then a clamorous lumber town. Developers and builders have yet to obscure the treasured vistas of hills and water. And, as a bracing lagniappe, you can experience troops of sentries in scarlet tunics and black shakos marching to drum and bagpipe to the morning changing of the guard, just as they do at Buckingham Palace.

Admittedly, Ottawa was an unlikely candidate for Canada's capital when it was chosen in the mid–19th century. The two provinces of Upper Canada (Ontario) and Lower Canada (Québec) were fused into the United Provinces of Canada, but their rivalry was so bitter the legislature had to meet alternately in Toronto and Montréal. Queen Victoria selected the village of Ottawa in 1858, no doubt in the hope that its location on the Ontario-Québec border would smooth the differences between French and English Canadas. Her choice wasn't met with much praise: Essayist Goldwin Smith called it "a sub-Arctic village, converted by royal mandate into a political cockpit." Other assessments weren't as kind.

For nearly a century the city languished in an undeniable provincialism and worked on its reputation for propriety. Even during its early days, though, it managed to nurture some colorful characters, not the least of whom was Canada's longest-serving prime minister, William Lyon Mackenzie King, who conducted World War II with the guidance of his dog, his deceased mother, and frequent consultations with his predecessor, Sir Wilfrid Laurier, who was by then 2 decades dead.

In the 1960s, perhaps because of Canada's burgeoning nationalism or because the government wished to create a real capital, Ottawa began to change. The National Arts Centre was built, ethnic restaurants multiplied, the Byward Market area and other historic buildings were renovated, and public parks and recreation areas were created—and the process has continued into the present with the building of the National Gallery of Canada. Hull, the Québecois city across the river, has been undergoing a similar transformation, highlighted by the opening of the superb Museum of Civilization and the Casino de Hull. Those twin cities are now full of unexpected pleasures—you can watch the debates and pomp of parliamentary proceedings, take in the street scene from a sidewalk terrace, ski or camp or hike in wilderness only 15 minutes away, and then put your feet up at the fireplace of a rustic French inn.

After visiting Ottawa, you may wish to explore **eastern Ontario** for a few days. The high points are covered here: **Kingston,** an appealing lakefront town with a 3-days-a-week farmers' market, is the principal gateway to the **Thousand Islands** of the St. Lawrence River and **St. Lawrence National Park.** East from **Port Hope**— a worthy stop for antiques hounds—stretches the **Bay of Quinte** and **Quinte's Isle,** a tranquil region of farms, orchards, quaint villages, and riverside parks. Still outside the usual tourist circuits, it was settled by colonials loyal to the Crown who fled the American Revolution.

1 Essentials

ARRIVING

BY PLANE **Ottawa International Airport** is about 20 minutes south of the city. **Air Canada** (☎ 800/361-8620; www.aircanada.ca) and **Canadian Airlines** (☎ 800/665-1177; www.cdnair.ca) are the main airlines serving Ottawa. Other choices are **US Airways** (☎ 800/428-4322; www.usairways.com), **Northwest** (☎ 800/225-2525; www.nwa.com), and **Delta Connection** (☎ 800/363-2857). A shuttle bus (☎ 613/736-9993) operates between the airport and downtown for C$9 (US$6) one-way or C$14 (US$9) adults and C$4 (US$2.65) seniors/students round-trip. A taxi from the airport to the city costs about C$20 (US$13).

BY TRAIN **VIA Rail** trains arrive at the station at 200 Tremblay Rd., at boulevard St-Laurent, in the southeastern area of the city. From here buses connect to downtown. For rail information, contact **VIA Rail Canada** at ☎ 613/244-1660 (www.viarail.ca) or call your local Amtrak office.

BY BUS Buses arrive at the **Central Bus Station,** 265 Catherine St., between Kent and Lyon. **Voyageur Colonial** (☎ 613/238-5900) provides service from other Canadian cities and the United States.

BY CAR Driving from New York, take Interstate 81 to Canada's Route 401 east to Route 16 north. From the west, come via Toronto, taking Route 401 east to Route 16 north. From Montréal, take Route 17 to Route 417.

Ottawa

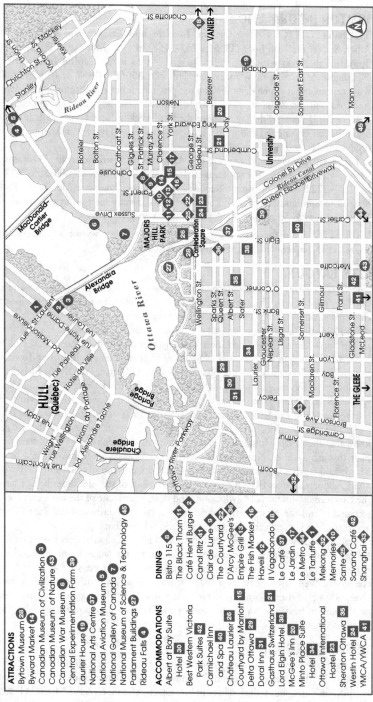

ATTRACTIONS
Bytown Museum 28
Byward Market 14
Canadian Museum of Civilization 3
Canadian Museum of Nature 43
Canadian War Museum 6
Central Experimentation Farm 39
Laurier House 19
National Arts Centre 37
National Aviation Museum 5
National Gallery of Canada 7
National Museum of Science & Technology 45
Parliament Buildings 27
Rideau Falls 4

ACCOMMODATIONS
Albert at Bay Suite Hotel 30
Best Western Victoria Park Suites 42
Carmichael Inn and Spa 40
Château Laurier 15
Courtyard by Marriott 26
Delta Ottawa 29
Doral Inn 31
Gasthaus Switzerland 21
Lord Elgin Hotel 38
McGee's Inn 20
Minto Place Suite Hotel 34
Ottawa International Hostel 23
Sheraton Ottawa 35
Westin Hotel 24
YMCA/YWCA 41

DINING
Bistro 115 8
The Black Thorn 17
Café Henri Burger 2
Canal Ritz 41
Clair de Lune 9
The Courtyard 22
D'Arcy McGee's 36
Empire Grill 13
The Fish Market 16
Haveli 12
Il Vagabondo 18
Le Café 47
Le Jardin 44
Le Metro 1
Le Tartuffe 46
Mekong 32
Memories 10
Sante 25
Savana Café 42
Shanghai 33

325

VISITOR INFORMATION

TOURIST OFFICES   The **Ottawa Tourism and Convention Authority,** 130 Albert St., on the 18th floor (☎ 613/237-5158), is open Monday to Friday 9am to 5pm, but the most convenient place to gather info is the **Capital Infocentre,** 90 Wellington St., across from Parliament Hill (☎ 800/465-1867 or 613/239-5000; www.capcan.ca); it's open daily 8:30am to 9pm in summer and 9am to 5pm in winter. An "Info-tent" on Parliament Hill lawn behind the West Block is where you book free tours of Parliament. Mid-May to about the third week in June, hours are daily 9am to 5pm; the rest of June to Labour Day, it's open Monday to Friday 9am to 8pm and Saturday, Sunday, and holidays 9am to 5pm.

For details about Hull, contact the **Association Touristique de l'Outaouais,** Maison du Tourisme, 103 rue Laurier, Hull, PQ J8X 3V8 (☎ 800/265-7822 or 819/778-2222; www.tourisme-outaouais.org). Summer hours are Monday to Friday 8:30am to 8pm and Saturday and Sunday 9am to 5pm; winter hours are Monday to Friday 8:30am to 5pm and Saturday and Sunday 9am to 4pm.

WEB SITES   On the Net, you may want to check out **www.ottawakiosk.com, www.festivalseeker.com,** and **www.tourottawa.org.**

CITY LAYOUT

The **Ottawa River**—Canada's second longest at over 700 miles—curves around the northern edge of city. The compact downtown area, where most major attractions are clustered within walking distance, is south of the river.

The **Rideau Canal,** sweeping past the National Arts Centre, divides the downtown area in two—Centre Town and Lower Town. In **Centre Town** are Parliament Hill, the Supreme Court, and the National Museum of Natural Sciences. In **Lower Town,** on the east side of the canal, are the National Gallery of Canada, the Byward Market (a vibrant center for restaurants and nightlife), and along Sussex Drive (which follows the Ottawa River's course), the Canadian War Museum, the Royal Canadian Mint, and (farther out) the Prime Minister's residence, diplomat's row, and finally Rockcliffe Park. The area south of the Queensway, west to Bronson and east to the canal, is known as the **Glebe,** containing some restaurants and clubs, on Bank Street from First to Fifth avenues. North across the river, in Québec, lies **Hull,** reached by the Macdonald-Cartier and Alexandra bridges from the east end of town and the Portage and Chaudière bridges from the west end. At the end of the Alexandra Bridge stands the curvaceous Museum of Civilization, and nearby are some of the city's best French restaurants and the most lively nightlife action (which continues until 2am). North and east of Hull stretch the Gatineau Hills and ski country.

Finding your way around is occasionally bewildering, since streets have a habit of halting abruptly and then reappearing a few blocks farther on, and some streets change names several times. For example, the main street starts in the west as Scott Street, changes to Wellington Street as it passes through downtown in front of Parliament, changes again to Rideau Street in downtown east, and finally becomes Montréal Road on the eastern fringes of town. So carry a map. The information office provides a serviceable one.

GETTING AROUND

Walking is the best way. The only public transportation is the 130-route bus network operated by the **Ottawa-Carleton Regional Transit Commission (OC Transpo).** For information about routes, where to buy tickets, and more, call ☎ 613/741-4390 (www.octtranspo.com) Monday to Friday 7am to 9pm, Saturday 8am to 9pm, and

A Few Orientation Tips

The main streets running east-west through center city are **Wellington, Laurier,** and **Somerset;** the **Rideau Canal** separates east from west and Centre Town from Lower Town, and the main north-south streets are **Bronson, Bank,** and **Elgin.**

Sunday 9am and 6pm. To inquire about schedules, call ☎ **560** plus the four-digit number of the nearest bus stop. **Exact-change fares** or **one-ride tickets** are C$2.25 (US$1.50) adults, C$1.25 (US85¢) ages 6 to 11; 5 and under are free. A C$5 (US$3.35) **DayPass** allows unlimited travel on all routes. Exact change, tickets, or the pass is required. You can buy tickets at 300 retail outlets, such as newsstands and PharmaPlus. All routes converge downtown at the Rideau Centre; they begin to close down at midnight, and there's no service 1 to 6am.

In Hull, buses are operated by the **Société de Transport l'Outaouais** (☎ **819/ 770-3242**). Transfers between the two systems are obtainable when you pay your fare on the bus.

You can hail a taxi on the street, but you'll find one more readily in front of major hotels and important buildings. And you can summon one by phone, something restaurant headwaiters are happy to do. One 24-hour company is **Blue Line** (☎ **613/ 238-1111**), with more than 600 cabs. Fares are C$2 (US$1.35) at the drop and C10¢ (US7¢) for each extra 85m (.05 mile). Most drivers accept credit cards, usually MasterCard or Visa.

In summer, athletic young men, mostly university students, pull one to two passengers around the tourist districts in **rickshaws.** Negotiate the fare before setting out.

You probably won't want to drive in Ottawa, but you may want to rent a car to explore the environs or continue elsewhere in Canada. Car-rental agencies based in Ottawa include **Avis** (☎ **613/238-3421**), **Budget** (☎ **613/729-6666**), **National Tilden** (☎ **613/232-3536**), and **Thrifty** (☎ **613/238-8000**), all with offices at the airport and various downtown locations. However, remember that you'll save money by arranging for the rental before leaving home.

Parking will cost about C$3 (US$2) per half hour, with about a C$9 (US$6) maximum at most local garages. The best parking bets are the municipal parking lots, marked with a large green "P" in a circle.

When driving, remember that Ontario has a compulsory seat-belt requirement, and pay careful attention to the city's system of one-way streets, which often have three or four streets in a row going in the same direction, rather than alternating. Know, too, that cars can turn right after stopping at a red light in Ottawa, but not across the river in Hull, Québec. The Queensway (Route 417) cuts right across the city, adding to the confusion. The downtown entrance to the highway is at O'Connor Street. Exit the highway at Kent Street for downtown.

Fast Facts: Ottawa

Area Code   The telephone area code for Ottawa is **613;** for Hull, **819.** When calling from Ottawa to Hull, you don't need to use the area code.

American Express   The office is at the **AMEX Bank of America,** 360 Albert St., Suite 1120 (☎ **819/246-0564**).

Doctors/Dentists   Check with the hotel front desk or with your consulate for the nearest doctor or dentist.

Embassies/High Commissions   The **U.S. Embassy** has moved to a large new building on Sussex Drive, north of Rideau Street (☎ **613/238-5335**). It's expected to be open Monday to Friday 8:30am to 5pm. The **U.K. Embassy** is at 80 Elgin (☎ **613/237-6537**). The **Australian High Commission** is at 50 O'Connor (☎ **613/236-4376**). And the **New Zealand High Commission** is at 99 Bank, Suite 727. Unlikely as it may seem, Ireland doesn't have an embassy in Canada. Consulates are primarily in Toronto, Montréal, and Vancouver.

Emergencies   Call ☎ **911** for police, fire, or ambulance.

Hospital   Your best bet is the **Ottawa Hospital General Campus,** 501 Smythe Rd. (☎ **613/737-6111**).

Internet Access   You can check on your mail and send messages at **The Internet Cafe,** 200 Bank St., at Somerset (☎ **613/230-9000**). It's open Monday to Friday 9:30am to 11pm, Saturday 11am to 11pm, and Sunday 11am to 8pm.

Liquor   The government controls liquor distribution, selling liquor and wine at certain LCBO stores and beer at others. Liquor stores generally open Monday to Saturday 10am to 6pm (to 9pm Thurs and Fri). Beer outlets open Monday to Saturday noon to 8pm (also to 9pm Thurs and Fri). The legal drinking age is 19 in Ottawa but 18 in Hull. Two convenient liquor stores are in the **Rideau Centre** (just inside the Rideau St. entrance) and in the **Byward Market area** at 140 George St., between Dalhousie and Cumberland, and there's a beer store at 1546 Scott St.

Newspapers/Magazines   A great variety of international publications, including the *New York Times, the Wall Street Journal,* and the *International Herald Tribune,* are sold at **Planet News,** 143 Sparks St.

Police   Call ☎ **911.**

Post Office   The most convenient post office is at 59 Sparks St., at Elgin Street (☎ **613/844-1545**), open Monday to Friday 8am to 6pm.

Taxes   In Ontario there's an 8% provincial sales tax (PST), a lodging tax of 5%, and a 16% tax on liquor, as well as the national 7% goods-and-services tax (GST). In Québec there's a 7½% tax on food, liquor, merchandise, and accommodations.

2 Accommodations

While reasonably priced doubles are available at a few B&B inns, you'll have to look to the outer districts for truly inexpensive lodgings, primarily in motels. There are ample choices for mid-priced to first-class rooms, however. Most hotels have no-smoking rooms. For more information and possibilities, try **www.all-hotels.com/canada**.

Add the 5% hotel tax and 7% GST to the rates quoted here.

Note: See the "Ottawa" map (p. 325) to locate most of the hotels in this section.

DOWNTOWN
VERY EXPENSIVE

✪ **Château Laurier.** 1 Rideau St. (at MacKenzie Ave.), Ottawa, ON K1N 8S7. ☎ **800/441-1414** or 613/241-1414. Fax 613/562-7030. www.chateaulaurier.com. E-mail reserve@clh.cphotels.ca. 426 units. A/C MINIBAR TV TEL. C$189–C$209 (US$126–US$139) double. Packages available. AE, DC, DISC, ER, MC, V. Parking C$15 (US$10).

Looking for a B&B?

Try **Ottawa Bed and Breakfast,** an organization that represents about 10 homes renting rooms for C$65 to C$80 (US$43 to US$53) double with breakfast. Contact Robert Rivoire, 488 Cooper St., Ottawa, ON K1R 5H9 (☎ **800/461-7889** or 613/563-0161). For more B&B possibilities in the Ottawa area, contact the **Ottawa Tourism and Convention Authority,** 130 Albert St., 18th Floor, Ottawa, ON K1P 5G4 (☎ **613/237-5150**).

Built at the same time (1912) and in the same Loire Valley Renaissance style as Québec City's Château Frontenac, the granite-and-sandstone Laurier has always attracted royalty and celebs to its ideal location beside the Rideau Canal at the east end of Parliament Hill. There was no stinting on materials or dimensions, as seen in its wide halls and acres of public lounges and lobbies. The high-ceilinged spacious guest rooms are decorated with mostly Louis XV reproductions, and the upper floors offer impressive views over the Ottawa River to the Gatineau Hills. The Entree Gold executive level has its own concierge and such extras as complimentary continental breakfast, honor bar, and overnight shoe shine.

Dining/Diversions: At Wilfrid's, you share a wonderful view of Parliament with government mandarins, and the chef uses Canadian ingredients in continental main dishes from C$15 to C$32 (US$10 to US$21). Recently renovated Zoe's, an atrium-lit room with chandeliers and potted palms, is the place for light meals, cocktails, afternoon tea, or a lavish Sunday brunch.

Amenities: Concierge, 24-hour room service, valet, twice-daily maid service; 20-yard-long indoor pool, sauna, steam room, massage salon, extensive exercise room, business center.

Westin Hotel. 11 Colonel By Dr. (a block south of Rideau St.), Ottawa, ON K1N 9H4. ☎ **800/228-3000** or 613/560-7000. Fax 613/234-5396. www.westin.com. E-mail ottaw@ westin.com. 515 units. A/C MINIBAR TV TEL. C$158–C$340 (US$105–US$227) double. AE, CB, DC, ER, MC, V. Parking C$19 (US$13). Pets allowed.

The Westin offers views over the canal from its atrium lobby and from many of its guest rooms. It also connects directly to both the Rideau Centre shopping complex and the Ottawa Congress Centre. The carefully furnished rooms contain oak furniture, brass lamps, and half-poster beds, with coffeemakers and hair dryers; 10 rooms are specially equipped for those with disabilities. Adult fitness swimmers have the pool to themselves daily 6:30 to 8am.

Dining/Diversions: The popular third-floor Daly's commands a close-up view of the canal and serves all meals. Hartwells, a bar and dance club just off the lobby, is a popular spot Tuesday to Saturday.

Amenities: Concierge, 24-hour room service, shoe shine, valet; health club with 12m (35-ft.) indoor pool, squash courts, whirlpool, massage, saunas; exercise area with lifecycles, treadmills, stairclimbers; business center.

EXPENSIVE

✪ **The Albert at Bay Suite Hotel.** 435 Albert St. (at Bay St.), Ottawa, ON K1R 7X4. ☎ **800/267-6644** or 613/238-8858. Fax 613/238-1433. www.albertatbay.com. E-mail info@albertatbay.com. 195 units. A/C TV TEL. C$99–C$139 (US$66–US$93) 1-bedroom suite; C$154–C$250 (US$103–US$167) 2-bedroom suite. Rates include continental breakfast. Weekend packages available. AE, CB, DC, DISC, ER, MC, V. Parking C$9 (US$6).

This conveniently located hotel, built as an apartment house, is one of Ottawa's best buys for long-stay businesspeople or families. All the units are suites, the smallest having one bedroom (including desk space off the living room) with a sofa bed, a fully furnished living room opening onto a terrace, two bathrooms, two TVs, and a kitchen with appliances and dishes. Dataports, voice mail, high-speed Internet access, coffeemakers, hair dryers, and irons and ironing boards are standard.

Dining: The independently operated Bay Street Bistro serves all meals.

Amenities: Room service (5 to 10pm), laundry/valet; exercise room with treadmill, exercycle, StairMaster, whirlpool, sauna; ATM, 24-hour convenience store.

○ **Carmichael Inn and Spa.** 46 Cartier St. (at Somerset St.), Ottawa, ON K2P 1J3. ☎ **613/236-4667.** Fax 613/563-7529. www.carmichaelinn.com. E-mail carmichael innAcyberus.ca. 10 units. A/C TV TEL. C$129–C$169 (US$86–US$113) double. Rates include continental breakfast. Weekend and spa packages available. AE, DC, ER, MC, V. Free parking.

Three blocks west of the Rideau Canal and a 15-minute walk south of Parliament Hill, this fetching retreat built in 1901 served as a Supreme Court judge's residence, a convent, and a senior-citizens' home before being converted to an inn. It's named after Group of Seven landscape artist Frank Carmichael, and the decor recalls their influential art as well as their early–20th-century life and times. Oak woodwork helps set that tone, and all the guest rooms are furnished uniquely with a mix of antiques and reproductions. Modern conveniences aren't neglected, including dataports. Guests can relax on the couches in front of the marble fireplace in the lounge or laze in Adirondack chairs on the veranda. The inn is full nearly all the time, so reserve for both room and spa treatments at least a month in advance or face the rather self-satisfied turnaway of the person handling the desk.

Amenities: Valet service, newspaper delivery, in-room massage and other spa treatments (herbal and mud wraps, hydrotherapy, aromatherapy, reflexology), secretarial services.

✪ **Delta Ottawa.** 361 Queen St. (at Bay St.), Ottawa, ON K1R 7S9. ☎ **800/268-1133** or 613/238-6000. Fax 613/238-2290. www.deltahotels.com. 328 units. A/C MINIBAR TV TEL. C$105–C$185 (US$70–US$123) double; C$160–C$210 (US$107–US$140) suite. Weekend packages available. AE, CB, DC, ER, MC, V. Parking C$12 (US$8).

The 1973 structure is beginning to look dated, but this member of the admirable Canadian chain has a skylit marble lobby with a welcoming fire in winter and island-style reception desks for a more personal welcome. The just-renovated guest rooms are in 14 configurations, spacious and refreshingly decorated, as with floral duvet covers on the beds; a substantial number are one- or two-bedroom suites with kitchenettes, and more than half have balconies. All have coffeemakers, Nintendo, irons and boards, hair dryers, and robes. While businesspeople rule during the week, every effort is made to make families welcome Friday to Sunday. At check-in kids receive bags of diverting goodies, and parents can leave them to supervised play in the "creative center" for C$6 (US$4) per hour (the parents are issued beepers).

Dining/Diversions: Facilities include the casual Gallery-Cafe, the Capital Club for more formal intimate dining, and Jester's lounge for cocktails and snacks.

Amenities: Concierge, room service (6am to 11pm), valet, twice-daily maid service; indoor pool with water slide, saunas, exercise room, game room, two self-service Laundromats.

Lord Elgin Hotel. 100 Elgin St. (at Queen St.), Ottawa, ON K1P 5K8. ☎ **800/267-4298** or 613/235-3333. Fax 613/235-3223. www.interconti.com. 312 units. A/C TV TEL. C$99–C$165 (US$66–US$110) double. Children under 19 stay free in parents' room. DC, DISC, ER, MC. Parking C$12 (US$8).

Only 3 blocks south of Parliament Hill and across from the National Arts Centre, the Lord Elgin offers good value. Built in 1941, the dignified stone edifice with its green copper roof was named after the eighth earl of Elgin, once Canada's governor-general. In recent years, the guest rooms have been enlarged and the decor has been lightened; the lobby has just been freshened. Many of the tile and faux-granite bathrooms have windows that open—a benefit bestowed by the building's age. About half the rooms have unstocked fridges, but all have coffeemakers and hair dryers.

Dining: The lobby bar is comfortably furnished with wingbacks and club chairs; the Connaught dining room is an airy galleria popular with Ottawans.

Amenities: Concierge, room service (6:30am to 11pm), dry cleaning; fitness room with exercise machines.

Minto Place Suite Hotel. 433 Laurier Ave. W. (at Lyon St.), Ottawa, ON K1R 7Y1. ☎ **613/232-2200.** Fax 613/232-6962. www.mintohotel.com. 417 units. A/C TV TEL. C$126–C$217 (US$84–US$145) suite. Children under 18 stay free in parents' room. Weekend rates available. AE, DC, ER, MC, V. Parking C$12 (US$8).

High-rise Minto Place has more than 400 studio and one- and two-bedroom suites, each attractively furnished. The upper-floor units boast sweeping views, and "studios" have kitchenettes and sofa beds. The full kitchens in larger suites contain fridges, microwaves, coffeemakers, and toasters, as well as pots, pans, and silverware; some also have electric stoves, dishwashers, and even clothes washers and dryers. The spacious living rooms are fully furnished, with desks, multiline phones with dataports, and dining tables. The bathrooms have phones and hair dryers, and there's an extra powder room in some suites.

Dining: Two restaurants are at the base of the tower.

Amenities: Room service (7:30am to 1am), 20m (66-ft.) lap pool, whirlpool, sauna, substantial fitness center.

Sheraton Ottawa. 150 Albert St. (at O'Connor St.), Ottawa, ON K1P 5G2. ☎ **800/489-8333** or 613/238-1500. Fax 613/235-2723. www.sheraton.com. 244 units. A/C TV TEL. C$133–C$314 (US$89–US$209) double. Packages available. Children under 18 stay free in parents' room; under 6 eat free. AE, CB, DC, ER, MC, V. Valet parking C$12 (US$8). Pets accepted.

Frequent travelers know what to expect of a downtown Sheraton—a middle-of-everything location, a health club and pool, executive floors, a business center, conference rooms, and spacious guest rooms with the usual electronics, including two phone lines, voice mail, modem links, coffeemakers, hair dryers, Nintendo, and irons and boards. This place meets the expectations of businesspeople, most of whom probably prefer not to deal with the eccentricities of many inns and boutique hotels, but leisure travelers will be satisfied too. Almost half the rooms are no-smoking.

Dining: The Carleton Restaurant is open daily 6:30am to 11pm.

Amenities: Laundry/valet, free newspaper, limited room service; indoor pool, saunas, fitness center with extensive exercise and weight equipment.

MODERATE

Auberge McGee's Inn. 185 Daly Ave. (at Nelson St.), Ottawa, ON K1N 6E8. ☎ **800/262-4337** or 613/237-6089. Fax 613/237-6201. www.coatesb.demon.co.uk/McGees/. 14 units. A/C TV TEL. C$88–C$198 (US$59–US$132) double. Rates include full breakfast. AE, MC, V. Free parking. From downtown, take Laurier Ave. E. and turn left at Nelson St.

On a quiet street only blocks from the University of Ottawa, this no-smoking inn occupies a handsome Victorian with a steep dormer roof and an awning-protected entrance. Each guest room is distinctively decorated, often with touches reflective of the owner's Anglo-Peruvian upbringing. All the rooms with queen-size beds have minibars and hair dryers, and two have Jacuzzis and fireplaces. Breakfast is served in an elegant room with a carved cherry-wood fireplace and Oriental rugs.

Best Western Victoria Park Suites. 377 O'Connor St. (at Gladstone St.), Ottawa, ON K2P 2M2. ☎ **800/465-7275** or 613/567-7275. Fax 613/567-1161. www.victoriapark.com. E-mail info@victoriapark.com. 100 units. A/C TV TEL. C$99–C$139 (US$66–US$93) suite. Rates include enhanced continental breakfast. Family packages available. AE, DC, ER, MC, V. Free parking.

It isn't glamorous and it's a bit too far south of the center city for easy walking, so this member of the well-known chain piles on several other incentives. Sixty rooms are studios and 40 are one-bedroom suites; all have kitchenettes with fridges, microwaves, and coffeemakers. The larger units have pullout sofas and two TVs with pay movies, so this is an economical choice for families arriving by car. Irons and boards, clock radios, and hair dryers are provided, and some floors have high-speed Internet access. The exercise room features a Universal machine, a StairMaster, exercycles, and two saunas. The Canadian Museum of Nature is a couple of blocks away.

Courtyard by Marriott. 350 Dalhousie St. (at York St.), Ottawa, ON K1N 7E9. ☎ **800/ 341-2210** or 613/241-1000. Fax 613/241-4804. 183 units. A/C TV TEL. C$119–C$139 (US$79–US$93) double. AE, DC, ER, MC, V.

Though this structure once housed another hotel, this is really a completely new facility, opened in 1999. The formula for this expanding chain sets it roughly midway between a roadside motel and a first-class hotel, with limited personal service but fairly complete facilities and a fitness center incorporating a weight machine, StairMaster, and treadmill. Adjacent are an indoor pool and whirlpool. The guest rooms are intentionally businesslike, with thoughtfully designed work areas, voice mail, and dataports, plus coffeemakers, irons, and hair dryers. A large parking lot adjoins, and all of Byward Market lies just beyond.

Doral Inn. 486 Albert St. (at Bay St.), Ottawa, ON K1R 5B5. ☎ **800/263-6725** or 613/ 230-8055. Fax 613/237-9660. www.doralinnottawa.com. E-mail doralinnottawa.com. 37 units. A/C TV TEL. C$80–C$135 (US$53–US$90) double. Extra person C$10 (US$7). Children under 12 stay free in parents' room. Rates include continental breakfast. AE, DC, DISC, ER, MC, V. Free parking.

A good choice on the price-value scale, this amiable inn occupies an expanded brick town house characteristic of many residential blocks in Ottawa. The guest rooms have brass bedsteads, floral wallpaper, desks, and armchairs, plus coffeemakers, hair dryers, and unstocked fridges. On the ground floor, two bay-windowed rooms serve as a lounge/sitting room and a breakfast area. You have use of a nearby pool and health club and laundry facilities. There's a cafe on the premises. No-smoking rooms are available.

✪ Gasthaus Switzerland. 89 Daly Ave. (at Cumberland St.), Ottawa, ON K1N 6E6. ☎ **888/663-0000** or 613/237-0335. Fax 613/594-3327. infoweb.magi.com/ ~switzinn. E-mail switzinn@magi.com. 22 units. A/C TV TEL. C$88–C$118 (US$59– US$79) double; C$128–C$198 (US$85–US$132) suite. Rates include full breakfast. AE, CB, DC, ER, MC, V. Free parking.

In an old stone building, this B&B possesses the familiar hallmarks of red gingham and country pine associated with rustic Swiss hospitality. There's a welcoming sitting room with cable TV, and you can use the garden and its barbecue in summer. Puffy duvets cover the beds of the no-smoking guest rooms; four have fireplaces. A Swiss-style breakfast buffet of breads, eggs, french toast, cheese, and cereal is served. The Gasthaus is east of Rideau Centre and 2 blocks south of the Byward Market area.

INEXPENSIVE

Ottawa International Hostel. 75 Nicholas St. (at Daly Ave.), Ottawa, ON K1N 7B9.
☎ **613/235-2595.** Fax 613/569-2131. infoweb.magi.com/~hicoe. E-mail hicoe@magi.com.
150 beds. C$17 (US$11) members, C$21 (US$14) nonmembers. MC, V Parking C$7
(US$4.65).

Originally the Carleton County Jail (1862 to 1972) and the site of Canada's last public
hanging, this hostel near the Byward Market and Parliament Hill certainly qualifies as
unusual lodging. The former lockup's chapel is now a dining room, and the walls
between cells have been removed to create small dorms housing anywhere from two
to eight beds per room. They've added three rooms for families. An attractive lounge
with TV and VCR, a fully equipped kitchen, a laundry, and bike and skate rentals are
offered.

YMCA/YWCA. 180 Argyle St. (at O'Connor St.), Ottawa, ON K2P 1B7. ☎ **613/237-1320.**
Fax 613/788-5095. 264 units, 26 with bathroom. A/C TEL. C$44 (US$29) single without bathroom, C$51 (US$34) single with bathroom; C$54 (US$36) double without bathroom. Children under 12 stay free in parents' room. MC, V. Parking C$3 (US$2).

This exceptional 15-story Y has mostly single rooms with shared washroom facilities,
though a few have private bathrooms; some doubles are available. There are TV
lounges and laundry facilities, plus the added attractions of an indoor pool, a gym,
exercise rooms, handball and squash courts, a cafeteria, and free local phone calls.
And, of course, the price is right.

A RESORT IN THE GATINEAU HILLS

✪ Château Cartier Sheraton. 1170 chemin d'Aylmer, Aylmer, PQ J9H 5E1. ☎ **819/
777-1088.** Fax 819/777-7161. www.sheraton.com. 129 units. A/C TV TEL. C$154–
C$185 (US$103–US$123) double. Packages available. AE, DC, DISC, ER, MC, V. Free
parking. Take the Champlain Bridge across the river and turn left on bd. Alexandre-Taché,
which becomes chemin d'Aylmer.

This 152-acre resort is only 15 minutes from Ottawa across the river in the Gatineau
Hills, and on entering the gracious pink-marble lobby you'll know this will be a stress-
free experience. Active options include working up an invigorating sweat in the well-
equipped fitness center to a round or two of chasing pebbly balls down the fairways
right outside. The spacious guest rooms have couches and carefully thought-out work
areas, plus tile and marble bathrooms with hair dryers. Most rooms are king- or
queen-size suites with parlor and bedroom separated by French doors, and they have
two TVs and two phones. In addition, four suites have fireplaces and two have
Jacuzzis. Over a third are no-smoking. Children can use supervised play centers.

Dining/Diversions: The dining room has French windows opening onto the patio,
which overlooks the golf course. A lounge with a circular bar, club chairs, and a small
dance floor features a pianist on weekends.

Amenities: Room service (to 10pm), same day laundry/dry cleaning; 18-hole golf
course that serves as cross-country ski trail in winter, one racquetball and one squash
court, two tennis courts, indoor pool with wraparound terrace, health club with Nautilus machines.

3 Dining

To experience a true Ottawa tradition, stop at the **Hooker's** stand (closed weekdays in
Jan and Feb) at the corner of George and William streets in the center of the Byward
Market and purchase a **beaver tail.** No, really. Furry rodents aren't involved. This
beaver tail is actually a deep-fried pastry about the size of a Ping-Pong paddle, served

either sweet, with cinnamon and sugar or raspberry jam, or savory, with garlic butter and cheese or cream cheese and scallions. Tasty and cheap.

Nearby, and in commercial districts around town, step up to one of the rolling grill carts and order a **hot Polish** or **German sausage.** Cooked to your request, it's cradled in a bun for you to slather with mustard and heap with sauerkraut, pickles, peppers, and onions. Another inexpensive solution for the munchies are the **chip wagons** found in parking lots and vacant spaces around the city and out in the Ontario countryside. Similar to the *casse-croutes* of Québec, they serve limited menus of sandwiches, soft drinks, and the namesake french fries. And you'll find units of the national coffeehouse chain, **Second Cup,** at strategic locations around town (usually a Starbucks will be nearby).

Note: See the "Ottawa" map (p. 325) to locate most of the restaurants in this section.

CENTRE TOWN
MODERATE

D'Arcy McGee's. 44 Sparks St. (at Elgin St.). ☎ **613/230-4433.** Main courses C$7–C$19 (US$4.65–US$13). AE. MC, V. Daily 11am–1am. IRISH.

If this avowed Irish pub looks like an unadulterated replica of the real thing (albeit less plagued with smoke and chill drafts), that's because the whole thing was shipped over from the Emerald Isle. The etched and stained-glass panels, dark wood partitions, and mosaic tiled floor were installed in a Dublinesque building near the Arts Center. Some feel that the result is a little formulaic, and that isn't unfair comment. But the menu has "Dublin Coddle" (sausage, smoked bacon, and roasted root vegetables atop mashed potatoes), fish-and-chips, and chicken cottage pie for tastes of the Auld Sod, along with daily specials less slavishly evocative of the homeland. No one leaves hungry with these man-sized portions, including the burgers and other sandwiches (C$6 to C$8/US$4 to US$5). Imported and domestic brews are on tap, as are single-malt scotches and Irish whiskeys. Live music fills the place Wednesday to Saturday nights, most of it Celtic, of course, but with a little New World folk and rock squeezed in. In warm weather, tables wrap around the exterior.

Le Café. In the National Arts Centre, 53 Elgin St. (at Confederation Sq.). ☎ **613/594-5127.** Reservations recommended. Main courses C$16–C$27 (US$11–US$18). AE, DC, ER, MC, V. June–Sept Mon–Sat 11:30am–11pm, Sun 11:30am–8pm; Oct–May Mon–Sat 11:30am–11pm. ECLECTIC.

Finding it is a bit of a challenge (in back, at canal level), but the National Arts Centre's Le Café commands an enticing view from its long summer terrace and offers imaginatively executed food year-round in its glass-enclosed main dining room. Featured are dishes employing such prime Canadian ingredients as Petrie Island mussels, Nova Scotia scallops, Broome Lake duck, and Alberta beef and lamb. Atlantic salmon usually figures in both appetizers and main dishes. The lunch and dinner menus are similar, but with lower prices at midday. Sample dishes are the seafood chowder of scallops, clams, and salmon; Muscovy duck breast with blueberries deglazed in vinegar; and sautéed white shrimp on seven-grain rice with tomato-cucumber vinaigrette. Several wines are available by the glass, and the interesting wine list is decently priced, most in the C$28 to C$32 (US$19 to US$21) range. To keep with the Canadian theme, try the Mission Hill chardonnay from the Niagara Frontier.

✪ **Le Metro.** 315 Somerset St. W. (between Bank and O'Connor sts.). ☎ **613/230-8123.** Reservations recommended. Main courses C$17–C$22 (US$11–US$14); table d'hôte lunch C$19 (US$13). AE, ER, MC, V. Mon–Fri 11:30am–2:30pm and 6–10:30pm, Sat 6–10:30pm. CLASSIC FRENCH.

Pubbing It Outside Ottawa

For both of these pubs, take Route 417 west to Route 5, and then go north to Carp.

This side of the Big Briney, English country pubs don't get more authentic than the **Cheshire Cat,** 2193 Richardson Side Rd. (☎ **613/831-2183**). In an 1883 stone cottage that once housed a school, it boasts a wood-burning stove, horse brasses, dimpled mugs, cool (not icy) bitter on draft, snatches of Cockney rhyming slang among the regulars at the bar—and even that requisite indifferent food. A variety of adequate sandwiches is available, as well as such traditional main courses as liver and bacon, fish-and-chips, mixed grill, steak-and-kidney pie, and shepherd's pie. The new cook has introduced a number of slightly more creative dishes. The beers are mostly British, along with a few Canadian microbrews. On summer days the garden is a happy spot to idle. The kitchen is open Tuesday to Saturday 11:30am to 9pm and Sunday noon to 9pm; the bar is open to 11pm Sunday to Wednesday and to 1am Thursday to Saturday.

If you're looking for accommodations, the pub is associated with a nearby B&B, **Kirkstone House** (☎ **613/831-8805;** www.bbcanada.com/1585.html).

Another corner of Blighty waits at the **Swan at Carp,** Falldown Lane (☎ **613/ 839-7926**), in a Victorian-style brick pile that was a Presbyterian rectory built in 1902. It was converted to a pub in 1987, complete with separate public and lounge bars, and was named after a pub the owners had managed back in Stoke, England. There are no videos or TVs, so conversation flows, real ale is drawn at cellar temperature, and British events and special days like the Dambusters Anniversary are celebrated. The characteristic pub fare includes bangers and mash, Guinness stew, fish-and-chips, and "afters" like sherry trifle, but go for the atmosphere and companionability. It's open Monday to Saturday 11am to midnight and Sun 11am to 11pm.

The owner's all-embracing welcome is signaled in the juxtaposed autographed photos of Bill Clinton and Fidel Castro in the vestibule of this south center-city town house. The pictures turn out to be a joke, but not the food or the setting. The cerulean walls set off the gold picture frames and moldings, bronze and silver candelabra, maroon napery, and lavish flowers. At lunch, small hurricane lamps flicker on the tables. The menu changes daily, the better to highlight market-fresh ingredients and to remind us what true French cooking was before it became the trampoline that launched pan-oceanic fusion cuisine. Begin with a definitive vichyssoise or pheasant terrine and proceed to breast of Brôme Lake duck with olive sauce; veal escalope with wild mushrooms; or shrimp, lobster, and scallops in puff pastry. The chef is the wife of the Parisian who runs the front. She doesn't diddle with tried-and-true recipes and cooks meats to the edge of moist perfection. And to make clear whence the inspiration for all this comes, if it's your birthday, a slice of cake with a sparkler in it will arrive to the first glorious bars of "La Marseillaise."

Mekong. 637 Somerset St. W. (near Bronson Ave.). ☎ **613/237-7717.** Reservations recommended on weekends. Main courses C$7–C$14 (US$4.85–US$9). AE, DC, ER, MC, V. Daily 11am–midnight. SZECHUAN/CANTONESE.

This modest restaurant started as a Vietnamese eatery in what passes for Ottawa's Chinatown. That cuisine didn't attract patrons, so they started phasing in Chinese dishes. That worked, and only a few Southeast Asian options remain on the substantial menu. Enter up a few stairs past a goldfish aquarium to the greetings of the outgoing staff. You write your own order on a scratch pad, perhaps the vermicelli with pork in a bowl bedded with slivers of lemongrass, lettuce strips, and bean sprouts. Whatever your choice, the price is right—spring rolls, a main course, tea, and beer should be under C$15 (US$10), including tax.

Savana Café. 431 Gilmour (between Bank and Kent sts.). ☎ 613/233-9159. Reservations recommended. Main courses C$11–C$15 (US$7–US$10). AE, DC, ER, MC, V. Tues–Fri 11:30am–3pm, Mon–Sat 5–10pm. CARIBBEAN FUSION.

Its tropical flavor, splashy Caribbean art, and peppery cuisine have kept this place super-heated for over 13 years. Start with the fabulous kalaloo soup—the real thing, with okra, spinach, thyme, Congo peppers, and lime. Among main-course favorites are fresh grilled marlin with wasabi mousseline, cubana chicken stuffed with bananas and cream cheese and served with jalapeño salsa, lamb glazed with guava and served with two chutneys, and (just to show they won't be hemmed in by arbitrary geographical borders) spicy Thai noodles and chicken satays. They have daily fish specials. The bar and front terrace fill early each night, usually with young to 40-ish professional types intent on unwinding as fast as easy companionship and rum drinks will allow. You can order most dishes mild, medium, or hot (and they mean hot!). In winter, the fire on the hearth adds a welcome touch.

Shanghai. 651 Somerset St. W. (near Bronson Ave.). ☎ 613/233-4001. Reservations recommended on weekends. Main courses C$9–C$12 (US$6–US$8). AE, MC, V. Tues–Fri 11am–2pm and 4:30–11pm (to 1am Fri), Sat 4:30pm–1am, Sun 4:30–11pm. SHANGHAI/ SZECHUAN.

A few doors west of Mekong (above), this long-established restaurant distinguishes itself with monthly art exhibits, from rock sculptures to watercolors to photographs. From the kitchen issue dishes drawn from a gastronomic crescent arching from Shanghai to Bangkok. A hot-and-sour soup might be followed by such tempting specialties as "spicy crispy" fish with ginger sauce, noodles with Asian veggies and cashews, and beef with Shanghai bok choy and roasted garlic. Instead of the usual uninspired Chinese desserts, there are mandarin mousse cake and litchi cheesecake.

LOWER TOWN & BYWARD MARKET AREA
EXPENSIVE

✪ **Le Jardin.** 127 York St. (east of Dalhousie St.). ☎ 613/241-1424. Reservations recommended. Main courses C$16–C$30 (US$11–US$20); table d'hôte dinner C$43 (US$29). AE, DC, ER, MC, V. Daily 5:30–11pm (lunch Mon–Fri Dec 1–23 only). FRENCH.

In a 19th-century brick house with gingerbread trim outside the Byward Market area, Le Jardin impresses with rooms of gilt-framed mirrors and paintings, tabletops of marble and mahogany, and lush sprays of fresh flowers; there's a fireplace in one room. (No garden, despite the name.) The main dining room is upstairs, subdued and seductively lit. The waiters are in tuxedos, a signal of their professionalism in a city where amateur status is more often the rule. They dole out chewy warm balls of bread, bring perfect cocktails, and remain attentive but unobtrusive. Even the simplest dishes are intensely flavored and aromatic, certainly the beef fillet in reduced claret sauce topped with escargots, the perimeter of the plate occupied by snow peas, baby carrots, cauliflower florets, and small roast potatoes. The lobster blanquette with morels and the same vegetables is also good, and the rack of lamb certainly seems popular. After cheesecake or chocolate terrine, espresso is poured in ornate demitasse cups.

MODERATE

Bistro 115. 110 Murray St. (east of Dalhousie St.). ☎ **613/562-7244.** Reservations recommended. Main courses C$15–C$22 (US$10–US$15); weekday table d'hôte lunch C$18 (US$12); 3-course prix-fixe dinner C$25–C$32 (US$17–US$21). AE, MC, V. Mon–Fri 11:30am–10pm, Sat–Sun 10:30am–10pm. FRENCH.

Though it's in the Byward Market area, this casual bistro is out of the clutch of the more frenetic streets. Lace tablecloths and a fireplace make the dining room inviting in winter, while the patio with its roof of trellised grapevines promotes an echo of sun-splashed southern France. The seasonal menu changes weekly, but starters have included shrimp provençal with aioli toast triangles followed by duck confit with baked goat cheese on wilted spinach. On warmer days, watch for the vegetable-scallop phyllo-wrapped spring rolls propped against a mound of rice ringed with honeyed curry sauce. Weekend brunch is a treat, but the best deal is the weekday table d'hôte lunch (C$4/US$2.65 less if you skip dessert). More than a dozen wines are available by the glass and half-bottle.

Clair de Lune. 81B Clarence St. (west of Dalhousie St.). ☎ **613/241-2200.** Reservations recommended. Main courses C$9–C$13 (US$6–US$9) at lunch, C$15–C$24 (US$10–US$16) at dinner. AE, DC, ER, MC, V. Mon–Fri 11:30am–10pm, Sat–Sun 11am–10pm. CONTEMPORARY FRENCH.

This long-running bistro is a favorite of many regulars to the market area. Main courses at lunch, such as the cold half-lobster with two salads of greens and pickled cabbage or smoked salmon rillettes, often show up as appetizers at dinner. That meal might be beef tenderloin with Jack Daniel's portobello jus or cumin-scented pork cutlet marinated in buttermilk. The two- and three-cheese plates are good choices to follow. Weight watchers have choices of three or four seasonal salads and a few designated low-fat main dishes. The restaurant has a glass-block bar and dividers, mahogany tabletops, and stamped tin ceiling and ducts overhead. Live jazz is on offer Saturday nights, and in summer, the sidewalk and rooftop terraces fill with diners watching the stars and passersby. Let's assume that the inept waiter who served my last meal here was an aberration.

The Courtyard. 21 George St. (east of Sussex St.). ☎ **613/241-1516.** Reservations recommended. Main courses C$15–C$22 (US$10–US$15). AE, DC, ER, MC, V. Daily 11:30am–11pm (closed 2–5:30pm in winter). CONTEMPORARY/CONTINENTAL.

Installed in a heritage building with a stone-walled dining room and outdoor tables on the cobblestoned courtyard from which it takes its name, this place has the air of an Old Montréal cafe. The menu lists war-horses like veal Oscar and filet mignon with béarnaise, but lighter, more up-to-date items increasingly shoulder them aside. The Outdoor Café is a popular meeting spot, and Sunday brunch is accompanied by live classical music.

Empire Grill. 47 Clarence St. (at Parent St.). ☎ **613/241-1343.** Reservations recommended in evening. Main courses C$16–C$32 (US$11–US$21). AE, MC, V. Mon–Fri 11:30am–1pm, Sat–Sun 10:30am–1am. ECLECTIC.

It says something that a lot of area chefs and waiters make this booming New York–ish bistro/bar/club a stop on their after-work circuit. The martinis are the driest, the company is congenial, and the food is piquant and mildly venturesome. Attractive young servers bring chicken quesadillas and fried calamari starters that segue to the likes of spicy seafood paella, Asian braised duck breast, and strips of lamb tenderloin glazed with rosemary-balsamic jus. The bar, in a question-mark shape that encourages conversation, is rimmed around with tables, augmented in warm weather with a dining deck. Customers range from those barely over drinking age to well past retirement with no apparent social unease. A DJ works the turntables after late dinner, and they have live jazz Sunday 6 to 10pm. All this and fair prices too (every main course but steak is less than C$30/US$20).

The Fish Market. 54 York St. (at Byward St.). ☎ **613/241-3474.** Reservations not accepted. Main courses C$12–C$23 (US$8–US$15); fixed-price dinner C$21 (US$14). AE, DC, ER, MC, V. Mon–Fri 11:30am–2pm and 4:30–10pm, Sat 11:30am–2:30pm and 4:30–11pm, Sun 11:30am–3pm and 4:30–11pm. SEAFOOD.

In an 1875 heritage building on a prominent Market corner are this sprawling fish restaurant; the casual, less expensive upstairs cafe, **Coasters,** which stays open through the afternoon and offers pastas, pizzas, and fish-and-chips; and the basement tavern, **Vineyards,** which features boutique wines and microbrews. The main room is enclosed by rough wood and brick and faintly nautical trappings amid old advertising signs. Fish cooked without artifice or complications is often the most satisfying, not to mention fast out of the kitchen, and waits between courses aren't long. So you don't expire from hunger, though, a plate of tuna salad and crackers tides you over until your appetizer arrives. The dauntingly large menu includes just about any marine creature available at the docks that day, cooked to your preference. One Brobdingnagian repast called the "Marine Platter" incorporates a whole lobster, Alaskan crab legs, two jumbo tiger shrimp, a smoked salmon fillet, sea scallops, crabmeat-stuffed mushroom caps, two thick onion rings, and rice pilaf—for C$40 (US$27). They're proud of their wine list, with bottles from every major producing country, many by the reasonably priced glass. The French Rieslings go well with most any of these dishes.

Haveli. 39 Clarence St. (at Sussex St.). ☎ **613/241-1700.** Reservations recommended. Main courses C$10–C$17 (US$7–US$11). AE, MC, V. Mon–Fri 11:30am–2pm and 5:30–9pm, Sat 5:30–9pm, Sun noon–2:30pm and 5–9pm. INDIAN.

This popular place finds itself in an odd physical situation: Most of the sidewalk tables belong to a neighboring restaurant, and when you go looking for the washrooms, you find yourself in an adjoining sports bar. But this shouldn't discourage admirers of exemplary Indian food. Everything is characterized by bold, simple, clean, intense flavors. A good sampler (and no appetizer will be needed if you order it) is thal-e-Haveli, a tray of tandoori chicken, lamb curry, vegetables, raita, chutney, and rice, with pillowy Nan bread on the side. Other possibilities are chicken tika masala and *bhaingan bharta* (roasted pureed eggplant, tomatoes, and onions). The most expensive item is marinated lobster tails broiled in the tandoor oven, while the best deals are the lunch and Sunday buffets. The cheerful owner and his staff are happy to advise on selections and solicitous about your reactions. But when they ask how you like your food spiced, don't say "hot" if you don't really mean it.

Sante. 45 Rideau St. (at Sussex St.). ☎ **613/241-7113.** Reservations recommended. Main courses C$15–C$20 (US$10–US$13). AE, DC, ER, MC, V. Mon–Sat 11:30am–3pm and 5–10pm. In summer, Sante often closes for Sat lunch. FUSION.

This second-floor restaurant overlooking one of the busiest downtown corners promotes an overtly multicultural approach to cooking, skipping from Thailand to California to the Caribbean to the Mediterranean. The tables are set with flowers, the walls are hung with works by local artists, and you may be seated at a table with armchairs. Start with the delicious callaloo soup, chicken satay, or Bali spring rolls. Follow with a sizzling-hot plate like the seafood with basil-coconut-cream sauce or with the Thai spicy shrimp stir-fried in tamarind, garlic, lemongrass, and chiles. The menu also lists specialties like chicken escabeche steeped in raspberry vinegar with bell peppers, red onion, and chiles and Java scallops spiced and sautéed with coconut, tamarind, and cinnamon.

INEXPENSIVE

The Black Thorn. 15 Clarence St. (west of Parent St.). ☎ **613/562-0705.** Reservations not accepted. Pizzas and other dishes C$8–C$12 (US$5–US$8). AE, ER, MC, V. Sun–Thurs 11:30am–11pm, Fri–Sat 11:30am–midnight. MEDITERRANEAN.

This used to be La Folie, replaced by this equally popular enterprise that isn't really all that different. The converted 19th-century brick house continues to draw substantial crowds to its fenced sidewalk terrace, to the terrace in back beside a courtyard fountain, and to the small dining room centered around an impressive mahogany bar. The kitchen turns out creative food that includes a dozen pizzas from the wood-burning oven, one version of which has toppings of smoked salmon, red onion, capers, and dill. Belgian beer stew and Cajun chicken pasta are winners, and there are a number of vegetarian dishes. Always available are a market catch of the day, wraps, specials, and desserts baked on the premises.

Memories. 7 Clarence St. (east of Sussex St.). ☎ **613/232-1882.** Reservations not accepted. Main courses C$9–C$15 (US$6–US$10); fixed-price lunch C$7 (US$4.65). AE, MC, V. Mon 11:30am–11pm, Tues–Fri 11:30am–midnight, Sat 10:30am–1am, Sun 11am–11pm. BISTRO.

Next door to The Black Thorn (above), this popular cafe offers a menu of snacks and mostly light meals. The fixed-price lunch is composed of soup or salad and a main course like Malaysian lamb curry. Options are sandwiches like ham and cheese with marinated mushrooms and Dijon mustard on a croissant, plus salads, soups, pâtés, and pastas. Weekend brunch brings the usual croissants, quiches, and eggs, as well as waffles with a choice of fruit toppings. Smoking is allowed only on the patio out front, which fills up quickly. Last time I was there, a palm reader appeared to be in permanent possession of one of the tables.

VANIER
MODERATE

Il Vagabondo. 186 Barrette St. (off Beechwood Ave.). ☎ **613/749-4877.** Reservations recommended. Main courses C$10–C$26 (US$7–US$17). AE, DC, ER, MC, V. Tues–Fri noon–2:30pm; Mon–Sat 5–11pm, Sun 5–10pm. ITALIAN.

A short hop across the bridge in Vanier, this trattoria in an 1890 corner house has a lot going for it. The modest bi-level dining room has an oak bar, colorful tablecloths, and a tiled floor. Chalkboard daily specials include the likes of *pollo a basilico* (basil chicken) or *fettuccine con erbe* (fettuccine with herb sauce)—but they disappear early. The à la carte menu features top-drawer veal, usually in fillets that can be prepared *al limone* (in reduced lemon sauce), marsala, or *alla Maltese* (in butter, white wine, cream, and fresh orange juice). Standards include lasagna, fettucini carbonara, and cannelloni fiorentina. Fresh herbs are judiciously deployed, and the pasta is made on the premises—but I'm not talking culinary innovation here. Everything comes in somewhat-daunting portions with vegetable garnishes that rarely vary from dish to dish. Wines are available by the glass.

THE GLEBE
INEXPENSIVE

Canal Ritz. 375 Queen Elizabeth Dr. (on the Rideau Canal). ☎ **613/238-8998.** Reservations recommended. Pizzas, pastas, and main courses C$8–C$15 (US$5–US$10). AE, ER, MC, V. Daily 11am–11:30pm. Shorter hours in winter. ITALIAN/INTERNATIONAL.

This outpost of a small local chain occupies a converted boat house with an airy two-story interior and a dining terrace a foot or two above the water. Houseboats and powerboats glide by. There are a few non-Italian selections, but the specialty is pizza baked in the wood-burning oven. Some versions reach for the designer edges: pears and Brie on braised onions? Forgive them that detour and look to the less bizarre choices: the shrimp, cappicola ham, figs, and mozzarella, or the mozzarella and plum tomato dressed with pesto. They're thin-crusted and uncut, requiring the use of the provided fork and serrated knife. Grilled chicken, shrimp, and sausage on penne highlight the pasta selections, most of which are available in small or full versions for C$10 to C$13 (US$7 to US$9). Charcoal-grilled fish and brochettes are other options. Among the desserts are caramel pecan cheesecake and numerous chocolate fancies. The waitstaff is always pleasant, if occasionally a little ditzy.

HULL
EXPENSIVE

✪ **Café Henri Burger.** 69 rue Laurier. ☎ **819/777-5646.** Reservations recommended. Main courses C$15–C$25 (US$10–US$17); table d'hôte menu C$14–C$17 (US$9–US$11) at lunch, C$40 (US$27) at dinner. AE, DC, ER, MC, V. Mon–Fri noon–3pm; daily 6–11pm. Terrace May–Sept daily noon–11pm. FRENCH.

Henri Burger, once the chef at Château Laurier, founded his eponymous restaurant across the river in the 1920s. He died in 1936, but his dining landmark continues to attract loyal patrons and visitors to the Museum of Civilization, across the street. Its reputation still holds up. The seasonally altered menu might offer chilled berry soup and lobster salad out on the covered terrace in July or bouillabaisse and grilled leg of lamb with roast garlic and rosemary in January. At night, one version of the fixed-price dinner of appetizer, soup, entree, and dessert can start with a napoleon of roasted peppers and goat cheese or smoked salmon with celery-root remoulade. Follow those with spicy grilled breast of capon bedded on smoked corn risotto or rack of pork glazed with Dijon mustard and maple syrup. Meat and game prevail, but salmon and shrimp are regulars. There's a fat book of judiciously chosen wines, those from the Loire Valley among the best values. For dessert, the classic tarte au citron (lemon tart) is a must.

✪ **Le Tartuffe.** 133 rue Notre-Dame (at rue Papineau). ☎ **819/776-6424.** Reservations recommended. Table d'hôte menu C$13–C$16 (US$9–US$10) at lunch, C$23–C$31 (US$15–US$20) at dinner. AE, DC, ER, MC, V. Mon–Fri 11:30am–2pm; Mon–Sat 5–10pm. Closed Mon Oct–May. FRENCH.

What a delight is this almost-hidden town-house restaurant and its inspired kitchen. (To find it, walk 2 blocks west on rue Laurier from the Museum of Civilization and turn right on rue Papineau.) The 42 seats in the two newly decorated dining rooms are matched by another 40 on the shaded terrace. The price of a fixed-price three-course lunch or dinner—soup, appetizer, and entree—is determined by the cost of the main course selected. Choices are unusually generous in number and composition. Of the eight dinner mains, for example, you can have roasted Barbarie duck breast with foie gras and truffle sauce or emu steak with pink peppercorns and Cahors wine sauce gelée. Starters (of seven) can be terrine with onion compote or lentil and smoked sturgeon with lovage oil dressing. One recent lunch choice was shredded duck confit atop a potato pancake that rested on mixed greens. The service is genial and attentive.

4 Seeing the Sights

Most of Ottawa's major sights are clustered downtown, so it's not difficult to walk from one to another.

   Paul's Boat Lines Ltd., 219 Colonnade Rd., Nepean (☎ **613/225-6781,** or 613/235-8409 in summer), offers two cruises. One departs from the dock in Hull, east of Alexandra Bridge in Jacques Cartier Park; carries you along the Ottawa River; and picks up additional passengers at the Ottawa Locks 30 minutes later. The other, along the Rideau Canal, leaves from the docks opposite the Arts Centre and goes down the canal to the Experimental Farm and Carleton University. The 1¼-hour river cruises leave at 11am and 2, 4, and 7:30pm; the 1¼-hour canal trip leaves at 10 and 11:30am and 1:30, 3, 4:30, 7, and 8:30pm. Each is C$12 (US$8) adults, C$10 (US$7) seniors, and C$6 (US$4) children.

The *Sea Prince II* also cruises daily along the Ottawa River from both the Ottawa and the Hull docks. The adult fare is C$14 (US$9), students and seniors C$12 (US$8), and children ages 6 to 12 C$7 (US$4.35). The boat also hosts dinner-dance cruises, theme events, and day cruises to Château Montebello. For details, contact the **Ottawa Riverboat Company,** 30 Murray St., Suite 100 (☎ **613/562-4888**). An intriguing variation kids love is offered by the "amphi-bus" of **Lady Dive,** 90 Wellington St. (☎ **613/852-1132** or 613/524-5235). The boat-shaped wheeled red vehicle lumbers around the land-based sights, then eases into the river and cruises past the waterside attractions. You'll find it beside the Info-Centre or in front of the Museum of Civilization in Hull. It leaves daily: May, June, September, and October 10am to 4pm and July and August 10am to 9pm. Fares are C$22 (US$15) adults, C$20 (US$13) students, and C$18 (US$12) children 14 and under.

Note: See the "Ottawa" map (p. 325) to locate the sights in this section.

THE TOP ATTRACTIONS

Discover the Hill Walking Tours, exploring the events and personalities that shaped Parliament Hill and the nation, are given daily late June to September 1. Make reservations at the Info-tent (see below).

✪ **Parliament Buildings.** On Parliament Hill, a bluff jutting into the Ottawa River. ☎ **613/992-4793** for tours. Free tours (English and French) of the grounds and 4 rooms each of the Centre and East Blocks given daily: late May–Labour Day 9am to 8pm (to 5pm the rest of the year). In summer, tours leave as often as every 10 min., but check at the Info-tent behind the West Block for the current schedule. In cooler months, tours depart at the front of the Centre Block. The last tour excludes the Peace Tower. No tours New Year's Day, Canada Day (July 1), Christmas Day. Free tours of the East Block historic offices given daily July–Labour Day 10am–6pm.

The Parliament buildings, with their steeply pitched copper roofs, dormers, and towers, are truly impressive, especially on first sighting from river or road. In 1860, Prince Edward (later Edward VII) laid the cornerstone for the buildings, which were finished in time to host the inaugural session of the first Parliament of the new Dominion of Canada in 1867. Entering through the south gate off Wellington Street, you'll pass the **Centennial Flame,** lit by Lester Pearson on New Year's Eve 1966 to mark the passing of 100 years since that historic event.

THE BUILDINGS Parliament is composed of three sprawling building blocks—the **Centre Block,** straight ahead, and the flanking **West Block** and **East Block.** They're at the heart of Canadian political life, containing the House of Commons and the Senate. You can attend sessions of the **House of Commons** to observe the 295 elected members debating in their handsome green chamber with tall stained-glass windows. Parliament is usually in recess from late June to early September and occasionally between September and June, including the Easter and Christmas holidays. Otherwise, the House usually sits Monday 11am to 6:30pm, Tuesday and Thursday 10am to 6:30pm, Wednesday 2 to 8pm, and Friday 10am to 4pm. The 104 appointed members of the **Senate** sit in an opulent red chamber with murals depicting Canadians fighting in World War I.

The imposing 302-foot campanile dominating the Centre Block's facade is the **Peace Tower.** It houses a 53-bell carillon, a huge clock, an observation deck, and the Memorial Chamber, commemorating Canada's war dead, most notably the 66,650 who lost their lives in World War I. Stones from the deadliest battlefields are lodged in the chamber's walls and floors. Atop the tower is a 35-foot bronze mast flying a Canadian flag. When Parliament is in session, the tower is lit. When you go up to the tower, you'll likely notice something strange about the elevator. For the first 98 feet of the journey it travels at a 10° angle.

A 1916 fire destroyed the original Centre Block; only the Library at the rear was saved. A glorious 16-sided dome, supported outside by flying buttresses and paneled inside with Canadian white pine, features a marble statue of the young Queen Victoria and splendid carvings—gorgons, crests, masks, and hundreds of rosettes. The West Block, containing parliamentary offices, is closed to the public, but you can visit the East Block, housing offices of prime ministers, governors-general, and the Privy Council. Four historic rooms are on view: the original governor-general's office, restored to the period of Lord Dufferin (1872 to 1878); the offices of Sir John A. Macdonald and Sir Georges-Etienne Cartier (the principal Fathers of Confederation); and the Privy Council Chamber with anteroom.

Stroll the grounds clockwise around the Centre Block—they're dotted with statues honoring such prominent figures as Queen Victoria, Sir Georges-Etienne Cartier, William Lyon Mackenzie King, and Sir Wilfrid Laurier. Behind the building is a promenade with sweeping views of the river. Here too is the old Centre Block's bell, which crashed to the ground shortly after tolling midnight on the eve of the 1916 fire. At the bottom of the cliff behind Parliament (accessible from the entrance locks on the Rideau Canal), a pleasant path leads along the Ottawa River.

✪ **CHANGING OF THE GUARD**   Late June to late August, a colorful half-hour ceremony is held daily on the Parliament Hill lawn (weather permitting). Two historic regiments—the Governor-General's Foot Guards and the Canadian Grenadier Guards—compose the Ceremonial Guard. The parade of 125 soldiers in busbies and scarlet jackets (guard, color party, and band) assembles at Cartier Square Drill Hall (by the canal at Laurier Avenue) at 9:30am and marches up Elgin Street to reach the hill at 10am. On arrival on the hill, the Ceremonial Guard splits, one division of the old guard positioned on the west side of the Parliament Hill lawn and two divisions of the new guard, or "duties," on the east side. The ceremony includes the inspection of dress and weapons of both groups. The colors are then marched before the troops and saluted, and the guards compliment each other by presenting arms. Throughout, sergeant-majors bellow unintelligible commands that prompt the synchronized stomp and clatter of boots and weapons. Finally, the outgoing guard commander gives the key to the guard room to the incoming guard commander, signifying that the process has been completed. The relieved unit marches back down Wellington Street to the beat of their drums and the skirl of bagpipes.

✪ **SOUND & LIGHT SHOW**   For years, May to August, Canada's history has unfolded in a dazzling half-hour display of sound and light against the dramatic backdrop of the Parliament buildings. Weather permitting, two performances are given per night, one in English, the other in French. There's bleacher seating for the free show. The shows were cancelled in 1999 to permit technical upgrading but are expected to be renewed in 2000. For details, contact the **National Capital Commission** at ☎ 613/239-5000.

Byward Market. Contained within the square formed by Sussex, Rideau, St. Patrick, and King Edward sts. May–Nov Mon–Sat 9am–6pm, Sun 10am–6pm; Dec–Apr daily 10am–6pm.

A traditional farmers' market here still sells all manner of foods, flowers, plants, and vegetables, while the central market building houses two floors of boutiques displaying a wide variety of wares and crafts. During market season, enjoy a snack or meal at more than 70 indoor and outdoor stand-up counters and cafes or watch life surge past over a cold beer or glass of wine. The neighborhood is a mix of rehabilitated 19th-century brick buildings and some undistinguished contemporary commercial structures. Street performers and balloon manipulators provide brief diversion (though someone seems to have rounded up the mimes).

The many stalls of carefully arranged gleaming produce invite inspection of the diverse offerings of regional farmers and food artisans. Pick up some cheese or cold cuts from **International Cheese & Deli,** 40 Byward Market St.; bread from **Le Boulanger Français,** 119 Murray St.; a bottle of wine at **Vintages Wines & Spirits,** 299 Dalhousie St.; and perhaps some desserts at **Aux Délices,** 32 Byward Market St. Then take your picnic back down to the canal.

Explore too the **Sussex courtyards,** which extend from George to St. Patrick streets along Sussex Drive.

✪ **Canadian Museum of Civilization.** 100 Laurier St., Hull. ☎ **819/776-7000.** Admission C$8 (US$5) adults, C$7 (US$4.65) seniors, C$6 (US$4) ages 13–17, C$3 (US$2) children 2–12. Free to all Sun 9am–noon. Tickets to CINEPLUS C$6–C$8 (US$3.65–US$5), combination museum and CINEPLUS tickets C$7–C$13 (US$4.65–US$9). July to mid-Oct Sun–Wed 9am–6pm, Thurs–Fri 9am–9pm; rest of the year Fri–Wed 9am–6pm, Thurs 9am–9pm.

Canadian Indian architect Douglas Cardinal designed this spectacular museum rising from the banks of the Ottawa River as though its curvilinear forms had been sculpted by wind, water, and glacier. The exhibits within tell the history of Canada, starting with the **Grand Hall,** the high windows of which provide fine views of the skyline. It's devoted to the "First Nations"—in this case, Native-Canadian bands of the west coast—featuring a ranked collection of huge totem poles and facades representing lodges. Behind these are small galleries of utensils, tools, weavings, and other artifacts. From there, take escalators to the third floor and its **Canada Hall.** Laid out in chronological order is the history of the country, starting with the arrival of the Vikings. There are effective tableaux of shipboard life through the whaling period, with human-sized models, moving images, and recorded shrieks of gulls and creaks of hawsers. Replications of fortified settlements of 18th-century New France follow, on through the military past to the rise of cities, including a walk along an early-1900s street. On the second floor are a **Children's Museum** and a **Postal Museum,** but the principal attraction is the **CINEPLUS** theater, containing an IMAX screen and an OMNIMAX (dome-shaped) screen that propel the viewer giddily into the film's action. There are also a cafeteria and a restaurant, **Les Muses** (☎ 819/776-7009).

✪ **National Aviation Museum.** At Rockcliffe Airport. ☎ **613/993-2010.** Admission C$5 (US$3.35) adults, C$4 (US$2.65) seniors/students, C$1.75 (US$1.15) children 7–15; children 6 and under free. Free to all Thurs 5–9pm. May–Labour Day daily 9am–5pm (to 9pm Thurs); rest of the year Tues–Sun 10am–5pm (to 9pm Thurs). From Sussex Dr., take Rockcliffe Pkwy. and exit at the National Aviation Museum.

This collection of more than 115 aircraft is one of the best of its kind in the world. In the main exhibit hall, a "Walkway of Time" traces aviation history from the start of the 20th century through the two world wars to the present. All the planes are either the real thing or full-sized replicas, starting with the Silver Dart, a biplane built by a consortium headed by Alexander Graham Bell. It took off from the ice of Baddeck Bay, Nova Scotia, in February 1909, performing Canada's first powered flight. It flew for 9 minutes—not bad, considering it looks as though it were built out of bicycle parts and kites. The other sections are concerned with specific uses, including the often-amphibious craft of bush pilots so critical in servicing the roadless outer reaches of monster Canada and the development of the airlines and of military and naval aircraft from World War I through the jet age. Examples are partially stripped of their outer skins to reveal their construction, and there are cockpit mock-ups with videos simulating takeoffs, a hit with kids.

✪ **National Gallery of Canada.** 380 Sussex Dr. (at St. Patrick St.). ☎ **613/ 990-1985.** Admission C$12 (US$8) adults, C$10 (US$7) seniors/students; under age 18 free. Special exhibits are extra. May to early Oct Wed–Sun 10am–6pm (to 8pm Thurs); mid-Oct to Apr Wed–Sun 10am–5pm (to 8pm Thurs). Guided tours daily at 11am and 2pm. Register at the information desk. Closed major holidays.

Architect Moshe Safdie, famed for his Habitat apartment block and Musée des Beaux-Arts in Montréal, designed this rose-granite crystal palace that gleams from a promontory overlooking the Ottawa River. A dramatic long glass concourse leads to the Grand Hall, commanding glorious views of Parliament Hill. Natural light also fills the galleries, thanks to ingeniously designed shafts with reflective panels. The museum displays about 800 examples of Canadian art, part of the 10,000 works in the permanent collection. A good way to take it all in is to go to the second floor and proceed down counterclockwise. Among the highlights are Benjamin West's famous 1770 history painting of General Wolfe's death at Québec; the fabulous Rideau Convent Chapel (1888), a rhapsody of wooden fan vaulting, cast-iron columns, and intricate carving created by architect/priest Georges Bouillon; the works of early Québecois artists like Antoine Plamondon, Abbé Jean Guyon, and Frère Luc; Tom Thomson and the Group of Seven landscapists; and the Montréal Automatistes Paul-Emile Borduas and Jean-Paul Riopelle. The European masters are also represented, from Corot and Turner to Chagall and Picasso, and contemporary galleries feature pop art and minimalism, plus later abstract works, both Canadian and American. Pause for a contemplative moment on the balcony of the central atrium looking down on a garden of triangular flower beds and a grove of trees that repeat the lines of the pyramidal glass roof. Each year, three or four major traveling exhibits are displayed, including recent ones on Monet and van Gogh. Facilities include two restaurants, a gift shop/bookstore, and an auditorium.

MORE ATTRACTIONS

Canadian Museum of Nature. 240 McLeod St. (at Metcalfe). ☎ **613/566-4700.** Admission C$5 (US$3.35) adults, C$4 (US$2.65) seniors/ages 13 and up, C$2 (US$1.35) ages 3–12, C$12 (US$8) families; children under 3 free. Half price on Thurs 9:30am–5pm, free 5–8pm. May–Labour Day daily 9:30am–5pm (to 8pm Thurs); rest of the year daily 10am–5pm (to 8pm Thurs).

Seven permanent exhibit halls trace the history of life on Earth from its beginnings 4,200 million years ago. A huge tree of life traces the evolutionary threads of life from 500 million years ago to the present. The third-floor dinosaur hall is a popular highlight, with fossils, skulls, and the intact skeleton of a mastadon. In an opposite gallery is a variety of snails, bugs, spiders, and other "creepy critters," some of them live. Down one floor are mineral galleries and exhibits of Canadian birds and large mammals preserved by taxidermy and placed in natural settings. Kids enjoy the Discovery Den activity area.

National Museum of Science & Technology. 1867 St. Laurent Blvd. (at Lancaster Rd.). ☎ **613/991-3044.** Admission C$6 (US$4) adults, C$5 (US$3.35) seniors/students, C$2 (US$1.35) ages 6–15; C$12 (US$8) family maximum (2 adults, 2 children). May 1–Labour Day daily 9am–5pm (to 9pm Fri); rest of the year Tues–Sun 9am–5pm. Closed Dec 25. Appointments needed to enter the observatory (call ☎ 613/991-3053 8am–4pm).

Take Time for a Scenic Drive

For a picturesque outing, drive east on Wellington Street past Parliament Hill, through Confederation Square. After Château Laurier, on the left, turn left (north) on Sussex Drive. After passing the new **American Embassy,** glorious views open up to the left over the islands.

Proceed along Sussex Drive to St. Patrick Street, turning left into **Nepean Point Park.** Here share a fine river view with the statue of Samuel de Champlain. Across the road is **Major's Hill Park,** between Château Laurier and the National Gallery, where the noonday gun is fired (at 10am on Sun to avoid disturbing church services). Return to Sussex Drive, continuing in the same direction. Just beyond the Macdonald-Cartier Bridge stands **Earnscliffe,** once the home of Sir John A. Macdonald, first Prime Minister of the Dominion of Canada, and now the residence of the British High Commissioner.

Farther along, Sussex Drive crosses the Rideau River, passing the contemporary **Ottawa City Hall,** in the middle of Green Island near Rideau Falls, to the left. The parkway proceeds past the Prime Minister's house, shielded by trees at 24 Sussex Dr., and on to **Rideau Hall,** at no. 1, also known as Government House, the Governor-General's residence. On the 88-acre grounds are scores of ceremonial trees planted by visiting dignitaries and heads of state, from Queen Victoria to John F. Kennedy, Richard Nixon, and Princess Diana. They're identified by nameplates at the base of the trees. In summer, a brief changing-of-the-guard ceremony is held at noon at the main gate. Tours of the grounds and the interior public rooms are conducted daily in July and August and on weekends the rest of the year. For information, stop in at the **Visitor Centre** (open daily 9:30am to 5:30pm) or call ☎ **613/998-7113.**

Continuing, the drive becomes **Rockliffe Driveway,** a beautiful route along the Ottawa River and through **Rockcliffe Park.** Where the road splits in the park, follow the right fork to Acacia Avenue to reach the **Rockeries,** where April blossoms herald spring. If you wish, continue on Rockliffe Driveway to reach the **Aviation Museum.** Or proceed on Acacia, which doubles back and connects once again with the Driveway back to the city.

Interactive displays encourage you to participate in demonstrations of such physical principles as viscosity, climb aboard a steam locomotive, launch a Black Brant rocket from a mini–control room, observe the heavens in the evening through Canada's largest refracting telescope (appointments necessary), see chicks hatching, and walk through the Crazy Kitchen, where everything looks normal but the floor is tilted at a sharp angle. The permanent exhibits deal with Canada in space, land and marine transportation, communications, and all kinds of modern industrial and household technology. The adjacent outdoor technology park features machines and devices from the windmill and lighthouse to radar and rocket.

Royal Canadian Mounted Police Musical Ride. 8900 St. Laurent Blvd. N. ☎ **613/ 993-3751.** At St. Laurent Blvd. N., take Sussex Dr. east past Rideau Hall and pick up Rockville Driveway; turn left at Sandridge Rd. and continue to the corner of St. Laurent.

The famous Musical Ride mounted drill team first performed in Regina in 1878. Horses and riders practice at the Canadian Police College, and the public is welcome to attend. Check before you go, though, because the ride is often on tour, especially during the warmer months, and schedules are extremely tentative.

Billings Estate Museum. 2100 Cabot St. ☎ **613/247-4830.** Admission C$2.50 (US$1.65) adults, C$2 (US$1.35) seniors, C$1 (US65¢) ages 5–17; children under 5 free. May–Oct Tues–Sun noon–5pm. Go south on Bank St., cross the Rideau River at Billings Bridge and take Riverside East; turn right on Pleasant Park and right on Cabot.

This imposing manse allows you to peer into the social life of the period from 1829, when Braddish Billings, head of one of Ottawa's founding families, oversaw its construction, to the 1970s, when the home was turned into a museum. You may use the picnic area and stroll the 8-acre grounds, and the experience is heightened when tea and scones are served on the lawn June 1 to September 1, 2 or 3 days a week (call ahead for current details).

Bytown Museum. 540 Wellington St. (at Commissioner St.). ☎ **613/234-4570.** Admission C$2.50 (US$1.65) adults, C$1.25 (US85¢) seniors/students, C50¢ (US35¢) children. Apr to mid-May and mid-Oct to Nov Mon–Fri 10am–4pm; mid-May to mid-Oct Mon–Sat 10am–5pm, Sun 1–5pm. Closed Dec–Mar.

Housed in Ottawa's oldest stone building (1827), which served as the Commissariat for food and material during construction of the Rideau Canal, this museum displays possessions of Lieutenant-Colonel By, the canal's builder and one of young Ottawa's most influential citizens. In addition, artifacts reflect the social history of the pioneer era of Bytown/Ottawa in three period rooms and a number of changing exhibits. The museum is beside the Ottawa Locks, between Parliament Hill and Château Laurier.

Canadian War Museum. 330 Sussex Dr. (at Bruyere St.). ☎ **819/776-8627.** Admission C$4 (US$2.65) adults, C$3 (US$2) seniors/ages 13–17, C$2 (US$1.35) children 2–12; free for everyone Sun 9:30am–noon. May to mid-Oct daily 9:30am–5pm (to 8pm Thurs), mid-Oct to Apr Tues–Sun 9:30am–5pm (to 8pm Thurs). Closed Christmas Day.

Kids love to clamber over the tanks outside this museum, and they enjoy almost as much imagining themselves in firefights in the life-size replica of a World War I trench. They seem unaffected by the innate solemnity of the collection, which traces Canada's long and often-tragic military history. The country has lost more than 115,000 men and women in 20th-century wars, more than 60,000 killed in World War I alone, and its population is one-tenth that of the United States. On display are intact airplanes, military equipment, antique and modern weaponry, a Mercedes used by Adolf Hitler, ephemera like General Wolfe's chess set, and uniforms (among them that of Canadian air ace Billy Bishop, credited with shooting down the Red Baron). There are several large mock-ups of famous battle scenes, including the D-Day landings at Normandy, with martial music and other sound effects. Exhibits begin at the beginning, taking note of skirmishes between Vikings and Canadian Natives circa 1000, and proceed chronologically through the War of 1812, the disaster at Dieppe in World War II, and Korea. It ends with an outline of the military's more recent role in peacekeeping missions, of which Canadians are especially proud.

Laurier House. 335 Laurier Ave. E. (at Chapel St.). ☎ **613/992-8142.** Admission C$2.25 (US$1.50) adults, C$1.75 (US$1.15) seniors, C$1.25 (US85¢) ages 6–16. Apr–Sept Tues–Sat 9am–5pm, Sun 2–5pm; Oct–Mar call ahead for hours.

This comfortable 1878 brick home is filled with mementos of the two Canadian prime ministers who lived here over a span of 50 years. From 1897 to 1919, it was occupied by Sir Wilfrid Laurier, Canada's seventh Prime Minister and the first French-Canadian elected to that office. He was followed by William Lyon Mackenzie King, who held the same post for 21 years and lived here from 1923 to 1950. King is said to have held seances in the library; on display is the crystal ball he supposedly coveted in London but said he couldn't afford—an American bought it for him when he overheard King's remarks. A portrait of the PM's mother is here, in front of which

King used to place a red rose daily. You'll also find a copy of the program Abraham Lincoln held on the night of his assassination, plus copies of his death mask and hands. Lester B. Pearson's library has also been re-created and contains the Nobel Peace Prize medal he won for his role in the 1956 Arab-Israeli dispute.

PARKS & GARDENS

The **Central Experimental Farm,** at Experimental Farm Drive and Prince of Wales Drive (☎ 613/991-3044), isn't a traditional park, as is obvious by the name—but with its 1,200 acres, it qualifies as the largest green space of all. Though now surrounded by suburban Ottawa, the farm has livestock barns housing various breeds of cattle, pigs, chickens, sheep, and horses. Milking time is 4pm. The greenhouses shelter a noted chrysanthemum show every November, and there are also an ornamental flower garden and an arboretum with 2,000 varieties of trees and shrubs. May to early October, you can ride in wagons drawn by brawny Clydesdales, weather permitting, Monday to Friday 10 to 11:30am and 2 to 3:30pm. Adults are charged C$2.50 (US$1.65) and children/seniors C$2 (US$1.35). In winter there are sleigh rides. Admission is C$3 (US$2) adults and C$2 (US$1.35) students/seniors/children 3 to 15. March to October, the agricultural museum, barns, and tropical greenhouse are open daily 9am to 5pm; November to February, except Christmas and New Year's Day, the barns and tropical greenhouse are open daily 9am to 4pm, but the museum's exhibits are closed.

Another star attraction in the Ottawa area is **Gatineau Park,** across the river in Québec, north of Hull. Only 3km (1.9 miles) from Parliament lie 88,000 acres of woodland and lakes named after notary-turned-explorer Nicolas Gatineau of Trois-Rivières. The park was inaugurated in 1938, when the federal government bought land in the Gatineau Hills to stop forest destruction. Black bear, timber wolf, otter, marten, and raccoon are joined by white-tailed deer, beaver, and more than 100 species of birds. Also resident, but rarely glimpsed, are lynx and wolverines.

Park facilities include 90 miles of **hiking trails** and supervised **swimming beaches** at Meech Lake, Lac Philippe, and Lac la Pêche. Vehicle access fees to beach areas are C$7 to C$9 (US$4.65 to US$6). You can rent boats (canoes, kayaks, and rowboats) at Lac Philippe and Lac la Pêche for C$28 (US$19) a day. Call ☎ 819/456-3555 to make reservations. Motorboats aren't permitted on park lakes except on Lac la Pêche, where motors up to 10 horsepower may be used for fishing. Most lakes can be fished (if it's not allowed, it's posted). A Québec license is required and can be obtained at many convenience stores around the park.

Camping facilities are at or near Lac Philippe, accessible by highways 5, 105, and 366; there are also 35 canoe camping sites at Lac la Pêche. For details on this and other camping facilities, contact the **Gatineau Park Visitor Centre,** 318 Meech Lake Rd., Old Chelsea, PQ J0X 1N0 (☎ 819/827-2020), or write the **National Capital Commission,** 40 Elgin St., Suite 202, Ottawa, ON K1P 1C7. Reservations are vital. Call ☎ 819/456-3016 mid-May to September 9am to 4pm. Fees are C$15 to C$20 (US$10 to US$13) per site per day (C$9/US$6 for seniors).

In winter, hiking trails become **cross-country ski trails,** marked by numbers on blue plaques, with chalets along the way. Winter camping is available at Lac Philippe.

In the middle of the park is the summer retreat of Mackenzie King at **Kingsmere.** Serving as Prime Minister for a record 22 years, King collected the architectural fragments on view at the estate, transported here from the Centre Block Parliament building after the 1916 fire and from London's House of Commons after the 1941 Blitz. Linger over a beverage and snack in a cottage called the Moorside Tearoom; May 1 to Oct 31 it's open daily 11am to 6pm. For reservations, call ☎ 819/827-3405.

There are several routes to the park: Cross over to Hull and take boulevard Taché (Route 148) to the Gatineau Parkway, which leads to Kingsmere, Ski Fortune, and eventually Meech Lake. Or take Route 5 (Autoroute de la Gatineau) north, take Exit 12 for Old Chelsea, turn left, and proceed 1.2km (0.7 mile) on Meech Lake Road to the Gatineau Park Visitor Centre. To reach Lac Philippe, take Route 5 north out of Hull and then Route 105 to the intersection of Route 366 west. Just before reaching Ste-Cecile-de-Masham, turn off to Lac Philippe; to reach Lac la Pêche, keep going along the Masham road to St-Louis-de-Masham and enter the park just beyond.

ESPECIALLY FOR KIDS

Kids love the bands, rifles, and uniforms at the **Changing of the Guard** on Parliament Hill. The **National Aviation Museum** is a fantasyland for budding pilots, especially the mock-ups of cockpits where they can pretend to be pilots. The perennial favorites at the **Canadian Museum of Nature** are the dinosaurs, the animals, and the Discovery Den, especially created for children. Extra-special attractions at the **Canadian Museum of Civilization** are the Children's Museum and CINEPLUS for action movies. Kids enjoy petting the animals at the **Agriculture Museum,** as well as picnicking or taking a hayride at the **Central Experimental Farm.** At the **National Museum of Science and Technology,** the hands-on exhibits manage to entertain while learning. Kids also love the tanks and weaponry on display at the **Canadian War Museum** and the Musical Ride practices at the **Canadian Police College.** All these attractions are described in detail earlier in this chapter.

When it's time to let off some steam, there's **canoeing** or **boating** at Dow's Lake; **biking** along the canal or **ice skating** on it; plus activities outside the city in Gatineau Park.

Outside Ottawa is the **Storyland Family Park,** Storyland Road (RR #5), off Route 17 about 6 miles northwest of Renfrew (☎ 613/432-2222), with a puppet theater, paddleboats, minigolf, a petting zoo, and more. Admission is C$9 (US$6) adults, C$8 (US$5) children 5 and over, and C$6 (US$4) seniors/children 2 to 4. Early June to mid-September, it's open daily 9:30am to 6pm. And the **Logos Land Resort,** Route 17 (RR #1), Cobden (☎ 613/646-9765), has five water slides, minigolf, paddleboats, and sleigh rides and cross-country skiing in winter. Admission is C$13 (US$9). June to August, it's open daily 9am to 8pm (to 5pm the rest of the year).

5 Special Events & Festivals

On weekends in February, it's **Winterlude** (☎ 613/239-5000; www.capcan.ca), an extravaganza bursting with parades, ice-sculpture competitions, fireworks, speed skating, snowshoe races, ice boating, curling, and more. One offbeat contest is the bed race on the frozen canal, while the most exciting event may be the harness racing on ice.

Ottawa's biggest event is the **Canadian Tulip Festival** (☎ 888/465-1867; www.capcan.ca) for about 2 weeks in mid-May, when the city is ablaze with 200 varieties of tulips enlivening public buildings, monuments, embassies, homes, and driveways. (Among the best viewing points is Dow's Lake.) The festival began in 1945, when the Netherlands sent 100,000 tulip bulbs to Canada in appreciation of the role Canadian troops played in liberating Holland. Queen Juliana, who'd spent the war years in Canada, arranged for an annual bulb presentation to celebrate the birth of her daughter, Princess Margriet, in Ottawa in 1943 (to ensure that the princess was born a Dutch citizen, the Canadian government proclaimed her room in the Ottawa Civic Hospital part of the Netherlands). Festival events include fireworks, concerts, parades, and a flotilla on the canal.

At the end of May is the **R.C.M.P. Musical Ride Sunset Ceremony** (☎ 613/ 993-3751; www.rcmp-grc.gc.ca), with outdoor evening performances of music and horsemanship, including jumping and dressage, as well the ride itself. In early June, the Canadian Museum of Nature holds a **Children's Festival** (☎ 613/728-5863; www.childfest.ca), an extravaganza of dance, mime, puppetry, and music. Late June brings the **Festival Franco-Ontarien** (☎ 613/741-1225; www.leroux.ca), a 5-day celebration of Francophone Canada, featuring classical and other musical concerts, fashion shows, street performers, games and competitions, crafts, and French cuisine.

On July 1, Canadians flock to the city to celebrate **Canada Day** (☎ 800/ 465-1867; www.capcan.ca), a huge birthday party with many kinds of entertainment, including fireworks. For 10 days in mid-July, the city is filled with the mainstream and cutting-edge sounds of the **Ottawa International Jazz Festival** (☎ 613/241-2633; www.jazz.ottawa.com). Local, national, and international artists give more than 125 performances at more than 20 venues. That event is followed by the 2-week **Ottawa Chamber Music Festival** (☎ 613/234-8008; www.chamberfest.com), North America's largest, with 74 concerts in the city's churches.

On Labour Day weekend, scores of brilliantly colored balloons fill the skies over Ottawa, while on the ground, people flock to musical events and midway rides during the **Gatineau Hot Air Balloon Festival** (☎ 819/243-2330; www.ville.gatineau. qc.ca/g_welcome.htm). Other major events include the **National Capital Air Show** in late May (☎ 613/526-1030; www.ncas.ottawa.com), the **National Capital Dragon Boat Race Festival** in late June (☎ 613/238-7711; www.dragonboat.net), and the 10-day **Central Canada Exhibition** (☎ 613/237-7222; www.the-ex.com) in mid- to late August.

6 Outdoor Activities & Spectator Sports

OUTDOOR ACTIVITIES

BIKING   Ottawans are enthusiastic cyclists, fully utilizing the more than 160km (99 miles) of bike paths running along the Ottawa and Rideau rivers, along the Rideau Canal, and in Gatineau Park—and more miles are being added. A blue, black, and white cyclist logo marks all bikeways. April to Canadian Thanksgiving in October, bicycles are available at **Rent a Bike,** 1 Rideau St., in the parking lot behind Château Laurier (☎ 613/241-4140). Town bikes, sport bikes, mountain bikes, and in-line skates are available, with standard bikes from C$7 (US$4.65) per hour to C$25 (US$17) for 24 hours or C$95 (US$63) per month, and performance bikes from C$30 (US$20) per day to C$145 (US$97) per month. Take the kids along in a bike trailer with two seats and a harness for another C$6 (US$4) per hour. The company will also provide maps of the self-guided day trips around the city, as well as guided tours. You can rent bikes and in-line skates at **Dow's Lake Marina** (☎ 613/232-5278).

BOATING/CANOEING   You can rent paddleboats and canoes at the marina (☎ 613/232-5278) at **Dow's Lake Pavilion,** 1001 Queen Elizabeth Dr., for C$11 (US$7) per hour or C$40 (US$27) per day. The C$3 million (US$2 million) glass-and-steel complex, which looks like a cluster of sails from a distance, has several restaurants and provides a welcome haven after a winter skate or a summer running or biking jaunt. You can also rent boats in Gatineau Park at Lac la Pêche and Lac Philippe (☎ 819/827-2020) for C$7 (US$4.65) per hour or C$25 (US$17) per day.

GOLF   The Ottawa metro region has over 60 courses, including the one on the premises of the **Château Cartier Sheraton** (☎ 819/778-0000) in Québec. Other

Ottawa's Pride & Joy: The Rideau Canal

Built in the early 19th century under the leadership of Lt. Colonel John By, a civil and military engineer, the **Rideau Canal** was meant to bypass the Thousand Islands section of the St. Lawrence River, thought to be vulnerable to American attack in the hostile atmosphere following the War of 1812. It connected Kingston with the Ottawa River, allowing the transporting of troops and supplies to Canada's capital and from there on to Montréal. The fear of invasion never came to fruition, railroads soon became the desired mode of transportation, and the quickly outmoded canal was left to evolve over time from neglected historical artifact into one of eastern Ontario's most impressive visual and recreational assets. In summer, walk or cycle along the canal paths or row a canoe or boat on a gentle journey before stopping at the canal-side cafe at the National Arts Centre. You can rent houseboats to navigate its entire length. In winter, it's turned into a 5-mile-long skating course worthy of Hans Brinker, as people glide to and from work, briefcases in hand, and families take to the ice with children perched atop their backs or drawn on sleighs.

Construction of the 123-mile canal began in 1826 and ended in 1832. Starting in Ottawa, it follows the course of the Rideau River to its summit on Upper Rideau Lake, which is connected to Newboro Lake, where the canal descends the Cataraqui River through a series of lakes controlled by dams to Kingston. In Ottawa, a flight of eight locks allows boats to negotiate the 80-foot difference between the artificially constructed portion of the canal and the Ottawa River—a sight not to be missed. You can observe this fascinating maneuver between Parliament Hill and Château Laurier.

desirable courses in the area are the **Emerald Links Golf & Country Club** (☎ 613/822-4653); **Canadian Golf and Country Club** (☎ 613/780-3565); **Le Club de Golf Heritage** (☎ 800/561-4707); and **Manderley on the Green** (☎ 613/489-2066). Greens fees for these run C$25 to C$35 (US$17 to US$23).

HIKING & NATURE WALKS   A band of protected wetlands and woodlands surrounds the capital on the Ontario side of the Ottawa River, and here you can find ideal hiking areas. At **Stony Swamp Conservation Area** in the region's west end are 39km (24 miles) of trails, including the Old Quarry Trail, the Jack Pine Nature Trail, and the Sasparilla Trail. Call ☎ 613/239-5000 for information. It's also good for cross-country skiing and snowshoeing. Regional maps are available from the Capital InfoCentre downtown at 14 Metcalfe St. **Gatineau Park** has a network of hiking trails, some long enough for a genuine day hike. For details, call the visitor center at ☎ 819/827-2020. West of the city in Kanata, **Riverfront Park** has nature trails along the Ottawa River. Call ☎ 613/592-4281. On the Québec side in Luskville, a trail leads to Luskville Falls from the Chemin de Hôtel de Ville. **The Rideau Trail,** running from Ottawa to Kingston, is the area's major serious hiking trail.

HORSEBACK RIDING   Near Edelweiss Valley, **Captiva Farm,** RR #2, Wakefield (☎ 819/459-2769), offers trail rides year-round on 40km (25 miles) of trails through the Gatineau Hills. Hourly charges are C$24 (US$16) adults and C$12 (US$8) children, and you can go with or without a guide. Reservations are required. About 40km (25 miles) west of the city, **Pinto Valley Ranch,** Fitzroy Harbour (☎ 613/623-3439), offers trail rides for C$20 (US$13) per hour, as well as pony riding and a petting zoo for children.

SKATING   Usually late December to late February, the **Rideau Canal** becomes the world's longest and most romantic skating rink, stretching from the National Arts Centre to Dow's Lake and Carleton University; every morning the radio news reports ice conditions. You can rent skates at several locations for C$12 to C$15 (US$8 to US$10) for 2 hours. The canal is serviced with heated huts, sleigh rentals, boot-check and skate-sharpening services, food concessions, and rest rooms. In-line skates are available at the Rent a Bike facility behind Château Laurier and from Dow's Lake Marina.

SKIING   Few visitors ski the areas around Ottawa, heading instead for Québec's more sophisticated resorts. In many ways, the following ski resorts are more compelling summer attractions with their water parks and other fun facilities. (See "St-Jovite & Mont-Tremblant," in chapter 7, and "Mont Ste-Anne: Skiing & Summer Sports," in chapter 8, for two of Québec's most popular ski resorts.)

   Mont Cascades, just 30 minutes north of Ottawa across the Gatineau River, outside of Cantley on Highway 307 (☎ **819/827-0301**), has 13 trails, one triple- and three double-chair lifts, and two T-bars. The longest run is 2,200 feet. There are two day lodges with a cafeteria and a restaurant/bar at the hill. Night skiing is available. During summer, there are six water slides in the state-of-the-art water park. **Mont Ste-Marie,** 89km (55 miles) north of Ottawa at Lac Ste-Marie (☎ **819/467-5200**), offers skiing on twin hills, with a 1,250-foot drop, and a 3km (1.9-mile) ski run. There are two quads and a Poma. Mont Ste-Marie also offers cross-country skiing. **Gatineau Park,** with 185km (115 miles) of groomed trails, offers the best cross-country skiing. In town, you can also ski along the bike paths paralleling the Eastern or Western parkways.

SWIMMING   Pools that are open to the public include those at **Carleton University** (☎ **613/520-5631**) on Colonel By Drive, the University of Ottawa (☎ **613/562-5789**) at 125 University Dr., and the YMCA-YWCA (☎ **613/788-5000**) at 180 Argyle Dr. Lake swimming is available in **Gatineau Park, Meech Lake, Lac la Pêche,** and **Lac Philippe.**

WHITE-WATER RAFTING   You can enjoy the exhilaration of a day of white-water rafting and be back in your hotel bed that night. Outings are available from mid-May to September, depending on the river. **Owl Rafting,** Box 29, Foresters Falls, ON K0J 1V0 (☎ **613/646-2263** in summer or 613/238-7238 in winter), offers 1- and 2-day white-water rafting trips within 90 minutes of the city, pounding over extensive rapids for the fit and adventurous and floating on gentler stretches for families. Prices start at C$75 (US$50) per person per day during the week, meals included. Companies operating similar trips and facilities are **Esprit Rafting Adventures,** Box 463, Pembroke, ON K8A 6X7 (☎ **800/596-7238** or 819/683-3241); **Ottawa Adventures Rafting,** Box 212, Bryson, QC J0X 1H0 (☎ **800/690-7238** or 819/647-3625); **River Run,** P.O. Box 179, Beachburg, ON K0J 1C0 (☎ **800/267-8504** or 613/646-2501); and **Wilderness Tours,** Foresters Falls, ON K0J 1V0 (☎ **800/267-9166** or 613/646-2291).

SPECTATOR SPORTS

The **Ottawa Senators** (☎ **613/599-0300**) are one of the youngest teams in the National Hockey League (a previous incarnation won a string of Stanley Cups earlier in this century) and currently play at the Corel Centre in Kanata. Tickets cost C$28 to C$80 (US$19 to US$53); call **Ticketmaster** at ☎ **613/755-1166.** The **Ottawa Lynx** (☎ **613/747-5969**), the Triple A affiliate of the Montréal Expos, play baseball at Jetform Park, 300 Coventry Rd. Tickets, which are generally available, cost C$4.25 to C$8 (US$2.85 to US$6); call ☎ **613/749-9947.**

7 Ottawa After Dark

Ottawa's culture and nightlife offerings aren't up to those of Toronto or Montréal, extending largely to the National Arts Centre, several bars, the Byward Market area, and a few dance clubs, the raciest of which are concentrated across the river in Hull. Still, there's certainly enough to occupy the evenings of a long weekend.

The biggest recent news in this regard was the opening of the **Casino de Hull,** 1 bd. du Casino (☎ **800/665-2274** or 819/772-2100), under 3 miles from Parliament Hill and open daily 11am to 3am. It imposes a dress code forbidding tank tops, jogging outfits, motorcycle boots, cutoffs, shorts, and beachwear. Both the exterior and the interior are dramatically landscaped with tropical plants, pools, and waterfalls. There are more than 1,300 slot machines and more than 50 gambling tables, including blackjack, roulette, baccarat, and stud poker (no craps, though, and alcoholic drinks aren't allowed in gambling areas). A dance-and-music revue provides respite from losing for C$28 to C$38 (US$19 to US$25) per show. The complex also has two lounges and three restaurants—fine dining in Le Baccara, a buffet in Banco, and a snack bar. Shuttles operate from Ottawa hotels to the casino for C$9 (US$6) per round-trip.

For Ottawa entertainment information, pick up a copy of *Where,* a free guide usually provided in your hotel; *Ottawa* magazine; the free *X-Press* weekly newspaper; or the Friday edition of the *Ottawa Citizen.*

THE PERFORMING ARTS

Canadian and international musical, dance, and theater artists—including the resident National Arts Centre (NAC) Orchestra—perform at the elaborate **National Arts Centre,** 53 Elgin St., at Confederation Square (☎ 613/947-7000). The building, created by architect Fred Lebensold, is made of three interlocking hexagons beside the Rideau Canal, its terraces tendering excellent views of Parliament Hill and the Ottawa River. There are three auditoriums: the European-style **Opera,** seating 2,300; the 950-seat **Theatre,** with its innovative apron stage; and the 350-seat **Studio,** employed for experimental works. The **National Arts Centre Orchestra** (☎ 613/996-5051) performs in seven or eight main concert series per year. The center also offers classic and modern drama in English and French. For reservations, call Ticketmaster at ☎ 613/755-1111 or visit the NAC box office Monday to Saturday noon to 9pm and Sunday and holidays when performances are scheduled noon to curtain time. Guided tours are available. A free monthly *Calendar of NAC Events* is available from the **NAC Marketing and Communications Department,** Box 1534, Station B, Ottawa, ON K1P 5W1 (☎ 613/996-5051; www.nac-cna.ca). See "Dining," above, for a review of the Centre's canal-side restaurant, Le Café.

Augmenting the main events at the National Arts Centre, the ensemble at the **Great Canadian Theatre Company,** 910 Gladstone Ave. (☎ 613/236-5196), presents contemporary drama and comedy with Canadian themes September to May. Tickets are C$22 (US$15).

LIVE-MUSIC CLUBS

Barrymore's Music Hall, 323 Bank St. (☎ 613/594-0003), is a suitably disreputable-looking rock palace utilizing a former cinema. It showcases bands bearing names like Buskerbash, Goo Fang Goo, and Man or Astroman. On Sundays, it switches to "retro" 1980s sounds. Next door is the smaller and even more ragged **Zaphod Beeblebrox 2,** 363 Bank St. (☎ 613/562-1010), which opens Thursday to Saturday for live underground and alternative rock and DJs the other nights.

A rollicking scene in Byward Market is **Molly McGuire's,** 130 George St. (☎ 613/ 241-1972), a cavernous pub where a variety of musical tastes—rock, folk, jazz—play into the small hours Friday and Saturday. For acoustic folk leavened with New Age melodies and unpredictable open-mike nights, all in a relaxed atmosphere, go to **Rasputin's,** 696 Bronson Ave. (☎ 613/230-5102). Blues action energizes the upstairs lounge at the **Rainbow Bistro,** 76 Murray St. (☎ 613/241-5123), featuring live music nightly. It has hosted such artists as k.d. lang, Colin James, and Buckwheat Zydeco, and though acts aren't often that noteworthy, there's always someone worth hearing. Cover charges run C$2 to C$8 (US$1.35 to US$5) as the week rolls on, but there are free matinees Thursday, Friday, and Saturday 3 to 7pm.

Also in the Byward Market area, beneath The Fish Market restaurant, is **Vineyards,** 54 York St. (☎ 613/241-4270). It's one of the city's cozier hangouts, with a rusticated cellar setting, stone floors, and red-and-white–checked tablecloths. Several house wines are featured every night (beginning C$6/US$4 a glass), from among more than 60 varieties, and there's an ample roster of imported beers. Sunday and Wednesday bring live jazz. Light meals and snacks are available. Fridays and Saturdays, jazz by duos and trios comes with the gelati, coffee, and snacks at **Café Quo Vadis,** 521 Sussex Dr. (☎ 613/789-1819). Piano soloists and jazz combos enhance the more sedate surroundings at **Zoe's,** in Château Laurier, 1 Rideau St. (☎ 613/241-1414, ext. 3213), and **The Lounge,** in the Westin Hotel, 11 Colonel By Dr. (☎ 613/ 650-7000).

BARS & PUBS

Sooner or later, every Ottawan of drinking age squeezes into **Patty's Pub,** 1186 Bank St. (☎ 613/730-2434), to raise a pint or three, tuck into fish-and-chips or Irish stew, and listen to the stirring Irish ballads rendered by a folk singer (resident Thurs to Sat). It's the kind of place where a brave leap into the fray will have you playing darts, chatting, and singing with the regulars in no time. Also popular is **Tramps,** on William Street (☎ 613/241-5523).

Elgin Street, from Gladstone to about Somerset, has bloomed with bars and eating places. Dominating them all is the muscular **Big Daddy's,** 339 Somerset St. (☎ 613/ 569-5200), which enjoys a reputation for attracting large numbers of striking young women, accounting for the striking numbers of young men. Frozen margaritas don't come any bigger, and other drinks are generously poured for the heavy traffic in the bar and out on the terrace. It's a good place to start an evening, and with inertia or a bit of luck connecting, you can stay on for the Creole-Cajun crawfish boil, gumbo, catfish, or oysters from the raw bar. Nearby, open-fronted **Maxwell's,** 340 Elgin St. (☎ 613/232-5771), also has a shellfish bar, with karaoke Tuesday and (often) live bands Wednesday to Saturday; call ahead to be sure. Not far away, the **Bravo Bar-Ristorante,** 292 Elgin St. (☎ 613/233-0057), is a fun place to drop in for a drink and some pool and has decent Italian food and Sunday brunch. For quiet drinking with a piano background, **Friday's Victorian Music Parlour,** 150 Elgin St. (☎ 613/ 237-5353), with its clubby atmosphere, old London engravings, and wingback chairs, plus an inviting fire in winter, is a good choice, especially for single women who just want to have a quiet drink. The pianist entertains nightly. A similar parlor upstairs at the **Full House,** 337 Somerset St. W. (☎ 613/238-6734), provides piano entertainment and a playful atmosphere Wednesday to Saturday. For an even more relaxing atmosphere, sink into plush upholstery and enjoy the lilting piano strains of the lobby bar in the **Delta Ottawa Hotel,** 361 Queen St. (☎ 613/238-6000).

Ottawa has an abundance of English and Irish pubs of varying degrees of authenticity (for the two best choices nearby, see the "Pubbing It Outside Ottawa" box earlier in this chapter). Crammed almost every night from the bar to the wraparound deck is the **Heart & Crown,** 67 Clarence St. (☎ 613/562-0674). The live music Wednesday to Saturday is usually composed of rousing Celtic tunes joined in with infectious enthusiasm by patrons who know every word. Many English, Irish, and Canadian brews are on tap, with Harp and Guinness prominent. Similar, but with a more pronounced English flavor, is **The Earl of Sussex,** 431 Sussex Dr. (☎ 613/562-5544), diagonally across from the new U.S. Embassy. Wingbacks huddle around the fireplace and are arranged by the front windows. They have darts, of course, and folk and pop music are staged Friday and Saturday. In addition to daily chalkboard specials of pastas and quiches, menu standards include steak-and-kidney pie, liver and onions, bangers and mash, and Cornish pasties. There are 27 ales, stouts, and lagers on draft. For even more pub-style conviviality, check out the **Brig,** 23 York St. (☎ 613/562-6666), in the Byward Market area, and the **Elephant and Castle,** 50 Rideau St. (☎ **613/234-5544**).

GAY & LESBIAN BARS

Capital XTRA! is Ottawa's gay/lesbian news-and-events magazine. Ottawa's oldest gay bar, the **Coral Reef Club,** 30 Nicholas St. (☎ **613/234-5118**), is underneath a parking garage (no flashy entrance here). You'll find lots of theme parties, and the cover is C$3 to C$5 (US$2 to US$3.35). *The* hot spot for dancing, the **Club Polo Pub,** 65 Bank St., second floor (☎ **613/235-5995**), features free pool and Internet access, with no cover and a full gamut of age ranges. **Icon,** 366 Lisgar St. (☎ **613/235-4005**), is an open-concept bar and dance floor with pounding techno and industrial sounds. There's live music on the first Thursday of each month. The cover runs C$2 (US$1.35).

DANCE CLUBS

Nightlife used to close down at 1am (11pm on Sun) in Ottawa but thumped on until 3am across the river in Hull. In recent years, though, the strip where most of the popular bars and clubs were located developed a reputation for late-night fights, muggings, and even near riots. The authorities on both sides of the river moved in and agreed to synchronize closing times at 2am. That's taken the heat off, and the area is both calmer and less exciting.

In Ottawa, **Hartwells,** in the Westin Hotel, 11 Colonel By Dr. (☎ **613/560-7000**), fills with a 25-plus crowd for dancing to DJ selections Tuesday to Saturday (cover charged). And on Saturday there's dancing to live entertainment at **Zoe's** in Château Laurier, 1 Rideau St. (☎ **613/241-1414**). In Hull, tucked away off promenade du Portage, is the still-warm disco/bar **Le Bop,** 9 Aubry St. (☎ **819/777-3700**), with a new Italian menu to enhance its appeal to 30-somethings. And farther along is **Au Zone,** 117 promenade du Portage (☎ **819/771-6677**), where the decor evokes an off-kilter Camelot and a hip-hop emphasis ensures crowds of decidedly younger revelers.

8 Exploring Eastern Ontario: Kingston & More

From Port Hope, about 105km (65 miles) east of Toronto, the coast of Lake Ontario incorporates the Bay of Quinte and Quinte's Isle. Once off the main highway, Route 401, you'll discover a tranquil region of farms and orchards largely settled by United Empire Loyalists, who fled the new republic to the south during and after the American Revolution. It's still off the beaten track—except to those in the know, who come to explore the attractive villages; go antiquing; or enjoy the beaches, dunes, and waterfront activities of its provincial parks. Kingston, a most appealing lakefront town with

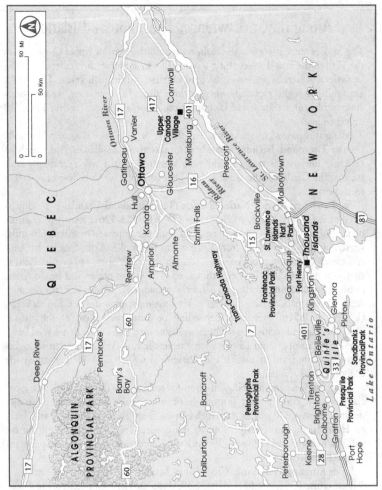

a thrice-weekly market, is intriguing architecturally and historically. It's also the gateway to the mighty St. Lawrence River, the Thousand Islands, and the St. Lawrence National Park.

To get from Ottawa to this region, take Route 16/416 south to 401 west, which connects the towns, parks, and townships from Brockville to Port Hope. From Toronto, take Route 401 east. An especially beguiling detour is the Thousand Islands Parkway, running between Brockville and Kingston parallel to Route 401. That expressway, while swift, is heavily trafficked and often stressful—if you're looking for relaxation, avoid it when possible. The more scenic Route 2, while slower, is a desirable alternative, where available.

KINGSTON

A 2-hour drive from Ottawa and about 3 hours from Toronto (172km/107 miles southwest of Ottawa, 255km/158 miles northeast of Toronto), **Kingston** stands at the

Along the St. Lawrence: The Thousand Islands

The St. Lawrence River was the main route into the heart of Upper Canada from the 17th to the mid–19th century, traveled first by explorers, fur traders, and missionaries and later by settlers en route to Ontario and the plains west. The river is a magnificent sight, especially where it flows around the outcroppings and pine-covered islets of the Thousand Islands region; in some stretches it's over 19km (12 miles) wide.

Along this part of its substantial length, the St. Lawrence is known primarily for the **Thousand Islands.** According to a Native-Canadian legend, petals of heavenly flowers fell to earth and were scattered on the river, creating Manitouana, the Garden of the Great Spirit. That isn't difficult to believe once you've seen them.

St. Lawrence Islands National Park (The Thousand Islands) is headquartered at 2 County Rd. 5, Mallorytown (☎ **613/923-5261;** www.parkscanada. pch.gc.ca/sli). Canada's smallest national park encompasses an 80km (50-mile) stretch of the St. Lawrence, from Kingston to Brockville. Along that length are a sufficiency of motels, cabin colonies, campgrounds, RV sites, and boat-launching sites, but development has been contained. The visitor center and headquarters is on the mainland, where you'll find a picnic area, beach, and nature trail. Access to the park's island facilities is via boat only; mooring is C$14 to C$24 (US$9 to US$16) overnight, depending on boat size. Most of the islands have docking and picnicking facilities, available on a first-come, first-served basis. The largest campground has 18 sites; the smallest, 2. Three consecutive nights is the docking limit at each island. Parking is C$5 (US$3.35) per car at the Mallorytown Landing.

Kingston is a good jumping-off point for touring the Thousand Islands, especially if you're coming from Toronto. In summer, **cruise boats** circulate through the more than 1,800 islands, past such extraordinary sights as **Boldt Castle,** built on Heart Island in the early 1900s by millionaire George Boldt as a gift for his wife. (When she died suddenly, the work was abandoned, and it stands a poignant relic of lost love.)

From Kingston Harbour at City Hall in May to mid-October, you can take a 3-hour cruise (C$17/US$11 adults, C$9/US$6 children 4 to 12) on the *Island Queen,* a triple-deck paddle wheeler. The 90-minute cruises (C$12/US$8 adults,

---

confluence of Lake Ontario, the Rideau Canal, and the St. Lawrence Seaway. This makes for splendid scenery, best viewed by taking the **free ferry trip to Wolfe Island.** Ferries leave at frequent intervals for this sparsely populated island that doubles as a quiet offshore retreat of pronounced rural character. (See the box "Along the St. Lawrence: The Thousand Islands," below, for details about other seagoing sightseeing voyages.) A stroll along Kingston's waterfront, site of many hotels and restaurants as well as marinas, pocket parks, gardens, and a maritime museum, is also a must.

Kingston boasts more than 300 years of history. That rich heritage, which includes a brief tenure as capital of Canada, lingers in the grand old limestone public buildings and private residences lining the downtown streets and giving the city a gracious air, in the four martello towers that once formed a string of defense works guarding the waterways along the U.S.-Canadian border, and the Christopher Wren–style St. Georges Church, which contains a Tiffany window.

C$6/US$4 children 4 to 12) aboard its sister boat, the *Island Belle,* take in the Kingston Harbour and waterfront. Both boats are used for 2-hour sunset cruises. For details, call ☎ **613/549-5544** or 613/549-5545 or check out **www.1000 islandscruises.on.ca**. In season, the nimble catamaran *Sea Fox II* also cruises the islands and the harbor from the bottom of Brock Street in Kingston. The 2-hour islands tour is C$12 (US$8) adults and C$6 (US$4) children 6 to 12. For details, call ☎ **613/542-4271** or check out **www.travelinx.com**.

From Kingston, you can also cruise the Rideau Canal or explore the Thousand Islands aboard a houseboat. Contact any of the following: **Aquaventures,** P.O. Box 70, Brockville, ON K6V 5T7 (☎ **888/498-2727**); **Houseboat Holidays,** RR #3, Gananoque, ON K7G 2V5 (☎ **613/382-2842**); or **St. Lawrence River Houseboat and Cruiser Rentals,** c/o Halliday Point, Wolfe Island, ON K0H 2Y0 (☎ **613/385-2290**). Most houseboats sleep up to six and have fully equipped kitchens, hot and cold running water, and propane systems for heat and light. Weekly summer rentals on the canal system average C$1,000 to C$1,200 (US$667 to US$800). On the St. Lawrence, in August, the cost starts at about C$600 (US$400) for a weekend and C$900 to C$1,250 (US$600 to US$834) for a week. Prices are higher in July but lower in May, June, and September, as well as during the week. You need to bring only sleeping bags and towels.

From the waterfront in **Gananoque** in May to mid-October, the **Thousand Islands Gananoque Boat Line** (☎ **613/382-2144** or 613/382-2146; www.ganboatline.com) offers 3-hour and 1-hour cruises at C$16 and C$11 (US$11 and US$7), respectively; children 7 to 12 on both are C$6 (US$4). The longer cruise stops at the fantastical Boldt Castle (extra C$6/US$3.75 adults, C$3.75/US$2.50 children). Note, though, that to visit the castle, which is in U.S. territory, you'll need the same ID you showed when crossing the Canada/U.S. border. Call ahead for the schedule. The same company operates 1-hour trips from **Ivy Lea,** leaving from west of the International Bridge on the Thousand Islands Parkway. The cost is C$11 (US$7) adults and C$6 (US$4) children 7 to 12. For a dramatic view from above, climb the Skydeck on Hill Island near Ivy Lea, which soars 400 feet above the river. On clear days, the reward is splendid 40-mile panoramic vista.

During summer, **Confederation Park** at the harbor is the site for band concerts and other performances, while in winter you might catch a local ice-hockey contest. In **Market Square** on Tuesday, Thursday, and Saturday, a farmers' market is held, and on Sunday it's the place to rummage for antiques and old stuff.

ESSENTIALS

GETTING THERE   If you're driving from Ottawa, take Route 16 south to 401 and drive west to the Kingston exits. Or, with a little more time, take the more scenic Route 2 instead of 401. From Toronto, take 401E to the Kingston exits. Several daily trains come from Ottawa (☎ **613/244-8289**), Toronto (☎ **416/366-8411**), and Montréal (☎ **514/989-2626**) to Kingston.

VISITOR INFORMATION   Contact the **Kingston Tourist Information Office,** 209 Ontario St., Kingston, ON K7L 2Z1 (☎ **613/548-4415**), on the waterfront across from the City Hall. Its attendants sell tickets for the bus tours that start out front and can help you find lodging.

EXPLORING THE TOWN

A good way to get acquainted with the town is aboard the **tour bus** made to look like a trolley that leaves from in front of the Kingston Tourist Information Office (above), every hour on the hour May to September 10am to 5pm (to 7pm in July and Aug). The tour lasts 50 minutes and costs C$8 (US$5) adults and C$6 (US$4) seniors/youths. If you want to explore **Wolfe Island,** there's a free 25-minute trip aboard the **car ferry** from downtown Kingston; it departs frequently from the dock near the intersection of Queen and Ontario streets. For serious hiking, the Rideau Trail runs 388km (241 miles) along the canal from Kingston to Ottawa. For details, contact the **Rideau Trail Association** at ☎ 613/545-0823.

Kingston spent decades of its early years anticipating an attack that never came, the reason for its still-evident defenses. You can view some of these along the waterfront, where **Confederation Park** stretches from the front of the old 19th-century town hall down to the yacht basin. Several blocks west of the park is one of the finest martello towers, built during the Oregon Crisis of 1846 to withstand the severest of naval bombardments. The **Murney Tower** (☎ 613/544-9925) is now a museum where you can see the basement storage rooms, the barrack room, and the gun platform. Mid-May to Labour Day, it's open daily 10am to 5pm, charging C$2 (US$1.35); children under 6 are free.

When exploring downtown and ambling along the waterfront, visit the **City Hall,** 2162 Ontario St. (☎ 613/546-4291), where guided tours are offered Monday to Friday 10am to 4pm and Saturday and Sunday 11am to 3pm. If there isn't enough time, at least take a look at the stained-glass windows upstairs in Memorial Hall, each one commemorating a World War I battle. It's open weekdays 8:30am to 4:30pm.

Fort Henry. On Rte. 2, just east of Kingston. ☎ 613/542-7388. Admission C$10 (US$6) adults, C$4.95 (US$3.30) children 5–16, C$1 (US65¢) children 2–4. Sunset Ceremonies, C$13 (US$9) adults, C$7 (US$4.35) children 5–16, C$1 (US65¢) children 2–4. Mid-May to Sept daily 10am–5pm.

Fort Henry, erected in 1812 and largely unchanged since its reconstruction in the 1830s, commands a high promontory overlooking the harbor and town. May 23 to Labour Day, the Fort Henry Guard and their goat mascot, David, perform 19th-century drills, musters, and parades. Regular programming includes music and marching displays by the fife-and-drum band, exhibitions of infantry drill, and mock battles of tall ships, many of them brought to a close with the firing of the garrison artillery and the lowering of the Union Jack. The most imposing events are the "Sunset Ceremonies," elaborate military tattoos with exhilarating music performed Wednesdays at 7:30pm in July and August. Part of the fort—the officers' quarters, men's barracks, kitchens, and artisans' shops—has been restored to show the military way of life circa 1867.

Royal Military College. On Point Frederick. ☎ 613/541-6000, ext. 6664. Free admission. Museum July–Labour Day daily 10am–5pm.

The Royal Military College, Canada's West Point, is next to Fort Henry. The campus occupies the site of a Royal Navy Dockyard, which played a key role in the War of 1812. Though you can tour the grounds year-round, the museum, in a large martello tower, is open only in summer. It houses displays about the college's history and Kingston's Royal Dockyard, plus the Douglas collection of small arms and weapons.

Bellevue House. 35 Centre St. ☎ 613/545-8666. Admission C$3 (US$2) adults, C$2.50 (US$1.65) seniors/students over 16, C$1.50 (US$1) children 6–15. June–Labour Day daily 9am–6pm; Apr–May and Labour Day–Oct daily 10am–5pm.

On July 1, 1867, the Canadian Confederation was proclaimed in Kingston's Market Square. The chief architect of that momentous political construction was Canada's first Prime Minister, Sir John A. Macdonald, closely identified with the city of Kingston, his home for most of his life. The most notable site in the city is Bellevue House, a stucco-faced, vaguely Italianate villa with green trim and a red roof, jokingly referred to as the "Pekoe Pagoda" and "Tea Caddy Castle" by many locals. Apple trees and hollyhocks fill the front yard, and costumed docents greet visitors. It has been restored to the period of 1848 to 1849, when Macdonald lived there as a young lawyer and rising member of Parliament.

Agnes Etherington Art Centre. University Ave. at Queen's Crescent. ☎ **613/533-2190.** Free admission. Tues–Fri 10am–5pm, Sat–Sun 1–5pm.

On the campus of Queen's University, the Agnes Etherington Art Centre displays a comparatively extensive collection in seven galleries. The collection's emphasis is Canadian, though it also contains European old masters and African sculpture. The center's heart is the original 19th-century home of benefactor Agnes Richardson Etherington (1880 to 1954) and features three rooms furnished in period style. The gallery was closed during most of 1999 for major expansion, and its schedule and hours continue to change frequently; so call ahead before making a special trip.

Marine Museum of the Great Lakes. 55 Ontario St. ☎ **613/542-2261.** Admission C$5 (US$3.65) adults, C$4.95 (US$3.30) seniors/students; children under 6 free. Mid-Apr to mid-Dec daily 10am–5pm; Jan–Mar Mon–Fri 10am–4pm.

For an understanding of the shipping days on the Great Lakes, so critical to the development of central Canada, stop by the Maritime Museum. It documents the change from sail in the 17th century to steam in the 19th century and from the great schooners in the 1870s to today's bulk carriers that still ply the Great Lakes. Other exhibits recapture the region's shipbuilding industry.

SIDE TRIPS TO FRONTENAC PROVINCIAL PARK & UPPER CANADA VILLAGE

Frontenac Provincial Park (☎ 613/376-3489), near Sydenham about 143km (89 miles) from Kingston and 72km (45 miles) from Ottawa, is a wilderness park with more than 182km (113 miles) of hiking trails that explore such intriguing areas as Moulton Gorge, the Arkon Lake bogs, and the Connor-Daly mine.

There are also terrific opportunities here to combine camping with self-propelled water journeys. The adventure might include sea-kayaking among the Thousand Islands. Local outfitters can provide all the equipment—canoes, kayaks, paddles, life jackets, car-top carriers, tents, sleeping bags, stoves, and utensils—for relatively modest fees, ranging from C$22 to C$29 (US$15 to US$19) per person per day. Trips run April to November. For details, contact **Frontenac Outfitters** at ☎ 613/376-6220 (in season) or 613/382-1039 (off-season).

About 50km (31 miles) east of Brockville along Route 2, **Upper Canada Village,** just east of Morrisburg (☎ 613/543-3704), is Ontario's effort to preserve its pre-Dominion past, a riverfront museum village representing frontier life in the 1860s. Some 40 brick-and-stone structures and interiors have been accurately restored using hand-forged nails and wooden pegs. They appear as if still inhabited, especially because they're occupied by costumed bilingual docents who perform the chores and crafts of the time (sew quilts, mill lumber, fashion tinware, conduct church services) and answer questions. In the woolen mill, the waterwheel turns the old machinery weaving wool into blankets, the bellows wheeze and hammers clang on anvils in the blacksmith's shop, and the heady aroma of fresh bread drifts from the bake shop near Willard's Hotel (early Apr to late Oct, stop at the hotel for lunch or high tea). "True

Canadian" draft horses draw both tour wagons and the barge on the carp-filled canal cutting through from the river to a small lake behind the village. Admission is C$13 (US$9) adults, C$12 (US$8) seniors, C$9 (US$6) students, and C$6 (US$4) children 6 to 12; children under 6 are free, and families get a 10% discount. May to Canadian Thanksgiving, it's open daily 9:30am to 5pm.

WHERE TO STAY

For B&Bs, contact **Kingston Area Bed and Breakfast** (☎ 613/542-0214) for a selection of homes throughout the area. Rates are C$60 to C$65 (US$40 to US$43) double; children 1 to 10 are charged C$10 (US$7) and children 11 and over C$15 (US$10).

Three chains have commandeered prime positions beside the harbor—the **Holiday Inn,** 1 Princess St. (☎ 800/549-8400 or 613/549-8400), charging C$110 to C$190 (US$73 to US$127) double; the **Howard Johnson Confederation Place,** 237 Ontario St. (☎ 800/446-4656 or 613/549-6300), charging C$69 to C$179 (US$46 to US$119); and the **Ramada Plaza Kingston Harbourfront,** 1 Johnson St. (☎ 800/272-6232 or 613/549-8100), charging C$130 to C$170 (US$87 to US$113). And there's a **Comfort Inn** at 1454 Princess St. (☎ 800/228-5150 or 613/549-5550), charging C$69 to C$115 (US$46 to US$77) double.

✪ **Best Western Fireside Inn.** 1217 Princess St., Kingston, ON K7M 3E1. ☎ **800/567-8800** in Ontario and Québec, 800/528-1234 elsewhere, or 613/549-2211. Fax 613/549-4523. www.bestwestern.kingston.on.ca. E-mail fireside@kos.net. 76 units. A/C TV TEL. C$106 (US$71) double; C$179–C$279 (US$119–US$186) suite. Corporate rates include full breakfast Mon–Fri. AE, DC, ER, MC, V.

Put aside preconceptions about motels with the Best Western logo. The lounge off the lobby looks like a Yukon cabin, with log siding, a moose head, and wing chairs. *Every* room has a fireplace, Canadiana pine furnishings, an unstocked fridge, a coffeemaker, and a hair dryer. Spring for a fantasy suite and your bed might be in a real Rolls-Royce, in the basket of a 2½-story-high hot air balloon, or in a simulated "Tranquility Moon Base." Lesser suites have whirlpools next to the fireplaces. Even the most ordinary rooms trump most big-city hotels for comfort (not counting the thin towels), equipped with puffy quilts, sofas, and shelves of old books. An outdoor pool is available, and the Bistro Stefan is unexpectedly capable.

General Wolfe Hotel. On Wolfe Island, ON K0H 2Y0. ☎ **800/353-1098** or 613/385-2611. Fax 613/385-1038. 6 units. A/C TV TEL. C$50–C$95 (US$33–US$63) double. AE, MC, V.

This small white clapboard hotel on Wolfe Island is known primarily for dining, though it also has notably economical guest rooms. The reasonably priced food is essentially continental—pheasant bourguignonne or leg of lamb à la moutarde. Many rooms afford views of the ferry landing and waterfront—great for sunset viewing. It's open mid-May to Labour Day daily for lunch and dinner; at other times the restaurant closes Monday. When the river is frozen, usually January to early April, the owners operate a shuttle to Dawson's Point connecting to the mainland. The cocktail lounge has dancing on weekends.

✪ **Hochelaga Inn.** 24 Sydenham St. S., Kingston, ON K7L 3G9. ☎ **800/267-0525,** or ☎ and fax 613/549-5534. www.someplacesdifferent.com. E-mail hochelaga@icos.net. 23 units. A/C TV TEL. C$135–C$190 (US$90–US$127) double. Extra person C$15 (US$10). Rates include continental breakfast. AE, MC, V.

All the guest rooms are furnished uniquely in this converted Victorian. A favorite is no. 301, an oddly shaped space with a carved bed set on a diagonal, a large armoire, and a love seat; three steps lead to an 11-sided tower with windows, and a stepladder reaches into a tiny sitting area. Other rooms are furnished with oak pieces as well as wing chairs and brass table lamps. You can enjoy the large sitting room with a carved ebony fireplace, or sit on the veranda viewing the garden. The buffet breakfast is served in a welcoming room with mismatched chairs.

✪ **Hotel Belvedere.** 141 King St. E., Kingston, ON K7L 2Z9. ☎ **800/559-0584** or 613/548-1565. Fax 613/546-4692. www.hotelbelvedere.com. 20 units. TV TEL. C$109–C$209 (US$73–US$139) double. Rates include continental breakfast. AE, DC, ER, MC, V.

Many regulars consider this *the* place to stay in Kingston. The carefully restored mansard-roofed brick Belvedere is on a residential street several blocks west of the downtown hubbub. All the rooms have king- or queen-sized beds, most have air-conditioning and pleasant sitting areas, and some have Jacuzzis. Typical of the diversity and thoughtfulness of the decor is no. 204, with a marine-blue tile fireplace, tasseled curtains, a kneehole dresser, and a bed with a lace-embroidered coverlet. You can relax in the elegant sitting room boasting a turquoise marble coal-burning fireplace and tall French windows opening onto a porch with plants in classical urns.

Prince George Hotel. 200 Ontario St., Kingston, ON K7L 2Y9. ☎ **613/547-9037.** Fax 613/542-5297. 26 units. A/C TV TEL. C$70–C$175 (US$47–US$117) double. AE, DC, ER, MC, V.

Often overlooked due to its modest entrance between terrace tables, this most satisfactory hotel (no elevator) has origins dating all the way to 1809. There have been many face-lifts since then, and it has taken in guests since the mid–19th century. The guest rooms are easily large enough to contain king or queen beds, armoire closets, and spacious sitting areas. Carpeting is wall-to-wall, and coffeemakers and clock radios are at hand. It's right in the middle of things, downtown next to City Hall, and there are entrances from the lobby to a martini-and-cigar lounge and a sprawling pub/restaurant, Tir na n'Og. The front desk isn't manned at all times, which can be frustrating after a long drive.

WHERE TO DINE

✪ **Chez Piggy.** 68R Princess St. ☎ **613/549-7673.** Reservations recommended on weekends. Main courses C$11–C$23 (US$7–US$15). AE, DC, MC, V. Mon–Fri 11:30am–2pm, Sat 11:30am–2:30pm, Sun 11am–2:30pm; daily 5:30–10pm. CONTINENTAL/ ECLECTIC.

Just off Princess Street in a complex of renovated buildings, Chez Piggy occupies an 1820s building that probably once was a stable. In front is a paved courtyard for dining outdoors, and inside are a long bar with high director's chairs and an upstairs dining room enhanced by two glorious Tunisian rugs. The printed menu listing seven or so dinner entrees also has daily specials. Fixed possibilities include duck leg confit with braised red cabbage, monkfish with spicy cilantro sauce and potatoes and preserved lemons, and any one of the half-dozen pastas (linguini with spinach salsa verde, for example). To begin, there are several salads and such dishes as mussels *piri piri* (steamed with perky Portuguese chili oil) and Stilton pâté. Brunch dishes, most under C$10 (US$7), deviate from the usual, like teriyaki salmon fillet with wasabi mayo or fried chorizo with black-bean cakes and eggs.

Hoppin' Eddie's. 393 Princess St. ☎ **613/531-9770.** Main courses C$10–C$16 (US$7–US$11). AE, MC, V. Daily 11:30am–10pm (to 11pm Fri–Sat). CREOLE/CAJUN.

This funky-as-all-get-out interior looks as if it had been airlifted intact from the lip of the Gulf of Mexico, out on a bayou a quick hop from the Big Easy. Since the food wears that cloak too, this isn't a place for you if you don't like your eats spicy-hot.

What issues from the open kitchen are jambalaya, blackened catfish, and several po' boy sandwiches. Oysters are opened to order and served on ice, with lemon wedges and shaved horseradish (no cocktail sauce). They're prepared at the big bar, where more eating than boozing goes on, at least until late. Fans of hot sauce will want to stop by the kitchen, where a dozen shelves display more bottled brands than they knew existed, with names like Global Warming, Endorphin Rush, After Death, and Scorned Woman.

Kingston Brewing Company. 34 Clarence St. ☎ **613/542-4978.** Burgers, sandwiches, and main courses under C$10 (US$7). AE, DC, ER, MC, V. Mon–Sat 11am–1am, Sun 11:30am–1am. PUB FARE.

In one of Ontario's earliest microbrew pubs, peer through the window behind the bar at the huge brewing tanks. Beer, several ales, and a pleasant lager are produced there, the best-known of which is Dragon's Breath ale, so rich as to be almost syrupy. Locals come here for substantial victuals of the brew house kind—monster burgers, fat onion rings, smoked beef and ribs, and charbroiled chicken wings with fiery barbecue sauce, as well as curries and pastas. All is served inside at polished wood tables, in the rear courtyard, or on the sidewalk terrace.

QUINTE'S ISLE

Prince Edward County is an island surrounded by Lake Ontario and the Bay of Quinte, 265km (159 miles) southwest of Ottawa. Much of its frontier character and relaxed pace have been retained. Its citizens are proud of their United Empire Loyalist settlers, those American colonists who were faithful to the Crown and fled the Revolution in the 1780s. Their descendants' fidelity to that past shows in the quiet streets of such historic villages as Picton, Bloomfield, and Wellington. Many of them still live, work, and farm here, and the Loyalist label is applied to a local college, pleasure boats, farms, a car dealership, and the road running around the island's edge. Much of Quinte is devoted to corn and cows, attested by the substantial presence of silos and dairy barns. Backyards on the south side of the road dip down to Lake Ontario. And though it's a popular vacation destination, even its largest resort is little more than a cottage colony.

ESSENTIALS

GETTING THERE   If you're driving from Trenton, take Route 33 south; from Belleville, Route 62 south off the 401; and from Kingston, Route 49 south off the 401.

VISITOR INFORMATION   Contact the **Prince Edward County Chamber of Tourism & Commerce,** 116 Main St. (Box 50), Picton, ON K0K 2T0 (☎ **613/ 476-2421** or www.pec.on.ca).

WELLINGTON & BLOOMFIELD

Driving through **Wellington,** you'll be impressed by the pride with which residents maintain their houses and gardens. Loyalists were among the first settlers, and their continuing enthusiasm for their historical connections to England is evidenced in the Union Jacks flapping proudly among the Maple Leaf flags. If lodgings have been hard to find, a drive along its main street will reveal more than half a dozen B&Bs.

Bloomfield, settled in the early 1800s, has been strongly influenced by Methodists and Quakers. The latter were harassed in their native New York for their pacifism during the American Revolution and fled to Canada with the Loyalists. Two Quaker cemeteries in town are part of that legacy. Today this attractive town has become a haven for retirees, artists, and craftspeople. The several potteries, craft shops, and antiques stores include **Bloomfield Pottery,** 274 Main St. (☎ **613/393-3258**), and the **Village Art Gallery,** 313 Main St. (☎ **613/393-2943**).

Where to Stay

Cornelius White House. 8 Wellington St., Bloomfield, ON K0K 1G0. ☎ **613/393-2282.** www.pec.on.ca. E-mail cwh@netreach.com. 4 units. A/C. C$80 (US$53) double. Extra person in suite C$20 (US$13). Rates include breakfast. MC, V. Pets accepted.

This 19th-century red-brick house offers views over meadows dotted with grazing Holsteins. A full breakfast (or continental, if you prefer) is served in the 1867 dining room, which has wide pine floors and a brick fireplace. You also have use of a lounge with TV, a billiards table, books, and a piano. A cottage with a small kitchen is also available.

Tara Hall. 146 Main St., Wellington, ON K0K 3L0. ☎ **613/399-2801.** Fax 613/399-1104. www.intranet.ca/~tarahall. E-mail tarahall@intranet.ca. 4 units. A/C TV. C$78 (US$52) double. Extra person C$25 (US$17). Rates include breakfast. V. Free parking.

Tara Hall is an 1839 home built by a wealthy merchant, one of the grander edifices in this village of unassuming houses. Originally the whole upper front floor served as a ballroom; today it has been divided into three guest rooms. Each room is furnished pleasantly with some antiques. A full formal breakfast is served, the table set with linen. No smoking.

Where to Stay & Dine

✪ **Angeline's.** In the Bloomfield Inn, 29 Stanley St. W., Bloomfield. ☎ **613/393-3301.** Fax 613/393-3301. www.pec.on.ca/angelines. E-mail angeline@connect.reach.net. Reservations recommended. Table d'hôte dinners C$30 or C$37 (US$20–US$25); main courses C$19–C$21 (US$13–US$14). MC, V. Dining room July–Aug daily 5:30–9pm; Sun 11:30am–2pm; patio July–Aug daily 3–9pm. Sept–June Thurs–Sun 5:30–9pm. FRENCH/REGIONAL CANADIAN.

While it has rooms for rent, the Bloomfield Inn is mainly known for its restaurant, Angeline's. Located in an 1869 house, it's operated by a young Austrian chef who's constantly conjuring ways to enhance the experience. His cuisine is seasonal and prepared largely from island products; he grows his own herbs, has inaugurated a popular Sunday lunch buffet, and has opened a cafe for light meals and a case-full of his delectable Viennese pastries. Dinner entrees might include roast rabbit in black olive sauce or Quinte Isle lamb with rosemary jus, both with Swiss potatoes, or trout served with bouillabaisse-style broth, saffron potatoes, and a mélange of vegetables on the side. Wines are available by the glass. The service is cheerful, if sometimes forgetful.

Across the parking lot are nine small but otherwise perfectly adequate guest rooms, all with TVs, phones, and hair dryers. They cost C$85 to C$95 (US$57 to US$63) double in summer and C$65 to C$75 (US$43 to US$50) the rest of the year.

FROM BLOOMFIELD TO PICTON

On an island where towns number their populations in dozens or hundreds, **Picton** is a metropolis, the hub and seat of Prince Edward County. East of the town lies the **Lake on the Mountain,** a small clear body of water 200 feet above Lake Ontario of mysterious origin. Volcanic? A meteor cavity? A simple sinkhole? No one knows for certain, not that it matters to those on a day's outing—this is a sublime spot for a picnic beneath the trees. From one side of the escarpment you get a fabulous view of the ferries crossing Picton Bay, indigo water, and islands stretching over the horizon.

The other major attractions, 18km (11 miles) west of Picton, are **Sandbanks** and **North Beach provincial parks.** Sandbanks Park has freshwater dunes over 80 feet high, among the tallest found anywhere. Consisting of two dune systems linked by fields and woods, it also fosters diverse plant and animal life. Some of the more unusual plants are hoary puccoon, butterfly weed, sea rocket, and spurge. Among the bird species that have been recorded here are the long-billed marsh wren, pileated woodpecker, northern oriole ruby, and golden crowned kinglet.

The park has prime sandy beaches and facilities for swimming, windsurfing, sailing, canoeing, and boating (rentals available). There are several self-guided nature trails in the park. Camping (549 sites) is available in four areas for C$18 to C$22 (US$12 to US$15) per day in peak months. Entry to the park is C$8 (US$5) per vehicle. Park officials begin taking reservations April 1 (it's open May to Oct). For information, call ☎ **800/668-2746** or log on to **www.ontarioparks.com**. For reservations, call ☎ **888/668-7275.**

The best way off Quinte's Isle is to take the rewarding 15-minute **ferry trip** from Glenora across to Adolphustown. The ferry departs every 15 minutes in summer, less frequently in winter, and has been operating since settlement began.

Where to Stay

Isaiah Tubbs Resort. RR #1 West Lake Rd., Picton, ON K0K 2T0. ☎ **800/724-2393** or 613/393-2090. Fax 613/393-1291. www.someplacesdifferent.com. E-mail itr@someplaces different.com. 64 units, 14 cottages. A/C TV TEL. C$99–C$179 (US$66–US$119) double; C$119–C$219 (US$79–US$146) suite; C$700–C$1,000 (US$467–US$667) per week lakeside cottage. AE, DC, ER, MC, V.

This miniresort spread beside West Lake offers a wide variety of accommodations in multi-unit dwellings scattered among the trees of a 30-acre property. It more nearly resembles an old-fashioned bungalow colony than the standard beach resort, and families, rather than singles and couples, are most likely to be happy here. The Carriage House rooms, in the original building's oldest section, have kitchenettes, pine furnishings, beamed ceilings, fireplaces, and microwaves. Standard rooms are also furnished in country style. Two lodges each feature a living room with fieldstone fireplace and two bedrooms, one upstairs with skylights and a Jacuzzi tub. Some lodges have sun porches. Facilities include outdoor and indoor pools, two tennis courts, a beach, windsurfing equipment and lessons, canoes and paddleboats, bike rentals, and nature trails.

Merrill Inn. 343 Main St. E., Picton, ON K0K 2T0. ☎ **800/567-5969** or 613/476-7451. Fax 613-476-8283. www.pgsm.com/merrill. 14 units. A/C TV TEL. C$95–C$135 (US$63–US$90) double. Extra person C$10 (US$7). Rates include continental breakfast. AE, ER, MC, V.

Pitched gables identify this established inn a block west of downtown Picton. The guest rooms are decorated in the conventional B&B manner, mixing true antiques with simply well-used pieces in floor plans of charming eccentricity. Room no. 101, for one, features a high-backed bed, wing chairs, and bay windows. One room has a Jacuzzi, another a fireplace; most have coffeemakers, and all have TV/VCRs. A cellar bar/restaurant called The Local has eight brews on tap to go with pub fare like shepherd's pie and bangers and mash and wine to complement more ambitious dishes like osso buco, poached salmon with dill cream, and mussels Provençale.

Ramada on the Bay. 11 Bay Bridge Rd. (at Rte. 2), Belleville, ON K8P 3P6. ☎ **800/272-6232** or 613/968-3411. Fax 613/968-5036. 125 units. A/C TV TEL. C$87–C$110 (US$58–US$73). Children under 18 stay free. AE, DC, ER, MC, V.

A reassuring stop after the quirks of alternative lodgings, this member of the middle-brow chain has a heated year-round pool with indoor access, three restaurants with a lounge, tennis courts, and a fitness center with a StairMaster, a lifecycle, free weights, and a whirlpool. The guest rooms have queen or king beds, cable TV with in-room movies, voice mail and dataports, irons and boards, and hair dryers. A complimentary paper is delivered to the door in the morning. The only significant annoyance are the cumbersome telephone-booth-style showers.

Where to Stay & Dine

Waring House. Rte. 33, west of Picton. ☎ **800/621-4956** or 613/476-7492. Fax 613/476-6648. www.pec.on.ca/waringhouse. E-mail waringhouse@sympatico.ca. Reservations recommended. Main courses C$17–C$24 (US$11–US$16). MC, V. Summer daily 11am–2pm and 5–9:30pm; winter usually Tues–Sun 11:30am–2pm and 5–9pm. CONTINENTAL.

This popular restaurant and inn is on the Loyalist Parkway in a fetching old stone house surrounded by shrubbery. Pine floors, archival photographs, and other regional memorabilia set the country tone. The kitchen sometimes applies alien techniques to local products (as with Cajun pickerel), but pastas, rosemary-scented lamb, and chicken with Dijon-apricot sauce are the more conventional norm. The waitresses are sweetly pleasant. In summer, they claim that the vegetables on your plate were picked that day. The bi-level Barley Room pub has a substantial brick-and-beam fireplace, a big-screen TV, and live entertainment on summer weekends.

A separate late–19th-century board-and-batten building on the property offers 12 no-smoking guest rooms. Antiques are scattered throughout, but they also have TVs, radios, hair dryers, and air-conditioning; three rooms have Jacuzzis, and several have walkout decks. Rates are C$100 to C$140 (US$67 to US$93) double.

Where to Dine

The Glenbridge. 106 Bridge St. (east of Picton). ☎ **613/476-7057.** Main courses C$10–C$19 (US$7–US$13). AE, MC, V. Summer daily 11:30am–10pm; the rest of the year Wed–Mon 11:30am–9pm. ECLECTIC.

Looking a mite too urbane for this rural setting, this essentially two-person operation delivers a touch of city savoir faire, underlined by the ripple of live piano music heard Thursday to Sunday nights. While there are no surprises on the plate—chicken parmigiana, steak au poivre, and poached salmon with hollandaise—each dish is prepared and presented well. The prices are more than fair, especially the two-course fixed-price dinners for as little as C$11 (US$7).

PORT HOPE, PRESQU'ÎLE PROVINCIAL PARK & TRENTON

Driving from Ottawa, take Route 16 south to 401 west, bringing you to the engaging old lakefront town of **Port Hope,** where antiques stores line the main street. It's at the mouth of the Ganaraska River, 117km (73 miles) east of Toronto. From Toronto, take 401 east. If you'd like to stay here, **The Carlyle,** 86 John St. (☎ **905/885-8686**), occupies the old 1857 Bank of Upper Canada. Rates are C$95 (US$63) in the main building, while those in the annex in back have fireplaces and go for C$125 (US$83). The casual dining room, open daily for lunch and dinner, offers moderately priced food along the lines of lasagna, chicken Kiev, and burgers.

Sixty-five kilometers (40 miles) east of Port Hope lies **Trenton,** the starting point for the Trent-Severn Canal, a 386km-long (239-mile-long) waterway traveling northeast via 44 locks to Georgian Bay on Lake Huron. It's also the western entrance to the Loyalist Parkway (Route 33), leading to Quinte's Isle.

Halfway between Port Hope and Trenton on Route 401 is **Brighton,** the gateway town to **Presqu'île Provincial Park.** This 2,000-acre area of marsh and woodland offers excellent camping and a mile-long beach. Flocks of migratory birds from the Atlantic and the Mississippi flyways inspire the major bird-watching weekends held in spring and fall. The visitor center is open Victoria Day to Labour Day. For details, call ☎ **613/475-2204;** for reservations, call ☎ **800/668-7275** or log on to **www.ontarioparks.com**. Admission is C$8 (US$5) per car.

Serpent Mounds Park, RR #3 (☎ **705/295-6879**), is in Keene, which you can reach by driving north from Port Hope on Highway 28. The park has 120 campsites and offers swimming and self-guided nature trails. The name comes from the Indian burial mounds it contains—one is shaped like a snake. Admission is C$7 (US$4.65) per car.

Farther north on Route 28 is **Peterborough,** at the center of the Kawartha Lakes—the series of lakes connected by the Trent-Severn Waterway from Trent to Georgian Bay. Here you can watch the boats moving through the locks and being lifted 62 feet from one water level to another at the **visitor center** (☎ **705/750-4900**) on the waterway on Hunter Street East.

Continuing northeast on Route 28 from Peterborough, you'll come to Stony Lake. At its eastern end, on Northey's Bay Road near the town of Stonyridge, is **Petroglyphs Provincial Park** (☎ **705/877-2552**). Although the hiking trails, two lakes, and forests are appealing, the petroglyphs themselves—hundreds of symbolic shapes and figures—are what attract visitors. It's believed that these images were carved by an Algonquin-speaking people between 1,100 and 6,500 years ago. About 300 distinct carvings have been identified alongside 600 indecipherable figures. Members of the Ojibwa Anishinabe Nation still revere this as a sacred site. The second Friday in May to Canadian Thanksgiving, it's open daily 10am to 5pm, costing C$8 (US$5) per car.

10

Toronto & the Golden Horseshoe

by Hilary Davidson

Chances are that even if you've never set foot in **Toronto** you've seen the city a hundred times. Known for the past decade as Hollywood North, it has become the film stand-in for everything from European capitals to New York, but rarely does it ever take center stage playing itself. Self-deprecating Torontonians find themselves in a paradox—proud of their city's architectural, cultural, and culinary charms but nonetheless unsure whether it's all up to international snuff.

After spending a single afternoon wandering around the city, you might wonder why this is a question at all. Toronto boasts lush parks throughout its sprawling borders, renowned architecture, and excellent galleries. And while there's no shortage of skyscrapers, particularly in the downtown core, it's an unending source of amazement to many visitors how so many Torontonians live in houses on tree-lined boulevards a walk or a bike ride away from work.

But Torontonians aren't so sure if visitors, recalling the stuffiness of the city's past, can see the fun side of the place. Often called Toronto the Good, it was a town where you could walk down any street in safety but couldn't get a drink on Sunday. Then a funny thing happened in the 1970s: Canada opened up its immigration policies and welcomed waves of Italians, Greeks, Chinese, Vietnamese, Jamaicans, Indians, Somalians, and others, many of whom settled in Toronto. And Québec's political unrest drove Anglophones out en masse, many into Toronto's waiting arms. The city's economic life flourished, giving its cultural side a boost.

Both natives and visitors reap the benefits of this rich cultural mosaic. More than 5,000 restaurants dot the city, serving every taste from simple Greek souvlakis to five-star Asian-accented fusion cuisine. Festivals like Caribana and Caravan celebrate heritage through music and dance, drawing tremendous crowds. Toronto's newfound cosmopolitanism has made it a key player on the arts scene too. September's Toronto International Film Festival and October's International Festival of Authors draw top stars of the film and publishing worlds. The theater scene rivals London's and New York's. Toronto now ranks at or near the top of any international urban quality-of-life study you'll read. It has accomplished something very rare: While expanding and developing its daring side, the city has held onto its traditional strengths.

In this chapter I first cover Toronto and then my favorite parts of the stretch of the Ontario lakefront often called the **Golden**

Metropolitan Toronto

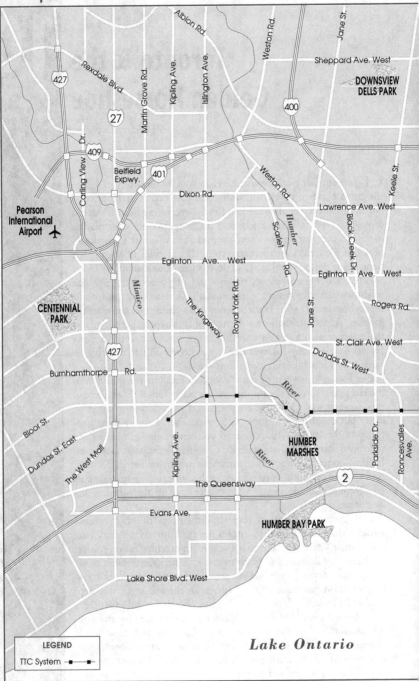

Pearson International Airport ✈

DOWNSVIEW DELLS PARK

CENTENNIAL PARK

HUMBER MARSHES

HUMBER BAY PARK

Lake Ontario

LEGEND

TTC System ■—■

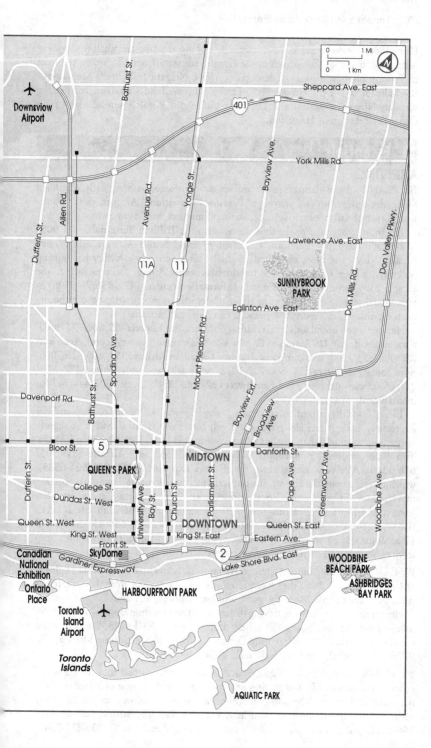

Horseshoe. *Golden* because the communities along the lake are wealthy, *horseshoe* because of its shape. This stretch of the Ontario lakefront from Niagara-on-the-Lake to Toronto offers you some golden opportunities: **Niagara Falls** itself; **Niagara-on-the-Lake,** home of the famous Shaw Festival; the **Welland Canal,** an engineering wonder; Niagara **wineries;** and Dundurn Castle and Royal Botanical Gardens in Canada's steel town of **Hamilton.**

1 Essentials

ARRIVING

BY PLANE   More than 20 major airlines serve Toronto, with regularly scheduled flights departing from and arriving at **Pearson International Airport,** in the northwest corner of metropolitan Toronto, about 30 minutes from downtown.

The most spectacular of the three terminals is the **Trillium Terminal 3** (☎ 905/612-5100), used by American, Canadian Airlines, British Airways, Air France, Alitalia, KLM, and most of United's flights. This supermodern facility has moving walkways, a huge food court, and hundreds of stores. Airport facilities include the exceptionally useful **Transport Canada Information centers** (☎ 905/676-3506) in all terminals, where a staff fluent in 10 languages will answer questions about the airport, the airlines, transportation services, and tourist attractions.

Here are a few useful airline reservation numbers: **Air Canada** (☎ 800/776-3000; www.aircanada.ca); **US Airways** (☎ 800/428-4322; www.usairways.com); **American** (☎ 800/433-7300; www.americanair.com); **Canadian Airlines** (☎ 800/426-7000; www.cdnair.ca); **Delta** (☎ 800/221-1212; www.delta-air.com); **United** (☎ 800/241-6522; www.ual.com); and **Northwest** (☎ 800/225-2525, or 800/444-4747 for international; www.nwa.com).

To get from the airport to downtown, take Highway 427 south to the Gardiner Expressway East. A taxi along this route will cost about C$40 (US$27). A slightly sleeker way to go is by flat-rate limousine, costing C$37 to C$38 (US$24 to US$25). Two limo services are **Aaroport** (☎ 416/745-1555) and **AirLine** (☎ 905/676-3210). Also very convenient is the **Airport Express** bus (☎ 905/564-6333), which travels among the airport, the bus terminal, and all major downtown hotels—the Harbour Castle Westin, Royal York, Crown Plaza Toronto Centre, Sheraton Centre, and Delta Chelsea Inn—every 20 minutes all day. The adult fare is C$13 (US$8) one-way or C$22 (US$14) round-trip; the service is free for children under 11 accompanied by an adult. In addition, most first-class hotels run their own limo services, so check when you make your reservation.

BY CAR   From the United States, you're most likely to enter Toronto via Highway 401 or via Highway 2 and the Queen Elizabeth Way if you come from the west. If you come from the east via Montréal, you'll also use Highways 401 and 2.

Here are a few approximate driving distances to Toronto: from Boston, 566km (351 miles); from Buffalo, 96km (60 miles); from Chicago, 534km (331 miles); from Cincinnati, 501km (311 miles); from Detroit, 236km (146 miles); from Minneapolis, 972km (603 miles); and from New York, 495km (307 miles).

BY TRAIN   Both VIA Rail's and Amtrak's passenger trains pull into the classically proportioned massive **Union Station** on Front Street, a block west of Yonge opposite the Royal York Hotel. The station has direct access to the subway, so you can easily reach any Toronto destination from here. For **VIA Rail** information, call ☎ 416/366-8411; in the United States, call your travel agent or **Amtrak** at ☎ 800/872-7245.

BY BUS   Out-of-town buses arrive at and depart from the **Metro Toronto Coach Terminal,** 610 Bay St., at Dundas Street, and provide frequent and efficient service from Canadian and American destinations. **Greyhound** (☎ 800/231-2222; www.greyhound.ca) services Buffalo, Niagara Falls, Windsor, Detroit, Ottawa, and Western Canada; **Trentway-Wagar** (☎ 416/393-7911) travels west from Montréal and Québec; and **Ontario Northland** (☎ 416/393-7911) has service from towns like North Bay and Timmins.

VISITOR INFORMATION

TOURIST OFFICES   Contact **Tourism Toronto,** 207 Queen's Quay W., Suite 509, in the Queen's Quay Terminal at Harbourfront (P.O. Box 126), Toronto, ON M5J 1A7 (☎ 800/363-1990 or 416/203-2600; www.tourism-toronto.com; e-mail mtcvaadm@pathcom.com). Take the Harbourfront LRT down to the terminal building. It's open Monday to Friday 9am to 5pm. There's also an **information center** in the Metro Toronto Convention Centre, 255 Front St. W., open the same hours.

More conveniently located is the drop-in **Travel Ontario Visitor Information Centre,** on Level 1 in the Eaton Centre on Yonge Street at Dundas (Subway: Dundas). It's open Monday to Friday 10am to 9pm, Saturday 9am to 6pm, and Sunday noon to 5pm. It has city and Ontario travel information.

You can also contact **Ontario Travel,** Queen's Park, Toronto, ON M7A 2R9 (☎ 800/ONTARIO or 416/314-0944).

WEB SITES   You can log on to *Toronto Life's* site at **www.torontolife.com**; it's heavily trafficked by locals looking for restaurant advice. Toronto.com (**www.toronto.com**) is operated by the Toronto Star newspaper and has listings for events, shops, and services. The My Toronto site (**www.myto.com**) has a comprehensive database that includes information about restaurants, events, and nightlife, as well as feature articles about the city.

CITY LAYOUT

Toronto is laid out in a grid system. **Yonge Street** (pronounced "Young") is the main south-north street, stretching from Lake Ontario in the south to well beyond Highway 401 in the north (it's the longest street in the world); the main east-west artery is **Bloor Street,** cutting right through the heart of downtown. Yonge Street divides western cross streets from eastern cross streets.

Downtown usually refers to the area stretching south from Eglinton Avenue to the lake between Spadina Avenue in the west and Jarvis Street in the east. I've divided this large area into **downtown** (from the lake to College/Carlton streets), **midtown** (College/Carlton streets to Davenport Road), and **uptown** (north from Davenport Road). In the first area, you'll find all the lakeshore attractions—Harbourfront, Ontario Place, Fort York, Exhibition Place, the Toronto Islands—plus the CN Tower, City Hall, SkyDome, Chinatown, the Art Gallery, and Eaton Centre. Midtown includes the Royal Ontario Museum, the University of Toronto, Markham Village, and chic Yorkville, a prime place to browse and dine alfresco. Uptown is a fast-growing residential and entertainment area for the young, hip, and well heeled.

Because **metropolitan Toronto** is spread over 634km² (245 sq. miles) and includes East York and the cities of (from west to east) Etobicoke, York, North York, and Scarborough, some primary attractions exist outside the central core, such as the Ontario Science Centre, the Metropolitan Zoo, and Canada's Wonderland—so be prepared to journey somewhat.

It's not enough to know Toronto's streets; you also need to know the warren of **sub-terranean walkways** enabling you to go from Union Station to Atrium on Bay at Dundas. Currently, you can walk from Yonge and Queen Street Station west to the Sheraton Centre, then south through the Richmond-Adelaide Centre, First Canadian Place, and Toronto Dominion Centre all the way (through the dramatic Royal Bank Plaza) to Union Station. En route, branches lead off to the Stock Exchange, Sun Life Centre, and Metro Hall. Additional passageways link Simcoe Plaza to 200 Wellington West and to the CBC Broadcast Centre. Other walkways exist around Bloor and Yonge and elsewhere in the city (ask for a map at the tourist office). So if the weather's bad, you can eat, sleep, dance, and go to the theater without even donning a coat.

2 Getting Around

The **Toronto Transit Commission (TTC)** operates an interconnecting subway, bus, and streetcar system (☎ **416/393-4636** 7am to 10pm). Adult fares (including transfers to buses or streetcars) are C$2 (US$1.35) for 1 token and C$8 (US$5) for 5; student/senior fares are C$1.35 (US90¢) for 1 token and C$11 (US$7) for 10; fares for children 2 to 12 are C50¢ (US35¢) for 1 token and C$4 (US$2.65) for 10. From any subway collector you can buy a C$7 (US$4.35) pass good for unlimited travel for one person after 9:30am weekdays and good for up to six persons anytime Saturday, Sunday, and holidays (maximum of two adults). To use surface transportation, you need a ticket, a token, or exact change. You can buy tickets and tokens at subway entrances or stores displaying the sign TTC TICKETS MAY BE PURCHASED HERE.

BY SUBWAY

The **subway** is a joy to ride—fast, quiet, and sparkling clean. It's a very simple system, designed basically in the form of a cross: The Bloor Street line runs from Kipling Avenue in the west to Kennedy Road in the east, where it connects with Scarborough Rapid Transit traveling from Scarborough Centre to McCowan. The Yonge Street line runs from Finch Avenue in the north to Union Station (Front Street) in the south. From here, it loops north along University Avenue and connects with the Bloor line at the St. George Station. A Spadina extension runs north from St. George to Wilson. The subway operates Monday to Saturday 6am to 1:30am and Sunday 9am to 1:30am. For route information, pick up a *Ride Guide* at subway entrances or call ☎ **416/393-4636.**

A **Light Rapid Transit (LRT)** streetcar service connects downtown to Harbourfront. It operates from Union Station along Queen's Quay to Spadina, stopping at Queen's Quay ferry docks, York Street, Simcoe Street, and Rees Street, then continuing up Spadina to the Spadina/Bloor subway station. A transfer isn't required, because the LRT links up underground with the Yonge–University subway line.

Smart commuters (and visitors!) park their cars for a low all-day parking fee at subway terminal stations—Kipling, Islington, Finch, Wilson, Warden, Kennedy, and McCowan; or at smaller lots at Sheppard, York Mills, Eglinton, Victoria Park, and Keele. You'll have to get there early, though.

BY BUS & STREETCAR

Where the subway leaves off, buses and streetcars take over to carry you east-west or north-south along the city's arteries. When you pay your fare (on streetcar, bus, or subway), always pick up a transfer—if you want to transfer to another mode of transportation, you won't have to pay another fare.

The TTC Subway System

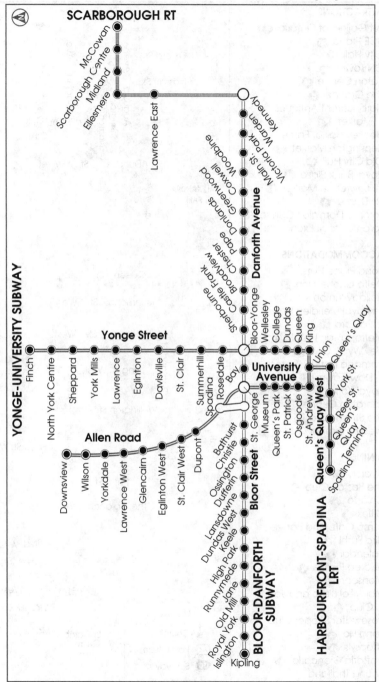

Downtown Toronto

ATTRACTIONS

Art Gallery of Ontario **4**
BCE Place **28**
City Hall **17**
CN Tower **22**
Eaton Centre **15**
The Grange **5**
Harbourfront Antiques
   Market **10**
Hockey Hall of Fame **28**
Kensington Market **2**
Old City Hall **18**
Royal Bank Plaza **27**
St. Lawrence Market **33**
SkyDome **9**
Toronto Dominion Centre **26**
Toronto Stock Exchange **20**

ACCOMMODATIONS

Bond Place Hotel **16**
Delta Chelsea Inn **13**
Holiday Inn on King **8**
Le Royal Meridien King
   Edward **30**
Metropolitan Hotel **14**
Neil Wycik College Hotel **11**
Ramada Hotel & Suites
   Downtown **12**
Royal York **24**
Sheraton Centre **19**
The Strathcona **25**
Westin Harbour Castle **23**

DINING

Avalon **7**
The Boston Club **32**
Chiado **1**
Cities **6**
Jump Café and Bar **29**
Hiro Sushi **34**
Kalendar **1**
Mildred Pierce **6**
Monsoon **21**
Montréal Bistro and Jazz
   Club **37**
Rosewater Supper Club **35**
Sang Ho **3**
Shopsy's **31**
Trattoria Giancarlo **1**
Young Thailand **36**

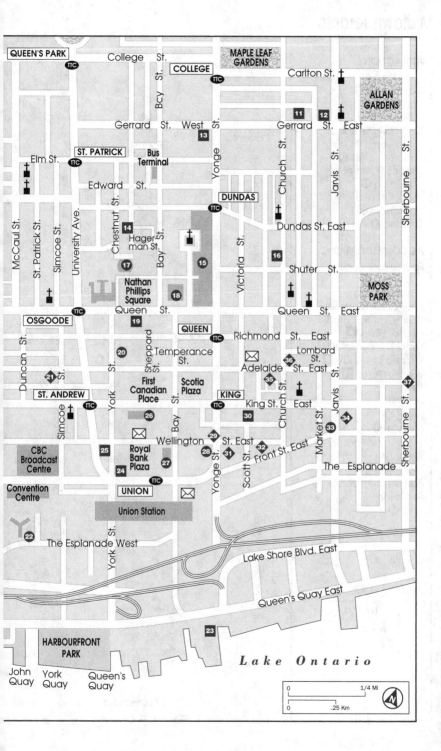

Midtown Toronto

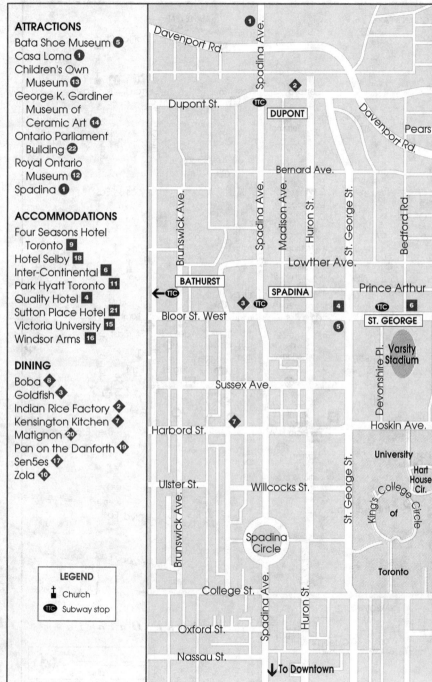

ATTRACTIONS
Bata Shoe Museum ⑤
Casa Loma ❶
Children's Own
 Museum ⑬
George K. Gardiner
 Museum of
 Ceramic Art ⑭
Ontario Parliament
 Building ㉒
Royal Ontario
 Museum ⑫
Spadina ❶

ACCOMMODATIONS
Four Seasons Hotel
 Toronto ⑨
Hotel Selby ⑱
Inter-Continental ⑥
Park Hyatt Toronto ⑪
Quality Hotel ④
Sutton Place Hotel ㉑
Victoria University ⑮
Windsor Arms ⑯

DINING
Boba ⑧
Goldfish ❸
Indian Rice Factory ❷
Kensington Kitchen ❼
Matignon ⑳
Pan on the Danforth ⑲
Sen5es ⑰
Zola ⑩

LEGEND
† Church
TTC Subway stop

Davenport Rd.
Spadina Ave.
Davenport Rd.
Pears
Dupont St.
TTC
DUPONT
Bernard Ave.
Brunswick Ave.
Spadina Ave.
Madison Ave.
Huron St.
St. George St.
Bedford Rd.
Lowther Ave.
BATHURST
TTC
SPADINA
Prince Arthur
TTC
Bloor St. West
ST. GEORGE
Devonshire Pl.
Varsity
Stadium
Sussex Ave.
Harbord St.
Hoskin Ave.
Ulster St.
Willcocks St.
University
Hart
House
Cir.
King's College Circle
of
Brunswick Ave.
St. George St.
Spadina
Circle
Toronto
College St.
Spadina Ave.
Huron St.
Oxford St.
Nassau St.
↓ To Downtown

376

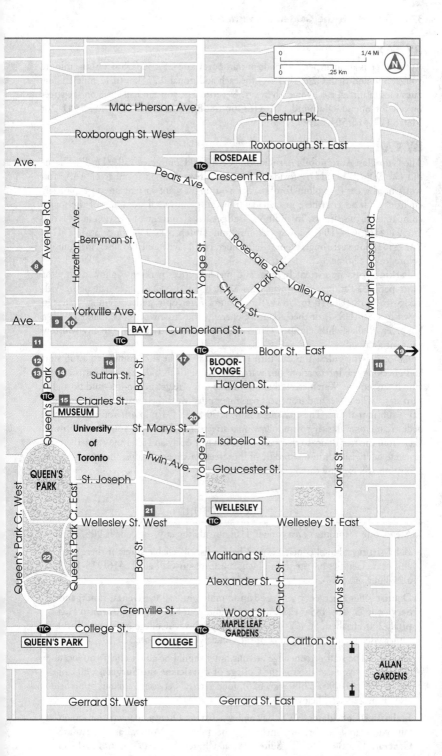

0   1/4 Mi
0   .25 Km

Mac Pherson Ave.

Chestnut Pk.

Roxborough St. West

Roxborough St. East

Ave.

ROSEDALE TTC

Pears Ave.

Crescent Rd.

Avenue Rd.

Hazelton Ave.

Berryman St.

Yonge St.

Rosedale Valley Rd.

Park Rd.

Mount Pleasant Rd.

8

Scollard St.

Church St.

Yorkville Ave.

Ave.

9 10

BAY   Cumberland St.

TTC

11

Bloor St.   East

19

12

13   14   16

Sultan St.

Bay St.

17

BLOOR-YONGE TTC

18

Hayden St.

TTC

15   Charles St.

MUSEUM

Charles St.

University

St. Marys St.

Isabella St.

Jarvis St.

of

20

Toronto

Irwin Ave.

Gloucester St.

QUEEN'S PARK

St. Joseph

Yonge St.

Queen's Park

Queen's Park Cr. West

Queen's Park Cr. East

21

WELLESLEY

Wellesley St. West

TTC

Wellesley St. East

Maitland St.

22

Bay St.

Alexander St.

Church St.

Jarvis St.

Grenville St.

Wood St.

MAPLE LEAF GARDENS

College St.

TTC

TTC

Carlton St.

QUEEN'S PARK

COLLEGE

ALLAN GARDENS

Gerrard St. West

Gerrard St. East

BY TAXI

As usual, taxis are an expensive mode of transportation: C$2.50 (US$1.65) the minute you step in and then C25¢ (US18¢) for each additional 0.275km (0.17 mile). These fares mount up, especially in rush hours. Nevertheless, you can hail a cab on the street or call for one at **Diamond** (☎ 416/366-6868), **Yellow** (☎ 416/504-4141), or **Metro** (☎ 416/504-8294).

BY CAR

The **Canadian Automobile Association** (CAA), 60 Commerce Valley Dr. E., Thornhill (☎ 905/771-3111), provides aid to any driver who's a member of AAA. You won't need a car to explore Toronto, but you might want to rent one to explore its environs or head elsewhere in Canada. You can get a rental from any of the major companies at the airport. In addition, **Budget** has a convenient location at 141 Bay St. (☎ 416/364-7104; Subway: Union), and **Tilden** is at 930 Yonge St. (☎ 416/925-4551; Subway: Yonge/Bloor). Remember, you'll save money by reserving your car before leaving home.

Parking costs are extremely high, and metered street parking is allowed only for short periods. Parking downtown runs about C$4 (US$2.65) per half hour, with C$15 to C$18 (US$10 to US$12) maximum. After 6pm and on Sunday, rates go down to C$6 (US$4) or thereabouts. Generally, the city-owned lots, marked with a big green *P,* are slightly cheaper. Observe the parking restrictions—the city will tow your car away.

As for **driving rules:** You can turn right on a red light after coming to a full stop and checking the intersection, but watch out for signs forbidding such turns at specific intersections. Watch carefully also for one-way streets and no-left- and no-right-turn signs. The driver and front-seat passenger must wear their seat belts or, if caught, pay a substantial fine. The city speed limit is 50kmph (31 m.p.h.). You must stop at pedestrian crosswalks. If you're following a streetcar and it stops, you must stop well back from the rear doors so that passengers can exit easily and safely. (Where there are concrete safety islands in the middle of the street for streetcar stops, this rule does not apply, but still exercise care.)

Fast Facts: Toronto

Area Code   Toronto's area code is **416;** outside the city, the code is **905.**

Baby-sitting   Hotel concierges will have a list of reliable sitters if there aren't child-care facilities on-site. In a pinch, call **Care-on-Call** at ☎ 416/975-1313, a 24-hour service.

Dentist   For emergency services 8am to midnight, call the **Dental Emergency Service** at ☎ 416/485-7121. After midnight, your best bet is the **Toronto Hospital,** 200 Elizabeth St. (☎ 416/340-3948; Subway: College or Queen's Park). Otherwise, ask at the front desk or the concierge at your hotel.

Doctor   The staff or concierge at your hotel should be able to help you locate a doctor, but you can also call the **College of Physicians and Surgeons,** 80 College St. (☎ 416/967-2600, ext. 626), for a referral between 9am and 5pm. See also "Emergencies," below.

Embassies/Consulates   While all embassies are in Ottawa, many nations maintain consulates in Toronto, including the following: **Australian Consulate-General,** 175 Bloor St. E., Suite 314, at Church Street (☎ 416/323-1155;

Subway: Yonge/Bloor); **British Consulate-General,** 777 Bay St., Suite 2800, at College Street (☎ **416/593-1290;** Subway: College); and the **U.S. Consulate,** 360 University Ave. (☎ **416/595-1700;** Subway: St. Patrick).

Emergencies Call ☎ **911** for fire, police, and ambulance. If you run into trouble once you arrive, call the **Travelers Aid Society** at ☎ **416/366-7788;** the organization will provide shelter for people in crisis situations.

Hospitals Try **Toronto General,** 200 Elizabeth St. (☎ **416/340-4611** or emergency 416/340-3946; Subway: Queen's Park).

Internet Access Open 24 hours, **Insomnia,** 563 Bloor St. W. (☎ **416/ 588-3907;** Subway: Bathurst), has computer terminals you can curtain off for privacy. If you're feeling social, there are also comfy couches and a big-screen TV.

Liquor Laws The minimum drinking age is 19, and drinking hours are daily 11am to 2am. Liquor, wine, and some beers are sold at **Liquor Control Board of Ontario** (LCBO) stores, open Monday to Saturday; most are open 10am to 6pm (some stay open evenings).

True wine lovers will want to check out **Vintages** stores (also operated by the LCBO), which carry a more extensive and specialized selection of wines. The most convenient downtown locations are in the lower-level concourse of **Hazelton Lanes** (☎ **416/924-9463;** Subway: Bay) and at Queen's Quay (☎ **416/ 864-6777;** Subway: to Union Station, then LRT to Queen's Quay). Look also for the **Wine Rack,** 560 Queen St. W. (☎ **416/504-3647;** Subway: Osgoode), and at 77 Wellesley St. E., at Church Street (☎ **416/923-9393;** Subway: Wellesley). This last chain sells only Ontario wines. Beer is sold at the chain **The Beer Store,** most of which are open Monday to Friday 10am to 10pm and Saturday 10am to 8pm. There's a downtown location at 614 Queen St. W. (☎ **416/ 504-4665;** Subway: Osgoode).

Newspapers/Magazines The four daily newspapers are the *Globe and Mail,* the *National Post,* the *Toronto Star,* and the *Toronto Sun. Eye* and *Now* are both free arts-and-entertainment weeklies. *Xtra!* is a free weekly targeted to the gay/lesbian community. *Toronto Life* is the major monthly city magazine; its sister publication is *Toronto Life Fashion,* which displays the best of the Canadian style scene. *Where Toronto* is usually provided free of charge by local hotels.

Pharmacies One big chain is **Pharma Plus,** with a store at 68 Wellesley St., at Church Street (☎ **416/924-7760;** Subway: Wellesley), open daily 8am to midnight. Other Pharma Plus branches are in College Park, Manulife Centre, Commerce Court, and First Canadian Place.

Post Office Postal services are available at convenience stores and drugstores. Look for the sign in the window indicating such services. There are also post-office windows open throughout the city in **Atrium on Bay** (☎ **416/506-0911;** Subway: Dundas), **Commerce Court** (☎ **416/956-7452;** Subway: King), and the **TD Centre** (☎ **416/360-7105;** Subway: St. Andrew).

Safety As large cities go, Toronto is generally safe, but be alert and use common sense, particularly at night. The Yonge/Bloor, Dundas, and Union subway stations are favorites with pickpockets. In the downtown area, Moss Park is considered one of the toughest areas to police. Avoid Allan Gardens and other parks at night.

Taxes The provincial retail sales tax is 8% in Ontario (on accommodations it's only 5%). There's also a national goods-and-services-tax (called the GST) of 7%.

These taxes are almost invariably added to the price of an item when you pay for it—they're not included in the price tag.

3 Accommodations

Toronto has no shortage of hotels, but finding inexpensive accommodations is a challenge. In exchange for proximity to top attractions like the Harbourfront Centre, Sky-Dome, and Eaton Centre, even budget hotels charge more than C$100 (US$67) a night in the high season, which runs April to October. Factor in the 5% accommodations tax and the 7% GST, and you're looking at spending a sizable sum.

If you're having trouble finding a hotel, call **Accommodations Toronto** (☎ **800/363-1990** or 416/203-2500), which represents more than 100 member properties throughout the city.

DOWNTOWN
Note: See the "Downtown Toronto" map (p. 374) to locate the hotels in this section.

VERY EXPENSIVE
Le Royal Meridien King Edward. 37 King St. E., Toronto, ON M5C 2E9. ☎ **416/863-9700.** Fax 416/367-5515. 315 units. A/C MINIBAR TV TEL. C$210–C$330 (US$140–US$220) double; from C$385 (US$257) suite. AE, DC, MC, V. Parking: C$25 (US$17). Subway: King.

The fortunes of the King Eddy have been quixotic. At one time it was the only Toronto choice for Hollywood royalty like Elizabeth Taylor and Richard Burton, but it then fell into neglect for years. It was rescued in the 1980s by local investors who plunked C$40 million (US$27 million) into a restoration of the hotel's former glory, with rosy marble columns and a glass-domed rotunda dominating the lobby. The sense of grandeur carries into the guest rooms and suites. Not every room is spacious, but they're all charmingly appointed; unlike those in many of its uptown competitors, the King Eddy's rooms feel personally designed rather than cut to pattern. The bathrooms are particularly nice, with generously portioned marble tubs, plush bathrobes and towels, makeup mirrors, and hair dryers.

Dining/Diversions: The formal dining room, Chiaro's, has been winning raves for its seafood starters. But with those lovely goldfish swimming in bowls on many tables, you might wish to stick to the nonseafood main courses, like the veal medallions with green-peppercorn sauce, avocado, and banana, and the decadent desserts, like the peach melba upside-down cake. The mirrored Lobby Lounge serves a traditional English afternoon tea, with clotted cream, jams, and finger sandwiches. The wood-paneled Consort Bar is wonderfully clubby, and its 8-foot-high windows afford fun people watching. The Café Victoria offers light, casual fare all day long.

Looking for a B&B?

B&Bs can be an excellent—and inexpensive—alternative to standard hotels. **Toronto Bed & Breakfast,** 253 College St., P.O. Box 269, Toronto, ON M5T 1R5 (☎ **416/588-8800;** www.torontobandb.com), keeps a lengthy list of accommodations at roughly C$65 to C$95 (US$43 to US$63) double. It's open Monday to Friday 9am to noon and 2 to 7pm. The **Downtown Association of Bed-and-Breakfast Guesthouses,** P.O. Box 190, Station B, Toronto, ON M5T 2W1 (☎ **416/368-1420;** www.bnbinfo.com), includes only no-smoking B&Bs; doubles range from C$60 to C$130 (US$40 to US$87).

Amenities: Concierge, 24-hour room service, laundry/valet, complimentary newspaper and shoeshine, nightly turndown; fitness center.

EXPENSIVE

✪ **Metropolitan Hotel.** 108 Chestnut St. (off Dundas St. W.), Toronto, ON M5G 1R3. ☎ **416/977-5000.** Fax 416/977-9513. www.metropolitan.com. 495 units. A/C MINIBAR TV TEL. C$210–C$250 (US$140–US$167) double; from C$325 (US$217) suite. Children under 16 stay free in parents' room. AE, DC, DISC, ER, EURO, JCB, MC, V. Parking: C$16 (US$11). Subway: St. Patrick.

One of Toronto's few major hotels that isn't part of a large chain, the Metropolitan caters to businesspeople and is a 5-minute stroll north of the business district and west of the Eaton Centre. But why walk when you can take advantage of the complimentary limo service to any downtown core address? That perk is just one of the ways in which the Metropolitan attempts to compete with its pricier competitors. Its guest rooms are furnished with comfort in mind but are nonetheless work ready. Standard features include phones with jacks for computer and fax use and in-closet safes. The luxury and executive suites boast Jacuzzis, Dolby Surround Sound TVs, CD players, and cordless phones.

Dining/Diversions: The modern-themed Hemispheres boasts a continental menu with Asian-inspired flourishes. Lai Wah Heen serves classic Cantonese cuisine; it's a top choice for business entertaining. (Both restaurants are rated Four Diamond by the AAA.) The Mezzanine Cafe turns into a candlelit piano bar come evening.

Amenities: Gold Key concierge, 24-hour room service, laundry/valet, complimentary limousine transportation in downtown core; 24-hour business center with PC and Mac computers; indoor pool; fitness center with sauna, whirlpool, massage.

Royal York. 100 Front St. W., Toronto, ON M5J 1E3. ☎ **800/441-1414** or 416/863-6333. 1,365 units. A/C MINIBAR TV TEL. C$175–C$250 (US$117–US$167) double; from C$300 (US$200) suite. Many special packages available. AE, DC, DISC, MC, V. Parking: C$20 (US$13). Subway: Union.

Looming across from Union Station, the Royal York was built by the Canadian-Pacific Railroad in 1929. The lobby is old-world magnificent, with an inlaid coffered ceiling punctuated by oversized bronze chandeliers. It's an event in itself to sit on one of the plush lobby couches and watch the crowd. Still, you have to decide whether you want to stay under the same roof with more than 1,000 others—the service is remarkably efficient but necessarily impersonal. The guest rooms are furnished with charming antique reproductions but are a mixed bag: Some are reasonably airy, though there's generally not much spare space. The well-equipped rooms for visitors with disabilities are designed for wheelchair users as well as those with hearing or visual impairments. Entrée Gold members enjoy several perks, including a private floor with superior rooms and separate check-in, a private lounge, complimentary breakfast and newspaper, and nightly turndown.

Dining/Diversions: You'll find 10 eateries and lounges. The main dining room, the Acadian Room, boasts dark paneling and an attentive staff. Other restaurants include the Benihana for Japanese food; the Gazebo for lunch; and Piper's Bar & Eatz, for pub grub. The posh Library Bar is renowned for its martinis.

Amenities: Concierge, 24-hour room service, laundry/valet; skylit indoor lap pool; fitness center with exercise equipment, saunas, steam rooms, whirlpool; barbershop and salon; shopping arcade with Am Ex travel center; business center.

Sheraton Centre. 123 Queen St. W., Toronto, ON M5H 2M9. ☎ **800/325-3535** or 416/361-1000. Fax 416/947-4854. 1,382 units. A/C MINIBAR TV TEL. C$260–C$295 (US$173–US$263) double; from C$345 (US$230) suite. Extra person C$20 (US$13). Two children under 18 stay free in parents' room. Special packages available. AE, CB, DC, ER, EURO, JCB, MC, V. Parking: C$25 (US$17). Subway: Osgoode.

A favorite with conventioneers, the Sheraton is across from New City Hall, a block from the Eaton Centre, and a short stroll from Queen Street West's trendy restaurant/boutique area. It's possible to stay here and never venture outside: In addition to the Sheraton complex with its half a dozen restaurants and bars and a cinema, the building is linked to Toronto's underground city, stretching over several miles. And if you long for a patch of green, the hotel provides that too—part of the lobby contains a manicured garden with a soothing waterfall. A C$50 million (US$33 million) renovation in the early 1990s completely refurbished the uniformly well-sized guest rooms. Most lack a serious view, though as you near the top of the 46-story complex the sights are inspiring. Those who have a lot of business to take care of may wish to upgrade to the Club-level rooms, with mini–business centers that include all-in-one fax/printer/copiers and two-line speaker phones.

Dining/Diversions: The Good Queen Bess in the shopping concourse is a true English pub (it was shipped over the pond in sections) where you can find excellent dark ales and standard pub grub for lunch and dinner. The Long Bar and Lounge has gorgeous City Hall views to go with its chichi drink menu. The Reunion is your basic sports bar, complete with pool tables. Postcards Cafe and Grill gives a good breakfast if you're in a hurry.

Amenities: Concierge, 24-hour room service, laundry/valet, supervised play center and baby-sitting services; gigantic indoor/outdoor pool, sundeck; fitness center with exercise rooms, sauna, hot tub; business center.

Westin Harbour Castle. 1 Harbour Sq., Toronto, ON M5J 1A6. ☎ **800/228-3000** or 416/869-1600. Fax 416/361-7448. 980 units. A/C MINIBAR TV TEL. C$180–C$290 (US$120–US$193) double; from C$325 (US$217) suite. Extra person C$20 (US$13). Children stay free in parents' room. Weekend packages and special long-term rates available. AE, DC, ER, MC, V. Parking: C$23 (US$15). Subway: Union, then LRT.

The Westin is on the lakefront, across from the Toronto Islands ferry docks and down the road from the Harbourfront Centre and Queen's Quay. Not surprisingly, the views are among the best in the city. The trade-off is that it's somewhat out of the way, but a shuttle bus and public LRT transportation means it's not too far from civilization. The guest rooms are divided between two towers, linked only at their base. They're modern in terms of decor and amenities; about half are no-smoking.

Dining/Diversions: The Grand Yatt Dynasty boasts menus in English and Chinese; the latter sometimes features shark's-fin or five-snake soup, which somehow never make it onto the English menu. The all-you-can-eat dim sum lunch is C$13 (US$8), making for a mob scene on weekends. The 38th-floor Lighthouse revolving restaurant depends on its view more than its kitchen to satisfy customers, and the Chartroom is a comfy piano bar. Afternoon tea and evening cocktails are served in the Lobby Lounge.

Amenities: 24-hour room service, concierge, laundry/valet, guest-room voice mail, beauty shop; fitness center with indoor pool, whirlpool, sauna, steam room; two squash courts, two outdoor tennis courts, massage clinic, shopping arcade.

MODERATE

Bond Place Hotel. 65 Dundas St. E., Toronto, ON M5B 2G8. ☎ **416/362-6061.** Fax 416/360-6406. 286 units. A/C TV TEL. C$130 (US$87) double in high season, C$69 (US$46) double in low season. Extra person C$15 (US$10). Weekend packages available. AE, DC, DISC, ER, MC, V. Parking: C$10 (US$7). Subway: Dundas.

ℹ️ Family-Friendly Hotels

Delta Chelsea Inn *(see below)*   At this perennial family favorite, there's a children's creative center, and baby-sitting services are available 9:30am to 10pm. Kids enjoy the in-room family movies, Super Nintendo, cookie jar that's replenished daily, and nightly turndown gift. Further reducing the strain on the family purse, kids have their own half-price menu at the hotel's restaurants.

Four Seasons Hotel Toronto *(see p. 385)*   A hop and a skip from the Children's Own Museum and the Royal Ontario Museum, this hotel has its own attractions. There are free bikes and video games for borrowing and an indoor/outdoor pool for splashing around. On your arrival, room service delivers complimentary cookies and milk to kids. The concierge and housekeeping staff are able to work magic, including conjuring up excellent baby-sitting services.

Sheraton Centre *(see p. 381)*   The endless attractions of this complex—including a supervised play center, half a dozen restaurants (some with a special menu for tykes), and a cinema—means there's a lot to keep the kiddies entertained. Kids also enjoy in-room video games and a welcome gift; parents like the baby-sitting service.

The Bond Place's location is right: a block from the Eaton Centre and around the corner from the Pantages and Elgin theaters. The guest rooms are on the small side and can best be described as quaint, but the price is right given its downtown proximity. Laundry/valet and concierge services are available. The recently spruced-up Freddy's restaurant serves lunch and dinner, as well as complimentary happy-hour hors d'oeuvres.

✪ **Delta Chelsea Inn.** 33 Gerrard St. W., Toronto, ON M5G 1Z4. ☎ **800/243-5732** or 416/595-1975. Fax 416/585-4362. 1,591 units. A/C TV TEL. C$129–C$235 (US$86–US$157) double with standard service; C$155–C$245 (US$103–US$163) double with signature service; C$15 (US$10) extra on business floor; from C$280 (US$187) suite. Extra person C$20 (US$13). Children under 18 stay free in parents' room. Weekend packages available. AE, DC, DISC, MC, V. Parking: C$19 (US$13) (575 spaces). Subway: College.

Though not a budget hotel, the Delta Chelsea offers bang for the buck. Its downtown location draws heaps of tour groups and a smattering of businesspeople, its family-friendly facilities lure those with little tykes, and its weekend packages capture cost-conscious vacationers. All in all, this hotel succeeds in being many things to many people. The guest rooms are bright and cheery; a few have kitchenettes. The special floor for business travelers offers cordless speaker phones, in-room fax machines, well-stocked desks, and ergonomic chairs. Many rooms have been designed for those with disabilities. Provided are 24-hour room service and laundry/valet service, as well as baby-sitting for children 3 to 8 between 9:30am and 10pm (nominal charge). The dining options include the charming but unstuffy Wittles; the Market Garden cafeteria, with soups, salads, and sandwiches; the Chelsea Bun, with daily live entertainment, usually jazz or R&B; and Deck 27, with great skyline views. Facilities include two pools (one for adults only, one for the whole family); a fitness center with an exercise room, a whirlpool, and a sauna; a billiards room; a beauty salon; a children's creative center; and a business center.

Holiday Inn on King. 370 King St. W. (at Peter St.), Toronto, ON M5V 1J9. ☎ **800/263-6364** or 416/599-4000. Fax 416/599-7394. www.hiok.com. 431 units. A/C TV TEL. C$169–C$299 (US$113–US$199) double. Extra person C$15 (US$10). AE, DISC, ER, MC, V. Parking: C$20 (US$13). Subway: St. Andrew.

The blinding white facade of this building suggests that some architect mistook Toronto for the tropics. No matter, the Holiday Inn's location *is* hot: The theater district, gourmet ghetto, Chinatown, and SkyDome are all nearby. Half of the floors contain office space; the guest rooms start at the 9th floor and go up to the 20th. The pastel-coated rooms are vintage Holiday Inn, with clock radios and hair dryers. Great food is just steps away, but for those who want to stick close to the hotel, there are a Japanese restaurant, a jazzy lounge, and a deli. Facilities include a small outdoor pool and a fitness center with an exercise room, a whirlpool, and a sauna.

Ramada Hotel & Suites Downtown. 300 Jarvis St. (just south of Carlton St.), Toronto, ON M5B 2C5. ☎ **800/567-2233** or 416/977-4823. Fax 416/977-4830. 102 units. A/C TV TEL. C$159–C$279 (US$106–US$186) double; from C$249 (US$166) suite. AE, DISC, ER, JCB. Parking: C$15 (US$10). Subway: College.

Popular with tour groups because of its proximity to the Eaton Centre and other downtown attractions, the Ramada is on a rather seedy (yet not unsafe) strip. For years this has been a moderately priced, comfortable hotel, but its 1999 renovations bring the hotel close to boutique status. Each attractive guest room boasts a queen- or a king-sized bed and a sofa, desk, and coffee table. Extras include refrigerators, coffeemakers, hair dryers, and complimentary newspaper delivery. The ground-floor restaurant is open all day, with room service 7am to 9pm. Facilities include an indoor pool, an exercise room, a whirlpool, a sauna, squash courts, and a sundeck.

INEXPENSIVE

Neil Wycik College Hotel. 96 Gerrard St. E. (between Church and Jarvis sts.), Toronto, ON M5B 1G7. ☎ **800/268-4358** or 416/977-2320. Fax 416/977-2809. 304 units, none with bathroom. TEL. C$41–C$51 (US$27–US$34) double; C$45–C$58 (US$30–US$39) family room (2 adults plus children). MC, V. Closed Sept to mid-May. Parking C$10 (US$7) nearby. Subway: College.

During the school year, this is a student residence for nearby Ryerson Polytechnic University. Some of those same students work here May to August, when the Neil Wycik morphs into a guest house. Travelers on tight budgets won't mind the minimalist approach: The rooms have beds, chairs, desks, and phones, but no air-conditioning or TVs. Areas are grouped so five rooms share two bathrooms and one kitchen with a refrigerator and stove. There are two roof decks, one on the 5th floor and one on the 23rd. Elsewhere are a TV lounge, a sauna, a 24-hour laundry room, and a cafe open for breakfast 7 to 11am.

The Strathcona. 60 York St., Toronto, ON M5J 1S8. ☎ **416/363-3321.** Fax 416/363-4679. 193 units. A/C TV TEL. May–Oct C$90–C$149 (US$60–US$99) double; Nov–Apr C$75–C$129 (US$50–US$86) double. AE, DC, MC, V. Parking C$12 (US$8) nearby. Subway: Union.

Completely renovated in 1999, the Strathcona remains one of the best buys in the city. It stands in the shadow of the Royal York, a short walk from all the major downtown attractions. The guest rooms are small but efficiently designed, and the ground-floor cafe is open all day (room service 6am to 8pm). Services include laundry/valet and a concierge.

MIDTOWN

Note: See the "Midtown Toronto" map (p. 376) to locate the hotels in this section.

VERY EXPENSIVE

✪ **Four Seasons Hotel Toronto.** 21 Avenue Rd., Toronto, ON M5R 2G1. ☎ **800/ 268-6282** or 416/964-0411. Fax 416/964-2301. 380 units. A/C MINIBAR TV TEL. C$305–C$410 (US$203–US$273) double; from C$435 (US$290) suite. Weekend rates available. AE, CB, DC, ER, JCB, MC, V. Parking: C$20 (US$13). Subway: Bay.

Firmly planted in the ritzy Yorkville district, the Four Seasons is the favored haunt of visiting celebs and has earned a reputation for offering fine service and complete comfort. It's not even close to being the city's largest hotel, but the building, with its myriad ballrooms, meeting rooms, and restaurants, is monolithic—it's easy to get lost inside (I've done it myself). Even if you do get lost, it's an interesting place to tread through. The public areas are like French parlors, with marble floors, patterned carpets, and dramatic floral arrangements. Once you make it to your room, you'll find that while it may not be especially spacious (a standard is about 325 sq. ft.), it's well designed and easy on the eye; corner rooms enjoy balconies. Extras include two-line phones, fax/modem hookups, and windows that open. The marble bathrooms come with hair dryers, makeup mirrors, and plush robes. There are also specially designed rooms for travelers with disabilities.

Dining/Diversions: The formal dining room, Truffles, is a Toronto institution. The second-floor Studio Cafe is open for all meals and is a favorite with the business crowd; its menu features many health-conscious, low-fat dishes. La Serre, which doubles as a piano bar in the evening and a spot for brunch on weekends, is the perfect perch for people watching, because it overlooks Yorkville Avenue. The Lobby Bar serves the best afternoon tea in the city.

Amenities: 24-hour concierge, 24-hour room service and valet pickup, 1-hour pressing, complimentary shoe shine, twice-daily maid service, in-room massage, babysitting, weekday courtesy limo to downtown, complimentary coffee and newspaper; business center; health club with indoor/outdoor pool, whirlpool, treadmills; free use of bicycles and video-game units for children.

Inter-Continental. 220 Bloor St. W., Toronto, ON M5S 1T8. ☎ **416/960-5200.** Fax 416/960-8269. 209 units. A/C MINIBAR TV TEL. C$275–C$345 (US$183–US$230) double; from C$360 (US$240) suite. AE, DC, JCB, MC, V. Parking: C$22 (US$15). Subway: St. George.

On the edge of Yorkville, the Inter-Continental is less than a 5-minute walk from the ROM, the Bata Shoe Museum, and one of the best shopping districts. It's favored by businesspeople, who appreciate its attentive personalized service. The building may look rather nondescript from the street but is filled with European and art deco details that give it more character. The guest rooms are spacious, boasting stylish love seats and roomy desks, as well as two-line phones, fax/modem hookups, windows that open, and luxe bathrobes.

Dining/Diversions: Signatures overlooks a small courtyard, where in warm weather a few dining tables sprout; the globe-trotting menu boasts many imported ingredients. The Harmony Lounge is for afternoon tea by day and cocktails by night; a piano player entertains there until the wee hours.

Amenities: Concierge, 24-hour room service, laundry/valet, twice-daily maid service, nightly turndown, complimentary shoe shine and newspaper; lap pool with adjacent patio; fitness room with treadmill, bikes, StairMaster; sauna and massage room; business center.

✪ **Park Hyatt Toronto.** 4 Avenue Rd., Toronto, ON M5R 2E8. ☎ **800/268-4927** or 416/924-5471. Fax 416/924-4933. 348 units. A/C MINIBAR TV TEL. C$255–C$435 (US$170–US$290) double; from C$305 (US$203) suite. Children under 18 stay free in parents' room. Weekend packages available. AE, DC, DISC, MC, V. Parking: C$20 (US$13). Subway: Museum or Bay.

Following a recent C$60 million (US$40 million) renovation by its new owners, the Chicago-based Hyatt Corp., the Park Hyatt has cemented its reputation as the last word in luxe. The art deco hotel is in the posh Yorkville district, with the ROM and the Children's Own Museum steps away. If the nearby Four Seasons is home-away-from-home for the glitterati, this official hotel of the Toronto International Film Festival prides itself on luring the literati. The north and south towers are linked by a glamorous lobby dotted with Eastern-inspired objets d'art. The guest rooms and suites have been appointed with oak and cherry woods, and glass walls now cover the terraces, increasing floor space so that even the smallest room boasts 500 square feet. Extras include two-line phones, fax machines, Internet hookup, and ironing boards and irons. The bathrooms have their own phones, plush terry robes, and hair dryers. The hotel is "dog friendly," so there's no need to leave your best friend at home.

Dining/Diversions: The 18th-floor Roof Restaurant provides stunning views, and the adjacent Roof Lounge is a favorite meeting spot for journalists; the martini is the drink of choice (the James Bond vodka with a drop of lillet is a must-try). Morton's of Chicago, an upscale steakhouse, is in the North Tower and open for dinner only. The Mezzanine Bar serves afternoon tea and evening drinks and canapés, with piano music at night.

Amenities: Concierge, 24-hour room service featuring many spa-inspired dishes, twice-daily maid service, laundry/valet, baby-sitting, complimentary newspaper and shoe shine; 24-hour business center with secretarial services; fitness center with indoor lap pool, treadmills, sauna, whirlpool, treatment rooms for massage and other spa-like pampering.

Windsor Arms. 18 St. Thomas St., Toronto, ON M5S 3E7. ☎ **416/971-9666.** Fax 416/971-3303. 28 units. A/C MINIBAR TV TEL. From C$375 (US$250) double; from C$575 (US$384) suite. Weekend rates available. AE, DC, DISC, MC, V. Subway: Bay.

Take one exquisite neo-Gothic building, tear it down, and build in its place an identical structure incorporating some of the original's elements. That's the recipe the new owner of the Windsor Arms followed in re-creating the hotel, which was first built in 1927 and closed in 1991. The result is a stunning mix of new and old, with state-of-the-art technology alongside leaded-glass windows. Only 4 of the 15 stories offer hotel rooms; the rest house million-dollar condos. The guest rooms and suites are exquisite confections of ivory, celadon, and silver, each featuring a butler's cupboard, with one door that opens from the hall and another that opens into the room (in case you want to enjoy room service but don't feel like answering the door). Extras include two-line phones, fax/modem hookups, large closets with built-in dressers, and CD players. The generously proportioned bathrooms have Jacuzzi jets in the tubs, plush robes, and phones.

Dining/Diversions: The ground-floor Courtyard Cafe, open for lunch and dinner, isn't really outside, though the glass-roof skylight, mirrored windows, and greenery add to the airy feel. The French-inspired menu is full of fish and gamy meats. The Club 22 lounge includes both a caviar-and-champagne bar (where a 4-oz. glass of Cristal goes for C$35/US$23) and a 9- by 9-foot humidor.

Amenities: Concierge, 24-hour room service, laundry/valet, twice-daily maid service, nightly turndown; lap pool, sauna, spa with massage, aromatherapy, and aquatherapy treatments.

EXPENSIVE

Sutton Place Hotel. 955 Bay St., Toronto, ON M5S 2A2. ☎ **800/268-3790** or 416/924-9221. Fax 416/924-1778. www.suttonplace.com. 292 units. A/C MINIBAR TV TEL. C$235–C$300 (US$157–US$200) double; from C$400 (US$267) suite. Extra person C$20

(US$13). Children under 18 stay free in parents' room. Weekend rates available. AE, DC, JCB, MC, V. Parking: C$25 (US$17) valet. Subway: Museum or Wellesley.

The hotel may tower over the intersection of Bay and Wellesley streets, but the Sutton Place boasts the advantages of a small hotel. In addition to more than its share of celebrities, it draws sophisticated business and leisure travelers who desire personalized service and serious pampering. The Sutton aims for European panache, scattering antiques and tapestries through the public spaces. The ambiance is carried through the spacious guest rooms, decorated in a similar, though scaled-down, style. Each boasts a substantial desk, a two-line phone with voice mail, a fax/modem hookup, bathrobes, and a hair dryer. A few suites have full kitchens. Pets are welcome.

Dining/Diversions: Accents, the elegant but unstuffy dining room, is open all day; it's a popular spot for locals as well as guests. The adjoining Accents Bar boasts live music and a multitude of wines by the glass.

Amenities: Concierge, 24-hour room service, laundry/valet, complimentary newspaper and shoe shine, twice-daily maid service, limo to the financial district; indoor pool with spacious sundeck, sauna, massage, fully equipped fitness center, business center.

MODERATE

Quality Hotel. 280 Bloor St. W. (at St. George), Toronto, ON M5S 1V8. ☎ **416/968-0010.** 210 units. A/C TV TEL. C$139–C$179 (US$93–US$119) double. Weekend and other packages available. AE, DC, DISC, MC, V. Parking: C$12 (US$8). Subway: St. George.

Considering the hotel's tony location (steps from Yorkville and several museums, including the ROM), the price is hard to beat. The guest rooms are small but comfortable, with well-lit work tables. Choice Club members receive a complimentary daily newspaper and have access to in-house secretarial services; Executive rooms have fax/modem hookups. There are a restaurant and coffee shop, with room service 7am to noon and 5 to 10pm. Laundry/valet services are available, and guests have access to a nearby health club.

INEXPENSIVE

Hotel Selby. 592 Sherbourne St., Toronto, ON M4X 1L4. ☎ **800/387-4788** or 416/921-3142. Fax 416/923-3177. 67 units, 59 with bathroom. A/C TV TEL. C$85–C$90 (US$57–US$60) double without bathroom, C$100 (US$67) double with bathroom; C$110–C$135 (US$73–US$90) suite. Rates include continental breakfast. AE, MC, V. Limited free parking on first-come, first-served basis; otherwise C$10 (US$7).

The Selby is one of Toronto's better-kept secrets. The charm of this 1890s Victorian building is enhanced by its ornate chandeliers, stucco moldings, and high ceilings. In a predominantly gay neighborhood, the hotel attracts couples both gay and straight, as well as students and seniors (both groups enjoy special rates). The rooms are individually decorated and often boast elaborate moldings, and the bathrooms usually come with good-sized clawfoot tubs. There's an on-site coin laundry, and guests can use a nearby fitness center for a small fee.

Victoria University. 140 Charles St. W., Toronto, ON M5S 1K9. ☎ **416/585-4524.** Fax 416/585-4530. 700 units, none with bathroom. C$60 (US$40) double. Rate includes breakfast. Discounts available for seniors/students. MC, V. Closed Sept to early May. Parking: C$12 (US$8) nearby. Subway: Museum.

This is a summer steal: Mid-May to late August, Victoria University (federated with the University of Toronto) makes its student accommodations available to travelers. Furnishings are simple—a bed, desk, and chair are standard—but the surroundings are splendid. Many of the rooms are in Burwash Hall, which overlooks a peaceful, leafy green quad; all rooms are just down the street from the ROM and up the street from Queen's Park. Guests are supplied with linens, towels, and soap; a self-service Laundromat is on-site. Athletic facilities, including tennis courts, are nearby.

4 Dining

With more than 5,000 restaurants around the city and cooking styles from any nationality you could name, Toronto's culinary scene is eclectic, palate teasing, and affordable. You'll find some of the best and least expensive dining in ethnic enclaves like Little Italy, Little Portugal, Chinatown, and Greektown.

Although dining out in Toronto doesn't have to be an expensive venture by any means (unless you frequent the four- and five-star restaurants exclusively), the level of taxation is high. All meals are subject to the 8% **provincial sales tax** and to the 7% **GST.** In other words, tax and tip together can add 30% to your bill (tips are normally left to diners' discretion, unless there are six or more people at the table; 15% is the usual amount tipped). The price of a bottle of wine is generally high because of the tax on such imports; get around this by ordering an Ontario vintage—the local wines enjoy a rising international reputation. Remember that there'll be a 10% tax on alcohol, whatever grape you're sipping.

DOWNTOWN WEST

This is where you'll find the greatest concentration of great restaurants in the city. **Little Italy,** which runs along **College Street,** and **Chinatown,** which radiates from **Spadina Avenue,** boast more restaurants from which to choose than anywhere else in the city.

Note: See the "Downtown Toronto" map (p. 374) to locate the restaurants in this section.

VERY EXPENSIVE

Another great pricey choice is **Avalon,** 270 Adelaide St. W., at John Street (☎ **416/ 979-9918;** Subway: St. Andrew), boasting one of the most inventive kitchens in the city. Of course, reservations are required. It's open Thursday noon to 2:30pm, Monday to Thursday 5:30 to 10pm, and Friday and Saturday 5:30 to 11pm.

Monsoon. 100 Simcoe St. ☎ **416/979-7172.** Reservations required. Main courses C$21–C$37 (US$14–US$25). AE, DC, MC, V. Mon–Fri noon–2:30pm, Mon–Sat 5:30–11pm. Subway: Osgoode. FUSION.

Monsoon is actually more famous for its award-winning interior design than for its food. That's a pity, because while the brown-on-black Zen-like setting is easy on the eye (especially with that fabulously flattering lighting), the cooking is subtly sensual. Sophisticated palates are familiar with Thai, Chinese, Japanese, and Indian flavors, but it's unusual to find them so seductively intertwined with North American staples. Veal goes vindaloo accompanied by a mango glaze, curried cauliflower, and grilled okra, and beef and prawns meet up in a cabernet-teriyaki reduction with wasabi mashed potatoes. The wine list hits all the right new- and old-world notes.

EXPENSIVE

✪ **Chiado.** 484 College St. (at Concorde Ave.). ☎ **416/538-1910.** Reservations recommended. Main courses C$17–C$30 (US$11–US$20). AE, DC, ER, MC, V. Mon–Sat noon–3pm, Mon–Thurs 5–10pm. Subway: Queen's Park, then streetcar west. PORTUGUESE.

Alone in this Mediterranean-obsessed part of town, Chiado serves modern Portuguese cuisine. Evoking opulence with its marble floors, oil paintings, and fresh orchids, it draws a sophisticated crowd. The servers are models of Euro professionalism, attentive without hovering. The menu favors seafood, from starters, like grilled squid with roasted peppers, to entrees, like poached or grilled salted cod (fresh fish is flown in daily). There's also a choice of braised rabbit or capon, among fowl and gamy dishes. Don't skimp on the sweets, which are lovingly prepared. The wine list is a treat, including many unfamiliar but rich and complex wines, most priced in the bargain-basement region.

Jump Café and Bar. 1 Wellington St. W. ☎ **416/363-3400.** Reservations recommended for lunch and dinner. Main courses C$19–C$28 (US$13–US$19). AE, DC, ER, JCB, MC, V. Mon–Fri 11:30am–11pm, Sat 4:30–11pm. Subway: King. AMERICAN.

Appropriately, Jump is always hopping. A sprawling space in Commerce Court, one of the financial district's monoliths, this is one of the city's most popular watering holes and restaurants. It's such a scene-and-be-seen spot you might suspect it's all show and no substance, yet the food is anything but an afterthought. The lunch and dinner menus are almost identical, both featuring dishes like grilled 10-ounce Black Angus steak, New York cut, with Yukon Gold fries, salsa, and mushroom gravy. For the more gastronomically adventurous there are roasted sea bass with fragrant coconut basmati rice and green curry and osso buco with spinach-and-lemon risotto. Starters stick to seafood for the most part, with steamed mussels in ginger-and-coconut-milk broth and grilled tiger shrimps atop a Thai mango-peanut salad. The wine list favors the New World, and there are a fair number of selections by the glass. The luxe desserts will put your diet back by about a month.

✪ Trattoria Giancarlo. 41–43 Clinton St. (at College). ☎ **416/533-9619.** Reservations strongly recommended. Main courses C$16–C$26 (US$11–US$17). AE, DC, MC, V. Mon–Sat 6–11pm. Subway: Queen's Park, then streetcar west. ITALIAN.

Everybody comes to Trattoria Giancarlo: lovers of exquisitely rendered Italian food, romantic couples in search of a candlelit rendezvous, and even the rich and famous. Sophia Loren made a splash here when she passed through town to promote her cookbook. But the real thrill comes from food like Nonna never made. Efficient, friendly staff keep the meal going at a steady pace. First, the antipasti: maybe *luna di camembert,* which bakes and wraps the cheese in Parma prosciutto and pairs it up with fresh fruit, or *polpi grigliati,* a tender octopus awash in braised onion and balsamic vinegar. Next on deck are the pasta plates (like linguine with shrimp, roasted tomatoes, and sweet onions) or meat dishes (like quail flavored with marsala and sage, served with creamy polenta). Traditional Italian sweets round out the meal: Try the delicious tiramisu or the decadent chocolate tartufo.

MODERATE

Cities. 859 Queen St. W. ☎ **416/599-7720.** Main courses C$12–C$20 (US$8–US$13). AE, MC, V. Daily noon–2:30pm and 5–10:30pm. Subway: Osgoode, then streetcar west. BISTRO.

This charming bistro—in which a rococo Elvis presides over the bar—evinces all the pleasures and problems of metropolitan life. Overcrowding is the first thing you notice: Nineteen tables for two cram the narrow room, forcing neighbors to rub elbows. The room is divided into smoking and no-smoking sections, though in such a minute space, there's little difference. The food, however, is what makes it all worthwhile. The menu is deliberately short, allowing the kitchen to focus hothouse-flower care on its featured selections: rack of lamb, Atlantic salmon, veal tenderloin, and more. Starters, like the three-mushroom salad, get equal care.

Mildred Pierce. 99 Sudbury St. ☎ **416/588-5695.** Reservations not accepted. Main courses C$14–C$22 (US$9–US$15). AE, DC, ER, MC, V. Mon–Fri noon–2pm, Sun 10am–3pm,

Sun–Thurs 6–10pm, Fri–Sat 6–11pm. Subway: Osgoode, then streetcar west to Dovercourt; walk south on Dovercourt and turn right at Sudbury. ECLECTIC.

Named after the Joan Crawford film, this restaurant is appropriately theatrical, with organza drapes tumbling down from the high ceiling. The walls are covered with murals of a Roman feast (a local in-joke, because they depict characters like the owner and a few food critics). The menu fits right in, rich in inspiration and dramatic flourishes borrowed from different countries. Grilled salmon is paired with saffron risotto and ragout of fennel, baby beets, and bok choy, while a Thai hot pot boasts tiger shrimp, scallops, mussels, and clams brewing in coconut-lime-cilantro sauce. The wine list is short but does touch on the pulse points of Italy, Spain, South Africa, and California. The lush desserts include maple crème brûlée and a rustic cranberry-and-walnut tart. Because the place doesn't accept reservations, getting in on a Friday or Saturday night is a challenge, even if you arrive early; other nights, there's rarely much of a wait. The dining room is entirely smoke free; smokers can lay claim to the small outdoor patio and enjoy the view of the city's skyline.

Sang Ho. 536 Dundas St. W. ☎ **416/596-1685.** Reservations not accepted. Main courses C$8–C$18 (US$5–US$12). MC, V. Sun–Thurs noon–10pm, Fri–Sat noon–11pm. Subway: St. Patrick. CHINESE.

There's no end of eateries along this eastward expanse of Chinatown, but Sang Ho will be the one with the longest queue out front. This restaurant boasts not only a top-notch kitchen but also a lovely dining room with several teeming aquariums. The regular menu never changes its 100-plus dishes, but there are many specials of the day listed on wall-mounted boards. Seafood is the obvious choice, whether shrimp, clams, or red snapper. The service is speedy and responsive. Try to go on a weeknight, when there's no more than a short wait for a table.

INEXPENSIVE

Kalendar. 546 College St. (just west of Bathurst). ☎ **416/923-4138.** Main courses C$10–C$13 (US$7–US$9). MC, V. Mon–Fri 11am–4pm. Subway: Queen's Park, then streetcar west. LIGHT FARE.

I can't go to this restaurant without snickering at the menu—pizzas are called "nannettes," for example—but the food itself inspires satisfied sighs. You'll find sandwiches stuffed with portobello mushrooms, havarti, and roasted red peppers, as well as five "scrolls," phyllo pastries filled with delights like artichoke hearts, eggplant, and hummus. The aforementioned nannettes are baked nan breads topped with ingredients like smoked salmon, capers, and red onions. The restaurant is divided into two

---

ⓘ Family-Friendly Restaurants

Kensington Kitchen *(see p. 394)*   This place is whimsically decorated with colorful toys and model airplanes amid the Oriental rugs. It seems to be easier to get kids to eat their greens when veggies are tucked into pita sandwiches, like the ones here.

Millie's Bistro *(see p. 395)*   This is a perennially popular spot with families. There's a special menu for tykes, and most of the Mediterranean food can be eaten without cutlery. The entire restaurant is smoke free.

Shopsy's *(see p. 392)*   When the kids are sick of eating out and craving comfort food, this is where to take them. Homestyle chili and the macaroni and cheese hit the spot, and there's a whole section of the menu devoted to ice cream.

mirrored rooms, one of which boasts an antique apothecary's cabinet behind the bar. The ambiance is very like a French bistro. In summer, the sidewalk sprouts a patio that's just the place to sit and watch the world go by.

DOWNTOWN EAST
VERY EXPENSIVE

✪ **The Boston Club.** 4 Front St. E. ☎ **416/860-0086.** Reservations required. Main courses C$23–C$38 (US$15–US$25). AE, DC, ER, MC, V. Mon–Fri noon–2:30pm, Mon–Sat 5:30–11:30pm. Subway: Union. SEAFOOD.

Toronto has never enjoyed a reputation as a great place for seafood. The deck was stacked against it—look at how far the city is from the nearest ocean. But The Boston Club is set to change all that. Sure, there are landlubber main courses (beef tenderloin makes a few appearances on the menu), but this restaurant devotes itself to cooking imported sea critters with uncommon finesse. The dining room eschews aquariums and lobster bibs in favor of refined elegance. The walls are paneled in rich wood, the gilt-framed portraits could've been lifted from an English lord's country home, and a jazz pianist serenades the chic crowd. The menu is really just a guideline, since the chef works with whatever fish happens to be flown in fresh that day. There might be grilled Ahi tuna with Asian-flavored jus, swordfish with citrus butter, or whole steamed lobster. The desserts depart from the rarefied mains (Boston cream pie, anyone?). The sleek service knows its way around the impressive wine list.

EXPENSIVE

✪ **Hiro Sushi.** 171 King St. E. ☎ **416/304-0550.** Reservations recommended. Main courses C$20–C$30 (US$13–US$20). AE, DC, MC, V. Mon–Fri noon–2:30pm, Mon–Sat 6–10:30pm. Subway: King. JAPANESE.

Widely regarded as the city's best sushi chef, Hiro Yoshida draws a horde of financial district types at lunch, though the dinner scene is mainly couples. The monochromatic setting is comfortably minimalist, and diners are encouraged to relax and leave their meal in Hiro's capable hands. The varieties of sushi range from the expected to the inventive, and there are also sashimi, tempura, and bento box combinations to choose from. Keep in mind that the service can be rather slow. Forget the few wines listed in favor of sake or beer.

Rosewater Supper Club. 19 Toronto St. (at Adelaide St.). ☎ **416/214-5888.** Reservations strongly recommended. Main courses C$20–C$32 (US$13–US$21). AE, DC, ER, MC, V. Mon–Fri 11:30am–2:30pm and 5:30–10:30pm, Sat 5:30–11:30pm. Subway: King. INTERNATIONAL.

This triple-decked pleasure dome is packed almost every night with dressed-up diners who pass the time checking one another out. Personally, I'm still caught on the scenery: Marble, moldings, and a three-story waterfall make quite an impression. So does the menu, which casually tours the globe. First up on deck are delectables like sweetbread tarte tatin in an apple reduction. Main courses include a potato-zucchini millefeuille with truffle oil and an asparagus salad and pan-baked pork with honey and cloves. The can't-miss desserts include a ganache-topped chocolate-caramel cake, as well as baked mascarpone pear with caraway ice cream. The serious wine list hails mainly from France and California, though there are some excellent Ontario vintages too.

MODERATE

Montréal Bistro and Jazz Club. 65 Sherbourne St. (at Adelaide St.). ☎ **416/363-0179.** Reservations recommended, especially on weekends. Main courses C$10–C$18 (US$7–US$12). AE, MC, V. Mon–Fri 11:30am–3pm; Mon–Thurs 6–11pm, Fri–Sat 6pm–midnight. Subway: King, then streetcar east. QUÉBECOIS.

Ontario and Québec may share a border, but it's no mean feat to find top-notch *tour-tière* in Toronto. Anyone who craves Québecois staples like pea soup and smoked-meat sandwiches can return their train ticket and stop by this bistro. The venue is divided into two rooms, the restaurant and one of the city's premier jazz clubs, so you can treat your ears while satisfying your palate.

INEXPENSIVE

Shopsy's. 33 Yonge St. ☎ **416/365-3333.** Sandwiches and main courses C$7–C$14 (US$4.65–US$9). AE, DC, MC, V. Mon–Wed 6:30am–11pm, Thurs–Fri 6:30am–midnight, Sat–Sun 8am–midnight. Subway: Union. DELI.

This Toronto institution has been in business for more than three-quarters of a century. Its large patio, festooned with giant yellow umbrellas, draws crowds for breakfast, lunch, and dinner and for tide-me-overs in-between. This is where you go for heaping corned beef or smoked-meat sandwiches served on fresh rye. There's also a slew of comfort foods like macaroni and cheese and chicken pot pie. Shopsy's also boasts one of the largest walk-in humidors in the city.

Young Thailand. 81 Church St. (south of Lombard St.). ☎ **416/368-1368.** Reservations recommended. Main courses C$8–C$16 (US$5–US$11). AE, DC, MC, V. Mon–Fri 11:30am–2pm; daily 4:30–11pm. Subway: Queen or King. THAI.

Wandee Young was one of the first chefs to awake Toronto's taste buds to the joys of Thai cuisine. That was more than 2 decades ago, and Young Thailand is still going strong with several locations around the city. The large dining room contains a few Southeast Asian decorative elements, but it's the low-priced, high-quality cuisine that attracts the hip-but-broke and the boomers alike. The bargain buffet at lunch is always a mob scene. The dinner menu is à la carte, with popular picks like spiced chicken and bamboo shoots in coconut milk, satays with fiery peanut sauce, and the ever-present pad thai. Soups tend to be sinus-clearing, though the mango salads offer a sweet antidote.

MIDTOWN WEST
VERY EXPENSIVE

Zola. 162 Cumberland St. ☎ **416/515-1222.** Reservations recommended. Main courses C$25–C$38 (US$17–US$25). AE, DC, MC, V. Daily noon–midnight. Subway: Bay. FRENCH.

Maybe you're in Toronto, but your heart is really set on, say, Paris. Dinner at Zola could give you the French fix you need. This ambitious bistro re-creates a train-station setting with its steel beams and girders. Along one wall, glassed like a window, is the skyline of Gay Paree with the Eiffel Tower rising triumphant. Tear your eyes away to consider the menu, and you'll find it brimming with Left Bank fare. The ingredients are rich—most first courses contain foie gras, caviar, lobster, or some combination thereof. The main courses are a mix of seafood (like fillet of grouper in red-wine sauce with Swiss chard) and meat (like angus tenderloin in truffle jus with green beans and *more* foie gras). Waistline watchers had best skip to the next stop. One hint that you're still in Toronto: The waiters aren't snobby at all.

EXPENSIVE

Boba. 90 Avenue Rd. ☎ **416/961-2622.** Reservations strongly recommended. Main courses C$20–C$29 (US$13–US$19). AE, DC, ER, MC, V. Mon–Sat 5:30–10pm. Subway: Bay. FUSION.

There's no shortage of stunning early-1900s houses in this part of town, and Boba happens to be located in one of the most charming, set back from the street. The interior's pastel-hued walls and tasseled lamp shades exude warmth Provençal style, and the patio up front is perfect for summer dining. Boba is a scene every night, with a mix of dressed-up and dressed-down professionals table-hopping with abandon. What draws them in is the inventive Fusion cuisine that has turned co-chefs Barbara Gordon and Bob Bermann into local celebrities. One of the highlights of the menu is Gordon's Muscovy duck two ways, which cooks the breast rare and braises the leg, with wonderful results. The grilled salmon is also just-so but nicely mated with curried vegetable risotto. The desserts are overwhelming, particularly the Valrhona chocolate triangle with crème fraîche ice cream, raspberries, and berry coulis (don't try to eat this alone!). There are several award-winning Ontario ice wines on the menu. The entire restaurant is smoke free.

Sen5es. 15 Bloor St. W. ☎ **416/935-0400.** Reservations required. Main C$18–C$36 (US$12–US$24). AE, DC, MC, V. Subway: Yonge/Bloor. CONTINENTAL.

Harry Wu, not content to rest on his laurels with two successful restaurants at the Metropolitan Hotel, recently opened Sen5es (forget the "5" and pronounce it *senses*), a bakery, gourmet food emporium, and restaurant rolled into one sophisticated space. Dining here is an experience for all the senses: The serene sandy tones are serious eye-candy, the background music soothes, and the velvety banquettes rub you the right way. Smell and taste get revved up with starters like the delicately rich asparagus risotto or the crabmeat salad with apple, scallions, and mustard sprouts. Main courses make for some clever pairings, such as grilled salmon with roasted fennel and spinach atop couscous and lemon-ginger cream, as well as duck breast spiked with sun-dried cherries and star anise jus. Do save room for dessert—the seven choices are all solid performers, but my favorite is the elegantly simple raspberry tart.

MODERATE

Goldfish. 372 Bloor St. W. ☎ **416/513-0077.** Reservations recommended. Main courses C$12–C$20 (US$8–US$13). AE, DC, ER, MC, V. Mon–Fri noon–10:30pm, Sat noon–11pm. Subway: Spadina. ECLECTIC.

With its floor-to-ceiling front window revealing all to passersby, dining at this new hot spot is like being in a fishbowl. The cool, crisp lines of Scandinavian design mix with miniature Japanese plants for an upscale Zen ambiance. While the look may be trendier-than-thou, the staff's attitude is consistently considerate. The menu is far less austere than the surroundings, and the simplest dishes receive full attention. Main courses run the gamut from ostrich tenderloin with orange-peppercorn sauce and beet salad to grilled salmon with an okra cake and coconut vinaigrette. Even the simplest green salad is refreshed with dollops of pumpkin seeds and a light dressing that contains a hint of lavender emulsion. And the short dessert list includes some inventive pairings, like a delicious apple tart with rosemary ice cream. The wine list is short but contains 10 selections by the glass.

Matignon. 51 St. Nicholas St. ☎ **416/921-9226.** Reservations recommended. Main courses C$14–C$18 (US$9–US$12). AE, MC, V. Mon–Fri 11:30am–2:30pm, Mon–Thurs 5–10pm, Fri–Sat 5–11pm. Subway: Wellesley. FRENCH.

Because this small restaurant is a bit off the beaten track, dining here gives a thrill of discovery. The intimately sized rooms, spread over two floors, are festooned with all things French. The crowd includes a large number of regulars, and the ambiance is that of a low-key bistro. The short menu is filled with classics from the old county, including Angus steak rolled in crushed pepper and flambéed with cognac and rack of lamb with mustard and herbs of Provence. The desserts stay on the same track, like vanilla ice cream under hot chocolate sauce. *Bon appétit!*

INEXPENSIVE

Indian Rice Factory. 414 Dupont St. ☎ **416/961-3472.** Reservations recommended. Main courses C$8–C$16 (US$5–US$11). AE, DC, MC, V. Mon–Sat noon–11pm, Sun 5–10pm. Subway: Dupont. INDIAN.

A Toronto institution since the late 1970s, the Indian Rice Factory is still in a league of its own. The corduroy banquettes and macramé wall hangings still draw boomers who started coming here 20 years ago. The Punjabi-influenced menu serves up heaping helpings of beef *dhansak,* in which braised beef meets up with lentil-eggplant-tomato curry, and chicken *khashabad,* which features a chicken breast stuffed with almonds, cashews, and raisins in coconut milk cream. There are many beers from local microbreweries and a small but well-chosen wine list.

✪ **Kensington Kitchen.** 124 Harbord St. ☎ **416/961-3404.** Reservations recommended. Main courses C$10–C$14 (US$7–US$9). AE, CB, DC, ER, MC, V. Mon–Sat 11:30am–11pm, Sun 11:30am–10pm. Subway: Spadina, then LRT south. MEDITERRANEAN.

Drawing a crowd of regulars—students and profs—from the nearby University of Toronto, Kensington Kitchen is a perennial gem. The decor hasn't changed in years, with the same Oriental carpets on the walls, painted wood floor, and decorative objects scattered about. The tradition of big portions at small cost stays constant too. The menu ventures to and fro among the ports of the Mediterranean. There are angel-hair pasta with heaps of shrimp, scallops, and mussels in tomato-coriander sauce; saffron paella with chicken and sausage; and Turkish-style braised lamb stuffed with raisins, eggplant, apricots, and figs. In clement weather, head to the rooftop patio, which is shaded by a mighty Manitoba maple.

MIDTOWN EAST/THE EAST END

Just about everything *will* be Greek to you in East End along Danforth Avenue. Known appropriately enough to locals as Greektown, this is where to come for low-cost but delicious dining, or for a midnight meal—the tavernas along this strip generally stay open till the wee hours, even on weeknights.

MODERATE

✪ **Pan on the Danforth.** 516 Danforth Ave. ☎ **416/466-8158.** Reservations accepted for parties of 6 or more only. Main courses C$13–C$19 (US$9–US$13). AE, MC, V. Sun–Thurs 5pm–midnight, Fri–Sat 5pm–1am. Subway: Chester or Pape. GREEK.

To the best of my knowledge, Pan was a god of music, not of food. I must've mixed it up, because if he's the inspiration for this restaurant, he certainly knows his way around a kitchen. This long-established eatery takes classic Greek dishes and updates them with panache. Grilled swordfish is wrapped in vine leaf and mated with spinach orzo, and a smoked and baked pork chop is served up with feta scalloped potatoes and zucchini relish. The well-chosen wine list favors the New World. The crowd is fairly sophisticated, which may explain the cryptic message over the bar: "You've done it already."

UPTOWN

This area is too large to consider a neighborhood, stretching as it does from north of Davenport Road to Steeles Avenue. While it doesn't have the concentration of restaurants Downtown enjoys, it has a number of stellar performers that make the trip north worthwhile.

VERY EXPENSIVE

Centro. 2472 Yonge St. ☎ **416/483-2211.** Reservations recommended. Main courses C$24–C$39 (US$16–US$26). AE, DC, MC, V. Mon–Sat 5–11:30pm. Subway: Eglinton. CONTINENTAL.

The palatial main room with its oxblood walls is always bustling. The dressed-up, all-ages crowd often starts out schmoozing at the wine bar downstairs, moving up to the main floor for dinner, then back downstairs for R&B and a nightcap (the wine bar stays open to 2am). French-born executive chef Marc Thuet is a motorcycle-riding local celebrity, though he takes his food no less seriously for it. The seasonal menu pays tribute to the restaurant's Northern Italian origins with pasta mains like pennette with Parma prosciutto and roasted sage. Still, many choices lean to contemporary Canadiana, like caribou chops with cloudberries and crabapple compote, or French modern, like rack of lamb with a Provençal honey-mustard crust served with ratatouille. The delish desserts run the gamut from traditional tiramisu to chocolate-vanilla baked Alaska. The stellar wine list is sure to thrill oenophiles.

✪ **North 44.** 2537 Yonge St. ☎ **416/487-4897.** Reservations recommended. Main courses C$27–C$40 (US$18–US$27). AE, DC, MC, V. Mon–Sat 5–11pm. Subway: Eglinton. INTERNATIONAL.

This is the one restaurant even people who've never set foot in Toronto have heard a bundle about—it has been profiled extensively in food and travel magazines. Can it possibly live up to its reputation? The spare art deco decor recently got a facelift, and the results are stunning: sleek glamour without a hint of trying too hard. The soft lighting and strategically situated mirrors wrap the dining room and its occupants in a gorgeous glow. People dress up to go here, though they don't have to, and if you scan the room you'll be able to pick out several couples obviously on a first date. The menu changes with the seasons, borrowing from Mediterranean, American, and Asian sources. The results are inspiring to the palate and to the eye (think of it as architectural food). On the list of main courses you might find grilled veal tenderloin with orange peppercorns, toasted barley, and root veggies, or roasted Muscovy duck breast with orange-soy marinade and foie gras. There are always a few pasta and pizza choices, such as caramelized squash ravioli with black truffle essence. The desserts, like the lemon meringue millefeuille, are among the best in the city, and there's a wide selection of accompanying ice wines. The wine list is comprehensive, though most of the prices veer off into the stratosphere. What really sets North 44 apart is its seamless service: Those who don't like to be pampered should stay away.

EXPENSIVE

Millie's Bistro. 1980 Avenue Rd., south of York Mills. ☎ **416/481-1247.** Reservations recommended. Main courses C$10–C$22 (US$7–US$15). AE, MC, V. Subway: York Mills, then walk west or take a taxi. MEDITERRANEAN.

Subtle as its signage is, it's hard to miss Millie's: The sole gastronomic draw in this neighborhood, it's splendid enough to lure even jaded downtowners. Divided into two sunny, skinny rooms (both no-smoking), the crowd is an unusual mix of young-to-middle-age courting couples, families with tiny tykes, and groups gearing up for a night on the town. The sprawling main menu includes dishes from Spain, southern France, Italy, Turkey, and Morocco (there's a shorter just-for-kids menu too). Start with tapas, perhaps a Catalan-style goat cheese with basil and olive oil; a Turkish flatbread with a topping of lamb, yogurt, and mint; or a *b'stilla* (aromatic chicken wrapped in herbed semolina). Better still, try them all—the cheery staff will arrange them on ceramic platters for sharing. Main courses include a must-try chicken-and-shrimp paella; a garlicky, spicy rib steak; and vegetarian lasagne with portobello mushrooms, sweet roasted peppers, and leeks. The sweets are seductive, though the generous tapas and main portions make saving room almost impossible. The wide-ranging wine list offers new- and old-world selections, with Spanish wines a particularly good value.

5 Seeing the Sights

First the good news: Toronto has amazing sights to see and places to be that'll appeal to travelers of all stripes. The bad news? No matter how long your stay, you just won't be able to fit everything in. Toronto is a sprawling city, and while there's a sizable collection of attractions downtown and midtown, some truly wonderful attractions are in less accessible areas.

Another difficulty is that many of the sights could take up a day of your visit: Ontario Place, the Harbourfront Centre, the Ontario Science Centre, and Paramount Canada's Wonderland all come to mind. This isn't even to mention the expansive parks, the arts scene, or the shopping possibilities. My best advice? Relax and bring a good pair of walking shoes. There's no better way to appreciate the kaleidoscopic metropolis that is Toronto than on foot.

THE TOP ATTRACTIONS
ON THE LAKEFRONT

Ontario Place. 955 Lakeshore Blvd. W. ☎ **416/314-9811,** or 416/314-9900 for a recording. Free admission, with some exceptions (like the Canadian National Exhibition). Gate admission C$10 (US$7); summer play-all-day pass C$22 (US$15) adults, C$11 (US$7) children 4–5. IMAX movies after Labour Day (included in play-all-day pass) C$9 (US$6) adults, C$4.50 (US$3) seniors/children 12 and under. Mid-May to Labour Day, daily 10am–dusk (except evening events and dining spots). Parking C$9 (US$6). Subway: Bathurst or Dufferin, then bus south to Exhibition Place; call TTC Information at ☎ **416/393-4636** for special bus service details.

When this 96-acre recreation complex on Lake Ontario opened in 1971, it seemed futuristic—and all these years later, it still does (the 1989 facelift no doubt helped). From a distance, you'll see five steel-and-glass pods suspended on columns 105 feet above the lake, three artificial islands, and a huge geodesic dome. The five pods contain a multimedia theater, a children's theater, a high-technology exhibit, and displays telling the story of Ontario in vivid kaleidoscopic detail. The dome houses **Cinesphere,** where a 60- by 80-foot screen shows specially made IMAX movies.

Under an enormous orange canopy, the **Children's Village** is the most creative playground anywhere. In a well-supervised area, children 12 and under can scramble over rope bridges, bounce on an enormous trampoline, explore a foam forest, slide down a twisting chute, or (most popular of all) squirt water pistols and garden hoses, swim, and generally drench one another in the water-play section. Afterward, parents can just pop them in the convenient dryers before moving on to other kids' amusements.

A stroll around the complex reveals **two marinas** full of yachts and other craft; the **HMCS** *Haida* (a destroyer, open for touring, that served in both World War II and the Korean War); an 18-hole **miniature golf course;** plenty of **grassland** for picnicking and romping; and a wide variety of **restaurants** and **snack bars** serving everything from Chinese, Irish, and German foods to hot dogs and hamburgers. And don't miss the wildest rides in town—the **Hydrofuge,** a tube slide allowing you to reach speeds over 30 m.p.h.; the **Rush River Raft Ride,** which carries you along a lengthy flume in an inflatable raft; the **pink twister** and **purple pipeline** (water slides); plus **bumper boats** and **go-karts.** For something more peaceful, you can navigate **pedal boats** or **remote-control boats** between the artificial islands.

At night, the outdoor **Molson Amphitheatre** accommodates 16,000 under a copper canopy and outside on the grass. It features top-line entertainers like Kenny G, James Taylor, The Who, and Hank Williams. For information, call ☎ **416/ 260-5600.** For tickets, call **Ticketmaster** at ☎ **416/870-8000.**

✪ **Harbourfront Centre.** Queen's Quay W. ☎ **416/973-3000** for info on special events, or 416/973-4000 for the box office. www.harbourfront.on.ca. Take the LRT from Union Station.

In 1972, the federal government took over this 96-acre strip of prime land to preserve the waterfront vista—and since then Torontonians have rediscovered their lakeshore. Abandoned warehouses, shabby depots, and crumbling factories were refurbished, and a tremendous urban park now stretches on and around the old piers. Today it's one of the most popular hangouts for locals and visitors—a great place to spend a day sunbathing, picnicking, biking, shopping, and sailing.

Queen's Quay, at the foot of York Street, is the first quay you'll encounter as you approach from the Westin Harbour Castle. From here, boats depart for tours of the harbor and ferries leave for the Toronto Islands. In this renovated warehouse you'll find the **Premiere Dance Theatre** (specially designed for dance performances) and two floors of shops, restaurants, and waterfront cafes.

After exploring Queen's Quay, walk west along the glorious waterfront promenade to **York Quay,** passing the **Power Plant,** a contemporary art gallery, and behind it, the **Du Maurier Theatre Centre.** At **York Quay Centre** you can secure a lot of information on Harbourfront programming, as well as entertain yourself at one of several galleries, including **The Craft Studio,** where you can watch artisans blow glass, throw pots, and make silk-screen prints. On the other side of the center, you can attend a free Molson Dry Front Music outdoor concert, held all summer long at Molson Place. Also on the quay is the **Water's Edge Cafe,** overlooking a small pond for electric model boats (there's skating in winter) and a children's play area.

From here, take the footbridge to John Quay, crossing over the sailboats moored below, to the stores and restaurants on **Pier 4—Wallymagoo's Marine Bar** and the **Pier 4 Storehouse.** Beyond on Maple Leaf Quay lies the **Nautical Centre.**

At the **Harbourside Boating Centre,** 283 Queen's Quay W. (☎ **416/203-3000**), you can rent sail- and powerboats or sign up for sailing lessons. A 3-hour sailboat rental costs C$60 (US$40) and up, depending on the boat size. Powerboats cost C$95 (US$63) and up. Weeklong and weekend sailing courses are also offered.

The **Harbourfront Antiques Market,** 390 Queen's Quay W., at the foot of Spadina Avenue (☎ **416/260-2626**), will keep antiques lovers busy browsing for hours. More than 100 antiques dealers spread out their wares—jewelry, china, furniture, toys, and books. Indoor parking is adjacent to the market, and a cafeteria serves fresh salads, sandwiches, and desserts. It's open Tuesday to Sunday 10am to 6pm.

At the west end of the park stands **Bathurst Pier,** with a large sports field for romping around, plus two adventure playgrounds, one for older kids and the other (supervised) for 3- to 7-year-olds.

More than 4,000 events take place annually at the Harbourfront, including the **Harbourfront Reading Series** in June and the **International Festival of Authors** in October, both of which have attracted top writers like Salman Rushdie, Margaret Atwood, and A. S. Byatt. Other happenings include films, dance, theater, music, children's events, multicultural festivals, and marine events.

⚫ Toronto Islands. ☎ **416/392-8193** for ferry schedules. Round-trip fare C$4 (US$2.65) adults, C$2 (US$1.35) seniors/ages 15–19, C$1 (US$65¢) children 14 and under. Ferries operate all day, leaving from the docks at the bottom of Bay St. Subway: Union Station, then the LRT south.

In only 7 minutes, an 800-passenger ferry will take you across to 612 acres of island parkland crisscrossed by shaded paths and quiet waterways—a glorious spot to walk, play tennis, bike, feed the ducks, putter around in boats, picnic, or lap up the sun. There are 14 islands in total, but the 3 major ones are **Centre, Ward's,** and **Algonquin.** The first is the busiest; the other two are home to about 600 people living in modest cottages. Originally, the land was a peninsula, but in the mid-1800s a series of storms shattered the finger of land into islands.

On Centre Island, families enjoy **Centreville** (☎ 416/203-0405), a 19-acre old-fashioned amusement park. You won't see the usual neon signs and shrill hawkers or smell the aroma of greasy hot-dog stands. Instead you'll find an early-1900s village complete with a Main Street, tiny shops, a firehouse, and even a small working farm where the kids can pet lambs and chicks and enjoy pony rides. They'll also love trying out the antique cars, fire engines, old-fashioned train, authentic 1890s carousel, flume ride, and aerial cars. Individual rides (19 of them) cost from C$1.30 to C$3.50 (US85¢ to US$2.35). An all-day pass is C$12 (US$8) for those 4 feet tall and under and C$18 (US$12) for those over 4 feet. Mid-May to Labour Day, Centreville is open daily 10:30am to 6pm (plus weekends early May and Sept).

Downtown

CN Tower. 301 Front St. W. ☎ **416/360-8500.** www.cntower.ca. Admission C$16 (US$11) adults, C$14 (US$9) seniors, C$11 (US$7) children 5–12. Motion simulator rides C$8 (US$5). Combination tickets available from C$22 (US$15). May–Sept daily 8am–11pm; Oct–Apr daily 9am–10pm.

As you approach the city, whether by plane, train, or auto, the first thing you'll notice is this slender structure shooting toward the sky. Glass-walled elevators glide up the 1,815-foot tower—still the tallest freestanding structure in the world. First, the elevators stop at the Look Out Level, 1,136 feet up from the ground (it takes just under a minute, so prepare for popping ears). From here, on a clear day you can't quite see forever, but the sweeping vista stretches to Niagara Falls and even to Buffalo in the south and to Lake Simcoe in the north. For an extra C$4 (US$2.65), you can take the elevator up to the Sky Pod, hovering 1,465 feet above ground. The view is even more dramatic than that at the Look Out Level, but C$4 per person seems like a steep price to pay for it.

Attractions are often revamped at the tower. Among the most recent new draws are the **IMAX theater,** which shows a film of a cross-Canada journey; two **simulator airplane trips,** one gentle and calm, the other rocketing riders through caves and over mountains; and a series of **interactive displays** showcasing the CN Tower along with such forerunners as the Eiffel Tower and the Empire State Building. The pod also contains broadcasting facilities, a nightclub, and **360,** a revolving restaurant (for lunch, dinner, or Sunday brunch reservations, call ☎ 416/362-5411).

Atop the tower sits a 335-foot antenna mast that took 31 weeks to erect with the aid of a giant Sikorsky helicopter. It took 55 lifts to complete the operation. Above the sky pod is the world's highest public observation gallery, the **Space Deck,** 1,465 feet above the ground (C$4/US$2.65 extra charge). The **Observation Deck** one floor below has a nerve-jangling glass floor. But don't worry about the elements sweeping the tower into the lake: It's built of contoured reinforced concrete covered with thick glass-reinforced plastic designed to keep ice accumulation to a minimum. The structure can withstand high winds, snow, ice, lightning, and earth tremors.

○ Art Gallery of Ontario. 317 Dundas St. W., between McCaul and Beverley sts. ☎ **416/977-0414.** Admission is pay what you can with suggestion of C$5 (US$3.35) per adult; up to C$12 (US$8) for special exhibits. Art Gallery: Tues–Fri noon–9pm, Sat–Sun 10am–5:30pm. The Grange: Tues–Sun noon–4pm, Wed noon–9pm. Closed Dec 25 and Jan 1. Subway: St. Patrick.

The exterior gives no hint of the light and openness inside this beautifully designed gallery. The space is dramatic, the paintings are imaginatively displayed, and throughout are audiovisual presentations and interactive computer presentations providing details on particular paintings or schools of painters.

The European collections are fine, but the **Canadian galleries** are the real treat. The collection of paintings by the Group of Seven—which includes Tom Thomson, F. H. Varley, and Lawren Harris—is extraordinary. In addition, other galleries show the genesis of Canadian art from earlier to more modern artists. And don't miss the extensive collection of Inuit art.

The **Henry Moore Sculpture Centre,** with more than 800 pieces (original plasters, bronzes, maquettes, woodcuts, lithographs, etchings, and drawings), is the largest public collection of his works. They were given to Toronto by the artist because he was so moved by the citizens' enthusiasm for his work (public donations bought his sculpture *The Archer* to decorate Nathan Phillips Square at City Hall after politicians refused to free up money for it). In one room, under a glass ceiling, 20 or so of his large works stand like silent prehistoric rock formations. Along the walls flanking a ramp are color photographs showing Moore's major sculptures in their natural locations, fully revealing their magnificent dimensions.

The collection of European old masters ranges from the 14th century to the French impressionists and beyond. An octagonal room is filled with works by Pissarro, Monet, Boudin, Sisley, and Renoir. De Kooning's *Two Women on a Wharf* and Karel Appel's *Black Landscape* are just two of the more modern examples. There are several works of particular interest to admirers of the pre-Raphaelite painters, including one by Waterhouse. Among the sculptures are Picasso's *Poupée* and Brancusi's *First Cry,* two beauties.

Behind the gallery and connected by an arcade stands **The Grange** (1817), Toronto's oldest surviving brick house and the gallery's first permanent space. Originally the home of the Boulton family, it was a gathering place for many of the city's social and political leaders, as well as for such eminent guests as Matthew Arnold, Prince Kropotkin, and Winston Churchill. Today it's a living museum of mid–19th-century Toronto life, having been meticulously restored and furnished to reflect the 1830s. Entrance is free with admission to the art gallery.

The gallery has an attractive restaurant, Agora (open for lunch), as well as a cafeteria and a gallery shop; there's also a full program of films, concerts, and lectures.

MIDTOWN

○ Royal Ontario Museum. 100 Queen's Park Crescent. ☎ **416/586-8000.** www.rom.on.ca. Admission C$10 (US$7) adults, C$5 (US$3.35) seniors/students/children 4–17, C$22 (US$15) families; children 3 and under free; pay what you can Tues 4:30–8pm. Mon–Sat 10am–6pm (to 8pm Tues), Sun 11am–6pm. Closed Dec 25 and Jan 1. Subway: Museum.

The ROM, as it's affectionately called, is Canada's largest museum, with more than 6 million objects in its collections. Among the many highlights are the world-renowned **T. T. Tsui Galleries of Chinese Art,** including priceless Ming and Qing porcelains, embroidered silk robes, and jade and ivory objects. One of the collection's treasures is the procession of 100 **earthenware figures,** with ox-drawn carts, soldiers, musicians, officials, and attendants from the early 6th to the late 7th century. Another is the

14 monumental **Buddhist sculptures** from the 12th to the 16th century. You can also see outstanding examples of early weapons and tools, oracle bones, bronzes, ceramic vessels, human and animal figures, and jewelry.

The **Sigmund Samuel Canadiana Galleries** display a premier collection of early Canadian decorative arts and historical paintings. The more than 1,200 objects show-cased in elaborate period-room settings reveal in a concrete way the French and English contributions to Canadian culture. Other must-sees are the **Ancient Egypt Gallery** (with several mummies), the **Roman Gallery** (the most extensive collection in Canada), the excellent **textile collection,** nine **life-science galleries** (devoted to evolution, mammals, reptiles, and botany), and the **Gallery of Indigenous Peoples** (with changing exhibits exploring the past and present cultures of Canada's indigenous peoples). Two recent additions are the **Gallery of Korean Art** (the largest exhibit of its kind in North America, with more than 200 works from the Bronze Age to today) and the **Joey and Toby Tanenbaum Gallery** (devoted to Byzantine art, with more than 300 objects—icons, frescoes, mosaics, gold jewelry, coins, and glassware).

A kids' favorite is the **Bat Cave Gallery,** a miniature replica of the St. Clair bat cave in Jamaica, complete with more than 3,000 lifelike bats roosting and flying through the air amid realistic spiders, crabs, a wildcat, and snakes. Kids also enjoy the spectac-ular **Dinosaur Gallery,** with 13 dinosaur skeletons realistically displayed, and the **Discovery Gallery,** a minimuseum where kids and adults alike can touch authentic artifacts from Egyptian scarabs to English military helmets.

George R. Gardiner Museum of Ceramic Art. 111 Queen's Park. ☎ **416/586-8080.** Suggested donation C$5 (US$3.35). Mon–Sat 10am–5pm (to 8pm Tues), Sun 11am–5pm. Closed Dec 25 and Jan 1. Subway: Museum or St. George.

Across from the ROM (above), North America's only specialized ceramics museum houses a great collection of 15th- to 18th-century European ceramics in four galleries. The pre-Columbian gallery contains fantastic Olmec and Maya figures, as well as objects from Ecuador, Colombia, and Peru. The majolica gallery displays spectacular 16th- and 17th-century salvers and other pieces from Florence, Faenza, and Venice, plus a Delftware collection of fine 17th-century chargers and other examples. Upstairs, the galleries are given over to 18th-century continental and English porce-lain—Meissen, Sèvres, Worcester, Chelsea, Derby, and other great names. Among the highlights are pieces from the Swan Service—a 2,200-piece set that took 4 years (1737 to 1741) to make—and an extraordinary collection of *commedia dell'arte* figures.

ON THE OUTSKIRTS

✪ **Ontario Science Centre.** 770 Don Mills Rd. (at Eglinton Ave. E.). ☎ **416/696-3127,** or 416/696-1000 for Omnimax tickets. www.osc.on.ca. Admission C$10 (US$7) adults, C$7 (US$4.65) seniors/youths 13–17, C$6 (US$4) children 5–12; children 4 and under free. Omnimax admission C$9 (US$6) adults, C$6 (US$4) seniors/youth 13–17, C$6 (US$3.65) children 5–12. Special discounts apply if you attend both. Daily 10am–5pm. Closed Dec 25. Parking C$5 (US$3.35). Take the Yonge St. subway to Eglinton, then the Eglinton bus going east; get off at Don Mills Rd. If you're driving from downtown, take the Don Valley Pkwy. and follow the signs from Don Mills Rd. north.

Described as everything from the world's most technical fun fair to a hands-on museum for the 21st century, the Science Centre really does hold a series of wonders for adults and children—800 interactive exhibits in 10 cavernous exhibit halls. With more than a million people visiting every year, it's best to arrive promptly at 10am so you'll be able to get around with less hassle.

Everywhere you look are things to touch, push, pull, or crank. Test your reflexes, balance, heart rate, or grip strength; surf the Internet; walk through a tropical rain forest; watch frozen-solid liquid nitrogen shatter into thousands of icy shards; study slides of butterfly wings, bedbugs, fish scales, or feathers under the microscope; tease your brain with optical illusions; land a spaceship on the moon; watch bees making honey; see how many lights you can light or how high you can elevate a balloon with your own pedal power. The fun goes on and on. Throughout are small theaters with film and slide shows, plus regular 20-minute demonstrations of lasers, metal casting, and high-voltage electricity (watch your friend's hair stand on end). And the Omnimax Theatre features a 24-meter domed screen that creates spectacular effects. Facilities include a licensed restaurant and lounge, cafeteria, and science shop.

✪ **Toronto Zoo.** Meadowvale Rd. (north of Hwy. 401 and Sheppard Ave.), Scarborough. ☎ **416/392-5900.** www.torontozoo.com. Admission C$12 (US$8) adults, C$9 (US$6) seniors/children 12–17, C$7 (US$4.65) children 4–11; children 3 and under free. Summer daily 9am–7:30pm; spring and fall daily 9am–5pm; winter daily 9:30am–4:30pm. Last admission 1 hour before closing. Closed Dec 25. Take the subway to Kennedy on the Bloor–Danforth line. Then take bus no. 86A north. Check with the TTC for schedules at ☎ **416/393-4636.** Driving from downtown, take the Don Valley Pkwy. to Hwy. 401 east and exit on Meadowvale Rd.

Covering 710 acres of Scarborough parkland is a unique zoological garden containing some 5,000 animals, plus an extensive botanical collection. The plants and animals are housed either in pavilions—including Africa, Indo-Malaya, Australasia, and the Americas—or in outdoor paddocks. It's a photographer's dream. The latest excitement here is at the **African Savannah** project, which re-creates an African market bazaar and safari through Kesho (meaning "tomorrow") National Park past such special features as a bush camp, a rhino midden, an elephant highway, and several watering holes. Six miles of walkways offer access to all areas. During the warm months, the Zoomobile takes you around the major walkways to view the animals contained in the outdoor paddocks.

Facilities include restaurants, a gift shop, first aid, and a family center; strollers, wagons, and wheelchairs are available. The zoo is equipped with ramps and washrooms for those with disabilities, and the African pavilion is equipped with an elevator for strollers and wheelchairs. There are ample parking and plenty of picnic areas with tables.

McMichael Canadian Art Collection. 10365 Islington Ave., Kleinburg. ☎ **905/893-1121.** www.mcmichael.com. Admission C$8 (US$5) adults, C$6 (US$4) seniors/students; children under 5 free. May–Oct daily 10am–5pm; Nov–Apr Tues–Sat 10am–4pm, Sun 10am–5pm. From downtown, take the Gardiner Expwy. to Hwy. 427 north, following it to Hwy. 7. Go east at Hwy. 7 and turn left (north) at the first light onto Hwy. 27. Turn right (east) at Major Mackenzie Dr. and left (north) at the first set of traffic lights to Islington Ave. and the village of Kleinburg. Or take the 401 to Hwy. 400 north. At Major Mackenzie Dr., go west to Islington Ave. and take a right to get to the gallery. Buses travel to the Gallery from Bay and Dundas station and the Yorkdale GO station. Bus service (C$20/US$13 adult, C$17/US$11 youth, under 4 free) is available from key downtown hotels.

In Kleinburg, 25 miles north of the city, the McMichael is worth a visit—for the setting as well as the art. The gallery began in 1965 when Robert and Signe McMichael donated their property, home, and collection to Ontario. Since then, the collection has expanded to include more than 6,000 works displayed in a log-and-stone gallery amid quiet stands of trees on 100 acres of conservation land. Specially designed for the landscape paintings it houses, the gallery is a work of art itself: The lobby has a pitched roof soaring to 27 feet on massive Douglas fir rafters; throughout, panoramic windows look south over white pine, cedar, ash, and birch.

The work of Canada's famous group of landscape painters, the Group of Seven, as well as David Milne, Emily Carr, and their contemporaries, is displayed. These artists, inspired by the early-1900s Canadian wilderness, particularly in Algonquin Park and northern Ontario, recorded the rugged landscape in highly individualistic styles. An impressive collection of Inuit and contemporary Native Canadian art and sculpture is also shown. In addition, four galleries are dedicated to changing exhibits of works by contemporary artists. The museum has a good book and gift store and a fine restaurant serving Canadian cuisine.

Paramount Canada's Wonderland. 9580 Jane St., Vaughan. ☎ **905/832-7000,** or 905/832-8131. www.canadaswonderland.com. Pay-One-Price Passport, including a day's unlimited rides and shows (excluding parking, special attractions, and the Kingswood Music Theatre) C$43 (US$29) adults, C$21 (US$14) seniors/children 3–6; children 2 and under free. Grounds admission only (no rides) C$25 (US$17). June 1–25 Mon–Fri 10am–8pm, Fri–Sat 10am–10pm. June 26–Labour Day daily 10am–10pm; Mid- and late May to early Oct weekends only 10am–8pm. Closed early Oct to early May. Parking: C$7 (US$4.35). Take subway to Yorkdale or York Mills, then GO Express Bus directly to Wonderland. If you're driving, take Yonge St. north to Hwy. 401 and travel west to Hwy. 400. Go north on Hwy. 400 to the Rutherford Rd. exit and follow the signs. Exit at Major MacKenzie, if you're going south.

Thirty minutes north of Toronto lies Canada's answer to Disney World. The 300-acre park features more than 140 attractions, including 50 rides, the 20-acre Splash Works water park, a participatory play area called Kid's Kingdom, and live shows. Because the park relies on the local audience, new rides are introduced every year. The newest addition is the **Fly** roller coaster, designed to make every seat feel like it's in the front car (the faint-of-heart can't hide at the back!). Other stomach-churners are the **Drop Zone,** in which you free-fall 230 feet in an open cockpit, and the **Xtreme Skyflyer,** a hang-gliding and skydiving hybrid that plunges you 150 feet in a free fall. The most popular rides are the nine **roller coasters,** ranging from a nostalgic, relatively tame wooden version to the looping inverted **Top Gun,** the stand-up looping **Sky Rider,** and the suspended **Vortex. Splash Works** offers a huge wave pool and 16 water rides from speed slides and tube rides to special scaled-down slides and a water-play area. To add to the thrills for *Star Trek*–loving kids and adults, Klingons, Vulcans, Romulans, and Bajorans (along with Hanna-Barbera characters) stroll around the park. Other attractions include the **Speedcity Raceway** (with two-seater go-karts), minigolf, batting cages, restaurants, shops, and the **Kingswood Theatre** (hosting top-name entertainers).

MORE ATTRACTIONS
ARCHITECTURAL HIGHLIGHTS

✪ **Casa Loma.** 1 Austin Terrace, next to Spadina (below). ☎ **416/923-1171.** www. casaloma.org. Admission C$9 (US$6) adults, C$6 (US$3.65) seniors/youths, C$5 (US$3.35) children 4–13. Daily 9:30am–4pm. Closed Dec 25 and Jan 1. Subway: Dupont, then walk 2 blocks north.

Every city has its folly, and Toronto's is a charming one—complete with Elizabethan-style chimneys, Rhineland turrets, secret passageways, an 800-foot underground tunnel, and a mellifluous-sounding name: Casa Loma. Sir Henry Pellatt, who built it between 1911 and 1914 at a cost of C$3.5 million (US$2.3 million) (plus C$1.5 million/US$1 million for furnishings), had a lifelong romantic fascination with castles. He studied medieval palaces and gathered materials and furnishings from around the world, bringing marble, glass, and paneling from Europe; teak from Asia; and oak and walnut from prime areas of North America. He imported Scottish stonemasons to build the massive walls surrounding the 6-acre site.

It's a fascinating place to explore: the majestic **Great Hall,** with a 60-foot-high hammer-beam ceiling; the **Oak Room,** where three artisans took 3 years to fashion the paneling; the **Conservatory,** with elegant bronze doors, a stained-glass dome, and pink and green marble; the **battlements** and **tower; Peacock Alley,** designed after Windsor Castle; **Sir Henry's suite,** containing a shower with an 18-inch-diameter shower head; the 1,700-bottle **wine cellar;** and the 800-foot **tunnel** to the **stables,** where horses were quartered amid the luxury of Spanish tile and mahogany. The tour is self-guided; you'll be given an audio cassette, available in eight languages, on arrival. May to October, the gardens are open too. Special events are scheduled in March, July, and December.

✪ **City Hall.** Queen St. W. ☎ **416/338-0338.** www.city.toronto.on.ca. Free admission. Mon–Fri 8:30am–4:30pm. Subway: Queen; then walk west to Bay or take the Queen St. streetcar west 1 stop.

Daringly designed in the late 1950s by Finnish architect Viljo Revell, City Hall consists of a low podium topped by the flying saucer–shaped Council Chamber, enfolded between two curved towers. Its interior is as dramatic as its exterior, and it houses the mayor's office and the city's administrative offices, as well as a cafeteria and a dining room. In front stretches **Nathan Phillips Square** (named after the mayor who initiated the project), where in summer you can sit and contemplate the gardens, fountains, and reflecting pool (which doubles as a skating rink in winter) and listen to concerts. Here also stands Henry Moore's *Three-Way Piece No. 2,* locally referred to as *The Archer,* bought through a public subscription fund, and the **Peace Garden,** commemorating Toronto's sesquicentennial in 1984. In contrast, to the east stands the **Old City Hall,** a green copper–roofed Victorian Romanesque building.

Royal Bank Plaza. Front and Bay sts. Free admission. Year-round. Subway: Union.

Shimmering in the sun, the Royal Bank Plaza looks like a pillar of gold—and with good reason. During its construction, 2,500 ounces of gold were used as a coloring agent in the building's 14,000 windows. It's an architectural masterpiece: Two triangular towers of bronze mirror glass flank a 130-foot-high glass-walled banking hall. The towers' external walls are built in a serrated configuration so they reflect a phenomenal mosaic of color from the skies and surrounding buildings. In the banking hall, hundreds of aluminum cylinders hang from the ceiling, the work of Venezuelan sculptor Jesus Raphael Soto. Two levels below are a waterfall and a pine-tree setting naturally illuminated from the hall above.

Fort York. Garrison Rd., off Fleet St. (between Bathurst St. and Strachan Ave.). ☎ **416/392-6907.** Admission C$5 (US$3.35) adults, C$3.25 (US$2.15) seniors/ages 13–18, C$3 (US$2) children 6–12. June–Oct Mon–Wed and Fri 10am–5pm, Thurs 10am–7pm, Sat–Sun noon–5pm; Nov–May Tues–Fri 10am–5pm, Sat–Sun noon–5pm. Subway: Bathurst; then streetcar no. 511 south.

Established by Lieutenant Governor Simcoe in 1793 to defend "little muddy York," as Toronto was then known, Fort York was sacked by Americans in 1813. You can tour the soldiers' and officers' quarters and clamber over the ramparts, as well as view demonstrations. In summer, the fort really comes to life, with daily demonstrations of drill, music, and cooking. It's a few blocks west of the CN Tower and 2 blocks east of Exhibition Place.

Osgoode Hall. 130 Queen St. W. ☎ **416/947-3300.** Free admission. Tours given July–Aug Mon–Fri at 1:15pm. Subway: Osgoode.

To the west of City Hall extends an impressive wrought-iron fence in front of an equally gracious public building, Osgoode Hall. Construction began in 1829, troops were billeted here after the Rebellion of 1837, and it's now the home of the Law Society of Upper Canada and Ontario's Court of Appeal. Folklore has it the fence was built to keep cows from trampling the flower beds. Tours of the interior show the splendor of the grand staircase, the rotunda, the Great Library, and the portrait and sculpture collection. The several magnificent courtrooms include one built with materials from London's Old Bailey. The courts are open to the public.

Spadina. 285 Spadina Rd., next to Casa Loma (above). ☎ **416/392-6910.** Admission C$5 (US$3.35) adults, C$3.25 (US$2.15) seniors/youth, C$3 (US$2) children 12 and under. Tues–Fri noon–4pm, Sat–Sun noon–5pm. Subway: Dupont.

If you want to know how the leaders of the Family Compact lived, visit this historic home of financier James Austin. The exterior isn't that imposing, but the interior contains a remarkable collection of art, furniture, and decorative objects. The same family, the Austins, occupied the house from 1866 to 1980, which accounts for the richness of the collections. Tours are mandatory. In summer, you can also tour the gardens; during the Christmas season the house is decorated authentically.

MUSEUMS

Black Creek Pioneer Village. 1000 Murray Ross Pkwy., Downsview (Steeles Ave. and Jane St.). ☎ **416/736-1733.** Admission C$8 (US$5) adults, C$6 (US$4) seniors, C$4 (US$2.65) children/students; children under 4 free. May–June weekdays 9:30am–4:30pm, weekends and holidays 10am–5pm; July–Sept daily 10am–5pm; Oct–Dec weekdays 9:30am–4pm, weekends and holidays 10am–4:30pm. Closed Dec 25 and Jan 1–Apr 30. Subway: Finch; then take bus no. 60 to Jane St.

Life here moves at the gentle pace of rural Ontario as it was a hundred years ago. You can watch the authentically dressed villagers going about their chores, spinning, sewing, rail splitting, sheepshearing, and threshing; enjoy their cooking; wander through the cozily furnished homesteads; visit the working mill; shop at the general store; or rumble past the farm animals in a horse-drawn wagon. There are more than 30 restored buildings to explore in this beautifully landscaped village. Special events are offered throughout the year, from a great Easter-egg hunt to Christmas by lamplight.

The Pier: Toronto's Waterfront Museum. 245 Queens Quay W. ☎ **416/338-PIER.** Admission C$9 (US$6) adults, C$7 (US$4.35) seniors/teenagers 13–18, C$6 (US$3.65) children 12 and under. Tues–Fri 10am–4pm, Sat–Sun noon–5pm. Subway: Union, then take the LRT.

This new museum explores the history of nautical travel. Many of its exhibits are strictly hands-on, so it's popular with kids. You can explore a shipwreck, guide a ship through a series of canals, or watch special exhibits about the ancient art of shipbuilding.

SPORTS HIGHLIGHTS

Air Canada Centre. 40 Bay St. (at Lakeshore Blvd.). ☎ **416/815-5500.** Tours C$9 (US$6) adults, C$7 (US$4.65) students/seniors, C$6 (US$4) children 12 and under. Tours on the hour Mon–Sat 10am–3pm and Sun 11am–3pm; events can disrupt this schedule, so call ahead. Subway: Union, then take the LRT.

Toronto's newest sports-and-entertainment complex is now home to the Toronto Maple Leafs and the Toronto Raptors. While longtime hockey fans were crushed when the Leafs moved here from Maple Leaf Gardens—the arena that had housed the team since 1931—the Air Canada Centre has quickly become a fan favorite. Seating 18,700 for hockey games, 19,500 for basketball, and an even 20,000 for concerts, the center was designed with comfort in mind. Seats are on a steeper-than-usual grade so even the "nosebleed" sections have decent sight lines; and the cushions are wider and upholstered.

Canada Sports Hall of Fame. Exhibition Place. ☎ **416/260-6789.** Free admission. Mon–Fri 10am–4:30pm. Subway: Bathurst; then take streetcar no. 511 south to the end of the line.

In the center of Exhibition Place, this three-floor sports hall is devoted to the country's greatest athletes in all major sports. It offers displays complemented by touch-screen computers that tell you everything you could want to know about particular sports personalities and Canada's sports heritage.

✪ **Hockey Hall of Fame.** 30 Yonge St. at Front St. in BCE Place. ☎ **416/360-7765.** Admission C$10 (US$7) adults, C$6 (US$3.65) seniors/children 3–13; children 2 and under free. Summer Mon–Sat 9:30am–6pm, Sun 10am–6pm; winter Mon–Fri 10am–5pm, Sat 9:30am–6pm, Sun 10:30am–5pm. Closed Dec 25 and Jan 1. Subway: Union.

Ice-hockey fans will be thrilled to see the original Stanley Cup (donated in 1893 by Lord Stanley of Preston), a replica of the Montréal Canadiens' locker room, Terry Sawchuck's goalie gear, Newsy Lalonde's skates, and the stick Max Bentley used, along with photographs of the personalities and great moments in hockey history. The best fun is at the shooting and goalkeeping interactive displays, where you can take a whack at targets with a puck or don goalie gear and face down flying video or sponge pucks.

SkyDome. 1 Blue Jays Way. ☎ **416/341-2770.** www.skydome.com. Tours C$10 (US$6) adults, C$7 (US$4.65) seniors/students 16 and under, C$6 (US$4) children 4–11; children 3 and under free. Tour schedule depends on events/sports schedule, so call ahead (tours usually begin on the hour). Subway: Union.

In 1989, the opening of the 53,000-seat SkyDome, home to the Toronto Blue Jays baseball team and the Toronto Argonauts football team, was a gala event. In 1992, the SkyDome became the first Canadian stadium to host the World Series, with the Blue Jays winning the championship for the first of two consecutive years. The stadium itself represents an engineering feat, featuring the world's first fully retractable roof, spanning more than 8 acres, and a gigantic video scoreboard. It's so large you could fit a 31-story building inside the complex when the roof is closed. Indeed, there's already an 11-story hotel with 70 rooms facing directly onto the field.

PARKS & GARDENS

The **Allan Gardens,** bordered by Jarvis, Sherbourne, Carlton, and Gerrard streets (☎ **416/392-7259;** Subway: Dundas), is now just a small grassy park because the gardens are gone. However, the glass-domed Palm House still stands in all its radiant Victorian glory. Be aware that the area is rather seedy and should be avoided at night. Admission is free, and the park is open daily dawn to dusk.

The quiet, formal 35-acre **Edwards Gardens,** Lawrence Avenue and Leslie Street (☎ **416/397-1340;** Subway: Eglinton, then take the Leslie or Lawrence bus), with a creek cutting through it, is part of a 600-acre series of parks stretching along the Don Valley. Gracious bridges arch over the creek, rock gardens abound, and rose and other seasonal flower beds add color and scent. The garden is famous for its rhododendrons. Admission is free, and it's open daily dawn to dusk. The 400-acre **High Park,** in the West End, extending south of Bloor Street to the Gardiner Expressway (Subway: High Park), contains a large lake called Grenadier Pond (great for skating in winter), a small zoo, a pool, tennis courts, sports fields, bowling greens, and vast expanses of green for baseball, jogging, picnicking, bicycling, and more. Admission is free, and it's open daily dawn to dusk.

ESPECIALLY FOR KIDS

The city puts on a fabulous array of special events for children at the **Harbourfront Centre.** In March, the **Children's Film Festival** screens 40 films from 15 countries. In April, **Spring Fever** celebrates the season with egg decorating, puppet shows, and more; on Saturday mornings in April, **cushion concerts** are given for the 5-to-12 set. And in May, the **Milk International Children's Festival** brings 100 international kids' performers to the city for a week of great entertainment. For details, call ☎ **416/ 973-3000.**

For the past 30 years, the **Young Peoples Theatre,** 165 Front St. E., at Sherbourne Street (☎ **416/862-2222** box office or 416/363-5131 administration), has been entertaining young people. Its season runs August to May.

Look in the sections above for the following Toronto-area attractions that have major appeal for kids of all ages. The first five on the list are tied for best venue, at least from a kid's point of view. The others will appeal to more specialized interests.

- **Ontario Science Centre**   Kids race to be the first at this paradise of fun hands-on games, experiments, and push-button demonstrations—800 of 'em.
- **Paramount Canada's Wonderland**   The kids can't wait to get on the roller coasters and daredevil rides in this theme park. But watch out for those video games—an unanticipated extra cost.
- **Harbourfront**   Kaleidoscope is an ongoing program of creative crafts, active games, and special events on weekends and holidays. There are also a summer pond, winter ice skating, and a crafts studio.
- **Ontario Place**   The Children's Village, water slides, a huge Cinesphere, a futuristic pod, and other entertainment are the big hits at this recreational/cultural park on three artificial islands on the edge of Lake Ontario. In the Children's Village, kids 12 and under can scramble over rope bridges, bounce on an enormous trampoline, or drench one another in the water-play section.
- **Toronto Zoo**   This is one of the best in the world, modeled after San Diego's—the animals in this 710-acre park really do live in a natural environment.
- **Toronto Islands—Centreville**   Riding a ferry to this early-1900s amusement park is part of the fun.
- **CN Tower**   The tower is especially popular for the interactive simulator games and the terror of the glass floor.
- **Royal Ontario Museum**   The top hits are always the dinosaurs and the spooky bat cave.
- **Fort York**   Head here for reenactments of battle drills, musket and cannon firing, and musical marches with fife and drum.
- **Hockey Hall of Fame**   Who wouldn't want the chance to goalkeep against Mark Messier and Wayne Gretzky (with a sponge puck) and to practice scoring and keeping up with the fun and challenging video pucks?
- **Black Creek Pioneer Village**   The craft and other demonstrations here will appeal to most kids.
- **Casa Loma**   The stables, secret passageway, and fantasy rooms really capture children's imaginations.
- **The Pier: Toronto's Waterfront Museum**   Here's a perfect place for any child fascinated by boats and shipwrecks.
- **Art Gallery of Ontario**   A big draw here is its hands-on kids' exhibit.

Children's Own Museum. 90 Queen's Park, in the McLaughlin Planetarium Building. ☎ **416/542-1492.** Admission C$3.75 (US$2.50). Tues 10am–8pm, Wed–Sat 10am–5pm, Sun noon–5pm. Subway: Museum.

The ROM's next-door neighbor is another favorite with tykes. At the Children's Own Museum, everything is designed with kids 1 to 8 in mind. This interactive learn-while-you-play center includes a sensory tunnel, a construction site, a garden, an animal clinic, and a theater. The museum has well-trained staff on hand to answer kiddies' endless questions.

◑ Riverdale Farm. 201 Winchester St., off Parliament, 1 block north of Carlton. ☎ **416/392-6794.** Free admission. Daily 9am–5pm.

Idyllically situated on the edge of the Don Valley Ravine, this working farm right in the city is a favorite with small tots who enjoy watching the cows and pigs and petting the other farm animals. There are farming demonstrations daily at 10:30am and 1:30pm.

Wild Water Kingdom. Finch Ave., 1 mile west of Hwy. 427, Brampton. ☎ **416/369-0774** or 905/794-0565. Admission C$19 (US$13) adults, C$15 (US$10) children 4–9. May 31 to mid-June weekends 10am–6pm, Late June–Labour Day daily 10am–8pm. Note that openings are weather-dependent.

This huge water-theme park comes complete with a 20,000-square-foot wave pool, tube slides, speed slides, giant hot tubs, and the super-thrilling Cyclone water ride. There are bumper boats, pedal boats, canoes, batting cages, and minigolf too.

6 Special Events & Festivals

February is a busy month. The **Chinese New Year** is ushered in with traditional and contemporary performances of Chinese opera, dancing, music, and more; for Harbourfront events, call ☎ 416/973-3000, or for the SkyDome, call ☎ 877/ 666-3838. The 3-day **Winterfest** celebration is spread over various neighborhoods and features ice-skating shows, snow play, midway rides, performances, and ice sculpting; for details, call ☎ 416/338-0338. During the last weekend of the month is the **Toronto Festival of Storytelling** at the Harbourfront Centre, which features 60 storytellers imparting legends and fables from around the world; call ☎ 416/ 973-3000 for details.

In late April, the **Sante—The Bloor-Yorkville Wine Festival** is a 4-day gourmet extravaganza bringing together the award-winning Ontario vintages, food from the city's top-rated chefs, and live jazz; call ☎ 416/504-3977 for details. May brings the **Milk International Children's Festival** at Harbourfront, a 9-day celebration of the arts for kids—from theater and music to dance, comedy, and storytelling.

June boasts the **Harbourfront Reading Series,** celebrating the best of Canadian literature. Top writers like Timothy Findley, Anne Michaels, and Barbara Gowdy flock here to read from their latest works; call ☎ 416/973-3000 for details. Alternative music fans flock to the 3-day **North by Northeast Festival,** featuring rock and indie bands at 28 venues around Toronto; call ☎ 416/469-0986 for details. Toronto's multicultural diversity is celebrated at the 9-day **Toronto International Festival Caravan,** with more than 40 themed pavilions, craft demonstrations, opportunities to sample authentic dishes, and traditional dance performances by 100 cultural groups; call ☎ 416/977-0466 for details. The last week in June is **Gay and Lesbian Pride Celebration,** and the week of events, performances, symposiums, and parties culminates in an extravagant Sunday parade; call ☎ 416/92PRIDE or 416/927-7433 for details. For sports lovers, there is the **Queen's Plate** at the Woodbine Race Track, in which the world's best thoroughbreds compete in the second leg of the Triple Crown; for details, call ☎ 416/675-7223.

July's most important event is the 2-week **Caribana.** Toronto's version of Carnival features traditional foods from the Caribbean and Latin America, ferry cruises, island picnics, children's events, concerts, and arts-and-crafts exhibits. It draws more than a million people from across North America and Britain; call ☎ 416/465-4884 for details. On the third weekend of July is the **Molson Indy** at the Exhibition Place Street circuit, one of Canada's major races on the IndyCar circuit; call ☎ 416/ 922-7477 for details.

August brings the **Canadian National Exhibition** at Exhibition Place. One of the world's largest fairs, this 18-day extravaganza features midway rides, display buildings, free shows, and grandstand performers; call ☎ **416/393-6000** for details. In September, the city is lit by stars at the ✪ **Toronto International Film Festival.** Second only to Cannes, the 10-day festival features more than 250 films from 70 countries; call ☎ **416/967-FILM** for details. October boasts the **International Festival of Authors** at Harbourfront, a renowned 11-day literary festival drawing more than 100 authors from 25 countries to perform readings and on-stage interviews. Among the literary luminaries who've appeared are Salman Rushdie, Margaret Drabble, Thomas Kenneally, Joyce Carol Oates, A. S. Byatt, and Margaret Atwood; call ☎ **416/ 973-3000** for details.

In November there's fun for the whole family at the 12-day **Royal Agricultural Winter Fair and Royal Horse Show** at Exhibition Place. It's the largest indoor agricultural and equestrian competition in the world, and the horse show is traditionally attended by a member of the British royal family; call ☎ **416/393-6400** for details. There's also the **Santa Claus Parade,** which has been a favorite with kids since 1905, with its marching bands, magical floats, and clowns. It's usually the third Sunday of November so that jolly St. Nick can avoid driving his reindeer through slushy snow; call ☎ **416/249-7833** for details. In December, the **Canadian Aboriginal Festival** at SkyDome attracts more than 1,500 Native American dancers, drummers, and singers. There are literary readings, an arts-and-crafts marketplace, and traditional foods to savor; call ☎ **519/751-0040** for details.

Call **Tourism Toronto** at ☎ **800/363-1990** or 416/203-2600 for more info on festivals and events.

7 Outdoor Activities & Spectator Sports

For general info on facilities in the parks, golf courses, tennis courts, swimming pools, beaches, and picnic areas, call **Metro Parks** at ☎ **416/392-8186** or **City Parks** at ☎ **416/392-1111.**

OUTDOOR ACTIVITIES

BEACHES The neighborhood running along Queen Street East from Coxwell Avenue to Victoria Park is called **The Beaches** because of its wealth of sandy stuff. A charming boardwalk connects the beaches in this area, starting at **Ashbridge's Bay Park,** which has a sizable marina. There's also **Woodbine Beach,** which connects to **Kew Gardens Park** and is a favorite with sunbathers and volleyball players.

The **Toronto Islands** are where you'll find the city's favorite beaches. The ones on **Centre Island** are the busiest and are favored by families because of nearby attractions like **Centreville.** The beaches on **Wards Island** are more secluded, and they're connected by the loveliest boardwalk in the city (it's bordered by masses of fragrant flowers and raspberry bushes). **Hanlan's Point** is Toronto's one-and-only nude beach.

BOATING/CANOEING At the **Harbourside Boating Centre,** 283 Queen's Quay W. (☎ **416/203-3000;** Subway: Union), you can rent sailboats or powerboats and take sailing lessons. For 3 hours, depending on the boat's size, sailboats cost C$60 (US$40) and up; powerboats, C$95 (US$63) and up. Weeklong and weekend sailing courses are also offered. The **Harbourfront Canoe and Kayak School,** 283A Queens Quay W. (☎ **416/203-2277;** Subway: Union), rents kayaks for C$40 to C$50 (US$27 to US$33) per day, depending on whether it's a weekend. Canoes go for C$35 to C$45 (US$23 to US$30). You can also rent canoes, rowboats, and pedal boats on the **Toronto Islands** just south of Centreville.

CROSS-COUNTRY SKIING   Just about every park in Toronto becomes possible prey for cross-country skiers as soon as there's snowfall. Best bets are **Sunnybrook Park** and **Ross Lord Park,** both in North York. For more information, call **Metro Parks** at ☎ **416/392-8186.** For skis, call the **Trakkers Cross Country Ski Club** at ☎ **416//63-0173;** it rents ski equipment and organizes day trips for cross-country skiers.

CYCLING   Favorite pathways include the **Martin Goodman Trail,** running from the Beaches to the Humber River along the waterfront; the **Lower Don Valley** bike trail, starting in the east end of the city and running north to Riverdale Park; **High Park,** with winding trails over 400 acres; and the **Toronto Islands,** where bikers roam free without fear of cars. For cycling trail advice, call **Ontario Cycling** at ☎ **416/426-7242** or **Toronto Parks and Recreation** at ☎ **416/392-8186.** Official bike lanes are marked on College and Carlton streets, the Bloor Street Viaduct leading to the Danforth, Beverly and St. George, and Davenport Road. The Convention and Visitors Association has more details on these bike lanes. There's no shortage of bike-rental depots either. Renting a bike usually runs about C$8 to C$10 (US$5 to US$7) per hour, with daily rates from C$24 (US$16) and up; try **Wheel Excitement,** 5 Rees St., near the Harbourfront Centre (☎ **416/260-9000;** Subway: Union).

GOLF   More than 75 public courses are within an hour's drive of the downtown core. Here are some of the best links: **Don Valley,** at Yonge Street south of Highway 401 (☎ **416/392-2465**), designed by Howard Watson, is a par-71 scenic course with some challenging elevated tees and a par-3 13th hole nicknamed the Hallelujah Corner (it takes a miracle to get through it with par). Greens fees are C$30 (US$20) on weekdays and C$35 (US$23) on weekends. **Humber Valley** (☎ **416/392-2488**) is a par-70 course that's relatively flat and easy to walk and gets lots of shade from towering trees. It does have three final holes requiring major concentration (the 16th and 17th holes are both par 5). Greens fees are C$26 to C$30 (US$17 to US$20).

One of the most famous golf greens in Canada is the championship course at the **Glen Abbey Golf Club** in Oakville (☎ **905/844-1800;** www.glenabbey.com). This par-73 course where the Canadian Open is most often played was designed by Jack Nicklaus himself. Greens fees are C$115 (US$77) in early spring and fall and C$225 (US$150) in summer. The **Lionhead Golf Club** in Brampton (☎ **905/455-8400**) has two 18-hole par-72 courses, charging C$120 (US$80) for the tougher course and C$110 (US$73) for the other. In Markham, the **Angus Glen Golf Club** (☎ **905/887-5157**) has a Doug Carrick–designed par-72 course and charges a C$130 (US$87) greens fee.

ICE-SKATING   **Nathan Phillips Square** in front of City Hall becomes a free ice rink in winter, as does an area at the Harbourfront Centre. Rentals are available. You'll also find artificial rinks in more than 25 parks, including Grenadier Pond in High Park—a romantic spot with its bonfire and vendors selling roasted chestnuts. They're open November to March.

IN-LINE SKATING   In summer, Toronto's streets (and sidewalks) are packed with in-line skaters, especially around the Beaches, the Harbourfront, and the Islands. Go with the flow and rent some blades at **Wheel Excitement** (see "Cycling" above).

ROCK CLIMBING   The dilemma: indoors or outdoors? Toronto has several climbing gyms, including **Joe Rockhead's,** 29 Fraser Ave. (☎ **416/538-7670;** Subway: St. Andrew then streetcar west to Dufferin), and the **Toronto Climbing Academy,** 100 Broadview Ave. (☎ **416/406-5900;** Subway: Broadview), where you can pick up the finer points of knot tying and belaying. Both gyms also rent equipment. But for the real thing, you need to head outdoors. Weekend excursions to the

Elora Gorge are organized through **Humber College** (☎ **416/675-5097;** Subway: Kipling).

SWIMMING   There are a dozen or so outdoor pools (open June to Sept) in the municipal parks, including High and Rosedale Parks, plus indoor pools at several community recreation centers. For **pool information,** call ☎ **416/392-1111.** The **University of Toronto Athletic Centre,** 55 Harbord St., at Spadina Avenue (☎ **416/ 978-4680;** Subway: Spadina), opens its pool free to the public Sunday noon to 4pm. You can use the pool at the **YMCA,** 20 Grosvenor St. (☎ **416/975-9622;** Subway: Wellesley or College), on a day pass costing C$14 (US$9).

TENNIS   There are tennis facilities in more than 30 municipal parks. The most convenient locations are the courts in High Park, Rosedale, and Jonathan Ashridge Parks, open in summer only. At Eglinton Flats Park, west of Keele Street at Eglinton, you can use six of the courts in winter. Call the city at ☎ **416/392-1111** or **Metro Parks** at ☎ **416/392-8186** for details.

SPECTATOR SPORTS

BASEBALL   The **SkyDome,** on Front Street beside the CN Tower (see "Seeing the Sights" above), is the home of the **Toronto Blue Jays** (World Series champs in 1992 and 1993). For details, contact the Toronto Blue Jays, P.O. Box 7777, Adelaide St., Toronto, ON M5C 2K7 (☎ **416/341-1000**). For tickets, which run C$15 to C$60 (US$10 to US$40), call ☎ **888/654-6529** or 416/341-1234.

BASKETBALL   Toronto's basketball team, the **Raptors,** has generated an urban fever. The team's home ground is the **Air Canada Centre** (see "Seeing the Sights"), and they play there October to April. The center seats 19,500 basketball fans. For details, contact the **Raptors Basketball Club,** 40 Bay St. (☎ **416/815-5600**). For tickets, C$25 to C$125 (US$17 to US$83), call **Ticketmaster** at ☎ **416/870-8000.**

FOOTBALL   Remember Kramer on *Seinfeld*? He would watch only Canadian football—now here's your chance to catch a game. The **SkyDome** is home to the **Argonauts** football team, which plays in the Canadian Football League June to November. For details, contact the club at SkyDome, Gate 3, Suite 1300, Toronto, ON M5V 1J3 (☎ **416/341-5151**). Argos tickets cost C$10 to C$35 (US$7 to US$23); call ☎ **888/654-6529** or 416/341-1234.

HOCKEY   While basketball is still in its honeymoon phase in Toronto, hockey is a longtime love. The **Air Canada Centre** is the new home of the **Toronto Maple Leafs,** replacing the revered Maple Leaf Gardens, which housed the team since 1931. Though there are 18,700 seats for hockey fans, tickets are still not easy to come by because many are sold by subscription. The rest, C$25 to C$100 (US$17 to US$67), are available through **Ticketmaster** at ☎ **416/870-8000.**

HORSE RACING   Horse racing takes place at **Woodbine Racetrack,** Rexdale Boulevard and Highway 427 in Etobicoke (☎ **416/675-6110** or 416/675-7223), famous for the Queen's Plate (contested in June/July); the Canadian International, a world-classic turf race (contested in Sept or Oct); and the North America Cup (mid-June). Woodbine also hosts harness racing in spring and fall.

8 Shopping

Toronto's major shopping districts are the **Bloor/Yorkville area** for designer boutiques and top-name galleries; **Queen Street West** for a more funky mix of fashion, antiques, and bookstores; and a number of **shopping malls/centers,** like Queen's Quay down on the waterfront and the 2-block-long Eaton Centre at 220 Yonge St.

Most stores open at 10am Monday to Saturday; closing hours are usually around 6pm, though many shops stay open to 8pm or later Thursday and Friday. Sunday shopping hours are usually noon to 5pm. Most art galleries are open Tuesday to Saturday 10:30am to 5:30pm, so don't come around on Sunday or Monday.

SHOPPING A TO Z

ANTIQUES   You'll find the finest antiques in the **Bloor/Yorkville area** and in the **Mount Pleasant/St. Clair area** along the 500 to 700 blocks of Mount Pleasant Road. For more eclectic and often more recent collectibles, try the various stores along **Queen Street West. Markham Village** also has several antiques stores. For a good introduction, try the **Harbourfront Antique Market,** 390 Queen's Quay W. (☎ 416/260-2626; Subway: Union), boasting more than 100 dealers selling everything from furniture to jewelry.

ART   The ✪ **Isaacs/Innuit Gallery of Eskimo Art,** 9 Prince Arthur Ave. (☎ 416/921-9985; Subway: Bay or St. George), sells museum-quality Inuit sculpture, prints, drawings, wall hangings, and antiquities from across the Arctic. The gallery also specializes in early native-Canadian art and artifacts. The bilevel **Kinsman Robinson,** 14 Hazelton Ave. (☎ 416/964-2374; Subway: Bay), exhibits such contemporary Canadian artists as Norval Morrisseau, Henri Masson, Robert Katz, and Stanley Cosgrove, plus sculptors Esther Wertheimer, Maryon Kantaroff, Joseph Jacobs, and many others.

BOOKS   Some of the best bookstores are part of large chains, most notably **Indigo Books Music & More,** 55 Bloor St. W. (☎ 416/925-3536; Subway: Bay), and **Chapters,** 110 Bloor St. W. (☎ 416/920-9299; Subway: Bay or Museum)—both offer a wide selection of merchandise, tables and chairs to encourage browsing, special events, and cafes. For a delightful old-fashioned bookshop, head to **Nicholas Hoare,** 45 Front E. (☎ 416/777-2665; Subway: Union), whose wooden shelves are piled high with Canadian and international fiction, art books, and children's stories; there's also a fireplace to lend a cozy feel in winter. The **Glad Day Bookshop,** 598A Yonge St., second floor (☎ 416/961-4161; Subway: Wellesley), offers gay fiction, biography, and other nonfiction of interest to the gay/lesbian community. It also stocks calendars, journals and magazines, and other items.

A DEPARTMENT STORE   There's only one real department store left in Toronto: **The Bay,** whose flagship is at Queen and Yonge streets (☎ 416/861-9111; Subway: Queen).

FASHION   Called for many years Canada's answer to the Gap, ✪ **Club Monaco,** 157 Bloor St. W. (☎ 416/591-8837; Subway: Museum), has emerged as a top purveyor of casual wear and sportswear, with a smattering of work-ready clothes mixed in. It also has its own accessories and makeup lines. There are 19 other outlets around the city, including the shop at 403 Queen St. W. (☎ 416/979-5633; Subway: Osgoode). **Roots,** at 95A Bloor St. W. (☎ 416/323-3289; Subway: Bay), is one Canadian retailer beloved by Hollywood types. The clothes are casual, from hooded sweats to polar fleece jackets, and there's a good selection of leather footwear. The slouchy Roots hat (in red or black) is known far and wide. Don't overlook the tykes' department, which has the same stuff in tiny sizes. Other locations include a bilevel store at the Eaton Centre, 220 Yonge St. (☎ 416/593-9640; Subway: Dundas).

FOOD   The specialty bakery ✪ **Dufflet Pastries,** 787 Queen St. W., near Bathurst Street (☎ 416/504-2870; Subway: Osgoode, then streetcar west), supplies many restaurants with its pastries and desserts. The special Dufflet cakes include a white- and dark-chocolate mousse, almond meringue, and many other singular creations. Fine coffees and teas are served too. In Chinatown is the fascinating **Ten Ren Tea,**

454 Dundas St. W., at Huron Street (☎ **416/598-7872;** Subway: St. Patrick, then streetcar west), where you can pick up some fine Chinese tea.

The colorful and lively ✪ **Kensington Market,** bounded by Dundas Street, Spadina Avenue, Baldwin Street, and Augusta Avenue (Subway: St. Patrick, then the streetcar west), shouldn't be missed. If you can struggle out of bed to get here around 5am, you'll see the squawking chickens being carried from their trucks to the stalls. You'll hear the accents of Caribbean Islanders, Portuguese, Italians, and merchants of other nationalities, who spread their wares before them—squid and crabs in pails, chickens, pigeons, bread, cheese, apples, pears, peppers, ginger, mangoes, salted fish, lace, fabrics, and other colorful remnants. There's no market on Sunday. The handsome **St. Lawrence Market,** 92 Front St. E. (☎ **416/392-7219;** Subway: Union), is housed in a vast building constructed around the facade of the second city hall, built in 1850. Vendors sell fresh meat, fish, fruit, vegetables, and dairy products, as well as other foodstuffs. The best time to visit is early Saturday morning, shortly after the farmers have brought their wares into town. It's open Tuesday to Thursday 9am to 7pm, Friday 8am to 8pm, and Saturday 5am to 5pm.

JEWELRY   Among the crystal and china at **Birks,** in the Manulife Centre, 55 Bloor St. W. (☎ **416/922-2266;** Subway: Bay), is an extensive selection of top-quality jewelry, including exquisite pearls and knockout diamond engagement rings. There are also branches at the Eaton Centre (☎ **416/979-9311;** Subway: Dundas) and First Canadian Place at Bay and Kings streets (☎ **416/363-5663;** Subway: King).

TOYS   Yo-yos and wind-up gadgets are the specialty at **Kidding Awound,** 91 Cumberland St. (☎ **416/926-8996;** Subway: Bay). There are also some antique toys (which you won't let the kids near) and gag gifts. Kids and adults alike will love the tiny **Science City,** 50 Bloor St. W. (☎ **416/968-2627;** Subway: Yonge/Bloor), filled with games, puzzles, models, kits, and books related to science. Whether your interest is in astronomy, biology, chemistry, archaeology, or physics, you'll find something here.

9 Toronto After Dark

The major companies to see in Toronto are the **National Ballet of Canada,** the **Canadian Opera Company,** the **Toronto Symphony Orchestra,** the **Toronto Dance Theatre,** and **Tafelmusik.** You can also catch major Broadway shows or a performance by one of the many small theater companies that make Toronto one of North America's leading theater centers. For additional entertainment, there are enough bars, clubs, cabarets, comedy clubs, and other entertainment to keep anyone spinning.

For local happenings, check *Where Toronto* and *Toronto Life,* as well as the *Globe and Mail,* the *Toronto Star,* the *Toronto Sun,* and the two free weeklies *Now* and *Eye.* Events of interest to the gay and lesbian community are listed in *Xtra!,* another free weekly.

For **Ticketmaster's** telecharge service, call ☎ **416/872-1111.** It also runs the **T O Tix** booth, selling half-price day-of-performance tickets. The booth is currently at Yonge and Dundas streets outside the Eaton Centre on the southwest corner, though plans are afoot to move it to a new unspecified location; call ☎ **416/870-8000** for the latest. Discount tickets are also available from the **Toronto Theatre Alliance,** 720 Bathurst St. (☎ **416/536-6468**), for a limited number of shows.

THE PERFORMING ARTS

The major performing-arts venues include **Massey Hall,** 178 Victoria St. (☎ **416/ 593-4828;** Subway: Queen), a Canadian musical landmark hosting a variety of music from classical to rock. The **Hummingbird Centre,** 1 Front St. E. (☎ **416/872-2262;**

Subway: Union), is home to the Canadian Opera Company and the National Ballet; it also presents Broadway musicals, headline entertainers, and other national and international theater, music, and dance companies. **Roy Thomson Hall,** 60 Simcoe St. (☎ 416/593-4828; Subway: St. Andrew), is the premier concert hall and home to the Toronto Symphony Orchestra, performing September to June. The **St. Lawrence Centre,** 27 Front St. E. (☎ 416/366-7723; Subway: Union), hosts musical and theatrical events and is home to the Canadian Stage Theatre Company in the Bluma Appel Theatre and to Music Toronto and public debates in the Jane Mallett Theatre. And then there's the **Premiere Dance Theatre,** 207 Queen's Quay W. (☎ 416/973-4000; Subway: Union, then LRT to Queen's Quay), home to a leading contemporary dance season featuring local companies—the Toronto Dance Theatre, the Danny Grossman Dance Company, and other Canadian and international companies, including the Desrosiers Dance Theatre.

OPERA & CLASSICAL MUSIC   The **Canadian Opera Company** began in 1950 with 10 performances of three operas and now stages eight operas a season (Sept to Apr) at the Hummingbird Centre and the Elgin Theatre. Call ☎ 416/872-2262 for tickets or 416/363-6671 for administration.

September to June, the **Toronto Symphony Orchestra** performs at Roy Thomson Hall, 60 Simcoe St. (☎ 416/593-4828 for tickets or 416/593-7769 for administration; Subway: St. Andrew). In June and July, concerts are also given at outdoor venues around the city. The world-renowned **Toronto Mendelssohn Choir** also appears at Roy Thomson Hall (☎ 416/598-0422). This choir, founded in 1895, performs the great choral works not only of Mendelssohn but also of Bach, Handel, Elgar, and others. Its most famous recording, though, is undoubtedly the soundtrack from Steven Spielberg's *Schindler's List.*

The **Tafelmusik Baroque Orchestra,** 427 Bloor St. W. (☎ 416/964-6337 for tickets or 416/964-9562 for administration), celebrated in England as "the world's finest period band," plays baroque music on authentic period instruments. Concerts featuring Bach, Handel, Telemann, Mozart, and Vivaldi are given at **Trinity–St. Paul's United Church,** 427 Bloor St. W. (Subway: Spadina or Bathurst), and also at **Massey Hall,** 178 Victoria St. (Subway: Dundas or Queen).

DANCE   One of the most beloved and famous of all Toronto's cultural icons is the ✪ **National Ballet of Canada,** 157 King St. E. (☎ 416/872-2262 for tickets or 416/366-4846). It was launched at Eaton Auditorium in Toronto on November 12, 1951, by English ballerina Celia Franca, who served initially as director, dancer, choreographer, and teacher. Among the highlights of its history have been its 1973 New York debut (with Nureyev's full-length *Sleeping Beauty*), Baryshnikov's appearance with the company soon after his 1974 defection, and the emergence of such stars as Karen Kain and Kimberly Glasco. The company performs its regular seasons in Toronto at the Hummingbird Centre in the fall, winter, and spring, as well as giving summer appearances at the open-air theater at Ontario Place. The repertory includes works by Glen Tetley, Sir Frederick Ashton, William Forsythe, and Jerome Robbins. James Kudelka was appointed artist in residence in 1991 and has created *The Miraculous Mandarin, The Actress,* and *Spring Awakening.* Tickets run C$14 to C$90 (US$9 to US$60).

Nightlife on the Web

If you have Internet access, surf over to *Toronto Life*'s Web site at **www.torontolife. com** or the *Toronto Star*'s site at **www.toronto.com** for lengthy lists of performances.

Toronto's Landmark Theaters

The following major theaters all offer guided tours, usually for a charge of C$5 (US$3.35) or less; call ahead for schedules.

Opened in 1913, the **Elgin Theatre** and the **Winter Garden Theatre,** 189 Yonge St. (☎ **416/872-5555** for tickets, 416/314-2871 for tour info; Subway: Queen), have been restored to their original gilded glory. The downstairs Elgin is the larger, seating 1,500 and featuring a lavish domed ceiling and gilded decoration on the boxes and proscenium. The 1,000-seat Winter Garden possesses a striking interior adorned with hand-painted frescoes; suspended from its ceiling and lit with lanterns are more than 5,000 branches of beech leaves, which were harvested, preserved, painted, and fireproofed. Both theaters offer everything from Broadway musicals and dramas to concerts and opera. Tickets run C$15 to C$85 (US$10 to US$57).

A giant complex, the **Ford Centre for the Performing Arts,** 5040 Yonge St. (☎ **416/872-2222;** Subway: North York Centre), is home to the North York Symphony and the Amadeus Choir. It's several venues in one: the 1,850-seat Apotex theater, which has featured award-winning musicals like *Sunset Boulevard* and *Ragtime*; the 1,025-seat George Weston Recital Hall, for music events; a 250-seat studio theater; and an art gallery covering 5,000 square feet. Tickets run C$40 to C$110 (US$27 to US$73). Opened in 1920, the glamorous **Pantages Theatre,** 244 Victoria St. (☎ **416/872-2222;** Subway: Queen), has been restored to the tune of C$18 million (US$12 million); it was originally a silent film house and vaudeville theater. Tickets run C$60 to C$110 (US$40 to US$73); discount seats are available 2 hours before the performance.

The spectacular 2,000-seat state-of-the-art **Princess of Wales Theatre,** 300 King St. W. (☎ **416/872-1212;** www.onstagenow.com; Subway: St. Andrew), was built for the production of *Miss Saigon* and has a stage large enough to accommodate the landing of the helicopter in that production. The exterior and interior walls have been spectacularly decorated by Frank Stella. Tickets run C$25 to C$115 (US$17 to US$77). When shows from Broadway migrate north, they usually head for the **Royal Alexandra Theatre,** 260 King St. W. (☎ **416/872-1212;** www.onstagenow.com; Subway: St. Andrew). Tickets are often snapped up by subscription buyers, so your best bet is to call or write ahead to the theater at the above address. Recent favorites have included *Master Class, Oliver,* and *Fame.* The Royal Alex itself is magnificent: Built in 1907, it's a riot of plush reds, gold brocade, and baroque ornamentation. Tickets run C$25 to C$115 (US$17 to US$77).

The **Toronto Dance Theatre** (☎ 416/973-4000 for tickets or 416/967-1365), the city's leading contemporary dance company, burst onto the scene about 30 years ago, bringing an inventive spirit and original Canadian dance to the stage. Today Christopher House directs the company; he joined in 1979 and has contributed 30 new works to the repertoire. Exhilarating, powerful, and energetic—don't miss their *Handel Variations, Artemis Madrigals, Sacra Conversazione,* and *Cactus Rosary.* Tickets run C$15 to C$75 (US$10 to US$50), sometimes higher for special performances.

THEATER With theaters and theater companies galore, Toronto has a very active scene, with a reputation second only to that of Broadway's in all North America. Many small theater groups are producing exciting offbeat drama—a burgeoning Toronto equivalent of Off Broadway. I've picked only the few whose reputations have been established rather than bombarding you with a list of all the offerings. Your choice will be made by what's scheduled while you're in town, so do your own talent scouting, checking the local newspaper or magazine for listings.

The **Canadian Stage Company** (☎ 416/368-3110) performs comedy, drama, and musicals in the St. Lawrence Centre and presents free summer Shakespeare performances in High Park. Since 1970, the experimental **Factory Theatre,** 125 Bathurst St. (☎ 416/504-9971; Subway: Bathurst, then streetcar south), has been a home to Canadian playwriting, showcasing the best new authors as well as established playwrights.

The intimate **Tarragon Theatre,** near Dupont and Bathurst at 30 Bridgman Ave. (☎ 416/536-5018; Subway: Bathurst or Dupont), opened in 1971 and continues to produce original works by such famous Canadian literary figures as Michael Ondaatje, Michel Tremblay, and Judith Thompson. Set in a warehouse, the **Theatre Passe Muraille,** 16 Ryerson Ave. (☎ 416/504-7529; Subway: Osgoode), started in the late 1960s when a pool of actors began experimenting and improvising original Canadian material. There's a main space seating 220 and a back space for 70. Take the Queen Street streetcar to Bathurst. **Buddies in Bad Times,** 12 Alexander St. (☎ 416/975-8555; Subway: Wellesley), is Canada's premier gay theater. Its cutting-edge reputation has been built by American Sky Gilbert. In addition to plays pushing social boundaries, the theater operates a popular bar and cabaret called Tallulah's.

DINNER THEATER & COMEDY

For the art of campy impersonation, there's **La Cage Dinner Theatre,** 278 Yonge St. (☎ 416/364-5200; Subway: Queen), which hosts a concert given by the shades of Buddy Holly, Roy Orbison, and Elvis, among others. For a unique show that can be likened only to Disney's *Fantasia* performed live on stage, go to the **Famous Players Dinner Theatre,** 110 Sudbury St. (☎ 416/532-1137; Subway: Osgoode, then streetcar west).

Top comedy clubs include ✪ **Second City,** 56 Blue Jays Way (☎ 416/343-0011; Subway: Union), which has been and still is the cauldron of Canadian comedy. If you enjoyed *Saturday Night Live* in its heyday or *SCTV,* you'll love the improvisational comedy here. Dan Aykroyd, John Candy, Bill Murray, Martin Short, Mike Myers, Andrea Martin, and Catherine O'Hara all got their start here. Another popular spot is **Yuk-Yuk's,** 2335 Yonge St. (☎ 416/967-6425 Subway: Eglinton), which has nurtured comedians like Jim Carrey, Harland Williams, Howie Mandel, and Norm MacDonald and has hosted such major American stars as Jerry Seinfeld and Robin Williams.

LIVE-MUSIC CLUBS

Colorful confusion reigns at the **BamBoo,** 312 Queen St. W. (☎ 416/593-5771; Subway: Osgoode). The granddaddy of Toronto's reggae scene, the 'Boo also beats out calypso, salsa, jazz, soul, and R&B. The teensy dance floor is bordered by tables set for dinner, and the menu is as diverse as the music, with pad thai, barbecued burgers, and jerk chicken top choices. Forget trying to have a quiet conversation, even if you score a seat on the rooftop patio—you're here for the music. Cover runs C$5 to C$10 (US$3.35 to US$7). The rock institution **El Mocambo,** 464 Spadina Ave. (☎ 416/968-2001; Subway: Spadina, then LRT south), has played peekaboo in recent years— it closes and reopens on a regular basis. But it can never really die: It's where the Rolling Stones rocked in the 1970s and Elvis Costello jammed in the 1980s, and today it hosts alternative diva Liz Phair. The rough-and-tumble atmosphere won't suit all comers; the genteel are advised to steer clear of the washrooms. Cover varies from C$2 to C$15 (US$1.35 to US$10) and maybe higher on occasion.

The **Horseshoe Tavern,** 370 Queen St. W. (☎ **416/598-4753;** Subway: Osgoode), is a traditional Toronto venue that has showcased the sounds of the decade: blues in the 1960s, punk in the 1970s, New Wave in the 1980s, and everything from ska, rock-abilly, celtic, and alternative rock in the 1990s. It's the place that launched Blue Rodeo, the Tragically Hip, the Band, and Prairie Oyster and hosted the Toronto debuts of The Police and Hootie & the Blowfish. It attracts a cross section of 20- to 40-year-olds. There's no cover, but admission is C$10 (US$7) and up for special concerts. **Lee's Palace,** 529 Bloor St. W. (☎ **416/532-1598;** Subway: Bathurst), ain't Versailles, but that hasn't kept the crème de la crème of the alternative-music scene from appearing: Nirvana, Red Hot Chili Peppers, the Tragically Hip, and Alanis Morrisette. The audience is young and rarely tires of slam-dancing in the mosh pit in front of the stage. Cover is sometimes C$10 (US$7).

Currently the **Rivoli,** 332 Queen St. W. (☎ **416/597-0794;** Subway: Osgoode), is the club for an eclectic mix of performances, including grunge, blues, rock, jazz, comedy, and poetry reading. Holly Cole launched her career here, Tori Amos made her Toronto debut in the back room, and The Kids in the Hall got started here and still consider it home. Shows begin at 8pm and continue to 2am. People dance if so inspired. One of the classiest jazz joints in town, the long, narrow **Top O' the Senator,** 249 Victoria St. (☎ **416/364-7517;** Subway: Dundas), is home away from home to top performers like vocalist Molly Johnson and sax goddess Jane Bunnett. Leathery couches and banquettes add to the lounge-lizard ambiance. For those who still care, the third-floor humidor has a premium collection of Cuban smokes. Cover is C$15 (US$10) and up.

THE BAR SCENE

HOTEL BARS   Some of the best bars are in hotels. **Accents,** at the Sutton Place, 955 Bay St. (☎ **416/924-9221;** Subway: Museum or Wellesley), boasts a pianist and a great selection of wines by the glass. The **Chelsea Bun,** at the Delta Chelsea Inn, 33 Gerrard St. W. (☎ **416/595-1975;** Subway: College), has a fine selection of single-malt whiskeys and jazz bands on weekends. The **Consort Bar** at the King Edward Hotel, 37 King St. E. (☎ **416/863-9700;** Subway: King), is a wonderfully clubby old-fashioned bar. **La Serre** at the Four Seasons, 21 Avenue Rd. (☎ **416/964-0411;** Subway: Bay), is a charming piano bar that welcomes cigar aficionados. The **Library Bar** at the Royal York, 100 Front St. W. (☎ **416/863-6333;** Subway: Union), specializes in "fishbowl" martinis. And **The Roof** at the Park Hyatt, 4 Avenue Rd. (☎ **416/924-5471;** Subway: Bay), is an old literary haunt, with comfortable couches in front of a fireplace and excellent drinks; the view from the terrace is splendid, one of the best in the city.

OTHER BARS & PUBS   A brew pub, the **Amsterdam,** 600 King St. W., at Portland Street (☎ **416/504-6882;** Subway: St. Andrew, then streetcar west), is a beer drinker's heaven, serving more than 200 labels as well as 30 types on draft. By 8pm, the tables in back are filled and the long bar is jammed. Downstairs at **Bar Italia & Billiards,** 582 College St. (☎ **416/535-3621;** Subway: Queen's Park, then streetcar west), a young, trendy, good-looking crowd quaffs drinks or coffee and snacks on Italian sandwiches. Upstairs, the six pool tables are the draw. Affectionately known as the Brunny House, the **Brunswick House,** 481 Bloor St. W. (☎ **416/964-2242;** Subway: Spadina or Bathurst), has been described as a cross between a German beer hall and an English north-country workingmen's club. Impromptu dancing to background music and pool and shuffleboard playing drown out the sound of at least two of the large-screen TVs, if not the other 18.

Despite the ominous-sounding name, the **Devil's Martini,** 136 Simcoe St. (☎ 416/591-7541; Subway: St. Andrew), is a great spot to slurp up a generous martini. The scene aims for hip but is actually fairly relaxed. Fashion-conscious singles in their 30s gather in the Moroccan-inspired **Fez Batik,** 129 Peter St. (☎ 416/977-7544; Subway: Osgoode), filling the sidewalk patio and downstairs bar area. For fun, you can have your Tarot cards read. An unpretentious place with pool tables and a wonderful rooftop patio, the **Pilot,** 22 Cumberland St. (☎ 416/923-5716; Subway: Yonge/Bloor), dates back to the early years of World War II.

Smokeless Joe's, 125 John St. (☎ 416/591-2221; Subway: St. Andrew), is Toronto's only smoke-free bar. It offers a list of more than 175 brews from around the globe and a patio where the desperate can get a nicotine fix. At **Wayne Gretzky's,** 99 Blue Jays Way (☎ 416/979-7825; Subway: Union), forget the food; instead, enjoy a drink at the long bar or head up to the rooftop **Oasis,** which is scented with hibiscus and affords a fine view of the CN Tower.

WINE BARS   The name **Sottovoce,** 537 College St. (☎ 416/536-4564; Subway: Queen's Park, then streetcar west), must be some kind of in-joke, because the decibel level is outrageous. This wine bar is still a great find, not least because it serves some truly inspired focaccia sandwiches and salads. **Vines,** 38 Wellington St. E. (☎ 416/955-9833; Subway: King), provides a pleasant atmosphere in which to sample a glass of champagne or any one of 30 wines, priced from C$6 to C$10 (US$4 to US$7) for a 4-ounce glass. Salads, cheeses, and light meals, served with fresh French sticks, are available.

DANCE CLUBS

A vast waterfront party complex, **The Docks,** 11 Polson St. (☎ 416/461-DOCKS; Subway: Union, then take a taxi to Lakeshore Blvd. East and Cherry St.; Polson runs off Cherry St.), hosts live entertainers like James Brown, Blue Rodeo, and the Pointer Sisters. The dance club (cover C$5 to C$10/US$3.35 to US$7 most nights) boasts more than a dozen bars, the latest in lighting, and other party effects. Thursday night is foam fun. There are a restaurant and a full raft of sports facilities too. Around for ages, in dance-club time, the **Fluid Lounge,** 217 Richmond St. W. (☎ 416/593-6116; Subway: Osgoode), is still hot. Only the dressed-to-kill gain entry to this haven for the beautiful and hip, with moody lighting and a simulated underwater decor. Sports and music celebs often drop by to groove to the neo-funk, industrial, and mainstream dance sounds. No running shoes or sportswear permitted. Cover is C$10 (US$7).

GAY & LESBIAN BARS

A popular spot for cruising, **Crews,** 508 Church St. (☎ 416/972-1662; Subway: Wellesley), is a complex with two patios. Fridays and Saturdays bring drag shows. The adjoining **Tango** bar draws a lesbian crowd; it hosts Tuesday and Sunday karaoke. A friendly and very popular local bar, **Woody's,** 467 Church St., south of Wellesley (☎ 416/972-0887; Subway: Wellesley), is frequented mainly by men but welcomes women. It's considered a good meeting place. Next door is **Sailor,** 465 Church St. (☎ 416/972-0887), a bar/restaurant.

Pope Joan, 547 Parliament St., at Winchester Street (☎ 416/925-6662; Subway: Wellesley, then streetcar east), is the city's most popular lesbian bar, with a pool table and game room downstairs, furnished with old cozy couches, and a restaurant and dance area upstairs. In summer, the fenced-in patio is the place to cool off. The incredibly popular **Slack Alice,** 562 Church St. (☎ **416/969-8742;** Subway: Wellesley), draws a gay/lesbian crowd. The menu features home-style comfort food; on weekend evenings, a DJ gets the crowd on its feet.

10 Niagara-on-the-Lake & the Shaw Festival

Only 1½ hours from Toronto, **Niagara-on-the-Lake** is one of North America's best-preserved and prettiest 19th-century villages, with its lakeside location and tree-lined streets bordered by handsome clapboard and brick period houses. Such is the setting for one of Canada's most famous events, the **Shaw Festival.** The town is the jewel of the Ontario wine region.

ESSENTIALS
VISITOR INFORMATION   The **Niagara-on-the-Lake Chamber of Commerce,** 153 King St. (P.O. Box 1043), Niagara-on-the-Lake, ON L0S 1J0 (☎ **905/468-4263**), will provide information and help you find accommodations at one of the 120 local B&Bs. It's open Monday to Friday 9am to 5pm and Saturday and Sunday 10am to 5pm.

GETTING THERE   Niagara-on-the-Lake is best seen by car. Driving from Toronto, take the QEW Niagara via Hamilton and St. Catharines and exit at Highway 55.

   Amtrak and **VIA** operate trains between Toronto (☎ **416/366-8411**) and New York that stop in St. Catharines and Niagara Falls. Call ☎ **800/361-1235** in Canada or **800/USA-RAIL** in the United States (www.amtrak.com). From either destination, you'll need to rent a car and exit at Highway 55. Rental locations in St. Catharines include **National Tilden,** 162 Church St. (☎ **905/682-8611**), and **Hertz,** 404 Ontario St. (☎ **905/682-8695**). In Niagara Falls, there's a **National Tilden** at 4523 Drummond Rd. (☎ **905/374-6700**).

EXPLORING THE TOWN
A stroll along Queen Street will take you by some entertaining shops. The **Niagara Apothecary Shop,** at no. 5 (☎ **905/468-3845**), dates to 1866, and the original glass and ceramic apothecary ware is on display. **Loyalist Village,** at no. 12 (☎ **905/468-7331**), has distinctively Canadian clothes and crafts, including Inuit art, Native Canadian decoys, and sheepskins. And **Maple Leaf Fudge,** at no. 14 (☎ **905/468-2211**), offers more than 20 varieties you can watch being made on marble slabs.

Niagara Historical Society Museum. 43 Castlereagh St., at Davy St. ☎ **905/468-3912.** Admission C$3 (US$2) adults, C$2 (US$1.35) seniors, C$1 (US65¢) students, C50¢ (US35¢) children 5–12. Jan–Feb weekends 1–5pm; Mar, Apr, Nov, Dec daily 1–5pm; May–Oct daily 10am–5pm.

A Driving Tip

The best way to see Niagara Falls, Niagara-on-the-Lake, St. Catharines, Port Colborne, and Hamilton is to take the Niagara Parkway from Niagara-on-the-Lake to Niagara Falls, drive to Port Colborne on Lake Erie, and follow the Welland Canal north to Port Dalhousie on Lake Ontario. Though this is, for the most part, a densely populated area with a tangled network of roads, there are several scenic routes: the parkway and the Wine Route, which takes you from Stoney Creek to Niagara Falls.

A Festival of Shaw & Company

The **Shaw Festival** is devoted to the dramatic and comedic works of George Bernard Shaw and his contemporaries. Opening in April and running through October, the festival offers a dozen plays in three theaters: the historic **Court House,** the exquisite **Festival Theatre,** and the **Royal George Theatre.** Some recent performances have included *All My Sons* by Arthur Miller, *Uncle Vanya* by Anton Chekhov, *Easy Virtue* by Noël Coward, and *Heartbreak House* by G. B. Shaw himself.

The Shaw announces its festival program in mid-January. Tickets are invariably difficult to obtain on short notice, so book in advance. Prices range from C$25 to C$70 (US$17 to US$47). For more information, contact the **Shaw Festival,** P.O. Box 774, Niagara-on-the-Lake, ON L0S 1J0 (☎ **800/511-7429** or 905/468-2172).

The Niagara Historical Society Museum houses more than 20,000 artifacts pertaining to local history, including many possessions of United Empire Loyalists who first settled the area at the end of the American Revolution.

Fort George National Historic Park. Niagara Pkwy. ☎ **905/468-6614.** Admission C$6 (US$4) adults, C$5 (US$3.35) seniors, C$4 (US$2.65) ages 6–16, C$20 (US$13) families; children 5 and under free. Apr–Oct daily 10am–5pm (to 8pm Sat July–Aug).

South along the Niagara Parkway at the Fort George National Historic Park lies an important historic site. The fort played a key role in the War of 1812 until the Americans invaded and destroyed it in May 1813. Though rebuilt by 1815, it was abandoned in 1828 and not reconstructed until the 1930s. You can view the guard room with its hard plank beds, the officers' quarters, the enlisted men's quarters, and the sentry posts. Those who believe in ghosts, take note: The Fort is one of Ontario's favorite "haunted" sites.

TOURING THE LOCAL WINERIES

Visiting a local winery is one of the loveliest (and tastiest) ways to pass an hour or two in this region. For area maps and information about the region's vintners, contact the **Wine Council of Ontario,** 110 Hanover Dr., Suite B-205, St. Catharines, ON L2W 1A4 (☎ **888/5-WINERY** or 905/684-8070; www.wineroute.com). The vintners below are all close to Niagara-on-the-Lake.

If you take Highway 55 (Niagara Stone Road) out of Niagara-on-the-Lake, you'll come to the **Hillebrand Estates Winery** just outside Virgil (☎ **905/468-7123;** www. hillebrand.com). It hosts a variety of special events (like a weekend concert series that features jazz and blues rhythms) and offers bike tours. Hillebrand's Vineyard Café, which enjoys views of both the barrel-filled cellar and the Niagara Escarpment, is a delightful spot for lunch or dinner. Winery tours are given daily 10am to 6pm on the hour.

If you turn off Highway 55 and go down York Road, you'll reach **Château des Charmes,** west of St. Davids (☎ **905/262-5202**), built to resemble a French manor house rather than an industrial winery, making it unique in the region. One-hour tours are given daily 10am to 6pm. You can reach the **Konzelmann Winery,** Lakeshore Road (☎ **905/935-2866**), by taking Mary Street out of Niagara-on-the-Lake. This vintner is famous for its award-winning ice wines (sweet dessert wines from grapes picked after a frost). May to late September, tours are given Monday to Saturday 10am to 6pm.

WHERE TO STAY

In summer, hotel space is much in demand; if you're having trouble finding a room, contact the chamber of commerce (above), which provides an accommodations-reservations service.

Gate House Hotel. 142 Queen St. (P.O. Box 1364), Niagara-on-the-Lake, ON L0S 1J0. ☎ **905/468-3263.** www.gatehouse-niagara.com. 10 units. A/C TV TEL. C$160–C$180 (US$107–US$120) double. AE, ER, MC, V.

Unlike many of the Canadiana-influenced hotels around town, the Gate House is decorated in clean-lined Milanese style. The guest rooms have a marbleized look accented with ultramodern black lamps, block marble tables, leatherette couches, and bathrooms with sleek Italian fixtures. The effect is quite glamorous. Ristorante Giardino, one of the best restaurants in town, is in the hotel (see "Where to Dine" below).

Moffat Inn. 60 Picton St. (at Queen and Picton sts.). Niagara-on-the-Lake, ON L0S 1J0. ☎ **905/468-4116.** Fax 905/468-4747. 22 units. A/C TV TEL. Apr 15–Oct 31 and Christmas/New Year's C$85–C$135 (US$57–US$90) double; Nov–Apr 14 C$65–C$119 (US$43–US$79) double. Packages available. AE, MC, V.

This is a fine and convenient no-smoking choice. Most of the guest rooms come with brass-framed beds and furnishings in traditional-style wood, wicker, and bamboo. They have built-in closets, and extra amenities include hair dryers, as well as a tea kettle and supplies. Seven rooms have fireplaces. Free coffee is available in the lobby, and there's also a restaurant and bar on-premises.

✪ Oban Inn. 160 Front St. (at Gate St.), Niagara-on-the-Lake, ON L0S 1J0. ☎ **905/468-2165.** 22 units. A/C TV TEL. C$160 (US$107) standard double, C$220 (US$147) double with lake view. Winter midweek and weekend packages available. AE, DC, MC, V.

Overlooking the lake, *the* place to stay is the Oban, a charming white Victorian with a green dormer-style roof and windows, plus a large veranda (the house is a re-creation of the 1824 structure, which burned down in 1992). The gardens are a joy to behold and the source of the bouquets throughout the house. The guest rooms are furnished with comfortable antique reproductions—corn-husk four-poster beds with candlewick spreads, ginger-jar lamps, and club-style sofas. Pets are welcome. Bar snacks and light lunches and dinners are available down in the pubby piano bar, with its leather Windsor chairs and hunting prints over the fireplace. The dinner menu choices run C$20 to C$25 (US$13 to US$17).

Old Bank House. 10 Front St. (P.O. Box 1708), Niagara-on-the-Lake, ON L0S 1J0. ☎ **905/468-7136.** 8 units, 6 with bathroom. A/C. C$100 (US$67) double without bathroom, C$115–C$135 (US$77–US$90) double with bathroom; C$145 (US$97) 1-bedroom suite; C$230 (US$153) 2-bedroom suite. Rates include breakfast. AE, MC, V.

Beautifully situated down by the river, this two-story Georgian was built in 1817 as the first branch of the Bank of Canada. All the guest rooms are tastefully decorated, and several have private entrances, like the charming Garden Room, which also has a private trellised deck. All but one have a refrigerator and coffee or tea supplies. The most expensive suite can accommodate four in two bedrooms, a sitting room, and a bathroom. The sitting room, with a fireplace, is extraordinarily comfortable and furnished with eclectic antique pieces.

Pillar & Post Inn. 48 John St. (at King St.), Niagara-on-the-Lake, ON L0S 1J0. ☎ **888/669-5566** or 905/468-2123. Fax 905/468-1472. www.vintageinns.com. 123 units. A/C

MINIBAR TV TEL. C$235–C$250 (US$157–US$167) double; C$275–C$335 (US$183–US$223) suite. Extra person C$20 (US$13). AE, DC, ER, MC, V.

The discreetly elegant Pillar & Post is a couple of blocks from the madding crowds on Queen Street. In recent years it has been transformed into one of the most sophisticated accommodations in town, complete with a spa featuring the latest in luxe treatments. The airy lobby boasts a fireplace, lush plantings, and comfortable seating. The style is classic Canadiana: The spacious guest rooms contain old-fashioned furniture, Windsor-style chairs, pine cabinets (albeit with color TVs tucked inside), and historical engravings. In the back is a secluded pool (some rooms facing the pool on the ground level have bay windows and window boxes). Warmed by fires on cool evenings, the two dining rooms offer an eclectic menu with everything from prime rib and Yorkshire pudding to Szechuan roast duck and bourbon-marinated beef tenderloin with smoky bacon jus. Entrees run C$17 to C$30 (US$11 to US$20). The adjoining wine bar features a curvaceous bar and a large selection of local and international wines. The spa offers a full range of body treatments and massage therapies, with prices starting at C$45 (US$30), plus a Japanese-style warm mineral-spring pool, complete with cascading waterfall. Other facilities include an indoor pool and an attractively landscaped outdoor pool, a sauna, a whirlpool, and bike rentals.

Prince of Wales Hotel. 6 Picton St., Niagara-on-the-Lake, ON L0S 1J0. ☎ **888/669-5566** or 905/468-3246. Fax 905/468-1310. www.vintageinns.com. 108 units. A/C TV TEL. C$350 (US$233) and up double. Extra person C$20 (US$13). Special packages available. AE, MC, V.

For a lively atmosphere retaining the elegance and charm of a Victorian inn, the Prince of Wales has it all: a main-street location across from the lovely gardens of Simcoe Park; full recreational facilities; lounges, bars, and restaurants; and attractive guest rooms decorated with antiques or reproductions, most with minibars. The bathrooms have bidets. The hotel's original section was built in 1864; in 1999, the hotel was restored to its original glory, and it is now unrivaled as the most luxurious in the district. An impressive old oak bar from Pennsylvania dominates the quiet bar off the lobby. Royals, the elegant main dining room, is decorated in French style. Its menu offers a dozen classics like mustard-crusted rack of lamb or salmon with thyme beurre blanc, priced C$18 to C$28 (US$12 to US$19). Three Feathers is a luxurious greenhouse cafe perfect for breakfast, lunch, or tea. The Queen's Royal lounge, furnished with wingback chairs and armchairs, is pleasant for cocktails or light evening fare. Facilities include an indoor pool, a whirlpool, a fitness center, and bike rental; aerobics classes and massage therapy are offered.

Queen's Landing Inn. P.O. Box 1180, 155 Byron St. (at Melville St.), Niagara-on-the-Lake, ON L0S 1J0. ☎ **888/669-5566** or 905/468-2195. 138 units. A/C MINIBAR TV TEL. C$260 (US$173) double without fireplace, C$275–C$310 (US$183–US$207) double with fireplace, from C$420 (US$280) double with fireplace and Jacuzzi. AE, DC, ER, MC, V.

Overlooking the river but also within walking distance of the theater, the Queen's Landing Inn is a modern Georgian-style mansion offering 71 guest rooms with fireplaces and 32 with fireplaces and Jacuzzis. The spacious rooms are comfortably furnished with half-canopy or brass beds, wingback chairs, and large desks. This hotel attracts a business crowd, in part because of its excellent conference facilities, including 20 meeting rooms. The cozy Bacchu lounge has a fieldstone fireplace, a copper-foil bar, and velvet-cushioned seating. The circular Tiara dining room looks out in summer over the yacht-filled harbor. It's elegantly styled with a grand stained-glass ceiling—a suitable foil for the fine cuisine. At dinner, about a dozen dishes are offered. Priced C$24 to C$36 (US$16 to US$24), they might include parsley-crusted sea bass slow-roasted with Estate chardonnay or roasted rack of lamb with tomato bread pudding, leaf spinach, and warm arugula oil. Breakfast, lunch, and Sunday brunch are served here too. Room service is provided 7am to 11pm, and facilities include an indoor pool, a whirlpool, a sauna, an exercise room, a lap pool, and bicycle rentals.

White Oaks Inn and Racquet Club. Taylor Rd., Niagara-on-the-Lake, ON L0S 1J0. ☎ **905/688-2550.** Fax 905/688-2220. 90 units. A/C TV TEL. July–Aug C$155–C$170 (US$103–US$113) double; C$175–C$240 (US$117–US$160) suite. Off-season, rates drop slightly. AE, DC, ER, MC, V. Take the QEW to Glendale Ave.; the exit ramp leads directly to the resort.

Not far from Niagara-on-the-Lake, the White Oaks is a sports enthusiast's paradise. It's entirely possible to arrive here, be caught in a flurry of athletic activity all weekend, and yet not set foot outside the resort. The guest rooms are as good as the facilities, each featuring oak furniture, vanity sinks, and niceties like a phone and hair dryer in the bathroom. Suites also have brick fireplaces, marble-top desks, Jacuzzis (some heart-shaped), and bidets. Deluxe suites have sitting rooms. Enjoy the restaurant/wine bar, the outdoor terrace cafe, or the pleasantly furnished cafe/coffee shop. Facilities include four outdoor and eight indoor tennis courts, six squash courts, two racquet-ball courts, a Nautilus room, jogging trails, a sauna, suntanning beds, bike rentals, massage therapist, and day-care center with a fully qualified staff.

ALONG THE WINE ROAD
The Vintner's Inn. 3845 Main St., Jordan, ON L0R 1S0. ☎ **905/562-5336.** 9 suites. A/C TEL. C$225–C$315 (US$150–US$210) suite. AE, DC, ER, MC, V.

Right in the village of Jordan, this modern inn boasts handsome suites, each containing an elegantly furnished living room with a fireplace and a bathroom with a whirlpool tub. Seven of the suites are duplexes—one of them, the deluxe loft, has two double beds on its second level—and three are single-level suites with high ceilings. The inn's restaurant, On the Twenty, is across the street (see "Where to Dine Along the Wine Road," below).

WHERE TO DINE
In addition to the listings below, don't forget the dining rooms at the **Pillar & Post, Queen's Landing,** and the **Prince of Wales,** all above.

You can enjoy light meals and lunches at the stylish **Shaw Cafe and Wine Bar,** with an outside patio, at 92 Queen St. (☎ **905/468-4772**). At 84 Queen St., the **Epicurean** offers hearty soups, quiches, sandwiches, and other fine dishes in a sunny Provence-inspired dining room. Service is cafeteria-style. Half a block off Queen, the **Angel Inn,** 224 Regent St. (☎ **905/468-3411**), is a delightfully authentic English pub. For an inexpensive down-home breakfast, go to the **Stagecoach Family Restaurant,** 45 Queen St. (☎ **905/468-3133**).

The Buttery. 19 Queen St. ☎ **905/468-2564.** Reservations recommended (required for Henry VIII feast). Henry VIII feast C$49 (US$33); tavern menu main courses C$8–C$15 (US$5–US$10); dinner main courses C$14–C$22 (US$9–US$15). MC, V. Summer daily 10am–11:30pm; other months daily noon–8pm except Fri and Sat when the Henry VIII feast takes place. Afternoon tea daily 2–5pm. CANADIAN/ENGLISH/CONTINENTAL.

The Buttery has been a main-street dining landmark for years, known for its weekend Henry VIII feasts, when "serving wenches" will "cosset" you with food and wine while jongleurs and musickers entertain. You'll be served "four removes"—four courses involving broth, chicken, roast lamb, roast pig, sherry trifle, syllabub, and cheese, all washed down with wine, ale, and mead. A full tavern menu is served 11am to 5:30pm and Monday all day, featuring spareribs, an 8-ounce New York strip, shrimp in garlic sauce, and such English pub fare as steak, kidney, and mushroom pie and lamb curry. Take home some of the fresh-baked goods—pies, strudels, dumplings, cream puffs, or scones.

Fans Court. 135 Queen St. ☎ **905/468-4511.** Reservations recommended. Main courses C$10–C$21 (US$7–US$14). AE, DC, MC, V. Daily noon–10pm. CHINESE.

Some of the best food in town is served at this comfortable Chinese spot, decorated with fans, cushioned bamboo chairs, and round tables with golden cloths. In summer, the courtyard has tables for outdoor dining. The cuisine is primarily Cantonese and Szechuan. Singapore beef, moo shu pork, Szechuan scallops, and lemon chicken are just a few of the dishes available. If you wish, you can order Peking duck 24 hours in advance.

Ristorante Giardino. In the Gate House Hotel, 142 Queen St. ☎ **905/468-3263.** Main courses C$20–C$30 (US$13–US$20). AE, ER, MC, V. Summer daily noon–2:30pm and 5–10pm; winter daily 5:30–9pm. ITALIAN.

On the ground floor of the Gate House is this sleek, ultramodern restaurant with a gleaming marble-top bar and brass accents throughout. The food is Northern Italian with fresh American accents. Main courses might include baked salmon with olive paste and tomato concasse, veal tenderloin marinated with garlic and rosemary, and braised pheasant in juniper berry/vegetable sauce. There are several pasta dishes too, plus such appealing appetizers as langoustine medallions garnished with orange-and-fennel salad. Desserts include a fine tiramisu.

ALONG THE WINE ROAD

On the Twenty Restaurant & Wine Bar. 3836 Main St., Jordan. ☎ **905/562-7313.** Main courses C$22–C$32 (US$15–US$21). AE, DC, MC, V. Daily 11:30am–3pm and 5–10pm. CANADIAN.

At Cave Spring Cellars, this restaurant is a favorite among foodies, its gold-painted dining rooms casting a warm glow. The cuisine features ingredients from many producers, giving On the Twenty a small-town feel: For example, the quail is from Joe Speck, and the guinea fowl originates at Keyhole Ranch. Naturally, there's an extensive selection of Ontario wines, including some wonderful ice wines to accompany desserts like lemon tart and fruit cobbler. On the Twenty is associated with the Vintner's Inn across the street (see "Where to Stay Along the Wine Road," above).

✪ Vineland Estates. 3620 Moyer Rd., Vineland. ☎ **905/562-7088.** Reservations strongly recommended. Main courses C$19–C$29 (US$13–US$19). AE, DC, MC, V. Daily 11am–3pm and 5–9pm. INTERNATIONAL.

Vineland Estates serves up some of the most innovative food. On warm days you can dine on a deck under a spreading tree or stay in the airy dining room furnished with white cloth–covered tables. The kitchen makes using local ingredients its mission wherever possible. Main courses start off strong with a goat-cheese soufflé resting atop local Cookstown greens, caramelized onions, and sweet-pepper coulis. Dinners can follow up with one of four pastas, including a radiatore with sautéed sweetbreads and marinated artichokes in mustard jus. Those craving a meatier main could choose venison with wild rice and mashed veggie in juniper-thyme reduction. For dessert, there's a wonderful tasting plate of Canadian farm cheeses, including the wonderful Abbey St. Benoit blue Ermite.

11 Niagara Falls: A Honeymoon Haven

Niagara Falls was for decades the region's honeymoon capital. I say this in an attempt to explain its endless motels (each boasting at least one suite with a heart-shaped pink bed). Today, it's better known for its casino, amusement parks, and wax museums. Nonetheless, nothing can steal the thunder of the falls . . . well, almost nothing—long-time locals fondly reminisce about the time when Marilyn Monroe came here to film *Niagara* in 1953.

ESSENTIALS

VISITOR INFORMATION Contact the **Niagara Falls Canada Visitor and Convention Bureau,** 5433 Victoria Ave., Niagara Falls, ON L2G 3L1 (☎ **905/ 356-6061**), or the **Niagara Parks Commission,** Box 150, 7400 Portage Rd. S., Niagara Falls, ON L2E 6T2 (☎ **905/356-2241**). **Summer information centers** are open at Table Rock House, Maid of the Mist Plaza, Rapids View parking lot, and Niagara-on-the-Lake.

GETTING THERE If you're driving from Toronto, take the QEW Niagara. **Amtrak** and **VIA Rail** operate trains between Toronto (☎ **416/366-8411**) and New York, stopping in St. Catharines and Niagara Falls. Call ☎ **800/361-1235** in Canada or 800/USA-RAIL in the United States (www.amtrak.com).

GETTING AROUND The best way to get around is aboard the **People Movers** (☎ **905/357-9340**). Park at Rapid View, several kilometers from the falls. The parking is free, and from here you can take the People Mover for C$4.50 (US$3) per person. Or park in Preferred Parking (overlooking the falls) for C$8 (US$5) with no in/out privileges. The People Mover is an attraction in itself. It travels in a loop, making nine stops from Rapid View to the Spanish Aero Car. Shuttles to the falls also operate from downtown and Lundy's Lane; an all-day pass is C$5 (US$3.35) adults and C$2.50 (US$1.65) children 6 to 12.

SEEING THE FAMOUS FALLS

You simply can't do anything else before you've seen ✪ **Niagara Falls,** the seventh natural wonder of the world. The most exciting way to do that is from the decks of the ✪ *Maid of the Mist,* 5920 River Rd. (☎ **905/358-5781**). This sturdy boat takes you right in—through the turbulent waters around the American Falls, past the Rock of Ages, and to the foot of the Horseshoe Falls, where in a minute 34.5 million Imperial gallons (41.4 million US gallons) of water tumble over the 176-foot-high cataract. You'll get wet and your glasses will mist, but that won't detract from the thrill. Mid-May to mid-October, boats leave daily from the dock on the parkway just down from the Rainbow Bridge. Fares are C$10 (US$7) adults and C$7 (US$4.35) children 6 to 12; it's free for children 5 and under.

Go down under the falls via the elevator at Table Rock House, which drops you 150 feet through solid rock to the **Journey Behind the Falls** (☎ **905/354-1551**). You'll appreciate the yellow biodegradable mackintosh you're given. The tunnels and viewing portals are open all year, and admission is C$6 (US$4.15) adults and C$3 (US$2) children 6 to 12; children under 6 are free.

Get Outta Town!

If the tacky commercial side of Niagara Falls starts to grate on your nerves, get out of town by driving along the Niagara Parkway; with its endless parks and gardens, the area is an oasis for nature lovers. See below.

A Money-Saving Pass

For C$19 (US$13) adults and C$10 (US$6) children 6 to 12, buy an **Explorer's Passport** securing admission to the Journey Behind the Falls, the Great Gorge Adventure, and the Niagara Spanish Aero Car, plus all-day transportation aboard the People Movers.

To view the falls from a spectacular angle, take a 9-minute spin (C$175/US$117 for two) in a chopper over the whole Niagara area. Helicopters leave from the heliport, adjacent to the whirlpool at the junction of Victoria Avenue and Niagara Parkway, daily 9am to dusk, weather permitting. Contact **Niagara Helicopters,** 3731 Victoria Ave. (☎ **905/357-5672**).

Or you can ride up in the external glass-fronted elevators 520 feet to the top of the **Skylon Tower Observation Deck,** 5200 Robinson St. (☎ **905/356-2651**). June to Labour Day, the observation deck is open daily 8am to midnight (call in other seasons). Adults pay C$8 (US$5), seniors C$7 (US$4.35), and children 6 to 12 and under C$4.50 (US$3).

You can get a similar perspective from the observation floors atop the 325-foot **Minolta Tower Centre,** 6732 Oakes Dr. (☎ **905/356-1501**). On-site attractions include the Volcano Mine Ride, the Galaxian Space Adventure, the Cybermind Virtual Reality, and the free *Waltzing Waters* (a computerized music, light, and water show given May to October nightly every 30 minutes 9pm to midnight). The tower is open daily 9am to 9pm (to 1am June to Sept, to 10pm Mar to Apr and Oct to Dec). Admission is C$6 (US$4) adults and C$5 (US$3.35) students/seniors; free for children under 10. A day pass for the observation deck and unlimited entry to the games costs C$20 (US$13) adults only. An unlimited play pass for the games only is C$15 (US$10).

For a thrilling introduction to Niagara Falls, stop by the **IMAX Theater,** 6170 Buchanan Ave. (☎ **905/358-3611**), and view the raging, swirling waters in *Niagara: Miracles, Myths, and Magic,* shown on a six-story-high screen. Admission is C$8 (US$5) adults, C$7 (US$4.65) seniors/children 12 to 18, and C$6 (US$3.65) children 5 to 11; children under 5 are free.

In winter, the falls are also thrilling to see, for the ice bridge and other formations are quite remarkable.

THE FALLS BY NIGHT Don't miss seeing the falls lit by 22 xenon gas spotlights (each producing 250 million candlepower of light), in shades of rose pink, magenta, amber, blue, and green. Call ☎ **800/563-2557** in the U.S., or 905/356-6061 for schedules. The show starts around 5pm in winter, 8:30pm in spring and fall, and 9pm in summer. In addition, July to early September, free fireworks are set off every Friday at 11pm to illuminate the falls.

MORE NIAGARA FALLS ATTRACTIONS

The biggest crowds aren't here for the falls anymore; instead, they head to **Casino Niagara,** 5705 Falls Ave. (☎ **905/374-3598**). This 24-hour monolithic complex features 123 gambling tables that offer blackjack, roulette, baccarat, and several different pokers, plus 3,000 slot and video poker machines. The casino contains five restaurants, including the Hard Rock Café; seven lounges; and several shops.

Founded in 1827, the **Niagara Falls Museum,** 5651 River Rd. (☎ **905/356-2151**), has exhibits ranging from Egyptian mummies to an odd mix of Indian and Asian artifacts, shells, fossils, and minerals, plus the Freaks of Nature display. It's open daily: summer 8:30am to 11pm and winter 10am to 5pm. Admission is C$8 (US$5) adults,

C$7 (US$4.35) seniors, C$5 (US$3.35) students 11 to 18, and C$4 (US$2.65) children 5 to 10; under 5 are free.

A popular family attraction is **White Water,** 7430 Lundy's Lane (☎ **905/ 357-3380**), where you don your swimsuit and swoop around the corkscrew turns of the five slides into the heated pools at the bottom or frolic in the wave pool. If you prefer to wallow in the hot tub, you can do that too. Tiny tykes can ride three small slides designed for them. Take a picnic and spend the greater part of the day (there's also a snack bar). Admission is C$16 (US$11) adults and C$11 (US$7) children 12 and under. It's open daily: July and August 9am to 6pm and May, June, September, and early October 10am to 4pm.

Another don't-miss spot for families is **Marineland,** 7657 Portage Rd. (☎ **905/ 356-9565**). At the aquarium/theater, King Waldorf, Marineland's mascot, presides over performances given by killer whales, talented dolphins, and sea lions. Friendship Cove, a 4½-million-gallon breeding and observation tank, lets the little ones see killer whales up close. Another aquarium features displays of freshwater fish. At the small wildlife display, kids enjoy petting and feeding the deer and seeing bears and Canadian elk. Marineland also has theme-park rides, including a roller coaster, a Tivoli wheel, Dragon Boat rides, and a fully equipped playground. The big thriller is Dragon Mountain, a roller coaster that loops, double-loops, and spirals its way through 1,000 feet of tunnels. There are three restaurants, but you can picnic at one of several tables provided. In summer, admission is C$25 (US$17) adults and C$22 (US$15) children 5 to 9/seniors; children 4 and under are free. It's lower in other seasons. The park is open daily: July to August 9am to 6pm, mid-April to mid-May and September to mid-October 10am to 4pm, mid-May to June 10am to 5pm. Rides open in late May and close the first Monday in October. In town, drive south on Stanley Street and follow the signs; from the QEW take the McCleod Road exit.

ALONG THE NIAGARA PARKWAY

If you're driving into Canada from the American side of the falls, you're in for a pleasant surprise. Whatever you think of the tourist-oriented town, you can't help but love the ✪ **Niagara Parkway** on the Canadian side of the falls. Unlike the American side, it's filled with natural wonders, including vast expanses of parkland. This 35-mile parkway with bike path is a refreshing respite from the neon glow that envelops the town both day and night.

You can drive all the way from Niagara Falls to Niagara-on-the-Lake on the parkway, taking in attractions en route. The first you'll come to is the **Great Gorge Adventure,** 4330 River Rd. (☎ **905/374-1221**). Stroll along the scenic boardwalk beside the raging white waters of the Great Gorge Rapids and wonder how it must have felt to challenge this mighty torrent, where the river rushes through the narrow channel at an average speed of 22 m.p.h. Admission is C$5 (US$3.50) adults and C$2.75 (US$1.85) children 6 to 12; kids under 6 are free. May to October, it's open daily 9am to 6pm.

Half a mile farther north you'll arrive at the **Niagara Spanish Aero Car** (☎ **905/ 354-5711**), a red-and-yellow cable-car contraption that'll whisk you on a 3,600-foot jaunt between two points in Canada, high above the whirlpool, providing excellent views of the landscape. Admission is C$5 (US$3.35) adults and C$2.50 (US$1.65) children 6 to 12; kids under 6 are free. It's open daily: May 9am to 6pm, June 9am to 8pm, July and August 9am to 9pm, September 10am to 7:30pm, and October 9am to 5pm.

At **Ride Niagara,** 5755 River Rd. (☎ **905/374-7433**), you can experience what it must be like going over the falls without risking your life. Before going over the

Niagara Falls

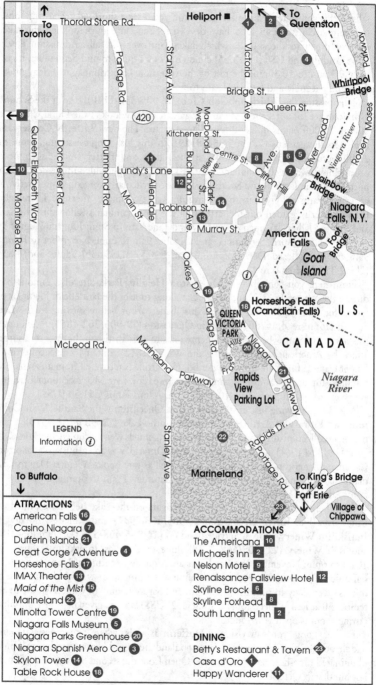

LEGEND
Information ⓘ

ATTRACTIONS
American Falls ⑯
Casino Niagara ⑦
Dufferin Islands ㉑
Great Gorge Adventure ④
Horseshoe Falls ⑰
IMAX Theater ⑬
Maid of the Mist ⑮
Marineland ㉒
Minolta Tower Centre ⑲
Niagara Falls Museum ⑤
Niagara Parks Greenhouse ⑳
Niagara Spanish Aero Car ③
Skylon Tower ⑭
Table Rock House ⑱

ACCOMMODATIONS
The Americana ⑩
Michael's Inn ②
Nelson Motel ⑨
Renaissance Fallsview Hotel ⑫
Skyline Brock ⑥
Skyline Foxhead ⑧
South Landing Inn ②

DINING
Betty's Restaurant & Tavern ㉓
Casa d'Oro ❶
Happy Wanderer ⓫

falls in this computerized motion simulator, you'll see a short video showing some of the weirder contraptions folks have devised for the same journey. Then you take an elevator down to the shuttle, which takes you over the falls. Admission is C$10 (US$7) adults and C$6 (US$3.65) children 5 to 12. June to mid-September, it's open daily 9:15am to 10:30pm; the rest of the year, hours are Monday to Friday noon to 5pm and Saturday and Sunday 11am to 5pm.

After passing the **Whirlpool Golf Club** (☎ **905/356-1140**), stop at the **School of Horticulture** for a free view of the vast gardens, plus a look at the Floral Clock, containing 25,000 plants in its 40-foot-diameter face. The new **Butterfly Conservatory** is also in the gardens (☎ **905/356-8119**). In this lush tropical setting, more than 2,000 butterflies (50 international species) float and flutter among such nectar-producing flowers as lantanas and pentas. The large bright blue luminescent Morpho butterflies from Central and South America are particularly gorgeous. Interpretive and other programs are given in the auditorium and two smaller theaters. There's also a native butterfly garden outside, attracting the more familiar swallowtails, fritillaries, and painted ladies. It's open daily: May and June 9am to 8pm; July and August 9am to 9pm; March, April, September, and October 9am to 6pm; November to February 9am to 5pm (closed Dec 25). Admission is C$7 (US$4.35) adults and C$3.50 (US$2.35) children 6 to 12.

From here you can drive to **Queenston Heights Park,** site of a famous battle during the War of 1812. You can take a walking tour of the battlefield. Picnic or play tennis for C$6 (US$4) per hour in this shaded arbor before moving to the **Laura Secord Homestead,** Partition Street in Queenston (☎ **905/262-4851**). The home of this heroic woman, who threaded enemy lines to alert British authorities to a surprise attack by American soldiers during the War of 1812, contains a fine collection of Upper Canada furniture from the period, plus artifacts recovered from an archaeological dig. Stop at the candy shop and ice-cream parlor. Late May to Labour Day, tours are given every half hour daily 10am to 6pm. Admission is C$1.50 (US$1).

Also worth viewing just off the parkway in Queenston is the **Samuel Weir Collection and Library of Art,** RR #1, Niagara-on-the-Lake (☎ **905/262-4510**), a small personal collection displayed as it was when Samuel Weir occupied the house. Mr. Weir (1898 to 1981), a lawyer from London, Ontario, was an enthusiastic collector of Canadian, American, and European art, as well as rare books. Victoria Day to Canadian Thanksgiving, it's open Wednesday to Saturday 11am to 5pm and Sunday 1 to 5pm. Admission is free.

From here the parkway continues into Niagara-on-the-Lake (see above), lined with fruit farms like **Kurtz Orchards** (☎ **905/468-2937**) and wineries, notably the **Inniskillin Winery,** Line 3, Service Road 66 (☎ **905/468-3554** or 905/468-2187), and **Reif Winery** (☎ **905/468-7738**). June to October, Inniskillin is open daily 10am to 6pm; November to May, hours are Monday to Saturday 10am to 5pm. The self-guided free tour has 20 stops explaining the process of wine making. A guided tour is given daily in summer at 2:30pm and Saturday only in winter. May 1 to September 30 at Reif Winery, tours costing C$2 (US$1.35) are given daily at 1:30pm; the tasting room is open year-round.

Farther along, you can visit the **Dufferin Islands,** where you can swim, rent a paddle boat, explore the surrounding woodland areas, and play a round of golf on the illuminated nine-hole par-three course. Open from the second Sunday in April to the last Sunday in October.

A little farther on, stop for a picnic in **King's Bridge Park** and stroll along the beaches before driving on to **Fort Erie,** 350 Lakeshore Rd., Fort Erie (☎ **905/ 871-0540**), a reconstruction of the fort that was seized by the Americans in July 1814, besieged later by the British, and finally blown up as the Americans retreated across the river to Buffalo. Guards in period costume stand sentry duty, fire the cannons, and demonstrate drill and musket practice. The first Saturday in May to mid-September and weekends only to Canadian Thanksgiving (U.S. Columbus Day), it's open daily 10am to 6pm. Admission is C$5 (US$3.35) adults and C$3 (US$2) children 6 to 16; kids under 6 are free.

WHERE TO STAY

Every other sign in Niagara Falls advertises a motel. In summer, rates go up and down according to the traffic, and some proprietors won't even quote rates ahead of time. So be warned. You can secure a reasonably priced room if you're lucky enough to arrive on a "down night," but with the casino in town that's becoming a rare occurrence. Still, always request a lower rate.

EXPENSIVE

Renaissance Fallsview Hotel. 6455 Buchanan Ave., Niagara Falls, ON L2G 3V9. ☎ **800/ 363-3255** or 905/357-5200. Fax 905/357-3422. www.niagara.com/nf-renaissance. 262 units. A/C MINIBAR TV TEL. C$109–C$349 (US$73–US$233) double; C$189–C$315 (US$126–US$210) whirlpool rooms. AE, DC, DISC, ER, MC, V. Free parking.

The Renaissance features tasteful yet colorful guest rooms decorated with wooden furniture (TVs are tucked away in cabinets). The bathrooms have double sinks and all the modern accoutrements. Some rooms have an excellent view of the falls; city views are less pricey. Renaissance Club rooms come with three phones and a Jacuzzi tub. Mulberry's restaurant serves continental fare, and there's a cafe on the 18th floor. Facilities include an indoor pool, a whirlpool, a health club with saunas, squash and racquetball courts, and a fitness and weight room.

Skyline Brock. 5685 Falls Ave., Niagara Falls, ON L2E 6W7. ☎ **800/263-7135** or 905/ 374-4444. 233 units. A/C TV TEL. Mid-June to Sept C$139–C$239 (US$93–US$159) double; Oct–Dec and Apr to mid-June C$99–C$160 (US$66–US$107) double; winter C$80–C$115 (US$53–US$77) double. Children under 18 stay free in parents' room. Extra person C$10 (US$7). Special packages available. AE, DC, DISC, ER, MC, V. Parking C$7 (US$4.65).

For an unmarred view of the falls, try the Skyline Brock, which has been hosting honeymooners and falls visitors since 1929. It still has a certain air of splendor, with a huge chandelier and marble walls in the lobby. About 150 of the guest rooms face the falls; city-view rooms are slightly smaller and less expensive. The 10th-floor Rainbow Room, with a lovely view, serves a popular continental menu that includes half a roast chicken with cranberry sauce, salmon hollandaise, and prime rib, priced at C$15 to C$27 (US$10 to US$18). Isaac's Bar is available for drinks, and there's also the Lobby Cafe.

Skyline Foxhead. 5875 Falls Ave., Niagara Falls, ON L2E 6W7. ☎ **800/263-7135** or 905/374-4444. 400 units. A/C TV TEL. Mid-June to Sept C$189–C$299 (US$126–US$199) double; Oct–Dec and Apr to mid-June C$125–C$175 (US$83–US$117) double; winter C$90–C$130 (US$60–US$87) double. Extra person C$10 (US$7). Children under 18 stay free in parents' room. Special packages available. AE, DC, DISC, ER, MC, V. Valet parking C$10 (US$7).

The Foxhead is another hotel to consider if you're looking for a room with a view (about half with balconies). In the past few years, the guest rooms have been renovated in a tasteful manner. The 14th-floor penthouse dining room takes fair advantage of the view with its large glass windows and serves a daily buffet for breakfast, lunch, and dinner, with nightly dancing to a live band (in season). Or there's the Steak and Burger for reasonably priced fare. The outdoor rooftop pool is a great place to relax.

MODERATE

The Americana. 8444 Lundy's Lane, Niagara Falls, ON L2H 1H4. ☎ **905/356-8444.** Fax 905/356-8576. 120 units. A/C TV TEL. Late June to late Aug C$130–C$170 (US$87–US$113) double; Sept to mid-June C$80–C$120 (US$53–US$80) double. Extra person C$10 (US$7). AE, DISC, ER, MC, V. Free parking.

The Americana is one of the nicer moderately priced hotels on this strip, set in 25 acres of grounds with a pleasant shady picnic area, a tennis court, indoor and outdoor pools, a whirlpool, a sauna, and a squash court. The large guest rooms are pleasantly decked out in muted colors and have good-sized windows. Some suites have whirlpool tubs and fireplaces. A dining room, lounge, and coffee shop are on the premises.

Michael's Inn. 5599 River Rd., Niagara Falls, ON L2E 3H3. ☎ **800/263-9390** or 905/354-2727. Fax 905/374-7706. www.michaelsinn.com. 130 units. A/C TV TEL. June 16–Sept 15 C$98–C$208 (US$65–US$139) double; Sept 16–June 15 C$59–C$178 (US$39–US$119) double. AE, CB, DC, ER, MC, V. Free parking.

At this four-story white building overlooking the Niagara River gorge, the large guest rooms are nicely decorated with modern conveniences. Many of the rooms have whirlpools; some also have special themes, like the Garden of Paradise and the Scarlett O'Hara. There's a solarium pool out back. The Ember's Open Hearth Dining Room is just that: The charcoal pit is enclosed behind glass so you can see all the cooking action. There's a lounge too.

INEXPENSIVE

Nelson Motel. 10655 Niagara River Pkwy., Niagara Falls, ON L2E 6S6. ☎ **905/295-4754.** 25 units. A/C TV. Mid-June to mid-Sept C$60–C$100 (US$40–US$67) double; late Sept to mid-Nov and mid-Mar to mid-June C$45–C$55 (US$30–US$37) double. Closed mid-Nov to mid-Mar. Rollaways and cribs extra. MC, V. Free parking.

For budget accommodations, try the Nelson, run by John and Dawn Pavlakovich, who live in the large adjacent house. The units have character, especially the family units with a double bedroom adjoined by a twin-bedded room for the kids. Regular units have modern furniture. None has a phone, and singles have a shower only. All units face the fenced-in pool and neatly trimmed lawn with umbrellaed tables and shrubs. The Nelson is a short drive from the falls overlooking the Niagara River, away from the hustle and bustle of Niagara itself.

IN NEARBY QUEENSTON

✪ **South Landing Inn.** At the corner of Kent and Front sts. (P.O. Box 269), Queenston, ON L0S 1L0. ☎ **905/262-4634.** Fax 905/262-4639. 23 units. A/C TV. Mid-Apr to Oct C$90–C$110 (US$60–US$73) double; Nov to mid-Apr C$60–C$70 (US$40–US$47) double. AE, MC, V. Free parking.

The original section of Queenston's South Landing Inn was built in the 1800s and today has five attractive rooms furnished with early Canadian furnishings, including four-poster beds. Other rooms are across the street in the modern annex. There's a distant view of the river from the inn's balcony. In the original inn you'll also find a cozy dining room with gingham-covered tables, where breakfast is served for C$4 (US$2.65).

WHERE TO DINE

Betty's Restaurant & Tavern. 8921 Sodom Rd. ☎ **905/295-4436.** Main courses C$8–C$16 (US$5–US$11). AE, MC, V. Mon–Sat 7am–10pm, Sun 9am–9pm. CANADIAN.

Betty's is a local favorite for honest food at fair prices. It's a family dining room where the staff will attempt to stuff you to the gills with massive platters of fish-and-chips, roast beef, and seafood, all including soup or juice, vegetable, and potato. There are burgers and sandwiches too. It's all but impossible to save room for the enormous portions of home-baked pies. Breakfast and lunch also offer good low-budget eating.

Casa d'Oro. 5875 Victoria Ave. ☎ **905/356-5646.** Reservations recommended. Main courses C$15–C$24 (US$10–US$16). AE, DC, DISC, ER, MC, V. Mon–Fri noon–3pm and 4–11pm, Sat 4pm–1am, Sun 4–10pm. ITALIAN.

Don't be intimidated by the wealth of kitsch: For Italian dining amid gilt busts of Caesar, Venetian-style lamps, statues of Roman gladiators, and murals of Roman and Venetian scenes, go to Casa d'Oro. Start with clams casino or the brodetto Antonio (a giant crouton topped with poached eggs, floating on a savory broth garnished with parsley and accompanied by grated cheese). Follow with specialties like saltimbocca alla romana or sole basilica (flavored with lime juice, paprika, and basil). Finish with a selection from the dessert wagon or really spoil yourself with cherries jubilee or bananas flambé.

Happy Wanderer. 6405 Stanley Ave. ☎ **905/354-9825.** Main courses C$10–C$26 (US$7–US$17). AE, MC, V. Daily 9am–11pm. GERMAN.

Warm hospitality reigns at the chalet-style Happy Wanderer, which offers a full selection of schnitzels, wursts, and other German specialties. Transport yourself back to the Black Forest among the beer steins and the game trophies on the walls. The several rooms include the Black Forest Room, with a huge intricately carved sideboard and cuckoo clock, and the Jage Stube, with solid wood benches and woven tablecloths. At lunch there are omelets, cold platters, sandwiches, and burgers. Dinner might start with goulash soup and proceed with bratwurst, knockwurst, rauchwurst (served with sauerkraut and potato salad), or a schnitzel-wiener, Holstein, or jaeger. All entrees include potatoes, salad, and rye bread. Desserts include, naturally, Black Forest cake and apple strudel.

Niagara Parkway Commission Restaurants

The Niagara Parkway Commission has commandeered the most spectacular scenic spots, where it operates some reasonably priced dining outlets. The **Table Rock Restaurant** (☎ **905/354-3631**) and **Victoria Park Restaurant** (☎ **905/356-2217**) are both on the Parkway right by the falls and are pleasant, if crowded. The **Diner on the Green** (☎ **905/356-7221**) is also on the Parkway but at the Whirlpool Golf Course near Queenston. It's very plain. The listing below offers the best dining experience.

Queenston Heights. 14276 Niagara Pkwy. ☎ **905/262-4274.** Reservations recommended. Main courses C$21–C$30 (US$14–US$20). AE, MC, V. Daily 11:30am–3pm; Sun–Fri 5–9pm, Sat 5–10pm. Closed Jan to mid-Mar. CANADIAN.

The star of the Niagara Parkway Commission's eateries stands dramatically atop Queenston Heights. Set in the park among fir, cypress, silver birch, and maple, the open-air balcony affords a magnificent view of the lower Niagara River and the rich fruit-growing land through which it flows. Or you can sit under the cathedral ceiling with its heavy cross beams where the flue of the stone fireplace reaches to the roof. At dinner, among the selections might be Atlantic salmon fillet with Riesling-chive hollandaise, prime rib, or grilled pork with apples and cider-dijon mustard sauce. Afternoon tea is served 3 to 5pm in summer. If nothing else, go for a drink on the deck and the terrific view.

12 St. Catharines to Port Colborne & Hamilton

ST. CATHARINES & THE WELLAND CANAL

In the heart of wine country and the Niagara fruit belt, the historic city of **St. Catharines** is home to two major events: the **Royal Canadian Henley Regatta** in early August and the 10-day **Niagara Grape and Wine Festival** in late September.

Year-round you can also observe the operations of the **Welland Canal,** running through the town of Port Colborne, south of St. Catharines. Built to circumvent Niagara Falls, the Welland Canal connects Lake Ontario to Lake Erie, 327 feet higher than Lake Ontario. Some 27 feet deep, the canal enables large ocean vessels to navigate the Great Lakes. The 26-mile-long canal has seven locks, each with an average lift of 46½ feet. The average transit time for any vessel is 12 hours. More than a thousand oceangoing vessels travel through in a year, the most common cargoes being wheat and iron ore.

The best places to observe the canal are at the **Welland Canal Viewing and Information Centres,** at Lock 3 in St. Catharines (on Government Road, north of Glendale Avenue off the QEW) and at Lock 8 in Port Colborne. At the first, from a raised platform you can watch ships from more than 50 countries passing between Lake Ontario and Lake Erie. The Canal Parkway allows you to walk beside the canal and follow the vessels. From the road below the canal you can observe only the funnels moving along above the top of the bank. It's also fun to bike along the canal between Locks 1 and 3.

Also at Lock 3, the **St. Catharines Museum** (☎ **905/984-8880**) houses displays illustrating the construction and working of the Welland Canal, as well as pioneer and War of 1812 memorabilia. Kids enjoy the Discovery Room, where they can operate a telephone switchboard or dress up in pioneer clothing and enjoy other hands-on fun. Admission is C$3 (US$2) adults, C$2 (US$1.35) students/seniors, C$1 (US65¢) children 5 to 13, and C$7 (US$4.65) families. It's open daily: Labour Day to Victoria Day 9am to 5pm and Victoria Day to Labour Day 9am to 9pm (closed December 25 and 26 and New Year's Day).

If you drive to St. Catharines from Niagara-on-the-Lake, on the right just before you enter St. Catharines is the free **Happy Rolph Bird Sanctuary and Children's Petting Farm** (☎ **905/935-1484**), which the kids will love. Late May to mid-October, it's open daily 10am to dusk.

At Port Colborne, the southern end of the canal opens into Lake Erie. You can gain a good sense of the area's history and development at the free **Port Colborne Historical and Marine Museum,** 280 King St. (☎ **905/834-7604**). The six-building complex downtown has a fully operational blacksmith shop and a tearoom. May to December, it's open daily noon to 5pm.

In Vineland, **Prudhomme's Landing–Wet 'n' Wild,** off Victoria Avenue (☎ **905/ 562-7304**), features water slides, a wave pool, go-karts, kids' rides, and miniature golf. An all-day pass costs C$11 (US$7) adults/children 5 or over. Mid-June to Labour Day, it's open daily 10am to 8pm (water park closes at 7pm).

ATTRACTIONS NEAR HAMILTON

On a landlocked harbor spanned at its entrance by the Burlington Skyway's dramatic sweep, **Hamilton** has long been known as "Steeltown." Although it has steel mills and smoke-belching chimneys, the town has received an extensive facelift in the past decade, but, more important, it's home to a couple of worthwhile attractions.

On the northern approaches to the city, the ✪ **Royal Botanical Gardens,** Highway 6 (☎ **905/527-1158**), spreads over 3,000 acres. The Rock Garden features spring bulbs in May, summer flowers in June to September, and chrysanthemums in October. The Laking Garden blazes during June and July with irises, peonies, and lilies. The arboretum fills with the heady scent of lilac from the end of May to early June, and with the exquisite color bursts of rhododendrons and azaleas thereafter. The Centennial Rose Garden is at its best late June to mid-September. Admission is C$7 (US$4.65) adults, C$6 (US$4) seniors/students, and C$2 (US$1.35) children 5 to 12; children 4 and under are free. The outdoor garden areas are open daily 9:30am to 6pm; the Mediterranean Garden is open daily 9am to 5pm.

Forty kilometers (25 miles) of nature trails crisscross the area, while nearby, and still part of the gardens, is **Cootes Paradise,** a natural wildlife sanctuary with trails leading through some 18,000 acres of water, marsh, and wooded ravines. For a trail-guide map, stop in at either the **Nature Centre** (open daily 10am to 4pm) or **headquarters** at 680 Plains Rd. W. (Highway 2), Burlington. Two teahouses—one overlooking the Rock Garden, the other the Rose Garden—serve refreshments.

Dundurn Castle, Dundurn Park, York Boulevard (☎ **905/546-2872**), affords a glimpse of the opulent life as it was lived in this part of southern Ontario in the mid–19th century. It was built between 1832 and 1835 by Sir Allan Napier MacNab, prime minister of the United Provinces of Canada in the mid-1850s and a founder of the Great Western Railway; he was knighted by Queen Victoria for the part he played in the Rebellion of 1837. The 35-plus–room mansion has been restored and furnished in the style of 1855. The gray stucco exterior, with its classical Greek portico, is impressive enough, but inside, from the formal dining rooms to Lady MacNab's boudoir, the furnishings are rich. The museum contains a fascinating collection of Victoriana. In December, the castle is decorated splendidly for a Victorian Christmas. From downtown Hamilton, take King Street West to Dundurn Street, turn right, and Dundurn will run into York Boulevard. Admission is C$6 (US$4) adults, C$6 (US$3.65) seniors, C$4.50 (US$3) students, and C$2.50 (US$1.65) children 6 to 14; children 5 and under are free. June to Labour Day, it's open daily 10am to 4pm; the rest of the year, it's open Tuesday to Sunday noon to 4pm (closed Christmas and New Year's Day).

Just a half-hour drive northwest of Hamilton, off Highway 8 between Hamilton and Cambridge, is the **African Lion Safari** (☎ **519/623-2620**). You can drive your own car or take the guided safari bus through this 750-acre wildlife park containing rhino, cheetah, lion, tiger, giraffe, zebra, vultures, and many other species. There are scenic railroad and boat rides, plus special kids' jungle and water (bring bathing suits) play areas. Admission, including a tour of the large game reserves plus the rides and shows, costs C$17 (US$11) adults, C$13 (US$9) seniors/youths 13 to 17, and C$11 (US$7) children 3 to 12. July to Labour Day, it's open daily 10am to 5:30pm (day after Labour Day to Oct and Apr to June it closes earlier).

WHERE TO DINE

Café Garibaldi. 375 St. Paul St., St. Catharines. ☎ **905/988-9033.** Reservations recommended for dinner. Main courses C$13–C$27 (US$9–US$18). AE, DC, ER, MC, V. Tues–Sat 11:30am–2:30pm and 5–11pm. ITALIAN.

This relaxed spot is a favorite among locals. The menu is filled with Italian staples like zuppa di pesce and veal scaloppine; the homemade lasagne is its most-requested dish. The wine list features both the local vintners' goods and some fine bottles from Italy.

Hennepin's. 1486 Niagara Stone Rd. (Hwy. 55) at Creek Rd., Virgil. ☎ **905/468-1555.** Tapas C$4–C$8 (US$2.65–US$5); main courses C$13–C$25 (US$9–US$17). AE, ER, MC, V. Sun–Wed 11:30am–9pm, Fri–Sat 11:30am–11pm. CONTEMPORARY.

The region's first tapas bar, Hennepin's still stands out. The specialty of the house is Mediterranean- and Asian-inspired tapas—coconut shrimp, olive-stuffed meatballs, chicken satay, samosas—which is served all day. At dinner, there are always temptations like escargots in pernod and pan-seared game pâté with blueberry kirsch sauce to start. The desserts are seriously rich: As evidence, I present the Death by Chocolate cake.

Iseya. 22 James St. (between St. Paul and King sts.), St. Catharines. ☎ **905/688-1141.** Reservations recommended for dinner. Main courses C$12–C$27 (US$8–US$18). AE, MC, V. Mon–Fri 11:30am–2:30pm; Mon–Sat 5–11pm. JAPANESE.

Chef Yasutoshi Hachoitori has had a virtual monopoly since he opened this eatery: Iseya is one of the region's few traditional Japanese restaurants, serving fresh sushi/sashimi, as well as teriyaki, tempura, and sukiyaki dishes.

Rinderlin's. 24 Burgar St., Welland. ☎ **905/735-4411.** Reservations recommended. Main courses C$17–C$30 (US$11–US$20). AE, DC, ER, MC, V. Tues–Fri 11:30am–2pm; Tues–Sat 6–9pm. FRENCH.

An intimate town-house restaurant, Rinderlin's has a good reputation for traditional French cuisine. On the dinner menu, you might find house-smoked trout with horse-radish sauce, roast pork tenderloin with honey-mustard bacon sauce, rack of lamb with minted onion-garlic sauce, and local venison with wild mushrooms and game sauce.

Wellington Court Restaurant. 11 Wellington St., St. Catharines. ☎ **905/682-5518.** Reservations recommended. Main courses C$11–C$23 (US$7–US$15). ER, MC, V. Mon–Sat 11:30am–2:30pm; Tues–Sat 5:30–9:30pm. CONTINENTAL.

In an Edwardian town house with a flower trellis, the dining rooms here feature contemporary decor with modern lithographs and photographs. The menu features daily specials—the fish and pasta of the day, for example—along with such items as beef tenderloin in shallot- and red-wine reduction, roasted breast of chicken on gingered plum preserves, and grilled sea bass with cranberry vinaigrette.

Southwestern Ontario

by Hilary Davidson

The lush, temperate region of **southwestern Ontario** brushes up against three Great Lakes, making for some of Canada's best farmland. A mix of Carolinian forests, rolling hills, and fertile plains, this region can claim more rare flora and fauna than anywhere else in the country. It attracted Canada's early pioneers, and different ethnic groups built their own towns here—these early influences are still felt in local traditions and celebrations. The Scots built towns like **Elora, Fergus,** and **St. Mary's;** the Germans, **Kitchener-Waterloo;** the Mennonites, **Elmira** and **St. Jacobs;** and the English Loyalists, **Stratford** and **London.** This cultural heritage feeds festivals like Oktoberfest, the Highland Games, and the Mennonite quilt sale, but the biggest draw is the world-famous theater festival at Stratford.

1 Exploring the Region

Windsor sits across from Detroit on the Canadian side of the border. From here, you can travel along either Highway 401 east or the more scenic Highway 3 (called the Talbot Trail, running from Windsor to Fort Erie), stopping along the way to visit some major attractions on the Lake Erie shore.

East of Windsor lies London, and from London it's an easy drive to Stratford. From Stratford, you can turn west to Goderich and Bayfield on the shores of Lake Huron or east to Kitchener-Waterloo and then north to Elmira, Elora, and Fergus.

VISITOR INFORMATION

Contact **Ontario Travel/Travelinx Ontario,** Queen's Park, Toronto, ON M7A 2E5 (☎ **800/ONTARIO** 9am to 8pm, or 416/314-0944). The offices are open Monday to Friday 8:30am to 5pm (daily mid-May to mid-Sept). You can also contact them on the Web at **www.travelinx.com**.

THE GREAT OUTDOORS

Ontario's 260 provincial parks offer a staggering array of opportunities for recreation. The daily in-season entry fee for a vehicle is C$6 or C$7 (US$4 or US$4.65) depending on the park; campsites cost anywhere from C$13 to C$20 (US$9 to US$13). For details, contact the **Ontario Ministry of Natural Resources** at ☎ **416/314-2000.**

Point Pelee National Park, southeast of Windsor, offers year-round hiking and (Apr to Oct) bicycle and canoe rentals. For details, contact

---

Staying on a Farm

A farm stay is a unique way to experience Ontario. You'll enjoy home-cooked meals, the peace of the countryside, and the rhythm of daily life on a dairy or mixed farm. You can choose farms in many locations. Rates average C$45 to C$75 (US$30 to US$50) double per night or C$240 (US$160) per week, all meals included. For information, write the **Ontario Vacation Farm Association,** RR #2, Alma, ON N0B 1A0, or contact **Ontario Travel** (above) for its free *Farm Vacation Guide.*

---

the Superintendent, Point Pelee National Park, RR #1, Leamington, ON N8H 3V4 (☎ 519/322-2365). If you're driving from Windsor, take Highway 3 east to reach Pelee Island. At Ruthven, get on Highway 18 and follow the signs to the park.

BIKING   The South Point and Marsh trails in **Rondeau Provincial Park,** near Blenheim (☎ 519/674-1750), are great for cycling. The nearest bike shop is **Reynold Cycle,** 400 St. Clair St., Chatham (☎ 519/354-6084).

BIRD WATCHING   **Point Pelee National Park,** southeast of Windsor (☎ 519/ 322-2371), is one of the continent's premier bird-watching centers. The spring and fall migrations are spectacular; you can spot more than 300 species here. In late summer, it's also the gathering place for flocks of monarch butterflies, which cover the trees before taking off for their migratory flight down south. At the southernmost tip of Canada, which juts down into Lake Erie at the same latitude as northern California, it features some of the same flora—white sassafras, sumac, black walnut, and cedar.

Another good bird-watching outpost is **Jack Miner's Bird Sanctuary,** Road 3 West, 3.2km (2 miles) north of Kingsville off Division Road (☎ 519/733-4034). The famed naturalist established the sanctuary to protect migrating Canada geese; the best time to visit is late October and November, when thousands of migrating waterfowl stop over. At other times you can see the 50 or so Canada geese and the few hundred ducks, plus wild turkeys, pheasant, and peacocks. The museum displays artifacts and photographs relating to Jack Miner. Admission is free; it's open Monday to Saturday 8am to 5:30pm.

BOATING & CANOEING   Companies offering trips on the Grand River include the **Grand River Canoe Company,** 132 Rawdon St., Brantford (☎ 519/759-0040), and **Canoeing the Grand,** 3734 King St. E., Kitchener (☎ 519/896-0290, or 519/893-0022 off-season). Rentals average C$40 to C$50 (US$27 to US$33) per day and C$150 to C$170 (US$100 to US$113) per week. There are also canoe rentals in **Point Pelee National Park** (☎ 519/322-2371).

GOLF   There are a few good courses in Windsor, and in Leamington you'll find the **Erie Shores Golf and Country Club** (☎ 519/329-4231). London offers half a dozen good courses, and Bayfield and Goderich have a couple of nine-hole courses. In Stratford check out the 18-hole course at the **Stratford Country Club** (☎ 519/ 271-3891), and in St. Mary's, the **Science Hill Country Club** (☎ 519/284-3621).

HIKING   The 60km (37-mile) **Thames Valley Trail** follows the Thames River through London, past the University of Western Ontario, and into farmlands all the way to St. Mary's. For details, contact the **Thames Valley Trail Association,** Box 821, Terminal B, London, ON N6A 4Z3 (no phone).

The 100km (62-mile) **Avon Trail** follows the Avon River through Stratford, cuts through the Wildwood Conservation Area, and spans farmlands around Kitchener. It links up with the Thames Valley Trail at St. Mary's and the Grand Valley Trail at

144
Sudbury
11
17
Sturgeon
Falls
17
Espanola
17
North Bay
6
Mattawa
Lake Nipissing
Ottawa River
Killarney
Provincial
Park
Little
Current
see Northern Ontario map 11
ALGONQUIN
*Manitoulin
Island*
6
PROVINCIAL
PARK
South
Baymouth
69
G e o r g i a n
McKellar
Oxtongue
Lake
Fathom Five
Prov. Park
*Lake
Rosseau*
Parry
Sound
*Lake
Joseph*
Huntsville
Tobermory
Bruce Peninsula
Nat. Park
B a y
Port Carling
11
Dorset
Georgian Bay
Islands
Nat. Park
*Lake
Muskoka*
Bracebridge
6
Gravenhurst
L a k e
Wiarton
Penetanguishene
69
Owen
Sound
Midland
12
Orilla
H u r o n
Wasaga
Beach
400
11
12
Port Elgin
Collingwood
26
*Lake
Simcoe*
Lindsay
21
Barrie
Lindsay
Kincardine
6
400
see Muskoka Lake Region map
Newcastle
Goderich
Oshawa
401
Elora
Fergus
★ **Toronto**
Bayfield
Elmira
21
Lake
8
St. Jacobs
6
401
Mississauga
Ontario
Waterloo
Kitchener
QEW
Stratford
7
8
Cambridge
Burlington
Niagara-on-
the-Lake
21
401
8
Hamilton
St. Marys
Woodstock
Brantford
2
QEW
Niagara Falls
7
St. Catharines
*Welland
Canal*
QEW
402
London
3
Fort
Erie
Buffalo
To Windsor &
Leamington/
Point Pelee
Nat. Park
401
St. Thomas
Nanticoke
Port
Colborne
90
N.Y.

0   50 Mi
0   50 Km
N

L a k e   E r i e

Conestoga. For details, contact **Avon Trail,** Box 20018, Stratford, ON N5A 7V3 (no phone). The 124km (77-mile) **Grand Valley Trail** follows the Grand River from Dunnville, north through Brantford, Paris, and farmlands around Kitchener-Waterloo to the Elora Gorge (below), connecting with the Bruce Trail at Alton. For details, contact **Grand Valley Trails Association,** Box 1233, Kitchener, ON N2G 4G8 (no phone).

HORSEBACK RIDING   The **Cinch Stables,** 43 Capulet Lane, London (☎ **519/ 471-3492**), offers hour-long trail rides for C$17 (US$12) per person. West of London in Delaware, the **Circle R Ranch,** RR #1 (☎ **519/471-3799**), leads 1-hour trail rides in the Dingman Creek Valley for C$19 (US$13) per person. Reservations are necessary.

ROCK CLIMBING   The Elora Gorge is the climber's destination of choice in this region. Tours and weekend excursions are organized through **Humber College** at ☎ **416/675-5097.**

SWIMMING   The Elora Gorge is a favorite swimming spot. So is **Rondeau Provincial Park** (☎ **519/674-1750**), located on Lake Erie (off Highway 21 near Blenheim); lots of other water sports are available there as well.

2 London: A Great Stop for Families

If you're driving into Canada from the U.S. Midwest, you certainly should plan on stopping in the pretty university town of **London,** sitting on the Thames River just like its namesake—particularly if you have children in tow. Its attractions include gorgeous scenery, hands-on museums for kids, and many family-friendly restaurants.

ESSENTIALS

VISITOR INFORMATION   Contact **Tourism London,** 300 Dufferin Ave. (P.O. Box 5035), London, ON N6A 4L9 (☎ **519/661-5000;** www.city.london.on.ca). It's open daily 10am to 5pm.

GETTING THERE   If you're driving, London is about 192km (119 miles) from Detroit via Highway 401, 110km (68 miles) from Kitchener via Highway 401, 195km (121 miles) from Niagara Falls via QEW and Highways 403 and 401, and 65km (40 miles) from Stratford via Highways 7 and 4.

You can also fly to London on **Canadian Airlines** (☎ **519/455-8385;** www.cdnair.ca). A taxi from the airport into town will cost about C$17 (US$11). **VIA** operates a Toronto-Brantford-London-Windsor route and, in conjunction with **Amtrak,** a Toronto-Kitchener-Stratford-London-Sarnia-Chicago route. Both offer several trains a day. The **VIA Rail** station in London is at 197 York St. (☎ **519/ 434-2149;** www.viarail.ca).

GETTING AROUND   For bus schedules, contact the **London Transit Commission** (☎ **519/451-1347**). The exact fare of C$2 (US$1.35) is required (C$1/US65¢ for children 6 to 12). Or you can buy five tickets for C$7 (US$4.65) adults and C$4 (US$2.65) children 6 to 12.

Taxis charge an initial C$2.40 (US$1.60), plus C10¢ (US7¢) each nine-tenths of a kilometer (half a mile) thereafter. There's an additional charge 11pm to 6am. You can hail a cab on the street, but it's best to call a taxi company like **Abouttown Taxi** (☎ **519/432-2244**) or **U-Need-A-Cab** (☎ **519/438-2121**).

SPECIAL EVENTS   The **London International Air Show,** Canada's largest military air show, ushers in summer each June. It's followed by the **Royal Canadian Big**

Band Festival, held over the July 1 weekend. The **Great London Rib-Fest and Hot Air Balloon Fiesta** usually takes place on August 1 (an Ontario holiday). In September, the 10-day **Fair** at the Western Fairgrounds is the seventh largest in Canada.

EXPLORING THE TOWN

Eldon House/London Regional Art Museum & London Historical Museum. 401 Ridout N. ☎ **519/661-5169.** Admission C$3 (US$2) adults, C$2 (US$1.35) seniors, C$1 (US65¢) children 5 to 16. Tues–Sun noon–5pm.

The city's oldest remaining house (1834) now contains the **London Historical Museum,** featuring ever-changing exhibits about the city's early life. There's information about the daily life of the first settlers as well as about London's "dark side" of fire, flood, and pestilence. Also in the building is the **London Regional Art Museum,** where you'll find works by local artists and students

Nearby at nos. 435, 441, and 443 Ridout N. are the original **Labatt Brewery** buildings.

Banting House Museum. 442 Adelaide St. N. ☎ **519/673-1752.** Admission C$3 (US$2) adults, C$2 (US$1.35) seniors/students; kids 5 and under free. Tues–Sat noon–4:30pm. Closed Dec 21–Jan 5 and public holidays.

Sir Frederick G. Banting won the Nobel Prize for his discovery of insulin, and this museum is dedicated to his life and work as a doctor and as an artist. There are displays about his medical research at the University of Toronto, his years as a soldier, and his drawings.

✪ **London Regional Children's Museum.** 21 Wharncliffe Rd. S. ☎ **519/434-5726.** Admission C$4 (US$2.65) 3 and over; children 2 and under free. Tues–Sat 10am–5pm, Sun noon–5pm; also open on holiday Mon; closed Dec 25–26 and Jan 1.

This interactive museum for both kids and adults occupies several floors of an old school. A family can easily spend a whole day here, for in every room children can explore, experiment, and engage their imaginations. For example, on "The Street Where You Live," kids can dress up in fire fighters' uniforms, don the overalls of those who work under the streets, and assume the role of a dentist, doctor, or construction worker. Some rooms contrast how people lived long ago with how they live today. Children can stand in a train station, send a Morse-code message, shop in a general store, and sit in a schoolhouse—all experiences they can share with their grandparents. Kids can enjoy more up-to-the-minute experiences at the photosensitive wall, at the zoetrobe, or in the kitchen, where they can see exactly how the appliances work. In the garden out back is a fun tree house with a spiral slide.

Museum of Indian Archaeology & Lawson Prehistoric Indian Village. 1600 Attawandaron Rd. (off Wonderland Rd. N., just south of Hwy. 22). ☎ **519/473-1360.** Admission C$3.50 (US$2.35) adults, C$2.75 (US$1.85) seniors/students, C$1.50 (US$1) children 5 to 12, C$8 (US$5) families; children 4 and under free. May–Labour Day daily 10am–5pm; Sept–Dec Tues–Sun 10am–5pm; Jan–Apr Wed–Sun 1–4pm.

The museum contains artifacts from various periods of native-Canadian history—projectiles, pottery shards, effigies, turtle rattles, and more. The most evocative exhibit is the reconstruction of a 500-year-old Attawandaron village. Behind the elm palisades, longhouses built according to original specifications and techniques have been erected on the 5 acres where archaeological excavations are taking place. About 1,600 to 1,800 people once lived in the community, about 70 sharing one longhouse. The houses have been constructed of elm, sealed with the pitch from pine trees, and bound together with the sinew of deer hide.

Guy Lombardo Music Centre & Bandshell. 205 Wonderland Rd. S. ☎ **519/473-9003.** Admission C$2 (US$1.35) adults, C$1.75 (US$1.15) seniors; children under 12 free. Mid-May to Labour Day Thurs–Mon 11am–5pm. Limited winter hours; call ahead.

Stroll back along memory lane in this outdoor bandshell where bandleader Guy Lombardo began playing in the 1930s (concerts are still given in the bandshell, including the annual Royal Canadian Big Band Festival in June or July). This local kid made good once he hit the big time with his band, the Royal Canadians, and he became famous for ringing in every new year at the Waldorf-Astoria in New York City. The Guy Lombardo Music Centre is filled with memorabilia, including outfits, instruments, and photographs.

Springbank Park Storybook Gardens. Off Commissioners Rd. W. ☎ **519/661-5770.** Admission C$6 (US$3.85) adults, C$4.25 (US$2.85) seniors, C$3.25 (US$2.15) children 3–14; children under 3 free. May–Labour Day daily 10am–8pm; Labour Day–early Oct Mon–Fri 10am–5pm, Sat–Sun 10am–6pm. Closed late Oct–Apr.

The Springbank Park Storybook Gardens is a children's zoo with a storybook theme. Special daily events include the seal feeding at 3:30pm and a variety of live entertainment. There are also a maze, a petting zoo, live entertainment, and Playworld, with many activities for children, including a tower slide. You can also hop on the boat *London Princess* for a short cruise of the Thames River.

Fanshawe Park & Fanshawe Pioneer Village. Park entrance off Fanshawe Park Rd., east of Clarke Rd. ☎ **519/451-2800** for park or 519/457-1296 for village. Admission to park C$6 (US$3.65) per vehicle; Pioneer Village C$5 (US$3.35) adults, C$4 (US$2.65) seniors/students, C$3 (US$2) children 3–12; children under 3 free. Park May–Nov 9:30am–sundown; Village May–Nov Wed–Sun 10am–4:30pm, Dec 1–Dec 20 daily 10am–4:30pm.

The **Pioneer Village** is a complex of 25-plus restored and reconstructed buildings where you can see craft demonstrations (broom making, candle dipping, and the like), enjoy wagon rides, and imagine what life was like during the 18th century. The period-costumed guides will explain the exhibits and answer your questions. In **Fanshawe Park** there's a large pool and beach at the 6km-long (3.7-mile-long) lake.

WHERE TO STAY

For B&Bs at C$45 to C$70 (US$30 to US$47), contact the **London and Area Bed and Breakfast Association,** 2 Normandy Gardens, London, ON N6H 4A9 (☎ **519/673-6797**). London also has several modest hotel chains: **Best Western Lamplighter Inn,** 591 Wellington Rd. S. (☎ **519/681-7151**), C$83 to C$109 (US$55 to US$73) double; **Ramada Inn,** 817 Exeter Rd. (☎ **519/681-4900**), C$72 to C$119 (US$48 to US$79) double; **Travelodge London South,** 800 Exeter Rd. (☎ **519/681-1200**), C$87 to C$106 (US$58 to US$71) double; and **Comfort Inn,** 1156 Wellington Rd. S. (☎ **519/685-9300**), C$85 (US$57) double.

Delta London Armouries Hotel. 325 Dundas St., London, ON N6B 1T9. ☎ **519/679-6111.** Fax 519/679-3957. 250 units. A/C MINIBAR TV TEL. C$175–C$220 (US$117–US$147) double; from C$285 (US$190) suite. Extra person C$10 (US$7). Children under 18 stay free in parents' room. Special weekend rates available. AE, CB, DC, DISC, ER, MC, V. Parking C$7 (US$4.65).

Built into the facade of a castle-like armory, this hotel is an impressive example of architectural conservation and conversion. The armory's 12-foot-thick walls form the building's main floor and base, and above the crenellated turrets and ramparts soars a modern glass tower. The guest rooms are furnished with Federal reproductions, and some (C$15/US$10 extra) have been outfitted for businesspeople with fax machines, laser printers, cordless speakerphones, halogen-lit desks, and ergonomically designed chairs (computers on request). Dining facilities include a restaurant and lounge, providing 24-hour room service. A pool and an exercise area occupy the former drill parade area, and there are a squash court and kid's activity center. Guests and locals alike are drawn to the Sunday jazz brunch.

Idlewyld Inn. 36 Grand Ave., London, ON N6C 1K8. ☎ and fax **519/433-2891.** 27 units. A/C TV TEL. C$130 (US$87) double; from C$145 (US$97) suite; from C$185 (US$123) Jacuzzi room. Rates include continental breakfast. AE, DC, MC, V. Free parking.

In a house a leather industrialist built in 1878, the inn is filled with fine details— 8-foot-tall windows, oak and cherry carved fireplaces, casement windows, oak-beamed ceilings, and wallpaper crafted to look like tooled leather in the dining room. The guest rooms are furnished uniquely: Room no. 302 has a tiny Romeo and Juliet balcony, room no. 202 has a marvelous fireplace of green cabbage-leaf tiles and a scallop-shell marble sink stand, and room no. 101 is the largest, with huge carved cherry columns separating the sitting area from the bedroom (boasting a comfortable chaise and a glazed tile fireplace). At breakfast you help yourself in the large kitchen equipped with toasters, coffeemakers, and refrigerators and then sit on the porch to eat.

WHERE TO DINE

Anthony's. 434 Richmond St. ☎ **519/679-0960.** Reservations recommended. Main courses C$17–C$24 (US$11–US$16). AE, DC, ER, MC, V. Mon–Fri 11:30am–2:30pm; Mon–Sat 5–10pm. SEAFOOD.

Anthony's uses the freshest ingredients and presents dishes so well it stimulates the appetite—the salmon with dill sauce often comes with lime wedges cut into tiny petals placed around a center of caviar. The dinner menu might include a warm salad of smoked tiger shrimp, followed by perch with pine nuts, provincial seafood stew, or beef tenderloin with tarragon sauce. The open kitchen (with gleaming copper pots) and the dining-room mural depicting tropical fish enhance the ambiance. The desserts change daily and are made on the premises, as are the handmade chocolates that conclude the meal.

Caribou Creek. 557 Wellington Rd. ☎ **519/686-1113.** Main courses C$7–C$12 (US$4.65–US$8). AE, MC, V. Daily 11am–3pm and 5–10:30pm. LIGHT FARE.

This cottage-themed restaurant is a favorite with kids. The rambling main room is paneled with rough-hewn wood and decorated with everything from canoe paddles to fisherman's nets; up front is a sunny patio that fills up fast in clement weather. The menu is packed with old-faithful standbys like sandwiches, burgers, and salads, but there's also a choice of chicken and steak main courses.

Michael's on the Thames. 1 York St. ☎ **519/672-0111.** Reservations recommended. Main courses C$12–C$22 (US$8–US$15). AE, DC, ER, MC, V. Mon–Fri 11:30am–2:30pm; daily 5–11pm. CONTINENTAL.

The restaurant boasts a lovely location overlooking the river. In winter, a blazing fire makes the dining room cozy. Among the main dishes, you might find pan-seared chicken breast with sun-dried tomato/basil/cashew pesto and cream sauce, rack of lamb roasted with mint finished with demi-glace and port wine, or salmon with hollandaise. Desserts include a flamboyant cherries jubilee. The wine list is impressive.

Mongolian Grill. 645 Richmond St. ☎ **519/645-6400.** All-you-can-eat C$10 (US$7). AE, DC, MC, V. Daily noon–2:30pm and 5–10:30pm. ASIAN.

This is cooking as performance art. Diners assemble their own meal-in-a-bowl with raw ingredients ranging from chicken to shrimp, broccoli to bok choy, and ginger to coriander. The bowl is presented to the cooks, who labor at a huge wheel-shaped grill that sizzles and steams. The young cooks know how to put on a good show, though I couldn't get past wondering how they could stand the intense heat. A one-bowl meal costs C$8 (US$5), but if you opt for the all-you-can-eat plan (most diners do), you can experiment with various combinations till you get it right.

Wonderland Riverview Dining Room. 284 Wonderland Rd. S. ☎ **519/471-4662.** Reservations recommended. Main courses C$13–C$28 (US$9–US$19). AE, MC, V. Daily 11:30am–2:30pm and 5–9pm. Closed Mon–Tues Jan–Mar. CONTINENTAL.

Still a favorite venue for special family occasions, the Wonderland offers such dishes as rack of lamb with Dijon mustard sauce, charbroiled beef tenderloin, prime rib, and surf and turf. Around the walls are framed clips of events that took place here in the 1930s and 1940s—dancing to Ozzie Williams, Shep Fields, and Mart Kenney. There are a lovely outdoor dining terrace under the trees and an outdoor dancing area overlooking the river.

LONDON AFTER DARK

September to June, the **Grand Theatre,** 471 Richmond St. (☎ **519/672-9030**), features drama, comedy, and musicals. The theater itself, built in 1901, has been described as one of the country's most beautiful. **Harness racing** takes place October to June at the Western Fairgrounds track (☎ **519/438-7203**) Wednesday, Friday, and Saturday. Races usually start at 7:45pm.

London also has a few bars and clubs: **Barneys,** 671 Richmond St. (☎ **519/ 432-1232**), attracts a young professional crowd and has a popular summer patio; **Jo Kool's,** 595 Richmond at Central (☎ **519/663-5665**), is a popular site for students.

3 Goderich & Bayfield

It's best to explore **Goderich** on foot. The town's most striking feature is the central octagonal space with the **Huron County Courthouse** at its hub. Another highlight is the **Historic Huron Gaol,** with walls 18 feet high and 2 feet thick. This also houses the **Huron County Museum,** 110 North St. (☎ **519/524-2686**), open daily 10am to 4:30pm. Admission is C$4 (US$2.65) adults, C$3 (US$2) seniors, and C$2.25 (US$1.50) children 6 to 13. For **Goderich information,** call the visitor center at ☎ **519/524-6600** or go by its premises on Hamilton Street, open daily from 10am to 4pm in summer; the town's Web site is **www.town.goderich.on.ca**.

Bayfield is a well-preserved, pretty 19th-century town about 13 miles from Goderich and 40 miles from Stratford. Once a major grain-shipping port, it became a quiet backwater when the railroad passed it by. Today the main square, High Street, and Elgin Place are part of a **Heritage Conservation District.** Walk around and browse in the appealing stores—the **information center** on Main Street (☎ **519/ 565-2021**) has a helpful walking-tour pamphlet and is open daily 10am to 5pm.

WHERE TO STAY

Benmiller Inn. RR #4, Goderich, ON N7A 3Y1. ☎ **519/524-2191.** 47 units. A/C TV TEL. C$112–C$205 (US$75–US$137) double; C$305 (US$203) deluxe suite. Rates include breakfast buffet; some plans include dinner. AE, DC, ER, MC, V.

The inn's heart is an 1877 wool mill and now contains the dining room, the bar, the reception area, and 12 guest rooms. When the mill was turned into an inn in 1974, many mechanical parts were refashioned into decorative objects—mirrors made from pulley wheels and lamps from gears. The guest rooms feature barn-board siding, desks, floor lamps, heated ceramic tile in the bathrooms, and handmade quilts. The 17 rooms in Gledhill House, the mill-owner's home, are generously proportioned, while the four suites have fireplaces, bidets, and Jacuzzi tubs. Ground-floor rooms have pressed-tin ceilings. There are more rooms in the River Mill, attached to a silo style building containing the pool, whirlpool, and running track. The dining room serves fine continental cuisine. The brick patio overlooking the gardens is a pleasant place to sit and look at the totem pole, brought from British Columbia. Facilities include two tennis courts, billiards, table tennis, and cross-country ski trails.

✪ **Clifton Manor Inn.** 19 The Square, P.O. Box 454, Bayfield, ON N0M 1G0. ☎ **519/565-2282.** 4 units. C$110–C$150 (US$79–US$107) double. No credit cards.

This elegant house was built in 1895 for the reve (bailiff or governor) of Bayfield. The interior features ash wood, etched-glass door panels, and other attractive period details. Today owner Elizabeth Marquis has added many touches—Oriental rugs and comfortable sofas and love seats in the living room and elegant silver and sideboards in the dining room. Each guest room is named after an artist or a composer and comes with cozy touches like mohair throws, sheepskin rugs, wingback chairs, and fresh flowers. The bathroom in the charming Renoir room has a 6-foot-long deep tub. Marquis provides candles and bubble bath—a lovely romantic touch. Lilac bushes and fruit trees fill the yard. Breakfast consists of egg dishes like omelets or crêpes, plus fresh fruit often plucked from the trees in the garden.

The Little Inn at Bayfield. Main St., P.O. Box 100, Bayfield, ON N0M 1G0. ☎ **519/565-2611.** Fax 519/565-5474. www.littleinn.com. 30 units. A/C TV. C$115–C$155 (US$77–US$103) double; from C$235 (US$157) suite. Special packages available. AE, DC, MC, V.

The inn, built in 1832, has been thoroughly modernized. The older guest rooms in the main building are small and have only showers, but they're comfortably furnished with oak or sleigh beds. The rooms in the newer section are larger and feature platform beds and modern furnishings. The suites across the street in the carriage house have platform beds, pine hutches, whirlpool bathtubs, propane-gas fireplaces, and verandas. The popular restaurant is open for lunch and dinner daily.

WHERE TO DINE

The **Benmiller Inn** (above) has an impressive formal dining room. For casual dining, Bayfield offers several choices. The **Albion Hotel** on Main Street (☎ 519/565-2641) features a wall-length bar decorated with hundreds of baseball hats and other sports paraphernalia. The fare consists of English specialties, plus ribs, pizza, and sandwiches, served daily noon to 2:30pm and 5:30 to 9:30pm. It also has seven rooms available starting at C$60 (US$40) double, sharing a bathroom. **Admiral Bayfield's,** 5 Main St. (☎ 519/565-2326), is fun too. A converted general store, it serves diner, deli, and pub fare, with occasional jazz and other entertainment, and it's open Monday to Saturday noon to 3pm and 5 to 10pm.

✪ **Red Pump.** Main St., Bayfield. ☎ **519/565-2576.** Reservations recommended. Main courses C$15–C$28 (US$10–US$19). AE, MC, V. Daily noon–3pm and 5–9pm. Closed Jan–Mar and Mon–Tues in late fall and winter. INTERNATIONAL.

This charming restaurant boasts an inviting patio and some of the area's most innovative cooking. Typical main dishes may include steamed chicken breast and scallops with pine-nut, red-pepper, tomato, and balsamic-vinegar sauce; barbecued fish; and tiger shrimp stuffed with crab and served with risotto cakes. The decor is plush and comfortable.

4 Stratford & the Stratford Festival

The ✪ **Stratford Festival** was born in 1953 when director Tyrone Guthrie lured renowned actor Alec Guinness to perform here. The festival has since become one of the most famous in North America, and it has put this scenic town on the map. While you'll notice the Avon River and other sights named in honor of the Bard himself, you may not realize that Stratford is also home to one of the best cooking schools in the country, making it a delight to dine at many of the spots in town.

ESSENTIALS

VISITOR INFORMATION For first-rate visitor info, go to the **Information Centre** by the river on York Street at Erie (☎ **519/273-3352**). May to early November, it's open daily 9am to 5pm (to 8pm Thurs to Sat). At other times, contact **Tourism Stratford,** 88 Wellington St., P.O. Box 818, Stratford, ON N5A 6W1 (☎ **800/561-SWAN** or 519/271-5140). It's open Monday to Friday 9am to 5pm.

GETTING THERE Driving from Toronto, take Highway 401 west to Interchange 278 at Kitchener. Follow Highway 8 west onto Highways 7 and 8 to Stratford. **Amtrak** (☎ **800/872-7245;** www.amtrak.com) and **VIA Rail** (☎ **800-561-3949;** www. viarail.ca) operate several trains daily along the Toronto-Kitchener-Stratford route.

EXPLORING THE TOWN

Stratford offers a wealth of attractions that complement the theater offerings. Within sight of the Festival Theatre, **Queen's Park** has picnic spots beneath tall shade trees or down by the Avon River. There are also some superb dining and good shopping prospects.

Past the Orr Dam and the nearly 100-year-old stone bridge, through a rustic gate, lies a very special park, the **Shakespearean Garden.** In this formal English garden, where a sundial measures out the hours, you can relax and contemplate the herb and flower beds and the tranquil river lagoon and muse on a bust of Shakespeare by Toronto sculptor Cleeve Horne.

If you turn right onto Romeo Street North from Highways 7 and 8 as you come into Stratford, you'll find the **Gallery/Stratford,** 54 Romeo St. (☎ **519/271-5271**), in a historic building on the fringes of Confederation Park (below). Since it opened in 1967, it has mounted fine Canadian-focused shows, often oriented to the theater arts. If you're an art lover, do stop in, for you're sure to find an unusual, personally satisfying show in one of the four galleries. Summer hours are daily 9am to 6pm; off-season hours are Tuesday to Sunday 9am to 6pm. Admission is C$4 (US$2.65) adults and C$3 (US$2) seniors/students 12 and up. **Confederation Park** itself is worth a visit—its Japanese garden was designed in 1967 to commemorate the 100th anniversary of Canada's confederation; admission is free.

Popular with history buffs is the **Stratford Perth Museum,** 270 Water St. (☎ **519/271-5311**), covering the history of the region from the first settlement in the area in the early 19th century. There are exhibits about everything from the building of the railroad to hockey. May to September 30, it's open Tuesday to Saturday 10am to 4pm and Sunday noon to 4pm; off-season hours are Thursday to Sunday noon to 4pm. Admission is C$2 (US$1.35); children 5 and under get in free.

Stratford is a historic town, dating back to 1832. July to Labour Day, 1-hour **guided tours of early Stratford** are given Monday to Saturday leaving at 9:30am from the visitors booth by the river. There are also many **fine shops** worth browsing along Ontario and Downie streets and tucked down along York Street. Antiques lovers

Stratford

To Hwys.
7 & 8 to
Kitchener

To Hwy. 8
to Goderich

To Hwys. 7 & 8 to
Kitchener

To Hwys. 7 & 19
to London

LEGEND

(i) Information

✉ Post Office

ATTRACTIONS

Arena ⑨
Avon Boat Rentals ⑳
Avon Theatre ⑱
City Hall / Bus Depot ⑲
Confederation Park ②
Festival Theatre ③
Gallery/Stratford ①
Shakespearean
    Garden ㉑
Stratford Perth Museum ⑧
Third Stage ⑩

ACCOMMODATIONS

Ambercroft ⑬
Bentley's ⑦
Brunswick House ⑭
Deacon House ⑮
Festival Inn ⑤
The Queen's Inn ④
Swan Inn ㉓
23 Albert Place ⑫
Woods Villa ㉒

DINING

Bentley's ⑦
The Church ⑯
Keystone Alley Cafe ⑰
The Old Prune ⑥
Rundles ⑪

will want to visit the nearby town of **Shakespeare** (7 miles out of town on Highway 7/8), which has several stores.

Paddleboat and canoe rentals are available at the **Boathouse,** behind and below the information booth. It's run by Avon Boat Rentals and is open daily 9am to dark in summer. For advance info, contact Avon at 40 York St. (☎ **519/271-7739**).

A COUPLE OF DAY TRIPS

Only half an hour or so away, the twin cities of **Kitchener** and **Waterloo** have two drawing cards: the **Farmer's Market** and the famous 9-day **Oktoberfest;** for Oktoberfest information, contact K-W Oktoberfest, P.O. Box 1053, 17 Benton St., Kitchener, ON N2G 4G1 (☎ **519/570-4267**). These cities still have a German-majority population, and many of their citizens are Mennonites. Starting at 6am you can sample shoofly pie, apple butter, kochcase, and other Mennonite specialties at the Saturday market in the Market Square complex at Duke and Frederick streets in Kitchener. For details, contact the **Kitchener-Waterloo Area Visitors and Convention Bureau,** 2848 King St. E., Kitchener, ON N2A 1A5 (☎ **519/748-0800**). It's open 9am to 5pm: daily in summer and Monday to Friday the rest of the year.

People enjoy visiting the town of **St. Jacobs,** 5 miles north of Kitchener, drawn there by close to 100 shops located in venues like converted mills, silos, and other factory buildings. For those interested in learning more about the Amish-Mennonite way of life, **The Meetingplace,** 33 King St. (☎ **519/664-3518**), shows a short film about it (May to Sept open daily 9am to 5pm; winter open Sat and Sun only noon to 5pm). St. Jacob's also boasts one of the best restaurants in the area, the skylit **Vidalia's Market Dining,** 39 King St. (☎ **519/664-2575**), which serves a bill of international fare. It's open daily noon to 9pm.

WHERE TO STAY

When you book your theater tickets, you can also, at no extra charge, book your accommodations. The festival can reserve you any type of accommodation and price category you prefer, from guest homes for as little as C$40 (US$27) to first-class hotels charging more than C$125 (US$83). Call or write the **Festival Theatre Box Office,** P.O. Box 520, Stratford, ON N5A 6V2 (☎ **800/567-1600** or 519/273-1600).

HOTELS & MOTELS

Another good choice is the **Swan Motel,** Rte. 2, Downie Street, Stratford, ON N5A 6S3 (☎ **519/271-6376**). Rates are about C$80 (US$53) double.

Bentleys. 107 Ontario St., Stratford, ON N5A 3H1. ☎ **519/271-1121.** 13 units. A/C TV TEL. Late Apr to mid-Nov C$145 (US$97) double; late Nov to mid-Apr C$90 (US$60) double. Extra person C$20 (US$13). AE, DC, ER, MC, V.

The soundproof guest rooms here are in fact luxurious duplex suites, each with an efficiency kitchen. Period English furnishings and attractive drawings, paintings, and costume designs on the walls make for a pleasant ambiance. Five of the suites have skylights. The adjoining British-style pub is popular with festival actors (see "Where to Dine" below).

Festival Inn. 1144 Ontario St. (P.O. Box 811), Stratford, ON N5A 6W1. ☎ **519/273-1150.** Fax 519/273-2111. 182 units. A/C TV TEL. C$95–C$155 (US$63–US$103) double. Extra person C$10 (US$7). Winter rates about 30% lower. AE, DC, MC, V. Free parking.

With its black-and-white motel-style units, the Festival is set back off Highways 7 and 8 on 20 acres of landscaped grounds. The place has an old-English air with its stucco walls, Tudor-style beams, and high-back red settees in the lobby. The Tudor style is

The Play's the Thing at the Stratford Festival

Since its modest but ambitious beginnings on July 13, 1953, when Sir Alec Guinness made his Stratford debut in *Richard III* staged in a huge tent, the Stratford Festival's artistic directors have all built on the innovative yet classic base first provided by Tyrone Guthrie to create a repertory theater with a glowing international reputation.

World famous for its Shakespearean productions, the festival also offers both classic and modern theatrical masterpieces. Recent productions have included *West Side Story, Oedipus Rex, Death of a Salesman, Dracula,* and *Glenn* (the latter about legendary eccentric Canadian pianist Glenn Gould). Offerings from the Bard have included *The Taming of the Shrew, The Tempest, Macbeth,* and *A Midsummer Night's Dream*. Among the company's famous alumni are Dame Maggie Smith, Sir Alec Guinness, Sir Peter Ustinov, Alan Bates, Christopher Plummer, Irene Worth, Julie Harris, and Uta Hagen. Present company members include Brian Bedford, Cynthia Dole, Martha Henry, Brent Carver, Lucy Peacock, and Benedict Campbell.

Theatergoers may also enjoy "Meet the Festival," a series of informal discussions with members of the acting company or the production or administrative staff; "Post Performance Discussions" that follow Thursday-evening performances; and backstage or warehouse tours, offered every Wednesday, Saturday, and Sunday morning early June to mid-October. The tours cost C$5 (US$3.35) adults and C$3 (US$2) seniors/students; they should be reserved when you buy tickets.

Stratford has three theaters: the **Festival Theatre,** 55 Queen St. in Queen's Park, with a dynamic thrust stage; the **Avon Theatre,** 99 Downie St., with a classic proscenium; and the **Tom Patterson Theatre,** an intimate 500-seat theater on Lakeside Drive.

The season usually begins early in May and continues through October, with performances Tuesday to Sunday and matinees Wednesday, Saturday, and Sunday. Ticket prices are C$39 to C$64 (US$26 to US$43), though there are special prices for students and seniors. For tickets, call ☎ **800/567-1600** or 519/273-1600; or write to the Stratford Festival, P.O. Box 520, Stratford, ON N5A 6V2. Tickets are also available in the United States and Canada at Ticketmaster outlets. The box office opens for mail and fax orders only in late January; telephone and in-person sales begin late February.

maintained throughout the large modern guest rooms, all with reproductions of old masters on the walls. Some have charming bay windows with sheer curtains, and all rooms in the main building, north wing, and annex have refrigerators. Other facilities include a dining room, a coffee shop, and an indoor pool with an outdoor patio.

The Queen's Inn. 161 Ontario St., Stratford, ON N5A 3H3. ☎ **800/461-6450** or 519/271-1400. Fax 519/271-7373. 31 units. A/C TV TEL. May–Nov 15 C$105–C$130 (US$70–US$87) double, C$165–C$190 (US$110–US$127) suite. Nov 16–Apr C$65 (US$43) double, from C$85 (US$57) suite. AE, DC, MC, V. Free parking.

Conveniently located in the town center, The Queen's Inn has recently been restored. The guest rooms have been pleasantly decorated in pastels and pine and have large windows. Facilities include the Boar's Head Pub, which carries a wide selection of light and dark ales, as well as standard pub grub.

23 Albert Place. 23 Albert St., Stratford, ON N5A 3K2. ☎ **519/273-5800.** Fax 519/ 273-5008. 34 units. A/C TV TEL. C$95–C$105 (US$63–US$70) double; C$115 (US$77) minisuite; from C$140 (US$93) suite. MC, V.

Right around the corner from the Avon Theatre, the Albert Place sports large guest rooms with high ceilings and simple modern furnishings. Some rooms have separate sitting rooms and minirefrigerators. This three-story building has never had an elevator, so you'll have to climb a flight of stairs or two to get to your room. Complimentary coffee, tea, and donuts are available in the lobby for guests in the early morning.

A PICK OF THE B&Bs

For more information on the Stratford B&B scene, contact **Tourism Stratford,** P.O. Box 818, 88 Wellington St., Stratford, ON N5A 6W1 (☎ **519/271-5140**). It's open Monday to Friday 9am to 5pm.

Ambercroft. 129 Brunswick St., Stratford, ON N5A 3L9. ☎ **519/271-5644.** 4 units. A/C. C$95–C$105 (US$63–US$70) double. Rates include continental breakfast. MC, V.

This inviting 1878 home in a quiet downtown area is convenient to the theaters and restaurants. There's a comfy front parlor, a small TV room, and a front and rear porch. Guests have the use of a refrigerator. The rooms aren't large but they abound with architectural detail and are tastefully decorated. An extended continental breakfast is served—seasonal fruits, cereals, homemade baked goods, and more. There's no smoking.

Brunswick House. 109 Brunswick St., Stratford, ON N5A 3L9. ☎ **519/271-4546.** 6 units, none with bathroom. From C$65 (US$43) double. Rates include full breakfast. No credit cards.

If you stay here you'll enjoy the very literate surroundings created by owners Geoff Hancock and Gay Allison—there are portraits of Canadian authors and poetry on the walls and books everywhere. The six nicely decorated guest rooms, with ceiling fans, share two bathrooms. One is a family room with a double and two single beds. Each room has a personal decorative touch—a Mennonite quilt, posters by an artist friend, or a parasol atop a wardrobe. It's within walking distance of the center of town and theaters. Smoking is restricted to the veranda.

Deacon House. 101 Brunswick St., Stratford, ON N5A 3L9. ☎ **519/273-2052.** 6 units. A/C. C$103–C$125 (US$69–US$83) double. Extra person C$20 (US$13). Rates include breakfast. Off-season packages available. MC, V.

Shingle-style Deacon House, built in 1907, has been restored by Dianna Hrysko and Mary Allen. The guest rooms are decorated in a country style, with iron-and-brass beds, quilts, pine hutches, oak rockers, and rope-style rugs. You'll be able to relax in the living room, with a fireplace, a TV, wingback chairs, and a sofa. The guest kitchen and the second-floor sitting/reading room are welcome conveniences. This is a great location, within walking distance of everything.

Woods Villa. 62 John St. N., Stratford, ON N5A 6K7. ☎ **519/271-4576.** Fax 519/ 271-7173. www.woodsvilla.orc.ca. 6 units. A/C TV TEL. C$115–C$185 (US$77–US$123) double. Rates include breakfast. DISC, MC, V.

This handsome 1870 house set on an acre is home to Ken Vinen, who collects and restores the Wurlitzers, Victrolas, and player pianos found throughout. In the large drawing room are six—and they all work. Ken will happily demonstrate, drawing on his vast library of early paper rolls and records. The large guest rooms, five with fireplaces, include a handsome suite with a canopied bed. In the morning, coffee is delivered to your room, followed by a full breakfast prepared to order and served in the dining room. You're welcome to use the attractively landscaped outdoor pool and terrace.

WHERE TO DINE
EXPENSIVE

✪ **The Church.** At the corner of Brunswick and Waterloo sts. ☎ **519/273-3424.** Reservations required. Summer fixed-price dinner C$55 (US$37); main courses C$21–C$33 (US$14–US$22). AE, DC, MC, V. Tues–Sat 11:30am–1am; Sun 11:30am–10pm. May be open Mon if there's a musical performance or some other special event at the theaters. CONTINENTAL.

The Church is simply stunning. The organ pipes and altar of the 1873 structure are still intact, along with the vaulted roof, carved woodwork, and stained-glass windows, and you can sit in the nave or the side aisles and dine to the appropriate sounds of, usually, Bach. Fresh flowers, elegant table settings, and a huge table in the center graced with two silver samovars further enhance the experience. In summer, there are a special four-course fixed-price and an à la carte dinner menu, a luncheon on matinee days, and an after-theater menu. Appetizers may include asparagus with black morels in their juices, white wine, and cream or sauté of duck foie gras with leeks and citron-mango-ginger sauce. Among the selection of eight or so entrees, you may find Canadian caribou with port-and-blackberry sauce, cabbage braised in cream with shallots and glazed chestnuts, or lobster salad with green beans, new potatoes, and truffles scented with caraway. The desserts are equally exciting, like the charlotte of white chocolate mousse with summer fruit and dark chocolate sauce or the nougat glace with kiwi sauce.

If you want to dine here during the festival, make reservations in March or April when you buy your tickets; otherwise, you'll be disappointed. The upstairs **Belfry Bar** is a popular pre- and posttheater gathering place.

The Old Prune. 151 Albert St. ☎ **519/271-5052.** Reservations required. 3-course fixed-price dinner C$53 (US$35). AE, MC, V. Wed–Sun 11:30am–1:30pm; Tues–Sat 5–9pm, Sun 5–7pm. After-theater menu available Fri–Sat from 9pm. Call ahead for winter hours. CONTINENTAL.

Set in a lovely Edwardian home, the Old Prune has three dining rooms and an enclosed garden patio and is run by the charming, whimsical Marion Isherwood and Eleanor Kane. Former Montréalers, they brought with them some French flair, as reflected in both the decor and the menu. Artist Marion created the subdued, dreamy palette of the walls, graced with her own inspired paintings. Chef Bryan Steele selects the freshest local ingredients, many from the region's organic farmers, and prepares them simply to reveal their abundant flavor. Among the appetizers might be an outstanding house-smoked salmon with lobster-potato salad topped with Sevruga caviar or a refreshing tomato consommé with saffron and sea scallops. Among the main courses, you may find Perth County pork loin grilled with tamari-and-honey glaze and served with shiitake mushrooms, pickled cucumbers, and sunflower sprouts; steamed bass in Napa cabbage with curry broth and lime leaves; or rack of Ontario lamb with smoky tomatillo-chipotle pepper sauce. The desserts are always inspired too, like rhubarb-strawberry napoleon with vanilla mousse. The Old Prune is lovely for lunch or a late supper, when light specialties like sautéed quail with grilled polenta with Italian greens, mushrooms, roasted tomatoes, and balsamic jus and smoked trout terrine are offered for C$7 to C$14 (US$4.65 to US$9).

Rundles. 9 Cobourg St. ☎ **519/271-6442.** Reservations required. 3-course fixed-price dinner C$54 (US$36). AE, ER, MC, V. Wed and Sat–Sun 11:30am–1:30pm; Tues 5–7pm, Wed–Sat 5–8:30pm, Sun 5–7pm. Closed in winter. INTERNATIONAL.

Overlooking the river, Rundles provides a premier dining experience in a serene room with whimsical contemporary art by Victor Tinkl. Proprietor Jim Morris eats, sleeps, thinks, and dreams food, and chef Neil Baxter delivers the exciting cuisine to the table. The three-course fixed-price dinner will always offer a full selection of palate-pleasing flavor combinations. The appetizers are delightful, from the shaved fennel, arugula, artichoke, and Parmesan salad to the warm seared Québec foie gras with caramelized endive, garlic-flavored fried potatoes, and tomato-and-basil oil. Among the five main dishes might be poached Atlantic salmon garnished with Jerusalem artichokes, wilted arugula, and yellow peppers in light carrot sauce or pink roast rib eye of lamb with ratatouille and rosemary aioli. My dessert choice is the glazed lemon tart with orange sorbet, but the hot mango tart with pineapple sorbet is also a dream.

MODERATE

Bentley's. 107 Ontario St. ☎ **519/271-1121.** Reservations not accepted. Main courses C$8–C$13 (US$5–US$9). AE, DC, ER, MC, V. Daily 11:30am–1am. CANADIAN/ENGLISH.

Bentley's is *the* local watering hole and a favorite theater company gathering spot. The popular pastime here is darts, but you can also watch the big game on TV or relax in one of the wingbacks. In summer, you can sit on the garden terrace and enjoy light fare—grilled shrimp, burgers, gourmet pizzas, fish-and-chips, shepherd's pie, and pasta dishes. More substantial dishes—like lamb curry, sirloin steak, and salmon baked in white wine with peppercorn-dill butter—are offered at dinner. Beer drinkers appreciate the 16 drafts on tap.

✪ **Keystone Alley Cafe.** 34 Brunswick St. ☎ **519/271-5645.** Reservations recommended. Main courses C$16–C$25 (US$11–US$17). AE, DC, MC, V. Mon 11am–3pm, Tues–Sat 11am–3pm and 5–9pm. CONTINENTAL.

Theater actors often stop in for lunch—perhaps sandwiches, like the maple-grilled chicken and avocado club, or a main dish like cornmeal-crusted Mediterranean tart. At dinner, entrees range from breast of Muscovy duck with stir-fried Asian vegetables and egg noodles in honey-ginger sauce to escalopes of calves' liver accompanied by a garlic-potato purée and creamed savoy cabbage with bacon. The short wine list is reasonably priced.

PICNICKING IN STRATFORD

Stratford is really a picnicking place. Take a hamper down to the banks of the river or into the parks; plenty of places cater to this business. **Rundles** (above) will make you a super-sophisticated hamper. Or go to **Picnics Gourmet Food Shop,** 40 Wellington St. (☎ **519/273-6000**), which offers all kinds of salads—pasta, grains, and vegetables—and pâtés; fish, chicken, and meat dishes; soups; and breads and pastries. It's open Tuesday to Friday 10am to 6pm and Saturday 10am to 4pm (closed 2 weeks in Jan).

WHERE TO STAY & DINE NEARBY

✪ **Langdon Hall.** RR #3, Cambridge, ON N3H 4R8. ☎ **800/268-1898** or 519/740-2100. Fax 519/740-8161. 49 units. A/C TV TEL. C$259–C$699 (US$173–US$466) double. Rates include continental breakfast. AE, DC, ER, MC, V.

The elegant house at the head of the curving drive was completed in 1902 by Eugene Langdon Wilks, youngest son of Matthew and Eliza Astor Langdon, a granddaughter of John Jacob Astor. It remained in the family until 1987; today its 200 acres of lawns,

gardens, and woodlands make for an ideal retreat. The main house, of red brick with
classical pediment and Palladian-style windows, is beautifully symmetrical. A similar
harmony is achieved inside, with the emphasis on comfort rather than grandiosity,
whether in the conservatory, the veranda where tea is served, or Wilks' Bar. Most of
the individually decorated guest rooms are set around the cloister garden; most have
fireplaces. The furnishings consist of handsome antique reproductions, mahogany
wardrobes, ginger-jar lamps, armchairs upholstered with luxurious fabrics, fine oriental rugs, pictures, and such nice touches as live plants and terry bathrobes. The airy
dining room overlooking the lily pond offers fine regional cuisine, with main courses
at C$22 to C$30 (US$15 to US$20). The on-site spa offers a complete range of treatments, with spa packages starting at C$180 (US$120). Beyond the cloister, down a
trellis arcade, and through a latched gate lies the herb-and-vegetable garden, and
beyond that are the pool (with pool house), tennis court, and croquet lawn.

Westover Inn. 300 Thomas St., St. Mary's, ON N4X 1B1. ☎ **519/284-2977.** Fax 519/
284-4043. www.westoverinn.com. 22 units. A/C TV TEL. C$95–C$175 (US$63–US$117)
double; C$180–C$225 (US$120–US$150) suite. AE, ER, MC, V.

This Victorian manor house (1867) features carved gingerbread decoration and
leaded-glass windows. The house is set on 19 acres, making for a secluded retreat, and
there's an outdoor pool. The guest rooms have been furnished in modern antique style
with reproductions; some have balconies. Six are located in the manor itself, including
a luxury suite with a whirlpool bathtub. The least expensive and smallest rooms
(12 of them) are found in the Terrace, built in the 1930s as a dorm for the priests
who attended what was then a seminary. The Thames Cottage, a modern building,
contains two two-bedroom suites. Downstairs in the manor, you may use the comfortable lounge.

5 Elora & Fergus: The Elora Gorge & More

If you're driving from Toronto, take Highway 401 west to Highway 6 north to 7 east,
then back to 6 north into Fergus. From Fergus, take Highway 18 west to Elora.

Elora has always been a special place. To the natives, the gorge was a sacred site,
home of spirits who dwelt within the great cliffs. Early explorers and Jesuit missionaries also wondered at the natural spectacle, but it was Scotsman William Gilkinson
who put the town on the map in 1832 when he bought 14,000 acres on both sides of
the Grand River and built a mill and a general store. He named the town Elora, after
the Ellora Caves in India. Most of the houses the settlers built in the 1850s stand
today. You'll want to browse the stores along picturesque Mill Street. For real insight
into the town's history, pick up a walking-tour brochure from the tourist booth on
Mill Street.

The **Elora Gorge** is a 350-acre park on both sides of the 70-foot limestone gorge.
Nature trails wind through it. Overhanging rock ledges, small caves, a waterfall, and
the evergreen forest on its rim are some of the gorge's scenic delights. The park
(☎ **519/846-9742**) has camping and swimming facilities, plus picnic areas and
playing fields. It's a favorite with rock climbers. Just west of Elora at the junction of
the Grand and Irvine rivers, it's open May 1 to October 15 daily 10am to sunset.
Admission is C$4 (US$2.65) adults and C$1.75 (US$1.15) children 6 to 14; children
under 6 are free. To camp, for unserviced campsites, it's C$10 (US$7) per day, C$13
(US$9) with water and electricity, plus the admission fee. For information, write
or call the **Grand River Conservation Authority,** 400 Clyde Rd. (P.O. Box 729),
Cambridge, ON N1R 5W6 (☎ **519/621-2761**).

An additional attraction mid-July to early August is the **Elora Festival,** a 3-week music celebration. For more information, contact **The Elora Festival,** P.O. Box 990, Elora, ON N0B 1S0 (☎ 519/846-0331).

Fergus (pop. 7,500) was founded by Scottish immigrant Adam Ferguson. There are more than 250 fine old 1850s buildings to see—examples of Scottish limestone architecture—including the Foundry, which now houses the Fergus market. The most noteworthy Fergus event is the **Fergus Scottish Festival,** which includes Highland Games, featuring pipe-band competitions, caber tossing, tug-of-war contests, and Highland dancing, and the North American Scottish Heavy Events, held usually on the second weekend in August. For more information on the games, contact **Fergus Scottish Festival and Highland Games,** P.O. Box 25, Fergus, ON N1M 2W7 (☎ 519/787-0099).

WHERE TO STAY & DINE

✪ **Breadalbane Inn.** 487 St. Andrew St. W., Fergus, ON N1M 1P2. ☎ **519/ 843-4770.** 6 units. C$75–C$175 (US$50–US$117) double. Rates include continental breakfast. AE, MC, V.

In the heart of Fergus, this inn is an excellent example of 1860s architecture. The stone imported from Scotland is complemented by intricate ironwork and walnut banisters and newel posts. It was built by the Honorable Admiral Ferguson as a residence but also served as a nursing home and rooming house before it was converted over 20 years ago. The comfortable guest rooms are elegantly furnished with early Canadian-style furniture. In back, the Coach House contains a suite with a fireplace, Jacuzzi tub, and private patio. Reservations are recommended for the two dining areas (open Tues to Sun 11:30am to 10pm), which have French doors leading into the garden. At darkly polished tables set with Royal Doulton china, you can dine to the strains of classical music. Chef/owner Peter Egger bakes his own bread and takes pains with everything. At dinner, start with the smooth chicken-liver pâté with brandy and peppercorns or the baked escargots with garlic-and-herb butter, and follow with such dishes as oven-roasted salmon with ginger-cucumber sauce or grilled venison medallions in black-currant/juniper-berry sauce. Prices range from C$18 to C$27 (US$12 to US$18). The pub, serving typical pub fare, is open daily.

Elora Mill Inn. 77 Mill St. W., Elora, ON N0B 1S0. ☎ **519/846-5356.** Fax 519/846-9180. 32 units. A/C TV TEL. C$160–C$175 (US$107–US$117) double; from C$190 (US$127) suite. Extra person C$25 (US$17). Rates include breakfast. AE, DC, MC, V.

This inn is in a five-story gristmill built in 1870 and operated until 1974. Downstairs, a lounge with the original exposed beams and a huge stone fireplace overlooks the falls. Upstairs are similarly rustic dining areas. Each guest room is furnished individually, some with four-posters, others with cannonball pine beds. Most beds are covered with quilts, and each room has a comfy rocker or hoop-back chair. Some rooms in adjacent buildings are duplexes with decks and river views; many inn rooms have gorge views, and some have fireplaces. The dining room's eight or so appetizers might include Bermuda chowder, a spicy broth of fish, vegetables, spiced sausage, dark rum, and sherry pepper. The main dishes are C$18 to C$32 (US$12 to US$21); the most popular option is the prime-rib cart, followed by a dessert—chocolate decadence or shoofly pie are popular. It's open daily for lunch and dinner.

North to Ontario's Lakelands & Beyond

by Hilary Davidson

If southern Ontario is marked by its sprawling cities and picturesque towns, the northern part of the province is remarkable for its vast wilderness. You'll be struck by the rugged beauty of the landscape, the forests of old-growth pine, and the thousands of lakes in the region. The most popular destinations are **Georgian Bay, Algonquin Provincial Park,** and the cottage country of **Huronia** and the **Muskoka Lakes.**

1 Exploring the Region

On weekends, many Torontonians head north to the cottage or to a resort to unwind. But if you want to explore the whole region, drive out from Toronto via Highway 400 north to Barrie. Here you can either turn west to explore Georgian Bay, the Bruce Peninsula, and Manitoulin Island or continue due north to the Muskoka Lakes, Algonquin Provincial Park, and points farther north.

VISITOR INFORMATION

Contact **Ontario Travel/Travelinx Ontario,** Queen's Park, Toronto, ON M7A 2E5 (☎ **800/ONTARIO** 9am to 8pm, or 416/314-0944). The offices are open Monday to Friday 8:30am to 5pm (daily mid-May to mid-Sept). You can also contact them on the Web at **www.ravelinx.com**.

THE GREAT OUTDOORS

In the parts of northern Ontario covered by this chapter, you'll find plenty of terrific places to canoe, hike, bike, or fish. Some 260 provincial parks in Ontario offer ample opportunities for outdoor recreation. The daily in-season entry fee for a vehicle is C$5 to C$10 (US$3.35 to US$7); campsites cost C$13 to C$21 (US$9 to US$14). For details, contact the **Ontario Ministry of Natural Resources** at ☎ **416/314-2000.**

Topographic maps are vital on extended canoeing/hiking trips and can be secured from the **Canada Map Office,** 130 Bentley Ave., Nepean, ON K1A 0E9 (☎ **613/952-7000**).

BIKING You'll find networks of biking and hiking trails in the national and provincial parks. Contact the individual parks directly for more information. One good route is the **Georgian Cycle and Ski Trail,** running 32km (20 miles) along the southern shore of Georgian

Bay from Collingwood via Thornbury to Meaford. The **Bruce Peninsula** and **Manitoulin Island** also offer good cycling opportunities. In the Burk's Falls–Magnetawan area, the **Forgotten Trail** has been organized along old logging roads and railroad tracks. For details, contact the **Huronia Travel Association** in Midhurst at ☎ **705/726-9300.**

CANOEING & KAYAKING   Northern Ontario is a canoeist's paradise. You can enjoy exceptional canoeing in **Algonquin, Killarney,** and **Quetico provincial parks;** along the rivers in the **Temagami** (Lady Evelyn Smoothwater Provincial Park) and **Wabakimi** regions; along the **Route of the Voyageurs** in Algoma Country (Lake Superior Provincial Park); and along the rivers leading into James Bay, like the **Missinaibi. Killbear Provincial Park, Georgian Bay,** and **Pukaskwa National Park** also are good places to paddle.

Alas, many places are getting overcrowded. One of the quietest, least-trafficked areas is the **Missinaibi River** in the Chapleau Game Reserve. Another truly remote canoeing area, accessible by plane only, is in **Winisk River Provincial Park,** where you're likely to see polar bears who establish their dens in the park. These areas are for advanced canoeists who can handle white water and orient themselves in the wilderness. For details on all these areas and detailed maps, contact the **Ministry of Natural Resources** at ☎ **416/314-2000** or the provincial parks themselves. Also see the individual park entries in this chapter.

Around Parry Sound and Georgian Bay, canoeing and kayaking trips are arranged by **White Squall,** RR #1, Nobel, ON P0G 1G0 (☎ **705/342-5324**). Day trips are C$100 (US$67); 4-day trips start at C$510 (US$340), including instruction, meals, and equipment. In Algonquin Provincial Park, several outfitters serve park visitors, including **Algonquin Outfitters,** Oxtongue Lake (RR #1), Dwight, ON P0A 1H0 (☎ **705/635-2243**), and **Opeongo Algonquin Outfitting Store,** Box 123, Whitney, ON K0J 2M0 (☎ **613/637-5470**). Complete canoe outfitting runs C$45 to C$55 (US$30 to US$37) per day, depending on the length of the trip and extent of the equipment. Canoe rentals are C$15 to C$30 (US$10 to US$20) per day and C$90 to C$210 (US$60 to US$140) per week.

Killarney Outfitters, on Highway 637, 5km (3 miles) east of Killarney (☎ **705/287-2828,** or 705/287-2242 off-season), offers complete outfitting for C$60 (US$40) per day or C$360 (US$240) per week. Canoe and kayak rentals range from C$18 to C$25 (US$12 to US$17) and C$25 to C$35 (US$17 to US$23), respectively. There's a 10% discount on rentals of 5 or more days. In the Quetico area, contact **Canoe Canada Outfitters,** Box 1810, 300 O'Brien St., Atikokan, ON P0T 1C0 (☎ **807/597-6418**).

North of Thunder Bay are excellent wilderness camping, fishing, hunting, and canoeing in the Wabakimi (accessed from Armstrong), with plenty of scope for beginning, intermediate, and advanced paddlers. Contact **Mattice Lake Outfitters** at ☎ **807/583-2483** for a 3- to 7-day trip priced at C$910 (US$607) and C$1,106 (US$738) per person, respectively. It'll also rent canoes for around C$1,000 (US$667) per week. In the Cochrane area, contact **Polar Bear Performance** at ☎ **705/272-5890** for details about trips along the Missinaibi, Mattagami, and Abitibi rivers. For other outfitters, call the **Northern Ontario Tourist Outfitters Association** at ☎ **705/472-5552.**

Note: In most provincial parks you must register with park authorities and provide them with your route.

FISHING Ontario is one of the world's largest freshwater fishing grounds, with more than 250,000 lakes and 60,000 miles of rivers supporting more than 140 species. The northern area covered in this chapter is the province's best fishing region. In summer, on **Manitoulin Island,** fishing for Chinook, coho, rainbow, lake trout, perch, and bass is excellent in Georgian Bay or any of the island lakes—**Mindenmoya, Manitou, Kagawong,** and **Tobacco,** to name a few. Trips can be arranged through **Timberlane Lodge** at ☎ **800/890-4177** or 705/377-4078.

Around **Nipissing** and **North Bay** there's great fishing for walleye, northern pike, smallmouth bass, muskie, whitefish, and perch. In addition to these, the **Temagami** region offers brook, lake, and rainbow trout. You can find more remote fishing in the **Chapleau** and **Algoma** regions, the **James Bay Frontier,** and north of **Lake Superior.**

Some outfitters will rent lakeside log cabins equipped with a propane stove and refrigerator and motorboat to go along with it. The cost varies from C$900 to C$1,150 (US$600 to US$767) per person for 3 to 7 days. Two outfitters to contact are **Smooth Rock Camps** at ☎ **807/583-2617** and **Mattice Lake Outfitters** at ☎ **807/583-2483** (see above). **Konopelky,** Box 1870, Cochrane, ON P0L 1C0 (☎ **705/272-4672**), rents cabins fully equipped with propane stoves, fridges, Coleman lights, and wood stoves (some on lakes accessible only by aircraft and some in drive-in locations). They offer fishing, moose and bear hunting, and canoe packages on the Missinaibi, Mattagami, and Abitibi rivers. **Polar Bear Camp,** P.O. Box 2436, Cochrane, ON P0L 1C0 (☎ **705/272-5680**), offers similar packages. For additional suggestions, contact **Ontario Tourism** or the **Northern Ontario Tourist Outfitters Association** (see above).

Note: You must follow fishing limits and regulations. Licenses are required, costing about C$15 (US$10). These licenses are usually available at boat shops and sporting-goods stores; or contact the **Ministry of Natural Resources** at ☎ **416/314-2000.**

GOLF Barrie has two exceptional courses—the **National Pines Golf and Country Club** (☎ **705/431-7000**) and the **Horseshoe Resort** golf course (☎ **705/835-2790**). Collingwood offers the scenic **Cranberry Resort** course (☎ **705/446-0000**). In the Huronia region, there's the **Bonaire Golf and Country Club** (☎ **705/835-2082**), in the town of Coldwater. In Bracebridge, you'll find the **Muskoka Highlands Golf Course** (☎ **705/646-1060**) and, farther north near North Bay, the **Mattawa Golf Resort** (☎ **705/744-5818**). Thunder Bay has five par-71 or -72 courses, while Timmins and Kenora have one each.

HIKING & BACKPACKING The region is a hiker's paradise. The **Bruce Trail,** starting at Queenston, runs for 782km (485 miles), crossing the Niagara escarpment and Bruce Peninsula and ending up in Tobermory. The Bruce Trail Association publishes a map you can get from sporting-goods stores specializing in outdoor activities. In the Bruce Peninsula National Park are four trails, three linked to the Bruce Trail. There's also a hiking trail around Flowerpot Island in Fathom Five National Park.

Manitoulin Island, particularly the **Cup and Saucer Trail,** is popular with hikers. South of Parry Sound, hikers can follow the 66km (41-mile) **Seguin Trail,** which meanders around several lakes. In the Muskoka region, trails abound in **Arrowhead Provincial Park** at Huntsville and the Resource Management Area on Highway 11, north of Bracebridge, and in **Algonquin Park.** Algonquin is a great choice for an extended backpacking trip, along the Highland Trail or the Western Uplands Hiking Trail, which combines three loops for a total of 170km (105 miles).

You can do a memorable 7- to 10-day backpacking trip in **Killarney Provincial Park** on the 97km (60-mile) La Cloche Silhouette Trail, which takes in some stunning scenery. **Sleeping Giant Provincial Park** has more than 81km (50 miles) of trails. The Kabeyun Trail provides great views of Lake Superior and the 800-foot-high cliffs of the Sleeping Giant. And the **Pukaskwa National Park** offers a coastal hiking trail between the Pic and Pukaskwa rivers along the northern shore of Lake Superior.

For additional hiking information, see the park entries later in this chapter.

HORSEBACK RIDING   Harmony Acres, RR #1, Tobermory (☎ 519/596-2735), offers overnight trail rides to the shores of Georgian Bay, as well as 1-hour and day rides. On Manitoulin Island, **Honora Bay Riding Stables,** RR #1, Little Current, ON P0P 1K0 (☎ 705/368-2669), operates an overnight trail ride May to October.

In Collingwood, there's **Braeburn Farms Limited,** RR #1 (☎ 705/446-2262), which has 1-hour guided trail rides as well as day rides. Near Sault Ste. Marie, **Cedar Rail Ranch,** RR #3, Thessalon (☎ 705/842-2021), offers both hourly and overnight trail rides with stops for swimming breaks along the route. Riding fees run C$20 to C$25 (US$13 to US$17) for an hour's guided trail ride to C$75 to C$100 (US$50 to US$67) for a day on horseback.

SKIING & SNOWMOBILING   Ontario's largest downhill-skiing area is the **Blue Mountain Resorts** in Collingwood. In the Muskoka region there's downhill skiing at **Hidden Valley Highlands** (☎ 705/789-1773 or 705/789-5942). Up north around Thunder Bay try **Loch Lomond** (☎ 807/475-7787), **Big Thunder** (☎ 807/475-4402), and **Mount Baldy** (☎ 807/683-8441).

You can cross-country ski at Big Thunder and in several provincial parks, such as **Sleeping Giant** and **Kakabeka Falls.**

One of the top destinations is the **Parry Sound** area, which has an extensive network of cross-country ski trails and more than 1,047km (649 miles) of well-groomed snowmobiling trails. There are nine snowmobiling clubs in the area, and the **Chamber of Commerce** (☎ 705/746-4213) can put you in touch with them. For details on cross-country skiing, contact the **Georgian Nordic Ski and Canoe Club,** Box 42, Parry Sound, ON P2A 2X2 (☎ 705/746-5067), which permits day use of its ski trails.

You'll also find groomed cross-country trails at **Sauble Beach** on the Bruce Peninsula and in many of the provincial parks farther north. Along the mining frontier, contact the **Porcupine Ski Runners** at ☎ 705/360-1444 in Timmins.

2   From Collingwood/Blue Mountain to Tobermory/Bruce Peninsula National Park

If you head west from Barrie, northwest from Toronto, you'll go along the west Georgian Bay coast from Collingwood up to the Bruce Peninsula. Driving from Toronto, take Highway 400 to Highway 26 west.

Nestled at the base of Blue Mountain, **Collingwood** is the town closest to Ontario's largest skiing area. Collingwood first achieved prosperity as a Great Lakes port and shipbuilding town that turned out large lake carriers. Many mansions and the Victorian main street are reminders of those days. And just east of Blue Mountain sweep 9 miles of golden sands at **Wasaga Beach.**

North beyond Collingwood stretches the **Bruce Peninsula National Park,** known for its limestone cliffs, wetlands, and forest. From Tobermory, you can visit an underwater national park.

For visitor information, contact **Georgian Triangle Tourism,** 601 First St., Collingwood, ON L9Y 4L2 (☎ **705/445-7722**). It's open daily 9am to 5pm.

BLUE MOUNTAIN SKI TRAILS, SLIDES, RIDES & MORE

In winter, skiers flock to **Blue Mountain Resort,** at RR #3, Collingwood (☎ **705/445-0231**). Ontario's largest resort has 16 lifts, 98% snowmaking coverage on 35 trails, and three base lodges. In addition, there are three repair, rental, and ski shops; a ski school; and day care. Lift rates are C$37 (US$25) daily.

In summer, you can board a minibobsled and zoom down the **Great Slide Ride,** 3,000 feet of asbestos-cement track, weaving in and out of trees and careening around high-banked hairpin curves. Naturally, you don't have to go at breakneck speed. The 10-minute ride to the top aboard the triple-chair lift treats you to a glorious panoramic view over Georgian Bay. Victoria Day (late May) to Canadian Thanksgiving (U.S. Columbus Day), the slide is open daily 9:30am to dusk. Admission for the Great Slide Ride is C$3.50 (US$2.35) adults and C$2.50 (US$1.60) children 7 and above; a book of four tickets is C$11 (US$7) and C$8 (US$5), respectively.

Other attractions at the resort include the **Tube Ride,** in which you take an inner tube down a series of waterfalls, ponds, and rapids stretching over 400 feet. Even more thrilling is the **Slipper Dipper water slide,** consisting of three flumes that loop and tunnel down 400 feet into a splash-down pool. For either of these exhilarating pleasures, adults pay C$4.75 (US$3.15) for five rides, children 8 to 12 cost C$4 (US$2.65), and children under 8 cost C$2.75 (US$1.85). Mid-June to Labour Day, they're open daily 9:30am to dusk. Children must be at least 8 years old and 42 inches tall for both. An all-day pass for unlimited rides on the Great Slide Ride, the Tube Ride, and the Slipper Dipper is C$17 (US$11) adults, C$14 (US$9) kids 8 to 12, and C$8 (US$5) children under 8.

Blue Mountain is also famous for its dark-hued **pottery,** and you can take a free factory tour and perhaps buy a few seconds. A pottery outlet is at 2 Mountain Rd., on Highway 26 in Collingwood (☎ **705/445-3000**).

Three miles east of Collingwood on Highway 26, at Fairgrounds Road, kids can enjoy testing their mettle and skills at **Blue Mountain Go-Kart Rides** (☎ **705/445-2419**). For the really small fry there are minicarts, costing C$4.50 (US$3) for 5 minutes, plus bumper boats (C$10/US$7 for about 10 min.), a batting cage, a pitching machine, minigolf, a small touch-and-pet animal park (C$3/US$2), and a game arcade. It's open daily 10am to midnight.

BRUCE PENINSULA NATIONAL PARK

Bruce Peninsula National Park features limestone cliffs, abundant wetlands, quiet beaches, and forest sheltering more than 40 species of orchids, 20 species of ferns, and several insectivorous plants. About 100 species of bird also inhabit the park. Three campgrounds (one trailer, two tent) offer 242 campsites (no electricity).

The **Bruce Trail** winds along the Georgian Bay Coastline, while Route 6 cuts across the peninsula; both end in Tobermory. It's one of Ontario's best-known trails, stretching 700km (434 miles) from Queenston in Niagara Falls to Tobermory. The most rugged part of the trail passes through the park along the Georgian Bay shoreline. **Cypress Lake Trails,** from the north end of the Cyprus Lake campground, provide access to the Bruce Trail and lead to cliffs overlooking the bay. You can use canoes and nonpowered craft on Cyprus Lake. The best swimming is at **Singing Sands Beach** and **Dorcas Bay,** both on Lake Huron on the west side of the peninsula. Winter activities include cross-country skiing, snowshoeing, and snowmobiling. For more **information,** contact the Superintendent, Bruce Peninsula National Park, Box 189, Tobermory, ON N0H 2R0 (☎ **519/596-2233**).

AN UNDERWATER NATIONAL PARK

From Tobermory you can visit an underwater national park, the **Fathom Five National Marine Park,** P.O. Box 189, Tobermory, ON N0H 2R0 (☎ **519/ 596-2233**), where at least 21 known shipwrecks lie waiting for diving exploration around the 19 or so islands in the park. The most accessible is **Flowerpot Island,** which you can visit by tour boat to view its weird and wonderful rock pillar formations. Go for a few hours to hike and picnic. Six campsites are available on the island on a first-come, first-served basis. Boats leave from Tobermory harbor. For more **information,** contact the Superintendent, Fathom Five National Marine Park, Box 189, Tobermory, ON N0H 2R0 (☎ **519/596-2233**).

WHERE TO STAY

Beaconglow Motel. RR #3, Collingwood, ON L9Y 3Z2. ☎ **705/445-1674.** Fax 705/ 445-7176. 33 units. A/C TV TEL. Motel and efficiency units from C$59 (US$39) double; C$45 (US$30) per person 2-bedroom standard suite weekends; C$75 (US$50) per person luxury 2-bedroom suite. Midweek and other packages available. Special weekly rates available. AE, MC, V.

The Beaconglow has nicely furnished efficiency units ranging from a compact one-bedroom with a kitchenette to a two-bedroom/two-bathroom suite with a fully equipped kitchen (including coffeemaker, microwave, and dishwasher), a living room with a wood-burning fireplace and VCR, and a bathroom with a Jacuzzi. For fun, there are an indoor pool, a whirlpool, a sauna, shuffleboard, a game room with a pool table, and a library of 375 movies. Reserve at least 3 months ahead for weekend or holiday stays.

✪ **Beild House.** 64 Third St., Collingwood, ON L9Y 1K5. ☎ **705/444-1522.** Fax 705/ 444-2394. A/C. 12 units. C$360–C$400 (US$240–US$267) for 2 on weekends, meals included; C$309–C$365 (US$206–US$243) midweek for same 2-night package for 2. Rates include breakfast. AE, MC, V.

Bill Barclay and his wife, Stephanie, are the enthusiastic owners of this handsome 1909 house. Bill prepares the breakfasts and gourmet dinners, while Stephanie is responsible for the inviting decor. The downstairs public areas are personalized by their collections of folk art, quill boxes from Manitoulin, and sculptures by Stephanie's mother. Two fireplaces make the place cozy in winter. The guest rooms are individually furnished with elegant pieces. Room no. 4 contains a bed once owned by the duke and duchess of Windsor, royal portraits, and a souvenir program of Prince Edward's 1860 trip to Canada. The five third-floor rooms have canopied beds and fireplaces. The hotel offers a sumptuous breakfast and a five-course dinner that's even more so, with such dishes as beef fillet with bordelaise sauce and salmon in phyllo with tarragon mayonnaise.

Blue Mountain Inn. RR #3, Collingwood, ON L9Y 3Z2. ☎ **705/445-0231.** 98 units. A/C TV TEL. Ski season from C$109 (US$73) per person midweek, C$139 (US$93) per person weekends; off-season from C$99 (US$66). Condos from C$179 (US$119). Special packages available. AE, MC, V.

Stay here right at the mountain base and you can beat the winter lift lines. The guest rooms are simply furnished, with little balconies facing the mountain and overlooking the tennis courts. You can also rent one- to three-bedroom condos, either slopeside or overlooking the fairway. The inn's facilities include three lounges, a dining room, an outdoor and an indoor pool, squash courts, 12 tennis courts, an 18-hole golf course, mountain-bike and kayak rentals, and a fitness center. Children's programs are offered.

WHERE TO DINE

✪ **Alphorn Restaurant.** Hwy. 26 W., Collingwood. ☎ **705/445-8882.** Reservations not accepted. Main courses C$14–C$20 (US$9–US$13). AE, MC, V. Mon–Fri 4–10pm, Sat–Sun 3–11pm; summer daily 11:30am–3pm. SWISS.

Bratwurst, Wiener schnitzel, chicken Ticino, and cheese fondue are just some of the favorites served at this chalet-style restaurant, which is loaded with Swiss atmosphere. It's a very popular place, always crowded winter and summer. Save room for the Swiss crêpes with chocolate and almonds.

✪ **Chez Michel.** Hwy. 26 W., Craigleith. ☎ **705/445-9441.** Reservations recommended. Main courses C$13–C$21 (US$9–US$14). AE, MC, V. Wed–Mon 11:30am–2pm; daily 5–9pm. FRENCH.

Small and charming, Chez Michel possesses a very French air created by chef/proprietor Michel Masselin, who hails from Normandy. The food is excellent and carefully prepared. Among the specials you may find Cornish hen with cassis sauce or rack of lamb with Dijon crust, along with more traditional favorites like coquilles St-Jacques. There's a good wine list too, and the desserts are worth waiting for, like the strawberries romanoff.

Christopher's. 167 Pine St. ☎ **705/445-7117.** Reservations recommended. Main courses C$13–C$19 (US$9–US$13). AE, MC, V. Daily 11am–2:30pm and 5–10pm. FRENCH/CONTINENTAL.

Dinner in this handsome Victorian town house might find you sampling such dishes as grilled lamb tenderloin with cider mint sauce or spinach fettuccine with shrimp, sun-dried tomatoes, and tomato-cream sauce. In summer, afternoon tea is served.

Spike & Spoon. 637 Hurontario St. ☎ **705/446-1629.** Reservations recommended. Main courses C$13–C$23 (US$9–US$15). MC, V. Tues–Fri noon–2pm; Tues–Sun 5:30–9pm. CONTINENTAL.

In an elegant mid–19th-century red-brick house that once belonged to a Chicago millionaire, this restaurant offers food prepared with fresh ingredients and herbs grown out back. There are three dining rooms, each with a different atmosphere, plus a closed-in porch for pleasant summer dining. The bread and the desserts are all freshly made on the premises. Main courses may be poached salmon with roasted–red-pepper cream or rack of lamb with fresh mint glaze au jus, and there's always a vegetarian dish.

3 Manitoulin Island: A Spiritual Escape

Manitoulin Island, named after the Great Indian Spirit Gitchi Manitou, is for those who seek a quiet, remote, and spiritual place where life is slow.

ESSENTIALS

VISITOR INFORMATION   Contact the **Manitoulin Tourism Association,** P.O. Box 119, Little Current, ON P0P 1K0 (☎ **705/368-3021**), open daily 10am to 4pm, or stop by the **information center** at the Swing Bridge in Little Current, open May to September daily 10am to 4pm.

GETTING THERE   By road, you can cross over the swing bridge connecting Little Current to Great Cloche Island and via Highway 6 to Espanola. You can also reach the island via the **Chi-Cheemaun ferry,** which transports people and cars from

Tobermory to South Baymouth on a 1¾- to 2-hour trip. Ferries operate early May to mid-October, with four a day in summer. Reservations are strongly recommended. One-way fare is C$11 (US$7) adults and C$6 (US$3.65) children 5 to 11; an average-size car costs C$24 (US$16) one-way, and bicycles cost C$4.75 (US$3.15). For information, call the **Northland Transportation Company** at ☎ **800/265-3163** or 519/376-6601 or the **Tobermory terminal** at ☎ **519/596-2510.**

EXPLORING THE ISLAND

Native peoples have lived on this land for centuries, and you can visit the **Ojibwa Indian Reserve,** occupying the large peninsula on the island's eastern end. It's home to about 2,500 people of Odawa, Ojibwa, and Potawotami descent; the area was never ceded to the government. The reserve isn't a tourist attraction but might appeal to anyone genuinely interested in modern life on a reservation. Try to time your visit for the big **Wikwemikong Powwow** in August. Other powwows are held during the year around the island. It's worth seeking out the few native art galleries, like the **Kasheese Studios,** outside West Bay at Highways 540 and 551 (☎ 705/377-4141), operated by artists in residence Blake Debassige and Shirley Cheechoo, and the **Ojibwa Cultural Foundation,** also outside West Bay (☎ 705/377-4902), open erratically and then only to 4pm. You can also visit individual artists' studios.

Although there are several communities on the island, the highlights are scenic and mostly outside their perimeters, like the **Mississagi Lighthouse,** at the western end outside Meldrun Bay. Follow the signs that'll take you about 4 miles down a dirt road past the limestone/dolomite quarry entrance (from which materials are still shipped across the Great Lakes) to the lighthouse. There you can see how the lightkeeper lived in this isolated area before the advent of electricity. The dining room is open in summer. From the lighthouse, several short trails lead along the shoreline.

One gallery worth a visit is the **Perivale Gallery,** RR #2, Spring Bay (☎ 705/377-4847), open the May holiday to mid-September, daily 10am to 6pm. Owners Sheila and Bob McMullan scour the country searching for the remarkable artists and craftspeople whose work they display in their log-cabin gallery overlooking Lake Kagawong. Glass, sculpture, paintings, engravings, fabrics, and ceramics fill the space. From Spring Bay, follow Perivale Road east for about 2 miles; turn right at the lake and keep following the road until you see the gallery on the right.

The island is great for hiking, biking, bird watching, boating, cross-country skiing, and just plain relaxing. Charters also operate from Meldrun Bay. You'll find golf courses in Mindemoya and Gore Bay. Fishing is excellent either in Georgian Bay or in the island's lakes and streams. You can arrange trips through **Timberlane Lodge** at ☎ **800/890-4177** or 705/377-4078. May to October, **Honora Bay Riding Stables,** RR #1, Little Current, ON P0P 1K0 (☎ **705/368-2669**), 27km (17 miles) west of Little Current on Highway 540, offers trail rides, including an overnight program. A 3-hour ride is C$30 (US$20).

There are several nature trails on the island. Among the more spectacular is the **Cup and Saucer Trail,** starting 18km (11 miles) west of Little Current at the junction of Highway 540 and Bidwell Road. Also off Highway 540 lies the trail to **Bridal Veil Falls** as you enter the village of Kagawong. Halfway between Little Current and Manitowaning, stop at **Ten Mile Point** for the view over the North Channel, dotted with 20,000 islands. The best beach with facilities is at **Providence Bay** on the island's south side.

WHERE TO STAY

Your best bet is to seek out one of several B&Bs, which will most likely be plain and simple but clean. Contact **Manitowaning Tourism Association,** Box 119, Little Current, ON P0P 1K0 (☎ 705/368-3021).

✪ **Manitowaning Lodge Golf & Tennis Resort.** Box 160, Manitowaning, ON P0P 1N0. ☎ **705/859-3136.** Fax 705/859-3270. 9 units, 13 cottages. C$105 (US$70) per person in standard room; C$155 (US$103) per person in 1-bedroom cabin with fireplace. Rates include breakfast and dinner. Special tennis packages available. AE, MC, V. Closed Canadian Thanksgiving (U.S. Columbus Day) to second Fri in May.

This idyllic place, a lodge and cottages on 11 acres of spectacularly landscaped gardens, lacks the pretension of so many resorts. Artists were employed to create a whimsical decor with trompe l'oeil painting and furniture sporting hand-painted scenes and designs. The buildings themselves have a delightful rustic air created by their beamed ceilings; in the lodge is a large fieldstone fireplace with a carved mask of the Indian Spirit of Manitowaning looming above. The cottages are comfortably furnished with wicker or painted log furniture, beds with duvets and pillows, dhurries, log tables, and hand-painted furnishings; all have fireplaces. None has a TV or phone—it's a real retreat. The dining room is airy, serving food that features fine local meats like lamb and fish. You might find Manitowaning poached trout, smoked pork loin with plum sauce, or tiger shrimp with coconut couscous. Lunch is served on the terrace overlooking the water. Facilities include an 18-hole golf course, four tennis courts with a pro, a pool surrounded by a deck and gardens with chaises, a gym, mountain bikes, water sports (canoes, motorboats, and sailboats), and great fishing.

Rock Garden Terrace Resort. RR #1, Spring Bay, ON P0P 2B0. ☎ **705/377-4652.** 18 motel units, 4 chalet suites. TV. Summer and winter C$86–C$105 (US$57–US$70) per person, including breakfast and dinner. Spring and fall rates slightly lower. Weekend and weekly packages available. MC, V.

This typical family resort, on the rocks above Lake Mindemoya, has a Bavarian flair. Most accommodations are in motel-style units furnished in contemporary style, but there are also four log-cabin–style suites. The dining room seems like an Austrian hunting lodge, with trophies displayed on the oak-paneled walls and a cuisine featuring German-Austrian specialties like Wiener schnitzel, sauerbraten, goulash, and beef rolladen. Facilities include a kidney-shaped pool, a whirlpool, a sauna, fitness facilities, a fishing dock, and games like outdoor shuffleboard and chess, as well as bicycle, boat, and canoe rentals.

WHERE TO DINE

The food on the island is simple and homey. For more sophisticated palate-pleasers, go to the **Manitowaning Lodge Golf & Tennis Resort** (☎ 705/859-3136) or the **Rock Garden Terrace Resort** (☎ 705/377-4642), both near Spring Bay. In Little Current, one of the nicest casual spots on the island for breakfast, lunch, or dinner is **The Old English Pantry,** Water Street (☎ 705/368-3341). At dinner you'll find a pasta and fish dish of the day, as well as English specialties like roast beef and Yorkshire pudding and baked pot pies, at C$11 to C$17 (US$7 to US$11). Afternoon cream teas and takeout are also available. Only a smaller selection of dishes like quiche, stuffed baked potato, and steak pie is offered after Labour Day. In summer, it's open Sunday to Thursday 9am to 9pm and Friday and Saturday to 11pm; winter hours are Monday to Wednesday 9am to 5pm and Thursday to Saturday 9am to 8pm.

4 Along Georgian Bay: Midland & Parry Sound

MIDLAND

Midland is the center for cruising through the thousands of beautifully scenic Georgian Islands, and **30,000 Island Cruises** (☎ **705/526-0161**) offers 2½-hour cruises following the route of Brélé, Champlain, and La Salle up through the inside passage to Georgian Bay. May to Canadian Thanksgiving (U.S. Columbus Day), boats usually leave the town dock twice a day. Fares are C$14 (US$9) adults, C$13 (US$9) seniors, and C$8 (US$5) children 2 to 12.

Midland lies 33 miles east of Barrie and 90 miles north of Toronto. If you're driving from Barrie, take Highway 400 to Highway 12W to Midland.

EXPLORING THE AREA

See the box below for details on **Sainte Marie Among the Hurons.** Across from the Martyrs' Shrine, the **Wye Marsh Wildlife Centre** (☎ **705/526-7809**) is a 150-acre wetland/woodland site offering wildlife viewing, guided and self-guided walks, and canoe excursions in the marsh. A floating boardwalk cuts through the marsh, fields, and woods, where trumpeter swans have been reintroduced into the environment and now number 40 strong. Reservations are needed for the canoe trips (call the number above), offered in July and August and occasionally September. In winter, cross-country skiing and snowshoeing are available. For information, write Highway 12 (P.O. Box 100), Midland, ON L4R 4K6. Admission is C$6 (US$4) adults and C$4 (US$2.65) students/seniors; children under 3 are free. Victoria Day (late May) to Labour Day (first Mon in Sept), the center is open daily 10am to 6pm; other months, hours are daily 10am to 4pm.

In town, **Freda's,** in an elegant home at 342 King St. (☎ **705/526-4851**), serves traditional continental cuisine, with main courses at C$9 to C$28 (US$6 to US$19). You can choose from a variety of meat and seafood dishes—steaks, beef Stroganoff, chicken Kiev, coquilles St-Jacques, and more.

EN ROUTE TO THE MUSKOKA LAKES: ORILLIA

Traveling to the Muskoka lakeland region, you'll probably pass through **Orillia** (from Barrie, take Highway 11). Here you can visit Canadian author/humorist **Stephen Leacock**'s summer home (☎ **705/329-1908**), a green-and-white mansard-roofed and turreted structure with a central balcony overlooking the beautiful lawns and garden sweeping down to the lake. The interior is filled with heavy Victorian furniture and mementos of this Canadian Mark Twain, author of 35 volumes of humor, including *Sunshine Sketches of a Little Town*, which caricatured many of the residents of Mariposa—a barely fictionalized version of Orillia. Admission is C$7 (US$4.65) adults,

Bright Lights in the Wilderness

While most visitors to northern Ontario are drawn by the peaceful expanses of wilderness, increasing numbers are gravitating to the **Casino Rama,** RR #6, Rama, ON L0K 1T0 (☎ **888/817-7262** or 705/329-3325), the 195,000-square-foot state-of-the-art casino just east of Orillia. Open 24 hours, the casino boasts more than 2,100 slot machines and 109 gaming tables. There are also three full-service restaurants, a food arcade, and a smoky lounge with live entertainment. So when all that peace and quiet starts getting to you, you know where to turn.

The Tragic Tale of Sainte Marie Among the Hurons

Midland's history dates from 1639, when Jesuits established a fortified mission here, **Sainte Marie Among the Hurons,** to bring Christianity to the Huron tribe. However, the mission retreat lasted only a decade, for the Iroquois, jealous of the Huron-French trading relationship, stepped up their attacks in the area. By the late 1640s, the Iroquois had killed thousands of Hurons and several priests and had destroyed two villages within 6 miles of Sainte Marie. Ultimately the Jesuits burned down their own mission and fled with the Hurons to Christian Island, about 20 miles away. But the winter of 1649 was harsh, and thousands of Hurons died. In the end, only a few Jesuits and 300 Hurons were able to make the journey back to the relative safety of Québec. The Jesuits' mission had ended in martyrdom. It was 100 years before the native Canadians in the region saw Europeans again, and those newcomers spoke a different language.

Today, local history is recaptured at the **mission** (☎ 705/526-7838), 5 miles east of Midland on Highway 12 (follow the HURONIA HERITAGE signs). The blacksmith stokes his forge, the carpenter squares a beam with a broadax, and the ringing church bell calls the missionaries to prayer, while a canoe enters the fortified water gate. A film depicts the life of the missionaries. Special programs given in July and August include candlelight tours and a 1½-hour canoeing trip (at extra cost). Admission is C$7 (US$4.85) adults and C$4.50 (US$3) students; children under 6 are free. Mid-May to mid-October, it's open daily 10am to 5pm.

Just east of Midland on Highway 12 rise the twin spires of the **Martyrs' Shrine** (☎ 705/526-3788), a memorial to the eight North American martyr saints. Because six were missionaries at Sainte Marie, this imposing church was built on the hill overlooking the mission, and thousands make pilgrimages here each year. The bronzed outdoor stations of the cross were imported from France. Admission is C$2 (US$1.35) adults; children under 16 are free. Mid-May to mid-October, it's open daily 8:30am to 9pm.

C$7 (US$4.35) seniors, C$2 (US$1.35) students, and C$1 (US65¢) children 5 to 13. The end of June to Labour Day, it's open daily 10am to 7pm; in other months, you need to make an appointment.

GEORGIAN BAY ISLANDS NATIONAL PARK

The park consists of 59 islands in Georgian Bay and can be reached via water taxi from Honey Harbour, a town north of Midland right on the shore. (As you're taking Highway 400 north, branch off to the west at Port Severn to reach Honey Harbour.) Hiking, swimming, fishing, and boating are the name of the game in the park. In summer and on weekends and holidays, the boaters really do take over—but it's a quiet retreat weekdays, late August, and off-season. The park's center is on the largest island, **Beausoleil,** with camping and other facilities. For more information, contact the Superintendent, **Georgian Bay Islands National Park,** Box 28, Honey Harbour, ON P0E 1E0 (☎ 705/756-2415).

THE PARRY SOUND AREA

Only 225km (140 miles) north of Toronto and 161km (100 miles) south of Sudbury, the Parry Sound area is the place for active vacations. For details, contact the **Parry**

Sound Area Chamber of Commerce, 70 Church St. (☎ **705/746-4213**), open Monday to Friday 10am to 4pm, or the **information center** at 1 Church St. (☎ **705/378-5105**), open daily 10am to 4pm.

There's excellent canoeing and kayaking; if you need an outfitter, contact **White Squall,** RR #1, Nobel, ON P0G 1G0 (☎ **705/342-5324**), which offers both day trips and multiday excursions. Run by **30,000 Island Cruise Lines,** 9 Bay St., Parry Sound, ON P2A 1S4 (☎ **705/746-2311**), the *Island Queen* cruises through the 30,000 islands for 3 hours. It leaves the town dock once or twice a day and charges C$16 (US$11) adults and C$8 (US$5) children.

And there are many winter diversions as well—loads of cross-country ski trails and more than 1,000km (620 miles) of well-groomed snowmobiling trails. For details on cross-country skiing, contact the **Georgian Nordic Ski and Canoe Club,** Box 42, Parry Sound, ON P2A 2X2 (☎ **705/746-5067**), which permits day use of their ski trails.

Nature lovers will head for **Killbear Provincial Park,** P.O. Box 71, Nobel, ON P0G 1G0 (☎ **705/342-5492,** or 705/342-5227 for reservations), farther north up Highway 69; it offers 4,000 glorious acres set in the middle of 30,000 islands. There are plenty of water sports—swimming at a 3km (1.9-mile) beach on Georgian Bay, snorkeling or diving off Harold Point, and fishing for lake trout, walleye, perch, pike, and bass. The climate is moderated by the bay, which explains why trillium, wild leek, and hepatica bloom. Among the more unusual fauna are the Blandings and Map turtles that inhabit the bogs, swamps, and marshes.

There are three **hiking trails,** including 3.5km (2.2-mile) Lookout Point, leading to a commanding view over Blind Bay to Parry Sound; and the Lighthouse Point Trail, crossing rocks and pebble beaches to the lighthouse at the peninsula's southern tip. There's also **camping** at 883 sites in seven campgrounds, costing C$16 to C$20 (US$11 to US$13). The daily vehicle entry fee is C$7 (US$4.65).

WHERE TO STAY

The inn below is exquisite and expensive, but there are other places to stay in the area. Contact the **Parry Sound and District Bed and Breakfast Association,** P.O. Box 71, Parry Sound, ON P2A 2X2 (☎ **705/746-5399**), for its listings at C$50 (US$33) and up double. There's also a **Comfort Inn,** 112 Bowes St. (☎ **705/746-6221**), where the rates are C$80 to C$100 (US$53 to US$67) double. And at the edge of Otter Lake, the modest, family-oriented **Tapatoo Resort,** Box 384, Parry Sound, ON P2A 2X5 (☎ **705/378-2208**), rents cottages, rooms, and suites and offers boating, windsurfing, waterskiing, canoeing, fishing, and swimming in an indoor pool. Rates are C$98 to C$150 (US$65 to US$100), with C$22 (US$15) per person extra for meals.

✪ **Inn at Manitou.** McKellar, ON P0G 1C0. ☎ **705/389-2171.** Fax 705/389-3818. 32 units, 1 3-bedroom country house. A/C TEL. Units: July–Aug C$219–C$319 (US$146–US$213) per person double; June and Sept C$200–C$239 (US$133–US$159) per person double; May and early Oct C$179–C$209 (US$119–US$139) per person double. Country house: July–Aug C$369 (US$246) per person; June and Sept C$300 (US$200) per person; rest of the year C$275 (US$183) per person. Rates include breakfast, lunch, afternoon tea, and dinner. Special packages available; special musical, cooking, and other events scheduled. AE, ER, MC, V. Closed late Oct to early May.

The Inn at Manitou is a stunner. Everything about the foyer glows; the space is opulently furnished in French style with elegant touches of chinoiserie. Beyond the foyer and a sitting area, a veranda stretches around the building's rear, with wicker and bamboo chairs overlooking the tennis courts. To the foyer's left is the very inviting Tea Room with a view of the lake. A steep staircase leads down to the swimming and boating dock. The accommodations are up the hill in several cedar lodges overlooking the lake. The standard rooms are small and simple; the deluxe units contain fireplaces, small sitting areas, and private sundecks, while the luxury rooms feature sizable living rooms with fireplaces, whirlpool bathtubs, saunas, and private decks.

Dining/Diversions: Downstairs in the main building is the Club Lounge night-club, a billiards room, and an open-to-view wine cellar, filled with fine vintages, where twice-weekly wine tastings are held. The resort's cuisine is renowned and is part of the reason the Relais and Châteaux organization awarded the property the distinguished Gold Shield. At dinner, a casual three-course bistro menu and a more elaborate four-course gourmet menu are offered along with a special spa menu. Afterward, you can retire to the Tea Room for coffee, petit fours, and truffles.

Amenities: Room service; spa facilities with full range of body treatments; outdoor heated pool, 20 tennis courts (including one indoor), bikes, sailboats, canoes, Wind-surfers, exercise equipment, pitch-and-putt facilities, instructional golfing range.

5 The Muskoka Lakes: A Land of Resorts

To settlers coming north in the 1850s, this region, with its 1,600-plus lakes north of the Severn River, was impossible to farm and difficult to traverse. But even then the wilderness attracted sports people and adventurers like John Campbell and James Bain, who explored the three major lakes—Rosseau, Joseph, and Muskoka. They later started the Muskoka Club, purchased an island in Lake Joseph, and began annual excursions here. Roads were difficult to cut, and waterways became the main trans-portation routes. It wasn't until the late 1800s that a fleet of steamers was running on the lakes and the railway arrived. Muskoka was then finally effectively linked by water and rail to the urban centers in the south.

The ✪ **Muskoka Lakes** area was wired for tourism. Some folks gambled that people would pay to travel to the wilderness if they were wined and dined once they got there. The idea caught on, and grand hotels like Clevelands House, Windermere House, and Deerhurst opened. The lakes became the enclave of the well-to-do from Ontario and the United States. By 1903, there were eight big lake steamers, countless steam launches, and supply boats (floating grocery stores) serving a flourishing resort area.

And though the advent of the car ended the era of the steamboats and grand hotels, the area still flourishes. The rich have been joined by families in their summer cottages and sophisticated young professionals from Toronto. You'll note that many resorts don't look impressive from the road—but just take a look at the other side and remember they were built to be approached by steamship.

ESSENTIALS

VISITOR INFORMATION   For information on the region, contact **Muskoka Tourism,** on Highway 11 at Severn Bridge, RR #2, Kilworthy, ON P0E 1G0 (☎ 705/689-0660). It's open daily 10am to 5pm.

GETTING THERE   You can drive from the south via Highway 400 to Highway 11, from the east via highways 12 and 169 to Highway 11, and from the north via Highway 11. It's about 160km (99 miles) from Toronto to Gravenhurst, 15km (9.3 miles) from Gravenhurst to Bracebridge, 25km (15½ miles) from Bracebridge to Port Carling, and 34km (21 miles) from Bracebridge to Huntsville. **VIA Rail** (☎ 416/366-8411; www.viarail.ca) services Gravenhurst, Bracebridge, and Huntsville from Toronto's Union Station.

Finding a B&B

If you don't want to pay resort rates or restrict yourself to staying at an American Plan resort, contact the **Muskoka Bed and Breakfast Association,** 175 Clairmont Rd., Gravenhurst, ON P1P 1H9 (☎ **705/687-4511**), which represents 28 or so B&Bs throughout the area. Prices range from C$45 to C$100 (US$30 to US$67) double.

GRAVENHURST

Gravenhurst is Muskoka's first town—the first you reach if you're driving from Toronto and the first to achieve town status (in 1887 at the height of the logging boom).

The **Norman Bethune Memorial House** is the restored 1890 birthplace of Dr. Norman Bethune, 235 John St. N. (☎ **705/687-4261**). In 1939, this surgeon, inventor, and humanitarian died tending the sick in China during the Chinese Revolution. Tours of the historic house include a modern exhibit on Bethune's life. A visitor center displays gifts from Chinese visitors, and an orientation video is shown. In summer, the house is open daily 10am to noon and 1 to 5pm (weekdays only in winter). Admission is C$2.25 (US$1.50) adults, C$1.75 (US$1.15) seniors, and C$1.25 (US85¢) children 6 to 16.

Mid-June to mid-October, you can also cruise aboard the old steamship **RMS *Segwun*** (1887), leaving from Gravenhurst and Port Carling. Aboard you'll find two lounges and a dining salon. The cruises on the lake vary from 1 hour at a cost of C$10 (US$7) to a full day's outing for C$50 (US$33). For details, call ☎ 705/687-6667.

Year-round theater performances are given in the **Gravenhurst Opera House** (☎ 705/687-5550) and, summer only, at the **Port Carling Community Hall** (☎ 705/765-5221). Tickets are C$20 to C$25 (US$13 to US$17) adults.

WHERE TO STAY

Severn River Inn. Cowbell Lane off Hwy. 11 (P.O. Box 44), Severn Bridge, ON P0E 1N0. ☎ **705/689-6333.** Fax 705/689-2691. 10 units. A/C. C$85 (US$57) double; C$120 (US$80) suite. Rates include breakfast. V.

The Severn River Inn (19km/12 miles north of Orillia and 14km/8.7 miles south of Gravenhurst) occupies a 1906 building that has served as a general store, post office, telephone exchange, and boardinghouse. The guest rooms are individually furnished with pine and oak pieces, brass beds, flounce pillows, lace curtains, and quilts; the suite contains a sitting room and the original old bathtub and pedestal sink. The intimate restaurant, with a Victorian ambiance, is candlelit at night. In summer, the screened-in porch and outdoor patio overlooking the river are favored dining spots. The menu features contemporary continental cuisine, with dishes at C$14 to C$19 (US$9 to US$13). The dining room/lounge is open daily: Sunday to Thursday 8am to 10pm and Friday and Saturday 8am to 1am.

WHERE TO DINE

Ascona Place. Bethune Dr., Gravenhurst. ☎ **705/687-5906.** Reservations recommended. Main courses C$17–C$23 (US$11–US$15). AE, ER, MC, V. Summer daily 11:30am–2pm and 5–9pm. Closed Mon–Tues Labour Day to Victoria Day. FRENCH/CONTINENTAL.

Named after a small picturesque village in southern Switzerland, Ascona Place offers a pretty courtyard for outside dining in July and August. The menu features classic

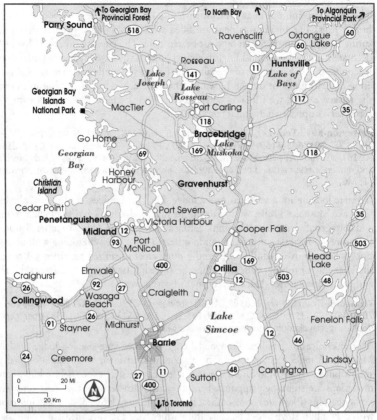

continental cuisine plus one or two Swiss specialties, such as an *émincé* of veal Swiss-style in white wine and cream sauce with mushrooms. You may dine in the wine cellar, a cozy nook hung with wine bottles, or the larger Ascona Room, hung with Swiss banners, wicker lampshades, and a set of Swiss cow bells. The desserts are exquisite—double-chocolate mousse cake, apple strudel, homemade meringues and sorbets, or iced soufflé with French Marc de Bourgogne.

BRACEBRIDGE: SANTA'S WORKSHOP

Halfway between the equator and the North Pole, **Bracebridge** bills itself as Santa's summer home, and **Santa's Village** (☎ 705/645-2512) is an imaginatively designed fantasyland full of delights—pedal boats and bumper boats on the lagoon, a roller-coaster sleigh ride, a Candy Cane Express, a carousel, and a Ferris wheel. At Elves' Island, kids can crawl on a suspended net and over or through various modules—the Lunch Bag Forest, Cave Crawl, and Snake Tube Crawl. Rides, water attractions, and roving entertainers are all part of the fun. Mid-June to Labour Day, it's open daily 10am to 6pm. Admission is C$16 (US$11) ages 5 and up and C$11 (US$7) seniors/children 2 to 4; children under 2 are free.

WHERE TO STAY & DINE

✪ **Inn at the Falls.** 1 Dominion St., P.O. Box 1139, Bracebridge, ON P1L 1V3. ☎ **705/645-2245.** Fax 705/645-5093. 37 units. A/C TV TEL. C$82–C$150 (US$55–US$100) double; C$195 (US$130) suite. Rates include breakfast. AE, DC, MC, V.

This attractive inn occupies a Victorian house on a quiet street overlooking Bracebridge Falls. The inviting gardens are filled with delphiniums, peonies, roses, and spring flowers, plus there's an outdoor heated pool. The guest rooms are individually decorated, with antiques and English chintz. Some units have fireplaces, Jacuzzis, and balconies; others have views of the falls. The Fox and Hounds is a popular local gathering place at lunch or dinner. In winter, the fire crackles and snaps, but in summer the terrace is filled with flowers and umbrella-shaded tables. The more elegant Victoria's serves upscale continental fare.

Patterson-Kaye Lodge. Golden Beach Rd. (off Hwy. 118), RR #1, Bracebridge, ON P1L 1W8. ☎ **705/645-4169.** Fax 705/645-5720. 30 units. TV. High season C$92–C$150 (US$61–US$100) per person, depending on type of accommodation. Rates include breakfast and dinner. Special weekend packages available; also special reductions during certain weeks. AE, MC, V.

If you're looking for a secluded casual lodge, ideal for families, this one fits the bill. On Lake Muskoka 3 miles west of town, the main lodge has a variety of guest rooms, and cottages of various sizes accommodating a total of 100 people are scattered around the property. Facilities include an outdoor heated pool, free waterskiing with instruction, a hot tub, two tennis courts, and a number of organized activities. Of course, there's plenty of fishing, golf, and riding nearby, and use of canoes, sailboats, kayaks, and paddleboats is free. You can rent motorboats as well.

Tamwood Resort. Hwy. 118, RR #1, Bracebridge, ON P1L 1W8. ☎ **800/465-9166** or 705/645-5172. 35 units. A/C MINIBAR TV TEL. C$80–C$130 (US$53–US$87) per person double. Special discount weekly rates available. MC, V.

A great choice for families, Tamwood Lodge is a moderate-size log lodge on Lake Muskoka, 6 miles west of town. The air-conditioned main lodge has 35 units, all simply but nicely decorated, and there are a few cottages. The four deluxe loft accommodations are stunningly appointed in pine, and each features two bedrooms with skylights, plus a loft area, two bathrooms, an efficiency kitchen, and a living room with a Franklin stove and a balcony from which you can dive into Lake Muskoka. Three new waterfront units come with fireplaces. Knotty-pine furnishings and large granite fireplaces imbue the lounge and main dining room with character. Facilities include indoor and outdoor swimming, fishing, tennis, volleyball, badminton, and shuffleboard, plus free waterskiing and boating, and all the winter sports imaginable. There's also lots of organized family fun—such as baseball games, marshmallow roasts, and bingo. Kids are also supervised, and there's a game room.

AN EAGLE LAKE HIDEAWAY

✪ **Sir Sam's Inn.** Eagle Lake P.O., ON K0M 1M0. ☎ **705/754-2188.** Fax 705/754-4262. 25 units. Summer C$125–C$155 (US$83–US$103) per person weekdays, C$265–C$310 (US$177–US$207) per person weekends. Rates include breakfast and dinner. Weekly rates and room-only rates available. Off-season rates drop about 10%. AE, ER, MC, V. Follow the signs to Sir Sam's ski area. From Hwy. 118, take Rte. 6 to Sir Sam's Rd.

Sir Sam's takes some finding, but that's the way politician/militarist Sir Sam Hughes probably wanted it when he built his stone-and-timber mansion in 1917 in the woods above Eagle Lake. The atmosphere is friendly yet sophisticated. A comfy sitting room with a large stone fireplace serves as its focal point. Accommodations are in the inn or in a series of new chalets or in two lakefront suites. The chalets have fetching bed-sitting rooms with light-pine furnishings, wood-burning fireplaces, small private decks, minirefrigerators, and kettles; some have whirlpool bathtubs. The inn rooms are a bit more old-fashioned, except in the Hughes Wing, where they're similar to the chalets, with whirlpools and fireplaces. The suites come with full kitchens and whirlpools.

Dining/Diversions: The pretty dining room serves upscale continental cuisine and offers a fixed-price dinner for C$33 (US$22). Among the decor of the Gunner's Bar is Sir Sam's gun rack; the bar has a small dance floor.

Amenities: Exercise room with rowing machine and stationary bicycle, two tennis courts, outdoor pool, beach; sailing, windsurfing, waterskiing, canoeing, paddleboats, mountain bikes; massage available by appointment; Sir Sam's ski area and cross-country skiing close by.

PORT CARLING

As waterways became the main means of transportation in the region, **Port Carling** grew into the hub of the lakes. It became a boat-building center when a lock was installed connecting lakes Muskoka and Rosseau, and a canal between lakes Rosseau and Joseph opened all three to navigation. The **Muskoka Lakes Museum** on Joseph Street (☎ 705/765-5367) captures the flavor of this era. July and August, it's open Monday to Saturday 10am to 5pm and Sunday noon to 4pm; June, September, and October, hours are Tuesday to Saturday 10am to 4pm and Sunday noon to 4pm. Admission is C$2.25 (US$1.50) adults and C$1.25 (US85¢) seniors/students.

WHERE TO STAY

Clevelands House. Minett P.O., near Port Carling, ON P0B 1G0. ☎ **888/567-1177** or 705/765-3171. Fax 705/765-6296. 107 units, 30 bungalows, several cottages. A/C TV TEL. C$150–C$200 (US$100–US$133) per person per day double, C$850–C$1,100 (US$567–US$734) per person per week double; from C$200 (US$133) daily per person suite, from C$1,100 (US$734) per person per week suite; C$4,000 (US$2,668) minimum per week cottages and bungalows. Rates depend on the number of people in the room and the type of accommodation. Rates include all meals. Special family week, off-season discounts, and packages available. AE, DC, MC, V.

The very name has a gracious ring, and indeed this resort has been providing the ultimate in luxury since 1869. Ontario's largest privately owned resort, it's very much a full-facility center. The lodge is a magnificent clapboard structure with a veranda running around the lakeside giving views over the well-kept flower gardens. A dance floor is set out on the dock with a sundeck on top. Accommodations vary in size and location and have solid old-fashioned furniture; the luxury suites, though, are super-modern, with private sundecks. Facilities include 16 tennis courts (two lighted), two racquetball courts, a nine-hole golf course, bike rentals, a huge children's playground and full children's program, an outdoor pool plus several kids' pools, and a fitness center. There are good fishing, swimming, boating, and waterskiing on Lake Rosseau.

Sherwood Inn. P.O. Box 400, Lake Joseph, Port Carling, ON P0B 1J0. ☎ **705/765-3131.** Fax 705/765-6668. 40 units. C$75–C$180 (US$50–US$120) per person in inn; C$159–C$242 (US$106–US$161) per person in cottage. Rates include breakfast and dinner. B&B rates and special packages available. AE, ER, MC, V. From Hwy. 400, take Hwy. 69 north to Foot's Bay. Turn right and take 169 south to Sherwood Rd. Turn left just before the junction of Hwy. 118. Or you can arrive via Gravenhurst and Bala or Bracebridge and Port Carling.

Accommodations here are either in the lodge or in beachside cottages. The latter are very appealing, with fieldstone fireplaces, comfortable armchairs, TVs, phones, and screened porches overlooking the lake. Some are more luxurious than others and have additional features like VCRs or private docks. The older rooms in the lodge feature painted wood paneling, while the newer wing has air-conditioning and wicker furnishings.

✪ Windermere House. Off Muskoka Rte. 4 (P.O. Box 68), Windermere, ON P0B 1P0.
☎ **800/461-4283** or 705/769-3611. Fax 705/769-2168. 78 units. TEL. C$115–C$180
(US$77–US$120) per person. Rates include breakfast and dinner. Weekly rates and European Plan also available. AE, ER, MC, V.

This striking 1864 stone-and-clapboard turreted building overlooks lawns that sweep
down to Lake Rosseau. It was renovated in 1986. Out front stretches a broad veranda
furnished with Adirondack chairs and geranium-filled window boxes. The guest
rooms are variously furnished, with some in the main house and others in cottages and
buildings scattered around the property. Some have air-conditioning; some, only overhead fans. All are furnished in modern style, some with a bamboo/rattan look. The
dining room, open to the public, offers fine modern continental cuisine. There's
nightly entertainment in the lounge. Services include room service (7am to 10pm)
and laundry/dry cleaning. A full children's program is offered in July and August.
Among the facilities are an outdoor pool, tennis courts, golf, and all kinds of water
sports (fishing, windsurfing, sailing).

HUNTSVILLE

Since the late 1800s, lumber has been the name of the game in Huntsville, and today
it's Muskoka's biggest town, with major manufacturing companies.

You can see some of the region's early history at the **Muskoka Pioneer Village and
Museum,** 88 Brunel Rd., Huntsville (☎ **705/789-7576**). June to Canadian Thanksgiving (U.S. Columbus Day), it's open daily 11am to 4pm; October hours are
Saturday and Sunday 11am to 4pm. Admission is C$6 (US$4) adults and C$4
(US$2.65) children 6 to 12; children under 6 are free. In nearby Brunel you can also
visit the **Brunel Locks,** a system of gates and sluices that can raise or lower the water
level on this key link in the Mary-Fairy-Vernon lake chain.

Robinson's General Store (☎ **705/766-2415**) on Main Street in Dorset (a
15-min. drive east of Huntsville) is so popular it was voted Canada's best country
store. Wood stoves, dry goods, hardware, pine goods, and moccasins—you name it,
it's here. The store is open Monday to Saturday 10am to 6pm.

WHERE TO STAY

Cedar Grove Lodge. P.O. Box 996, Huntsville, ON P0A 1K0. ☎ **705/789-4036.** Fax 705/
789-6860. www.cedargrove.on.ca. 8 units, none with bathroom; 19 cabins. C$90–C$160
(US$60–US$107) per person double in main lodge; C$200–C$240 (US$133–US$160)
per person in cabin. Rates include all meals. Weekly rates and special packages available.
AE, MC, V. Take Grassmere Resort Rd., off Hwy. 60.

On Peninsula Lake, 12km (7.4 miles) from Huntsville, Cedar Grove Lodge is a very
attractive and well-maintained resort. The main lodge contains eight rooms sharing
three bathrooms; the rest of the accommodations are one-, two-, or three-bedroom log
cabins like the Hermit Thrush, which contains pine furnishings, a fieldstone fireplace,
a porch overlooking the lake, a bar/sink and refrigerator, and conveniently stored firewood; or the Chickadee, a smaller version of the same, for two only. The main lodge
contains a comfortable, large sitting room with a stone fireplace, a TV, and a piano,
along with the pretty lakeside dining room. Facilities include two tennis courts, a hot
tub, a kid's beach, and a game room. There's free waterskiing, plus sailboarding,
canoeing, and windsurfing for an extra charge; cross-country skiing and skating on the
lake are offered in winter.

✪ Deerhurst Resort. 1235 Deerhurst Dr., Huntsville, ON P1H 2E8. ☎ **800/
441-1414** or 705/789-6411. Fax 705/789-2431. 350 units. A/C TV TEL. C$109–C$279

(US$73–US$186) double; C$209–C$750 (US$139–US$500) suite. AE, CB, DC, DISC, ER, MC, V. Take Canal Rd. off Hwy. 60 to Deerhurst Rd.

Catering to well-heeled families and a slick, mainly Toronto crowd, the Deerhurst opened in 1896 but has expanded over the past 2 decades, scattering building units all over the property. It's on 900 acres of rolling landscape fronting on Peninsula Lake. The accommodations range from hotel rooms in the Terrace and Bayshore buildings to fully appointed one-, two-, or three-bedroom suites, many with fireplaces and/or whirlpools. The suites come with all the comforts, including stereos, TVs, and VCRs; some have full kitchens with microwaves, dishwashers, and washer/dryers. The most expensive suites are the three-bedroom units on the lake.

Dining/Diversions: The lounge features a massive stone fireplace and comfortable furnishings. The adjacent dining room offers romantic dining overlooking the lake (prix-fixe dinner C$33/US$22, à la carte C$19 to C$27/US$13 to US$18), while the Cypress Lounge provides a chic cocktail environment. Another dining option is Steamers Restaurant and Pub at the golf course. Live entertainment includes a musical show in the theater as well as in the lounge.

Amenities: Indoor sports complex with three tennis courts, three squash courts, one racquetball court, indoor pool, whirlpool, sauna, full-service spa; pool, eight tennis courts, beach, canoes, kayaks, sailboats, paddleboats, waterskiing, windsurfing, horseback riding, two 18-hole golf courses; full winter program with on-site cross-country skiing, snowmobiling, dogsledding, downhill skiing at nearby Hidden Valley Highlands; children's activity program in summer and on weekends year-round.

✪ Grandview Inn & Resort. RR #4, Huntsville, ON P0A 1K0. ☎ **705/789-4417.** Fax 705/789-6882. 200 units. A/C TV TEL. Late July to Aug C$164–C$258 (US$109–US$172) double; Sept to mid-July C$100 (US$67) and up double. Outdoors and other packages, plus meal plans available. Children under 19 stay free in parents' room. AE, ER, MC, V.

If the Deerhurst is for the folks on the fast track, the Grandview is for those looking for a more measured pace. This smaller resort retains the natural beauty and contours of the original farmstead even while providing the latest resort facilities. Eighty accommodations are traditional hotel-style rooms, but most units are suites in a series of buildings, some down beside the lake and others up on the hill with a lake view. All are spectacularly furnished. Each executive suite contains a kitchen, a dining area, a living room with a fireplace and access to an outside deck, a large bedroom, and a large bathroom with a whirlpool bathtub.

Dining/Diversions: The Mews contains a reception area, a comfortable lounge/entertainment room with sofas and wingbacks, and conference facilities. The main dining room, in the old farmhouse, is decorated in paisleys and English chintz and has an awninged patio overlooking the gardens. Snacks are served in summer at the Dockside Restaurant right on the lake and at the golf clubhouse year-round.

Amenities: Outdoor and indoor pools, a nine-hole golf course, one indoor and two outdoor tennis courts, exercise room, waterskiing, windsurfing, sailing, canoeing, and cross-country skiing. Mountain bikes are also available, and boat cruises are offered aboard a yacht. Nature trails cross the property and a resident naturalist leads guided walks.

6 Algonquin Provincial Park

Immediately east of Muskoka lie **Algonquin Provincial Park**'s 7,770km^2 (2,973 sq. miles) of wilderness—a haven for the naturalist, camper, and fishing and sports enthusiast. It's an especially memorable destination for the canoeist, with more than 1,610km (998 miles) of canoe routes for paddling. One of Canada's largest provincial parks, it served as a source of inspiration for the famous Group of Seven artists. Algonquin Park is a sanctuary for moose, beaver, bear, and deer and offers camping, canoeing, backpacking trails, and plenty of fishing for speckled, rainbow, and lake trout and smallmouth black bass (more than 230 lakes have native brook trout and 149 have lake trout).

There are eight **campgrounds** along Highway 60. The most secluded sites are at **Canisbay** (248 sites) and **Pog Lake** (281 sites). **Two Rivers** and **Rock Lake** have the least secluded sites; the rest are average. Four remote wilderness campgrounds are set back in the interior: **Rain Lake** (with only 10 sites); **Kiosk** (17 sites) on Lake Kioshkokwi; **Brent** (28 sites) on Cedar Lake, great for pickerel fishing; and **Achray** (39 sites), the most remote site on Grand Lake, where Tom Thomson painted many of his great landscapes (the scene that inspired his Jack Pine is a short walk south of the campground). Call the **Visitor Centre** at ☎ **613/637-2828** for details. It's open daily: May to October 9am to 6pm and November to April 10am to 5pm.

Among the **hiking trails** is the 2.4km (1½-mile) self-guided trail to the 325-foot-deep Barron Canyon on the park's east side. In addition, there are 16 day trails. The shortest is the 1km (0.6 mile) **Hardwood Lookout Trail,** which goes through the forest to a fine view of Smoke Lake and the surrounding hills. Other short walks are the **Spruce Bog Boardwalk** (1.5km/0.9 mile) and the **Beaver Pond Trail,** a 2km (1.2-mile) walk with good views of two beaver ponds.

For longer backpacking trips, the **Highland Trail** extends from Pewee Lake to Head, Harness, and Mosquito lakes for a round-trip of 35km (22 miles). The **Western Uplands Hiking Trail** combines three loops for a total of 169km (105 miles), beginning at the Oxtongue River Picnic Grounds on Highway 60. The first 32km (20-mile) loop will take 3 days; the second and third loops take longer. There's also a **mountain bike trail.** Call the visitor center below for more details on all trails.

Fall is a great time to visit—the maples usually peak in the last week of September. Winter is wonderful too; you can **cross-country ski** on 80km (50 miles) of trails. Three trails lie along the Highway 60 corridor with loops ranging from 5km (3.1 miles) to 24km (15 miles). Mew Lake Campground is open in winter, and you can rent skis at the west gate. Spring offers the best **trout fishing** and great **moose viewing** in May and June. During summer, the park is most crowded, but it's also when park staff lead expeditions to hear the timber wolves howling in response to naturalists' imitations. More than 250 **bird species** have been recorded in the park, including the rare gray jay, spruce grouse, and many varieties of warbler. The most famous bird is the common loon, found nesting on nearly every lake.

Information centers are located at both the west and east gates of the park, plus there's a super **Visitor Centre** (☎ **613/637-2828**), about 43km (27 miles) from the west gate and 10km (6.2 miles) from the east gate; it houses exhibits on the park's flora and fauna and history and also has a restaurant, bookstore, and theater. You can sign up here for conducted walks and canoe outings.

For additional **information,** contact the park at P.O. Box 219, Whitney, ON K0J 2M0 (☎ **705/633-5572**).

WHERE TO STAY

✪ **Arowhon Pines.** Algonquin Park, ON P0A 1B0. ☎ **705/633-5661** in summer or 416/483-4393 in winter. Fax 705/633-5795 in summer or 416/483-4429 in winter. 50 units. From C$135–C$187 (US$90–US$125) per person, double occupancy, in standard accommodations; from C$200 (US$133) per person in cabin. 20% discount in spring and 5% in fall, except on weekends. Rates include all meals. V. Closed mid-Oct to mid-May.

Operated by charming Eugene and Helen Kates, Arowhon is 8km (5 miles) off Highway 60 down a dirt road, so you're guaranteed total seclusion and serenity. The cabins are dotted around the pine forests surrounding the lake, and each is furnished uniquely with assorted Canadian pine antiques; they vary in layout but all have bedrooms with private bathrooms and sitting rooms with fireplaces. You can opt for a private cottage or one containing anywhere from 2 to 12 bedrooms and sharing a communal sitting room with a stone fireplace. Sliding doors lead onto a deck. There are no TVs or phones—just the sound of the loons, the gentle lap of the water, the croaking of the frogs, and the sound of oar paddles cutting the smooth surface of the lake. You can swim in the lake or canoe, sail, row, or windsurf. There are also two tennis courts, a sauna, a game room where a film is shown in the evening, and miles of hiking trails.

At the heart of the resort is a hexagonal dining room beside the lake with a spacious veranda. A huge fireplace is at the room's center. Helen and Eugene pay close attention to the details, so everything is artfully done, right down to the bark menus at mealtimes. The food is good, with fresh ingredients, and there's plenty of it. No alcohol is sold in the park, so if you wish to have wine with dinner you'll need to bring your own. Dinner begins with soup and a buffet spread of appetizers—pâtés, salads, garlic chicken wings, and so on—and follows with dishes like salmon with sorrel sauce or pork stuffed with apples and prunes. The desserts are arranged on a harvest table—a wonderful spread of trifle, chocolate layer cake, almond tarts, fresh-fruit salad, and more. Breakfast brings a full selection, all cooked to order.

Killarney Lodge. Algonquin Park, ON P1H 2G9. ☎ **705/633-5551.** Fax 705/633-5667 (summer only). 26 cabins. High season C$160–C$220 (US$107–US$147) per person double. Off-season rates about 30% less. Rates include all meals. MC, V. Closed mid-Oct to mid-May. Enter the park on Hwy. 60 from either Dwight or Whitney.

The Killarney isn't as secluded as Arowhon (the highway is still visible and audible), but it too has charm. The pine-log cabins, with decks, stand on a peninsula jutting out into the Lake of Two Rivers. Furnishings include old rockers, country-house–style beds, desks, chests, and braided rugs. A canoe comes with every cabin. Home-style meals are served in an attractive rustic log dining room. You can relax in the log-cabin lounge warmed by a wood stove.

WHERE TO DINE OR STAY

Spectacle Lake Lodge. Barry's Bay. ☎ **613/756-2324.** Reservations recommended in summer. Main courses C$12–C$17 (US$8–US$11). MC, V. Daily 8am–8pm. Closed last 2 weeks of Nov. Head 17km (11 miles) west of Barry's Bay, 35km (22 miles) east of Algonquin Park, south off Hwy. 60. CANADIAN.

The lodge's rustic dining room looks out over the lake. Traditional fare includes salmon trout and orange roughy, as well as Italian favorites like spaghetti with meatballs and veal parmigiana. Breakfast and lunch are served too. Nine nicely kept cottages are available for rent, some with housekeeping facilities including fridge and stove. The rates are C$45 to C$60 (US$30 to US$40) per person. Canoe and pedal boats are available, as are snowmobiles. Facilities include a comfortable sitting room with a hearth and games available, a decent wine cellar, a health club, bikes, and a tennis court; all kinds of water sports are available, as is cross-country skiing in winter.

Northern Ontario

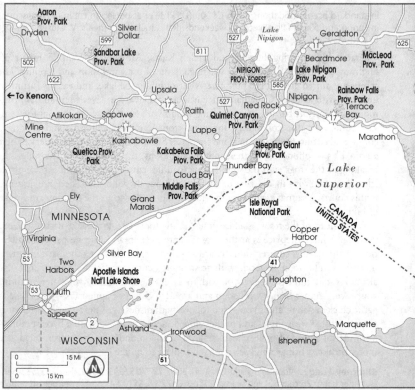

7 Some Northern Ontario Highlights: Driving Along Highways 11 & 17

From the Muskoka region, **Highway 11** winds up toward the province's northernmost frontier via North Bay, Kirkland Lake, Timmins (using Route 101), and Cochrane before sweeping west to Nipigon. There it links up briefly with **Highway 17,** the route traveling the northern perimeters of the Great Lakes from North Bay via Sudbury, Sault Ste. Marie, and Wawa, to Nipigon. At Nipigon, highways 11 and 17 combine and lead into Thunder Bay. They split again west of Thunder Bay, with Highway 17 taking a more northerly route to Dryden and Kenora and Highway 11 proceeding via Atikokan to Fort Frances and Rainy River.

TRAVELING HIGHWAY 11 FROM HUNTSVILLE TO NORTH BAY, COBALT & TIMMINS

From Huntsville, Highway 11 travels north past **Arrowhead Provincial Park** (☎ 705/789-5105), with close to 400 campsites. The road heads through the town of Burk's Falls, at the head of the Magnetawan River, and the town of South River, the access point for **Mikisew Provincial Park** (☎ 705/386-7762), with sandy beaches on the shore of Eagle Lake.

From South River, the road continues to **Powassan,** famous for its excellent cedar-strip boats. Stop in at B. Giesler and Sons to check out these reliable specimens. The

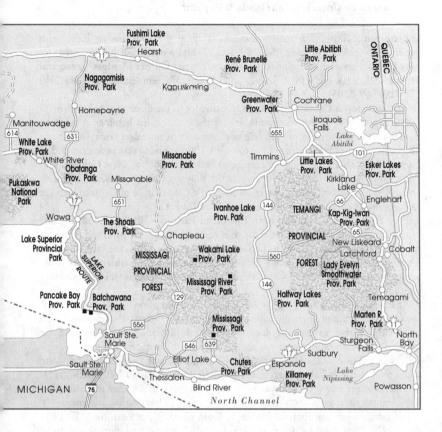

next stop is **North Bay,** on the northeast shore of Lake Nipissing. The town originated on the northern Voyageurs route traveled by fur traders, explorers, and missionaries. Noted for its nearby hunting and fishing, North Bay became world famous in 1934, when the Dionne quintuplets were born in nearby Corbeil; their original home is now a local museum.

From North Bay, Highway 11 continues north toward New Liskeard. Along the route you'll pass **Temagami,** at the center of a superb canoeing region. Its name is Ojibwa for "deep waters by the shore." The region is also associated with the legendary figure Grey Owl, who first came to the area in 1906 as a 17-year-old named Archie Belaney. Archie had always dreamed of living in the wilderness among the Indians; eventually he learned to speak Ojibwa and became an expert in forest and wilderness living. He abandoned his original identity and name, renamed himself Grey Owl, married an Indian woman, and became accepted as a native trapper. He subsequently published a series of books that quickly made him a celebrity.

Finlayson Point Provincial Park (☎ 705/569-3205) is on Lake Temagami. The small park—only 232 acres—is a great base for exploring the lake and its connecting waterways. Steep rugged cliffs, deep clear waters dotted with 1,300 islands, and magnificent stands of tall pines along its shore make for an awesome natural display. The park offers 113 secluded campsites (many on the lakeshore), plus canoeing, boating, swimming, fishing, hiking, and biking.

Lady Evelyn Smoothwater Provincial Park is 45km (28 miles) northwest of Temagami and encompasses the highest point of land in Ontario Maple Mountain and Ishpatina Ridge. Waterfalls are common along the Lady Evelyn River, with Helen Falls cascading more than 80 feet. White-water skills are required for river travel. There are no facilities. For details, contact District Manager, **Temagami District,** Ministry of Natural Resources, P.O. Box 38, Temagami, ON P0H 2H0 (☎ 705/569-3205).

The next stop is **Cobalt,** which owes its existence to the discovery of silver here in 1903. Legend has it that blacksmith Fred LaRose threw his hammer at what he thought were fox's eyes, but he hit one of the world's richest silver veins. Cobalt was also in the ore; hence the name of the town. By 1905 a mining stampede extended to Gowganda, Kirkland Lake, and Porcupine. A little farther north, **New Liskeard** is at the northern end of Lake Timikaming at the mouth of the Wabi River. Strangely enough, this is a dairy center, thanks to the "Little Clay Belt," a glacial lake bed that explains the acres of farmland among the rock and forest.

Even farther north, **Kap-kig-iwan Provincial Park** (☎ 705/544-2050) lies just outside **Englehart,** also the name of the river rushing through the park, and is famous for its "high falls," which give the park its name. Recreational facilities are limited to 64 campsites and self-guided trails. Farther along Highway 11, **Kirkland Lake** is the source for more than 20% of Canada's gold. One original mine is still in production after more than half a century.

At **Iroquois Falls,** a town on the Abitibi River, it's said some Iroquois once raided the Ojibwa community near the falls. After defeating the Ojibwa, the Iroquois curled up to sleep in their canoes tied along the riverbank. But when the Ojibwa cut the canoes loose, the Iroquois were swept over the falls to their deaths. From Iroquois Falls, you can take Route 101 southwest to **Timmins.** Along the way you'll pass the access road to **Kettle Lakes Provincial Park,** 896 Riverside Dr. (☎ 705/363-3511). The park's name refers to the depressions that are formed as a glacier retreats. It has 137 camping sites, five trails, three small beaches, and 22 lakes to fish and enjoy.

In Timmins, you can tour the **Hollinger Gold Mine,** James Reid Road (☎ 705/267-6222). Discovered by Benny Hollinger in 1909, it produced more than C$400 million (US$267 million) worth of gold in its day. You don helmets, overalls, and boots and grab a torch before walking down into the mine to observe a scaling bar, slusher, mucking machine, and furnace at work and to view the safety room to which the miners rushed in the event of a rockfall. At the surface is a panoramic view from the Jupiter Headframe and ore samples to be inspected along the Prospector's Trail. Admission is C$17 (US$11) adults, C$15 (US$10) students, and C$6 (US$4) surface tours only. July to August, it's open daily 10am to 4pm; May to June and September to October, hours are Wednesday to Sunday noon to 4pm (call ahead at other times).

For additional city information, contact the **Timmins Convention and Visitors Bureau,** 54 Spruce St. S. (☎ 705/264-0811). It's open daily: June to August 10am to 4pm and September to May noon to 3pm.

COCHRANE: STARTING POINT OF THE *POLAR BEAR EXPRESS*

Back on Highway 11, the next stop is **Cochrane,** at the junction of the Canadian National Railway and the Ontario Northland Railway. From here, the famous ✪ *Polar Bear Express* departs to Moosonee and Moose Factory, making one of the world's great railroad/nature excursions. The train travels 4½ hours, 299km (185 miles) from Cochrane along the Abitibi and Moose rivers (the latter, by the way, rises and falls 6 feet twice a day with the tides) to Moosonee on James Bay, gateway to the Arctic.

Your destination, **Moosonee** and **Moose Factory,** on an island in the river, will introduce you to frontier life—still challenging, though it's easier today than when native Cree and fur traders traveled the rivers and wrenched a living from the land 300 years ago. You can take the cruiser *Polar Princess* or a freighter-canoe across to Moose Factory (site of the Hudson's Bay Company, founded in 1673) and see the 17th-century Anglican church and other sights. If you stay over, you can also visit **Fossil Island**, where you can see 350-million-year-old fossils in the rocks, and the **Shipsands Waterfowl Sanctuary,** where you might see rare birds, including the Gyrfalcon.

Trains operate the end of June to Labour Day, but tickets are limited because priority is given to the excursion passengers. Round-trip fares are C$48 (US$32) adults and C$24 (US$16) children 5 to 12. Various 3-day/2-night and 4-day/3-night packages are also offered from North Bay and Toronto. Contact **Ontario Northland** at 555 Oak St. E., North Bay, ON P1B 8L3 (☎ **705/472-4500**), or at Union Station, 65 Front St. W., Toronto, ON M5J 1E6 (☎ **416/314-3750**). From June to Labour Day, you'll need to make lodging reservations well in advance.

For additional information, contact the **Cochrane Board of Trade,** P.O. Box 1468, Cochrane, ON P0L 1C0 (☎ **705/272-4926**). It's open Monday to Friday 9am to 4pm.

WHERE TO STAY

The **Chimo Motel** on Highway 11 (☎ **705/272-6555**) offers one- or two-bedroom efficiencies and Jacuzzi rooms at C$65 to C$75 (US$43 to US$50) double. Another option is the **Westway Motel,** 21 First St. (☎ **705/272-4285**), at only C$65 (US$43) double.

EN ROUTE FROM COCHRANE TO NIPIGON

From Cochrane, Highway 11 loops farther north past the turnoff to **Greenwater Provincial Park** (☎ **705/272-6335**). This 13,215-acre park has good camping (90 sites in three campgrounds), swimming, boating (rentals available), hiking, and fishing on 26 lakes. One of the park's more challenging trails goes along Commando Lake. Spectacular views of the northern lights are an added attraction.

Highway 11 continues west past **Rene Brunelle Provincial Park** (☎ **705/367-2692**) and **Kapuskasing,** where General Motors has its cold-weather testing facility, to **Hearst,** Canada's "moose capital," at the northern terminus of the Algoma Central railway. It continues all the way to **Lake Nipigon Provincial Park** (☎ **807/887-5000**) on the shores of Lake Nipigon. The lake is famous for its black-sand beaches. Facilities include 60 camping sites, boat rentals, and self-guided trails.

The nearby town of **Nipigon** stands on Lake Superior at the mouth of the Nipigon River. It's where the world-record brook trout, weighing 14½ pounds, was caught. At this point Highways 17 and 11 join and run all the way into Thunder Bay.

TRAVELING HIGHWAY 17 ALONG THE PERIMETER OF THE GREAT LAKES

Instead of traveling north from North Bay up Highway 11 to explore the northern mining frontier, you could choose to take Highway 17 along the perimeter of the Great Lakes. I consider this the more scenic and interesting route.

SUDBURY

The road travels past Lake Nipissing through Sturgeon Falls to **Sudbury,** a nickel-mining center. With a population of 160,000, this is northern Ontario's largest metro area, a rough-and-ready mining town with a landscape so barren that U.S. astronauts were trained here for lunar landings.

Sudbury's two major attractions are **Science North,** 100 Ramsey Lake Rd. (☎ **705/522-3701,** or 705/522-3700 for recorded info), and the **Big Nickel Mine** (below). The first occupies two giant stainless-steel snowflake-shaped buildings dramatically cut into a rock outcrop overlooking Lake Ramsey. You can conduct experiments like simulating a hurricane, monitoring earthquakes on a seismograph, or observing the sun through a solar telescope. In addition to the exhibits, a 3-D film/laser experience, *Shooting Star*, takes you on a journey 5 billion years into the past, charting the formation of the Sudbury Basin. A performance in another theater tells the story of naturalist Grey Owl. There's also a water playground (kids can play and adults can build a sailboat), space-exploration and weather command centers, and a fossil-identification workshop. It's open daily: May and June 9am to 5pm and July to Canadian Thanksgiving (U.S. Columbus Day) 9am to 6pm; call ahead for winter hours (usually 10am to 4pm). Admission is C$9 (US$6) adults and C$7 (US$4.35) students/seniors; children under 5 are free. A combined admission with the mine will save money (C$14/US$9 adults and C$10/US$7 students/seniors).

At the **Big Nickel Mine,** 100 Ramsey Lake Rd. (☎ **705/522-3701**), you're taken underground for a 30-minute tour. On the surface you can view a mineral-processing station, measure your weight in gold, and enjoy some other video programs. It's open May to Canadian Thanksgiving, the same hours as Science North, with the same admission. A combined admission with Science North will save money.

The **Path of Discovery** is a 2-hour bus tour providing the only public access to INCO Ltd., the biggest nickel producer in the Western world. On the tour, given July to Labour Day daily at 10am and 2pm, you observe the surface processing facilities and one of the world's tallest smokestacks. Contact **Science North** at ☎ **705/ 522-3701.**

For further information on Sudbury, contact either the **Sudbury and District Chamber of Commerce,** 166 Douglas St. W. (☎ **705/673-7133**), open Monday to Friday 9am to 4:30pm, or the **Community Information Service and Convention and Visitors Service,** Tom Davies Square (☎ **705/674-3141**), open daily 9am to noon and 1 to 4pm.

Where to Stay
Your best bets for lodgings are the chains—**Comfort Inn,** 2171 Regent St. S. (☎ **705/522-1101**), and 440 2nd Ave. N. (☎ **705/560-4502**); **Ramada Inn,** 85 St. Anne Rd. (☎ **705/675-1123**); or **Venture Inn,** 1956 Regent St. S. (☎ **705/ 522-7600**). There's also the **Sheraton Four Points,** 1696 Regent St. S. (☎ **705/ 522-3000**). Rates for all these are about C$60 to C$95 (US$40 to US$63) double.

A CROWN JEWEL: KILLARNEY PROVINCIAL PARK
Less than an hour's drive southwest of Sudbury is **Killarney Provincial Park** (☎ **705/ 287-2900**), called the "crown jewel" of the province's park system. This 119,795-acre park on the north shore of Georgian Bay, accessible only on foot or by canoe, features numerous lakes and a fabulous range of quartzite ridges. More than 100 species of birds breed here, including kingfishers and loons on the lakes in summer. Four members of the Group of Seven painted in the region: Frank Carmichael, Arthur Lismer, A. Y. Jackson, and A. J. Casson. The park has 122 campsites at the George Lake campground near the entrance.

Killarney is a paradise for the canoeist (rentals are available in the park). Compared to Algonquin Park, it's much quieter—you have to cross only one lake to find total privacy at Killarney, while at Algonquin you may have to canoe across three lakes. Three hiking trails loop from the campground and can be completed in 3 hours.

For a more ambitious backpacking tour, the park's **La Cloche Silhouette Trail** winds for more than 97km (60 miles) through forest and beaver meadows past crystal-clear lakes. The trail's main attraction is Silver Peak, towering 1,214 feet above

Georgian Bay and offering views of 81km (50 miles) on a clear day. This is a serious undertaking; it'll take 7 to 10 days to complete the whole trail.

The best fishing is in Georgian Bay; sadly, acid rain has killed off most of the fish in the lakes.

DRIVING WEST FROM SUDBURY

From Sudbury it's 305km (189 miles) west along Highway 17 to Sault Ste. Marie, or the Soo, as it's affectionately called. At Serpent River you can turn off north to the town of Elliot Lake and **Mississagi Provincial Park** (☎ 705/848-2806), and the river of the same name. The park has 90 campsites and swimming and offers some fine canoeing. Hikers will find short self-guided trails, as well as trails from 6km to 16km (3.7 miles to 9.9 miles) long.

Continuing along Highway 17, bordering the North Channel, will bring you past the access point to **Fort St. Joseph National Park** (☎ 705/941-6203) on St. Joseph Island (between Michigan and Ontario) and into the Soo, 305km (189 miles) west of Sudbury.

SAULT STE. MARIE

The highlights of any visit to **Sault Ste. Marie** are the **Soo locks,** the **Agawa Canyon Train,** and the **Bon Soo,** one of North America's biggest winter carnivals, celebrated in late January and early February.

The **Soo,** at the junction of lakes Superior and Huron, actually straddles the border. The twin cities, one in Ontario and the other in Michigan, are separated by the St. Marys River rapids and now are joined by an international bridge. The Northwest Fur Trading Company founded a post here in 1783, building a canal to bypass the rapids from 1797 to 1799. That canal was replaced later by the famous **Soo locks**—four on the American side and one on the Canadian. The locks are part of the St. Lawrence Seaway system, enabling large international cargo ships to navigate from the Atlantic along the St. Lawrence to the Great Lakes. Lake Superior is about 23 feet higher than Lake Huron, and the locks raise and lower the ships. You'll find a viewing station at both sets of locks. June to about October 10, you can take a 2-hour cruise through the lock system daily for C$17 (US$11) adults, C$13 ($9) youths, and C$9 (US$6) children. For information, contact **Lock Tours Canada,** Roberta Bondar Park Dock off Foster Drive, Box 325, Sault Ste. Marie, ON P6A 5L8 (☎ 705/253-9850).

The Algoma Central Railway, which operates the ✪ **Agawa Canyon Train Tours,** was established in 1899. The Canadian artists known as the Group of Seven used to shunt up and down the track in a converted boxcar they used as a base camp for canoe excursions into the wilderness. Today the tour train takes you on a 184km (114-mile) trip from the Soo to the Agawa Canyon, where you can enjoy a 2-hour stop to view the waterfalls, walk the nature trails, or enjoy a picnic. The train snakes through a vista of deep ravines and lakes, hugging the hillsides and crossing gorges on skeletal trestle bridges. The most spectacular time to take the trip is mid-September to mid-October. The train operates daily early June to mid-October; on weekends only January to March. June to August, fares are C$50 to C$60 (US$33 to US$40) adults and C$15 (US$10) children/students; September to October, fares are C$59 (US$39) adults, C$34 (US$23) children 5 to 18, and C$10 (US$7) children under 5; January to March, fares are C$53 (US$35) adults, C$27 (US$18) children 5 to 18, and C$11 (US$7) children under 5. You can, of course, ride the passenger train from the Soo to Hearst, though there are no stops en route. Round-trip fares are C$125 (US$83). For information, contact the **Algoma Central Railway,** Passenger Sales, P.O. Box 130, 129 Bay St., Sault Ste. Marie, ON P6A 6Y2 (☎ 800/242-9287 or 705/946-7300).

The surrounding area offers great fishing, snowmobiling, cross-country skiing, and other sports opportunities. For cross-country skiing info, call the **Stokely Creek Ski Touring Centre,** at **Stokely Creek Lodge,** Karalash Corners, Goulais River (☎ 705/ 649-3421). Contact the **Sault Ste. Marie Chamber of Commerce,** 360 Great Northern Rd. (☎ 800/242-9287 or 705/949-7152), for more sports information; it's open Monday to Friday 9am to 5pm.

Where to Stay

Whatever you do, make your reservations in advance. If you're taking the Algoma Train, the most convenient hotel is the **Quality Inn,** 180 Bay St. (☎ 705/945-9264), across from the train station. It offers 128 units (6 with Jacuzzi tubs), as well as an indoor pool, an exercise room, and an Italian restaurant. Rates are C$98 to C$150 (US$65 to US$100) double and C$180 (US$120) for a suite.

You can also try the other chains: the **Holiday Inn,** 208 St. Marys River Dr., on the downtown waterfront (☎ 705/949-0611), or **Comfort Inn,** 333 Great Northern Rd. (☎ 705/759-8000). The **Ramada Inn,** 229 Great Northern Rd. (☎ 705/ 942-2500), has great facilities for families—a water slide, bowling, indoor golf, and more. Rates at these run C$60 to C$120 (US$40 to US$80).

LAKE SUPERIOR PROVINCIAL PARK

Alona and Agawa bays are in ✪ **Lake Superior Provincial Park** (☎ 705/ 856-2284). The 1,540km² (595-sq.-mile) park, one of Ontario's largest, offers the haunting shoreline and open waters of Longfellow's "Shining Big-Sea Water," cobble beaches, rugged rocks, and limitless forests. Dramatic highlights include rock formations like Lac Mijinemungsing, the Devil's Chair, and Old Woman Bay. At the park's east end, the Algoma Central Railway provides access to the park along the Agawa River. At Agawa Rock, you can still see traces of the early Ojibway people—there are centuries-old paintings depicting animals and scenes from their legends.

The magnificent scenery has attracted artists for years, including the Group of Seven. Among the most famous paintings of the park are Frank Johnston's *Canyon and Agawa,* Lawren Harris's *Montreal River,* A. Y. Jackson's *First Snows,* and J. E. H. Mac-Donald's *Algoma Waterfall and Agawa Canyon.* As for wildlife, you may see moose as well as caribou, which once were common here and have been reintroduced along the coast areas and offshore islands. More than 250 bird species have been identified here; about 120 types nest in the area.

Some 269 camping sites are available at three **campgrounds.** The largest, at Agawa Bay, has a 3km (1.9-mile) beach. Crescent Lake, at the southern boundary, is the most basic, while Rabbit Blanket Lake is well located for exploring the park's interior.

The park has eight canoe routes, ranging in length from 3km to 56km (1.9 miles to 35 miles) and in difficulty from easy to challenging, with steep portages and white water. Rentals are available at the campgrounds, but outfitter services are limited. Contact the **Wawa Chamber of Commerce,** P.O. Box 858, Wawa, ON P0S 1K0 (☎ 705/856-4538).

The 11 ✪ **hiking trails** range from short interpretive trails to rugged overnight trails up to 55km (34 miles) long. The most accessible is the **Trapper's Trail,** featuring a wetlands boardwalk from which you can watch beaver, moose, and great blue heron. The 16km (9.9-mile) **Peat Mountain Trail** leads to a panoramic view close to 500 feet above the surrounding lakes and forests. The 26km (16-mile) **Toawab Trail** takes you through the Agawa Valley to the 81-foot Agawa Falls. The **Orphan Lake Trail** is popular due to its moderate length and difficulty, plus its panoramic views over Orphan and Superior lakes, a pebble beach, and Baldhead Falls. The **Coastal Trail,** along the shoreline, is the longest at 55km (34 miles), stretching from Sinclair Cove to Chalfant Cove, and will take 5 to 7 days to complete. Fall is the best time to hike, when the colors are amazing and the insects are few.

In winter, though no formal facilities or services are provided, you can cross-country ski, snowshoe, and ice fish at your own risk.

WAWA & THE CHAPLEAU GAME RESERVE

From the park, it's a short trip into **Wawa,** 230km (143 miles) north of the Soo, the site of the famous salmon derby. Wawa serves as a supply center for canoeists, fishermen, and other sports folks.

East of Wawa is the **Chapleau Game Reserve,** where there's some of Ontario's best canoeing and wildlife viewing in **Chapleau Nemegosenda River Provincial Park**—200km (124 miles) northeast of the Soo and 100km (62 miles) west of Timmins. It's accessible from Chapleau or by Emerald Lake on Highway 101 to Nemegosenda Lake. There are no facilities. Nonresidents need a permit to camp, costing C$10 (US$7) per person per night. For additional info, contact **Ontario Parks,** Ministry of Natural Resources, 190 Cherry St., Chapleau, ON P0M 1K0 (☎ **705/864-1710,** ext. 237).

PUKASKWA NATIONAL PARK

Southwest of White River on the shores of Lake Superior is Ontario's only national park in the wilderness, **Pukaskwa National Park,** Hattie Cove, Heron Bay, ON P0T 1R0 (☎ **807/229-0801**), reached via Highway 627 from Highway 17. The interior is accessible only on foot or by boat.

In this 1,878km² (725-sq.-mile) park survives the most southerly herd of **woodland caribou**—only 40 of them. Lake Superior is extremely cold, and for this reason rare Arctic plants are also found here. **Hattie Cove** is the center of most park activities and services, including a 67-site campground, a series of short walking trails, access to three sand beaches, and parking facilities and a visitor center.

The 60km (37-mile) **Coastal Hiking Trail** winds from Hattie Cove south to the North Swallow River and requires proper planning and equipment (camping areas are every half- to full-day's hike apart). A 15km (9.3-mile) day hike along this trail can be taken to the White River Suspension Bridge. There are also backcountry trails. In winter, cross-country skiers can use 6km (3.7 miles) of groomed trails or hazard the fast slopes and sharp turns created by the topography. Snowshoers are welcome too.

CANOEING THE WHITE & PUKASKWA RIVERS

The White and Pukaskwa rivers offer white-water adventure. You can paddle the easily accessed **White River** any time during the open-water season. Many wilderness adventurers start from nearby **White Lake Provincial Park** and travel 4 to 6 days to the mouth of the White River and then paddle about an hour north on Lake Superior to Hattie Cove.

Where Winnie-the-Pooh Was Born

Ninety-eight kilometers (61 miles) from Wawa on Highway 17 is **White River,** birthplace of Winnie-the-Pooh. In 1916, Winnipeg soldier Harry Colebourne, on his way to Europe from his hometown, bought a mascot for his regiment here and named it Winnie. When he shipped out from London he couldn't take the bear cub, so it went to the London Zoo, where it became the inspiration for A. A. Milne's classic character. Just outside White River are the spectacular **Magpie High Falls.**

The **Pukaskwa River** is more remote, more difficult (with rugged and long portages and an 850-foot drop between the headwaters at Gibson Lake and the river mouth at Lake Superior), and navigable only during the spring runoff. It's best to start where the river crosses Highway 17 near Sagina Lake and paddle to Gibson Lake via Pokei Lake, Pokei Creek, and Soulier Lake. Otherwise, you'll have to fly in from White River or Wawa.

Outfitters include **Pukaskwa Country Outfitters,** P.O. Box 603, Marathon, ON P0T 2E0 (☎ **807/229-0265**); **Naturally Superior Adventures,** RR #1, Lake Superior, Wawa, ON P0S 1K0 (☎ **800/203-9092** or 705/856-2939); and **U-Paddle-It,** P.O. Box 374, Pinewood Drive, Wawa, ON P0S 1K0 (☎ **705/856-1493**).

MORE PROVINCIAL PARKS

From White River it's 270km (167 miles) to **Nipigon** and **Nipigon Bay,** offering fine rock, pine, and lake vistas. It's another 12km (7.4 miles) to **Ouimet Canyon Provincial Park** (☎ **807/977-2526**), at the location of a spectacular canyon 330 feet deep, 500 feet wide, and a mile long. When you stand on the edge of the canyon and gaze out over the expanse of rock and forest below, you can sense the power of the forces that shaped, built, and split the earth's crust and then gouged and chiseled this crevasse—one of Eastern Canada's most striking canyons. The park is for day use only.

About 25km (15½ miles) on, the next stop is **Sleeping Giant Provincial Park** (☎ **807/977-2526**), named after the rock formation the Ojibwa Indians say is Nanabosho (the Giant), turned to stone after disobeying the Great Spirit. The story goes that Nanabosho, who had led the Ojibwa to the north shore of Lake Superior to save them from the Sioux, discovered silver one day, but fearing for his people, he told them to bury it on an islet at the tip of the peninsula and keep it a secret. But vanity got the better of one of the chieftains, who made silver weapons for himself. Subsequently, he was killed in battle against the Sioux. Shortly afterward, Nanabosho spied a Sioux warrior leading two white men in a canoe across Lake Superior to the source of the silver. To keep the secret, he disobeyed the Great Spirit and raised a storm that sank and drowned the white men. For this, he was turned into stone.

Take Route 587 south along the Sibley Peninsula, which juts into the lake. Among the park's natural splendors are bald eagles, wild orchids, moose, and more than 190 species of birds. Facilities include 168 campsites at Marie Louise Campground plus about 40 interior sites. There's a beach at the campground.

The trail system consists of three self-guided nature trails, three walking trails, and a network of about 70km (43 miles) of hiking trails, including the 2-day Kabeyun Trail, which originates at the Thunder Bay lookout and follows the shoreline south to Sawyer Bay. The park has great cross-country skiing with 30km (19 miles) of trails.

THUNDER BAY

Just before you enter Thunder Bay, stop and honor Terry Fox at the **Monument and Scenic Lookout.** Not far from this spot he was forced to abandon his heroic cross-Canada journey to raise money for cancer research. To access the remote **Wabakimi region,** take Route 527 north just east of Thunder Bay. It'll take you to Armstrong, the supply center for this wilderness region.

From the port city of **Thunder Bay**—an amalgam of Fort William and Port Arthur—wheat and other commodities are shipped out via the Great Lakes all over the world. Fifteen grain elevators still dominate the skyline. You can't really grasp the city's role and its geography unless you take the **Harbor Cruise.** Other highlights include **Old Fort William** (☎ **807/473-2344**), about 10 miles outside the city on the Kaministiquia River. From 1803 to 1821, this reconstructed fort was the headquarters of the North West Fur-Trading Company, which was later absorbed by the Hudson's Bay Company.

Where to Stay

For B&B accommodations, contact the **North of Superior B&B Association** at ☎ **807/475-4200.** Your best bets are the chains: **The Best Western NorWester,** 2080 Hwy. 61, RR #4, ON P7C 4Z2 (☎ **807/473-9123**), which has rooms for C$74 to C$95 (US$49 to US$63) double, plus an indoor pool and lounge/restaurant; **Comfort Inn by Journey's End,** 660 W. Arthur St. (☎ **807/475-3155**), where rooms are C$75 to C$120 (US$50 to US$80) double; and the **Venture Inn,** 450 Memorial Ave. (☎ **807/345-2343**), which also has a lounge/restaurant and an indoor pool and rents rooms for C$78 to C$100 (US$52 to US$67) double.

Airlane Hotel. 698 W. Arthur St., Thunder Bay, ON P7E 5R8. ☎ **807/473-1600.** 154 units. A/C MINIBAR TV TEL. C$100–C$108 (US$67–US$72) double; C$160 (US$107) suite. AE, MC, V.

The Airlane has modern guest rooms with amenities like coffeemakers. Facilities include an indoor pool and fitness center, as well as a lounge/restaurant and dance club. Suites with whirlpools are available too.

White Fox Inn. RR #4, 1345 Mountain Rd., Thunder Bay, ON P7C 4Z2. ☎ **807/577-3699.** 9 units. A/C TV TEL. C$110–C$220 (US$73–US$147) double. AE, DC, MC, V.

On 15 acres with a view of the Norwester Mountain range, this inn was once a lumber magnate's home. The individually decorated guest rooms have fireplaces and VCRs, while the three largest rooms have in-room Jacuzzis. There's also a fine-dining room serving Mediterranean cuisine. Nearby you'll find a variety of outdoor activities.

FROM THUNDER BAY TO FORT FRANCES/RAINY RIVER VIA HIGHWAY 11

From Thunder Bay it's 480km (298 miles) along the Trans-Canada Highway to **Kenora.** Several provincial parks line the route.

Kakabeka Falls Provincial Park, 435 James St. S., Suite 221, Thunder Bay (☎ **807/473-9231**), with its fantastic 130-foot-high waterfall, is 29km (18 miles) along the Trans-Canada Highway. The gorge was carved out of the Precambrian Shield when the last glaciers melted, and fossils dating back 1.6 billion years have been found here. The park has several nature trails, plus safe swimming at a roped-off area above the falls. Two campgrounds provide 166 sites (C$10 to C$17/US$7 to US$11, depending on season and site). In winter, there are 13km (8 miles) of groomed cross-country ski trails.

Atikokan is the gateway to ☼ **Quetico Provincial Park** (☎ **807/597-2737**), primarily a wilderness canoeing park. The 4,662km² (1,800-sq.-mile) park has absolutely no roads, and only two of the six entrance stations are accessible by car (those at French Lake and Nym Lake, both west of Thunder Bay). Instead, there are miles of interconnecting lakes, streams, and rivers with roaring white water dashing against granite cliffs. It's one of North America's finest canoeing areas. **Dawson Trail Campgrounds,** with 133 sites at French Lake, is the only accessible site for car camping. Extended hikes are limited to the 13km (8-mile) trip to Pickerel Lake; there are also six short trails in the French Lake area (three interpretive). The park can be skied, but there are no groomed trails. Also in the park on some rocks near Lac la Croix, you can see 30 ancient pictographs representing moose, caribou, and other animals, as well as hunters in canoes.

Fort Frances is an important border crossing to the United States and the site of a paper mill. Another 90km (56 miles) will bring you to **Rainy River** at the extreme western point of Ontario across from Minnesota. The district abounds in lake-land scenery, much of it in **Lake of the Woods Provincial Park,** RR #1, Sleeman (☎ **807/ 488-5531**), 43km (27 miles) north of Rainy River. This shallow lake has a 185-yard-long beach and is good for swimming and waterskiing. In spring you can fish for walleye, northern pike, and large- and smallmouth bass. You can rent canoes and boats in nearby Morson. The park has 100 campsites, as well as a couple of easy nature trails to hike.

Almost due north of Thunder Bay via Route 527 lies **Wabakimi Provincial Park,** which has some fine canoeing and fishing. It's accessible from Armstrong.

FROM THUNDER BAY TO KENORA VIA HIGHWAY 17

Instead of taking Highway 11 west from Thunder Bay as described above, you can take Highway 17, which follows a more northerly route. Just follow 17 where it branches off at Shabaqua Corners, about 56km (35 miles) from Thunder Bay. Continue northwest to **Ignace,** the access point for two provincial parks.

At Ignace, turn off onto Highway 599 to **Sandbar Lake** (☎ **807/934-2995,** or 807/934-2233 for local Natural Resources office), which offers more than 12,350 acres of forest with nine smaller lakes plus the large one from which it takes its name. The park's most notable inhabitants are the painted turtle, whose tracks you can often see in the sand; the spotted sandpiper; the loon; the common merganser; and several species of woodpecker. The campground has 75 sites; the beach has safe swimming; and there are several short and long canoe routes plus several hiking trails, including the 2km (1.2-mile) **Lookout Trail,** which begins on the beach.

Turtle River Provincial Park is a 120km-long (74-mile-long) waterway from Ignace to Mine Centre. The canoe route begins on Agimak Lake at Ignace and follows a series of lakes into the Turtle River, ending on Turtle Lake just north of Mine Centre. The park also includes the famous log castle built by Jimmy McQuat in the early 1900s on White Otter Lake. Follow Highway 599 farther north to the remote Albany and Apawapiskat rivers, which drain into James Bay.

Back on Highway 17 from Ignace, it's another 40km (25 miles) to the turnoff on Highway 72 to **Ojibway Provincial Park** (☎ **807/737-2033**), which has only 45 campsites but offers swimming, boating, and self-guided trails. Back on Highway 17, it's only a short way beyond Highway 72 to **Aaron Provincial Park** (☎ **807/ 938-6534,** or 807/223-3341 for Natural Resources office), where you'll find close to 100 campsites, facilities for boating and swimming, plus some short nature trails. Nearby Dryden is the supply center for Aaron.

From Dryden it's about 43km (27 miles) to Vermilion Bay, where Route 105 branches off north to Red Lake, the closest point to one of the province's most remote provincial parks, **Woodland Caribou** (☎ **807/727-2253**). Offering superb fishing, the 1,111,500-acre park has no facilities except picnic tables and boat rentals nearby. It's home to one of the largest herds of woodland caribou south of the Hudson Bay lowlands. It's also inhabited by black bear, great blue heron, osprey, and bald eagles. There are 1,600km (992 miles) of canoe routes. Contact the **Northern Ontario Tourist Outfitters Association** at ☎ 705/472-5552 for details on fly-in camps. Back on Highway 17 from Vermilion Bay, it's only 72km (45 miles) until the road links up with Highway 71 outside Kenora, just shy of the Manitoba border.

Where to Stay & Dine Near Kenora

Totem Resorts. Box 180, Sioux Narrows, ON P0X 1N0. ☎ **807/226-5275.** Fax 807/ 226-5187. www.totemresorts.com. 27 cabins, 3 units. A/C TV. C$160 (US$107) per person per night; cabins without meals from C$1,600 (US$1,067) per week. Weekly and special packages available. MC, V. Access is off Hwy. 71, 1 mile north of Sioux Narrows.

At the end of Long Bay on Lake of the Woods, this lodge caters to outdoor enthusiasts and families who come for the superb fishing and hunting. The main lodge is an A-frame featuring a dining room, a lounge, and decks with umbrella-shaded tables overlooking the water. The timber-and-stone decor is appropriately rustic. The cabins have full modern bathrooms, beds with Hudson's Bay blankets, fireplaces, and screened-in porches or outdoor decks, plus cooking facilities. The rooms above the boathouse lack cooking facilities but do have fridges. Facilities include 16-foot fishing boats, canoes, Windsurfers, and wet jets, and the management will arrange fly-out fishing trips. Fish-cleaning facilities and freezer service are available.

Wiley Point Lodge. Box 180, Sioux Narrows, ON P0X 1N0. ☎ **807/543-4090.** 3 units, 7 cabins. Fishing packages C$160 (US$107) per person per night based on 2 per boat (includes boat, gas, and bait). Hunting packages also available. MC, V.

This lodge is accessible only by boat and therefore offers more of a wilderness experience. The main lodge has three suites, plus there are seven cabins (two- or three-bedroom), all with full bathroom, fridge, and screened-in porch. The lodge contains a dining room, lounge, and deck overlooking the lake. Facilities include a beach with a diving raft, paddleboats, windsurfers, and wet skis; a hot tub; a sauna; and an exercise room. Spring and fall bear hunts are offered, as well as more traditional hunting.

13 Manitoba & Saskatchewan

by Bill McRae

Visitors don't exactly flock to central Manitoba and Saskatchewan, but that can be a plus if you like unpopulated wide-open spaces. Part of the great prairies, these two provinces boast some beautiful wilderness and parkland and an almost infinite chain of lakes, making them terrific choices for fishing, canoeing, wildlife watching, and more.

Manitoba is famous for its friendly people, who not only brave long, harsh winters but also till the southern prairie lands in summer, making the region a breadbasket for the nation and the world. Along the southern border outside Winnipeg, wheat, barley, oats, and flax wave at the roadside, the horizon is limitless, and grain elevators pierce the skyline. Beyond the province's southern section, punctuated by Lake Winnipeg and Lake Manitoba, stretches one of the last wilderness frontiers, a paradise for anglers and outdoors enthusiasts of all sorts. Here you'll find many of the province's 100,000 lakes, which cover about 20% of Manitoba. You'll also see polar bears and beluga whales and hear the timber wolves cry on the lonesome tundra surrounding the Hudson Bay port of Churchill.

Five times the size of New York State, with a population of about a million, **Saskatchewan,** another of Canada's prairie provinces, produces 60% of Canada's wheat. Here you'll find a hunting and fishing paradise in the northern lakes and forests; several summer playgrounds (including Prince Albert National Park and 31 provincial parks); and the cities of Regina, the capital, and Saskatoon.

1 Exploring the Provinces

The **Trans-Canada Highway** (Highway 1) cuts across the southern part of both provinces. In Manitoba, you can stop along Highway 1 at Whiteshell Provincial Park in the east. You can return to the highway or visit the shores of Lake Winnipeg at Grand Beach Provincial Park and then head south via Selkirk and Lower Fort Garry to Winnipeg, the provincial capital. From Winnipeg, you can take the train north to Churchill to explore the Northern tundra around Hudson Bay. On your return trip to Winnipeg, you can pick up Highway 1 again and drive west across the province, stopping for a detour to Riding Mountain National Park or to Spruce Woods Provincial Park before exiting into Saskatchewan.

Highway 1 leads from Manitoba to Regina, with a stop perhaps at Moose Mountain Provincial Park along the way. From Regina it's a 2½-hour or so drive to Saskatoon, and about another 2½-hour drive

Manitoba

Thompson

6

Flin Flon

10

Snow Lake

Grass River
Provincial Park

39

Clearwater Lake
Provincial Park

10

The Pas

6

Cedar
Lake

60

Grand Rapids

*Lake
Winnipeg*

10

Swan
River

*Lac
Winnipegosis*

Berens River

Maintoba
Ontario

Duck Mountain
Provincial
Park

*Lac
Manitoba*

*Dauphin
Lake*

6

Atikaki Provincial
Wilderness Park

Dauphin

Riding Mountain
National Park

Hecla Provincial
Heritage Park

Wasagaming

8

16

10

5

*Lake
Manitoba*

Gimli

Grand Beach
Provincial Park

Nopiming
Provincial Park

Minnedosa

16

Winnipeg
Beach

9

59

11

Whiteshell
Provincial Park

Brandon

Carberry

Portage la
Prairie

Selkirk

12

1

Spruce Woods
Provincial Park

Winnipeg

44

17

10

5

75

12

Steinbach

1

CANADA

281

69

UNITED

29

STATES

313

487

to Prince Albert National Park (you can stop at Batoche en route). From Prince Albert you can return via Fort Battleford National Historic Park to Saskatoon and then to Highway 1 at Swift Current, or you can take Route 4 directly from Battleford to Swift Current. From here, the Trans-Canada Highway heads west to the Alberta border.

VISITOR INFORMATION

Contact **Travel Manitoba,** Department SV6, 7-155 Carlton St., Winnipeg, MB R3C 3H8 (☎ **800/665-0040;** www.travelmanitoba.com). Or you can visit the information center at 31 Forks Market Rd., open Monday, Tuesday, Wednesday, and Friday 8:30am to 4:30pm and Thursday 10am to 4:30pm. For taped info on the latest happenings, call ☎ **204/942-2535.** For information on Manitoba's provincial parks, call ☎ **800/214-6497** or 204/945-6784.

In Saskatchewan, contact **Tourism Saskatchewan,** 500-1900 Albert St., Regina, SK S4P 4L9 (☎ **877/237-2273** or 306/787-2300; www.sasktourism.com; e-mail travel.info@sasktourism.com); it's open Monday to Friday 8am to 7pm and Saturday and Sunday 10am to 4pm.

THE GREAT OUTDOORS

Manitoba's major playgrounds are **Riding Mountain National Park** and the provincial parks of **Whiteshell, Atikaki, Spruce Woods, Duck Mountain,** and **Grass River.** Call ☎ **800/214-6497** or 204/945-6784 for details.

Saskatchewan boasts 80,290km² (30,889 sq. miles) of water, and 3 million acres are given over to parks—1 million alone constitute Prince Albert National Park. In addition, there are 31 provincial parks. The major ones are **Cypress Hills** (☎ **306/662-4411**), **Moose Mountain** (☎ **306/577-2600**), **Lac La Ronge** (☎ **306/425-4234**), and **Meadow Lake** (☎ **306/236-7680**). At the parks you can camp for C$10 to C$20 (US$7 to US$13), plus a C$4 to C$6 (US$2.65 to US$4) entry fee. Some parks, such as Cypress Hills and Moose Mountain, also have cabins for an average of C$40 to C$65 (US$27 to US$43) for a one-bedroom cabin and C$65 to C$100 (US$43 to US$67) for a two-bedroom cabin.

Summers can be simply magnificent, with warm sunny days and cool refreshing evenings and nights. Average winter temperatures are pretty harsh at –18°C to –12°C (0°F to 10°F), but that doesn't stop winter-sports enthusiasts.

BIRD WATCHING   In Manitoba, you'll find a goose sanctuary at **Whiteshell Provincial Park.** Gull Harbour's **Hecla Provincial Park,** on Lake Winnipeg, has a wildlife-viewing tower; the Grassy Narrow Marsh there is home to a wide variety of waterfowl. **Riding Mountain National Park** boasts more than 200 species of birds. And many varieties stop near **Churchill** on their annual migrations.

In Saskatchewan, **Moose Mountain Provincial Park** is home to many waterfowl and songbirds, including the magnificent blue heron and the red-tailed hawk. As you might expect, **Prince Albert National Park** has a wide variety of bird life, with the highlight being an enormous colony of white pelicans at Lavallee Lake. And there's even a waterfowl park right in the middle of downtown **Regina,** where you can see more than 60 species. A naturalist is on duty weekdays.

CANOEING   In Manitoba, the best places to canoe are **Riding Mountain National Park, Whiteshell Provincial Park,** and the chain of lakes around **Flin Flon,** which is right on the border between the two provinces.

In Saskatchewan, **Prince Albert National Park** has some fine canoeing, and plenty of other northern water routes offer a challenge to both novice and expert. Some 55 canoe routes have been mapped, traversing terrain that hasn't changed since the era of explorers and fur traders. You can get to all but three of the routes by road. Various

Saskatchewan

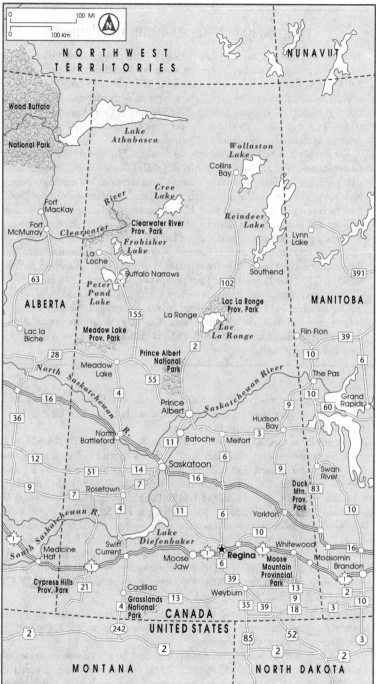

NORTHWEST TERRITORIES

NUNAVUT

Wood Buffalo National Park

Lake Athabasca

Fort MacKay

Fort McMurray

Clearwater River

Clearwater River Prov. Park

Cree Lake

Wollaston Lake

Collins Bay

Reindeer Lake

Frobisher Lake

La Loche

Buffalo Narrows

Southend

Lynn Lake

391

63

Peter Pond Lake

102

MANITOBA

ALBERTA

Lac La Ronge Prov. Park

155

La Ronge

Lac La Ronge

Flin Flon

39

Lac la Biche

Meadow Lake Prov. Park

2

10

6

28

Meadow Lake

Prince Albert National Park

The Pas

16

North Saskatchewan

4

55

10

60

Grand Rapids

36

Prince Albert

Saskatchewan River

North Battleford

9

Hudson Bay

11

Batoche

Melfort

3

12

14

Saskatoon

6

51

16

9

Swan River

9

7

Rosetown

7

Duck Mtn. Prov. Park

83

4

11

6

Yorkton

10

7

South Saskatchewan R.

Lake Diefenbaker

10

Whitewood

16

Medicine Hat

Swift Current

1

Regina

Moose Mountain Provincial Park

Moosomin

Brandon

1

Moose Jaw

6

1

2

10

Cypress Hills Prov. Park

21

Cadillac

39

Weyburn

13

Grasslands National Park

13

35

39

9

18

3

4

242

CANADA

UNITED STATES

85

52

3

2

2

MONTANA

2

2

NORTH DAKOTA

Farm & Ranch Vacations on the Prairies

There's no better way to really get the feel of the prairies than to stay on a farm or ranch. Contact the **Manitoba Country Vacations Association,** Box 53, Grp. 374, RR 3, Winnipeg, MB R3C 2E7 (☎ **204-667-3526;** www.countryvacations.mb.ca), for details about farm accommodations. Rates average C$75 (US$50) per day and C$450 (US$300) per week for adults and C$25 (US$17) per day and C$150 (US$105) per week for children—a very reasonable price for such an exciting authentic experience.

Just outside Riding Mountain National Park, the 720-acre **Riding Mountain Guest Ranch,** Box 11, Lake Audy, MB R0J 0Z0 (☎ **204/848-2265;** fax 204/848-4658), offers much more than a simple farm vacation. You can enjoy horseback riding, hiking, and loon watching at the lake. Accommodations consist of four rooms, plus a dorm room with 12 beds and a bunkhouse accommodating another 12. The ranch also features a lounge with a stone fireplace, a sunroom veranda, a billiards room, a sauna, and a hot tub. In summer, you can take trail rides. Evenings are given over to campfire sing-alongs. In winter, the ranch has 20km (12 miles) of cross-country ski trails. There's a 2-day minimum stay, at C$85 to C$95 (US$57 to US$63) per person per day, including all meals.

In Saskatchewan, farm vacations average C$50 to C$75 (US$33 to US$50) double for a bed and a real farm breakfast (additional meals can be arranged). For information, contact the **Saskatchewan Country Vacations Association,** 1308 5th Ave. N., Saskatoon, SK S7K 2S2 (☎ **306/664-3278;** www.bbcanada.com/saskcountry.html).

outfitters will supply tents, camping equipment, and canoes; look after your car; and transport you to your trip's starting point. Most are in either Flin Flon or Lac La Ronge, 400km (248 miles) north of Saskatoon.

Churchill River Canoe Outfitters in La Ronge, Saskatchewan (☎ **306/635-4420;** www.lights.com/waterways/crco/index.html), offers a selection of packages. Canoes and kayaks go for about C$30 (US$20) per day, or they can outfit you for a real wilderness expedition. You can also rent cabins for C$20 to C$27 (US$13 to US$18) per person per night, with a C$80 to C$180 (US$53 to US$120) minimum. The **Canoe Ski Discovery Company,** 1618 9th Ave. N., Saskatoon, SK S7K 3A1 (☎ 306/653-5693), offers several canoeing and cross-country skiing wilderness eco-tours in Prince Albert National Park, in Lac La Ronge Provincial Park, and along the Churchill and Saskatchewan rivers. The trips last 3 to 12 days, cost C$250 to C$1,550 (US$167 to US$1,034), and are led by qualified eco-interpreters. For additional info, contact **Tourism Saskatchewan,** 500-1900 Albert St., Regina, SK S4P 4L9 (☎ **877/237-2273** or 306/787-2300).

FISHING   The same clear, cold northern lakes that draw canoeists hold out the chance of catching walleye, northern pike, four species of trout, and Arctic grayling. Licenses are required in both provinces.

Since Manitoba has strong catch-and-release and barbless-hook programs, the number of trophy fish is high. In 1994, 8,272 Master Angler Fish were recorded and nearly 75% released. The province is also known as the North American mecca for channel catfish, particularly along the Bloodvein River. Good fishing abounds in **Whiteshell, Duck Mountain,** the lake chains around **The Pas** and **Flin Flon,** and in fly-in areas up north. For a selection of outfitters, contact the **Manitoba Lodges and**

Outfitters Association, 23 Sage Crescent, Winnipeg, MB R2Y 0X8 (☎ 204/
889-4840; www.mloa.com). In Saskatchewan, **La Rouge, Wollaston,** and **Reindeer**
are just a few of the lakes so densely inhabited by northern pike and walleye you can
practically pluck them from the clear waters.

More than 300 northern outfitters—both fly-in and drive-in camps—offer equipment, accommodations, and experienced guides to take you to the best fishing spots.
Rates for packages vary—C$1,000 to C$3,000 (US$667 and US$2,001) per person
per week, including transportation, meals, boat, guide, and accommodations. Contact
the **Saskatchewan Outfitters Association,** P.O. Box 2016, Prince Albert, SK S6V
6R1 (☎ 306/763-5434). A boat and motor will cost about C$100 to C$250 (US$67
to US$167) per day, and guide services run about C$80 to C$150 (US$53 to
US$100) per day. For more info, contact **Tourism Saskatchewan,** 500-1900 Albert
St., Regina, SK S4P 4L9 (☎ 877/237-2273 or 306/787-2300).

WILDLIFE VIEWING   Manitoba's **Riding Mountain National Park** is a prime
destination for wildlife enthusiasts, who might be able to spot moose, coyote, wolf,
lynx, black bear, beaver, and more—there's even a bison herd. **Grass River Provincial
Park** is home to moose and woodland caribou. **Churchill,** in the far northern part of
the province, is a fantastic place for viewing polar bears; you can even see white beluga
whales in the mouth of the Churchill River. **Kaskattama Safari Adventures** (☎ 204/
667-1611) offers pricey but memorable organized trips to see the bears and the other
wildlife in the north, including Cape Tatnam Wildlife Management Area.

In Saskatchewan, **Prince Albert National Park** is the place to be; you'll be able to
spot and photograph moose, elk, caribou, shaggy bison, lumbering black bears, and
more. It'll come as no surprise that moose live in **Moose Mountain Provincial Park,**
where their neighbors include deer, elk, beaver, muskrat, and coyote. You can also spot
adorable black-tailed prairie dogs in **Grasslands National Park.**

2 Winnipeg: Capital of Manitoba

Tough, sturdy, muscular, midwestern—that's **Winnipeg,** Manitoba's capital. The cast-
iron warehouses, stockyards, railroad depots, and grain elevators all testify to its historical role as a distribution-and-supply center, first for furs and then for agricultural
products. It's a toiling city where about 600,000 inhabitants sizzle in summer and
shovel in winter.

That's one side. The other is a city and populace that have produced a symphony
orchestra that triumphed in New York, the first royal ballet company in the British
Commonwealth, and a theater-and-arts complex worthy of any national capital.

ESSENTIALS
VISITOR INFORMATION   Contact **Travel Manitoba,** 7-155 Carlton St.,
Winnipeg, MB R3C 3H8 (☎ 800/665-0040). For specific Winnipeg information,
contact **Tourism Winnipeg,** 279 Portage Ave., Winnipeg, MB R3B 2B4 (☎ 800/
665-0204 or 204/943-1970), open Monday to Friday 8:30am to 4:30pm, or the **Airport InfoCentre,** Winnipeg International Airport (☎ 204/982-7543), open daily
8am to 9:45pm.

GETTING THERE   **Winnipeg International Airport** (☎ 204/982-7547) is only
about 20 minutes west-northwest of the city center (allow 30 to 40 min. in rush
hours). **Air Canada** (☎ 800/776-3000; www.aircanada.ca) and **Canadian Airlines**
(☎ 800/426-7000 in the U.S. or 800/665-1177 in Canada; www.cdnair.ca) serve the
city. You can get from the airport to downtown by taxi, costing C$12 to C$15 (US$8
to US$10), or by the city bus, costing C$1.55 (US$1.05) and running to Portage and
Garry about every 15 minutes during the day and every 22 minutes during the night.

If you're driving, Winnipeg is 697km (432 miles) from Minneapolis, Minnesota, and 235km (146 miles) from Grand Forks, North Dakota. The **VIA Rail Canada** depot is at Main Street and Broadway (☎ 204/949-7400; www.viarail.ca).

CITY LAYOUT A native Winnipegger once said to me, "I still can't get used to the confined and narrow streets in the east." When you see Portage and Main, each 132 feet wide (that's 10 yd. off the width of a football field), and the eerie flatness that means no matter where you go, you can see where you're going, you'll understand why.

Portage and Main is the city's focal point, at the junction of the Red and Assiniboine rivers. The Red River runs north-south, as does Main Street; the Assiniboine and Portage Avenue run east-west. Going north on Main from the Portage-Main junction will bring you to the City Hall, the Exchange District, the Manitoba Centennial Centre (including the Manitoba Theatre Centre), the Museum of Man and Nature, the Ukrainian Museum, and on into the North End, once a mosaic of cultures and still dotted with bulbous church domes and authentic delis.

From Portage and Main, if you go 6 blocks west along Portage (a major shopping district) and 2 blocks south, you'll hit the Convention Centre. From here, going 1 block south and 2 blocks west brings you to the Legislative Building, the art gallery, and south, just across the Assiniboine River, Osborne Village.

GETTING AROUND For information, contact **City of Winnipeg Transit,** 421 Osborne St. (☎ 204/986-5700). For regular buses, you need C$1.55 (US$1.05) in exact change (C$1.25/US85¢ children/seniors) to board. Call ☎ 204/986-5700 for route and schedule info, or visit the information booth in the Portage and Main concourse, open Monday to Friday 9:30am to 5:30pm.

You can find taxis at the downtown hotels. They charge C$2.55 (US$1.70) when the meter drops and C$1.80 (US$1.20) per mile thereafter. Try **Duffy's Taxi** (☎ 204/772-2451 or 204/775-0101) or **Unicity Taxi** (☎ 204/925-3131).

SPECIAL EVENTS The **Red River Exhibition,** usually starting the third week of June, celebrates the city's history, showcasing agricultural, horticultural, commercial, and industrial achievements. There are also a midway, a photography show, and other themed features like a lumberjack show. For more information, contact the Red River Exhibition, 3977 Portage Ave., Winnipeg, MB R3G 3J7 (☎ 204/888-6990).

Folklorama, a Festival of Nations, is a 2-week cultural festival in August featuring more than 35 pavilions celebrating ethnic culture, with traditional food, dancing, music, costumes, entertainment, and crafts. It attracts more than 400,000 guests yearly. For more information, contact Folklorama, 56 The Promenade, Winnipeg, MB R3B 3G8 (☎ 800/665-0234 or 204/982-6210).

The 10-day **Festival du Voyageur,** held in mid-February, celebrates French Métis culture in St. Boniface (☎ 204/237-7692).

EXPLORING THE CITY
THE TOP ATTRACTIONS

At the junction of the Red and Assiniboine rivers, the **Forks Market Area** is a major attraction created in the late 1980s when the old rail yard was redeveloped. The draw is the market—a wonderful display of fresh produce and specialty foods. There are also restaurants and specialty stores, with programs, exhibits, and events scheduled throughout the year. In summer, you can stroll on the river walks along the Red and Assiniboine rivers; in winter, there's free public skating on outdoor artificial ice or along groomed river trails. From the Forks National Historic site you get a view across to St. Boniface, where all kinds of special events and interpretive programs are held. It's also a great place for a picnic. The **Manitoba Children's Museum** (☎ 204/956-5437) and the new **Manitoba Theatre for Young People** (☎ 204/947-0394)

Winnipeg

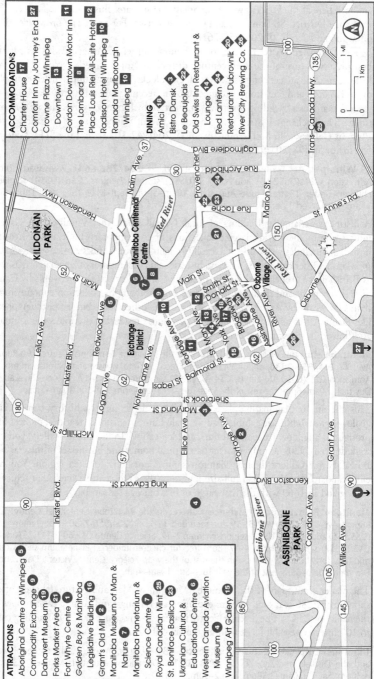

are both here at the Forks as well. Fun Splash Dash Water Buses link the forks to The Exchange District, St. Boniface, and Osborne Village. For an update on what's going on at the Forks, call ☎ **204/957-7618.**

The **Exchange District,** close to the famous corner of Portage and Main, is the best-preserved turn-of-the-20th-century district in North America. Now a national historic site, the area encompasses over 30 city blocks, featuring unparalleled examples of terra-cotta and cut-stone architecture. In recent years, the area has been in great demand as a backdrop for movie production by filmmakers from across the continent. The Exchange District is also home to two of Winnipeg's best art galleries: the **Plug In Gallery,** 286 McDermott Ave. (☎ **204/942-1043**), and the **SITE Gallery,** 55 Arthur St. (☎ **204/942-1618**).

✪ **Winnipeg Art Gallery.** 300 Memorial Blvd. ☎ **204/786-6641.** www.wag.mb.ca. Admission C$4 (US$2.65) adults, C$3 (US$2) students/seniors, C$6 (US$4) families; children under 13 free. June–Aug daily 10am–5pm. Sept–May Tues and Thurs–Sun 11am–5pm, Wed 11am–9pm.

A distinctive triangular building of local Tyndall stone, the Winnipeg Art Gallery houses one of the world's largest collections of contemporary Inuit art—a treasure house that includes wry works like Leah Qumaluk Povungnituk's *Birds Stealing Kayak from Man.* Other collections focus on historic and contemporary Canadian art, as well as British and European artists. The decorative art collections feature works by Canadian silversmiths and studio potters, while the photography collection contains more than 200 works by Andre Kertesz and represents other 20th-century photographers, like Diane Arbus and Irving Penn. The penthouse restaurant overlooks the fountain and flowers in the sculpture court.

Manitoba Museum of Man and Nature. In the Manitoba Centennial Centre, 190 Rupert Ave. ☎ **204/956-2830,** or 204/943-3139 for recorded info. www.manitobamuseum.mb.ca. Admission C$5 (US$3.35) adults, C$4 (US$2.65) seniors/children 3–17. Victoria Day–Labour Day daily 10am–6pm; the rest of the year Tues–Fri 10am–4pm, Sat–Sun 10am–5pm.

This museum is a fascinating place, with galleries depicting local history, culture, and geology through life-size exhibits like a buffalo hunt, prehistoric creatures, pioneer life, pronghorn antelope, teepees, sod huts, and log cabins. In the Urban Gallery, you can walk down a 1920s Winnipeg street past typical homes and businesses of the era. The Boreal Forest Gallery depicts Manitoba's most northerly forested region. You can climb aboard the *Nonsuch,* a full-size replica of the 17th-century ketch that returned to England in 1669 with the first cargo of furs out of Hudson Bay.

Manitoba Planetarium & Science Centre. In the Manitoba Centennial Centre, 190 Rupert Ave. ☎ **204/943-3139** for recorded info, or 204/956-2830. Planetarium C$4 (US$2.65) adults, C$3 (US$2) seniors/children 4–17. Science Centre C$2.60 (US$1.75) adults, C$3 (US$2) seniors/children 4–17. Both free for children under 2. Planetarium shows daily mid-May to Labour Day; Tues–Sun the rest of the year. Science Centre, Victoria Day–Labour Day daily 10am–6pm; rest of the year Tues–Sun 10am–4pm.

The planetarium, part of the Manitoba Museum of Man and Nature (above), offers shows in its 280-seat Star Theatre exploring everything from cosmic catastrophes to the reality of UFOs. The Science Centre is a hands-on science gallery containing close to 100 interactive exhibits explaining the laws of nature.

Ukrainian Cultural & Educational Centre. 184 Alexander Ave. E. (at the corner of Main and the Disraeli Freeway). ☎ **204/942-0218.** Donations requested. Mon–Fri 9:30am–4:30pm, Sat 10:30am–3:30pm, Sun 2–5pm.

The Oseredok, or Ukrainian Centre, one of the largest such institutions in North America, conserves the artifacts and heritage of the Ukrainian people. The art gallery and museum feature changing exhibits on such subjects as 18th-century icons,

A Taste of France Across the River: The Historic District of St. Boniface

Across the river in **St. Boniface,** a street becomes a *rue* and a hello becomes *bonjour.* Here you'll find the largest French-speaking community in western Canada, dating from 1783, when Pierre Gaultier de Varennes established Fort Rouge at the junction of the Red and Assiniboine rivers. The junction became the center of a thriving fur trade for the North West Company, which rivaled and challenged the Hudson's Bay Company. A basilica built in 1819 was dedicated to Boniface, and in 1846 four Grey Nuns arrived and began their ministry.

The original basilica was replaced in 1908 by a beautiful church that was subsequently destroyed by fire in 1968. The massive Gothic arches remain, and cradled within the shell of the old building is the new basilica, built in 1972. In front of the cathedral, the cemetery is the resting place of Louis Riel, whose grave is marked by a replica of a Red River cart. Riel, leader of the Métis uprising and president of the provincial government formed from 1869 to 1870, tried to prevent the transfer of the Red River settlement to Canada. For walking tours of St. Boniface, call the chamber of commerce at ☎ 204/235-1406.

embroidery, weaving, painted eggs, wood carving, ceramics, clothing, and other folk arts. The gift shop stocks traditional and contemporary folk art and crafts.

Royal Canadian Mint. 520 Lagimodière Blvd. ☎ **204/257-3359** or 204/983-6429. Admission C$2 (US$1.35) adults; children under 6 free. May–Aug tours given every 30 min. Mon–Fri 8:30am–4pm; self-guided tours at other times of the year. Take Main St. south over the Assiniboine/Red rivers, turn left onto Marion St., and then right onto Lagimodière. You'll see the mint rise up just beyond the Trans-Canada Hwy. (Rte. 135).

The process of making money is mind-boggling, and this tour will prove it to you. Dies are produced; a roof crane lifts 4,000-pound strips of bronze and nickel; three 150-ton presses stamp out up to 8,800 coin blanks per minute; and coining presses turn out up to 18,000 coins per hour to the telling machines that count the number for bagging. The whole process from start to finish represents an extraordinary engineering feat streamlined by conveyor belts and an overhead monorail.

MORE ATTRACTIONS

In addition to the following sights, visit the **Aboriginal Centre of Winnipeg,** 181 Higgins Ave. (☎ **204/989-6395**), in a beautifully restored late–19th-century CP Rail station. The building is a community center for Winnipeg's First Nation citizens and has a restaurant; the excellent Canadian Plains Gallery offers for sale some of the finest Native art in Canada. The center is open daily 8:30am to 4:30pm.

The Golden Boy & Manitoba Legislative Building. 450 Broadway. ☎ **204/945-5813.** July–Sept tours given hourly Mon–Sun 9am–6pm; by reservation at other times.

There he stands, 240 feet above ground atop the Legislative Building's dome, clutching a sheaf of wheat under his left arm and holding aloft in his right an eternally lit torch symbolizing the spirit of progress. French sculptor Charles Gardet created his 5-ton, 13½-foot bronze statue during World War I. The building below, a magnificent classical Greek structure, was designed in 1919 by British architect Frank Worthington Simon. The building's focal point is, of course, the Legislative Chamber, where the 57 members of Manitoba's legislative assembly meet.

Dalnavert Museum. 61 Carlton St. (between Broadway and Assiniboine Ave.). ☎ **204/943-2835.** Admission C$4 (US$2.65) adults, C$3 (US$2) seniors/students, C$20 (US$1.35) ages 6–18, C$8 (US$5) families; children under 6 free. June–Aug Tues–Thurs and Sat–Sun 10am–6pm; Sept–Dec and Mar–May Tues–Thurs and Sat–Sun noon–5pm; Jan–Feb Sat–Sun noon–5pm.

Just 2 blocks east of the Legislative Building (above) stands the Victorian home built in 1895 for Hugh John Macdonald, the only son of Canada's first prime minister. It's a fine example of a late-Victorian gingerbread house with a wraparound veranda and the latest innovations of the time—electric lighting, indoor plumbing, central hot-water heating, and walk-in closets.

Commodity Exchange. On the 5th floor of the Commodity Exchange Tower, 360 Main St. ☎ **204/925-5000.** Viewing gallery open Mon–Fri 9:30am–1:15pm. Tours at 9:10am and 12:50pm daily, but call ahead to arrange.

Organized in 1887 as a grain exchange, the Commodity Exchange is the only exchange in Canada that trades in agricultural commodities. Once this was the heart and soul of Winnipeg: the world's premier grain market until World War II. Today it has about 240 members and 77 companies registered for trading privileges. It's best to come around 9:15am or right near closing at 12:45pm, when you're more likely to see some feverish action on the floor.

Western Canada Aviation Museum. 958 Ferry Rd. ☎ **204/786-5503.** www.wcam. mb.ca. Admission C$3 (US$2) adults, C$2 (US$1.35) students 3–17. Mon–Sat 10am–4pm, Sun 1–4pm. Closed Dec 25–26, Jan 1, and Good Friday.

Among the historic flying treasures at the Western Canada Aviation Museum is Canada's first helicopter, designed and test-flown between 1935 and 1939. The children's interactive area is also popular.

Grant's Old Mill. 2777 Portage Ave. (mailing address 20072, Winnipeg MB R3K 2E5; at the corner of Booth Dr.). ☎ **204/986-5613.** Admission by donation. June–Aug daily 10am–6pm; the rest of year by appointment only.

Grant's Old Mill is a reconstruction of the water mill built on Sturgeon Creek in 1829, believed to be the first water mill west of the Great Lakes and the first instance of the use of hydropower in Manitoba. Grist is ground daily during summer, and you can take away a souvenir bag of whole wheat or buckwheat.

Fort Whyte Centre. 1961 McCreary Rd., Fort Whyte. ☎ **204/989-8355,** or 204/989-8350 for recorded info. Admission C$4 (US$2.65) adults, C$3 (US$2) students/seniors/children over 2. Mon–Tues and Thurs–Fri 9am–5pm, Wed 9am–9pm, Sat–Sun and holidays 10am–5pm.

About 15 minutes from downtown, some old cement quarries have been converted into lakes at Fort Whyte Centre and now serve as an environmental educational facility. The freshwater aquarium has many local Manitoba specimens, like the northern pike and walleye. There are self-guided nature trails, waterfowl gardens, and an interpretive center and gift shop.

PARKS & GARDENS

Comprising 393 acres for playing, picnicking, or biking, **Assiniboine Park,** at 2355 Corydon Ave. (☎ 204/986-6921), contains a miniature railway, a duck pond, an English garden (which opens in June), and a conservatory. In winter there are skating on the pond and tobogganing. The park also contains a 98-acre **zoo** (see "Especially for Kids"). Art lovers will also want to visit the **studio of Leo Mol** (☎ 204/986-6531) and see the sculpture garden containing his works. The park is open daily dawn to dusk. The elegant new **Tavern in the Park** (☎ 204/896-7275) offers lunch 11:30am to 2:30pm (C$8 to C$12/US$5 to US$8) and dinner 5 to 10pm (C$16 to

C$24/US$11 to US$16). Reservations are suggested. The free **Pavilion Gallery** houses a permanent collection of works by three Manitoba artists. And the new **Lyric outdoor theater** (☎ 204/888-5466, ext. 5) provides free entertainment in summer with performances by the Winnipeg Symphony, The Royal Winnipeg Ballet, local jazz combos, and so on.

Kildonan Park is quite delightful, with landscaped gardens, picnic spots, biking paths, outdoor swimming, and wading pools, as well as a restaurant and dining room overlooking a small artificial lake. Also look for the Witch's House from *Hansel and Gretel* in the park. Rainbow Stages musical comedies are performed here in July and August.

CRUISES & A STEAM-TRAIN EXCURSION

During summer, the cruise ships **MS** *River Rouge* and **MS** *Paddlewheel Queen* depart from their dock at Water and Gilroy at the foot of the Provencher Bridge on a variety of cruises, including a sunset dinner-dance cruise beginning at 7pm and a moonlight version on weekends leaving at 10pm. Both cost C$13 (US$9). Two-hour sightseeing trips costing C$12 (US$8) depart at 1pm and provide fine views of the city from the Red and Assiniboine rivers. Occasionally the company offers longer cruises to Lake Winnipeg. For details, call ☎ **204/942-4500.**

A 1900 steam-era train, the *Prairie Dog Central,* takes you on a 2½-hour, 58km (36-mile) round-trip from Winnipeg north on the Oak Point line. En route you really get a feel for the prairie and what the late–19th-century immigrants might've seen when they arrived. The train operates weekends June to September. Admission is C$13 (US$9) adults, C$11 (US$7) seniors/youths 12 to 17, and C$7 (US$4.65) children 2 to 11. For details, contact the **Vintage Locomotive Society** at ☎ **204/832-5259.**

ESPECIALLY FOR KIDS

At the Forks, there's a **Children's Museum** (☎ 204/956-1888), specially designed with participatory exhibits for 2- to 13-year-olds. At Under the Big Top they can run away to the circus and devise a show of their very own; and in the TV studio they can create their own television shows, as performers or as technicians. Admission is C$4 (US$2.65) adults and C$3.50 (US$2.35) seniors; children 2 and under are free. It's open Monday, Tuesday, and Wednesday 9am to 5pm; Thursday and Friday 9am to 8pm; Saturday 10am to 8pm; and Sunday and holidays 10am to 5pm.

Assiniboine Park, 2355 Corydon Ave. (☎ 204/986-6921), is a great place to picnic or play. Its top attraction, however, is the 98-acre **zoo** where the animals—bear, tiger, zebra, flamingo, bison, elk, and deer—are kept in as natural an environment as possible. Some exotic species on display are snow leopards, ruffed lemurs, and Irkutsk lynx. Many spectacular birds live and breed in the Tropical House. A special Discovery Centre with a barnful of young farm animals is fun. March to October, admission is C$3 (US$2) adults, C$2.75 (US$1.85) seniors, C$1.50 (US$1) youths 13 to 17, and C$1 (US65¢) children 2 to 12; November to February, it's C$1 (US65¢) for everyone. The park is open daily dawn to dusk, the zoo daily 10am to dusk. To get there, take Portage Avenue west, exit onto Route 90 south, and then turn right onto Corydon.

Darkzone, 230 Osborne St. (☎ 204/287-8710), is the hippest game at the moment for kids and adults—an advanced laser game in which as many as 30 players and three teams compete against one another in trying to deactivate the opposing players and their bases using a phaser and computerized vest. It's open Monday to Thursday 4pm to midnight, Friday 4pm to 1am, Saturday 10am to 1am, and Sunday 10am to 10pm. Admission is C$5 (US$3.35) or C$14 (US$9) for three games.

Kids love the thrills at **Fun Mountain Water Slide Park,** 6km (3.7 miles) east of the mint on Highway 1 east (☎ 204/255-3910). There are 10 slides, as well as rides, including bumper boats, a giant hot tub, and a kids' playground with a wading pool. All-day admission is C$12 (US$8) adults and C$9 (US$6) children 4 to 12; children under 4 are free. June to August, it's open daily 10am to 8pm, weather permitting.

The **Manitoba Theatre for Young People,** in the CanWest Global Performing Arts Centre at Forks Market (☎ 204/947-0394), presents plays for children and teens. The season runs October to May, and tickets are C$9 (US$6).

WHERE TO STAY
EXPENSIVE

Crowne Plaza, Winnipeg Downtown. 350 St. Mary's Ave., Winnipeg, MB R3C 3J2. ☎ **204/942-0551.** Fax 204/943-8702. www.crownplaza.mb.ca. 389 units. A/C MINIBAR TV TEL. C$150 (US$100) double. Children under 18 stay free in parents' room. Weekend packages available. AE, CB, DC, DISC, ER, MC, V. Parking C$8 (US$5).

The 17-story Holiday Inn Crowne Plaza is right downtown and connected by a sky-walk to the Convention Centre. The pleasantly decorated guest rooms feature the usual amenities, plus two phones with fax modem capacity, coffeemakers, and irons/ironing boards. Poolside rooms are a couple of dollars more than standard rooms, while club-floor rooms include such extras as breakfast and evening hors d'oeuvres, overnight shoeshine, in-room trouser presses, and heated tiles in the bathrooms.

Dining/Diversions: The Elephant and Castle pub is for all-day dining and the Chef's Table for fine contemporary cuisine. There's also a piano bar, Ticker's Lounge.

Amenities: 24-hour room service, laundry/valet; skylit indoor pool, outdoor pool, exercise facilities.

The Lombard. 2 Lombard Place, Winnipeg, MB R3B 0Y3. ☎ **800/441-1414** or 204/957-1350. Fax 204/949-1486. www.cphotels.ca. 350 units. A/C MINIBAR TV TEL. C$159 (US$106) double. Weekend packages available. AE, DC, DISC, ER, MC, V. Parking C$8 (US$5), valet parking C$16 (US$11).

At the corner of Portage and Main rises the 21-story white concrete Lombard, a member of the Canadian Pacific chain, a few minutes' walk from the Manitoba Centennial Centre. Its rooms are furnished with white colonial-style pieces and the usual amenities, plus such extras as three phones, hair dryers, and irons/ironing boards.

Dining: The Velvet Glove features luxurious dining amid gilt-framed portraits, wood paneling, and brass torchières. You might choose an entree such as pepper-roasted wild boar with apple-turnip compote or roast cedar-plank salmon and onion marmalade. Prices are C$16 to C$25 (US$11 to US$17). If you want that C$100-plus (US$67-plus) bottle of wine, it's available. The self-serve Cafe Express offers deli sandwiches and hot specials.

Amenities: Concierge, 24-hour room service, laundry/valet, free local phone calls; indoor pool, whirlpool, sauna, fitness center.

Radisson Hotel Winnipeg. 288 Portage Ave. (at Smith St.), Winnipeg, MB R3C 0B8. ☎ **800/268-1133** or 204/956-0410. Fax 204/947-1129. www.radisson.com. E-mail reserv@mts.net. 272 units. A/C MINIBAR TV TEL. Weekdays C$194 (US$129) double. Weekend packages available. AE, CB, DC, DISC, ER, MC, V. Parking C$9 (US$6).

The guest rooms here occupy floors 15 to 29. All offer good views of the city and are well equipped, with hair dryers and coffeemakers. The hotel is right next door to a promenade accessing the 300-plus shops in Eaton Place and Portage Place. A business lounge is on the P-level.

Dining/Diversions: The oak-paneled candlelit Signatures offers fine dining and piano entertainment. In Tillie's, sports events are shown on a big-screen TV.

Amenities: 24-hour room service; indoor pool with outdoor deck, whirlpool, sauna, exercise room, twin cinemas, free Children's Creative Centre (supervised on weekends).

MODERATE

Charter House. York and Hargrave sts., Winnipeg, MB R3C 0N9. ☎ **800/782-0175** or 204/942-0101. Fax 204/956-0665. 86 units. A/C TV TEL. C$125–C$135 (US$83–US$90) double. Extra person C$10 (US$7). Children under 16 stay free in parents' room. Packages available. AE, DC, DISC, MC, V. Free parking.

A block from the Convention Centre, the Charter House offers attractively decorated guest rooms. The top-floor rooms are designed for business travelers, featuring ergonomically designed furniture, fax/Internet access, coffeemakers, and hair dryers. The other rooms have modern amenities like voice mail, and about half have balconies. There are an outdoor pool and a deck/patio. The Rib Room is well-known locally for good prime rib, steaks, and seafood, with main courses at C$13 to C$24 (US$9 to US$16). There's a coffee shop too.

✪ **Place Louis Riel All-Suite Hotel.** 190 Smith St. (at St. Mary's), Winnipeg, MB R3C 1J8. ☎ **204/947-6961.** Fax 204/947-3029. www.placelouisriel.com. E-mail info@ placelouisriel.com. 277 units. A/C TV TEL. C$100–C$110 (US$67–US$73) double. Extra person C$10 (US$7). Children under 16 stay free in parents' room. Weekend package available. Three wheelchair-accessible suites. AE, DC, MC, V. Parking C$4.50 (US$3).

In the heart of downtown is a bargain you shouldn't pass up. Here you can stay in a studio (with a sleeping/living area partitioned from the kitchen) or a beautifully furnished one- or two-bedroom suite. All units come with fully equipped kitchens (including microwaves and coffeemakers) and dining areas. For convenience, a Laundromat, grocery store, and restaurant and lounge are on the ground floor of the 23-floor building.

Ramada Marlborough Winnipeg. 331 Smith St. (at Portage), Winnipeg, MB R3B 2G9. ☎ **800/667-7666** or 204/942-6411. Fax 204/942-2017. 148 units. A/C TV TEL. C$105 (US$70) double. Children under 18 stay free in parents' room. Special Fri–Sun rates available. AE, DC, DISC, ER, MC, V. Free parking.

This isn't your average Ramada. Built in 1914, the Marlborough retains its vaulted ceilings, stained-glass windows, and Victorian Gothic exterior but now offers all the modern amenities, including a fine-dining room, Victor's. There are also a coffee shop and a club with live entertainment on weekends. The recently renovated rooms feature tasteful decor that maintain the period charm of the building while offering every modern comfort. If you're looking for extra space, ask for one of the Club Rooms, which are somewhat larger.

INEXPENSIVE

For reliable, clean, and attractively decorated rooms, the **Comfort Inn by Journey's End,** 3109 Pembina Hwy. (☎ **204/269-7390**), is hard to beat. Doubles are C$78 to C$84 (US$52 to US$56). Local phone calls are free.

Gordon Downtowner Motor Hotel. 330 Kennedy St., Winnipeg, MB R3B 2M6. ☎ **204/943-5581.** Fax 204/338-4348. 40 units. A/C TV TEL. C$57 (US$38) double. Extra person C$7 (US$4.65). Children under 16 stay free in parents' room. AE, DC, ER, MC, V.

Probably the best budget hotel downtown is the Gordon Downtowner, part of Portage Place. The guest rooms were all renovated recently and boast touches like extra phones in the bathrooms. Amenities include a pub and a comfortable restaurant (open 7am to 9pm).

WHERE TO DINE

An excellent place to go looking for a good Mediterranean restaurant is along **Corydon Avenue,** south of downtown across the Assiniboine River. Known as Little Italy, the area was settled by Italian immigrants and still has a strong continental feel, with lots of cafes and streetside restaurants.

EXPENSIVE

✪ **Le Beaujolais.** 131 Provencher Blvd. (at Tache), St. Boniface. ☎ **204/237-6276.** Reservations recommended. Main courses C$20–C$35 (US$13–US$23). AE, ER, MC, V. Mon–Fri 11:30am–2:30pm; daily 5pm to variable closing times, depending on the number of reservations. FRENCH.

Le Beaujolais is a comfortable place serving such traditional dishes as roast duck with cassis, veal tenderloin with Roquefort-and-leek sauce, and rack of lamb Nicoise (made with ratatouille). At night, the room, which features etched glass and glass-brick partitions, takes on a romantic air when candles are lit. Roasted ostrich is also a specialty. It's raised locally and served with portobello mushrooms and a balsamic-vinegar glaze.

✪ **Restaurant Dubrovnik.** 390 Assiniboine Ave. ☎ **204/944-0594.** Reservations recommended. Main courses C$16–C$25 (US$11–US$17). AE, MC, V. Mon–Sat 11am–2pm; daily 5–11pm. CONTINENTAL.

Dubrovnik offers a romantic setting for fine continental cuisine and Eastern European specialties. It occupies a beautiful Victorian brick town house with working fireplaces, leaded-glass windows, and an enclosed veranda. Each dining area is decorated tastefully with a few plants and colorful gusle (beautifully carved musical instruments, often inlaid with mother-of-pearl). Start with the traditional Russian borscht, wild-game pâté, or Caribbean shrimp cocktail with tomato, lemon, and cognac. Then follow with the chicken breast with caramelized cranberries, crisp-roasted duck with hoisin-and-plum glaze, or Atlantic salmon seared with a vinaigrette of basil, garlic, olive oil, and fresh dill. Finish with a coffee Dubrovnik (sljivovica, kruskovac bitters, coffee, whipped cream, and chopped walnuts).

MODERATE

✪ **Amici.** 326 Broadway. ☎ **204/943-4997.** Reservations recommended. Main courses C$14–C$28 (US$9–US$19). AE, DC, ER, MC, V. Mon–Fri 11:30am–2:30pm; Mon–Sat 5–11pm. CONTINENTAL/ITALIAN.

The atmosphere is plush and comfortable and the northern Italian cuisine is tops in the city. You have your choice of 12 or more pastas, with selections like fettucini alla boscaiola (with wild mushrooms, veal, and lingonberries) and spaghetti alla carbonara. Or you can have such richly flavored meat and fish dishes as venison with wild mushrooms and potato gnocchi, lamb loin with spinach and mushrooms wrapped in puff pastry, medallions of beef with Barolo wine sauce, and sea bass in saffron broth with Mediterranean vegetables.

✪ **Bistro Dansk.** 63 Sherbrook St. ☎ **204/775-5662.** Reservations recommended. Main courses C$8–C$14 (US$5–US$9). AE, V. Mon–Sat 11am–3pm; Mon–Sat 5–9:30pm. DANISH.

In this warm chalet-style bistro, bright-red gateback chairs complement the wooden tables and raffia place mats. Main courses include seven superlative Danish specialties, such as *frikadeller* (Danish meat patties, made from ground veal and pork, served with red cabbage and potato salad), and *aeggekage* (a Danish omelet with bacon, garnished with tomatoes and green onions, served with home-baked Danish bread). At lunch, specialties include nine or so open-face sandwiches, served on homemade rye or white bread, most at C$3 to C$7 (US$2 to US$4.65).

Old Swiss Inn Restaurant & Lounge. 207 Edmonton St. ☎ **204/942-7725.** Reservations recommended. Main courses C$12–C$27 (US$8–US$18). AE, DC, ER, MC, V. Mon–Fri 11:30am–2:30pm; Mon–Sat 5–9:30pm. Free parking after 5pm. SWISS.

This restaurant lives up to its name with unpretentious alpine warmth, wood paneling, pictures of mountain scenery, and Swiss specialties. At dinner, you might start with Swiss onion soup or cheese fondue and follow with veal Zurich (with white wine and mushrooms) accompanied by delicious Swiss rösti potatoes, or the house specialty, fondue bourguignonne. At lunch, you'll find wiener schnitzel, *bratwurst mit rösti* (Swiss fried potatoes), and more central European specialties.

Red Lantern. 302 Hamel Ave., St. Boniface. ☎ **204/233-4841.** Reservations recommended. Main courses C$13–C$28 (US$9–US$19). AE, CB, MC, V. Mon–Fri 11:30am–2pm; Sun–Thurs 5–9pm, Fri–Sat 5–10pm. CONTINENTAL.

A red lantern stands outside the small house occupied by this restaurant, which offers a cozy dining room. The food is excellent, nicely presented, graciously served, and very reasonably priced. French background music adds to the atmosphere. Among the specialties are veal Oscar; trout meunière; steak Madagascar (with red wine, green peppercorn, and tomato demi-glace); and chicken breast stuffed with brie, spinach, and carrots served with thyme cream sauce.

River City Brewing Co. 437 Stradbrook Ave. ☎ **204/452-2739.** Reservations not accepted. Main courses C$7–C$19 (US$4.65–US$13). AE, MC, V. Mon–Wed 11:30am–midnight, Thurs–Sat 11:30am–2am, Sun 4pm–midnight. PUB FARE.

Winnipeg's first brew pub, the River City serves up good handcrafted beers plus excellent food. The usual pub grub suspects are here—burgers, ribs, and fish-and-chips—plus steaks, grilled chicken and fish, and vegetarian dishes that verge on fine dining.

WINNIPEG AFTER DARK

THE PERFORMING ARTS The **Manitoba Centennial Centre,** 555 Main St. (☎ 204/956-1360), is a complex that includes the Centennial Concert Hall (home to the Royal Winnipeg Ballet, the Winnipeg Symphony, and the Manitoba Opera). Nearby are the Manitoba Theatre Centre, the Warehouse Theatre, and Pantages Playhouse Theatre.

Other spaces offering frequent concerts and performances include the **Winnipeg Art Gallery** (☎ 204/786-6641), with blues/jazz, chamber music, and contemporary music groups; the **Pantages Playhouse Theatre,** 180 Market Ave. E. (☎ 204/191-5047); and the **Convention Centre,** 375 York Ave. (☎ 204/956-1720), with popular, folk, and light orchestral musical concerts.

The world-renowned ✪ **Royal Winnipeg Ballet,** 380 Graham Ave., at Edmonton Street (☎ 204/956-0183, or 204/956-2792 for the box office), was founded in 1939 by two British immigrant ballet teachers, making it North America's second-oldest ballet company (after San Francisco's). By 1949, it was a professional troupe and in 1953 it was granted a royal charter. Today its repertoire includes both contemporary and classical works, such as Ashton's *Thais, Giselle,* and *Sleeping Beauty.* The company performs at the Centennial Concert Hall, usually for a week in October, November, December, March, and May. Tickets are C$9 to C$45 (US$6 to US$30), with discounts for students, seniors, and children.

Established in 1947, the **Winnipeg Symphony Orchestra,** 555 Main St. (☎ 204/949-3950, or 204/949-3999 for the box office), made its debut in 1978 at Carnegie Hall in New York City. The orchestra's prestige has attracted guest artists like Itzhak Perlman, Isaac Stern, Tracey Dahl, and Maureen Forrester. The season usually runs September to mid-May, and tickets are C$12 to C$40 (US$8 to US$27).

The **Manitoba Opera,** 380 Graham, (☎ **204/942-7479,** or 204/957-7842 for the box office), features a season of three operas each year at the Centennial Concert Hall, with performances in November, February, and April. English subtitles are used. Tickets begin at C$16 (US$11).

THEATER   You can enjoy theater in the park at the **Rainbow Stage,** 2021 Main St., in Kildonan Park (☎ **204/989-5261**), Canada's largest and oldest continuously operating outdoor theater. The stage presents two musical classics running about 3 weeks each in July and August. On the banks of the Red River, the Rainbow is easily accessible by bus or car. For tickets, C$10 to C$23 (US$7 to US$15), write Rainbow Stage, 201-320 Sherbrook St., Winnipeg, MB R3B 2W6.

The **MTC Warehouse,** at 140 Rupert Ave. at Lily (☎ **204/943-4849**), presents more cutting-edge, controversial plays in an intimate 300-seat theater. Its four-play season runs mid-October to mid-May, and tickets are C$25 to C$35 (US$17 to US$23). Since its founding by Tom Hendry and John Hirsch, the **Manitoba Theatre Centre,** 174 Market Ave. (☎ **204/942-6537**), has been dedicated to producing good serious theater, and this is indeed one of Canada's best regional companies. A recent season's offerings included *Hamlet* starring Keanu Reeves. The season usually features six productions and runs October to April, with tickets at C$20 to C$50 (US$13 to US$33).

A CASINO   The tropical-themed **Club Regent,** 1425 Regent Ave. (☎ **888/ 957-4652** or 204/957-2700), offers slots, electronic blackjack, bingo, poker, keno, and breakopen games, plus traditional bingo and the Fountain of Fortune, a series of progressive slot machines. It's open Monday to Saturday 10am to 3am and Sunday noon to 3am.

DANCE CLUBS   Country-western dance bars are a large part of the nightlife in Winnipeg. Sample the cowboy boot and line dance scene at **Longhorn's Saloon,** 1011 Henderson Hwy. (☎ **204/338-5585**), with both live bands and DJs spinning country hits. **Silverado's,** 2100 McPhillips Ave., in the Canad Inn Garden City (☎ **204/633-0024**), has three floors of dancing to country bands and classic rock acts.

For a more straightforward dance club, go to **8-Trax,** 441 Main St. (☎ **204/ 942-TRAX**), with funk and rock in a historic bank building. **Die Maschine Cabaret,** 108 Osborne St. (☎ **204/284-6766**), is one of the most popular dance clubs in Winnipeg—every night's a theme night, from Brit pop, hip-hop to hits of the 1970s. **Scandals,** 1792 Pembina Hwy. (☎ **204/269-6955**), is a dance bar popular with students from nearby University of Manitoba.

SIDE TRIPS FROM WINNIPEG

LOWER FORT GARRY NATIONAL HISTORIC SITE   The oldest intact stone fur-trading post in North America is **Lower Fort Garry** (☎ **204/785-6050**), only 32km (20 miles) north of Winnipeg on Highway 9. Built in the 1830s, Lower Fort Garry was an important Hudson's Bay Company trans-shipment and provisioning post. Within the walls of the compound are the governor's residence; several warehouses, including the fur loft; and the Men's House, where male employees lived. Outside the compound are company buildings—a blacksmith's shop, the farm manager's home, and so on. The fort is staffed by costumed volunteers who make candles and soap; forge horseshoes, locks, and bolts; and demonstrate the ways of life of the 1850s. In a lean-to beside the fur-loft building stands an original York boat; hundreds of these once traveled the waterways from Hudson Bay to the Rockies and from the Red River to the Arctic carrying furs and trading goods.

Mid-May to Labour Day, the site is open daily 10am to 6pm. Admission is C$6 (US$4) adults, C$3.75 (US$2.50) seniors, and C$2.75 (US$1.85) children 6 to 16; children 5 and under are free.

STEINBACH MENNONITE HERITAGE VILLAGE   About 48km (30 miles) outside Winnipeg is the **Steinbach Mennonite Heritage Village,** 2.4km (1½ miles) north of Steinbach on Highway 12 (☎ **204/326-9661**). This 40-acre museum complex is worth a detour. Between 1874 and 1880, about 7,000 Mennonites migrated here from the Ukraine, establishing settlements like Kleefeld, Steinbach, Blumenort, and others. After World War I, many moved to Mexico and Uruguay when Manitoba closed all unregistered schools between 1922 and 1926, but they were replaced by another surge of emigrants fleeing the Russian Revolution. Their community life is portrayed here in a complex of about 20 buildings. In the museum building, dioramas display daily life and community artifacts, like woodworking and sewing tools, sausage makers, clothes, medicines, and furnishings. Elsewhere in the complex, you can view the windmill grinding grain, ride in an ox-drawn wagon, watch the blacksmith at work, or view any number of homes, agricultural machines, and more. The restaurant serves Mennonite food—a full meal of borscht, thick-sliced homemade brown bread, coleslaw, pirogies, and sausage, plus rhubarb crumble, at very reasonable prices.

The village is open Monday to Saturday: May and September 10am to 5pm; June, July, and August 10am to 7pm. On Sunday the gates don't open until noon. October to April, the museum is open Monday to Friday 10am to 4pm. Admission is C$5 (US$3.35) adults, C$4 (US$2.65) seniors, C$3 (US$2) students grades 1 to 12, and C$15 (US$10) families (all day for adults and dependent children).

3 Whiteshell Provincial Park & Lake Winnipeg

WHITESHELL PROVINCIAL PARK

Less than a 2-hour drive east of Winnipeg (144km/89 miles) lies a network of a dozen rivers and more than 200 lakes in the 2,590km² (1,000-sq.-mile) ✪ **Whiteshell Provincial Park** (☎ **204/369-5232**). Among the park's natural features are Rainbow and Whitemouth falls; a lovely lily pond west of Caddy Lake; West Hawk Lake, Manitoba's deepest lake, created by a meteorite; and a goose sanctuary (best seen mid-May to July, when the goslings are about). You can also view petroforms, stone arrangements fashioned by an Algonquin-speaking people to communicate with the spirits. In fall, you can witness an ancient ritual—the Indians harvesting wild rice. One person poles a canoe through the rice field while another bends the stalks into the canoe and knocks the ripe grains off with a picking stick.

In July and August, the **Manitoba Naturalist's Society,** headquartered at 401-63 Albert St. in Winnipeg (☎ **204/943-9029**), operates wilderness programs and other workshops at their cabin on Lake Mantario. There are six self-guided trails, plus several short trails you can complete in less than 2 hours. For serious backpackers, the **Mantario Trail** is a 3- to 6-day hike over 60km (37 miles) of rugged terrain. There are also all-terrain biking trails. You can canoe the Frances Lake route, which covers 18km (11 miles) of pleasant paddling with 12 beaver-dam hauls and three portages and takes about 6 hours. There are swimming at Falcon Beach; scuba diving in West Hawk Lake; and sailing, windsurfing, waterskiing, and fishing in other places.

Horseback riding is offered at **Falcon Beach Riding Stables** (☎ 204/349-2410). In winter, there are downhill skiing, cross-country skiing, snowmobiling, snowshoeing, and skating. Most recreational equipment, including skis, canoes, snowshoes, and fishing gear, is available from the **Falcon Trail Resort** (☎ 204/349-8273).

Within the park, **Falcon Lake** is the center of one of Canada's most modern recreational developments, including various resorts with tennis courts, an 18-hole par-72 golf course, hiking trails, horseback riding, fishing, canoeing, and skiing. Most park resorts and lodges charge C$70 to C$110 (US$47 to US$73) double or C$450 to C$750 (US$300 to US$500) per week for a cabin. Most resorts offer recreational equipment rentals. Camping facilities abound. For more info, call the park at ☎ 204/369-5232 or contact **Travel Manitoba,** Dept. SV8, 155 Carlton St., Winnipeg, MB R3C 3H8 (☎ 800/665-0040, ext. SV8, or 204/945-3777, ext. SV8).

LAKE WINNIPEG

The continent's seventh largest, **Lake Winnipeg** is 425km (264 miles) long, and its shores shelter some interesting communities and attractive natural areas. At its southern end, **Grand Beach Provincial Park** (☎ 204/754-2212) has white-sand beaches backed by 30-foot-high dunes in some places. This is a good place to swim, windsurf, and fish. There are three self-guided nature trails. Campsites are available in summer only.

About 97km (60 miles) north of Winnipeg, on the western shore, the farming-and-fishing community of **Gimli** is the hub of Icelandic culture in Manitoba. Established a century ago as the capital of New Iceland, it had its own government, school, and newspapers for many years. It still celebrates an Icelandic festival known as Islendingadagurinn, on the first long weekend in August.

Hecla Island, 185km (115 miles) northeast of Winnipeg, was once a part of the Republic of New Iceland and was until recently home to a small Icelandic-Canadian farming-and-fishing community. Today it's the site of **Hecla/Grindstone Provincial Park,** Box 70, Riverton, MB R0C 2R0 (☎ 204/378-2945). Open year-round, it's an excellent place to hike (with five short trails), golf, fish, camp, bird-watch, canoe, swim, windsurf, play tennis (two courts), hunt, cross-country ski, snowshoe, or snowmobile and toboggan. (Gull Harbour Resort has bicycle, tennis, ski, toboggan, and other sports equipment rental.) Camping is available in summer. For reservations, call ☎ 888/482-2267. Photographers and wildlife enthusiasts appreciate the park's wildlife-viewing tower and the **Grassy Narrow Marsh,** which shelters many species of waterfowl. There are a campground and 15 cabins available (for reservations call **Destinet** at ☎ 888/482-2267), plus the Gull Harbour Resort (below).

WHERE TO STAY IN GULL HARBOUR

Gull Harbour Resort Hotel. Box 1000, Riverton, MB R0C 2R0. ☎ 800/267-6700 or 204/475-2354. Fax 204/279-2000. 93 units. A/C TV TEL. C$111 (US$74) double. Extra person C$10 (US$7). Children under 18 stay free in parents' room. Watch for specials year-round. AE, MC, V.

This is an ideal place to take the family. Though it boasts first-class resort facilities, it also reflects a concern for the environment. The beaches and woods have been left intact. Facilities include an indoor pool, a whirlpool, and a sauna; activities include badminton, volleyball, a game room with a pool table, an 18-hole golf course, a putting green, minigolf, two tennis courts, a skating rink, shuffleboard, and more. The resort also has a full line of rental equipment, from bicycles, skis, toboggans, and snowmobiles. The lodge buildings all reflect an Icelandic style, with carved doors, shuttered windows, and steeply sloped rooflines. The Icelandic touches end at the guest rooms, which are comfortably furnished and fully modern, but lack some of the flair applied to the rest of this marvelous resort.

4 West Along the Trans-Canada Highway to Spruce Woods Provincial Park & Brandon

About 67km (42 miles) west of Portage la Prairie, before reaching Carberry, turn south on Highway 5 to **Spruce Woods Provincial Park,** Box 900, Carberry, MB R0K 0H0 (☎ **204/827-2543** in summer, or 204/834-8803). The park's unique and most fragile feature is Spirit Sands, large stretches of open sand that are the remains of the once-wide Assiniboine Delta. Only a few hardy creatures such as the Bembix wasp and one type of wolf spider live here. The rest of the park is forest and prairie grasslands inhabited by herds of wapiti (elk).

There's camping at Kiche Manitou as well as at hike-in locations. The park is on the Assiniboine River canoe route, which starts in Brandon and ends north of Holland. You can rent canoes at Pine Fort IV in the park. The park's longest trail is the 40km (25-mile) **Epinette Trail,** but its most fascinating is the **Spirit Sands/Devil's Punch Bowl,** accessible from Highway 5. It loops through the Dunes and leads to the Devil's Punch Bowl, which was carved by underground streams. There are also bike and mountain-bike trails; swimming at the campground beach; and in winter, cross-country skiing, skating, tobogganing, and snowmobiling.

Brandon is Manitoba's second-largest city, with a population of 40,000. This university town features the **Art Gallery of Southwestern Manitoba;** the **B. J. Hales Museum,** with mounted specimens of birds and mammals; plus interesting tours of the **Agriculture and Agri Food Research Centre.** During summer, families flock to the **Thunder Mountain Water Slide,** 8km (5 miles) west of Brandon on the Trans-Canada Highway.

5 Riding Mountain National Park & Duck Mountain Provincial Park

RIDING MOUNTAIN NATIONAL PARK

About 248km (154 miles) northwest of Winnipeg, **Riding Mountain National Park,** Wasagaming, MB R0J 2H0 (☎ **204/848-7275**), is set in the highlands atop a giant wooded escarpment sheltering more than 260 species of birds, plus moose, wolf, coyote, lynx, beaver, black bear, and a bison herd at Lake Audy.

The park has more than 400km (248 miles) of **hiking trails.** Twenty are easily accessible, short, and easy to moderate in difficulty; another 20 are long backcountry trails. Call the number above for more info. You can ride many trails on mountain bike and horseback and can rent bikes in Wasagaming. The **Triangle Ranch Ltd.,** P.O. Box 275, Onanole (☎ **204/848-4583**), offers 1-hour and day rides for C$18 and C$65 (US$12 and US$43), respectively.

You can rent canoes and other boats at **Clear Lake Marina.** As for **fishing,** northern pike is the main game fish and specimens up to 30 pounds have been taken from Clear Lake. Rainbow and brook trout populate Lake Katherine and Deep Lake. The park also has one of the province's best **golf courses;** greens fees are C$30 (US$20). In winter, there's **cross-country** and **downhill skiing** at Mount Agassiz on the east side of the park, plus ice fishing in Clear Lake.

The **visitor center** is open daily in summer 9am to 9pm. For information, call or write: Superintendent, Riding Mountain National Park, Wasagaming, MB R0J 2H0

(☎ 204/848-7275). The park is easily accessed from Brandon, about 95km (59 miles) north along Highway 10. Entry is C$3.25 (US$2.15) adults and C$8 (US$5) families; multiday passes are also available.

WHERE TO STAY

At the **Shawenequanape Kipi-Che-Win** (Southquill Camp), you can stay in a traditional teepee for C$50 (US$33) double and learn about the traditional ceremonies, arts, crafts, and culture of the Anishinabe. Each interpretive program is C$5 (US$3.35). For information, contact Kathy Boulanger or Richard Gaywish at **Shawenequanape Camp and Cultural Tours,** 704-167 Lombard Ave., Winnipeg, MB R3B 0V3 (☎ 204/925-2030). Summer only.

In Wasagaming, you can stay at five park **campgrounds** or in motel and cabin accommodations for C$45 to C$130 (US$30 to US$87) double. Wasagaming also has six tennis courts, lawn-bowling greens, a children's playground, and a log-cabin movie theater in the Wasagaming Visitor Centre beside Clear Lake. There are also a dance hall, picnic areas with stoves, and a band shell down by the lake for Sunday-afternoon concerts. At the lake itself you can rent boats and swim at the main beach.

Wasagaming Campground has more than 500 sites, most unserviced. Facilities include showers and toilets, kitchen shelters, and a sewage-disposal station nearby. Rates range from C$9 (US$6) unserviced to C$20 (US$13) for full service. Other outlying campgrounds (93 sites) are at **Moon Lake, Lake Audy, Whirlpool,** and **Deep Lake.** None of these is serviced. For reservations, call ☎ 800/707-8480. Outlying campgrounds are C$11 (US$7), site only. Advance recommendations are strongly recommended.

Elkhorn Resort & Conference Centre. Mooswa Dr. E., Clear Lake, MB R0J 2H0. ☎ **204/848-2802.** Fax 204/848-2109. 57 units. A/C TV TEL. C$139 (US$93) lodge room double; extra person C$15 (US$10); children under 17 stay free in parents' room. Lower off-season rates available. C$249 (US$166) chalet per night; less mid-week and off-season (Mar to mid-May and mid-Oct to mid-Dec). AE, DC, ER, MC, V.

This year-round lodge is on the edge of Wasagaming with easy access to Riding Mountain, overlooking quiet fields and forest. The guest rooms are large, comfortable, and nicely appointed with modern pine furnishings; some have fireplaces and private balconies. At the ranch's common room, you can join a game of bridge or cribbage in the evening. There are also an indoor pool, an exercise room, a game room with a pool table, and a nine-hole golf course. In summer, facilities include a riding stable; winter pleasures include sleigh rides, cross-country skiing, outdoor skating, and tobogganing. Also on the property are several fully equipped two- and three-bedroom chalets (with fireplaces, fire extinguishers, toasters, dishwashers, microwaves, and balconies with barbecues) designed after Quonsets.

DUCK MOUNTAIN PROVINCIAL PARK

Northwest of Riding Mountain via Highway 10, off Route 367, **Duck Mountain Provincial Park** (no phone) is popular for fishing, camping, boating, hiking, horseback riding, and biking. **Baldy Mountain,** near the park's southeast entrance, is the province's highest point at 2,727 feet. **East Blue Lake** is so clear the bottom is visible at 30 to 40 feet.

For accommodations in Duck Mountain, the place to stay is **Wellman Lake Lodge and Outfitters,** Box 249, Minitonas, MB R0L 1G0 (☎ 204/525-4422), which has cabins. Some are rustic, with outdoor washrooms and cold water only, but with fridges, ovens, and electricity, while others are more modern with full bathrooms and fully equipped kitchenettes, plus a covered deck with picnic table. Two have fireplaces or pellet stoves. Full services for anglers and hunters are offered. There's also a beach for swimming. There are three campgrounds in Duck Mountain that offer various levels of service. For reservations, call ☎ **888/482-2267.**

6 On to the Far North & Churchill, the World's Polar-Bear Capital

The best way to explore the north is aboard **VIA Rail's** *Hudson Bay* on a 2-night, 1-day trip from Winnipeg to Churchill, via **The Pas,** a mecca for fishing enthusiasts, and the mining community of Thompson. You can also drive to Thompson and take the train from there. No other land route has yet penetrated this remote region, which is covered with lakes, forests, and frozen tundra. The train leaves Winnipeg at about 10pm and arrives 34 hours later in Churchill. A round-trip ticket (including a bedroom) costs C$1,149 (US$766) for two June to October or C$894 (US$596) at other times. Semiprivate (facing seats with berths) rooms cost C$1,244 (US$830) in season or C$745 (US$497) otherwise. For more information, contact your travel agent or VIA Rail at ☎ **800/561-8630.** You can also fly into Churchill on **Canadian Airlines** (☎ **800/426-7000;** www.cdnair.ca).

If you're up this way in February, The Pas hosts the annual ✪ **Northern Trappers' Festival,** with world-championship dogsled races, ice fishing, beer fests, moose calling, and more. It's usually held the third week in February. Call ☎ **204/623-2912** for information.

Churchill is the polar-bear capital of the world. To the south and east of the city lies one of the largest polar-bear maternity denning sites. The area was placed under government protection in 1996 when the **Wapusk National Park** was established. Visit October to early November to see these awesome creatures. The area is also a vital habitat for hundreds of thousands of waterfowl and shorebirds. More than 200 species, including the rare Ross Gull, nest or pass through on their annual migration. In summer, white beluga whales frolic in the mouth of the Churchill River, and you can sight seals and caribou along the coast. You can also see the aurora borealis from here. For additional info, contact **Parks Canada,** Box 127, Churchill, MB R0B 0E0 (☎ **204/675-8863**).

Churchill, population 1,100, is a grain-exporting terminal, and grain elevators dominate its skyline. You can watch the grain being unloaded from grain cars onto ships—25 million bushels of wheat and barley clear the port in only 12 to 14 weeks of frantic nonstop operation. You can also take a boat ride to **Fort Prince of Wales** (☎ **204/675-8863**), a partially restored large stone fort open in July and August. Construction was started in 1730 by the Hudson's Bay Company and took 40 years. Yet after all that effort, Gov. Samuel Hearne and 39 clerks and tradesmen surrendered the fort to the French without resistance in 1782, when faced with a possible attack by three French ships. From here you can observe beluga whales. May 15 to November 10, the park is open daily 1 to 5pm and 6 to 9pm. Admission to the grounds is free, though there's a $3 fee for any special interpretive programs that may be scheduled.

Cape Merry, at the mouth of the Churchill River, is also an excellent vantage point for observing beluga whales and is a must for birders (it's open continuously June to Aug). The town's **Visitor Centre** is open daily mid-May to mid-November, weekdays only otherwise. For Churchill information, contact the **Churchill Chamber of Commerce,** Box 176, Churchill, MB R0B 0E0 (☎ **888/389-2327** or 204/678-2022). In town, the **Eskimo Museum,** 242 Laverendrye St., Box 10 (☎ **204/675-2030**), has a collection of fine Inuit carvings and artifacts; June to mid-November, it's open Tuesday to Saturday 9am to noon and 1 to 5pm, and admission is free.

Some 240km (149 miles) southeast of Churchill, the very remote **York Factory National Historic Site** was established by the Hudson's Bay Company in 1682 as a fur-trading post. It operated for nearly 2 centuries until it was abandoned in 1957. Several generations of structures have been built near or on the site. The current site referred to as York Factory III was developed after 1788. The depot building is the oldest wood structure still standing on permafrost; its unattached walls and floors allow for the buckling of the earth due to frost heaves. Across Sloop Creek are the remains of a powder magazine and a cemetery with headstones dating from the 1700s. Guided tours are C$5 (US$3.35). The site is staffed only June to September. Access is limited to charter planes or by canoe down the Hayes River. For more info on these sites, contact **Parks Canada,** Box 127, Churchill, MB R0B 0E0 (☎ 204/675-8863).

North of The Pas are two provincial parks. The first is **Clearwater Lake Provincial Park,** at the junction of highways 10 and 287; the lake lives up to its name because the bottom is visible at 35 feet. It offers great fishing, plus swimming, boating, hiking, and camping. The second is **Grass River Provincial Park** (no phone), on Highway 39, a wilderness home to woodland caribou, moose, and plenty of waterfowl. The Grass River is good for fishing and canoeing.

Kaskattama Safari Adventures, 170 Harbison W., Hudson Bay, Manitoba (☎ 204/667-1611), offers a comfortable way to view the polar bears. Their 6-day/5-night trip starts in Winnipeg, where you stay at the Radisson before flying to Kaskattama, built as a fur-trading post in 1923 by the Hudson's Bay Company. Today, the storeroom and warehouse serve as the main visitor lodge and dining room. Two four-bedroom/four-bathroom cabins, each with a screened porch, accommodate a maximum of 16. A naturalist introduces you to the **Cape Tatnam Wildlife Management Area,** home to more than 200 species of birds, caribou, moose, black bear, Arctic wolves, fox, and the great white bears who head to land in July and can be seen foraging along the grasslands, with cubs in tow. Four days are spent at Kaska. The trip costs C$2,810 (US$1,874) per person double. If you like, for an extra C$282 (US$188) per person you can take a helicopter trip to York Factory.

WHERE TO STAY

In Churchill, the 26-room **Churchill Motel,** at Kelsey and Franklin (☎ 204/675-8853), charges C$90 (US$60) double and has a restaurant. Additional amenities, like room service and a bar, are offered at the **Seaport Hotel,** 299 Kelsey Blvd. (☎ 204/675-8807), with 21 rooms at C$95 (US$63) double. The **Tundra Inn,** 34 Franklin St. (☎ 204/675-8831), has 31 comfortable rooms for C$90 (US$60) double.

For nearby accommodations, try **Grassy River Lodge,** Box 1680, The Pas, MB R9A 1L4 (☎ 204/358-7171, or 800/6379852 or 918/455-2324 in winter), open mid-May to October. There's also **Peterson's Reed Lake Lodge,** Box 1648, The Pas, MB R9H 1L4 (☎ YLS-3078 mobile phone).

7 Regina: Capital of Saskatchewan

Originally named "Pile O'Bones" after the heap of buffalo skeletons the first settlers found (native Canadians had amassed the bones in the belief they would lure the vanished buffalo back again), the city of **Regina** (pronounced Re-*jeye*-na) has Princess Louise, daughter of Queen Victoria, to thank for its more regal name. She named the city in her mother's honor in 1882 when it became the capital of the Northwest Territories. Despite the barren prairie landscape and the infamous Regina mud, the town grew.

Today the provincial capital of Saskatchewan, with a population of 193,652, Regina still has a certain prairie feel, though it's becoming more sophisticated, with some good hotels and some rather interesting attractions.

ESSENTIALS

VISITOR INFORMATION   Contact **Tourism Saskatchewan,** 500-1900 Albert St., Regina, SK S4P 4L9 (☎ **877/237-2273** or 306/787-2300; www.sasktourism. com), open Monday to Friday 8am to 5pm. For on-the-spot Regina info, contact **Tourism Regina,** P.O. Box 3355, Regina, SK S4P 3H1 (☎ **800/661-5099,** ext.227, or 306/789-5099; www.tourismregina.com), or visit the **Visitor Information Centre,** Highway 1 East, just west of CKCK-TV, open daily 8:30am to 4:30pm (to 7pm mid-May to Labour Day).

GETTING THERE   **Air Canada** (☎ **800/776-3000;** www.aircanada.ca) and **Canadian Airlines** (☎ **800/426-7000;** www.cdnair.ca) serve Regina. The airport is west of the city, only 15 minutes from downtown. If you're driving, Regina is right on the Trans-Canada Highway. **VIA Rail** trains pull into the station at 1880 Saskatchewan Dr., at Rose Street (☎ **800/561-8630** in Canada, 800/561-3949 in the U.S.; www.viarail.ca).

CITY LAYOUT   The two main streets are **Victoria Avenue,** which runs east-west, and **Albert Street,** which runs north-south. South of the intersection lies the **Wascana Centre.** Most of the downtown hotels stretch along Victoria Avenue between Albert Street on the west and Broad Street on the east. The **RCMP barracks** are to the north and west of the downtown area. **Lewvan Drive** (also called the Ring Road) allows you to circle the city by car.

GETTING AROUND   **Regina Transit,** 333 Winnipeg St. (☎ **306/777-7433**), operates nine bus routes that make it easy to get around. For schedules and maps, go to the **Transit Information Centre** at 2124 11th Ave., next to Eatons. Fares are C$1.50 (US$1) adults, C$1.05 (US70¢) high-school students, and C95¢ (US65¢) elementary-school students. Exact fare is required.

For car rentals, try **Hertz,** at the airport (☎ **800/263-0600** or 306/791-9131); **Tilden,** 2627 Airport Rd. (☎ **306/757-5757**); or **Avis,** 2010 Victoria Ave. (☎ **306/ 757-1653**). You can most easily find **taxis** at downtown hotels. They charge C$2.55 (US$1.70) when you get in and C10¢ (US7¢) per 89m (292 ft.) thereafter. **Regina Cab** (☎ **306/543-3333**) is the most used.

SPECIAL EVENTS   During the first week of June, **Mosaic** celebrates the city's multiethnic population. Special passports entitle you to enter pavilions and experience the food, crafts, customs, and culture of each group. Regina's **Buffalo Days,** usually held the first week in August, recall the time when this noble beast roamed the west. Throughout the city, businesses and individuals dress in Old West style, while the fair itself sparkles with a midway, grandstand shows, big-name entertainers, livestock competitions, beard-growing contests, and much more. For details, contact **Buffalo Days,** P.O. Box 167, Exhibition Park, Regina, SK S4P 2Z6 (☎ **888/734-3975** or 306/781-9200).

EXPLORING THE WASCANA CENTRE

This 2,300-acre park in the city center contains a **waterfowl park,** frequented by 60 or more species of marsh and water birds. There's a naturalist on duty Monday to Friday 9am to 4pm; call ☎ **306/522-3661** for information. Another delightful spot is **Willow Island,** a picnic island reached by a small ferry from the overlook west of Broad Street on Wascana Drive.

Wascana Place, the headquarters building for Wascana Centre Authority (☎ **306/ 522-3661**), provides public information. You can get a fine view from its fourth-level observation deck. Victoria Day to Labour Day, it's open daily 9am to 6pm; winter hours are Tuesday to Saturday 10am to 6pm.

The center also contains the Legislative Building, the University of Regina, the Royal Saskatchewan Museum, the Norman MacKenzie Art Gallery, and the Saskatchewan Centre of the Arts. Also in the park stands the **Diefenbaker Homestead** (☎ **306/522-3661**), the unassuming one-story log home of John Diefenbaker, prime minister from 1957 to 1963, which has been moved from Borden, Saskatchewan. John Diefenbaker helped his father build the three-room house, which is furnished in pioneer style and contains some original family articles. Victoria Day to Labour Day, it's open daily 9am to 6pm. Admission is free.

Legislative Building. Wascana Centre. ☎ **306/787-5357** or 306/787-5358. Tours daily every half hour 8am–5pm in winter, 8am–9pm in summer. Tours can be arranged through the visitor services office. On sessional nights, tours available 6–9pm. Groups please call ahead. Free admission.

This splendid, stately edifice built from 1908 to 1912 boasts 30 kinds of marble in the interior. Check out the mural *Before the White Man Came,* depicting aboriginal people in the QuAppelle Valley preparing to attack a herd of buffalo on the opposite shore. See also the Legislative Assembly Chamber, the 400,000-volume library, and the art galleries in the basement and on the first floor.

Norman MacKenzie Art Gallery. Wascana Centre, 3475 Albert St. (at Hillsdale). ☎ **306/ 522-4242.** www.MackenzieArtGallery.sk.ca. Free admission. Daily 11am–6pm (Wed–Thurs to 10pm).

The art gallery's approximately 1,600 works concentrate on Canadian artists, particularly such Saskatchewan painters as James Henderson and Inglis Sheldon-Williams; contemporary American artists; and 15th- to 19th-century Europeans who are represented with paintings, drawings, and prints.

Royal Saskatchewan Museum. Wascana Centre, College Ave. and Albert St. ☎ **306/ 787-2815.** Free admission. May–Labour Day daily 9am–8:30pm; day after Labour Day–Apr daily 9am–5:30pm. Closed Christmas.

This museum focuses on the province's anthropological and natural history, displaying a life-size mastodon and a robotic dinosaur that comes roaring to life, plus other specimens. A video cave, a rock table, and a laboratory with a resident paleontologist are all found in the interactive Paleo Pit. A new life-sciences gallery is scheduled to open in 2000.

MORE ATTRACTIONS

Saskatchewan Science Centre. Winnipeg St. and Wascana Dr. ☎ **800/667-6300** or 306/791-7914; 306/522-4629 for IMAX. www.sciencecentre.sk.ca. Admission to Powerhouse of Discovery C$7 (US$4.65) adults, C$4.75 (US$3.15) seniors/children 4–13; children 3 and under free. IMAX theater C$7 (US$4.65) adults, C$5 (US$3.35) seniors/children 4–13, C$3.75 (US$2.50) children 3 and under. Combination tickets C$12 (US$8) adults, C$9 (US$6) youths/seniors, C$3.75 (US$2.50) children. Summer Mon–Fri 9am–6pm, Sat–Sun 11am–6pm; winter Tues–Fri 9am–5pm, Sat–Sun and holidays noon–6pm.

The Saskatchewan Science Centre is home to the Powerhouse of Discovery and the Kramer IMAX Theatre. The first houses more than 80 thought-provoking and fun hands-on exhibits demonstrating basic scientific principles, ranging from a hot-air balloon that rises three stories in the central mezzanine to exhibits where you can test your strength, reaction time, and balance. The Kramer IMAX Theatre shows films on a five-story screen accompanied by thrilling six-channel surround-sound. Call for show times (most are in the afternoon).

♦ RCMP Training Academy & Museum. Off Dewdney Ave. W. ☎ **306/780-5838.** www.rcmpmuseum.com. Free admission. Victoria Day weekend–Labour Day weekend daily 8am–6:45pm; the rest of the year daily 10am–4:45pm. Tours at 9am, 10am, 11am, 1:30pm, 2:30pm, and 3:30pm. Closed Christmas and New Year's Day.

This fascinating museum traces the history of the Royal Canadian Mounted Police since 1874, when they began the Great March West to stop liquor traffic and enforce the law in the Northwest Territories, using replicas, newspaper articles, artifacts, uniforms, weaponry, and mementos to document the lives of the early Mounties and the pioneers. It traces the Mounties' role in the 1885 Riel Rebellion, the Klondike Gold Rush (when the simple requirements they laid down probably saved the lives of many foolhardy gold diggers who came pitifully ill-equipped), the Prohibition era (when they sought out stills), World Wars I and II, the 1935 Regina labor riot, and the capture of the mad trapper (who was chased in Arctic temperatures for 54 days from 1931 to 1932). Kids and even adults will love to role-play in the cockpit of the de Havilland single-engine Otter from the Air Services Division and see an audiovisual presentation of training.

A tour also goes to the chapel and, when possible, allows you to see cadets in training. The highlight is the Sergeant Majors Parade, which normally takes place around 12:45pm Monday to Friday. The schedule is tentative, so call before you go. In July and early August, the Sunset Ceremony takes place on Tuesdays just after 6:30pm; it's an exciting 45-minute display of horsemanship by the Mounties accompanied by pipe and bugle bands and choir.

WHERE TO STAY
EXPENSIVE

Delta Regina Hotel. 1919 Saskatchewan Dr., Regina, SK S4P 4H2. ☎ **800/268-1133** or 306/525-5255. Fax 306/781-7188. www.deltahotels.com. 255 units. A/C MINIBAR TV TEL. C$123 (US$82) double. Extra person C$15 (US$10). Children under 16 stay free in parents' room. Weekend and senior rates available. AE, DC, ER, MC, V. Adjacent parking C$5 (US$3.35).

Conveniently located downtown in the Saskatchewan Trade and Convention Centre, the Delta Regina is adjacent to two large retail malls, the Cornwall Centre and the Galleria. The modern guest rooms are elegantly appointed with marble vanities, sitting areas, and desks.

Dining/Diversions: There's the casual Summerfields Cafe, as well as Capers Lounge for cocktails.

Amenities: Room service (7am to 11pm); Waterworks Recreation Complex with three-story indoor water slide, pool, and whirlpool.

Hotel Saskatchewan–Radisson Plaza. 2125 Victoria Ave. (at Scarth St.), Regina, SK S4P 0S3. ☎ **800/333-3333** or 306/522-7691. Fax 306/522-8988. www.hotelsask.com. E-mail info@hotelsask.com. 217 units. A/C MINIBAR TV TEL. C$185 (US$123) double. Extra person C$15 (US$10). Children under 12 stay free in parents' room. Group, senior, and package rates offered. AE, CB, DC, DISC, ER, MC, V.

The hotel's ivy-covered limestone exterior has a rather solid old-world air about it, a satisfying prelude to the modern comfort within. The large, almost heart-shaped clock in the lobby is original to the 1927 Georgian-style building. The guest rooms have elegant high ceilings and decorative moldings; each bathroom contains a hair dryer and an additional phone.

Dining: Cortlandt Hall—boasting terraced seating, stately windows, and a coffered oak ceiling with brass chandeliers—specializes in grills, seafood, veal, and chicken dishes. Entrees are C$15 to C$23 (US$10 to US$15) at dinner.

Amenities: Room service to midnight; fully equipped fitness center with sauna.

Ramada Hotel & Convention Centre (The Sands). 1818 Victoria Ave., Regina, SK S4P 0R1. ☎ **306/569-1666.** Fax 306/525-3550. 251 units. A/C TV TEL. C$140–C$180 (US$93–US$120) double. Children under 18 stay free in parents' room. Weekend packages available. AE, DC, MC, V. Parking C$3.50 (US$2.35).

You notice the Ramada's organic natural quality in the lobby with its earth-color stone walls and plant-filled coffee plaza. The attractive guest rooms have modern furnishings and the usual amenities. Dining facilities include a restaurant and a lounge. You'll also find an indoor pool, a sauna, a sundeck, a whirlpool, an exercise room, and a children's play area.

Regina Inn. 1975 Broad St., Regina, SK S4P 1Y2. ☎ **800/667-8162** in Canada, or 306/525-6767. Fax 306/352-1858. 235 units. A/C TV TEL. C$139 (US$93) double. Extra person C$10 (US$7). Children under 18 stay free in parents' room. Weekend family rates from C$65 (US$43). Group and senior rates available. AE, DC, ER, MC, V.

This inn occupies an entire block and offers numerous facilities. Its guest rooms, most with balconies, have a contemporary decor and louvered closets. Guests enjoy the sundeck and health club. The hotel offers a restaurant, a lounge, and a nightspot.

MODERATE

Chelton Suites Hotel. 1907 11th Ave., Regina, SK S4P 0J2. ☎ **800/667-9922** in Canada, or 306/569-4600. Fax 306/569-3531. 56 units. A/C TV TEL. C$119–C$175 (US$79–US$117) suites. Weekend rates available. Free parking and local phone calls. AE, DC, ER, MC, V.

Located downtown, the Chelton is small enough to provide friendly personal service. The large guest rooms sport modern furnishings. A bedroom/sitting room will contain a table, chairs, drawers, and a couch, as well as a sink, a fridge, a microwave, and a coffeemaker. Even the smallest rooms are bright and spacious compared to most other accommodations. Suites have separate bedrooms and living areas. Facilities include a casual restaurant and lounge.

INEXPENSIVE

✪ **Turgeon International Hostel.** 2310 McIntyre St., Regina, SK S4P 2S2. ☎ **800/467-8357** or 306/791-8165. Fax 306/721-2667. E-mail hihostels.sask@sk.sympatico.ca. 50 beds. A/C. C$13 (US$9) members, C$18 (US$12) nonmembers. Group rates available. MC, V. Closed Dec 25–Jan 31. Lights out at 11:30pm.

Regina is fortunate to have one of Canada's best youth hostels, located in a handsome 1907 town house adjacent to the Wascana Centre. Accommodations are in dorms with three or four bunks; the top floor has two larger dorms, and each dorm has access to a deck. Downstairs is a comfortable sitting room worthy of any inn, with couches in front of the oak fireplace and plenty of magazines and books. The basement contains an impeccably clean dining and cooking area with electric stoves, as well as a laundry. Picnic tables are available in the backyard.

WHERE TO DINE

In addition to the places below, try **Neo Japonica,** 2167 Hamilton St., at 14th Avenue (☎ **306/359-7669**), for good Japanese cuisine; it's open Monday to Thursday 11am to 2pm and 5 to 10pm, Friday 11am to 2pm and 5 to 11pm, Saturday 5 to 11pm, and Sunday 5 to 10pm. Although this is beef country, the **Heliotrope Whole Food Vegetarian Restaurant,** 2204 McIntyre St. (☎ **306/569-3373**), serves ethnic vegan cooking prepared from organic produce. It's open daily 8am to 10pm (closed January 1 to March 1).

The Diplomat Steak House. 2032 Broad St. ☎ **306/359-3366.** Reservations recommended. Main courses C$13–C$40 (US$9–US$27). AE, DC, ER, MC, V. Mon–Fri 11:30am–2pm; Mon–Sat 4pm–midnight. CANADIAN.

This old-style steak house boasts semicircular banquettes and tables set with pink cloths, burgundy napkins, and tiny lanterns. Around the room hang portraits of eminent-looking prime ministers; there are a fireplace and lounge up front. The menu's main attractions are the steaks—20-ounce porterhouse, 18-ounce T-bone—along with coq au vin, veal marsala, poached salmon, and other traditional favorites.

Golf's Steak House. 1945 Victoria Ave. (at Hamilton St.). ☎ **306/525-5808.** Reservations required. Main courses C$12–C$29 (US$8–US$19). AE, DC, ER, MC, V. Mon–Fri 11:30am–2pm; Mon–Sat 4:30pm–midnight, Sun and holidays 4–11pm. CANADIAN.

In this venerable Regina institution, the atmosphere is decidedly plush (note the large fireplace, the piano and antique organ, the heavy gilt-framed paintings, and the high-backed carved-oak Charles II–style chairs). The menu offers traditional steak house fare.

Saje Gourmet Cafe. 2330 Albert St. ☎ **306/569-9726.** Reservations recommended. Main courses C$12–C$22 (US$8–US$15). AE, DC, MC, V. Mon–Sat 11:30am–2pm and 5–9pm. NEW CANADIAN.

Saje is a low-key, almost nonchalant little cafe with quite good food and a pleasantly unfocused atmosphere. There are two menus: The small fine-dining menu offers innovative preparations of beef, chicken, seafood, and wild game; the other menu is almost more inviting, featuring several pages of salads, sandwiches, and bagel creations. Both are available at dinner, making this a good place to go if there are different levels of appetite in your group. The desserts and breads are homemade and very good. The wine list is small but thoughtful.

REGINA AFTER DARK

The focus of the city's cultural life is the **Saskatchewan Centre of the Arts,** on the southern shore of Wascana Lake (☎ **800/667-8497** or 306/565-4500, and 306/525-9999 for the box office). With two theaters and a large concert hall, the Centre is home to the Regina Symphony Orchestra and features many other performance companies. Ticket prices vary depending on the show. The box office at 200 Lakeshore Dr. (☎ **306/525-9999**) is open Monday to Saturday 10am to 6pm.

October to April, the **Globe Theatre,** Old City Hall, 1801 Scarth St. (☎ **306/525-6400**), a theater-in-the-round, presents six plays. Productions run the gamut from classics (Shakespeare, Molière, Shaw, and others) to modern dramas, musicals, and comedies. Tickets are C$12 to C$22 (US$8 to US$15). Box-office hours are Monday to Saturday 10am to 5pm and 10am to 9pm show nights.

The **Casino Regina,** at Broad Street and Saskatchewan Drive (☎ **800/555-3189** or 306/565-3000), is the latest year-round amusement. It has 40 gaming tables plus 500 slots and is open daily 9am to 4am (closed Christmas). The college crowd favors **Checkers,** at the Landmark Inn, 4150 Albert St. (☎ **306/586-5363**), a comfortable, rustic, and relaxed dance spot. In summer, the outdoor area called **Scotland Yard** is also crowded.

A slightly older crowd (25 to 35) frequents the **Manhattan Club and Island Pub** at 2300 Dewdney St. (☎ **306/359-7771**). The upstairs dance club here is open Thursday and Saturday only. For more relaxed entertainment, there's the **Regina Inn Lounge,** 1975 Broad St. (☎ **306/525-6767**), or the **Ramada's Mulligan Lounge,** 1818 Victoria Ave. (☎ **306/569-1666**).

8 Saskatchewan Highlights Along the Trans-Canada Highway

MOOSE MOUNTAIN PROVINCIAL PARK & WEST TO REGINA

Just across the Manitoba/Saskatchewan border at Whitewood, you can turn south down Highway 9 to **Moose Mountain Provincial Park** (☎ 306/577-2600); it's also accessible from highways 16 and 13. About 106km (66 miles) southeast of Regina, this 388km² (150-sq.-mile) park is dotted with lakes and marshes. The park harbors a variety of waterfowl and songbirds—blue-winged teal, red-necked ducks, blue heron, red-tailed hawk, ovenbird, rose-breasted grosbeak, and Baltimore oriole—and animals, including deer, elk, moose, beaver, muskrat, and coyote.

In summer, park rangers lead guided hikes. The Beaver Youell Lake and the Wuche Sakaw trails are also easy to follow. You can hike or bike along the **nature trails;** swim at the **beach** south of the main parking lot and at several of the lakes; cool off at the super-fun **giant water slides** on Kenosee Lake, which include an eight-story free-fall slide (open mid-May to Labour Day); **golf** at the 18-hole course; go **horseback riding;** or play **tennis.** In winter, the park has more than 56km (35 miles) of **cross-country ski trails** and more than 120km (74 miles) of **snowmobiling trails.**

The modern, no-nonsense **Kenosee Inn** (☎ 306/577-2099; fax 306/577-2465) offers 30 rooms and 23 cabin accommodations (with air-conditioning, TV, and phone) overlooking Kenosee Lake in the park. Facilities include a restaurant, a bar, an indoor pool, and a hot tub. Rates are C$82 (US$55) double for a room, C$69 (US$46) for a one-bedroom cabin, and C$89 to C$110 (US$59 to US$73) for a two-bedroom cabin, depending on its age and size. The park also has two **campgrounds.**

MOOSE JAW

Moose Jaw gained notoriety as Canada's rum-running capital; today some restored buildings still retain the underground tunnels used for the illicit trade, and you can tour them (call ☎ 306/693-8097). The **Moose Jaw Art Museum, Gallery & Historical Museum** in Crescent Park (☎ 306/692-4471) has a fine collection of Cree and Sioux beadwork and clothing, plus art-history and science exhibits. It's open Tuesday to Sunday noon to 5pm and Tuesday and Wednesday 7 to 9pm. The town is also known for its **26 outdoor murals** depicting aspects of the city's heritage. For information, call Murals of Moose Jaw at ☎ 306/693-4262.

The **Western Development Museum History of Transportation,** at highways 1 and 2 (☎ 306/693-5989 or 306/693-6556), showcases the roles that air, rail, land, and water transportation played in opening up the West. One gallery pays tribute to the Snowbirds, Canada's famous air demonstration squadron. You can see a large-screen film about the squadron and experience the thrills for yourself on the flight simulator. Museum admission is C$5 (US$3.35) adults, C$4 (US$2.65) students/seniors, C$1.75 (US$1.15) children under 12, and C$12 (US$8) families; preschoolers enter free. **Wakamow Valley** (☎ 306/692-2717), which follows the course of the river through town, includes six parks with walking and biking trails, canoeing, and skating facilities. Free guided walking tours are available to groups on request.

If you stop in Moose Jaw, the place to stay is the **Temple Gardens Mineral Spa Hotel and Resort** (☎ 800/718-7727 or 306/694-5346), offering 96 rooms and 24 spa suites with private mineral-water Jacuzzis. It's a full-facility resort with special mineral pools where you can take the waters. The spa offers a full range of body treatments. Rates are C$90 (US$60) double and C$210 (US$140) for spa Jacuzzi suites.

For more information, contact **Tourism Moose Jaw,** 99 Diefenbaker Dr., Moose Jaw, SK S6H 0V4 (☎ 306/693-8097; fax 306/694-1882).

SWIFT CURRENT, CYPRESS HILLS PROVINCIAL PARK & FORT WALSH

Swift Current, Saskatchewan's base for western oil exploration and a regional trading center for livestock and grain, is 16/km (104 miles) along the Trans-Canada Highway from Moose Jaw. It's known for its **Frontier Days** in June and **Old Tyme Fiddling Contest** in September. From Swift Current it's about another 201km (125 miles) to the Alberta border.

Straddling the border is **Cypress Hills Provincial Park,** P.O. Box 850, Maple Creek, SK S0N 1N0 (☎ **306/662-5411**), and the **Fort Walsh National Historic Site.** En route to Cypress Hills, off the Trans-Canada Highway, is **Maple Creek,** a thoroughly Western cow town with many heritage storefronts on the main street. On the Saskatchewan side, the provincial park is divided into a Centre Block, off Route 21, and a West Block, off Route 271. Both blocks are joined by Gap Road, which is impassable when wet. The park's core is in the Centre Block, where there are six campgrounds; an outdoor pool; canoe, row/paddleboat, and bike rentals; a nine-hole golf course; tennis courts; a riding stable; and swimming at the beach on Loch Leven. In winter there are 24km (15 miles) of **cross-country skiing trails.** Entry to the park costs C$5 (US$3.35); camping costs C$13 to C$22 (US$9 to US$15).

The **Cypress Four Seasons Resort** (☎ **306/662-4477**) offers hotel-style rooms starting at C$75 (US$50), as well as cabins starting at C$65 (US$43) and condominium accommodations from C$99 (US$66) in high season.

Fort Walsh National Historic Site can be accessed from Route 271 or directly from the park's West Block by gravel and clay roads. Built in 1875, the fort's soldiers tried to contain the local native tribes and the many Sioux who sought refuge here after the Battle of Little Bighorn in 1876, as well as keep out American criminals seeking sanctuary. It was dismantled in 1883. Today the reconstruction consists of five buildings and a trading post staffed with folks in period costume. May to mid-October, it's open daily 9am to 5:30pm. Admission is C$6 (US$4) adults, C$4.50 (US$3) seniors, and C$3 (US$2) children.

GRASSLANDS NATIONAL PARK

About 121km (75 miles) south of Swift Current along the U.S. border stretches **Grasslands National Park,** P.O. Box 150, Val Marie, SK S0N 2T0 (☎ **360/298-2257**)—2 blocks of protected land separated by about 27km (17 miles). On this mixed prairie- and grassland there's no escape from the sun and the wind. The Frenchman River cuts deep into the West Block, where you can spot pronghorn antelope. Black-tailed **prairie dogs,** which bark warnings at intruders and reassure each other with kisses and hugs, also make their home here. In the East Block, the open prairie is broken with coulees and the adobe hills of the Killdeer Badlands, so called because of their poor soil.

Although the park doesn't have facilities, there are two self-guided **nature trails,** and you can also climb to the summit of 70 Mile Butte and no-trace camp. The **information center** (☎ **306/298-2257**) is in Val Marie at the junction of Highway 4 and Centre Street (closed weekends in winter).

9 Saskatoon: The Progressive City on the Plains

Saskatoon (pop. 219,056) is the progressive city on the plains. The town still retains a distinctly Western air. The downtown streets are broad and dusty and dotted in summer with many a pickup truck. Those same downtown streets just seem to disappear on the edge of town into the prairie, where grain elevators and telegraph poles become the only reference points and the sky your only company.

Scenically, Saskatoon possesses some distinct natural advantages. The Lower Saskatchewan River cuts a swath through the city. Spanned by several graceful bridges, its banks are great for strolling, biking, and jogging. Much of the city's recent wealth has come from the surrounding mining region that yields potash, uranium, petroleum, gas, and gold; Key Lake is the largest uranium mine outside Russia.

ESSENTIALS

VISITOR INFORMATION Around May 1 to the end of August, a booth is open at Avenue C North at 47th Street. Otherwise, contact **Tourism Saskatoon,** 6-305 Idylwyld Dr. N. (P.O. Box 369), Saskatoon, SK S7K 0Z1 (☎ **800/567-2444** or 306/242-1206; www.city.saskatoon.sk.ca/tourism). Summer hours are Monday to Friday 8:30am to 7pm and Saturday and Sunday 10am to 7pm; winter hours are Monday to Friday 8:30am to 5pm.

GETTING THERE **Air Canada** (☎ **800/776-3000;** www.aircanada.ca) and **Canadian Airlines** (☎ **800/426-7000;** www.cdnair.ca) fly in and out of the one-terminal airport. If you're driving, Highway 16 leads to Saskatoon from the east or west. From Regina, Route 11 leads northwest to Saskatoon, 257km (159 miles) away. **VIA Rail** trains arrive in the west end of the city on Chappel Drive. For information and reservations, call ☎ **800/561-8630** in Canada or 800/561-3949 in the United States (www.viarail.ca).

CITY LAYOUT The South Saskatchewan River cuts a diagonal north-south swath through the city. The main downtown area lies on the west bank; the **University of Saskatchewan** and the long neon-sign–crazed **8th Street** dominate the east bank. Streets are laid out in a numbered grid system—**22nd Street** divides north- and south-designated streets; **Idylwyld Drive** divides, in a similar fashion, east from west. **First Street** through **18th Street** lie on the river's east side; **19th Street** and up, on the west bank in the downtown area. **Spadina Crescent** runs along the river's west bank, where you'll find such landmarks as the Bessborough Hotel, the Ukrainian Museum, and the art gallery.

GETTING AROUND You may need to use transportation only when you visit the University of Saskatchewan and the Western Development Museum. **Saskatoon Transit System,** 301-226 23rd St. E. (☎ **306/975-3100**), operates buses to all city areas Monday to Saturday 6am to 12:30am and Sunday 9:15am to 9pm for an exact-change fare of C$1.50 (US$1) adults, C$1 (US65¢) high-school students, and C75¢ (US50¢) grade-school students.

Car-rental companies include **Avis,** 2625 Airport Dr. (☎ **306/652-3434**); **Budget,** 234 1st Ave. S. and 2215 Ave. C N. (☎ **800/844-7888** or 306/244-7925); and **Hertz,** 16-2625 Airport Dr. (☎ **800/263-0600** or 306/373-1161). Taxis cost C$2.10 (US$1.40) when you step inside and C10¢ (US7¢) every 90m (295 ft.). Try **Saskatoon Radio Cab Ltd.** (☎ **306/242-1221**) or **United Cabs Ltd.** (☎ **306/652-2222**), which also operates the limousine to the airport for C$7 (US$4.65) from downtown hotels.

SPECIAL EVENTS Saskatoon's 8-day **Exhibition,** usually held the second week of July, provides some grand agricultural spectacles, like the threshing competition in which steam power is pitted against gas—sometimes with unexpected results—and the tractor-pulling competition, when standard farm tractors are used to pull a steel sled weighted down with a water tank. The pay-one-price admission of C$8 (US$5) adults and C$5 (US$3.35) seniors/youths 10 to 15 (children under 10 are free) lets you in all the entertainments—a craft show, talent competitions, thoroughbred racing, midway, and Kidsville, which features clowns, games, and a petting zoo. Parking is C$2.50 (US$1.65). For more information, contact **Saskatoon Prairieland Exhibi tion Corporation,** P.O. Box 6010, Saskatoon, SK S7K 4E4 (☎ 306/931-7149).

In mid-August, a **Folkfest** celebrates the city's many ethnic groups. The **Prairieland Pro Rodeo** is held at the Exhibition Stadium in October.

EXPLORING THE CITY

Housed in a striking modern building overlooking the South Saskatchewan River, a short walk from downtown, the **Mendel Art Gallery and Civic Conservatory,** 950 Spadina Crescent E. (☎ 306/975-7610), has a good permanent collection of Canadian paintings, sculpture, watercolors, and graphics. Admission is free. The gallery is open daily: Victoria Day to Thanksgiving 9am to 9pm and the rest of the year noon to 9pm (closed Christmas).

Nearby is the **Ukrainian Museum of Canada,** 910 Spadina Crescent E. (☎ 306/ 244-3800). Reminiscent of an early-1900s Ukrainian home in western Canada, this museum preserves the Ukrainian heritage in clothing, linens, tools, books, photographs, documents, wooden folk art, ceramics, *pysanky* (Easter eggs), and other treasures and art forms brought from the homeland by Ukrainian immigrants to Canada. Admission is C$2 (US$1.35) adults, C$1 (US65¢) seniors, and C50¢ (US35¢) children 6 to 12. It's open Monday to Saturday 10am to 5pm and Sunday 1 to 5pm.

At the **Saskatoon Zoo,** 1903 Forest Dr. (☎ 306/975-3382), 300 species of Canadian and Saskatchewan wildlife are on view—wolves, coyotes, foxes, bears, eagles, owls, hawks, deer, caribou, elks, and bison. There's a children's zoo too. During winter you can cross-country ski the 4km (2½-mile) trail. Admission is C$4 (US$2.65) adults, C$2.50 (US$1.65) seniors/children 6 to 18, and C$8 (US$5) families. May 1 to Labour Day there's a C$2 (US$1.35) vehicle charge. The zoo is open daily: May 1 to Labour Day 9am to 9pm and the rest of the year 10am to 4pm. It's in northeast Saskatoon; follow the signs on Attridge Drive from Circle Drive.

The **University of Saskatchewan** (☎ 306/966-4399 or 306/966-4462) occupies a dramatic 2,550-acre site overlooking the South Saskatchewan River and is attended by some 20,000 students. The actual campus buildings are set on 360 acres while the rest of the area is largely given over to the university farm and experimental plots. The Diefenbaker Canada Centre contains the papers and memorabilia of one of Canada's best-known prime ministers and is open Monday and Friday 9:30am to 4:30pm; Tuesday to Thursday 9:30am to 8pm; and Saturday, Sunday, and holidays 12:30 to 5pm. The observatory (open Sat evenings after dusk) houses the Duncan telescope. The Little Stone Schoolhouse, built in 1887, served as the city's first school and community center (open May and June, Mon to Fri 9:30am to 4pm and Sat and Sun 12:30 to 5pm; July to Labour Day, Sat and Sun hours only). Admission is by donation. You can arrange special tours of the research farm and many of the colleges. Contact the **Office of Public Relations,** University of Saskatchewan (☎ 306/966-6607). To get there, take bus no. 7 or 19 from downtown at 23rd Street and 2nd Avenue.

Western Development Museum. 2610 Lorne Ave. S. ☎ 306/931-1910. Admission C$5 (US$3.35) adults, C$4 (US$2.65) seniors, C$1.75 (US$1.15) children 5–12, C$12 (US$8) families; children under 5 free. Daily 9am–5pm. Take Idylwyld Dr. south to the Lorne Ave., exit and follow Lorne Ave. south until you see the museum on the right. Bus 1 from the 23rd St. Bus Mall between 2nd and 3rd aves.

The energetic years of Saskatchewan settlement are vividly portrayed by Boomtown 1910, an authentic replica of prairie community life in that year. When you step onto the main street of Boomtown, the memories of an earlier age flood your senses. Browse through the shops, crammed with the unfamiliar goods of days gone by; savor the past through the mysterious aromas that permeate the drugstore; step aside as you hear the clip-clop of a passing horse and buggy; or wander down to Boomtown Station drawn by the low wail of an approaching steam locomotive. The museum truly comes to life during Pion-Era on the last weekend in July, when volunteers in authentic costume staff Boomtown and many pieces of vintage equipment are pressed into service once again.

✪ **Wanuskewin Heritage Park.** RR #4, 5km (3.1 miles) north of Saskatoon on Hwy. 11. ☎ **306/931-6767.** Admission C$6 (US$4) adults, C$2.50 (US$1.65) children 5–12. Victoria Day to Labour Day daily 9am–9pm; the rest of the year daily 9am–5pm.

This park is built around the archaeological discovery of 19-plus Northern Plains Indian sites. Walking along the trails, you'll see archaeological digs in progress, habitation sites, stone cairns, teepee rings, bison jumps, and other trace features of this ancient culture. At the amphitheater, native performers present dance, theater, song, and storytelling, while at the outdoor activity area you can learn how to build a teepee, bake bannock, tan a hide, or use a travois (a transportation device). The main exhibit halls feature computer-activated displays and artifacts, multimedia shows exploring the archaeology and culture of the Plains peoples, contemporary art, and a Living Culture exhibit that tells the stories behind the daily headlines.

SHOPPING

For Canadian merchandise, stop in at **The Trading Post,** 929 Railway Ave. (☎ **800/653-1769** or 306/653-1769), which carries Inuit soapstone carvings, native-Canadian art, Cowichan sweaters, mukluks, beadwork, and more. Some galleries showing local artists that are worth browsing include the **A. K. A. Gallery,** 12 23rd St. E. (☎ **306/652-0044**); the **Photographers Gallery,** also at 12 23rd St. E. (☎ **306/244-8018**); the **Arlington Art Gallery,** 265 2nd Ave. S. (☎ **306/244-5922**); the **Collectors Choice Art Gallery,** 625D 1st Ave. N. (☎ **306/665-8300**); and the **Handmade House Handcraft Store,** 710 Broadway Ave. (☎ **306/665-5542**), which specializes in crafts.

WHERE TO STAY

The **Sheraton Cavalier,** 612 Spadina Crescent E. (☎ **800/325-3535** or 306/652-6770), offers a special executive floor for businesspeople, plus a complete resort complex with adult and kiddie pools and 250-foot-long water slides that attract many happy families. A double is C$99 (US$66). The **Ramada Hotel Saskatoon City Centre,** 1st Avenue and 22nd Street East (☎ **800/668-4442** or 306/244-2311), has a very convenient location, opposite the Eatons complex and Centennial Auditorium. A double costs C$77 to C$110 (US$51 to US$73).

The **Saskatoon Travelodge,** 106 Circle Dr. W. at Idylwyld (☎ **800/578-7878** or 306/242-8881; www.travelodge.com), has doubles for C$72 to C$120 (US$48 to US$80). There's an especially attractive pool area, plus a 250-foot-long water slide and whirlpool. For a pleasant, fairly priced room, the 80-room **Comfort Inn,** 2155 Northridge Dr. (☎ **800/228-5150** or 306/934-1122; www.choicehotels.ca), is a good choice. Rates are C$77 (US$51) double.

Delta Bessborough. 601 Spadina Crescent E., Saskatoon, SK S7K 3G8. ☎ **800/268-1133** or 306/244-5521. Fax 306/653-2458. 225 units. A/C TV TEL. C$119 (US$79) double; C$225 (US$150) suite. Extra person C$10 (US$7). Children under 18 stay free in parents' room. Weekend packages available. AE, MC, V. Parking C$4 (US$2.65).

A gracious hostelry built in 1930 and finished in 1935, the Bessborough looks like a French château, with a copper roof and turrets. Each guest room is unique, though all have venerable oak entrance doors and antique or traditional furniture. Front rooms are large and most have bay windows. Riverside rooms are smaller but have lovely views across the Saskatchewan River. There are a river-view coffee shop and the Samurai Japanese Steakhouse. Facilities include an indoor pool with whirlpool, a sauna, and an exercise room.

Radisson Hotel Saskatoon. 405 20th St. E., Saskatoon, SK S7K 6X6. ☎ **800/333-3333** or 306/665-3322. Fax 306/665-5531. www.radisson.com. 291 units. A/C TV TEL. From C$129 (US$86) double. Extra person C$10 (US$7). Children under 16 stay free in parents' room. Weekend packages available. AE, DC, MC, V. Parking C$6 (US$4).

Offering a riverside location in the heart of downtown, the Radisson is a luxury property, with well-decorated guest rooms. About a third of the units offer river views; the corner rooms are particularly attractive. Summerfields serves three meals daily, and guests enjoy a three-story recreation complex containing a large indoor pool, two indoor water slides, a sauna, and a whirlpool. Bike rentals are available, and jogging and cross-country ski trails adjoin the property.

WHERE TO DINE

Black Duck Freehouse. 154 2nd Ave. S. ☎ **306/244-8850.** Reservations not accepted. Main courses C$7–C$14 (US$4.65–US$9). MC, V. Daily 11am–midnight. PUB FARE.

The Black Duck is Saskatoon's great meeting place, where students, office workers, and travelers come together for a drink (there's a hefty selection of regional ales, as well as 30-odd brands of Scotch), as well for good bar meals, which range from burgers to fish-and-chips to daily specials. The Duck has a friendly publike atmosphere where you'll find it easy to find someone local to talk to—exactly what you may be looking for after a few days on the road.

✪ **Cousin Niks.** 1110 Grosvenor Ave. (between 7th and 8th sts.). ☎ **306/374-2020.** Reservations recommended. Main courses C$15–C$26 (US$10–US$17). AE, MC, V. Daily 5–11pm. GREEK/CANADIAN.

If you have only one dinner in Saskatoon, seek out the not-to-be-missed Cousin Niks. Here you'll find a delightful setting: an open courtyard garden lit from above and made even more charming by the sound of the splashing fountain. Greek rugs add color to the predominantly white background. Various steak and seafood dishes are offered, from baked salmon with lemon butter to rack of lamb with mint sauce. Main-course prices include *avgolemono* (egg-and-lemon) soup, Greek salad, and fresh seasonal fruit. On weekends there's entertainment in the lounge.

St. Tropez Bistro. 243 3rd Ave. S. ☎ **306/652-1250.** Reservations recommended. Main courses C$9–C$18 (US$6–US$12). AE, MC, V. Sun–Thurs 5–10pm and Fri–Sat 5–11pm. CONTINENTAL.

This is one of my favorite downtown restaurants, where the background music is classical or French and the tables are covered in Laura Ashley–style floral-design prints. For dinner, you can choose from a variety of pastas and stir-fries or such dishes as sweet garlic veal or blackened chicken. For dessert, go for the rich chocolate fondue with fresh fruit. This is one place where you can find out what's happening culturally in Saskatoon.

Saskatoon Station Place. 221 Idylwyld Dr. N. ☎ **306/244-7777.** Reservations recommended. Main courses C$10–C$20 (US$7–US$13). AE, DC, MC, V. Mon–Fri 11:30am–2pm and 5–10pm, Sat 5–10pm. GREEK/STEAK HOUSE.

This is a restaurant with a lot of thematic convergence going on. The dining room faces into a real vintage rail dining car, and the decor reflects Golden Age of Rail nostalgia. However, about half the menu (the better half?) is Greek, with excellent souvlaki and grilled ribs. Otherwise, there's a good selection of steaks and seafood available if the Greek and rail themes don't charm. This is a nice place to come for a drink and nibbles.

SASKATOON AFTER DARK

There's not an awful lot of nightlife, but the **Saskatoon Centennial Auditorium,** 35 22nd St. E. (☎ **306/975-7777**), provides a superb 2,003-seat theater, with a range of shows. The **Saskatoon Symphony** (☎ **306/665-6414**) regularly performs in a September-to-April season. Tickets are C$20 to C$31 (US$13 to US$20).

Among local theater companies, the **Persephone Theatre,** 2802 Rusholme Rd. (☎ **306/384-2126** or 306/384-7727), offers six shows per fall-to-spring season (dramas, comedies, and musicals); tickets are C$12 to C$24 (US$8 to US$16). **Shakespeare on the Saskatchewan,** Box 1646, Saskatoon, SK S7K 3R8 (☎ **306/653-2300;** www.zu.com/shakespeare), produces the Bard in two tents overlooking the river from July to mid-August. Three Shakespeare plays are performed, plus a special Festival Frolics during the season. Tickets are C$20 (US$13) adults, C$17 (US$11) seniors/students, and C$12 (US$8) children 6 to 12; children under 6 are free.

For quiet drinking and conversation, you can't beat the Samurai lounge in the **Bessborough Hotel,** 601 Spadina Crescent E. (☎ **306/244-5521**), or **Cousin Niks** (see "Where to Dine," above). For a more pubby atmosphere, try the **Black Duck,** 154 2nd Ave. S. (☎ **306/244-8850**).

The **Marquis Downs racetrack,** at the corner of Ruth Street and St. Henry Avenue (☎ **306/242-6100**), is open for live and simulcast racing. The live season goes mid-May to mid-October. The racetrack has a lounge, a cafeteria, and terrace dining overlooking the paddock and home stretch. Admission is free. The other place to wager is the **Emerald Casino,** Prairieland Exhibition Centre (☎ **306/683-8840** or 306/931-7149), where you can play five or so table games. It opens at 5:30pm weekdays and at 2pm weekends. Take the Ruth Street exit off Idylwyld Freeway.

SIDE TRIPS FROM SASKATOON

FORT BATTLEFORD NATIONAL HISTORIC PARK   About 138km (86 miles), a 1½-hour drive, northwest of Saskatoon on Highway 16, **Fort Battleford** served as the headquarters for the Northwest Mounted Police from 1876 to 1924. Outside the interpretive gallery, a display relates the role of the mounted police from the fur-trading era to the events that led to the rebellion of 1885. You'll see a Red River cart, the type used to transport police supplies into the West; excerpts from the local Saskatchewan *Herald;* a typical settler's log-cabin home, which is amazingly tiny; articles of the fur trade; and an 1876 Gatling gun.

Inside the palisade, the Visitor Reception Centre shows two videos about the 1885 Uprising and the Cree People. From there, proceed to the guardhouse (1887), containing a cell block and the sick-horse stable (1898), and the Officers Quarters (1886), with police documents, maps, and telegraph equipment.

Perhaps the most interesting building is the Commanding Officer's Residence (1877), which, even though it looks terribly comfortable today, was certainly not so in 1885 when nearly 100 women took shelter in it during the siege of Battleford. Admission is C$4 (US$2.65) adults, C$3 (US$2) seniors, C$2 (US$1.35) students, and C$10 (US$7) families. It's open daily 9am to 5pm. Call ☎ **306/937-2621** for further information.

BATOCHE NATIONAL HISTORIC SITE   In spring 1885, the Northwest Territories exploded in an armed uprising led by the Métis Louis Riel and Gabriel Dumont. Trouble had been brewing along the frontier for several years. The Indians

The Trial of Louis Riel

Louis Riel was tried and hanged in Regina in 1885 Bitter arguments have been fought between those who regard Riel as a patriot and martyr and those who regard him as a rebel. Whatever the opinion, Riel certainly raises some extremely deep and discomforting questions. As G. F. Stanley, professor of history at the Royal Military College, Kingston, has written, "The mere mention of his name bares those latent religious and racial animosities which seem to lie so close to the surface of Canadian politics."

Even though he took up the cause of the mixed-blood population of the west, French-speaking Canadians often regarded him as a martyr and English-speaking Canadians damned him as a madman. Written by John Coulter, *The Trial of Louis Riel* is a play based on the actual court records of the historical trial. It's presented Wednesday to Friday at the Norman MacKenzie Art Gallery during August. Nothing if not provocative, the play raises such issues as language rights, prejudice, and justice. Tickets are C$12 (US$8) adults, C$10 (US$7) seniors/students, and C$9 (US$6) children 12 and under. For information or reservations, call ☎ **306/525-1185.**

were demanding food, equipment, and farming assistance that had been promised to them in treaties. The settlers were angry about railway development and protective tariffs that meant higher prices for the equipment and services they needed.

The Métis were the offspring of the original French fur traders, who had intermarried with the Cree and Saulteaux women. Initially they'd worked for the Hudson's Bay and North West companies, but when the two companies merged, many were left without work and returned to buffalo hunting or became independent traders with the Indians in the west. When Riel was unable to obtain guarantees for the Métis in Manitoba from 1869 to 1870, even when he established a provisional government, it became clear the Métis would have to adopt the agricultural ways of the whites to survive. In 1872, they established the settlement at **Batoche** along the South Saskatchewan River; but they had a hard time acquiring legal titles and securing scrip, a certificate that could be exchanged for a land grant or money. The Métis complained to the government but received no satisfactory response. So they called on Riel to lead them in what became known as the Northwest Rebellion.

Of the rebellion's five significant engagements, the Battle of Batoche was the only one government forces decisively won. From May 9 to May 12, 1885, fewer than 300 Métis and Indians led by Riel and Dumont defended the village against the Northwest Field Force commanded by Gen. Frederick Middleton and numbering 800. On the third day, Middleton succeeded in breaking through the Métis lines and occupying the village. Dumont fled to the United States but returned and is buried at the site; Riel surrendered, stood trial, and was executed (see the box above).

At the park you can view four battlefield areas and see a film at the visitor center. It'll take 4 to 6 hours to walk to all four areas or 2½ hours to complete areas 1 and 2. For more information, contact **Batoche National Historic Park,** P.O. Box 999, Rosthern, SK S0K 3R0 (☎ **306/423-6227**). Admission is C$4 (US$2.65) adults, C$3 (US$2) seniors, C$2 (US$1.35) children 6 to 16, and C$10 (US$7) families. May to October, it's open daily 10am to 5pm. The site is about an hour from Saskatoon via Highway 11 to 312 to 225.

10 Prince Albert National Park: A Jewel of the National Park System

The million-acre wilderness area of ✪ **Prince Albert National Park,** 240km (149 miles) north of Saskatoon and 91km (56 miles) north of the town of Prince Albert, is one of the jewels of Canada's national park system. Its terrain is astoundingly varied, since it lies at the point where the great Canadian prairie grasslands give way to the pristine evergreen forests of the north. Here you'll find clear, cold lakes, ponds, and streams created thousands of years ago as glaciers receded. It's a hilly landscape, forested with spruce, poplar, and birch.

The park offers outdoor activities from canoeing and backpacking to nature hikes, picnicking, swimming, and great wildlife viewing. You can see and photograph moose, caribou, elk, black bear, bison, and loons. (The moose and caribou tend to wander through the forested northern part of the park, while the elk and deer graze on the southern grasslands.) Lavallee Lake is home to Canada's second-largest white-pelican colony.

In the 1930s, this park's woods and wildlife inspired famed naturalist Grey Owl, an Englishman adopted by the Ojibwa who became one of Canada's pioneering conservationists and most noted naturalists. For 7 years, he lived in a simple one-room cabin called Beaver Lodge on Ajawaan Lake; many hikers and canoeists make a pilgrimage to see his cabin and nearby grave site.

Entry fees are C$4 (US$2.65) adults, C$3 (US$2) seniors, and C$2 (US$1.35) children. The park is open year-round, but many campgrounds, motels, and facilities are closed after October. There are a handful of winter campsites, though, if you've come to ice fish or to cross-country ski on the more than 150km (93 miles) of trails.

The town of **Waskesiu,** which lies on the shores of the lake of the same name, is the supply center and also has accommodations. At the **Visitor Service Centre** at park headquarters in Waskesiu, you'll find an 18-hole golf course, tennis courts, bowling greens, and a paddle wheeler that cruises Waskesiu Lake. The staff can tell you about the weather and the condition of the trails; check in with them before undertaking any serious canoe or backcountry trip. The park's **Nature Centre** (☎ 306/663-4512) presents an audiovisual program called "Up North" daily in July and August.

The park has 10 short **hiking trails,** plus 4 or so longer trails for backpackers, ranging from 10km to 41km (6.2 to 25 miles). Several easier ones begin in or near Waskesiu, though the best begin farther north. From the northwest shore of Lake Kingsmere, you can pick up the 20km (12-mile) trail leading to Grey Owl's cabin. **Canoeing** routes wind through much of the park through a system of interconnected lakes and rivers. Canoes can be rented at three lakes, including Lake Waskesiu, and paddled along several routes, including the Bagwa and Bladebone routes. There's terrific **fishing** in the park, but anglers must have a national-park fishing license you can buy at the information center.

The park offers six **campgrounds,** two with more than 100 sites and two with fewer than 30. They fill up fast on summer weekends; rates are C$10 to C$20 (US$7 to US$13). The information office in Waskesiu can issue backcountry camping permits to backpackers and canoeists. Other accommodations are available in Waskesiu, including hotels, motels, and cabins, with rates starting at C$45 (US$30) double and rising to C$180 (US$120) for a suite sleeping six to eight. Most cabins and lodges are rustic in style and often contain stone fireplaces. You could also base yourself in the town of Prince Albert and come into the park on a long day trip.

For additional info, contact **Prince Albert National Park,** P.O. Box 100, Waskesiu Lake, SK S0J 2Y0 (☎ 877/255-7267).

Alberta & the Rockies

14

by Bill McRae

Stretching from the Northwest Territories to the U.S. border of Montana in the south, flanked by the Rocky Mountains in the west and Saskatchewan in the east, **Alberta** is a big, beautiful, empty chunk of North America. At 661,188km² (255,291 sq. miles), the province has just 2 million inhabitants.

Culturally, Alberta is a beguiling mix of big-city swagger and affluence and rural Canadian sincerity. Its cities, Calgary and Edmonton, are models of modern civic pride and hospitality; in fact, an anonymous behavioral survey recently named Edmonton Canada's friendliest city.

Early settlers came to Alberta for its wealth of furs; the Hudson's Bay Company established Edmonton House on the North Saskatchewan River in 1795. The Blackfoot, one of the West's most formidable Indian nations, maintained control of the prairies until the 1870s, when the Royal Canadian Mounted Police arrived to enforce the white man's version of law and order. Open-range cattle ranching prospered on the rich grasslands, and agriculture is still the basis of the rural Alberta economy. Vast oil reserves were discovered in the 1960s, introducing a tremendous 30-year boom across the province.

More than half the population lives in Edmonton and Calgary, leaving the rest of the province a tremendous amount of elbow room, breathing space, and unspoiled scenery. The **Canadian Rockies** rise to the west of the prairies and contain some of the finest mountain scenery on earth. Between them, Banff and Jasper national parks preserve much of this mountain beauty, but vast and equally spectacular regions of the Rockies, as well as portions of the nearby Columbia and Selkirk mountain ranges, are protected by other national and provincial parks.

All this wilderness makes outdoor activity Alberta's greatest draw. Hiking, biking, and pack trips on horseback have long pedigrees in the parks, as does superlative skiing—the winter Olympics were held in Calgary in 1988. Outfitters throughout the region offer white-water and float trips on mighty rivers; and calmer pursuits like fishing and canoeing are also popular.

In addition, some of Canada's finest and most famous hotels are in Alberta. The incredible mountain lodges and châteaux built by early rail entrepreneurs are still in operation, offering unforgettable experiences in luxury and stunning scenery. These grand hotels established a standard of hospitality that's observed by hoteliers across the province. If you're looking for a more rural experience, head to one of Alberta's many guest ranches, where you can saddle up, poke some doggies, and end the evening at a steak barbecue.

1 Exploring the Province

It's no secret that Alberta contains some of Canada's most compelling scenery and outdoor recreation. Mid-June to August, this is a very busy place; Banff is generally acknowledged to be Canada's single-most-popular destination for foreign travelers. A little planning is essential, especially if you're traveling in summer or have specific destinations or lodgings in mind.

Skiers should know that heavy snowfall closes some mountain roads in Alberta in winter. However, major passes are maintained and usually remain open. Highways 3, 1, and 16 are open year-round, though it's a good idea to call to check road conditions. You can inquire locally or call **Travel Alberta** at ☎ **800/661-8888** or the **Alberta Motor Association** at ☎ **403/474-8601** or check their Web site at **www. ama.ab.ca**. If you're a member of **AAA** or **CAA,** call their information line at ☎ **800/ 642-3810.** Always carry traction devices like tire chains in your vehicle, plus plenty of warm clothes and a sleeping bag if you're planning winter car travel.

VISITOR INFORMATION

For information about the entire province, contact **Travel Alberta,** Box 2500, Edmonton, AB T5J 2Z4 (☎ **800/661-8888;** www.explorealberta.com). Be sure to ask for a copy of the accommodations and visitors guide, as well as the excellent *Traveler's Guide* and a road map. There's a separate guide for campers, which you should ask for if you're considering camping at any point during your trip.

Alberta has no provincial sales tax. There's only the national 7% goods-and-services tax (GST), plus a 5% accommodations tax.

THE GREAT OUTDOORS

Banff and Jasper national parks have long been Alberta's center of mountain recreation. If you're staying in Banff, Jasper, or Lake Louise, you'll find that outfitters and recreational rental operations in these centers are pretty sophisticated and professional: They make it easy to get outdoors and have an adventure. Most hotels will offer a concierge service that can arrange activities for you; for many, you need little or no advance registration. Shuttle buses to more distant activities are usually available as well.

You don't even have to break a sweat to enjoy the magnificent scenery—hire a horse and ride to the backcountry or take an afternoon trail ride. Jasper, Banff, and Lake Louise have gondolas to lift you from the valley floor to the mountaintops. Bring a picnic or plan a ridge-top hike. If you're not ready for white water, the scenic cruises on Lake Minnewanka and Maligne Lake offer a more relaxed waterborne adventure.

A Warning

Accommodations are very tight throughout the province, especially so in the Rockies. Make room reservations for Banff and Jasper as early as possible; likewise, Calgary is solidly booked for the Stampede, as is Edmonton for Klondike Days. Advance reservations are mandatory for these events, so call ☎ **888/800-PARK** or 780/471-7210.

Alberta

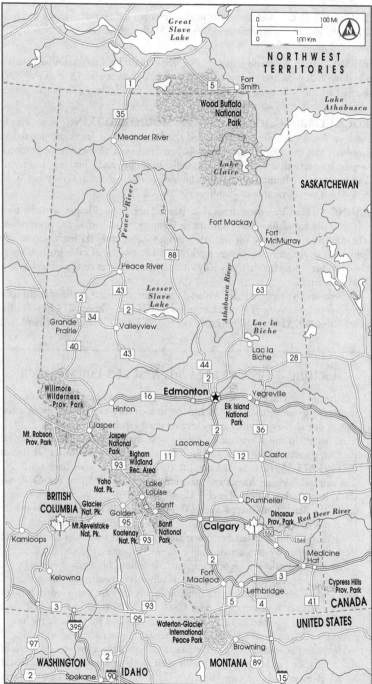

BACKPACKING   Backcountry trips through high mountain meadows and remote lakes provide an unforgettable experience; Banff Park alone has 3,059km (1,897 miles) of hiking trails.

BIKING   Both Banff and Jasper provide free maps of local mountain-bike trails; the ✪ **Bow Valley Parkway** between Banff and Lake Louise and ✪ **Parkway 93A** in Jasper Park are both good less-trafficked roads for road biking. Bike rentals are easily available nearly everywhere in the parks.

ROCK CLIMBING, ICE CLIMBING & MOUNTAINEERING   The sheer rock faces on Mount Rundle near Banff and the Pallisades near Jasper are popular with climbers, and the area's many waterfalls become frozen ascents for ice climbers in winter. Instruction in mountaineering skills, including rock climbing, is offered by **Yamnuska Inc. Mountain School,** a climbing outfitter based in Canmore (☎ **403/ 678-4164;** e-mail yamnuska@banffnet.net).

SKIING   There are downhill areas at Banff, Lake Louise, Jasper, and the former Olympic site at Nakiska in the Kananaskis Country. At its best, skiing is superb here: The snowpack is copious, the scenery is beautiful, the après-ski festivities are indulgent, and the accommodations are world-class. There's a lot of value in an Alberta ski holiday—lift tickets here are generally cheaper than those at comparable ski areas in North America.

   Heli-skiing isn't allowed in the national parks but is popular in the adjacent mountain ranges near Golden in British Columbia. **CMH Heli-Skiing,** 217 Bear St., Banff (☎ **800/661-0252** or 402/762-7100; fax 403/762-5879; www.cmhski.com), is the

---

Getting a Taste of the Old West at a Guest Ranch

Alberta has been ranch country for well over a century, and the Old West lifestyle is deeply ingrained in its culture. Indulge in a cowboy fantasy and spend a few days at one of the province's many historic guest ranches.

   At Seebe, in the Kananaskis Country near the entrance to Banff National Park, are a couple of the oldest and most famous guest ranches. **Rafter Six Ranch** (☎ **403/673-3691**), with its beautiful log lodge, can accommodate up to 60. The original Brewster homestead was transformed in 1923 into the ✪ **Brewster's Kananaskis Guest Ranch** (☎ **403/673-3737**). Once a winter horse camp, the **Black Cat Guest Ranch** (☎ **800/865-8486** or 403/865-3084) near Hinton is another long-established guest ranch in beautiful surroundings.

   At all these historic ranches, horseback riding and trail rides are the main focus, but other Western activities, like rodeos, barbecues, and country dancing, are usually on the docket. Gentler pursuits, like fishing, hiking, and lolling by the hot tub, are equally possible. Meals are usually served family-style in the central lodge, while accommodations are either in cabins or in the main lodge. A night at a guest ranch usually ranges from C$80 to C$100 (US$53 to US$67) and includes a ranch breakfast. Full bed-and-board packages are available for longer stays. There's usually an additional hourly fee for horseback riding.

   Homestays at smaller working ranches are also possible. Here you can pitch in and help your ranch-family hosts with their work or simply relax. For a stay on a real mom-and-pop farm, obtain a list of member ranches from **Alberta Ranch & Farm Holidays,** P.O. Box 396, Sangudo, AB T0E 2A0 (☎ and fax **403/785-3700;** www.comcept.ab.ca/cantravel/vacation.html).

Bed & Breakfast Networks

B&Bs are abundant in Alberta and cheaper than most hotels. These agencies make it easy to shop for B&Bs province-wide: **Alberta and Pacific Bed and Breakfast,** P.O. Box 15477, M.P.O., Vancouver, BC V6B 5B2 (☎ **604/944-1793;** fax 604/ 552-1659), is a reservation service that maintains a network of B&Bs throughout Alberta and BC; rates start at C$55 (US$37) for doubles. The **Alberta Bed and Breakfast Association** (www.bbalberta.com) provides listings of inspected and approved B&Bs throughout the province.

Alberta is rich with hostels as well, especially in the Rocky Mountain national parks, where they're often the only affordable lodging option. All **Hostelling International** hostels in Alberta welcome guests of all ages. To find out more, check out their Web site at **www.hostellingintl.ca/alberta.**

---

leader in this increasingly popular sport, which uses helicopters to deposit skiers on virgin slopes far from the lift lines and runs of ski resorts. CMH offers 7- and 10 day trips to eight locations; prices begin at C$3,700 (US$2,468), all lodging, food, equipment, and transport from Calgary inclusive.

Cross-country skiers will also find a lot to like in the Canadian Rockies. A number of snowbound mountain lodges remain open throughout winter and serve as bases for adventurous Nordic skiers. The historic ✪ **Emerald Lake Lodge** in Yoho National Park (☎ **800/663-6336** or 250/343-6321) is one of the finest.

WHITE-WATER RAFTING & CANOEING The Rockies' many glaciers and snowfields are the source of mighty rivers. Outfitters throughout the region offer white-water rafting and canoe trips of varying lengths and difficulty—you can spend a single morning on the river or plan a 5-day expedition. Jasper is central to a number of good white-water rivers; **Maligne Rafting Adventures Ltd.** (☎ **780/852-3370;** www.mra.ab.ca) has three packages for rafters of all experience levels.

WILDLIFE VIEWING If you're thrilled by seeing animals in the wild, you've turned to the right chapter. No matter which one you choose, the Rocky Mountain national parks are all teeming with wildlife—bighorn sheep, grizzly and black bears, deer, mountain goats, moose, coyotes, lynxes, wolves, and more. See "Introducing the Canadian Rockies," later in this chapter, for important warnings about how to handle wildlife encounters in the parks responsibly and safely. Aside from the Rockies, there's also ✪ **Elk Island National Park** just outside Edmonton, which harbors the tiny pygmy shrew and the immense wood buffalo.

2 Calgary: Home to the Annual Stampede

Historically, **Calgary** dates back just over a century, to the summer of 1875, when a detachment of the Northwest Mounted Police reached the confluence of the Bow and Elbow rivers. The solid log fort they built had attracted 600 settlers by the end of the year. Gradually the lush prairie lands around the settlement drew tremendous beef herds, many of them from overgrazed U.S. ranches in the south. Calgary grew into a cattle metropolis and a large meat-packing center. When World War II ended, the placid city numbered barely 100,000.

The oil boom erupted in the late 1960s, and in one decade the pace and complexion of the city changed utterly. The population shot up at a pace that made statisticians dizzy. In 1978 alone, C$1 billion (US$667 million) worth of construction was added to the skyline, creating office high rises, hotel blocks, walkways, and shopping centers so fast even locals weren't sure what was around the next corner. In the mid-1990s, the oil market heated up again, and Alberta's probusiness political climate tempted national companies to build their headquarters here.

In February 1988, Calgary was the site of the Winter Olympics, giving it the opportunity to roll out the welcome mat on a truly international scale. The city outdid itself in hospitality, erecting a whole network of facilities, including the Canada Olympic Park, by the Trans-Canada Highway, some 15 minutes west of downtown.

Calgary (population 850,000) has an imposing skyline boasting dozens of business towers topping 40 stories. Despite this, the city doesn't seem urban. With its many parks and convivial populace, Calgary retains the atmosphere of a much smaller, friendlier town.

ESSENTIALS

VISITOR INFORMATION The **Visitor Service Centres** at Tower Centre, 9th Avenue SW and Centre Street, and at the airport, provide you with free literature, maps, and info about the city. These are run by the **Calgary Convention and Visitors Bureau,** whose head office is at 237 8th Ave. SE, Calgary, AB T2G 0K8. Included in their phone services is a useful no-charge accommodations bureau (☎ **800/661-1678** or 403/263-8510; e-mail destination@visitor.calgary.ab.ca; www. tourismcalgary.com).

GETTING THERE **Calgary International Airport** lies 16km (9.9 miles) northeast of the city. You can go through U.S. Customs right here if you're flying home via Calgary. The airport is served by **Air Canada** (☎ 800/776-3000; www.aircanada.ca), **Canadian Airlines** (☎ 800/426-7000; www.cdnair.ca), **Delta** (☎ 800/221-1212; www.delta-air.com), **American Airlines** (☎ 800/433-7300; www.americanair.com), **United** (☎ 800/241-6522; www.ual.com), **KLM** (☎ 800/374-7747), and Air B.C., Horizon, and several commuter lines. A shuttle service to and from Edmonton is run almost hourly by Air Canada and Canadian Airlines. Cab fare to downtown hotels from the airport comes to around C$25 (US$17). The **Airporter bus** (☎ **403/ 531-3909**) takes you downtown from the airport for C$9 (US$6).

From the U.S. border in the south, Highway 2 runs to Calgary. The same road continues north to Edmonton (via Red Deer). From Vancouver in the west to Regina in the east, you take the Trans-Canada Highway.

The nearest **Via Rail** station is in Edmonton. You can, however, take a scenic train ride from Vancouver on the *Rocky Mountaineer* service, operated by the **Great Canadian Rail Tour Company** (☎ **800/665-7245**). The lowest-priced tickets begin at C$539 (US$360) for 2 days of daylight travel, which includes meals and overnight accommodation in Kamloops. Trains depart every 5 days.

Greyhound Buses (☎ **800/661-8747** or 403/260-0877; www.greyhound.ca) link Calgary with most other points in Canada, including Banff and Edmonton, as well as points in the United States. The depot is at 877 Greyhound Way SW.

CITY LAYOUT Central Calgary lies between the Bow River in the north and the Elbow River to the south. The two rivers meet at the eastern end of the city, forming **St. George's Island,** which houses a park and the zoo. South of the island stands **Fort Calgary,** birthplace of the city. The Bow River makes a bend north of downtown, and in this bend nestles **Prince's Island Park** and **Eau Claire Market.** The Canadian Pacific Railway tracks run between 9th and 10th avenues, and **Central Park** and **Stampede Park,** scene of Calgary's greatest annual festival, stretch south of the tracks. Northwest, just across the Bow River, is the **University of Calgary**'s lovely campus. The airport is just northwest of the city.

A Walking Warning

The first thing you'll note about Calgary is how long the east-west blocks are. Allow 15 minutes to walk 5 blocks. You'll also like the "Plus-15" system, a series of enclosed walkways 15 feet above street level connecting downtown buildings. These walkways enable you to shop in living-room comfort, regardless of the weather. Watch for the little "+15" signs on the streets for access points.

Calgary is divided into four segments: **northeast** (NE), **southeast** (SE), **northwest** (NW), and **southwest** (SW), with avenues running east-west and streets north-south. The north and south numbers begin at Centre Avenue, the east and west numbers at Centre Street—a recipe for confusion if ever there was one.

GETTING AROUND   Within the city, transportation is provided by the **Calgary Transit System** (☎ **403/276-1000**). The system uses buses and a light-rail system called the C-Train. You can transfer from the light rail to buses on the same ticket. The ride costs C$1.60 (US$1.05) adults and C$1 (US65¢) children; the C-Train is free in the downtown stretch between 10th Street and City Hall (buses aren't). Tickets are good only for travel in one direction.

Car-rental firms include **Tilden,** 114 5th Ave. SE (☎ **403/263-6386**); **Budget,** 140 6th Ave. SE (☎ **403/226-1550**); and **Hertz,** 227 6th Ave. SW (☎ **403/ 221-1300**). Each of these, as well as other international agencies, have bureaus at the airport. Remember, though, that you'll save money if you reserve your car before leaving home.

To summon a taxi, call **Checker Cabs** (☎ **403/299-9999**), **Red Top Cabs** (☎ **403/974-4444**), or **Yellow Cabs** (☎ **403/974-1111**).

SPECIAL EVENTS

Every year during July, Calgary puts on the biggest, wildest, woolliest Western fling on earth: the ✪ **Calgary Stampede.** To call the stampede a show would be a misnomer. The whole city participates by going mildly crazy for the occasion, donning Western gear, whooping, hollering, dancing, and generally behaving uproariously.

Many of the organized events spill out into the streets, but most take place in Stampede Park, a show/sports/exhibition ground just south of downtown built for just that purpose. Portions of the park become amusement areas, whirling, spinning, and rotating with the latest rides. Other parts are set aside especially for the kids, who romp through Kids' World and the Petting Zoo. Still other areas have concerts, livestock shows, food and handicraft exhibits, free lectures, and dance performances.

The top attractions, though, are the rodeo events, the largest and most prestigious of their kind in North America. Cowboys from all over the world take part in such competitions as riding bucking broncos and bulls, roping calves, and wrestling steers for prize money totaling C$1.1 million (US$734,000). At the world-famous Chuckwagon Race you'll see old-time Western cook wagons thundering around the track in a fury of dust and pounding hooves. At night the arena becomes a blaze of lights when the Stampede Grandstand—the largest outdoor extravaganza in the world—takes over with precision-kicking dancers, clowns, bands, and spectacles. On top of that, the Stampede offers a food fair, an art show, dancing exhibitions, an international bazaar, a gambling casino, lotteries, and free entertainment on several stages.

The whole city is absolutely packed for the occasion, not just to the rafters but way out into the surrounding countryside. Reserving accommodations well ahead is essential—as many months ahead of your arrival as you can possibly foresee. (For help with

lodging, call **Calgary's Convention and Visitors Bureau** at ☎ **800/661-1678.**)
Some downtown watering holes even take reservations for space at their bar; that
should give you an idea of how busy Calgary gets.

The same advice applies to reserving tickets for all the park events. Tickets cost
C$18 (US$12) to C$49 (US$33), depending on the event, the seats, and whether it's
afternoon or evening. For mail-order bookings, contact the **Calgary Exhibition and
Stampede,** P.O. Box 1860, Station M, Calgary, AB T2P 2M7 (☎ **800/661-1678;**
fax 403/223-9736; www.calgary-stampede.com).

FAST FACTS   American Express   There's an office at 421 7th Ave. SW (☎ **403/
261-5085**).

Doctors   If you need nonemergency medical attention, check the phone number
for the closest branch of **Medicentre,** a group of walk-in clinics open daily 7am to
midnight.

Emergency   For medical, fire, or crime emergencies, dial ☎ **911.**

Hospitals   If you need medical care, try **Foothills Hospital,** 1403 29th St. NW
(☎ **403/670-1110**).

Newspapers   Calgary's two dailies, the *Calgary Herald* and the *Calgary Sun,* are both
morning papers. The local arts and events newspapers are *Avenue* and *Cityscope. Ffwd*
is more youth-oriented and a good place to look for information on the local music
scene.

Pharmacies   Check the phone book for **Shoppers Drug Mart,** which has more than
a dozen stores in Calgary, most open till midnight. The branch at the Chinook Centre,
6455 Macleod Trail S. (☎ **403/253-2424**), is open 24 hours.

Police   The 24-hour number is ☎ **403/266-1234.** Dial ☎ **911** in emergencies.

Post Office   The main post office is at 207 9th Ave. (☎ **403/974-2078**). Call
☎ **403/292-5434** to find other branches.

EXPLORING CALGARY
THE TOP ATTRACTIONS

✪ **Glenbow Museum.** 130 9th Ave. SE (at 1st St.). ☎ **403/268-4100.** www.
glenbow.org. E-mail glenbow@glenbow.org. Admission C$8 (US$5) adults, C$6 (US$4)
seniors/students, C$25 (US$17) families; children under 6 free. May to mid-Oct daily
9am–5pm; late Oct to Apr Tues–Sun 9am–5pm. LRT: 1st St. E.

One of Canada's finest museums, the Glenbow is a must for anyone with an interest
in the history and culture of western Canada. What sets this apart from other
museums chronicling the continent's native cultures and pioneer settlement is the
excellence of its interpretation. Especially notable is the third floor, with its vivid evocation of Canada's native cultures and compelling description of western Canada's
exploration and settlement. The chronology isn't so strictly adhered to that there isn't
time for brief asides into whimsy, like the display of early washing machines. Other
floors contain displays of West African carvings, gems and minerals, and a cross-
cultural look at arms and warfare. The second floor is reserved for special shows and
changing displays of paintings and artwork from the permanent collection.

Fort Calgary Historic Park. 750 9th Ave. SE. ☎ **403/290-1875.** Admission C$5
(US$3.35) adults, C$4.25 (US$2.85) seniors, C$2.50 (US$1.65) youths; children under 7 free.
May to mid-Oct daily 9am–5pm. LRT: Bridgeland.

On the occasion of the city's centennial in 1975, Fort Calgary became a public park
of 40 acres, spread around the ruins of the original Mounted Police stronghold. At
the moment, volunteers are reconstructing an exact replica of the original fort, using

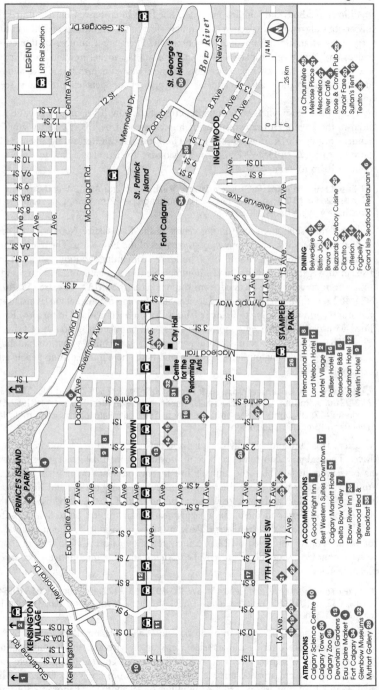

Calgary

LEGEND
🚉 LRT Rail Station

ATTRACTIONS
Calgary Science Centre 🔟
Calgary Tower 🕥
Calgary Zoo 🕥
Devonian Gardens 🔞
Eau Claire Market 🕓
Fort Calgary 🕥
Glenbow Museums 🕥
Muttart Gallery 🕥

ACCOMMODATIONS
A Good Knight Inn 1️⃣
Best Western Suites Downtown 🔳
Calgary Marriott Hotel 7️⃣
Delta Bow Valley 🔳
Elbow River Inn 🕥
Inglewood Bed & Breakfast 🕥
International Hotel 8️⃣
Lord Nelson Hotel 🔳
Motel Village 2️⃣
Palliser Hotel 🔳
Rosedale B&B 🔳
Sandman Hotel 🔳
Westin Hotel 9️⃣

DINING
Belvedere 🔳
Bistro JoJo 🔳
Brava 🔳
Buzzards Cowboy Cuisine 🕥
Cilantro 🕥
Criterion 🕥
Fogbelly 🕥
Grand Isle Seafood Restaurant 6️⃣
La Chaumière 🕥
Melrose Place 🕥
Mescalero 🕥
River Café 🕥
Rose & Crown Pub 🕥
Savoir Fare 🕥
Sultan's Tent 🕥
Teatro 🕥

traditional methods and building materials. The fort's Interpretive Centre captures the history of Calgary, from its genesis as a military fort to the beginnings of 20th-century hegemony as an agricultural-and-oil boomtown. There are a number of interesting videos and docent-led displays; always in focus are the adventures and hardships of the Mounties a century ago. The rigors of their westward march and the almost-unbelievable isolation and loneliness these pioneer troopers endured now seem incredible.

If all this history whets your appetite, cross the Elbow River on 9th Avenue and head to the **Deane House.** This historic home was built by a Fort Calgary superintendent nearly 100 years ago and is now **The Dean House Restaurant** operated by Fort Calgary (☎ **403/269-7747**), open Monday to Saturday 11am to 2pm and Sunday 10am to 2pm.

✪ **Eau Claire Market & Prince's Island Park.** Near 2nd Ave. SW and 3rd St. SW. ☎ **403/264-6450.** Free admission. Market building open 9am–9pm, shops and restaurants have varying hours. LRT: 3rd St. W.

Calgary's new shopping/social/dining center is the **Eau Claire Market,** a car-free pedestrian zone north of downtown on the banks of the Bow River. The market itself is a huge two-story warehouse of a building, containing boutique shops; fresh fish, meat, vegetable, and fruit stalls; innumerable casual restaurants and bars; and a four-screen cinema. Also accessed from the market is the **IMAX Theatre** (☎ **403/974-4629**) with its five-story domed screen. Surrounding the market are lawns, fountains, and pathways leading to **Prince's Island Park,** a bucolic island in the Bow River lined with paths, shaded by cottonwood trees, and populated by hoards of Canada geese. The market is where much of downtown Calgary comes to eat, drink, shop, sunbathe, jog, and hang out—it's easy to spend hours here just watching people and exploring.

✪ **Calgary Zoo, Botanical Garden & Prehistoric Park.** 1300 Zoo Rd. NE. ☎ **403/232-9300.** Admission C$8 (US$5) adults, seniors half price Tues–Thurs, C$4 (US$2.65) children 2–17; discounts off season. Late May to Sept daily 9am–6pm; Oct to mid-May daily 9am–4pm. LRT: Zoo station.

Calgary's large and thoughtfully designed zoo lies on St. George's Island in the Bow River. The **Calgary Zoo** comes as close to providing natural habitats for its denizens as is technically possible—the animals live in environments rather than confines. You'll particularly want to see the troop of majestic lowland gorillas and the African warthogs. The flora and fauna of western and northern Canada is on display in the **Botanical Garden,** and there's an amazing year-round tropical butterfly enclosure. Adjoining the zoo is the **Prehistoric Park,** a three-dimensional textbook of ancient dinosaur habitats populated by 22 amazingly realistic replicas. Call to inquire about special summer events, like Thursday Jazz Nights and free interpretive talks called "Nature Tales."

Calgary Tower. 9th Ave. and Centre St. SW. ☎ **403/266-7171.** Elevator ride C$6 (US$4) adults, C$2.95 (US$1.95) children. June 15–Sept 15 daily 7:30am–11pm; Sept 16–June 14 daily 8am–10pm. LRT: 1st St. E.

Reaching 626 feet (762 steps) into the sky, this Calgary landmark is topped by an observation terrace offering unparalleled views of the city and the mountains and prairies beyond. A stairway from the terrace leads to the cocktail lounge, where you can enjoy drinks and a panoramic view. Photography from up here is fantastic. The high-speed elevator whisks you to the top in just 63 seconds. The **Panorama Restaurant** (☎ **403/266-7171**) is the near-mandatory revolving restaurant; it's open daily 8am to 10pm, and reservations are suggested.

Olympic Hall of Fame and Museum. 88 Canada Olympic Park Rd. SW. ☎ **403/ 247-5452.** www.coda.ab.ca. E-mail info@coda.ab.ca. Admission C$7 (US$4.65) families. Summer daily 8am–9pm; off-season daily 8am–5pm. Take Hwy. 1 west.

This lasting memento of Calgary's role as host of the 1988 Winter Olympic Games stands in the Olympic Park. Three floors of exhibits contain the world's largest collection of Olympic souvenirs, such as the torch used to bring the flame from Greece, costumes and sporting equipment used by the athletes, superb action photographs, and a gallery of all medal winners since the revival of the Olympic Games in 1924. Also shown is a video presentation of the games and their history. Activities include summer luge rides for C$13 (US$9), a new mountain-bike course, and chairlift rides up to the ski-jump tower.

MORE ATTRACTIONS

Devonian Gardens. 8th Ave. and 3rd St. SW, 4th floor. ☎ **403/268-3830.** Free admission. Daily 9am–9pm. LRT: 3rd St. W.

The gardens are a patch of paradise in downtown, an enclosed 2½-acre park 46 feet above street level. Laid out in natural contours with 1.6km (1 mile) of pathways and a central stage for musical performances, they contain 20,000 plants (mostly imported from Florida), a reflecting pool, a sun garden, a children's playground, a sculpture court, and a water garden.

Fish Creek Provincial Park. Canyon Meadows Dr. and Macleod Trail SE. ☎ **403/ 297-5293.** Bus: 52, 11, 78.

On the outskirts of town but easily accessible, Fish Creek Park is one of the largest urban parks in the world—actually, a kind of metropolitan wildlife reserve. Spreading over 2,900 acres, it provides a sheltered habitat for a vast variety of animals and birds. You can learn about them by joining in the walks and slide presentations given by park interpreters. For information on their schedules and planned activities, visit the administration office or call the number above.

Museum of the Regiments. 4520 Crowchild Trail SW (at Flanders Ave.). ☎ **403/ 974-2850.** www.nucleus.com/~regiments. Suggested donations C$5 (US$3.35) adults, C$3 (US$2) seniors, C$2 (US$1.35) youth; 12 and under free. Thurs–Tues 10am–4pm. Bus: 20 to Flanders Ave., then 1 block south.

The largest military museum in western Canada tells the story of four famous Canadian regiments from the early 1900s to today. A series of lifelike miniature and full-size displays re-create scenes from the Boer War in 1900 to World War II; contemporary peacekeeping operations are also depicted. You also see videos, weapons, uniforms, medals, and photographs relating the history of the regiments and hear the actual voices of the combatants describing their experiences.

Muttart Gallery. 1221 2nd St. SW, in the Memorial Library. ☎ **403/266-2764.** www. culturenet.ca/muttart. Free admission. Tues–Wed and Fri noon–5pm, Thurs noon–8pm, Sat 10am–5pm. LRT: 4th St. W.

The Muttart is a contemporary art gallery housed in the handsome old Calgary Library building. The Muttart places a special emphasis on the contribution of local and regional talent and is a good place to see Calgary's contribution to the modern-art scene. National and regional shows also travel to the Muttart.

ESPECIALLY FOR KIDS

Calgary Science Centre. 701 11th St. SW. ☎ **403/221-3700.** www.calgaryscience.ca. Admission (exhibits and star shows) C$9 (US$6) adults, C$7 (US$4.65) youths/seniors, C$6 (US$4) children 3–12; under 3 free. Summer daily 10am–8pm; off-season Wed 1–9pm, Thurs–Fri 1–9:30pm, Sat 10am–9:30pm, Sun 10:30am–5pm. LRT: 10th St. W.

The Calgary Science Centre features a fascinating combination of exhibits, a planetarium, films, laser shows, and a live theater all under one roof. The hands-on, science-oriented exhibits change but always invite you to push, pull, talk, listen, and play. The 360° Star Theatre opens windows to the universe.

TOURS & EXCURSIONS

For tours of the city, contact **White Stetson Tours** (☎ **403/274-2281**), whose 4-hour narrated van tour is C$35 (US$23). The company also offers day trips to Banff and Lake Louise for C$79 (US$53). **Lone Wolf Tours** (☎ **403/246-9586**) also offers tours of Calgary for C$35 (US$23) and trips to Banff, Lake Louise, and the Kananaskis Country. **Hammer Head Scenic Tours** (☎ **403/260-0940;** www.hammerheadtours.com) has 9-hour tours to the Drumheller badlands and the Royal Tyrell Museum for C$55 (US$37). Once weekly, the company runs its van to Head-Smashed-In Buffalo Jump for C$55 (US$37).

   Brewster Transportation (☎ **403/221-8242**), in conjunction with Gray Line Bus Lines, offers a wide variety of bus tours. In addition to a 4-hour Calgary tour for C$45 (US$30), destinations include Banff, Lake Louise, Jasper, the Columbia Icefield, and Waterton Lakes.

SHOPPING

DOWNTOWN   The city's main shopping district is along **8th Avenue SW,** between 5th and 1st streets SW. The lower part of 8th Avenue has been turned into a pedestrian zone called the **Stephen Avenue Mall,** closed to most vehicles and lined with trees, buskers, shops, and outdoor cafes. Major shopping venues lining 8th Avenue between 1st Street SW and 4th Street SW include **Eatons,** the **Hudson's Bay Company, Holt Renfrew, TD Square, Penny Lane,** and **Scotia Centre. Banker's Hall** is another upscale boutique mall on 8th Avenue at 2nd Street SW.

   The **Eau Claire Market,** at the river's end of 2nd Street SW, is a food market with lots of stalls selling produce, fish, meats, wine, and all manner of edibles. The market also has small clothing and accessory boutiques, plus plenty of gift shops.

KENSINGTON VILLAGE   A hip hangout for Calgary's young at heart, Kensington is just northwest of downtown across the Bow River, centered at 10th Street NW and Kensington Road. Crowded between the ubiquitous coffee shops are bicycle shops, trendy new- and used-clothing shops, bookstores, and decor boutiques.

INGLEWOOD   Calgary's principal antiques-shop area is just east of downtown, in the little neighborhood of Inglewood. Lining 9th Avenue SE near 12th Street are historic storefronts that now house dozens of shops devoted to **antiques and collectibles.**

17TH AVENUE SW   The stretch of 17th Avenue approximately between 4th and 10th streets SW has developed a mix of specialty shops, boutiques, cafes, bars, restaurants, and delis that makes strolling and browsing a real pleasure. Many of Calgary's art galleries and interior-decorating shops are also here.

WHERE TO STAY

If you enjoy B&Bs, try **Alberta B&B Association**'s Web site at **www.bbalberta.com,** which has several dozen listings for Calgary. The visitors bureau at ☎ **800/661-1678** can also book a B&B for you.

DOWNTOWN
Very Expensive
Delta Bow Valley. 209 4th Ave. SE, Calgary, AB T2G 0C6. ☎ **403/266-1980.** Fax 403/266-0007. 398 units. A/C MINIBAR TV TEL. C$225 (US$150) double, from

C$215–C$285 (US$145–US$192) suite. Special weekend rate C$99 (US$66), including complimentary gifts for children. Children under 18 stay free in parents' room; children under 6 eat free from children's menu. AE, DC, DISC, ER, MC, V. Valet parking C$11 (US$7) weekdays; free on weekends.

Completely renovated in 1995, the Delta is one of Calgary's finest hotels, with excellent restaurants and an attractive large lobby. These are some of the best facilities in the city if you're a business traveler. In the corner business suites are large desks completely set up for work, with printers, in-room fax machines, cordless phones, and ergonomic chairs; some rooms even have a phone in the bathroom. And after all this there's still room for a king-size bed and a couch and chair to relax in. The standard rooms are also spacious and equipped with all the niceties you'd expect in this class of hotel.

Dining/Diversions: Besides the classy Conservatory restaurant, there are a coffee shop and comfortable lobby bar.

Amenities: Room service, laundry/dry cleaning; complete children's activity center in summer and on weekends, pool, hot tub, sauna area, rooftop deck.

✪ **Palliser Hotel.** 133 9th Ave. SW., Calgary, AB T2P 2M3. ☎ **800/441-1414** or 403/262-1234. Fax 403/260-1260. www.cphotels.ca. 421 units. A/C MINIBAR TV TEL. C$180–C$289 (US$120–US$193) double; from C$225 (US$150) suite. AE, DC, DISC, ER, MC, V. Valet parking C$16 (US$11) per day; self-parking C$12 (US$8).

Opened in 1914 as one of the Canadian Pacific Railroad hotels, the Palliser is Calgary's landmark historic hotel. The vast marble-floored lobby, surrounded by columns and lit by gleaming chandeliers, is the picture of Edwardian sumptuousness. The guest rooms are large for a hotel of this vintage—the Pacific Premier rooms would be suites at most other hotels—and they preserve the period charm while incorporating all the modern luxuries and facilities. All rooms feature cordless phones, voice mail, and business desks with easy-to-reach electrical outlets and modem jacks. Entree Gold rooms come with their own concierge service, express check-in, and cozy private lounge with complimentary breakfast, drinks, and hors d'oeuvres. The Palliser's C$30 million (US$20 million) renovation continues, with new carpets, upholstery, and furniture throughout.

Dining/Diversions: The Rimrock Room has vaulted ceilings, period Western murals, a massive stone fireplace, and hand-tooled leather panels on real teakwood beams. The lounge bar, with its towering windows, looks like a gentlemen's West End club.

Amenities: Concierge, 24-hour room service, secretarial services; new indoor lap pool, health club, whirlpool, steam room, sauna, staffed business center with computer and Internet access.

Expensive

Calgary Marriott Hotel. 110 9th Ave. SE (at Centre St.), Calgary, AB T2G 5A6. ☎ **800/ 228-9290** or 403/266-7331. Fax 403/262-8442. www.marriotthotels.com. 384 units. A/C TV TEL. From C$179–C$229 (US$116–US$149) double. Extra person C$20 (US$13). Ask about "Two for Breakfast" packages. AE, CB, DC, DISC, ER, MC, V. Valet parking C$13 (US$8); self-parking C$10 (US$7).

The newly renovated Marriott is about as central as things get: Linked to the Calgary Convention Centre and convenient to the Centre for the Performing Arts and the Glenbow Museum, it's also connected via skywalk with Palliser Square, Calgary Tower, and loads of downtown shopping. The first- and second-floor lobbies have been redesigned. The guest rooms are large and nicely and subtly decorated, with new furniture, carpets, and upholstery. All have windows that open, voice mail, lots of mirrors, desks set up for business travelers, and ironing boards/irons. The suites are especially nice—the French Parlour suites could pass for elegant apartments.

Dining/Diversions: The Wheatsheaf offers casual family dining; Traders is the fine-dining restaurant. A fireside cocktail bar, the Plaza Lounge, is the spot for cocktails and conversation.

Amenities: Concierge, room service, free newspapers; pool, whirlpool, sauna, health club complex.

International Hotel. 220 4th Ave. SW, Calgary, AB T2P 0H5. ☎ **800/637-7200** or 403/265-9600. Fax 403/265-6949. www.intlhotel.com. 247 units. A/C MINIBAR TV TEL. C$200–C$225 (US$130–US$146) 1-bedroom suite; C$210–C$245 (US$137–US$159) 2-bedroom suite. Children under 16 stay free in parents' room. AE, CB, DC, ER, MC, V. Parking C$8 (US$5).

This soaring tower with a breathtaking view from the upper balconies is an all-suite hotel. Just out the back door is Chinatown and the Eau Claire Market area; the hotel is also convenient to adjacent business towers. The hotel was built as an apartment building, so the suites are up to 800 square feet and contain bedrooms and living rooms, private balconies, and large bathrooms. The decor is low-key, but you get the expected extras, like huge minibars, two TVs and phones, and modem hookups. The very large two-bedroom suites are great for families. Some units have full kitchens. Recent renovations have added new carpets and furniture and a face-lift to all bathrooms. The downside? The elevators date from the days when this was an apartment building; in summer, when tour buses hit, it can be exasperating to wait for the three elevators to serve guests on all 35 floors.

Dining/Diversions: There's a family-dining restaurant and a lobby lounge.

Amenities: Room service, on-call massage treatment, newspaper delivery, courtesy car; indoor pool, Jacuzzi, fitness room, sauna.

✪ **Westin Hotel.** 320 4th Ave. SW, Calgary, AB T2P 2S6. ☎ **800/937-8461** or 403/266-1611. 514 units. A/C MINIBAR TV TEL. C$129–C$230 (US$84–US$150) double; C$247–C$380 (US$161–US$247) suite. Extra person C$20 (US$13). Weekend packages bring the rates under C$100 (US$65), with C$37 (US$24) worth of in-hotel coupons. Family and senior rates available. AE, DC, DISC, ER, MC, V. Parking C$9 (US$6).

The Westin is a massive modern luxury block in the heart of the financial district and probably the single nicest hotel in Calgary. It has undergone a major renovation (C$1 million was spent on the lobby alone) over the past 5 years. Gone is the anonymous business-hotel atmosphere, replaced with a subtle Western feel reflected in the super-comfortable Mission-style furniture, Navajo-look upholstery, feather duvets, and in-room period photos commemorating the city's bronco-busting and oil-boom past. Beautiful barn-wood breakfronts and lowboys dispel the feeling you're in one of the city's most modern hotels. Each guest room has two phones and dataports, voice-mail, and iron/ironing boards. For C$20 (US$14), upgrade to a Westin Guest Office Room and you'll get a fax machine, printer, and copier.

Dining: There are no fewer than seven venues, from a buffet to the Owl's Nest, one of Calgary's favorite special-occasion restaurants.

Amenities: Room service; streamlined check-in for families, baby-sitting service, special kid's menu; strollers, potty chairs, playpens, room service delivery of fresh diapers; rooftop indoor pool with sauna and whirlpool.

Moderate

Travelers on a budget have excellent though limited choices downtown. Luckily, Calgary's light-rail system makes it easy to stay outside the city center yet have easy access to the restaurants and sites of downtown.

Best Western Suites Downtown. 1330 8th St. SW, Calgary, AB T2R 1B3. ☎ **800/ 981-2555** or 403/228-6900. Fax 403/228-5535. 123 units. A/C TV TEL. C$125–C$145

(US$81–US$98) junior suite, C$165 (US$111) 1-bedroom suite, C$185 (US$124) 2-bedroom suite. Extra person C$10 (US$7). Senior, weekly, and monthly rates available. AE, DISC, ER, MC, V. Free parking.

This all-suites hotel is an excellent value. You have a choice of standard, one-, or two-bedroom units; some come with efficiency kitchens (microwaves and refrigerators). The rooms are quite large, almost apartment sized, and fitted with quality furniture and fixtures. The Best Western is a few blocks from downtown but is near the trendy street life of 17th Avenue. The hotel has its own lounge and restaurant.

✪ Sandman Hotel. 888 7th Ave. SW, Calgary, AB T2P 3J3. ☎ **800/726-3626** or 403/237-8626. Fax 403/290-1238. 301 units. A/C TV TEL. C$99–C$135 (US$66–US$90) double; C$175 (US$117) suite. Children under 16 stay free in parents' room. Off-season rates available. AE, DC, DISC, MC, V. Parking C$4 (US$2.65).

This 23-story hotel on the west end of downtown is one of Calgary's best deals. It's conveniently located on the free rapid-transit mall, just west of the main downtown core. The standard rooms are good-sized, but the real winners are the extra-large corner rooms, with great views on two sides and small kitchens. All rooms were renovated throughout in 1997. The hotel's fitness facility is the most complete of any in Calgary; it houses a private health club, available free to all guests, with a large pool, three squash courts, aerobic exercise groups, and weight training. A massage therapist is available by appointment. Room service is available 24 hours, and there are three restaurants and two bars on the premises.

Inexpensive

Lord Nelson Inn. 1020 8th Ave. SW, Calgary, AB T2P 1J3. ☎ **800/661-6017** or 403/269-8262. Fax 403/269-4868. 57 units. A/C TV TEL. C$95 (US$63) double; C$105 (US$70) suite. Extra person C$10 (US$7). Children under 18 stay free in parents' room. AE, ER, MC, V. Free parking.

One of the city's best deals, the modern nine-story Lord Nelson has recently renovated its guest rooms and suites. Though on the edge of downtown, it's just a block from the free C-Train, which will put you in the heart of things in 5 minutes. The inn has a small cozy lobby with red-brick pillars and comfortable armchairs. Adjoining are a coffee shop and the Pub, a tavern with an outdoor patio. The rooms come with two 25-inch TVs, couches, desks, refrigerators, and balconies; the suites come with Jacuzzis.

IN INGLEWOOD

Inexpensive

✪ Inglewood Bed & Breakfast. 1006 8th Ave. SE, Calgary, AB T2G 0M4. ☎ **403/262-6570.** www.cadvision.com/schoderh. E-mail inglewood.bb@cadvision.com. 3 units. C$70 (US$47) double. Rates include breakfast. MC, V.

It's a great location: minutes from downtown, on a quiet residential street backed up to a park and the swift waters of the Bow River. The Inglewood is a rambling modern structure in Queen Anne style built as a B&B. The three guest rooms are simply but stylishly furnished with handmade pine furniture and antiques. Two of the turret rooms have great views over the river. If you're in Calgary with a family or on an extended stay, ask about the newly completed suite, with full kitchen facilities, a fireplace, and TV. Both of the owners are professional chefs, so expect an excellent breakfast.

ALONG THE MACLEOD TRAIL

Once this was a cattle track, but now it's the main expressway heading south toward the U.S. border. The northern portions of the Macleod Trail are lined with inns and motels—from upper-middle range to economy. Here's an example of what you'll find.

Inexpensive

Elbow River Inn. 1919 Macleod Trail S., Calgary, AB T2G 4S1. ☎ **800/661-1463** or 403/ 269-6771. Fax 403/237-5181. www.casino-hotel.com. 73 units. A/C TV TEL. C$89 (US$59) double. AE, DC, ER, MC, V. Free parking.

Directly opposite the Stampede grounds and the only hotel on the banks of the little Elbow River, this inn has a pleasantly furnished lobby and a dining room with a view of the water. There are also a restaurant offering hearty home-style cooking and a casino operating 6 days a week until midnight. The guest rooms are simply furnished; it's a good comfortable hostelry with near-budget rates.

NORTH OF DOWNTOWN

Moderate

A Good Knight B&B. 1728 7th Ave. NW, Calgary, AB T2N 0Z4. ☎ **800/261-4954** or 403/270-7628. E-mail kknight@calgary-stampede.com. 3 units. C$110–C$150 (US$73– US$100). Lower off-season rates. V.

North of the trendy Kensington district in a quiet tree-lined neighborhood, the Good Knight is a modern home built to resemble the Victorian homes surrounding it. The guest rooms have cable TVs and coffeemakers and are decorated according to whimsical themes. The nicest room is the large Buttons and Bows Suite, with a private balcony, arched ceilings, a jetted tub, and a two-person shower. The owners are avid collectors, and you'll smile at their large collection of teapots.

Rosedale B&B. 1633 7A St. NW, Calgary, AB T2M 3K2. ☎ **403/284-0010** or 403/ 284-9568. 3 units. C$90–C$130 (US$60–US$87). AE, MC, V.

This rambling modern place has a pleasingly ersatz quality. Built as a trophy home by a recent central European immigrant, it included such oddities as a huge two-story foyer with wraparound mezzanines and a pool in the basement. That was then. Now the Rosedale is a friendly B&B—sans indoor pool—with three large comfortable guest rooms and two very spacious guest lounges, one with a pool table, a fireplace, a fridge and microwave, couches and chairs, and a hot tub.

MOTEL VILLAGE

Northwest of downtown, **Motel Village** is a triangle of more than a dozen large motels, plus restaurants, stores, and gas stations, forming a self-contained hamlet near the University of Calgary. Enclosed by Crowchild Trail, the Trans-Canada Highway, and Highway 1A, the village is arranged so most of the costlier places flank the highway; the cheaper ones lie off Crowchild Trail. If you're driving and don't want to deal with downtown traffic, just head here to find a room: Except during the Stampede, you'll be able to find a room without reservations; on C-Train, use either the Lions Park or the Banff Park stop. A number of chain hotels are located here, including **Travelodge North,** 2304 16th Ave. NW (☎ **800/578-7878** or 403/ 289-0211), and the **Quality Inn Motel Village,** 2359 Banff Trail NW (☎ **800/ 661-4667** or 403/289-1973).

WHERE TO DINE

Calgary has very stylish and exciting restaurants. The city is going through an unparalleled period of prosperity, and the citizenry's average age is 30. Put these two factors together and you've got the ingredients for a vibrant bar-and-restaurant scene. In general, you'll find fine dining downtown, while more casual bistros and restaurants tend to be found along 17th Avenue.

DOWNTOWN
Expensive
✪ **Belvedere.** 107 8th Ave. SW. ☎ **403/265-9595.** Reservations recommended. Main courses C$21–C$30 (US$14–US$20). AE, DC, MC, V, Mon–Fri 11:30am–10pm, Sat–Sun 5:30–10pm. NEW CANADIAN.

The stylish Belvedere is one of the most impressive of Calgary's many new restaurants. The dining room is shadowy, dominated by couchlike banquettes in black and burgundy. This elegant 1930s steakhouse atmosphere is counterpointed by exposed ductwork, brick walls, and dozens of mirrors, giving the restaurant a faint *Lady from Shanghai* look. The menu blends traditional North American favorites with stand-up-and-take-notice preparations. An outstanding appetizer is the seared fois gras with ouzo-poached pear with mango glaze. Also excellent is a molten Shropshire Blue cheese soufflé with rye-bread toasts and heirloom tomatoes. As an entree, choose from rack of lamb with green-olive crust or the superlative veal tenderloin with potato, apple, and thyme gallette. The service is cordial and professional. The front bar is a sophisticated spot for a drink and a predinner snack.

✪ **River Cafe.** Prince's Island Park. ☎ **403/261-7670.** Reservations recommended. Main courses C$12–C$32 (US$8–US$21). AE, MC, V. Mon–Fri 11am–11pm, Sat–Sun 10am–11pm. Closed Jan–Feb. NEW CANADIAN.

To reach the aptly named River Cafe, take a short walk through the Eau Claire Market area and over the footbridge to lovely Prince's Island Park in the Bow River. On a lovely summer evening, the walk is a plus; the other attractions of the River Cafe are the lovely parkside decks (no vehicles hurtling by) and the excellent food. Wood-fired free-range and wild-gathered foods teamed with organic whole breads and freshly baked desserts form the backbone of the menu. There's a wide range of appetizers and light dishes—many vegetarian—as well as pizza-like flat breads topped with zippy cheese, vegetables, and fruit. Specialties from the grill include venison chop with wild rice and asparagus and pink peppercorn-crusted pork loin with grilled nectarine. Menus change seasonally and read like tasty adventure novels.

Teatro. 200 8th Ave. SE. ☎ **403/290-1012.** www.teatro-rest.com. Reservations recommended. Main courses C$15–C$23 (US$10–US$15). AE, DC, ER, MC, V. Mon–Fri 11:30am–11pm, Sat 5pm–midnight, Sun 5–10pm. ITALIAN.

In the handsome and historic Dominion Bank Building across from the Centre for the Performing Arts, Teatro delivers the best New Italian cooking in Calgary. The high-ceilinged dining room is dominated by columns and huge panel windows, bespeaking class and elegance. The extensive menu is based on "Italian Market Cuisine," featuring what's seasonally best and freshest in the market, which is then cooked skillfully and simply to preserve natural flavors; some of the best dishes come from the wood-fired oven dominating one wall. Lighter appetites can choose from the large selection of antipasti, boutique pizzas, and salads; the entrees, featuring Alberta beef, veal, pasta, and seafood, are prepared with flair and innovation. The service is excellent.

Moderate
Buzzards Cowboy Cuisine. 140 10th Ave. SW. ☎ **403/264-6959.** www.cowboy cuisine.com. Main courses C$10–C$20 (US$7–US$13). AE, MC, V. Daily 11:30am–10pm. STEAK/WESTERN.

The chuck wagon of the cattle-drive days of the 1880s may seem an unlikely place to go searching for fine cuisine, but at Buzzards—surely one of Calgary's most unusual restaurants—the foods of the early Canadian West serve as the inspiration for up-to-the-minute dining. Appetizers include grilled buffalo marrow bones, julienned buffalo tongue with cranberry ketchup, and even "prairie oysters" (calf testicles) sautéed with lemon, white wine, and pickled garlic. (Out here, testicles are becoming a popular novelty meat, and "Testicle Festivals" are common events in small western towns.) If the above dishes don't appeal, other appetizers are Indian smoked salmon, Caesar salad, and traditional soups. Steaks—both prime beef and buffalo—lead out the entree menu. The traditional "Son of a Bitch" stew is also served, as are more familiar dishes like meat loaf, ribs, and fried chicken; watch for Dutch oven specials. The Old West dining room is charming, and there's patio seating in summer.

Criterion. 121 8th Ave. SW. ☎ **403/232-8080.** Reservations recommended. Main courses C$16–C$18 (US$11–US$12). AE, MC, V. Mon 11am–3:30pm, Tues–Wed 11am–11pm, Thurs–Fri 11am–midnight, Sat 4pm–2am. FUSION.

If you enjoy high-concept design, you'll need to make a pilgrimage to this lively late-night restaurant and watering hole. The high-ceilinged dining room is wrapped in mirrors and banks of etched glass that slowly shift color, from orange to yellow and back to orange. The look is somewhere between a 1930s cruise ship and a 1968 Summer of Love. The extensive menu offers lots of small plates and finger food to go with drinks, plus boutique pizza, like a thin-crust Chinese lacquered duck pizza. For entrees, there's sake-marinated grilled scallops in a nest of purple potatoes with jicama salsa or beef tenderloin stuffed with sun-dried tomatoes and chevre.

Grand Isle Seafood Restaurant. 128 2nd Ave. SE. ☎ **403/269-7783.** Reservations recommended on weekends. Most dishes under C$12 (US$8). AE, MC, V. Daily 10am–midnight. CANTONESE/SEAFOOD.

This is one of Chinatown's best restaurants, and the Grand Isle's beautiful dining room overlooks the Bow River. Pick your entree from the saltwater tanks, then enjoy the view. Dim sum is served daily; there are a huge lunch buffet on weekdays and a weekend brunch service.

Mescalero. 1315 1st St. SW. ☎ **403/266-3339.** Fax 403/265-0607. Reservations recommended. Most dishes around C$12–C$22 (US$8–US$15). AE, DC, ER, MC, V. Mon–Fri 11:30am–11pm, Sat–Sun 11am–2am, Sun brunch from 11:30am. SOUTHWESTERN.

Mescalero specializes in tapas—small dishes of salad, tiny sandwiches, grilled meats, zesty dips, cheese, minipizzas, and more. Assemble them into a meal as you see fit. As long as you're lucky enough to score a table, just order some wine and an ongoing series of tapas. Most dishes will provide a good-sized nibble for a table of four. More standard lunch and dinner entrees—usually Southwestern in derivation—are also available.

Inexpensive

Budget diners have two strongholds in downtown Calgary: Chinatown and the Eau Claire Market. There are dozens of inexpensive restaurants in **Chinatown,** not all Chinese: check out Vietnamese and Thai options. Dim sum is widely available and inexpensive. **Eau Claire Market,** just north of downtown along the river, is a food grazer's dream. Two floors of food stalls and tiny restaurants in the market itself only begin to paint the picture. Put together a picnic with fresh bread, cheese, and wine or grab an ethnic takeout, and mosey on over to the park like everyone else in Calgary.

ON 17TH AVENUE

Seventeenth Avenue, roughly between 4th Street SW and 10th Street SW, is home to many of Calgary's best casual restaurants and bistros. Take a cab or drive over and walk the busy cafe-lined streets, perusing the menus; the restaurants listed below are just the beginning.

A good place to go and get a feel for the avenue is **Melrose Place,** 730 17th Ave. SW (☎ **403/228-3566**), a bar/restaurant that has the best deck seating in the area (sit by the street or by a waterfall). Also check out **Fogbelly,** 719 17th Ave. SW (☎ **403/ 228-7898**), an amazing deli and gourmet takeout joint run by the same folks who operate Brava (below).

Expensive

☉ La Chaumière. 139 17th Ave. SW. ☎ **403/228-5690.** www.calgarymenus.com/ lachaumiere. Reservations recommended. Main courses C$18–C$28 (US$12–US$19). AE, DC, MC, V. Mon–Fri noon–2pm; Mon–Sat 6pm–midnight. FRENCH.

Winner of half a dozen awards for culinary excellence, La Chaumière is a discreetly luxurious temple of fine dining. Dining here is an occasion to dress up, and this is one of the few spots in town that enforce a dress code—men must wear jackets and ties. The impressively broad menu is based on classic French preparations but features local Alberta meats and produce. In its new location, La Chaumière has more room than ever and offers plenty of patio seating in summer. If you want a special-occasion restaurant in Calgary, this is it.

Moderate

Bistro Jo Jo. 917 17th Ave. SW. ☎ **403/245-2382.** Reservations recommended on week-ends. Main courses C$14–C$19 (US$9–US$13). AE, DC, MC, V. Mon–Fri 11:30am–2pm (except summer) and 5:30–10:30pm, Sat 5:30–10:30pm. PROVENÇAL.

Jo Jo's is a classic French bistro, right down to the tiled floor, mirrors, banquettes, fan-back chairs, and tiny tables. The food is moderately priced for the quality and atmos-phere. All your French favorites are here: duck breast, escargot, lamb, and even seafood *marmite* (saffron-infused sea bass, tuna, and mussels in fennel-and-carrot broth). The desserts are worth a trip in themselves.

☉ Brava. 723 17th Ave. SW. ☎ **403/228-1854.** Reservations recommended. Main courses C$15–C$21 (US$10–US$14). AE, DC, MC, V. Mon–Tues 11am–11pm, Wed–Sat 11am–midnight. NEW CANADIAN.

One of Calgary's most exciting new restaurants, Brava is an offshoot of one of the city's most successful catering companies. The beautifully lit relaxed dining room serves a variety of dishes, from elegant appetizers and boutique pizzas to traditional main courses with contemporary zest. For an appetizer, try the beef carpaccio with gor-gonzola nuggets and chokecherry vinaigrette. For an entree, try the venison schnitzel with lemon-oregano cream or grilled salmon with guava barbecue sauce. Eighty vari-eties of wine are available by the glass.

Cilantro. 338 17th Ave. SW. ☎ **403/229-1177.** Reservations recommended on weekends. Main courses C$9–C$20 (US$6–US$13). AE, DC, MC, V. Sun–Thurs 11am–11pm, Fri–Sat 11am–midnight. INTERNATIONAL.

Cilantro has an attractive stucco storefront, plus a pleasant garden patio with a veranda bar. The food is eclectic (some would call it Californian). The pasta dishes are as various as beef tenderloin with wild mushrooms in Zinfandel sauce and ginger radi-atore with julienned vegetables and chili sauce. Chicken breasts come stuffed with roasted peppers and dressed with green-onion sauce. The wood-fired pizzas—with mostly Mediterranean ingredients—seem almost tame in comparison. However, the food is excellent and the setting casual and friendly.

Rose and Crown Pub. 1503 4th St. SW. (just off 17th Ave. SW). ☎ **403/244-7757.** Reser-vations not accepted. Main courses C$7–C$13 (US$4.65–US$9). MC, V. Mon–Sat 11am–2am, Sun 10am–2pm. PUB FARE.

This traditional English pub has lots of quiet outdoor seating, good ales, and a menu featuring sandwiches, fish-and-chips, and other light entrees. This is a good place to gather if you find the scene on 17th Avenue a little too precious.

Savoir Fare. 907 17th Ave. SW. ☎ **403/245-6040.** Reservations recommended. Main courses C$13–C$26 (US$9–US$17). AE, DC, MC, V. Mon–Thurs 11am–11pm, Fri–Sat 11am–midnight, Sun 11am–10pm (May to late Aug 5–10pm only). NEW CANADIAN.

One of 17th Avenue's most coolly elegant places, Savoir Fare offers a tempting selection of seasonally changing and inventive menus. Preparations tend to mix classic technique with nouveau ingredients, producing very tasty results. You don't have to overindulge to enjoy yourself—there's a good selection of interesting salads and sandwiches—but the entrees are hard to resist. The vegetable napoleon and beef tenderloin crusted with pepper and ground coffee beans are sure to please. The wine list is quite good.

Sultan's Tent. 909 17th Ave. SW. ☎ **403/244-2333.** Reservations recommended on weekends. Main courses C$11–C$17 (US$7–US$11). AE, DC, MC, V. Mon–Sat 5:30–11pm. MOROCCAN.

Though the Sultan's Tent is in a modern Western building, the interior has been transformed by carpets and tapestries into a pretty good imitation of a Saharan tent. If you like great couscous or tangines, then you definitely should make this a stop. Go all out and order the C$28 (US$19) per-person Sultan's Feast, which includes all the trimmings and provides an evening's worth of eating and entertainment.

CALGARY AFTER DARK

THE PERFORMING ARTS   The **Calgary Centre for Performing Arts,** 205 8th Ave. SE (☎ **403/294-7455;** www.culturenet.ca/cpa), gives the city the kind of cultural hub many places twice as big still lack. The center houses the 1,800-seat Jack Singer Concert Hall, home of the Calgary Philharmonic Orchestra; the Max Bell Theatre; the Theatre Calgary; the Alberta Theatre Projects; and the Martha Cohen Theatre, which puts on some avant-garde and innovative performances. Call the center, check the Web sites, or consult the newspapers for info on what's currently being performed.

The magnificent **Jubilee Auditorium,** 14th Avenue and 14th Street NW on the Southern Alberta Institute of Technology campus (☎ **403/297-8000**), seats 2,700. An acoustical marvel, the performance hall is high on a hill with a panoramic view. The Calgary Opera performs three operas yearly here, and periodic productions by the Alberta Ballet Company are also part of the auditorium's varied programs.

A DINNER THEATER   Calgary loves dinner theater, and **Stage West,** 727 42nd Ave. SE (☎ **403/243-6642**), puts on polished performances as well as delectable

Summer Jazz & Shakespeare

Every Thursday evening late June to August, the Calgary Zoo sponsors **Jazzoo,** with live bands. The concerts start at 6pm, and tickets are usually C$5 (US$3.35). You can buy dinner from concessionaires or bring your own. For information, call ☎ 403/232-9300.

Early July to mid-August, **Shakespeare in the Park** (☎ 403/240-6374) presents the Bard's works Thursday to Saturday at 7pm at Prince's Island Park in the Bow River. Admission is free (donations are appreciated, though).

buffet fare. The buffet functions 6 to 8pm, then the show starts. Performances are Tuesday to Sunday, and tickets are C$42 to C$73 (US$28 to US$49).

THE CLUB & BAR SCENE Cover charges at most clubs are C$5 (US$3.35) to C$10 (US$7) for live music. Pick up a copy of *Ffwd* or *Calgary Straight* for up-to-date listings.

There are three major centers for nightlife in central Calgary. The **Eau Claire Market** area, parklike and car free, is also the home of the **Hard Rock Cafe,** 101 Barclay Parade SW (☎ **403/263-7625**), with its Beatles stained-glass window and 70-foot-long guitar suspended from the ceiling. The **Barleymill Neighbourhood Pub,** 201 Barclay Parade SW (☎ **403/290-1500**), is just across the square and is a cross between a collegiate hangout and a brew pub. **The Garage,** in the Eau Claire Market (☎ **403/262-6762**), is the hip place to play billiards and listen to really loud alternative rock.

If you're looking for the dance clubs, there's a knot of five or so venues near the corner of 1st Street SW and 12th Avenue. **Crazy Horse,** 1315 1st St. SW (☎ **403/266-3339**), is an immensely popular, slightly precious nightclub with lines out the door; it's open Thursday, Friday, and Saturday only. The **Tasmanian Ballroom,** or the Taz, upstairs at 12th Avenue SW and 1st Street (☎ **403/266-1824**), is a bit grittier and even louder. The **Night Gallery,** 1209B 1st St. SW (☎ **403/264-4484**), has alternative bands and theme nights; it's open from 9pm to 3am.

Among the cafes and galleries on 17th Avenue are more nightclubs. **Republik,** 219 17th Ave. SW (☎ **403/244-1884**), is the main alternative music venue in Calgary. **Arena,** 318 17th Ave. SW (☎ **403/228-5730**), is another hot spot for dancing, as is the basement at **The Mercury,** 801B 17th Ave. SW (☎ **403/541-1175**). **Kaos Jazz and Blues Bistro,** 718 17th Ave. SW (☎ **403/228-9997**), is one of western Canada's top jazz clubs, frequently hosting international bands. **The Ship and Anchor Pub,** 534 17th Ave. SW (☎ **403/245-3333**), is a youthful hangout with eclectic alternative music and two outdoor patios; expect lines out the door on summer nights. **Detour,** 318 17th Ave. SW (☎ **403/244-8537**), a lively disco, is a good place to begin exploring gay Calgary. The best gay dance bar is **Boyztown,** 213 10th Avenue SW (☎ **403/265-2028**), with three dance floors, but you'll need to buy a membership (around C$20/US$13) to get in.

Put on your cowboy boots and swing your partner out to **Ranchman's,** 9615 Macleod Trail S. (☎ **403/253-1100**), the best country-western dance bar in the city; it offers free dance lessons during the week at 7pm. **Dusty's,** 1088 Olympic Park Way SE, 4 blocks north of the Saddledome (☎ **403/263-5343**), has the city's largest floating dance floor, with live country bands on weekend evenings and free line-dancing lessons on Wednesday and Thursday.

If you're just looking for a convivial drink, head to **Bottlescrew Bill's Old English Pub,** 1st Street and 10th Avenue SW (☎ **403/263-7900**), a friendly neighborhood pub with outdoor seating and Alberta's widest selection of beers, including many from the local Big Rock microbrewery. Upstairs early in the evening, **The Mercury** (see above) is a great spot for a cocktail.

CASINOS There are several legitimate casinos whose proceeds go wholly to charities. None imposes a cover charge. **Cash Casino Place,** 4040B Blackfoot Trail SE (☎ **403/243-4812**), operates with a restaurant on the premises Monday to Saturday noon to midnight. The **Elbow River Inn Casino,** 1919 Macleod Trail S. (☎ **403/266-4355**), is part of a hotel by the same name (see above). It offers the usual games plus a variation called Red Dog. The minimum stake is C$2 (US$1.35) and the maximum C$500 (US$334). It's open Monday to Saturday 10am to 3am.

On the Trail of Dinosaurs in the Alberta Badlands

The Red Deer River slices through Alberta's rolling prairies east of Calgary, revealing underlying sedimentary deposits that have eroded into badlands. These expanses of desert-like hills, strange rock turrets, and banded cliffs were laid down about 75 million years ago, when this area was a low coastal plain in the heyday of the dinosaurs. Erosion has incised through these deposits spectacularly, revealing a vast cemetery of Cretaceous life. Paleontologists have excavated here since the 1880s, and the Alberta badlands have proved to be one of the most important dinosaur-fossil sites in the world.

Two separate areas have been preserved and developed for research and viewing. Closest to Calgary (145km/90 miles northeast) is the ✪ **Royal Tyrrell Museum of Palaeontology,** P.O. Box 7500, Drumheller, AB T0J 0Y0 (☎ **888/440-4240** or 403/823-7707; fax 403/823-7131; www.tyrrellmuseum.com; e-mail info@tyrrellmuseum.com). North of Drumheller, this is one of the world's best paleontology museums and educational facilities. It offers far more than just impressive skeletons and life-sized models, though it has dozens of them. The entire fossil record of the earth is explained, era by era, with an impressive variety of media and educational tools. You walk through a prehistoric garden, watch numerous videos, use computers to "design" dinosaurs for specific habitats, watch plate tectonics at work, and see museum technicians preparing fossils. The museum is also a renowned research facility where scientists study all forms of ancient life. Summer hours are daily 9am to 9pm and winter hours Tuesday to Sunday 10am to 5pm. Admission is C$7 (US$4.65) adults, C$6 (US$4) seniors, C$3 (US$2) children, and C$15 (US$10) families.

Radiating out from Drumheller and the museum are a number of interesting side trips. Pick up a map from the museum and follow an hour's loop drive into the badlands along **North Dinosaur Trail.** The paved road passes two viewpoints over the badlands and crosses a free car-ferry on the Red Deer River before returning to Drumheller along the **South Dinosaur Trail.** A second loop passes through Rosedale to the south, past a ghost town, hoodoo formations, and a historic coal mine.

DAY TRIPS FROM CALGARY: THE OLD WEST

The Old West isn't very old in Alberta. If you're interested in the life and culture of the cowboy and rancher, stop at one of the following sights. Both are short and very scenic detours on the way from Calgary to the Rocky Mountains.

The **Western Heritage Centre** (☎ **403/932-3514;** www.whcs.com) is 15 minutes west of Calgary in the little ranching town of Cochrane. This new museum and interpretive center is at the Cochrane Ranch Provincial Historic Site, which preserves Alberta's first large-scale cattle ranch, established in 1881. The center commemorates traditional farm and ranch life, contains a rodeo hall of fame, and offers insights into this most Western of sporting events. Special events—often rodeo-related—are scheduled throughout summer; call for a schedule. To reach Cochrane, follow Crowchild Trail (which becomes Highway 1A) out of Calgary; from Highway 1 to Banff, take Highway 22 north to Cochrane. Admission is C$8 (US$5) adults, C$6 (US$4) students/seniors, C$3.50 (US$2.35) children, and C$20 (US$13) families. It's open late May to mid-October daily 9am to 5pm.

Dinosaur Provincial Park is in Red Deer River Valley near Brooks (about 225km/140 miles east of Calgary and 193km/120 miles southeast of Drumheller) and contains the world's greatest concentration of fossils from the late Cretaceous period. More than 300 complete dinosaur skeletons have been found in the area, which has been named a World Heritage Site. Park excavations continue from early June to late August, based out of the Field Station of the Royal Tyrrell Museum. Much of the park is a natural preserve, with access restricted to guided interpretive bus tours and hikes. Tours run daily mid-May to Labour Day and on weekends to mid-October. May to August, lab tours run so you can view fossil preparation. Other programs include evening hikes and campfire and amphitheater presentations in July and August. Prices for tours and hikes are C$4.50 (US$3) adults and C$2.25 (US$1.50) youths 6 to 15; children under 6 are free. Space is limited, so be prepared to be flexible with your choices. "Rush" tickets are sold at 8:30am for that day's events. Reservations are strongly encouraged in July and August. Five self-guiding trails and two outdoor fossil displays are also available. Facilities at the park include a campground, a picnic area, and a service center.

For more information, contact **Dinosaur Provincial Park,** P.O. Box 60, Patricia, AB T0J 2K0 (☎ **403/378-4342;** fax 403/378-4247; www.gov.ab.ca/env/parks/prov_parks/dinosaur/). To make tour reservations, call ☎ **403/378-4344** during the week.

If you're really keen on dinosaurs, you can **participate in one of the digs.** Day programs only are offered at the Royal Tyrrell Museum and include a half-day kids' event, a dig watch at C$12 (US$8) adults, or a day spent helping with the dig at C$85 (US$57) adults. Weeklong programs only are offered at Dinosaur Provincial Park. On the Field Experience Program, you get to be part of the dig crew for 7 days for C$875 (US$584), including bed and board. For all programs, contact the Bookings Officer at the **Royal Tyrrell Museum,** P.O. Box 7500, Drumheller, AB T0J 0Y0 (☎ **403/823-7707;** fax 403/823-7131).

An hour southwest of Calgary, the **Bar U Ranch National Historic Site** (☎ **403/395-2212**) is a well-preserved and still-operating cattle ranch that celebrates both the past and the present of the area's ranching traditions. Tours of the ranch's 35 original buildings (some from the 1880s) are available; a video of the area's ranching history is shown in the interpretive center. Special events include displays of ranching activities and techniques; this is a real ranch, so you might get to watch a branding or roundup—at the very least you'll get to see some horseplay! To reach the Bar U, follow Highway 22 south from Calgary to the little community of Longview. Admission is C$6 (US$4) adults, C$4.60 (US$3.05) seniors, and C$2.90 (US$1.95) children. It's open mid-May to mid-October daily 10am to 6pm.

3 Southern Alberta Highlights

South of Calgary, running through the grain fields and prairies between Medicine Hat and Crowsnest Pass in the Canadian Rockies, Highway 3 roughly parallels the

U.S.-Canadian border. This rural connector links several smaller Alberta centers and remote but interesting natural and historic sites.

MEDICINE HAT & CYPRESS HILLS PROVINCIAL PARK

Medicine Hat (291km/180 miles southeast of Calgary) is at the center of Alberta's vast natural-gas fields. To be near this inexpensive source of energy, a lot of modern industry has moved to Medicine Hat, making this an unlikely factory town surrounded by grain fields. In the early 1900s, the primary industry was fashioning brick and china from the local clay deposits. Consequently, the town's old downtown is a showcase of handsome frontier-era brick buildings; take an hour and explore the historic city center, flanked by the South Saskatchewan River.

Eighty-one kilometers (50 miles) south of Medicine Hat is **Cypress Hills Provincial Park,** 316km² (122 sq. miles) of highlands—outliers of the Rockies—that rise 1,500 feet above the flat prairie grasslands. In this preserve live many species of plants and animals, including elk and moose, that are usually found in the Rockies.

LETHBRIDGE

East of Fort Macleod (105km/65 miles north of the U.S. border, 216km/134 miles southeast of Calgary) lies **Lethbridge,** a delightful garden city and popular convention site (it gets more annual hours of sunshine than most places in Canada). Lethbridge started out as Fort Whoop-up, a notorious trading post that traded whiskey to the Plains Indians in return for buffalo hides and horses. The post boomed during the 1870s, until the Mounties arrived to bring order. Today Lethbridge is a pleasant prairie city and Alberta's third largest, with a population of 66,000. For details, contact the **Lethbridge Visitor Centre,** 2805 Scenic Dr., Lethbridge, AB T1K 5B7 (☎ **800/661-1222** or 403/320-1222), open daily 9am to 5pm.

Lethbridge has two good art centers that display regional and touring art. The **Southern Alberta Art Gallery,** 601 3rd Ave. S. (☎ **403/327-8770**), has a number of changing art shows throughout the year; the gift shop is a good place to go for local crafts. It's open Tuesday to Saturday 10am to 5pm and Sunday 1 to 5pm. The **Bowman Arts Centre,** 811 5th Ave. (☎ **403/327-2813**), is housed in an old school and is the fine-arts hub of Lethbridge, with studios, classes, offices for arts organizations, and two galleries featuring the works of area artists; it's open Monday to Friday 9am to 5pm and Saturday 10am to 4pm.

The **Sir Alexander Galt Museum and Archives,** at the west end of 5th Avenue S. (☎ **403/320/3898**), is an excellent regional museum located in a historic former hospital. Exhibit galleries focus on the local Native culture, the city's coal-mining past, and the role of immigrants in the region's growth. Two of the galleries are devoted to the works of regional artists. The back windows of the museum overlook the impressive Oldman River Valley with its natural park systems. It's open daily 10am to 4:30pm, with free admission.

The city's heritage as a frontier whiskey-trading center is commemorated at the **Fort Whoop-Up Interpretive Center** (☎ **403/329-0444**) in Indian Battle Park (follow 3rd Avenue South toward the river). A replica of the fort—built by Montana-based traders of buffalo skins and whiskey in the 1870s—stands in the park, with costumed docents providing horse-drawn carriage tours, interpretive programs, and historic reenactments. Mid-May to September, it's open Monday to Saturday 10am to 6pm and Sunday noon to 6pm; the rest of the year, it's open Tuesday to Friday 10am to 4pm and Sunday 1 to 4pm. In summer, admission is C$2.50 adults (US$1.65), C$1 (US65¢) seniors/students, with children under 6 free. In winter, admission is C$1 (US65¢) per adult.

The pride of Lethbridge is the **Nikka Yuko Japanese Garden** (☎ 403/328-3511) in Henderson Lake Park on Mayor Mangrath Drive, east of downtown. Its pavilion and dainty bell tower were built by Japanese artisans without nails or bolts. The garden is one of the largest Japanese gardens in North America; Japanese-Canadian women in kimonos give tours and explain the philosophical concepts involved in Japanese garden design. In summer, the gardens are open daily 9am to 5pm; May 11 to 31 and September 11 to October 15, it's open Thursday to Saturday noon to 5pm. Admission is C$4 (US$2.65) adults, C$3 (US$2) seniors, and C$2 (US$1.35) youths 6 to 17; children under 6 are free.

WHERE TO STAY & DINE

Heritage House B&B. 1115-8 Ave. S., Lethbridge, AB T1J 1P7. ☎ **403/328-3824.** Fax 403/328-9011. www.ourheritage.net/bb.html. E-mail haigba@uleth.ca. 2 units, neither with bathroom. TV. C$50 (US$33) double. Rates include breakfast. No credit cards.

This wonderful B&B will come as an architectural surprise: In an otherwise early-1900s neighborhood, this art deco jewel really stands out. Considered one of the finest examples of International Art Moderne in the province, the house is a designated provincial historic site. The interior retains the look of 1930s, including some original wall murals. The comfortable guest rooms are spacious and share a bathroom and a half.

Ramada Hotel & Suites. 2375 Mayor Magrath Dr. S., Lethbridge, AB T1K 7M1. ☎ **800/272-6232** or 403/380-5050. Fax 403/380-5051. www.ramada.ca/leth.html. 119 units. A/C TV TEL. C$85–C$115 (US$55–US$75) double. AE, DC, DISC, MC, V.

New in 1999, the Ramada is the nicest lodging in Lethbridge. The spacious rooms come with two-line speaker phones with dataports, hair dryers, coffeemakers, microwaves, fridges, irons/ironing boards, and voice mail. Facilities include an indoor water park with waterslides, a wave pool, a Jacuzzi, and a regular pool, plus a convenience store, an exercise room, and a business center.

WHERE TO DINE

For breakfast pastries or lunchtime sandwiches, the **Penny Coffee House,** 331 5th St. S. (☎ **403/320-5282**), is a friendly hangout open Monday to Saturday 7am to 10pm and Sunday 9am to 5pm. **Dionysios,** 635 13th St. N. (☎ **403/320-6554**), has slow service but tasty Greek food and is daily open 5 to 11pm. With good food and a lively atmosphere, **Coco Pazzo,** 1264 3rd Ave. S. (☎ **403/329-8979**), is probably one of the best places to eat in town, with a menu focusing on pizza and specialties from the wood-fired oven; it's open daily 11am to midnight.

FORT MACLEOD

Forty-four kilometers (27 miles) west of Lethbridge stands what was in 1873 the western headquarters of the Northwest Mounted Police. Named after Colonel MacLeod, the redcoat commander who brought peace to Canada's west, the reconstructed **Fort Macleod** is now a provincial park (☎ **403/553-4703**). It's still patrolled by Mounties in their traditional uniforms; precision riding drills are performed daily at 10am, 11:30am, 2pm, and 3:30pm.

The rebuilt fort is filled with fascinating material on the frontier period. Among its treasured documents is the rule sheet of the old Macleod Hotel, written in 1882: "All guests are requested to rise at 6am. This is imperative as the sheets are needed for tablecloths. Assaults on the cook are prohibited. Boarders who get killed will not be allowed to remain in the house." The fort grounds also contain the Centennial Building, a museum devoted to the history of the local Plains Indians. A highlight of visiting the fort in summer is the Mounted Patrol Musical Ride at 10am, 11:30am, 2pm, and 3:30pm, with eight horseback Mounties performing a choreographed equestrian program to music.

March to December 23, Fort Macleod Provincial Park is open daily 9am to 4pm (to 8pm July and Aug). Admission is C$4.50 (US$3) adults, C$4 (US$2.65) seniors, C$2.50 (US$1.65) children 12 to 17, and C$1.50 (US$1) kids 6 to 11; children under 6 are free.

HEAD-SMASHED-IN BUFFALO JUMP

One of the most interesting sights in southern Alberta is the curiously named ✪ **Head-Smashed-In Buffalo Jump** (☎ 403/553-2731) on Spring Point Road, 19km (12 miles) west of Fort Macleod on Highway 2 (187km/116 miles southwest of Calgary, 109km/68 miles north of the U.S. border). This excellent interpretive center/museum is built into the edge of a steep cliff over which the native Canadians used to stampede herds of bison, the carcasses then providing them with meat, hides, and horns. The multimillion-dollar facility tells the story of these ancient harvests by means of films and native-Canadian guide-lecturers. Other displays illustrate and explain the traditional life of the prairie-dwelling natives in precontact times and the ecology and natural history of the northern Great Plains. Hiking trails lead to undeveloped jump sites.

Designated a World Heritage Site, the center is open daily 9am to 7pm in summer and 9am to 5pm in winter. Admission is C$7 (US$4.65) adults, C$6 (US$4) seniors, and C$3 (US$2) children 17 and under.

4 Waterton Lakes National Park

In the southwestern corner of the province, ✪ **Waterton Lakes National Park** is linked with Glacier National Park in neighboring Montana; together these two beautiful tracts of wilderness compose Waterton-Glacier International Peace Park. Once the hunting ground of the Blackfoot, 526km² (203-sq.-mile) Waterton Park contains superb mountain, prairie, and lake scenery and is home to abundant wildlife.

During the last ice age, the park was filled with glaciers, which deepened and straightened river valleys; those peaks that remained above the ice were carved into distinctive thin, finlike ridges. The park's famous lakes also date from the ice ages; all three of the Waterton Lakes nestle in glacial basins.

The park's main entrance road leads to Waterton Townsite, the only commercial center, with a number of hotels, restaurants, and tourist facilities. Other roads lead to more remote lakes and trailheads. Akamina Parkway leads from the townsite to Cameron Lake, glimmering beneath the crags of the Continental Divide. At the small visitors center, you can rent canoes; this is a great spot for a picnic. Red Rock Parkway follows Blackiston Creek past the park's highest peaks to Red Rock Canyon. From here, three trails lead up deep canyons to waterfalls.

The most popular activity in the park is the **International Shoreline Cruise** (☎ 403/859-2362), which leaves from the townsite and sails Upper Waterton Lake past looming peaks to the ranger station at Goat Haunt, Montana, in Glacier Park. These tour boats leave five times daily; the cruise there and back usually takes 2 hours, including the stop in Montana. The round-trip price is C$20 (US$13) adults, C$12 (US$8) youths 13 to 17, and C$8 (US$5) children 4 to 12; children 3 and under are free.

For more information, contact the **Waterton Park Chamber of Commerce and Visitors Association,** P.O. Box 5599, Waterton Lakes National Park, AB T0K 2M0

(☎ **403/859-5133** summer or 403/859-2224 winter; www.parkscanada.pch.gc.ca/ waterton or www.discoverwaterton.com). The per-day park entry fee is C$4 (US$2.65) adults, C$3 (US$2) seniors, and C$2 (US$1.35) children.

WHERE TO STAY

Kilmorey Lodge. P.O. Box 100, Waterton Park, AB T0K 2M0. ☎ **888/859-8669** or 403/859-2334. Fax 403/859-2342. www.agt.net/public/kilmorey/waterton.html. E-mail kilmorey@telusplanet.net. 25 units. C$86–C$133 (US$57–US$89) double. Extra person C$10 (US$7). Children under 16 stay free in parents' room. AE, DC, ER, MC, V.

Beloved by oft-returning guests, the Kilmorey is a rambling old lodge from the park's heyday. One of the few lodgings with direct lake views, it has small but elegantly appointed guest rooms. Expect down comforters, antiques, squeaky floors, and loads of character and charm. The Lamp Post is one of Waterton's most acclaimed restaurants; there are also the Gazebo Cafe and the Ram's Head Lounge.

✪ **The Lodge at Waterton Lakes.** P.O. Box 4, Waterton Park, AB T0K 2M0. ☎ **888/ 98LODGE** or 403/859-2151. Fax 403/859-2229. www.watertonresort.com. 80 units. TV. C$135–C$175 (US$90–US$117) double. Extra person C$12 (US$8). Off-season rates available. AE, ER, MC, V.

This new classy lodging complex sits on 4 acres in the heart of Waterton Townsite. The guest rooms are in nine lodgelike buildings flanking a central courtyard. Also part of the complex is a guest and community sports facility, with a large indoor pool, a fitness center, and a spa. There are three types of rooms: large standard rooms with queen beds; deluxe rooms with two queen beds and a sofa bed, gas fireplaces, and two-person showers and jetted tubs; and kitchenettes with all the features of deluxe rooms plus dining rooms and kitchens. All rooms are decorated with an environmental theme and appointed with handsome pine furniture. Dining options include the Wildflower Dining Room, the Good Earth Deli, and the Wolf's Den Lounge.

Prince of Wales Hotel. Waterton Lakes National Park, AB T0K 2M0. ☎ **403/226-5551.** (Off-season 1225 N. Central Ave., Phoenix, AZ 85077; ☎ 602/207-6000). 87 units. C$175–C$700 (US$115–US$467) double. Extra person C$15 (US$10). Children under 12 stay free in parents' room. MC, V. Open May 14–Sept 26.

Built in 1927 by the Great Northern Railway, this beautiful mountain lodge perched on a bluff above Upper Waterton Lake is reminiscent of the historic resorts in Banff Park on a smaller scale. The guest rooms have been totally renovated, though many are historically authentic (rather small). Operated by the same dilatory Greyhound/Dial Soap consortium that manages the historic lodges in Glacier National Park in Montana, the Prince of Wales is in need of some reinvestment (at these prices, you don't expect water-stained acoustic ceiling tiles in the bar). However, you won't be able to resist visiting this landmark for the views and perhaps for a meal in the Garden Court Restaurant or afternoon tea in Valerie's Tea Room; there are also a pub and a lobby bar.

5 Introducing the Canadian Rockies

Few places in the world are more dramatically beautiful than the **Canadian Rockies.** Banff and Jasper national parks are famous for their mountain lakes, flower-spangled meadows, spirelike peaks choked by glaciers, and abundant wildlife. Nearly the entire spine of the Rockies—from the U.S. border north for 1,127km (699 miles)—is preserved as parkland or wilderness.

The Canadian Rockies

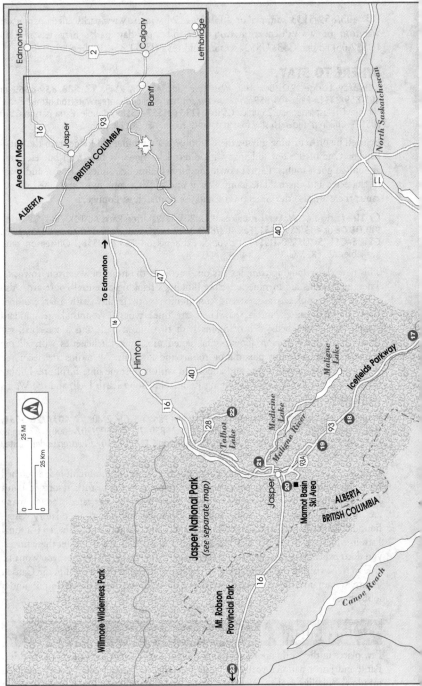

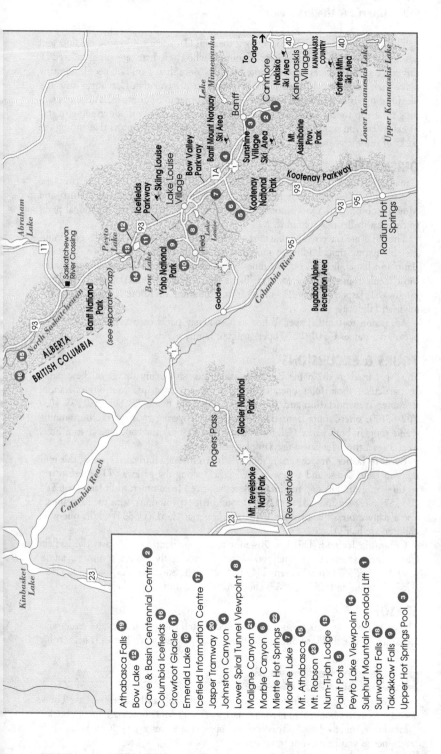

Athabasca Falls ❿

Bow Lake ⓬

Cave & Basin Centennial Centre ❷

Columbia Icefields ⓰

Crowfoot Glacier ⓫

Emerald Lake ❿

Icefield Information Centre ⓱

Jasper Tramway ⓴

Johnston Canyon ❹

Lower Spiral Tunnel Viewpoint ❽

Maligne Canyon ㉑

Marble Canyon ❻

Miette Hot Springs ㉒

Moraine Lake ❼

Mt. Athabasca ⓯

Mt. Robson ㉓

Num-Ti-jah Lodge ⓭

Paint Pots ❺

Peyto Lake Viewpoint ⓮

Sulphur Mountain Gondola Lift ❶

Sunwapta Falls ⓲

Takakkaw Falls ❾

Upper Hot Springs Pool ❸

That's the good news. The bad news is that this Canadian wilderness, the flora and fauna that live in it, and the lovers of solitude who come here, are going to need all this space as the Rockies become more popular. More than 5 million people annually make their way through Banff National Park. But it seems that Draconian measures like limiting visitors are as yet brought up only in order to be dismissed. Advance planning for a trip to the Canadian Rockies is absolutely necessary if you're going to stay or eat where you want or if you want to evade the swarms of visitors that throng the parks in summer.

ORIENTATION

Canada's Rocky Mountain parks include Jasper and Banff, which together comprise 17,519km² (6,764 sq. miles); the provincial parklands of the Kananaskis Country and Mount Robson; and Yoho, Kootenay, Glacier, and Mount Revelstoke national parks to the west in British Columbia.

The parks are traversed by one of the finest highway systems in Canada, plus innumerable nature trails leading to more remote valleys and peaks. The two "capitals," Banff and Jasper, lie 287km (178 miles) apart, connected by Highway 93, one of the most scenic routes you'll ever drive. Banff lies 128km (79 miles) from Calgary via Highway 1; Jasper, 375km (233 miles) from Edmonton on Route 16, the famous Yellowhead Highway.

Admission to Banff, Jasper, Yoho, and Kootenay parks costs C$5 (US$3.35) per person per day or C$10 (US$7) per group or family per day.

TOURS & EXCURSIONS

You'll get used to the name Brewster, associated with many things in these parts. In particular, these folks operate the park system's principal tour-bus operation. **Brewster Transportation and Tours,** 100 Gopher St., Banff, AB T0L 0C0 (☎ **403/ 762-6767**), offers tours from Banff and Jasper, covering most of the outstanding scenic spots in both parks. Call for a full brochure or ask the concierge at your hotel to arrange a trip. Here are a few sample packages:

Banff to Jasper (or vice versa): Some 9½ hours through unrivaled scenery, this tour takes in Lake Louise and a view of the ice field along the parkway. (The return trip requires an overnight stay, not included in the price.) In summer, adult fares are C$85 (US$57) one-way and C$118 (US$79) round-trip. If you don't want the tour, there's also a daily express bus between Banff and Jasper at C$51 (US$34) adults one-way; children are half price.

Columbia Icefield: This is a 9½-hour tour from Banff. You stop at the Icefield Centre and get time off for lunch and a Snocoach ride up the glacier. In summer, adults pay C$85 (US$57) and children C$43 (US$29). The Snocoach ride is an extra C$25 (US$17) adults and C$10 (US$7) children, and you must buy tickets in advance.

SEASONS

The parks have two peak seasons during which hotels charge top rates and restaurants are jammed. The first is summer, mid-June to late August, when it doesn't get terribly

---

Warning: Reserve Far Ahead

If you're reading this on the day you plan to arrive in Banff, Jasper, or Lake Louise and haven't yet booked your room, start worrying. Most hotels are totally booked for the season by July 1. To avoid disappointment, reserve your room as far in advance as you know your travel dates.

A Wildlife Warning

Whenever you come across wildlife in the Rockies, avoid the temptation to get up-close and personal. Don't feed the animals and don't touch them! You can get fined—or worse.

hot, rarely above 80°F, though the sun's rays are powerful at this altitude. The other peak time is winter, the skiing season from December to February; this is probably the finest skiing terrain in all Canada. March to May is decidedly off-season: Hotels offer bargain room rates, and you can choose the best table in any eatery. There's plenty of rain in the warmer months, so don't forget to bring some suitable rainwear.

LODGING IN THE ROCKIES

On any given day in high season, up to 50,000 people wind through the Canadian Rocky national parks. Because growth in the parks is strictly regulated, there's not an abundance of hotel rooms waiting. The result is strong competition for a limited number of very expensive rooms. Adding to the squeeze is the fact that many hotels have 80% to 90% of their rooms reserved for coach tours in summer.

Regarding price, it seems that lodgings can ask for and get just about any rate they want in high season. For the most part, hotels are well kept up in the parks, but few would justify these high prices anywhere else in the world. Knowing that, there are a few choices. You can decide to splurge on one of the world-class hotels here, actually only a bit more expensive than the midrange competition. Camping is another good option, because the parks have dozens of campgrounds with varying degrees of facilities. There are also a number of hostels throughout the parks.

Outside high season, prices drop dramatically, often as much as one-half. Most hotels will offer ski packages in winter, as well as other attractive getaway incentives. Be sure to ask if there are any special rates, especially at the larger hotels, which have trouble filling their rooms off-season.

PARK WILDLIFE & YOU

The parklands are swarming with wildlife, with some animals meandering along and across highways and hiking trails, within easy camera range. However tempting, **don't feed the animals and don't touch them!** For starters, you can be fined up to C$500 (US$334) for feeding any wildlife. There's also the distinct possibility you may end up paying more than cash for disregarding this warning.

It isn't easy to resist the blithely fearless bighorn sheep, mountain goats, elk, soft-eyed deer, and lumbering moose you meet. (You'll have very little chance of meeting the coyotes, lynx, and occasional wolves, since they give humans a wide berth.) But the stuff you feed them can kill them. Bighorns get accustomed to summer handouts of bread, candy, potato chips, and marshmallows when they should be grazing on the high-protein vegetation that'll help them survive through the winter. Moose involve additional dangers. They've been known to take over entire picnics after being given an initial snack, chase off the picnickers, and eat up everything in sight—including cutlery, dishes, and the tablecloth.

Portions of the parks may sometimes be closed to hikers and bikers during elk calving season. A mother elk can mistake your recreation for an imminent attack on her newborn; or an unsuspecting hiker could frighten a mother from her calf, separating the two for good. Pay attention to—and obey—postings at trailheads.

Bears pose the worst problems. The parks contain two breeds: the big grizzly, standing up to 7 feet on its hind legs, and the smaller black bear, about 5 feet long.

The grizzly spends most of the summer in high alpine ranges, well away from tourist haunts. As one of North America's largest carnivores, its appearance and reputation are awesome enough to make you beat a retreat on sight. But the less formidable black bear is a born clown with tremendous audience appeal and takes to human company like a squirrel. The black bear's cuddly looks and circus antics, plus its knack for begging and rummaging through garbage cans, tend to obscure the fact that these are wild animals: powerful, faster than a horse, and completely unpredictable.

Hiking in bear country (and virtually all parkland is bear country) necessitates certain precautions—ignore them at your own peril. Never hike alone and never take a dog along. Dogs often yap at bears, then when the animal charges, they run toward their owners for protection, bringing the pursuer with them. Use a telephoto lens when taking pictures. Bears in the wild have a set tolerance range that, when encroached upon, may bring on an attack. Above all, never go near a cub. The mother is usually close by, and a female defending her young is the most ferocious creature you'll ever face—and possibly the last.

6 Kananaskis Country & Canmore

Kananaskis Country is the name given to three Alberta provincial parks on the Rocky Mountains' eastern slope. Once considered only a gateway region to more glamorous Banff, the Kananaskis has developed into a recreation destination on a par with more famous brand-name resorts in the Canadian Rockies.

Just west of the Kananaskis and outside the eastern boundary of Banff National Park, **Canmore** is a sprawl of condominium/resort development in a dramatic location beneath the soaring peaks of Three Sisters Mountain. Only 20 minutes from Banff, Canmore hasn't yet topped the list of Canadian resort destinations, but the scenery is magnificent and the accommodations are generally much less expensive and considerably less overbooked than those in Banff. If you can't locate affordable lodgings in Banff, give Canmore a try.

The weather is generally warmer and sunnier here, which is conducive to golfing; the championship course at Kananaskis is one of the best in North America. When the 1988 Olympics were held in Calgary, the national park service wouldn't allow the alpine ski events to be held at the ski areas in the parks. **Nakiska,** in the Kananaskis, became the venue instead, vaulting this ski area to international prominence.

The main road through the Kananaskis Country is Highway 40, which cuts south from Highway 1 at the gateway to the Rockies and follows the Kananaskis River. Kananaskis Village, a collection of resort hotels and shops, is the center of activities in the Kananaskis and is convenient to most recreation areas. Highway 40 eventually climbs up to 7,239-foot Highwood Pass, the highest pass in Alberta, before looping around to meet Highway 22 south of Calgary.

For more details, try the Web site at **www.gov.ab.ca/env/parks/prov_parks/ kananaskis/KCINFO** or write **Barrier Lake Visitor Information Centre,** Box 32, Exshaw, AB G0L 2C0 (☎ **403/673-3985**). There's **Travel Alberta Visitor Information Centre** at the Bow Valley Trail exit off Highway 1 at Canmore (☎ **403/ 678-5277**). This province-wide center also has lots of information on Canmore.

ADVENTURE SPORTS

It's the excellent access to outdoor recreation that makes Canmore and the Kananaskis such a prime destination. Recreation here is highly organized and easy to indulge in. From its office in the Lodge at Kananaskis and in Canmore at #3, 999 Bow Valley Trail Canmore (mailing address: P.O. Box 8097, Canmore, AB T1W 2T8 (☎ **888/312-7238** or 403/678-4919; fax 403/609-3210; www.miragetours.com/

home.html; e-mail info@miragetours.com), **Mirage Adventure Tours** represents most local outfitters and most activities available in the area. Bicycle trips, horseback trail rides, rafting, hiking, sightseeing tours, and other recreational opportunities are offered. Mirage also rents cross-country skis and equipment.

DOWNHILL SKIING   Kananaskis gained worldwide attention when it hosted the alpine ski events for the 1988 Winter Olympic Games. At world-famous **Nakiska,** you can follow in the tracks of winter Olympians past. A second ski area, **Fortress Mountain,** is 19km (12 miles) south of Kananaskis Village. Though overshadowed by Nakiska's Olympic reputation, Fortress Mountain offers an escape from the resort crowd and features accommodations in a dormitory. Both areas offer terrain for every age and ability and are open early December to mid-April. Adult lift tickets cost C$39 (US$26) at Nakiska and C$29 (US$19) at Fortress; tickets are completely transferable between the two areas. For more details on the ski areas, call ☎ **800/258-7669** or 403/591-7777 or write **Ski Nakiska,** P.O. Box 1988, Kananaskis Village, AB T0L 2H0.

The **Canmore Nordic Centre** (mailing address: 1988 Olympic Way, Canmore, AB T1W 2T6), south of town off Spray Lakes Road (☎ **403/678-2400**), was developed for the Olympic's cross-country skiing competition, though now the facility is open year-round. In winter, it offers 70km (43 miles) of scenic cross-country trails, plus the on-site Trail Sports shop (☎ **403/678-6764**) for rentals, repairs, and sales. In summer, the trails are used for hiking and mountain biking; Trail Sports also offers bike rentals, plus skill-building courses and guided rides.

GOLF   Kananaskis also features three championship golf courses and one of Canada's premier golf resorts. Rated one of the top courses in Canada, the **Kananaskis Country Golf Course** boasts two 18-hole, par-72 championship courses set among alpine forests and streams; they features water hazards on 20 holes, 140 sand traps, and four tee positions. Contact **Golf Kananaskis,** The Kananaskis Country Golf Course, P.O. Box 1710, Kananaskis Village, AB T0L 2H0 (☎ **403/591-7154**). Greens fees are C$50 (US$33). Near Canmore, the 18-hole **Canmore Golf Course** is along the Bow River at 2000 8th Ave. (☎ **403/678-1600**). Greens fees are C$42 (US$28). The **Golf Course at Silvertip** is a Les Furber–designed 18-hole, par-72 course high above Canmore off Silvertip Drive. Boasting a length of 7,300 yards, the course has sand bunkers on all holes and water on eight. Greens fees plus a cart rental are C$105 (US$70).

HORSEBACK TRIPS   The Kananaskis is noted for its dude ranches (see "Guest Ranches," below), which offer a variety of horseback adventures from short trail rides to multiple-day pack trips into the wilderness. **Mirage Adventure Tours** (above) is a good clearinghouse for information, or you can contact the guest ranches themselves.

RAFTING   The Kananaskis and Bow rivers are the main draw here. In addition to half-day (C$49/US$33), full-day (C$99/US$66), and 2-day white-water trips (C$229/US$153), there are also trips combining a half day of horseback riding or mountain biking with an afternoon of rafting (both C$119/US$79 per person). Contact **Mirage Adventure Tours** (above) for details on these packages.

WHERE TO STAY

Kananaskis is a major camping destination for families in Calgary, and the choice of campgrounds is wide. There's a concentration of campgrounds at **Upper and Lower Kananaskis lakes,** some 32km (20 miles) south of Kananaskis Village. A few campgrounds are scattered nearer to Kananaskis Village, around Barrier Lake and Ribbon Creek. For a full-service campground with RV hookups, go to **Mount Kidd RV Park** (☎ **403/591-7700**), just south of the Kananaskis golf course.

KANANASKIS VILLAGE

The lodgings in Kananaskis Village were built for the Olympics, so all are new and well maintained. There's no more than a stone's throw between them, and to a high degree, public facilities are shared among all the hotels.

Best Western Kananaskis Inn. Kananaskis Village, AB T0L 2H0. ☎ **800/528-1234** or 403/591-7500. Fax 403/591-7500. 96 units. TV TEL. C$160 (US$107) double; C$325 (US$217) suite. AE, DC, DISC, ER, MC, V.

This handsome wood-fronted hotel is the most affordable place to stay in Kananaskis—though that doesn't mean it's inexpensive. The hotel offers a wide variety of guest-room types, including many loft rooms with kitchenettes, which can sleep six. There are a pool, whirlpool, and steam room.

Lodge at Kananaskis. Kananaskis Village, AB T0L 2H0. ☎ **800/441-1414** or 403/591-7711. Fax 403/591-7770. 321 units. MINIBAR TV TEL. Peak season C$225–C$330 (US$150–US$220) double. Ski/golf package rates and discounts available. Parking C$6 (US$4), valet parking C$10 (US$7). AE, CB, DC, ER, MC, V.

This resort hotel is operated by Canadian Pacific and has two buildings facing each other across a pond at the center of Kananaskis Village. The Lodge is the larger building, with a more rustic facade, a shopping arcade, and a number of drinking and dining choices. Its guest rooms are spacious and well furnished; many have balconies and some have fireplaces. The smaller Manor is quieter, and its rooms are generally larger and more expensive than the Lodge's. Together the buildings offer seven dining venues, from the upscale l'Escapades to the tapas-style nibbling in Brady's Market, plus coffee shops and light entree service in the lounges. There's also a full range of exercise facilities, with a pool, indoor/outdoor whirlpools, aerobic studios, and a health/beauty spa.

Ribbon Creek Hostel. At Nakiska Ski Area. ☎ **403/762-3441** reservations or 403/591-7333 hostel itself. Sleeps 44. C$12 (US$8) members, C$16 (US$11) nonmembers. MC, V.

This is a great place for a traveler on a budget; there are also four family rooms. The hostel is located right at the ski area, within walking distance of Kananaskis Village, and has showers, laundry facilities, and a common room with a fireplace.

CANMORE

Best Western Pocaterra Inn. 1725 Mountain Ave., Canmore, AB T1W 2W1. ☎ **800/661-2133** or 403/678-4334. Fax 403/678-2670. www.pocaterrainn.com. E-mail info@pocaterrainn.com. 83 units. A/C TV TEL. C$139–C$159 (US$93–US$106) double. Rates include continental breakfast. AE, DISC, MC, V. Children under 18 stay free in parents' room.

This is one of the nicest of the hotels along the Bow Valley Trail strip. All the guest rooms are spacious and have gas fireplaces, queen-size beds, coffeemakers, and fridges. Facilities include a waterslide and an indoor pool, a whirlpool, a fitness room, and a guest laundry.

An Eagle's View B&B. 6 Eagle Landing, Canmore, AB T1W 2Y1. ☎ **403/678-3264.** www.aneaglesview.com. E-mail eaglean@telusplanet.net. 2 units. TV. C$95 (US$63) double. AE, MC, V.

An Eagle's View is in one of the new developments high above Canmore, providing eye-popping views onto the Three Sisters and the Bow Valley. The large guest rooms are on the main floor of the house (which guests have to themselves). The guest lounge has a TV and VCR and tea and coffee makings. Guests share a garden patio, plus a sunny second-floor deck overlooking the mountains.

○ **McNeill Heritage Inn.** 500 Three Sisters Dr., Canmore, AB T1W 2P3. ☎ **877/MCNEILL** or 403/678-4884. www.mcneillinn.ab.ca. E-mail info@mcneillinn.ab.ca. 5

units. TV. C$125–C$150 (US$83–US$100) double. Rates include breakfast. Extra person C$25 (US$17). MC, V.

Built in 1907 as a trophy home for the manager of the local coal mine, this inn is a marvelous bit of historic architecture combined with modern comfort. Just west of downtown Canmore, the rambling house sits on an outcrop of rock above the Bow River. The guest rooms (four with queen-size beds, one with a king-sized bed) are decorated with uncluttered yet handsome simplicity. The ceilings are 10 feet high throughout, making the spacious rooms feel even larger. Guests share a living room with a fireplace, a library stocked with outdoor guides, and a veranda running along the length of the house. You'll find a friendly welcome and professional service, plus an excellent breakfast. This is a good lodging for cross-country skiers, because it's adjacent to the Canmore Nordic Centre.

✪ **Quality Inn Chateau Canmore.** 1720 Bow Valley Trail, Canmore, AB T1W 1P7. ☎ **800/228-5151** or 403/678-6699. Fax 403/678-6954. www.chateaucanmore.com. E-mail info@chateaucanmore.com. 120 units. C$185 (US$123) standard suite; from C$259 (US$173) deluxe suite. A/C TV TEL. AE, CB, DISC, ER, JCB, MC, V.

You can't miss this enormous complex along the hotel strip. Like a series of 10 four-story conjoined chalets, the Chateau Canmore offers some of the largest guest rooms in the area, nicely decorated in a comfortable rustic style; the lobby and common rooms look like they belong in a log lodge. The standard suites have fireplaces, fridges, microwaves, and sitting-bedrooms, while the deluxe one- or two-bedroom suites include all the previous plus living rooms, dining rooms, and en suite washer/dryers. Guests enjoy a full-service spa, an indoor pool, an outdoor hot tub, and a fitness center.

GUEST RANCHES

✪ **Brewster's Kananaskis Guest Ranch.** (30 min. east of Banff on Hwy. 1), P.O. Box 964, Banff, AB T0L 0C0. ☎ **800/691-5085** or 403/673-3737. Fax 403/673-2100. www.brewsteradventures.com. 33 units. C$90–C$110 (US$60–US$73) double. Extra person C$15 (US$10). AE, MC, V. Full board is available.

The Brewsters were movers and shakers in the region's early days, playing a decisive role in the formation of Banff, Jasper, and Montana's Glacier national parks, and they were the first outfitters (and transport providers) in the parks. The Kananaskis Ranch was the original Brewster family homestead in the 1880s and was transformed into a guest ranch in 1923. On the Bow River near the mouth of the Kananaskis River, the original lodge buildings remain as common areas. The guest rooms, in chalets or cabins, are fully modern. Activities include horseback riding, river rafting, canoeing, hiking, and more. Long-distance backcountry horseback rides are a specialty—a 3-day trip is under C$400 (US$267)—and backcountry campsites have new sleeping cabins.

Rafter Six Ranch Resort. Box 6, Seebe, AB T0L 1X0. ☎ **888/26RANCH** or 403/673-3622. Fax 403/673-3961. www.raftersix.com. E-mail vacations@raftersix.com. Accommodates 30 in log lodge and cabins. C$110–C$250 (US$72–US$163) double in lodge; cabins from C$125–C$250 (US$81–US$163) double. Extra person C$15 (US$10). June–Sept 14, 3- and 4-day packages available. AE, DC, ER, MC, V.

Rafter Six is in a meadow right on the banks of the Kananaskis River. Another guest ranch with a long pedigree, it's a full-service resort ranch. The huge old log lodge, with a restaurant, barbecue deck, and lounge, is especially inviting. Casual horseback and longer pack trips are offered, as well as raft and canoe trips. Facilities include hot tubs, an outdoor pool, a playground, and a game room. Seasonal special events are offered, like rodeos, country dances, and hay or sleigh rides.

WHERE TO DINE

The dining rooms at both **Rafter Six** and **Kananaskis guest ranches** are open to nonguests with reservations. For Creole and Cajun food, go to the **French Quarter,** 102 Boulder Crescent, Canmore (☎ **403/678-3612**), open Monday to Saturday 6:30am to 10pm and Sunday 4 to 10pm. A popular pub with good food is the **Rose and Crown,** 749 Railway Ave., Canmore (☎ **403/678-5168**), open Sunday to Thursday 11am to midnight and Friday and Saturday 11am to 1am.

Boccallino Grotto. 838 10th St., Canmore. ☎ **403/678-6424.** Reservations recommended. Main courses C$11–C$19 (US$7–US$13). AE, MC, V. Tues–Sun 5–10pm. CONTINENTAL.

The cooking at this pleasant Alpine-look restaurant straddles the boundary between Switzerland and Italy. There's a good selection of pastas, including vermicelli Arrabiato, strips of beef in spicy tomato-pepper sauce. Veal is a house specialty and comes in a variety of preparations; veal mince Zurichoise, thin slices of veal tenderloin with wine-and-mushroom cream, is one of the signature dishes. Boccallino Grotto is also a good spot for pizza.

Sherwood House. At Main and 8th Ave., Canmore. ☎ **403/678-5211.** Reservations accepted. Main courses C$13–C$29 (US$9–US$19). AE, MC, V. Daily 7am–10pm. CANADIAN.

This handsome log restaurant on the busiest corner of downtown (which isn't *that* busy) is a long-time favorite. The wide-ranging and well-executed menu offers everything from pizza and pasta to prime Angus steaks, but what makes this one of Canmore's favorite gathering spots is the wonderful landscaped deck. In summer, there's no better place to spend the afternoon. In winter, you'll enjoy the traditional lodge building with its cozy fireplace.

✪ **Sinclairs.** 637 Main St., Canmore. ☎ **403/678-5370.** Reservations recommended. Main courses C$12–C$20 (US$8–US$13). AE, MC, V. Daily 11am–10pm. NEW CANADIAN.

Downtown in a converted heritage home, Sinclairs is the most ambitious of the new restaurants in Canmore. The menu is very broad and offers an excellent selection of appetizers and small plates if you'd like to snack around a number of dishes rather than have a traditional dinner. There are also a number of individual pizzas and pasta dishes for lighter appetites. However, the entrees are hard to resist. Seared pancetta-wrapped salmon comes with a warm horseradish lemon lentil salad, and broiled marinated lamb chops are served with chili-glazed apple sauce and wild mushroom polenta tortilla. Jasmine tea–steamed halibut with pomegranate juice, beef tenderloin and squid with goat cheese crème fraiche—there's nothing ordinary about the food here. The wine list is very good and the service excellent.

Zona's Late Night Bistro. 710 9th St. ☎ **403/609-2000.** Reservations not accepted. Main courses C$10–C$14 (US$7–US$9). MC, V. Daily 11:30pm–midnight. INTERNATIONAL.

Zona's is where you want to go if you don't want to spend a fortune but do want sophisticated food with some zip. This friendly little hangout looks more like a coffeehouse, but the warm and casual atmosphere only makes the spicy and unusual fare seem that much more beguiling. The menu trots the globe: Moroccan pomegranate-molasses lamb curry, coconut-lime chicken lasagne, and *salmonkepita* (filo-wrapped salmon, spinach, and cheese) are a few of the main dishes. The menu also has a number of smaller tapas dishes and wraps, plus ample vegetarian choices.

7 Banff National Park: Canada's Top Tourist Draw

Banff is Canada's oldest national park, founded in 1885 as a modest 26km² (10-sq.-mile) reserve by the country's first prime minister, Sir John A. Macdonald. The park is now 6,641km² (2,564 sq. miles) of incredibly dramatic mountain landscape, glaciers, high moraine lakes, and rushing rivers. Its two towns, Lake Louise and Banff, are both splendid counterpoints to the wilderness, with beautiful historic hotels, fine restaurants, and lively nightlife.

If there's a downside to all this sophisticated beauty, it's that Banff is *incredibly* popular—it's generally considered Canada's number-one tourist destination. About 4 million people visit Banff yearly, with the vast majority squeezing in during June, July, and August.

Happily, the wilderness invites visitors to get away from the crowds and from the congestion of the developed sites. Banff Park is blessed with a great many outfitters who make it easy to get on a raft, bike, or horse and find a little mountain solitude. Or consider visiting the park off-season, when prices are lower, the locals are friendlier, and the scenery is just as stunning.

SPORTS & OUTDOOR ACTIVITIES IN THE PARK

Lots of great recreational activities are available in Banff National Park, so don't just spend your vacation shopping the boutiques on Banff Avenue. Most day trips require little advance booking—a day in advance is usually plenty—and the easiest way to find a quick adventure is just to ask your hotel's concierge to set one up. Multiday rafting and horseback trips do require advance booking, because places are limited and keenly sought after. There are many more outfitters in Banff than the ones I list, but the offerings and prices below are typical of what's available.

BICYCLING **Cycling the Rockies,** Box 25, Lake Louise, AB T0L 1E0 (☎ **888/ 771-9453** or 403/522-2211), makes it easy to get out on two wheels and explore the beautiful Bow Valley. Regularly scheduled guided bike trips include half-day trips around Lake Louise for C$59 (US$39) and a full-day journey between Banff and Lake Louise for C$89 (US$59). More adventuresome travelers can check out the "Peddles & Paddles" option, combining a half day of cycling with a half day of white-water rafting on the Kicking Horse River for C$113 (US$75). Prices include cycle and helmet rental, plus snacks and meals.

If you'd prefer a **self-guided tour,** simply rent a bike in Banff or Lake Louise (dozens of outfitters offer rentals) and peddle along the Bow Valley Parkway—Highway 1A—between Banff and Lake Louise. Hardier cyclists may want to challenge themselves with the longer Icefields Parkway between Lake Louise and Jasper. Most cyclists will need 3 days to make the trip, stopping at night in the numerous charming hostels found along this amazing mountain road.

FISHING **Banff Fishing Unlimited** (☎ 403/762-4936) offers a number of fly-fishing expeditions on the Bow River, as well as fishing at Lake Minnewanka. All levels of anglers are accommodated, and packages include part- or whole-day trips.

GOLFING The **Banff Springs Golf Course** in Banff, which rolls out along the Bow River beneath towering mountain peaks, offers 27 holes of excellent golf. Although associated with the resort hotel, the course is open to the public. Call ☎ 403/762-6801 for a tee time.

HELICOPTER TOURS **Alpine Helicopters** (☎ 403/678-4802), operating out of Canmore, offers flights over the Canadian Rockies starting at C$110 (US$73).

HIKING One of the great virtues of Banff is that many of its most dramatic and scenic areas are easily accessible by day hikes. The park has more than 80 maintained hiking trails, from interpretive nature strolls to long-distance backpacking expeditions (you'll need a permit if you're planning on camping in the backcountry). For a good listing of popular hikes, pick up the free *Banff/Lake Louise Drives and Walks* brochure.

One of the best day hikes is up ✪ **Johnston Canyon,** 24km (15 miles) north of Banff on Highway 1A. This relatively easy hike up a limestone canyon passes seven waterfalls before reaching a series of jade-green springs known as the **Inkpots.** Part of the fun of this trail is the narrowness of the canyon—the walls are more than 100 feet high and only 18 feet across; the path skirts the cliff face, tunnels through walls, and winds across wooden footbridges for more than 1.6km (1 mile). The waterfalls plunge down through the canyon, soaking hikers with spray; watch for black swifts diving in the mist. The hike through the canyon to Upper Falls takes 1½ hours; all the way to the Inkpots will take at least 4 hours.

It's easy to strike out from Banff Townsite and find any number of satisfying short hikes. Setting off on foot can be as simple as following the footpaths along both sides of the **Bow River.** From the west end of the Bow River Bridge, trails lead east to Bow Falls, past the Banff Springs Hotel, to the Upper Hot Springs. Another popular hike just beyond town is the **Fenlands Trail,** which begins just past the train station and makes a loop through marshland wildlife habitat near the Vermilion Lakes. Two longer trails leave from the Cave and Basin Centennial Centre. The **Sundance Trail** follows the Bow River for nearly 5km (3.1 miles) past beaver dams and wetlands, ending at the entrance to Sundance Canyon. Keen hikers can continue up the canyon another 2.4km (1½ miles) to make a loop past Sundance Falls. The **Marsh Loop** leaves the Cave and Basin area to wind 2.4km (1½ miles) past the Bow River and marshy lakes.

If you'd prefer a **guided hike,** several are offered daily by Parks Canada. Ask at the Banff Information Centre or check the chalkboard outside to find out what options are currently offered. Some walks are free, while others (like the popular evening **Wildlife Research Walks**) charge a small fee; both require preregistration. For details and preregistration, call ☎ 403/762-9818.

HORSEBACK RIDING See Banff on horseback with **Warner Guiding and Outfitting** (☎ 403/762-4551; fax 403/762-8130; www.horseback.com; e-mail warner@telusplanet.net). Multiday trail rides start at C$437 (US$291) for 3 days and peak at C$992 (US$662) and explore some of the park's most remote and scenic areas. Some rides climb up to backcountry lodges, which serve as base camps for further exploration; other trips involve a backcountry circuit with lodging in tents. Shorter day rides are also offered from two stables near the townsite: just west of the Banff Springs Hotel and near the Cave and Basin Centennial Site. A morning ride with brunch is C$61 (US$40), and a full-day ride along the scenic Spray River Valley is C$115 (US$77).

Operating out of Lake Louise, **Timberline Tours** (☎ 888/858-3388 or 403/522-3743) offers day trips to some of the area's more prominent beauty sites—starting at C$35 (US$23) for 90 minutes. From their Bow Lake Corral at Num-Ti-Jah Lodge, hourlong rides start at C$20 (US$13). Three- to 10-day pack trips are also offered.

RAFTING & CANOEING One-hour family float trips on the Bow River just past Banff are available from the **Rocky Mountain Raft Company** (☎ 403/762-3632).

Banff Town & Banff National Park

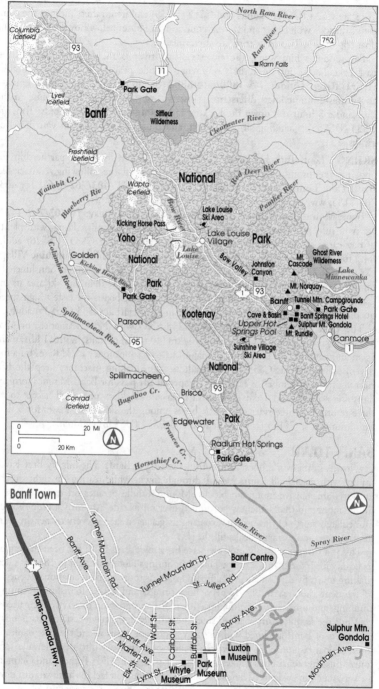

Trips are C$24 (US$16) adults and C$12 (US$8) children; rafters meet at the company's dock at Wolf Street and Bow Avenue and take buses below Bow Falls, where the float trip begins. Two-hour trips are also available.

For serious white water, the closest rafting river is the Kicking Horse River, past Lake Louise just over the Continental Divide near Field, British Columbia. **Hydra River Guides** (☎ **800/644-8888** or 403/762-4554; e-mail email@ adventures-unlimited.net) offers free transport from Banff and Lake Louise to the river and a 3-hour run down the Kicking Horse through Grade IV rapids. Trips are C$83 (US$55), including all gear, lunch, and transport to and from your hotel or campsite.

SKIING　Banff Park has three ski areas, and they've formed a partnership for booking and promotional purposes. For details on all the following, contact **Ski Banff/Lake Louise,** Box 1085, Banff, AB T0l 0C0 (☎ **403/762-4561;** fax 403/ 762-8185; www.skibanfflakelouise.com; e-mail skibll@banff.net).

Banff Mount Norquay (formerly Mystic Ridge and Norquay; ☎ **403/762-4421**) are twin runs just above the town of Banff. They cater to family skiing, with plenty of day care, ski instruction, and night skiing. Rates start at C$39 (US$26) adults for a full day. Skiers must ski or take a gondola to the main lifts at **Sunshine Village** (☎ **403/762-6500**) and the Sunshine Inn, a ski-in/ski-out hotel. Sunshine, 15 minutes west of Banff off Highway 1, receives more snow than any ski area in the Canadian Rockies (more than 30 ft. per year!). Sunshine boasts the fastest high-speed quad chairlifts in the world. Lift tickets for Sunshine start at C$53 (US$35) adults.

The **Lake Louise Ski Area** (☎ **800/258-SNOW** in North America, or 403/ 552-3555) is the largest in Canada, with 64km (40 miles) of trails. With 11 lifts, management guarantees no long lines on major lifts—or your money back! Rates for a full day of skiing start at C$53 (US$35) adults. Snowmaking machines keep the lifts running from November to early May. A **special lift pass** for Banff Mount Norquay, Sunshine Village, and Lake Louise Ski Area allows skiers unlimited access to all three resorts (and free rides on shuttle buses among the ski areas). Passes for 3 days (minimum) cost C$153 (US$102) adults and C$57 (US$38) children.

BANFF TOWN

Few towns in the world boast as beautiful a setting as **Banff.** The mighty Bow River, murky with glacial till, courses right through town, while rearing up right on the outskirts are massive mountain blocks. Mount Rundle parades off to the south, a finlike mountain that somehow got tipped over on its side. Mount Cascade rises up immediately north of downtown, exposing its glaciered face at every corner. In every direction, yet more craggy peaks fill the sky.

This is a stunning, totally unlikely place for a town, and Banff has been trading on its beauty for more than a century. The Banff Springs Hotel was built in 1888 as a destination resort by the Canadian Pacific Railroad. As tourists and recreationalists began to frequent the area for its scenery, hot springs, and access to fishing, hunting, climbing, and other activities, the little town of Banff grew up to service their needs.

While the setting hasn't changed since the early days, the town certainly has. Today, the streets of Banff are lined with exclusive boutique malls where the best names in international fashion offer their wares; trendy cafes spill out into the sidewalks, and tourist bus after tourist bus chokes the streets. Japanese, English, French, and Germans are very much in evidence. There's a vital and cosmopolitan feel to the town; just don't go here expecting a bucolic Alpine village. Banff in summer is a very busy place.

ESSENTIALS

VISITOR INFORMATION   The **Banff Information Centre,** 224 Banff Ave., houses both the **Banff Tourism Bureau** and a **national-park info center.** Contact the office at P.O. Box 1298, Banff, AB T0L 0C0 (☎ 403/762-0270; fax 403/762-8545). It's open daily June 15 to October 15 9am to 9pm and the rest of the year 9am to 5pm. Be sure to ask for the *Official Visitors Guide,* absolutely packed with info about local businesses and recreation.

GETTING THERE   If you're driving, the **Trans-Canada Highway** takes you right to Banff's main street; the town is 129km (80 miles) west of Calgary. There's no air or rail service. **Greyhound buses** pass through Banff on their way from Calgary to Vancouver; the depot is at 100 Gopher St. (☎ 403/762-6767; www.greyhound.ca). The one-way fare between Banff and Calgary is C$20 (US$13). The closest **VIA Rail** train service is at Jasper, 287km (178 miles) north; **Brewster Transport** (☎ 403/762-6767) offers an express bus between the two park centers five times weekly at C$51 (US$34) adult one-way.

If you're flying into Calgary and heading straight to Banff, call and reserve a seat on the **Banff Airporter** (☎ 403/762-3330; www.banffairport.com). Vans depart from the Calgary Airport roughly every 2 hours; one-way tickets are C$30 (US$20).

ORIENTATION   Getting your bearings is easy. The **Greyhound and Brewster Bus Depot** is at the corner of Gopher and Lynx streets (☎ 403/762-2286). The main street—**Banff Avenue**—starts at the southern end of town at the Bow River and runs north until it's swallowed by the Trans-Canada Highway. Along this broad and bustling thoroughfare, you'll find most of Banff's hotels, restaurants, stores, office buildings, and nightspots. Just beyond the river stands the park administration building amid a beautifully landscaped public garden. Here the road splits: Banff Springs Hotel and the **Sulphur Mountain Gondola** are to the left; to the right are the **Cave and Basin Hot Springs,** Banff National Park's original site. At the northwestern edge of town is the old rail station, and a little farther northwest the road branches off to Lake Louise and Jasper. In the opposite direction is the highway going to Calgary.

GETTING AROUND   Banff offers local bus service along two routes designed to pass through downtown and by most hotels. Service on **The Banff Bus** is pretty informal, but there's generally a bus every half hour. One route runs between the Banff Springs Hotel and down Banff Avenue to the northern end of town; the other runs between the train station and the Banff Hostel on Tunnel Mountain; the fare is C$1 (US65¢). The bus operates summer only; call ☎ 403/760-8294 for details.

For a taxi, call **Banff Taxi and Limousine** at ☎ 403/762-4444. For a rental car, contact **Tilden Rent-A-Car,** at the corner of Caribou and Lynx streets (☎ 403/762-2688), or **Banff Rent A Car,** 204 Lynx St. (☎ 403/762-3352), for a less expensive but reliable used vehicle. **Avis, Budget,** and **Hertz** also have offices in Banff.

SPECIAL EVENTS   The **Banff Centre,** St. Julien Road (☎ 800/413-8368 or 403/762-6300; www.banffcentre.ab.ca), is a remarkable year-round institution devoted to art and entertainment in the widest sense. June to August annually, the center hosts the ✪ **Banff Arts Festival,** offering a stimulating mix of drama, opera, jazz, ballet, classical and pop music, singing, and the visual arts. Highlights include the International String Quartet Competition, with 10 world-class quartets vying for a cash prize and a national tour; the Digital Playgrounds series brings performance artists to the stage. Tickets for some of the events cost C$8 to C$22 (US$5 to US$15); many are free. In November, the center shows the **Festival of Mountain Films.** Find out what's currently on by getting the program at the Banff Tourism Bureau or by checking out the Banff Centre Web site at **www.banffcentre.ab.ca/CFA**.

EXPLORING BANFF

Apart from helicopter excursions, the best way to get an overall view of Banff's mountain landscape is by the **Sulphur Mountain Gondola Lift** (☎ 403/762-5438), whose lower terminal is 6km (3.7 miles) southeast of Banff on Mountain Avenue. The gondolas are roomy, safe, and fully enclosed; the panoramas are stunning. At the upper terminal is the Summit Restaurant for dining with a view, and hiking trails are along the mountain ridges. Rides cost C$12 (US$8) adults and C$6 (US$4) children 5 to 11; children under 5 ride free.

    Lake Minnewanka Boat Tours (☎ 403/762-3473; fax 403/762-2800) offers scenic and wildlife-viewing trips in glassed-in motor cruisers on the lake, just 24km (15 miles) north of Banff. Trips are usually 1½ hours long and cost C$26 (US$17) adults and C$11 (US$7) children 11 and under. During high season, five trips depart daily; these cruises are popular, so reservations are suggested. Buses run from the Banff bus station to the lake in conjunction with the boat departure schedules.

    The **Buffalo Nations Luxton Museum** (☎ 403/762-2388) is devoted to the history of native Canada and housed in a log fort south of the Bow River, just across the bridge. The Luxton offers realistic dioramas, a sun-dance exhibit, artifacts, weaponry, and ornaments. Admission is C$6 (US$4) adults, C$3.75 (US$2.50) seniors/students, and C$2.25 (US$1.50) children. The museum is open daily 9am to 7pm.

    Part art gallery, part local-history museum, the **Whyte Museum of the Canadian Rockies,** 111 Bear St. (☎ 403/762-2291), is the only museum in North America that collects, exhibits, and interprets the history and culture of the Canadian Rockies. Two large furnished heritage homes on the museum grounds are open during summer and stand as a memorial to the pioneers of the Canadian Rockies. Interpretive programs and tours run year-round. Mid-May to mid-October, the Elizabeth Rummel Tea Room offers light lunches, desserts, and coffee. Admission is C$4 (US$2.65) adults and C$2 (US$1.35) seniors/students; children under 5 are free. It's open daily 10am to 6pm in high season, with limited hours at other times.

    Housed in a lovely wood-lined building from the 1910s, the **Banff Park Museum,** beside the Bow River Bridge (☎ 403/762-1558), is largely a paean to taxidermy, but there's a lot to learn here about the wildlife of the park and how the various ecosystems interrelate. The real pleasure, though, is the rustic lodge-style building, now preserved as a National Historic Site. Admission is C$2.25 (US$1.50) adults, C$1.75 (US$1.15) seniors, and C$1.25 (US85¢) youths 6 to 16; children 6 and under are free. Summer, it's open daily 10am to 6pm.

    Though most people now associate Banff with skiing or hiking, in the early days of the park, travelers streamed in to visit the curative hot springs. In fact, it was the discovery of the hot springs now preserved as the **Cave and Basin National Historic Site** (☎ 403/762-1566) that spurred the creation of the national park in 1888. During the 1910s, these hot mineral waters, which rise in a limestone cave, were piped into a rather grand natatorium. The Cave and Basin springs are no longer open for swimming or soaking, but the old pool area and the original hot springs cave have been preserved along with interpretive displays and films. Entrance is C$2.25 (US$1.50) adults, C$1.75 (US$1.15) seniors, and C$1.25 (US85¢) youths 6 to 18; children under 6 are free. It's open daily 9am to 6pm. The Cave and Basin is 1.6km (1 mile) west of Banff; turn right at the west end of the Bow River Bridge.

    If you want a soak in mountain hot springs, drive up to **Upper Hot Springs Pool** (☎ 403/762-1515), at the top of Mountain Avenue, 5km (3.1 miles) west of Banff.

The pool/spa complex has recently undergone a complete renovation. In addition to the redesigned pool filled with hot sulfurous waters, there are a restaurant, snack bar, and home spa boutique. If you're looking more for a cure than a splash, go to the adjacent **Upper Hot Springs Spa** (☎ 403/760-2500), where you get access to a steam room, massage therapists, plunge pools, and various aromatherapy treatments. Admission to the pool is C$7 (US$4.65) adults, C$6 (US$4) seniors, C$3.50 (US$2.35) children 3 to 16, and C$20 (US$13) families. The spa is open to adults only and costs C$30 (US$20).

The **Natural History Museum**, 112 Banff Ave. (☎ 403/762-4747), has displays of early forms of life on earth, dating from the Canadian dinosaurs of 350 million years ago, plus an "authentic" model of a Sasquatch, or "Bigfoot." Summer hours are daily 11am to 8pm, and admission is free.

SHOPPING

The degree to which you like the town of Banff will depend largely on your taste for shopping. **Banff Avenue** is increasingly an open-air boutique mall, with throngs of shoppers milling around, toting their latest purchases. Of course, you'd expect to find excellent outdoor gear and sporting-good stores here, as well as the usual T-shirt and gift emporiums. What's more surprising are the boutiques devoted to Paris and New York designers, the upscale jewelry stores, and the high-end art galleries. What's most surprising is that it seems most visitors actually prefer to while away their time in this masterpiece of nature called Banff by shopping for English soaps or Italian shoes.

There are no secrets to shopping in Banff: Arcade after arcade opens out onto Banff Avenue; you'll find everything you need. Quality and prices are both quite high.

WHERE TO STAY

Banff National Park offers hundreds of campsites within easy commuting distance of Banff. The closest are the three ✪ **Tunnel Mountain campgrounds,** just past the youth hostel west of town. Two of the campgrounds are for RVs only and have both partial and full hookups, costing C$19 (US$13); the third has showers and is usually reserved for tenters, costing C$16 (US$11). For more details, call the park's visitor center at ☎ 403/762-1500. Campsites within the park can't be reserved in advance.

All prices below are for high season. Call for reduced off-season rates.

Very Expensive

Banff Park Lodge Resort & Conference Centre. 222 Lynx St., Banff, AB T0L 0C0. ☎ **800/661-9266** or 403/762-4433. Fax 403/762-3553. www.banffparklodge.com. E-mail info@banffparklodge.com. 212 units. A/C TV TEL. C$229–C$299 (US$153–US$199) double. Extra person C$10–C$15 (US$7–US$10). Children 16 and under stay free in parents' room. Off-season and ski rates available. AE, CB, DC, ER, MC, V. Free heated parking underground.

A large cedar-and-oak structure with a cosmopolitan air, the Banff Park Lodge is a quiet block and a half off the main street, near the Bow River. Calm and sophisticated are the key words here: All the guest rooms are soundproofed, and après-ski cavorting isn't the norm or even much encouraged. The lodge seems like a tranquil retreat after a day in antic Banff. The rooms are spacious and exceptionally well furnished, all with balconies and twin vanities (one inside, one outside the bathroom). The lodge, with its abundant ground-floor rooms and wide halls, is popular with travelers with mobility concerns.

Dining/Diversions: The lodge has one formal and one family-style restaurant, plus a cocktail lounge.

Amenities: Concierge, room service, laundry/dry cleaning; indoor pool with whirlpool and steam room, 10 convention rooms, shopping arcade, beauty salon, heated parking.

Banff Springs Hotel. Spray Ave. (P.O. Box 960), Banff, AB T0L 0C0. ☎ **800/441-1414** or 403/762-2211. Fax 403/762-5755. www.cphotels.com. E-mail bshres@cphotels.ca. 875 units. MINIBAR TV TEL. C$233–C$449 (US$155–US$299) double; C$609–C$1,257 (US$406–US$838) suite. Rates include full breakfast. AE, DC, DISC, ER, MC, V. Valet parking C$11 (US$7); self-parking C$7 (US$4.65).

Standing north of Bow River Falls like a Scottish baronial fortress, the Banff Springs Hotel is one of North America's most beautiful and famous hotels. The Canadian Pacific Railroad founded this stone castle in 1888 as an opulent destination resort, and it's still the best address in Banff—especially after the full 1997 renovation. The hotel doesn't offer the largest rooms in Banff, but with the views, the spa, and the near-pageantry of service, it's still the most amazing resort in an area blessed with great hotels. The Springs greets you with a reception hall of such splendor you won't be surprised to learn it maintains a staff of 1,200 and holds medieval banquets for convention groups.

Dining/Diversions: The hotel boasts 15 food outlets, from palatial to functional, and three cocktail lounges.

Amenities: Concierge, 24-hour room service, dry cleaning, twice-daily maid service, secretarial service, courtesy car; Solace, a European-style health and beauty spa, with therapeutic mineral baths, massage treatments, aerobic and fitness training, and nutritional consultation; 50 stores and boutiques, Olympic-size indoor pool, tennis courts, business center; 27-hole golf course considered one of the world's most scenic.

✪ **Buffalo Mountain Lodge.** P.O. Box 1326, Banff, AB T0L 0C0. ☎ **800/661-1367** or 403/762-2400. Fax 403/762-4495. www.crmr.com. E-mail bmll@telusplanet.net. 108 units. TV TEL. C$255 (US$170) double; C$325 (US$217) 1-bedroom apt. AE, ER, MC, V.

The most handsome of the hotel/condominium developments on Tunnel Mountain, just 1.6km (1 mile) west of Banff, the Buffalo Mountain is the perfect place to stay if you'd rather avoid the frenetic pace of downtown Banff and yet remain central to restaurants and activities. Its quiet location, beautiful central lodge, and choice of room types make this a good alternative to equally priced lodgings in the heart of Banff.

The lodge building itself is an enormous log cabin right out of your fantasies. The three-story lobby is supported by massive log rafters and filled with warm Navajo-style carpets and comfortable Western-style furniture. A huge fieldstone fireplace dominates the interior, separating the lovely dining room and cozy lounge. The guest rooms are located in units scattered around the forested 8-acre holding. There are three room types: from cozy one-bedroom apartments with full kitchens to exceptionally handsome rooms in brand-new lodge buildings. The nicest rooms are the Premiers, which feature VCRs and beautiful slate-floored bathrooms, with clawfoot tubs and slate-walled showers. The quality pine-and-twig furniture lends a rustic look to the otherwise-sophisticated decor. All rooms have fireplaces (wood is free and stacked near your door) and balconies or patios, and the beds have feather duvets and pillows. These are some of the most attractive rooms in Banff.

Dining: The lodge restaurant is one of the best in Banff, and in summer the excellent Cilantro Cafe opens with deck seating.

Amenities: Baby-sitting, dry cleaning; steam room, outdoor hot tub.

✪ **Rimrock Resort Hotel.** Mountain Ave. (5km/3.1 miles south of Banff; P.O. Box 1110), Banff, AB T0L 0C0. ☎ **800/661-1587** or 403/762-3356. Fax 403/762-1842.

www.rimrock@banff.net. E-mail rimrock@banff.net. 366 units. A/C MINIBAR TV TEL. C$240–C$340 (US$160–US$227) double; from C$350–C$1,200 (US$233–US$800) suite. AE, DC, DISC, JCB, MC, V. Valet parking C$10 (US$7); self-parking C$6 (US$4); heated garage.

If you want modern luxury and views, this should be your hotel. This enormous stunning hotel (completed in 1993) drops nine floors from its roadside lobby entrance down a steep mountain slope, affording tremendous views from nearly all rooms. Aiming for the same quality of architecture and majesty of scale as venerable older lodges, the Rimrock offers a massive glass-fronted lobby, lined with cherry wood, tiled with unpolished marble floors, and filled with soft inviting chairs, couches, and Oriental carpets. The limestone fireplace, open on two sides, is so large that staff members just step inside to ready the kindling. The large guest rooms boast handsome furniture; some have balconies. Standard room prices vary only by view; all rooms are the same size. The suites are truly large, with balconies, wet bars, and loads of cozy couches.

Dining/Diversions: There are two restaurants, including the four-star Ristorante Classico (see "Where to Dine" below), and a lobby lounge.

Amenities: Concierge, 24-hour room service, laundry/dry cleaning, secretarial service, free shuttle bus to and from downtown Banff; fitness facilities like indoor pool, squash court, hot tub, workout room with regularly scheduled aerobics, weight training, and fitness devices; shopping arcade, beauty salon.

Expensive

Brewster's Mountain Lodge. 208 Caribou St., Banff, AB T0L 0C0. ☎ **888/762-2900** or 403/762-2900. Fax 403/762-2970. www.brewsteradventures.com. E-mail bml@ brewsteradventures.com. 63 units. TV TEL. C$179–C$199 (US$119–US$133) double. AE, MC, V. Free heated parking.

This new lodgelike hotel is in the heart of Banff and operated by the Brewster family, which dominates a lot of local recreation, guest ranching, and transportation. The Brewster affiliation makes it simple to take advantage of lodging/adventure packages involving horseback riding and hiking. This modern hotel does its best to look rustic: peeled-log post and beams fill the lobby and foyer, and quality pine furniture and paneling grace the large guest rooms.

Dining: There's no restaurant in the hotel but plenty are adjacent in central Banff.

Amenities: Concierge; whirlpool, sauna, steam room, rooms accessible for travelers with disabilities.

Caribou Lodge. 521 Banff Ave., Banff, AB T0L 0C0. ☎ **800/563-8764** or 403/762-5887. Fax 403/762-5918. 207 units. TV TEL. C$193–C$200 (US$125–US$133) double; C$250–C$300 (US$167–US$200) suite. Up to 2 children under 16 stay free in parents' room. AE, DC, DISC, ER, MC, V. Free heated parking.

Built in 1993, the Caribou, with its gabled green roof, outdoor patio, bay windows, and wooden balconies, has a Western-lodge look that blends well with the alpine landscape. The interior is equally impressive, including a vast lobby with a slate tile floor, peeled log woodwork, and a huge stone fireplace. The finely furnished bedrooms continue the Western theme with rustic pine chairs and beds with snug down comforters. The bathrooms are spacious. Some of the rooms have balconies. The lodge is long on service and friendliness; although it's not in the absolute center of town (about 10 min. on foot), a free shuttle bus ferries guests to destinations throughout Banff.

Dining: The Keg restaurant is a favorite with locals, serving hand-cut steaks for C$14 to C$17 (US$9 to US$11).

Amenities: Concierge, room service, free downtown shuttle; three hot tubs, sauna, steam room.

Dynasty Inn. P.O. Box 1018, 501 Banff Ave., Banff, AB T0L 0C0. ☎ **800/667-1464** or 403/762-8844. Fax 403/762-4418. 99 units. A/C TV TEL. C$189 (US$126) double. Extra person C$10 (US$7). Children under 12 stay free in parent's room. Early-bird specials available. AE, MC, V. Free heated underground parking.

One of the newest accommodations in Banff, about a mile from downtown along the Banff Avenue strip, the Dynasty is a very handsome mountain lodge with very nicely furnished guest rooms. All have private balconies and some have fireplaces. Facilities include a steam room and a whirlpool.

○ **Thea's House.** 138 Otter St. (Box 661), Banff, AB T0L 0C0. ☎ **403/762-2499.** Fax 403/762-2496. www.theashouse.com. E-mail theas@telusplanet.net. 3 units. TV TEL. C$225–C$245 (US$150–US$163) double. MC, V.

Banff's most upscale B&B, Thea's is a striking modern log-and-stone home just a couple minutes' walk from downtown. It boasts 25-foot ceilings, antiques and exquisite artwork, and friendly, discreet service. The guest rooms are all very large and beautifully furnished, with vaulted pine ceilings, fir floors, rustic pine and antique furniture, fireplaces, sitting areas, cassette and CD players, and private balconies. "Elegant Alpine" is how Thea's describes itself, and you'll have no trouble imagining you're in a fairy-tale mountain lodge while here. A perfect spot for a romantic getaway.

Moderate

Blue Mountain Lodge. Box 2763, Banff, AB T0L 0C0. ☎ **800/313-6203** or 403/762-5134. Fax 403/762-8081. www.bluemtnlodge.com. E-mail info@bluemtnlodge.com. 10 units. TV. From C$74 (US$49) double. Extra person C$10 (US$7). Rates include continental breakfast. MC, V.

This rambling lodging just east of downtown began in 1908 as a boarding house. As you might expect in an older building built at the edge of the wilderness, the guest rooms were never exactly palatial, and when they were redesigned for en suite bathrooms, they got even smaller. That's the bad news. The good news is that the Blue Mountain Lodge is full of charm and funny nooks and crannies and that the small rooms mean you'll be spending time with new friends in the guest lounge and open kitchen. The owner admits that guests refer to the lodge as an upscale hostel, and that's accurate. The Blue Mountain is certainly one of the least expensive and friendliest places to stay in central Banff. Breakfast is served buffet style, or eggs are provided if you prefer to cook them on your own. Complimentary hot beverages and homemade cookies are served in the afternoon. Many of the guests who stay here are avid outdoorspeople, and this is a great place to stay if you're on your own and would appreciate meeting others to hike with. The staff is young, friendly, and eager to help you get out on the trails.

○ **Eleanor's House.** 125 Kootenay Ave., Box 1553, Banff, AB T0L 0C0. ☎ **403/760-2457.** Fax 403/762-3852. www.bbeleanor.com. E-mail info@bbeleanor.com. 2 units. TV TEL. C$135 (US$90) double. Rates include continental breakfast and evening drinks. Closed Nov–Jan. MC, V.

One of the most spacious and comfortable B&Bs in Banff, Eleanor's is on the south side of the Bow River, an easy walk from downtown. The large guest lounge has a Western feel, complete with stuffed game heads, and each guest room reflects the lives of the owners: a childhood on the prairies and a career as a park ranger. They're quite large and have full four-piece bathrooms, plus sitting areas. The welcome is gracious and the service very professional.

Homestead Inn. 217 Lynx St., Banff, AB T0L 0C0. ☎ **800/661-1021** or 403/762-4471. Fax 403/762-8877. 27 units. TV TEL. C$139 (US$93) double. Extra person C$10 (US$7). Children under 12 stay free in parents' room. AE, MC, V.

One of the best lodging deals in Banff is the Homestead Inn, only a block from all the action on Banff Avenue. Though the amenities are modest compared to what you'll find at the upscale alternatives, the guest rooms are tastefully furnished and come with couches, armchairs, and stylish bathrooms.

✪ **Mountain Home Bed & Breakfast.** 129 Muskrat St. (P.O. Box 272), Banff, AB T0L 0C0. ☎ **403/762-3889.** Fax 403/762-3254. www.banff.net/mountainhome/. E-mail mountainhome@banff.net. 3 units. TV. C$135 (US$90) double. Rates include breakfast. Extra person C$20 (US$13). MC, V.

If you're looking for a bit of historic charm yet all the modern comforts, this excellent B&B may be it. It was built as a tourist lodge in the 1940s and was a private home for years before being restored and turned back into a guesthouse. The rooms are large and nicely furnished with high-quality furniture and antiques. The decor manages to be evocative without being too fussy. Especially nice is the cozy Rundle Room, with its own slate fireplace. Breakfast is a full cooked meal with homemade baked goods. Downtown Banff is just a 2-minute walk away.

Pension Tannenhof. 121 Cave Ave. (Box 1914), Banff, AB T0L 0C0. ☎ **877/999-5011** or 403/762-4636. Fax 403/762-5660. pensiontannenhof.com. E-mail riedinger@hotmail.com. 10 units, 8 with bathroom. TV. C$85–C$135 (US$57–US$90) double. Rates include full breakfast. Extra person C$20 (US$13). MC, V.

Built during World War II by a Calgary businessman with 10 children, this rambling historic home is the result of an elaborate remodel of two preexisting cabins. During the war, no new construction was allowed, so the owner "remodeled" by building around the cabins, eventually tearing them down from the inside. The rooms have a mix of shared and en suite bathrooms; most rooms are quite large and are simply but adequately furnished. In a separate chalet at the back of the inn are two king suites, each with a fireplace, a jetted tub, and lots of room to spread out. Pension Tannenhof is an excellent value and is a good place to stay if you want clean, unfussy accommodations.

Red Carpet Inn. 425 Banff Ave., Banff, AB T0L 0C0. ☎ **800/267-3035** or 403/762-4184. Fax 403/762-4894. 52 units. TV TEL. C$110–C$125 (US$73–US$83) double. AE, MC, V.

A handsome three-story brick building with a balcony along the top floors, the Red Carpet is located along the long hotel-lined street leading to downtown. Well maintained and more than adequately furnished, it's one of the best lodging deals in Banff. The beds and furniture are ample and new; the rooms have easy chairs and a desk. There's no restaurant on the premises, but there's an excellent one next door. The entire facility is shipshape and clean—just the thing if you don't want to spend a fortune in Banff.

Inexpensive

Banff B&B. 440 Muskrat St. (Box 2932), Banff, AB T0L 0C0. ☎ **403/762-8806.** 2 units. C$75–C$100 (US$50–US$67) double. Rates include continental breakfast. V.

This modern home is just east of downtown in a quiet residential neighborhood. The guest rooms have queen-size beds, private or en suite bathrooms, and lots of natural light. Clean and unfussy, this is a good place if you're looking for a friendly, uncomplicated place to stay.

Banff International Hostel. On Tunnel Mountain Rd. (1.6km/1 mile west of Banff; P.O. Box 1358), Banff, AB T0L 0C0. ☎ **403/762-4122.** Fax 403/762-3441. E-mail banff@ HostellingIntl.ca. Sleeps 214 people. C$20 (US$13) members, C$24 (US$16) nonmembers. MC, V.

With a mix of two-, four-, and six-bed rooms, this new youth hostel is by far the most pleasant budget lodging in Banff. Couple and family rooms are also available. Reserve a place at least a month in advance during summer. Facilities include a recreation room, a kitchen area, a laundry, and a lounge area with a fireplace. Meals are available at the hostel's Cafe Alpenglow.

YWCA. 102 Spray Ave., Banff, AB T0L 0C0. ☎ **800/813-4138** or 403/762-3560. Fax 403/760-3202. E-mail info@ymcabanff.ab.ca. C$20 (US$13) bunk in a dorm (sleeping bag required); C$55–C$95 (US$37–US$63) double. Free parking. MC, V.

The YWCA is a bright modern building with good amenities just across the Bow River bridge from downtown. The Y welcomes both genders—singly, in couples, or in family groups—with accommodations in private or dorm rooms, as required. Some units have private bathrooms. There are also an assembly room with a TV and a guest laundry on the premises.

WHERE TO DINE

Food is generally good in Banff, though you pay handsomely for what you get. The difference in price between a simply okay meal in a theme restaurant and a nice meal in a classy dining room can be quite small. Service is often very indifferent, as most food servers have become used to waiting on the in-and-out-in-a-hurry tour-bus crowds.

An abundance of restaurants line **Banff Avenue;** most hotels have at least one dining room. You'll have no problem finding something good to eat in Banff, and the following recommendations are just the beginning of what's available in a very concentrated area.

Expensive

✪ **Buffalo Mountain Lodge.** 1.6km (1 mile) west of Banff on Tunnel Mountain Rd. ☎ **403/762-2400.** Reservations recommended on weekends. Main courses C$19–C$33 (US$13–US$22). Daily 6–10pm. AE, DC, ER, MC, V. INTERNATIONAL NOUVELLE.

One of the most pleasing restaurants in Banff, the dining room at the Buffalo Mountain Lodge occupies half the lodge's soaring three-story lobby in a quiet wooded location just outside town. As satisfying as all this is to the eye and the spirit, the food is even more notable. The chef brings together the best of regional ingredients—Albertan beef, lamb, pheasant, venison, trout, and BC salmon—and prepares each in a seasonally changing international style. For example, salmon trout is baked in a potato/saffron crust and roast free-range chicken is served with hazelnut couscous and creamed spinach. The fireplace-dominated lobby bar is a lovely place to come for an intimate cocktail.

Ristorante Classico. In the Rimrock Resort, 5km (3.1 miles) south of Banff on Mountain Ave. ☎ **403/762-3356.** Reservations required. Main courses C$26–C$39 (US$17–US$26); 5-course table d'hôte C$48 (US$32). AE, DC, DISC, JCB, MC, V. Tues–Sun 6–10pm. FINE ITALIAN.

This is Banff's dining room with the best views, and the four-star rating will appeal to serious gastronomes. The artfully prepared and aggressively flavored dishes featuring fresh seafood, veal, fowl, and up-to-the-minute ingredients are almost as impressive as the view. Even the table settings merit a mention: Paloma Picasso designed the china—the display plates are rumored to be worth more than C$500 (US$334). The menu features a mix of updated Italian favorites, along with more inventive dishes featuring local beef, lamb, and game. Unusual combinations include venison medallions served on barley risotto with a maple-mustard-whiskey sauce and a salad of arugula and baby lettuce garnished with quail eggs and blood oranges.

Moderate

Balkan Restaurant. 120 Banff Ave. ☎ **403/762-3454.** Main courses C$8–C$19 (US$5–US$13). AE, MC, V. Daily 11am–11pm. GREEK.

Up a flight of stairs is this airy blue and white dining room with windows overlooking the street. The fare consists of reliable Hellenic favorites, well prepared and served with a flourish; Canadian dishes and burgers are also available. The Greek platter (for two) consists of a small mountain of beef souvlaki, ribs, moussaka, lamb chops, tomatoes, and salad for C$45 (US$30). If you're dining alone, you can't do better than the *logo stifado* (rabbit stew) with onions and red wine.

✪ Coyotes Deli & Grill. 206 Caribou St. ☎ **403/762-3963.** Reservations accepted. Main courses C$14–C$22 (US$9–US$15). AE, DC, MC, V. Daily 7:30am–11pm. SOUTH-WEST/MEDITERRANEAN.

One of the few places in Banff where you can get lighter, healthier food, Coyotes is an attractive bistro-like restaurant with excellent contemporary Southwestern cuisine. There's a broad selection of vegetarian dishes, as well as fresh fish, grilled meats, and multiethnic dishes prepared with an eye to spice and full flavors. In addition, there's a deli where you can get the makings for a picnic and head to the park. This is a very popular place, so go early or make reservations if you don't want to stand in line.

Giorgio's Trattoria. 219 Banff Ave. ☎ **403/762-5114.** Reservations accepted only for groups of 8 or more. Pasta courses C$12–C$15 (US$8–US$10); pizza C$12–C$17 (US$8–US$11). MC, V. Daily 4:30–10pm. ITALIAN.

Giorgio's is a cozy no-smoking eatery dimly lit by low-hanging pink-gleaming lamps over the tables. Divided into a counter section and table portion (both comfortable), Giorgio's serves authentic old-country specialties at eminently reasonable prices. Wonderful crisp rolls—a delicacy in themselves—come with your meal. Don't miss the *gnocchi alla piemontese* (potato dumplings in meat sauce) or the Sicilian *cassata* (candied fruit ice cream).

Magpie & Stump Restaurant & Cantina. 203 Caribou St. ☎ **403/762-4067.** Reservations not accepted. Main courses C$8–C$12 (US$5–US$8). AE, ER, MC, V. Daily noon–2am. MEXICAN.

The false-fronted Magpie & Stump doesn't really match up architecturally with the rest of smart downtown Banff—and thank goodness, neither does the food or atmosphere. The food is traditional Mexican, done up with style and heft: Someone in the kitchen sure knows how to handle a tortilla. This isn't high cuisine, just well-prepared favorites like enchiladas, tamales, tacos, and the like. But the dishes are well priced compared to those elsewhere in town, and you won't go away hungry. The interior looks like a cozy dark English pub, except there are buffalo heads and cactus plants everywhere (plus a lot of Southwest kitsch). This is also a good place for a lively late-night drink, because the town's young summer waitstaff likes to crowd in here to unwind with an after-shift beverage—usually a beer in a jam jar.

St. James Gate Irish Pub. 205 Wolf St. ☎ **403/762-9355.** Reservations not accepted. Main courses C$10–C$17 (US$7–US$11). MC, V. Mon–Fri 11am–2pm, Sat–Sun 10am–2pm. IRISH.

The St. James Gate is owned by Guinness, which knows a thing or two about Irish pubs. Newly created to resemble a traditional draught house, this lively pub also has a very extensive menu of bar meals to accompany its selection of draft beers and ales. Halibut fish-and-chips is a specialty, as are traditional meat pies and sandwiches. Full meals are also available. This is a lively place, and in the Irish tradition, you never know when a table full of dislocated Finnians will break into a heartfelt ballad or two.

Inexpensive

If you're really on a budget, then you'll probably get used to the deli case at **Safeways,** at Martin and Elk streets, because even inexpensive food is costly in Banff. Here are a few suggestions for fun places where you don't have to spend a fortune to fill up.

Cafe Alenglow, at the Banff International Hostel, Tunnel Mountain Road (☎ 403/762-4122), offers healthy and inexpensive food with youthful flair; it has an outdoor patio and a liquor license and is open daily 7am to 9pm. **Bruno's Cafe and Grill,** 304 Caribou St. (☎ 403/762-8115), is a coffee shop with Italian sandwiches, salads, and lunch and dinner specials; it's open daily 7am to 11pm (to 2am in summer). The **Jump Start Coffee and Sandwich Place,** 206 Buffalo St. (☎ 403/ 762-0332), offers sandwiches, soup, salads, and pastries; it'll also pack a picnic for you. It's open daily 7am to 6pm. For great home-baked muffins and rolls, go to **Evelyn's Coffee Bar,** 201 Banff Ave. (☎ 403/762-0352); light meals are available daily 7am to 11pm. For all-day and all-night pizza, head to **Aardvark Pizza,** 304a Caribou St. (☎ 403/762-5500), open daily 11am to 4am.

BANFF AFTER DARK

Most of Banff's larger hotels and restaurants offer some manner of nightly entertainment. However, for a more lively selection, head to downtown's Banff Avenue. One of the best spots is **Wild Bill's,** the "legendary saloon" at 203 Banff Ave. (☎ 403/ 762-0333), where you can watch Asian tourists in cowboy hats learning to line dance, and **The Barbary Coast,** 119 Banff Ave. (☎ 403/762-4616), a "California-style" bar/restaurant that features live music among the potted plants. The **Rose and Crown Pub,** 202 Banff Ave. (☎ 403/762-2121), brings in live entertainers all week; English-style pub grub is available late.

The new focus of young club-goers is the three-floor extravaganza at the corner of Banff Avenue and Caribou Street. **The Hard Rock Cafe,** 137 Banff Ave. (☎ 403/ 760-2347), takes up the main floor, while immediately below is **Outabounds** (☎ 403/762-8434), a dance club. Topping all is **King Eddy Billiards** (☎ 403/ 762-4629), the hip place to smoke cigars and shoot pool. **St. James Gate Irish Pub,** 205 Wolf St. (☎ 403/762-9355), is the place if you're looking for a pint and a conversation.

LAKE LOUISE

Lake Louise (56km/35 miles northwest of Banff), deep green and surrounded by forest-clad snowcapped mountains, is one of the most famed beauty spots in a park renowned for its fabulous scenery. The village that's grown up in the valley below the lake has developed in the past few years into a resort destination in its own right. Lake Louise boasts the largest ski area in Canada and easy hiking access to the remote high country along the Continental Divide.

The lake may be spectacular, but probably as many people wind up the road to Lake Louise to see its most famous resort, the Chateau Lake Louise. Built by the Canadian Pacific Railroad, the Chateau is, along with the Banff Springs Hotel, one of the most celebrated in Canada. More than just a lodging, this storybook castle perched 1.6km (1 mile) high in the Rockies is the center of recreation, dining, shopping, and entertainment for the Lake Louise area.

There's a reason the water in Lake Louise is as green as an emerald: The stream water tumbling into the lake is filled with minerals, ground by the glaciers that hang above the lake. Sunlight refracts off the glacial "flour," creating vivid colors. You'll want at least to stroll around the shore of the lake and gawk at the glaciers and back at the massive Chateau. The gentle **Lakeshore Trail** follows the northern shore of the lake to the end of Lake Louise. If you're looking for more exercise and even better views, continue on the trail as it begins to climb. Now called the ✪ **Plain of Six Glaciers Trail,** the path passes a teahouse (5km/3.1 miles from the Chateau and open summers only) on its way to a tremendous viewpoint over Victoria Glacier and Lake Louise.

SEEING THE SIGHTS

Early June to mid-September, the **Lake Louise Summer Sightseeing Lift** (☎ **403/522-3555**) offers a 10-minute ride up to the Whitehorn Lodge, midway up the Lake Louise Ski Area. From here the views onto Lake Louise and the mountains along the Continental Divide are magnificent. Hikers can strike out and follow one of many trails into alpine meadows or join a free naturalist-led walk and explore the delicate ecosystem. The restaurant at the Whitehorn Lodge is much better than you'd expect at a ski area, and specially priced ride-and-dine tickets are available for those who'd like to have a meal at 7,000 feet; the Canadian BBQ buffet is especially fun. The round-trip costs C$11 (US$7) adults, C$10 (US$7) seniors/students, and C$8 (US$5) children 6 to 15.

To many visitors, ✪ **Moraine Lake** is an even more dramatic and beautiful spot than its more famous twin, Lake Louise. Ten spirelike peaks over 10,000 feet rise precipitously from the shores of a tiny gem-blue lake. It's an unforgettable sight, definitely worth the short 13km (8-mile) drive from Lake Louise. There's a lodge on the shore of the lake with meals and refreshments, and a hiking trail follows the lake's north shore to the mountain cliffs. If the panorama looks familiar, you might've seen it on the back of a Canadian $20 bill.

WHERE TO STAY

✪ **Chateau Lake Louise.** Lake Louise, AB T0L 1E0. ☎ **800/441-1414** or 403/522-3511. Fax 403/522-3834. 513 units. A/C MINIBAR TV TEL. High season C$579–C$719 (US$386–US$480) double; C$779–C$919 (US$519–US$613) suite. Rates depend on lake view or mountain view. Off-season rates and packages available. Children under 17 stay free in parents' room. AE, CB, DC, DISC, ER, MC, V. Parking C$6 (US$4).

The Chateau is one of the best-loved hotels in North America. If you want to splurge on only one hotel in the Canadian Rockies, make it this massive formal structure, blue-roofed and turreted, furnished with Edwardian sumptuousness and alpine charm—you won't be sorry. Built by the Canadian Pacific Railroad in stages over the course of a century, the hotel was remodeled and upgraded in 1990 and now stays open year-round. The cavernous grand lobby, with its curious figurative chandeliers, gives way to a sitting room filled with overstuffed chairs and couches; these and other common areas overlook the gardens and the deep blue-green lake in its glacier-hung cirque. The marble-tiled bathrooms, crystal barware, and comfy down duvets in your room are indicative of the attention to detail and luxury you can expect.

Dining/Diversions: The Chateau offers nine restaurants and eateries in the high season (including the exquisite Edelweiss room), as well as two lounge and bar areas. Guests can enjoy afternoon tea and cabaret entertainment at night.

Amenities: Indoor pool, whirlpool, steam room, tanning salon, shopping arcade.

Deer Lodge. 109 Lake Louise Dr., Lake Louise (mailing address: P.O. Box 1598, Banff, AB T0L 0C0). ☎ **800/661-1595** or 403/522-3747. www.crmr.com/dl/deer.html. E-mail info@crmr.com. 73 units. C$150–C$220 (US$100–US$147) double. AE, ER, MC, V.

The Chateau Lake Louise isn't the only historic lodge at Lake Louise. Built in the 1920s, the Deer Lodge was a tea house for the early mountaineers who came to the area to hike (the original tea room is now the very handsome and rustic Mt. Fairview Dining Room). Although Lake Louise itself is a short stroll away, the charming Deer Lodge offers a sense of privacy and solitude the busy Chateau Lake Louise can't offer.

There are three types of rooms: cozy lodge rooms with either a double bed or twin beds in the original lodge, larger rooms with double beds in the newer Tower Wing, and Heritage Rooms in the newest wing with the largest rooms. All have feather duvets and handsome mountain-style furniture. If you're looking for a quiet mountain getaway, choose this over the Chateau.

Dining/Diversions: The Mt. Fairmont Dining Room offers Northwest cuisine, and the Caribou Lounge is open for drinks and three meals daily.

Amenities: Rooftop hot tub, billiards table, games room, TV and VCR area, sauna.

Lake Louise Inn. 210 Village Rd. (P.O. Box 209), Lake Louise, AB T0L 1E0. ☎ **800/ 661-9237** or 403/522-3791. Fax 403/522-2018. www.lakelouiseinn.com. E-mail llinn@ telusplanet.net. 232 units. TV TEL. High season C$128–C$264 (US$85–US$176) double. Free parking. AE, DC, MC, V.

The Lake Louise Inn stands in a wooded 8-acre estate, a 7-minute drive from the fabled lake at the base of the moraine, with forest all around and snowcapped mountains peering over the trees outside your window. The inn consists of five buildings— a central lodge (with a pool, whirlpool, steam room, restaurant, bar, and lounge) and four lodging units. There are five room types, beginning with standard twin rooms with double beds. The superior queen and executive rooms are the newest and nicest, with pine-railed balconies and sitting areas; for families, the superior lofts are capable of sleeping eight, each with two bathrooms, a complete kitchen (including dishwasher), a living room and fireplace, and two bedrooms and a foldout couch.

WHERE TO DINE

Lake Louise Station. 200 Sentinel Rd. ☎ **403/522-2600.** Reservations recommended on weekends. Pizzas to C$15 (US$10); steaks and seafood C$12–C$22 (US$8–US$15). AE, MC, V. Daily 11:30am–midnight. PIZZA/STEAKS.

This log building served as the Lake Louise train station for nearly a century, before rail service ceased in the 1980s. Now the handsome and historic building has been converted into a bar/restaurant. Dining is accommodated in the old waiting room, and the ticketing lobby is where to go for a quiet drink. Two old dining cars sit on the sidings beside the station and are open for fine dining in the evenings. Excellent steaks and grilled meat are the specialties here.

✪ **Post Hotel Dining Room.** In the Post Hotel, Lake Louise. ☎ **403/522-3989.** www.posthotel.com. Reservations required. Main courses C$26–C$39 (US$17–US$26). AE, MC, V. Daily 7–11am, 11:30am–2pm, and 5–10pm. INTERNATIONAL.

Here you'll find some of the finest dining in the Canadian Rockies, in a long rustic room with wood beams and windows looking out onto glaciered peaks. The dinner menu focuses on full-flavored meat and fish preparations. For an appetizer, you might try scampi, served on asparagus with both an orange and a lemon sauce; rack of lamb is served with grilled portobello mushrooms and a rosemary sauce. The desserts are equally imaginative. The service is excellent, as is the very impressive wine list, with some good values discreetly hidden in the mostly French selection.

✪ **Walliser Stube Wine Bar.** In Chateau Lake Louise. ☎ **403/522-1817.** Reservations required. Main courses C$13–C$20 (US$9–US$13); fondues C$32–C$43 (US$21– US$29). AE, DISC, ER, MC, V. Daily 5–11:30pm. SWISS.

While the Chateau Lake Louise operates four major restaurants, including the formal Edelweiss Room, the most fun and relaxing place to eat is the Walliser Stube, a small dining room that serves excellent Swiss-style food and some of the best fondue ever. The back dining room is called the Library and is indeed lined with tall wood cases and rolling library ladders. Happily, the cases are filled with wine, not books: Part of the Chateau's huge wine selection is stored here. The cheese fondue is fabulous; forget the stringy glutinous experience you had in the 1970s. Hot-meat fondues are also available, as is an excellent veal-and-vegetable fondue cooked in spicy wine broth. For the raclettes, heat lamps melt chunks of cheese until bubbly, and the aromatic, molten result is spread on bread. It's all great fun in a great atmosphere—go with friends and you'll have a blast.

THE ICEFIELDS PARKWAY

Between Lake Louise and Jasper winds one of the most spectacular mountain roads in the world: the ✪ **Icefields Parkway,** climbing through three deep river valleys, beneath soaring glacier-notched mountains, and past dozens of hornlike peaks shrouded with permanent snowfields. Capping this 287km (178-mile) route is the **Columbia Icefields,** a massive dome of glacial ice and snow straddling the top of the continent. From this mighty cache of ice—the largest nonpolar ice cap in the world—flow the Columbia, Athabasca, and North Saskatchewan rivers.

Though you can drive the Icefields Parkway in 3 hours, plan to take enough time to stop at eerily green lakes, hike to a waterfall, and take an excursion up onto the Columbia Icefields. There's also a good chance you'll see wildlife: ambling bighorn sheep, mountain goats, elks with huge shovel antlers, momma bears with cubs—all guaranteed to halt traffic and set cameras clicking.

After Lake Louise, the highway divides: Highway 1 continues west toward Golden, British Columbia, while Highway 93 (the Icefields Parkway) continues north along the Bow River. **Bow Lake,** the river's source, glimmers below enormous **Crowfoot Glacier;** when the glacier was named, a third "toe" was more in evidence, lending a resemblance to a bird's claw. Roadside viewpoints look across the lake at the glacier; **Num-Ti-Jah Lodge,** on the shores of Bow Lake, is a good place to stop for a bite to eat and some photographs.

The road mounts Bow Summit and drops into the North Saskatchewan River drainage. Stop at the **Peyto Lake Viewpoint** and hike up a short but steep trail to glimpse this startling blue-green body of water. The North Saskatchewan River collects its tributaries at the little community of Saskatchewan River Crossing; thousands of miles later, the Bow and the Saskatchewan rivers join and flow east through Lake Winnipeg to Hudson Bay.

The parkway then begins to climb up in earnest toward the Sunwapta Pass. Here, in the shadows of 11,450-foot **Mount Athabasca,** the icy tendrils of the **Columbia Icefields** come into view. However impressive these glaciers may seem from the road, they're nothing compared to the massive amounts of centuries-old ice and snow hidden by mountain peaks; the Columbia Icefields cover nearly 518km^2 (200 sq. miles) and are more than 2,500 feet thick. From the parkway, the closest fingers of the ice field are Athabasca Glacier, filling the horizon to the west of the **Columbia Icefields Centre** (☎ 780/852-7032), a newly rebuilt lodge with a restaurant open daily 8am to 10pm and accommodations (with doubles starting at C$195/US$131). The **Icefield Information Centre** (☎ 780/852-7030), a park service office that answers questions about the area, stands beside the lodge. The center is open daily: May to June 14 and September 8 to October 15 9am to 5pm and June 15 to September 7 9am to 6pm.

From the **Brewster Snocoach Tours ticket office** (☎ 403/762-6735), specially designed buses with balloon tires take you out onto the face of the glacier. The 90-minute excursion includes a chance to hike the surface of Athabasca Glacier. The Snocoach Tour is C$25 (US$17) adults and C$10 (US$7) children 6 to 15; children under 6 are free. If you don't have the time or cash (no credit cards are accepted) for the Snocoach Tour, you can drive to the toe of the glacier and walk up onto the surface. *Use extreme caution* when on the glacier—tumbling into a crevasse can result in broken limbs or even death.

From the Columbia Icefields, the parkway descends steeply into the Athabasca River drainage. From the parking area for **Sunwapta Falls,** you can decide to crowd around the chain-link fence and peer at this turbulent falls or to take the half-hour hike to equally impressive but less crowded Lower Sunwapta Falls. **Athabasca Falls,** farther north along the parkway, is another must-see. Here, the powerful wide Athabasca River constricts into a roaring torrent before dropping 82 feet into a narrow canyon. A mist-covered bridge crosses the chasm beyond the falls; a series of trails leads to more viewpoints. The parkway continues along the Athabasca River, through a landscape of meadows and lakes, before entering the Jasper Townsite.

Facilities are few along the parkway. Hikers and bikers will be pleased to know that there are rustic **hostels** at Mosquito Creek, Rampart Creek, Hilda Creek, Beauty Creek, Athabasca Falls, and Mount Edith Cavell. Reservations for all the Icefield Parkway hostels can be made by calling ☎ **403/439-3215.** A **shuttle** runs among the Calgary International Hostel and hostels in Banff, in Lake Louise, and along the Icefield Parkway to Jasper. You must have reservations at the destination hostel to use the service. Call ☎ **403/283-5551** for more information.

8 Jasper National Park: Canada's Largest Mountain Park

Jasper, now Canada's largest mountain park, was established in 1907. Slightly less busy than Banff to the south, Jasper Park attracts a much more outdoors-oriented crowd, with hiking, biking, climbing, horseback riding, and rafting the main activities. Sure, there are shopping and fine dining in Jasper, but it's not the focus of activity, as in Banff. Travelers seem a bit more determined and rugged-looking, as if they've just stumbled in from a long-distance hiking trail or off the face of a rock—certainly there's no shortage of outdoor recreation here.

For more details about the park, contact **Jasper National Park,** P.O. Box 10, Jasper, AB T0E 1E0 (☎ **780/852-6176**).

SPORTS & OUTDOOR ACTIVITIES IN THE PARK

A clearinghouse of local outfitters and guides is the **Jasper Adventure Centre,** 604 Connaught Dr. (☎ **800/565-7547** in western Canada, or 780/852-5595; www. jasperadventurecentre.com; e-mail tours@telusplanet.net). White-water raft and canoe trips, horseback rides, guided hikes, and other activities can be ticketed out of this office. June to October 1, it's open 9am to 9pm.

A number of shops rent most of the equipment you'll need for an adventure. Rent a mountain bike for C$8 (US$5) per hour or C$20 (US$13) per day from **On-Line Sport and Tackle,** 600 Patricia St. (☎ **780/852-3630**); it also rents canoes and rafts, tents, fishing gear, and skis. They can also set you up with guided rafting and fishing trips. Snowboards, cross-country ski equipment, and more bikes are available from **Freewheel Cycle,** 618 Patricia St. (☎ **780/852-3898**).

CLIMBING   The **Jasper Climbing School,** 806 Connaught Dr. (☎ **780/ 852-3964**), offers beginner, intermediate, and advanced climbing in 1-day private courses. Basics are taught at the foot of Mount Morro, 19km (12 miles) from Jasper. The personal guided climbing fee is C$250 (US$167) per day. For C$30 (US$20), beginners can sample rappelling in a 3-hour workshop. Food, transport, and accommodations (in private homes) are extra.

Jasper Town & Jasper National Park

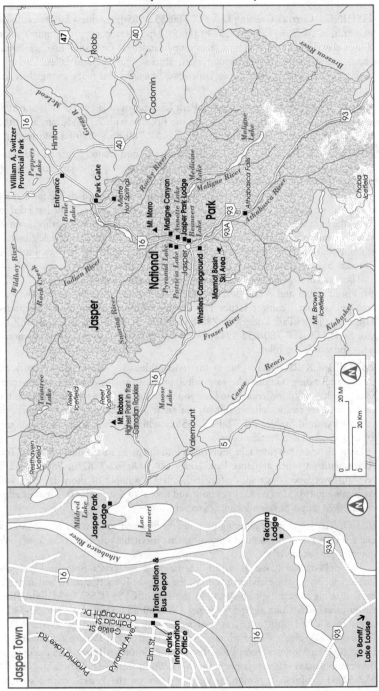

Brazeau River

47

Robb

40

Cadomin

93

McLeod

Creek

Greg R

16

Hinton

William A. Switzer
Provincial Park

Peppers
Lake

40

Rocky River

Maligne
Lake

Maligne River

Athabasca Falls

Athabasca River

Chaba
Icefield

Entrance

Park Gate

Miette
Hot Springs

Brule
Lake

Mt. Morro

Maligne Canyon

Medicine
Lake

Jasper Park Lodge

Annette Lake

93

93A

Wildhay River

Indian River

Rock Creek

Snaring River

16

Jasper

National

Pyramid Lake

Patricia Lake

Beauvert
Lake

Whistlers Campground

Marmot Basin
Ski Area

Park

Fraser River

Mt. Brown
Icefield

Kinbasket

Jasper

Twintree
Lake

Reef
Lake

Reef
Icefield

Mt. Robson
Highest Point in the
Canadian Rockies

16

Moose
Lake

Valemount

5

Canoe

Reach

Resthaven
Icefield

N

20 MI

20 Km

0

0

Jasper Town

Mildred
Lake

Jasper Park
Lodge

Lac
Beauvert

Athabasca River

Tekarra
Lodge

93A

Pyramid Lake Rd.

Gelkie St.

Patricia St.

Connaught Dr.

16

Train Station &
Bus Depot

Elm St.

Pyramid Ave.

Parks
Information
Office

16

93

To Banff/
Lake Louise

N

FISHING **Currie's Guiding Ltd.** (☎ 780/852-5650) conducts fishing excursions to beautiful Maligne Lake at C$149 (US$99) per person (two minimum) for an 8-hour day. Tackle, bait, and boat rentals are included, as well as full lunches. Inquire about the special single and group rates. Patricia and Pyramid lakes, just north of Jasper, are more convenient to Jasper-based anglers who fancy trying their luck at trout fishing.

GOLF The 18-hole course at **Jasper Park Lodge,** east of Jasper Town, is one of the most popular and challenging courses in the Rockies, with 73 sand traps and other, more natural hazards like visiting wildlife. Call ☎ 780/852-6090 for information.

HIKING Overnight and long-distance hikers will find around Jasper an abundance of backcountry trails that reach into some of the most spectacular scenery in the Rockies. There are fewer but still good choices for day hikers.

The complex of trails around **Maligne Canyon** makes a good choice for a group, because there are a number of access points (across six footbridges). The less keen can make the loop back and meet fellow hikers (after getting the vehicle) farther down the canyon. Trails ring parklike Beauvert and Annette lakes (the latter is wheelchair accessible), both near Jasper Park Lodge. Likewise, Pyramid and Patricia lakes, just north of town, have loop trails but more of a backcountry atmosphere.

The brochure *Day Hikers' Guide to Jasper National Park* costs C$1 (US65¢) at the visitor center and details dozens of hikes throughout the park. Several outfitters lead guided hikes; contact **Jasper Park Lodge Mountaineering and Interpretive Hiking,** at Jasper Park Lodge (☎ 780/852-3301), or **Walk and Talks Jasper,** 614d Connaught Dr. (☎ 780/852-4945; e-mail walktalk@incentre.net), for a selection of half- and whole-day hikes.

HORSEBACK RIDING One of the most exhilarating experiences the park can offer is trail riding. Guides take your riding prowess (or lack of it) into account and select foothill trails slow enough to keep you mounted. And the special mountain trail horses used are steady, reliable animals not given to sudden antics. For a short ride, contact **Pyramid Stables** (☎ 780/852-3562), which offers short 1- to 3-hour trips around Pyramid and Patricia lakes.

Long-distance trail rides take keen riders into the park's backcountry. **Skyline Trail Rides,** with an office at Jasper Park Lodge (☎ 888/582-7787 or 780/852-4215; www.discoverjasper.com/trailrides/skyline), offers a number of short day trips with costs at roughly C$25 (US$17) per hour and also 3- to 4-day trips to a remote albeit modernized lodge. Sleigh rides are offered in winter.

RAFTING Jasper is the jumping-off point for float and white-water trips down several rivers. A raft trip is a good option for that inevitable drizzly day, because you're going to get wet anyway.

The mild rapids (Class II to III) of the wide Athabasca River make a good introductory trip, while wilder runs down the Maligne River (Class III) will appeal to those needing something to brag about, at a cost of C$55 (US$37). **Maligne River Adventures,** 626 Connaught Dr., Jasper (☎ 780/852-3370; fax 780/852-3405), offers trips down both rivers, as well as a 3-day wilderness trip on the Kakwa River (Class IV-plus). Wilder white-water runs (Class III to IV) are available on the Fraser River in Mount Robson Park from **Sekani Mountain Tours,** who maintain an information/ticket office in Jasper at the Work World Store, 618 Patricia St. (☎ 780/852-5211). "Salmon spawning" floats take place on the Fraser's calmer stretches during mid-August and mid-September.

Trips generally include most equipment and transportation. Jasper is loaded with rafting outfitters; a stroll along the main streets of town reveals a half-dozen outfitters.

Or just ask your hotel concierge for advice booking a trip. You'll have no trouble getting out onto a river.

SKIING   Jasper's downhill ski area is **Ski Marmot Basin,** 19km (12 miles) west of Jasper on Highway 93. Marmot is generally underrated as a ski resort; it doesn't get the crowds of Banff or the infamous Chinook winds. The resort has 52 runs and seven lifts and rarely any lines. Lift tickets start at C$42 (US$28). Call ☎ **780/852-3816** for more information.

GETTING AROUND THE PARK

Some of the principal outfitters and guides also offer transportation to outlying beauty spots. Organized tours of the park's major sites—notably the **Athabasca snowfields** (C$78/US$52) and a **Maligne Lake cruise** (C$56/US$37)—are offered by both **Brewster,** in the train station (☎ **780/852-3332**), and **Maligne Tours,** 626 Connaught Dr. (☎ **780/852-3370**). **Beyond the Beaten Path,** 414 Connaught Dr. (☎ **780/852-5650**; e-mail curries@ycs.ab.ca), offers trips to these popular destinations as well as to **Miette Hot Springs** (C$42/US$28) and more intimate sightseeing, photography, wildlife viewing, and picnic trips. They also offer a shuttle service for hikers and rafting parties.

JASPER TOWN

Jasper isn't Banff, and to listen to most Jasper residents, that's just fine with them. Born as a railroad division point, Jasper Town lacks the glitz of its southern neighbor and Banff's slightly precious air of an internationalized alpine fantasyland. Jasper has a lived-in, community-oriented sense largely lacking in Banff. The streets are thronged with avid young hikers and mountain bikers, giving Jasper a recreational focus that Banff has lost to the shopping hordes. Chances are the people you meet on the streets will be a little muddy or wet, as if they've just gotten in from the river or the mountain.

But development is rapidly approaching. New nightclubs, restaurants, and tourist shops are springing up along Patricia Street, and that sound in the distance is the thunder of tour buses.

ESSENTIALS

VISITOR INFORMATION   For information on the town, contact **Jasper Tourism and Commerce,** P.O. Box 98, Jasper, AB T0E 1E0 (☎ **780/852-3858;** fax 780/852-4932).

GETTING THERE   Jasper is on the Yellowhead Highway System—linking it with Vancouver, Prince George, and Edmonton—and is an important transportation hub. The town is 287km (178 miles) northwest of Banff. **VIA Rail** connects Jasper to Vancouver and Edmonton with three trains weekly; the train station is at town center (☎ **780/852-4102;** www.viarail.ca), along Connaught Street. The train tracks run due north before they start the long easterly sweep leading to Edmonton. Also headquartered at the train station is the **Greyhound** bus station (☎ **780/852-3926;** www.greyhound.ca) and **Brewster Transportation** (☎ **780/852-3332**), which offers express service to Banff, as well as a large number of sightseeing excursions to scenic spots in the park.

ORIENTATION   Jasper is much smaller than Banff. The main street, **Connaught Drive,** runs alongside the Canadian National Railway tracks and is the address of the majority of hotels. **Patricia Street,** 1 block west, is quickly becoming the boutique street, with new shops and cafes springing up. Right in the center of town, surrounded by delightful shady gardens, is the **Parks Information Offices** (☎ **780/852-6146**). The post office is at the corner of Patricia and Elm streets. At the northern end of

Connaught and Geike streets, a quarter mile from downtown, is another complex of hotels.

GETTING AROUND **Tilden Rental Cars** is at 638 Connaught Dr. (☎ **780/ 852-3798**). Call a **taxi** at ☎ **780/852-5558** or 780/852-3600.

EXPLORING JASPER & ENVIRONS

The **Jasper Tramway** (☎ 780/852-3093; www.worldweb.com/JasperTramway) starts at the foot of Whistler's Mountain, 6km (3.7 miles) south of Jasper off Highway 93. Each car takes 30 passengers (plus baby carriages, wheelchairs, or dogs) and hoists them 2km (1¼ miles) up to the summit (7,400 ft.) in a breathtaking sky ride. At the upper terminal you step out into alpine tundra, the region above the tree line where some flowers take 25 years to blossom. A wonderful picnic area carpeted with mountain grass is alive with squirrels. You'll also see the "whistlers"—actually hoary marmots—the mountain is named for. The ride costs C$16 (US$11) adults and C$9 (US$6) children; cars depart every 10 to 15 minutes. Or consider a sunset ride followed by a three-course dinner at the terminal's restaurant for C$30 (US$20); buffet breakfast and lunch are also available.

Just northeast of Jasper, off the Jasper Park Lodge access road, the Maligne River drops from its high mountain valley to cut an astounding canyon into a steep lime-stone face on its way to meet the Athabasca River. The chasm of **Maligne Canyon** is up to 150 feet deep at points and yet only 10 feet across; the river tumbles through the canyon in a series of powerful waterfalls. A sometimes-steep hiking trail follows the canyon down the mountainside, bridging the gorge six times. Interpretive signs describe the geology. A teahouse operates at the top of the canyon in summer.

An incredibly blue mountain lake buttressed by a ring of high-flying peaks 45 min-utes east of Jasper, **Maligne Lake** is one of the park's great beauty spots. The lake is the largest glacier-fed lake in the Rockies and the second largest in the world. The native Canadians, who called the lake Chaba Imne, had a superstitious awe of the region. Settlers (in this case, a white woman, Mary Schäffer) didn't discover Maligne until 1908. Today droves of tour buses go to the "hidden lake," and the area is popular with hikers, anglers, trail riders, and white-water rafters. No matter what else they do, most people who visit Maligne Lake take a boat cruise to Spirit Island, at the head of the lake. The 90-minute cruise leaves from below the Maligne Lake Lodge, an attractive summer-only facility with a restaurant, bar, and gift shop (no lodging, though). Cruise tickets are C$32 (US$21) adults, C$29 (US$19) seniors (65-plus), and C$16 (US$11) children.

Maligne Lake waters are alive with rainbow and eastern brook trout, and the Maligne Lake Boathouse is stocked with licenses, tackle, bait, and boats. **Guided fishing trips** include equipment, lunch, and hotel transportation with half-day excur-sions starting at C$120 (US$80). You can rent a boat, canoe, or sea kayak to ply the waters. Morning and afternoon **rides on horseback** up the Bald Hills depart from the Chalet at Maligne Lake. The cost is C$55 (US$37).

All the facilities at Maligne Lake, including the lake cruises, fishing, trail rides, and a white-water raft outfitter that offers tours down three Jasper Park rivers, are operated by **Maligne Tours.** There's an office at the lake, next to the lodge, and also in Jasper at 626 Connaught Dr. (☎ **780/852-3370;** www.jaspertravel.com/malignelake; e-mail maligne@ycs.ab.ca), and at the Jasper Park Lodge (☎ **780/852-4779**). Maligne Tours also operates a shuttle bus between Jasper and the lake.

Downstream from Maligne Lake, the Maligne River flows into **Medicine Lake.** This large body of water appears regularly every spring, grows 8km (5 miles) long and 60 feet deep, then vanishes in the fall, leaving only a dry gravel bed through winter.

The reason for this annual wonder is a system of underground drainage caves. The local Indians believed that spirits were responsible for the lake's annual disappearance, hence the name.

The **Miette Hot Springs** (☎ **780/866-3939**) lies 60km (37 miles) northeast of Jasper off Highway 16, one of the best **animal-spotting routes** in the park. Watch for elk, deer, coyotes, and moose en route. You can enjoy the hot mineral springs in a beautiful pool or two soaker pools, surrounded by forest and an imposing mountain backdrop. Nearby are campgrounds and an attractive lodge with refreshments. In summer, the pool is open daily 8:30am to 10:30pm. Admission is C$5 (US$3.65) adults, C$4.50 (US$3) children/seniors, or C$15 (US$10) families.

SHOPPING

Weather can be unpredictable in Jasper. If it's raining, you can while away an afternoon in the town's shops and boutiques. The shopping arcade at the Jasper Park Lodge, called the **Beauvert Promenade,** has a number of excellent clothing and gift shops. In Jasper itself, **Patricia Street** contains most of the high-quality shops. A number of galleries feature Inuit and native arts and crafts: Check out **Our Native Land,** 601 Patricia St. (☎ 780/852-5592). Fashionable yet functional outdoor gear is the specialty of **Wild Mountain Willy's,** 610 Patricia St. (☎ 780/852-5304).

WHERE TO STAY

As in Banff, there's a marked difference between high-season prices and the rest of the year, so if you can avoid June to September, you'll find that most accommodations have reduced their prices by 50%. Note that all prices below are for high season. Call for reduced off-season rates. You'll want to make reservations as soon as you can, because most rooms are booked well in advance. If you can't find a room or don't want to bother with the details, contact **Reservations Jasper** (☎ 780/852-5488; fax 780/852-5489; e-mail resjas@incentre.net). There's a fee for using the service.

If you find the prices too astronomical in Jasper or just can't find a room, consider staying just east of the park near **Hinton,** where there's a growing abundance of B&Bs and motels.

Very Expensive

✪ **Chateau Jasper.** 96 Geikie St., Jasper, AB T0E 1E0. ☎ **800/661-9323** or 780/852-5644. Fax 780/852-4860. E-mail chjasper@agt.net. 119 units. A/C TV TEL. C$290 (US$180) double; C$335–C$390 (US$223–US$260) suite. AE, CB, DC, DISC, MC, V. Free covered heated parking.

Jasper Town's best hotel, the Chateau Jasper is a refined three-story lodging with some of the best staff and service in town. The grounds are beautifully landscaped, with colorful floral patches scattered through the courtyards. The guest rooms are nicely decorated and come with all the amenities you'd expect at a four-star lodging. All the standard rooms have two double beds; all suites have Jacuzzi tubs, and the truly large King Suites come with both Jacuzzis and shower stalls, huge 36-inch TVs, wet bars, and sitting areas. About half the hotel is no-smoking (separated by floors).

Dining/Diversions: The noted Beauvallon Dining Room and lounge (see "Where to Dine" below) is just off the lobby.

Amenities: Concierge, room service, dry cleaning/laundry, baby-sitting; complimentary shuttle bus to train and bus station; pool, hot tub, ski lockers.

Jasper Park Lodge. P.O. Box 40, Jasper, AB T0E 1E0. ☎ **800/465-7547** in Alberta, 800/441-1414 elsewhere in North America, or 780/852-3301. Fax 780/852-5107. www.cphotels.ca. 446 units. C$149–C$459 (US$99–US$306) double; from C$289–C$689 (US$193–US$460) suite; cabins from C$1677 (US$1118) per night. Free parking. AE, DC, DISC, ER, JCB, MC, V.

Jasper's most exclusive lodging, the Jasper Park Lodge was built by the Canadian Pacific Railroad and has the same air of luxury and gentility as their other properties, but with a more woodsy feel. The wooded elk-inhabited grounds are along Lac Beauvert, about 8km (5 miles) east of Jasper proper. The lodgings are all extremely comfortable, though a bit hard to characterize, because there are a wide variety of cabins, lodge rooms, chalets, and cottages—all from different eras, all set amid the forest, and all within easy walking distance of the beautiful central lodge. All rooms have the same amenities, but they vary widely in style, size, and price; it's a good idea to call and talk to the staff and find out what's available for your money, needs, and size of group. Friends or family traveling together may opt for one of the enormous housekeeping cabins, some of which have up to eight bedrooms.

Dining/Diversions: There are four restaurants, including the famed four-star Edith Cavell Dining Room, with four-course dinners at C$60 (US$40), and the Moose's Nook Dining Room (see "Where to Dine" below); the Tent City Lounge is one of Jasper's youthful hangouts.

Amenities: 24-hour room service, dry cleaning/laundry, secretarial service, babysitting; stables, tennis courts, outdoor pool, health club, one of the best golf courses in Canada; shopping arcade.

Expensive

Amethyst Lodge. 200 Connaught Dr. (P.O. Box 1200), Jasper, AB T0E 1E0. ☎ **800/661-9935** or 780/852-3394. Fax 780/852-5198. 97 units. A/C TV TEL. C$196–C$206 (US$131–US$137) double. AE, CB, DC, MC, V.

If you're sick of the faux alpine look prevalent in the Canadian Rockies, then you may be ready for the Amethyst Lodge, a comfortable and unabashed motor inn. All guest rooms come with two double or two queen beds; half have balconies. The Amethyst is more central to downtown Jasper than most lodgings.

Dining/Diversions: There's a large restaurant and a lounge; afternoon tea is served daily in the lounge.

Amenities: Laundry/dry cleaning; two hot tubs.

✪ **Jasper Inn.** 98 Geikie St. (P.O. Box 879), Jasper, AB T0E 1E0. ☎ **800/661-1933** or 780/852-4461. Fax 780/852-5916. www.jasperinn.com. E-mail jasperin@telusplanet.net. 157 units. TV TEL. C$175–C$202 (US$117–US$135) double; C$212–C$325 (US$141–US$217) suite. Extra person C$10 (US$7). Children under 17 stay free in parents' room. AE, DC, ER, MC, V. Free parking.

The Jasper Inn is on the northern end of town but set back off the main road. Guest rooms are available in four buildings and in many different size and bed configurations. If you're looking for a good value, ignore the standard and efficiency units (which are perfectly nice, mind you); pay C$10 (US$7) more, C$212 (US$141), and reserve a one-bedroom suite, a large with a fireplace and fully equipped kitchen. Even nicer are the extra-large no-smoking rooms in the Maligne Suites unit (the marble- and granite-lined bathrooms are enormous); all come with fireplaces, wet bars, Jacuzzis, nice furniture, balconies, and two beds. (The top of the line is Elke Sommers's former room; ask for it by name.) Also available are two-bedroom chalet-style rooms (which can sleep up to seven); these are perfect for families, with full kitchens, balconies, and fireplaces.

Dining: The Inn Restaurant, in a garden-like atrium, offers tasty Canadian fare, with good prime rib, salmon, and pasta.

Amenities: Coin laundry, sauna, steam room, hot tub, small pool, ski wax room, small meeting facility.

✪ **Lobstick Lodge.** 96 Geikie St. (P.O. Box 1200), Jasper, AB T0E 1E0. ☎ **888/852-7737** or 780/852-4431. Fax 780/852-4142. www.mtn-park-lodges.com. 139 units.

TV TEL. C$196 (US$131) double; C$211 (US$141) kitchenette unit. Children under 15 stay free in parents' room. Free parking. AE, DC, ER, MC, V.

The Lobstick Lodge was totally renovated in 1995 and now features a lounge and elevators, good additions to one of Jasper's most popular hotels. The standard rooms are the largest in Jasper, all with two double beds. Even more impressive are 43 huge kitchen units, each with a complete kitchen, including a full-size fridge, four-burner stove, and microwave, plus a double and twin-size bed and a foldout couch. These are perfect for families and go fast—reserve them early. The upstairs meeting room has great mountain views, and guests can use it for playing cards or lounging if it's not in use.

Dining/Diversions: A family restaurant and a cocktail lounge with great views.

Amenities: Dry cleaning/laundry; indoor pool, whirlpool, two outdoor hot tubs, patio.

Marmot Lodge. 86 Connaught Dr., Jasper, AB T0E 1E0. ☎ **800/661-6521** or 780/852-4471. Fax 780/852-3280. 107 units. TV TEL. C$190 (US$127) double; C$206 (US$137) kitchen unit. Children under 15 stay free in parents' room. AE, DC, MC, V.

At the northern end of Jasper's main street, the Marmot Lodge offers pleasant rooms in three buildings, each with different types of rooms. One building has all-kitchen units with fireplaces, popular with families. The building facing the street has smaller, less expensive rooms with two singles or one queen bed, while the third building has very large "deluxe" rooms with two queen beds. All rooms have been decorated with a Native-American theme; some have tapestry-like weavings on the walls.

Dining/Diversions: The Marmot has a barbecue patio, a newly renovated dining room, and a fireside lounge.

Amenities: Heated picture-windowed pool with sauna and whirlpool.

Moderate

During high season, it seems that nearly half the dwellings in Jasper let rooms B&B fashion; contact **Jasper Home Accommodation Association,** P.O. Box 758, Jasper, AB T0E 1E0, for a full list of such accommodations. B&Bs listed with the local visitors association have little signs in front; if you arrive early enough in the day, you can comb the streets looking for a likely suspect. B&Bs in Jasper are much less grand and less expensive than those in Banff. Due to antiquated restrictions, some can't even serve cooked breakfast. Double-occupancy accommodations are about C$50 to C$75 (US$33 to US$50) at most homes. You'll need to pay cash for most; there's no central booking agency in Jasper, so you'll need to contact your host directly.

Athabasca Hotel. 510 Patricia St., Jasper, AB T0E 1E0. ☎ **800/563-9859** or 780/852-3386. Fax 780/852-4955. 61 units, 39 with bathroom. TV TEL. C$89 (US$59) double without bathroom, C$135 (US$90) double with bathroom. AE, DC, MC, V.

The Athabasca has a lobby like a hunting lodge, with a stone fireplace; trophy heads of deer, elk, and bighorn; and a great bar with its own huge fireplace. A gray stone corner building with a homey old-fashioned air, the hotel was built in 1929 as a destination hotel and has a large attractive dining room and a small coffee shop. Each of the fair-sized guest rooms has a mountain view and tasteful simple furniture (armchairs, writing table), plus a walk-in closet. The Athabasca is one of the few good values in Jasper.

✪ **Becker's Chalets.** Hwy. 95 (5km/3.1 miles south of Jasper; P.O. Box 579), Jasper, AB T0E 1E0. ☎ **780/852-3779.** Fax 780/852-7202. 96 chalets. TV. C$75–C$150 (US$50–US$100) 1-bedroom cabin; C$130–C$205 (US$87–US$137) 2-bedroom cabin; C$180–C$325 (US$120–US$217) 3-bedroom cabin. MC, V.

This very attractive log-cabin resort offers a variety of lodging options in freestanding chalets in a glade of trees along the Athabasca River. While the resort dates from the 1940s and retains the feel and atmosphere of an old mountain retreat, most of the chalets have been built in the past 5 years and are thoroughly modernized. They come with river-stone fireplaces and full kitchens. The dining room, open for breakfast and dinner, is one of Jasper's best (see "Where to Dine" below).

Tekarra Lodge. P.O. Box 669, Jasper, AB T0E 1E0 (1.6km/1 mile east of Jasper off Hwy. 93A). ☎ **888/404-4540** or 780/852-3058. Fax 780/852-4636. www.tekarralodge.com. 52 units. C$139 (US$93) lodge room; C$139–C$189 (US$93–US$126) cabin for 2. Extra person C$10 (US$7). 2-night minimum in summer. Lodge rates include continental breakfast. AE, DC, MC, V.

This charming log-cabin resort is just east of Jasper, above the confluence of the Miette and Athabasca rivers. Accommodations are in the lodge or cabins that can sleep from two to seven people. The cabins are rustic-looking and nicely furnished, with kitchenettes or full kitchens, but it's the location that really sets Tekarra Lodge apart. Just far enough from the bustle of Jasper and off a quiet road in the forest, it offers the kind of venerable charm you dream of in a mountain cabin resort. To make the isolation more complete, none of the rooms has a phone or TV. One of Jasper's best restaurants is in the lodge.

Inexpensive

HOSTELS   Two **Hostelling International** hostels are near Jasper and are the best alternatives for budget travelers. Both locations have the same reservations number (reservations are strongly advised in summer) and same addresses: P.O. Box 387, Jasper, AB T0E 1E0 (☎ **780/852-3215;** e-mail jihostel@telusplanet.net).

The **Jasper International Hostel** is on Skytram Road, 6km (3.7 miles) west of Jasper. It sleeps 80 and charges C$15 (US$10) members and C$20 (US$13) nonmembers. The closest hostel to Jasper, it's open year-round but especially popular in summer, when 2-week advance reservations are a good idea. There are two family rooms. The hostel rents mountain bikes, so you can get down to town and around; there are a barbecue area and indoor plumbing and hot showers. In winter, ski packages are available. The **Maligne Canyon Hostel** is off Maligne Lake Road, 18km (11 miles) east of Jasper. It sleeps 24 and charges C$9 (US$6) members and C$14 (US$9) nonmembers. This convenient hostel is just above the astonishing Maligne Canyon and an easy hitchhike from Jasper. Facilities include a self-catering kitchen and dining area.

PARK CAMPGROUNDS   There are 10 campgrounds in Jasper National Park. The closest to Jasper Town is **The Whistlers,** up the road toward the gondola, providing some 700 campsites. You need a special permit to camp anywhere in the parks outside the regular campgrounds—a regulation necessary because of fire hazards. Contact the **parks information office** at ☎ 780/852-6176 for permits. The campgrounds range from completely unserviced sites to those providing water, power, sewer connections, laundry facilities, gas, and groceries.

A Local Guest Ranch

Black Cat Guest Ranch. P.O. Box 6267, Hinton, AB T7V 1X6. ☎ **800/859-6840** or 780/865-3084. Fax 780/865-1924. www.telusplanet.net/public/bcranch. E-mail bcranch@ telusplanet.net. 16 units. High season C$82–C$85 (US$55–US$57) per person double. Rates include all meals. MC, V.

Established in 1935 by the Brewsters, this guest ranch is a historic wilderness retreat 56km (35 miles) northeast of Jasper. The rustic two-story lodge, built in 1978—guests don't stay in the original old cabins—offers unfussy guest units with large windows affording unspoiled views of the crags in Jasper Park across a pasture filled with horses and birds. There's a large fireplace room with couches, easy chairs, and game tables. The big home-cooked lunch, dinner, and breakfast are served family-style by the friendly staff. Activities include hikes, horseback riding (C$16/US$11 per hour for guided trips), canoe rentals, murder-mystery weekends, and fishing. The ranch staff will meet your train or bus at Hinton.

WHERE TO DINE
Expensive
Beauvallon Dining Room. In the Chateau Jasper, 96 Geike St. ☎ **780/852-5644.** Reservations recommended. Main courses C$17–C$32 (US$11–US$21); table d'hôte C$34 (US$23); Sun brunch C$16 (US$11) adults, C$10 (US$7) seniors/youths. AE, DC, ER, MC, V. Daily 6:30am–2pm and 5:30–11pm. CANADIAN.

Offering one of the most ambitious menus in Jasper, the Beauvallon specializes in "classic" European preparations with Canadian meats, fish, and an extensive selection of game. The menu changes seasonally and includes complex eclectic dishes like Caribou Normandy (grilled caribou loin with calvados sauce); braised venison, chanterelle mushrooms, and creamy red-wine sauce; northern Pacific seafood fricassee; and gingered duck breast. The service is excellent, and the dining room—filled with high-back chairs—is cozy. The wine list is extensive and well priced.

Becker's Gourmet Restaurant. At Becker's Chalets, Hwy. 93 (5km/3.1 miles south of Jasper). ☎ **780/852-3779.** Reservations required. Main courses C$12–C$25 (US$8–US$17). MC, V. Daily 8am–2pm and 5:30–10pm. CANADIAN.

Though the name's not very elegant, it's highly descriptive. This high-quality inventive restaurant serves what could only be termed gourmet food at one of the nicest log-cabin resorts in Jasper (above). The dining room is an intimate log-and-glass affair overlooking the Athabasca River. The menu includes such choices as four-nut crusted lamb chops, chèvre Mornay sauce and dill on grilled chicken breast, and grilled venison loin with Saskatoon-berry compote.

Moose's Nook Dining Room. In the Jasper Park Lodge, 8km (5 miles) east of Jasper. ☎ **780/852-6052.** Main courses C$17–C$26 (US$11–US$17). AE, CB, DISC, ER, JCB, MC, V. Daily 6–10pm. CANADIAN.

This new restaurant in the Jasper Park Lodge (above) features "Canadiana" specialties. With equal parts tradition and innovation, the Moose's Nook serves hearty presentations of native meats, fish, and game. Pheasant breast is grilled and served with a compote of local Saskatoon berries; buffalo steak is served with a wild-mushroom, shallot, and whiskey sauce. Lighter appetites will enjoy the seafood hot pot and vegetarian cabbage rolls. Sautéed veal kidneys are offered as an appetizer, as is goose liver pâté. This hearty fare is served in a charming wood-beamed room that could double as a hunting lodge.

Moderate
✪ **Fiddle River.** 620 Connaught Dr. ☎ **780/852-3032.** Reservations required. Main courses C$13–C$23 (US$9–US$15). AE, MC, V. Daily 5pm–midnight. SEAFOOD.

This rustic-looking upstairs retreat has panoramic windows viewing the Jasper railroad station and the mountain range beyond. The specialty is fresh fish, though a number of pasta dishes and red-meat entrees will complicate your decision process. Fiddle River offers as many daily specials: Waiters bring a chalkboard tripod to your table to give you some predinner reading. They could include grilled salmon (one special was served with red-pepper purée and dill-cream sauce), half a dozen oysters on the half shell, Caribbean chicken breast breaded in crushed banana chips and coconut and served with mango and yogurt, and pepper steak with blue cheese demi-glace. There's a small but interesting wine list.

Something Else. 621 Patricia St. ☎ **780/852-3850.** Reservations accepted. Main courses C$10–C$18 (US$7–US$12). AE, DC, ER, MC, V. Daily 11am–midnight. INTERNATIONAL/ PIZZA.

Something Else is accurately named: Folded together here are a good Greek restaurant and a pizza parlor, to which a high-quality Canadian-style restaurant has been added. In short, if you're with a group that can't decide where to eat, this is the place to go. Prime Alberta steaks, fiery Louisiana jambalaya and mesquite chicken, Greek saganaki and moussaka, an array of 21 pizza varieties—all the food is very well prepared and fresh, and the welcome is friendly.

Tekarra Lodge Restaurant. Hwy. 93A (1.6km/1 mile east of Jasper). ☎ **780/852-4624.** Reservations recommended on weekends. Main courses C$13–C$20 (US$9–US$13). AE, DC, MC, V. Daily 5–11pm. STEAK/INTERNATIONAL.

At the confluence of the Miette and Athabasca rivers, this longtime favorite of the locals has excellent leg of lamb, as well as steaks and other intriguing dishes like pan-seared chicken with roast grapes. The charming fireplace-dominated lodge dining room is one of Jasper's hidden gems, with friendly service. In addition to the meat entrees, the Tekarra offers lighter dishes like specialty stir-fries and pasta dishes. It may be a little confusing to find; ask directions before you set out.

Inexpensive

For fresh bakery goods like muffins or fresh-cut sandwiches, coffee, drinks, and desserts, soup, and salads, go to the **Soft Rock Cafe,** 622 Connaught Dr. (☎ 780/ 852-5850), a pleasant little deli in the Connaught Square Mall, in the center of town. There's also rotisserie chicken to go or eat in; and you can log on to the Web or check your e-mail at one of their computers. June to October 15, it's open daily 8am to 9pm; the rest of the year, hours are daily 8am to 6pm. Another casual cafe is **Spooner's Coffee Bar,** upstairs at 601 Patricia St. (☎ 780/852-4046), with a juice bar, coffee drinks, burritos, soup, sandwiches, and other deli items. June to October 1, it's open daily 8:30am to 9pm; the rest of the year, hours are daily 8:30am to 5pm.

Jasper Pizza Place. 402 Connaught Dr. ☎ **780/852-3225.** Reservations not accepted. Pizza C$7–C$13 (US$4.65–US$9). MC, V. Daily 7am–midnight. PIZZA.

One of Jasper's most popular eating spots, the highly redesigned Pizza Place agreeably combines the features of an upscale boutique pizzeria with a traditional Canadian bar. The pizzas are baked in a wood-fired oven and come in some very unusual—some would say unlikely—combinations. If you're not quite ready for a sour-cream and Dijon-mustard pizza or an escargot pizza, then maybe the smoked salmon, caper, and black-olive pizza will please. Standard-issue pizzas are also available, as are a selection of sandwiches and a mammoth helping of lasagna. The bar side of things is lively, with pool tables and a lively crowd of summer resort workers on display.

Malowney's Wine Cafe. 606 Patricia St. ☎ **780/852-4559.** Reservations not accepted. Main courses C$6–C$12 (US$4–US$8). MC, V. Daily 11:30am–10pm. INTERNATIONAL.

Jasper is just *packed* with wine and liquor stores for some reason. However, Mal-owney's goes the extra distance and offers tasty light entrees to accompany their wines and liquors. This isn't a big place—only a handful of lucky guests score a table or a stool—but it's worth it to sit back and enjoy a toothsome light meal with a favorite beverage. Most entrees change daily and are featured on a chalkboard as you enter; lunchtime sandwiches and soups give way to pasta, grilled chicken, fish, or beef dishes at dinner. You can also come here and snack your way through some appetizers while sampling the 35 specialty martinis.

✪ **Mountain Foods Cafe.** 606 Connaught Dr. ☎ **780/852-4050.** Main courses C$5–C$8 (US$3.35–US$5). MC, V. Daily 8am–10pm. DELI.

This small deli/cafeteria is bright and friendly, just the antidote to the stodgy food pervasive in much of the park. Most meals are light and healthful—salads, soups, and quick ethnic dishes—and specialties include burrito "wraps," sandwich "melts," and breakfast "scrambles." The deli case is filled with items available to take out. Nothing costs much over C$6 (US$4). Beer and wine are served.

JASPER AFTER DARK

Nearly all Jasper's nightlife can be found in the bars and lounges of hotels, motels, and inns. **O'Shea's,** at the Athabasca Hotel, 510 Patricia St. (☎ 780/852-3386), is usually just called the Atha'B, or simply The B, and has a changing lineup of Top-40s bands, catering to a young crowd. There's a dance floor, and movies are shown on the large-screen TV in the Trophy room. Jasper's newest hot spot is **Pete's Night Club,** 610 Patricia St. (☎ 780/852-6262), presenting live alternative and blues bands. Another youthful gathering place is **Tent City,** at the Jasper Park Lodge, where you'll find billiards, loud music, and a preponderance of the JPL's 650 employees. The **D'ed Dog Bar and Grill,** 404 Connaught Dr. (☎ 780/852-3351), is the place to find the young river and hiking guides who gather in Jasper to work every summer; Friday-night happy hour here can get pretty rowdy.

9 British Columbia's Rockies: Mount Robson Provincial Park & Yoho, Glacier, Mount Revelstoke & Kootenay National Parks

MOUNT ROBSON PROVINCIAL PARK

The highlight of beautiful **Mount Robson Provincial Park,** just west of Jasper National Park along the Yellowhead Highway, is 12,972-foot-high Mount Robson, the highest peak in the Canadian Rockies. This massive sentinel fills the sky from most vantage points in the park, making it a certainty you'll easily run through a roll of film if the weather is good. One of the best viewpoints is from the visitor center, where the mountain looms above a wildflower meadow.

The mighty Fraser River rises in the park and is a popular and challenging white-water adventure for experienced rafters. A number of Jasper-area outfitters offer trips down the Fraser (see the Jasper listings above). Short 2- to 4-hour park tours are offered by **Mount Robson Adventure Holidays,** Valemount, British Columbia (☎ 250/566-4386; fax 250/556-4351). For C$42 (US$28), you can choose a guided nature tour by raft, canoe, or van. Longer hiking or backpacking excursions are also available.

For more information about the park, contact P.O. Box 579, Valemount, BC V0E 2Z0 (☎ 250/566-4325).

YOHO NATIONAL PARK & GOLDEN

Just west of Lake Louise and east of Golden on the western slopes of the Rockies in British Columbia, **Yoho National Park** preserves some of the most famous rocks in Canada, as well as a historic rail line and the nation's second-highest waterfall. Yoho Park is essentially the drainage of the Kicking Horse River—famed for its white-water rafting—and is traversed by the Trans-Canada Highway.

The first white exploration of this area was by scouts looking for a pass over the Rockies suitable for the Canadian Pacific's transcontinental run. Kicking Horse Pass, at 5,333 feet, was surveyed and the railroad began its service in 1884. However, the grade down the aptly named Big Hill, on the west side of the pass, was near precipitous. The steepest rail line in North America, it descended the mountain at 4.5%. The first train to attempt the descent went out of control and crashed, killing three men. In 1909, after decades of accidents, the Canadian Pacific solved its problem by curling two spiral rail tunnels into the mountains facing Big Hill. Together, the two tunnels were over 6,100 feet long. At the **Lower Spiral Tunnel Viewpoint** are interpretive displays explaining this engineering feat, and you can still watch trains enter and emerge from the tunnels.

Thirteen kilometers (8 miles) from the Kicking Horse Pass, turn north onto Yoho Valley Road to find some of the park's most scenic areas. Past another viewpoint onto the Spiral Tunnels, continue 13km (8 miles) to ✪ **Takakkaw Falls,** Canada's second highest, cascading 1,248 feet in two drops. A short all-abilities trail leads from the road's end to a picnic area, where views of this amazing waterfall are even more eye-popping. Another impressive waterfall is **Wapta Falls** on the rushing Kicking Horse River. The falls is reached by an easy 2.4km (1½-mile) hike near the park's western entrance.

The Kicking Horse River descends between Mount Fields and Mount Stephen, famous in paleontological circles for Burgess Shale, fossil-rich deposits from the Cambrian era that were the subject of Stephen Jay Gould's 1988 bestseller, *A Wonderful Life.* Interpretive displays about these fossil digs, which have produced organisms that seem to challenge some established evolutionary tenets, are found at the park's visitor center in Fields. If you're interested enough in the fossil digs to face a daylong 19km (12-mile) round-trip hike, you can join a guided hike to the quarries. The **Yoho-Burgess Shale Foundation,** P.O. Box 148, Field, BC V0A 1G0 (☎ **800/ 343-3006;** www.burgess-shale.bc.ca), offers earth-science educational hikes July to mid-September. The 20km (12-mile) round-trip Burgess Shale Hike (Walcott Quarry) is a moderately difficult 10-hour hike. Departure time is 8am and the cost is C$45 (US$30) per person and C$25 (US$17) per child (under 12). Note that collecting fossils in these areas, or in the national park in general, is prohibited.

Emerald Lake, a jewel-toned lake in a glacial cirque, is one of the Yoho Park's most popular stops. Hiking trails ring the lake, and the popular **Emerald Lake Lodge** (see "Where to Stay & Dine" below) is open for meals and lodging year-round; this area is popular for cross-country skiing. In summer, this is a very busy place, but it's worth the drive; plan to stay for lunch or dinner. **Lake O'Hara** is another beautiful mountain lake nestled below the soaring peaks of the Continental Divide. To protect the fragile alpine ecosystem, access to the lake is restricted. Although you can hike into the lake basin—13km (8 miles) one-way—most people reserve a seat on the four-times-daily bus that travels the gravel road leading to the lake. Reservations are essential, and in high season difficult to obtain. The buses run mid-June to September 30, and tickets are C$11 (US$7); the reservation fee is another C$10 (US$7). For information and reservations, call ☎ **250/343-6433.**

Just west of Yoho National Park, the town of **Golden** is increasingly a major player as a Canadian Rockies destination. It sits in a breathtaking location in the trenchlike Columbia River Valley between the massive Rocky Mountains and the soaring Purcell Range, within a 90-minute drive from five major national parks. The fact that Golden is near—and not in—the parks is in large part the reason for the area's recent phenomenal growth. Types of recreation (like heli-skiing and heli-hiking, below) that aren't allowed in the national parks for conservation reasons make Golden their base. And with park towns like nearby Banff trying to limit further development, businesses, outfitters, and retirees that want a Rocky Mountain hub find Golden a convenient and congenial center. Golden won't win any awards for charm, but it's a functional little town with lots of motel rooms in a magnificent location.

HELI-HIKING & HELI-SKIING

Golden is at the center of some of the world's best terrain for helicopter-assisted skiing and hiking. The Bugaboo, Purcell, Selkirk and Cariboo Mountains all rear up behind Golden, and since they're unencumbered with national-park status (unlike the Canadian Rockies), they're available to licensed helicopter-assisted recreationalists. Banff-based **CMH Heli-Skiing,** Box 1660, Banff, AB T0L 0C0 (☎ **800/661-0252** or 403/762-7100; fax 403/762-5879; www.cmhski.com), has in the ranges near Gol-den eight high-country lodges that serve as bases for weeklong heli-skiing and -hiking holidays. Rates include all lodging, food, nonalcoholic drinks, helicopter transport, use of equipment, and ground transport from the nearest large airport (usually Calgary). Prices vary greatly depending on the lodge and time of year, but heli-skiing trips range between C$3,700 (US$2,468) and C$6,000 (US$4,002) per week.

WHITEWATER RAFTING

The Kicking Horse River, which enters the Columbia at Golden, is one of the most exciting whitewater-rafting trips in Canada, with constant Class III and Class IV rapids as it tumbles down from the Continental Divide through Yoho National Park. Rafting trips are usually offered mid-May to mid-September.

Alpine Rafting (☎ **888/599-5299** or 250/344-6778; www.recnet.ca/alpineraft) offers daylong trips for C$80 (US$53) per person, including a barbecue steak lunch. Half-day trips are also available. **Canadian Whitewater Adventures** (☎ **888/ 577-8118** or 403/720-8745; www.canadianwhitewater.ca) offers rafting trips and combination rafting and hiking or rafting and rappelling trips. Rafting packages include Upper Kicking Horse Canyon for C$69 (US$46), Lower Canyon for C$49 (US$33), and the Upper and Lower Combo for C$99 (US$66).

The **service center** for Yoho Park is the little town of Fields, with a half-dozen modest accommodations and a few casual restaurants. The park's visitor center is just off Highway 1 near the entrance to town. For more information, contact **Yoho National Park,** P.O. Box 99, Fields, BC V0A 1G0 (☎ 250/343-6324).

WHERE TO STAY & DINE

There are a lot of exceptional aspects to Golden, but fine dining isn't one of them. If you're staying at one of the lodges with the option of American plan dining, you should take advantage of it. If not, a number of places offer hearty Canadian-style fare at inexpensive prices. **Norberts & Doris Bakery Cafe,** 505 9th Ave. (☎ 250/ 344-5506), is a continental-style bakery with pastries and lunch soup, salads, and deli sandwiches; it's open daily 8am to 5pm. **Sisters & Beans,** 1122 10th Ave. S. (☎ 250/344-2443), is a coffeehouse with a largely vegetarian light-dining menu; it's open Tuesday to Sunday 11am to 9pm. The **Mad Trapper Pub,** 1203 9th St. S. (☎ 250/344-6661), is a congenial place for ale and a burger open daily 11am to 1pm. The **Kicking Horse Cafe,** 1105 9th St. (☎ 250/344-2330), is the only fine-dining option in Golden. It's a historic log cabin near downtown that features an international menu with "the tastes of the world"—dishes from Japan to Mexico to India.

✪ **Alpine Meadows Lodge.** 717 Elk Rd., Golden, BC V0A 1H0. ☎ **888/700-4477** or 250/344-5863. Fax 250/344-5853. www.alpinemeadowslodge.com. E-mail alpmeadow@redshift.bc.ca. 9 units. C$89 (US$59) double. Rates include breakfast. American Plan available. AE, MC, V.

High above Golden, looking across onto the face of the Rockie Mountains, this family-owned and family-friendly lodge enjoys a great location removed from the bustle of Golden yet only 10 minutes from skiing, golf, and town services. The large wooden lodge boasts a three-story central Great Room flanked by wraparound balconies and open staircases (it was built from timber felled on the property). A huge two-sided stone fireplace dominates the living area, surrounded by overstuffed chairs and couches. Sharing the main floor is a dining room, where home-style dinners are served to American plan guests, plus a lounge and gift shop. The guest rooms are light-filled and airy, with a simple unfussy decor. Outdoor recreation is literally right out the door, with paths from the lodge leading to hiking trails in neighboring federal forest land. The owner is very knowledgeable about local lore and activities and will make it easy to get you out into the wilderness or onto the fairways. Alpine Meadows offers a number of very well-priced packages that include lodging, golfing, skiing, whitewater rafting, and flightseeing.

✪ **Emerald Lake Lodge.** Box 10, Field, BC V0A 1G0. ☎ **800/663-6336** or 403/ 609-6199. www.crmr.com. E-mail info@crmr.com. 85 units. C$285–C$445 (US$190– US$297) double. Extra person C$25 (US$17). Children 12 and under stay free in parents' room. AE, DC, MC, V.

The Emerald Lake Lodge sits in a spectacular setting: within forests at the base of a placid aquamarine lake beneath towering cliff-faced mountains. The lake was discovered in 1882 when the Canadian Pacific pushed over Kicking Horse Pass, and by 1902 the railway had built a lodge on the lakeshore. The original lodge has expanded since but retains a marvelous sense of woodsy venerability and rustic charm. It houses a formal dining room, a bar, reading and sitting rooms, conference facilities, and a games room. Accommodations are in 24 new cabin-style buildings designed to harmonize with the historic lodge and the dramatic setting. Each of the guest units features a fieldstone fireplace, bent-willow chairs, queen or double beds with down comforters, and a private balcony commanding a superb lake view.

Dining/Diversions: Fine dining is offered in the elegant lodge dining room, with lighter cuisine at Cilantro, in the new lodge cafe building. The lounge features an oak back bar salvaged from an 1890s Yukon saloon.

Amenities: Outdoor hot tub, sauna; canoe rental, horseback riding, cross-country ski rentals.

Golden Rim Motor Inn. 1416 Golden View Rd., Golden, BC V0A 1H0. ☎ **250/344-2216.** Fax 250/344-6673. 69 units. A/C TV TEL. C$80 (US$53) double. AE, MC, V.

There are dozens of moderately priced motels in Golden, but this is the pick of the litter. Standing above the precipitous Kicking Horse River valley just 1km (0.6 miles) east of Golden, with sweeping views of the Rockies and the Columbia Valley, the Golden Rim has standard queen-bed motel accommodations with some housekeeping and Jacuzzi units. Facilities include a licensed dining room, indoor and outdoor pools, waterslides, a sauna, a whirlpool, and a recreation center.

Prestige Inn Golden. 1049 Trans-Canada Hwy., Golden, BC V0A 1H0. ☎ **877/737-8443** or 250/344-7990. Fax 250/344-7902. 82 units. From C$110 (US$73) double. AE, DISC, ER, MC, V.

Easily the swankest place to stay in Golden, the new Prestige Inn is luxurious, with excellent facilities, a variety of room types, and a good family-dining restaurant. The guest rooms are spacious and richly appointed, each with two phones and voice mail, an iron/ironing board, a coffeemaker, and a hair dryer. Some kitchenettes are available. Dining is offered in the ABC Country Restaurant. Facilities include an indoor pool, a hot tub, a fitness center, and meeting and convention facilities; services include room service, a concierge, and turndown service.

GLACIER NATIONAL PARK

Amid the highest peaks of the Selkirk Mountains, Canada's **Glacier National Park** amply lives up to its name. More than 400 glaciers repose here, with 14% of the park's 2,168km² (837 sq. miles) lying under permanent snowpack. The reason this high country is so covered with ice is the same reason this is one of the more unpopulated places to visit in the mountain West: It snows and rains a lot here.

The primary attractions in the park are the viewpoints onto craggy peaks and hiking trails leading to wildflower meadows and old-growth groves; heavy snow and rainfall lend a near–rain-forest feel to forest hikes. Spring hikers and cross-country skiers should beware of avalanche conditions, an intrinsic problem in areas with high snowfall and steep slopes. Call park information at ☎ 250/837-7500 for weather updates.

Glacier Park is crossed by the Trans-Canada Highway and the Canadian Pacific rail tracks. Each has had to build snowsheds to protect these transportation systems from the effects of heavy snows and avalanches. **Park headquarters** are just east of 4,100-foot Rogers Pass; stop here to watch videos and learn from the displays on natural and human history in the park; there are new exhibits on the role of the railroads in opening up this rugged area. Sign up for ranger-led interpretive hikes. On a typically wet gray day, the center may be the driest place to enjoy the park. Several easy hiking trails leave from the center. The **Abandoned Rails Trail** follows a rails-to-trails section of the old CPR track for an hourlong round-trip with a gentle grade through a wildflower-studded basin. The **Balu Pass Trail** is a more strenuous 5km (3.1-mile) hike up to the base of the glaciers on 2,728m (8,950-feet) Ursus Major.

The other important trailhead is at Illecillewaet Campground west of Rogers Pass along Highway 1. Seven major trails head up into the peaks from here, including the **Asulkan Valley Trail,** which follows a stream up a narrow valley to a hiker's hut. These trails require more exertion than the trails at Rogers Pass and will take most of a day to complete.

For more information about the park, contact **Glacier National Park,** P.O. Box 350, Revelstoke, BC V0E 2S0 (☎ 250/837-7500; e-mail revglacier_reception@ pch.gc.ca). No fee is charged if you pass through the park on Highway 1 without stopping, but if you stop to hike or picnic, there's a charge of C$4 (US$2.65) adults, C$3 (US$2) seniors, C$2 (US$1.35) children 6 to 16, and C$10 (US$7) families.

MOUNT REVELSTOKE NATIONAL PARK

Just west of Glacier National Park is **Mount Revelstoke National Park,** a glacier-clad collection of craggy peaks in the Selkirk Range. Comprising only 417km² (161 sq. miles), Mount Revelstoke can't produce the kind of awe its larger neighbor, Glacier National Park, can in good weather; but Revelstoke offers easier access to the high country and alpine meadows.

The most popular activity in the park is driving up to the top of 6,000-foot **Mount Revelstoke,** with great views onto the Columbia River and the peaks of Glacier Park. To reach Mount Revelstoke, take the paved Meadows in the Sky Parkway north from the town of Revelstoke and follow it 23km (14 miles) to Balsam Lake. The road is closed to trailers and motor coaches, because it's a very narrow mountain road with 16 steep switchbacks.

At Balsam Lake, at the Meadows in the Sky area, free shuttle buses operated by the parks department make the final ascent to the top of Mount Revelstoke, but only after the road is clear of snow, usually early July to late September. If the shuttle isn't running, you have a choice of several easy hiking trails around Balsam Lake leading past rushing brooks through wildflower-spangled meadows. The **Eagle Knoll Trail** and the **Parapets** are two easy trails that take less than an hour to complete. At the summit are longer trails, including the 6km (3.7-mile) **Eva Lake Trail.**

If you don't make the trip up to the Meadows in the Sky area, you can enjoy a short hike in the park from along Highway 1. The **Skunk Cabbage Trail** is a boardwalk winding through a marsh that explodes with bright yellow and odiferous flowers in early summer. Another popular hike is the **Giant Cedars Trail,** a short boardwalk out into a grove of old-growth cedars that are over 1,000 years old.

The park is flanked on the south by Highway 1, the Trans-Canada Highway. The park has no services or campgrounds. However, all services are available in the neighboring town of Revelstoke. **Revelstoke** (pop. 8,507) sits on a shelf of land above confluence of the Columbia and Illecillewaet rivers. Founded in the 1880s, the town center retains a number of original storefronts and buildings and is very pleasant to explore. You'll find plenty of coffeehouses, galleries, and cafes, plus some standout architectural jewels, like the domed Revelstoke Courthouse, 1123 Second St. W. Near the corner of Victoria Road and Campbell Avenue, Grizzly Plaza is a courtyard lined with red-brick storefronts; this is the site for the Saturday-morning farmers' market and free live music Monday to Saturday 7 to 10pm from July through Labor Day.

For more information about the park, contact **Mount Revelstoke National Park,** P.O. Box 350, Revelstoke, BC V0E 2S0 (☎ **250/837-7500;** e-mail revglacier_reception@pch.gc.ca). Entry to the park is C$4 (US$2.65) adults, C$3 (US$2) seniors, C$2 (US$1.35) children 6 to 16, and C$10 (US$7) families.

WHERE TO STAY & DINE

○ **Mulvehill Creek Wilderness Inn & B&B.** 4200 Hwy. 23 S. (P.O. Box 1220), Revelstoke, BC V0E 2S0. ☎ **877-837-8649** or 250/837-8649. www.mulvehillcreek.com. E-mail mulvehil@junction.net. 8 units. C$85 (US$57) double; C$115–C$195 (US$77–US$130) suite. Rates include breakfast. MC, V.

One of the most superlative inns in all BC, the Mulvehill Creek Wilderness Inn is on Arrow Lake 19km (12 miles) south of Revelstoke on Highway 23. It sits in a clearing in the deep forest, steps from the lake and a magnificent 300-foot waterfall. The long cedar-shake–sided lodge has three rooms with queen beds, two with twin beds, and one with a king bed, plus a family suite with a king bed and a queen sofa bed and a honeymoon suite with a king bed, two-person Jacuzzi tub, and private deck. The rooms are all beautifully decorated with rich colors, locally made pine furniture, and original folk art. The comfortable guest lounge is lined with bookcases; grab a novel and curl up by the fireplace. From the wraparound deck, look onto the 20- by 40-foot pool and the large organic garden, which produces much of the fruit and vegetables served at the inn; the inn's hens provide the eggs. Children are welcome at Mulvehill, and there's even a playground. Guests have free use of canoes on the lake. Your hosts—the epitome of Swiss hospitality—serve a Swiss-style breakfast buffet with fresh breads and baked goods and homemade jams and jellies and are happy to arrange cross-country ski or snowshoe excursions, horseback riding, fishing, and motorboat trips. In its first year of operation, the word *paradise* appeared 106 times in guest-book comments.

Regent Inn. 112 First St. E., Revelstoke, BC V0E 2S0. ☎ **888/245-5523** or 250/837-2107. Fax 250/837-9669. E-mail regent@regentinn.com. 50 units. A/C TV TEL. C$88–C$129 (US$59–US$86) double. AE, MC, V. Rates include breakfast.

The finest lodging in downtown Revelstoke, the Regent is a refurbished heritage hotel facing onto historic Grizzly Plaza. The large guest rooms are nicely furnished. Fine dining is offered in the One Twelve Restaurant, drinks and light meals are served in

Dapper Dan's Pub, and cocktails are served in the Grizzly Lounge. Facilities include an outdoor heated pool, a hot tub, and a sauna.

KOOTENAY NATIONAL PARK & RADIUM HOT SPRINGS

Kootenay National Park, just west of Banff on the western slopes of the Rockies, preserves the valleys of the Kootenay and Vermilion rivers. The park contains prime wildlife habitats and a number of hiking trails. Though Kootenay's scenery is as grand as anywhere else in the Rockies, the trails are considerably less thronged than the neighboring parks.

The park is linked to the other Canadian Rocky Mountain parks by Highway 93, which departs from Highway 1 at Castle Junction to climb over the Vermilion Pass and descend to Radium Hot Springs, the park's western entrance. The town of Radium Hot Springs sits at the junction of highways 93 and 95. Not an especially attractive place, it nonetheless offers ample motel rooms along the 0.8km (half-mile) stretch of Highway 93 just before the park gates.

Kootenay has the fewest facilities of the four major Rocky Mountain national parks, and day-hiking options are limited. The drive through the park on Highway 93 does offer spectacular scenery, and if you have binoculars along, chances are good you'll see a mountain goat. Much of the area around Vermillion Pass, the eastern entrance to the park, was burned in a massive forest fire in 1968; from the parking area at the pass, the interpreted 15-minute **Fireweed Trail** leads out into the still-devastated forest, describing the process of revegetation.

Seven kilometers into the park is another dramatic stop. **Marble Canyon** is a narrow 200-foot-deep chasm cut through a formation of limestone. A short hiking trail winds over and through the canyon, bridging the canyon in several places. Just 5 minutes down the road are the **Paint Pots.** Here, cold spring water surfaces in an iron-rich deposit of red and yellow clay, forming intense colored pools. Early native Canadians journeyed here to collect the ochre-colored soil for body paint; for them, this was an area filled with "great medicine."

The highway leaves the Vermilion River valley and climbs up to a viewpoint above the Hector Gorge, into which the river flows before meeting the Kootenay River. From the viewpoint, also look for mountain goats, which can often be seen on the rocky cliffs of Mount Wardle to the north (the goat is the symbol of the park). The highway passes through one of these narrow limestone canyons after it mounts Sinclair Pass and descends toward Radium Hot Springs. Called **Sinclair Canyon,** the chasm is about 10km (6.2 miles) long and in places is scarcely wide enough to accommodate the roadbed.

The **Radium Hot Springs Pool** (☎ **250/347-9485**), a long-established hot springs spa/resort, sits at the mouth of Sinclair Canyon. As the name suggests, the mineral waters are slightly radioactive, but not enough to be a concern to casual soakers. Stop for a swim or a soak or a therapeutic massage. Mid-May to mid-October, the hot springs facilities are open daily 9am to 11pm; late October to early May, hours are daily noon to 9pm. Day passes are C$8 (US$5) adults, C$7 (US$4.85) seniors/children, and C$23 (US$16) families; each extra child is C$4.50 (US$3). The park user fee is included in the admission price. Also here is the **Radium Hot Springs Massage Clinic** (☎ **250/347-9714**), which offers therapeutic and relaxation massage, foot baths, and reflexology.

For more information about the park, contact **Kootenay National Park,** P.O. Box 220, Radium Hot Springs, BC V0A 1M0 (☎ **250/347-9505;** fax 250/347-9980; e-mail kootnay_reception@pch.gc.ca).

WHERE TO STAY & DINE

The **Old Salzburg Restaurant,** 4943 Hwy. 93 (☎ **250/347-6553**), a Tyrol-themed restaurant, is one of the most authentic looking of all Radium's ersatz Alpine structures. The menu features six varieties of schnitzels. April 15 to December 31, it's open daily 11am to 10pm. **Back Country Jack's,** 7555 West Main St. (☎ **250/347-0097**), is a lively bar/restaurant that stresses a mountain-man theme and is open daily 11am to 1pm.

The Chalet. 5063 Madsen Rd., Radium Hot Springs, BC V0A 1M0. ☎ **888/428-9998** or 250/347-9305. Fax 250/347-9306. www.radiumhotsprings.com/chalet. E-mail chalet@radiumhotsprings.com. 17 units. C$95–C$125 (US$63–US$83) suite. Extra person C$10 (US$7). AE, MC, V.

One of the few places to stay in Radium that doesn't have busy Highway 93 as its front yard, The Chalet is perched high above the Columbia Valley, just above the entrance to Kootenay Park. Each suite consists of a master bedroom with a queen bed and a galley kitchen with a microwave, fridge, sink, and dining table; the sitting area includes a dining table, queen hide-a-bed sofa, and TV. Off the sitting area are French doors leading onto a private balcony with superlative views of the Rocky Mountains and Columbia Valley. Facilities include a guest laundry, a whirlpool, an exercise room, and a gift shop.

10 Edmonton: Capital of Alberta

Edmonton is Alberta's capital and has the largest metropolitan population in the province, currently around 850,000. On the banks of the North Saskatchewan River, it's an outgoing and sophisticated city noted for its easygoing friendliness—a trait that's been scientifically proven. In 1995, an independent study of Canadians' altruistic behavior found that Edmonton was the most friendly and helpful city in the nation.

Edmonton grew in spurts, following a boom-and-bust pattern as exciting as it was unreliable. During World War II, the boom came in the form of the Alaska Highway, with Edmonton as the material base and temporary home of 50,000 American troops and construction workers. The ultimate boom, however, gushed from the ground on a freezing afternoon in February 1947. That was when a drill at Leduc, 40km (25 miles) southwest of the city, sent a fountain of dirty-black crude oil soaring skyward. Some 10,000 other wells followed, all within a 161km (100-mile) radius of the city. In their wake came the petrochemical industry and the major refining and supply conglomerates. In 2 decades, the population of the city quadrupled, its skyline mushroomed with glass-and-concrete office towers, a rapid-transit system was created, and a C$150 million (US$100 million) civic center rose. Edmonton had become what it is today—the oil capital of Canada.

ESSENTIALS

VISITOR INFORMATION   For guidance on Edmonton and its attractions, contact **Edmonton Tourism,** 9797 Jasper Ave. NW, Edmonton, AB T5J 1N9 (☎ **800/463-4667** or 780/496-8400; www.tourism.ede.org). There are also **visitor centers** at City Hall and at Gateway Park, both open daily 9am to 6pm, and on the Calgary Trail at the southern edge of the city, open daily 9am to 9pm.

GETTING THERE   Edmonton is served by most major airlines, including **Air Canada** (☎ **800/776-3000;** www.aircanada.ca) and **Canadian Airlines** (☎ **800/426-7000;** www.cdnair.ca), which also operates the shuttle to Calgary, a no-reservation service with more than a dozen flights a day. The **Edmonton International Airport** (☎ **800/268-7134**) lies 29km (18 miles) south of the city on Highway 2, about a 45-minute drive away. By cab, the trip costs about C$35 (US$23); by Airporter bus, C$11 (US$7).

Edmonton straddles the **Yellowhead Highway,** western Canada's new east-west interprovincial highway. Just west of Edmonton, the Yellowhead is linked to the Alaska Highway. The city is 515km (319 miles) north of the U.S. border and 283km (175 miles) north of Calgary.

Passenger trains arrive at and depart from the **VIA Rail Station,** 104th Avenue and 100th Street (☎ **800/561-8630** or 780/422-6032; www.viarail.ca). **Greyhound buses** link Edmonton to all points in Canada and the United States from the depot at 10324 103rd St. (☎ **780/413-8747;** www.greyhound.ca).

CITY LAYOUT   The winding North Saskatchewan River flows right through the heart of the city, dividing it into roughly equal halves. One of the capital's greatest achievements is the way in which this river valley has been kept out of the grasp of commercial developers. Almost the entire valley has been turned into public parklands, forming 27km (17 miles) of greenery, sports, picnic, and recreation grounds.

The founding fathers decided to begin the street-numbering system at the corner of 100th Street and 100th Avenue, which means downtown addresses have five digits and suburban homes often have smaller addresses than businesses in the very center of town. Edmonton's main street is **Jasper Avenue** (actually 101st Avenue), running north of the river. The "A" designations you'll notice for certain streets and avenues downtown add to the confusion; they're essentially old service alleys between major streets, many of which now are pedestrian areas with sidewalk cafes. Get a good map and give yourself time to puzzle the city's layout; it's not entirely straightforward.

At 97th Street, on Jasper Avenue, rises the massive pink **Canada Place,** the only completely planned government complex of its kind in Canada. Immediately across the street is the **Edmonton Convention Centre,** which stair-steps down the hillside to the river. Beneath the downtown core stretches a network of pedestrian walkways—called **Pedways**—connecting hotels, restaurants, and shopping malls with the library, City Hall, and the Citadel Theatre. These Pedways not only avoid the surface traffic but also are climate controlled.

At the northern approach to the High Level Bridge, surrounded by parkland, stand the buildings of the **Alberta Legislature,** seat of the provincial government. Across the bridge, to the west, stretches the vast campus of the **University of Alberta.** Just east is **Old Strathcona,** a bustling neighborhood of cafes, galleries, and hip shops that's now a haven for Edmonton's student and more "alternative" population. The main artery through Old Strathcona—which used to be its own town—is **Whyte Avenue,** or 82nd Avenue. Running south from here in a straight line is **104th Street,** which becomes Calgary Trail and leads to the Edmonton International Airport.

West of downtown Edmonton, Jasper Avenue shifts and twists to eventually become **Stony Plain Road,** which passes near **West Edmonton Mall,** the world's largest shopping-and-entertainment center, before merging with Highway 16 on its way to Jasper National Park.

GETTING AROUND   Public transport is handled by **Edmonton Transit** (☎ **780/ 496-1611**), which operates a family of services including the city buses and the LRT (Light Rail Transit), a partly underground/partly aboveground electric rail service connecting downtown Edmonton with Northlands Park to the north and the University of Alberta to the south. The LRT and the Transit buses have the same fares: C$1.60 (US$1.05) adults and C$1 (US65¢) seniors/children; a day pass is C$4.75

(US$3.15) adults and C$3.75 (US$2.50) children. You can transfer from one to the other at any station on the same ticket. On weekdays 9am to 3pm, downtown LRT travel is free among Churchill, Central, Bay, Corona, and Grandin stations.

In addition to the following downtown locations, **Tilden,** 10131-100A St. (☎ 780/422-6097; LRT: Central); **Budget,** 10016-106th St. (☎ 780/448-2000; Bus: 8); and **Hertz,** 10815 Jasper Ave. (☎ 780/423-3431; LRT: Corona), have bureaus at Edmonton International Airport. Call **CO-OP Taxi** at ☎ 780/425-2525 or 780/425-8310 for a ride in a driver/owner-operated cab.

FAST FACTS   American Express   There's an office at 10180 101st St., at 102nd Avenue (☎ 780/421-0608; LRT: Corona).

CAA   The **Alberta Motor Association,** affiliated with the Canadian Automobile Association, reciprocates with the AAA, offering members free travel information, advice, and services. The Edmonton office is at 11220 109th St. (☎ 780/471-3550; Bus: 8).

Doctors   If you need nonemergency medical care while in Edmonton, check the phone book for the closest branch of **Medicentre,** which offers walk-in medical services daily.

Emergency   For fire, medical, or crime emergencies, dial ☎ **911.**

Hospitals   The closest hospital with emergency service to downtown Edmonton is the **Royal Alexandra Hospital,** 10240 Kingsway Ave. (☎ 780/477-4111; Bus: 9).

Newspapers   The *Edmonton Journal* and *Edmonton Sun* are the local daily papers. Arts, entertainment, and nightlife listings can be found in the *See* weekly.

Pharmacies   Shoppers Drug Mart has more than a dozen locations in Edmonton, most open till midnight. One central location is 8210 109th St. (☎ 780/433-2424; Bus 6).

Post Office   The main post office is at 103A Avenue and 99th Street (LRT: Churchill).

KLONDIKE DAYS & OTHER SPECIAL EVENTS

The gold rush that sent an army of prospectors heading for the Yukon in 1898 put Edmonton "on the map." Although the actual gold fields lay 2,415km (1,497 miles) to the north, the little settlement became a giant supply store, resting place, and "recreation" ground for thousands of men stopping there en route before tackling the hazards of the Klondike Trail that led overland to Dawson City in the Yukon. Edmonton's population quickly doubled, and its merchants, saloon keepers, and ladies of easy virtue waxed rich in the process.

Since 1962, Edmonton has been celebrating the event with one of the greatest and most colorful extravaganzas staged in Canada. The ✪ **Klondike Days** (☎ 888/800-PARK or 780/471-7210) are held annually in late July. Street festivities last 10 days, as does the great Klondike Days Exposition at Northlands Park. Locals and visitors dress in period costumes, street corners blossom with impromptu stages featuring anything from country bands to cancan girls, stagecoaches rattle through the streets, and parades and floats wind from block to block.

The 16,000-seat Coliseum holds nightly spectaculars of rock, pop, variety, or Western entertainment. Northlands Park turns into Klondike Village, complete with the Chilkoot Gold Mine, the Silver Slipper Saloon, and a gambling casino (legal for this occasion only). The Walterdale Playhouse drops serious stage endeavors for a moment and puts on hilarious melodramas with mustachioed villains to hiss and dashing heroes to cheer. Immense open-air "Klondike breakfasts" are served, massed marching bands compete in the streets, and down the North Saskatchewan River float more than 100 of the weirdest-looking home-built rafts ever seen, competing in the "World Championship Sourdough River Raft Race."

Edmonton

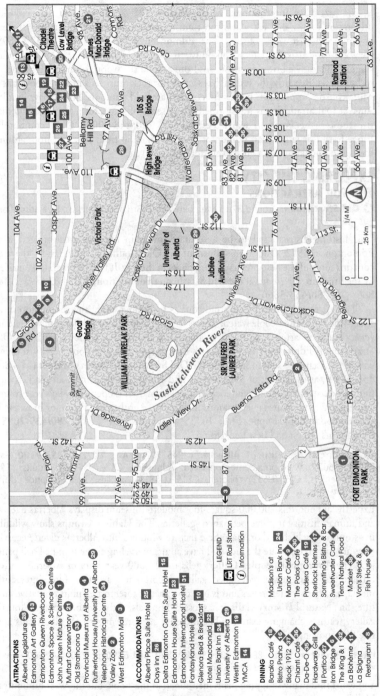

ATTRACTIONS
Alberta Legislature 28
Edmonton Art Gallery 13
Edmonton Queen Riverboat 20
Edmonton Space & Science Centre 5
John Janzen Nature Centre 1
Muttart Conservatory 21
Old Strathcona 35
Provincial Museum of Alberta 4
Rutherford House/University of Alberta 29
Telephone Historical Centre 34
Valley Zoo 2
West Edmonton Mall 3

ACCOMMODATIONS
Alberta Place Suite Hotel 25
Days Inn 26
Delta Edmonton Centre Suite Hotel 15
Edmonton House Suite Hotel 23
Edmonton International Hostel 31
Fantasyland Hotel 3
Glenora Bed & Breakfast 10
Hotel Macdonald 22
Union Bank Inn 24
University of Alberta 29
Westin Edmonton 19
YMCA 14

LEGEND
LRT Rail Station
ⓘ Information

DINING
Baraka Café 18
Bistro Praha 16
Block 1912 55
Chianti Café 45
Da-De-O 45
Hardware Grill 42
Il Portico 21
Iron Bridge 9
The King & I 17
La Bohème 11
La Spigna 6
Restaurant 8

Madison's at
Union Bank Inn 24
Manor Café 9
The Palos Café 59
Pradera Café 19
Sherlock Holmes 17
Sorrentino's Bistro & Bar 17
Sweetwater Café 7
Terra Natural Food
Market 48
Von's Steak &
Fish House 59

The **Jazz City International Music Festival** (☎ 780/432-7166) is a citywide celebration of jazz that takes over most music venues in Edmonton for the last week of June and first week of July. The **Edmonton Folk Fest** (☎ 780/429-1899; www.efmf.ab.ca) is the largest folk-music festival in North America. Held in mid-August, the festival brings in musicians from around the world, from the Celtic north to Indonesia. Recently, the festival has seen major rock musicians making appearances with acoustic "unplugged" bands. All concerts are held outdoors. For 10 days in mid-August, Old Strathcona is transformed into a series of stages for a festival of alternative theater, the **Fringe Theatre Festival** (☎ 780/448-9000). Only Edinburgh's fringe festival is larger than Edmonton's—more than 60 troupes attend from around the world—making this a great event for theater lovers.

EXPLORING THE CITY
THE TOP ATTRACTIONS

✪ **Old Strathcona.** Around 82nd Ave., between 103rd and 105th sts. Free admission. Bus: 46.

This historic district used to be a separate township but was amalgamated with Edmonton in 1912. Due to the efforts of the Old Strathcona Foundation, the area contains some of the best-preserved landmarks in the city. It's best seen on foot, guided by the brochures given out at the **Old Strathcona Foundation,** 10324 82nd Ave., 4th floor (☎ 780/433-5866).

The best reason to visit Old Strathcona is to wander along the shops, stop in at street-side cafes, and people watch. This is "hipster central" for Edmonton, where university students, artists, and the city's alternative community come to hang out: Old Strathcona is Edmonton's Left Bank. It's easy to spend an afternoon here, just being part of the scene. Be sure to stop in at the **Old Strathcona Farmers Market** (☎ 780/439-1844), at the corner of 83rd Avenue and 103rd Street, an open-air market with fresh produce, baked goods, and local crafts. The market is open Saturdays year-round and Tuesday and Thursday afternoons in summer. Another good stop for browsers is **Greenwoods' Bookshoppe Ltd.,** 10355 Whyte Ave. NW (☎ 780/439-2005), Edmonton's largest and best bookstore.

✪ **Provincial Museum of Alberta.** 12845 102nd Ave. ☎ 780/453-9100. Fax 780/454-6629. www.pma.edmonton.ab.ca. Admission C$7 (US$4.65) adults, C$6 (US$4) seniors, C$3 (US$2) children, C$15 (US$10) families. Tues half-price. Daily 9am–5pm. Bus: 1.

Expertly laid out, this 200,000-square-foot modern museum displays Alberta's natural and human history in three permanent galleries. The **Habitat Groups** show wildlife in astonishingly lifelike dioramas; these picture windows into Alberta's diverse ecosystems are sure to captivate the kids and have adults marveling at the trompe l'oeil paint job. The **Aboriginal Peoples Gallery** tells the 11,000-year story of Alberta's native inhabitants. This newly redesigned gallery incorporates artifacts, film, interactive media, and native interpreters and is one of Canada's foremost exhibits on native culture. The **Natural History Gallery** has fossils, minerals, and a live-bug room. A fourth gallery features changing exhibits. The museum also presents artists and artisans and free film showings.

West Edmonton Mall. 8882 170th St. ☎ 800/661-8890 or 780/444-5200. www.westedmontonmall.com. Free admission. Bus: 10.

You won't find many shopping malls mentioned in this book, but the West Edmonton Mall is something else. Though it contains 800 stores and services, including 90 popular eateries, it looks and sounds more like a large slice of Disneyland that has somehow broken loose and drifted north. Locals modestly call it the "Eighth Wonder of the World." More theme park than mall, the 5.2-million-square-foot West Edmonton Mall houses the world's largest indoor amusement park, including a titanic indoor roller coaster, a bungee-jumping platform, and an enclosed wave-lake, complete with a beach and enough artificial waves to ride a surfboard on. It has walk-through bird aviaries, a huge ice-skating palace, 19 movie theaters, a lagoon with performing dolphins, and several absolutely fabulous adventure rides (one of them by submarine to the "ocean floor," another simulating a white-water raft journey; some are fairly expensive). In the middle of it all, an immense fountain with 19 computer-controlled jets weaves and dances in a musical performance.

Of course, you can go shopping and dining at the mall, and an increasingly large share of the city's nightlife is opening here. On Saturdays at 2pm, you can even tour the rooms at the mall's excellent "theme" hotel, Fantasyland. Roll your eyes all you want, but do go. You have to see the West Edmonton Mall to believe it.

✪ **Fort Edmonton Park.** On the Whitemud Dr. at Fox Dr. ☎ **780/496-8787.** www.gov.edmonton.ab.ca/fort. Admission C$7 (US$4.65) adults, C$5 (US$3.35) seniors/youths, C$3.50 (US$2.35) children, C$21 (US$14) families. Mid-May to late June Mon–Fri 10am–4pm, Sat–Sun 10am–6pm; late June to early Sept daily 10am–6pm. LRT: University, then bus 32.

Fort Edmonton Park is a large complex of townscapes re-creating various eras of Edmonton's lengthy history. Perhaps the most interesting of the four sections of the park is the complete reconstruction of the old Fort Edmonton fur-trading post from the turn of the 18th century. This vast wooden structure is a warren of rooms and activities: Blacksmiths, bakers, and other docents ply their trades throughout. Other sections re-create Edmonton in later periods. On 1885 Street it's Frontier Edmonton, complete with a blacksmith shop, a saloon, a general store, and the Jasper House Hotel serving hearty pioneer meals. On 1905 Street you'll see an antique photographic studio and a fire hall with appropriate engines. On 1920 Street, sip an old-fashioned ice-cream soda at Bill's "confectionery." You can ride Edmonton streetcar no. 1, a stagecoach, or a steam locomotive among the various "streets."

Adjoining Fort Edmonton, the **John Janzen Nature Centre** (☎ 780/496-2939) offers historic exhibits, hiking trails, and lessons in nature lore. You can go bird watching, "shake hands" with a garter snake, observe a living beehive, and take courses from professionals in everything from building a log cabin to game stalking and tracking. May 18 to June 30, it's open Monday to Friday 9am to 4pm and Saturday, Sunday, and holidays 11am to 4pm; July 1 to September 7, it's open Monday to Friday 9am to 6pm and Saturday, Sunday, and holidays 11am to 6pm. Admission is by donation.

Muttart Conservatory. Off James MacDonald Bridge at 98th Ave. and 96A St. ☎ **780/496-8755.** Admission C$4.75 (US$3.15) adults, C$3.75 (US$2.50) seniors/youths, C$2.25 (US$1.50) children. Mon–Fri 9am–6pm, Sat–Sun and holidays 11am–6pm. Bus: 51.

The conservatory, in four pavilions that look like I. M. Pei pyramids, houses one of the finest floral displays in North America. Each pyramid contains a different climatic zone—the tropical one has an 18-foot waterfall. The Arid Pavilion has desert air and shows flowering cacti and their relatives. The temperate zone includes a cross section of plants from this global region. The fourth pyramid features changing ornamental displays of plants and blossoms; an orchid greenhouse has newly opened. For good measure, there's also the Treehouse Cafe.

***Edmonton Queen* Riverboat.** 9734 98th Ave. ☎ **780/424-2628.** Cruise only C$6–C$15 (US$4–US$10); meal packages C$16–C$40 (US$11–US$27). Call for hours. Bus: 12, 45.

Moored just outside the convention center, this riverboat plies the North Saskatchewan River as it runs through the city's many parks. A number of packages are offered, usually the cruise itself or a meal package that includes lunch or dinner.

MORE ATTRACTIONS

Alberta Legislature Building. 109th St. and 97th Ave. ☎ **780/427-7362.** www.assembly.ab.ca. Free tours daily every hour 9am–4pm, Sat–Sun and holidays noon–5pm. LRT: Grandin.

The Alberta Legislature rises on the site of the early trading post from which the city grew. Surrounded by lovingly manicured lawns, formal gardens, and greenhouses, it overlooks the river valley. The seat of Alberta's government was completed in 1912; it's a stately Edwardian structure open to the public throughout the year. Free conducted tours tell you about the functions of provincial lawmaking: who does what, where, and for how long.

Edmonton Art Gallery. 2 Sir Winston Churchill Sq. ☎ **780/422-6223.** www.eag.org. Admission C$3 (US$2) adults, C$1.50 (US$1) seniors/students; children under 12 free. Mon–Wed 10:30am–5pm, Thurs–Fri 10:30am–8pm, Sat–Sun and holidays 11am–5pm. LRT: Churchill.

The Edmonton Art Gallery occupies a stately building in the heart of downtown, east of City Hall. The interior, however, is state-of-the-art modern, subtly lit, and expertly arranged. Exhibits consist partly of contemporary Canadian art, partly of international contemporary art, partly of changing works on tour from every corner of the globe. The Gallery shop sells an eclectic array of items, from art books to handmade yo-yos.

Rutherford House. 11153 Saskatchewan Dr., on the campus of the University of Alberta. ☎ **780/427-3995.** E-mail lmp@mcd.gov.ab.ca. Admission C$2 (US$1.35) adults, C$1.50 (US$1) seniors/youths, C$5 (US$3.65) families. High season daily 10am–6pm; winter Tues–Sun noon–5pm. LRT: University.

The home of Alberta's first premier, Alexander Rutherford, this lovingly preserved Edwardian gleams with polished silver- and gilt-framed oils. Around 1915, this mansion was the magnet for the social elite of the province: Today, guides dressed in period costumes convey some of the spirit of the times. There's also a charming restaurant/tearoom, the **Arbour** (☎ **780/422-2697**), open daily 11:30am to 4pm.

Telephone Historical Centre. 10437 83rd Ave. ☎ **780/441-2077.** www.discoveredmonton.com/telephonemuseum. Admission C$3 (US$2) adults, C$2 (US$1.35) children, C$5 (US$3.35) families. Tues–Fri 10am–4pm, Sat noon–4pm. Bus: 44.

North America's largest museum devoted to the history of telecommunications is located in the 1912 Telephone Exchange Building. Multimedia displays tell the history of words over wire and hints at what your modem will get up to next.

ESPECIALLY FOR KIDS

Edmonton Space & Science Centre. 11211 142nd St., Coronation Park. ☎ **780/451-3344.** www.edmontonscience.com. E-mail essc@planet.eon.net. Admission C$7 (US$4.65) adults, C$6 (US$4) youths, C$6 (US$4) seniors, C$5 (US$3.65) children 3–12, C$26 (US$17) families. Summer daily 10am–10pm; winter Tues, Sun, and holidays 10am–10pm. Bus: 17, 22. Free parking.

This is one of the most advanced multipurpose facilities of its kind in the world. It contains, among other wonders, a giant-screen IMAX theater (☎ **780/493-4250,** separate admission), the largest planetarium theater in Canada, and many high-tech exhibit galleries (including a virtual-reality showcase and a robotics display) and an observatory open on clear afternoons and evenings. The show programs include star shows, laser-light music concerts, and the special IMAX films that have to be seen to be believed.

Valley Zoo. In Laurier Park, 13315 Buena Vista Rd, ☎ **780/496-6911.** Admission C$5 (US$3.50) adults, C$3.75 (US$2.50) seniors/youths, C$2.75 (US$1.85) children under 13, C$16 (US$11) families. Summer daily 9:30am–8pm; winter daily 9:30am–4pm. Bus: 12.

In this charming combination of reality and fantasy, real live animals mingle with fairy-tale creations. More than 500 animals and birds are neighbors to the Three Little Pigs, Humpty Dumpty, and the inhabitants of Noah's Ark.

SHOPPING

There are more shops per capita in Edmonton than in any other city in Canada. Go for it!

DOWNTOWN   Most of downtown's shops are contained in a few large mall complexes; all are linked by the Pedway system, which provides pedestrians protection from summer heat and winter cold. The following malls each face onto 102nd Avenue, between 103rd and 100th streets. The **Edmonton Centre** has 140 stores and shares the block with the **Hudson's Bay Company.** The Eaton Centre contains more than 100 stores, including the flagship Eatons. Across the street is **Manulife Place,** with 60 stores, anchored by Holt Renfrew.

OLD STRATHCONA   If you don't like mall shopping, then wandering the **galleries and boutiques** along Whyte Avenue in Old Strathcona might be more your style. About the only part of Edmonton that retains any historic structures, Old Strathcona is trend central for Edmonton's student population and the bohemian left. Shop for antiques, imported clothes, gift items, books, and crafts amid buskers and crowded streetside cafes. Be sure to stop by the **Farmers Market** at 103rd Street and 102nd Avenue.

HIGH STREET   This small district, running from 102nd to 109th avenues along 124th Street, has Edmonton's greatest concentration of art galleries, interior-design and housewares shops, small fashion boutiques, and bookstores. Great restaurants too.

WEST EDMONTON MALL   The **world's largest shopping mall,** the West Ed Mall (as it's known), covers 48 square blocks near 87th Avenue and 170th Street. This is Edmonton's greatest tourist draw, with more than 800 shops, a hotel, a water park and slide, performing dolphins, an amusement park, an ice-skating rink, a casino, dozens of bars and restaurants, and just about every other form of entertainment. Not for the faint of heart.

WHERE TO STAY
VERY EXPENSIVE

✪ **Hotel Macdonald.** 10065 100th St., Edmonton, AB T5J 0N6. ☎ **800/441-1414** or 780/424-5181. Fax 780/429-6481. www.hotelmacdonald.ca. 198 units. A/C MINIBAR TV TEL. High season C$229–C$249 (US$153–US$166) deluxe standard room, C$265–C$277 (US$177–US$185) Pacific Premier suite, C$349 (US$233) executive suite, C$429–C$699 (US$286–US$466) specialty suite. Buffet breakfast included for premiere suites guests. Discounts on weekends and off-season. AE, DC, DISC, ER, MC, V. Parking C$15 (US$10). LRT: Central.

The palatial Hotel Macdonald, named after Canada's first prime minister, opened in 1915. After a long colorful career, it was bought by the Canadian Pacific chain in 1988 and became a masterwork of sensitive renovation. With its limestone facade and gargoyles, the Mac, as it's known locally, looks like a feudal château—right down to the kilted service staff. The courtly public rooms were left intact, and the guest rooms were completely rebuilt to modern luxury standards. While the renovation brought the rooms up-to-date with important additions like new plumbing and individual temperature controls, it retained all the original charm (old deep bathtubs, brass door plates, high ceilings, handsome paneled doors). Each Pacific Premier suite has a sitting area with a couch and two chairs and a handy dressing area off the bathroom with a vanity table. Free coffee, local phone calls, and buffet breakfast are included. Each Executive suite has two TVs and phones, with a separate bedroom and a large sitting area. The eight specialty suites—which take up the entire eighth floor—are simply magnificent. Even pets get special treatment: a gift bag of treats and a map of pet-friendly parks. Needless to say, there aren't many hotels like this in Edmonton—or in Canada for that matter.

Dining/Diversions: The Library Bar resembles an Edwardian gentlemen's club. The Harvest Room restaurant offers views of the panoramic backdrop of the North Saskatchewan River valley, as well as an outdoor garden terrace for summer dining.

Amenities: Concierge, 24-hour room service, dry cleaning/laundry; pool, wading pool for children; health club with pro shop, juice bar, weight room, sauna, steam room, squash courts, massage therapy area, exercise room with personal trainers; business center.

EXPENSIVE

Delta Edmonton Centre Suite Hotel. In the Eaton Centre, 10222 102nd St., Edmonton, AB T5J 4C5. ☎ **780/429-3900.** Fax 780/428-1566. 169 units. A/C MINIBAR TV TEL. C$132–C$250 (US$88–US$167) standard business suite; C$218 (US$145) deluxe executive suite, or C$147 (US$98) if you're here on business. Ask about summer family and low weekend package rates. AE, DC, ER, MC, V. Parking C$9 (US$6), valet parking C$12 (US$8). LRT Central.

This all-suite hotel forms part of the upscale Eaton Centre Mall in the heart of downtown. Three-quarters of the windows look into the mall, so you can stand behind the tinted one-way glass (in your pajamas, if you like) and watch the shopping action outside. Most units are deluxe executive suites, each with a large sitting area with a couch, chairs, a TV, and a wet bar, plus a bedroom of equal size with more easy chairs, another TV, a large desk, and a plate-glass wall looking into the seven-story mall atrium. Each suite has two phones. If you need lots of room or have work to do, these very spacious rooms are just the ticket. All rooms have jetted tubs. The entire hotel is nicely furnished and well decorated.

Dining/Diversions: Cocoa's is the Delta's casual restaurant and lounge, just off the shopping mall.

Amenities: Concierge, dry cleaning/laundry, baby-sitting; business center; health center with exercise machines, steam bath, whirlpool; 140 retail shops in the mall, movie theaters, entertainment pub, indoor nine-hole putting green.

Fantasyland Hotel. 17700 87th Ave., Edmonton, AB T5T 4V4. ☎ **800/737-3783** or 780/444-3000. Fax 780/444-3294. 354 units. A/C TV TEL. C$138–C$165 (US$92–US$110) standard room, C$225–C$295 (US$150–US$197) double. Extra person C$10 (US$7). Weekend and off-season packages available. AE, ER, MC, V. Free parking. Bus: 1 or 100.

From the outside, this solemn brown brick tower at the end of the West Edmonton Mall reveals little of the wildly decorated and luxurious rooms inside. The Fantasyland is what you might expect to find in Las Vegas. It contains 116 "themed" rooms decorated in nine styles (as well as 238 large and well-furnished regular rooms)—they're exceedingly clever, very comfortable, and way over the top. Take the Truck Room: Your bed is in the back end of a real pickup (you can choose a Ford or Chevy); the pickup's bench seats fold down into a bed for a child, the lights on the vanity are real stoplights, and the lights on the roll bar are actually reading lights; traffic signs

---

Fantasyland Tours

If you have any doubt about the rooms at the Fantasyland or just want a break from routine sightseeing, the hotel offers tours of all the different theme types on Saturdays at 2pm. After you complete the tour, you'll wish you were staying there.

---

decorate the walls. In the Igloo Room, a round bed is encased in a shell that looks like ice blocks, keeping company with you are statues of sled dogs, and all the walls are painted with amazingly lifelike Arctic murals; the dogsleds even become beds for children. Then there's the Canadian Rail Room (train berths for beds), African Room, Roman Room. . . . The theme rooms come with four-person Jacuzzi tubs, lots of sitting room (albeit usually disguised as something else), and all the amenities you'd expect at a four-star hotel. The nontheme rooms are divided into superior rooms (each with either a king or two queen beds) or executive rooms (each with a king bed, a four-person Jacuzzi, and masses of sitting room).

Dining: The hotel's fine-dining restaurant is quite good.

Amenities: Room service; business work area with desks, modems, printers; small workout room; passes are offered to the mall's Waterpark; all-weather access to the world's largest shopping mall.

Westin Edmonton. 10135 100th St., Edmonton, AB T5J 0N7. ☎ **800/937-8461** or 780/426-3636. Fax 780/428-1454. www.westin.ab.ca. E-mail sales@westin.ab.ca. 413 units. A/C MINIBAR TV TEL. From C$135 (US$90) double. Parking C$14 (US$9), valet parking C$17 (US$11). AE, CB, DC, DISC, ER, MC, V. LRT: Central.

In the heart of Edmonton's downtown shopping-and-entertainment district, the Westin—a modern bow-shaped building—offers some of the city's largest rooms. Though the lobby is a bit austere, the guest rooms are comfortably furnished and come with nice touches like coffeemakers, two phones, voice mail, and irons/ironing boards. The rooms in the premier wing have a second TV in the bathroom! For an extra C$20 (US$13), you can request a Westin Guest Office, a room with a printer, a fax, an ergonomic chair, and a proper business desk. Seventy percent of the rooms are no-smoking.

Dining/Diversions: There are two restaurants, including the Pradera Cafe, one of Edmonton's most inventive restaurants (see "Where to Dine" below), as well as two lounges.

Amenities: Concierge, 24-hour room service, valet laundry; complete exercise facilities with indoor pool, sauna, whirlpool.

MODERATE

Alberta Place Suite Hotel. 10049 103rd St., Edmonton, AB T5J 2W7. ☎ **800/661-3982** or 780/423-1565. Fax 780/426-6260. 86 units. TV TEL. C$81–C$120 (US$54–US$80) double bed-sitter; C$104 (US$69) double one-bedroom suite. Extra person C$8 (US$5). Children under 17 stay free in parents' room. AE, DC, ER, MC, V. Free parking. LRT: Corona.

This downtown apartment-hotel is an excellent choice for those who need a little extra space or a family that wants cooking facilities. Everything is supplied to set up housekeeping. The apartments, of various sizes, are very well furnished and comfortable, and each has a full kitchen (including a microwave) and a large desk and working area. There's also a pool (with hot tub and sauna).

Days Inn. 10041 106th St., Edmonton, AB T5J 1G3. ☎ **800/267-2191** or 780/423-1925. Fax 780/424-5302. www.daysinn.com. E-mail daysinn@compusmart.ab.ca. 76 units. A/C TV TEL. C$59–C$89 (US$39–US$59) double. Children under 12 stay free in parents' room. Senior, AAA, and corporate discounts available. AE, CB, DC, DISC, ER, MC, V. Free parking. LRT: Corona.

For the price, this is one of downtown Edmonton's best deals. Located just 5 minutes from the city center, this motor inn has everything you need for a pleasant stay, including guest laundry and king- or queen-size beds in comfortably furnished guest rooms.

✪ **Edmonton House Suite Hotel.** 10205 100th Ave., Edmonton, AB T5J 4B5. ☎ **800/661-6562** or 780/420-4000. Fax 780/420-4008. www.edmontonhouse.com. 300 units. TV TEL. C$69–C$140 (US$46–US$93) 1-bedroom suite. Extra person C$5 (US$3.35). Weekend, weekly, and monthly rates. AE, DC, ER, MC, V. Free parking. Bus: 7 or 9.

This is a great alternative to pricier downtown hotels, with big well-decorated guest rooms, free parking, and (given its location above the North Saskatchewan River) one of the best views in Edmonton. The suites are large; each comes with a full kitchen and dining area, a bedroom, a separate sitting area with a foldout couch and chairs, and a balcony from which to take in the view; two-bedroom suites are also available. Each room has two phones and a computer jack; room service is available. Facilities include a pool and sauna, an exercise room, a game room, and a laundry, plus a lounge and a restaurant.

Glenora Bed & Breakfast. 12327 102nd Ave. NW, Edmonton, AB T5N 0L8. ☎ **780/488-6766.** Fax 780/488-5168. 18 units. C$70–C$140 (US$47–US$93) double. Rates include deluxe continental breakfast. AE, MC, V.

In the heart of the High Street district just west of downtown, the Glenora occupies the upper floors of a 1912 heritage boarding house. There's an array of room types, from simple rooms with a mix of shared and private bathrooms, to studios, suites, and rooms that are best thought of as apartments. The rooms are all pleasantly furnished with period antiques and rich designer fabrics.

Union Bank Inn. 10053 Jasper Ave., Edmonton, AB T5J 1S5. ☎ **780/423-3600.** Fax 780/423/4623. www.unionbankinn.com. 29 units. A/C MINIBAR TV TEL. C$125–C$145 (US$83–US$97) double. Rates include full breakfast. AE, DC, ER, MC, V. Free parking. LRT: Central.

The stylish Union Bank, built in 1910, has seen many uses during its long life; however, the building had sat vacant for years before a young businesswoman bought it and redeveloped it into an elegant restaurant and intimate boutique hotel. In order to make each of the guest rooms unique, she asked each of Edmonton's top interior designers to design a room. The results are charming—each room with its own style, colors, furniture, fabrics, and layout; if you're coming here with work to do, ask for one of the larger rooms. All the rooms have the same amenities, including fireplaces, voice mail and modem jacks, goose-feather pillows and duvets, and bathrooms full of nice toiletries. The service is very friendly and professional. The main lobby restaurant/bar, Madison's (see "Where to Dine" below), is a great place to meet friends. If you're weary of anonymous corporate hotels and would like a cozy place in central Edmonton, then this is a wonderful choice.

INEXPENSIVE

In summer, 1,200 dorm rooms in Lister Hall at the **University of Alberta,** 87th Avenue and 116th Street (☎ **780/492-4281;** fax 780/492-7032; www.hfs.ualberta.ca; e-mail conference@ualberta.ca; LRT: University), are thrown open to visitors. Most are standard bathroom-down-the-hall rooms with two twin beds for C$33 (US$22). Available year-round are guest suites, two-bed dorms sharing a bathroom with only one other suite, costing C$40 (US$27). The university is right on the LRT line and not far from trendy Old Strathcona. Parking is C$3 (US$2).

The **Edmonton International Hostel** has a new location in Old Strathcona at 10647 81st Ave., Edmonton, AB T6E 1Y1 (☎ **780/988-6836;** fax 780/988-8698; e-mail eihostel@hostellingintl.ca; Bus: 6). Right in the thick of things in Edmonton's most exciting neighborhood, the hostel sleeps 104. Rates are C$15 (US$10) members and C$20 (US$13) nonmembers.

The **YMCA,** 10030 102A Ave. (☎ **780/421-9622;** fax 780/428-9469; LRT: Churchill), offers 106 rooms for C$42 (US$28) double. It has a cafeteria, pool, weight room, gymnasium, and racquetball court, plus a TV lounge; it accommodates men, women, and couples. Only a few rooms have private bathrooms.

WHERE TO DINE

Edmonton has a vigorous dining scene, with lots of hip new eateries joining traditional steak and seafood restaurants. In general, special-occasion and fine dining is found downtown and on High Street, close to the centers of politics and business. Over in Old Strathcona, south of the river, is an area of trendy—and less expensive—cafes and bistros with up-to-the-minute cosmopolitan menus.

If you're staying downtown, one place you'll get to know well is the **Baraka Cafe,** 10088 Jasper Ave. (☎ 780/423-1819). Baraka's has expertly made espresso drinks, two cases full of exquisite pastries and sweets, and a large selection of magazines and newspapers. With cafe tables to lounge at, this is the perfect place to caffeinate in the morning or have a late-night dessert.

DOWNTOWN
Expensive

✪ **Hardware Grill.** 9698 Jasper Ave. ☎ **780/423-0969.** www.hardwaregrill.com. Reservations suggested. Main courses C$20–C$30 (US$13–US$20). AE, MC, V. Mon–Fri 11:30am–2pm; Mon–Thurs 5–9:30pm, Fri–Sat 5–10pm. Closed 1st week of July and 1st week of Jan. Bus: 120. NEW CANADIAN.

In what was Edmonton's original hardware store, the Hardware Grill is easily one of the city's most savvy and exciting restaurants. The menu reflects new cooking styles, regional ingredients, and wonderful presentation. There are as many appetizers as entree selections, making it tempting to graze through a series of smaller dishes. Sautéed sweetbreads are served with a hearty potato hash, wild-mushroom ragout spills over grilled polenta, and smoked duck comes in crispy spring rolls. However, it's hard to resist entrees like maple-smoked pork loin with sweet corn sauce and lamb sirloin with herb gnocchi and mint aioli. The wine list is extensive and witty—after the mandatory listing of chardonnays, the substantial list of other white wines is listed under "Anything but Chardonnay." The building may be historic, but there's nothing antique about the dining room. Postmodern without being stark, it's edged with glass partitions, with exposed pipes and ducts painted a smoky rose. The kitchen is open to the dining room and contains a fearsome squadron of cooks.

La Bohème. 6427 112th Ave. ☎ **780/474-5693.** Reservations required. Main courses C$15–C$29 (US$10–US$19). AE, MC, V. Mon–Sat 11am–3pm, Sun 11am–3:30pm; daily 5–11pm. Bus: 2. FRENCH.

La Bohème consists of two small lace-curtained dining rooms in a historic building northeast of downtown. There's a wide selection of appetizers and light dishes, including a number of intriguing salads. The entrees are hearty, classic French preparations like rack of lamb, chicken breast, and seafood. The restaurant also features daily changing vegetarian entrees. The wine selection has a particular accent on Rhône Valley vintages, and the desserts are outstanding.

Madison's at Union Bank Inn. 10053 Jasper Ave. ☎ **780/423-3600.** Reservations suggested. Main courses C$14–C$21 (US$9–US$14); table d'hôte C$25 (US$17). AE, ER, MC, V. Daily 7am–11pm. LRT: Central. NEW CANADIAN.

This is one of the loveliest dining rooms and casual cocktail bars in Edmonton. It was an early-1900s bank, and the formal architectural details remain—columns and big moldings—but they share the light and airy space with modern art, light-wood floors, avant-garde furniture, and excellent food. The menu is up-to-date, with grilled and roast fish and meats, pasta dishes, interesting salads (one special featured rose petals, baby lettuce, and shaved white chocolate), and several specials daily. Many dishes boast an international touch, like prawns with cilantro and tequila-lime cream served over pasta, and grilled salmon served with cranberry-citrus salsa.

Pradera Cafe. In the Westin Edmonton, 10135 100th St. ☎ **780/426-3636.** Fax 780/428-1454. Reservations recommended. Main courses C$15–C$25 (US$10–US$17). AE, DC, DISC, MC, V. Mon–Fri 6:30am–2pm, Sat–Sun 7am–2pm; daily 5–11pm. LRT: Central. INTERNATIONAL.

One of downtown Edmonton's most inventive restaurants features creative fusion cooking. Pradera's menu free-associates across several cuisines, notably Asian, Italian, and Canadian, to arrive at new dishes that succeed at being more than the sum of their parts. The herb-crusted rack of lamb is served with polenta and Sambuca coffee jus, the grilled mahimahi comes with a potato spring roll and papaya relish, and the prime rib is served with a horseradish profiterole. The service is excellent.

Sorrentino's Bistro and Bar. 10162 100th St. ☎ **780/424-7500.** Reservations suggested. Main courses C$17–C$25 (US$11–US$17). AE, DC, MC, V. Mon–Fri 7–11am, 11:30am–2:30pm, and 5:30pm–midnight; Sat 5pm–midnight. LRT: Central. ITALIAN.

This new upscale branch of a local chain is a good addition to the downtown dining scene. The coolly sophisticated dining room and bar—flanked by the Havana Room, where Cuban cigars are available with port and single-malt Scotch—is a popular meeting place for the captains of the city's business and social life. The food is excellent: You can't do better than a plate from the daily appetizer table, which features grilled vegetables, bean salads, and marinated anchovies. Entrees range from risottos to pasta and wood-fired–oven pizza to imaginative entrees like tournedos of salmon and scallops, veal and chicken dishes, and several rotisserie specials daily.

Moderate

Bistro Praha. 10168 100A St. ☎ **780/424-4218.** Reservations recommended on weekends. Main courses C$13–C$18 (US$9–US$12). AE, DC, ER, MC, V. Mon–Fri 11am–2am, Sat noon–2am, Sun 4pm–midnight. LRT: Central. CENTRAL EUROPEAN.

Bistro Praha is one of several side-by-side casual restaurants—all with summer street-side seating—that take up the single block of 100A Street (formerly a service alley). It's also the best of these restaurants and features a charming wood-paneled interior, a mural-covered wall, and great Eastern European cooking. The menu offers a wide selection of light dishes, convenient for a quick meal or a midafternoon snack. The entree menu centers on schnitzels (there are three kinds), as well as a wonderful roast goose with sauerkraut. The desserts tend toward fancy confections like Sachertorte. The service is friendly and relaxed and the crowd cosmopolitan and mainly young.

✪ **Il Portico.** 10012 107th St. ☎ **780/424-0707.** Reservations recommended on weekends. Main courses C$11–C$23 (US$7–US$15). AE, DC, DISC, MC, V. Mon–Fri 11:30am–2pm; Mon–Sat 5:30–11pm, Sun 5–10pm. LRT: Corona. ITALIAN.

One of the most popular Italian restaurants in Edmonton, Il Portico has a wide menu of well-prepared traditional but updated dishes. This is seriously good Italian food, with excellent selections of grilled meats, pastas, and pizza: It's one of those rare restaurants where you want to try everything. Have the Caesar salad and remember how wonderful these salads can be if prepared properly. The service is impeccable and the wine list one of the best in the city. Remarkably, they'll open any bottle on the list (except reserve bottles) if you buy a half liter. The dining room is nicely informal but classy; there's outdoor seating in summer.

Inexpensive

At the corner of 101A Avenue and 100A Street, in the heart of downtown, are a number of street cafes with moderate to inexpensive menus. The actual restaurants seem to change frequently, but the venues remain. This is a good place to go and shop the menus for pasta, sandwiches, and burgers. There are also inexpensive food options in the **Eaton Mall,** at 102nd Avenue and 101st Street, and in Edmonton's compact **"Chinatown"** centered at 102nd Avenue and 96th Street.

Sherlock Holmes. 10012 101A Ave. ☎ **780/426-7784.** www.thesherlockhomes.com. Main courses C$7–C$10 (US$4.65–US$7). AE, ER, MC, V. Mon–Sat 11:30am–2am, Sun noon–8pm. LRT: Central. ENGLISH.

The Sherlock Holmes is a tremendously popular English-style pub with good local and regional beers on tap (as well as Guinness) and a very good bar menu. The pub is housed in a charming building with black crossbeams on whitewashed walls and a picket fence around the outdoor patio. The menu has a few traditional English dishes—like fish-and-chips and steak-and-kidney pie—but there's a strong emphasis on new pub grub like chicken-breast sandwiches, beef curry, burgers, and salads. There are two other Sherlock Holmeses in Edmonton, one in the West Edmonton Mall and the other in Old Strathcona at 10341 82nd Ave.

HIGH STREET

High Street is a small neighborhood with galleries, classy shops, and several good restaurants, centered at 102nd Avenue and 124th Street, just west of downtown. In addition to the restaurants below, there's a lively bar and bistro called the **Iron Bridge,** 12520 102nd Ave. (☎ **780/482-5620**), with a popular summer patio.

Moderate

La Spiga Restaurant. 10133 125th St. ☎ **780/482-3100.** Fax 780/488-3225. Reservations recommended on weekends. Main courses C$13–C$23 (US$9–US$15). AE, DC, MC, V. Mon–Fri 11:30am–2pm; Mon–Sat 5–11pm. Bus: 1 or 100. ITALIAN.

One of Edmonton's best Italian restaurants, La Spiga is along the gallery row in the trendy High Street neighborhood. This is nouveau Italian cooking, with an emphasis on fresh ingredients and unusual tastes and textures. The rack of lamb is marinated in fresh herbs and grappa; prawns and scallops are paired with a white-wine lemon sauce and served over angel-hair pasta.

Manor Cafe. 10109 125th St. ☎ **780/482-7577.** Fax 780/488-7763. Reservations recommended on weekends. Main courses C$9–C$15 (US$6–US$10). AE, DC, ER, MC, V. Sun–Thurs 11am–11pm, Fri–Sat 11am–midnight, Sun 5–11pm. Bus: 1 or 100. PACIFIC RIM.

Housed in a stately two-story mansion overlooking a park, the Manor Cafe offers one of the most fashionable outdoor dining patios in town and one of the most interesting menus. Recently renamed and redesigned, this longtime favorite now offers Pacific Rim cuisine, which brings the tastes and spices of Asian food together with international ingredients and cooking techniques. Duck breast is stuffed with apricots and served with shallot, pesto, and port sauce; hoisin lamb tenderloin is served on a bed of couscous. Smoked duck wontons are among the intriguing appetizers. The food is eclectic but always delicious.

Sweetwater Cafe. 12427 102nd Ave. ☎ **780/488-1959.** Main courses C$5–C$12 (US$3.35–US$8). AE, MC, V. Mon–Thurs 11am–10pm, Fri 11am–midnight, Sat 9am–midnight, Sun 10am–5pm. Bus: 1 or 100. INTERNATIONAL/SOUTHWESTERN.

Here's a bright and lively bistro with good inexpensive food; in summer you can sit on the charming outdoor deck in the back, thankfully far from the roar of traffic. The food is international, leaning toward Southwestern—sandwiches are served in tortillas, and there are several types of quesadillas. Pizza and pastas are also available, and everything here—except for a handful of steak and chicken entrees—is in the C$5-to-C$7 (US$3.35-to-US$4.65) range.

OLD STRATHCONA

South of downtown, across the river, along **Whyte Avenue (82nd Avenue)** in the old center of Strathcona village, is a dynamic youthful business district dominated by artists, students, and Edmonton's other bohemian elements. Also here, amid the busy street life, are a great many cafes, bistros, and small restaurants. This is an excellent place to come to browse your way past dozens of good places to eat. In addition to the full-service restaurants below, you may want to explore the **Terra Natural Good Market,** 10313 82nd Ave. (☎ 780/433-6807), a health-food store with a cafe, open Monday to Friday 9:30am to 8pm, Saturday 9:30am to 6pm, and Sunday noon to 5pm. ✪ **Block 1912,** 10361 82nd Ave. (☎ 780/433-6575), is a friendly cafe with one refrigerated case full of great-looking salads, one full of eye-popping desserts, and an array of deli sandwiches. It's open Monday to Thursday 9am to 11pm, Friday and Saturday 9 to midnight, and Sunday 10am to 11pm.

Expensive

✪ **The Polos Cafe.** 8405 112th St. ☎ **780/432-1371.** Reservations suggested. Main courses C$10–C$24 (US$7–US$16). AE, DC, MC, V. Mon–Fri 11am–2:30pm; Mon–Thurs 5–10pm, Fri–Sat 5pm–midnight. Bus: 6. ITALIAN/CHINESE/FUSION.

The Polo in question is Marco Polo, the first European to travel between Italy and China. The menu brings together classic Italian and Chinese cooking in a new cuisine loftily hailed as "Orie-ital"—and it's always interesting and delicious. Rack of lamb with cilantro-garlic pesto and marsala-wine reduction is a typical hybrid; Italian pasta and Shanghai noodles are tossed together with a variety of Sino-Italian sauces; tea-smoked duck comes with caramelized apples in merlot. Food doesn't get much more exotic than this, and chances are you'll never see these dishes again on a menu. The dining room has art-hung mauve walls, cool pools of light, and eager diners.

Von's Steak & Fish House. 10309 81st Ave. ☎ **780/439-0041.** Reservations recommended on weekends. Main courses C$13–C$40 (US$9–US$27). AE, MC, V. Mon–Sun 11am–midnight. Bus: 6. STEAK/SEAFOOD.

One of the best steak houses in Edmonton, Von's is a comfortable supper club with good Alberta beef; the prime rib is excellent, as are the various steaks. If you've had your fill of red meat, try the pasta or fresh-fish dishes.

Moderate

Chianti Cafe. 10501 82nd Ave. ☎ **780/439-9829.** Reservations required. Main courses C$7–C$15 (US$4.65–US$10). AE, DC, DISC, MC, V. Sun–Thurs 11am–11pm, Fri–Sat 11am–midnight. Bus: 6. ITALIAN.

Chianti is a rarity among Italian restaurants: The food is very good and very inexpensive. Pasta dishes begin at C$6 (US$4) and run to C$10 (US$7) (for fettuccine with scallops, smoked salmon, curry, and garlic), and even veal dishes (more than a dozen!) and seafood specials barely top C$12 (US$8). Soups and salads start at C$3 (US$2), so you can assemble a full meal for the cost of appetizers at a pricier restaurant. Chianti is in a handsomely remodeled post-office building; the restaurant isn't a secret, so it can be a busy and fairly crowded experience.

Da-De-O. 10548A 82nd Ave. ☎ **780/433-0930.** Main courses C$6–C$18 (US$4–US$12). MC, V. Mon–Wed 11·30am–11pm; Thurs–Sat 11am–11:30pm. Bus: 6. CAJUN/SOUTHERN.

This New Orleans–style diner is authentic right down to the low-tech, juke-box-at-your-table music system. The food is top-notch, with good and goopy po'boy sandwiches, fresh oysters, five kinds of jambalaya, and a big selection of blackened and *toufe* meats and seafood. Especially good is the Sorochan Angel, seafood in Pernod cream over angel-hair pasta. There's a whole page of appetizers and salads, so you can also relax in the vinyl-covered booths, listen to Billie Holiday, and graze through some chicken wings or crab fritters with a glass of beer.

The King & I. 8208 107 St. ☎ **780/433-2222.** Main courses C$11–C$19 (US$7–US$13). AE, MC, V. Mon–Thurs 11:30am–10:30pm, Fri 11:30am–11:30pm, Sat 4:30–11:30pm. Bus: 6. THAI.

This is the place for excellent, zesty Thai food, which can be a real treat after the beef-rich heavy cooking of western Canada. Many dishes are vegetarian, almost a novelty in Alberta. Various curries, ranging from mild to sizzling, and rice and noodle dishes are the house specialties. For a real treat, try the lobster in curry sauce with asparagus.

EDMONTON AFTER DARK

Tickets to most events are available through **Ticketmaster** (☎ 780/451-8000). For a complete listing of current happenings, check the Friday arts section of the *Edmonton Journal* or the alternative arts weekly *See.*

THE PERFORMING ARTS A masterpiece of theatrical architecture, the ✪ **Citadel Theatre,** 9828 101A Ave. (☎ 780/426-4811; LRT: Churchill), isn't a playhouse in the conventional sense but a community project encompassing virtually every form of show craft. The complex takes up the entire city block adjacent to Sir Winston Churchill Square and looks like a gigantic greenhouse—more than half is glass-walled, and even the awnings are glass. Apart from auditoriums, it also has a magnificent indoor garden with a waterfall and a restaurant. But the best feature of the complex is that it houses five theaters adapted for different productions and distinct audiences, plus workshops and classrooms. The Citadel today is one of the largest, busiest, and most prolific theaters in Canada.

The **Northern Alberta Jubilee Auditorium,** 11455 87th Ave. (☎ 780/427-2760; fax 780/422-3750; LRT: University), is the setting for a great variety of concert and ballet performances. The facility is a 2,678-seat multipurpose performing-arts center with another 250-seat theater on the lower level. The Jubilee is the resident home of the Edmonton Opera and the Alberta Ballet.

DINNER THEATER The charming **Mayfield Dinner Theatre,** 16615 109th Ave. (☎ 780/483-4051; Bus: 126), at the Mayfield Inn, combines excellent food with lighthearted, often sumptuously equipped stage productions. Shows go on at 8pm nightly and at brunch-time Sunday, with tickets at C$26 to C$64 (US$17 to US$43), meals included. Spoofy comedies and musical revues are the specialty at the lively **Celebrations Dinner Theatre,** in the O'Aces Entertainment Hotel at 13103 Fort Rd. (☎ 780/448-9339; LRT: Belvedere). Shows are mounted Wednesday to Sunday evenings, with tickets at C$49 (US$33), meals included.

THE CLUB & BAR SCENE   The upscale country-and-western scene is the name of the game, with new places opening up all the time. But there are plenty of options if you're not into Garth Brooks and line dancing. Most live-music clubs charge a cover on weekends, usually C$6 to C$8 (US$4 to US$5).

The hottest country dance bar in town is the **Cook County Saloon,** 8010 103rd St. (☎ 780/432-2665; Bus: 6), with a changing lineup of Western bands nightly. **Longriders Saloon,** 11733 78th St. (☎ 780/479-8700; LRT: Coliseum), has live country music 6 nights a week, as does the **Wild West Saloon,** 12912 50th St. (☎ 780/476-3388; LRT: Belvedere). For something uniquely Edmonton but without the twang, check out the **Sidetrack Cafe,** 10333 112th St. (☎ 780/421-1326; Bus: 2), the city's most versatile music venue. You get an Australian rock group one week, a musical comedy troupe the next, a blues band the following, progressive jazz after that, and so on.

Blues on Whyte, 10329 82nd Ave. (☎ 780/439-5058; Bus: 6), is Edmonton's best blues club, located in the vintage Commercial Hotel in Old Strathcona, with a popular billiards room. **The Rev,** 10032 102nd St. (☎ 780/424-2745; LRT: Central), is the premier club for the alternative-music scene. The **Rebar,** 10551 82nd Ave. (☎ 780/433-3600; Bus: 6), is a good student-oriented dance club in Old Strathcona. Edmonton's gay and lesbian bar of choice is **The Roost,** 10345 104th St. (☎ 780/426-3150; Bus: 8), with a large and pleasant outdoor patio.

Straighter and more predictable is the **Hard Rock Cafe,** Bourbon Street, 1638 West Edmonton Mall (☎ 780/444-1905; Bus: 1 or 100). Also in the mall is **Yuk Yuk's International,** Bourbon Street, 1646 West Edmonton Mall (☎ 780/481-YUKS; Bus: 1 or 100), the Edmonton branch of a national chain of live stand-up comedy clubs. Shows are Wednesday to Friday at 9pm and Saturday at 8:30 and 11pm. Admission is C$7 to C$11 (US$4.65 to US$7). The most romantic place for a drink is the **Library Bar** at the Hotel Macdonald, 10065 100th St. (☎ 780/424-5181; LRT: Central).

CASINOS   In Alberta, the money from casinos goes to charities. The casinos are privately owned and provide comfortable surroundings, full-service food and liquor service, and an amiable staff. The games are blackjack, roulette, baccarat, red dog, and sic bo; bets range from C$2 to C$500 (US$1.35 to US$334), and the play goes daily 10am to 3am. Try your luck at **Casino ABS,** City Centre, 10549 102nd St. (☎ 780/424-9467), or **Casino ABS,** Southside, 7055 Argyll Rd. (☎ 780/466-9467). The **Palace Casino,** 8770 170 St. (☎ 780/444-2112), operates in the West Edmonton Mall.

SIDE TRIPS FROM EDMONTON

✪ **Elk Island National Park** (☎ 780/992-5790), on the Yellowhead Highway, 32km (20 miles) east of Edmonton, is one of the most compact and prettiest in the national-parks system. It protects one of Canada's most endangered ecosystems and is the home and roaming ground to North America's largest and smallest mammals— the wood buffalo and the pygmy shrew (a tiny creature half the size of a mouse but with the disposition of a tiger). The park has hiking trails, campgrounds, golf courses, a lake, and a sandy beach. A 1-day vehicle permit costs C$4 (US$2.65) per person or C$8 (US$5) per group.

The ✪ **Ukrainian Cultural Heritage Village** (☎ 780/662-3640; e-mail hssuchv@oanet.com) is an open-air museum and a park of living history 25 minutes east of Edmonton on Yellowhead Highway 16. The village has 30 restored historic buildings arranged in an authentic setting; the adjacent fields and pastures are planted and harvested according to period techniques. You'll learn what life was like for Ukrainian pioneers in the 1892-to-1930 era through costumed interpreters who re-create the daily activities of the period. The village and interpretive center are defi-nitely worth the drive, especially in midsummer, when you can watch horse-drawn wagons gathering hay and harvesting grain. It's open daily: May 15 to early September 10am to 6pm and mid-September to mid-October 10am to 4pm. Admission is C$7 (US$4.65) adults, C$6 (US$4) seniors, and C$3 (US$2) children; children under 6 are free.

Located 40 minutes south of Edmonton off Highway 2, the **Reynolds Alberta Museum** (☎ 800/661-4726 or 780/352-5855; www.gov.ab.ca/~mcd/mhs/ram/ ram.htm; e-mail ram@mcd.gov.ab.ca) is a science-and-technology museum with spe-cialties in transport, industry, and agricultural engineering. The collection of vintage cars and period farm equipment is especially impressive, and there are hands-on activ-ities to keep children busy. Adjoining the museum is Canada's **Aviation Hall of Fame,** with a hangar full of vintage airplanes. Admission is C$7 (US$4.65) adults, C$6 (US$4) seniors, C$3 (US$2) youths 7 to 17, or C$15 (US$10) families. June to early September, the museum is open daily 9am to 5pm; mid-September to May, hours are Tuesday to Sunday 9am to 5pm.

11 Wood Buffalo National Park: The World's Second-Largest National Park

In the far northeastern corner of Alberta is **Wood Buffalo National Park,** the world's second-largest national park. Bigger than Switzerland, it measures 44,807km^2 (17,300 sq. miles). Two-thirds of the park lies inside Alberta and one-third in the Northwest Territories. The park was created for the specific purpose of preserving the last remaining herd of wood bison, who in the early 1900s were near extinction. Today some 6,000 of the creatures roam their habitat, where you can see and snap them in droves. The park is also the only known breeding ground for the whooping crane. Some 50 of these birds live here from April until October before migrating to their winter range along the Gulf of Mexico.

One of the problems faced by would-be visitors is simply getting to the park. By vehicle, it's 1,296km (804 miles) between Edmonton and Fort Smith, the park head-quarters, over mostly gravel roads. You'll find it easier to fly into Fort Smith on Cana-dian North Airlines, and once here, hook up with an outfitter who'll arrange transport to the park and activities. The tours offered by **Sub-arctic Wildlife Adventures,** P.O. Box 685, Fort Smith, NT X0E 0P0 (☎ 780/872-2467; fax 780/872-2126; www.subarcticwildlife.nt.ca), offer naturalist-led excursions to many of the park's best wildlife-viewing areas. The shortest excursion into the park is 4 days and explores the woods and wetlands near its famed salt plains, where wildlife gather to lick the natu-rally occurring minerals. Costs run about C$600 (US$400) per person; longer trips are also available.

For information, contact the **Park Superintendent,** P.O. Box 750, Fort Smith, NT X0E 0P0 (☎ 780/872-2349).

15

Vancouver

by Shawn Blore

If you really want to understand **Vancouver,** stand at the edge of the Inner Harbour (the prow of the Canada Place pavilion makes a good vantage point) and look up: past the float planes taking off over Stanley Park, around the container terminals, over the tony waterfront high rises, and then up the steep green slopes of the north-shore mountains to the twin snowy peaks of the Lions. All this—well, 90% of it anyway—is the result of a unique collaboration between God and the Canadian Pacific Railway (CPR).

It was the Almighty—or Nature (depending on your point of view)—who raised up the Coast range and then sent a glacier slicing along its foot, simultaneously carving out a deep trench and piling up a tall moraine of rock and sand. When the ice retreated, water from the Pacific flowed in and the moraine became a peninsula, flanked on one side by a deep natural harbor and on the other by a river of glacial meltwater. Some 10,000 years later, a CPR surveyor came by; took in the peninsula, the harbor, and the river; and decided he'd found the perfect spot for the railway's new Pacific terminus. He kept it quiet until the company had bought up most of the land around town, and then the railway moved in and set up shop. The city of Vancouver was born.

The resulting boom was pretty small. Though the port did a good business shipping out grain and sawmills and salmon canneries sprang up, the city was too far from the rest of North America for any serious manufacturing. Vancouver became a town of sailors, lumberjacks, and fishers. Cheap draught was a staple; gambling and whoring were the major service industries. And so it remained until the 1980s, when Vancouver decided to host Expo '86, a stunning success. The world came to visit, including many people from the newly emerging tiger economies of Hong Kong, Taiwan, and Malaysia. They looked at the mountains, the ocean, and the price of local real estate and were amazed. Many people moved here and settled new neighborhoods. On the Fraser river delta, the bedroom community of Richmond became a city, with a population more than half Chinese. In older neighborhoods, prices went ballistic, doubling and tripling overnight. And on the railyard-turned-Expo site, 40 new high-rise condo towers began to rise.

Unlike previous immigrants, these newcomers didn't worry about finding work; they made their own, founding financial services, software, international education, engineering, and architectural consulting businesses. A film industry sprang up. Vancouver became a postmodern town of Jags, Beemers, cell phones, and shining residential towers. The newcomers brought a love of dining out, so the steak house and the ubiquitous "Chinese and Canadian" diner gave way to a thousand little places offering sushi and Szechuan, tapas and bami, and, inevitably, fusion.

Working indoors, Vancouverites fell in love with the outdoor activities like mountain biking, windsurfing, kayaking, rock climbing, parasailing, snowboarding, and back-country skiing. When they mastered all these, they began experimenting with new sports, and strange summer-winter combinations were born: skiing-kayaking, mountain-biking snowboarding, and snowshoe-paragliding.

Splints and scrapes aside, folks seemed happy with the new state of affairs. And the rest of the world seemed to agree. *Outside* magazine voted Vancouver one of the 10 best cities in the world to live in. *Condé Nast Traveler* called it one of the 10 best cities to visit. And the World Council of Cities ranked it second only to Geneva for quality of life. Heady stuff, particularly for a spot that less than 20 years ago was derided as the world's biggest mill town. But then again, God—and the Canadian Pacific Railway—works in mysterious ways.

1 Essentials

GETTING THERE

BY PLANE   Daily direct flights between major U.S. cities and Vancouver are provided by **Air Canada** (☎ 800/661-3936 www.aircanada.ca), **Canadian Airlines** (☎ 800/363-7530 www.cdnair.ca), **United Airlines** (☎ 800/241-6522; www.ual. com), **American Airlines** (☎ 800/433-7300; www.americanair.com), **Continental** (☎ 800/231-0856; www.flycontinental.com), and **Northwest Airlines** (☎ 800/ 447-4747; www.nwa.com).

Vancouver International Airport is 13km (8 miles) south of downtown on uninhabited Sea Island. A massive expansion of this facility was completed in 1997. To pay for these improvements, the airport authority imposes an **international departure surcharge** of C$15 (US$10) per person for international travelers outside North America, C$10 (US$7) for passengers traveling within North America (including Hawaii and Mexico), and C$5 (US$3.35) for passengers departing on flights within BC or the Yukon. There's no surcharge on arrival. **Tourist Information Kiosks** on Levels 2 and 3 of the Main and International terminals (☎ 604/276-6101) are open daily 6:30am to 11:30pm.

Parking is available at the airport for both loading passengers and long-term stays (☎ 604/276-6106). **Courtesy buses** to the airport hotels are available, and a **shuttle bus** links the Main and International terminals to the South Terminal, where smaller and private aircraft are docked. Drivers heading into Vancouver take the Arthur Laing Bridge, which leads directly into Granville Street, the most direct route to downtown.

The pale-green **YVR Airporter** (☎ 604/946-8866) provides bus service to downtown Vancouver's major hotels. It leaves from Level 2 of the Main Terminal every 15 minutes daily 6:30am to 10:30pm and every 30 minutes 10:30pm on, with a final run at 12:15am. The 30-minute ride whisks you up the delta through central Vancouver before taking the Granville Street Bridge into downtown. The one-way fare is C$10 (US$7) adults, C$8 (US$5) seniors, and C$5 (US$3.35) children; the round-trip fare is C$17 (US$11) adults, C$16 (US$11) seniors, and C$10 (US$7) children. Bus service back to the airport leaves from selected downtown hotels every half an hour 5:35am to 10:55pm. Scheduled pickups serve the Bus Station, Four Seasons, Hotel Vancouver, Waterfront Centre Hotel, Georgian Court, Sutton Place, Landmark, and others.

Getting to and from the airport with public transit is a pain. The buses are slow, and you have to transfer at least once to get downtown. The hassle probably isn't worth the savings, but **bus no. 100** stops at both terminals. At the Granville/West 71st Street stop, get off and transfer to **bus no. 8** to downtown Vancouver. BC Transit fares are C$1.50 (US$1) during off-peak hours and C$2.25 (US$1.50) during weekdays up to 6:30pm. But transfers are free in any direction within a 90-minute period.

The average **taxi** fare from the airport to a downtown Vancouver hotel is about C$25 (US$17) plus tip. Nearly 400 taxis service the airport. Most major **car-rental firms** have airport counters and shuttles. Make advance reservations for fast check-in and guaranteed availability—especially if you want a four-wheel-drive vehicle or a convertible.

BY TRAIN   VIA Rail Canada, 1150 Station St. (☎ **800/561-8630;** www.viarail. ca), connects with Amtrak at Winnipeg, Manitoba. From there, you travel on a spectacular route running between Calgary and Vancouver. Lake Louise's beautiful alpine scenery is just part of this enjoyable journey. **Amtrak** (☎ **800/872-7245;** www.amtrak.com) has regular service from Seattle and also a direct route from San Diego to Vancouver. It stops at all major U.S. West Coast cities and takes a little under 2 days to complete the entire journey. The fare is US$440, but substantial seasonal discounts are available. Non-U.S. and non-Canadian travelers can buy a 15- to 30-day **USA Railpass** for US$340 to US$425 peak or US$229 to US$339 off-peak. You can use the pass for rail connections to Vancouver. **BC Rail,** 1311 W. First St., North Vancouver (☎ **604/631-3500;** www.bcrail.com/bcr/), also connects Vancouver to other cities in the province, including Whistler. The trip to Whistler is 2½ hours each way; including breakfast or dinner, a one-way ticket is C$31 (US$21) adults and C$25 (US$17) seniors/children under 12.

The main Vancouver rail station, **Pacific Central Station,** is at 1150 Station St., near Main Street and Terminal Avenue just south of Chinatown. You can reach downtown Vancouver from there by cab for about C$5 (US$3.35). A block from the station is the **SkyTrain's Main Street Station,** so within minutes you can be downtown. The Granville and Waterfront stations are two and four stops away, respectively. A one-zone SkyTrain ticket (covering the city of Vancouver) is C$1.50 (US$1).

BY BUS   Greyhound Bus Lines (☎ **604/482-8747;** www.greyhound.ca) and **Pacific Coach Lines** (☎ **604/662-8074**) have their terminals at the **Pacific Central Station,** 1150 Station St. Greyhound Canada's **Canada Pass** offers 10, 20, or 40 days of unlimited travel for C$246 to C$449 (US$164 to US$299). Pacific Coach Lines provides service between Vancouver and Victoria at C$26 (US$17) one-way per adult, including ferry; daily departures are 5:45am to 7:45pm. **Quick Coach Lines** (☎ **604/940-4428**) connects Vancouver to the Seattle-Tacoma International Airport. The bus leaving from Vancouver's Sandman Inn, 180 W. Georgia St., picks up from most major hotels and stops at the Vancouver International Airport. The 4-hour ride costs C$39 (US$26) one-way or C$70 (US$47) round-trip.

BY CAR You'll probably be driving into Vancouver along one of two routes. The 226km (140-mile) drive from Seattle along **U.S. Interstate 5** takes about 2½ hours. The road changes into **Highway 99** when you cross the border at the Peace Arch. You'll drive through the cities of White Rock, Delta, and Richmond; pass under the Fraser River through the George Massey Tunnel; and cross the Oak Street Bridge. The highway ends there and becomes Oak Street, a busy urban thoroughfare. Turn left onto 70th Avenue. (A small sign suspended above the left lane at the intersection of Oak Street and 70th Avenue reads CITY CENTRE.) Six blocks later, turn right onto Granville Street. This street heads directly into downtown Vancouver on the Granville Street Bridge.

Trans-Canada Highway 1 is a limited-access freeway running all the way to Vancouver's eastern boundary, where it crosses the Second Narrows bridge to North Vancouver. When coming on Highway 1 from the east, exit at Cassiar Street and turn left at the first light onto Hastings Street (Highway 7A), adjacent to Exhibition Park. Follow Hastings Street 6.5km (4 miles) into downtown. When coming to Vancouver from Whistler or parts north, take exit 13 (the sign says TAYLOR WAY, BRIDGE TO VANCOUVER) and cross the Lions Gate Bridge into Vancouver's West End.

BY SHIP & FERRY   The **Canada Place** cruise-ship terminal at the base of Burrard Street (☎ **604/665-9085**) is a city landmark. Topped by five eye-catching white Teflon sails, Canada Place pier juts out into the Burrard Inlet and is at the edge of the downtown financial district. **Princess Cruises, Holland America, Royal Caribbean, Crystal Cruises, Norwegian Cruise Lines, World Explorer Majesty Cruise Line, Hanseatic, Seabourn,** and **Carnival Cruise lines** dock at Canada Place and the nearby Ballantyne Pier to board passengers headed for Alaska via British Columbia's Inside Passage. Public-transit buses and taxis greet new arrivals, but you can also easily walk to many major hotels, like the Pan-Pacific, Waterfront Centre, and Hotel Vancouver.

BC Ferries (☎ **888/223-3779;** www.bcferries.bc.ca) has three routes between Vancouver and the Island. The one-way fare is C$9 (US$6) adults, C$4.25 (US$2.85) children 5 to 11, and C$29 (US$19) per car. The most direct route to Victoria is the **Tsawwassen-Swartz Bay ferry,** running every 2 hours daily 7am to 9pm. The Tsawwassen terminal is about 12 miles south of Vancouver. Take Highway 17 from Tsawwassen until it merges with Highway 99 just before the George Massey Tunnel, then follow the driving directions to Vancouver given in "By Car," above. The **Mid-Island Express** operates between Tsawwassen and Duke Point, just south of Nanaimo. The 2-hour crossing runs six times daily 5:30am to 11pm. The **Horseshoe Bay-Nanaimo ferry** has eight daily sailings, leaving Horseshoe Bay near West Vancouver and arriving 95 minutes later in Nanaimo. To reach Vancouver from Horseshoe Bay, take the Trans-Canada Highway (Highways 1 and 99) east and then take Exit 13 (Taylor Way) to the Lions Gate Bridge and downtown Vancouver's West End.

VISITOR INFORMATION

TOURIST OFFICES   The **Vancouver Tourist Info Centre,** 200 Burrard St. (☎ **604/683-2000;** www.tourism-vancouver.org; Bus: 22), is your best source for details about Vancouver and the North Shore. May to Labor Day, it's open daily 8am to 6pm; the rest of the year, hours are Monday to Friday 8:30am to 5:30pm and Saturday 9am to 5pm. If you plan to see more of this beautiful province, contact **Super Natural British Columbia** at ☎ **800/663-6000** or 604/663-6000 or on the Web (see below).

WEB SITES   Here are some of the best sites out there: **Tourism BC** (www.tourism-bc.ca), **Super Natural British Columbia** (www.iias.com/travel or www.snbc-res.com), **Tourism Vancouver** (www.tourism-vancouver.org), **Environment Canada** (www.weatheroffice.com), **BC Transit** (http://transitbc.com or www.cmbuslink.com), **BC Ferries** (www.bcferries.com), and *Vancouver* magazine (www.vanmag.com).

CITY LAYOUT

Think of Vancouver's downtown peninsula as being like an upraised thumb on the mitten-shaped Vancouver mainland. Stanley Park, the West End, Yaletown, and Vancouver's business-and-financial center are on the "thumb," bordered to the west by English Bay, to the north by Burrard Inlet, and to the south by False Creek. The mainland part of the city, the "mitten," is mostly residential, with a sprinkling of businesses

Greater Vancouver

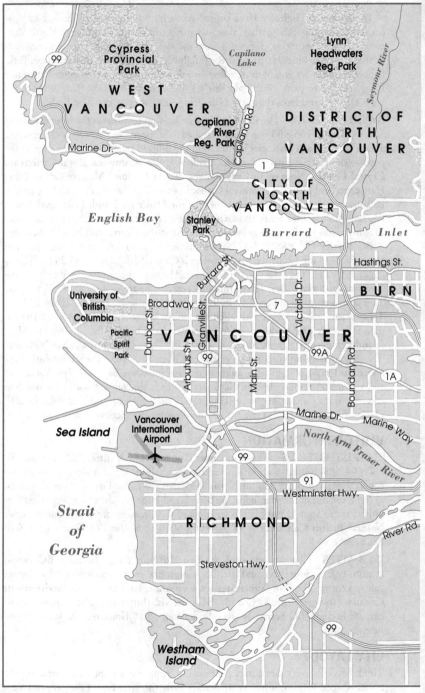

Cypress Provincial Park

Capilano Lake

Lynn Headwaters Reg. Park

Seymour River

99

W E S T

V A N C O U V E R

Capilano River Reg. Park

Capilano Rd.

D I S T R I C T O F

N O R T H

V A N C O U V E R

Marine Dr.

1

C I T Y O F

N O R T H

V A N C O U V E R

English Bay

Stanley Park

Burrard   *Inlet*

Burrard St.

Hastings St.

University of British Columbia

Broadway

7

Victoria Dr.

B U R N

Pacific Spirit Park

Dunbar St.

V A N C O U V E R

Granville St.

99

Main St.

99A

Boundary Rd.

1A

Arbutus St.

Sea Island

Vancouver International Airport

Marine Dr.

Marine Way

99

North Arm Fraser River

91

Westminster Hwy.

Strait of Georgia

R I C H M O N D

River Rd.

Steveston Hwy.

99

Westham Island

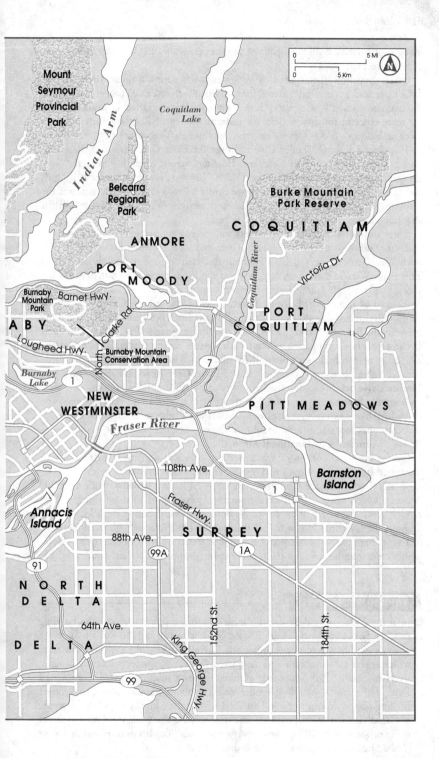

along main arteries. Both the mainland and the peninsula are covered by a simple rectilinear street pattern.

On the downtown peninsula are four key east-west streets. **Robson Street** starts at B.C. Place Stadium on Beatty Street, flows through the West End's touristed shopping district, and ends at Stanley Park's Lost Lagoon on Lagoon Drive. **Georgia Street**— far more efficient for drivers than the pedestrian-oriented Robson—runs from the Georgia Viaduct on downtown's eastern edge through Vancouver's commercial core and carries on through Stanley Park and over the Lions Gate Bridge to the North Shore. Three blocks north of Georgia is **Hastings Street,** which begins in the West End, runs east through downtown, and skirts Gastown's southern border as it heads east to the Trans-Canada Highway. **Davie Street** starts at Pacific Boulevard near the Cambie Street Bridge, travels through Yaletown into the West End's more residential shopping district, and ends at English Bay Beach.

Three **north-south downtown streets** will get you everywhere you want to go in and out of downtown. Two blocks east of Stanley Park is **Denman Street,** which runs from West Georgia Street at Coal Harbour to Beach Avenue at English Bay Beach. This main West End thoroughfare is where the locals go to dine out. It's also the shortest north-south route between the two ends of the Stanley Park Seawall. Eight blocks east of Denman is **Burrard Street,** which starts near the Canada Place Pier, runs south through downtown, crosses the Burrard Street Bridge, and then forks. One branch, still **Burrard Street,** continues south and intersects **West 4th Avenue** and **Broadway** before terminating at **West 16th Avenue** on the borders of Shaughnessy. The other branch becomes **Cornwall Avenue,** which heads due west through Kitsilano, changing its name two more times to **Point Grey Road** and then **Northwest Marine Drive** before entering the University of British Columbia campus.

Granville Street starts near the Waterfront Station on Burrard Inlet and runs the entire length of downtown, crosses over the Granville Bridge to Vancouver's West Side, and continues south across the breadth of the city before crossing the Arthur-Laing Bridge to **Vancouver International Airport.**

On the mainland portion of Vancouver, the city's east-west roads are successively numbered from 1st Avenue at the downtown bridges to 77th Avenue by the banks of the Fraser River. By far the most important east-west route is **Broadway** (formerly 9th Avenue), which starts a few blocks from the University of British Columbia and extends across the length of the city to the border with neighboring Burnaby, where it becomes the Lougheed Highway. In Kitsilano, **West 4th Avenue** is also an important east-west shopping-and-commercial corridor. Intersecting with Broadway at various points are a number of important north-south commercial streets, each of which

Finding an Address

In many Vancouver addresses, the suite or room number precedes the building number. For instance, 100-1250 Robson St. is Suite 100 at 1250 Robson St.

In downtown Vancouver, Chinatown's **Carrall Street** is the east-west axis from which streets are numbered and designated. Westward, numbers increase progressively to Stanley Park; eastward, numbers increase heading toward Commercial Drive. For example, 400 West Pender would be about 4 blocks from Carrall Street heading toward downtown; 400 East Pender would be 4 blocks on the opposite side of Carrall Street. Off the peninsula, the system works the same, but **Ontario Street** is the east-west axis. All east-west roads are avenues (like 4th Avenue), while streets (Main Street) run exclusively north-south.

defines a particular neighborhood. The most significant are (west to east) **Macdonald Street** in Kitsilano, then **Granville Street, Cambie Street, Main Street,** and **Commercial Drive.**

The Vancouver Tourist Info Centre (see "Visitor Information," above) and most hotels can provide you with detailed downtown maps. A good all-around metropolitan area map is the **Rand McNally Vancouver city map,** available for C$3 (US$2) at the Vancouver Airport Tourism Centre kiosk. If you're an auto-club member, the Canadian Automobile Association (CAA) map is also good. It's not for sale but is free to both AAA and CAA members and is available at AAA offices across North America. **International Travel Maps and Books,** 552 Seymour St. (☎ **604/687-3320**), has the city's most extensive selection of Vancouver and British Columbia maps and specialty guidebooks.

Neighborhoods in Brief

When figuring out what's where in Vancouver, keep in mind that this is a city where property is king and the word *west* has such positive connotations folks have gone to great lengths to associate it with their particular patch of real estate. Thus there's the **West End,** the **West Side,** and **West Vancouver,** which improbably enough is located immediately beside **North Vancouver.** The West End is a high-rise residential neighborhood on the downtown peninsula. The West Side is one-half of Vancouver, from Ontario Street west to the University of British Columbia. (The more working-class **East Side** covers the city's mainland portion, from Ontario Street east to Boundary Road.) The tony West Vancouver is a city to itself on the far side of Burrard Inlet. Together with its more middle-class neighbor North Vancouver, it forms an area called the **North Shore.**

DOWNTOWN   Vancouver's commercial-and-office core runs from Nelson Street north to the harbor, with Homer Street as the eastern edge and a more ragged boundary running roughly along Burrard Street forming the western border. The truly prime office space is on or near Georgia Street. Hotels stick mostly to the northern third of downtown, clustering especially thickly near the water's edge, but restaurants are sprinkled throughout. Walking is a good bet for transport downtown, day and night. Unlike in many North American cities, lots of people live in and around Vancouver's central business district, so the area is always populated.

THE WEST END   A fascinating neighborhood of high-rise condos mixed with Edwardian homes, the West End has within its borders all the necessities of life: great cafes and nightclubs, many and varied bookshops, and some of the city's best restaurants. The Pacific Ocean laps against the West End on two sides, in the form of Burrard Inlet to the north and English Bay to the south, while on the western edge spreads Stanley Park. Burrard Street forms the West End's eastern border.

GASTOWN   The city's oldest section, Gastown was named after Vancouver's first settler, riverboat skipper/saloon keeper Jack Deighton, nicknamed "Gassy" thanks to his longwinded habits of speech. It was rebuilt in brick after the 1886 fire wiped out the original wooden city. Gastown's cobblestone streets and late-Victorian architecture make it well worth a visit, despite an infestation of curio shops and souvenir stands. It lies east of downtown, in the 6 square blocks between Water and Hastings streets and Cambie and Columbia streets.

CHINATOWN   South of Hastings Street, between Gore and Carrall streets to the east and west and Keefer Street to the south, Vancouver's Chinatown isn't large but is intense. Fishmongers stand calling out their wares in Cantonese before a shop filled

Vancouver

ATTRACTIONS

B.C. Sports Hall of Fame and Museum 62
Canada Place 37
Canadian Craft Museum 55
Capilano Suspension Bridge & Park 1
Dr. Sun-Yat-sen Classical Garden 41
Granville Island's Kids Only Market 29
Granville Island's Water Park & Adventure Playground 29
Miniature Railway 3
Museum of Anthropology 20
Pacific Space Centre 17
Science World British Columbia 45
Stanley Park's Children's Farm 4
Vancouver Aquarium Marine Science Centre 2
Vancouver Art Gallery 53
Vancouver Centennial Police Museum 40
Vancouver Maritime Museum 19
Vancouver Museum 17

ACCOMMODATIONS

Best Western Downtown Vancouver 47
Blue Horizon 32
Canadian-Pacific Hotel Vancouver 54
Crowne Plaza Hotel Georgia 58
Four Seasons Hotel 57
Granville Island Hotel 30
Heritage Harbour Bed and Breakfast 18
Hostelling International Vancouver Downtown Hostel 14
Hostelling International Vancouver Jericho Beach Hostel 21
Johnson House Bed & Breakfast 24
Listel Vancouver 33
Metropolitan Hotel Vancouver 56
Pacific Palisades Hotel 31
Pan-Pacific Hotel Vancouver 36
Rosedale on Robson Suite Hotel 60
Sheraton Wall Centre Vancouver 49
Sutton Place Hotel 50
Sylvia Hotel 6
West End Guest House 11
YWCA Hotel/Residence 61

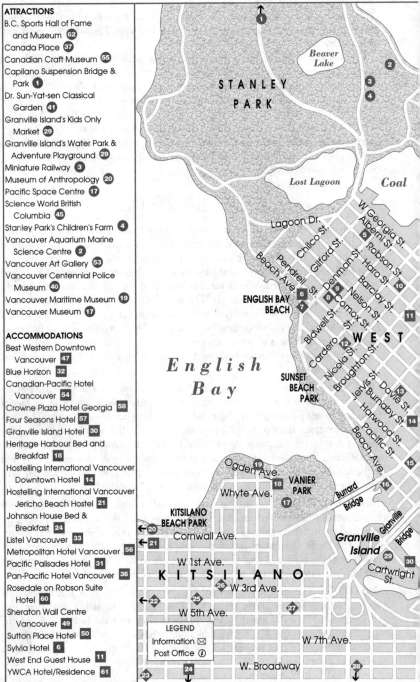

LEGEND
Information ✉
Post Office ⓘ

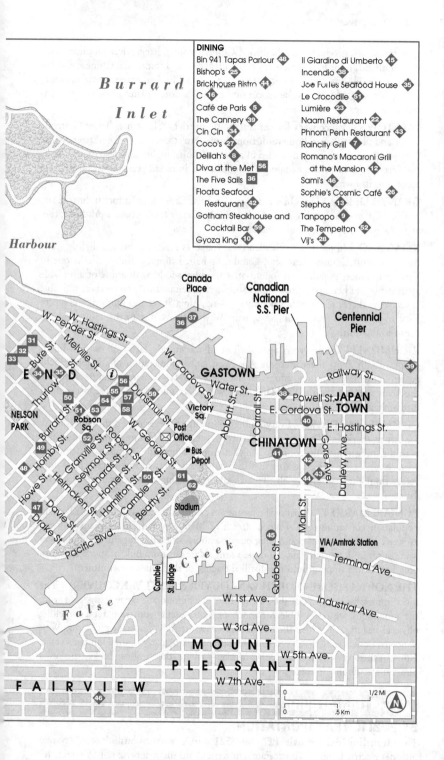

DINING

Bin 941 Tapas Parlour 48
Bishop's 25
Brickhouse Bistro 44
C 16
Café de Paris 5
The Cannery 39
Cin Cin 34
Coco's 27
Delilah's 8
Diva at the Met 56
The Five Sails 36
Floata Seafood
Restaurant 42
Gotham Steakhouse and
Cocktail Bar 59
Gyoza King 10

Il Giardino di Umberto 15
Incendio 38
Joe Fortes Seafood House 35
Le Crocodile 51
Lumière 23
Naam Restaurant 22
Phnom Penh Restaurant 43
Raincity Grill 7
Romano's Macaroni Grill
at the Mansion 12
Sami's 46
Sophie's Cosmic Café 26
Stephos 13
Tanpopo 9
The Tempelton 52
Vij's 28

Burrard Inlet

Harbour

Canada Place

Canadian National S.S. Pier

Centennial Pier

W. Hastings St.
W. Pender St.
Melville St.
Bute St.
Thurlow St.
Burrard St.
Homby St.
Hornby St.
Howe St.
Helmcken St.
Granville St.
Seymour St.
Richards St.
Homer St.
Hamilton St.
Cambie St.
Beatty St.
Davie St.
Drake St.
Pacific Blvd.

E N D

NELSON PARK

Robson Sq.
Dunsmuir St.
W. Georgia St.
W. Cordova St.
Water St.
Victory Sq.
Post Office
Bus Depot
Stadium

GASTOWN

Railway St.
Powell St.
E. Cordova St.
E. Hastings St.
JAPAN TOWN

CHINATOWN

Gore Ave.
Dunlevy Ave.
Main St.

VIA/Amtrak Station
Terminal Ave.
Industrial Ave.

Cambie St. Bridge
Creek
Québec St.
W 1st Ave.
W 3rd Ave.
W 5th Ave.
W 7th Ave.

False

M O U N T
P L E A S A N T

F A I R V I E W

0   1/2 Mi
0   .5 Km

with crabs, eels, geoducks, and bullfrogs. Chinese women haggle over produce, while their husbands hunt for deer antler or dried seahorse at a traditional Chinese apothecary. And inside any one of a dozen restaurants, you'll find an entire extended family sitting at a single big round table, consuming half a dozen plates of succulent Cantonese cooking.

YALETOWN   Vancouver's former warehouse district, Yaletown is below Granville Street and above Pacific Boulevard, from Davie Street over to Smithe Street. It has long since been converted to an area of apartment lofts, nightclubs, restaurants, high-end furniture shops, and a fledgling multimedia biz. In recent years the area has finally come into its own.

GRANVILLE ISLAND   On a peninsula on False Creek, this former industrial site is now a fun and fascinating mix of urban markets, craft fairs, artisan workshops, theaters, cafes, offices, parks, and restaurants.

KITSILANO   In the 1960s, Kitsilano was Canada's Haight-Asbury, a slightly seedy enclave of coffeehouses, head shops, and long-haired hippies. Today, Kits is one of Vancouver's most popular and sought-after neighborhoods, with a mix of affordable apartments and heritage homes, funky shops, great restaurants, and pleasant walkable streets. And there's Kits beach. Roughly speaking, Alma Street and Burrard Street form Kitsilano's east and west boundaries, with West 16th Avenue to the south and the ocean to the north.

RICHMOND   Twenty years ago, Richmond was mostly farmland, with a bit of sleepy suburb. Now it has become Asia West, an agglomeration of shopping malls geared to the new (read rich, educated, and successful) Chinese immigrants. Malls like the Aberdeen Mall and the Yao Han Centre will make you feel as if you've just stepped into Singapore.

COMMERCIAL DRIVE   Every immigrant group that ever passed through the city has left its mark on "The Drive," as Vancouverites call it. Combine those influences with the indigenous culture of left-wing activism and ongoing yuppification, and the result is a peculiar but endearing mix: the Italian cafe next to the Marxist bookstore across from the vegetarian deli that has taken to selling really expensive yeast-free Tuscan bread.

PUNJABI MARKET   Most of the businesses catering to Vancouver's sizable Punjabi population are found on a 4-block stretch of Main Street, from 48th up to 52nd avenues. The area is at its best during business hours, when the fragrant scent of spices wafts out from food stalls and Hindi pop songs blare out from hidden speakers. Shopping here is like sipping from the distilled essence of the Indian subcontinent.

THE NORTH SHORE (NORTH VANCOUVER & WEST VANCOUVER)   The most impressive thing about the North Shore is its mountain range. Huge and wild, the mountains are responsible for much of Vancouver's reputation for compelling physical beauty. The cities themselves, however, aren't without their charms. West Vancouver offers some fine waterfront restaurants, particularly in the Dundarave area. North Vancouver's Lonsdale Quay Market—where the SeaBus docks—makes a pleasant afternoon's outing.

2 Getting Around

BY PUBLIC TRANSPORTATION
The **Translink/BC Transit** (☎ 604/521-0400; www.cmbuslink.com) system includes electric buses, SeaBus catamaran ferries, and the magnetic-rail SkyTrain. It's

Key Bus Routes

Keep these routes in mind as you tour the city by bus: **no. 5** (Robson Street), **no. 22** (Kitsilano beach to downtown), **no. 50** (Granville Island), **nos. 35** and **135** (to Stanley Park bus loop), **no. 240** (North Vancouver), **no. 250** (West Vancouver–Horseshoe Bay), and **nos. 4** and **10** (UBC to Exhibition Park via Granville Street downtown). In summer, the Vancouver Parks Board operates a bus route through Stanley Park.

an ecologically friendly, highly reliable, and inexpensive system that allows you to get everywhere, including the beaches and ski slopes. Regular service on the main routes runs daily 5am to 2am, with less frequent "Owl" service operating on several downtown and suburban routes to 4:20am.

Schedules and routes are available at the Vancouver Tourist Info Centre, at many major hotels, online, and on buses. Pick up a copy of *Discover Vancouver on Transit* at the Vancouver Tourist Info Centre (see "Visitor Information," above). This publication gives transit routes for many city neighborhoods, landmarks, and attractions, including numerous Victoria sites.

Fares are the same for the bus, SeaBus, and SkyTrain. A one-way, all-zone fare is C$1.50 (US$1) after 6:30pm weekdays and all day weekends and holidays. Weekdays before 6:30pm, a one-zone fare (covering all Vancouver) is C$1.50 (US$1), a two-zone fare (required to travel to North Vancouver, Burnaby, or Richmond) is C$2.25 (US$1.50), and a three-zone fare (for travel to Surrey) is C$3 (US$2). Free transfers are available on boarding and good for travel in any direction and for the SkyTrain and SeaBus but have a 90-minute expiration. **DayPasses,** good anytime for unlimited travel on all public transit, are C$6 (US$4) adults and C$4 (US$2.65) seniors/students/children. Tickets and passes are available at the Vancouver Tourist Info Centre, both SeaBus terminals, convenience stores, drugstores, credit unions, and other outlets displaying the "FareDealer" symbol.

The **SkyTrain** is a computerized magnetic-rail train servicing 20 stations along its 35-minute trip from downtown Vancouver east to Surrey through Burnaby and New Westminster. The **SeaBus** catamaran ferries annually take more than 700,000 passengers, cyclists, and wheelchair riders on a scenic 12-minute commute between downtown's Waterfront Station and North Vancouver's Lonsdale Quay. Weekdays, a SeaBus leaves each stop every 15 minutes 6:15am to 6:30pm, then every 30 minutes to 1am. SeaBuses depart on Saturdays every half hour 6:30am to 12:30pm, then every 15 minutes to 7:15pm, then every half hour to 1am. On Sundays and holidays, runs depart every half hour 8:30am to 11pm.

BY TAXI

Cab fares are quite reasonable, starting at C$2.30 (US$1.55) and increasing at a rate of C$1.25 (US85¢) per kilometer, plus C30¢ (US20¢) per minute at stoplights. In the downtown area, you can expect to travel for less than C$6 (US$4) plus tip. The typical fare for the 8-mile drive from downtown to the airport is C$25 (US$17).

Taxis are easy to find in front of major hotels, but flagging one can be tricky. Most drivers are usually on radio calls. But thanks to built-in satellite positioning systems, if you call for a taxi, it usually arrives faster than if go out and hail one. Call for a pickup from **Black Top** at ☎ 604/731-1111, **Yellow Cab** at ☎ 604/681-1111, or **MacLure's** at ☎ 604/731-9211. **AirLimo** at ☎ 604/273-1331 offers flat-rate stretch limousine service. AirLimo charges C$29 (US$19) per trip to the airport (not per person), plus tax and tip. The drivers accept all major credit cards.

BY CAR

Vancouver's driving laws are similar to those of much of the United States: You may turn right on red after coming to a full stop, seat belts are mandatory, children under 5 must be in a child seat, and motorcyclists must wear helmets. (The only exception is the flashing green light, which in BC isn't a left turn signal but a sign to proceed with caution.) Gas is sold by the liter, averaging around C60¢ (US40¢). This may seem inexpensive until you consider that a gallon of gas is about C$2.70 (US$1.80). Speeds and distances are posted in kilometers.

You won't need a car to explore the city, but you may want one to explore the environs or continue on elsewhere in Canada. If you're over 25 and have a major credit card, you can rent a vehicle from **Avis,** 757 Hornby St. (☎ 800/879-2847 or 604/606-2847; Bus: 22); **Budget,** 450 W. Georgia St. (☎ **800/527-0700,** 800/268-8900, or 604/668-7000; Bus: 15); **Enterprise,** 585 Smithe St. (☎ **800/736-8222** or 604/688-5500; Bus: 15); **Hertz Canada,** 1128 Seymour St. (☎ **800/263-0600,** or 604/688-2411; Bus: 4); **National/Tilden,** 1130 W. Georgia St. (☎ **800/387-4747** or 604/685-6111; Bus: 22); and **Thrifty,** 1015 Burrard St. or 1400 Robson St. (☎ **800/367-2277** or 604/606-1666; Bus: 22). These firms all have counters and shuttle service at the airport as well.

All major downtown hotels have guest **parking;** rates vary from free to C$20 (US$13) per day. There's public parking at **Robson Square** (enter at Smithe and Howe streets), the **Pacific Centre** (Howe and Dunsmuir streets), and **The Bay** department store (Richards near Dunsmuir Street). You'll also find **parking lots** at Thurlow and Georgia streets, Thurlow and Alberni streets, and Robson and Seymour streets.

Metered **street parking** isn't impossible to come by, but it may take a trip or three around the block to find a spot. Rules are posted on the street and invariably are strictly enforced. Unmetered parking on side streets is often subject to neighborhood residency requirements. Check the signs. If you park in such an area without the appropriate sticker on your windshield, you'll get ticketed, then towed. If your car is towed away or if you need a towing service and aren't a member of AAA, call **Unitow** at ☎ **604/251-1255** or **Busters** at ☎ **604/685-8181.**

Members of the American Automobile Association (AAA) can get assistance from the **Canadian Automobile Association (CAA),** 999 W. Broadway, Vancouver (☎ **604/268-5600,** or for road service 604/293-2222; Bus: 9).

BY BICYCLE

Vancouver is decidedly bicycle friendly. There are plenty of places to rent a bike along Robson Street and Denman Street near Stanley Park. A trip around the Stanley Park seawall is one of Vancouver's premier sightseeing experiences, enjoyed by thousands of visitors every year, including President Bill Clinton, who jogged the seawall during his 1996 Vancouver stopover. Bike routes are designated throughout the city. Paved paths crisscross though parks and along beaches. Helmets are mandatory and riding on sidewalks is illegal except on designated bike paths.

Cycling BC (☎ **604/737-3034**) accommodates cyclists on the SkyTrain and buses by providing "Bike & Ride" lockers at all "Park & Ride" parking lots. The department also dispenses loads of information about events, bike touring, and cycle insurance. Many downtown parking lots and garages also have no-fee bike racks.

You can take a bike on the SeaBus anytime free. All the West Vancouver blue buses (including the bus to the Horseshoe Bay ferry terminal) can carry two bikes free, first come, first served. In Vancouver, only a limited number of suburban routes allow bikes on the bus, and space is limited. Bikes aren't allowed on the Skytrain or in the

George Massey Tunnel, but a tunnel shuttle operates four times daily mid-May to September to transport you across the Fraser; May 1 to Victoria Day (the third weekend of May), the service operates on weekends only.

BY FERRY

Crossing False Creek to Vanier Park or Granville Island on one of the blue miniferries is cheap and fun. The **Aquabus** docks at the foot of Howe Street. It takes you either to Granville Island's public market or east along False Creek to Science World and Stamps Landing. The **Granville Island Ferry** docks at Sunset Beach below the Burrard Street Bridge and the Aquatic Centre and goes to Granville Island and Vanier Park. Ferries to Granville Island leave every 5 minutes 7am to 10pm; those to Vanier Park, every 15 minutes 10am to 8pm. One-way fare on all routes is C$1.75 adults (US$1.15) and C75¢ (US50¢) seniors/children.

Fast Facts: Vancouver

American Express The office is at 1040 W. Georgia St. (☎ 604/669-2813; Bus: 22), open Monday to Friday 8:30am to 5:30pm and Saturday 10am to 4pm.

Area Codes The area code for Vancouver and the rest of the British Columbia Lower Mainland is **604.** The area code for all other parts of British Columbia, including Victoria, Vancouver Island, and the BC Interior, is **250.**

Business Hours Vancouver **banks** are open Monday to Thursday 10am to 5pm and Friday 10am to 6pm. Some banks, like Canadian Trust, are also open Saturday. **Office hours** are Monday to Friday 9am to 5pm (lunch is noon to 1pm). **Stores** are generally open Monday to Saturday 10am to 6pm. Last call at the city's **restaurant bars** and **cocktail lounges** is 2am.

Consulates The **U.S. Consulate** is at 1095 W. Pender St. (☎ 604/685-4311; Bus: 35). The **British Consulate** is at 800-1111 Melville St. (☎ 604/683-4421; Bus: 35). The **Australian Consulate** is at 1225-888 Dunsmuir St. (☎ 604/684-1177; Bus: 5). Check the yellow pages for other countries.

Currency Exchange Banks and ATMs have a better exchange rate than most foreign exchange bureaus (the latter charge transaction and service fees).

Dentists Most major hotels have a dentist on call. The **Vancouver Centre Dental Clinic,** Vancouver Centre Mall, 11-650 W. Georgia St. (☎ 604/682-1601; Bus: 4), is an option. You must make an appointment. The clinic is open Monday to Saturday with varying hours somewhere between 8:30am and 6pm.

Doctors Hotels usually have a doctor on call. The **Vancouver Medical Clinics,** Bentall Centre, 1055 Dunsmuir St. (☎ 604/683-8138; Bus: 22), is a drop-in clinic open Monday to Friday 8am to 5pm. Another drop-in medical center, **Carepoint Medical Centre,** 1175 Denman St. (☎ 604/681-5338; Bus: 5), is open daily 9am to 9pm. See also "Emergencies" below.

Emergencies Dial ☎ 911 for fire, police, ambulance, and poison control.

Hospitals St. Paul's Hospital, 1081 Burrard St. (☎ 604/682-2344; Bus: 22), is the closest facility to downtown and the West End. West Side Vancouver hospitals include **Vancouver General Hospital Health and Sciences Centre,** 855 W. 12th Ave. (☎ 604/875-4111; Bus: 9, 17), and **British Columbia's Children's Hospital,** 4480 Oak St. (☎ 604/875-2345; Bus: 17). In North

Vancouver, there's **Lions Gate Hospital,** 231 E. 15th St. (☎ **604/988-3131;** Bus: 250).

Internet Access   There's free Internet access at the **Vancouver Public Library Central Branch,** 350 W. Georgia St. (☎ **604/331-4000;** Bus: 5), open Monday to Thursday 10am to 8pm, Friday and Saturday 10am to 6pm, and Sunday 1 to 5pm. There's also **Dakoda's Internet Cafe,** 1602 Yew St. (☎ **604/731-5616;** Bus: 22), a pleasant small cafe in the pub/restaurant zone across from Kits Beach; it's open Monday to Friday 7am to 10pm and Saturday and Sunday 7:30am to 10pm. **Webster's Internet Cafe,** 340 Robson St. (☎ **604/915-9327;** Bus: 5), is across from the main public library and open daily 9am to 11pm.

Liquor Laws   The legal drinking age in British Columbia is 19. Spirits are sold only in government liquor stores, but you can buy beer and wine from specially licensed, privately owned stores and pubs. There are 22 LCBC (Liquor Control of British Columbia) stores scattered throughout Vancouver. Most are open Monday to Saturday 10am to 6pm, but some are open to 11pm. Call the **Liquor Distribution Branch** at ☎ **604/252-3000** for location details.

Newspapers/Magazines   The two local papers are the *Vancouver Sun* (Mon to Sat mornings) and *The Province* (Sun to Fri mornings). The free weekly entertainment paper *The Georgia Straight* comes out Thursday. The monthly *Vancouver* magazine is a glossy attitude-filled guide to the city's cultural scene, available on newsstands.

Pharmacies   Shopper's Drug Mart, 1125 Davie St. (☎ **604/685-6445;** Bus: 6), is open 24 hours. Several Safeway supermarkets have late-night pharmacies, including the one at the corner of Robson and Denman streets, which is open to midnight.

Police   For emergencies, dial ☎ **911.** Otherwise, the **Vancouver City Police** can be reached at ☎ **604/717-3535.**

Post Office   The **main post office,** 349 W. Georgia St., at Homer Street (Bus: 17), is open Monday to Friday 8am to 5:30pm. Postal outlets are located in souvenir stores and drugstores displaying the red-and-white Canada Post emblem.

Safety   Overall, Vancouver is a safe city; violent-crime rates are quite low. However, property crimes and crimes of opportunity (such as items being stolen from unlocked cars) do occur with troubling frequency, particularly downtown. Vancouver's Downtown East Side, between Gastown and Chinatown, is a troubled neighborhood and should be avoided at night.

Taxes   Hotel rooms are subject to a 10% tax. The provincial sales tax (PST) is 7% (excluding food, restaurant meals, and children's clothing). For specific questions, call the **B.C. Consumer Taxation Branch** at ☎ **604/660-4500.** Most goods and services are subject to a 7% federal goods and services tax (GST). You can get a refund on short-stay accommodations and all shopping purchases that total at least C$100 (US$67). (This refund doesn't apply to car rentals, parking, restaurant meals, room service, tobacco, or alcohol.) Hotels and the Info Centres can give you application forms. Save your receipts. For details on the GST, call ☎ **800/561-6990.**

Time Zone   Vancouver is in the Pacific time zone, as are Seattle and San Francisco. Daylight saving time applies April to October.

3   Accommodations

The past few years have seen a lot of activity in the Vancouver hotel business. Lots of new rooms have opened up, some in the high end but a lot more in the moderate-to-budget range. Most of the hotels are in the downtown and Yaletown areas or in the West End. Note that quoted prices below don't include the 10% provincial accommodations tax or the 7% goods and services tax (GST). Non-Canadian residents can get a GST rebate on short-stay accommodations by filling out the Tax Refund Application.

Reservations are highly recommended June to September and on holidays. If you arrive without a reservation or have trouble finding a room, call Super Natural British Columbia's **Discover British Columbia hot line** at ☎ **800/663-6000** or **Tourism Vancouver's hot line** at ☎ **604/683-2000.** Specializing in last-minute bookings, they can make arrangements using their large daily listing of hotels, hostels, and B&Bs.

Note: See the "Vancouver" map (p. 620) to locate most of the hotels in this section.

DOWNTOWN & YALETOWN

All downtown hotels are within 5 to 10 minutes' walking distance of shops, restaurants, and attractions. You can reach the downtown hotels by taking the SkyTrain to the Granville or Burrard stop, just a few blocks apart. The Waterfront station is close to the Pan-Pacific and Waterfront Centre hotels. The Stadium station is just a few blocks from the Georgian Court, Rosedale on Robson, and YWCA. The no. 1 or 5 bus will take you to the West End hotels; the no. 4 or 10 bus will get you to hotels near False Creek.

VERY EXPENSIVE

Another ultradeluxe choice is the 21-story **Sutton Place Hotel,** 845 Burrard St., Vancouver, BC V6Z 2K6 (☎ **800/961-7555** or 604/682-5511; fax 604/682-5513; Bus: 22). Don't let the big pink hospital-like exterior fool you: Once you enter the lobby of this central five-diamond hotel, you'll find that everything is pure luxury. High-season rates run C$289 to C$419 (US$193 to US$279) double and C$475 to C$1,700 (US$317 to US$1,134) suite.

✪ **Metropolitan Hotel Vancouver.** 645 Howe St., Vancouver, BC V6C 2Y9. ☎ **800/ 667-2300** or 604/687-1122. Fax 604/643-7267. www.metropolitan.com. 215 units. 9 no-smoking floors. A/C MINIBAR TV TEL. May–Sept C$365 (US$243) double weekdays, C$225 (US$150) double weekends; Oct–Apr C$285 (US$190) double. Year-round Business Class C$30 (US$20) extra per room/suite; C$1,500 (US$1,000) suite. Children stay free in parents' room; those under 6 eat free in the restaurant when accompanied by a paying adult. AE, DC, MC, V. Underground valet parking C$18 (US$12). Small pets accepted. Bus: 4, 7.

Between the financial district and downtown shopping areas, the Metropolitan underwent a C$4 million (US$2.65 million) renovation in 1997, and the result is uncompromising luxury in the guest rooms and public areas. Most units in the

Staying at a B&B

If you prefer to stay in a B&B, the **Beachside Bed & Breakfast Registry,** 4208 Evergreen Ave., West Vancouver, BC V7V 1H1 (☎ **800/563-3311** or 604/ 922-7773), can assist you. Rates average C$120 to C$200 (US$80 to US$133) for a double or C$250 to C$350 (US$167 to US$233) for a luxury room.

18-story hotel have small balconies; all have stately dark-wood furnishings, queen-size beds, marble bathrooms, fluffy bathrobes, and complimentary in-room coffee. I recommend the studio suites, much roomier and only slightly more expensive. Each of the Business Class rooms and studio suites has a fax machine, printer, modem hookup, cordless speaker phone, power strip, and other home-office amenities.

Dining: Diva at the Met is one of Vancouver's finest restaurants, serving innovative Pacific Northwest cuisine at lunch and dinner (see "Dining" below).

Amenities: Concierge, 24-hour room service, dry cleaning, newspaper delivery, baby-sitting, secretarial services, express checkout, courtesy car or limo, business center; lap pool, health club, Jacuzzi, men's steam room, squash and racquetball courts, exercise room, saunas, sundeck.

✪ Pan-Pacific Hotel Vancouver. 300-999 Canada Place Way, Vancouver, BC V6C 3B5. ☎ **800/937-1515** or 604/662-8111. Fax 604/685-8690. www.panpac.com. 506 units. A/C MINIBAR TV TEL. June–Oct C$359–C$419 (US$239–US$279) double; Nov–May C$219–C$259 (US$146–US$173) double; year-round C$455–C$2,500 (US$303–US$1,668) suite. AE, DC, ER, JCB MC, V. Valet parking C$23 (US$15). Bus: 4 or 7.

Apart from its natural surroundings, the city's most distinctive landmark is the Canada Place Pier with its five white Teflon sails. The pier houses the Vancouver Trade and Convention Centre, the Alaska cruise-ship terminal, and this spectacular 23-story hotel. (If you're taking an Alaskan cruise, this and the Canadian-Pacific Waterfront Centre Hotel are the closest accommodations.) All the modern guest rooms are spacious and comfortably furnished with soft colors, down duvets on the king-size beds, and elegant marble bathrooms. Many of the rooms look out over the harbor and up to the mountains; they're some of the most spectacular view rooms in town.

Dining: Whether you stay here or not, The Five Sails restaurant is one of the city's best and worth a visit (see "Dining" below).

Amenities: Concierge, 24-hour room service, valet, limo service; outstanding health club (extra C$10/US$7), outdoor pool.

✪ Sheraton Wall Centre Vancouver. 1088 Burrard St., Vancouver, BC V6Z 2R9. ☎ **800/325-3535** or 604/331-1000. Fax 604/893-7200. www.sheratonwallcentre.com. 434 units. No-smoking and wheelchair-accessible rooms. A/C MINIBAR TV TEL. C$400 (US$267) double; C$450–C$500 (US$300–US$334) suite; C$1,500 (US$1,000) loft penthouse. AE, DC, ER, MC, V. Free self-parking; valet parking C$17 (US$11). Bus: 22.

The 35-story Wall Centre's two distinctive blue-gray glass towers are built on downtown's highest point. The guest rooms are elegantly appointed with blond wood furnishings, luxury bathrooms, and king-sized or double beds with down duvets and Egyptian cotton sheets. Every room has stunning floor-to-ceiling windows that maximize the views. For an extra C$25 to C$40 (US$17 to US$27), you can upgrade to one of the 25th- or 26th-floor Crystal Club rooms, which bring added amenities as well as access to the bi-level Crystal Club lounge. The ultimate suite is the two-bedroom loft penthouse with stunning views.

Dining/Diversions: Indigo features innovative West Coast cuisine. The hotel's bar, Cracked Ice, offers an intimate atmosphere and a lighter menu.

Amenities: Concierge, 24-hour room service, dry cleaning/laundry, newspaper delivery, in-room massage, baby-sitting, secretarial services, express checkout, courtesy car or limo; indoor heated pool, health club, Jacuzzi, sauna, business center, conference rooms, beauty salon.

EXPENSIVE

✪ Canadian-Pacific Hotel Vancouver. 900 W. Georgia St., Vancouver, BC V6C 2W6. ☎ **800/441-1414** or 604/684-3131. Fax 604/662-1929. www.cphotels.ca. 579 units.

A/C MINIBAR TV TEL. Low season from C$215 (US$143) double, from C$300 (US$200) suite; high season C$275–C$454 (US$183–US$303) double, C$360–C$640 (US$240–US$427) suite. AE, DC, DISC, MC, V. Parking C$18 (US$12). Bus: 22.

With a C$50 million (US$33 million) renovation completed in 1996, the grande dame of Vancouver's hotels has been restored beyond her former glory. The guest rooms have marble bathrooms and mahogany furnishings and offer city, harbor, and mountain views; about 75% have been equipped to accommodate the needs of business travelers, with dedicated fax and modem lines, speakerphones, coffeemakers, and desk supplies. The best rooms are on the Entree Gold floors: Offering upgraded furniture, they include services like a private concierge, check-in/out service, continental breakfast, free local calls, shoeshine, and afternoon tea with hors d'oeuvres.

Dining/Diversions: Serving West Coast cuisine, 900 West is one of Vancouver's hottest new spots for fine dining. Griffins is the casual restaurant, serving all meals. The Lobby Bar also serves a light menu.

Amenities: Concierge, 24-hour room service, valet/laundry; indoor pool, wading pool, Jacuzzi, health club with weight room, sauna, tanning salon, day spa; shops like Louis Vuitton, Bally, and Aquascutum.

✪ **Crowne Plaza Hotel Georgia.** 801 W. Georgia St., Vancouver, BC V6C 1P7. ☎ **800/663-1111** or 604/682-5566. Fax 604/642-5579. www.hotelgeorgia.bc.ca. 313 units. A/C TV TEL. Jan–Apr C$209–C$269 (US$139–US$179) double; May–Oct C$299–C$399 (US$199–US$266) double; Nov–Dec C$219–C$279 (US$146–US$186) double. Children under 16 stay free in parents' room. AE, CB, DC, MC, V. Valet parking C$15 (US$10). Bus: 4, 7.

The Crowne Plaza Hotel Georgia has recently undergone major renovations to restore its 1920s glory. The guest rooms are decorated with custom-designed art deco furniture and lamps with a blue/gold or green/silver color scheme. They come with adequate workspace and modem access, tea/coffeemakers, and two phone lines. The 12th floor is dedicated to the Club Level rooms, well worth the C$30 surcharge because they offer CD players, speakerphones, robes, complimentary breakfast, afternoon hors d'oeuvres and drinks, a workstation with computer and office supplies, business publications, and meeting space. All Club Level guests also have access to the "Elvis Room," an executive lounge serving afternoon hors d'oeuvres and drinks and providing a workstation with a computer and office supplies, business publications, and meeting space. (Elvis stayed in this room when it used to be a suite, hence the blue suede lounge chairs.)

Dining/Diversions: The Casablanca lounge, with leopard-skin wallpaper, is open for drinks, light lunches, and snacks. The As Time Goes By restaurant serves breakfast, lunch, dinner, and afternoon tea. Also housed in the hotel is the funky downstairs Chameleon Lounge and the street-level Georgia Street Bar and Grill.

Amenities: Concierge, 24-hour room service, dry cleaning/laundry, newspaper delivery, express checkout; health club, business center, conference rooms, beauty salon.

✪ **Four Seasons Hotel.** 791 W. Georgia St., Vancouver, BC V6C 2T4. ☎ **800/332-3442** in the U.S., or 604/689-9333. Fax 604/684-4555, www.fshr.com. 385 units. A/C MINIBAR TV TEL. C$285–C$440 (US$190–US$293) double; C$335–C$510 (US$223–US$340) junior suite; C$370–C$580 (US$247–US$387) executive suite. AE, DC, ER, MC, V. Parking C$20 (US$13). Bus: 4 or 7.

This modern 28-story palace sits atop the Pacific Centre's 200 retail stores a few blocks from the financial district, a particularly appealing location for both shoppers and businesspeople. The guest rooms are tastefully appointed with French provincial furniture and marble bathrooms. The rooms aren't large, however, so for more space try

> ## ⓘ Family-Friendly Hotels
>
> Vancouver hotels offer a wide range of choices if you're bringing your kids, and
> you don't have to sacrifice service or quality. To add to their appeal, a lot of the
> downtown hotels offer baby-sitting.
>
> **Four Seasons Hotel** *(see p. 629)*   Kids get cookies and milk in the evening, as
> well as special room-service menus and warm terry robes.
>
> **Granville Island Hotel** *(see p. 633)*   Granville Island could've been made for
> kids. There are a park and playground right next door to this hotel, and a water
> park and kids-only mall are just a 5-minute walk away. Traffic moves at a snail's
> pace on the island, so parents can let kids run around in safety.
>
> **Rosedale on Robson Suite Hotel** *(see below)*   Dual TVs with in-room movies
> and Nintendo will have the kids cheering, while the full kitchenettes in
> the Rosedale's suites will let parents save the time and expense of one or more
> restaurant meals.

a deluxe room on one of the building's corners, a deluxe Four Seasons room (with a
separately partitioned sitting area), or a suite or junior suite. Wheelchair-accessible
rooms are available.

Dining/Diversions: Winston Churchill's country home was the inspiration for the
decor and the name of the hotel's restaurant, Chartwell's, which serves an eclectic
blend of continental, West Coast, and Asian dishes. For casual dining there are the
Garden Terrace and the Terrace Bar.

Amenities: Concierge, 24-hour room service, laundry/valet, twice-daily housekeeping, limo service; evening cookies and milk for children, special room-service
menus, terry robes; indoor/outdoor pool, weight and exercise room, whirlpool and
saunas, sundeck, florist, cigar store.

MODERATE

Best Western Downtown Vancouver. 718 Drake St. (at Granville St.), Vancouver,
BC V6Z 2W6. ☎ **888/669-9888** or 604/660-9888. Fax 604/669-3440. www.
bestwesterndowntown.com. 143 units. A/C TV TEL. C$139–C$209 (US$93–US$139)
double; C$280–C$350 (US$187–US$233) penthouse. AE, MC, V. Rates include continental
breakfast. Parking C$5 (US$3). Bus: 4 or 7.

The 12-story Best Western is a 5-block walk from the theater area at the south end of
downtown. The hotel is not overflowing with facilities, but the guest rooms are
well furnished and the location is convenient. The 32 rooms with full kitchens are
available for an extra C$20 to C$25 (US$13 to US$17). If you need a workspace,
ask for one of the corporate rooms, which include a full-size desk and activities table.
All rooms have voice-mail phones and dataports, safes, irons and ironing boards, and
hair dryers. In addition, there are a roof-top exercise room, a games area, a Ping-Pong
table, a VCR and movies, a sauna, a Jacuzzi, a sundeck, and a laundry. The deluxe
breakfast is served in the lounge in the lobby. Shuttle service to downtown is offered
7am to 7pm.

Rosedale on Robson Suite Hotel. 838 Hamilton St. (at Robson St.), Vancouver, BC V6B
6A2. ☎ **800/661-8870** or 604/689-8033. 275 units. A/C MINIBAR TV TEL. May–Oct C$215
(US$143) 1-bedroom suite, C$265 (US$177) 2-bedroom suite. Nov–Apr C$175 (US$117)
1-bedroom suite, C$225 (US$150) 2-bedroom suite. Extra adult C$20 (U$13); kitchen utensils C$5 (US$3.35). AE, DC, ER, JCB, MC, V. Parking C$8 (US$5). Bus: 5.

Across from Library Square, the Rosedale has a tower capped by a 15-foot-tall rose emblem. The one- and two-bedroom suites feature separate living rooms, two TVs, and full kitchenettes with microwaves, stoves, ovens, sinks, and half-size refrigerators (dishes and cooking utensils are available on request). The rooms are rather small, but ample bay windows and light wood furnishings scaled to the rooms' size provide a feeling of spaciousness. The corner suites have more windows, and upper-floor suites have furnished terraces and great city views. Guests on executive floors get bathrobes, free local calls, daily newspaper, nightly turndown, in-room movies, Nintendo games, and modem and fax access. Rosie's is a New York–style deli (without the attitude, of course), a rarity in this city filled with West Coast and Pacific Northwest cuisine. There's also a lounge off the lobby. Room service is available 6:30am to 11pm; there's a concierge. The hotel also has an indoor pool, a Jacuzzi, a sauna, a weight and exercise room, and a gift shop.

INEXPENSIVE

✪ **YWCA Hotel/Residence.** 733 Beatty St., Vancouver, BC V6B 2M4. ☎ **800/663-1424** or 604/895-5830. Fax 604/681-2550. 155 units, 53 with bathroom. A/C TEL. C$64–C$84 (US$43–US$56) double without bathroom, C$98–C$130 (US$65–US$87) double with bathroom. Weekly, monthly, group, and off-season discounts available. AE, MC, V. Parking C$5 (US$3.35). Bus: 5 or 8.

Built in 1995, this attractive 12-story residence is an excellent choice for male and female travelers, as well as for families with limited budgets. The guest rooms are simply furnished; some have TVs, all have minirefrigerators, and three communal kitchens are available for guests' use. (There are a number of small grocery stores nearby, as well as a Save-On Foods Super-market a 10-minute walk west on Davie Street.) There are also three TV lounges, a coin laundry, and free access to the best gym in town at the nearby co-ed YWCA Fitness Centre.

THE WEST END
EXPENSIVE

Listel Vancouver. 1300 Robson St., Vancouver, BC V6E 1C5. ☎ **800/663-5491** or 604/684-8461. Fax 604/684-8326. www.listel-vancouver.com. 130 units. A/C MINIBAR TV TEL. May–Sept C$240–C$300 (US$160–US$200) double, C$260–C$320 (US$173–US$213) suite; Oct–Apr C$150–C$190 (US$100–US$127) double, C$170–C$210 (US$113–US$140) suite. AE, DC, DISC, ER, JCB, MC, V. Parking C$14 (US$9). Bus: 5.

This hotel boasts a killer location at the western end of the Robson Street shopping strip, and for the past couple of years, the owners have been putting a lot of effort into making the interior match the address. The guest rooms have been extensively remodeled and now feature top-quality bedding and cherry-wood furnishings, including little window banquettes on which to sit and read or relax. Particularly noteworthy are the 54 Gallery Rooms on the top two floors; each of these rooms and suites is like a small art gallery, hung with original works borrowed from the Buschlen Mowatt Gallery, one of the city's leading private art dealers. They also feature Aveda toiletries and better views. The upper-floor rooms facing Robson Street are worth the price, because each has views of the lively shopping strip, as well as glimpses of the harbor and the mountains. The others face the alley and nearby apartment buildings. Soundproof windows eliminate traffic noise, which can be pretty loud on summer weekends.

Dining: O'Doul's restaurant is a good spot for people watching, and despite the sports-bar name the restaurant has been slowly re-inventing itself as a spot for fine dining. Breakfast, lunch, and dinner are served all day.

Amenities: Concierge, room service, valet/laundry, secretarial services, newspaper delivery, express checkout; indoor pool, exercise room, whirlpool, meeting and banquet space, access to nearby health club.

✪ **Pacific Palisades Hotel.** 1277 Robson St., Vancouver, BC V6E 1C4. ☎ **800/ 663-1815** or 604/688-0461. Fax 604/688-4374. www.pacificpalisadeshotel.com. 233 units. A/C MINIBAR TV TEL. May–Oct C$219 (US$146) studio suite, C$269 (US$179) executive suite; Nov–Dec 15 C$165 (US$110) studio suite, C$205 (US$137) executive suite; Dec 16–May C$165 (US$110) studio suite, C$205 (US$137) executive suite. AE, DC, MC, V. Parking C$13 (US$9). Bus: 5.

At press time, the Palisades had just been sold. The new management apparently intends to leave things more or less the same, but given the place's popularity, a rate hike wouldn't be surprising. Standing on the crest of Robson, it was converted from two luxury apartment towers in 1991 and is popular with visiting film and TV production companies who demand sterling service, privacy, spacious rooms, and great value. The well-appointed suites are divided into studio, executive, and penthouse, all with panoramic views. Most also have private terraces. The kitchenettes come with microwaves, coffeemakers, and minibars; fully equipped kitchens are C$10 (US$7) extra. Extended-stay accommodations are available in a new tower next door.

Amenities: Concierge, 24-hour room service, limousine service, laundry/valet, complimentary shoeshine, business center with full secretarial services, voice-mail message service, doctor on call, daily newspaper, modem access; complete fitness center with health bar, sauna, indoor Olympic lap pool, tanning room; bicycle rentals (mountain bikes available); gift shop; meeting and banquet rooms.

MODERATE

✪ **Blue Horizon.** 1225 Robson St., Vancouver, BC V6E 1C5. ☎ **800/663-1333** or 604/688-1411. Fax 604/688-4461. 214 units. No-smoking and wheelchair-accessible rooms. A/C MINIBAR TV TEL. C$159–C$199 (US$106–US$133) double; C$279 (US$186) suite. Off-season and senior discounts available. Children under 16 stay free in parents' room. Extra person C$15 (US$10). AE, DC, MC, V. Parking C$8 (US$5). Bus: 5.

This unmistakable blue-tiled 1960s high rise on Robson capitalizes on one of Vancouver's best assets—the view. The guest rooms are spacious, and thanks to the hotel layout, every one is a corner room, which maximizes light and window space. Standard rooms are from the 3rd to the 14th floors, while superior rooms are on the 15th to the 30th. Each features a safe, voice mail, dataport, a tea/coffeemaker, an ironing board, a sitting area, and a balcony. There's no concierge or room service, but all rooms have a refrigerator or a minibar. The exercise area includes a lap pool, a Jacuzzi, a sauna, and exercise equipment. Services include dry cleaning, laundry, daily maid service, baby-sitting, secretarial services, and express checkout. Facilities include an indoor heated lap pool and conference rooms.

✪ **West End Guest House.** 1362 Haro St., Vancouver, BC V6E 1G2. ☎ **604/ 681-2889.** Fax 604/688-8812. 7 units. TV TEL. C$145–C$225 (US$97–US$150) double. Rates include full breakfast. AE, MC, V. Free valet parking. Bus: 5.

A 1906 heritage home, this guesthouse is a fine example of what the West End looked like until the early 1950s. Decorated with beautiful 1930s antiques and an amazing collection of old photographs of Vancouver, this is a wonderful respite from the West End's hustle and bustle. The guest rooms provide the ultimate in bedtime luxury: feather mattresses, duvets, and pillows; robes; and your very own stuffed animal. Particularly indulgent is the Grand Queen Suite, an attic bedroom with skylights, a brass bed, a fireplace, a sitting area, and a clawfoot tub. Owner Evan Penner pampers you with a scrumptious breakfast and serves afternoon iced tea and sherry. Throughout the day, you have access to the parlor, sundeck, porch kitchen stocked with home-baked munchies and refreshments, and bikes; if you ask nicely, Penner will crank up the gramophone to provide some period background music.

INEXPENSIVE

Hostelling International Vancouver Downtown Hostel. 1114 Burnaby St. (at Thurlow St.), Vancouver, BC V6E 1P1 ☎ **888/203-4302** or 604/684-4565. Fax 604/684-4540. www.hihostels.bc.ca. 239 beds in 4-person units. Some double and triple units. Wheelchair accessible. Beds C$20 (US$13) IYHA members, C$24 (US$16) nonmembers; doubles C$55 (US$37) members, C$80 (US$53) nonmembers; triples C$70 (US$47) members, C$86 (US$57) nonmembers. Annual adult membership C$27 (US$18). MC, V. Limited free parking. Bus: 2 or 5.

In a converted nunnery, this new modern hostel makes an extremely convenient base of operations from which to explore downtown. The beach is a few blocks south and downtown is a 10-minute walk north. Most beds are in quad dorms, with a limited number of doubles and triples available. As with all hostels, there are common cooking facilities, as well as a patio and a games room. The hostel gets extremely busy in summer, so book ahead. It's open 24 hours.

✪ **Sylvia Hotel.** 1154 Gilford St., Vancouver, BC V6G 2P6. ☎ **604/681-9321.** Fax 604/682-3551. www.sylviahotel.com. 118 units. TV TEL. Oct–Mar C$75–C$100 (US$50–US$67) double, C$115–C$175 (US$77–US$117) suite; Apr–Sept C$75–C$125 (US$50–US$83) double, C$130–C$200 (US$87–US$133) suite. Children under 18 stay free in parents' room. Pets accepted. AE, DC, MC, V. Parking C$5 (US$3.35). Bus: 2 or 5.

The ivy-wreathed gray-stone Sylvia (built in 1912) stands on the shores of English Bay a few blocks from Stanley Park. One of Vancouver's oldest hotels, it has in recent years become deservedly trendy. The guest-room furnishings from the 1950s to the 1970s are appropriately mismatched, and the views from the upper floors are unparalleled. The suites feature fully equipped kitchens and are large enough for families. Sixteen rooms in the 12-year-old low-rise annex offer individual heating but have less atmosphere. Valet and room service are available in both sections. Make reservations a few months ahead for a summer stay.

THE WEST SIDE
EXPENSIVE

✪ **Granville Island Hotel.** 1253 Johnston St., Vancouver, BC V6H 3R9. ☎ **800/ 663-1840** or 604/683-7373. Fax 604/683-3061. www.granvilleislandhotel.com. 54 units. A/C TV TEL. C$219 (US$146) double. Off-season discounts available. AE, CB, DC, ER, MC, V. Parking C$6 (US$4). Bus: 4, 10, or 50.

Completely renovated in 1997 by its new owners, this small modern hotel is at the east end of Granville Island. Surrounded by artists' studios and galleries on one side and pleasure boats on the other, it enjoys a unique waterfront location and has a cozy lobby, attractively decorated with dark wood paneling and stone floors. In addition to its location near the Granville Island Public Market and its close-up views of False Creek, the hotel offers guest rooms with skylights and bathrooms with marble floors and oversize tubs.

Dining/Diversions: The Creek microbrewery restaurant/bar has a harbor-side patio and a large humidor stocked with Cuban and Dominican cigars.

Amenities: Concierge, room service, dry cleaning/laundry, newspaper delivery, in-room massage, baby-sitting, secretarial services, express checkout; rooftop health club with fitness equipment, sauna, Jacuzzi; staff can arrange boat charters at the marina.

MODERATE

Heritage Harbour Bed and Breakfast. 1838 Ogden Ave., Vancouver, BC V6J 1A1. ☎ **604/736-0809.** Fax 604/736-0074. www.vancouver-bc.com/HeritageHarbour. E-mail dhorner@direct.ca. 2 units. May–Oct 15 C$165 (US$110) double; Oct 16–Apr C$125 (US$83) double. No credit cards. Rates include breakfast. Street parking free. Bus: 22.

This B&B occupies a luxurious 1993 Kitsilano-style home in the upscale neighborhood of Kits Point, within walking distance of Kits Beach and Vanier Park. On the main floor, the elegant sitting room with a fireplace offers fine views of the water and the mountains. Upstairs, the Garden Room is light and airy, with a high ceiling, a fan, and a queen-size bed; there's also a balcony overlooking the back of the house and the garden. With pink and red luxury bedding, the Harbour Room is a bit smaller but makes up for it with a small balcony looking out at a fine view over English Bay. Guests share the use of the library. Oak panels, hardwood floors and rugs, black leather couches, a fireplace, and a big view window make this the perfect room to spend a rainy day or a quiet evening, browsing the bookshelves or watching a movie from the owner's video collection. A full breakfast is served at 9am in the dining room, adjacent to the sitting room.

Johnson House Bed & Breakfast. 2278 W. 34th Ave., Vancouver, BC V6M 1G6. ☎ **604/266-4175.** Fax 604/266-4175. 3 units, 1 with bathroom. C$85–C$155 (US$57–US$103) double. Rates include full breakfast. Weekly discounts and off-season rates available. No credit cards. Free parking. Bus: 14.

This charming white-shingled home in Vancouver's quiet residential Kerrisdale district is within a 15-minute drive from the airport and a 10-minute drive from the UBC campus. Outside, the rock garden and sculpture catch your eye; inside, there are wooden carousel animals and other antiques. The cozy guest rooms boast an eclectic array of antique trunks, biplane propellers, and gramophones and feature queen-size brass beds. In the spacious dining room overlooking the tree-shaded back garden, you're served a full breakfast accompanied by homemade muffins, breads, and jams.

INEXPENSIVE

Hostelling International Vancouver Jericho Beach Hostel. 1515 Discovery St., Vancouver, BC V6R 4K5. ☎ **888/203-4303** or 604/224-3208. Fax 604/224-4852. www.hihostels.bc.ca. 286 beds in 14 dorms; 10 family units. Wheelchair accessible. Dorms C$18 (US$12) IYHA members, C$22 (US$14) nonmembers; family units C$47–C$53 (US$32–US$35) members, C$56–C$62 (US$37–US$41) nonmembers. Annual adult membership C$27 (US$18). Family and group memberships available. MC, V. Parking C$3 (US$2). Bus: 4 or 22.

In an old military barracks, this hostel is surrounded by an expansive lawn next to Jericho Beach. Individuals, families, and groups are welcome, but there are no facilities for children under 5 or pets. The 10 private rooms can accommodate up to six, and the dorm-style arrangements are well maintained and supervised. Linens are provided. Basic inexpensive food is served in the cafe April to October. You also have the option of cooking for yourself year-round in the hostel's kitchen.

THE NORTH SHORE
EXPENSIVE

Lonsdale Quay Hotel. 123 Carrie Cates Court, North Vancouver, BC V6M 3K7. ☎ **800/836-6111** or 604/986-6111. Fax 604/986-8782. E-mail sales@lonsdalequayhotel.bc.ca, www.lonsdalequayhotel.bc.ca. 83 units. No-smoking rooms. A/C MINIBAR TV TEL. Low season C$140–C$165 (US$93–US$110) double or twin, C$250 (US$167) harbor-view or waterfront executive suite; high season C$220–C$225 (US$147–US$150) double or twin, C$350 (US$233) harbor-view or waterfront executive suite. Extra person C$25 (US$17). Senior discount available. AE, CB, DC, DISC, ER, MC, V. Parking C$7 (US$4.65), free on weekends and holidays. SeaBus: Lonsdale Quay.

This hotel is at the water's edge above the Lonsdale Quay Market at the SeaBus terminal. An escalator rises from the midst of the market's food, crafts, and souvenir stalls to the front desk on the third floor. The guest rooms are simply and tastefully decorated, with coffeemakers and water coolers but not the grand touches found in comparably priced downtown hotels. Nevertheless, the hotel has unique and fabulous harbor and city views and is only 15 minutes by bus or car from the Grouse Mountain Ski Resort and Capilano Regional Park. The Waterfront Bistro serves lunch, cocktails, and dinner, and the relaxed Q Cafe serves all meals daily. Guests have access to a whirlpool and a weight and exercise room.

MODERATE

✪ **Beachside Bed & Breakfast.** 4208 Evergreen Ave., West Vancouver, BC V7V 1H1. ☎ **800/563-3311** or 604/922-7773. 3 units. C$150–C$250 (US$100–US$167) double. Extra person C$30 (US$20). Rates include full breakfast. MC, V. Free parking. Bus: 250, 251, 252, or 253.

Bouquets of fresh flowers in every room are a signature touch at this lovely Spanish-style waterfront home at the end of a quiet cul-de-sac. Its all-glass southern exposure affords a panoramic view of Vancouver. The private beach is just steps from the door. You can watch the waves from the patio or from the outdoor Jacuzzi or just spend the afternoon fishing and sailing. Hosts Gordon and Joan Gibb are knowledgeable about local history and will direct you to Stanley Park, hiking, skiing, and other area highlights.

INEXPENSIVE

Mountainside Manor. 5909 Nancy Greene Way, North Vancouver, BC V7R 4W6. ☎ **604/990-9772.** Fax 604/985-8484. E-mail mtnside@ibm.net. 4 units. TV. May–Oct C$95–C$155 (US$63–US$103) double; Nov–Apr C$85–C$135 (US$57–US$90) double. Rates include breakfast. Off-season discounts available. DC, MC, V. Free parking. SeaBus: Lonsdale Quay, then Bus 241.

This is the closest house to both the ski slopes on Grouse Mountain and the 26-mile-long Baden-Powell hiking trail. High above the city on a tree-covered ridge, this spectacular modern home nestled in a peaceful alpine setting offers a magnificent view of the Coast Mountains and the Burrard Inlet from the rooms and the outdoor hot tub. The Panorama Room (the largest) has a queen-size bed, rosewood furniture, a Jacuzzi with a separate shower, and views of the mountains and the city. All rooms are stocked with fresh flowers and lots of amenities.

4 Dining

Vancouverites seem to dine out more than residents of any other Canadian city. Outstanding meals are available in all price ranges and in many ethnic cuisines—like Chinese, Japanese, Greek, French, Italian, Spanish, Mongolian, Ethiopian, Vietnamese, and even Canadian. Even better, over the past few years Vancouverites have come to expect top quality but absolutely refuse to pay the same kind of top dollar diners would in New York or San Francisco. Somehow, restaurateurs here have managed to square this circle. For discerning diners from elsewhere, Vancouver is a steal.

The cuisine buzz words here are *tapas* and *West Coast.* Justifiable pride in local produce, game, and seafood is combined with innovation and creativity. More and more restaurants are shifting to seasonal (even monthly) menus, giving their chefs greater freedom. While there are as many variations on this regional fare as there are fine chefs, the focus on freshness, flavor, and local ingredients makes this cuisine unique and unparalleled.

As for tapas, it seems that diners in Vancouver have grown more sociable, while also becoming more commitment shy. So they avoid ordering one big main dish by ordering two or three small tapas plates and sharing them with their friends.

Because they're so numerous, Vancouver restaurants aren't hard to find. If you're staying in downtown, you can walk to the West End and English Bay (west of downtown from Thurlow Street to Stanley Park), Gastown, or Chinatown. If you're willing to travel farther, you can venture to the West Side. Or if you'd like to head in the opposite direction, cross the Lions Gate Bridge and turn left and you'll be in West Vancouver. For something fun and casual, head east to a bistro on Main Street or Commercial Drive.

Note: See the "Vancouver" map (p. 620) to locate most of the restaurants in this section.

DOWNTOWN & YALETOWN
VERY EXPENSIVE

✪ **C.** 1600 Howe St. ☎ **604/681-1164.** Reservations recommended. Main courses C$15–C$32 (US$10–US$21). AE, DC, ER, JCB, MC, V. Daily 11:30am–11pm. Bus: 1 or 2. SEAFOOD.

C wins top marks for the sheer indulgent quality with which it serves fish. C's taster box—a kind of small wooden high-rise of appetizers—includes salmon gravlax cured in Saskatoon-berry tea, artichoke carpaccio, abalone tempura, and grilled garlic squid. A variety of seafood main courses is available, but for the ultimate dining experience, let chef Robert Clark show off (he's dying to) by ordering the seven-course sampling menu. The highlight is a huge Alaskan scallop wrapped in octopus bacon! Wine pairings throughout are brought to you by Peter, a sommelier of exceptional knowledge. Savor the exquisite cuisine and watch as the sun goes down over yet another yacht gliding into the marina.

Diva at the Met. 645 Howe St. ☎ **604/602-7788.** Reservations recommended. Main courses C$12–C$18 (US$8–US$12) at lunch, C$20–C$32 (US$13–US$21) at dinner. AE, DC, JCB, MC, V. Daily 8:30am–11:30pm. Bus: 4 or 7.

Since opening this place just a few years ago next to the revamped Metropolitan Hotel, chef Michael Noble has made a habit of walking off with city restaurant awards in categories like Best West Coast and Most Creative Menu. His dishes extol the virtues of fresh seasonal ingredients combined with a light approach to spices and seasonings. Starters include house-smoked salmon with Québec foie gras, and main courses include halibut with black olive tapenade. Diva's tasting menu is also very popular, and its weekend brunches are among the best in town.

✪ **The Five Sails.** In the Pan-Pacific Hotel, 999 Canada Place Way. ☎ **604/891-2892.** Reservations recommended. Main courses C$21–C$38 (US$14–US$25); tasting menu C$34–C$45 (US$23–US$30). AE, DC, ER, JCB, MC, V. Sun–Fri 6–10pm, Sat 6–11pm. SkyTrain: Waterfront. WEST COAST.

The view from the Five Sails is spectacular and so is the food. The hallmarks of the Five Sails approach are top-quality ingredients given just enough preparation to bring out their finest flavors. Think dry-aged Angus beef done to perfection or a perfect steak of freshly caught Pacific salmon, lightly grilled and served with fresh potatoes. The Five Sail's wine selection lists slightly toward hard-to-find Cascadian bottles, which is all to the good.

Gotham Steakhouse and Cocktail Bar. 615 Seymour St. ☎ **604/605-8282.** Reservations recommended. Main courses C$27–C$42 (US$18–US$28). AE, MC, V. Mon–Fri 11:30am–2:30pm; daily 5–11pm (cocktail bar somewhat later). Bus: 4 or 7. STEAK.

Vegetarians beware: This New York–style steak house serves USDA beef and little else but potatoes and a bit of fish flesh. The wine list—bound in thick black suede—is encyclopedic. And then there's the food. The deep-fried çalamari appetizer is light and tasty. The jumbo shrimps are sumo-sized, in a wonderful garlic-cream sauce. And the steaks are incredible: a porterhouse cut the size of a catcher's mitt; a petit filet mignon as tall as half a bread loaf. Gotham will cook these cuts however you prefer, but if you have it medium rare it'll come with a thin layer of broiling top and bottom, pink and ever so slightly warm in the middle, and so tender that after that initial crunch of flavor the meat melts on your tongue. The veggie side dishes are eminently forgettable.

EXPENSIVE

Il Giardino di Umberto. 1382 Hornby St. ☎ **604/669-2422.** www.umberto.com. Reservations required. Main courses C$14–C$33 (US$9–US$22). AE, DC, ER, MC, V. Mon–Fri noon–2:30pm; daily 5:30–11pm. Bus: 1 or 22. ITALIAN.

Decorated in burnt sienna with exposed wood beams, this restaurant re-creates the ambiance of an Italian seaside villa, down to the enclosed garden terrace for alfresco dining and Tuscan menu emphasizing pasta and game. Entrees include osso buco Milanese with saffron risotto, tortellini with portobello mushrooms in truffle oil, roasted reindeer loin with port-peppercorn sauce, and pheasant breast stuffed with wild mushrooms. After sampling the cuisine, more than a few devoted foodies have run off to enroll in Umberto's Tuscan cooking school.

✪ Joe Fortes Seafood House. 777 Thurlow St. (at Robson St.). ☎ **604/669-1940.** Reservations recommended. Main courses C$16–C$24 (US$11–US$16). AE, DC, DISC, ER, MC, V. Sun–Thurs 11:30am–11pm, Fri–Sat 11:30am–midnight. Bus: 5. SEAFOOD.

Named after the burly Caribbean seaman and popular local hero who became English Bay's first lifeguard in the early 1900s, Joe Fortes has been known for years as the place where the young and tanned would meet for mutual schmoozing over the oyster bar. Lately, under the direction of chef Brian Faulk, Joe's has grown into one of city's best seafood fusion spots. The rooftop patio comes with its own bar and strategically placed gas heaters.

Le Crocodile. 100-909 Burrard St. ☎ **604/669-4298.** Reservations recommended. Main courses C$12–C$25 (US$8–US$17) at lunch, C$18–C$28 (US$12–US$19) at dinner. AE, DC, MC, V. Mon–Fri 11:30am–2pm; Mon–Thurs 5:30–10pm, Fri–Sat 5:30–10:30pm. Bus: 22. FRENCH.

On the ground floor of a red-brick condo tower a block south of Robson Street, you'll find this dining room with sassy yellow walls. This is French as de Gaulle would've had it—onion tarte, calf's liver, grilled pheasant breast with port-wine sauce, tender Dover sole with beurre blanc, and crème brûlée. The wine list doesn't deign to acknowledge grapes unfortunate enough to have placed their roots outside the mother country, but the list of French vintages is vast.

MODERATE

Bin 941 Tapas Parlour. 941 Davie St. ☎ **604/683-1246.** Reservations not accepted. Main courses C$7–C$19 (US$4.65–US$13). AE, DC, MC, V. Daily 5:30pm–2am. Bus: 4, 5, or 8. TAPAS.

At press time, Bin 941 is the latest in trendy tapas dining. True, the music's too loud, the room too small, and the menu unbelievably pretentious. However, the food that alights on the bar or ever-so-tiny table is quite delicious, and like all tapas a lot of fun to eat. Look especially for local seafood offerings like scallops and tiger prawns in bonito butter sauce. Sharing is unavoidable in this sliver of a bistro—your food with your friends, your conversation with your neighbors, your jokes with the entire place.

ⓗ Family-Friendly Restaurants

Romano's Macaroni Grill at the Mansion *(see p. 640)*   The huge children's menu here offers numerous dinner choices, and the friendly staff will even let kids wander up the inviting mansion staircase to explore the upper rooms.

Sophie's Cosmic Cafe *(see p. 642)*   In Kitsilano, Sophie's offers great finger food, crayons and coloring paper, and lots and lots of eye-candy. In addition, almost any Chinese restaurant will be practiced in accommodating children, and given the size of most menus, there's guaranteed to be something they'll like.

INEXPENSIVE

The Tempelton. 1087 Granville St. ☎ **604/685-4612.** Main courses C$3.50–C$9 (US$2.35–US$6). Sun–Mon 10am–10pm, Tues–Thurs 10am–midnight, Fri–Sat 10am–4am. Bus: 4, 7, 8, or 10. AMERICAN.

It's a diner but not really a diner—more like a trendy retro commentary on the diner, except that this place has been in continuous operation since 1934. True, back then the green Hamilton Beach milk shake makers were the height of modern and the serving staff likely didn't go in for nose and nipple rings and tattooed belly-buttons—but other than that, what's changed? Well, the food for one. Hamburgers and fries aren't a staple here. Instead, expect jambalaya, chili, blackened chicken breast, or portobello-mushroom vegetarian burger. Saturday brunch is 10% off if you arrive in your pajamas. Staff already have them on.

GASTOWN & CHINATOWN
EXPENSIVE

The Cannery. 2205 Commissioner St., near Victoria Dr. ☎ 604/254-9606. www.canneryseafood.com. Reservations recommended. Main courses C$17–C$27 (US$11–US$18). AE, DC, DISC, MC, V. Mon–Fri 11:30am–2:30pm; daily 5:30–10pm. Bus: 7 to Victoria Dr. From downtown, head east on Hastings St., turn left on Victoria Dr. (2 blocks past Commercial Dr.), then right on Commissioner St. SEAFOOD.

The Cannery is hidden away on the Vancouver waterfront, and at least some of the joy of eating here comes from simply finding the place. The building itself, with its beam-laded warehouse interior, loaded with old nets and seafaring memorabilia, chips in another hefty portion of the charm. And the view is one of the best in Vancouver. So how about the food? It's good, solid, traditional seafood, often alder-grilled, with an ever-changing fresh sheet to complement the salmon and halibut basics. The wine list is stellar, with a few good bargains among the pricier selections.

MODERATE

✪ Floata Seafood Restaurant. 400-180 Keefer St. ☎ 604/602-0368. Reservations recommended. Main courses C$10–C$45 (US$7–US$30); dim sum dishes C$2.50–C$3.75 (US$1.65–US$2.50). AE, DC, ER, JCB, MC, V. Daily 8am–10pm. Bus: 19 or 22. CHINESE/DIM SUM.

In classic Hong Kong style, Floata is on the third floor of a shopping plaza/parking garage. (Look for the bright red building a stone's throw from the Dr. Sun-Yat-sen Garden.) Its dining area is nearly a full city block long. Dim sum is a traditional brunch/lunch buffet rolled out on numerous carts by friendly waitresses who stop at each table. Patrons make their selections right at their table from carts loaded with shumai and *hargow* (steamed dumplings), *dum bao* (buns filled with barbecued pork), sautéed vegetables, roast duck, roast pork, spring rolls, sausages rolled in sesame-crusted puff pastry, and other delicacies that ply the aisles to 2:30pm. Dinner dishes include shark-fin and bird's-nest soups, whole crisp sea bass in black-bean sauce, and crisp Peking duck.

INEXPENSIVE

Incendio. 103 Columbia St. ☎ **604/688-8694.** Main courses C$7–C$12 (US$4.85–US$8). AE, MC, V. Mon–Fri 11:30am–3pm and 5–10pm; Sat–Sun 5–11pm. Bus: 1 or 8. PIZZA.

The 22 combinations of pizza are served on fresh, crispy crusts baked in an old wood-fired oven. The pastas are homemade, and you're encouraged to mix and match sauces and pastas—try the mussels with spinach fettuccine, capers, and tomatoes in lime butter. The wine list is decent; the beer list is inspired. And now there's a patio. Sunday night features all-you-can-eat pizza for C$8 (US$5).

Phnom Penh Restaurant. 244 E. Georgia St., near Main St. ☎ **604/682-5777.** Reservations recommended. Dishes C$4.50–C$11 (US$3–US$7). DC, MC. Wed–Mon 10am–9:30pm. Bus: 8 or 19. CAMBODIAN/VIETNAMESE.

This family-run restaurant serves a mix of Vietnamese and slightly spicier Cambodian cuisine. Try the outstanding hot-and-sour soup, loaded with prawns and lemongrass suspended in a flavorful light broth. The deep-fried garlic squid served with rice is also delicious. For dessert, the fruit-and-rice pudding is an exotic treat. There's a second location at 955 Broadway at Oak Street (☎ **604/734-8898**).

THE WEST END
EXPENSIVE

Cin Cin. 1154 Robson St. ☎ **604/688-7338.** www.cincin.net. Reservations recommended. Main courses C$12–C$35 (US$8–US$23). AE, DC, MC, V. Mon–Sat noon–2:30pm; daily 5–11pm. Bus: 5 or 22. On-street parking. ITALIAN.

Cin Cin's dining room is built around the open kitchen that's built around a huge alderwood-fired oven. Nice. But it's a penne toss whether to eat here, have a drink at the big bar, or duck out onto the heated terrace overlooking Robson Street and spend an hour or three people watching. The dishes range from elegant pastas and pizzas—capellini alla pomodoro, penne puttanesca, and pizza Margherita—to more substantial dishes like rosemary-marinated rack of lamb, sea bass crusted with porcini mushrooms, and smoked chicken breast. The wine list is extensive, as is the selection of wines by the glass.

Delilah's. 1789 Comox St. ☎ **604/687-3424.** Limited reservations accepted for parties of 6 or more. Fixed-price menus C$21–C$34 (US$14–US$22). AE, DC, ER, MC, V. Daily 5:30pm–midnight. Bus: 5. CONTINENTAL.

The first order of business at Delilah's is ordering a martini—the restaurant's forte. The two-page martini list comes with everything from the basic Boston Tea Partini to the ultimate in southern excess, the Miranda. The menu offers some 20 dishes, listed vertically and divided into soups, salads, appetizers, and entrees. Order a small dinner and you get to tick off two courses (C$21/US$14). Order a full dinner (C$34/US$22) and the pencil ticks off four courses, with desserts listed separately but included in the price. The menu tends toward seafood, which Delilah's does well, sticking to freshness and simple sauces. The portions are small, the menu advises, and in bold type it says **HAVE FUN!** With a martini in hand and an ever-changing variety of campy tunes on the sound system (Sinatra at the Sands, Petula Clark's "Downtown"), this turns out not to be a difficult task at all.

✪ **Raincity Grill.** 1193 Denman St. ☎ **604/685-7337.** Reservations recommended. Main courses C$13–C$24 (US$9–US$16). AE, DC, ER, MC, V. Mon–Fri 11:30am–2:30pm; Sat–Sun brunch 10:30am–3pm; daily 5–10:30pm. Bus: 1 or 5. WEST COAST.

Raincity's room is long and low and hugs the shoreline, the better to let the early-evening sun pour in. In terms of food, the restaurant's forte is expertly sourced local ingredients done up West Coast style. That means appetizers of barbecued quail with sage and goat-cheese polenta, crispy jumbo spot prawns, and smoked steelhead salad, as well as main courses of grilled Fraser Valley free-range chicken and fresh-caught spring salmon. And then there's the huge wine list, which focuses on BC and the Pacific Northwest. Most varieties are available by the glass, allowing you to make an extended wine trip through the region.

MODERATE

Café de Paris. 751 Denman St. (at Robson St.). ☎ **604/687-1418.** Reservations recommended. Main courses C$14–C$17 (US$9–US$11); fixed-price menus C$27–C$29 (US$18–US$19). AE, MC, V. Mon–Fri 11:30am–2pm; daily 5:30–10pm. Bus: 5. FRENCH.

Enter this cafe and you're on the Left Bank. Edith Piaf's voice caresses a cozy room filled with linen-covered tables, and the big wood bar is stocked with fine French liquors and cognacs. The wine list never leaves the Fifth Republic and ranges from a C$24 (US$16) house red to a C$1,500 (US$1,000) bottle of Château Haut-Brion Bordeaux 1985. The cuisine is ever so French (though the friendly service is anything but). Dinner hors d'oeuvres include Burgundy snails in garlic butter, braised rabbit in Dijon mustard sauce, veal kidneys with mushrooms, and onion soup. The menu also includes classics like tournedos, pepper steak, and roasted chicken. Make sure you save some room for a dessert like frangellico-poached pears, fresh raspberry custard tart, or maraschino chocolate cake, any of which makes fine company with a tiny glass of chilled Muscat.

Romano's Macaroni Grill at the Mansion. 1523 Davie St. ☎ **604/689-4334.** Reservations recommended. Main courses C$8–C$16 (US$5–US$11); children's courses C$3.95–C$6 (US$2.65–US$3.65). AE, DC, MC, V. Daily 11:30am–10:30pm. Bus: 5. ITALIAN/FAMILY.

In a huge stone mansion built in the early 1900s, Romano's is fun and casual. The menu emphasizes Southern Italian fare, and the pastas are definitely the favorites. This isn't high-concept Italian; the food is simple, understandable, and consistently good. You're charged for the house wine based on how much you consume when you pour your portion from unlabeled bottles. Your kids will love the children's menu, which features lasagna and meat loaf and tasty pizzas, as well as the permissive staff, who burst into opera at the slightest provocation.

Tanpopo. 1122 Denman St. ☎ **604/681-7777.** Reservations recommended. Main courses C$8–C$19 (US$5–US$13). AE, DC, MC, V. Daily 11:30am–10:30pm. Bus: 5. JAPANESE.

Occupying the half-block-long second floor of a corner building, Tanpopo has a partial view of English Bay and a huge menu of hot and cold Japanese dishes. But the lines of people willing to wait 30 minutes or more for a table every single night are there for all-you-can-eat sushi. Call ahead, but they take only an arbitrary percentage of reservations for dinner each day. And if the restaurant is full or if they've stopped taking reservations, you can still show up and wait for a table or ask to sit at the sushi bar.

INEXPENSIVE

Gyoza King. 1508 Robson St. ☎ **604/669-8278.** Main courses C$6–C$13 (US$4–US$9). AE, DC, JCB, MC, V. Daily noon–2:30pm; Mon–Sat 5:30pm–2am, Sun 5:30pm–midnight. Bus: 5. JAPANESE.

Gyoza King features an entire menu of gyozas, succulent Japanese dumplings filled with prawns, pork, vegetables, and other combinations, as well as Japanese noodles and staples like *katsu-don* (pork cutlet over rice) and *o-den* (a rich, hearty soup). This is the gathering spot for hordes of young Japanese visitors, probably because it's the closest to home cooking and there are so many choices for less than C$10 (US$7). Seating is divided among Western-style tables, the bar (where you can watch the chef in action), and the Japanese-style front table, reserved for larger groups if the restaurant is busy. The staff is very courteous and happy to explain the dishes if you're not familiar with Japanese cuisine.

✪ **Stephos.** 1124 Davie St. ☎ **604/683-2555.** Reservations accepted for parties of 5 or more. Main courses C$4.25–C$10 (US$2.85–US$7). AE, MC, V. Daily 11:30am–11:30pm. Bus: 5. GREEK.

There's a reason Stephos is packed every day for lunch and dinner: The cuisine is simple Greek fare at its finest and cheapest. Customers line up outside and wait up to 30 minutes for a seat amid Greek travel posters, potted ivy, and whitewashed walls. (The average wait is 10 to 15 minutes.) Generous portions of delicious marinated lamb, chicken, pork, or beef over rice pilaf; *tzatziki* (a yogurt dip that's a garlic lover's dream come true); and heaping platters of calamari are just a few of the offerings. Beware of ordering too much food. It's easy to do here.

THE WEST SIDE
VERY EXPENSIVE

✪ **Bishop's.** 2183 W. 4th Ave. ☎ **604/738-2025.** www.settingsun.com/Bishops. Reservations required. Main courses C$24–C$30 (US$16–US$20). AE, DC, MC, V. Mon–Sat 5:30–11pm, Sun 5:30–10pm. Bus: 4 or 7. FRENCH.

The atmosphere in Bishop's features candlelight, white linen, and soft jazz playing in the background. The service is impeccable and the food even better, with the menu changing three or four times a year. Recent dishes have included roast duck breast with sun-dried Okanagan Valley fruits and candied ginger glacé, steamed smoked black cod with new potatoes and horseradish sabayon, and marinated sirloin of lamb with garlic mashed potatoes and a fresh mint, tomato, and balsamic vinegar reduction. If you have only one evening to dine in Vancouver and have room in your budget, spend it here.

✪ **Lumière.** 2551 W. Broadway. ☎ **604/739-8185.** Reservations recommended. Main courses C$24–C$35 (US$16–US$23); vegetarian tasting menu C$55 (US$37); chef's tasting menu C$70 (US$47), accompanying flight of wines by the glass C$40 (US$27). AE, DC, MC, V. Tues–Sun 5:30–9:30pm (to 10:30pm Fri–Sat). Bus: 9 or 10. FRENCH.

The success of this fine-dining experiment in the heart of Kitsilano has turned chef Rob Feenie into a hot commodity. He now regularly jets off to New York to teach folks back east how to do it right. And how is that? His preparation and presentation are immaculately French and his ingredients resolutely local, making for interesting surprises like fresh ginger popping up in the veal or raspberries in the foie gras. Everything is excellent, but particularly interesting are the tasting menu and the vegetarian menu. Dishes change with the seasons, so it's a little hard to make recommendations. Your best bet is to opt for the tasting menu and let Feenie show you what French cuisine can be.

EXPENSIVE

Vij's. 1480 W. 11th Ave. ☎ **604/736-6664.** Reservations not accepted. Main courses C$10–C$14 (US$7–US$9). AE, DC, ER, MC, V. Daily 5:30–10pm. Bus: 8 or 10. INDIAN.

During prime dining time there's a line outside every night. Patrons huddled under Vij's (pronounced *veeg*-is) violet neon sign are treated to complimentary tea and papadums. Inside, the decor is as warm and subtle as the seasonings, which are all roasted and ground by hand, then used with studied delicacy. The menu changes monthly, and recent offerings have included coconut curried chicken and saffron rice, as well as marinated pork medallions with garlic-yogurt curry and *naan* (flat bread). Vegetarian selections abound, including curried vegetable rice pilaf with cilantro-cream sauce and Indian lentils with naan and *raita* (yogurt-mint sauce).

MODERATE

Coco. 1684 W. 4th Ave. ☎ **604/731-1185.** Reservations not accepted. Main courses C$6–C$13 (US$4–US$9). AE, MC, V. Daily 5pm–1am. Bus: 4. TAPAS.

Coco's provides a welcome bit of evening energy in a neighborhood trending toward middle-age restraint. The regular menu includes grilled Japanese eggplant, spicy crusted oysters in coriander cream, littleneck clams in red-curry/coconut-milk sauce, and other such seafood fusion wonders, all priced around C$10 (US$7) and portioned big enough for generous sharing. Drinks include seasonal draughts from the Granville Island Brewing Company and a small wine list with a few carefully chosen BC and California vintages.

Sami's. 986 W. Broadway. ☎ **604/736-8330.** Reservations not accepted. Main courses C$6–C$11 (US$4–US$7). AE, MC, V. Daily 11am–11pm. Bus: 9. INDIAN.

In the long and honorable history of South Asian food in Vancouver, there was never a less promising location than this—a strip mall, by a 7-11, in the dull office corridor of West Broadway. But the food is fabulous, like beef shortribs braised in cumin and ginger and seafood poached in coconut nectar. The source of all this value is restaurateur Sami Lalji, who decided he'd had it with the big time and wanted a fun, manageable spot where he could cook up the Indian/Western mix that's his pride and joy. The result has been a stunning success, so much so that evening lineups often spill out of the warm little dining room and into the mall parking lot.

INEXPENSIVE

The Naam Restaurant. 2724 W. 4th Ave. ☎ **604/738-7151.** Reservations not accepted. Main courses C$3.95–C$8 (US$2.65–US$5). AE, ER, MC, V. Daily 24 hrs. Bus: 4 or 22. VEGETARIAN.

Back in the 1960s when Kitsilano was Canada's hippie haven, the Naam was tie-dye central. Things have changed a tad since, but this oldest of Vancouver's vegetarian/natural food restaurants retains a pleasantly granola feel. The decor is simple, earnest, and welcoming; the brazenly healthy fare ranges from open-face tofu melts, enchiladas, and burritos to tofu teriyaki, Thai noodles, and pita pizzas. The sesame spice fries are a Vancouver institution. The only real trick to eating here is arriving well before you're actually hungry: The waitstaff will invariably disappear on an extended search for personal fulfillment at some point during your meal.

Sophie's Cosmic Café. 2095 W. 4th Ave. ☎ **604/732-6810.** Main courses C$4.50–C$15 (US$3–US$10). MC, V. Daily 8am–10pm. Bus: 4. AMERICAN/FAMILY.

Sophie's is readily identifiable by the giant silver knife and fork bolted to the outside front walls. Inside, every available space has been crammed with toys and knickknacks from the 1950s and 1960s, creating an experience much akin to having lunch inside a McDonald's Happy Meal box. For that very reason, children are inordinately fond of Sophie's. Crayons and coloring paper are always on hand to keep their fingers off the toys. The menu is simple: pastas, burgers and fries without fancy names, great milk shakes, and a few classic Mexican dishes.

THE EAST SIDE
MODERATE

Brickhouse Bistro. 730 Main St. ☎ **604/689-8645.** Reservations accepted. Main courses C$9–C$15 (US$6–US$10). AE, MC, V. Mon–Sat 5:30–11pm, Sun 5:30–10pm. Bus: 3. CASUAL.

There were once two partners who opened a bar in a slightly seedy section of town. It did well. Encouraged, they refurbished the room above their bar and opened it as a bistro—a funky kind of place, all bricks and wood beams, staffed by a chef capable of cooking simple but superior food, like New Zealand rib eye in Madeira jus or specials of fresh fish. The restaurant was slower to catch on, so to lure customers, the partners kept their prices very low. Dinner, drinks, and dessert could all be had for less than C$30 (US$20). With the revenue from their thriving bar, the partners can afford to do this until word of the cuisine and ambiance spreads. And for those who arrive in the meantime, the bistro is an ever-so-tasty steal.

THE NORTH SHORE
EXPENSIVE

✪ **The Beach House at Dundarave Pier.** 150 25th St., West Vancouver. ☎ **604/922-1414.** Reservations recommended. Main courses C$12–C$16 (US$8–US$11) at lunch, C$22–C$31 (US$15–US$21) at dinner. AE, DC, ER, MC, V. Mon–Thurs 11:30am–3pm and 5–10pm; Fri–Sat 5–11pm; Sat–Sun brunch 11am–3pm. Light appetizers served 3–5pm. WEST COAST.

In a dramatic waterfront location, every seat in the House has a panoramic view of English Bay. The cuisine is consistently top quality—innovative but not so experimental it leaves the West Van burghers gasping for breath. Appetizers include soft-shell crab with salt-and-fire jelly; grilled scallops with baby spinach, crispy onions, and red-pepper cream; and grilled portobello mushrooms with Okanagan Valley goat cheese. Entrees have been known to encompass garlic-crusted rack of lamb with honey balsamic glaze and baked striped sea bass with basil mousse and rock prawns. The wine list is award winning.

✪ **The Salmon House on the Hill.** 2229 Folkstone Way, West Vancouver. ☎ **604/926-3212.** www.salmonhouse.com. Reservations recommended for dinner. Main courses C$6–C$14 (US$4–US$9) at lunch, C$14–C$24 (US$9–US$16) at dinner. AE, DC, ER, MC, V. Mon–Sat 11:30am–2:30pm; Sun brunch 11am–2:30pm; daily 5:30–10pm. WEST COAST.

High above West Vancouver, the Salmon House offers a spectacular view of the city and Burrard Inlet. Chef Dan Atkinson's menu reflects his extensive research into local ingredients and First Nations cuisine. An alderwood-fired grill dominates the kitchen, lending a delicious flavor to many of the dishes. Entrees include grilled BC salmon with local prawns, fiddlehead ferns, and Fraser Valley blueberry salsa; Fraser Valley free-range chicken with roasted onion jus; and smoked West Coast black cod with wasabi cream and balsamic mustard-seed vinaigrette. The wine list earned an award of excellence from *Wine Spectator*.

5 Seeing the Sights

A city perched on the edge of a great wilderness, Vancouver offers unmatched opportunities for exploring the outdoors: You can hike through old-growth forests, kayak an ocean fjord, and ski or snowboard fresh powder, all within view of the city. Paradoxically, Vancouver is also intensely urban. There are sidewalk cafes to match Paris's and shopping streets to rival London's. The forest of downtown residential high rises looks somewhat like New York's, while the buzz and movement in Chinatown are reminiscent of San Franciso's or even Canton. Comparisons with other places soon begin to pall, however, as you come to realize that Vancouver is entirely its own creation—a self-confident, sparklingly beautiful city, like no place else on Earth.

Note: See the "Vancouver" map (p. 620) to locate sights in this section.

DOWNTOWN & THE WEST END

B.C. Sports Hall of Fame and Museum. 777 Pacific Blvd. S. (B.C. Place Stadium, Gate A, Beatty and Robson sts.). ☎ **604/687-5520.** Admission C$6 (US$4) adults, C$4 (US$2.65) seniors/students; children under 5 free. Daily 10am–5pm. SkyTrain: Stadium. Bus: 15.

A great destination for sports-minded kids with endless energy, the museum's Participation Gallery features interactive running, climbing, throwing, riding, rowing, and racing competitions where they can pit themselves against video-simulated competitors. There are also a climbing wall, pitching cages, and stationary bikes. For parents, the Hall of Champions and Builders Hall document the achievements of British Columbia's most lauded athletes.

Canadian Craft Museum. 639 Hornby St. ☎ **604/687-8266.** Admission C$5 (US$3.35) adults, C$3 (US$2) seniors/students; children under 12 free. Mon–Wed and Fri–Sat 10am–5pm, Thurs 10am–9pm, Sun and holidays noon–5pm. Closed Tues Sept–May. SkyTrain: Granville. Bus: 3.

Hidden behind the Cathedral Place building at the edge of a beautiful outdoor courtyard, the Canadian Craft Museum presents a vast collection of Canadian and international crafts in glass, wood, metal, clay, and fiber. Recent shows have included an impressive display of carved Chinese signature seals and calligraphy, British Columbian artist Bill Reid's gold and silver jewelry, and furniture created by Canada's best industrial designers.

Vancouver Art Gallery. 750 Hornby St. ☎ 604/662-4719 or 604/662-4700. www.vanartgallery.bc.ca. Admission C$8 (US$5) adults, C$6 (US$4) seniors, C$4 (US$2.65) students, C$25 (US$17) families. Thurs 6–9pm by donation. Mon–Sun 10am–5:30pm, Thurs 10am–9pm, holidays noon–5pm. SkyTrain: Granville. Bus: 3.

The VAG is an excellent stop for anyone wanting to see what sets Canadian and West Coast art apart from the rest of the world. You'll find an impressive collection of paintings by BC native Emily Carr, as well as examples of a unique Canadian art style created during the 1920s by members of the "Group of Seven," who included Vancouver painter Fred Varley. Their bold style was strongly influenced by the dramatic Canadian landscapes they captured on canvas. On the contemporary side, the VAG hosts rotating exhibits of sculpture, graphics, photography, and video art, some from BC artists, many from around the world. Geared to younger audiences, the Annex Gallery features rotating presentations of visually exciting educational exhibits.

✪ **Vancouver Aquarium Marine Science Centre.** Stanley Park. ☎ **604/659-FISH** (3474). www.vanaqua.org. Admission C$13 (US$9) adults, C$11 (US$7) seniors/students/youths 13–18, C$9 (US$6) children 4–12, C$43 (US$29) families; children under 4 free. June 23–Sept 4 daily 9:30am–7pm; Sept 5–June 22 daily 10am–5:30pm. Bus: 135; "Around the Park" shuttle bus June–Sept only, parking C$5 (US$3.35) summer, C$3 (US$2) winter.

One of North America's largest and best aquariums, the Vancouver Aquarium houses more than 8,000 marine species, most in meticulously re-created environments, including the icy-blue Arctic Canada exhibit, the Amazon rain-forest gallery, and the Pacific Canada exhibit. On the Marine Mammal Deck are sea otters, Steller sea lions, beluga whales, an orca (killer whale), and a Pacific white-sided dolphin. During regularly scheduled shows, the aquarium staff explains marine mammal behavior while working with these impressive creatures. In addition to tours, the aquarium has a regular program of special events, including behind-the-scenes tours, sleepover programs for children and youths, and evening barbecues.

THE WEST SIDE

✪ Science World British Columbia. 1455 Quebec St. ☎ **604/268-6363.** www. scienceworld.bc.ca. Admission C$12 (US$8) adults; C$8 (US$5) seniors/students/ children 4 and up; children under 4 free. Combination tickets available for Omnimax film. Mon–Fri 10am–5pm, Sat–Sun 10am–6pm. SkyTrain: Main Street–Science World.

Science World is unmistakable—in the big blinking geodesic dome on the eastern end of False Creek. It's a hands-on scientific discovery center where you and your kids can light up a plasma ball, walk through a 1,700-square-foot maze, lose your shadow, walk through the interior of a camera, create a cyclone, blow square bubbles, and watch a zucchini explode as it's charged with 80,000 volts. In the Omnimax Theatre— a huge projecting screen equipped with Surround-Sound—you feel as though you're taking a death-defying flight through the Grand Canyon and performing other spine-tingling feats.

✪ Vancouver Maritime Museum. 1905 Ogden Ave., in Vanier Park. ☎ **604/ 257-8300.** www.vmm.bc.ca. Admission C$6 (US$4) adults, C$3 (US$2) seniors/ students, C$14 (US$9) families; children under 6 free. Daily 10am–5pm; closed Tues Sept to mid–May. Bus: 22, then walk 4 blocks north on Cypress St. Boat: False Creek Ferries dock at Heritage Harbour.

This museum houses the RCMP Arctic patrol vessel *St. Roch,* the first ship to traverse its way back and forth through the northwest passage. Tours of the *St. Roch* are particularly popular with children—they get to clamber around the boat poking and prodding stuff. The other half of the museum holds intricate ship models, antique wood and brass fittings, maps, prints, and a number of permanent exhibits including "Pirates!," a treasure chest of an exhibit filled with pirate lore, artifacts, a Jolly Roger, pieces of eight, and a miniature ship where kids can dress up and play pirate for the day.

Vancouver Museum. 1100 Chestnut St., in Vanier Park. ☎ **604/736-4431.** www. vanmuseum.bc.ca. Admission C$9 (US$6) adults, C$6 (US$3.65) youths. Group rates available. Daily 10am–5pm; closed Mon Sept–June. Bus: 22, then walk 3 blocks south on Cornwall Ave. Boat: Granville Island Ferry to Heritage Harbour.

Opened in 1894, the Vancouver Museum is dedicated to amassing evidence of the city's history, from its days as a Native settlement and European outpost to its early– 20th-century maturation into a modern urban center. The exhibits allow you to walk through the steerage deck of a 19th-century passenger ship, peek into a Hudson's Bay Company frontier trading post, or take a seat in an 1880s Canadian-Pacific Railway passenger car. Re-creations of Victorian and Edwardian rooms show how early Vancouverites decorated their homes. Rotating exhibits include a display of the museum's collection of neon signage.

Pacific Space Centre. 1100 Chestnut St., in Vanier Park. ☎ **604/738-STAR.** www. pacific-space-centre.bc.ca. Admission C$12 (US$8) adults, C$10 (US$6) seniors/youths 11–16, C$8 (US$5) children 5–10, C$4 (US$2.65) children under 5; C$38 (US$25) families (up to 5, maximum 2 adults). Extra family member C$8 (US$5). Extra Virtual Voyages experiences C$4 (US$2.65) each. Open daily 10am–5pm (to 8pm Fri); holidays (except Christmas) 10am–5pm. Bus: 22.

In the same building as the Vancouver Museum (above), the space center and observatory offers hands-on displays and exhibits that'll delight both kids and amateur astronomy, space, science, and computer buffs. In the Virtual Voyages Simulator you can go on a voyage to Mars or collide with an oncoming comet. In the interactive

Cosmic Courtyard, you can look at an Apollo 17 manned-satellite engine, try your hand at designing a spacecraft, or maneuver a lunar robot.

✪ Museum of Anthropology. 6393 NW Marine Dr. ☎ **604/822-3825.** Admission C$6 (US$4) adults, C$3.50 (US$2.35) seniors/students, C$15 (US$10) families; children under 6 free. Free Tues after 5pm. Mid-May to Sept Wed–Mon 10am–5pm, Tues 10am–9pm; Oct to mid-May Wed–Sun 11am–5pm, Tues 11am–9pm. Closed Dec 25–26. Bus: 4 or 10.

This isn't just any old museum. In 1976, architect Arthur Erikson re-created a classic Native post-and-beam structure out of modern concrete and glass to house one of the world's finest collections of West Coast native art. Haida artist Bill Reid's masterpiece, *Raven and the First Men,* is worth the price of admission all by itself. The huge carving in glowing yellow cedar depicts a Haida creation myth, in which Raven (the trickster) coaxes humanity out into the world from their birthplace in a clamshell. Some of Reid's creations in gold and silver are also on display. Don't forget to take a walk around the grounds behind the museum. Overlooking Point Grey are two longhouses built according to the Haida tribal style and 10 hand-carved totem poles.

GASTOWN & CHINATOWN

✪ Dr. Sun-Yat-sen Classical Garden. 578 Carrall St. ☎ **604/689-7133.** C$7 (US$4.35) adults, C$5 (US$3.35) seniors, C$4 (US$2.65) children/students. June 15–Sept 15 daily 9:30am–7pm; Sept 16–June 14 daily 10am–6pm. Bus 4 or 7.

The Classical Garden was built in the Suzhou province of northern China around 1492 and relocated to Vancouver just in time for Expo '86. It was packed in 950 crates, and 52 artisans took nearly 10 years to completely reassemble it, replant it, and stock it with turtles and ornamental carp. This serenely beautiful garden is the only one of its kind in the western hemisphere.

✪ Vancouver Centennial Police Museum. 240 E. Cordova St. ☎ **604/665-3346.** www.city.vancouver.bc.ca/police/museum. Admission C$5 (US$3.35) adults, C$3 (US$2) students/seniors; under 6 free. Year-round Mon–Fri 9am–3pm; May–Aug Sat 10am–3pm. Bus: 4 or 7.

This is a bizarre, macabre, and utterly delightful little museum, dedicated to memorializing some of the best crimes and crime stoppers in the city's short but colorful history. Housed in the old Vancouver Coroner's Court—where actor Errol Flynn was autopsied after dropping dead in the arms of a 17-year-old girl—the museum features photos, text, and vintage equipment from the files and evidence room of Vancouver's finest.

THE NORTH SHORE

Capilano Suspension Bridge & Park. 3735 Capilano Rd., North Vancouver. ☎ **604/985-7474.** www.capbridge.com. Admission C$11 (US$7) adults, C$9 (US$6) seniors, C$6 (US$4.25) students, C$3.25 (US$2.15) children 6–12; children under 6 free. Winter discounts. May–Sept daily 8:30am–dusk; Oct–Apr daily 9am–5pm. Closed Dec 25. Bus: 246 from downtown Vancouver, 236 from Lonsdale Quay SeaBus terminal.

Vancouver's first and oldest tourist trap (built in 1889), this attraction still works, mostly because there's still something inherently thrilling about standing on a narrow shaking walkway, 230 feet above the canyon floor, held up by nothing but a pair of miserable cables. In addition to the bridge, there are a carving center where native carvers show their skill, an exhibit explaining the region's natural history, a pair of restaurants, and a gift shop.

Grouse Mountain Resort. 6400 Nancy Greene Way, North Vancouver. ☎ **604/984-0661.** www.grousemountain. SkyRide C$17 (US$11) adults, C$15 (US$10) seniors, C$11 (US$7) youths, C$6 (US$4) children 6–12; under 6 free. SkyRide free with advance Grouse

Nest restaurant reservation. Daily 10am–10pm. SeaBus: Lonsdale Quay, then transfer to bus 236.

Once a small local ski hill, Grouse has been slowly developing itself into a year-round mountain recreation park, offering impressive views and instantaneous access to the North Shore mountains. Only a 20-minute drive from downtown, the SkyRide gondola transports you to the mountain's 3,700-foot summit in about 10 minutes. At the top is a bar, a restaurant, a large-screen theater, a ski and snowboard area, hiking and snowshoeing trails, a skating pond, a children's snow park, forest interpretive trails, a logger sports show, helicopter tours, mountain-bike trails, and a native feast house. Some of these are free with your SkyRide ticket, most aren't, but the view is free, and it's one of the best around.

PARKS & GARDENS

For general information about Vancouver's parks, call ☎ **604/257-8400.**

Stanley Park is a 1,000-acre rain forest near the busy West End. It's named after the same Lord Stanley whose name is synonymous with professional hockey success—the Stanley Cup. The park is filled with towering western red cedar trees, placid lagoons, walking trails, manicured lawns, and flower gardens. Stanley Park houses the Vancouver Aquarium, a petting zoo, three restaurants, a handful of snack bars, cricket greens, a pool, a miniature railway, and a water park. It also boasts abundant wildlife, including beavers, coyotes, bald eagles, raccoons, geese, ducks, and skunks, as well as pristine natural settings and amazing marine views.

In Chinatown, the **Dr. Sun-Yat-sen Classical Garden** is a small, tranquil oasis in the heart of the city (see entry above). On the West Side, **Queen Elizabeth Park** at Cambie Street and West 33rd Avenue sits atop a 500-foot-high extinct volcano and is the highest urban Vancouver vantage point south of downtown, offering panoramic views in all directions. It's Vancouver's most popular location for wedding-photo sessions, with well-manicured gardens and a profusion of colorful flora. The **Bloedel Conservatory** (☎ **604/257-8570**) stands next to the park's huge sunken garden, an amazing reclamation of an abandoned rock quarry. A 140-foot-high domed structure with a commanding 360° view, the conservatory houses a tropical rain forest with more than 100 plant species, as well as free-flying tropical birds. Admission is C$3 (US$2) adults and C$1.50 (US$1) seniors/children.

Nearby is the **VanDusen Botanical Garden,** 5251 Oak St., at 37th Avenue (☎ **604/878-9274**). Formerly the Shaughnessy Golf Course, the 55-acre formal garden features rolling lawns, lakes, Elizabethan hedge mazes, and marble sculptures. Admission is C$6 (US$3.65) adults, C$2.75 (US$1.85) seniors/students/children, and C$11 (US$8) families. Off-season admission is usually less. The garden opens daily at 10am but closes between 6 and 8pm, depending on the time of year.

The University of British Columbia campus incorporates a number of parks and gardens. Established nearly a century ago, the **UBC Botanical Garden,** 6250 Stadium Rd., Gate 8 (☎ **604/822-9666**), has 70 acres of formal alpine, herb, and exotic plantings. Nearby is the **Nitobe Memorial Garden,** 6565 NW Marine Dr., Gate 4 (☎ **604/822-6038**), a traditional Japanese garden. March 7 to October 4, both are open daily 10am to 6pm; October 5 to March 6, the Botanical Garden is open daily during daylight hours and the Nitobe Memorial Garden is open Monday to Friday about 10am to 2:30pm. Admission to the Botanical Garden is C$4.50 (US$3) adults and C$1.75 (US$1.15) seniors; admission for Nitobe Memorial Garden is C$2.50 (US$1.65) adults and C$1.50 (US$1) seniors. A dual pass for both is C$6 (US$3.85) adults. Out near UBC, **Pacific Spirit Park** (usually called the **Endowment Lands**) comprises 1,885 acres of temperate rain forest, marshes, and beaches and includes nearly 22 miles of trails suitable for hiking, riding, mountain biking, and beachcombing.

Across the Lions Gate Bridge are six provincial parks that delight outdoor enthusiasts year-round. The publicly maintained **Capilano River Regional Park,** 4500 Capilano Rd. (☎ 604/666-1790), surrounds the Capilano Suspension Bridge and Park. Hikers can follow the river for 4½ miles down the well-maintained **Capilano trails** to the Burrard Inlet and the Lions Gate Bridge, or about a mile upstream to **Cleveland Dam,** which serves as the launching point for whitewater kayakers and canoeists. The **Capilano Salmon Hatchery,** on Capilano Road (☎ 604/666-1790), is on the river's east bank about a quarter-mile below the Cleveland Dam. Approximately 2 million coho and Chinook salmon are hatched annually in glass-fronted tanks connected to the river by a series of channels. Admission is free, and the hatchery is open daily 8am to 7pm (to 4pm in winter).

ESPECIALLY FOR KIDS

Pick up copies of the free monthly newspapers *BC Parent,* 4479 W. 10th Ave. (☎ 604/221-0366), and *West Coast Families,* 81551 Johnston St. (☎ 604/ 689-1331). *West Coast Families'* centerfold "Fun in the City" and event calendar list everything currently going on, including IMAX and Omnimax shows and free children's programs. Both publications are available at Granville Island's Kids Only Market and at neighborhood community centers throughout the city.

Stanley Park offers a number of attractions for children. The **Stanley Park's Children's Farm** (☎ 604/257-8530) has peacocks, rabbits, calves, donkeys, and Shetland ponies. Next to the petting zoo is Stanley Park's **Miniature Railway** (☎ 604/ 257-8531). The diminutive steam locomotive with passenger cars runs on a circuit through the woods, carrying nearly as many passengers annually as all the Alaska-bound cruise ships combined. Also in Stanley Park, the **Vancouver Aquarium** has sea otters, sea lions, whales, and numerous other marine creatures, as well as many exhibits geared toward children (see above).

Right in town, **Science World** is a hands-on kids' museum where budding scientists can get their hands into everything. And at the **Vancouver Maritime Museum,** kids can dress up like a pirate or a naval captain for a day or board the RCMP icebreaker *St. Roch* (see above for both). **Granville Island's Kids Only Market,** 1496 Cartwright St. (☎ 604/689-8447), offers playrooms and 21 shops filled with toys, books, records, clothes, and food. Kids will also love taking the Aquabus or Granville Island Ferry to get there.

Across Burrard Inlet on the North Shore, **Maplewood Farm,** 405 Seymour River Place, North Vancouver (☎ 604/929-5610), has more than 200 barnyard animals living on its 5-acre farm, open daily year-round. The farm also offers pony rides. Three-quarters of an hour east of the city, the **Greater Vancouver Zoological Center,** 5048-264th St., Aldergrove (☎ 604/856-6825), is a lush 120-acre farm filled with lions, tigers, jaguars, ostriches, elephants, buffalo, elk, antelope, zebras, giraffes, a rhino, hippos, and camels. And the **Burnaby Heritage Village and Carousel,** 6501 Deer Lake Ave., Burnaby (☎ 604/293-6501), is a 9-acre re-creation of the Victorian era. You can walk along boardwalk streets among costumed townspeople, watch a blacksmith pounding horseshoes, shop in a general store, ride a vintage carousel, and visit an ice-cream parlor that's been at the same location since the early 1900s.

Athletic kids can work up a sweat at the Participation Gallery in the **B.C. Sports Hall of Fame and Museum** (see above), where they can run, jump, climb, race, throw fastballs, and attempt to beat world records. At **Granville Island's Water Park and**

Adventure Playground, 1496 Cartwright St., kids can really let loose with movable water guns and sprinklers. They can also have fun on the water slides or in the wading pool. The facilities are open in summer daily 10am to 6pm. Admission is free; changing facilities are nearby at the False Creek Community Center (☎ 604/257-8195).

6 Special Events & Festivals

The first event of the year is the annual New Year's Day **Polar Bear Swim** at English Bay Beach; thousands of hardy citizens show up in elaborate costumes to take a dip in the icy waters of English Bay. On the second Sunday in January, the **Annual Bald Eagle Count** takes place in Brackendale. The count starts at the **Brackendale Art Gallery** (☎ 604/898-3333).

In late February, the **Chinese New Year** is celebrated with 2 weeks of firecrackers, dancing dragon parades, and other festivities. The **International Wine Festival** in March is a major wine-tasting event featuring the latest international vintages. Each winery sets up a booth where you may try as many varieties as you like. The **Vancouver Sun Run,** in April, is Canada's biggest 10K race, featuring 17,000 runners, joggers, and walkers who race through 10 scenic kilometers. The run starts and finishes at B.C. Place Stadium.

The June **International Children's Festival** features plays and music; it's held in Vanier Park on False Creek. For information, call ☎ 640/708-5655. The **VanDusen Flower and Garden Show,** at the VanDusen Botanical Garden, 5251 Oak St. (☎ 604/878-9274), is Vancouver's premier flora gala. The late-June **Alcan Dragon Boat Festival** features more than 150 local and international teams racing huge dragon boats. Four stages of music, dance, and Chinese acrobatics also take place as part of the events at the **Plaza of Nations** (☎ 604/688-2382).

During the July **DuMaurier International Jazz Festival** (☎ 604/872-5200), more than 800 international jazz and blues players perform at 25 venues around town. Running July to September, the **Bard on the Beach Shakespeare Festival** in Vanier Park (☎ 604/739-0559) presents Shakespeare's plays in a tent overlooking English Bay. On **Canada Day,** July 1, Canada Place Pier hosts an all-day celebration including music and dance and an evening fireworks display over the harbor to top off the entertainment. The second or third weekend in July brings the **Vancouver Folk Music Festival** (☎ 604/602-9798). International folk music is played outdoors at Jericho Beach Park. During the ✪ **Benson & Hedges Symphony of Fire,** three international fireworks companies compete for a coveted title by launching their best displays timed to explode in time to accompanying music over English Bay Beach. Don't miss the grand finale on the fourth night.

Mid-August to Labour Day, the **Pacific National Exhibition** (☎ 604/253-2311) offers everything from big-name entertainment to a demolition derby, livestock demonstrations, logger sports competitions, fashion shows, and North America's finest all-wooden roller coaster. On the Labour Day weekend, the **Molson Indy** (☎ 604/684-4639) roars around the streets of False Creek, attracting more than 500,000 spectators. Later in September, the **Vancouver's Fringe Festival** (☎ 604/257-0350) highlights the best of Vancouver's independent theater.

Every October, the **Vancouver International Film Festival** (☎ 604/685-0260) features 250 new works, revivals, and retrospectives, representing filmmakers from 40 countries. All December, the **Christmas Carol Ship Parade** lights up Vancouver Harbour, as harbor cruise ships decorated with colorful Christmas lights sail around English Bay, while on-board guests sip cider and sing Christmas Carols.

7 Outdoor Activities & Spectator Sports

Just about every imaginable sport has a world-class outlet within the Vancouver city limits. Downhill and cross-country skiing, snowshoeing, sea kayaking, fly-fishing, diving, hiking, paragliding, and mountain biking are just a few of the options. Activities that can't really be practiced in metropolitan Vancouver, but can be done close by, include rock climbing, river rafting, and heli-skiing.

OUTDOOR ACTIVITIES

BEACHES   A great place for viewing sunsets, **English Bay Beach** lies at the end of Davie Street off Denman Street and Beach Avenue. South of English Bay Beach near the Burrard Street Bridge and the Vancouver Aquatic Centre is **Sunset Beach.** On **Stanley Park's** western rim, **Second Beach** is a quick stroll north from English Bay Beach. A playground, a snack bar, and an immense heated freshwater pool make this a convenient spot for families. Farther along the seawall lies secluded **Third Beach,** due north of Stanley Park Drive. At **Kitsilano Beach,** along Ogden Street, a heated saltwater pool is open in summer for people who don't enjoy the rather-bracing ocean temperatures. Farther west along Point Grey Road is **Jericho Beach,** followed by **Locarno Beach** and **Spanish Banks.** Below UBC's Museum of Anthropology, **Wreck Beach** is Vancouver's immensely popular nude beach. At the northern foot of the Lions Gate Bridge, **Ambleside Park** is a popular North Shore spot.

BICYCLING & MOUNTAIN BIKING   Helmets are legally required for cyclists, both off-road and on. Marked cycle lanes traverse Vancouver, including the cross-town Off-Broadway route, the Adanac route, and the Ontario route. One of the city's most scenic cycle paths has been extended and now runs all the way from Canada Place Pier to Pacific Spirit Park. Cycling maps are available at most bicycle retailers and rental outlets.

Local mountain bikers love the cross-country ski trails on **Hollyburn Mountain** in Cypress Provincial Park. Mount Seymour's very steep **Good Samaritan Trail** connects to the Baden-Powell Trail and the Bridle Path near Mount Seymour Road. Closer to downtown, both **Pacific Spirit Park** and **Burnaby Mountain** offer excellent beginner and intermediate off-road trails.

Rentals run around C$4 (US$2.65) for a one-speed "Cruiser" to C$10 (US$7) for a top-of-the-line mountain bike per hour or C$15 to C$40 (US$10 to US$27) per day. Bikes, helmets, locks, and child trailers are available by the hour or day at **Spokes Bicycle Rentals & Espresso Bar,** 1798 W. Georgia St. (☎ 604/688-5141; Bus: 23, 35). **Bayshore Bicycle and Rollerblade Rentals,** 745 Denman St. (☎ 604/688-2453; Bus: 5), and 1601 W. Georgia St. (☎ 604/689-5071; Bus: 23, 35), rents 21-speed mountain bikes, bike carriers, tandems, city bikes, and kids' bikes.

BOATING   You can find rentals of 15- to 17-foot powerboats for as little as a few hours or up to several weeks at **Stanley Park Boat Rentals Ltd.,** Coal Harbor Marina (☎ 604/682-6257; Bus: 23, 35). **Granville Island Boat Rentals, Ltd.,** 1696 Duranleau St., Granville Island (☎ 604/682-6287; Bus: 50), features hourly, daily, and weekly rentals of 15- to 19-foot speedboats and also offers sportfishing, cruising, and sightseeing charters. Rates on all the above begin at around C$30 (US$20) per hour and C$135 (US$90) per day for a sport boat that holds four. **Delta Charters,** 3500 Cessna Dr., Richmond (☎ 604/273-4211 or 800/661-7762; Bus: 100), has weekly and monthly rates for 32- to 58-foot powered craft. Prices begin around C$1,400 (US$934) per week for a boat sleeping four.

CANOEING & KAYAKING   Both placid, urban False Creek and the incredibly beautiful 19-mile North Vancouver fjord known as Indian Arm have launching points you can reach by car or bus. Rentals range from C$7 (US$4.65) per hour to C$32 (US$21) per day for kayaks and about C$25 (US$17) per day for canoes. Customized tours range from C$70 to C$110 (US$47 to US$73) per person. **Adventure Fitness,** 1510 Duranleau St. on Granville Island (☎ **604/687-1528;** Bus: 50), rents canoes and kayaks, offers lessons, and has a cool showroom filled with outdoor gear. In North Vancouver, **Deep Cove Canoe and Kayak Rentals,** Deep Cove (☎ **604/929-2268;** Bus: 240), offers an easy starting point for anyone planning an Indian Arm run. It offers hourly and daily rentals of canoes and kayaks, as well as lessons and customized tours. **Lotus Land Tours,** 2005-1251 Cardero St. (☎ **800/528-3531** or 604/684-4922; Bus: 5), runs guided kayak tours on Indian Arm, complete with transportation to and from Vancouver, a barbecue salmon lunch, and incredible scenery. One-day tours cost C$130 (US$87).

DIVING   BC's underwater scenery is stunning, but the water is chilly. Most local divers use dry suits. Cates Park in Deep Cove, Whytecliff Park and Porteau Cover near Horseshoe Bay, and Lighthouse Park are nearby dive spots. **The Diving Locker,** 2745 W. 4th Ave. (☎ **604/736-2681;** Bus: 4), rents equipment and offers courses and lots of free advice. Rentals cost around C$50 (US$33) per day or C$63 (US$42) with a second tank included; hiring a dive master to accompany you costs about C$60 (US$40) per dive, and a seat on a weekend dive boat runs about C$69 (US$46) per dive.

ECOTOURS   **Rockwood Adventures,** 1330 Fulton Ave. (☎ **604/926-7705**), offers guided hikes of the north shore rain forest, complete with a trained naturalist and a gourmet lunch. Tours cover Capilano Canyon, Bowen Island, or Lighthouse Park and cost C$75 (US$50). Pickups are at major hotels downtown.

FISHING   Five species of salmon, rainbow and Dolly Varden trout, steelhead, and even sturgeon abound in the local waters. To fish, you need a nonresident saltwater or freshwater license. **Hanson's Fishing Outfitters,** 102-580 Hornby St. (☎ **604/684-8988** or 684-8998; Bus: 22), and **Granville Island Boat Rentals,** 1696 Duranleau St. (☎ **604/682-6287;** Bus: 50), are outstanding outfitters as well as sources for tackle and licenses. Licenses for freshwater fishing are C$16 (US$11) for 1 day or C$32 (US$21) for 8 days. Saltwater fishing licenses cost C$8 (US$5) for 1 day, C$20 (US$13) for 3 days, and C$39 (US$26) for 5 days.

Bonnie Lee Fishing Charters Ltd., on the dock at the entrance to Granville Island, (mailing address: 744 W. King Edward Ave., Vancouver, BC V5Z 2C8; ☎ **604/ 290-7447;** Bus: 50), is another reputable outfitter. **Corcovado Yacht Charters Ltd.,** 1696 Duranleau St., Granville Island (☎ **604/669-7907;** Bus: 50), has competitive rates. *The Vancouver Sun* prints a daily **fishing report** in the B section that details which fish are in season and where they can be found.

GOLF   This is a year-round Vancouver sport. The public **University Golf Club,** 5185 University Blvd. (☎ **604/224-1818;** Bus: 4), is a great 6,560-yard, par-71 course with a clubhouse, a pro shop, locker rooms, a bar and grill, a sports lounge, and a 280-car parking lot. Or call **A-1 Last Minute Golf Hot Line** at ☎ **800/684-6344** or 604/878-1833 for substantial discounts and short-notice tee times at more than 30 Vancouver-area courses.

HIKING   Good trail maps are available from the **Greater Vancouver Regional Parks District** (☎ **604/432-6350**) and from **International Travel Maps and**

Books, 552 Seymour St. (☎ **604/687-3320;** Bus: 4), which also stocks guidebooks and topographical maps. If you're looking for a challenge without the time commitment, hike the aptly named **Grouse Grind** from the bottom of Grouse Mountain to the top, then buy a one-way ticket down on the Grouse Mountain SkyRide gondola. The one-way fare is C$5 (US$3.35) per person.

Lynn Canyon Park, Lynn Headwaters Regional Park, Capilano River Regional Park, Mount Seymour Provincial Park, Pacific Spirit Park, and Cypress Provincial Park have good easy-to-challenging trails that wind up through stands of Douglas fir and cedar and contain a few serious switchbacks. Pay attention to the trail warnings posted at the parks; some have bear habitats. Golden Ears, in Golden Ears Provincial Park, and The Lions, in West Vancouver, are for seriously fit hikers.

ICE SKATING   November to early April, Robson Square has free skating on a covered rink directly under Robson Street between Howe and Hornby streets (Bus: 5). Rentals are available in the adjacent concourse. The **West End Community Centre,** 870 Denman St. (☎ **604/257-8333;** Bus: 5), also rents skates at its enclosed rink, open October to March. The enormous **Ice Sports Centre,** 6501 Sprott, Burnaby (☎ **604/291-0626;** Bus: 110), is the Vancouver Canucks' official practice facility. It has eight rinks, is open year-round, and offers lessons and rentals.

IN-LINE SKATING   You'll find locals rolling along beach paths, streets, park paths, and promenades. If you didn't bring a pair of blades, try **Bayshore Bicycle and Rollerblade Rentals,** 745 Denman St. (☎ **604/688-2453;** Bus: 23, 35). Rentals generally run C$5 (US$3.35) per hour, with a 2-hour minimum, or C$15 (US$10) per day or overnight.

JOGGING   You'll find fellow runners traversing Stanley Park's **Seawall Promenade,** where the scenery is spectacular and cars aren't allowed.

RAFTING   A 2½-hour drive from Vancouver on the wild Nahatlatch River, **Reo Rafting,** 355-535 Thurlow St., Vancouver (☎ **800/736-7238;** www.reorafting.com; Bus: 4), offers some of the best guided white-water trips in the province at a reasonable price. One-day packages including breakfast, lunch, all your gear, and 4 to 5 hours on the river start at C$99 (US$66). Multiday trips and group packages are also available.

SAILING   **Cooper Boating Center,** 1620 Duranleau St. (☎ **604/687-4110;** Bus: 50), offers cruises, boat rentals, and sail instruction packages on 21- to 46-foot boats. Prices vary widely, from C$150 (US$100) for a 3-hour lesson to C$4,000 (US$2,668) or more for a week charter. Call for details.

SKIING & SNOWBOARDING   It seldom snows in the city's downtown and central areas, but Vancouverites can ski before work and after dinner at the three ski resorts in the North Shore mountains.

The **Grouse Mountain Resort,** 6400 Nancy Greene Way, North Vancouver (☎ **604/984-0661;** snow report 604/986-6262; Bus: 241), has four chairs, two beginner tows, and two T-bars to take you to 22 alpine runs. There's also a 300-foot half pipe for snowboarders. Full-day lift tickets are C$29 (US$19) adults, C$22 (US$15) youth 13 to 18, and C$16 (US$11) children 7 to 12; children under 7 are free. **Mount Seymour Provincial Park,** 1700 Mt. Seymour Rd., North Vancouver (☎ **604/986-2261;** snow report 604/986-3999), has the area's highest base elevation; it's accessible via four chairs and a tow. Lift tickets are C$18 (US$12) adults/children. A shuttle bus to Mt. Seymour departs daily from Rogers Avenue in Lonsdale Quay (accessible via SeaBus). On weekdays, the bus departs at 3:30 and 5:30pm, with return trips leaving at 4:30, 6:30, 8:30, and 10pm. On weekends and holidays, departures are at 8:30am, 10:30am, 12:30pm, 3pm, and 5pm, with return trips at 11:30am,

1:30pm, 4pm, 6pm, 8pm, and 10pm. The trip takes about 50 minutes one-way. Round-trip fares are C$7 (US$4.60) adults and C$5 (US$3.35) students/youth/seniors; one-way fares are C$4 (US$2.65) adults and C$3 (US$2) students/youth/seniors. **Cypress Bowl,** 1610 Mt. Seymour Rd. (☎ **604/926-5612;** snow report 604/419-7669), has the area's longest vertical drop (1,750 ft.), challenging ski and snowboard runs, and 10 miles of track-set cross-country skiing trails. Full-day lift tickets are C$35 (US$23) adults, C$29 (US$19) youth 13 to 18, C$17 (US$11) children 5 to 12, and C$2 (US$1.35) children under 5. A shuttle bus to Cypress departs daily from Lonsdale Quay (accessible via SeaBus). Departures are every 2 hours 7:15am to 5:15pm. The bus returns from the Cypress alpine area every 2 hours 12:15pm to 10:15pm, with the last departure at 11pm. A round-trip costs C$7 (US$4.65) adults and C$5 (US$3.35) youth; a one-way trip is C$5 (US$3.35) adults and $C3 (US$2) youth.

SWIMMING   Vancouver's midsummer saltwater temperature rarely exceeds 65°F (18°C). Some swimmers opt for fresh- and saltwater pools at city beaches (see "Beaches," above). Others take to indoor pools, including the **Vancouver Aquatic Centre,** 1050 Beach Ave. at the foot of Thurlow Street (☎ **604/665-3424;** Bus: 22); the **YWCA fitness center,** 535 Hornby St. (☎ **604/895-5777;** Bus: 22); and **UBC's Aquatic Centre,** 2075 Wesbrook Mall (☎ **604/822-4521;** Bus: 4, 7, or 10).

TENNIS   Vancouver maintains 180 outdoor hard courts that have a 1-hour limit and accommodate patrons on a first-come, first-served basis 8am to dusk. With the exception of the Beach Avenue courts, which charge a nominal fee, all city courts are free. **Stanley Park** has four courts near Lost Lagoon and 17 courts near the Beach Avenue entrance, next to the Fish House Restaurant. **Queen Elizabeth Park**'s 18 courts service the central Vancouver area, and **Kitsilano Beach Park**'s 10 courts service the beach area between Vanier Park and the UBC campus (Bus: 22). You can play at night at the **Langara Campus** of Vancouver Community College, on West 49th Avenue between Main and Cambie streets (Bus: 15). The **UBC Coast Club,** on Thunderbird Boulevard (☎ **604/822-2505;** Bus: 4), has 10 outdoor and 4 indoor courts. Indoor courts are C$10 (US$7) per hour, plus C$3 (US$2) per person; outdoor courts are C$3 (US$2) per person.

WILDLIFE WATCHING   During winter, thousands of ✪ **bald eagles** line the banks of **Indian Arm fjord** and the **Squamish, Cheakamus,** and **Mamquam** rivers to feed on spawning salmon (see chapter 16). The official January 1994 eagle count in Brackendale (a small community near Squamish) recorded 3,700—the largest number ever seen in North America. The annual summer salmon runs attract more than bald eagles. Tourists also flock to coastal streams and rivers to watch the waters turn red with leaping coho and sockeye. The salmon are plentiful at the **Capilano Salmon Hatchery** (see "Parks & Gardens," above), **Adams River** (see chapter 16), **Goldstream Provincial Park** (see chapter 16), and numerous other fresh waters.

Along the Fraser River delta, more than 250 bird species migrate to or perennially inhabit the **George C. Reifel Sanctuary's** wetland reserve. Nearby **Richmond Nature Park** has educational displays for young and first-time birders plus a boardwalk-encircled duck pond. **Stanley Park** and **Pacific Spirit Park** are both home to a heron rookery. You can see these large birds nesting just outside the Vancouver Aquarium. Ravens, dozens of species of waterfowl, raccoons, skunks, beavers, and even coyotes are also full-time residents.

WINDSURFING   Windsurfing isn't allowed at the mouth of False Creek near Granville Island, but you can bring a board to Jericho and English Bay beaches or rent one there. Equipment sales, rentals (including wet suits), and instruction can be found at **Windsure Windsurfing School,** 1300 Discovery St., at Jericho Beach (☎ **604/ 224-0615;** Bus: 4). Rentals start at C$17 (US$11) per hour.

SPECTATOR SPORTS

You can get schedule information on all major events at the **Vancouver Tourist Info Centre,** 200 Burrard St. (☎ **604/683-2000;** Bus: 22).

BASKETBALL   The **Grizzlies** currently play at **General Motors Place Stadium,** 800 Griffith Way (☎ **604/899-7469;** event hotline 604/899-7444; Bus: 2). At the completion of the 1999/2000 season, however, they're expected to be moved to St. Louis. Tickets run C$13 to C$89 (US$9 to US$59).

FOOTBALL   The Canadian Football League's **B.C. Lions** (☎ **604/930-5466**) play in the 60,000-seat **B.C. Place Stadium,** 777 Pacific Blvd. S. (Bus: 2). Tickets run C$25 to C$47 (US$17 to US$31).

HOCKEY   The National Hockey League's **Vancouver Canucks** play at **General Motors Place,** 800 Griffith Way (☎ **604/899-4600;** event hotline 604/899-7444; Bus: 2). Tickets are C$26 to C$95 (US$17 to US$63).

HORSE RACING   Mid-April to October, thoroughbreds run at **Hastings Park Racecourse,** Exhibition Park, East Hastings and Cassiar streets (☎ **604/254-1631;** www.hastingspark.com; Bus: 10).

SOCCER   The American Professional Soccer League's **Vancouver 86ers** (☎ **604/ 930-5466**) play at **Swangard Stadium,** at Boundary Road and Kingsway in Burnaby (☎ **604/435-7121;** Bus: 19). Admission is normally C$15 to C$25 (US$10 to US$17).

8 Shopping

Blessed with a climate that seems semitropical in comparison to that of the rest of Canada, Vancouverites tend to do their shopping on the street, browsing from one window to the next on the lookout for something new. **Robson Street** is the spot for high-end fashions. The 10-block stretch of **Granville Street** from 6th Avenue up to 16th Avenue is were Vancouver's old-money comes to shop for classic men's and women's fashions, housewares, and furniture. **Water Street** in Gastown features knickknacks, antiques, cutting-edge furniture, First Nations art, and funky basement retro shops. **Main Street** from 19th Avenue to 27th Avenue means antiques and lots of 'em. **Granville Island,** a rehabilitated industrial site beneath the Granville Street Bridge, is one of the best places to pick up salmon and other seafood. It's also a great place to browse for crafts and gifts.

SHOPPING A TO Z

ANTIQUES   The **Vancouver Antique Centre,** 422 Richards St. (☎ **604/ 669-7444;** Bus: 20), contains 15 shops, specializing in everything from china, glass, Orientalia, and jewelry to military objects, sports, toys, and watches. **Uno Langmann Ltd.,** 2117 Granville St. (☎ **604/736-8825;** Bus: 4), caters to upscale shoppers, specializing in European and North American paintings, furniture, and silver.

BOOKS   Since 1957, the locally owned chain **Duthie Books,** 2239 W. 4th Ave., Kitsilano (☎ **604/732-5344;** Bus: 4), has been synonymous with good books in Vancouver. On Granville Island, **Blackberry Books,** 1663 Duranleau St. (☎ **604/ 685-4113;** Bus: 50), stocks books about art, architecture, and fine cuisine, as well as a wide variety of more general categories. **Chapters,** 788 Robson St. (☎ **604/ 682-4066;** Bus: 5), is pleasant and well planned, with little nooks and comfy benches in which to browse at length; there are other locations around town. **Little Sister's Book & Art Emporium,** 1238 Davie St. (☎ 604/669-1753; Bus: 1), is the West End bookstore with the largest selection of lesbian, gay, bisexual, and transgender books, videos, and magazines. **International Travel Maps,** 552 Seymour St. (☎ 604/687-3320; Bus: 4), has the best selection of travel books, maps, charts, and globes.

DEPARTMENT STORES   From the establishment of its early trading posts during the 1670s to its modern coast-to-coast chain, **The Bay (Hudson's Bay Company),** 674 Granville St. (☎ 604/681-6211; Bus: 4), has built its reputation on quality goods. You can still buy a Hudson's Bay woolen "point" blanket (the colorful stripes originally represented how many beaver pelts each blanket was worth in trade), but you'll also find wares from Tommy Hilfiger, Polo, DKNY, Ellen Tracy, Anne Klein II, and Liz Claiborne.

FASHION   International designer outlets in Vancouver include **Chanel Boutique,** 103-755 Burrard St. (☎ 604/682-0522; Bus: 22); **Salvatore Ferragamo,** 918 Robson St. (☎ 604/669-4495; Bus: 5); **Gianni Versace Boutique,** 757 W. Hastings St. (☎ 604/683-1131; Bus: 4); **Versace's Versus,** 1008 W. Georgia St. (☎ 604/688-8938; Bus: 22); **Polo/Ralph Lauren,** The Landing, 375 Water St. (☎ 604/682-7656; Bus: 1); and **Plaza Escada,** Sinclair Centre, 757 W. Hastings St. (☎ 604/688-8558; Bus: 4).

For something uniquely West Coast, don't miss the one-of-a-kind First Nations designs of **Dorothy Grant,** 250-757 W. Hastings St. (☎ 604/681-0201; Bus: 4). Grant's exquisitely detailed Haida motifs are appliquéd onto coats, leather vests, jackets, caps, and accessories. The clothes are gorgeous and collectible. **Dream,** 311 W. Cordova (☎ 604/683-7326; Bus: 1), is one of the few places to find the early collections of local designers. **Zonda Nellis Design Ltd.,** 2203 Granville St. (☎ 604/736-5668; Bus: 4), offers imaginative handwoven separates, sweaters, vests, soft knits, and a new line of hand-painted silks.

FIRST NATIONS ART   You'll find First Nations art in abundance. **Images for a Canadian Heritage,** 164 Water St. (☎ 604/685-7046; Bus: 1), is a government-licensed First Nations art gallery, featuring traditional and contemporary works. The **Leona Lattimer Gallery,** 1590 W. 2nd Ave. (☎ 604/732-4556; Bus: 4), presents museum-quality displays of ceremonial masks, totem poles, argillite sculptures, and gold and silver jewelry, at a more affordable price than galleries downtown.

FOOD   At **Chocolate Arts,** 2037 W. 4th Ave. (☎ 604/739-0475; Bus: 4), the works are of such exquisite craftsmanship that they're sometimes a wrench to eat. Look for the all-chocolate diorama in the window—it changes every month or so. **Murchie's Tea & Coffee,** 970 Robson St. (☎ 604/669-0783; Bus: 5), is a Vancouver institution. You'll find everything from Jamaican Blue Mountain and Kona coffees to Lapsing, Souchong, and Kemun teas. **The Lobsterman,** 1807 Mast Tower Rd. (☎ 604/687-4531; Bus: 50), is one of the city's best spots to pick up seafood. Salmon and other seafood can be packed for air travel. And the **Salmon Village,** 779 Thurlow St. (☎ 604/685-3378; Bus: 4), specializes in salmon of all varieties.

GIFTS   For a good range of basic souvenirs, try **Canadian Impressions at the Station,** 601 Cordova St. (☎ 604/681-3507; Bus: 1). The store carries lumberjack shirts, Cowichan sweaters, T-shirts, and other trinkets.

JEWELRY   Opened in 1879, **Henry Birk & Sons Ltd.,** 698 W. Hastings St. (☎ 604/669-3333; Bus: 7), has a long tradition of designing and creating beautiful jewelry and watches and selling jewelry to international designers. On Granville Island, **The Raven and the Bear,** 1528 Duranleau St. (☎ 604/669-3990; Bus: 50), is a great spot to shop for West Coast native jewelry.

MALLS & SHOPPING CENTERS   The **Pacific Centre Mall,** 700 W. Georgia St. (☎ 604/688-7236; Bus: 7), is 3-block complex containing 200 shops and services, including Godiva, Benetton, Crabtree & Evelyn, and Eddie Bauer. For more upscale shopping, try the **Sinclair Centre,** 757 W. Hastings St. (☎ **604/659-1009;** Bus: 7), which houses elite shops like Armani, Leone, and Dorothy Grant, as well as smaller boutiques, art galleries, and a food court.

SPORTING GOODS   Everything you'll ever need for the outdoors is at **Mountain Equipment Co-op,** 130 W. Broadway (☎ **604/872-7858;** Bus: 9).

TOYS   The **Kids Only Market,** Cartwright St., Granville Island (☎ **604/ 689-8447;** Bus: 50), is a 24-shop complex that sells toys, games, computer software, and books for kids.

WINE   In addition to carrying a full range of British Columbian wines, **Marquis Wine Cellars,** 1034 Davie St. (☎ **604/684-0445** or 604/685-2246; Bus: 1), has a large international selection, plus a very knowledgeable staff.

9 Vancouver After Dark

For an overview of Vancouver's nightlife, pick up a copy of the weekly tabloid *The Georgia Straight,* the glossy *Vancouver* magazine, or *Xtra! West,* the free gay-and-lesbian biweekly tabloid. The **Vancouver Cultural Alliance Arts Hot Line** at ☎ 604/684-2787 or **www.culturenet.ca/vca** is a great source for all performing arts, music, theater, literary events, art films, and dance, including where and how to get tickets. **Ticketmaster** (Vancouver Ticket Centre), 1304 Hornby St. (☎ **604/ 280-3311;** www.info.ticketmaster.ca/tminfo/bc/vancouver/venue-info.htm; Bus: 4), has 40 outlets in the greater Vancouver area. With a credit card, you can buy tickets over the phone and pick them up at the venue.

Three major Vancouver theaters regularly host touring performances: the **Orpheum Theatre,** 801 Granville St. (☎ **604/665-3050;** Bus: 7); the **Queen Elizabeth Theatre,** 600 Hamilton St. (☎ **604/665-3050;** Bus: 5); and the **Vancouver Playhouse** (same number). They share a Web site at **www.city.vancouver.bc.ca/.**

In a converted early-1900s church, the **Vancouver East Cultural Centre** (the "Cultch" to locals), 1895 Venables St. (☎ **604/254-9578;** www.thedrive.net/vecc; Bus: 20), hosts avant-garde theater productions, children's programs, and art exhibits.

THE PERFORMING ARTS

Theater isn't only an indoor pastime here. There's an annual summertime Shakespeare series called **Bard on the Beach,** in Vanier Park (☎ 604/737-0625; Bus 22). You can also bring a picnic dinner to Stanley Park and watch **Theatre Under the Stars** (☎ 604/687-0174; Bus: 35), which features popular musicals and light comedies. For more original fare, don't miss **Vancouver's Fringe Festival** (☎ 604/257-0350; www.vancouverfringe.com). The Fringe features more than 500 innovative and original shows each September, all costing under C$10 (US$7).

The **Arts Club Theatre Company** presents live theater in two venues, the **Granville Island Stage** at the Arts Club Theatre, 1585 Johnston St. (Bus: 50), and the **Stanley Theatre,** 2750 Granville St. (Bus: 8). Phone and Web site for both theaters: ☎ 604/687-1644; www.culturenet.ca/vca/artscl.htm. Housed in Vancouver's Firehall No. 1, the **Firehall Arts Centre,** 280 E. Cordova St. (☎ **604/ 689-0926;** www.mcsquared.com/firehall/index.htm; Bus: 4), is home to three cutting-edge companies: the Firehall Theatre Company, Touchstone Theatre, and Axis Mime. Expect experimental and challenging plays.

OPERA   The **Vancouver Opera,** 500-845 Cambie St. (☎ **604/683-0222; **Bus: 17), alternates between obscure or new works and older, more popular favorites. English supertitles projected above the stage help audiences follow the dialogue of the lavish productions.

CLASSICAL MUSIC   The extremely active **Vancouver Symphony,** 601 Smithe St. (☎ **604/876-3434;** Bus: 7), presents a number of series: great classical works, light classics, modern classics and ethnic works, popular and show tunes, and music geared toward school-age children. The traveling summer concert series takes the orchestra from White Rock to the top of Whistler Mountain.

DANCE   For fans of modern and original dance, the time to be here is early July, when the **Dancing on the Edge Festival** (☎ **604/689-0691**) presents 60 to 80 envelope-pushing original pieces over a 10-day period. **Ballet British Columbia,** 502-68 Water St. (☎ **604/732-5003;** Bus: 4), is a young company that strives to present innovative works. For more about other festivals and dance companies around the city, call the **Dance Centre** at ☎ **604/606-6400.**

COMEDY & LIVE-MUSIC CLUBS

Performers with the **Vancouver TheatreSports League** (☎ **604/687-1644**) rely on a basic plot supplemented by audience suggestions the actors take and improvise on, often to hilarious results. Performances are in the Arts Club Theatre, 1585 Johnston St., Granville Island (Bus: 50), with shows costing C$13 (US$9) weekends and C$6 (US$4) weeknights. **Yuk Yuk's Komedy Kabaret,** Plaza of Nations, 750 Pacific Blvd. (☎ **604/687-5233;** Bus: 2), presents a constantly changing lineup of leading Canadian and American stand-up comics; the cover is C$10 (US$7).

Every June, the **du Maurier International Jazz Festival** (☎ **604/872-5200**) takes over several venues in Vancouver and outdoor locations around town. The festival includes a number of free concerts. The **Vancouver Folk Festival** (☎ **604/602-9798**) takes place outdoors in July on the beach at Jericho Park (Bus: 4). The **Coastal Jazz and Blues Society,** 316 W. 6th Ave. (☎ **604/872-5200;** Bus: 9), has information on current and upcoming events throughout the year.

Cover at the functional **Starfish Room,** 1055 Homer St. (☎ **604/682-4171;** Bus: 7), ranges from C$3 to C$30 (US$2 to US$20), depending on the act. Bands vary from jazz and blues to Celtic, lounge, funk, and even punk. For folk, the **WISE Hall,** 1882 Adanac (☎ **604/254-5858;** Bus: 20), is the place to be, with a cover running C$5 to C$15 (US$3.35 to US$10). And for blues, go to the smoky, sudsy old **Yale Hotel,** 1300 Granville St. (☎ **604/681-9253;** Bus: 4), with a Thursday-to-Saturday cover of C$5 to C$12 (US$3.35 to US$8).

BARS, PUBS & LOUNGES

The **Atlantic Trap and Gill,** 612 Davie St. (☎ **604/806-6393;** Bus 4), is an east-coast sea shanty of a place, where the regulars know the words to every song. **Fred's Tavern,** 1006 Granville St. (☎ **604/605-4350;** Bus: 4), features a steady stream of simulcast sports, but for some reason those in the beautiful young crowd are mostly interested in each other. Called a diamond in the rough, the **Brickhouse Bar,** 730 Main St. (☎ **604/689-8645;** Bus: 8), is a great bar in the slowly gentrifying neighborhood around Main and Terminal. The **Shark Club Bar and Grill,** 180 W. Georgia St. (☎ **604/687-4275;** Bus: 5), is the city's premier sports bar. If you're looking for a brew pub, **Steamworks Pub & Brewery,** 375 Water St. (☎ **604/689-2739;** Bus: 7), is your best bet. Choose from a dozen in-house beers, from dark Australian-style ales to light, refreshing wheat lagers. The **Yaletown Brewing Company,** 1111 Mainland St. (☎ **604/688-0039;** Bus: 2), also offers good home-brewed fare.

View junkies will think they've died and gone to heaven at **Cloud Nine,** 1400 Robson St., on the 42nd floor of the Empire Landmark Hotel (☎ 604/687-0511; Bus: 5). This sleek hotel-top lounge rotates six degrees a minute, offering an ever-changing and always-fabulous view of the city. The **Georgia Street Bar and Grill,** 801 W. Georgia St. (☎ 604/602-0994; Bus: 22), is a pleasant street-front lounge with great weekend jazz combos.

DANCE CLUBS

You get two venues for the price of one at Gastown's **The Purple Onion,** 15 Water St. (☎ 604/602-9442; Bus: 4). The Club room is a dance floor pure and simple; in the Lounge a house band squeals out funky danceable jazz for a slightly older crowd. The cover runs C$5 to C$7 (US$3.35 to US$4.65). The dance-oriented **Richards on Richards,** 1036 Richards St. (☎ 604/687-6794; Bus: 7), has been packing 'em in for close to 2 decades, and the cover is C$5 to C$40 (US$3.35 to US$27). **Sonar,** 66 Water St. (☎ 604/683-6695; Bus: 4), is Vancouver's purest hip-hop house joint; it was named one of world's top-20 nightclubs by Britain's *Ministry* magazine. The cover runs C$5 to C$9 (US$3.35 to US$6). And at the **Stone Temple Cabaret,** 1082 Granville St. (☎ 604/488-1333; Bus: 7), it's disco pure and simple. The moderate-size dance floor in the front room features lights, smoke, booming bass, and an early-20s collegiate crowd. The cover is C$5 to C$20 (US$3.35 to US$13).

GAY & LESBIAN BARS

Open Monday to Saturday noon to 6pm, the **Gay & Lesbian Centre,** 2-1170 Bute St. (☎ 604/684-6869; Bus: 1), has information on the current hot spots, but it's probably easier just to pick up a free copy of *Xtra West!,* available in most downtown cafes.

Celebrities, 1022 Davie St. (☎ 604/689-3180; Bus: 1), is the West End's largest gay dance club, with a cover running C$4 to C$7 (US$2.65 to US$4.65). Billed as a "neighborhood club," **Homers,** 1249 Howe St. (☎ 604/689-2444; Bus: 4), has a relaxed atmosphere, a few billiards tables, and a great pub menu. The **Dufferin Pub,** 900 Seymour St. (☎ 604/683-4251; Bus: 7), is home to the city's glitziest drag show, Buff at the Duff. The rest of the time (and before, during, and after many of the shows) the DJs play a mix of sounds to keep you grooving. **The Odyssey,** 1251 Howe St. (☎ 604/689-5256; Bus: 4), is the hippest, happeningest gay/mixed dance bar in town, with a cover of C$3 to C$5 (US$2 to US$3.35). The **Heritage House Hotel,** 455 Abbott St. (☎ 604/685-7777; Bus: 4), is home to two gay bars, **Charlie's Lounge** and the slightly seedy **Chuck's Pub,** and one lesbian locale, the **Lotus Cabaret.** Cover at the Lotus is C$4 to C$7 (US$2.65 to US$4.65). The Lotus offers a big bar, little alcoves for sitting, an adequate dance floor, and an upbeat atmosphere. The crowd is normally mixed, but on Fridays it's women only.

CASINOS

There's no alcohol and there are no floor shows, but on the other hand, you haven't really lived until you've sat down for some serious gambling with a room full of Far Eastern big shots trying to re-create the huge night they had in Happy Valley or Macau. At the Gateway Casino, 611 Main St., third floor (☎ 604/688-9412; Bus: 3), you can play pai gow poker, blackjack, roulette, and sic bo mini bac, and let it ride. It's open noon to 2am, with a C$500 (US$334) maximum bet. Similar games are on offer at the **Great Canadian Casino,** 1133 W. Hastings St. (☎ 604/682-8145; Bus: 23), and the **Royal Diamond Casino,** 750 Pacific Blvd., in the Plaza of Nations (☎ 604/685-2340; Bus: 2).

Victoria & British Columbia

16

by Shawn Blore & Bill McRae

British Columbia runs the length of Canada's west coast, from the Washington border to the Alaskan panhandle. Roughly 947,8000km^2 (588,935 sq. miles), it's more than twice the size of California, though the population (3.7 million) is roughly a quarter of Los Angeles's. Most residents live in the greater Vancouver and **Victoria** areas in the southwest, along a coast dotted with beachfront communities, modern cities, and belts of rich farmland. But just a few hours' drive to the north on any of BC's mostly two-lane highways, the communities are tiny, the sparse population is scattered, and the land is alternately towering forest, fields of stumps left by timber harvests, and high alpine wilderness. Between these extremes are the areas covered in this chapter.

British Columbia's outstanding feature is its variety: of scenery, climates, and cultures. The wide-open ranch lands of the High Country and Kamloops contain the last vestiges of North America's legendary Wild West, with cowboys riding herd, prospectors staking claims, cattle drives crossing the high plains, and Indians struggling to reclaim ancestral lands. The rough-hewn mountains of the Cariboo and Chilcotin regions are topped with glaciers running off into hidden lakes. Alpine meadows, buried under snow all winter, burst forth with a profusion of blossoms every summer. The rugged fjords and misty islands along the coast from the Queen Charlotte Islands to Howe Sound are home to the world's only resident population of orcas, most of the world's remaining old-growth temperate rain forests, and some of North America's earliest human settlements. The arid Okanagan Valley is filled with fruit trees and surrounded by vineyards and wineries on the hillsides, and it boasts sagebrush and sand deserts. And hundreds of lakes, sheltered beaches, and majestic mountains stretch across the province, separating each region from the others yet interlacing them all.

1 Exploring the Province

There's more to British Columbia than Vancouver's urban bustle. In fact, the other Vancouver—**Vancouver Island**—is 90 minutes from the city by ferry. On Vancouver Island is the province's capital, **Victoria.** It's a lovely seaport city that's proud of its English roots, lavish Victorian gardens, and picturesque port. It's also the ideal place to begin exploring the entire island, which stretches more than 450km (279 miles) from Victoria to the northwest tip of Cape Scott.

Southern British Columbia

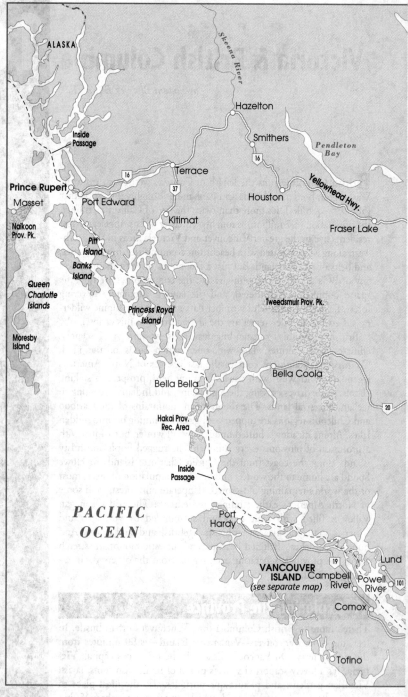

ALASKA

Skeena River

Hazelton

Smithers

Pendleton Bay

Inside Passage

16

Terrace

37

Prince Rupert

Masset

Port Edward

Houston

Yellowhead Hwy.

Naikoon Prov. Pk.

Kitimat

Fraser Lake

Pitt Island

Banks Island

Queen Charlotte Islands

Princess Royal Island

Tweedsmuir Prov. Pk.

Moresby Island

Bella Coola

Bella Bella

20

Hakai Prov. Rec. Area

Inside Passage

PACIFIC OCEAN

Port Hardy

Lund

VANCOUVER ISLAND Campbell River

19

Powell River

101

(see separate map)

Comox

Tofino

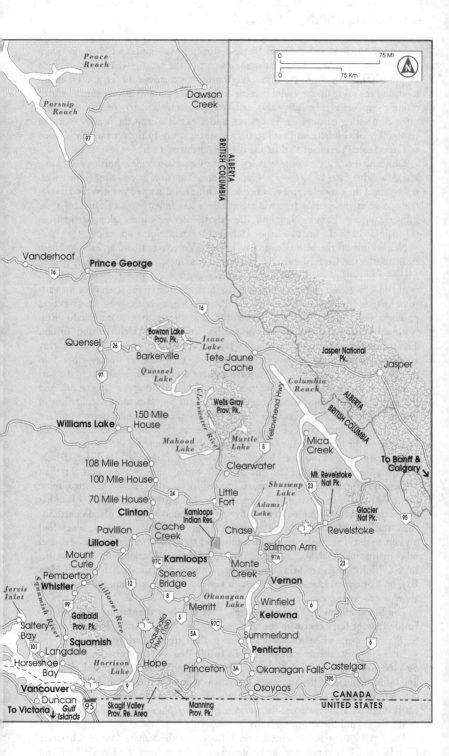

You can reach most Vancouver Island destinations via the Island Highway. From Victoria, which is Mile 0, to Nanaimo, it's part of the coast-to-coast Trans-Canada Highway (Highway 1). At Nanaimo, the Trans-Canada crosses the ferry to the mainland, and the route up the island becomes Highway 19 until its arrives at its northern terminus in Port Hardy. Along this route you encounter a variety of distinctive and often contrasting cultures, environments, and lifestyles—from the heavily touristed tranquillity of **Goldstream Provincial Park** in the south to the untamed wilderness of **Cape Scott Provincial Park** at the island's northwestern tip.

Duncan, the "City of Totem Poles" in the Cowichan Valley, north of Victoria, reveals another facet of Vancouver Island culture. This lush green valley is the ancestral home of the Cowichan tribe, famed for crafting hand-knitted sweaters, and it contains some of the island's best wineries. Only a few miles north of Duncan is the formerly industrial city of **Nanaimo,** the arrival center for visitors taking ferries from the mainland and the site of a major 19th-century coal-mining operation.

Nestled just off the island's east coast between Vancouver Island and the southern mainland lie the **Gulf Islands.** These islands—the most popular being Salt Spring, Mayne, and Galiano—are havens for artists and craftspeople attracted to the mild climate, slow pace, and pastoral landscapes. In sharp contrast to the serenity of the east-coast islands, the raging beauty of the Pacific Ocean on the west coast entices photographers, hikers, kayakers, naturalists, and divers to explore **Pacific Rim National Park, Long Beach,** and the neighboring towns of **Ucluelet** and **Tofino.** Thousands arrive between March and May to see as many as 20,000 **Pacific gray whales** pass close to shore as they migrate north to their summer feeding grounds in the Arctic Circle. More than 200 **shipwrecks** have occurred off the shores in the past 2 centuries, luring even more travelers to this eerily beautiful underwater world. And the park's world-famous **West Coast Trail** beckons an international collection of intrepid backpackers and "extreme" hikers to brave the 10-day hike over the rugged rescue trail—established after the survivors of a shipwreck in the early 1900s died from exposure on the beach because there was no land access route for the rescuers.

On east-central Vancouver Island, the towns of Parksville, Qualicum Beach, Courtenay, and Comox are famous for their warm sandy beaches and for their numerous championship golf courses. Campbell River—the "Salmon Fishing Capital of the World"—is dominated by fishing resorts, while just-offshore Quadra Island has one of the world's best museums of Native art. The waters along the island's northeast coast near **Port McNeil** are home to two species of orca whales: residents, which feed on salmon and live in the area consistently, and transients, which feed on seals and other marine mammals and move annually from **Johnstone Strait** to the open Pacific. In this vicinity are also two tiny unique communities: the native-Indian town of **Alert Bay,** on Cormorant Island, and **Telegraph Cove,** a boardwalk community on pilings above the rocky shore.

The Island Highway's final port of call, **Port Hardy** is the starting point for the **Inside Passage ferry cruise** up the northern coast. The ferry carries passengers bound for Prince Rupert, where it meets the ferries to the **Queen Charlotte Islands.**

Since 1966, BC Ferries has operated the **Inside Passage ferry** between Port Hardy on Vancouver Island and Prince Rupert. This rugged, thickly forested mainland coastline is the highlight of the Vancouver-to-Alaska cruises. It's also the ancestral home of native-Indian tribes who intrigued late–19th-century American photographer Edward Curtis so much he spent more than a decade photographing and filming the people, their villages, and their potlatch feasts.

The ferry system also connects Prince Rupert to the remote **Queen Charlotte Islands,** the ancestral home of the Haida tribe and the location of a UNESCO World

Heritage Site, **Haida Gwaii.** The remains of untouched Haida villages, abandoned more than 400 years ago, stand amid a thick rain forest of old-growth Sitka spruce. Cedar totem poles, sculptures, funerary boxes, and longhouses are all that remains of the culture that flourished there for nearly 10,000 years—and inspired Victoria-born artist Emily Carr's now-famous paintings and drawings, which you can see at the Vancouver Art Gallery.

Between Lillooet and Prince George in the Fraser River Valley, you'll discover that the Canadian Wild West hasn't changed too much in the past century. This is **Cariboo Country,** the scene of the 1860s Cariboo Gold Rush. The town of **Lillooet,** "Mile 0" of the Old Cariboo Highway, was the starting point of a 250-mile journey taken by prospectors and settlers who sought their fortunes in the northern Cariboo goldfields. The gold-rich town of **Barkerville** sprang up after a British prospector named Billy Barker struck it rich on Williams Creek. But gold isn't the only thing that attracts thousands to this area year-round. Cross-country skiers and snowmobilers explore the creekside paths during the winter.

It's only a 97km (60-mile) drive from Lillooet (and a 121km/75-mile drive from Vancouver) to North America's most popular ski resort—the glacial peaks of **Whistler and Blackcomb mountains.** Whistler is also a popular summer getaway, where you can ski or snowboard the Horstman Glacier at the top of Blackcomb Mountain, paddle the raging glacier-fed Green River or the placid River of Dreams, mountain bike down the slopes of Whistler Mountain, or fish in the icy waters of **Birkenhead Lake Provincial Park.**

Due east, on the opposite side of Cariboo Country, the High Country's arid and hilly lowlands attract fishers and boaters to the shores of the lower Thompson River and **Shuswap Lakes.** But rising up from this dry terrain as you head north to the town of **Clearwater** is a majestic 3,211,000-acre forested mountain wilderness formed by glaciers and volcanoes, **Wells Gray Provincial Park.** Due south of the High Country on Highway 97, the arid **Okanagan Valley** and its long chain of crystal-blue lakes lure sports enthusiasts and wine lovers to its **fruit orchards, vineyards, golf courses, waterskiing,** and **ski resorts** in and around the towns of **Kelowna, Penticton,** and **Vernon.**

VISITOR INFORMATION

TOURIST OFFICES   Contact **Tourism British Columbia,** 865 Hornby St., 8th Floor, Vancouver, BC V6Z 2G3 (☎ **604/663-6000**), and the **Tourism Association of Vancouver Island,** 302-45 Bastion Sq., Victoria, BC V8W 1J1 (☎ **250/ 382-3551**), for details about travel in the province. You can also call **Super Natural British Columbia** at ☎ **800/663-6000** or 604/663-6000 (see the Web addresses below). Contact the individual regional tourism associations and Visitor Info Centres listed in this chapter for more detailed local information.

WEB SITES   Here are some of the best sites currently out there: **Tourism BC** (www.tourism-bc.ca), **Super Natural British Columbia** (www.iias.com/travel or www.snbc-res.com), **Nature and Wildlife information** (www.travel.bc.ca), **Whistler and Blackcomb Resorts** (www.whistler.net), **Environment Canada** (www.weatheroffice.com), and **BC Ferries** (www.bcferries.com).

THE GREAT OUTDOORS

It's hard to believe the province's variety of sports and other outdoor activities. Even the most cosmopolitan British Columbians spend their leisure time mountain biking, windsurfing, skiing, or hiking in the surrounding mountains, rivers, and meadows. The varied and largely uninhabited terrain seems to lure visitors to get close to nature.

To find out what's happening in the great British Columbian outdoors, pick up a copy of the free bimonthly tabloid *Coast: The Outdoor Recreation Magazine* (☎ **604/876-1473**). It contains the latest info on mountain-bike races, kayaking competitions, eco-challenges (an international pentathlon-style competition encompassing kayaking, horseback riding, hiking, mountain biking, and skiing). It's available at outfitters, recreational-equipment outlets, and community centers throughout the province.

Members of the American Automobile Association (AAA) can get assistance from the **BC Automobile Association** (BCAA) by calling ☎ **800/222-4357** or 604/293-2222. Seat belts and daytime headlights must be used while driving in the province.

BIKING   Throughout British Columbia are countless marked mountain-bike trails and cycling paths. In **Victoria,** the 8-mile Scenic Marine Drive has an adjacent paved path following Dallas Road and Beach Drive, then returning to downtown via Oak Bay Avenue (see "Victoria," below). On **Newcastle Island Provincial Park,** off the Nanaimo coast, the Shoreline Trail circles the lovely island, which was once a holiday resort. There are plenty of marked trails to explore on **Salt Spring Island** in the Gulf Islands group between Vancouver Island and the mainland.

The best **Okanagan Valley** off-road bike trail is the incredible **Kettle Valley Railway** route. The **Myra Canyon** railway route near Kelowna crosses over 18 trestle bridges and passes through two tunnels carved through the mountains (see "The Okanagan Valley," below). In the **Shuswap Lakes** region of the High Country, off-road trails run through the hilly terrain surrounding the lakes and rivers that attract hordes of houseboaters and anglers. It's also the location of the world's largest salmon run (see "Wells Gray Provincial Park & the Shuswap Lakes," below).

The ski runs on the lower elevations of both **Whistler and Blackcomb Mountains** are transformed into mountain-bike trails during summer. Bikes are permitted on the gondola ski lift, allowing you to reach the peaks where the winding marked trails begin. From here, experts, intermediates, and novices barrel down through the colorful alpine slopes. June to September, bike challenges take place regularly on both mountains (see "Whistler," below). In town, the **Valley Trail** offers 20km (12 miles) of paved paths that pass through residential areas and around alpine lakes. Next to the Chateau Whistler Golf Course, the **Lost Lake Trails** feature numerous unpaved alternative routes that fan out from the main lakeside trail (see "Whistler," below).

BOATING & SAILING   While you're in **Victoria,** take a leisurely cruise south to Sooke Harbour or up the Strait of Georgia in a rental boat or a skippered vessel. There are many outfitters at the **Brentwood Bay** and **Oak Bay Marinas** (see "Victoria," below).

On the **Gulf Islands,** you can take the wheel of a 30-foot sailing craft or enjoy a skippered cruise on a power catamaran around the Gulf Islands. The remote **Queen Charlotte Islands** offer a world of marine beauty you can best discover by taking a guided cruise on a skippered schooner. The crews are familiar with the history and lore of the mysterious waters surrounding the home of the Haida Native-Indian tribe (see "The Inside Passage," below). On the mainland, more than a dozen **Okanagan Valley** lakes lure boaters, houseboaters, and water-sports enthusiasts. Whether you're into waterskiing, fishing, jet skiing, house-, or pleasure boating, local marinas offer full-service rentals (see "The Okanagan Valley," below).

CAMPING   British Columbia's national parks, provincial parks, marine parks, and private campgrounds are generally filled during summer weekends. Most areas are first-come, first-served, so stake your claim early in the afternoon (for weekends, arrive by Thurs). However, March 1 to September 15, you can book a campsite up to 3 months in advance by calling **Discover Camping** at ☎ **800/689-9025** in North America or 604/689-9025. It's open Monday to Friday 7am to 9pm and Saturday and Sunday 9am to 5pm. There's a nonrefundable service fee of C$6 (US$4.30), and reservations can be confirmed only with MasterCard or Visa.

The provincial park campgrounds charge C$9 to C$19 (US$6 to US$12) per site. There's a 2-week maximum for individual campsite stays. Facilities vary from rustic (walk-in or water-access) to basic (pit toilets and little else) to luxurious (hot showers, flush toilets, and sani-stations). All provincial drive-in campgrounds offer precut-wood piles, grill-equipped fire pits, bear-proof garbage cans, pumped well water, and well-maintained security. The rustic wilderness campgrounds provide minimal services—a covered shelter or simply a cleared patch of ground and little else.

CANOEING & KAYAKING   You'll quickly discover why sea kayakers rate **Vancouver Island's west coast** one of the world's best places to paddle. Novice and intermediate paddlers launch from the passenger ferry MV *Lady Rose* into the sheltered waters of **Barkley Sound.** Surf kayakers are drawn to the tidal swells that crash along the shores of **Long Beach,** part of Pacific Rim National Park. And the **Broken Island Group's** many islands offer paddlers an excellent site for overnight expeditions amid the rugged beauty of the outer coast.

On Vancouver Island's east coast, **Johnstone Strait** lures paddlers to one of the world's largest orca (killer whale) populations, and to ancient native-Indian villages (see "Northern Vancouver Island," below). In **Whistler,** paddlers are treated to an exhilarating stretch of glacial waters that runs behind the village itself. Some savvy kayakers and canoeists call it the "River of Dreams" (see "Whistler," below).

CLIMBING & SPELUNKING   Off Valleyview Road, east of Penticton in the Okanagan Valley, **Skaha Bluffs** has more than 400 bolted routes set in place. For info about organized climbing trips throughout the province, contact the **Federation of Mountain Clubs of BC,** 1367 W. Broadway, Vancouver, BC V6H 4A9 (☎ **604/ 737-3053**).

FISHING   Numerous fishing packages depart from the **Victoria** docks, where charters run to the southern island's best catch-and-release spots for salmon, halibut, cutthroat, and lingcod. About 134km (83 miles) north of Victoria, **Elk & Beaver Lakes Provincial Park's** Beaver Lake is stocked with steelhead, rainbow trout, kokanee, Dolly Varden char, and smallmouth bass. Year-round sportfishing for salmon, steelhead, trout, Dolly Varden char, halibut, cod, and snapper lures anglers to the waters near **Port Alberni** and **Barkley Sound.** Nearby **Long Beach** is great for bottom fishing (see "Vancouver Island's West Coast," below).

On Vancouver Island's east coast, **Campbell River** is the home of **Painter's Lodge.** A favorite Hollywood getaway for over 50 years, it has entertained Bob Hope, John Wayne (who was a frequent guest), and Goldie Hawn (see "Vancouver Island's East Coast," below). The **Queen Charlotte Islands** were only recently opened to sportfishers, and the fish stories about 70-pound tyee salmon and 125-pound halibut emanating from these misty shores are true. **Langara Island and Naden Harbour on Graham Island** are perfect salmon-fishing spots where anglers commonly release catches under 30 pounds as they aim for the big fish (see "The Inside Passage," below).

The desert-like **Okanagan Valley** summers are far too hot for fish and fishermen, but for the region's **Okanagan, Kalamalka, and Skaha Lakes,** spring and fall are bountiful seasons. The best summer fishing centers around the small hillside lakes surrounding the valley. These spots brim with trout, steelhead, Dolly Varden char, and

Three Trips of a Lifetime

Each of the following trips, within striking distance of Vancouver and Victoria, takes you to a place like no other on earth.

KAYAKING CLAYOQUOT SOUND   In 1993, environmentalists from across the province and around the world arrived in British Columbia to protect this pristine fjord on the West Coast of Vancouver Island. More than 1,000 were arrested before the government and logging companies gave in and agreed to leave Clayoquot (pronounced *kla*-kwat) Sound's temperate old-growth rain forest intact. This trip involves paddling a kayak for 4 or 5 days through the protected waters of the sound, from the funky former fishing village of Tofino to a natural hot-springs bath near a native village of the Hesquiaat people. Along the way you'll see thousand-year-old trees and glaciers and whales and bald eagles.

Three companies in Tofino can set you up with a kayak: **Pacific Kayak,** 606 Campbell St. (☎ **250/725-3232;** www.tofino-bc.com/pacifickayak); the **Tofino Sea Kayaking Company,** 320 Main St. (☎ **800/TOFINO-4;** www. island.net/~paddlers); and **Remote Passages,** 71 Wharf St. (☎ **800/863-4664** or 250/725-4222; www.island.net/~paddlers). Sea kayaking isn't hard, and the great advantage of a trip on Clayoquot Sound is that it's entirely in sheltered inshore waters, though the scenery and the feeling are those of being in a wide-open wilderness. If you're tentative about kayaking on your own, many companies, like the three above, can set you up on a guided trip.

The preferred route leaves Tofino and travels for 2 or 3 days through the protected waters of Clayoquot Sound up to the natural Hot Springs Cove. From there you can fly back—strapping your kayak to the floats of the plane—or retrace your route to Tofino. Whichever way you go, save some time and money for a memorable meal at the Pointe Restaurant in the Wickaninnish Inn (see "Where to Stay" later in this chapter); after a week in the wilderness, the food here will seem sublime.

SAILING THROUGH THE GREAT BEAR RAIN FOREST   If you look at a map of British Columbia, you'll see about halfway up the west coast an incredibly convoluted region of mountains, fjords, bays, channels, rivers, and inlets. There are next to no roads here—the geography's too intense. Thanks to that isolation,

smallmouth bass (see "The Okanagan Valley," later in this chapter). Sportfishing is the best reason to visit the **Cariboo Country lakes,** about 250 of which are accessible by road. Some lakes are nestled at altitudes as high as 6,000 feet and can be reached by booking a guided floatplane trip (see "Cariboo Country to Prince George," below).

In the **Shuswap Lakes** area, weed beds nurture the shrimp, sedge, and insects rainbow trout thrive on. Many of these lakes are considered trout factories. The area is close to civilization, but it's not hard to get away by helicopter or floatplane to isolated Bonaparte Plateau fishing resorts for even more excitement (see "Wells Gray Provincial Park & the Shuswap Lakes," below).

Whistler's **Green River** and nearby **Birkenhead Lake Provincial Park** have runs of steelhead, rainbow trout, Dolly Varden char, cutthroat, and salmon that attract sport anglers from around the world (see "Whistler," below).

GOLFING   Considering **Victoria**'s British heritage and its lush rolling landscape, it's no wonder golf is a popular pastime. The three local courses offer terrain—minus thistles—similar to Scotland's too (see "Victoria," below).

this is also one of the last places in the world where grizzly bear are still found in large numbers, not to mention salmon and large trees and killer whales and otters and porpoises. But to get there you'll need a boat. And if you're going to have to take a boat, why not take a 100-year-old fully rigged 92-foot sailing schooner?

Run by an ex-pilot turned naturalist and sailor, **Maple Leaf Adventures,** 2087 Indian Crescent, Duncan, BC V9L 5L9 (☎ **888/599-5323** or 250/715-0906; fax 250/715-0912), runs a number of trips to this magic area. Owner Brian Falconer is extremely knowledgeable and normally brings along a trained naturalist to explain the fauna (especially the whales, dolphins, and grizzlies). The trips vary from 4 days to 2 weeks and from C$1,250 to C$2,500 (US$834 to US$1,668), covering territory from the midcoast to the Queen Charlotte Islands (Haida Gwaii) to the coasts of Alaska. All include gourmet meals (more than you could ever eat) and comfortable but not luxurious accommodation aboard Brian's beautiful schooner, the *Maple Leaf.*

HORSE TREKKING ON THE CHILCOTIN PLATEAU The high plateau country of the BC interior boasts some of the most impressive scenery around. Soaring peaks rise above deep valleys, and mountain meadows come alive with flowers that bloom for just a few weeks in high summer. The advantage to taking in this territory on horseback are that the horse's feet get sore, not yours; if you come across a grizzly, you've got some height on him; and horses can carry far more and far better food.

While dude ranches abound in both Canada and the States, there's one key difference to certain British Columbia outfits. It's called a guide-outfitter tenure—one company is granted exclusive rights to run guided tours through that section of wilderness. In BC, the territories are typically 5,000km^2 (1,931 sq. miles), all high-country wilderness where you likely won't meet another horse team. One of the guide-outfitters closest to Vancouver is the **Chilcotin Holidays Guest Ranch,** Gun Creek Road, Gold Bridge, BC V0K 1P0 (☎ **250/238-2274;** www.chilcotinholidays.com). Their trips run 4 to 7 days, cost C$600 to C$900 (US$400 to US$600), and involve encounters with wildflowers, bighorn sheep, grizzlies, and wolves.

There are also a number of outstanding layouts in central **Vancouver Island,** including an 18-hole course designed by golf legend Les Furber. The **Morningstar** championship course is in Parksville. The **Storey Creek Golf Club** in Campbell River also has a challenging course design and great scenic views (see "Vancouver Island's East Coast," below). There are 9- and 18-hole golf courses in the **Okanagan Valley,** including the **Gallagher's Canyon Golf & Country Club** in Kelowna and **Predator Ridge** in Vernon (see "The Okanagan Valley," below). Visitors to **Whistler** can tee off at the **Chateau Whistler Golf Course,** at the base of Blackcomb Mountain, or the **Nicklaus North** golf course on the shore of Green Lake (see "Whistler," below).

The **Salmon Arm Golf Course** and **Shuswap Lakes Estates Golf & Country Club** offer beautiful terrain, great values on greens fees, and more than your fair share of bunkers, traps, and ascents (see "Wells Gray Provincial Park & the Shuswap Lakes," below).

HIKING Among the best short nature walks on Vancouver Island, the lush temperate rain forest of **Goldstream Provincial Park** offers hikes through centuries-old stands of Douglas fir (see "Side Trips from Victoria," below). Accessible by ferry from Nanaimo, **Newcastle Island Provincial Marine Park** has trails that meander through the wooded interior and along the sandy shoreline (see "Side Trips from Victoria," below).

On Vancouver Island's west coast, the world-famous ✪ **West Coast Trail** is considered by many seasoned hikers the challenge of a lifetime. The boardwalked **South Beach Trail** near Tofino provides a contemplative stroll through a Sitka-spruce temperate rain forest, as does the **Big Cedar Trail** on Meares Island. The trails following **Long Beach** allow hikers a close-up glimpse of the marine life that inhabits the tidal pools in the park's many quiet coves (see "Vancouver Island's West Coast," below). At Whistler, **Lost Lake Trails**'s 30km (19 miles) of marked trails around creeks, beaver dams, blueberry patches, and lush cedars are ideal for biking, Nordic skiing, or just quiet strolling and picnicking. The **Ancient Cedars** area of Cougar Mountain above Whistler's Emerald Estates is an awe-inspiring grove of towering old-growth cedars and Douglas firs.

Whistlers' **Singing Pass Trail** is a 4-hour moderately difficult hike winding from the top of Whistler Mountain down to the village via the Fitzsimmons Valley. North of Whistler, **Nairn Falls Provincial Park** features a gentle 1.6km (1 mile) trail leading to a stupendous view of the icy-cold Green River as it plunges 196 feet over a rocky cliff into a narrow gorge. There's also an incredible view of Mount Currie peaking over the treetops. In the High Country, **Shuswap Lakes Provincial Park** was the site of a gold-mining operation during the 1930s and 1940s. Today, the old-growth ponderosa pines and second-growth red cedar and Douglas fir form a towering canopy over an extensive network of trails. And nearby **Copper Island** has a pleasant circular trail leading to elevated views of the surrounding countryside.

HORSEBACK RIDING   Besides booking a trip to one of the **Cariboo Country guest ranches** (see "Cariboo Country to Prince George," below) or the outfitters and guest ranches near **Wells Gray Provincial Park** (see "Wells Gray Provincial Park & the Shuswap Lakes," below), you can take an afternoon ride along a wooded trail near Victoria's Buck Mountain. In Whistler, there are riding trails along the Green River and across the Pemberton Valley, and even up on Blackcomb Mountain itself (see "Whistler," below).

RAFTING   Whistler's **Green River** offers novices small rapids and views of snow-capped mountains for their first rafting runs (see "Whistler," below). Intermediate and expert rafters can take on the **Elaho and Squamish rivers,** which offer Class IV runs. Just a 2½-hour drive from Vancouver, the wild **Nahatlatch River** offers some of the best guided whitewater trips in the province (see "Outdoor Activities & Spectator Sports" in chapter 15). The Chilco-Chilcotin-Fraser river system near Williams Lake has sosme of the most challenging whitewater in the province (see "Cariboo Country to Prince George," below).

SKIING & SNOWBOARDING   Cross-country and powder skiing are the **Okanagan Valley's** main winter attractions. **Big White Ski Resort** gets an annual average of 18 feet of powder and has more than 20km (12 miles) of cross-country trails. **Apex Resort** maintains 56 downhill runs and extensive cross-country trails. And **Silver Star Mountain Ski Resort & Cross-Country Centre** offers cross-country skiers 93km (58 miles) of trails (including 6.6km/4 miles lit for night skiing), plus 50km (31 miles) of trails in the adjacent Silver Star Provincial Park. The ski-in/ski-out resort resembles a 19th-century mining town. For off-piste fanatics, some of Canada's most extreme verticals are here among the resort's 72 downhill runs. Nearby **Crystal**

Mountain caters to intermediate and novice downhill skiers and snowboarders (see "The Okanagan Valley," below).

There are 63 downhill runs and two snowboarding half pipes at the High Country's **Sun Peaks Resort.** Up in the mountains of **Wells Gray Provincial Park,** outfitters offer expert guidance through the miles of cross-country skiing trails surrounding Trophy Mountain (see "Wells Gray Provincial Park & the Shuswap Lakes," below). And then there's **Whistler Mountain.** With a 5,006-foot vertical and 100 marked runs, it's the cream of the province's ski resorts. And **Blackcomb Mountain,** which shares its base with Whistler, has a 5,280-foot vertical and 100 marked runs. Dual-mountain passes are available. **Helicopter skiing** makes another 100-plus runs accessible on nearby glaciers. **Lost Lakes Trails** are converted into miles of groomed cross-country trails, as are the **Valley Trail System, Singing Pass,** and **Ancient Cedars** (see "Whistler," below).

WILDLIFE WATCHING   Whether you're in search of the 20,000 **Pacific gray whales** that migrate to **Vancouver Island's** west coast (see "Vancouver Island's West Coast," below), resident ✪ **orcas** (killer whales) in the east coast's Johnstone Strait (see "Northern Vancouver Island," below), or thousands of ✪ **bald eagles** in Goldstream Provincial Park (see "Side Trips from Victoria," below), there are land-based observation points and numerous knowledgeable outfitters who can guide you to the best nature and bird-spotting areas the island has to offer.

If you take the ferry cruise up the **Inside Passage,** you have a great opportunity to spot **orcas, Dall porpoises, salmon, bald eagles,** and **sea lions.** While on the Queen Charlotte Islands, you can observe **peregrine falcons, Sitka deer, horned puffins, Cassin's auklets, Steller's sea lions,** and the world's largest **black bears** (see "The Inside Passage," below).

2 Victoria: Victorian England Meets Canadian Wilderness

In an Arcadian parkland of oak and fir at the edge of a natural harbor, **Victoria** spent the better part of the 20th century in a reverie, looking back to its glorious past as an outpost of England at the height of the Empire. It was a busy trading post and booming colonial city in the 19th century, but Victoria's lot began to fade soon after Vancouver was established in the 1880s. When its economy finally crashed early in the 20th century, shocked Victorians realized they were looking at a future with nothing much to live on but some fabulous Tudor and Victorian architecture, a beautiful natural setting, and a carefully cultivated sense of Englishness. So they decided to market that.

So successful was the sales job that the Victorians themselves began to believe they inhabited a little patch of England. They began growing elaborate rose gardens, which flourished in the mild Pacific climate, and cultivated a taste for afternoon tea with jam and scones. For decades, the reverie continued unabated. But the Victorians proved flexible enough to accommodate some changes as well. Early on it was discovered that few in the world shared the English taste for cooking, so Victoria's restaurants branched out into seafood and ethnic and fusion cuisines. And lately, as visitors have shown themselves more interested in exploring the natural world, Victoria has quietly added whale-watching and mountain-biking trips to its traditional tours on London-style double-decker buses. The result, at century's end, is that Victoria is the only city in the world where you can zoom out on a zodiac in the morning to see a pod of killer whales and make it back in time for a lovely afternoon tea with all the trimmings.

ESSENTIALS

GETTING THERE   By Plane   Air Canada (☎ 888/247-2262; www.aircanada. ca) and **Canadian Airlines** (☎ 800/363-7530; www.cdnair.ca) offer direct connections from Seattle, Vancouver, and other western cities. Provincial commuter airlines, including floatplanes that land in Victoria's Inner Harbour and helicopters, service the city as well. They include Air Canada affilliate **Air BC** (☎ 888/247-2262 or 604/688-5515), **Harbour Air** (☎ 604/688-1277), **Pacific Spirit Air** (☎ 800/665-2359), **Kenmore Air** (☎ 800/543-9595), and **Helijet Airways** (☎ 250/382-6222 in Victoria, or 604/273-1414 in Vancouver).

The **Victoria International Airport** (☎ 250/953-7500) is near the Sidney ferry terminal, 27km (17 miles) north of Victoria off the Patricia Bay Highway (Highway 17). The airport **bus service,** operated by AKAL Airport (☎ 250/386-2526), makes the 45-minute trip into town every 30 minutes 4:30am to midnight; the fare is C$13 (US$9) one-way and C$23 (US$15) round-trip. A cab ride from the airport into downtown Victoria takes about half an hour and costs about C$40 (US$27) plus tip. **Empress Cabs** and **Blue Bird Cabs** make airport runs. Several **car-rental firms** have desks at the airport, including **Avis** (☎ 250/656-6033), **Hertz** (☎ 250/656-2312), and **Tilden** (☎ 250/656-2541).

By Train   Travelers on the Horseshoe Bay–Nanaimo ferry can board a train that winds down the Cowichan River Valley through Goldstream Provincial Park into Victoria. The VIA Rail's **E&N Railiner** leaves Courtenay (about 210km/130 miles northwest of Victoria) at 1:15pm daily and arrives in Nanaimo at about 3:07pm and in Victoria at 5:45pm. The Victoria **E&N Station,** 450 Pandora Ave. (☎ 800/561-8630 in Canada), is near the Johnson Street Bridge. The one-way fare from Nanaimo to Victoria is C$20 (US$14) adults, C$18 (US$12) seniors/students, and C$12 (US$8) youth.

By Bus   Pacific Coach Lines (☎ 800/661-1725 in Canada, or 604/662-8074) operates bus service between Vancouver and Victoria. The 4-hour trip from the Pacific Central Station, 1150 Terminal Ave. in Vancouver, to the Victoria Depot, 710 Douglas St., includes passage on the Tsawwassen–Swartz Bay ferry. The adult fare is C$26 (US$17) one way, including the ferry, with daily departures 5:45am to 7:45pm.

By Ship & Ferry   See "Getting There" in chapter 15 for information about **BC Ferries** service between Vancouver and Victoria.

Three ferry services offer daily connections between Port Angeles, Bellingham, or Seattle, Washington, and Victoria. **Black Ball Transport** (☎ 250/386-2202 in Victoria, or 360/457-4491 in Port Angeles) operates between Port Angeles and Victoria, with one-way fares at C$9 (US$6) adults and C$29 (US$19) cars and drivers. The crossing takes 1½ hours, and there are at least two sailings per day (four in summer).

Clipper Navigation, 1000A Wharf St., Victoria (☎ 800/888-2535 in North America, or 250/382-8100 in Victoria), operates the *Princess Marguerite III,* a 1,070-passenger, 200-vehicle ferry. It leaves Seattle's Pier 48 at 1pm and arrives at Victoria's Ogden Point at 5:30pm. One-way fares start at US$29 adults, US$25 seniors, and US$15 children 1 to 11. Vehicles are an extra US$25. Also operated by Clipper Navigation, the *Victoria Clipper* is a high-speed catamaran running between Seattle and Victoria, with some sailings stopping in the San Juan Islands. It's a passenger-only service, and sailing time is about 3 hours with daily sailings. Adult fares are US$58 to US$66 one-way and US$94 to US$109 round-trip.

Victoria

ATTRACTIONS
- Beacon Hill Children's Farm 34
- Butchart Gardens 3
- Carr House 33
- Craigdarroch Castle 19
- Crystal Gardens 35
- Fisgard Lighthouse & Fort Rodd Hill 1
- Hatley Castle 1
- Helmcken House 20
- Maritime Museum of British Columbia 13
- Market Square 9
- Miniature World 22
- Pacific Undersea Gardens 23
- Parliament Buildings 24
- Royal British Columbia Museum 21
- Royal London Wax Museum 25
- Victoria Bug Zoo 11
- Victoria Butterfly Gardens 3

ACCOMMODATIONS
- Abigail's Hotel 18
- Admiral Motel 29
- The Aerie 4
- Andersen House Bed and Breakfast 26
- The Boathouse 4
- The Empress 32
- Hateleigh Heritage Inn 27
- Laurel Point Inn 28
- The Magnolia 16
- Ocean Pointe Resort 11
- Sooke Harbour House 2
- Swan's Hotel 8
- University of Victoria 5
- Victoria International Youth Hostel 10

DINING
- The Aerie 4
- Barb's Place 32
- Blue Crab Bar and Grill 8
- Cassis Bistro 35
- Don Mee 12
- Herald Street Caffè 6
- Millos 17
- Pablo's Dining Lounge 30
- Pagliacci's 15
- Re-bar 12
- Sooke Harbour House 2
- Restaurant 7

671

June to October, Victoria San Juan Cruises's **MV *Victoria Star*** (☎ **800/443-4552** in North America, or 360/738-8099) departs the Fairhaven Terminal in Bellingham, Washington, at 9am and arrives in Victoria at noon. It departs Victoria at 5pm, arriving in Bellingham at 8pm. Fares are US$42 one way or US$79 round-trip adult and include a free salmon dinner on the return Victoria-Bellingham run.

VISITOR INFORMATION   Across from the Empress hotel is the **Tourism Victoria Visitor Info Centre,** 812 Wharf St. (☎ 250/953-2033; info@tourismvictoria.bc.ca or www.travel.victoria.bc.ca; Bus 5, 30). If you didn't reserve a room before you arrived, you can go to this office or call its reservations hot line at ☎ **800/663-3883** or 250/953-2022 for last-minute bookings. The center is open daily 9am to 5pm (summer to 9pm).

CITY LAYOUT   Victoria is on the southeastern tip of Vancouver Island, across the Strait of Juan de Fuca from Washington state's snow-capped Olympic Peninsula. The areas of most interest to visitors, including the **downtown** and **Old Town,** lie along the eastern edge of the **Inner Harbour.** (North of the Johnson Street Bridge is the **Upper Harbour,** which is almost entirely industrial.) A little farther east, the **Ross Bay** and **Oak Bay** residential areas around Dallas Road and Beach Drive reach the beaches along the open waters of the Strait of Juan de Fuca.

Victoria's central landmark is the **Empress hotel** on Government Street, right across from the Inner Harbour wharf. If you turn your back to the hotel, the downtown and Old Town will be on your right, while the provincial **Legislative Buildings** and the **Royal BC Museum** will be on your immediate left.

Government Street goes through Victoria's main downtown shopping-and-dining district. **Douglas Street,** running parallel to Government Street, is the main business thoroughfare as well as the road to Nanaimo and the rest of the island.

GETTING AROUND   Strolling along the Inner Harbour's pedestrian walkways and streets is very pleasant. The terrain is predominantly flat, and with few exceptions, Victoria's points of interest are accessible in less than 30 minutes on foot.

By Bus   The **Victoria Regional Transit System (BC Transit),** 520 Gorge Rd. (☎ **250/382-6161**), operates 40 bus routes through greater Victoria, as well as the nearby towns of Sooke and Sidney. Regular service on the main routes runs 6am to just past midnight. Schedules and routes are available at the Tourism Victoria Visitor Info Centre. Fares are calculated on a per-zone basis. One-way single-zone fares are C$1.75 (US$1.15) adults and C$1.10 (US75¢) seniors/children 5 to 13; two zones are C$2.50 (US$1.65) and C$1.75 (US$1.15), respectively. Transfers are good for travel in one direction only with no stops. A **DayPass** (C$6/US$3.65 adults, C$4/US$2.65 seniors/children 5 to 13) covers unlimited travel throughout the day. You can buy passes at the Tourism Victoria Visitor Info Centre, as well as convenience stores and ticket outlets displaying the FareDealer symbol.

By Ferry   Crossing the Inner, Upper, and Victoria Harbors by one of the 12-passenger blue **Victoria Harbour Ferries** (☎ 250/708-0201) is cheap and fun. During the high summer season, ferries to the Empress hotel, Coast Harborside Hotel, and Ocean Pointe Resort Hotel run about every 15 minutes 9am to 9pm. Off-season, the ferries run only on sunny weekends 11am to 6pm. The cost is C$3 (US$2) adults and C$1.50 (US$1) children.

By Car   Make sure your hotel has parking. Metered **street parking** is hard to come by in the downtown area, and rules are strictly enforced. Unmetered parking on side streets is rare. All major downtown hotels have guest parking; rates vary from free to C$20 (US$13) per day. There are parking lots at **View Street** between Douglas and

Blanshard streets; **Johnson Street** off Blanshard Street; **Yates Street** north of Bastion Square; and **the Bay** on Fisgard at Blanshard Street. Car-rental agencies in Victoria include **ABC,** 2507 Government St. (☎ **800/464-6464** or 250/388-3153; Bus: 31); **Avis,** 1001 Douglas St. (☎ **800/879-2847** or 250/386-8468; Bus: 5); **Budget,** 757 Douglas St. (☎ **800/268-8900** or 250/253-5300; Bus: 5); **Hertz Canada,** 102-907 Fort St. (☎ **800/263-0600** or 250/388-4411; Bus: 11); and **Tilden International,** 767 Douglas St. (☎ **800/387-4747** or 250/386-1213; Bus: 11). Car rentals cost about C$25 to C$45 (US$17 to US$30) per day for a compact to mid-size vehicle. Remember that it's always cheaper to arrange the rental before you leave home.

By Bicycle   There are bike lanes throughout the city and paved paths along parks and beaches. You can rent bicycles for C$6 (US$4) per hour and C$20 (US$13) per day from **Budget,** 757 Douglas St. (☎ **250/953-5300;** Bus: 5).

By Taxi   Within the downtown area, you can expect to travel for less than C$6 (US$4) plus tip. It's best to call for a cab; drivers don't always stop on city streets for flag-downs, especially when it's raining. Call for a pickup from **Empress Cabs** at ☎ **250/381-2222** or **Blue Bird Cabs** at ☎ **250/382-8294.**

SPECIAL EVENTS & FESTIVALS   So many flowers bloom during the temperate month of February in Victoria and the surrounding area that the city holds an annual **Flower Count.** Call ☎ **250/383-7191** for details. In April, the city hosts the **TerrifVic Dixieland Jazz Party** (☎ **250/953-2011**) with bands from around the world playing swing, Dixieland, honky-tonk, and fusion. Toward the end of May, thousands of yachts sail into Victoria Harbor during the **Swiftsure Yacht Race;** call ☎ **250/953-2033** for details. In June, the **Jazz Fest International** (☎ **250/388-4423**) brings jazz, swing, bebop, fusion, and improv artists from around the world. The **Folkfest,** a free 8-day worldbeat music festival, takes place at the end of June.

The provincial capital celebrates **Canada Day** (July 1) with events centered around the Inner Harbour, including music, food, and fireworks. The August **First Peoples Festival** (☎ **250/384-3211**) highlights the culture and heritage of the Pacific Northwest First Nations tribes. In November, the **Great Canadian Beer Festival** (☎ **250/952-0360**) features samples from the province's best microbreweries. And Victoria rings in the New Year with **First Night** (☎ **250/380-1211**), a family-oriented New Year's Eve celebration with free performances at many downtown venues.

FAST FACTS   **American Express**   The office is at 1203 Douglas St. (☎ **250/385-8731;** Bus: 5), open Monday to Friday 8:30am to 5:30pm and Saturday 10am to 4pm.

Area Code   The telephone area code for all Vancouver Island, including Victoria and most of British Columbia, is **250.**

Dentist   Most major hotels have a dentist on call. **Cresta Dental Centre,** 3170 Tillicum Rd. at Burnside Street (☎ **250/384-7711;** Bus: 21), in the Tillicum Mall, is open Monday 8am to 5pm, Tuesday to Friday 8am to 9pm, Saturday 9am to 5pm, and Sunday noon to 5pm.

Doctor   Hotels usually have a doctor on call. The **James Bay Treatment Center,** 100-230 Menzies St. (☎ **250/388-9934;** Bus: 5), a medical facility, is open Monday to Friday 9am to 6pm and Saturday and statutory holidays 10am to 4pm.

Emergencies   Dial ☎ **911** for fire, police, ambulance, and poison control.

Hospitals   Local hospitals include the **Royal Jubilee Hospital,** 1900 Fort St. (☎ **250/370-8000;** emergency 250/370-8212; Bus: 11), and **Victoria General Hospital,** 1 Hospital Way (☎ **250/727-4212;** emergency 250/727-4181; Bus: 22).

Police   Dial ☎ **911.** The **Victoria City Police** can also be reached by calling ☎ **250/995-7654.** The **Royal Canadian Mounted Police** can be reached at ☎ **250/ 380-6261.**

Safety   Crime rates are quite low in Victoria, but transients panhandle throughout the downtown and Old Town areas. As in any city, stay alert to prevent crimes of opportunity.

Weather   Call ☎ **250/656-3978** for weather updates.

SEEING THE SIGHTS
Note: See the "Victoria" map (p. 671) to locate sights in this section.

THE TOP ATTRACTIONS
Maritime Museum of British Columbia. 28 Bastion Sq. ☎ **250/385-4222.** http:// mmbc.bc.ca. Admission C$5 (US$3.35) adults, C$4 (US$2.65) seniors, C$3 (US$2) students, C$2 (US$1.35) children 6–12; children under 6 free. Family discounts. Daily 9am–4:30pm. Closed Christmas. Bus: 5.

In the former provincial courthouse, this museum is dedicated to recalling the province's rich maritime heritage. The displays do a good job illustrating maritime history, from the early explorers to the fur-trading and whaling era to the days of grand ocean liners and military conflict. There's also an impressive collection on ship models and paraphernalia—uniforms, weapons, gear—along with photographs and journals. The gift shop offers an excellent selection of nautical books.

Parliament Buildings (Provincial Legislature). 501 Belleville St. ☎ **250/387-3046.** www.parl-bldgs.gov.bc.ca. Free admission. Daily 9am–5pm. Tours every 20 min. in summer, hourly in winter.

Designed by 25-year-old Francis Rattenbury and built between 1893 and 1898 at a cost of nearly C$1 million (US$667,000), the Parliament Buildings (a.k.a. the Legislature) are an architectural gem. The half-hour guided tour comes across at times like a Grade 8 civics lesson, but it's worth it just to see the fine mosaics, marble, woodwork, and stained glass.

✪ **Butchart Gardens.** 800 Benvenuto Ave., Brentwood Bay. ☎ **250/652-4422** or 250/652-8222 for dining reservations. www.butchartgardens.bc.ca/butchart. Admission C$16 (US$11) adults, C$8 (US$5) youths 13–17, C$2 (US$1.35) children 5–12. Spring, fall, and winter discounts. Daily from 9am; call for seasonal closing times. AE, MC, V. Take Blanshard St. (Hwy. 17) north toward the ferry terminal in Saanich, then turn left on Keating Crossroads, which leads directly to the gardens—about 20 min. from downtown Victoria. Bus: 75.

These internationally acclaimed gardens were born after Robert Butchart exhausted the limestone quarry near his Tod Inlet home. His wife, Jenny, gradually landscaped the deserted eyesore into the resplendent Sunken Garden, opening it to the public in 1904. A Rose Garden, an Italian Garden, and a Japanese Garden were added. As the fame of the 50 acres grew, the Butcharts also transformed their house into an attraction. The gardens—still in the family—now display more than a million plants throughout the year. On summer evenings, they're beautifully illuminated with a variety of softly colored lights, and fireworks displays are held on Saturdays in July and August. A very good lunch, dinner, and afternoon tea are served in the Dining Room Restaurant in the residence; casual family fare is served in the Blue Poppy Restaurant.

✪ **Royal British Columbia Museum.** 675 Belleville St. ☎ **800/661-5411** or 250/387-3701. http://rbcm1.gov.bc.ca. Admission C$7 (US$4.65) adults, C$4 (US$2.65) seniors/students/youth; C$18 (US$12) families. Higher rates sometimes in effect for temporary exhibits. Daily 9am–5pm. Closed Dec 25 and Jan 1. Bus: 5, 28, 30.

One of the world's best regional museums, the Royal BC features natural-history dioramas indistinguishable from the real thing, full-size re-creations of frontier towns and native longhouses, and a collection of native art and artifacts that'll really impress you. The second-floor Natural History Gallery shows the coastal flora, fauna, and geography, from the ice age to the present; it includes dioramas of a temperate rain forest, a seacoast, an underground ecology of giant bugs, and (particularly appealing to kids) a live tidal pool with sea stars and anemones. The third-floor First Peoples Gallery is an incredible showpiece of native art and also houses many artifacts showing everyday native life, a full-size re-creation of a longhouse, and many smaller village scenes. The museum also has an IMAX theater showing a variety of large-screen movies. On the way out (or in) be sure to stop by Thunderbird Park, beside the museum, where a cedar longhouse houses a workshop where native carvers work on new totem poles.

✪ **Victoria Butterfly Gardens.** 1461 Benvenuto Ave., Brentwood Bay. ☎ **250/ 652-3822.** www.victoriabc.com/attract/butterfly.htm. Admission C$8 (US$5) adults, C$7 (US$4.35) students/seniors, C$4.50 (US$3) children 3–12, C$25 (US$17) families; under 3 free. May–Oct daily 9:30am–5pm; Nov–Apr call in advance. Bus: 75.

Hundreds of exotic colorful butterflies flutter freely through this lush tropical green-house. You're provided with an identification chart and set free to roam around. Species range from the tiny Central American Julia (a brilliant orange butterfly about 3 inches across) to the Southeast Asian Giant Atlas Moth (mottled brown and red, with a wingspan approaching a foot). Other butterflies are brilliant blue, yellow, or a mix of colors and patterns. Naturalists are on hand to explain butterfly biology, and there's even a display where you can see the beautiful creatures emerge from their cocoons.

Royal London Wax Museum. 470 Belleville St. ☎ **250/388-4461.** Admission C$8 (US$5) adults, C$7 (US$4.35) seniors, C$3 (US$2) children. Daily 9am–7:30pm. Bus: 5, 27, 28, 30.

See the same royal family you already get too much of on TV. See other, older royals of even less significance. See their family pets. All courtesy of Madame Tussaud's 200-year-old wax technology. There's also the chamber of horrors, which rates well below a *Buffy the Vampire Slayer* episode on the scariness scale. Still not thrilled? The management of the wax museum seems to suspect as much—they've begun taking liberties with their wax figures' figures. Look especially for the Princess Diana mannequin with the Pamela Anderson implants.

Pacific Undersea Gardens. 490 Belleville St. ☎ **250/382-5717.** Admission C$7 (US$4.65) adults, C$6 (US$4) seniors, C$5 (US$3.35) children 5–11; children under 5 free. Family discounts. May–Sept 15 daily 9am–5pm; Sept 16–Apr daily 10am–5pm. Bus: 5, 27, 28, 30.

A gently sloping stairway leads down to this unique marine observatory's glass-enclosed viewing area, where you can observe the Inner Harbour's marine life up close. Some 5,000 creatures feed, play, hunt, and court in these protected waters. Sharks, wolf eels, poisonous stonefish, flowery sea anemones, starfish, sturgeon, and salmon are just a few of the organisms that make their homes in these waters. One of the harbor's star attractions is a remarkably photogenic octopus (reputedly the largest in captivity). Injured seals and orphaned seal pups are cared for in holding pens along-side the observatory as part of a provincial marine-mammal rescue program.

Fisgard Lighthouse National Historic Site & Fort Rodd Hill. 603 Fort Rodd Hill Rd. ☎ **250/478-5849.** http://parkscanada.pch.gc.ca. Admission C$3 (US$2) adults, C$2.25 (US$1.50) seniors, C$1.50 (US$1) children 6–16; children under 6 free. Family discounts. Mar–Oct daily 10am–5:30pm; Nov–Feb daily 9am–4:30pm.

Perched on an outcrop of volcanic rock, the **Fisgard Lighthouse** has guided ships toward Victoria's sheltered harbor since 1873. The light no longer has a keeper (the beacon has long been automated), but the site itself has been restored to its 1873 appearance. Two floors' worth of exhibits in the lightkeepers' house narrate stories of the lighthouse, its keepers, and the terrible shipwrecks that gave this coastline its ominous moniker, "the graveyard of the Pacific." Adjoining the lighthouse, **Fort Rodd Hill** is a perfectly preserved 1890s coastal artillery fort that—though in more than half a century it never fired a shot in anger—still sports camouflaged searchlights, underground magazines, and its original guns. Audiovisual exhibits bring the fort to life with the voices and faces of the men who served at this key outpost. Displays of artifacts, room re-creations, and videos of historic film footage add to the experience. It's so close to the lighthouse that concussion from the guns once blew out all the lighthouse's windows.

Miniature World. In the Empress hotel, 649 Humboldt St. ☎ **250/385-9731.** www. miniatureworld.com. Admission C$7 (US$4.65) adults, C$6 (US$4) students, C$5 (US$3.35) children. Summer daily 8:30am–9pm; winter daily 9am–5pm. Bus: 5, 27, 28, 30.

It sounds cheesy: Hundreds of dolls and miniatures and scenes from old fairy tales. And its brochure features bizarre photos of Brady Bunch clones in 1950s fashions grinning like idiots as they loom over yet another diorama. Yet this place is actually kinda cool. You walk in and are plunged into darkness, except for a moon and some planets and a tiny spaceship flying up to rendezvous with an orbiting mother ship. This is the most up-to-date display. Farther in are re-creations of battle scenes and 18th-century fancy-dress balls, a miniature CPR railway that runs all the way across a miniature Canada, a three-ring circus and midway, and scenes from Mother Goose and Charles Dickens stories. Better yet, most of the displays do something.

Aviation Museum. 1910 Norseman Rd., Sidney. ☎ **250/655-3300.** Admission C$4 (US$2.65) adults, C$3 (US$2) seniors; children under 12 free. Summer daily 10am–4pm; winter daily 11am–3pm. Closed Dec 25. Bus: Airport. This is a working museum inside a hangar at Victoria International Airport. Volunteers keep busy restoring vintage aircraft to add to the collection, which already includes World War II fighters and bombers, a 1929 Eastman Flying Boat, a Gibson Twin (built in Victoria in 1911), and much more.

ARCHITECTURAL HIGHLIGHTS & HISTORIC HOMES

For an excellent guide to many of Victoria's buildings, as well as short biographies of its most significant architects, pick up *Exploring Victoria's Architecture,* by Martin Segger and Douglas Franklin. You'll find copies in **Munro's Books,** 1008 Government St. (☎ **604/382-2464;** Bus: 5, 30).

Perhaps the most intriguing downtown edifice isn't a building at all but a work of art. The walls of **Fort Victoria,** which once covered much of downtown, have been demarcated in the sidewalk with bricks bearing the names of original settlers and fur traders. Look in the sidewalk on Government Street at the corner of Fort Street.

Most of the retail establishments in Victoria's Old Town area are housed in 19th-century shipping warehouses that have been carefully restored. You can take a **self-guided tour** of these buildings, most of which were erected between the 1870s and 1890s and whose history is recounted on easy-to-read outdoor plaques. The majority of the restored buildings are between Douglas and Johnson streets from Wharf Street to Government Street. The most impressive structure once contained a number of shipping offices and warehouses but is now the home of a 45-shop complex known as **Market Square,** 560 Johnson St./255 Market Sq. (☎ **250/386-2441;** Bus: 6).

What do you do when you're the richest man in British Columbia, when you've clawed and scraped and bullied your way up from indentured servant to coal baron and merchant prince? You build a castle, of course. So in the 1880s, Scottish magnate Robert Dunsmuir built ✪ **Craigdarroch Castle,** 1050 Joan Crescent (☎ **250/ 592-5323;** Bus: 11, 14). The 39-room Highland-style castle is topped with stone turrets and chimneys and filled with the opulent Victorian splendor you'd expect to read about in a romance novel. You're provided with a self-tour booklet, and for those with the urge to know more, there are volunteer docents on every floor. Admission is C$8 (US$5) adults, C$5 (US$3.35) students, C$2 (US$1.35) children 6 to 12; children under 6 are free. It's open daily: June 15 to August 9am to 7pm and September to June 14 10am to 4:30pm.

Dunsmuir's son, James, built his own palatial home, **Hatley Castle,** off Highway 14 in Colwood. The younger Dunsmuir reportedly commissioned architect Samuel Maclure with the words "Money doesn't matter; just build what I want." The bill, in 1908, came to over C$1 million. The grounds of the castle, now home to **Royal Roads University,** feature extensive floral gardens and are open to the public free of charge (☎ 250/391-2511; Bus: 50 to Western Exchange, then bus 56).

To get a taste of how upper-middle-class Victorians lived, visit the **Carr House,** 207 Government St. (☎ 250/383-5843; Bus: 5, 30), where painter Emily Carr was born in 1871. An artistic pioneer, Carr broke free of then-dominant European conventions about art to create a vibrant painting style all her own. Many of her works depict rugged west coast landscapes or people or scenes from native villages along the coast. Carr was also an accomplished writer, and her most popular book, *Klee Wyck,* tells of her travels among west coast natives. **Helmcken House,** 675 Belleville St. (☎ 250/ 386-0021; Bus: 5, 30), was the residence of a pioneer doctor who settled in the area during the 1850s; it still contains the original imported British furnishings and his medicine chest. **Craigflower Farmhouse,** 110 Island Hwy. (☎ 250/383-4621; Bus: 14), in the View Royal district, was built in 1856 by a Scottish settler who brought many of his furnishings from the old country. The Carr House, Helmcken House, and Craigflower Farmhouse are open in summer, Thursday to Monday 11am to 5pm. Admission is C$3.25 (US$2.15) adults, C$2.25 (US$1.50) seniors/students, and C$1.25 (US85¢) children 6 to 12; children under 6 are free. A three-site discount pass is available.

PARKS & GARDENS

The 154-acre **Beacon Hill Park** (Bus: 11) stretches from Southgate Street to Dallas Road between Douglas and Cook streets. Stands of indigenous Garry oaks (found only on Vancouver Island, Hornby Island, and Salt Spring Island) and manicured lawns are interspersed with floral gardens and ponds. Hike up Beacon Hill to get a clear view of the Strait of Georgia, Haro Strait, and Washington's Olympic Mountains. The children's farm (below), aviary, tennis courts, lawn-bowling green, putting green, cricket pitch, wading pool, playground, and picnic area make this a wonderful place to spend a few hours with the family.

Government House, the official residence of the Lieutenant Governor, is at 1401 Rockland Ave. (Bus: 1), in the Fairfield residential district. The house itself is closed to the public (and not worth touring anyway), but the formal gardens are open and well worth a wander. Round back, the hillside of Garry oaks is one of the last places to see what the area's natural fauna would've looked like before European settlers arrived. At the front, the rose garden is sumptuous.

Victoria has an indoor garden that first opened as a huge saltwater pool in 1925 (Olympic swimmer and original *Tarzan* star Johnny Weismuller competed here) and was converted into a big-band dance hall during World War II. The **Crystal Garden,** 731 Douglas St. (☎ 250/953-8800; Bus: 5, 30), is filled with rare and exotic tropical flora and fauna and is open daily 10am to 5:30pm (later in summer). Admission is C$8 (US$5) adults, C$7 (US$4.35) seniors, and C$4 (US$2.65) children 5–16; children under 5 are free. Family and group discounts are available.

ESPECIALLY FOR KIDS

Nature's the thing for kids in Victoria. At the **Beacon Hill Children's Farm,** Circle Drive, Beacon Hill Park (☎ **250/381-2532;** Bus: 11), kids can ride ponies; pet goats, rabbits, and other barnyard animals; and even cool off in the wading pool. Mid-March to September, the farm is open daily 10am to 5pm. Admission is by donation.

For a new take on this old concept, visit the **Victoria Butterfly Gardens** (above). The **Crystal Gardens** (☎ **250/381-1277;** Bus: 5, 11, 30) behind the Empress hotel also has butterflies, as well as macaws and pelicans. Closer to town and two shades creepier than the Butterfly Gardens is the **Victoria Bug Zoo,** 1107 Wharf St. (☎ **250/384-BUGS;** Bus: 6), home to praying mantises and giant African cockroaches, along with knowledgeable guides who can bring the bugs out and let you or your kids handle and touch them. Admission is C$6 (US$4) adults and C$4 (US$2.65) children 3 to 16; children 2 and under are free. Kids also love the creatures at the **Pacific Undersea Gardens** (above).

ORGANIZED TOURS

BUS TOURS   Gray Line of Victoria, 700 Douglas St. (☎ **250/388-5248;** Bus: 5, 11, 30), conducts tours of Victoria and Butchart Gardens. The 1½-hour "Grand City Tour" costs C$14 (US$9) adults and C$7 (US$4.65) children. In summer, tours depart every 30 minutes 9:30am to 7pm; December to mid-March, there are daily departures at 11:30am and 1:30pm. The same company operates a **trolley service** every 40 minutes 9:30am to 5:30pm on a circuit of 35 hotels, attractions, shops, and restaurants. A day pass, which allows you to stop and reboard at the destinations of your choice throughout the day, costs C$7 (US$4.65) adults and C$4 (US$2.65) children.

SPECIALTY TOURS   For C$12 (US$8), Victoria Harbour Ferries, 922 Old Esquimalt Rd. (☎ **250/708-0201),** offers a terrific 45-minute tour of the Inner and Outer Harbors. A 50-minute tour of the Gorge opposite the Johnson Street Bridge, where tidal falls reverse with each change of the tide, costs C$14 (US$9) adults, C$12 (US$8) seniors, and C$7 (US$4.65) children. Tours depart from seven stops around the Inner Harbour every 15 minutes daily 10am to 10pm. To get a bird's-eye view of Victoria, take a 30-minute tour with **Harbour Air Seaplanes,** 1234 Wharf St. (☎ **250/361-6786;** Bus: 6). Rates are C$72 (US$48) per person; flights depart at 10am, noon, and 4pm.

Heritage Tours and Daimler Limousine Service, 713 Bexhill Rd. (☎ **250/ 474-4332),** will pick you up and guide you through the city, Butchart Gardens, and Craigdarroch Castle in a six-passenger Daimler limo. Rates start at C$62 (US$41) per hour per vehicle (not per person). The bicycle-rickshaws operated by **Kabuki Kabs,** 15-950 Government St. (☎ **250/385-4243),** usually "park" in front of the Empress hotel, and a tour is C$60 (US$40) per hour for a two-person cab and C$90 (US$60) per hour for a four-person cab.

Tallyho Horse Drawn Tours, 2044 Milton St. (☎ **250/383-5067),** has conducted tours of Victoria in horse-drawn carriages since 1903. Excursions start at the corner of Belleville and Menzies streets; fares are C$14 (US$9) adults, C$12 (US$8) seniors, C$9 (US$6) students, and C$6 (US$4) children 17 and under. Family discounts are available. Tours operate every 30 minutes daily 9am to 10pm in summer (10am to 5:30pm in late March, Apr, May, and Sept). Tallyho also offers private tours (maximum six people) at C$35 (US$23) for 15 minutes and C$60 (US$40) for 30 minutes.

For a pleasant and informative summer-evening stroll, join a guided walk through downtown and Old Town. The **Old Cemetery Society of Victoria,** Box 40115, Victoria, BC V8W 3R8 (☎ 250/598-8870), presents **Lantern Tours in the Old Burying Ground,** which begin at the Cherry Bank Hotel, 845 Burdett St. (Bus: 5), at 9pm nightly in July and August. On Sundays at 2pm, the tour leaves from Bagga Pasta, in the Fairfield Plaza, 1516 Fairfield Rd. (Bus: 1), across from the cemetery gate. Both tours are C$5 (US$3.35) per person or C$12 (US$8) per family. The Society also offers tours of the Ross Bay Cemetery; cost is by donation. Phone for times and information; group tours of the Ross Bay Cemetery are also available for C$35 (US$23).

Victoria's Haunted Walk & Other Tours, 185-911 Yates St., Victoria, BC V8V 4Y9 (☎ 250/361-2619), introduces you to some of the city's nefarious ghosts and spirits. June to September, tours lasting 1½ hours begin nightly at 7 and 9pm at the Tourism Victoria Info Centre on the Inner Harbour. Cost is C$8 (US$5) adults and C$7 (US$4.65) students/seniors; children under 12 are free.

OUTDOOR ACTIVITIES

Specialized rental outfitters are listed with each activity below, but **Sports Rent,** 3084 Blanshard St. (☎ 250/385-7368; Bus: 30, 31), is a general-equipment and water-sport rental outlet to keep in mind if you forget to pack something.

BIKING The 8-mile **Scenic Marine Drive** bike path begins at Dallas Road and Douglas Street, at the base of Beacon Hill Park. The paved path follows the walkway along the beaches, winds up through the residential district on Beach Drive, and eventually turns left and heads south toward downtown Victoria on Oak Bay Avenue. The **Inner Harbour pedestrian path** has a bike lane for cyclists who want to take a leisurely ride around the entire city seawall. The new **Galloping Goose Trail** runs from Victoria west through Colwood and Sooke all the way up to Leechtown. If you don't want to cycle the whole thing, there are numerous places to park along the way, as well as several places where the trail intersects with public transit. Call **BC Transit** at ☎ 250/382-6161 to find out which bus routes take bikes.

Bikes, helmets, locks, and child trailers are available by the hour or day at **Budget Car Rentals,** 727 Courtenay St., behind the Empress (☎ 250/953-5333; Bus: 5, 11, 30), costing from C$5 (US$3.35) per hour and C$20 to C$25 (US$13 to US$17) per day. The **Pacific Rim Bicycle Tour Company** (☎ 250/881-0585) offers guided bike tours starting at C$29 (US$19).

BOATING You can book boat rentals and charters of a few hours to a couple of weeks at **Brentwood Inn Resort Boat Rentals,** 7176 Brentwood Dr., Brentwood Bay (☎ 250/652-3151; Bus: 75). There are also a number of independent charter companies docked at the **Oak Bay Marina,** 1327 Beach Dr. (☎ 250/598-3369; Bus: 2)— for example, the **Horizon Yacht Centre** (☎ 250/595-2628) offers sailboat charters, lessons, and navigational tips geared toward familiarizing you with the surrounding waters. The **Marine Adventure Centre** (☎ 250/995-2211), on the floatplane docks in the Inner Harbour, can arrange boat charters and almost anything else marine related. Skippered charters in the area run about C$600 (US$400) per day, and boat rentals average C$125 (US$83) for a couple of hours. If you're taking the wheel yourself, don't forget to check the **marine forecast** at ☎ 250/656-7515 before casting off.

CANOEING & KAYAKING **Ocean River Sports,** 1437 Store St., Victoria, BC V8W 3J6 (☎ 250/381-4233; Bus: 6), can equip you with everything from single-kayak, double-kayak, and canoe rentals to life jackets, tents, and dry-storage camping gear. Rental for a single kayak is C$14 (US$9) per hour and C$42 (US$28) per day. If you're a little tentative about renting a boat on your own, Ocean River also runs guided tours on the harbor and on the sheltered waters near Sidney, in sight of the Gulf Islands. Tours start at C$55 (US$37) for a 3-hour novice lesson and paddle. Sundown tours are especially popular.

FISHING　If you're looking to do saltwater fishing, **Adam's Fishing Charters** (☎ 250/370-2326) and the **Marine Adventure Centre** (☎ 250/995-2211) in Victoria are good places to look for a charter (see also "Boating," above). To fish, you need a nonresident saltwater or freshwater license. Licenses for freshwater fishing cost C$16 (US$11) for 1 day for those who live outside the province. Saltwater fishing licenses cost C$6 (US$3.75) for 1 day, plus a surcharge of C$6 (US$4.30) for salmon fishing. **Robinson's Sporting Goods Ltd.,** 1307 Broad St. (☎ 250/385-3429; Bus: 1, 5, 11, 30), is a reliable source for information, recommendations, lures, licenses, and gear.

GOLF　The **Cedar Hill Municipal Golf Course,** 1400 Derby Rd. (☎ 250/595-3103; Bus: 24), is an 18-hole public course 3.3km (2 miles) from downtown Victoria; daytime greens fees are C$30 (US$20) and twilight fees C$26 (US$17). The **Cordova Bay Golf Course,** 5333 Cordova Bay Rd. (☎ 250/658-4075; Bus: 75), is northeast of downtown. Designed by Bill Robinson, the 18-hole course features 66 sand traps and some tight fairways. Greens fees are C$45 (US$30) Monday to Thursday and C$48 (US$32) Friday to Sunday and holidays. The **Olympic View Golf Club,** 643 Latoria Rd. (☎ 250/474-3673; www.sunnygolf.com/ov/ov.html; Bus: 50 to CanWest Exchange, then bus 54), is one of the top-35 golf courses in Canada. Amid 12 lakes and a pair of waterfalls, this 18-hole, 6,414-yard course is open daily, with greens fees C$49 (US$33) Monday to Thursday and C$55 (US$37) Friday to Sunday and holidays. You can also call the **A-1 Last Minute Golf Hotline** at ☎ 800/684-6344 or 604/878-1833 for substantial discounts and short-notice tee times at courses around the area.

HIKING　For groups of 10 or more who want to learn more about the surrounding flora and fauna, book a naturalist-guided tour of the island's rain forests and seashore with **Coastal Connections Interpretive Nature Hikes** (☎ 250/480-9560) or **Nature Calls** (☎ 877/361-HIKE). Tours cost C$60 to C$110 (US$40 to US$73), transport included, and go to **Botanical Beach, East Sooke Park,** or the **Carmanah Valley.**

WATER SPORTS　The **Crystal Pool & Fitness Centre,** 2275 Quadra St. (☎ 250/380-7946; schedule 250/380-4636; Bus: 6), is Victoria's main aquatic facility. The 50m lap pool, children's pool, diving pool, sauna, whirlpool, and steam, weight, and aerobics rooms are open daily 6am to midnight. Drop-in admission is C$4.20 (US$2.80) adults, C$3.15 (US$2.10) seniors/students, and C$2.10 (US$1.40) children 6 to 12. **Beaver Lake** in Elk and Beaver Lake Regional Park (Bus: 70, 75) has lifeguards on duty, as well as picnicking facilities along the shore. **All Fun Recreation Park,** 650 Hordon Rd. (☎ 250/474-4546 or 250/474-3184; Bus: 52), operates a ¾-mile water-slide complex that's ideal for cooling off on hot summer days. It's open daily 11am to 7pm in season, and full-day passes are C$16 (US$11) for sliders over 6 years (nonsliders get in for C$6/US$4); after 3pm admission drops to C$12 (US$8) for sliders and C$5 (US$3.35) for nonsliders.

　　Windsurfers skim along the Inner Harbour and Elk Lake when the breezes are right. Though there are no specific facilities, French Beach, off Sooke Road on the way to Sooke Harbour, is a popular local windsurfing spot. **Ocean Wind Water Sports**

Rentals, 5411 Hamsterly Rd. (☎ **250/658-8171;** Bus: 70, 75), rents nearly every form of popular water-sports gear, including parasails.

WHALE WATCHING   The waters surrounding the southern tip of Vancouver Island teem with orcas (killer whales), as well as harbor seals, sea lions, bald eagles, and harbour and Dahl's porpoises. **Victoria Marine Adventures,** 950 Wharf (☎ **250/995-2211;** Bus: 6), is just one of many outfits offering whale-watching tours in both Zodiacs and covered boats. Fares are C$75 (US$50) adults and C$49 (US$33) children. March to October, **Pride of Victoria Cruises,** Oak Bay Beach Hotel, 1175 Beach Dr. (☎ **250/592-3474;** Bus: 1), offers daily 3½-hour whale-watching charters on a fully equipped 45-foot catamaran that can handle up to eight passengers. A picnic-style lunch is served. Fares are C$79 (US$53) adults and C$39 ($26) children; lunch is C$6 (US$4) per person in summer.

SHOPPING

Victoria has dozens of little specialty shops that appeal to every taste and whim, and because the city is built to such a pedestrian scale, you can wander from place to place seeking out whatever treasure it is you're after. Nearly all the areas below are within a short walk of the Empress hotel.

ANTIQUES   Many of the best stores are in **Antiques Row,** a 3-block stretch on Fort Street between Blanshard and Cook streets. Though farthest from downtown, **Faith Grant's Connoisseur Shop Ltd.,** 1156 Fort St. (☎ **250/383-0121;** Bus: 1, 10), is also the best. Other shops on the row that are worth poking your nose into are **Jeffries and Co. Silversmiths,** 1026 Fort St. (☎ **250/383-8315;** Bus: 1, 10); **Romanoff & Company Antiques,** 837 Fort St. (☎ **250/480-1543;** Bus: 1, 10); and for furniture fans **Charles Baird Antiques,** 1044A Fort St. (☎ **250/384-8809;** Bus: 1, 10).

ARTS & CRAFTS   Owned/operated by the Cowichan native band, the **Cowichan Native Village,** 200 Cowichan Way, Duncan (☎ **250/746-8119**), sells beautiful crafts and stocks an excellent selection of books and publications on First Nations history and lore. **Cowichan Trading Ltd.,** 1328 Government St. (☎ **250/383-0321;** Bus: 1, 5, 30), sells a mix of T-shirts and gewgaws in addition to fine Cowichan sweaters, masks, and fine silver jewelry.

BOOKS   All bookstores should look as good as **Munro's Book Store,** 1108 Government St. (☎ **250/382-2464;** Bus: 1, 5, 30), with its mile-high ceiling and wall murals. All bookstores should also stock so much over 35,000 titles, including an excellent selection of books about Victoria. **The Field Naturalist,** 1126 Blanshard St. (☎ **250/388-4174;** Bus: 1, 5, 30), is a smallish but incredibly well-stocked emporium of field guides, spotting charts, binoculars, and telescopes.

A DEPARTMENT STORE & SHOPPING MALL   The **Bay (Hudson's Bay Company),** 1701 Douglas St. (☎ **250/385-1311;** Bus: 5), sells camping and sports equipment, Hudson's Bay woolen point blankets, and fashions by Tommy Hilfiger, Polo, DKNY, and Liz Claiborne. Right in the center of town, the **Victoria Eaton Centre,** between Government and Douglas streets (☎ **250/382-7141;** Bus: 1, 5, 30), is a full modern shopping mall disguised as a block of heritage buildings. Inside are three floors of shops and boutiques.

FASHION   Voted best women's clothing store year after year in *Monday* magazine's best-of-annual poll, **Sunday's Snowflakes,** 1000 Douglas St. ☎ **250/381-4461;** Bus: 1, 5, 30), features exclusively Canadian designers and makes a point of stocking small sizes. More classic clothing lines are to be found at **W.&J. Wilson's Clothiers,** 1221 Government St. (☎ **250/383-7177;** Bus: 1, 5, 30), Canada's oldest family-run clothing store. **Prescott & Andrews,** 909 Government St. (☎ 250/953-7788; Bus: 1, 5, 30), is the place to pick up a sweater. For men's fashions, try **British Importers,** 1125 Government St. (☎ 250/386-1496; Bus: 1, 5, 30).

JEWELRY   Ian MacDonald of **MacDonald Jewelry,** 618 View St. (☎ 250/382-4113; Bus: 1, 2), designs and crafts all his own jewelry, which makes for some interesting creations. At the **Jade Tree,** 606 Humboldt St. (☎ 250/388-4326; Bus: 1, 5, 30), you'll find jewelry crafted from British Columbia jade into necklaces, bracelets, and other items.

NATIVE ART   All the coastal tribes are represented in the **Alcheringa Gallery,** 665 Fort St. (☎ 250/383-8224; Bus: 1, 2), along with a significant collection of pieces from Papau New Guinea. Presentation is museum quality, with prices to match. **Hill's Indian Crafts,** 1008 Government St. ☎ 250/385-3911; Bus: 1, 5, 30), features exquisite traditional native art, including wooden masks and carvings, Haida argillite, and silver jewelry.

OUTDOOR CLOTHES & EQUIPMENT   **Ocean River Sports,** 1437 Store St. (☎ 250/381-4233; Bus: 6), is the place to go to arrange a sea-kayak tour. It's also a good spot for outdoor clothing and camping knickknacks.

WHERE TO STAY

Reservations are absolutely essential in Victoria from May to September. If you arrive without a reservation and have trouble finding a room, **Tourism Victoria** (☎ 800/663-3883 or 250/382-1131) can make reservations for you at hotels, inns, and B&Bs.

Note: See the "Victoria" map (p. 671) to locate hotels in this section.

INNER HARBOUR

Very Expensive

✪ **The Empress.** 1 Government St., Victoria, BC V8W 1W5. ☎ **800/441-1414** or 250/384-8111. Fax 250/381-4334. www.cphotels.ca. 497 units. MINIBAR TV TEL. May–Oct C$295–C$490 (US$197–US$327) double; Nov–Apr C$200–C$395 (US$133–US$263) double. Year-round C$425–C$1,500 (US$283–US$1,000) suite. Wheelchair-accessible rooms available. AE, CB, DC, DISC, ER, MC, V. Underground valet parking C$15 (US$10). Bus: 5.

Francis Rattenbury's 1908 harborside creation is a joy to look at, but there are things you need to know before staying at the Empress. Some of the deluxe guest rooms and all the Entree Gold rooms are dreamy: large beds, wide windows, high ceilings, and natural light enough to illuminate Venice. The 36 Entree Gold rooms also include private check-in, a concierge, breakfast in the private lounge, and extras like CD players and TVs in the bathrooms. However, many of the other rooms are built to the "cozy" standards of 1908. If you can afford an Entree Gold or a deluxe regular room, go for it. If you can't, it may be better to admire the Empress from afar.

Dining: The Bengal Lounge serves curry buffets and an à la carte menu; the Empress Dining Room serves Pacific Northwest cuisine in an elegant formal setting; the more affordable Kipling's serves regional cuisine in a casual setting. The famous high tea (see the "Tea for Two" box, below) is served under the stained-glass dome of the Palm Court and in the Lobby Lounge.

Amenities: Concierge, room service, valet, laundry/dry cleaning, secretarial service, massage; indoor 40-foot lap pool, children's wading pool, health club, sauna, whirlpool, shopping arcade, conference center with meeting and banquet space for up to 1,500, car-rental desk.

✪ **Ocean Pointe Resort.** 45 Songhees Rd., Victoria, BC V9A 6T3. ☎ **800/667-4677** or 250/360-2999. Fax 250/360-1041. www.oprhotel.com. 284 units. Wheelchair-accessible units available. A/C MINIBAR TV TEL. Apr 16–May C$312–C$492 (US$208–US$328) double; June–Oct 11 C$412–C$628 (US$275–US$419) double; Oct 12–Apr 15 C$304–C$412 (US$203–US$275) double. Year-round C$399–C$595 (US$266–US$397) suite. Promotional rates available in all seasons. Pets one-time C$30 (US$20) fee. Children 16 and under stay free in parents' room. AE, DC, ER, MC, V. Underground valet parking C$9 (US$6). Bus: 24.

On the Inner Harbour's north shore, the luxurious "OPR" offers commanding views of downtown Victoria, the Legislature, and the Empress. The hotel also has all the little touches you'd expect in a four-diamond property, including fancy toiletries and fluffy robes. The beds are large, the linen is top quality, and the decor is refreshingly modern. The Inner Harbour rooms offer the best views, many with floor-to-ceiling windows; rooms facing the Outer Harbour top that with floor-to-ceiling bay windows.

Dining/Diversions: The Victorian Restaurant offers elegant West Coast cuisine; the Boardwalk Restaurant is more casual. Rick's Lounge & Piano Bar is a warm and friendly room.

Amenities: Concierge, 24-hour room service, dry cleaning/laundry, newspaper delivery, in-room massage, baby-sitting, secretarial services, express checkout; indoor pool, health club, Jacuzzi, sauna, sundeck, outdoor tennis courts, squash and racquetball courts, jogging path, business center, conference rooms, beauty salon.

Expensive

✪ **Haterleigh Heritage Inn.** 243 Kingston St., Victoria, BC V8V 1V5. ☎ **250/384-9995.** Fax 250/384-1935. www.haterleigh.com. 6 units. TEL. C$201–C$291 (US$134–US$194) double. Rates include full breakfast. MC, V. Free parking. Bus: 30.

Paul and Elizabeth Kelly run this exceptional B&B that captures the essence of Victoria's charm and romance with a combination of antique furniture, intricate stained-glass windows, and attentive personal service. All the Haterleigh's spacious guest rooms boast high arched ceilings, large windows, separate sitting areas, and enormous bathrooms with hand-painted tiles and Jacuzzi tubs. A full gourmet breakfast is served family-style daily at 8:30am sharp. There's also complimentary sherry in the drawing room each evening.

✪ **Laurel Point Inn.** 680 Montreal St., Victoria, BC V8V 1Z8. ☎ **800/663-7667** or 250/386-8721. Fax 250/386-9547. www.laurelpoint.com. 200 units. No-smoking and wheelchair-accessible rooms available. A/C TV TEL. Oct 16–May 15 C$125 (US$83) double, C$185 (US$123) junior suite, C$255 (US$170) bedroom suite, C$325 (US$217) full suite; May 16–June 15 C$155 (US$103) double, C$215 (US$143) junior suite, C$350 (US$233) bedroom suite, C$425 (US$283) full suite; June 16–Oct 15 C$190 (US$127) double, C$250 (US$167) junior suite, C$375 (US$250) bedroom suite, C$450 (US$300) full suite. Seasonal discounts available. Children under 12 stay free in parents' room. AE, CB, ER, JCB, MC, V. Free parking. Bus: 30.

The Laurel's original owners were deeply enamored of Japan, so the hotel design and lobby reflect Japanese artistic principles—elegant simplicity, blond wood surfaces, and the subtle integration of light and water and stone. The hotel consists of the original north wing and a new south wing: The latter is where you want to be. All the rooms there are suites, featuring blond wood with black marble accents, shoji-style sliding doors, Asian art pieces, and soaker tubs and floor-to-ceiling glassed-in showers in the bathrooms. In addition, all have stunning views. Thankfully, these studio-style junior suites cost only about 25% more than north-wing standard rooms. The deluxe and executive suites are more pricey, of course, but feature nice touches like Jacuzzis in glassed-in alcoves by the patio.

Dining/Diversions: The Terrace Room serves full meals in a glassed-in atrium by a formal Japanese garden. Cafe Laurel serves casuals fare, and Cooke's Landing is the lounge with a view of the Inner Harbour.

Amenities: Concierge, 24-hour room service, valet, laundry; heated indoor pool, Jacuzzi, sauna, exercise bikes, gift shop, meeting and banquet space for 250.

Moderate

✪ **Admiral Motel.** 257 Belleville St., Victoria, BC V8V 1X3. ☎ and fax **250/ 388-6267.** www.admiral.bc.ca. 29 units. A/C TV TEL. May–Sept C$105–C$155 (US$70–US$103) double, C$115–C$165 (US$77–US$110) suite with kitchen or harbor-view room; Oct–Apr C$69–C$89 (US$46–US$59) double, C$79–C$99 (US$53–US$66) suite with kitchen or harbor-view room. Extra person C$10 (US$7). Rates include continental breakfast. Children under 12 stay free in parents' room. Senior, weekly, and off-season discounts available. AE, ER, MC, V. Pets free. Free parking. Bus: 5.

The Admiral's guest rooms attract young couples, families, seniors, and other travelers in search of a harbor view at a price that doesn't break the bank. The rooms are pleasant and comfortably furnished, with balconies or terraces, coffeemakers, and small refrigerators. Full kitchen units are also available. Some rooms can sleep up to six (on two double beds and a double hide-a-bed), which is great for accommodating families. The owners are very friendly and can provide assistance with sightseeing.

Andersen House Bed & Breakfast. 301 Kingston St., Victoria, BC V8V 1V5. ☎ **250/ 388-4565.** www.islandnet.com/~andersen. 5 units; 1 yacht. TV TEL. C$85–C$195 (US$57–US$130) double; C$235 (US$157) yacht. Rates include breakfast. MC, V. Free parking on street. Bus: 30.

The 1891 Andersen House has the high ceilings, stained-glass windows, and ornate fireplaces typical of the Queen Anne style, but the art and decorations are far more eclectic: hand-knotted Persian rugs, Raku sculptures, cubist-inspired oil paintings, and carved-wood African masks. Each of the guest rooms has a unique style: The sun-drenched Casablanca room on the top floor is decorated with Persian rugs, a four-poster queen bed, and a lovely boxed window seat; the ground-floor Garden studio has a two-person Jacuzzi and a fireplace. If you're looking for something even more unconventional, there's the *Mamita,* a 50-foot yacht moored in the Inner Harbour that provides double-bed accommodation in the teak wheelhouse.

DOWNTOWN & OLD TOWN

Expensive

✪ **Abigail's Hotel.** 906 McClure St., Victoria, BC V8V 3E7. ☎ **800/561-6565** or 250/ 388-5363. Fax 250/388-7787. www.abigailshotel.com. 22 units. TEL. C$199–C$329 (US$133–US$219) double. Rates include full breakfast. Winter discounts up to 40% AE, MC, V. Free parking. Bus: 1.

In a Tudor mansion east of downtown, Abigail's began in the 1920s as a luxury apartment house before being converted to an elegant boutique hotel. Not all the guest rooms come with all the frills, but pampering is always an objective. In the original building, some of the 16 rooms are bright and beautifully furnished, with pedestal sinks and goose-down comforters. Others boast soaker tubs and double-sided fireplaces, so you can relax in the tub by the light of the fire. One room boasts a sundeck. The six Celebration Suites in the new Coach House are the apogee of indulgence. After a night spent there, you drift over to the sunny breakfast room in the main building, where the chef has prepared a multicourse gourmet breakfast. Services include a concierge, dry cleaning, free coffee or refreshments, and a gift shop.

✪ **The Magnolia.** 623 Courtney St., Victoria, BC V8W 1B8 ☎ **877/624-6654** or 250/ 381-0999. Fax 250/381-0988. www.magnoliahotel.com. 68 units. MINIBAR TV TEL. Apr 16–May C$159–C$199 (US$106–US$133) double, C$259 (US$173) suite; June–Oct 15 C$189–C$219 (US$126–US$146) double, C$319 (US$213) suite; Oct 16–Apr 15

C$139–C$179 (US$93–US$119) double, C$239 (US$159) suite. AE, ER, MC, V. Valet parking C$8 (US$5). Bus: 5.

A brand-new boutique hotel in the center of Victoria, the Magnolia offers luxurious accommodation at a surprisingly reasonable price. The two-poster beds have high-quality linen and down duvets, and the bathrooms feature walk-in showers and deep soaker tubs. The work desks are well lit and large enough to spread out several stacks of paper. Two phone lines run to every room, and the phone itself is cordless. The top-floor Diamond Suite features a sitting room with a fireplace, a couch chair, and a Murphy bed, along with the usual comfy queen bed in a separate bedroom.

Dining/Diversions: Reviews of the Capitol City Steakhouse show the food quality to be fluctuating wildly, not surprising in a kitchen so new. A brew pub, Hugo's Lounge, offers good beer in a hip room until late at night.

Amenities: Concierge, room service, dry cleaning, secretarial service.

Moderate

✪ Swan's Hotel. 506 Pandora Ave., Victoria, BC V8W 1N6. ☎ **800/668-7926** or 250/361-3310. Fax 250/361-3491. www.islandnet.com/~swans. 29 units. TV TEL. C$135–C$189 (US$90–US$126) suite. Off-season discounts available. AE, MC, V. Parking C$8 (US$5). Bus: 23, 24.

By the Johnson Street Bridge, this heritage property is one of Old Town's best-known and best-loved buildings. The suites are spacious; many are split-level, featuring open lofts and huge exposed beams. All have fully equipped kitchens, separate dining areas, living rooms, and queen-sized beds. The two-bedroom suites have the feel of little town houses—they're great for families, accommodating up to six comfortably. The fine-dining Fowl Fish Cafe is open daily for dinner. Swan's Pub has excellent pub grub, and the Buckerfield's Brewery produces half a dozen truly inspired lagers, ales, stouts, and bitters. The basement Millennium Jazz Club has live entertainment. Services include room service, a guest laundry, access to a nearby health club, baby-sitting referrals, secretarial services, and video rentals.

Inexpensive

✪ Victoria International Youth Hostel. 516 Yates St., Victoria, BC V8W 1K8. ☎ **250/385-4511.** Fax 250/385-3232. www.hostels.bc.ca. 104 beds. Wheelchair-accessible room available. C$16 (US$11) International Youth Hostel members, C$20 (US$13) nonmembers. MC, V. Street parking available. Bus: 70.

The location is perfect—right in the heart of Old Town. In addition, this hostel has all the usual accoutrements, including two kitchens, a dining room, a TV lounge with a VCR, a games room, a common room, a library, and laundry facilities. The dorms are on the large side (16 beds to a room) and strictly segregated by sex. There are also a couple of family rooms. An extensive ride board helps those in need of transportation, and the collection of outfitter and tour information rivals that of the local tourism office.

OUTSIDE THE CENTRAL AREA

Expensive

The Aerie. 600 Ebedora Lane, P.O. Box 108, Malahat, BC V0R 2L0. ☎ **250/743-7115.** Fax 250/743-4766. www.aerie.bc.ca. 24 suites. A/C TV TEL. Apr 25–June and Sept 5–Oct 14 C$180–C$240 (US$120–US$160) double, C$275–C$375 (US$183–US$250) suite; July–Sept 4 C$195–C$260 (US$130–US$173) double, C$295–C$425 (US$197–US$283) suite; Oct 15–Apr 24 C$150–C$200 (US$100–US$133) double, C$250–C$300 (US$167–US$200) suite. Rates include 7am breakfast hamper at the door and full breakfast later. Accommodation and dinner packages available. AE, MC, V. Free parking. Take Hwy. 1 to the Spectacle Lake turnoff; take the first right and follow the winding driveway up.

Set on a mountain by a fjord about half an hour from town, this Mediterranean-inspired villa was designed, built, and decorated by Austrian hotelier Marie Schuster. In the guest rooms, Christian Dior bedcovers and duvets half a foot thick are placed atop gargantuan four-poster beds. Overstuffed white leather couches await before gas or wood fireplaces, elaborately carved gilt mirrors shine back from the walls, and Persian carpets further soften the already-springy wall-to-wall carpeting. The Aerie offers six room configurations; all rooms contain wet bars, refrigerators, and coffeemakers, and all but the standard rooms include sexy soaker tubs for two. In the master and residence suites you'll find private decks and fireplaces.

Dining: The restaurant serves three meals daily but is open to the public only for dinner (see "Where to Dine" below).

Amenities: Concierge, 24-hour room service, laundry, helipad, heated indoor pool, outdoor hot tub, tennis courts (rackets and balls available), full spa treatments, outdoor wedding chapel, conference facilities for 20.

✪ **Sooke Harbour House.** 1528 Whiffen Spit Rd., Sooke, BC V0S 1N0. ☎ **250/642-3421.** Fax 250/628-6988. www.sookeharbourhouse.com. E-mail shh@islandnet. com. 28 units. TEL. C$260–C$465 (US$173–US$310) double. Rates include breakfast and lunch. Dinner C$56 (US$37). Off-season discounts. AE, ER, JCB, MC, V. Free parking. Take the Island Hwy. (Hwy. 1) to the Sooke/Colwood turnoff (Junction Hwy. 14). Follow Hwy. 14 to Sooke. About 1 mile past the town's only traffic light, turn left onto Whiffen Spit Rd.

This little inn/restaurant on the end of a sand spit about 30km (19 miles) west of Victoria has an international reputation for quality. Each suite is unique, decorated according to a particular northwest theme. For example, the Herb Garden Room is appointed in shades of mint and parsley, and the Thunderbird Room reflects the bold colors and striking design of this most famous of West Coast symbols. All suites boast wood-burning fireplaces, separate sitting areas, and wonderful water views; many have sundecks and Jacuzzi tubs.

Dining: Sooke Harbour House has one of the best restaurants in the area, perhaps in all Canada, where you can sample the outstanding cooking of owner/chef Sinclair Philip (see "Where to Dine" below).

Amenities: In-room breakfast, optional in-room dinner, baby-sitting referrals, free newspaper; two small meeting/banquet rooms, massage therapist by appointment.

Moderate

✪ **The Boathouse.** 746 Sea Dr., RR #1, Victoria, BC VM8 1B1. ☎ **250/652-9370.** www.members.home.net/boathouse. 1 unit. TEL. Pets accepted. C$165 (US$110) double. Rate includes continental breakfast. MC, V. Free parking. Bus: 75.

It's a short stroll (or row) to Butchart Gardens from this secluded tiny red cottage in the Brentwood Bay district. The converted boathouse is perched on pilings over the Saanich Inlet, and the only passersby you're likely to see are seals, bald eagles, otters, herons, and raccoons. Inside are a new queen-size bed, a dining table, a kitchen area with a small refrigerator and toaster oven, an electric heater, and a reading alcove overlooking the floating dock. Full toilet and shower facilities are in a separate bathhouse, 17 steps back uphill. All the makings for a delicious continental breakfast are provided, and you have use of a private dinghy.

Inexpensive

University of Victoria. Housing, Food, and Conference Services, P.O. Box 1700, Sinclair at Finerty Rd., Victoria, BC V8W 2Y2. ☎ **250/721-8395.** Fax 250/721-8930. www. hfcs.uvic.ca/uvichfcs.htm. 898 units. May–Aug C$50 (US$33) double; C$146 (US$98) suite. Room rates include full breakfast and taxes; suite rates include taxes. Closed Sept–Apr. Parking C$4 (US$2.65). Bus: 4, 14.

Here's one of the best deals going, price-wise. Victoria's major university opens its dorms to summer visitors for the 4 months when classes aren't in session. All rooms have single beds and basic furnishings, and there are bathrooms, pay phones, and TV lounges on every floor. The suites come with kitchens. Linens, towels, and soap are provided.

WHERE TO DINE

Though early Victoria settlers were intent on re-creating a little patch of the old country on their wild western island, the one thing they were never tempted to import was British cooking. Thankfully. Instead, following the traditional Canadian norm, each little immigrant group imported its own cuisine, so now Victoria is a cornucopia of culinary styles. With more than 700 restaurants, there's something for every taste and wallet.

But with all this variety, the one thing you're unlikely to find is a lot of late-night dining. Victorians time their meal to the setting of the sun. Try for a seat at 7pm and the restaurant will be packed. Try at 9pm and it'll be empty. Try at 10pm and it'll be closed, especially on weekdays. Reservations are strongly recommended for prime sunset seating in summer.

Note: See the "Victoria" map (p. 671) to locate restaurants in this section.

INNER HARBOUR & OLD TOWN
Expensive
Blue Crab Bar and Grill. In the Coast Hotel, 146 Kingston St. ☎ **250/480-1999.** Reservations recommended. Main courses C$16–C$30 (US$11–US$20). AE, DC, ER, MC, V. Daily 6:30am–10pm (dinner from 5pm). SEAFOOD.

Victoria's best seafood spot, the Blue Crab combines fresh ingredients, inventive recipes, and beautiful presentations with a killer view. The first order of business is to peruse the chalkboard of daily seafood specials. What's there is entirely dependent on what came in on the boats or floatplanes that day—salmon in season is a strong possibility, as are spotted prawns or crab or other such benthic creatures. Occasionally, little Salt Spring Island lambs also wander onto the board. The chefs are fond of unusual combinations: sea bass with taro root, grapefruit, and blood orange or foie gras with raspberries. The service is deft and smart and very obliging.

Pablo's Dining Lounge. 225 Quebec St. ☎ **250/388-4255.** Reservations recommended. Main courses C$14–C$29 (US$9–US$19). AE, MC, V. Daily 5–around 11pm. Bus: 30. CONTINENTAL.

Pablo Hernandez's paella valenciana saffron rice baked with a medley of meats, seafood, and vegetables has been a local favorite for nearly 20 years. This intimate restaurant is in an Edwardian house near Laurel Point. Special dinners for two include rack of Salt Spring Island lamb and chateaubriand forestière (with mushrooms). Try a seafood dish prepared in classic French style (the border between French and Spanish cuisines becomes a little fuzzy at Pablo's, but the fusion produces excellent results).

Moderate
Cassis Bistro. 253 Cook St. ☎ **250/384-1932.** Reservations recommended. Main courses: C$13–C$23 (U$9–U$15). Mon–Fri 5:30pm–9:30pm, Sat–Sun 5:30–10pm, Sun brunch 10am–2pm. MC, V. ECLECTIC ITALIAN.

In Cook Village, just off Beacon Hill Park, this neighborhood bistro has been making quite a name for itself. The owner describes the menu as eclectic Italian, but there are some French and Moroccan influences, as in the Harissa sauce served with the halibut. The menu changes frequently; the restaurant is still young and experimenting with

Tea for Two

The afternoon tea at the **Empress** hotel, 721 Government St. (☎ **250/ 384-8111;** Bus: 5, 30), is undoubtedly the best in town, served in the Palm Court or in the Lobby Lounge, both of which are beautifully ornate and luxurious. Tea runs C$30 (US$20) per person, with seatings at 12:30, 2, 3:30, and 5pm. The **Point Ellice House,** an old villa at 2616 Pleasant St. on the Gorge waterway just outside downtown (☎ **250/380-6506;** Bus: 14), also makes a fine destination for afternoon tea, especially on a sunny day, when tea is served on the lawn. Tea runs C$15 (US$10), including admission to the grounds, and seatings are at 12:30, 2, and 3:30pm. Reservations are required. The **Butchart Gardens Dining Room Restaurant,** 800 Benvenuto Ave. (☎ **250/652-4422;** Bus: 75), offers the impeccably groomed gardens as a backdrop to a memorable tea experience that runs C$25 (US$17). June to August, seatings are noon to 7pm; September to May, seatings are noon to 5pm.

different flavors. Considering how well they're doing now, time will only improve things. The emphasis is on fresh seafood and lots of it. Tapas are on the menu and are a great way to mix and match various dishes.

✪ **Herald Street Caffè.** 546 Herald St. ☎ **250/381-1441.** Reservations required. Main courses C$11–C$20 (US$7–US$13). AE, ER, MC, V. Wed–Sat 11:30am–3pm; Sun brunch 10am–3pm; Sun–Wed 5:30–10:30pm, Thurs–Sat 5:30pm–midnight. Bus: 5. PASTA/WEST COAST.

At this casual bistro, young hip locals flock to the excellent Sunday brunch, where the poached eggs on fresh cheese scones (all breads are baked on-premises), with back bacon and sun-dried tomatoes, is a wonderful twist on eggs Benedict. Located in a 19th-century heritage building, the dining room is filled with potted palms and floral arrangements. However, it's the chef's own creations—fresh pastas, venison, or steamed mussels with prawns, ginger, lemongrass, and roasted cashews—that make the place so wonderful. The award-winning wine list highlights the province's best vintages and has won the restaurant almost as much recognition as its inventive menu.

Millos. 716 Burdett Ave. ☎ **250/382-4422** or 250/382-5544. Reservations recommended. Main courses C$9–C$25 (US$6–US$17). AE, DC, ER, MC, V. Mon–Sat 11:30am–4:30pm; daily 4:30–11pm. Bus: 5. GREEK.

Millos isn't hard to find—look for the blue-and-white windmill behind the Empress hotel, or listen for the hand clapping and plate breaking as diners get into the swing of things. Flaming saganaki (a sharp cheese sautéed in olive oil and flambéed with Greek brandy), grilled halibut souvlaki, baby-back ribs, and succulent grilled salmon are just a few of the menu items at this lively five-level restaurant. Kids get their own menu. Folk dancers and belly dancers highlight the entertainment on Friday and Saturday nights, and the waitstaff is remarkably warm and entertaining every night.

✪ **Pagliacci's.** 1011 Broad St. ☎ **250/386-1662.** Reservations not accepted. Main courses C$11–C$19 (US$7–US$13). AE, MC, V. Daily 11:30am–midnight (light menu 3–6pm). ITALIAN.

Launched in 1979 by expatriate New Yorker Howie Siegal, Pagliacci's radiates an energy, an un-Victorian kind of big-city buzz. Tables jostle up against one another as diners ogle one another's food and eavesdrop on one another's conversations while

Howie works the room, dispensing a word or two to long-lost friends, many of whom he's only just met. The cuisine comes from the south of Italy—veal parmesan, tortellini, and 19 or 20 other à la carte pastas, many quite inventive and all made by hand. The service isn't blindingly fast, but then when you're having this much fun, who cares? Grab some wine, munch some hot focaccia, and enjoy the atmosphere.

Inexpensive

Barb's Place. 310 St. Lawrence St. ☎ **250/384-6515.** Reservations not accepted. Menu items C$2.25–C$9 (US$1.50–US$6). No credit cards. Daily 7am–sunset. FISH-AND-CHIPS.

The best chippie in town, Barb serves lightly breaded halibut and hand-hewn chips served in folded-newspaper pouches from a floating restaurant at Fisherman's Wharf. There are picnic tables to sit on, plus boats and seagulls and lots of other eye-candy to amuse the kids.

✪ **Don Mee Restaurant.** 538 Fisgard St. ☎ **250/383-1032.** Reservations accepted. Main courses C$4.95–C$10 (US$3.30–US$7); 4-course dinner for 2 C$17 (US$11). AE, DC, MC, V. Mon–Fri 11am–2:30pm, Sat–Sun and holidays 10:30am–2:30pm; daily from 5pm. Bus: 5. CANTONESE/SZECHUAN.

Since the 1920s, elegant Don Mee's has been serving up Victoria's best dim sum, chop suey, and chow mein, along with piquant Szechuan seafood dishes and delectable Cantonese sizzling platters. You can't miss this second-story restaurant, because a huge Chinese lantern made of neon looms above the small doorway. The dinner specials for two, three, or four people are particularly good deals if you want to sample lots of everything on the menu.

Re-bar. 50 Bastion Sq. ☎ **250/361-9223.** Main courses C$7–C$14 (US$4.65–US$9). AE, MC, V. Mon–Thurs and Sat 7:30am–8pm, Fri 7:30am–9pm, Sun 10am–3pm. Bus: 5. WEST COAST.

Even if you're not hungry, it's worth dropping down the steps from Bastion Square for a juice blend—say grapefruit, banana, melon, and pear combined with bee pollen or blue-green algae for added oomph. If you're hungry, then rejoice: Re-bar is the city's premier dispenser of vegetarian comfort food. Dishes include a vegetable-and-almond patty with red onions and sprouts on a multigrain kaiser roll, and crisp salads with toasted pine nuts, feta cheese, and sun-dried tomato vinaigrette. The juices are still the crown jewels on the menu, with more than 80 blends.

OUTSIDE THE CENTRAL AREA
Expensive

The Aerie. 600 Ebedora Lane, P.O. Box 108, Malahat. ☎ **250/743-7115.** Fax 250/743-4766. Reservations required. Main courses C$28–C$32 (US$18–US$21); 7-course set menu C$60 (US$40). AE, MC, V. Daily 5–10pm. Free parking. Take Hwy. 1 to the Spectacle Lake turnoff; take the first right and follow the winding driveway. FRENCH.

The dining room of this red-tile villa high up the on the Malahat boasts panoramic windows overlooking Finlayson Inlet, a 14-carat gold-leaf ceiling, crystal chandeliers, intricately carved high-backed gilt chairs, faux-marble columns, and a large open-hearth fireplace. The cuisine is resolutely French. Consider the appetizer of venison-and-pistachio pâté with dried-fruit compote, juniper-and-port glaze, and herbed sunflower croutons, or the millefeuille of British Columbian salmon pastrami, honey, and thyme mascarpone. Entrees include beef tenderloin with caramelized shallot crust in red wine/rosemary reduction, roasted lamb chop and loin with currant/cracked pepper glaze, and free-range chicken breast with forest mushroom/nut mousse and savory tarragon/onion bread-and-butter pudding in sherry-vinegar jus. The Aerie wine list includes vintage Margaux and Bordeaux.

✪ **Sooke Harbour House.** 1528 Whiffen Spit Rd., Sooke. ☎ **250/642-3421.** www.sookeharbourhouse.com. Reservations required. Main courses C$29–C$36 (US$19–US$24). AE, ER, MC, V. Daily 5–9pm. Take the Island Hwy. to the Sooke/ Colwood turnoff (Junction Hwy. 14). Continue on Hwy. 14 to Sooke. About a mile past the town's only traffic light, turn left onto Whiffen Spit Rd. WEST COAST.

In a rambling white house on a bluff overlooking Sooke's Whiffen Spit, this restaurant/hotel offers spectacular waterfront views and a quiet, relaxed atmosphere. Hosts Frederica and Sinclair Phillips will immediately make you feel at home as you dine on imaginatively prepared West coast cuisine, featuring local seafood and organically grown herbs and vegetables fresh from the Phillipses' garden. The halibut baked in an herb, sunflower-seed, and parmesan crust is accompanied by a roasted carrot, coriander, and parsley puree, and the roasted veal is served with a wild mushroom, port wine, and lovage sauce.

VICTORIA AFTER DARK

Victoria is never going to set the world on fire, but taken together the U Vic. students and the tourists and a small but dedicated cadre of Victoria revelers form a critical mass large enough to keep a number of small but steady reactions going in various parts of the city. You just have to know where to look.

Monday magazine's listings section provides near-comprehensive coverage of what's happening in town. If you can't find it in cafes or record shops, *Monday* also has a Web presence at **www.monday.com**.

The **Community Arts Council of Greater Victoria,** 511-620 View St. (☎ **250/ 381-ARTS** or 250/381-2787; Bus: 1, 2, 6), runs a 24-hour hotline that tells what's happening where in Victoria. You can buy tickets and get schedules from the **Tourism Victoria Travel Visitor Centre,** 812 Wharf St. (☎ **800/663-3883** or 250/382-1131; Bus: 5, 30), open daily 9am to 5pm (summer to 9pm).

THE PERFORMING ARTS   The **Royal Theatre,** 805 Broughton St. (☎ **250/ 361-0820;** box office 250/386-6121; Bus: 5, 30), hosts concerts like Victoria Symphony concerts, dance recitals, and touring stage plays. The box office is at the **McPherson Playhouse,** 3 Centennial Sq., at Pandora Avenue and Government Street (☎ **250/386-6121.** Bus: 5, 30), which is also home to Victoria's Pacific Opera and the Victoria Operatic Society. The box office is open Monday to Saturday 9:30am to 5:30pm.

The **Belfry Theatre,** 1291 Gladstone St. (☎ **250/385-6815;** Bus: 1, 2), is a nationally acclaimed theatrical group that stages four productions October to April and a summer show in August. The **Victoria Fringe Festival** (☎ **888/FRINGE2** or 250/383-2663) presents short, inexpensive original fare at six venues from late August to mid-September.

The **Pacific Opera Victoria,** 1316B Government St. (☎ **250/385-0222;** box office 250/386-6121; Bus: 5, 30), presents productions in October, February, and April. Performances are normally at the McPherson Playhouse and Royal Theatre. **The Victoria Operatic Society,** 798 Fairview Rd. (☎ **250/381-1021**), stages old-time Broadway musicals and other popular fare year-round at the McPherson Playhouse.

The **Victoria Symphony Orchestra,** 846 Broughton St. (☎ **250/385-9771;** Bus: 5, 30), kicks off its season on the first Sunday of August with Symphony Splash, a free concert performed on a barge in the Inner Harbour. Regular performances begin in October and last to May.

LIVE-MUSIC CLUBS   **Legends,** 919 Douglas St. (☎ **250/383-7137;** Bus: 5, 30), is the live-music venue below street level in the Strathcona Hotel. It covers the gamut from afro-pop to blues to zydeco. Another basement, this one below Swan's Pub, is home to the **Millennium Jazz Club,** 506 Pandora St. (☎ 250/360-9098; Bus: 6), which offers swing bands on Thursdays, disco DJs on Fridays, and soul and R & B bands on Saturdays. **Steamers,** 570 Yates St. (☎ 250/381-4340; Bus: 5, 30), is the city's premium blues bar. Cover hovers around C$5 (US$3.35).

LOUNGES, BARS & PUBS   A truly unique experience, the **Bengal Lounge** in the Empress hotel, 721 Government St. (☎ 250/384-8111; Bus: 5, 30), is one of the last outposts of the old empire, except the martinis are ice cold and jazz plays in the background (on weekends it's live in the foreground). **Rick's Lounge,** in the Ocean Pointe Resort, 45 Songhees Rd. (☎ 250/360-2999; Bus: 6 or harbor ferry), is without doubt the best place to watch as the last light of day fades.

The **Harbour Canoe Club,** 450 Swift St. (☎ 250/361-1940; Bus: 6), is one of the most pleasant spots going to hoist a pint after a long day's sightseeing. **Big Bad John's,** 919 Douglas St., in the Strathcona Hotel (☎ 250/383-7137; Bus: 5, 30), is Victoria's only hillbilly bar—a low, dark warren of a place, with inches of discarded peanut shells on the plank floor and a crowd of drunk and happy rowdies. Overlooking Victoria Harbour on the west side of the Songhees Point Development, **Spinnaker's Brew Pub,** 308 Catherine St. (☎ 250/386-BREW or 250/386-2739; Bus: 6 or harbor ferry), has one of the best views and some of the best beer in town.

DANCE CLUBS   Most dance clubs are open Monday to Saturday to 2am and Sunday to midnight. The **Ice House,** 1961 Douglas St., in the Horizon West Hotel (☎ 250/382-2111; Bus: 5, 30), is the place if house is your thing. **Uforia,** 1208 Wharf St. (☎ 250/381-2331; Bus: 6), is a waterfront club where the DJs play popular Top 40 dance tracks for a 20-something crowd; there's a C$4 (US$2.65) cover after 8pm on weekends. The **Jet Lounge,** 751 View St. (☎ 250/920-7797; Bus: 1, 5, 30), serves as a plush hangout for Victoria's small but oh-so-beautiful crowd of upscale Gen-Xers and their slightly younger siblings and dance partners. DJs spin house, rave, and acid jazz. The cover is C$4 (US$2.65).

GAY & LESBIAN BARS   The scene isn't large enough in Victoria for the homosexual nation to segregate by sex, so they all come to **Rumors,** 1325 Government St. (☎ 250/385-0566; Bus: 5, 30), where they pack the dance floor on weekends. **Friends of Dorothy's Cafe,** 615 Johnson St. (☎ 250/381-2277; Bus: 1, 2, 5), has *The Wizard of Oz* playing continuously, which adds to the kitschy glam without— surprisingly enough—driving you over the rainbow. **BJ's Lounge,** 642 Johnson St. (☎ 250/388-0505; Bus: 1, 2, 5), has a full menu and lounge decor.

A CASINO   At the **Great Canadian Casino,** 3075 Douglas St. (☎ 250/389-1136; Bus: 30), there are no floor shows, no alcohol, no dancing girls in glittering bikinis— just blackjack, roulette, sic bo, red dog (diamond dog), and Caribbean stud poker. Admission is free, and it's open daily noon to 3am.

3 Side Trips from Victoria: Goldstream Provincial Park, the Duncan Native Heritage Center & the Cowichan Valley Wineries

North of Victoria along the Island Highway are three sites worth visiting: Goldstream Provincial Park, the Duncan Native Heritage Centre, and the Cowichan Valley wineries. The drive along the east coast is pleasant, with mountain and ocean views, and the three sites are close enough together to do in a day trip from Victoria.

GOLDSTREAM PROVINCIAL PARK

The tranquil arboreal setting of **Goldstream Provincial Park** overflowed with prospectors during the 1860s gold-rush days. Trails take you past abandoned mine shafts and tunnels, as well as 600-year-old stands of towering Douglas fir, lodge pole pine, red cedar, indigenous yew, and arbutus trees. The **Gold Mine Trail** leads to Niagara Creek and the abandoned mine that was operated by Lt. Peter Leech, a Royal Engineer who discovered gold in the creek in 1858. The **Goldstream Trail** leads to the salmon spawning areas. (You might also catch sight of mink and river otters racing along this path.)

The park is 20km (12 miles) west of downtown Victoria along Highway 1; the drive takes about half an hour. For general information on this and all the other provincial parks on the South Island, contact **BC Parks** at ☎ 250/391-2300. Throughout the year, Goldstream Park's **Freeman King Visitor Centre** (☎ 250/478-9414) offers guided walks, talks, displays, and programs geared toward kids but interesting for adults too. It's open daily 9:30am to 6pm.

Three species of salmon (chum, Chinook, and steelhead) make **annual salmon runs** up the Goldstream River in October, November, December, and February. You can easily observe this natural wonder along the riverbanks. For details, contact the park's **Freeman King Visitor Centre** at ☎ 250/478-9414.

DUNCAN: THE CITY OF TOTEM POLES

Duncan, 64km (40 miles) north of Victoria along Highway 1, is named the "City of Totem Poles," and its main attraction is the Native Heritage Centre (below). However, don't be misled by its tag line. Duncan is a strip mall of a town, and the hundreds of totem poles plunked down in the parking lots of every third 7-11 do nothing to redeem it. Fortunately, the "City of Strip Malls" is very close to Cowichan Bay (below), so you can first visit the Native Heritage Centre, then immediately take off for somewhere pleasant.

The **Duncan-Cowichan Visitor Info Centre,** 381 Trans-Canada Hwy., Duncan, BC V9L 3R5 (☎ 250/746-4636), is open daily 9am to 6pm.

Created by the Cowichan Indian Band itself, the **Native Heritage Centre,** 200 Cowichan Way (☎ 250/746-8119), is an attempt to bring native culture to visitors in a way that's both commercially successful and respectful of native traditions. The longhouses built along the Cowichan River contain an impressive collection of cultural artifacts and presentations of life among the aboriginal tribes who've lived in the area for thousands of years. Regularly scheduled events include ceremonial dances and dinners, and master and apprentice carvers create poles and masks and feasting bowls in workshops open to the public. Two large gift shops in the complex sell some of those works, as well as native-made jewelry, clothing, silk-screened prints, and other items. The center and gift shops are open daily 9:30am to 5pm; admission is C$6 (US$4) adults, C$5 (US$3.35) seniors, and C$3 (US$2) children under 12. A family rate is also available.

THE COWICHAN VALLEY WINERIES

A gorgeous agricultural valley just 60km (37 miles) from Victoria, the **Cowichan Valley** is a little like the south of England, except for the mountains. Both the wineries and the seaside town of Cowichan Bay are worth a stop. The vintners of the Cowichan Valley have gained a solid reputation for producing fine wines. Just a couple hours' drive from Victoria, the wineries offer 1-hour tours that are a great introduction for novices. They usually include a tasting of the vintner's art, as well as a chance to purchase bottles or cases of your favorites.

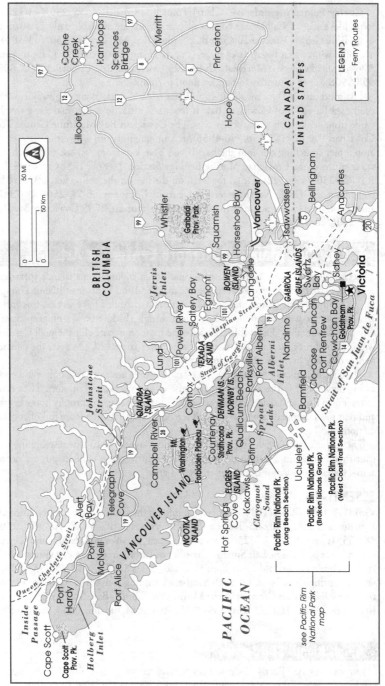

Vancouver Island

LEGEND
--- Ferry Routes

BRITISH COLUMBIA

CANADA
UNITED STATES

Cache Creek
Kamloops
Spences Bridge
Merritt
Princeton
Hope
Lillooet

Whistler
Garibaldi Prov. Park
Squamish
Horseshoe Bay
Vancouver
Tsawwassen
Bellingham
Anacortes

Jervis Inlet
Saltery Bay
Egmont
BOWEN ISLAND
Langdale

Powell River
Luna
TEXADA ISLAND
Malaspina Strait
Strait of Georgia

GABRIOLA
GULF ISLANDS
Swartz Bay
Sidney
Victoria
Goldstream Prov. Pk.

Johnstone Strait
QUADRA ISLAND
Comox
DENMAN IS.
HORNBY IS.
Qualicum Beach
Parksville
Port Alberni
Alberni Inlet
Nanaimo
Duncan
Port Renfrew
Cowichan Bay
Strait of San Juan de Fuca

Campbell River
Mt. Washington
Forbidden Plateau
Courtenay
Strathcona Prov. Pk.

FLORES ISLAND
Tofino
Kakawis
Clayoquot Sound
Hot Springs Cove
NOOTKA ISLAND

Sproat Lake
Bamfield
Clo-oose

Ucluelet
Pacific Rim National Pk. (Long Beach Section)
Pacific Rim National Pk. (Broken Islands Group)
Pacific Rim National Pk. (West Coast Trail Section)

see Pacific Rim National Park map

PACIFIC OCEAN

VANCOUVER ISLAND

Inside Passage
Queen Charlotte Strait
Cape Scott
Cape Scott Prov. Pk.
Holberg Inlet
Port Hardy
Port Alice
Port McNeill
Alert Bay
Telegraph Cove

N

50 MI
50 Km

693

Cherry Point Vineyards, 840 Cherry Point Rd., Cowichan (☎ **250/743-1272**), looks like a slice of California's Napa Valley, and tours are available daily 11:30am to 6pm. **Blue Grouse Vineyards,** 4365 Blue Grouse Rd., Mill Bay (☎ **250/743-3834**), a smaller winery that began as a hobby, is open Wednesday to Sunday 11am to 5pm. Another small winery is **Merridale Cider,** 1230 Merridale Rd., Cobble Hill (☎ **800/ 998-9908**), open Thursday to Sunday noon to 5pm.

Just southeast of Duncan, about 45 minutes from Victoria along Highway 1, is the pretty seaside town of Cowichan Bay. It has a few attractions that make it a worthwhile stop, in addition to the ocean view. The **Cowichan Bay Maritime Centre,** 761 Cowichan Bay Rd. (☎ **250/746-4955**), is a unique museum where the displays sit atop a pier stretching out into the bay. If you have kids along, go see and touch the sea creatures at the **Cowichan Marine Ecology Station,** Pier 66, 1751 Cowichan Bay Rd. (☎ **250/748-4522**). Or go for a sail on the bay on the sailing ketch *Meriah* by contacting the **Great Northwestern Adventure Company** at ☎ **250/748-7347.** Afterward, dine by the ocean at the **Masthead Restaurant,** 1705 Cowichan Bay Rd. (☎ **250/748-3714**).

4 The Gulf Islands: A Remote Center for Art

The **Gulf Islands** are a collection of several dozen mountainous islands sprawling across the Strait of Georgia between the BC mainland and Vancouver Island. Though only a handful of the islands are served by regularly scheduled ferry service, this entire area is popular with vacationers. Lying in the rain shadow of Washington State's Olympic Mountains, the Gulf Islands have the most temperate climate in all Canada, without the heavy rainfall that usually characterizes coastal BC. In fact, the climate here is officially listed as semi-Mediterranean!

The fact that these mountainous rock-faced islands are reachable only via a confusing network of ferries enhances their sense of remoteness and mystery. They exist in their own time and space: Part arty counterculture enclave, part trophy home exurb, and part old-fashioned farm and orchard territory, the Gulf Islands are full of contradictions and charm.

The major islands—Salt Spring, Galiano, and Mayne—boast fine restaurants, elegant small inns, and a multitude of art galleries. In fact, the Gulf Islands are noted across Canada as a major center for crafts and arts.

ESSENTIALS

VISITOR INFORMATION   For general info on the Gulf Islands, contact **Tourism Vancouver Island,** 302-45 Bastion Square, Victoria, BC V8W 1J1 (☎ **250/ 382-3551;** fax 250/382-3523; www.islands.bc.ca or www.gulfislands.com; e-mail tavi@islands.bc.ca). The **Salt Spring Chamber of Commerce** operates a visitor center at 121 Lower Ganges Rd., Salt Springs Island, BC V8K 2T1 (☎ **250/537-5252;** www.saltspringisland.bc.ca; e-mail chamber@saltspring.com). For Galiano Island, contact **Galiano Island Tourist/Visitor Info,** 2590 Sturdies Bay Rd., Box 73, Galiano Island, BC V0N 1P0 ☎ **250/539-2233;** www.galianoisland.com; e-mail info@

A Gulf Islands B&B Service

You can reserve B&Bs, lodges, resorts, and country inns in all price ranges free of charge through a centralized booking agency, the **Canadian Gulf Islands B&B Reservation Service** (☎ **888/539-2930** or 250/539-2930; www.gulfislandreservations.com; e-mail reservations@gulfislands.com).

galianoisland.com). For Mayne Island, contact the **Mayne Island Community Chamber of Commerce,** Box 2, Mayne Island, BC V0N 2J0 (www.gulfislands. com/mayne_chamber).

GETTING THERE   By Ferry   BC Ferries (☎ **888/223-3779** or 604/444-2890; www.bcferries.bc.ca) operates three ferry runs to the Gulf Islands—from Tsawwassen on the BC mainland and from Swarz Bay and Crofton on Vancouver Island.

Here are sample peak-season fares: A car and two passengers from Tsawwassen to Mayne Island is C$54 (US$36); a single foot passenger is C$9 (US$6). From Swartz Bay to Salt Spring Island for a car and two passengers is C$31 (US$21); a single foot passenger is C$6 (US$4). Inter-island fares are C$13 (US$9) for a car and two passengers or C$3 (US$2) for a walk-on. For payment, all Gulf Island ferry terminals take Visa and MasterCard in addition to cash and traveler's checks. You can take bikes aboard the ferries for usually less than C$1.50 (US$1).

By Plane   A number of small commuter airlines offer regularly scheduled floatplane service to the Gulf Islands from Vancouver Harbour and Vancouver International Airport's seaplane terminal. One-way tickets usually are C$60 to C$70 (US$40 to US$47). Make reservations early. Contact **Harbour Air** (☎ **800/665-0212** or 604/688-1277; www.harbour-air.com), **Seair** (☎ **800-447-3247** or 250-273-8900), or **Pacific Spirit Air** (☎ **800/665-2359** or 250/537-9359).

SPECIAL EVENTS   Early July to mid-September, the Gulf Islands Community Arts Council presents **ArtCraft,** a summerlong craft fair presenting the work of more than 250 Gulf Island artists and artisans. ArtCraft is held on Salt Spring Island at Mahon Hall, just north of Ganges at the corner of Park Drive and Lower Ganges Road.

EXPLORING THE GULF ISLANDS

The largest of the Gulf Islands, **Salt Spring Island** is a bucolic getaway filled with artisans, sheep pastures, and cozy B&Bs. It's also a busy cultural crossroads: The super rich, movie stars, economy-minded retirees, high-tech telecommuters, and hippie farmers all rub shoulders here.

Many people come to Salt Spring expressly to visit the galleries and studios of local artists and craftspeople—the island is famed across Canada as an artist's colony, and Ganges claims to be one of the top-10 small art towns in North America. At the visitor center (above), pick up a copy of the Studio Tour Map locating 35 artists— glassblowers, painters, ceramists, weavers, carvers, sculptors—around the island.

The center of Salt Spring Island life is **Ganges,** a village with gas stations, grocery stores, banks, and galleries, all overlooking a busy pleasure-boat harbor. April to October, Saturdays 8am to 4pm is Market in the Park, which brings together an infectious mix of craftspeople, farmers, musicians, bakers, and just about everyone else on the island who might plausibly be able to sell or buy something.

Galiano Island is perhaps the most physically striking of the Gulf Islands, particularly the mountainous southern shores. Mount Sutil, Mount Galiano, and the exposed cliffs above Georgeson Bay simply called The Bluffs rise above sheep-filled meadows, shadowy forests, and steep fern-lined ravines. Active Pass, the narrow strait separating Galiano from Mayne Island, is another scenic high spot: All the pleasure-boat and ferry traffic between Vancouver and Victoria negotiates this turbulent cliff-lined passage (tides churn through this cleft at speeds of 9 knots). Watch the bustle of the boats and ferries on Active Pass from the up-close-and-personal vantage point of Bellhouse Provincial Park, a picnicking area at the end of Jack Road.

Bucolic **Mayne Island** is a beautiful medley of rock-lined bays, forested hills, farm fields, and pastureland. Seemingly distant from the pressures of modern life, Mayne was once a center of early Gulf Island agriculture and is noted for its apple and tomato production. Many of the island's early farm homes remain, and a rural, lived-in quality is one of Mayne's most endearing features.

OUTDOOR ACTIVITIES

BIKING　　Salt Spring has the best network of paved roads. However, few roads have shoulders, and with 10,000 inhabitants and three ferries unleashing cars throughout the day, there's a lot more traffic here than you'd think. For bike rentals, contact **Salt Spring Kayaking** on the Ganges Harbour docks (☎ **250/537-4664**).

While you won't have to worry overly about traffic on Galiano's 31km (19-mile) paved road running up the island's west side, there are enough steep ascents to keep your attention focused. Mountain bikers can follow unmaintained logging roads that skirt the eastern shores. Contact **Galiano Bicycle Rental,** 36 Burrill Rd. (☎ **250/539-9906**), for a full range of options, including mountain, touring, and tandem bikes.

Mayne is one of the best islands for cyclists. The rolling hills provide plenty of uphill challenges, but the terrain is considerably less mountainous than that of the other islands. Bring your bike on the ferry or rent one from the **Bayview B&B,** 764 Steward Dr. (☎ **250/539-2924**).

KAYAKING & BOATING　　Home to otters, seals, and bald eagles, the gentle island-shielded waters of Montague Harbour on Galiano Island are a perfect kayaking destination. **Galiano Island Sea Kayaking** (☎ **888/539-2930** or 250/539-293) at Sutil Lodge, 637 Southwind Rd., Montague Harbour, offers guided 2- and 4-hour trips out onto the bay; a 2-hour wildlife-viewing paddle is C$19 (US$13). Rentals are also available. Another way to explore the bay and islands is with Sutil Lodge's **Catamaran Cruises.** The 4-hour sail cruise leaves from Montague Harbour Marina and travels across the bay to a remote uninhabited island. The rate for a 4-hour cruise plus picnic lunch or dinner is C$39 (US$26) adults and C$29 (US$19) children under 12.

Mayne Island Kayak & Canoe Rentals, at Seal Beach in Miner's Bay (☎ **250/539-2667**), rents kayaks and canoes for C$20 (US$13) for 2 hours or C$42 (US$28) for a full day. The company will drop off kayaks at any of six launching points on the island, and if you get stranded, they'll even pick up kayaks (and too-weary kayakers) from other island destinations.

On Salt Spring, **Sea Otter Kayaking,** 1168 North End Rd. (☎ **250/537-5678;** www.saltspring.com/kayaking), rents kayaks and canoes starting at C$20 (US$13) per hour. Guided tours begin at C$35 (US$23) for a 2-hour harbor exploration.

WHERE TO STAY

Ruckle Provincial Park, off Beaver Point Road on Salt Spring Island (☎ **250/391-2300**), has 70 walk-in–only camping sites at C$12 (US$8). Hiking, kayaking, and mountain biking are all popular pastimes in the park.

ON SALT SPRING ISLAND

✪ **The Old Farmhouse B&B.** 1077 North End Rd., Salt Spring Island, BC V8K 1L9. ☎ **250/537-4113.** Fax 250/537-4969. www.islandnet.com/~pixsell.bcbbd/1/ 1000182.html. E-mail Farmhouse@saltspring.com. 4 units. C$170 (US$113) double. Rates include breakfast. MC, V.

One of the best-loved of all the Gulf Islands accommodations, the Old Farmhouse B&B combines top-quality lodgings, great food, and two of the friendliest and most professional innkeepers you'll ever meet. The Old Farmhouse is in fact an 1894 homestead built at the center of 3 acres of grassy meadows, orchards, and specimen trees. The guest rooms, each with a balcony or patio, are in an adjoining stylistically harmonious guest house.

Seabreeze Inn. 101 Bittancourt Rd., Salt Spring Island, BC V8K 2K2. ☎ **800/434-4112** or 250/537-4145. Fax 250/537-4323. www.ferrytravel.com/seabreeze. E-mail seabreeze@saltspring.com. 28 units. TV TEL. C$79–C$89 (US$53–US$59) double. AE, DC, DISC, MC, V.

An excellent alternative to Salt Spring's expensive B&Bs, the Seabreeze is a well-maintained, attractive motel just south of Ganges. All the guest rooms are clean and nicely furnished, with extras like refrigerators and coffeemakers. The 16 kitchen units come with electric cooktops, full-size refrigerators, and microwaves.

Summerhill Guest House. 209 Chu-an Dr., Salt Spring Island, BC V8K 1H9. ☎ **250/537-2727.** Fax 250/537-4301. www.bestinns.net./canada/bc/summerhill.html. E-mail summerhill@saltspring.com. 3 units. C$100–C$125 (US$67–US$83) double. Rates include breakfast. MC, V.

A strategic remodel turned this rambling ranch-style home into a contemporary lodging filled with great natural light, intriguing colors, and quality furniture. Two of the guest rooms share a large second-story deck. The back patio and gardens are lovely; past banks of lavender, the arbutus-shaded lawn slopes down to a rocky cliff with incredible views over forested islands, boats, and deep-blue water.

On Galiano Island

Bellhouse Inn. 29 Farmhouse Rd., Galiano Island, BC V0N 1P0. ☎ **800/970-7464** or 250/539-5667. Fax 250/539-5316. www.Monday.com/bellhouse. 4 units. C$135–C$175 (US$90–US$117) double. Rates include breakfast. MC, V.

Built in 1890 as a farmhouse and converted in the 1920s to an inn, the Bellhouse sits in a grassy meadow above a private beach. The views onto Mayne Island across boat-filled Active Pass are stunning; pods of orcas sometimes swim up to frolic in front of the inn. Three of the guest rooms have private balconies. The inn's 6 acres of grounds retain the feel of the old farm, with heritage fruit trees lining the property and sheep grazing in the fields.

✪ **Woodstone Country Inn.** 743 Georgeson Bay Rd., RR #1, Galiano Island, BC V0N 1P0. ☎ **888/339-2022** or 250/539-2022. Fax 250/539-5198. www.gulfislands.com/woodstone. E-mail woodstone@gulfislands.com. 12 units. C$99–C$185 (US$66–US$123). Rates include full breakfast. AE, ER, MC, V.

A quintessential small country inn, the Woodstone sits in a stand of fir trees over-looking a series of meadows that serve as a de facto bird sanctuary (in fact, the inn was built as a retreat for birders). The Woodstone is beautifully decorated with restrained but hearty good taste, with the owners' collection of folk art and carvings from Arctic Canada and Southern Africa. The guest rooms are large and beautifully furnished, with writing tables, upholstered chairs, and intriguing art; each has a fireplace. The dining room's daily-changing menu is a blend of classic French cuisine enlivened with vivid international flavors, with a four- course dinner at C$22 to C$27 (US$15 to US$18). Reservations are required, and dinner is served Sunday to Thursday 5 to 9pm and Friday and Saturday 5 to 10pm.

On Mayne Island

Blue Vista Resort. 563 Arbutus Dr., Mayne Island, BC V0N 2J0. ☎ **250/539-2463.** 8 cottages. C$50–C$75 (US$33–US$50) one-bedroom cottage, C$80–C$110 (US$53–US$73) two-bedroom cottage. Closed mid-Jan to mid-Feb. MC, V.

This venerable resort is a good example of that rare Gulf Island lodging—a place where kids and pets are welcome. On the warm eastern side of Mayne Island (close to beaches, kayaking, and hiking), the Blue Vista's comfortable one- and two-bedroom cabins are all you need: With full kitchens, fireplaces, sundecks, barbecues, and complimentary bikes, these cottages represent one of the best values on any of the Gulf Islands.

✪ **Oceanwood Country Inn.** 630 Dinner Bay Rd., Mayne Island, BC V0N 2J0.
☎ **250/539-5074.** Fax 250/539-3002. www.oceanwood.com. E-mail oceanwood@
gulfislands.com. 12 units. C$149–C$299 (US$99–US$199). Rates include breakfast and
afternoon tea. Closed Dec–Feb. MC, V.

This superlative inn has grown from a home-style B&B in a beautiful location to
a luxury lodging with an excellent restaurant. The newer wing's guest rooms are
wonderfully well appointed: Best thought of as luxury suites, these multitiered rooms
have private water-view decks, large sitting areas with comfy couches and chairs,
queen-sized beds, and two-person jetted or soaker tubs facing wood-burning
fireplaces. All but one room has magnificent views over formal gardens to boat-flecked
Navy Channel. Refined yet robust, the cuisine at Oceanwood alchemizes the
rich bounty of Pacific Northwest fish, meat, game, fruit, and vegetables into richly
sophisticated food. The four-course prix-fixe menu is C$39 (US$26). Reservations
are required, and dinner is served Sunday to Thursday 5:30 to 9pm and Friday and
Saturday 5:30 to 10pm.

WHERE TO DINE
ON SALT SPRING ISLAND

✪ **Hastings House.** 160 Upper Ganges Rd. ☎ **250/537-2362.** Reservations required.
Prix-fixe 5-course dinner C$70 (US$47). AE, DC, ER, MC, V. Summer dinner sitting at
7:30pm, spring and fall sitting at 7pm. PACIFIC NORTHWEST.

Elegant and romantic, the dining room at Hastings House combines old-world
sophistication with the freshest of West Coast ingredients and up-to-the-moment
kitchen savvy. The menus change daily and are designed to incorporate local produce
and fish; most of the herbs and vegetables are grown on the grounds of this luxurious
country inn (accommodations are available, starting at C$400/US$267). The rose-
covered Manor House—the inn's original structure, built in the 1930s as a replica of
a medieval English country house—is now the restaurant/lounge area. Jackets are
required for men. You can experience the same five-course menu in less formal
ambiance by requesting seating in The Snug, a pleasant ground-level room tucked
below the main dining room.

✪ **House Piccolo.** 108 Hereford Ave., Ganges. ☎ **250/537-1844.** Reservations
required. Main courses C$18–C$29 (US$12–US$19). AE, DC, MC, V. CONTINENTAL.

The Northern European accents in House Piccolo's unusual menu reflect the Finnish
origins of the chef/owner, particularly the fresh fish specials that feature the best of the
local catch. Sole in sorrel sauce was one night's special, while the seasonal menu features baked chicken breast in persillade crust and local Camembert and grilled lamb
chops with aioli.

5 Vancouver Island's West Coast: Pacific Rim National Park, Tofino & Ucluelet

Vancouver Island's west coast is a magnificent area of old-growth forests, stunning
fjords (called sounds in local parlance), rocky coasts, and long sandy beaches.
And though **Pacific Rim National Park** was established back in 1971 as Canada's
first marine park, it wasn't until 1993—when thousands of environmentalists
gathered to protest the clear-cutting of old-growth forests in Clayoquot Sound—
that the area really exploded into the people's consciousness. Tourism here has never
looked back.

ESSENTIALS

VISITOR INFORMATION   March to September, the **Tofino Visitor Info Centre,** 380 Campbell St. (P.O. Box 476), Tofino, BC V0R 2Z0 (☎ 250/725-3414), is open Monday to Friday 11am to 5pm. July to September, the **Ucluelet Visitor Info Centre,** Junction Highway 4 (P.O. Box 428), Ucluelet, BC V0R 3A0 (☎ 250/726-4641), is open the same hours. Mid-March to September, the **Long Beach Visitor Information Centre,** about a mile from the Highway 4 junction to Tofino (☎ 250/726-4212), is open daily 10am to 6pm.

GETTING THERE   By Bus   Island Coach Lines (☎ 250/724-1266) operates regular daily service between Victoria and Tofino/Ucluelet. The 7-hour trip, departing Victoria at 7:30am and arriving in Tofino at 2:45pm, costs C$45 (US$30) to Ucluelet and C$48 (US$32) to Tofino. The bus also stops in Nanaimo and can pick up passengers arriving from Vancouver on the ferry.

By Car   Tofino, Ucluelet, and Long Beach all lie near the end of Highway 4 on the west coast of Vancouver Island. From Nanaimo, take the Island Highway (Highway 19) north for 52km (32 miles). Just before the town of Parksville is a turnoff for Highway 4, which leads first to the mid-island town of Port Alberni (38km/24 miles) and then to the coastal towns of Tofino (135km/84 miles west of Port Alberni) and Ucluelet (103km/64 miles west). The road is well paved the whole way but gets windy after Port Alberni.

By Ferry   A 4½-hour ride aboard the **Alberni Marine Transportation** (☎ 250/723-8313) passenger ferry MV *Lady Rose* takes you from Port Alberni through Alberni Inlet to Ucluelet. It makes brief stops along the way to deliver mail and packages to solitary cabin dwellers along the coast and to let off or pick up kayakers bound for the Broken Islands Group. The *Lady Rose* departs three times a week to each destination from Alberni Harbour Quay's Angle Street. The fare to Ucluelet is C$23 (US$15) one-way and C$45 (US$30) round-trip. The service is in summer only.

By Plane   May to September, **North Vancouver Air** (☎ 800/228-6608) operates twin-engine, turbo-prop plane service daily between Vancouver or Victoria and Tofino; October to April, it runs four times a week. One-way fare, including all taxes and airport fees, is C$165 (U$110); flying time is 45 minutes. **Northwest Seaplanes** (☎ 800/690-0086) and **Sound Flight** (☎ 800/825-0722) offer floatplane service between Seattle and Tofino mid-June to late September.

EXPLORING THE PACIFIC RIM NATIONAL PARK (LONG BEACH DIVISION)

The three main areas to this section of the island's west coast are Ucluelet, Tofino, and the Long Beach division of the Pacific Rim National Park. They lie along the outer edge of a peninsula about half-way up the western shore.

A Whale of a Festival

About 20,000 Pacific gray whales migrate to this area annually. During the second week of March, the **Pacific Rim Whale Festival** (☎ 250/726-4641) is held in Tofino and Ucluelet (March 18 to April 2, 2000). Live crab races, the Gumboot Golf Tournament, guided whale-watching hikes, and a Native Indian festival are just a few of the events celebrating the annual whale migration.

The town of **Ucluelet** (pronounced you-*clue*-let, meaning "safe harbor" in the local Nuu-chah-nulth dialect) sits on the southern end of this peninsula, on the edge of Barkely Sound. When fishing was the major industry on the coast, it was the big town. Though it now has a winter population of only 1,900, thousands of visitors arrive between March and May to see as many as 20,000 Pacific gray whales pass close to the shore as they migrate north to their summer feeding grounds in the Arctic Circle. At the moment, the town has a beautiful location and a couple of fine B&Bs but has yet to develop the range of restaurants and activities Tofino offers. On the plus side, Ucluelet is cheaper, just as close to Long Beach, and much less busy.

About a 15-minute drive north is ✪ **Long Beach,** part of the Pacific Rim National Park group. The beach is more than 16km (10 miles) long, broken here and there by rocky headlands and bordered by tremendous groves of cedar and Sitka spruce. The beach is popular with countless species of birds and marine life and lately also with wet-suited surfers.

At the far-northern tip of the peninsula, **Tofino** (population 1,300) borders on beautiful Clayoquot Sound and is the center of the west coast eco-tourism business. It's a schizophrenic kind of town: Half is composed of eco-tourism outfitters, nature lovers, activists, and serious granolas; the other half is composed of loggers and fishers. Conflict was common in the early years, but recently the two sides seem to have learned how to get along. Hikers and beachcombers come to Tofino simply for the scenery, while others use it as a base from which to explore Clayoquot Sound.

OUTDOOR PURSUITS

FISHING Sportfishing for salmon, steelhead, rainbow trout, Dolly Varden char, halibut, cod, and snapper is excellent off the west coast of Vancouver Island. **Chinook Charters,** 450 Campbell St., Tofino (☎ **800/665-3646** or 250/725-3431), organizes fishing charters throughout the Clayoquot Sound area. Fishing starts in March or April and goes to December. The company supplies all the gear, a guide, and a boat. Prices start at a minimum of C$85 (U$57) per hour, with a minimum of 4 hours. A 10-hour fishing trip for four people on a 25-foot boat costs C$750 (US$500).

GUIDED NATURE HIKES Owned/operated by Bill McIntyre, former chief naturalist of the Pacific Rim National Park, the ✪ **Long Beach Nature Tour Co.** (☎ **250/726-7099;** fax 250726-4282) offers guided beach walks, storm watching, land-based whale-watching tours, and rain-forest tours customized to suit your group's needs. Also excellent are the tours offered by wildlife author Adrienne Mason of **Raincoast Communications** (☎ **250/725-2878;** e-mail amason@port.island.net). A local naturalist/science writer, she can accommodate various group sizes and will greatly enhance your knowledge of the rain-forest ecology and local flora and fauna.

HIKING In and around **Long Beach,** numerous marked trails 0.8km to 3.3km (½ mile to 2 miles) long take you through the thick temperate rain forest edging the shore. The **Gold Mine Trail** (about 3.3km/2 miles long) near Florencia Bay still has a few artifacts from the days when a gold-mining operation flourished here. The partially boardwalked **South Beach Trail** (less than a mile long) leads through the moss-draped rain forest onto small quiet coves like Lismer Beach and South Beach, where you can see abundant life in the rocky tidal pools. The **Big Cedar Trail** (☎ **250/725-3233**) on Meares Island is a 3.3km (2-mile) boardwalked path built in 1993 to protect the old-growth temperate rain forest. Maintained by the Tla-o-qui-aht Native Indian Band, the trail has a long staircase leading up to the Hanging Garden Tree, the province's fourth-largest western red cedar.

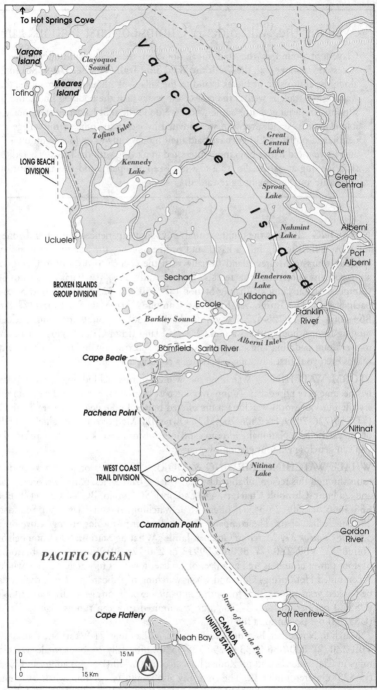

To Hot Springs Cove

Vargas Island

Clayoquot Sound

Meares Island

Tofino

Tofino Inlet

Vancouver Island

Great Central Lake

LONG BEACH DIVISION

Kennedy Lake

4

Sproat Lake

Great Central

Nahmint Lake

Alberni

Ucluelet

Port Alberni

BROKEN ISLANDS GROUP DIVISION

Sechart

Henderson Lake

Kildonan

Ecoole

Franklin River

Barkley Sound

Bamfield   Sarita River

Alberni Inlet

Cape Beale

Pachena Point

Nitinat

WEST COAST TRAIL DIVISION

Clo-oose

Nitinat Lake

Carmanah Point

Gordon River

PACIFIC OCEAN

Port Renfrew

14

Cape Flattery

CANADA
UNITED STATES

Strait of Juan de Fuc

Neah Bay

0   15 Mi
0   15 Km

N

Walking the Wild Side: A Glimpse of First Nations Life

Clayoquot Sound is the traditional home of the Nuu-chah-nulth peoples. Accessed via water taxi, the **Walk the Wild Side Trail** (☎ **888/670-9586**) runs along the south side of Flores Island to the village of Ahousat. There's a fee for walking the trail, as well as the cost of the water taxi; the booking line above is supposed to arrange both. Some who have done the trail have reported incredible experiences and afterward were invited by elders to come to the village to celebrate a potlatch. Others have paid their money only to be foisted off on 12- and 13-year-old native boys more interested in playing with their two-way radios than looking at nature. So it's a toss-up. Keep an open mind and the spirit of adventure and you might be rewarded.

KAYAKING   Perhaps the quintessential Clayoquot experience, and certainly one of the most fun, is to slip into a kayak and paddle out into the Sound. For beginners, half-day tours to Meares Island (usually with the chance to do a little hiking) are an especially good bet. For rentals, lessons, and tours, try **Pacific Kayak,** 606 Campbell St., at Jamie's Whaling Station (☎ **250/725-3232;** www.tofino-bc.com/pacifickayak). The **Tofino Sea-Kayaking Company,** 320 Main St., Tofino (☎ **800/863-4664** or 250/725-4222; www.island.net/~paddlers), offers kayaking packages ranging from 4-hour paddles around Meares Island (from C$52/US$35 per person) to weeklong paddling and camping expeditions. Instruction by experienced guides makes even your first kayaking experience a comfortable, safe, and enjoyable one.

STORM WATCHING   Watching the winter storms behind big glass windows has become very popular in Tofino over the past year or so. For a slight twist on this, try the outdoor storm-watching tours offered by the **Long Beach Nature Tour Co.** (☎ **250/726-7099;** fax 250/726-4282). Owner Bill McIntyre, former chief naturalist of the Pacific Rim National Park, can explain how storms work and where to stand so you can get close without getting swept away.

WHALE WATCHING, BIRDING & MORE   A number of outfitters conducts tours through this region inhabited by gray whales, bald eagles, porpoises, orcas, seals, and sea lions. **Chinook Charters,** 450 Campbell St., Tofino, BC V0R 2Z0 (☎ **800/665-3646** or 250/725-3431), offers whale-watching trips in Clayoquot Sound on 25-foot Zodiac boats. The company also conducts trips to Hot Springs Cove on its 32-foot *Chinook Key.* March to October, **Jamie's Whaling Station,** 606 Campbell St., Tofino, BC V0R 2Z0 (☎ **800/667-9913** or 250/725-3919), uses a glass-bottomed 65-foot power cruiser as well as a fleet of Zodiacs for tours to watch the gray whales. A combined Hot Springs Cove and whale-watching trip aboard a 32-foot cruiser can be booked year-round. Fares for both companies' expeditions generally start at C$75 (US$50) per person for a 3-hour tour; customized trips can run as high as C$200 (US$133) per person for a full day.

March to November, **Remote Passages,** Meares Landing, 71 Wharf St., Tofino, BC V0R 2Z0 (☎ **800/666-9833** or 250/725-3330), runs daily 2½-hour whale-watching tours in Clayoquot Sound on Zodiac boats, costing C$50 (US$33) adults and C$35 (US$23) children under 12. The company also conducts a 7-hour whale-watching/hot springs trip at C$75 (US$50) adults and C$50 (US$33) children under 12. Reservations are recommended.

For land-based bird watching, contact local naturalist/science writer Adrienne Mason of **Rainforest Communications** (☎ 250/725-2878). Adrienne knows the area and can customize a tour depending on your needs.

Hot Springs Cove, accessible only by water, is a natural hot spring about 67km (41 miles) north of Tofino. Take a water taxi, sail, canoe, or kayak up to Clayoquot Sound to enjoy swimming in the steaming pools and bracing waterfalls. A number of kayak outfitters and boat charters offer trips to the springs.

RAINY-DAY ACTIVITIES

You can browse books at the **Wildside Booksellers and Espresso Bar,** Main Street (☎ 250/745-4222), or get a massage or salt glow at the **Ancient Cedars Spa** at the Wickaninnish (☎ 250/725-3100).

You can also check out the galleries. The **Eagle Aerie Gallery,** 350 Campbell St. (☎ 250/725-3235), constructed in the style of a Native Indian Longhouse, features the innovative work of Tsimshian artist Roy Henry Vickers. The **House of Himwitsa,** 300 Main St. (☎ 250/725-2017), is also owned/operated by Native Indians. The quality and craftsmanship of the shop's artwork, masks, baskets, totems, gold and silver jewelry, and apparel are excellent. The **Island Folk Artisans Gallery,** 120 4th St. (☎ 250/725-3130), represents mainly art from Vancouver Island artists. The themes are often trees, wildlife, and crafts made out of wood or seashells, a lasting memory of your trip. You can find the new age side of Tofino in the **Reflecting Spirit Gallery,** 441 Campbell St. (☎ 250/725-4229), which offers medicine wheels, rocks, and crystals, as well as a great selection of native art, carvings, wood crafts, and pottery.

WHERE TO STAY

The 94 campsites on the bluff at **Green Point** are maintained by the Pacific Rim National Park (☎ 250/726-7721). The grounds are full every day in July and August, and the average wait for a site is 1 to 2 days. Leave your name at the ranger station when you arrive to be placed on the list. You're rewarded for your patience with a magnificent ocean view, pit toilets, fire pits, pumped well water, and free firewood (no showers or hookups). Sites in July and August are C$14 to C$20 (US$9 to US$13) and in the shoulder season C$12 to C$18 (US$8 to U$12). The campground is closed October to March.

The **Bella Pacifica Resort & Campground,** 3.3km (2 miles) south of Tofino on the Pacific Rim Highway (P.O. Box 413), Tofino, BC V0R 2Z0 (☎ 250/725-3400), is privately owned and has 165 campsites from which you can walk to Mackenzie Beach or take the resort's private nature trails to Templar Beach. Flush toilets, hot showers, water, laundry, ice, fire pits, firewood, and full and partial hookups are available. Rates are C$16 to C$33 (US$11 to US$22) per two-person campsite. Reserve at least a month in advance for a spot on a summer weekend.

IN UCLUELET

Ocean's Edge B&B. 855 Barkely Place, Box 557, Ucluelet, BC V0R 3A0. ☎ **250/726-7099.** www.oceansedge.bc.ca. 3 units. May–Sept C$120 (US$80) double; Oct–Apr C$95 (US$63) double. No credit cards. No pets or children. 2-night minimum on long weekends and holidays.

This remarkable B&B on its own tiny peninsula juts into the Pacific, with only a thicket of interwoven hemlocks sheltering it from the wind and the surf of the ocean, which roars up surge channels on either side. The guest rooms are pleasant and spotless without being opulent. The real attraction is the scenery and the wildlife. Owners

Bill and Susan McIntyre have installed a skylight in the kitchen so breakfasting guests can keep an eye on the pair of bald eagles and their chicks, nesting in a 200-year-old Sitka spruce in the driveway. Bill, former chief naturalist of the Pacific Rim National Park, is a font of information and also does nature tours (see above).

A Snug Harbour Inn. 460 Marine Dr., Box 357, Ucluelet, BC V0R 3A0. ☎ **250/726-2686.** www.ucluelet.com/asnugharbourinn. 4 units. June–Sept C$180–C$280 (US$120–US$187) double; Oct–May C$150–C$200 (US$100–US$133) double. MC, V.

A beautiful clifftop B&B overlooking its own little bay, A Snug Harbour Inn makes the most of its location. On the back of the inn are several large viewing decks, one with a hot tub. The guest rooms are spacious, with queen- or king-sized beds, opulent bathrooms, and jetted tubs. The heart-shaped tub with a waterfall may be a bit over the top, but who's complaining? Owner Skip Rowland had the inn built by a ship-wright, and the craftsmanship shows.

In Tofino

✪ **Clayoquot Wilderness Resort.** P.O. Box 728, Tofino, BC V0R 2Z0. ☎ **888/ 333-5405** in North America, or 250/725-2688. Fax 250/725-2689. www.wildretreat. com. 16 units, 4 camps. May–Oct C$249 (US$166) per person; Nov–Apr C$189 (US$126) per person. Rate includes three meals and transfer to/from Tofino. AE, MC, V. Parking provided in Tofino.

The latest in absolute luxury in the area, the Clayoquot Wilderness Resort (CWR) floats alone in splendid isolation on Quoit bay, about a half-hour boat ride from Tofino. Guests are encouraged to use the lodge as a base camp for exploring the natural beauty of the sound. The CWR has set up a number of forest walking trails nearby and runs trips to Hot Springs Cove, as well as horseback-riding excursions and mountain-biking trips. (Most of these activities are charged separately.) There are also spots to fly-fish or simply laze in the sun. The meals are prepared by noted West Coast chef Timothy May.

Inn at Tough City. 350 Main St., P.O. Box 8, Tofino, BC V0R 2Z0. ☎ **250/725-2021.** Fax 250/725-2088. E-mail cityinn@cedar.alberni.net. www.alberni.net/toughcity. 6 units. TEL. Mar–May 15 C$90–C$120 (US$60–US$80); May 16–Oct 15 C$140–C$165 (US$93–US$110); Oct 16–Feb C$75–C$100 (US$50–US$67). MC, V.

This is possibly the nicest small inn in Tofino and certainly the quirkiest. Built in 1996 from salvaged and recycled material, the inn is chockablock with antiques and bric-a-brac. The guest rooms are spacious, and several feature soaker tubs or fireplaces or both. Crazy Ron and Johanna are the innkeepers.

Middle Beach Lodge. P.O. Box 100, Tofino, BC V0R 2Z0. ☎ **250/725-2900.** Fax 250/ 725-2901. E-mail lodge@middlebeach.com. www.middlebeach.com. 7 units, 25 cabins. TEL. C$110–C$165 (US$73–US$110) double; C$165–C$275 (US$110–US$183) suite; C$175–C$370 (US$117–US$247) single cabin; C$160–C$295 (US$107–US$197) duplex cabin; C$110–C$210 (US$73–US$140) triplex cabin; C$125–C$195 (US$83–US$130) sixplex cabin. AE, MC, V. No smoking, no pets, children welcome.

This beautiful lodge/resort complex is on a headland overlooking the ocean. The rustic look was accomplished by using largely recycled beams, and the result is very pleasant. Accommodations range from simple lodge rooms to cabins with waterside decks, soaker tubs, gas fireplaces, and kitchenettes. All guests have access to a lofty common room overlooking the ocean, a good place to pour a coffee or something stronger and look out over the waves crashing in.

Red Crow Guest House. Box 37, 1084 Pacific Rim Hwy., Tofino, BC V0R 2Z0. ☎/fax **250/ 725-2275.** www.bedandbreakfast.com/Bbc/P613513.Asp. E-mail tofinoredcrow@hotmail.com.

3 units, 1 cottage. May–Sept C$100–C$135 (US$67–US$90) double, C$160 (US$107) cottage; Oct–Apr C$85–C$110 (US$57–US$73) double, C$135 (US$90) cottage. Extra person C$20 (US$13) year-round. V. Rates include substantial breakfast.

By the sheltered waters of Clayoquot Sound, this pleasant Cape Cod cottage looks as if it could be set on a lake—until you paddle 50 feet out in a canoe or rowboat (use of which is free for guests) and see the glaciers. Red Crow host/owner Cathy Whitcomb runs an extremely laid-back place. Guests are welcomed to their rooms with tea and cookies, then given the run of the extensive grounds, likely with one of two friendly large dogs for company. The guest rooms are large and pleasant, with queen-size beds and 1920s-style furnishings. Located on the lower level of the large house, they have their own porch and look out on a fabulous view of the Sound.

✪ **Wickaninnish Inn.** Osprey Lane at Chesterman Beach, P.O. Box 250, Tofino, BC V0R 2Z0. ☎ **800/333-4604** in North America, or 250/725-3300. Fax 250/725-3110. E-mail wick@island.net. 46 units. AC TV TEL. Mar–June 25 C$170–C$210 (US$113–US$140) double, C$325 (US$217) suite; June 26–Sept C$240–C$280 (US$160–US$187) double, C$395 (US$263) suite; Oct–Nov 1 C$180–C$220 (US$120–US$147) double, C$325 (US$217) suite; Nov 2–Feb 28 C$140–C$180 (US$93–US$120) double, C$375 (US$250) suite. Special packages available year-round. AE, MC, V. Drive 5km (3.1 miles) south of Tofino toward Chesterman Beach to Osprey Lane.

No matter which room or suite you book in this beautiful new cedar, stone, and glass lodge, you'll wake to a magnificent view of the untamed Pacific. The inn is on a rocky promontory, surrounded by an old-growth spruce and cedar rain forest and the sprawling sands of Chesterman Beach. You do have to make some choices: select a king- or queen-size bed and whether you want a room with an ocean view from the tub. Rustic driftwood, richly printed textiles, and local artwork highlight the decor. Every one of the spacious guest rooms features a fireplace, down duvet, soaker tub, and private balcony. Winter storm-watching packages have become so popular the inn is as busy then as it is in summer. The Pointe Restaurant (see "Where to Dine" below) and On-the-Rocks Bar serve three meals daily and feature an oceanfront view. The staff can arrange whale-watching, golfing, fishing, and diving packages. No-Stress Express packages include air transport and accommodations.

WHERE TO DINE
IN UCLUELET

Fine dining is only just beginning in this coast town, as urban refugees with a flair for cooking arrive and try to make a go of it. Two that have done so are the **Kingfisher Restaurant,** 1952 Peninsula Rd. (☎ 250/726-3463), open Monday to Saturday 6am to 8pm, and the **Matterson Teahouse and Garden,** 1682 Peninsula Rd. (☎ 250/726-2200), open daily noon to 8pm. Somewhat less ambitious but still good is the **Eagle's Nest Marine Pub,** 140 Bay St. (☎ 250/726-7515), open Monday to Saturday 10am to midnight and Sunday 10am to 10pm.

IN TOFINO

The Coffee Pod. 461 Campbell St. ☎ **250/725-4246.** Snacks and meals C$3–C$10 (US$2–US$7). Daily 5:30am–6pm. LIGHT FARE.

At this laid-back semigranola kind of place, you'll find excellent coffee. You can't miss it as you drive into Tofino—the Pod is on your left; you'll see the patio and people milling about. It's a great place to go for breakfast, have a steaming latté or cappuccino with a breakfast pannini, read the paper, and listen in on the local gossip.

Common Loaf Bakeshop. 181 First St. ☎ **250/725-3915.** Snacks and meals C$3–C$12 (US$2–US$8). Daily 8am–9pm. LIGHT FARE.

At the "far" end of town, the Common Loaf serves great baked goods: muffins, cookies, whole-grain breads, and huge sticky cinnamon buns. Lunch items include soups, curry, and pizza, accompanied by herbal teas, coffee, juices, and wine and beer. If it looks crowded downstairs, take the stairs to the loft where you can usually find a spot and have a bird's-eye view.

Pointe Restaurant. In the Wickaninnish Inn, Osprey Lane at Chesterman Beach. ☎ **250/ 725-3110.** Reservations recommended. Main courses C$18–C$30 (US$12–US$20). MC, V. Daily 8am–2:30pm, 2–5pm (snacks), 5–9:30pm. PACIFIC NORTHWEST.

Perched on the water's edge at Chesterman Beach is the Pointe, where a 280° view of the roaring Pacific is the backdrop to a fine dining experience. Chef Rodney Butters applies his talents to an array of local ingredients, including Dungeness crab, spotted prawns, halibut, salmon, quail, lamb, and rabbit. His signature version of bouill-abaisse, Wickaninnish Potlatch, is a chunky blend of soft and firm fish, shellfish, and vegetables simmered in a thick seafood broth. Delectable appetizers include goat-cheese tarts and shaved fennel salad and entrees like grilled lamb chops with new pota-toes, fresh artichokes, and sea asparagus. Butters' signature dessert—a double-chocolate, mashed-potato brioche—is superb when accompanied by a glass of raspberry wine.

Rain Coast Cafe. Off Campbell at 4th St. ☎ **250/725-2215.** Main courses C$11–C$20 (U$7–U$13). Daily 11:30am–3pm and 5–10pm. AE, MC, V. SEAFOOD.

This small cozy restaurant has developed a deserved reputation for some of the best seafood and vegetarian dishes in town. To start off, try one of the most popular appe-tizers, the Rain Coast salad—smoked salmon, sautéed mushrooms, and chevre cheese on a bed of greens, served with maple-balsamic vinaigrette. Fresh fish is a big part of the cuisine, and menu items are supplemented with a catch-of-the-day special.

6 Vancouver Island's East Coast: Parksville to Campbell River & Quadra Island

Vancouver Island's east coast is lined with long sandy beaches, world-class golf courses, and fishing resorts. Parksville and neighboring Qualicum Beach are longtime favorites for family vacations. With miles of beach for the kids and six local golf courses for the parents, these twinned towns are the perfect base for a relaxing vacation. Sixty-one kilometers (38 miles) north, Comox and Courtenay are another set of inter-grown beach towns with access to great sea kayaking and tours to fossil digs. Campbell River (pop. 29,000), 46km (29 miles) farther north, is by far the most famous salmon fishing center in British Columbia, with many long-established fishing resorts that have hosted everyone from the Shah of Iran to John Wayne to Goldie Hawn. A short ferry ride across Discovery Channel from Campbell River is Quadra Island, a moun-tainous island with one of the best First Nations museums in Canada.

ESSENTIALS

VISITOR INFORMATION   For info on Parksville and Qualicum Beach, contact the **Parksville–Qualicum Beach Tourism Association,** 174 Railway St., Box 374, Qualicum Beach, BC V9K 1S9 (☎ 888/799-3222 or 250/752-2388; fax 250/ 752-2392; www.oceanside-bc.com; e-mail info@oceanside-bc.com). For details on the Comox/Courtenay area, contact the **Comox Valley Visitor Info Centre,** 2040 Cliffe Ave., Courtenay, BC V9N 2L3 (☎ 888/357-4471 or 250/334-3234; www.vquest.com/cv.chamber or www.tourism-comox-valley.bc.ca; e-mail chamber@ mars.ark.com). The **Campbell River Visitor Info Centre** is at 1235 Shopper's Row,

Box 44, Campbell River, BC V9W 5B6 (☎ **250/287-4636;** www.vquest.com/ crtourism).

GETTING THERE   By Car   From Nanaimo, the Island Highway (Highway 19) links Parksville, Courtenay, and Campbell River with points north. Campbell River is 52km (32 miles) north of Courtenay and 266km (165 miles) north of Victoria.

By Bus   Laidlaw Coach Lines (☎ **250/385-4411**) operates four buses daily with service to and from Victoria and Port Hardy via Nanaimo, with stops in Parksville, Qualicum Bay, Courtenay, and Campbell River. One-way fare from Nanaimo to Campbell River is C$23 (US$15).

By Ferry   BC Ferries (☎ **888/724-5223** or 604/444-2890; www.bcferries.bc.ca) operates a 75-minute crossing from Powell River on the mainland to Campbell River. There's also a crossing to and from Little River, just north of Comox to Powell River. The one-way fare for both ferries is C$8 (US$5) per passenger and C$28 (US$19) per vehicle.

By Train   The **E&N Railiner** operates daily between Courtenay and Victoria, with stops in Parksville and Qualicum Beach.

By Plane   The **Campbell River and District Regional Airport,** south of Campbell River off of Jubilee Parkway, has regularly scheduled flights on conventional commuter planes to and from Vancouver and Seattle on **Canadian Regional Airlines** (☎ **800/665-1177**) and **Air BC** (☎ **800/663-3721** in BC, 800/776-3000 in the US). Harbor-to-harbor service between Vancouver and Campbell River is also available late June to Labor Day via **Air Rainbow** (☎ **250/287-8371**). **Comox Valley Regional Airport,** north of Comox off Ryan Road, has daily scheduled flights to and from Vancouver on Canadian Regional Airlines and Air BC.

EXPLORING THE EAST COAST

Parksville (pop. 9,576) and **Qualicum Beach** (pop. 6,874) are near the most popular beaches on Vancouver Island: Spending a week on the beach here is a family tradition for many longtime residents. Parksville claims to have the warmest ocean-water beaches in all Canada. **Rathtrevor Beach Provincial Park** is a popular place for swimming and sunbathing.

Facing each other across the Courtenay River Estuary, the twin towns **Comox** (pop. 11,847) and **Courtenay** (pop. 18,420) provide a bit of urban polish to a region rich in beaches, outdoor recreation, and dramatic land- and seascapes. The highlight of the **Courtenay Museum & Paleontology Centre,** 360 Cliffe Ave. (☎ **250/334-3611;** www.courtenaymuseum.bc.ca), is a 12m (39-foot) cast skeleton of an elasmosaur, a crocodile-like Cretaceous marine reptile. July and August, the museum leads 3-hour **fossil tours** of its paleontology lab and to a local fossil dig; they're held Tuesdays, Thursdays, and Sundays, and tickets are C$10 (US$7) adults, C$8 (US$5) seniors/ students, C$5 (US$3.35) children, or C$30 (US$20) families. Call ahead for tour times and reservations. Admission to the museum alone is C$2 (US$1.35). May to August, museum hours are daily 10am to 4:30pm; September to April, hours are Tuesday to Saturday 10am to 4:40pm.

The **Museum at Campbell River,** 470 Island Hwy. (☎ **250/287-3103;** www. island.net/~crm_chin), has an exhibit hall devoted to carvings and artifacts from the local First Nations; especially fine is the exhibit of contemporary carved wooden masks. Another compelling exhibit is the sound-and-light presentation *The Treasure of Siwidi,* which uses masks to retell an ancient native Indian myth. Admission is C$2.50 (US$1.65) adults, C$2 (US$1.35) seniors/students, and C$8 (US$5) families; children under 6 are free. Mid-May to September, the museum is open Monday to

Saturday 10am to 5pm and Sunday noon to 5pm; October to early May, hours are Tuesday to Sunday noon to 5pm.

Quadra Island sits right across Discovery Channel from Campbell River. The main reason to make the 10-minute ferry passage (C$4.50/US$3 per passenger, C$12/US$8 per vehicle) is to visit the excellent ۞ **Kwakiutl Museum and Cultural Center,** WeiWai Road in Cape Mudge Village (☎ **250/285-3733**). The museum has one of the world's best collections of artifacts, ceremonial masks, and tribal costumes once used by the Cape Mudge Band in elaborate potlatch ceremonies. The Canadian government outlawed the potlatch in 1922 as part of a short-lived enforced-assimilation policy. During this time, the artifacts in the Kwakiutl Museum were removed to museums and private collections in eastern Canada and England, where they were preserved and cataloged. The collection was repatriated to the Cape Mudge Band in the early 1990s, when the tribe built the present spectacular museum. It's open Monday to Saturday 10am to 4:30pm (summer also Sun noon to 4:30pm). Admission is C$3 (US$2) adults and C$2 (US$1.35) seniors/students. The road to the museum isn't well signposted. From the ferry, take Cape Mudge Road south about 5km (3.1 miles) and watch for the signs for WeiWai Road and a hand-painted sign saying MUSEUM.

SPORTS & OUTDOOR ACTIVITIES

DIVING   The decommissioned **HMCS *Columbia*** was sunk in 1996 near the sea-life–rich waters of Seymour Narrows off the Quadra Island's west coast. For information on diving to this artificial reef and on other diving sites in the Campbell River area, contact **Beaver Aquatics** at ☎ **250/287-7652.**

FISHING   Between Quadra Island and Campbell River, the broad Strait of Georgia squeezes down to a narrow mile-wide passage called Discovery Channel. All the salmon that entered the Strait of Juan de Fuca near Victoria to spawn in northerly rivers funnel down into this tight constriction, a churning waterway with 13-foot tides.

However, fishing isn't what it once was in Campbell River, when tyee and coho salmon regularly tipped the scales at 75 pounds. Some salmon runs are now catch-and-release only, while others are open for limited catches; many fishing trips are now billed as much as wildlife adventures as hunting-and-gathering expeditions.

If you'd like to get out onto the waters and fish, be sure to call ahead and talk to an outfitter or the tourist center to find out what fish are running during your visit and if the seasons have been opened. Because of plummeting numbers of salmon and of recent treaties with the United States, the next few years will see even more greatly restricted fishing seasons in the waters off Vancouver Island. Don't be disappointed if there's no salmon fishing when you visit or if the salmon you hook is catch-and-release only. For one thing, there are other fish in the sea: Not all types of salmon are as threatened as the coho and tyee, and fishing is also good for halibut and other bottom fish. And if you really just want to get out on the water and have an adventure, consider a wildlife-viewing boat tour, offered by many fishing outfitters.

There are dozens of fishing guides in the Campbell River area, with a range of services from basic to pure extravagance. Expect to pay around C$45 to C$50 (US$30 to US$33) per hour for 4 to 5 hours of fishing with a no-frills outfitter, while a flashier trip on a luxury cruiser can cost more than C$120 (US$80) per hour. To fish here, you need nonresident saltwater and freshwater licenses, which you can buy at recreation stores throughout Campbell River or at **Painter's Lodge Holiday & Fishing Resort,** 1625 MacDonald Rd., Box 560, Campbell River, BC V9W 5C1 (☎ **250/ 286-1102**). The most famous fishing guides are also associated with the Painter's Lodge and its sibling property April Point Lodge (see "Where to Stay" below).

GOLF   Greens fees at the following courses are C$35 to C$45 (US$23 to US$30) for 18 holes. For more information, check out the Web site at **www.golfvancouverisland. com**.

There are six courses in the Parksville–Qualicum Beach area, and more than a dozen within an hour's drive. Here are two favorites: The **Eagle Crest Golf Club,** 2035 Island Hwy. (☎ **250/752-6311**), is a 18-hole, par-71 course with an emphasis on shot making and accuracy; and the public **Morningstar Golf Club,** 525 Lowry's Rd. (☎ **250/248-8161**), is an 18-hole, 7,018-yard course with a par-72 rating.

One of the finest courses on Vancouver Island is the brand-new **Crown Isle Resort & Golf Community,** 339 Clubhouse Dr., Courtenay (☎ **888/338-8439** or 250/ 703-5050; www.crownisle.com). This lavish 18-hole links-style championship golf course has already hosted the Canadian Tour and Canadian Junior Men's Tournament. Because it was carved out of a dense forest, you may see wildlife grazing on the fairway and roughs at the **Storey Creek Golf Club,** Campbell River (☎ **250/923-3673**). Gentle creeks and ponds also wind through this course.

KAYAKING   With the Courtenay Estuary and Hornby, Tree, and Denman Islands an easy paddle away, sea kayaking is popular in Courtenay and Comox. **Comox Valley Kayaks,** 2020 Cliffe Ave. (☎ **888/545-5595** or 250/334-2628; www.island.net/ ~seakayak; e-mail seakayak@island.net), offers rentals, lessons, and tours. A 3-hour introductory lesson (includes all instruction and equipment) is given Tuesday and Thursday evenings at C$40 (US$27); a guided day trip to Tree Island costs C$60 (US$40), including lunch.

SKIING   In the Comox Valley, the **Mount Washington Ski Resort,** P.O. Box 3069, Courtenay (☎ **888/837-4663** or 604/619-0550; 250/338-1515 snow report), is British Columbia's third-largest ski area. A 1,600-foot vertical drop and 42 groomed runs are serviced by four chair lifts and a beginners' tow. Nineteen miles of track-set Nordic trails connect to Strathcona Provincial Park. Full-day rates are C$42 (US$28) adults, C$32 (US$21) seniors/students, and C$22 (US$15) kids 7 to 12.

WHERE TO STAY
IN PARKSVILLE & QUALICUM BEACH

✪ **Bahari B&B.** 5101 Island Hwy. W., Qualicum Beach, BC V9K 1Z1. ☎ **877/ 752-9278** or 250/752-9278. Fax 250/752-9038. www.baharibandb.com. E-mail lhooper@macn.bc.ca. 5 units. C$125–C$175 (US$83–US$117) double. AE, MC, V.

The Bahari, reached by an avenue flanked by forest and manicured gardens, could easily take pride of place in *Architectural Digest.* The four guest rooms, plus a two-bedroom apartment, are uniquely decorated but share a spare Danish-Modern-by-way-of-Tokyo aesthetic. Each room has original artwork, balconies, robes, and quality linens. Paths lead to the beach, frequented by seals and eagles.

Tigh-Na-Mara Resort Hotel. 1095 East Island Hwy., Parksville, BC V9P 2E5. ☎ **800/ 663-7373** or 250/248-2072. Fax 250/248-4140. www.tigh-na-mara.com. E-mail info@ tigh-na-mara.com. 142 units. C$104–C$189 (US$69–US$126) double. AE, DC, MC, V.

Opened in the 1940s on a forested waterfront beach, Tigh-Na-Mara has been added to over the years, adding cottages, lodge-style rooms, and most recently beautifully furnished condo-style suites with stunning ocean views—all log built. And there's more to do than just go to the beach, especially for kids. The list of supervised child-friendly activities (many of them free) is lengthy. All rooms, cottages, and condos have fireplaces and some form of kitchen. The restaurant serves an eclectic international-ized version of Northwest cuisine in the log-and-stone central lodge. Facilities include tennis courts, an indoor pool, a sauna, hot tubs, exercise rooms, watercraft and video rentals, children's playgrounds, and outdoor barbecues. There's an extra charge for the "Parent's Night Out" baby-sitting program.

IN COURTENAY

Kingfisher Oceanside Resort and Spa. 4330 S. Island Hwy., Courtney, BC V9N 8H9. ☎ **800/663-7929** or 250/338-1323. Fax 250/338-0058. www.kingfisher-resort-spa.com. E-mail stay@kingfisher-resort-spa.com. 45 units. TV TEL. C$99 double (US$66); C$170 (US$113) suite. AE, DC, MC, V.

Located 7km (4.3 miles) south of Courtenay, the Kingfisher is a long-established and comfortable beach resort that recently added a bank of splendid beachfront suites and a classy health, beauty, and fitness spa. The dining room brings together waterfront views of beach, island, and coastal mountains with high-quality seafood and continental specialties, plus spa cuisine; it's open daily 7 to 10:30am, 11:30am to 2pm, and 5 to 10pm. Facilities include an outdoor pool, a hot tub, a steam cave, a sauna, and canoe and kayak rentals. The Kingfisher Oceanside Spa offers a wide selection of beauty treatments and body works, plus a full exercise room.

IN CAMPBELL RIVER

Hotel Bachmair Suite Hotel. 492 S. Island Hwy., Campbell River, BC V9W 1A5. ☎ **888/923-2849** or 250/923-2848. Fax 250/923-2849. www.bctravel.com/ni/hotelbachmair.html. 23 units. TV TEL C$79–C$130 (US$53–US$87) suite. Extra person C$10 (US$7). AE, MC, V.

This hotel on the southern edge of Campbell River has very large and beautifully furnished guest rooms at very moderate prices. The styles range from hotel rooms to one- and two-bedroom suites, plus two penthouse suites, one of which can sleep eight, and a loft suite for two. The suites all come with large bedrooms, full kitchens, and sitting rooms with couches and chairs, plus a dining area. Most rooms have views of Discovery Passage, and all have balconies.

✪ **Painter's Lodge Holiday & Fishing Resort.** 1625 MacDonald Rd., Box 460, Campbell River, BC V9W 4S5. ☎ **800/663-7090** or 250/286-1102. Fax 250/598-1361. www.obmg.com. E-mail obmg@pinc.com. 90 units, 4 cottages. TV TEL. C$110–C$145 (US$73–US$97) double; C$150–C$360 (US$100–US$240) cottage. AE, MC, V. Closed Nov–Mar.

This has been a favorite fishing hideaway for film stars like John Wayne, Bob Hope, and Kurt Russell. You can see why, for the wooded coastal location is awe-inspiring. Built in 1924 on a point overlooking the Discovery Passage, this lodge retains a rustic grandeur, with spacious lodge rooms and suites decorated in natural wood and pastels. Secluded self-contained cottages nestled near the lodge are also available.

Dining/Diversions: The beautiful tiered Legends dining room at Painter's Lodge is entirely flanked by windows, allowing every table to have a view of busy Discovery Passage waterway. The menu features local seafood and international dishes like jambalaya, porterhouse of lamb, and Cuban-style pork chops (marinated in rum and tandoori spices). It's open daily 7am to 10pm (closed Nov to Mar). A lighter menu of burgers and pub food is available in the Tyee Pub. If you're having dinner at Legends, consider hopping the free water taxi to April Point Lodge for a cocktail or a predinner appetizer at its sushi bar.

Amenities: Guided fishing trips, tennis courts, fitness center, and airport shuttle.

ON QUADRA ISLAND

April Point Lodge & Fishing Resort. April Point Rd., Quadra Island (mailing address: Box 1, Campbell River, BC V9W 4Z9). ☎ **800/663-7090** or **250/285-2222.** www.obmg.com. E-mail obmg@pinc.com. 30 units, 6 guest houses. C$139–C$199 (US$93–US$133) double; C$189–C$249 (US$126–US$166) guest house. AE, MC, V.

The secluded April Point Lodge, world-famous for its saltwater fishing charters, has magnificent views of the Discovery Passage in a tranquil private setting. This luxury fishing resort is owned by the same partnership that owns Painter's Lodge just across the channel, and there's a free boat taxi between the two properties. The one- to six-bedroom guest houses at the water's edge have hot tubs, fireplaces, and kitchens. The lodge suites are also spacious and nicely appointed.

Dining: The waterfront restaurant at this beloved fishing resort has a stellar view across Discovery Passage and well-prepared Pacific Northwest cuisine. Daily-changing seafood specials are the highlight of the restaurant; there's also a sushi bar. Dining hours are daily 7 to 10:30am, 11am to 2pm, and 5 to 10pm.

Amenities: Kayak, bicycle, and scooter rentals; fishing and adventure tours; full-service marina.

7 Northern Vancouver Island: Port McNeill, Alert Bay, Telegraph Cove & Port Hardy

It's a winding 198km (123-mile) drive through thickly forested mountains along the Island Highway (Highway 19) from Campbell River to **Port McNeill** on northern Vancouver Island. But the majestic scenery, the crystal-clear lakes, and the unique wilderness along the way make it worthwhile. This area is home to a number of orca pods, which migrate annually from the Queen Charlotte Strait south to the adjoining salmon-rich waters of the **Johnstone Strait.** (Orcas, or killer whales, are actually the largest members of the oceanic dolphin family and live in groups from a few to 50 individuals, known as pods or herds.) There's plenty to see in the small nearby community of **Alert Bay** (pop. 615) and in **Telegraph Cove,** a boardwalk community with only five year-round residents.

The Island Highway's terminus, **Port Hardy,** is 52km (32 miles) north of Port McNeill. Though it's a remote community of only 5,500, Port Hardy is the starting point for two unique experiences: the **Inside Passage ferry cruise** to Prince Rupert and the **Discovery Coast ferry cruise** (see "The Inside Passage," below).

ESSENTIALS

VISITOR INFORMATION   The **Port McNeill Visitor Info Centre,** 1626 Beach Dr. (mailing address: Box 129), Port McNeill, BC V0N 2R0 (☎ **250/956-3131**), is open May 15 to September 15 daily 10am to 6pm. The **Alert Bay Visitor Info Centre,** 116 Fir St. (mailing address: Box 28), Alert Bay, BC V0N 1A0 (☎ **250/ 974-5213**), is near the ferry terminal. Summer, it's open daily 9am to 6pm; the rest of the year, hours are Monday to Friday 9am to 5pm. The **Port Hardy Visitor Info Centre** is at 7250 Market St. (mailing address: Box 249), Port Hardy, BC V0N 2P0 (☎ **250/949-7622,** e-mail chamber@capescott.bc.ca). It's open daily: June to Labour Day Monday 9am to 9pm and the rest of the year 9am to 5pm.

GETTING THERE   By Car   Telegraph Cove is 198km (132 miles) north of Campbell River along the Island Highway (Highway 19). Port McNeill is another 8.8km (5½ miles) north. Port Hardy is 238km (148 miles) north of Campbell River.

By Bus   Laidlaw Coach Lines (☎ **250/385-4411**) operates daily service among Nanaimo and Port McNeill and Port Hardy. The one-way fare to and from Port Hardy and Nanaimo is C$75 (US$50).

By Plane   Pacific Coastal Airlines (☎ **800/663-2872;** http://pacific-coastal. com/), a partner with Canadian Airlines, flies three times daily into Port Hardy Airport from Vancouver.

SPECIAL EVENTS   During the second week of June, the Nimpkish Reserve hosts **June Sports & Indian Celebrations** (☎ 250/974-5556) on the soccer field in Alert Bay. Traditional tests of strength and agility are demonstrated by the island's tribal members.

EXPLORING THE AREA: SPOTTING ORCAS & MORE

Port McNeill has ferry service to Malcolm Island and Alert Bay (a 45-min. crossing). This side trip offers you opportunity to explore this amazing wilderness and meet the people who have coexisted with its remarkable marine inhabitants for centuries. **BC Ferries** (☎ 888/724-5223 in BC; www.bcferries.bc.ca) operates between Port McNeill and Alert Bay 10 times daily; fares are C$6 (US$3.65) passengers and C$14 (US$9) vehicles.

Eight kilometers (5 miles) south of Port McNeill, **Telegraph Cove** is one of the few remaining elevated-boardwalk villages on Vancouver Island, overlooking Johnstone Strait and Robson Bight. This postcard-perfect fishing village's buildings are perched on stilts over the water, making it an entertaining destination for a stroll, especially since whales have been spotted close to shore many times. May to mid-October, a passenger-only ferry travels to and from Telegraph Cove and Alert Bay. Return tickets for the half-hour journey cost C$20 (US$13) adults and C$10 (US$7) children 3 to 12. In high season, the ferry departs Telegraph Cove every 2 hours on the hour 9am to 9pm.

Alert Bay on Cormorant Island has a rich native-Indian heritage you can see in the tiny island's proudly preserved architecture and artifacts. Alert Bay has been a Kwakiutl tribal village site for thousands of years. The integration of Scottish immigrants into the area during the 19th and 20th centuries is clearly depicted in the design of the **Anglican Church** on Front Street (☎ 250/974-5213). The cedar building was erected in 1881, and the stained-glass window designs reflect a fusion of native Kwakiutl and Scottish design motifs. Summer, it's open Monday to Saturday 8am to 5pm.

Walk 1.6km (1 mile) from the ferry terminal along Front Street to the island's two most interesting attractions. A 173-foot **totem pole** stands next to the Big House (the tribal community center), which isn't open to the public. Visitors are welcome, however, to enter the outside grounds to get a closer look. Erected in 1973, this cedar totem pole features 22 hand-carved figures of bears, orcas, and ravens, plus a sun at the top.

A few yards down the road from the Big House and totem pole is the **U'Mista Cultural Centre,** Front Street, Alert Bay (☎ 250/974-5403), which displays a collection of carved-wood ceremonial masks, cedar baskets, copper jewelry, and other potlatch artifacts confiscated by the Canadian government when the potlatch was banned in 1922. The items were only recently returned to the island's native-Indian community. Revolving exhibits explain the Kwakiutl tribe's culture and history. Admission is C$5 (US$3.35) adults, C$4 (US$2.65) seniors, and C$1 (US65¢) children under 12. The museum is open daily 9am to 6pm (on weekends and summer holidays it opens at noon).

The best way to closely observe the many **orca pods** (families of killer whales) inhabiting the Johnstone Strait is to kayak out to where you can also observe sea lions as they cavort along the shore. You can paddle to overnight campgrounds at any of the marine parks and explore abandoned Kwakiutl villages. This area is ideal for novice kayakers; the placid sheltered waters provide a safe entry to this growing sport (see "Tours & Excursions," below).

There's one very special observation point in this area. Sixteen and a half kilometers (10 miles) south of Telegraph Cove and accessible by boat charter, the ✪ **Robson**

Bight Ecological Reserve provides some of the most fascinating whale watching in the province. Orcas, some the size of small school buses, regularly beach themselves in the shallow waters of the Bight's world-famous pebbly "rubbing beaches" to remove the barnacles from their tummies.

Port Hardy is the final stop on the Island Highway. It's the point of departure for the Inside Passage and Discovery Coast ferry cruises, which transport residents and visitors to the remote villages on the mainland coast, the northern town of Prince Rupert, and the misty Queen Charlotte Islands.

TOURS & EXCURSIONS

Stubbs Island Charters Ltd. (☎ 800/665-3066 or 250/928-3185; e-mail stubbs@ island.net; mailing address: Box 7, Telegraph Cove, BC V0N 3J0) operates from Telegraph Cove June to September, conducting tours to Robson Bight and the Johnstone Strait on 60-foot cruisers outfitted with hydrophones so passengers can hear as well as see the orcas. Normally, several half-day trips are offered daily; call ahead for times. Costs are C$65 (US$43) adults and C$59 (US$39) seniors/children 1 to 12.

Seasmoke Tours (☎ 800/668-6722 or 250/974-5225; mailing address: Box 483, Alert Bay, BC V0N 1A0) offers sailing trips June to October. Trips through the Johnstone Strait aboard a 44-foot yacht include a seafood lunch and Devonshire tea. This boat is also outfitted with a hydrophone. A half-day tour costs C$70 (US$47) adults and C$40 (US$27) children 3 to 14.

You can also kayak out to Johnstone Strait on a guided sea-kayak tour. **Robson Bight Adventures** (☎ 877/956-2582 or 250/956-2581) offers year-round excursions along the Johnstone Bight, giving you a chance to get up-close-and-personal with the orcas.

WHERE TO STAY & DINE
IN PORT MCNEILL & TELEGRAPH COVE

Port McNeill has a number of modest homestay B&Bs and older motels. If you can't get into the recommended Telegraph Cove–area resorts and don't want to continue on to Port Hardy, try the **Dalewood Inn,** 1703 Broughton Blvd. (☎ 250/ 956-3304), a motor inn with rooms starting at C$66 (US$44) double, as well as a licensed dining room.

Hidden Cove Lodge. Lewis Point, Box 258, Port McNeill, BC V0N 2R0. ☎ **250/956-3916.** www.pixsell.bc.ca/bb/1263.htm. 8 units, 3 cabins. C$125–C$150 (US$83–US$100) double; C$250 (US$167) cabin. Rates include continental breakfast. MC, V. Closed Dec–Apr. Take the Island Hwy. (Hwy. 19) to Telegraph Cove/Beaver Cove; turn right and follow the signs. The lodge is 6.6km (4 miles) from Telegraph Cove.

This handsome lodge is nestled beside a secluded cove overlooking the Johnstone Strait. The split-level cathedral-ceilinged great room and dining room are comfortably furnished, and the lodge's five twin and three queen guest rooms are clean and simply decorated. Facing onto the strait are three new two-bedroom, one-bathroom cabins, each with an efficiency kitchen and a large deck. The resort's restaurant is open nightly (nonguests by reservation only).

Telegraph Cove Resorts. 8km (5 miles) south of Port McNeill, Box 1, Telegraph Cove, BC V0N 3J0. ☎ **800/200-HOOK** or 250/928-3131. www.telegraphcoveresort.com. E-mail tcrltd@island.net. 19 units. C$115–C$155 (US$77–US$103) double. Extra person C$5 (US$3.35). MC, V.

Most of the lodgings offered by Telegraph Cove Resorts are refurbished older homes from the early 20th century scattered along the bayside boardwalk. Each home is

The Lure of a Fishing Camp

One of the only fishing camps directly accessed from Port Hardy is **Duval Point Lodge,** Goletas Channel, Box 818, Port Hardy, BC V0N 2P0 (☎ **250/ 949-6667;** www.island.net/~duval; e-mail duval@island.net). Open June to September, Duval Point offers 3- and 4-day packages from its base camp on an island 5 miles north of Port Hardy. The emphasis is on fishing: You receive a short training on motorboat usage and fishing technique, and then groups are given their own boat and pointed to the channel, which is alive with halibut, cod, and (in season) salmon. Lodging is in two two-story floating lodges, each with four bedrooms and a mix of private and shared bathrooms. Each lodge has an ample kitchen, a dining area, and a sitting room with a fireplace. Brand new at Duval Point Lodge are two log cabins with three bedrooms and two bathrooms and shared kitchen, dining, and living room. Rates (including transportation from Port Hardy) are C$185 (US$123) per night, with a 4-night minimum; Visa is accepted. Duval Lodge also now offers kayaking adventures.

unique, and they range in size from small double rooms in a former fisherman's boarding house to large three-bedroom homes that can sleep up to nine. All these lodgings have private bathrooms and fully furnished kitchens; no phones or TV. There are also hotel-style rooms at the Wastell Manor, a large home built in 1912. Although none of the lodgings at Telegraph Cover Resort is exactly fancy, these historic buildings are clean, simply furnished, and charming, and they make for a unique lodging experience. The 121 wooded campsites at Telegraph Cove Resorts, C$23 (US$15), are a short walk from the cove and the boardwalk town. The Killer Whale Café offers a seafood-rich Canadian menu, and the Old Saltery Pub has burgers and lighter fare. Both have outdoor seating. Services: Moorage, fishing charters, kayak rentals.

IN PORT HARDY

Oceanview B&B. 7735 Cedar Place, Box 1837, Port Hardy, BC V0N 2P0. ☎ and fax **250/949-8302.** www.island.net/~oceanvue. E-mail oceanvue@island.net. 3 units. TV. C$85 (US$57) double. Rates include buffet breakfast. No credit cards.

Perched on a bluff overlooking Port Hardy Bay, Oceanview is a large and comfortably furnished modern home. A large room with two queen beds and an en suite bathroom overlooks the cul-de-sac and front gardens, while another large room with one queen bed offers views of the bay; this room shares a bathroom with a smaller queen room. The hostess is a longtime Port Hardy resident and offers a friendly welcome and advice on local travel; however, children aren't welcome.

Quarterdeck Inn. 6555 Hardy Bay Rd., P.O. Box 910, Port Hardy, BC V0N 2P0. ☎ **250/ 902-0455.** Fax 250/902-0454. www.capescott.net/~quarterdk/. E-mail quarterdk@ capescott.net. 40 units. C$102 (US$68) double. Rates include continental breakfast. AE, MC, V.

Opened in 1999, the Quarterdeck has more going for it than just its comparative youth. Above the busy Quarterdeck Marina, all the guest rooms have great views onto a large fishing and pleasure-boat port. They're very spacious (some are practically suites) and are fitted out with quality beds, furniture, and amenities; some have kitchenettes. The Quarterdeck also has an RV park (C$20/US$13 full hookup) and the adjacent IV's Quarterdeck Pub, with a full dinner menu.

8 The Inside Passage: Prince Rupert & the Queen Charlotte Islands

The ferry cruise along British Columbia's **Inside Passage** combines the best scenic elements of Norway's rocky fjords, New Zealand's majestic South Island, Chile's Patagonian range, and Nova Scotia's wild coastline. Once nearly inaccessible, this rugged 491km (304-mile) stretch of Pacific coast is now served by two BC Ferry lines. The **Inside Passage ferry** operates between **Port Hardy** on Vancouver Island and **Prince Rupert** on the mainland. Also departing from Port Hardy, the Discovery Coast's *Queen of Prince Rupert* connects with small, mostly First Nations communities along the fjords and islands of the central BC coast, including Namu, Bella Bella, Shearwater, Ocean Falls, and Klemtu.

The BC Ferries system also connects Prince Rupert to the remote **Queen Charlotte Islands,** the ancestral home of the Haida tribe. The misty archipelago known as **Haida Gwaii** has been designated as a UNESCO World Heritage Site and is managed by the Gwaii Haanas Reserve. Amid the lush old-growth Sitka spruce in this temperate rain forest are the remains of untouched Haida villages abandoned over 400 years ago.

ESSENTIALS

VISITOR INFORMATION   The **Prince Rupert Visitor Info Centre,** 100 1st Ave. E. (at the corner of McBride St.), Prince Rupert, BC V8J 3S1 (☎ **800/667-1994** in Canada, or 250/624-5637; e-mail prtravel@citytel.net; mailing address: Box 669), is open daily 9am to 5pm. The **Queen Charlotte Islands Visitor Info Centre,** 3220 Wharf St., Queen Charlotte, BC V0T 1S0 (☎ **250/559-8316;** www.qcinfo.com; e-mail qcvic@island.net; mailing address: Box 819), is open May 1 to September 4 daily 9am to 5pm. For more information on the **Gwaii Haanas Park,** write Box 37, Queen Charlotte City, BC V0T 1S0 (☎ **250/559-8818;** fas.sfu.ca/parkscan/gwaii; e-mail gwaiicom@qcislands.net).

GETTING THERE   By Car   The 1,518km (941-mile) drive from Vancouver to Prince Rupert begins on the Sea-to-Sky Highway (✪ **Highway 99**), which intersects the Cariboo Highway (Highway 97) after passing through Whistler, Pemberton, and Lillooet. The town of Prince George is 812km (503 miles) north of Vancouver. At this central junction, head east for 745km (462 miles) on the Yellowhead Highway (Highway 16).

By Ferry   ✪ BC Ferries's (☎ **888/223-3779** or 250/386-3431; www.bcferries.bc.ca) MV *Queen of the North* makes the daytime crossing from Port Hardy through the Inside Passage to Prince Rupert in 15 hours. Humpback whales, orcas, Dall porpoises, salmon, bald eagles, and sea lions line the route past the relatively uninhabited coast and around countless forested islands.

June to mid-October, the 410-foot *Queen of the North* ferry crosses every other day, leaving Port Hardy at 7:30am and arriving in Prince Rupert at 10:30pm. The *Queen of Prince Rupert* travels the Discovery Coast, the name given to the central BC coastline, stopping at Bella Coola, Ocean Falls, Shearwater, McLoughlin Bay, and Klemtu. Both ferries briefly encounter open ocean before passing behind Calvert Island and entering Fitz Hugh Sound.

The ferries carry up to 750 passengers and 157 vehicles. You can wander around the ferry and lounge on inside and outside deck seating or rest in a private dayroom or overnight cabin. On board you'll find buffet-style dining, a cafeteria, a snack bar, a playroom, a business center, and a gift shop.

Reservations are required. On the Inside Passage's *Queen of the North,* the one-way passenger fare is C$104 (US$69) adults and C$52 (US$35) children 5 to 11; children under 5 are free when accompanied by a paying passenger. For an extra charge of C$43 to C$52 (US$29 to US$35), you can reserve a dayroom or an overnight cabin. Cars cost an extra C$214 (US$143) each way; mountain bikes cost an extra C$7 (US$4.35) each way.

In summer, the Discovery Coast's *Queen of Prince Rupert* has two direct ferry runs on Tuesday and Thursday to Bella Coola, plus a Saturday-departing circular run that goes north to Klemtu before returning to Port Hardy via Bella Coola. These trips depart from Port Hardy at 9:30am; the Tuesday and Saturday departures require a night on the boat. High-season fares between Port Hardy and Bella Coola are C$110 (US$73) adults, C$55 (US$37) children 5 to 11, and C$214 (US$143) cars. Berths rent for C$43 to C$52 (US$29 to US$35).

From Prince Rupert, you can continue north to Skagway, Alaska, on the **Alaska Marine Highway System ferry** (☎ 800/642-0066), which docks at the same terminal. Or you can travel to the Queen Charlotte Islands on the **Prince Rupert–Skidegate ferry,** which leaves Prince Rupert late in the morning and arrives about 6½ hours later at Skidegate in the Queen Charlotte Islands. The one-way high season fare is C$24 (US$16) adults and C$12 (US$8) children. Car transport is an extra C$90 (US$60).

By Plane   **Air BC** (☎ 800/663-3721 in Canada, 800/766-3000 in the U.S.) and **Canadian Regional Airlines** (☎ 800/665-1177 in Canada, 800/426-7000 in the U.S.) provide air service to and from Vancouver and the Prince Rupert Airport. **Harbour Air** (☎ 800/665-0212 or 250/627-1341) departs from the seaplane base at Seal Cove with scheduled service to the Queen Charlotte Islands and many other smaller communities along the coast and islands.

By Train   The **VIA Rail** (☎ 888/842-7245 or 800/561-3949; www.viarail.ca) passenger train departs from Prince George on Monday, Thursday, and Saturday at 7:45am and arrives in Prince Rupert at 8:30pm. One-way fares start at C$63 (US$42) adults. The train follows the same route as the Yellowhead Highway. **BC Rail's** *Cariboo Prospector* route (☎ 604/984-5246; www.bcrail.com/bcr/) from North Vancouver to Prince George connects with this service (see "Cariboo Country to Prince George," below).

GETTING AROUND   In the Queen Charlotte Islands, the island-to-island **Skidegate–Alliford Bay ferry** operates 12 daily sailings between the main islands. The fare is C$4.50 (US$3) each way or C$12 (US$8) per vehicle. **Budget** (☎ 250/559-4675), **Rustic Car Rentals** (☎ 250/559-4641), **Tilden** (☎ 250/626-3318), and **Thrifty** (☎ 250/559-8050) have car-rental offices on the islands.

SPECIAL EVENTS   During the second week in June, Prince Rupert hosts **Seafest** (☎ 250/624-9118), which features a fishing derby, parades, games, food booths, the annual blessing of the fleet, and bathtub races.

EXPLORING PRINCE RUPERT

Prince Rupert gets more than 18 hours of sunlight a day during summer. And despite its northerly location, this coastal city of 17,700 residents enjoys a mild climate most of the year. Mountain biking, cross-country skiing, fishing, kayaking, hiking, and camping are just a few of the region's popular activities. And northern British Columbia's rich native-Indian heritage has been preserved in its museums and archaeological sites.

The **Museum of Northern British Columbia,** 100 1st Ave. (☎ 250/624-3207), displays artifacts created by the Tsimshian/Nisga'a and Haida tribes, who've inhabited this area for over 10,000 years. There are also artifacts and photographs from Prince Rupert's 19th-century European settlement. Admission is C$5 (US$3.35) adults, C$2 (US$1.35) students, C$1 (US65¢) children, and C$10 (US$7) families. May 23 to October, it's open Monday to Saturday 9am to 8pm and Sunday 9am to 5pm; November to May 22, hours are Monday to Saturday 9am to 5pm. In summer, the museum's Archaeological Harbour Tours allow you to see the area's many active dig sites at ancestral villages dating back more than 5,000 years. The historic **Cow Bay** district on the waterfront reminds you that both fishing and logging attracted European settlers to this remote outpost in the 1800s. The many art galleries, gift shops, and craft stores along the water invite browsers.

Twenty kilometers (12 miles) south of Prince Rupert, the province's oldest working salmon-cannery village, built in 1889, is located at **Port Edward** and has a picturesque boardwalk. Every summer, fishing fleets dropped off their catches at the cannery, which employed hundreds of native-Indian and Asian seasonal workers. Managed by the **North Pacific Cannery Village Museum** (☎ 250/628-3538; mailing address: Box 1104, Port Edward, BC V0V 1G0), the working museum allows visits to the manager's house, cannery store, workers' mess, canning buildings, and seasonal workers' cabins, which are open year-round. Admission is C$8 (US$5) adults, C$6 (US$4) seniors/students, and C$3 (US$2) children; May to mid-October, it's open Monday to Sunday 9am to 5pm.

Outdoor Activities

HIKING & BIKING   Kalen Sports, 344 2nd Ave. W. (☎ 250/624-3633), and **Far West Sports,** 221 3rd Ave. W. (☎ 250/624-2568), are the best sources for information about hiking and mountain-biking trails. Both of these outfitters can also supply clothing or camping, climbing, and skiing equipment, but it's advisable to call ahead with special requests.

KAYAKING & CANOEING   The waters surrounding Prince Rupert are tricky, and rough tidal swells and strong currents are common. **Eco Trek Adventures,** 824 Smithers St. in Cow Bay (☎ 250/624-8311; www.citytel.net/ecotreks; e-mail ecotrks@citytel.net), offers guided half-day trips for C$45 (US$30). Kayak rentals cost from C$25 (US$17) a half day.

Where to Stay

A mile from the ferry terminal, the **Park Avenue Campground,** 1750 Park Ave. (☎ 250/624-5861; fax 250/627-8009; mailing address: Box 612, Prince Rupert, BC V8J 4J5), has 97 full-hookup and tenting sites. Facilities include a laundry, hot showers, flush toilets, a playground, a mail drop, and pay phones. Make reservations in advance during summer because this campground is the best in the area. Rates are C$14 to C$19 (US$9 to US$13) per campsite.

✪ **Crest Hotel.** 222 1st Ave. W., Prince Rupert, BC V8J 3P6. ☎ **800/663-8150** or 250/624-6771. Fax 250/627-7666. www.cresthotel.bc.ca. E-mail info@cresthotel.com. 102 units. TV TEL. C$109–C$119 (US$73–US$79) double. AE, ER, MC, V.

On the bluff's edge overlooking Tuck Inlet, Metlakata Pass, and the busy Prince Rupert harbor, the Crest offers nicely furnished guest rooms and gracious, even opulent, common rooms. Rockwell's is a coffee shop open for three meals daily, and the Waterfront Restaurant, with incredible views and patio dining, serves the town's best

Northwest Cuisine. Facilities include a hot tub, a fitness center, a steam room, meeting rooms, and banquet facilities.

Eagle Bluff Bed & Breakfast. 201 Cow Bay Rd., Prince Rupert, BC V8J 1A2. ☎ **800/ 833-1550** in Canada or 250/627-4955. Fax 250/627-7945. E-mail eaglebed@citytel.net. 5 units. TV. C$55–C$65 (US$37–US$43). MC, V.

One of the best located B&Bs in the city—at least if you like Prince Rupert's maritime ambiance—the Eagle Bluff sits right on the wharf at Cow Bay. Step outside your door and directly into a tour boat or kayak; cafes and coffee shops are just steps away. The B&B has single, double, and family accommodations, with a mix of private and shared bathrooms.

WHERE TO DINE

For 60 years, **Smile's Seafood Cafe,** 113 Cow Bay Rd. (☎ 250/624-3072), has served seafood in every shape and form, from oyster burgers and seafood salads to heaping platters of fried fish. In the historic Cow Bay district, this small place is always busy during summer, but it's always worth the wait. Main courses range from C$7 to C$23 (US$4.65 to US$15). It's open daily: summer 10am to 10pm and the rest of the year 11am to 9pm.

Right next door is **Breakers Pub** (☎ 250/624-5990), a popular local pub with a harbor view and tasty fare like fish-and-chips, barbecued ribs, and stir-fries. It's open Monday to Saturday noon to 2am and Sunday noon to midnight.

EXPLORING THE QUEEN CHARLOTTE ISLANDS

The misty and mysterious Queen Charlotte Islands inspired 19th-century painter Emily Carr to document her impressions of the towering carved-cedar totem poles and longhouses at the abandoned village of **Ninstints on Anthony Island.** The islands still lure artists, writers, and photographers wishing to experience their haunting beauty.

On **South Moresby Island,** you'll discover an array of rare fauna and flora, including horned puffins, Cassin's auklets, waterfowl raptors, gray whales, harbor seals, Steller's sea lions, and the world's largest black bears—all framed by moss-covered Sitka spruces, western hemlocks, and red cedars.

Graham Island's **Naikoon Provincial Park** is a 180,000-acre wildlife reserve where whales can be spotted from the beaches, peregrine falcons fly overhead, and Sitka deer silently observe you as you walk along trails through the dense temperate rain forest. And just outside the town of Masset, the **Delkatla Wildlife Sanctuary** is a birder's paradise. It's the first landfall for the 113 migrating species of bird life that use the Pacific Flyway.

GWAII HAANAS: THE LAND WHERE TIME STOOD STILL

Ninstints on Anthony Island is an ancient native-Indian village revered as sacred ground by the modern-day Haida tribe. According to local legends, the Haida people were created on this island by the "Raven who captured the Sun" after he brought the life-giving light to the dark, ice-encrusted earth. Cedar totem poles and longhouses stand in mute testament to a culture that flourished here for nearly 10,000 years. An epidemic spread by European explorers in the 1890s wiped out 90% of the Kunghit Haida tribe. The village was abandoned in 1900.

The island and the surrounding area are a designated UNESCO World Heritage Site called **Gwaii Haanas** (also known as South Moresby National Park Marine Reserve). Gwaii Haanas is accessible only by sea kayak and sailboat. For permission to enter the area, contact the **Haida Gwaii Watchmen** (☎ 250/559-8225; mailing address: Box 609, Skidegate, Haida Gwaii, BC V0T 1S0), who act as site guardians and area hosts. Their office is at Second Beach, just north of Skidegate Landing on Highway 16.

TOURS & EXCURSIONS

Longtime sea kayak outfitters, **Ecosummer Expeditions,** 1516 Duranleau St., Vancouver, BC V6H 3S4 (☎ **800/465-8884** or 604/669-7741; www.ecosummer. com), offers 1-week trips to Gwaii Haanas for C$1,445 (US$964). **Pacific Rim Paddling Company,** P.O. Box 1840, 621 Discovery St., Victoria, BC V8W 2Y3 (☎ **250/384-6103;** www.islandnet.com/~prp; e-mail prp@islandnet.com), has both 7- and 14-day kayak trips to Gwaii Haanas, with prices starting at C$1,355 (US$904).

Sailing into Qwaii Haanas is another popular option, and most sailboat operators also have kayaks aboard for the use of guests. **Queen Charlotte Adventures,** Box 196, Queen Charlotte, BC V0T 1S0 (☎ **250/559-8990;** www.island.net/infobus/qca; e-mail qciadven@island.net), offers package tours to Ninstints on a 53-foot schooner. Prices include accommodations and meals on board. Tours range from a 2-day Gwaii Haanas sampler for C$1,100 (US$734) to a 5-day all-inclusive package for C$2,750 (US$1,834) per person.

WHERE TO STAY & DINE

After a long day of exploration, stop in at **Daddy Cool's Neighbourhood Pub,** Collison Avenue at Main Street, Masset (☎ **250/626-3210**), for a pint and a fish tale or two. It's open Monday to Saturday noon to 2am and Sunday noon to midnight. The **Cafe Gallery,** Collison Avenue at Orr Street, Masset (☎ **250/626-3672**), serves hearty portions of fresh seafood, steaks, pasta dishes, sandwiches, and salads. Main courses are C$12 to C$16 (US$8 to US$11). It's open Monday to Saturday 9:30am to 9pm.

Dorothy & Mike's Guest House. 3127 2nd Ave. (mailing address: Box 595), Queen Charlotte City, BC V0T 1S0. ☎ **250/559-8688.** Fax 250/559-8439. 5 units, 3 with bathroom. C$40–C$75 (US$27–US$50) suite. Rates include breakfast. No credit cards. Closed Oct–Mar. Drive 3.3km (2 miles) away from the Skidegate ferry terminal on 2nd Ave.

The atmosphere here has an island flavor: A large deck overlooks the Skidegate Inlet, and a serene garden surrounds the house. The warm, cozy guest suites are filled with local art and antiques, with full kitchen facilities. It's within walking distance of the ocean, restaurants, and shopping.

✪ Spruce Point Lodging. 609 6th Ave., Queen Charlotte City, Graham Island, BC V0T 1S0. ☎ **250/559-8234.** 7 units. TV TEL. C$65 (US$43) double or triple. Kitchen unit C$10 (US$7). Rates include breakfast. MC, V. Drive 0.8km (0.5 mile) away from the Skidegate ferry terminal on 6th Ave.

This rustic inn, overlooking the Hecate Strait, features guest rooms with private entrances, as well as excellent views. Each of the double-, twin-, and queen-bedded rooms has a refrigerator and a choice of a private shower or a bathtub. Some rooms even have full kitchen facilities, and all have complimentary tea and coffee service. The shared balcony is used as a guest lounge. Your hosts can also arrange kayaking packages to the surrounding islands.

9 Cariboo Country to Prince George

North of Lillooet and south of Prince George along Highway 97, the Canadian Wild West hasn't changed much in the past century. This is **Cariboo Country,** a vast landscape that changes from alpine meadows and thick forests of Douglas fir and lodgepole pine to rolling prairies and granite-walled arid canyons as it encounters the gigantic glacial peaks of Coastal Mountains.

The Sea-to-Sky Highway (Highway 99) from Vancouver through Whistler and the Cayoosh Valley eventually descends into the town of **Lillooet,** which was Mile 0 of the Old Cariboo Highway during the gold-rush days of the 1860s. Prospectors and settlers made their way north up what's now called the **Cariboo Gold Trail** (Highway 97).

Highway 97 follows the gold-rush trail through **70 Mile House, 100 Mile House, 108 Mile House, 150 Mile House, Williams Lake,** and **Quesnel,** to the gold-rich town of **Barkerville.** Many of these towns were named after the mile-marking road-houses patronized by prospectors and settlers headed north to the goldfields.

ESSENTIALS

VISITOR INFORMATION Contact the **Cariboo Chilcotin Coast Tourist Association,** 266 Oliver St., Williams Lake, BC V2G 1M1 (☎ 800/663-5885 or 250/ 392-2226; www.cariboocountry.org; e-mail cta@cariboocountry.org). For info on Prince George, contact the **Prince George Visitor Info Centre,** 1198 Victoria St., Prince George, BC V2L 2L2 (☎ 800/668-7646 or 250/562-3700; fax 250/ 563-3584; www.tourismpg.bc.ca).

GETTING THERE Whether you travel by train or by car, the trip from Whistler to Cariboo Country is a visually exhilarating experience.

By Car The shortest and most scenic route to the Cariboo from Vancouver is along Highway 99 past Whistler to Lillooet and continuing to Highway 97 and turning north to 100 Mile House and points north. From Vancouver to Quesnel is 600km (372 miles). If you want to bypass dramatic but slow-speed Highway 99 and head straight up to the central Cariboo district, you can also take the Highway 1 expressway east from Vancouver and jump onto Highway 97 at Merritt.

By Train BC Rail's (☎ 604/984-5246; www.bcrail.com/bcr/) *Cariboo Prospector* departs from the North Vancouver train station three times a week at 7am. The first section of the route (Vancouver to Lillooet) is extraordinarily scenic. The train continues north to 100 Mile House, Williams Lake, and Quesnel and terminates in Prince George. Prince George is a transfer point onto the mainline transcontinental VIA Rail system. From North Vancouver to Prince George, the fare is C$170 (US$113).

By Bus Greyhound buses (☎ 800/661-8747; www.greyhound.ca) travel from Vancouver through the Cariboo to Prince George via Highway 1 and Highway 97, passing through 100 Mile House, Williams Lake, and Quesnel. One-way fare to Prince George is C$91 (US$61). Greyhound also has two buses daily among Prince George, Jasper, and Edmonton. One-way fare to Jasper is C$47 (US$31).

By Plane Air BC (☎ 800/667-3721) offers three-times-daily service to and from Quesnel and Vancouver. Air BC and **Canadian Regional Airlines** (☎ 800/ 665-1177) both have air service between Prince George and Vancouver.

LILLOOET TO 100 MILE HOUSE

There's nothing subtle about the physical setting of **Lillooet** (pop. 2,058). To the west, the soaring glaciated peaks of the Coast Mountains are *right there,* filling up half the sky. To the east rise the steep desert walls of the Fountain Range, stained with rusty red and ochre. Cleaving the two mountain ranges is the massive and roaring Fraser River. From the Coast Range peaks immediately behind Lillooet to the surging river is a drop of nearly 9,000 feet, making an incredibly dramatic backdrop for a town.

Lillooet was Mile 0 of the 1860s **Cariboo Gold Rush Trail.** In 1858, a trail was established from the Fraser Valley goldfields in the south to the town of Lillooet. At the big bend on Main Street, a cairn marks MILE 0 of the original Cariboo Wagon Road.

From Lillooet, Highway 99 heads north along the Fraser River Canyon, affording lots more dramatic vistas before turning east to its junction with Highway 97. Immediately before the junction is the **Hat Creek Ranch** (☎ **800/782-0922** or 250/457-9722), built in 1861 as an inn for gold miners headed north during the Cariboo gold rush. The only extant roadhouse from this period, the Hat Creek remained a stagecoach inn until 1916. The grounds boast more than 20 restored period buildings, including a blacksmith shop, an 1894 barn, a wash house, and a stable. You can stroll the ranch grounds year-round; however, regular visitor services and guided tours are offered mid-May to Labour Day daily 10am to 6pm.

Named for the roadhouse inn that marked the hundredth mile north of Lillooet in the days of the Cariboo gold rush, **100 Mile House** (pop.1,978) is an attractive ranching community at the heart of a vast recreational paradise. There are thousands of lakes in the valleys ringing the town, and canoeing, fishing, and boating are popular activities. In winter, the gently rolling landscape, combined with heavy snowfalls, make 100 Mile House a major cross-country ski destination. Eight miles north of 100 Mile House is, naturally enough, **108 Mile Ranch,** another old-time community that sprung up during the Cariboo gold rush.

WHERE TO STAY & DINE
Near Lillooet
Tyax Mountain Lake Resort. Tyaughton Lake Rd., Gold Bridge, BC V0K 1P0. ☎ **250/238-2221.** Fax 250/238-2528. www.tyax.bc.ca. E-mail fun@tyax.bc.ca. 29 lodge units, 5 three- to six-bedroom log chalets, 12 campsites. TEL. C$98–C$129 (US$65–US$86) double lodge room; C$220–C$398 (US$147–US$265) chalet; C$24 (US$16) 2-person site. Drive 2 hours (86km/53 miles) from Lillooet up the unpaved Tyaughton Lake Rd. Follow signs to the resort.

Set high above the town of Lillooet, Tyaughton Lake is the perfect alpine setting for a romantic vacation. On its shores stands this huge log lodge, which offers luxurious accommodations and a host of activities ranging from heli-fishing and heli-skiing trips to barbecues on the lake. The guest rooms are comfortably furnished, with queen-size beds. The restaurant serves Pacific Northwest cuisine, and there's a cocktail lounge. Facilities include a sauna, a fitness center, an outdoor whirlpool, and a tennis court. Fly-out fishing charters, floatplane sightseeing, canoe rentals, horseback riding, cross-country ski trails, heli-skiing, heli-fishing, and mountain-bike rentals are available.

Near 100 Mile House
Best Western 108 Resort. 4618 Telqua Dr., Box 2, 108 Mile Ranch, BC V0K 2Z0. ☎ **800/667-5233** or 250/791-5211. Fax 250/791-6537. www.108resort.com. E-mail 108rst@bcinternet.net. 62 units, 11 camping sites. A/C TV TEL. C$125–C$155 (US$83–US$103) double; C$15 (US$10) campsite per vehicle with a C$5 (US$3.35) charge for electricity. AE, MC, V.

This upscale hotel/resort 8 miles north of 100 Mile House centers on its fantastic golf course, though even if you're not a duffer there's a lot to like here. The guest rooms are large and beautifully furnished, all with balconies overlooking either the golf course or a small lake. The dining room serves fine Northwest cuisine. Facilities include a golf course, ski and bike rental, stables, a heated pool, and a gift shop.

100 Mile Lodge B&B. 150 Hwy. 97, 100 Mile House, BC V0K 2E0. ☎ **888/667-7451** or 250/395-9099. www.bbcanada.com/2732.html. E-mail lodgebnb@bcinternet.net. 4 units, none with bathroom. C$70 (US$47) double. Rates include breakfast. MC, V.

"Roughing It" at a Guest Ranch

The **Hills Health & Guest Ranch,** Highway 97, 108 Mile Ranch, P.O. Box 26, BC V0K 2Z0 (☎ **250/791-5225;** fax 250/791-6384; www.grt-net.com/thehills; e-mail thehillls@bcinternet.net), is a full-service health/beauty spa with outdoor activities like horseback riding, hayrides, guided hikes, and cross-country skiing on more than 166km (103 miles) of private trails. The 46 guest rooms (C$100–C$120/US$68–US$81 double) are large, with ranch-style natural pine decor; the self-contained chalet accommodations (C$129–C$149/US$87–US$100) feature kitchens and full bathrooms and sleep up to six; and the 10 campsites go for C$15 (US$10). The restaurant serves guests and the public a unique blend of cowboy favorites and spa cuisine; it's open daily 8am to 9pm, and reservations are recommended. The health spa offers indoor exercise classes, health programs and wellness workshops, an aerobics studio, hydrotherapy pools, massage, herbal wraps, facials, reflexology, and body packs. Facilities include a sauna, an indoor pool, a hot tub, and a fully equipped fitness facility.

The **Big Bar Guest Ranch,** Big Bar Road (mailing address: Box 27), Clinton, BC V0N 1K0 (☎ and fax **250/459-2333;** www.bigbarranch.com), is just north of Clinton off Highway 97. The centerpiece of the property is the Harrison House, a hand-hewn log home built by pioneers in the 1800s. Besides taking horseback-riding and pack trips year-round, you can canoe, fish, hike, pan for gold, and cross-country ski on the beautiful grounds. The 12 guest rooms in the lodge have bathrooms (C$250/US$167 double, including meals); the four self-contained log cabins (C$144/US$96 double) have kitchens, bathrooms, and wood-burning fireplaces; the six campsites go for C$30 (US$20); and a number of tepees sleeping up to four cost C$79 (US$53) per person. The licensed family-style dining room serves hearty Western barbecue dishes. There are also a fireside lounge, a billiard room, and an outdoor hot tub. Two-hour horseback rides cost C$37 (US$25); lodging/activity packages are available.

The **Echo Valley Ranch Resort,** P.O. Box 16, Jesmond, Clinton, BC V0K 1K0 (☎ **800/253-8831** or 250/459-2386; www.evranch.com; e-mail evranch@ uniserve.com), is another upscale guest ranch, complete with a spa. Lodging is in the central Dove Lodge building or in the new Look-out Lodge containing nine rooms with king-sized beds. In addition, Echo Valley has three cabins, one a "honeymoon" cabin with a hot tub. Facilities include an excellent restaurant, an indoor pool, a sauna, an outdoor hot tub, and a complete spa with beauty treatments, massage, and fitness equipment. Activities include horseback riding, fishing, hiking, and whitewater rafting, plus unusual options like watching falcons being trained and visiting a remote native village where tribe members net fish in the Fraser River. The base rate of C$205 (US$137) per person per night includes all meals and access to all facilities on the ranch; you'll pay extra for horseback riding and any guided activities. A number of packages including riding and adventure activities start at C$275 (US$183) per person per day. In high season, there's a 3-night minimum stay.

The 100 Mile Lodge is a historic inn built in 1930 to replace the original roadhouse that gave the town its name. The large plank-sided inn occupies a quiet, shady location on Little Bridge Creek, within easy walking distance of both downtown and the Highway 97 strip. The guest rooms have comfortable period furnishings; the rooms share two bathrooms. There's a cozy fireside sitting area, and a full country-style breakfast is served.

WILLIAMS LAKE TO BARKERVILLE

Unabashedly a ranch town, **Williams Lake** (pop. 11,398) is known across the West for its large hell's-a-poppin' rodeo, the **Williams Lake Stampede,** held the first weekend of July. Begun in the 1920s as an amusement for area cowboys, the stampede has grown into a 4-day festival. Rodeo cowboys from across Canada and the western United States gather here to compete for prizes in excess of C$80,000 (US$53,360). For more information, contact the Williams Lake Stampede, P.O. Box 4076, Williams Lake, BC V2G 2V2 (☎ **250/392-6585;** www.imagehouse.com/rodeo). For tickets, call ☎ **800/717-6336.** Reserved seats are C$10 (US$7) adults and C$7 (US$4.65) children/seniors.

Williams Lake is also the Highway 20 gateway to the **Chilcotin,** the mountainous coastal area to the west. The Chilko-Chilcotin-Fraser river system running east from the Coast Mountains is a major whitewater-rafting destination, though not for the faint of heart—Lava Canyon on the Chilko River drops 1,500 feet in just 15 miles, with almost continuous Class IV rapids. **Chilko River Expeditions,** P.O. Box 4723, Williams Lake, BC V2G 2V7 (☎ **800-967-7238** or 250/398-6711; fax 250/398-8269; www.chilkoriverexpeditions.com; e-mail rapids@chilkoriverexpeditions.com), leads a variety of trips on the three rivers, including a 1-day trip on the Chilcotin for C$99 (US$66) adults and C$79 (US$53) youths.

Highway 20 continues through a wild and rugged land of lakes and towering glacier-hung mountains on its way to **Bella Coola,** a native village on a Pacific inlet. From here, BC Ferries Discovery Coast service connects to **Port Hardy** on Vancouver Island, making this an increasingly popular sightseeing loop (see "The Inside Passage," above).

Like most other towns throughout the Cariboo District, **Quesnel** (pop. 8,588) was founded during the gold-rush years in the 1860s. After the long overland journey from Lillooet, the prospectors turned east and followed the Quesnel River to the gold fields near Barkerville and Wells. From Quesnel on Highway 26 east, drive 87km (58 miles) deep into the moss-covered forests of the Cariboo Mountains, where moose, black bears, and deer are often seen on the road. At the end of the paved road is ✪ **Barkerville,** one of the most intact ghost towns in Canada.

The 1860 Cariboo Gold Rush was the reason thousands of miners made their way to this boom town on the banks of Williams Creek. Barkerville was founded after a British immigrant, Billy Barker, discovered one of the region's richest gold deposits 50 feet below the water line in the summer of 1862. The town sprang up practically overnight—and died almost as quickly when the gold ran out.

May to Labour Day, the "townspeople" dress in period costumes and bring Barkerville back to life. You can pan for gold outside the general store, learn about the big strikes and the miners' lives from the local miners, take a stagecoach ride, or attend a criminal trial. The Theatre Royal actors perform dramatic productions in the town hall. You can have a root beer at the town saloon or a meal in the Chinatown section.

Two-day admission to the town is C$7 (US$4.65) adults, C$4.25 (US$2.85) seniors/students, and C$1 (US65¢) children 6 to 12. Barkerville is open daily dawn to dusk year-round. For info on Barkerville, contact Barkerville Historic Town, Box 19, Barkerville, BC V0K 1B0 (☎ **250/994-3302;** www.heritage.gov.bc.ca).

WHERE TO STAY & DINE

There are three campgrounds in **Barkerville Provincial Park,** Highway 26, Barkerville (☎ **250/398-1414;** mailing address: 181 1st Ave. N., Williams Lake, BC V2G 1Y8), all open year-round. They cost C$12 to C$15 (US$8 to US$10). **Lowhee Campground** is the best and closest to the park entrance.

In Williams Lake

Fraser Inn. 285 Donald Rd., Williams Lake, BC V2G 4K4. ☎ **888/452-6789** or 250/ 398-7055. Fax 250/398-8269. www.Fraserinn.com. E-mail book@Fraserinn.com. 75 units. A/C MINIBAR TV TEL. C$69–C$92 (US$46–US$61) double. Extra person C$7–C$10 (US$4.65–US$7); kitchen C$10 (US$7). AE, MC, V.

The Fraser Inn overlooks Williams Lake from its hillside perch north of town along Highway 97. Large and modern, the Fraser has a level of facilities not usually found in small ranch towns, plus a good steakhouse restaurant. The Great Cariboo Steak Company is the town's leading place for steaks and prime rib (C$16/US$11) and grilled chicken, plus soup, salad bar, and a selection of pasta dishes. Also here you'll find the Billy Miner Saloon. Room and valet service are provided, and facilities include a Universal gym, a whirlpool, and a sauna.

In Wells

The Wells Hotel. Pooley St. (mailing address: Box 39), Wells, BC V0K 2R0. ☎ **800/ 860-2299** in Canada, or 250/994-3427. Fax 250/994-3494. www.wellshotel.com. E-mail goldcity.net. 16 units with shared bathroom, 24 units with private bathrooms. C$70–C$120 (US$47–US$80) double. Rates include breakfast. AE, MC, V.

Opened in 1933, this restored hotel is filled with lovely antique furnishings and offers guest rooms tastefully decorated in earth-tone textiles and locally executed artwork; some have fireplaces. The hotel added another 23 rooms in a new wing in 1999. On the premises are the fully licensed Pooley Street Café, an espresso shop, the Wells Hotel Pub, and the Fireplace Lounge. Facilities include mountain-bike rental, conference rooms, a hot tub, and a licensed massage therapist.

PRINCE GEORGE

The largest city in northern BC, **Prince George** (pop. 77,996) is a natural base for exploring the sites and recreation of the province's north central region, filled with forested mountains, lakes, and mighty rivers.

There has been settlement at the junction of the Fraser and the Nechako rivers for millennia, because the two river systems were as much a transportation corridor for the early First Nations people as for the European settlers who came later. What really put Prince George on the map was the building of the Grand Trunk Railroad, Canada's northerly transcontinental rail route, which passed through here in 1914.

Prince George is rightly proud of its parks, many of them linked by the Heritage Rivers trail system. Eighty-nine-acre **Fort George Park** is the site of the original fur trading post that established the city. On the grounds is a First Nations Burial Ground, a working miniature railway, and the original Fort George rail station. Also in the park, the outstanding **Fraser Fort George Regional Museum** (☎ **250/ 562-1612**) details the region's long history, starting with excellent exhibits on the customs and lifestyle of the native Carrier people and moving on through the region's fur-trading and logging past. Admission is C$7 (US$4.65) adults, C$6 (US$4) seniors, C$4.50 (US$3) children under 12, and C$10 (US$7) families. Fort George Park is on the Fraser River end of 20th Avenue.

WHERE TO STAY & DINE

Coast Inn of the North. 770 Brunswick St., Prince George, BC V2L 2C2. ☎ **800/663-1144** or 250/563-0121. Fax 250/563-1948. www.coasthotels.com. 150 units. A/C MINIBAR TV TEL. C$155 (US$103) double. Extra person C$10 (US$7). Family plan, corporate and off-season rates, and senior discounts offered. AE, MC, V.

The Coast Inn is right in the thick of things, such as these things are in downtown Prince George. It offers very nicely furnished guest rooms; ask for a corner room and you'll get a balcony. You have your choice of three restaurants: Shogun, a Japanese steakhouse; Winston's Dining Room; and the Coffee Garden. There are also a pub, a lobby lounge, and a dance club. Services include a travel agency, a fitness center, a tanning salon, a hair salon, a florist, and clothing boutique. Facilities include saunas, whirlpools, and an indoor pool.

10 Whistler: One of North America's Premier Ski Resorts

The premier ski resort in North America, according to *Ski* and *Snow Country* magazines, the ✪ **Whistler/Blackcomb complex** boasts more vertical, more lifts, and more varied ski terrain than any other on the continent. In winter, you can choose from downhill skiing, backcountry skiing, cross-country skiing, heli-skiing, snowboarding, snowmobiling, sleigh riding, and more. In summer there are rafting, hiking, golfing, and horseback riding.

And then there's **Whistler Village,** a resort town of 40,000 beds, arranged around a central village street in a compact-enough fashion you can park your car and remain a pedestrian for the duration of your stay.

ESSENTIALS

VISITOR INFORMATION   The **Whistler Visitor Info Centre,** 2097 Lake Placid Rd., Whistler, BC V0N 1B0 (☎ 604/932-5528), is open daily 9am to 5pm. An **information kiosk** on Village Gate Boulevard at the entry to Whistler Village is open mid-May to early September during the same hours. The **Whistler Resort Association** is at 4010 Whistler Way, Whistler, BC V0N 1B0 (☎ **604/932-3928**), open daily 9am to 5pm.

GETTING THERE   By Car   Whistler's about a 2-hour drive from Vancouver along Highway 99, also called the Sea to Sky Highway. The drive is spectacular, winding first along the edge of Howe Sound before climbing up through the mountains. Parking at the mountain is free for day skiers.

By Bus   Whistler Express, 8695 Barnard St., Vancouver (☎ 604/266-5386 in Vancouver; 604/905-0041 in Whistler), operates bus service from Vancouver International Airport to the Whistler Bus Loop. Buses depart five times daily in the summer and eight times in winter. The trip takes about 3½ hours; round-trip fares in summer are C$86 (US$57) adults and C$50 (US$33) children, and in winter they're C$98 (US$65) adults and C$58 (US$39) children. Reservations are required year-round. **Greyhound,** Pacific Central Station, 1150 Station St., Vancouver (☎ 604/662-8051 in Vancouver; 604/482-8747 in Whistler; www.greyhound.ca), operates service from the Vancouver Bus Depot to the Whistler Bus Loop. The trip takes about 2½ hours; one-way fares are C$18 (US$12) adults and C$9 (US$6) children 5 to 12.

By Train   BC Rail (☎ 604/984-5246; www.bcrail.com/bcr/) operates the *Cariboo Prospector* throughout the year. It leaves the North Vancouver train terminal daily at 7am and reaches the Whistler train station at 10:35am. The same train leaves Whistler at 6:10pm and returns to the North Vancouver train terminal at 8:45pm. The 2½-hour trip includes breakfast or dinner. A one-way ticket is C$31 (US$21) adults, C$28 (US$19) seniors, C$19 (US$13) children 2 to 12, and C$6 (US$4) children under 2.

GETTING AROUND   The walk between the Whistler Mountain (Whistler Village) and Blackcomb Mountain (Upper Village) resorts takes about 5 minutes.

By Bus   A year-round **public transit service** (☎ 604/932-4020) operates on frequent daily schedules from the Tamarisk district and the BC Rail Station to the neighboring districts of Nester's Village, Alpine Meadows, and Emerald Estates. Bus service from the Village to Village North and Upper Village accommodation is free. For other routes, one-way fares are C$1.50 (US$1) adults and C$1.25 (US85¢) seniors/students.

By Taxi   The village's taxis operate around the clock. Taxi tours, golf-course transfers, and airport transport are also offered by **Airport Limousine Service** (☎ 604/273-1331), **Whistler Taxi** (☎ 604/938-3333), and **Sea to Sky Taxi** (☎ 604/932-3333).

By Car   Rental cars are available from **Budget** at the Holiday Inn Sunspree, 4295 Blackcomb Way (☎ 604/932-1236), and **Thrifty** in the Listel Whistler Hotel, 4121 Village Green (☎ 604/938-0302).

SPECIAL EVENTS   Dozens of downhill ski competitions are held December to May. They include the **Whistler Snowboard World Cup** (Dec), **Owens-Corning World Freestyle Competition** (Jan), **Power Bar Peak to Valley Race** (Feb), **Kokanee Fantastic Downhill Race** (Mar), and **World Ski & Snowboard Festival** (Apr). Mountain bikers compete in the **Power Bar Garibaldi Gruel** (Sept) and the **Cheakamus Challenge Fall Classic Mountain Bike Race** (Sept).

During the third week in July, the villages host **Whistler's Roots Weekend** (☎ 604/932-2394). Down in the villages and up on the mountains, you'll hear the sounds of Celtic, zydeco, bluegrass, folk, and world-beat music at free and ticketed events. The **Whistler Summit Concert Series** (☎ 604/932-3434) is held during August weekends. The mountains provide a stunning backdrop for the on-mountain concerts.

The **Alpine Wine Festival** (☎ 604/932-3434) takes place on the mountaintop during the first weekend in September and features wine tastings and other events that highlight North America's finest vintages. And the second weekend in September ushers in the **Whistler Jazz & Blues Festival** (☎ 604/932-2394), featuring live performances in the village squares and the surrounding clubs.

WINTER ACTIVITIES

CROSS-COUNTRY SKIING   The 30km (19 miles) of easy to very difficult marked trails at **Lost Lake** start a block away from the Blackcomb Mountain parking lot. Passes are C$8 (US$5); a 1-hour cross-country lesson runs about C$35 (US$23) and can be booked at the same station where you purchase your trail pass. The **Valley Trail System** in the village becomes a well-marked cross-country ski trail during winter.

DOWNHILL SKIING   The **Whistler/Blackcomb Mountains,** 4545 Blackcomb Way, Whistler, BC V0N 1B4 (☎ 604/932-3434; snow report 604/687-1032;

www.whistler-blackcomb.com), are now jointly operated by Intrawest, so your pass gives access to both ski areas.

Whistler Mountain has 5,006 feet of vertical and 100 marked runs that are serviced by a high-speed gondola and eight high-speed chair lifts, plus four other lifts and tows. There are cafeterias and gift shops on the peak, as well as a fully licensed restaurant. **Blackcomb Mountain** has 5,280 feet (1 mile) of vertical and 100 marked runs that are serviced by nine high-speed chair lifts, plus three other lifts and tows. The cafeteria and gift shop aren't far from the peak. Both mountains also have bowls and glade skiing, with Blackcomb offering glacier skiing well into August.

During winter, daily lift tickets for both mountains are C$57 to C$59 (US$38 to US$39) adults, C$48 to C$50 (US$32 to US$33) youth/seniors, and C$29 (US$19) children. Lifts are open 8:30am to 3:30pm (to 4:30pm mid-Mar to closing, depending on weather and conditions). Whistler/Blackcomb offers ski lessons and guides for all levels and interests. (For skiers looking to try snowboarding, a rental package and a half-day lesson is a particularly attractive option.) Phone **Guest Relations** at ☎ **604/932-3434** for details. **Summit Ski** (☎ **604/938-6225** or 604/932-6225), at various locations, including the Delta Whistler Resort and Market Pavilion, rents high-performance and regular skis, snowboards, cross-country skis, and snowshoes.

HELI-SKIING   Whistler Heli-Skiing (☎ **888/HELISKI** or 604/932-4105; www. heliskiwhistler.com), is one of the more established operators. A three-run day, with 8,000 to 10,000 feet of vertical helicopter lift, costs C$430 (US$287) per person. A 6-run day with 15,000 feet of vertical helicopter lift costs C$660 (US$440) per person.

SLEIGH RIDING   For a sleigh ride with horses, contact **Blackcomb Horsedrawn Sleigh Rides,** 103-4338 Main St., Whistler, BC V0N 1B4 (☎ **604/932-7631;** www.whistlerweb.net/resort/sleighrides). In winter, tours go out every evening and cost C$45 (US$30) adults and C$25 (US$17) children under 12.

SNOWSHOEING   Outdoor Adventures@Whistler, P.O. Box 1054, Whistler, BC V0N 1B0 (☎ **604/932-0647;** e-mail outdoors@whistler.net; www.adventureswhistler. com), has guided tours for novices at C$39 (US$26) for 1½ hours. A 4-hour tour to a ghost town costs C$69 (US$46), including lunch. If you want to just rent the snowshoes and find your own way around, rentals are C$15 (US$10) per day.

SNOWMOBILING   The year-round ATV/snowmobile tours offered by **Canadian Snowmobile Adventures Ltd.,** Carleton Lodge (☎ **604/938-1616;** www. cdn-snowmobile.com), are a unique way to take to the Whistler Mountain trails. After a gondola ride up the mountain, a 1-hour tour costs C$59 (US$39) for a driver and C$39 (US$26) for a passenger. **Blackcomb Snowmobile** (☎ 604/905-7002; www.snowmobiling.bc.ca) offers 3- to 8-hour guided snowmobile tours on Blackcomb. A 3-hour tour costs C$139 (US$93) per person if you're alone or C$99 (US$66) per person for two people; an all-day tour costs C$299 (US$199) per person if you're alone or C$229 (US$153) per person for two people, lunch included.

SUMMER ACTIVITIES

BIKING   Some of the best mountain-bike trails in the village are on Whistler and Blackcomb Mountains. Lift tickets at both mountains are C$19 to C$30 (US$13 to US$20) per day, and discounted season mountain-bike passes are available. You can rent a mountain bike from **Blackcomb Ski & Sports,** Blackcomb Mountain Day Lodge, Upper Village (☎ **604/938-7788**); **Trax & Trails,** Chateau Whistler Hotel, 4599 Chateau Blvd., Upper Village (☎ **604/938-2017**); and the **Whistler Bike**

Company, Delta Whistler Resort, 4050 Whistler Way, Whistler Village (☎ **604/ 938-9511**). Prices range from C$10 (US$7) per hour to C$30 (US$20) per day.

CANOEING & KAYAKING The 3-hour River of Golden Dreams Kayak & Canoe Tour offered by **Whistler Sailing & Water Sports Center Ltd.,** P.O. Box 1130, Whistler, BC V0N 1B0 (☎ **604/932-7245**), is a great way to get acquainted with an exhilarating stretch of racing glacial water that runs between Green Lake and Alta Lake behind the village of Whistler. Packages range from C$29 (US$19) per person unguided to C$40 (US$27) per person unguided for a kayak or canoe.

FISHING Spring runs of steelhead, rainbow trout, and Dolly Varden char; summer runs of cutthroat and salmon; and fall runs of coho salmon attract anglers from around the world to the many glacier-fed lakes and rivers in the area and to **Birkenhead Lake Provincial Park,** 67km (44 miles) north of Pemberton. Bring your favorite fly rod and don't forget to buy a fishing license when you arrive at **Whistler Backcountry Adventures,** 36-4314 Main St., Whistler (☎ 604/932-3474). **Whistler River Adventures** (see "Jet Boating," below); **Sea to Sky Reel Adventures,** P.O. Box 776, Pemberton, BC V0N 2L0 (☎ 604/894-6928); and **Off the Beaten Track Wilderness Expeditions,** P.O. Box 1085, Whistler, BC V0N 1B0 (☎ **604/ 938-9282;** www.otbt.bc.ca), offer half-day and full-day catch-and-release fishing trips in the surrounding glacier rivers. Rates are C$99 to C$250 (US$66 to US$167) per person, which includes all fishing gear, round-trip transport to and from the Whistler Village Bus Loop, and a snack or lunch.

GOLF Robert Trent Jones's **Chateau Whistler Golf Club,** at the base of Blackcomb Mountain (☎ **604/938-2092,** pro shop 604/938-2095), is an 18-hole, par-72 course. Greens fees are C$110 to C$175 (US$73 to US$117), which includes powercart rental. A multiple-award-winning golf course, **Nicklaus North at Whistler** (☎ **604/938-9898**) is a 5-minute drive north of the village on the shores of Green Lake. The par-71 course's mountain views are spectacular. Greens fees are C$100 to C$125 (US$67 to US$83). The **Whistler Golf Club** (☎ **800/376-1777** or 604/ 932-4544), designed by Arnold Palmer, features nine lakes, two creeks, and magnificent vistas. In addition to the 18-hole, par-72 course, the club offers a driving range, putting green, sand bunker, and pitching area. Greens fees are C$125 (US$83).

The **A-1 Last Minute Golf Hotline** (☎ **800/684-6344** or 604/878-1833) can arrange a next-day tee time at Whistler golf courses. Savings can be as much as 40% on next-day, last-minute tee times. No membership is necessary. Call between 3 and 9pm for the next day or before noon for the same day.

HIKING There are numerous easy hiking trails in and around Whistler. You can take a lift up to Whistler and Blackcomb Mountains' trails during summer, but you have a number of other choices as well. The **Lost Lake Trail** starts at the northern end of the Day Skier Parking Lot at Blackcomb. The 30km (19 miles) of marked trails that wind around creeks, beaver dams, blueberry patches, and lush cedar groves are ideal for biking, cross-country skiing, or just strolling and picnicking.

The **Valley Trail System** is a well-marked paved trail connecting parts of Whistler. The trail starts on the west side of Highway 99 adjacent to the Whistler Golf Course and winds through quiet residential areas, as well as golf courses and parks. Garibaldi Provincial Park's **Singing Pass Trail** is a 4-hour hike of moderate difficulty. The fun way to experience this trail is to take the Whistler Mountain gondola to the top and walk down the well-marked path that ends in the village.

Nairn Falls Provincial Park is about 33km (21 miles) north of Whistler on Highway 99. It features a mile-long trail leading you to a stupendous view of the icy-cold Green River as it plunges 196 feet over a rocky cliff into a narrow gorge on its way downstream. On Highway 99 north of Mount Currie, **Joffre Lakes Provincial Park** is an intermediate-level hike leading past several brilliant-blue glacial lakes up to the very foot of a glacier. The **Ancient Cedars** area of Cougar Mountain is an awe-inspiring grove of towering cedars and Douglas firs. Some of the trees are over 1,000 years old and measure 9 feet in diameter.

HORSEBACK RIDING   **Whistler River Adventures** (see "Jet Boating," below) offers 2-hour (C$49/US$33) and 5-hour (C$109/US$73) trail rides along the Green River, through the forest, and across the Pemberton Valley from its 10-acre riverside facility in nearby Pemberton. The 5-hour ride goes up into the mountains and includes lunch.

JET BOATING   **Whistler River Adventures,** Whistler Mountain Village Gondola Base (P.O. Box 202), Whistler, BC V0N 1B0 (☎ **888/932-3532** or 604/932-3532; fax 604/932-3559; www.whistler-river-adv.com), takes you up the Green River just below Nairn Falls, where moose, deer, and bear sightings are common in the sheer-granite canyon. The Lillooet River tour goes past ancient petroglyphs, fishing sites, and the tiny Native Indian village of Skookumchuk. **Whistler Jet Boating Company Ltd.** (☎ **604/894-5200**) runs you down the icy rapids of the Green River or speed-cruising through the Lillooet River Valley throughout summer, water levels permitting. Tours by both companies range from hour-long trips for C$69 (US$46) to 4-hour cruises for C$135 (US$90).

RAFTING   **Whistler River Adventures** (see "Jet Boating," above) offers 2-hour and full-day round-trip rafting runs down the Green, Elaho, or Squamish River. They include equipment and ground transport for C$57 to C$125 (US$38 to US$83). The full-day trip includes a salmon barbecue lunch. The company also conducts 3-hour round-trip jet-boat tours on the Green river for C$69 (US$46) per person, which includes ground transport and a wet suit.

TENNIS   The **Whistler Racquet & Golf Resort,** 4500 Northland Blvd. (☎ **604/932-1991;** e-mail whisracq@whistler.net), features three covered courts, seven outdoor courts, and a practice cage, all open to drop-in visitors. Indoor courts are C$24 (US$16) per hour and outdoor courts C$12 (US$8) per hour. Adult and junior tennis camps are offered during summer. Camp prices range from C$250 to C$350 (US$167 to US$233) for a 3-day camp; kids camps cost C$36 (US$24) per day drop-in or C$150 (US$100) for a 5-day camp. The **Mountain Spa & Tennis Club,** Delta Whistler Resort, Whistler Village (☎ **604/938-2044**), and the **Chateau Whistler Resort,** Chateau Whistler Hotel, Upper Village (☎ **604/938-8000**), also offer courts to drop-in players. Prices run C$10 (US$7) per hour per court, with racquet rentals at C$5 (US$3.35) per hour.

There are **free public courts** at Myrtle Public School, Alpha Lake Park, Meadow Park, Millar's Pond, Brio, Blackcomb Benchlands, White Gold, and Emerald Park. Call ☎ **604/938-PARK** for details.

EXPLORING THE TOWN

SEEING THE SIGHTS   To learn more about Whistler's heritage, flora, and fauna, visit the **Whistler Museum & Archives Society,** 4329 Main St., off Northlands Boulevard (☎ **604/932-2019**). June to Labour Day, the museum is open daily 10am to 4pm; call ahead for winter opening hours. Admission is C$1 (US65¢) adults; children under 18 are free.

The **Whistler Inuit Gallery,** 4599 Chateau Blvd. (☎ **604/938-3366**), on the lower concourse of the Chateau Whistler Resort, specializes in Inuit, West Coast, and contemporary artists. **Gallery Row** in the Delta Whistler Resort consists of three galleries: the **Whistler Village Art Gallery** (☎ 604/938-3001), the **Northern Lights Gallery** (☎ 604/932-2890), and the **Adele Campbell Gallery** (☎ 604/938-0887). Their collections include fine art, sculpture, and glass.

Departing from the Whistler train station on Lake Placid Road at 8am, **BC Rail's Whistler Explorer** (☎ 604/984-5246; www.bcrail.com/bcr/) takes an 8½-hour round-trip ramble through Pemberton Valley before arriving at Kelly Lake, adjacent to the historic Cariboo Gold Rush Trail. After a 1-hour strolling break, you reboard the train, returning to Whistler at 5:30pm. The round-trip fare is C$114 (US$76) adults/seniors/children over 12 and C$78 (US$52) children 2 to 12.

Whistler Village and the Upper Village sponsor, near the base of the mountains, **daily activities** tailored for active kids of all ages. There are mountain-bike races, an in-line skating park, a trapeze, a trampoline, wall-climbing lessons, summer skiing, snowboarding, and snowshoeing. There's even a first-run multiplex movie theater.

Based at Blackcomb Mountain, the **Dave Murray Summer Ski Camp,** P.O. Box 98, Whistler, BC V0N 1B0 (☎ 604/932-5765), is North America's longest-running summer ski camp. Junior programs cost about C$1,200 (US$800) per week mid-June to Mid-July. The packages include food, lodging, and lift passes, as well as tennis, trapeze, and mountain-biking options.

SHOPPING   The **Whistler Marketplace,** in the center of Whistler Village, and the area surrounding the **Blackcomb Mountain lift** brim with clothing, jewelry, craft, specialty, gift, and equipment shops open daily 10am to 6pm. The **Horstman Trading Company** (☎ 604/938-7725), beside the Chateau Whistler at the base of Blackcomb, carries men's and women's casual wear to suit seasonal activities, from swimwear and footwear to polar-fleece vests and nylon jacket shells. The **Escape Route** (☎ 604/938-3228), at Whistler Marketplace and Crystal Lodge, has a great line of outdoor clothing and equipment.

GETTING THE SPA TREATMENT   The **Spa at Chateau Whistler Resort** (☎ 604/938-2086) is considered the best in Whistler. Open daily 8am to 9pm, it offers massage therapy, aromatherapy, skin care, body wraps, and steam baths. The **Whistler Body Wrap,** 210 St. Andrews House, next to the Keg in the Village (☎ 604/932-4710), can nurture you with shiatsu massage, facials, pedicures or manicures, waxings, sunbeds, and aromatherapy. The therapists at **Whistler Physiotherapy** (☎ 604/932-4001 or 604/938-9001) have a lot of experience with the typical ski, board, and hiking injuries. There are two locations: 339-4370 Lorimer Rd., at Marketplace, and 202-2011 Innsbruck Dr., next to Boston Pizza in Creekside.

WHERE TO STAY

South of Whistler on the Sea to Sky corridor is the very popular **Alice Lake Provincial Park.** You can reserve spots for Alice Lake by calling **Discover Camping** at ☎ 800/689-9025. About 27km (17 miles) north of Whistler, the well-maintained campground at **Nairn Falls,** Highway 99 (☎ 604/898-3678), is more adult-oriented, with pit toilets, pumped well water, fire pits, and firewood, but no showers. Prices for the 88 campsites are C$15 (US$10), on a first-come, first-served basis.

The 85 campsites at **Birkenhead Lake Provincial Park,** off Portage Road, Birken (☎ 604/898-3678), fill up very quickly during summer. To reserve a spot, call **Discover Camping** at ☎ 800/689-9025. Boat launches, great fishing, and well-maintained tent and RV sites make this an angler's paradise. Campsites are C$12 (US$8).

Prices for Whistler's studios, one- to five-bedroom fully furnished condos, town houses, and chalets are C$90 to C$1,400 (US$60 to US$934). **Whistler Central Reservations** (☎ 800/944-7853 or 604/664-5625; fax 604/938-5758;

www.whistler-resort.com) has more than 2,000 rental units to choose from and can book a wide range of accommodations in the Whistler area, from B&Bs to hotel rooms or condos. Other booking agencies are **Whistler Chalets and Accommodations Ltd.,** 4360 Lorimer Rd., Whistler, BC V0N 1B0 (☎ 800/663-7711 in Canada, or 604/932-6699; www.whistlerchalets.com), and **Rainbow Retreats Accommodations Ltd.,** 2129 Lake Placid Rd., Whistler, BC V0N 1B0 (☎ 604/932-2343; www.whistler.net/rainbow). Reservations for peak winter periods should be made by September.

IN THE VILLAGE

Canadian Pacific Chateau Whistler Resort. 4599 Chateau Blvd., Whistler, BC V0N 1B4. ☎ **800/441-1414** in the U.S., 800/606-8244 in Canada, or 604/938-8000. Fax 604/938-2055. 563 units. MINIBAR TV TEL. Summer C$299–C$335 (US$199–US$223) double, C$425–C$1,000 (US$283–US$667) suite; winter C$385–C$435 (US$257–US$290) double, C$570–C$1,200 (US$380–US$800) suite. Wheelchair-accessible rooms. AE, ER, MC, V. Underground valet parking C$15 (US$10).

The Canadian Pacific chain spared little expense re-creating the look and feel of an old-time country retreat at the foot of Blackcomb Mountain. Massive wooden beams support an airy peaked roof in the lobby, while in the hillside Mallard Bar, double-sided stone fireplaces cast a cozy glow on the couches and leather armchairs. The guest rooms and suites feature double, queen-, and king-size beds; duvets; bathrobes; and soaker tubs. Gold service guests can have breakfast or relax après ski in a private lounge with the warm and slightly musty feel of Victorian library.

Dining: Daily 7 to 11am, the Wildflower Restaurant offers the best buffet-style brunch in the village. It's also an excellent spot for fine dining. The Mallard Bar has a great view of the Blackcomb lifts.

Amenities: Concierge, room service; ski and bike storage, full-service spa, massage therapy, heated indoor/outdoor pool, sauna, whirlpool, steam room, weight room, terrace barbecue, tennis courts, 18-hole golf course.

Pan Pacific Lodge–Whistler. 4320 Sundial Crescent, Whistler, BC V0N 1B4. **888/905-9955,** or 604/905-2999. Fax 604/905-2995. www.panpac.com. 121 units. Summer C$109–C$199 (US$73–US$133) suite; winter C$155–C$375 (US$103–US$250) suite. Wheelchair-accessible rooms. AE, ER, MC, V. Underground valet parking C$15 (US$10).

The Pan's location is killer: right at the foot of the Whistler Mountain gondola. Swimming in the outdoor pool or soaking in one of two outdoor Jacuzzis, you can look up at the snow-covered runs and wonder at the ameliorative effects of warm water on aching muscles. The suites are light and pleasant, built according to the same basic pattern: Each studio suite comes with a full kitchen and dining area, a sitting area warmed by a gas fireplace, a sofa bed and Murphy bed, and a small balcony. It's a very comfortable space for two, but somewhat cramped for four. The larger suites feature one or two bedrooms opening off the main room.

Dining/Diversions: Fine dining is offered at Arthur's Restaurant. More fun and better value is the Dubh Linn Gate Irish Lounge/Pub, a convincing re-creation of a Dublin pub.

Amenities: Concierge, room service, laundry; heated outdoor pool, Jacuzzis, fitness center and steam room; ski, bike, golf-bag storage.

OUTSIDE THE VILLAGE

Cedar Springs Bed & Breakfast Lodge. 8106 Cedar Springs Rd., Whistler, BC V0N 1B8. ☎ **800/727-7547** or 604/938-8007. Fax 604/938-8023. www.whistlerinns.com\cedarsprings. 9 units, 7 with bathroom. C$80–C$199 (US$53–US$133) double; C$129–C$199 (US$86–US$133) suite. Rates include full breakfast. MC, V. Take Hwy. 99 north toward Pemberton 4km (2½ miles) past Whistler Village. Turn left onto Alpine Way. Drive 1 block to Rainbow Dr. and turn left. Drive 1 block to Camino St. and turn left. The lodge is 1 block down at the corner of Camino and Cedar Springs.

Guests at this charming lodge have a choice of king-, queen-, or twin-size beds in comfortably modern surroundings. The honeymoon suite boasts a fireplace and balcony. The guest sitting room has a TV, VCR, and video library. A sauna and hot tub on the sundeck overlooking the gardens add to the pampering. A gourmet breakfast is served in the dining room by the fireside, and you're welcome to enjoy afternoon tea. Complimentary Alpine Meadows bus provides transportation to and from the village.

✪ **Durlacher Hof Pension Inn.** 7055 Nesters Rd. (P.O. Box 1125), Whistler, BC V0N 1B0. ☎ **604/932-1924.** Fax 604/938-1980. www.durlacherhof.com. 8 units. June 19–Sept 30 C$120–C$199 (US$80–US$133) double; Dec 18–Mar 31 C$179–C$259 (US$119–US$173) double. Extra person C$30 (US$20). Spring and fall discounts available. Rates include full breakfast and afternoon tea. MC, V. Free parking. Take Hwy. 99 north about 0.8km (½ mile) north of Whistler Village to Nester's Rd. Turn left and the inn is immediately on the right.

You'll feel completely spoiled by the fine European service, decor, and cuisine at this Austrian-style inn. Each guest room has a goose-down duvet on the extra-long twin- or queen-size bed, fluffy robes, a bathroom (some with jetted tubs) with deluxe toiletries, and an incredible mountain view from a private balcony. The licensed cocktail lounge has a welcoming fireplace and offers complimentary après-ski appetizers. On selected nights, dinners are offered at an extra charge, and they're often prepared by a celebrated guest chef.

Hostelling International Whistler. 5678 Alta Lake Rd., Whistler BC V0N 1B0 ☎ **888/ 203-4303** or 604/932-5492. Fax 604/932-4687. www.hihostels.bc.ca. 33 beds in 4 to 6 bed dorms. Wheelchair accessible. C$19 (US$12) IYHA members, C$23 (US$15) nonmembers. Annual adult membership C$27 (US$18). Family and group memberships available. MC, V. Free parking.

One of the few inexpensive spots in Whistler, the hostel also happens to have one of the nicest locations: on the south edge of Alta Lake, with a dining room, deck, and lawn looking over the lake to Whistler Mountain. It's extremely pleasant, with a lounge with a wood-burning stove, a common kitchen, a piano, Ping-Pong tables, and a sauna, as well as a drying room for ski gear and storage for bikes and boards and skis. In summer, guest have use of a barbecue, canoe, and rowboat. As with all hostels, most rooms and facilities are shared.

WHERE TO DINE

Whistler literally overflows with dining spots. A quick meal for gourmets on the go can be found at **Chef Bernard's,** 4573 Chateau Blvd., Whistler Village (☎ **604/ 932-7051**). It serves full breakfasts, soups, salads, and sandwiches, as well as hot entrees for C$4.95 to C$8 (US$3.30 to US$5); it's open daily 7am to 9pm. **Ingrid's Village Café,** just off the Village Square (☎ **604/932-7000**), is another locals' favorite, for both quality and price. A large bowl of Ingrid's clam chowder costs just C$4.50 (US$3), while a veggie burger comes in at C$5 (US$3.35). It's open daily 8am to 6pm.

The **Citta Bistro,** in the Whistler Village Square (☎ **604/932-4177**), serves thin-crust pizzas like the Californian herb, topped with spiced chicken breast, sun-dried tomatoes, fresh pesto, and mozzarella, as well as gourmet burgers like the Citta Extra-ordinaire, topped with bacon, cheddar, and garlic mushrooms. Main courses are C$7 to C$11 (US$4.65 to US$7), and it's open daily noon to midnight. The **Dubh Linn**

Gate Irish Lounge/Bar in the Pan Pacific hotel offers solid pub grub and the atmosphere of the Emerald Isle; it's open Monday to Saturday 10am to midnight and Sunday 10am to 10pm. Brand new to Whistler but long known in Vancouver for its quality beef is **Hy's Steakhouse,** 4308 Main St. (☎ 604/905-5555), open daily 4pm to midnight.

⭐ **Araxi Restaurant & Bar.** 4222 Village Sq. ☎ **604/932-4540.** Main courses C$11–C$27 (US$7–US$18). Daily 11am–10:30pm. AE, MC, V. ITALIAN/WEST COAST.

This is one of the top places to dine in town—it consistently wins awards for its wine list and was voted "Best Restaurant in Whistler" in 1998 and 1999 by readers of *Vancouver* magazine. And thanks to a C$250,000 (US$166,750) renovation in the spring of 1999, Araxi's now has storage for its 12,000-bottle inventory of fine BC and foreign wines. The heated patio seats 80 amid barrels of flowers, while inside, the artwork, antiques, and terra-cotta tiles give a subtle Italian ambiance. The menu is less Italian than West Coast, with the emphasis on fresh regional products, including BC ostrich, salmon, and scallops. The locally caught trout is smoked in the Araxi kitchen. Appetizers include sweet chili-marinated prawns and grilled Fraser Valley quail. Main courses include seafood like ahi tuna, salmon fillet, and scallops. For meat lovers, the menu offers rack of lamb, tenderloin, and alder-smoked pork loin.

Caramba! Restaurant. 12-4314 Main St., Town Plaza. ☎ **604/938-1856.** Main courses C$11–C$17 (US$7–US$11). Daily noon–10:30pm. AE, MC, V. MEDITERRANEAN.

The room is bright and filled with the pleasant buzz of nattering diners. The kitchen is open, and the smells wafting out hint tantalizingly of fennel and artichoke and pasta. These are good signs. Caramba! may be casual dining, but its Mediterranean-influenced menu offers fresh ingredients prepared with a great deal of pizzazz. Try the pasta, the free-range chicken, or the roasted pork loin. Better still, if you're feeling especially good about your dining companions, order a pizza or two, a plate of grilled calamari, some hot spinach-and-cheese artichokes, and shallots and a plate of sliced prosciutto and bullfighters toast.

Uli's Flipside. 4433 Sundial Place (upstairs). ☎ **604/935-1107.** Main courses C$11–C$17 (US$7–US$11). Mon–Sat 3pm–1am, Sun 3pm–midnight. AE, DC, MC, V. PASTA/ITALIAN.

Few other spots in town offer the same combination of Uli's excellent pasta, good wine list, and warm and pleasant room with vaulted ceiling and intimate window-side booths—all at a very moderate price. Given that Whistler shares the West Coast affliction of early dining (few kitchens are open as late as 10pm), Uli's is also the best bet for late-night dining.

WHISTLER AFTER DARK

For a town of just 8,000, Whistler has a more-than-respectable nightlife scene. You'll find concert listings in the *Pique,* a free local paper available at cafes and food stores. **Tommy Africa's,** underneath the Pharmasave at the entrance to the Main Village (☎ 604/932-6090), and the dark and cavernous **Maxx Fish,** in the Village Square below the Amsterdam Cafe (☎ 604/932-1904), cater to the 18- to 22-year-old crowd; you'll find lots of beat and not much light. The crowd at **Garfinkel's,** at the entrance to Village North (☎ 604/932-2323), is similar, though the cutoff age can reach as high as 26 or 27. The **Boot Pub,** Nancy Green Drive just off Highway 99 (☎ 604/932-3338), is crammed with young Australian ski-lift operators. **Buffalo Bills,** across from the Whistler Gondola (☎ 604/932-6613), and the **Savage Beagle,** opposite Starbucks in the Village (☎ 604/938-3337), cater to the 30-something crowd. Bills is bigger, with a pool table, a video ski machine, and a smallish dance floor. The Beagle has a fabulous selection of beer and bar drinks, with a pleasant little pub upstairs and a house-oriented dance floor below.

11 Wells Gray Provincial Park & the Shuswap Lakes

The High Country's landscape is arid and hilly in the lowlands along the Trans-Canada Highway (Highway 1), which follows the shores of the lower Thompson River and Shuswap Lakes. The acres of undulating sheets of black mesh draped along the hillsides are actually shading field after field of cultivated ginseng.

The **Shuswap Lakes** are popular with houseboaters. It's easy to navigate the region's 1,000km (620 miles) of waterways, landing along the way at campsites and beaches accessible only by boat. The Adams River sockeye-salmon run is an annual event, but the dominant runs that occur every 4 years are worth the wait (the next one is due in 2002). Rent a houseboat in the nearby town of **Salmon Arm** (pop. 15,034), and then spend a relaxing vacation at one of the area's marine parks.

Rising up from this dry terrain, heading north along Highway 5, the road enters the cool green forests of the High Country. And high above the town of **Clearwater** (pop. 1,666) is the pristine wilderness of **Wells Gray Provincial Park.** The cascading waters of **Helmcken Falls** and **Dawson Falls** aren't the only natural wonders you'll find in the 3,211,000-acre wilderness. Drive up the winding dirt road to the **Green Point Observatory** for a perfect overview of the park from the three-story wooden observation tower.

ESSENTIALS

VISITOR INFORMATION   Contact the **Thompson Okanagan Tourism Association,** 1332 Water St., Kelowna, BC V1Y 9P4 (☎ **800/860-9993** or 250/860-5999; e-mail info@thompsonokanagan.com). The **Clearwater Visitor Info Centre** is at 425 E. Yellowhead Hwy. 5 (mailing address: Box 1988, RR #1), at the intersection of Highway 5 and Wells Gray Park Road, Clearwater, BC V0E 1N0 (☎ **250/674-2646**). October 16 to April 14, it's open Monday to Saturday 9am to 5pm; April 15 to June 30 and September 1 to October 15, hours are daily 9am to 6pm; July and August, hours are daily 8am to 8pm. At the **Salmon Arm Visitor Info Centre,** 751 Marine Park Dr. NE (mailing address: Box 999), Salmon Arm, BC V1E 4P2 (☎ **250/832-2230;** e-mail: sacofc@shuswap.net), the staff can help with travel plans throughout the Shuswap Lakes region. September 2 to May 30, it's open Monday to Friday 9am to 5pm; June 1 to September 1, hours are daily 9am to 5pm.

GETTING THERE   You need a car to explore the best areas of the High Country, especially Wells Gray Provincial Park.

By Car   To get to **Wells Gray Provincial Park** from Quesnel, take Highway 97 south to 100 Mile House. Follow the signs to Highway 24 east, which runs through the small towns of Lone Butte and Bridge Lake before arriving in Little Fort, 83km (52 miles) farther. At Little Fort, take the Yellowhead Highway (Highway 5) north 32km (20 miles) to Clearwater.

To get to the **Shuswap Lakes** from Vancouver, take the Trans-Canada Highway (Highway 1) through Cache Creek and Kamloops to Chase (about 420km/260 miles) or Salmon Arm (473km/293 miles), in the heart of the Shuswap Lakes region.

From the Okanagan Valley, take Highway 97 north, pick up the Trans-Canada Highway just outside Kamloops, and then head east 58km (36 miles) to Chase.

By Plane & Car   You can fly into Kamloops, a 50-minute flight from Vancouver, and rent a car at the airport. **Air BC** (☎ **800/667-3721**) and **Canadian Regional**

Airlines (☎ 800/426-7000 in the U.S. or 800/363-7530 in Canada) operate daily flights. The major car-rental firms have desks at the airport.

SPECIAL EVENTS   The Reino Keskl–Salmo Loppet (☎ 250/832-7740) attracts cross-country skiers from across North America to the Larch Hills Cross-Country Ski Hill in Salmon Arm during the second week in January. The **Wells Gray Loppet** (☎ 250/674-3657) in Wells Gray Provincial Park during the first week of February is a doubly enjoyable event for cross-country skiers. The hilly 42km (26-mile) course attracts more contestants in all age groups and levels each year, and the scenery is spectacular.

The annual **Salmon Arm Bluegrass Festival** (☎ 250/832-3258), in Salmon Arm's R. J. Haney Heritage Park during the first weekend in July, features performers from Canada, the United States, and Europe. Departing from a different Cariboo ranch each year, the annual ✪ **Kamloops Cattle Drive,** Box 1332, Kamloops, BC V2C 6L7 (☎ 250/372-7075; www.cattledrive.bc.ca), has grown immensely popular over the past decade. More than 1,000 people participate in the 6-day ride during the second week in July. Cattle, cowboys, and visitors from around the world ride through the High Country's rolling prairies for 5 days, finishing with a grand arrival and a big party in Kamloops. Horses, gear, and even seats on the chuck wagons are available for rent.

EXPLORING WELLS GRAY PROVINCIAL PARK

Established in 1939, **Wells Gray Provincial Park** (☎ 604/371-6400) is British Columbia's second-largest park, encompassing more than 1.3 million acres of virgin wilderness: mountains, rivers, volcanic formations and outcroppings, lakes, glaciers, forests, and alpine meadows. Wildlife abounds, including mule deer, moose, caribou, grizzly and black bears, beaver, coyote, rufous hummingbirds, timber wolves, mink, wolverine, marmot, and golden eagles.

Twice as tall as Niagara Falls, the park's **Helmcken Falls** are an awesome sight you can reach by paved road. In addition, a paved road leads to the broad cascade known as **Dawson Falls.** Boating, canoeing, kayaking, and fishing are popular pastimes on **Clearwater** and **Azure Lakes, Mahood Lake,** and **Murtle Lake.** The wilderness campgrounds along the lakes make perfect destinations for overnight canoe or fishing trips.

Multiday hiking destinations include exploring the area around **Ray Farm Homestead, Rays Mineral Spring** and the thickly forested **Murtle River Trail** that leads to **Majerus Falls, Horsehoe Falls,** and **Pyramid Mountain,** a volcanic upgrowth that was shaped when it erupted beneath miles of glacial ice that covered the park millions of years ago.

TOURS & EXCURSIONS

The **Wells Gray Guest Ranch,** Wells Gray Road (mailing address: RR #1, Box 1766), Clearwater BC V0E 1N0 (☎ 250/674-2792 or 250/674-2774), offers guided trips and packages that include hiking, canoeing, white-water rafting, fishing, mountain biking, and motorboating (on Clearwater and Azure Lakes) during summer, and dogsledding, cross-country skiing, downhill skiing, snowshoeing, snowmobiling, and ice fishing during winter. Excursions range from half-day to weeklong trips.

Crazy Moon Enterprises, Helmcken Falls Lodge, Wells Gray Road, Clearwater (☎ 250/674-3657), offers half- and full-day guided hikes and canoeing trips through the park and environs. And **Interior Whitewater Expeditions** (☎ 250/674-3727) conducts a variety of rafting and kayaking packages, ranging from half-day to 5-day trips, on some of the wildest, most beautiful stretches of the North Thompson River.

WHERE TO STAY

Most campers head to Wells Gray Provincial Park's ✪ **Spahats, Clearwater,** and **Dawson Falls Campgrounds** (☎ 250/851-3000). Only 88 sites are in the park, so check the sign outside the Clearwater Visitor Info Centre to make sure the grounds aren't full before driving all the way up to the park. Sites are C$12 (US$8). Facilities include fire pits, firewood, pumped well water, pit toilets, and boat launches at the lakes.

✪ **Nakiska Ranch.** Trout Creek Rd. (off Wells Gray Park Rd.), Clearwater, BC V0E 1N0. ☎ **250/674-3655.** Fax 250/674-3387. www.nakiskaranch.bc.ca. 3 units, 4 cabins. Summer C$105 (US$70) double; C$115–C$135 (US$77–US$90) cabin. Winter C$80 (US$53) double; C$89–C$95 (US$59–US$63) cabin. Small pets accepted. MC, V. Drive up Wells Gray Park Rd. for 42km (26 miles). The road actually takes about 40 min. to drive. Turn right at the ranch sign onto Trout Creek Rd.

Gorgeous log cabins, acres of mowed meadows, and Wells Gray's majestic forests and mountains surround the main log house on this working ranch. The RUSTIC CABINS sign at the entrance describes only the exteriors of these pristine hideaways. The immaculate interiors of both the lodge and the individual cabins are straight out of the pages of *House Beautiful,* featuring open kitchens, hardwood floors and walls, lots of windows, and Scandinavian-style wood furnishings. The two-story cabins can sleep up to six comfortably. Breakfast is served in the lodge house, but you must bring your own groceries for lunch and dinner. (It's a 30-min. drive to the nearest restaurant or store.)

✪ **Trophy Mountain Buffalo Ranch Bed & Breakfast & Campground.** RR #1 (mailing address: P.O. Box 1768), Clearwater, BC V0E 1N0. ☎ **250/674-3095.** Fax 250/674-3131. E-mail buffranch@hotmail.com. 4 units, 15 campsites, 4 camping cabins. C$45–C$60 (US$30–US$40) double; C$14–C$17 (US$9–US$11) campsite; C$11 (US$7) cabin. Rates include breakfast. MC, V. Drive up Wells Gray Park Rd. for 33km (21 miles). Turn left at the ranch sign.

You can't miss the small buffalo herd casually grazing in a fenced pasture (well, they're usually there) as you drive up the Wells Gray Park Road. Beyond this pastoral setting stand a log lodge, campsites, and cabins nestled in the woodlands. The lodge rooms are cozy and clean, featuring warm comforters and soft pillows. The camping cabins, tent sites, and separate RV sites are also extremely well kept. Dishwashing sinks are set up on the deck of the shower house, where hot water flows liberally. There's plenty of free firewood; fire-pit grills are available for a nominal fee. Hiking and horseback-riding trails surround the ranch. In fact, horses are available for rent, and guided trail rides run through the forest to the cliffs overlooking the Clearwater River valley and to the base of a secluded 115-foot waterfall. Prices start at C$48 (US$32) for a 2½-hour trip. If you get a sudden urge to venture deep into the woods near Trophy Mountain, your hosts can give you directions and outfit you with rental gear, from canoes and tents to cookware.

✪ **Wells Gray Backcountry Chalets.** Box 188B, Clearwater, BC V0E 1N0. ☎ **888/ SKI-TREK** or 250/587-6444. Fax 604/587-6446. 3 chalets. Summer C$35 (US$23) per person; winter C$40 (US$27) per person. MC, V. Drive up Wells Gray Park Rd. for 37km (23 miles). The road actually takes about 35 min. to drive. Turn left at the ranch sign.

Ian Eakins and Tay Briggs run a family-owned outdoor guiding company that maintains three year-round chalets nestled deep in the park. The chalets sleep up to 12 and are fully equipped with kitchens, furniture, bedding, books, a sauna, and propane-generated lighting and heat. It's the best of both worlds: You can experience untrammeled wilderness and great rural hospitality. The owners offer guided or self-catered hiking and cross-country ski packages, as well as guided 3-day and 6-day family canoe trips on Clearwater and Azure Lakes in Wells Gray Provincial Park. Fully catered and guided trips are available in 3- to 8-day packages. Summer hikes are C$125 (US$83) per person per day; winter cross-country ski trips are C$135 (US$90) per person per day.

WHERE TO DINE

The **Clearwater Country Inn,** 449 Yellowhead Hwy E. (☎ **250/674-3455**), has good home-style cooking like fried chicken and breaded veal cutlets and is open daily 4am to 9pm. The **Helmcken Falls Lodge,** Wells Gray Park Road, Clearwater (☎ **250/674-3657**), and the **Wells Gray Guest Ranch,** Wells Gray Park Road, Clearwater (☎ **250/674-2774**), offer buffet-style dinners at 7pm sharp daily for C$25 (US$17) per person. The guest ranch's saloon is a great place to share stories of world travels with the many Swiss and German hikers who frequent this area.

EXPLORING THE SHUSWAP LAKES

One of nature's most amazing phenomena, the **Adams River Salmon Run,** takes place annually in late October. Millions of crimson fish fight their way upstream from the Pacific Ocean to spawn in the placid Shuswap waters in Roderick Haig-Brown Provincial Park. "Dominant" runs occur every 4 years; the 2002 runs are projected to be the next dominant run, with an estimated 1.5 to 2 million sockeye salmon struggling upstream to spawn in the Adams River near Squilax. Park trails provide riverside viewing. The "Salute to Salmon" program has displays and trained staff in attendance to interpret this spectacle. Take the Trans-Canada Highway (Highway 1) to Squilax (about 10km/6.2 miles east of Chase). Follow the signs north to Roderick Haig-Brown Provincial Park.

Fishing and boating are the area's biggest lures. With 1,000km (620 miles) of shoreline filled with sandy beaches, private coves, and narrow channels, visitors come to while away the summer days aboard houseboats or fishing charters, enjoying the tranquil beauty of the lakes.

SPORTS & OUTDOOR ACTIVITIES

FISHING To fish here, you need a nonresident freshwater license. Pick up a copy of *BC Sport Fishing Regulations Synopsis for Non-Tidal Waters.* Independent anglers should also pick up a copy of the *BC Fishing Directory and Atlas.* For licenses, equipment, and advice, head to the **Westside Store,** 360 Hwy. 1, in Salmon Arm (☎ **250/832-8141**).

GOLF The **Salmon Arm Golf Club,** 3641 Hwy. 97B SE, Salmon Arm (☎ **250/832-4727;** e-mail: sagolf@jetstream.net), is an 18-hole, par-72, 6,738-yard course. Greens fees are C$45 (US$30). The **Shuswap Lakes Estate Golf & Country Club,** 2404 Centennial Rd., Sorrento (☎ **800/661-3955** in Canada, or 250/675-2315), offers an 18-hole, par-71, 6,438-yard course. Greens fees start at C$42 (US$28) per person.

HIKING On the northern shore of Shuswap Lake near the town of Squilax, **Shuswap Lake Provincial Park** (☎ **250/851-3000**) was the site of a gold-mining operation during the 1930s and 1940s. The original mineral-bearing creek no longer flows through this rich delta, but the area offers wonderful strolling, with abundant old-growth ponderosa pines and second-growth red cedar and Douglas fir. About a mile offshore, **Copper Island** has a pleasant circular trail leading to a high point where boaters looking for a dry-land hiking experience can survey the lake and surrounding countryside and catch a glimpse of the many mule deer that inhabit the island.

SKIING   Sun Peaks Resort, Tod Mountain Road, Heffley Creek, north of Kamloops off Highway 5 (☎ **250/578-7232,** or 250/578-7232 for snow reports), is a great powder-skiing and open-run area with a vertical rise of 2,891 feet. The 80 runs are serviced by one high-speed quad chair with bubble cover, one fixed-grip quad chair, one triple chair, one double chair, one T-bar, and one beginner platter. Snowboarders have a choice of two half pipes, one with a super-large boarder-cross. At the bottom of this 3,000-foot run are handrails, cars, a fun box, hips, quarter pipes, burly tabletops, transfers, and fat gaps that were designed by Ecosign Mountain Planners and some of Canada's top amateur riders. Cross-country and snowmobile trails are also available. Lift tickets are C$45 (US$30) adults, C$40 (US$27) children over 12, and C$26 (US$17) children 12 and under.

WHERE TO STAY & DINE

The best way to see the lakes is to rent a houseboat for a few days. After all, Shuswap is the "Houseboating Capital of Canada." For around C$2,000 (US$1,334) per week, you can rent a fully equipped houseboat sleeping up to 10. **Three Buoys Houseboat Vacations,** 710 Riverside (mailing address: Box 709), Sicamous, BC V0E 2V0 (☎ **250/836-2403**); **Twin Anchors Houseboat Vacations,** 101 Martin St. (mailing address: Box 318), Sicamous, BC V0E 2V0 (☎ **250/836-2450**); and **Bluewater Houseboats,** 110 Weddup (mailing address: Box 248), Sicamous, BC V0E 2V0 (☎ **250/836-2255;** www.shuswap.bc.ca/sunny/bluewtr.htm), are just a few of the area outfitters.

The 280 campsites at **Shuswap Lake Provincial Park** (☎ **250/851-3000**), 32km (20 miles) northeast of Highway 1 at Squilax, cost C$19 (US$13) per night. Facilities include free hot showers, flush toilets, a playground, and a nature house. The 35 sites at **Silver Beach Provincial Park** (☎ **250/851-3000**) are accessible by an unpaved road from the town of Anglemount, by ferry from Sicamous, or by boating to the north end of Seymour Arm. Facilities include pit toilets and fire pits; sites are C$8 (US$5) per night. And there are 51 campsites at **Herald Provincial Park** (☎ **250/851-3000**), 15km (9 miles) northeast of Highway 1 at Tappen. Facilities include free hot showers, pit toilets, a sani-station, and a boat launch. Sites are C$19 (US$13) per night.

Quaaout Lodge. Little Shuswap Lake Rd. (mailing address: Box 1215), Chase, BC V0E 1M0. ☎ **800/663-4303** or 250/679-3090. Fax 250/679-3039. E-mail quaaout@quaaout.com. 72 units. A/C TV TEL. C$119–C$175 (US$79–US$117) double. Free parking. AE, MC, V. On the Trans-Canada Hwy. (Hwy. 1), drive through the town of Chase. About 16km (10 miles) east, turn left at the Squilax Bridge underpass. Take the overpass and the lodge is on the first road on the left.

This gorgeous resort draws heavily on native-Indian tradition in its design and decor. Set on the sandy shores of Little Shuswap Lake, it's owned/operated by the Shuswap band of the Secwepemc tribe, who built it in 1992. Six of the well-appointed guest rooms have fireplaces and Jacuzzis. The hotel's excellent licensed restaurant offers a menu featuring many traditional dishes, including alder-smoked salmon, grilled duck breast with wild rice, venison, and a fluffy fried bread called bannock. Facilities include an indoor pool, a Jacuzzi, a fully equipped gym, and saunas. Hiking and biking trails, fishing, cross-country skiing, canoeing, and a playground (adventurous kids can opt to spend a night in a large teepee provided by the lodge) round out the fun. Rental canoes and mountain bikes are available.

12 The Okanagan Valley: A Taste of the Grape

Just south of the High Country on Highway 97, the arid **Okanagan Valley** with its long chain of lakes is the ideal destination for freshwater-sports enthusiasts, golfers, skiers, and wine lovers. The climate is hot and dry during the summer high season (when, one local told me, the valley's population increases five-fold from its winter average of about 35,000).

Ranches and small towns have flourished here for more than a century; the region's **fruit orchards and vineyards** will make you feel as if you've been transported to the Spanish countryside. Summer visitors get the pick of the fruit crop at insider prices from the many fruit stands that line Highway 97. Be sure to stop for a pint of cherries, a basket of apples, homemade jams, and other goodies.

An Okanagan region chardonnay won gold medals in 1994 at international competitions held in London and Paris. And more than three dozen other wineries produce vintages that are following right on its heels. Despite this coveted honor, the valley has received little international publicity. Most visitors are Canadian, and the valley isn't yet a major tour-bus destination. Get here before they do.

Many Canadian retirees have chosen **Penticton** as their home because it has relatively mild winters and dry, desert-like summers. It's also a favorite destination for younger visitors, drawn by boating, waterskiing, sportfishing, and windsurfing on 128km-long (79-mile-long) Lake Okanagan.

Remember to bring your camera when you head out on the lake. If you spot its legendary underwater resident, **Ogopogo,** take a picture. The shy monster (depicted in ancient petroglyphs found in the valley as a snakelike beast with a horselike head) is said to be a distant cousin of Scotland's Loch Ness monster.

The town of **Kelowna** in the central valley is the hub of the BC wine-making industry and the valley's largest city. And the town of **Vernon** is a favorite destination for cross-country and powder skiers, who flock to the northern valley's top resort— **Silver Star Mountain.**

ESSENTIALS

VISITOR INFORMATION   The **Penticton Visitor Info Centre** is at 888 Westminster Ave. W., Penticton, BC V2A 8R2 (☎ **800/663-5052** or 250/493-4055). The **Kelowna Visitor Info Centre** is at 544 Harvey Ave., Kelowna, BC V1Y 6C9 (☎ **250/861-1515**). And the **Vernon Visitor Info Centre** is at 701 Highway 97 S. (mailing address: Box 520), Vernon, BC V1T 6M4 (☎ **250/542-1514;** www.vernontourism.com). All are open daily 9am to 6pm.

GETTING THERE   **By Car**   The 395km (245-mile) drive from Vancouver to Penticton via the Trans-Canada Highway (Highway 1) and Highway 3 rambles through rich delta farmlands and the forested mountains of Manning Provincial Park and the Similkameen River region before descending into the Okanagan Valley's antelope-brush and sagebrush desert. For a more direct route to the valley, take the Trans-Canada Highway to the Coquihalla Toll Highway (C$10/US$7) via Merritt and Hope. Using this expressway allows drivers to make the journey from Kelowna to Vancouver in 4 hours.

By Plane   **Canadian Airlines** (☎ **800/426-7000** in the U.S. or 800/363-7530 in Canada; www.cdnair.ca) and **Air BC** (☎ **800/667-3721**) have frequent daily commuter flights from Calgary and Vancouver to Penticton and Kelowna.

SPECIAL EVENTS   Colorful balloons meet to fly the valley's air thermals during the first and second weeks in February at Vernon's **Annual Winter Carnival & Hot Air Balloon Festival** (☎ 250/545-2236). Indoor and outdoor events like arts and crafts exhibits, food stands, and live musical entertainment take place at locations throughout the city.

Be the first to taste the valley's best chardonnay, pinot noir, merlot, and ice wines at the **Okanagan Wine Festival** (☎ 250/861-6654), during the first and second weeks in October at wineries and restaurants throughout Penticton.

TASTING THE FRUITS OF THE VINEYARDS

British Columbia has a long history of producing wines, ranging from mediocre to really, truly bad. A missionary, Father Pandosy, planted apple trees and vineyards in 1859 and produced sacramental wines for the valley's mission. Other monastery wineries cropped up, but none of them worried about the quality of their bottlings, because they were subsidized by the BC government.

In the 1980s, the government threatened to pull its support of the industry unless it could produce an internationally competitive product. The vintners listened. Root stock was imported from France and Germany. European-trained master vintners were hired to oversee the development of the vines and the wine-making process. The climate and soil conditions turned out to be some of the best in the world for wine making, and today, British Columbian wines are winning international gold medals. Competitively priced, about C$7 to C$50 (US$4.65 to US$33) per bottle, they represent some great bargains in well-balanced chardonnays, pinot blancs, and gewürztraminers; full-bodied merlots, pinot noirs, and cabernets; and dessert ice wines that surpass the best muscat d'or.

Because U.S. visitors are allowed to bring back 33.8 oz. (1 liter) of wine per person without paying extra duty, Americans can bring a bottle of their favorite selection back home if they've visited Canada for more than 24 hours. Travelers from the United Kingdom can take back up to 2 liters of still wine without paying duty.

The valley's more than 3 dozen vineyards and wineries conduct free tours and wine tastings throughout the year. Here are a few favorite stops:

The town of **Okanagan Falls** is 20km (12 miles) south of Penticton along Highway 97. Adjacent to a wilderness area and bird sanctuary overlooking Vaseaux Lake, **Blue Mountain Vineyards & Cellars,** Allendale Road (☎ 250/497-8244; mailing address: RR #1, Site 3, Comp 4, Okanagan Falls, BC V0H 1R0), offers tours by appointment and operates a wine shop and tasting room. **Wild Goose Vineyards and Winery,** Sun Valley Way (☎ 250/497-8919; mailing address: RR #1, Site 3, Comp 11, Okanagan Falls, BC V0H 1R0), conducts daily tours and operates a wine shop and tasting room April to October daily 10am to 5pm; November to March, tours are conducted by appointment only.

The **Hester Creek Estate Winery,** Road 8 (☎ 250/498-4435; e-mail info@ hestercreek.com), has a wine boutique open daily 10am to 5pm, and tours of the wine-making area are available by appointment; especially nice here is the grapevine–shaded patio that invites picnickers. The superior growing conditions at Hester Creek produce intense fruit flavors that make the wines from here some of the best in all BC.

In and around **Kelowna** are some of the biggest names in British Columbia's wine-making industry. **Calona Wines,** 1125 Richter St., Kelowna, BC V1Y 2K6 (☎ 250/762-3332), conducts tours through western Canada's oldest (since 1932) and largest winery. Many antique wine-making machines are on display alongside the state-of-the-art equipment the winery now uses. May to September, tours are given daily on the hour 11am to 5pm. The wine shop is open daily: May to September 10am to 7pm and October to April 10am to 5pm. At **Summerhill Estate Winery,** 4870 Chute Lake Rd., Kelowna, BC V1W 4M3 (☎ **800/667-3538** in Canada, or 250/764-8000), the wine shop and tasting room are open daily 10am to 6pm year-round.

Another experience worth savoring even if you're not an oenophile is the **Quail's Gate Estate,** 3303 Boucherie Rd., Kelowna, BC V1Z 2H3 (☎ **250/769-4451**). If ice wines (made with grapes that have been allowed to stay on the vine through several frosts, dyhydrating them and intensifying the sugars) are your favorite dessert potable, you'll want to taste the vintages here. May 30 to late June, tours are conducted daily at 11am, 1pm, and 3pm; from the last weekend in June to Labour Day, they're given daily on the hour 11am to 4pm. The wine shop and tasting room are housed in the restored log home of the Allison family, pioneers who arrived in the valley during the 1870s. The shop is filled with historic regional artifacts. It's open daily: May 30 to Labour Day 10am to 6pm and the rest of the year 10am to 5pm.

The neighboring town of **Westbank** is home to **Mission Hill Wines,** 1730 Mission Hill Rd., Westbank, BC V4T 2E4 (☎ **250/768-7611;** e-mail kmoul@ markanthony.com), established in 1981. July and August, tours are given daily on the hour 10am to 5pm; the rest of the year, tours are Saturday and Sunday on the hour 10am to 5pm. July and August, the wine shop is open daily 9am to 7pm; the rest of the year, it's open Saturday and Sunday 10am to 5pm.

Located 43km (27 miles) north of Penticton, the **Hainle Vineyards Estate Winery,** 5355 Trepanier Bench Rd. (☎ **250/767-2525;** www.hainle.com; mailing address: Box 650, Peachland, BC V0H 1X0), was the first Okanagan winery to produce ice wine. May to October, the wine shop is open Tuesday to Sunday 10am to 5pm; November to April, it's open for tastings Thursday to Sunday noon to 5pm. **Amphora,** the winery's bistro, is open Tuesday to Sunday noon to 3pm.

North of Penticton along Highway 97 is another wine-producing area, where you'll find the **Sumac Ridge Estate Winery,** 17403 Hwy. 97 (☎ **250/494-0451;** www. sumacridge.com; mailing address: Box 307, Summerland, BC V0H 1Z0). May to mid-October, winery tours are daily 10am to 4pm on the hour. Besides operating a wine shop and tasting room, the winery features a fine dining room, the Cellar Door Bistro.

SPORTS & OUTDOOR ACTIVITIES

BIKING   The best **Okanagan Valley** off-road bike trail is the old **Kettle Valley** railway route. The tracks and ties have been removed, making way for some incredibly scenic biking. The **Myra Canyon** railway route between Kelowna and Penticton crosses over 18 trestle bridges, and passes through two tunnels were carved through the mountains. **Sun Country Cycle,** 533 Main St. (☎ **250/493-0686**), has bike rentals and lots of friendly advice. Guided biking tours are organized by **Silver Star Mountain Resort** (see "Skiing & Snowboarding" at the beginning of this chapter).

BOATING & WATER SPORTS   The Okanagan Valley's numerous local marinas offer full-service boat rentals. **Okanagan Boat Charters,** 291 Front St., Penticton (☎ 250/492-5099), rents houseboats with fully equipped kitchens that can accommodate up to 10 people. Prices for a weeklong rental begins at C$1,295 (US$864). The **Marina on Okanagan Lake,** 291 Front St., Penticton (☎ 250/ 492-2628), rents ski-boats, Tigersharks (similar to Jet-Skis or Sea-Doos), fishing boats, and tackle.

GOLF   The greens fees throughout the Okanagan Valley range from C$30 to C$85 (US$20 to US$57) and are a good value not only because of the beautiful locations but also for the quality of service you'll find at each club. Les Furber's **Gallagher's Canyon Golf and Country Club,** 4320 McCulloch Rd., Kelowna (☎ 250/861-4240), has an 18-hole course that features a hole overlooking the precipice of a gaping canyon and another that's perched on the brink of a ravine. It also has a nine-hole course, a midlength course, and a new double-ended learning center. Resting high on a wooded ridge between two lakes, Les Furber's **Predator Ridge,** 360 Commonage Rd., Vernon (☎ 250/542-3436), has hosted the BC Open Championship in recent years. The par-5 fourth hole can be played only over a huge mid-fairway lake; it's a challenge even for seasoned pros.

A-1 **Last Minute Golf Hotline** (☎ 800/684-6344 or 604/878-1833) can arrange a next-day tee time at local golf courses. Savings can be as much as 40% on next-day, last-minute tee times. No membership is necessary. Call between 3 and 9pm for the next day or before noon for the same day.

SKIING Cross-country and powder skiing are the Okanagan Valley's main winter attractions. Intermediate and expert downhill skiers frequent the **Apex Resort,** Green Mountain Road, Penticton (☎ 800/387-2739, 250/492-2880, 250/292-8111, or 250/492-2929, ext. 2000 for snow report), where 56 runs are serviced by one quad chair, one triple chair, one T-bar, and one beginner tow/platter. The 52km (32 miles) of cross-country ski trails are well marked and well groomed, offering both flat stretches and hilly ascents. Facilities include an ice rink, snow golf, sleigh rides, casino nights, and racing competitions.

Only a 15-minute drive from Westbank, **Crystal Mountain Resorts Ltd.** (☎ 250/768-5189, or 250/768-3753 for snow report; mailing address: Box 26044, Westbank, BC V4T 2J9), has a range of ski programs for all types of skiers, specializing in clinics for children, women, and seniors. This friendly family-oriented resort lets you ski free on your birthday as one of its regular promotions. The resort's 20 runs are 80% intermediate-to-novice grade and are serviced by one double chair and two T-bars. The runs are equipped for day and night skiing. There's also a half pipe for snowboarders. Lift tickets start at C$32 (US$21) adults, C$26 (US$17) youths, and C$20 (US$13) juniors. Half-day and nighttime discounts are available.

If you yearn for hip-deep dry powder, then head to **Big White Ski Resort,** Parkinson Way, Kelowna (☎ 250/765-3101, or 250/765-SNOW for snow report, or 250/765-8888 for lodge reservations). The resort spreads over a broad mountain, featuring long, wide runs. Skiers cruise open bowls and tree-lined glades. There's an annual average of 18 feet of fluffy powder, so it's no wonder the resort's 57 runs are so popular. There are three high-speed quad chairs, one fixed-grip quad, one triple quad, one double chair, one T-bar, one beginner tow, and one platter lift. The resort also offers more than 25 miles of groomed cross-country ski trails, a recreational racing program, and night skiing 5 nights a week.

WHERE TO STAY

The **BC Provincial Parks Service/Okanagan District** (☎ 250/494-6500) maintains a number of provincial campgrounds in this area. They're open April to October, and fees are C$12 to C$19 (US$8 to US$13) per night. There are 41 campsites at **Haynes Point Provincial Park** in Osoyoos, which has flush toilets, a boat launch, and visitor programs. This campground is popular with naturalists interested in hiking the "pocket desert." **Vaseaux Lake Provincial Park,** near Okanagan Falls, offers 12 campsites and great wildlife-viewing opportunities; deer, antelope, and even a number of California bighorn sheep live in the surrounding hills. And **Okanagan Lake**

Provincial Park has 168 campsites nestled amid 10,000 imported trees. Facilities include free hot showers, flush toilets, a sani-station, and a boat launch.

In Penticton

The Penticton Lakeside Resort. 21 West Lakeshore Dr., Penticton, BC V2A 7M5. ☎ **800/663-9400** or 250/493-8221. Fax 250/493-0607. www.rpbhotels.com. E-mail lakeside@rpbhotels.com. 204 units. A/C TV TEL. C$155 (US$103) double; C$159–C$205 (US$106–US$137) suite. Free parking. Pets C$10 (US$7) extra. AE, CB, DC, DISC, MC, V. Follow the signs to Main St. when you arrive in town. Lakeshore Dr. is at the north end of Main St.

On the water's edge, the Penticton Lakeside Resort has its own stretch of sandy Lake Okanagan beachfront where you can sunbathe or stroll along the adjacent pier. This year-round resort is also close to great golf courses and the Apex Mountain ski area. The deluxe suites feature Jacuzzis, and the lakeside rooms are highly recommended for their view.

Dining: The menus at the fully licensed Okanagan Surf N' Turf Company Restaurant and the Barking Parrot Bar & Patio feature locally grown ingredients.

Amenities: Indoor pool, sauna, whirlpool, fitness center with complete Nautilus circuit, tennis courts, hair salon, gift shop, volleyball, running trails.

In Kelowna

The Grand Okanagan Lakefront Resort & Conference Centre. 1310 Water St., Kelowna, BC V1Y 9P3. ☎ **800/465-4651** or 250/763-4500. Fax 250/763-4565. www.grandokanagan.com. E-mail sales@grandokanagan.com. 325 units. A/C TV TEL. C$199–C$265 (US$133–US$177) double; C$240–C$420 (US$160–US$280) suite/condo. Extra person C$15 (US$10). Off-season discounts. AE, DC, MC, V. Free parking. On Hwy. 97, cross the Lake Okanagan Bridge. At the first set of lights, turn left onto Abbott St. At the second set of lights turn onto Water St.

This elegant lakeshore resort is on 25 acres of beach and parkland, and the atmosphere is reminiscent of Miami Beach in the 1920s. The atrium lobby of the modern hotel has a fountain with a sculpted dolphin as its centerpiece. The rooms, suites, and condos (with kitchens) are decorated in salmon, sea blue, and shell white and exude a relaxed yet elegant atmosphere. It's an ideal location for those who want to feel pampered.

Dining/Diversions: The Dolphins Restaurant and Vines cocktail lounge overlook the resort's private marina.

Amenities: Heated outdoor pool, salon, shops, fitness center, motorized swans and kid-sized boats in protected waterway.

Lake Okanagan Resort. 2751 Westside Rd., Kelowna, BC V1Z 3T1. ☎ **800/663-3273** or 250/769-3511. Fax 250/769-6665. www.lakeokanagan.com. 140 units. A/C TV TEL. C$160–C$215 (US$107–US$145) 1-bedroom suite, C$325 (US$219) 3-bedroom suite. Off-season discounts and packages available. Free parking. AE, MC, V. Drive 18km (11 miles) up Westside Rd., which overlooks the lake.

The long, winding coastline road leading to this secluded hideaway is a sports-car driver's dream come true. And there are many more activities to keep you interested once you arrive. Located on 300 acres of Okanagan Lake's hilly western shore, the resort offers one-bedroom units with kitchenettes, as well as suites and rooms. Because the resort is built on a hillside, every room has a terrific view of the lake.

Dining/Diversions: You'll find a patio cafe, two elegant restaurants, and a poolside bar.

Facilities: Three heated outdoor pools, indoor and outdoor Jacuzzis, cabana, fitness center, par-3 golf course, seven tennis courts (including three nighttime courts), horseback riding, mountain-bike and hiking trails, sandy private beach, marina, nature program, a summer kids' camp.

WHERE TO DINE
IN KELOWNA

✪ **de Montreuil.** 368 Bernard Ave. ☎ **250/860-5508.** Reservations recommended. Main courses C$18–C$24 (US$12–US$16). AE, MC, V. Mon–Fri 11am–10pm, Sat–Sun 5–11pm. CONTEMPORARY CANADIAN.

This low-key, high-performance restaurant produces the Okanagan's most exciting and delicious cooking. The menu is simply divided into four sections: Appetizers, Bowls, Salads, and Main Plates. Of course you can order à la carte, or better yet follow the simple pricing where any two-course meal (main course plus an appetizer, a salad, or a bowl of soup) is C$28 (US$19) and a three-course meal is C$34 (US$23). The menu changes weekly, but expect everything to be fresh and bright tasting yet filled with hearty earthiness.

IN & AROUND PENTICTON

The Historic 1912 Restaurant. Lakehill Rd., Kaleden. ☎ **250/497-6868.** Reservations recommended. Main courses C$19–C$35 (US$13–US$23). MC, V. Tues–Sun 5:30–10pm. Drive 5 min. south of Penticton on Hwy. 97. Take the 2nd left after the Okanagan Game Farm onto Lakehill Rd. CONTINENTAL.

This is a quintessential romantic hideaway. At the end of a long, winding road, the lakeside restaurant is in a stone building that served as a general store when it was built in 1912. The decor is Victorian, featuring dark-wood paneling, white linens, and soft lights. The menu offers seafood specialties like lemon vodka prawns, pasta dishes, steaks, lamb, and chocolaty desserts.

Three Mile House. 1507 Naramata Rd., Penticton. ☎ **250/492-5152.** Reservations recommended. Main courses C$13–C$24 (US$9–US$16). AE, MC, V. Tues–Sun 6–11pm. FRENCH.

Hosts George and June McLeod have created a haven for lovers of fine country-style French dishes like pâté de maison and grilled tenderloins of filet mignon. And they've added a few local touches as well, creating combinations like oysters Florentine, Okanagan fruit soup, halibut steak au poivre, wild-boar cutlets in red-wine sauce, and roast pheasant. Save room for the signature Belgian chocolate mousse.

The Yukon, the Northwest Territories & Nunavut: The Great Northern Wilderness

by Bill McRae

The **Far North** of Canada is one of North America's last great wilderness areas. The Yukon, the Northwest Territories, Nunavut, and the far north of British Columbia are home to the native Inuit and northern Indian tribes like the Dene, vast herds of wildlife, and thousands of square miles of tundra and stunted subarctic forest. For centuries, names like the Klondike, Hudson's Bay, and the Northwest Passage have had the power to conjure up powerful images. For an area so little visited and so distant, the North has long played an integral role in the history and imagination of the Western world.

Yet the North is changing before our eyes, creating a whole pattern of paradoxes. The Arctic is a hotbed of mineral, oil, gas, and diamond exploration. Jobs and schools have brought Inuit and Indian natives from the hunting camps to town, where they live in prefabs instead of igloos and drive trucks and snowmobiles out to their trap lines. But the money they spend in supermarkets is earned by ancestral hunting skills, and their lifestyle remains based on the pursuit of migrating game animals and marine creatures.

The **native Canadians** (Indians) and the **Inuit** make up the majority of the North's population, particularly when you add the **Métis** offspring of white and native-Canadian couples. All the natives were originally nomadic, covering enormous distances in pursuit of migrating game animals. Today nearly all First Nation people, as native Canadians are often called, have permanent homes in settlements, but many of them spend part of the year in remote tent camps hunting, fishing, and trapping. And though nobody lives in igloos anymore, these snow houses are still built as temporary shelters when the occasion arises.

Survival is the key word for the native Canadians. They learned to survive in conditions unimaginably harsh for southern societies, by means of skills that become more wondrous the better you know them. The early white explorers soon learned that in order to stay alive, they had to copy those skills as best they could. Those who refused to "go native" rarely made it back.

The first white man known to have penetrated the region was **Martin Frobisher.** His account of meeting the Inuit, written 400 years ago, is the earliest on record. About the same time, European whalers, hunting whales for their oil, were occasionally forced ashore by storms or shipwrecks and depended on Inuit hospitality for survival. This almost-legendary hospitality, extended to any stranger who came to them, remains an outstanding characteristic of the Inuit. Whites began to move into the Canadian Arctic in greater number during the "fur rush" of the late 18th century. In the wake of the fur hunters and traders came Roman Catholic and Anglican missionaries, who built churches and opened schools.

For most of its recorded history, the Far North was governed from afar, first by Great Britain, then by the Hudson's Bay Company, and from 1867 by the new Canadian government in Ottawa. At that time the Territories included all the Yukon, Saskatchewan, Alberta, and huge parts of other provinces. Then, in 1896, **gold** was discovered on Bonanza Creek in the Klondike. Tens of thousands of people descended in a matter of months, giving birth to Dawson City, Whitehorse, and a dozen other tent communities that went bust along with the gold veins. The Yukon gold rush was the greatest in history; more than C$500,000 (US$333,500) in gold was washed out of the gravel banks along the Klondike before industrial mining moved in. With its new wealth and population, the Yukon split off from the rest of the Northwest Territories in 1898.

The rest of the Northwest Territories didn't receive its own elected government until 1967, when the center of government was moved from Ottawa to Yellowknife and a representative assembly was elected. However, with 3.4 million km^2 (1.3 million sq. miles), the territory has proved an unwieldy piece of real estate to govern, and the process of self-determination continues. In 1999, the eastern section of the Northwest Territories became a separate and autonomous territory, known as **Nunavut** (meaning "our land"). The rump Northwest Territories, which roughly speaking consists of the drainage of the Mackenzie River, including Yellowknife, and the Arctic coast west of Coppermine, has retained the Northwest Territory name.

1 Exploring the North

The Arctic isn't like any other place. That observation may seem elementary, but even a well-prepared first-timer will experience many things here to startle—and perhaps offend—the senses.

No matter where you start from, the Arctic is a long way away. By far the easiest way to get there is by plane. Whitehorse, Yellowknife, and Iqaluit all have an airport with daily service from major Canadian cities. Each of these towns is a center for a network of smaller airlines with regularly scheduled flights to yet smaller communities; here you'll also find charter services to take you to incredibly out-of-the-way destinations.

VISITOR INFORMATION

For information, write **Tourism Yukon**, P.O. Box 2703, Whitehorse, YT Y1A 2C6 (☎ **867/667-5340;** fax 867/667-3546; www.touryukon.com; e-mail info@ touryukon.com). Be sure to ask for a copy of the official vacation guide *Canada's Yukon.*

For the Northwest Territories, contact **NWT Arctic Tourism**, P.O. Box 1320, Yellowknife, NT X1A 2L9 (☎ **800/661-0788** or 867/873-7200; fax 867/873-0294; www.nwttravel.nt.ca). Ask for the free map of the province (it's almost impossible to find a map of the Territories elsewhere) and *The Explorers' Guide,* with full listings of accommodations and outfitters.

For Nunavut and Baffin Island, contact **Nunavut Tourism**, P.O. Box 1450, Iqaluit, NT X0A 0H0 (☎ **800/491-7910** or 867/979-6551; www.nunanet.com/~nunatour; e-mail nunatour@nunanet.com). Ask for the *Arctic Traveller,* with full listings of destinations, accommodations, and outfitters.

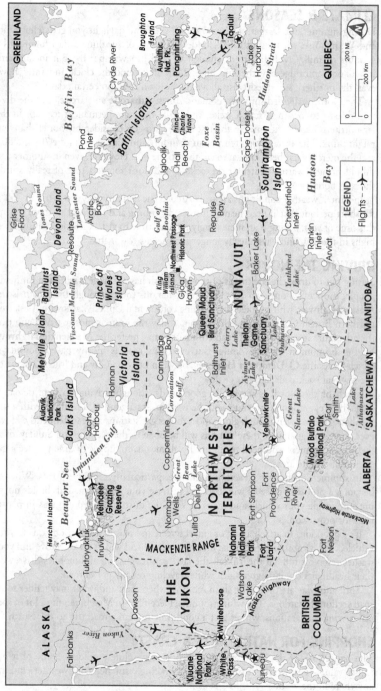

CLIMATE & SEASONS

During summer, the farther north you travel, the more daylight you get. Yellowknife and Whitehorse, in the south, bask under 20 hours of sunshine a day, followed by 4 hours of milky twilight bright enough to read a newspaper by. But in northern Inuvik or Cambridge Bay, the sun shines 24 hours around the clock. In winter, however, the northern sun doesn't rise above the horizon at all on certain days.

The North is divided into two climatic zones: **subarctic** and **arctic,** and the division doesn't follow the Arctic Circle. And while there are permanent ice caps in the far-northern islands, summer in the rest of the land gets considerably hotter than you might think. The average high temperatures in July and August are in the 70s and 80s, and the mercury has been known to climb into the 90s. However, even in summer you should bring a warm sweater or ski jacket—and don't forget a pair of really sturdy shoes or boots.

In winter, weather conditions are truly Arctic. The mercury may dip as low as –60°F for short periods. You'll need heavily insulated clothing and footwear to travel during this time of year. Spring is an increasingly popular time to visit, with clear sunny skies, highs in the 20s, and days already longer than seems reasonable.

DRIVING THE NORTH

Setting out to drive the backroads of the Far North has a strange fascination for many people, most of whom own RVs. The most famous route through the North is the **Alaska Highway,** which linked the wartime continental United States with Alaska via northern British Columbia and the Yukon. Today the route is mostly paved and isn't the adventure it once was. Off-road enthusiasts may prefer the **Mackenzie Highway,** linking Edmonton to Yellowknife. But even this road is mostly paved nowadays, which leaves the ✪ **Dempster Highway,** between Dawson City and Inuvik, as one of the few real backroads left.

Much of the North is served by good roads, though driving up here demands different preparations than you might be used to. It's a good idea to travel with a full 5-gallon gas can, even though along most routes gas stations appear frequently. However, there's no guarantee these stations will be open in the evenings, on Sunday, or at the precise moment you need to fill up. By all means, fill up every time you see a gas station in remote areas.

In summer, dust can be a serious nuisance, particularly on gravel roads. When it becomes a problem, close all windows and turn on your heater fan. This builds up air pressure inside your vehicle and helps to keep the dust out. Keep cameras in plastic bags for protection.

It's a good idea to attach a bug or gravel screen and plastic headlight guards to your vehicle. And it's absolutely essential that your windshield wipers are operative and your washer reservoir full. In the Yukon, the law requires that all automobiles drive with their headlights on; it's a good idea while traveling on any gravel road.

April and May are the spring slush months, when mud and water may render some road sections hazardous. The winter months, December to March, require a lot of special driving preparations; winter isn't a good time to plan a road trip to the North.

SHOPPING FOR NATIVE ARTS & CRAFTS

The handiwork of the Dene and Inuit people is absolutely unique. Some of it has utility value—you won't get finer, more painstakingly stitched cold-weather clothing anywhere in the world.

The Baffin Island communities are famous worldwide for their **stone, bone,** and **ivory carvings.** Inuit artists also produce noted weavings, prints, and etchings with native themes; clothing articles made of sealskin are also common. The Dene produce caribou-skin moccasins and clothing, often with beaded decoration.

Most arts-and-crafts articles are handled through community cooperatives, thus avoiding the cut of the middleman. Official documentation will guarantee that a piece is a genuine native-Canadian object. Don't hesitate to ask retailers where a particular object comes from, what it's made of, and who made it. They'll be glad to tell you and frequently will point out where the artist lives and works. In the eastern Arctic particularly, artists will often approach tourists in the streets or in bars and restaurants, seeking to sell their goods. While these articles may lack the official paperwork, the price is often right; use your judgment when deciding to buy.

Before investing in native art, make sure you know what the **import restrictions** are in your home country. In many countries, it's illegal to bring in articles containing parts of marine mammals (this includes walrus or narwhal ivory, as well as whale bones or polar-bear fur). Sealskin products are commonly prohibited. Consult a customs office to find out what restrictions are in place.

FOOD, DRINK & ACCOMMODATIONS

Northerners traditionally lived off the land by hunting and fishing (many still do), and Arctic specialties have now worked their way onto many fine dining menus. **Caribou** and **musk ox** appear on almost all menus in the North and offer a different taste and texture for meat eaters. Good caribou, sometimes dressed in sauces made from local berries (wild blueberries or Saskatoonberries) tastes like mild venison and is usually cheaper than beef or lamb in the North. Musk ox is rather stronger tasting, with a chewy texture, and is often served with wild mushrooms. **Arctic char** is a mild pink-fleshed fish, rather like salmon but coarser grained and less oily. You won't find the mainstays of the Inuit diet—seal and whale meat—on most restaurant menus, but in outlying communities you won't have to look hard to find someone able to feed you some *muktuk* (seal meat). **Bannocks,** a type of baking-powder biscuit, and **Eskimo doughnuts,** a cousin of Indian fry bread, are popular snacks to feed tourists. You may want to keep your distance from what's called **Eskimo ice cream,** a concoction made of whipped whale fat.

Vegetarians aren't going to find much to eat in the North. The traditional Arctic diet doesn't include much in the way of fruits or vegetables, and green stuff that's been air-freighted in is pretty sad-looking by the time it reaches the table. *Bring your own dietary supplements if you have a restricted diet.*

No matter what you eat in the North, it's going to be expensive. In towns like Yellowknife, Inuvik, and Iqaluit, a normal entree at a decent hotel restaurant will cost at least C$25 (US$17); at outlying villages, where hotels offer full board, a sandwich with fries will run C$20 (US$13). Chances are excellent that, for the money, your food will be very pedestrian in quality. In most towns, the grocery-store chain The Northern shelters a few fast-food outlets, usually the only other dining option.

Alcohol is banned or highly restricted in most native communities. Some towns are completely dry: no one, not even visitors in the privacy of their hotel rooms, is allowed to possess or consume alcohol. In some locales, RCMP officers will check the baggage of incoming travelers and confiscate alcohol. In other communities, alcohol is legal but regulated to such a degree the casual visitor will find it impossible to get hold of a drink. In other communities, alcohol is available in hotel bars or restaurants but not in stores (or even by room service). Alcohol is a major social problem in the North, so by all means respect the local laws regulating alcohol consumption.

Accommodations are the most expensive day-to-day outlay in the North. Almost every community, no matter how small, will have a hotel, but prices are very high. You

---

Warning: Get Thee to an Outfitter

Outdoor enthusiasts in many parts of the world can simply arrive at a destination and put together a recreational trip when they get there. That isn't the case in the North. If you want to get out onto the land, the water, or the glacier, you'll need to have the assistance of an outfitter or a local tour provider. There are no roads to speak of here, so you'll need help simply to get wherever you're going; this usually involves a boat or an airplane trip. Sports-equipment rental is all but unheard of; and it's very foolish to head out into the wilds (which start at the edge of the village) without the advice and guidance of someone who knows the terrain, weather, and other general conditions. For all these reasons—and for the entree you'll get into the community—you should hire an outfitter. You'll end up saving money, time, and frustration.

---

can save some money with B&Bs or homestays, which also have the advantage of introducing you to the locals.

THE GREAT OUTDOORS

SEASONAL TRAVEL   Hiking and naturalist trips are popular in late July, August, and early September. The ice is off the ocean, allowing access by boat to otherwise-remote areas. Auyuittuq National Park, with its famed long-distance hiking and rock climbing, is popular with experienced recreationalists. Float trips on the Soper River in Katannilik Park are popular with those seeking adventures that are a bit softer. Naturalist-led hikes out onto the tundra make great day trips. The South Nahanni River, in Nahanni National Park, is popular for weeklong raft or canoe trips below massive 316-foot Virginia Falls.

While it may seem natural to plan a trip to the Arctic in summer, the Far North is a year-round destination. Late-winter dogsledding trips out into the frozen wilderness are popular with adventurous souls. In May and June from Pond Inlet, dogsled or snow-machine trips visit the edge of the ice floe, where wildlife viewing is superb. And in the dead of winter, there are the 24-hour darkness and the northern lights, which lure people north to have a look.

MOSQUITOES, DEERFLIES & OTHER CRITTERS   During summer especially, two of the most commonly heard sounds in the North are the rhythmic buzzing of winged biting insects and the cursing of their human victims. **Insect repellent** is a necessity, as is having a place you can get away from the mosquitoes for a while. Some hikers wear expedition hats or head nets to ward off the worst attacks. Mosquitoes can go through light fabric, which is why it's better to wear sturdy clothes even on the hottest days. Wasps, hornets, and other stinging insects are common. If you're allergic, be ready with your serum.

CANOEING & DOGSLEDDING   If you want to see the land as early explorers and natives did, try exploring the North via these two traditional methods. The following outfitters usually offer recreation in more than one part of the North or different recreational pursuits depending on the season.

Canoeing   The early French-Canadian trappers, or *voyageurs,* explored the North—particularly the Yukon—by canoe, and outfitters now offer multiday expeditions down the region's wide powerful rivers. A good place to go for advice and a wide range of guided tours on Northwest Territory rivers is the **Canadian Recreational Canoeing Association,** P.O. Box 398, 446 Main St. W., Merrickville, ON K0G 1N0

(☎ **888/252-6292** or 613/269-2910; fax 613/269-2908; www.crca.ca; e-mail staff@ crca.ca). **Kanoe People,** P.O. Box 5152, Whitehorse, YT Y1A 4S3 (☎ **867/ 668-4899;** fax 867/668-4891; www.kanoe.yk.net; e mail kanoe@yknet.yk.ca), offers a number of guided canoe trips down several of the Yukon's most historic rivers, past mining ghost towns and native-Canadian villages. Trips are offered on the Teslin, Yukon, and Big Salmon rivers and range from 7 days at C$1,279 (US$853) to 8 days at C$1,469 (US$980). Bring your own sleeping bag; everything else, like transportation from Whitehorse, is included.

In southern Baffin Island, the Soper River, flowing past innumerable waterfalls in Katannilik Park, is the most famous canoeing river. **NorthWinds,** P.O. Box 849, Iqaluit, NT X0A 0H0 (☎ **867/979-0551;** fax 867/979-0573; www. northwinds-arctic.com), offers 8-day trips down the beautiful Soper—gentle enough for family groups—starting at C$2,200 (US$1,467).

Dogsledding An even more indigenous mode of transport in the north is travel by dogsled. While few people run dogs as their sole means of getting around any longer, the sport of dogsledding is hugely popular, and dogsledding trips to otherwise-snowbound backcountry destinations make a great early-spring adventure. On Baffin Island, **NorthWinds** (see above) offers a variety of dogsled trips, ranging from day trips to 5-day expeditions, costing C$2,500 (US$1,668), out to see the northern lights; you'll also get a chance to learn how to run the dogs!

In the Yukon, **Michie Creek Mushing,** P.O. Box 10104, Whitehorse, YT Y1A 7A1 (☎ **867/333-1364;** fax 867/668-2633; www.michiemushing.com), offers 6-day guided backcountry trips out into the wilderness, where you, your hosts, and the sled team stay in old trappers' cabins. Six-day trips are available for C$2,000 (US$1,334).

WILDLIFE VIEWING It's easy to confuse **caribou** with reindeer because the two species look very much alike. Actually, caribou are wild and still travel in huge migrating herds stretching to the horizon, sometimes numbering 100,000 or more. They form the major food and clothing supply for many of the native people, whose lives are cycled around the movements of caribou herds.

The mighty **musk ox** is indigenous to the Arctic. About 12,000 of them live on the northern islands—immense and prehistoric looking, the bulls weigh up to 1,300 pounds. They appear even larger because they carry a mountain of shaggy hair. Underneath the coarse outer coat, musk oxen have a silky-soft layer of underwool, called *qiviut* in Inuit. One pound of qiviut can be spun into a 40-strand thread 25 miles long! As light as it is soft, a sweater made from the stuff will keep its wearer warm in subzero weather. And it doesn't shrink when wet. Qiviut is extremely expensive: Once spun, it sells for C$70 (US$47) an ounce.

The monarch of the Arctic, the **polar bear** roams the coast and the shores of Hudson Bay; you'll have to travel quite a way over mighty tough country to see one in its habitat. Weighing up to 1,450 pounds, they're the largest predators in North America. **Grizzly bears** are found in the boreal forests and river basins. Both animals are very dangerous; if you encounter them, give them a wide berth. The North is full of other animals much easier to observe than the bears. In the wooded regions, you'll come across **wolves** and **wolverines** (harmless to humans, despite the legends about them), **mink, lynx, otter, ptarmigan,** and **beaver.** The sleek and beautiful white or brown **Arctic foxes** live in ice regions as well as beneath the tree line and near settlements.

Mid-July to late August, **seals, walruses, narwhals,** and **bowhead** and **beluga whales** are in their breeding grounds off the coast of Baffin Island and in Hudson Bay. And in the endless skies above there are **eagles, hawks, huge owls, razor-billed auks,** and **ivory gulls.**

2 The Alaska Highway: On to the Last Frontier

Constructed as a military freight road during World War II to link Alaska to the Lower 48, the **Alaska Highway** (a.k.a. the Alcan Highway) is now a popular tourist route to the Last Frontier. Now as much a phenomenon as a road, it has become something of a pilgrimage route. The vast majority of people who make the trip are recent retirees, who take their newly purchased RVs and head up north—it's a rite of passage.

Strictly speaking, the Alaska Highway starts at the Mile 1 marker in **Dawson Creek,** on the eastern edge of British Columbia, and travels northwest for 2,452km (1,635 miles) to **Fairbanks, Alaska,** passing through the Yukon along the way. Even a decade ago, much of the talk of the Alaska Highway had to do with conditions of the road itself: where the really torn-up sections were, making it through soupy roads during freak rain and snowstorms, and how to make it between far-flung gas pumps. However, for the road's 50th anniversary in 1992, the final stretches were paved.

You should consider several things before setting out to drive this road. First, it's a very *long* road. Popular wisdom states that if you drive straight out, it's a 3-day drive between Fairbanks and Dawson Creek. If you're in that big of a hurry to get to Fairbanks, consider flying: Much of the road is winding, slow-moving RV traffic is heavy, and a considerable amount of the road is under reconstruction every summer. If you try to keep yourself to a 3-day schedule, you're going to be miserable.

Summer is the only opportunity to upgrade or repair the road, so construction crews really go to it; depend on lengthy delays and some very rugged detours. Visitor centers along the way get faxes of daily construction schedules and conditions. Stop and ask about any delays or call ☎ 867/667-5893 for **24-hour highway information.**

While gasoline availability isn't the problem it once was, there are a couple of things to remember. Gas prices are high, about a third higher than in Edmonton or Calgary. While there's gasoline at most of the little communities that appear on the provincial road map, most close early in the evening, and some outfits are less than friendly. There are 24-hour gas stations and plenty of motel rooms at Dawson City, Fort St. John, Fort Nelson, Watson Lake, and Whitehorse.

Try to be patient when driving the Alaska Highway. During the high season, the entire route is one long caravan of RVs. Many people have their car in tow, a boat on the roof, and several bikes chained to the spare tire. Thus encumbered, they lumber up the highway at top speeds of 70kmph (43 m.p.h.).

DRIVING THE ALASKA HIGHWAY

The route begins (or ends) at **Dawson Creek** in British Columbia and before long crosses the Peace River and passes through **Fort St. John.** There are ample tourist facilities along this stretch of the highway. It continues north, parallel to the Rockies. The forests thin, with pointy spruce trees replacing pine and fir trees. Wildlife viewing is good; you can often see moose from the road.

From Fort St. John to **Fort Nelson,** there are gas stations and cafes every 65km to 81km (40 to 50 miles), though lodging options are pretty dubious. At Fort Nelson, the Alaska Highway turns west and heads into the Canadian Rockies; from here too, graveled Highway 7 continues north to Fort Liard and Fort Simpson, the gateway to **Nahanni National Park.** Fort Nelson is thick with motels and gas stations; hours from any other major service center, this is a good place to spend the night.

The road through the Rockies is mostly narrow and winding; you can pretty much depend on finding a construction crew working along this stretch. The Rockies are relatively modest mountains in this area, not as rugged or scenic as they are farther south in Jasper Park. Once over the Continental Divide, the Alaska Highway follows tributaries of the Liard River through **Stone Mountain Provincial Park** and **Muncho Lake Provincial Park.** Attractive rustic lodges and cabin resorts are scattered along the road for accommodations; this is also a good place to find a campsite.

At the town of **Liard River,** be sure to stop and stretch your legs or go for a soak at **Liard Hot Springs.** The provincial parks department maintains two nice soaking pools in the deep forest; the boardwalk out into the mineral water marsh is pleasant even if you don't have time for a dip. As you get closer to **Watson Lake** in the Yukon, you'll notice that mom-and-pop gas stations along the road will advertise they have cheaper gas than in Watson Lake. Believe them and fill up: Watson Lake is an unappealing town whose extortionately priced gasoline is probably its only memorable feature. If you don't plan your trip well, you may end up spending the night here.

The long road between Watson Lake and **Whitehorse** travels through rolling hills and forest to **Teslin and Atlin lakes,** where the landscape becomes more mountainous and the gray clouds of the Gulf of Alaska's weather systems hang menacingly in the western horizon. Whitehorse is the largest town along the route of the Alaska Highway, and unless you're in a great hurry, plan to spend at least a day here. You'll want to wash the dust off the car at the very least and eat a decent meal before another day of driving on the way to Alaska.

Hope for good weather as you leave Whitehorse, since the trip past **Kluane National Park** is one of the most beautiful parts of the entire route. The two highest peaks of Canada straddle the horizon, while glaciers push down mountain valleys. The road edges by lovely Kluane Lake before passing Beaver Creek and crossing over into Alaska. From the border crossing to Fairbanks is another 481km (298 miles).

A number of guidebooks deal exhaustively with driving the Alaska Highway; particularly good is the mile-by-mile classic, the annual *Alaska Milepost.*

3 Whitehorse: Capital of the Yukon

Once part of the Northwest Territories, the Yukon is now a separate territory bordering on British Columbia in the south and Alaska in the west (when locals refer to the United States, they nearly always mean Alaska). Compared with the old Northwest Territories, it's a mere midget in size, but with 518,000km^2 (200,000 sq. miles), it's immense by most other standards.

The entire territory has a population of only 41,000—over half of them living in **Whitehorse.** The capital of the Yukon is a late arrival on the scene. It was established only in the spring of 1900, fully 2 years after the stampeders had swarmed into Dawson City. But Whitehorse, on the banks of the Yukon River, is the logical hub of the Territory, and it became the capital in 1953 after Dawson fizzled out along with the gold.

ESSENTIALS

GETTING THERE   The airport, on a rise above the city, is served by **Canadian Airlines** (☎ (☎ 800/426-7000; www.cdnair.ca) from Vancouver; flights range from C$741 to C$1,600 (US$494 to US$1,067) round-trip. **Air North** (☎ 867/668-2228; www.airnorth.yk.net) flies from Juneau to Whitehorse for C$174 to C$284 (US$116 to US$189) round-trip; their Klondike Explorer Pass (good for 21 days of travel) allows you to travel to many Yukon and Alaska destinations for C$429 (US$286). **Cab fare** to downtown is around C$8 (US$5). Whitehorse is 458km (284 miles) southeast of Beaver Creek (the Alaskan border).

VISITOR INFORMATION   Your first stop should be the **Whitehorse Visitor Reception,** 2nd and Hanson streets (☎ 867/667-3084). The third week in May to

Labour Day, the center is open daily 8am to 8pm; winter hours are Monday to Friday 9am to 4:30pm.

GETTING AROUND　　Public transit is handled by **Whitehorse Transit** (☎ 867/668-7433). Car rental is available from **Tilden** (☎ 867/668-6872), **Avis** (☎ 867/667-2847), **Budget** (☎ 867/667-6200), and **Norcan** (☎ 867/668-2137). If you need a taxi, try **Yellow Cabs** at ☎ 867/668-4811.

SPECIAL EVENTS　　February is a happening month in Whitehorse. One of the top dogsled races in North America, the **Yukon Quest** begins in Whitehorse and runs to Fairbanks. The town is filled with hundreds of yapping dogs and avid mushers, eager to vie for the C$100,000 (US$66,700) top prize. Making even more noise is the **Frostbite Music Festival,** which attracts musicians and entertainers from across Canada. Immediately afterward is the **Yukon Sourdough Rendezvous,** a midwinter festival commemorating the days of the gold rush with various old-fashioned competitions, like dog pulls, fiddling and costume contests, and a "mad trapper" competition.

EXPLORING WHITEHORSE

✪ **Yukon Transportation Museum.** Adjacent to the Yukon Visitor Centre, Mile 915 on the Alaska Hwy. ☎ **867/668-4792.** Admission C$4.25 (US$2.85) adults, C$3.25 (US$2.15) seniors/students, C$2 (US$1.35) children 5 and older, C$9 (US$6) families; children under 5 free. Mid-May to Aug daily 10am–7pm; Sept to early May daily noon–4pm.

In a remote area like the Yukon, the history of white settlement is essentially the story of its transportation systems. In this fascinating museum, the development of travel, from dogsled to railway to bush plane and through the building of the Alaska Highway, is presented. You'll come away with a new appreciation of what it was to travel to the Yukon in the past. The exhibits and vintage photos on travel by dogsled are especially interesting. There's a replica of the historic aircraft *Queen of the Yukon,* the sister aircraft of *The Spirit of St. Louis,* plus a film on the building of the White Pass Railroad from Skagway to Whitehorse.

SS *Klondike.* Anchored at the Robert Campbell Bridge. ☎ **867/667-3910.** Admission C$3.50 (US$2.35) adults, C$2.50 (US$1.65) seniors, C$2 (US$1.35) students, C$8 (US$5) families. Tours on the half hour: May 15–June 15 daily 9am–6pm; June 16–Aug 15 daily 9am–7pm.

The largest of the 250 riverboats that chugged up and down the Yukon River between 1866 and 1955, the *Klondike* is now permanently dry-docked beside the river. The boat has been restored to its 1940s glory.

✪ **MacBride Museum.** First Ave. at Wood St. ☎ **867/667-2709.** Admission C$4 (US$2.65) adults, C$3.50 (US$2.35) seniors, C$2.50 (US$1.65) students, C$2 (US$1.35) children 6–12, C$9 (US$6) families; children under 6 free. Daily 10am–6pm.

The MacBride covers half a city block, with four galleries, open-air exhibits, and a gift shop. Within the museum compound you'll also find Sam McGee's Cabin (read Service's poem on the cremation of same) and the old Whitehorse Telegraph Office. The log-cabin museum is crammed with relics from the gold-rush era and has a large display of Yukon wildlife and minerals. It's interesting material, lovingly arranged by a nonprofit society.

Yukon Art Centre. Yukon Place at Yukon College, off Range Rd. N. ☎ **867/667-8575.** Admission by donation. Mon–Fri 9:30am–5pm, Sat–Sun 1–4pm.

The gallery at the Yukon Art Centre has changing exhibits that feature regional artists, photographers, and themes. The art center also houses a tearoom and a theater that functions as Whitehorse's performing-arts center.

Yukon Beringia Interpretive Centre. Adjacent to the Yukon Transportation Museum, Mile 915 on the Alaska Hwy. ☎ **867/667-8855.** www.touryukon.com. E-mail info@ touryukon.com. C$6 (US$4) adults, C$5 (US$3.35) seniors, C$4 (US$2.65) students. Late May to mid-Sept daily 8am–9pm.

During the last ice age, a land bridge joined Asia to Alaska and the Yukon. These lands, and the exposed Bering Sea floor, formed a subcontinent now known as Beringia. Bordered on all sides by glaciers, the region was home to woolly mammoths and other Pleistocene-era animals, as well as cave-dwelling humans. This new museum highlights the archaeological and paleontological past of this part of North America, with exhibits on the prehistoric ecosystem, skeletons and other remains of ancient life, multimedia displays, and films.

Old Log Church. Elliott St. at Third Ave. ☎ 867/668-2555. Admission C$2.50 (US$1.65) adults, C$2 (US$1.35) seniors, C$1 (US65¢) children, C$6 (US$4) families. Mon–Sat 9am–6pm, Sun noon–4pm.

When Whitehorse got its first resident priest in 1900, he lived and held services in a tent. By the next spring, the Old Log Church and rectory were built, and they're now the only buildings of that date in town still in use. The Old Log Church was once the Roman Catholic cathedral for the diocese—the only wooden cathedral in the world—and it now contains artifacts on the history of all the Yukon's churches. Mass is every Sunday at 10:30am. (On the next block over are two "log skyscrapers"—old two- and three-story log cabins used as apartments and offices.)

Takhini Hot Springs. On the Klondike Hwy., 27km (17 miles) north of Whitehorse. ☎ **867/633-2706.** Admission C$4.50 (US$3) adults, C$3.50 (US$2.35) seniors/students, C$3 (US$2) children. Daily 8am–10pm.

A swimming pool fed by natural hot springs and surrounded by rolling hills and hiking trails, the developed Takhini Hot Springs might be just what you need after days on the Alaska Highway. After swimming, you can refresh yourself at the coffee shop. Horseback riding is also available.

Whitehorse Rapids Dam. At the end of Nisutlin Dr., in suburban Riverdale. Free admission. Daily 8am–10pm.

The native chinook salmon that pass by Whitehorse are completing one of the longest fish migrations in the world, and to bypass the Whitehorse Rapids Dam, they climb the world's longest wooden fish ladder. Interpretive displays and an upper viewing deck show you the entire process by which the dam has ceased to be an obstruction to the salmon migration.

TOURS & EXCURSIONS

HISTORICAL WALKING TOURS   The **Yukon Historical and Museums Association,** Donnenworth House, 3126 Third Ave., behind the Chamber of Commerce Visitors Centre (☎ **867/667-4704**), offers Whitehorse Heritage Buildings Walking Tours in June, July, and August. Monday to Saturday, the 45-minute tours are at 9am, 11am, 1pm, and 3pm and cost C$2 (US$1.35); they pass many of the gold-rush–era structures and historic sites and are a good introduction to the town.

WILDLIFE TOURS   The **Yukon Wildlife Preserve** covers hundreds of acres of forests and meadows. Roaming freely throughout are bison, moose, musk ox, elk, snowy owls, and the rare peregrine falcon. Tours of the preserve depart daily at 10:30am and 6:30pm and cost C$18 (US$12) adults and C$9 (US$6) children. Book through **Gray Line,** 208G Steele St. (☎ **867/668-3225**).

RIVER CRUISES   The **MV** *Schwatka* is a river craft that cruises the Yukon River through the famous Miles Canyon. This stretch—once the most hazardous section of water in the Territory—is now dammed and tamed, though it still offers fascinating wilderness scenery. The cruise takes 2 hours, accompanied by narration telling the story of the old "wild river" times. Adults pay C$18 (US$12), children half price. For reservations, call ☎ 867/668-4716; the boat leaves 5km (3.1 miles) south of White-horse; follow the signs for Miles Canyon.

A more authentic river experience is offered by the *Emerald May,* a steel pontoon raft that closely duplicates (but this one is completely safe and motorized) the style of boat used by the original 98ers, the gold-rush prospectors who stormed through the Yukon on their way to the Klondike in 1898. Instead of shooting dangerous rapids, today's trips focus on wildlife viewing and historic sites. Excursions are offered by **Taste of 98 Tours** (☎ 867/633-4767) and leave daily from the log cabin on First Avenue, across from the MacBride Museum; tickets are C$50 (US$33) with a max-imum of 8 people per group for each 3-hour tour.

SHOPPING

The **Yukon Gallery,** 2093 Second Ave. (☎ 867/667-2391), is Whitehorse's best commercial visual-arts gallery, featuring a large show space devoted to Yukon and regional artists. There's an extensive display of paintings and prints, as well as some ceramics and Northern crafts, like moose-hair tufting. **Northern Images,** 311 Jarvis St. (☎ 867/668-5739), is the best gallery in the Yukon for native-Canadian art, in particular Inuit carvings and native masks. **Mac's Fireweed Books,** 203 Main St. (☎ 867/668-2434), is the best bookstore in town.

SPORTS & OUTDOOR ACTIVITIES

CANOEING   Many of these rivers were explored by French-Canadian *voyageurs* in canoes, and the Yukon's swift-flowing wide rivers still make for great canoe trips. In addition to their multiday expeditions (see "The Great Outdoors" above), **Kanoe People** (☎ 867/668-4899) offers 3-hour trips on the Yukon River for C$30 (US$20) per person; it also rents canoes and sea kayaks. For day rentals at C$25 (US$17) as well as a selection of easy day canoe trips, contact **Up North** (☎ 867/667-7905; www.upnorth.yk.ca), on the Yukon River across from the MacBride Museum. You can also rent a canoe for a day and shoot the once-harrowing 25-mile Miles Canyon—C$45 (US$30) pays for two shuttles and the canoe rental.

HIKING   The **Yukon Conservation Society,** 302 Hawkins St. (☎ 867/668-5678), offers free guided nature walks in the Whitehorse area. Hikes are given Monday to Friday, and on most days several destinations are offered (most walks are only a couple of hours long). Self-transport is necessary; bring comfortable shoes and insect repellent.

If you're looking for a nice hike on your own, cross the Second Avenue Bridge and follow the riverside path past the Whitehorse Dam and up to **Miles Canyon.** Here the Yukon River cuts a narrow passage through the underlying basalt. Though not deep, the canyon greatly constricts the river, forming rapids that were an object of dread to the greenhorn 98ers in their homemade boats. Three kilometers (1.9 miles) up the canyon, a footbridge crosses the canyon, leading to both the Miles Canyon Road (arrange a pickup here) and a series of footpaths on the opposite side of the canyon.

HORSEBACK RIDING   The **White Horse Riding Stable** (☎ 867/663-3086) is 8km (5 miles) south of Whitehorse, just before the Miles Canyon turnoff. Riding costs C$20 (US$13) per hour.

WHERE TO STAY

There are a great number of campgrounds in and around Whitehorse; they represent the best alternative for travelers watching their money.

Tenters will like the **Robert Service Campground,** South Access Road (☎ 867/668-3721), close to downtown and free of RVs. There are 48 unserviced tent sites, plus fire pits, washrooms, showers, and a picnic area. The rate is C$11 (US$7) per tent. Just north of Whitehorse on the Dawson City road are a number of lakeside territorial parks with campgrounds. At Lake Laberge Park, you can camp "on the marge of Lake Lebarge" with the creatively spelled verses of Robert Service filling your thoughts.

Most convenient for RVers is **Downtown Sourdough Park,** on Second Avenue north of Ogilvie (☎ 867/668-7938), with 146 campsites, most of them full-service, with showers, laundry, and a gift shop. Sites range from C$16 to C$19 (US$11 to US$13).

Whitehorse has more than 20 hotels, motels, and chalets in and around the downtown area, including a couple opposite the airport. This is far more than you'd expect in a place its size, and the standards come up to big-city levels in every respect.

EXPENSIVE

Edgewater Hotel. 101 Main St., Whitehorse, YT Y1A 2A7. ☎ **877/484-3334** or 867/667-2572. Fax 867/668-3014. www.edgewaterhotel.yk.ca. E-mail theedge@internorth.com. 30 units. A/C TV TEL. C$119–C$159 (US$79–US$106) double. AE, DC, ER, MC, V. Free parking.

At the end of Main Street, overlooking the Yukon River, this small vintage hotel has a distinct old-fashioned charm of its own. The lobby and guest rooms are cozy, and there's a well-appointed lounge. The rooms are newly renovated, in soft pastel colors, and equipped with extra-long beds, individual heating/air-conditioning units, and kitchenettes with coffeemakers and refrigerators.

Dining: There are two dining rooms, including the excellent Cellar Dining Room (see "Where to Dine" below).

Amenities: Room service, newspaper delivery.

✪ **Westmark Whitehorse Hotel.** 201 Wood St. (P.O. Box 4250), Whitehorse, YT Y1A 3T3. ☎ **800/544-0970** or 867/668-4700. Fax 867/668-2789. www.westmarkhotels. com. E-mail perry@whitehorse.net. 181 units. TV TEL. C$125 (US$83) double. Children under 12 stay free in parent's room. AE, ER, JCB, MC, V. Free parking.

Centrally located in downtown Whitehorse, this representative of a national chain has one of the busiest lobbies in town, nicely fitted with armchairs and settees. There's a small arcade alongside, housing a gift shop, barber, and hairdresser, plus a travel agency. The spacious guest rooms, including rooms for nonsmokers and travelers with disabilities, are well furnished and decorated.

Dining/Entertainment: The Westmark has a combination dining room, coffee shop, and cocktail lounge. The hotel is also host to one of Whitehorse's popular musical revues, the Frantic Follies.

Amenities: Most complete conference facilities in the Yukon, guest laundry.

MODERATE

✪ **Best Western Gold Rush Inn.** 411 Main St., Whitehorse, YT Y1A 2A7. ☎ **800/661-0539** in western Canada, 800/764-7604 in Alaska, or 867/668-4500. Fax 867/668-4432. www.goldrushinn.com. E-mail goldrush@yknet.yk.ca. 106 units. A/C TV TEL. C$119 (US$79) double. AE, DISC, MC, V. Free parking.

Modern but with a Wild West motif, the Gold Rush Inn is one of the most comfortable and central lodgings in Yellowknife, within easy walking distance of attractions and shopping. All the guest rooms, recently remodeled, have refrigerators and hair dryers; some come with kitchenettes. There are meeting facilities and a Jacuzzi. The restaurant is good and the convivial tavern is the scene of one of Yellowknife's evening theaters.

Hawkins House. 303 Hawkins St., Whitehorse, YT Y1A 1X5. ☎ **867/668-7638.** Fax 867/668-7632. www.hawkinshouse.yk.ca. E-mail cpitzel@internorth.com. 4 units. TV TEL. C$96–C$163 (US$64–US$109) double. AE, DC, MC, V. Free on-site parking.

All the guest rooms have balconies in this modern but stylishly retro Victorian home. The rooms are decorated according to theme, but tastefully so: The Fireweed Room has rustic pine furniture à la Klondike, while the Fleur de Lys Room recalls belle époque France. They have worktables and computer jacks, and there are free laundry facilities. Breakfast is available for C$7 (US$4.65).

River View Hotel. 102 Wood St., Whitehorse, YT Y1A 2E3. ☎ **867/667-7801.** www.riverview.ca. E-mail hotel@riverview.ca. Fax 867/668-6075. 53 units. TV TEL. C$80–C$100 (US$53–US$67) double. Extra person C$10 (US$7). DC, DISC, ER, MC, V. Heated underground parking C$5 (US$3.35).

One of the oldest establishments in the Yukon, completely rebuilt in 1970, the River View breathes territorial tradition. Don't judge by the rather-plain exterior; the guest rooms are large and fully modern and represent a good deal in an otherwise-expensive town. The lobby is crowded with Old Yukon memorabilia, from hand-cranked phones to moose antlers. You can't beat the location either: It's on the Yukon River, across from the MacBride Museum, and only 1 block from Main Street.

WHERE TO DINE

Food generally is more expensive in Whitehorse than in the provinces, and this goes for wine as well. Be happy you didn't come during the gold rush, when eggs sold for C$25 (US$17) each—in 1899 money!

EXPENSIVE

Cellar Dining Room. In the Edgewater Hotel, 101 Main St. ☎ **867/667-2572.** Reservations recommended. Main courses C$19–C$40 (US$13–US$27). AE, MC, V. Mon–Fri 11:30am–1:30pm; daily 5–10pm. CANADIAN.

This plush lower-level place has a big local reputation. You'll enjoy whatever you order, but expect to pay top dollar. Pasta dishes start at C$19 (US$13); you can't go wrong selecting either the king crab, lobster, and prawns or the excellent prime rib (C$28/US$19). Dress casually, but not too casually. For good food—including steaks and prime rib—at a cheaper price point, eat at the Gallery, just upstairs from the Cellar.

Panda's. 212 Main St. ☎ **867/667-2632.** Reservations recommended. Main courses C$18–C$45 (US$12–US$30). AE, DC, MC, V. Mon–Fri 11:30am–1:30pm; Mon–Sat 5–10pm (July–Aug also Sun 5–10pm). INTERNATIONAL.

Panda's is possibly the finest and certainly the most romantic restaurant in the Yukon. The decor is a mix of restrained elegance enlivened by traditional Klondike touches, and the service is smoothly discreet. This is one of the few places in town to offer daily specials apart from the regular menu. Dishes are classic European, like beef Wellington, pheasant breast with juniper berries, and veal Chanterelle, with a seafood curry dish thrown in for spice.

MODERATE

If you're looking for a moderately priced copious lunch, try the Asian buffet at **China Garden Restaurant,** 309 Jarvis St. (☎ **867/668-2899**), served Monday to Friday 11:30am to 2pm for C$9 (US$6). China Garden also serves full dinners from its extensive menu.

✪ **Antonio's Vineyard.** 202 Strickland St. ☎ **867/668-6266.** Reservations recommended. Pasta C$14–C$19 (US$9–US$13); pizzas (medium) C$15–C$20 (US$10–US$13); main courses C$19–C$39 (US$13–US$26). AE, MC, V. INTERNATIONAL.

This is one of Whitehorse's most popular restaurants, with good reason. The menu is extensive, ranging from pizzas to pasta (there are nearly 20 choices, including some vegetarian options) and on to lamb, seafood, and steaks. If the restaurant has a specialty, it's Greek souvlaki, which comes in six meat choices. What's more, the preparations are tasty, and the staff does a good job of table service—when they're not called on to enforce crowd control (word is out on the tour-bus circuit).

✪ **No Pop Sandwich Shop.** 312 Steele St. ☎ **867/668-3227.** Reservations recommended. Sandwiches C$4–C$7 (US$2.65–US$4.65); dinner main courses C$10–C$15 (US$7–US$10). MC, V. Mon–Thurs 8am–9:30pm, Fri 9am–10pm, Sat 10am–9pm, Sun 10am–4pm. COFFEE SHOP/SANDWICHES.

Whitehorse's hip "alternative" eating spot is No Pop, part bakery, part espresso shop, and part evening bistro. The baked goods are especially notable (try a raisin cinnamon roll) and the midday sandwiches meaty and happily retro. At night, the extensive sandwich menu is available, as well as a number of daily changing special entrees, usually featuring fresh fish. On Sunday, this is the place for brunch, with omelets and crêpes leading the menu.

INEXPENSIVE

Pasta Palace. 209 Main St. ☎ **867/667-6888.** Main courses C$8–C$13 (US$5–US$9). MC, V. Daily 11:30am–10pm. ITALIAN/TAPAS.

This is one of the few inexpensive restaurants in Whitehorse where you don't feel you're eating on a budget. The best thing about the menu is the extensive selection of tapas and appetizers, available throughout the day. The selection includes bruschettas, salads, and satays, all between C$5 and C$6 (US$3.35 and US$4). Full entrees are also good bargains, with full-flavored pasta dishes starting at C$8 (US$5) and steaks, chops, and kebobs topping out at C$11 (US$7). Everything is à la carte, but you can still have a full meal and get change back from C$12 (US$8). The dining room isn't fancy, but the service is prompt and friendly.

WHITEHORSE AFTER DARK

The top-of-the-bill attraction in Whitehorse is the ✪ **Frantic Follies,** a singing, dancing, clowning, and declaiming gold-rush revue that has become famous throughout the North. The show is an entertaining melange of skits; music-hall drollery; whooping, high-kicking, garter-flashing cancan dancers; sentimental ballads; and deadpan corn, interspersed with rolling recitations of Robert Service's poetry. Shows take place nightly at the **Westmark Whitehorse Hotel,** 201 Wood St.; for reservations call ☎ **867/668-2042.** Tickets are C$18 (US$12) adults and C$9 (US$6) children.

4 Kluane National Park

Tucked into the southwestern corner of the Yukon, a 2-hour drive from Whitehorse, these 22,015km² (8,500 sq. miles) of glaciers, marshes, mountains, and sand dunes are unsettled and virtually untouched. Bordering on Alaska in the west, **Kluane National Park** contains **Mount Logan** and **Mount St. Elias,** respectively the second- and third-highest peaks in North America.

The park also contains an astonishing variety of **wildlife.** Large numbers of moose, wolves, red foxes, wolverines, lynx, otters, and beavers abound, plus black bears in the forested areas and lots of grizzlies in the major river valleys.

Designated as a **UNESCO World Heritage Site,** Kluane Park lies 158km (98 miles) west of Whitehorse—take the Alaska Highway to Haines Junction. There, just outside the park's boundaries, you'll find the **Visitor Reception Centre,** open year-round (☎ **867/634-2345**). The center has information on hiking trails and canoe routes and shows an award-winning audiovisual presentation on the park. Admission to the park is free.

OUTDOOR ADVENTURES

Because this park is largely undeveloped and is preserved as a wilderness, casual exploration of Kluane is limited to a few day-hiking trails and to aerial sightseeing trips on small aircraft and helicopters.

The shortest hike up to one of Kluane's glaciers follows the **Slims East Trail,** leaving from south of the Sheep Mountain Information Centre. To reach Kaskawulsh Glacier and return will take at least 3 days, but this is an unforgettable hike into very remote and dramatic country. If you're interested in exploring the backcountry, you'll need to be in good shape and have experience with mountaineering techniques.

Day hikers have a few options, mostly near Haines Junction and south along Haines Road. Stop at lovely **Kathleen Lake,** where there's an easy interpreted hike or else a longer trail along the lake's south bank. Stop at the visitor center for more information on hikes in Kluane.

KLUANE AREA OUTFITTERS

The vast expanse of ice and rock in the wilderness heart of Kluane is well beyond the striking range of the average outdoor enthusiast. The area's white-water rafting is world-class but likewise not for the uninitiated. The Tatshenshini and Alsek rivers are famous for cold and wild white water that flows through magnificent mountain and glacier scenery. Some raft trips pass through iceberg-filled lakes just below huge glaciers!

To explore this part of Kluane, contact an outfitter. **Ecosummer Expeditions,** 5640 Hollybridge Way, Unit #130, Richmond, BC V7C 4N3 (☎ **800/465-8884** or 604/214-7484; www.ecosummer.com; e-mail trips@ecosummer.com), takes guided backpacking, mountaineering, and white-water rafting parties to Kluane National Park. Individual trips can feature trekking or rafting, while others combine the two in one trip. Trekking expeditions include an 8-day naturalist tour and a 12-day expedition across the park; both are C$1,650 (US$1,101). Rafting trips include an 11-day trip down the Alsek and Tatshenshini for C$2,695 (C$1,798). Ecosummer also offers Sila Sojourns, backcountry trips—some for women only—combining adventure travel and components of artistic creativity, such as writing, sketching, or photography workshops.

Also offering white-water trips is **Tatshenshini Expediting,** 1602 Alder St., Whitehorse, YT Y1A 3W8 (☎ **867/633-2742;** fax 867/633-6184; www. tatshenshiniyukon.com). Trips range from a 1-day run down the Tatshenshini at

C$100 (US$67) to an 11-day trip down the Tatshenshini from Dalton Post and down the Alsek River to the Pacific at C$2,500 (US$1,668). Four- and 6-day trips down the Alsek are also available. Call ahead because trip offerings vary from year to year and fill up fast.

AERIAL SIGHTSEEING

Purists may object, but the only way the average person is going to have a chance to see the backcountry of Kluane Park is by airplane or helicopter. The most popular glacier-viewing trip is flown by **Trans North Helicopters** (☎ 867/668-2177; www. tntaheli.com/tours.htm). Three trips are offered, ranging from C$45 (US$30) per person for 10 minutes in the air to C$250 (US$167) per person for an hour in the air. Short trips provide a panorama of Kluane Lake and the foothills of the park; longer trips explore the glaciers. **Sifton Air** (☎ 867/634-2916) also has three airplane flights over the park; two fly over Kaskawulsh or Lowell glacier for C$100 (US$67) per person (which one you fly over may depend on the weather); the longer trip, C$135 (US$90) per person, loops over both.

5 The Chilkoot Trail & White Pass

South of Whitehorse, massive ranges of glacier-chewed peaks rise up to ring the Gulf of Alaska; stormy waters reach far inland as fjords and enormous glaciers spill into the sea (the famed Glacier Bay is here). This spectacularly scenic region is also the site of the **Chilkoot Trail,** which in 1898 saw 100,000 gold-rush stampeders struggle up its steep slopes. Another high mountain pass was transcribed in 1900 by the White Pass and Yukon Railroad on its way to the goldfields; excursion trains now run on these rails, considered a marvel of engineering.

To see these sites, most people embark on long-distance hiking trails, rail excursions, or cruise boats. Happily, two highways edge through this spectacular landscape; if you use the **Alaska Marine Highway ferries** (☎ 800/642-0066; www.dot.state. ak.us/external/amhs/home.html), this trip can be made as a loop from either Whitehorse or Haines Junction. Because the ferries keep an irregular schedule, you'll need to call to find out what the sailing times are on the day you plan to make the trip.

THE CHILKOOT TRAIL

In 1896, word of the great gold strikes on the Klondike reached the outside world, and nearly 100,000 people set out for the Yukon to seek their fortunes. There was no organized transportation into the Yukon, so the stampeders resorted to the most expedient methods. The **Chilkoot Trail,** long an Indian trail through one of the few glacier-free passes in the Gulf of Alaska, became the primary overland route to the Yukon River, Whitehorse, and the goldfields near Dawson City.

The ascent of the Chilkoot became the stuff of legend, and pictures of men and women clambering up the steep snowfields to Chilkoot Summit are one of the enduring images of the stampeder spirit. The North Western Mounted Police demanded that anyone entering the Yukon carry a ton of provisions (literally); there were no supplies in the newly born gold camps on the Klondike, and malnutrition and lack of proper shelter were major problems. People were forced to make up to 30 trips up the trail in order to transport all their goods into Canada. Once past the RCMP station at Chilkoot Summit, the stampeders then had to build some sort of boat or barge to ferry their belongings across Bennett Lake and down the Yukon River.

Today, the Chilkoot Trail is a national historic park jointly administered by the Canadian and U.S. parks departments. The original trail is open year-round to hikers who wish to experience the route of the stampeders. The route also passes through marvelous glacier-carved valleys, coastal rain forest, boreal forest, and alpine tundra.

However, the Chilkoot Trail is as challenging today as it was 100 years ago. Though the trail is a total of 53km (33 miles) in length, the vertical elevation gain is nearly 3,700 feet (1128m); much of the trail is very rocky. Weather, even in high summer, can be extremely changeable, making this always-formidable trail sometimes a dangerous one.

Most people make the trip from **Dyea,** 15km (9.3 miles) north of Skagway in Alaska over the Chilkoot Summit (the U.S.-Canadian border) to **Bennett** in northwest British Columbia, in 4 days. The third day is the hardest, with a steep ascent to the pass and a 12km (7.4-mile) distance between campsites. At Bennett, there's no road or boat access; from the end of the trail, you'll need to make another 6km (3.7-mile) hike out along the rail tracks to Highway 2 near Fraser, British Columbia (the least expensive option), or you can ride the White Pass and Yukon Railway (☎ **800/343-7373**) from Bennett for C$25 (US$17) out to Fraser or for C$65 (US$43) down to Skagway.

The Chilkoot Trail isn't a casual hike; you'll need to plan and provision for your trip carefully. And it isn't a wilderness hike, because between 75 and 100 people start the trail daily. Remember that the trail is preserved as a historic park; leave artifacts of the gold-rush days—the trail is strewn with boots, stoves, and other effluvia of the stampeders—as you found them.

For details on the Chilkoot Trail, contact the **Klondike Gold Rush National Historic Park,** P.O. Box 517, Skagway, AK 99840 (☎ **907/983-2921**), or the **Canadian Parks Service,** P.O. Box 5540, Whitehorse, YT Y1A 5H4 (☎ **867/667-0486**).

WHITE PASS & THE YUKON ROUTE

In 1898, engineers began the task of excavating a route up to **White Pass.** Considered a marvel of engineering, the track edged around sheer cliffs on long trestles and tunneled through banks of granite. The train effectively ended traffic on the Chilkoot Trail, just to the north.

The White Pass and Yukon Route railroad now operates between Skagway, Alaska, and Bennett, British Columbia. Several trips are available on the historic line. Trains travel twice daily from Skagway to the summit of White Pass, a 3-hour return journey for C$80 (US$53) adults. Roughly twice a month, a train makes an 8-hour roundtrip from Skagway to Lake Bennett, the end of the Chilkoot Trail, for C$128 (US$79); hikers on the Chilkoot Trail can catch this train on its downhill run. Connections between Fraser and Whitehorse via motor coach are available daily. Prices for children are half the adult fare.

The White Pass and Yukon excursion trains operate mid-May to the last weekend of September. Advance reservations are suggested; for details, contact the **White Pass and Yukon Route,** P.O. Box 435, Skagway, AK 99840 (☎ **800/343-7373** or 907/983-2217; www.whitepassrailroad.com; e-mail info@whitepass.net).

6 Dawson City: An Authentic Gold-Rush Town

Dawson City is as much of a paradox as a community today. Once the biggest Canadian city west of Winnipeg, with a population of 30,000, it withered to practically a ghost town after the stampeders stopped stampeding. In 1953 the seat of territorial government was shifted to Whitehorse, which might've spelled the end of Dawson—but didn't. For now, every summer the influx of tourists more than matches the stream of gold rushers in its heyday. The reason for this is the remarkable preservation and restoration work done by Parks Canada. Dawson today is the nearest thing to an authentic gold-rush town the world has to offer.

However, Dawson City is more than just a gold-rush theme park; it's a real town with 2,000 year-round residents, many still working as miners (and many as sourdough wannabes). The citizens still like to party, stay up late, and tell tall tales to strangers, much as they did 100 years ago.

ESSENTIALS

VISITOR INFORMATION The **Visitor Reception Centre,** Front and King streets (☎ **867/993-5566;** fax 867/993-7298), provides details on all historic sights and attractions; the national park service also maintains an information desk here. It's open mid-May to mid-September daily 9am to 8pm. A walking tour of Dawson City, led by a highly knowledgeable guide, departs from the center once a day, costing C$5 (US$3.35). A good Web site for info on Dawson City is **www.dawsoncity.com**.

GETTING THERE From Whitehorse you can catch an **Air North** plane for the 1-hour hop (☎ **867/668-2228;** www.airnorth.yk.net); with 7-day advance purchase, tickets are roughly C$200 (US$133).

If you're driving from Alaska, take the **Taylor Highway (Top of the World)** from Chicken to Dawson. The **Klondike Highway** runs from Skagway, Alaska, to Whitehorse, and from there north to Dawson City via Carmacks and Stewart Crossing. The 537km (333 miles) from Whitehorse to Dawson City is a very long and tiring drive even though the road is fine.

SPECIAL EVENTS **Discovery Days** in mid-August commemorates the finding of the Klondike gold a century ago with dancing, music, parades, and canoe races. The winter's big party, in mid-March, is the **Percy De Wolfe Memorial Race and Mail Run,** a 210-mile dogsled race from Dawson City to Eagle, Alaska.

EXPLORING DAWSON CITY & ENVIRONS

All of Dawson City and much of the surrounding area is preserved as a National Historic Site, and it's easy to spend a day wandering the boardwalks, looking at the old buildings, shopping the boutiques, and exploring vintage watering holes. About half of the buildings in the town are historic; the rest are artful contemporary reconstructions. **Klondike National Historic Sites** (☎ 867/993-7200; fax 867/993-7299) preserves eight buildings and sites in and around Dawson City. The Parks Service has recently instituted a fee, usually C$5 (US$3.35) adults, for most of its sites and services. However, you can get a yearlong pass to all the Park Service's Dawson City sites for C$15 (US$10). For current Parks Canada program information and tickets, head over to the local Visitor Reception Centre.

Between the town and the mighty Yukon River are a **series of dikes** channeling the once-devastating floodwaters. A path follows the dikes and makes for a nice stroll. The **SS Keno,** a Yukon riverboat, is berthed along the dikes. Built in Whitehorse in 1922, it was one of the last riverboats to travel on the Yukon—there were once more than 200 of them.

✪ **Dawson City Museum.** Fifth Ave. ☎ **867/993-5291.** E-mail dcmuseum@yknet.yk.ca. Admission C$4 (US$2.65) adults, C$3 (US$2) students/seniors; small children free. Mid-may to Mid-Sept daily 10am–6pm. MC, V.

In the grand old Territorial Administration building, this excellent museum should be your first stop on a tour of Dawson City. Well-curated displays explain the geology and paleontology of the area (this region was on the main migratory path between Asia and North America during the last ice age), as well as the history of the native

Han peoples. The focus, of course, is the gold rush, and the museum explains various mining techniques; one of the galleries is dedicated to demonstrating the day-to-day life of early-1900s Dawson City. Various tours and programs are offered on the hour, including two video programs. Costumed docents are on hand to answer questions and recount episodes of history. On the grounds are early rail steam engines that served in the mines.

Robert Service Cabin. Eighth Ave. ☎ **867/993-7200.** Admission C$6 (US$4) adults, C$2.50 (US$1.65) children. Mid-May to Sept daily 9am–5pm; recitals daily at 10am and 3pm.

Poet Robert Service lived in this two-room log cabin from 1909 to 1912. Backed up against the steep cliffs edging Dawson City, Service's modest cabin today plays host to a string of pilgrims who come to hear an actor recite some of the most famous verses in the authentic milieu. In this cabin, Service composed his third and final volume of *Songs of a Rolling Stone,* plus a middling-awful novel entitled *The Trail of Ninety-eight.* Oddly enough, the bard of the gold rush neither took part in nor even saw the actual stampede. Born in England, he didn't arrive in Dawson until 1907—as a bank teller—when the rush was well and truly over. He got most of his plots by listening to old prospectors in the saloons, but the atmosphere he soaked in at the same time was genuine enough—and his imagination did the rest.

Jack London's Cabin. Eighth Ave. ☎ **867/993-5575.** Admission C$2 (US$1.35). Daily 10am–5pm; recitations daily.

Jack London lived in the Yukon less than a year—he left in June 1898 after a bout with scurvy—but his writings immortalized the North, particularly the animal stories like *The Call of the Wild, White Fang* and "The Son of Wolf."

Bonanza Creek. West on Bonanza Creek Rd., 5km (3.1 miles) south of Dawson City.

The original Yukon gold strike and some of the richest pay dirt in the world were found on **Bonanza Creek,** an otherwise-insignificant tributary flowing north into the Klondike River. A century's worth of mining has left the streambed piled into an orderly chaos of gravel heaps, the result of massive dredges. The national park service has preserved and interpreted a number of old prospecting sites; however, most of the land along Bonanza Creek is owned privately, so don't trespass, and by no means should you casually gold-pan.

The **Discovery Claim,** 16km (9.9 miles) up Bonanza Creek Road, is the spot, now marked by a National Historic Sites cairn, where George Carmack, Skookum Jim, and Tagish Charlie found the gold that unleashed the Klondike Stampede in 1896. They staked out the first four claims (the fourth partner, Bob Henderson, wasn't present). Within a week, Bonanza and Eldorado creeks had been staked out from end to end, but none of the later claims matched the wealth of the first. Fifteen kilometers (9.3 miles) up Bonanza Creek is **Dredge no. 4** (☎ 867/993-7200), one of the largest gold dredges ever used in North America; it's open June to late August daily 9am to 6pm, with tours offered hourly to 5pm at C$3 (US$2). Dredges—which augured up the permafrost, washed out the fine gravel, and sifted out the residual gold—were used after placer miners had panned out the easily accessible gold along the creek. Dredge no. 4 began operation in 1913 and could dig and sift 18,000 cubic yards in 24 hours, thus doing the work of an army of prospectors. You can do some free panning yourself at Claim 6, 14km (9 miles) up Bonanza Road.

The next drainage up from Bonanza Creek is **Bear Creek,** which became the headquarters for the dredge gold mining that dominated the Klondike area from 1905 to 1965, after the bloom went off placer mining. Parks Canada has developed a 65-building interpretive site that explores the history of industrial mining, including

The Klondike Gold Rush

The Klondike gold rush began with a wild war whoop from the throats of three men—two native Canadians and one white—that broke the silence of Bonanza Creek on the morning of August 17, 1896: "Gold!" they screamed, "Gold, gold, gold!" That cry rang through the Yukon, crossed to Alaska, and rippled down into the United States. Soon the whole world echoed with it, and people as far away as China and Australia began selling their household goods and homes to scrape together the fare to a place few of them had ever heard of before.

Some 100,000 men and women from every corner of the globe set out on the Klondike Stampede, descending on a territory populated by a few hundred souls. Tens of thousands came by the Chilkoot Pass from Alaska—the shortest route but also the toughest. Canadian law required each stampeder to carry 2,000 pounds of provisions up over the 3,000-foot (914m) summit. Sometimes it took 30 or more trips up a 45° slope to get all the baggage over, and the entire trail—with only one pack—takes about 3½ days to hike. Many collapsed on the way, but the rest slogged on—on to the Klondike and the untold riches to be found there.

The riches were real enough. The Klondike fields proved to be the richest ever found anywhere. Klondike stampeders were netting C$300 to C$400 (US$200 to US$267) in a single pan (and gold was then valued at around C$15/US$10 an ounce)! What's more, unlike some gold that lies embedded in veins of hard rock, the Klondike gold came in dust or nugget forms buried in creek beds. This placer gold, as it's called, didn't have to be milled—it was already in an almost-pure state!

The trouble was that most of the clerks who dropped their pens and butchers who shed their aprons to join the rush came too late. By the time they had completed the backbreaking trip, all the profitable claims along the Klondike creeks had been staked out and were defended by grim men with guns in their fists.

Almost overnight, Dawson boomed into a roaring, bustling, gambling, whoring metropolis of 30,000 people, thousands of them living in tents. And here gathered those who made fortunes from the rush without ever handling a pan: the supply merchants, saloonkeepers, dance-hall girls, and cardsharps. There were also some oddly peripheral characters: A bank teller named Robert Service who listened to the tall tales of prospectors and set them to verse (he never panned gold himself). And a stocky 21-year-old former sailor from San Francisco who adopted a big mongrel dog in Dawson, then went home and wrote about him a book that sold half a million copies. The book was *The Call of the Wild;* the sailor, Jack London.

By 1903, more than C$500 million (US$334 million) in gold had been shipped south from the Klondike, and the rush petered out. A handful of millionaires bought mansions in Seattle, tens of thousands went home with empty pockets, and thousands more lay dead in unmarked graves along the Yukon River. Dawson—"City" no longer—became a dreaming backwater haunted by 30,000 ghosts.

a dredge, a hydraulic monitor, and a gold mill, where the gold nuggets were cleaned, melted down, and cast into bullion. The turnoff for Bear Creek is 16km (9.9 miles) south of Dawson City, off the Klondike Highway. The site is open dawn to dusk, and the tours of the gold mill are on the hour 9am to 5pm, costing C$3 (US$2).

TOURS & EXCURSIONS

The national park service offers a C$5 (US$3.35) **daily walking tour** of Dawson City; sign up at the information center. **Gold City Tours** (☎ 867/993-5175) offers a 3½-hour minibus tour of Dawson City and the Bonanza goldfields, as well as a late-evening trip up to Midnight Dome for a midnight-sun panorama of the area. The office is on Front Street, across from the riverboat *Keno*.

The *Yukon Queen II* is a new "fast cat" catamaran that can carry 104 passengers over the 108-mile stretch of river from Dawson City to Eagle, Alaska. Tickets include meals; mid-May to mid-September, the daylong journey runs daily. Adults pay C$198 (US$132) round-trip and C$120 (US$80) one-way. Book at **Gray Line Yukon** on Front Avenue near the visitor center (☎ 867/993-5599); tickets go quickly, so try to reserve well in advance.

WHERE TO STAY

There are about a dozen hotels, motels, and B&Bs in Dawson City. Most are well appointed, but none is particularly cheap. Only the Eldorado and downtown hotels and a couple of the B&Bs remain open year-round.

EXPENSIVE

Downtown Hotel. At the corner of Second and Queen sts., Dawson City, YT Y0B 1G0. ☎ **867/993-5346.** Fax 867/993-5076. 60 units. TV TEL. C$124 (US$83) double. Senior discount offered. AE, DC, DISC, ER, MC, V.

One of Dawson City's originals, the Downtown has been completely refurbished and updated with all modern facilities, yet it preserves a real Western-style atmosphere. The Jack London Grill and Sourdough Saloon look right out of the gold-rush era; they're definitely worth a visit. Free airport pickup is offered. Facilities include a Jacuzzi and winter plug-ins for car head-bolt heaters.

Eldorado Hotel. Third Ave. and Princess St., Dawson City, YT Y0B 1G0. ☎ **867/993-5451.** Fax 867/993-5256. 52 units. TV TEL. C$129 (US$86) double. AE, DC, DISC, MC, V.

Another vintage hotel made over and modernized, the Eldorado offers guest rooms in its original building or in an adjacent modern motel unit. Some rooms feature kitchenettes. There are a licensed dining room and a separate lounge, plus a guest laundry. Free airport pickup is offered. Facilities include winter plug-ins for car head-bolt heaters.

Westmark Inn. Fifth and Harper sts., Dawson City, YT Y0B 1G0. ☎ **800/544-0970** or 867/ 993-5542 (summer only). 136 units. TV TEL. C$169 (US$113) double. AE, MC, V.

The Westmark only looks old; on the inside, it reveals itself to be a modern hotel. Facilities include a Laundromat, a cafe with a courtyard deck, a gift shop, and a traditional cocktail lounge.

MODERATE

Dawson City B&B. 451 Craig St., Dawson City, YT Y0B 1G0. ☎ **867/993-5649.** Fax 867/ 993-5648. www.yukon.net/dawsonBB. E-mail dawsonBB@dawsoncity.net. 7 units, 3 with bathroom. TV. C$85–C$95 (US$57–US$63) double. Senior discounts. DC, MC, V. Free parking.

This nicely decorated large home fronted by two stories of decks is on the outskirts of Dawson City, overlooking the Klondike and Yukon rivers. Rooms are ample sized, very clean, and simply but attractively furnished. Breakfasts are bounteous. Your hosts will also provide use of bicycles and fishing rods.

Dawson City Bunkhouse. Front and Princess sts., Dawson City, YT Y0B 1G0. ☎ **867/ 993-6164.** Fax 867/993-6051. E-mail bunkhouse@yknet.yk.ca. 32 units, 20 with bathroom. TV TEL. C$50–C$95 (US$33–US$63) double; C$95 (US$63) suite. Senior discounts. MC, V. Free parking.

One of the few good lodging values in town, this handsome hotel looks Old West but is brand new. The guest rooms are small but bright and clean; the beds come with Hudson's Bay Company wool blankets. The cheapest rooms have their own toilets, but showers are down the landing. Only the queen (sleeps three) and king (sleeps four) suites have private bathrooms.

WHERE TO DINE

Food is generally good in Dawson City and, considering the isolation and transport costs, not too expensive. The hotels have good dining rooms and are open for three meals a day. Many restaurants close in winter or keep shorter hours. The **River West Food & Health,** at Front and York streets. (☎ **867/993-6339**), is a health-food shop and cafe that's a good place to get a decent cup of coffee and order sandwiches either to eat in or take out for picnics. It's open daily 9am to 8pm.

Klondike Kate's Restaurant. At the corner of Third Ave. and King St. ☎ **867/993-6527.** Main courses C$5–C$22 (US$3.35–US$15). MC, V. Daily 7am–11pm. CANADIAN.

This friendly and informal cafe is near the theaters and casino and serves tasty uncomplicated meals from a small but dependable menu. The atmosphere is Old Dawson, and weather permitting, there's dining on the veranda.

✪ **Marina's.** Fifth Ave. (between Princess and Harper sts.). ☎ **867/993-6800.** Main courses C$13–C$27 (US$9–US$18). MC, V. Daily 11am–10pm. PIZZA/STEAKS/PASTA.

Housed in an attractive historic-looking building, Marina's offers Dawson City's best dining, with a wide menu offering everything from salads to fine seafood. The pasta and steaks are truly good, and the pizza's not bad either. The bow-tied waitstaff give prompt and professional service.

DAWSON CITY AFTER DARK

Dawson City is still full of honky-tonks and saloons, and most have some form of nightly live music. On warm summer evenings all the doors are thrown open and you can sample the music by strolling through town on the boardwalks; the music is far better than you'd expect for a town of 2,000 people. A couple of favorites: Both the lounge bar and the pub at the **Midnight Sun,** at Third Avenue and Queen Street, have live bands nightly; the bar at the **Westminster Hotel,** between Queen and Princess on Third, often features traditional Yukon fiddlers.

Canada's only legal gambling casino north of the 60th parallel, **Diamond Tooth Gertie's,** Fourth and Queen streets (☎ 867/993-5575), has an authentic gold-rush decor, from the shirt-sleeved honky-tonk pianist to the wooden floorboards. The games are blackjack, roulette, 21, red dog, and poker, as well as slot machines; the minimum stakes are low, and the ambiance is friendly rather than tense. There's a maximum set limit of C$100 (US$67) per hand. The three nightly floor shows combine cancan dancing, throaty siren songs, and ragtime piano. May to September, Gertie's is open daily 7pm to 2am, and admission is C$6 (US$4).

Built at the height of the stampede by "Arizona Charlie" Meadows, the original **Palace Grand Theatre,** King Street (☎ 867/993-6217), had its slam-bang gala premier in July 1899. Now totally rebuilt according to the original plans, it serves as a showcase for the *Gaslight Follies,* a spoofy musical-comedy revue. May to September, performances are Wednesday to Monday at 8pm, with tickets at C$15 to C$17 (US$10 to US$11).

7 The Top of the World Highway

The scenic **Top of the World Highway** links Dawson City to Tetlin Junction in Alaska. After the free Yukon River ferry crossing at Dawson City, this 175-mile gravel road rapidly climbs above the tree line, where it follows meandering ridge tops—hence the name. The views are wondrous: Bare green mountains undulate for hundreds of miles into the distance; looking down, you can see clouds floating in deep valley clefts.

After 106km (66 miles), the road crosses the U.S.-Canadian border; the border crossing is open in summer only, 8am to 8pm Pacific time (note that the time in Alaska is an hour earlier). There are no rest rooms, services, or currency exchange at the border. The quality of the road deteriorates on the Alaska side.

The free ferry at Dawson City can get very backed up in high season; delays up to 3 hours are possible. Commercial and local traffic have priority and don't have to wait in line. The Top of the World Highway isn't maintained during winter; it's generally free of snow April to mid-October.

8 North on the Dempster Highway

Forty kilometers (25 miles) east of Dawson City, the famed ✪ **Dempster Highway** heads north 735km (456 miles) to Inuvik, Northwest Territories, on the Mackenzie River near the Arctic Ocean. The most northerly public road in Canada, the Dempster is another of those highways that exudes a strange appeal to RV travelers; locals in Inuvik refer to these tourists as "end of the roaders." It's a beautiful drive, especially early in the fall, when frost brings out the color in tiny tundra plants and migrating wildlife is more easily seen. The Dempster passes through a wide variety of landscapes, from tundra plains to rugged volcanic mountains; in fact, between Highway 2 and Inuvik the Dempster crosses the Continental Divide three times. **North Fork Pass** in the Ogilvie Mountains, with the knife-edged gray peaks of Tombstone Mountain incising the horizon to the west, is especially stirring. The Dempster crosses the Arctic Circle—one of only two roads in Canada to do so—at Mile 252.

The Dempster is a gravel road open year-round. It's in good shape in most sections, though very dusty; allow 12 hours to make the drive between Inuvik and Dawson City. There are services at three points only: Eagle Plains, Fort McPherson, and Arctic Red River. Don't depend on gas or food outside of standard daytime business hours. At the Peel and the Mackenzie rivers are free ferry crossings in summer; in winter, vehicles simply cross on the ice. For 2 weeks, during the spring thaw and the fall freeze up, through-traffic on the Dempster ceases. For details on ferries and road conditions, call ☎ **800/661-0750.** For more on Inuvik, see "The Arctic North," below.

9 Yellowknife: Capital of the Northwest Territories

The capital of the Northwest Territories and the most northerly city in Canada, **Yellowknife** lies on the north shore of Great Slave Lake. The site was originally occupied by the Dogrib tribe, and the first white settlers didn't arrive until 1934, following the discovery of gold on the lakeshores.

This first **gold boom** petered out in the 1940s, and Yellowknife dwindled nearly to a ghost town in its wake. But in 1945 came a second gold rush that put the place permanently on the map. The local landmarks are the two operating gold mines flanking Yellowknife: **Miramar Con** and **Giant Yellowknife.**

Most of the old gold-boom vestiges are gone—the bordellos, gambling dens, log-cabin banks, and never-closing bars are merely memories now. But the original **Old Town** is there, a crazy tangle of wooden shacks hugging the lakeshore rocks, surrounded by bush-pilot operations that fly sturdy little planes—on floats in summer, on skis in winter.

Yellowknife is a vibrant, youthful place. The white population of Yellowknife is mostly made up of people in their late 20s and 30s. Yellowknife attracts young people just out of college looking for high-paying public-sector jobs, wilderness recreation, and the adventure of living in the Arctic. However, after a few years, most people head back south to warmer climes; not many stay around to grow old. Yellowknife is also the center for a number of outlying native communities, which roots the city in a more long-standing traditional culture.

People are very friendly and outgoing and seem genuinely glad to see you. The party scene here is just about what you'd expect in a town surrounded by native villages and filled with miners and young bureaucrats. There's a more dynamic nightlife here than the size of the population could possibly justify.

ESSENTIALS

VISITOR INFORMATION   For information about the territory in general or Yellowknife in particular, contact one of the following: the **Northern Frontier Regional Visitors Centre,** No. 4, 4807 49th St., Yellowknife, NT X1A 3T5 (☎ 867/873-4262; fax 867/873-3654; www.northernfrontier.com; e-mail nfva@ssimicro.com); or **NWT Arctic Tourism,** P.O. Box 610, Yellowknife, NT X1A 2N5 (☎ 800/661-0788 or 867/873-7200; fax 867/873-0294; www.nwttravel.nt.ca).

A useful phone number for motorists is the **ferry information line** at ☎ 800/661-0751, which lets you know the status of the various car ferries along the Dempster and Mackenzie highways. At breakup and freeze-up time, there's usually a month's time when the ferries can't operate and the ice isn't yet thick enough to drive on.

GETTING THERE   NWT Air, a division of Air Canada (☎ 800/776-3000 in the U.S. or 800/332-1080 in Alberta; www.aircanada.ca), and **Canada North,** a division of Canadian Airlines (☎ 800/426-7000; www.cdnair.ca), fly into Yellowknife from Edmonton; flights range from C$500 to C$1,250 (US$334 to US$834). Canada North also provides daily flights to and from Ottawa and Toronto; round-trip tickets are C$1,400 to C$2,800 (US$934 to US$1,868). Yellowknife Airport is 5km (3.1 miles) northeast of the town.

If you're driving from Edmonton, take Highway 16 to Grimshaw. From there the **Mackenzie Highway** leads to the Northwest Territories border, 475km (295 miles) north, and on to Yellowknife via Fort Providence. The total distance from Edmonton is 1,524km (945 miles). Most of the road is now paved, though construction continues throughout summer.

CITY LAYOUT   The city's expanding urban center, **New Town**—a busy hub of modern hotels, shopping centers, office blocks, and government buildings—spreads above the town's historic birthplace, called **Old Town.** Together the two towns count about 20,000 inhabitants, by far the largest community in the Territories.

Most of New Town lies between rock-lined Frame Lake and Yellowknife Bay on Great Slave Lake. The main street in this part of town is **Franklin Avenue,** also called **50th Avenue.** Oddly, early town planners decided to start the young town's numbering system at the junction of 50th Avenue and 50th Street; even though the downtown area is only 10 blocks square, the street addresses give the illusion of a much larger city.

The junction of 48th Street and Franklin (50th) Avenue is pretty much the center of town. A block south are the post office and a number of enclosed shopping arcades (very practical up here, where winter temperatures would otherwise discourage shopping). Turn north and travel half a mile to Old Town and **Latham Island,** which stick out into Yellowknife Bay. This is still a bustling center for boats, floatplanes, B&Bs, and food and drink.

South of Frame Lake is the modern residential area, and just west is the airport. If you follow 48th Street out of town without turning onto the Mackenzie Highway, the street turns into the **Ingraham Trail,** a bush road heading out toward a series of lakes with fishing and boating access, hiking trails, and a couple of campgrounds. This is the main recreational playground for Yellowknifers, who love to canoe or kayak from lake to lake or all the way back to town.

GETTING AROUND   Monday to Saturday, the **City Bus** (Cardinal Coach Lines; ☎ 867/873-4693) makes a loop through Yellowknife once an hour. The fare is C$2 (US$1.35).

For car rentals, **Avis** (☎ 867/920-2491) and **Budget** (☎ 867/873-3366) both have offices at the airport. **Rent-A-Relic,** 356 Old Airport Rd. (☎ 867/873-3400; e-mail xferrier@ssimicro.com), offers older models at substantial savings—and they'll deliver a vehicle to your hotel or campsite. **Tilden,** 5118 50th St. (☎ 867/ 873-2911), has a range of rentals from full-size cars to half-ton four-speed vans. At all these operations, the number of cars available during summer is rather limited and the demand very high. You may have to settle for what's to be had rather than what you want. Try to book ahead as far as possible. To rent an RV, contact **Frontier RV Rentals,** P.O. Box 1088, Yellowknife, NT X1A 2N7 (☎ 867/873-5413).

Taxis are pretty cheap in Yellowknife; call **City Cabs** at ☎ 867/873-4444 or **Gold Cabs** at ☎ 867/873-8888 for a lift. A ride to the airport costs about C$10 (US$7).

SPECIAL EVENTS   The **Caribou Carnival,** in late March, is a burst of spring fever after a very long, very frigid winter (one of the fever symptoms consists of the delusion that winter is over). For a solid week Yellowknife is thronged with parades, igloo-building contests, and Inuit wrestling. The competition highlight is the Canadian Championship Dog Derby, a 3-day, 240km (149-mile) dogsled race. The **Festival of the Midnight Sun** is an arts festival in mid-July. There are a one-act play competition, various arts workshops (including lessons in native beading and carving), and fine art on display all over town.

EXPLORING YELLOWKNIFE

Stop by the **Northern Frontier Regional Visitor Centre** (☎ 867/873-4262), on 48th Street on the west edge of town, to see a number of exhibits explaining the major points of local history and native culture; you'll want to put the kids on the "bush flight" elevator, which simulates a flight over Great Slave Lake while slowly rising to the second floor. Also pick up a free parking pass, enabling you to escape the parking meters. It's open daily 8:30am to 6pm.

The ✪ **Prince of Wales Northern Heritage Centre,** on the shore of Frame Lake (☎ 867/873-7551), is a museum in a class all its own. You'll learn the history, background, and characteristics of the Dene and Inuit peoples (the Métis and pioneer whites) through dioramas; artifacts; and talking, reciting, and singing slide presentations. It depicts the human struggle with an environment so incredibly harsh that survival alone seems an accomplishment. Admission is free. Labour Day to September, it's open daily 10:30am to 5:30pm; October to May, it's open Tuesday to Friday 10:30am to 5:30pm.

Rising above Old Town, the **Bush Pilot's Memorial** is a stone pillar paying tribute to the little band of airmen who opened up the Far North. The surrounding cluster of shacks and cottages is the original Yellowknife, built on the shores of a narrow peninsula jutting into Great Slave Lake. It's not exactly a pretty place, but definitely intriguing. Sprinkled along the inlets are half a dozen bush-pilot operations, minuscule airlines flying charter planes as well as scheduled routes to outlying areas. The little floatplanes shunt around like taxis, and you can watch a landing or takeoff every hour of the day. About 100 yards off the tip of the Old Town peninsula lies **Latham Island,** which you can reach by a causeway. The island has a small native-Canadian community, a few luxury homes, and a number of B&Bs.

TOURS & EXCURSIONS

Operating out of the visitor center, **Raven Tours** (☎ 867/873-4776; fax 867/873-4856; e-mail raventours@yellowknife.com) offers a standard 3-hour city tour, as well as a number of more specialized trips (boat, waterfall, and wildlife tours and more). The standard tour costs C$20 (US$13); call to find out what other tours are offered during your visit.

Natural-history tours of the Yellowknife area, with an emphasis on subarctic ecology, bird watching, and geology, are offered by **Cygnus Ecotours** (☎ 867/873-4782; e-mail cygnus@internorth.com). Some tours focus on the ecosystem near town, while others journey out along the Ingraham Trail to more distant lakes; hikes to Cameron Falls are also available.

Cruise Canada's Arctic in the **MS *Norweta,*** a modern diesel-engine craft equipped with radar and owned by the NWT Marine Group, 5414 52nd St., Yellowknife, NT X1A 3K1 (☎ 867/873-2489). For part of the summer, the *Norweta* is in Yellowknife and offers a number of day excursions and dinner cruises. Call ahead to make reservations and to make sure the boat is available. Twice a summer, the *Norweta* conducts 5-day cruises of the scenic East Arm of Great Slave Lake, costing C$1,700 to C$2,000 (US$1,134 to US$1,334). The *Norweta* also makes one trip up and back on the mighty Mackenzie River to Inuvik, costing C$4,000 (US$2,668).

SHOPPING

Yellowknife is a principal retail outlet for Northern artwork and craft items, as well as the specialized clothing the climate demands. Some of it is so handsome that sheer vanity will make you wear it in more southerly temperatures.

Northern Images, in the Yellowknife Mall, 50th Avenue (☎ 867/873-5944), features authentic native-Canadian articles: apparel and carvings, graphic prints, silver jewelry, ornamental moose-hair tuftings, and porcupine quill work. The log cabin–style **Trappers Cabin,** 4 Lessard Dr., Latham Island (☎ 867/873-3020), is the nearest thing to an old-time frontier store Yellowknife can offer. You drop in there not just to buy goods but to have coffee and snacks, book cruises and excursions, listen to gossip, and collect information.

SPORTS & OUTDOOR ACTIVITIES

The town is ringed by hiking trails, some gentle, some pretty rugged. Most convenient for a short hike or a jog is the trail ringing **Frame Lake,** accessible from the Northern Heritage Centre and other points.

The other major focus of recreation in the Yellowknife area is the **Ingraham Trail,** a paved and then gravel road starting just west of town and winding east over 73km (45 miles) to Tibbet Lake. En route lie a string of lakes, mostly linked by the Cameron River, making this prime canoe and kayak country. Ingraham Trail also crosses by several territorial parks, two waterfalls, the Giant Mine, and waterfowl habitat, plus lots of picnic sites, camping spots, boat rentals, and fishing spots.

One of the largest lakes along the trail is **Prelude Lake,** 32km (20 miles) east of town; it's a wonderful setting for scenic boating and trout, pike, and Arctic-grayling fishing. The **Prelude Lake Lodge** (☎ 867/920-4654) rents motorboats and rowboats.

CANOEING & KAYAKING   When you fly into Yellowknife, you'll notice that about half the land surface is composed of lakes, so it's no wonder that kayaking is really catching on here. **Above and Below Sports,** 4100 Franklin Ave. (☎ 867/ 669-9222), offers canoe and kayak rentals and instruction, as well as guided tours of Great Slave and Prelude lakes. The visitor center offers maps of seven canoe paths through the maze of lakes, islands, and streams along the Ingraham Trail; with a few short portages, it's possible to float all the way from Prelude Lake to Yellowknife, about a 5-day journey. A daylong rental is around C$50 (US$33).

FISHING TRIPS   Traditionally, fishing has been the main reason to visit the Yellowknife and the Great Slave Lake area. Lake trout, Arctic grayling, northern pike, and whitefish grow to storied size in these Northern lakes; the pristine water conditions and general lack of anglers mean fishing isn't just good, it's great. **Bluefish Services** (☎ 867/873-4818) offer fishing trips on Great Slave Lake directly from town, but most serious anglers fly in floatplanes to fishing lodges, either on Great Slave or on more remote lakes, for a wilderness fishing trip.

One of the best of the lodge outfitters on Great Slave Lake is the **Frontier Fishing Lodge** (☎ 780/465-6843; fax 780/466-3874). A 3-day all-inclusive guided fishing trip will cost around C$1,450 (US$967). Nearly two dozen fishing-lodge outfitters operate in the Yellowknife area; contact the visitor center or consult the *Explorers' Guide* for a complete listing.

HIKING   The most popular hike along the **Ingraham Trail** is to **Cameron River Falls.** The well-signed trailhead is 48km (30 miles) east of Yellowknife. Although not a long hike—allow 1½ hours for the round-trip—the trail to the falls is hilly. An easier trail is the **Prelude Lake Nature Trail,** winding along Prelude Lake through wildlife habitat. The 90-minute hike begins and ends at the lakeside campground. Closer to Yellowknife, the **Prospectors Trail** at Fred Henne Park is an interpreted trail through gold-bearing rock outcroppings; signs tell the story of Yellowknife's rich geology.

WHERE TO STAY

The campground most convenient to Yellowknife is **Fred Henne Park** (☎ 867/ 920-2472), just east of the airport on Long Lake. Both RVs and tents are welcome; there are showers and kitchen shelters but no hookups. Campsites are C$12 (US$8). At **Prelude Lake Territorial Park** (☎ 867/920-4674), 29km (18 miles) east of Yellowknife, there are rustic campsites without camping fees; though there are no facilities beyond running water, boat rental and food service is available at the nearby **Prelude Lake Lodge** (☎ 867/920-4654).

The **visitor center** (☎ 867/873-4262) also operates as a room-reservation service, which is especially handy for locating rooms at local B&Bs.

EXPENSIVE

✪ **Explorer Regency International Hotel.** 4825 49th Ave., Yellowknife, NT X1A 2R3. ☎ **800/661-0892** or 867/873-3531. Fax 867/873-2789. www.explorerhotel. nt.ca. 128 units. A/C TV TEL. C$172 (US$115) double; from C$225 (US$150) suite. AE, ER, MC, V.

The Explorer is a commanding eight-story snow-white structure overlooking both the city and a profusion of rock-lined lakes. It has long been Yellowknife's premier hotel—Queen Elizabeth herself has stayed here. The lobby is large and comfortable, with indoor greenery and deep armchairs and sofas. The guest rooms are spacious and uncluttered, all with writing desks and tables. A no-smoking floor is available. Barkley's Eats & Drinks is one of the Territories' finest restaurants (see "Where to Dine" below). Services include room service, dry cleaning, and laundry. There are also conference rooms and a gift shop.

✪ **Yellowknife Inn.** 5010 49th St., Yellowknife, NT X1A 2N4. ☎ **800/661-0580** or 867/873-2601. Fax 867/873-2602. 130 units. www.yellowknifeinn.com. TV TEL. C$150 (US$100) double. Rates include breakfast. AE, DC, ER, MC, V.

This inn is right in the center of Yellowknife and has recently been completely refurbished and updated. The new lobby is joined to a large shopping-and-dining complex, making this the place to stay in winter. The guest rooms are fair-sized, some with minibars, and offer amenities that have won an International Hospitality award. The walls are decorated with Inuit art. Guests receive a pass to local fitness facilities and complimentary shuttle rides to and from the airport. The fourth floor is reserved for nonsmokers.

MODERATE

Captain Ron's. 8 Lessard Dr., Yellowknife, NT X1A 2G5. ☎ **867/873-3746.** 4 units, none with bathroom. TV TEL. C$90 (US$60) double. Rates include breakfast. MC, V.

Located on Latham Island on the shores of the Great Slave Lake, Captain Ron's is reached by causeway. It's a cozy and picturesque place with four guest rooms and a reading lounge with a fireplace and TV. Each room has a double bed, radio, phone, and picture windows to take in the lake view.

Igloo Inn. 4115 Franklin Ave. (P.O. Box 596), Yellowknife, NT X1A 2N4. ☎ **867/873-8511.** Fax 867/873-5547. E-mail iglooinn@internorth.com. 44 units. TV TEL. C$99 (US$66) double. AE, DC, MC, V.

An attractive two-story wood structure, the Igloo sits at the bottom of the hill road leading to Old Town. Complimentary coffee and morning pastries are served in its breakfast room. Thirty-three of the units have pleasantly spacious kitchenettes stocked with electric ranges and all the necessary utensils. Altogether, it's a great value for your money.

INEXPENSIVE

Eva and Eric's B&B. 114 Knutsen Ave., Yellowknife, NT X1A 2Y4. ☎ **867/873-5779.** Fax 867/873-6160. 4 units, none with bathroom. TEL. C$70 (US$47) double. Rates include breakfast. No goods-and-services tax (GST) added to room rates. No credit cards.

Near the airport, Eva and Eric Henderson have four rooms available for nonsmokers. There are a shared lounge with a color TV, a shared bathroom, a kitchen for guests, a library, and Northern foods for breakfast (if requested). The Hendersons are some of the nicest and most welcoming people around; you'll enjoy staying here.

WHERE TO DINE
EXPENSIVE

Barkley's Eats & Drinks. In the Explorer Regency International Hotel, 4825 49th Ave. ☎ **867/873-3531.** Reservations recommended. Main courses C$10–C$25 (US$7–US$17). AE, DC, ER, MC, V. Daily 6am–midnight. INTERNATIONAL/NORTHERN.

Barkley's offers some of the best Northern cooking in the Northwest Territories. The menu lists a number of game dishes peculiar to the region (caribou and musk ox) but prepared with French sauces and finesse. Other dishes—steaks, pasta, and seafood—have a more international provenance.

The Office. 4915 50th St. ☎ **867/873-3750.** Reservations recommended. Main courses C$9–C$26 (US$6–US$17). AE, MC, V. Mon–Sat 11:30am–10pm. CANADIAN/NORTHERN.

This sophisticated retreat sports an elegant decor and paintings by local artists. House specialties include Northern fare, like the frozen thinly sliced Arctic char and caribou steak. Otherwise the menu is top-grade Anglo: roast lamb, beef with Yorkshire pudding, roast duckling, great steaks, and a large selection of seafood. The eggs Benedict is famous among the lunchtime crowd. And The Office puts on possibly the best salad bar in the North.

MODERATE

L'Attitudes Restaurant & Bistro. Center Square Mall, 5010 49th St. ☎ **867/920-7880.** Pizza C$10–C$12 (US$7–US$8); pasta C$12–C$15 (US$8–US$10); main courses C$12–C$26 (US$8–US$17). MC, V. Daily 7:30am–8pm. INTERNATIONAL/NORTHERN.

L'Attitudes is one of Yellowknife's newest and most attractive restaurants and reflects its youth with lighter, more eclectic offerings. The menu ranges from boutique pizzas to pasta, barbecued ribs, and chicken and on to intriguing Northern specialties like rack of caribou with rosemary mint sauce. If you're more interested in grazing through several dishes, there's a snack menu, with salads and nibbles available all day; you can also caffeinate on espresso drinks. There are more vegetarian selections here than anywhere else in Yellowknife.

✪ **Wildcat Café.** Wiley Rd., Old Town. ☎ **867/873-8850.** Reservations not accepted. Main courses C$7–C$17 (US$4.65–US$11). MC, V. Mon–Sat 7am–9:30pm, Sun 10am–9pm. Closed in winter. NORTHERN.

The Wildcat Café is a tourist site as much as an eatery. A squat log cabin with a deliberately grizzled frontier look, it's actually refurbished in the image of the 1930s original. The atmospheric interior is reminiscent of Yellowknife in its pioneer days, and the cafe has been photographed, filmed, painted, and caricatured often enough to give it star quality. The menu changes daily but focuses on local products like caribou and lake fish, in addition to steaks. Seating is along long benches, and you'll probably end up sharing your table with other diners.

INEXPENSIVE

The coffee shop at the **Northern Heritage Centre,** on Frame Lake (☎ 867/873-7551), has a good selection of inexpensive lunch items; this is a good place to go for soup, salad, or sandwiches, whether or not you plan on visiting the museum. For good and inexpensive family dining, go to the **Country Corner,** 4601 Franklin Ave. (☎ **867/873-9412**), a log cafe just north of downtown. Come here for breakfast when the line snakes out the door at the Wildcat. Brand-name fast food is present in Yellowknife, and for people on a tight budget, this is probably the way to avoid the otherwise rather high cost of dining. All the downtown shopping arcades have inexpensive food outlets as well.

YELLOWKNIFE AFTER DARK

By and large, people in Yellowknife aren't scared of a drink, and nightlife revolves around bars and pubs. Increasingly, there's a music scene in Yellowknife; a number of local bands have developed national followings.

The Float Base, at the corner of 50th Avenue and 51st Street (☎ 867/873-3034), is a jolly neighborhood basement pub with polished cedar tables and upholstered swivel chairs. Floatplane bits and photos are used for decoration. Yellowknife's first brew pub, the ✪ **Bush Pilot,** 3502 Wiley Rd. (☎ 867/920-2739), is where Arctic Ales are served up on a bar made from the wing of a plane. On Sunday it becomes a teahouse: Darjeeling and cream cakes share the billing with clairvoyants and tarot-card readers. This fun pub has a great location on the water in Old Town.

Officially called Bad Sam's, the **Gold Range Tavern,** in the Gold Range Hotel, 5010 50th St. (☎ 867/873-4441), is better known by its local nickname—"Strange Range." The Range is an occasionally rip-roaring tavern that attracts the whole gamut of native and visiting characters in search of some after-dinner whoopee. You don't come here for a quiet evening, but you can't say you've seen Yellowknife if you haven't seen the Strange Range.

10 Nahanni National Park

A breathtaking, unspoiled wilderness of 4,766km² (1,840 sq. miles) in the southwest corner of the Territories, **Nahanni National Park** is accessible only by foot, motorboat, canoe, or charter aircraft. The park preserves 295km (183 miles) of the **South Nahanni River.** One of the wildest rivers in North America, the South Nahanni claws its path through the rugged Mackenzie Mountains, at one point charging over incredible **Virginia Falls,** twice as high as Niagara (at 105m/344 ft.) and carrying more water. Below the falls, the river surges through one of the continent's deepest gorges, with canyon walls up to 1,333m (4,373 ft.) high.

White-water rafting from Virginia Falls through the canyon is the most popular, but not the only, white-water trip in the park. The trip from the falls (you'll need to fly in, because this is a roadless park) to the usual takeout point takes 6 days or more, depending on the amount of time spent hiking or relaxing en route. The best white water in the park is actually far above the falls, beginning at Moose Ponds and continuing to Rabbitkettle Lake, near an impressive hot-springs formation.

A number of outfitters are licensed to run the South Nahanni River. For a full listing and for details about the park, contact the Superintendent, **Nahanni National Park,** Postal Bag 300, Fort Simpson, NT X0E 0N0 (☎ 867/695-3151). As an example, **Nahanni and Whitewolf River Adventures,** P.O. Box 4869, Whitehorse, YT Y1A 4N6 (☎ 800/297-6927 or 867/668-3180; fax 867/668-3056; www.nahanni.com; e-mail nahanni@yknet.yk.ca), operates a 6- to 10-day trip from the falls through the canyon with either canoes or inflatable rafts for C$2,495 (US$1,664).

A number of charter airlines also offer daylong aerial sightseeing trips into the park. **Deh Cho Air** (☎ 867/770-4103), operating out of Fort Liard, offers half-day charters to Virginia Falls for C$250 (US$167), minimum numbers required.

11 The Arctic North: Getting Away From It All

Canada's **Arctic North** is one of the world's most remote and uninhabited areas, but one that holds many rewards for the traveler willing to get off the beaten path. Arctic landscapes can be breathtaking: the 72km-wide (45-mile-wide) wildlife-filled delta of the **Mackenzie River** or the awesome fjords and glaciers of **Baffin Island.** In many areas, traditional Indian or Inuit villages retain age-old hunting and fishing ways but welcome respectful visitors to their communities. The **artwork** of the North is famous worldwide; in almost every community, artists engage in weaving, print-making, or stone, ivory, and bone carving. Locally produced artwork is available from community co-ops, galleries, or the artists themselves.

Traveling the wilds of the Canadian Arctic is a great adventure, but frankly it isn't for everyone. Most likely the Arctic isn't like anywhere you've ever traveled before, and while that may be exciting, there are some realities of Arctic travel you need to be aware of before you start making plans.

PRICES   The Arctic is an *expensive* place to travel. Airfare is very high (many tourists travel here on frequent-flier miles, one of the few ways to get around the steep ticket prices). While almost every little community has a serviceable hotel/restaurant, room prices are shockingly high; a hostel-style rustic room with full board costs as much as a decent room in Paris. Food costs are equally high (remember that all your food was air-freighted in) and the quality is poor. And don't plan on having a drink anywhere except Inuvik or Iqaluit, where you'll spend C$5 (US$3.35) a bottle for beer.

FLYING IN THE BUSH   Except for the Dempster Highway to Inuvik, there's no road access to any point in the Arctic. *All public transportation is by airplane.* To reach the most interesting points in the North, you'll need to fly on floatplanes, tiny commuter planes, and aircraft that years ago passed out of use in the rest of the world. Of course, all aircraft in the Arctic are regularly inspected and regulated for safety, but if you have phobias about flying, you might find the combination of rattling aircraft and changeable flying conditions unpleasant.

CULTURE SHOCK   The Arctic is the homeland of the Inuit. Travelers are made welcome in nearly all native villages, but it must be stressed that these communities aren't set up as holiday camps for southern visitors. Most people aren't English speakers; except for the local hotel, there may not be public areas open for non-natives. You're definitely a guest here; while people are friendly and will greet you, you'll probably feel very much an outsider.

The Inuit are hunters: On long summer nights, you'll go to sleep to the sound of hunters shooting seals along the ice floes. Chances are good you'll see people butchering seals or whales along the beaches. You may be lucky enough to visit an Inuit village during a traditional feast. All the meat, including haunches of caribou, entire seals, and slabs of whale, will be consumed raw. And the Arctic isn't a pristine place, for garbage and carcasses litter the shoreline and town pathways. Don't come to the North expecting to find a sanitized feel-good atmosphere.

If these realities are a problem for you, then you should reconsider a trip here. If not, then traveling to a traditional Inuit village under a 24-hour summer sun to partake of native hospitality is a great adventure; this is surely one of the last truly traditional cultures and unexploited areas left in North America.

INUVIK: END OF THE ROAD

Inuvik, 771km (478 miles) from Dawson City, is the town at the end of the long Dempster Highway—the most northerly road in Canada—and the most-visited center in the western Arctic. Because of its year-round road access and frequent flights from Yellowknife, Inuvik is becoming a tourist destination in itself and is the departure point for many tours out to more far-flung destinations. However, don't come looking for history: The town was built by the Canadian government in the 1950s and improved on by the oil boom in the 1970s. While there's not much charm to the town beyond its many-colored housing blocks, it does have lots of comforts and facilities: good hotels and restaurants, hospitals, schools, banks (and ATMs), shops, a Laundromat, and one traffic light. All this 2° north of the Arctic Circle!

Inuvik is on the Mackenzie River, one of the largest rivers in the world. Here, about 129km (80 miles) from its debouchment into the Arctic Ocean, the Mackenzie flows into its vast delta, 88km (55 miles) long and 65km (40 miles) wide. This incredible waterway, where the river fans out into a maze containing thousands of lakes, dozens of channels, and mile after mile of marsh, is a rich preserve of wildlife, especially waterfowl and aquatic mammals. Inuvik is also right at the northern edge of the taiga, near the beginning of the tundra, making this region a transition zone for a number of the larger Northern animals.

The town is home to a population of 3,500, composed of near-equal parts of **Inuvialuit,** the Inuit people of the western Arctic; of **Gwich'in,** a Dene tribe from south of the Mackenzie River delta; and of more recent white settlers, many of whom work at public-sector jobs.

ESSENTIALS

GETTING THERE   The drive from Dawson City along the Dempster usually takes 12 hours, and most people make the drive in 1 day (remember, in summer, there's no end of daylight). It's best to drive the road after July 1, when the spring mud has dried up. One flight a day links Inuvik to Yellowknife on **Canadian North** (☎ **800/426-7000**). Staying over Saturday night, the fare is C$800 (US$534); otherwise, expect to pay around C$1,400 (US$934).

VISITOR INFORMATION   For more information about Inuvik and the surrounding area, contact the **Western Arctic Tourism Association,** P.O. Box 2600, Inuvik, NT X0E 0T0 (☎ **800/661-0788** or 867/777-4321; fax 867/777-2434; www.inuvik.net).

WEATHER   Weather can change rapidly in Inuvik. In summer, a frigid morning, with the winds and rains barreling off the Arctic Ocean, can change to a very warm and muggy afternoon in seemingly minutes. (Yes, it does get hot up here.) During summer, there's nearly a month when the sun doesn't set at all, and 6 months when there's only a short dusk at night. Correspondingly, there are about 3 weeks in winter when the sun doesn't rise.

SPECIAL EVENTS   July is festival season in Inuvik. The **Great Northern Arts Festival,** the third week of July through August, is a celebration of the visual and performing arts, with most regional artists displaying works for sale; artists also give workshops on traditional craft techniques. The festival also includes **Musicfest,** a weekend of traditional fiddling, drumming, and jigging. The last week of July, Inuvik hosts the **Northern Games,** a celebration of traditional native sports and competitions, including drumming, dancing, high-kicking, craft displays, and the unique "Good Woman" contest, in which Inuit women show their amazing skill at seal and muskrat skinning, bannock baking, sewing, and other abilities that traditionally made a "good woman."

WHAT TO SEE IN INUVIK

The most famous landmark in Inuvik is **Our Lady of Victory Church,** a large round structure with a glistening dome, usually referred to as the Igloo Church. You should definitely stop at the **Northwest Territories Arctic Tourism** (☎ **800/661-0788** or 867/873-7200) on the south end of town. Exhibits provide a good overview of the human and natural history of the area and of recreation and sightseeing options. June 15 to Labour Day, it's open 10am to 5pm.

Several art and gift shops offer local Inuit and Indian carvings and crafts; probably the best is **Northern Images,** 4801 Franklin Ave. (☎ **867/873-5944**). Don't miss the

Boreal Bookstore, 181 Mackenzie Rd. (☎ 867/777-3748), for a great selection of books on all things Northern.

EXPLORING OUTSIDE INUVIK

The best of the local tour operators is **Arctic Nature Tours,** P.O. Box 1530, Inuvik, NT X0E 0T0 (☎ 867/777-3300; www.arcticnaturetours.com; e-mail arcticnt@ permafrost.com). This family-operated business also owns a charter airline, so there's no problem lining up planes and pilots for expeditions. Trips to all the following destinations are offered. The **Arctic Tour Company,** P.O. Box 325, Tuktoyaktuk, NT X0E 1C0 (☎ 867/977-2230; fax 867/977-2276; www.auroranet.nt.ca/atc/), also offers tours to many of the same destinations, plus an imposing list of more specialized tours, all with native guides. However, because minimum numbers are necessary for all tours, don't count on specific trips to run while you're visiting.

TUKTOYAKTUK   On the shores of the Beaufort Sea, 161km (100 miles) south of the permanent polar ice cap in the Arctic Ocean and popularly known as "Tuk," this little native town is reached by a short flight from Inuvik (in winter, the frozen Mackenzie River becomes an "ice road" linking the two towns by vehicle). Most tour operators in Inuvik offer 2-hour tours of Tuk (including the flight) for around C$160 (US$107), focusing on the curious "pingos" (volcano-like formations made of buckled ice that occur only here and in one location in Siberia) and the Inuvialuit culture. Stops are made at the workshops of stone carvers and other artisans, and you'll get the chance to stick your toe in the Arctic Ocean. Though there are a couple of hotels in Tuk, there's really no reason to spend more than a couple of hours up here; even as Arctic towns go, Tuk is pretty desolate.

MACKENZIE DELTA TRIPS   When the Mackenzie River meets the Arctic Ocean, it forms an enormous basin filled with a multitude of lakes, river channels, and marshlands. River trips on the mazelike delta are fascinating: One popular trip visits a fishing camp for tea, bannock, and conversations with local fishers who prepare Arctic char by age-old methods; the cost is C$55 (US$37). Other river tours include a dinner or a midnight-sun champagne cruise. (You can also arrange to fly to Tuk and return by boat to Inuvik up the Mackenzie River.)

HERSCHEL ISLAND   This island, 241km (149 miles) northwest of Inuvik, sits just off the northern shores of the Yukon in the Beaufort Sea. Long a base for native hunters and fishers, in the late 1800s Herschel Island became a camp for American and then Hudson's Bay Company whalers. Today, it's a territorial park, preserving both the historic whaling camp and abundant tundra plant- and wildlife (including Arctic fox, caribou, grizzly bear, and many shorebirds).

Tours of the island are generally offered mid-June to mid-September, when the Arctic ice floes move away from the island sufficiently to allow floatplanes to land in **Pauline Cove,** near the old whaling settlement. This is a great trip to an otherwise completely isolated environment. A day trip to the island, costing C$275 (US$183), includes a brief tour of the whaling station and a chance to explore the tundra landscape and Arctic shoreline. On the flight to the island, there's a good chance of seeing musk ox, nesting Arctic swans, caribou, and grizzly bear. Camping expeditions to the island can be arranged.

WHERE TO STAY & DINE

Rooms are expensive in Inuvik. It's not cheap to operate a hotel up here, and realistically, you're not likely to drive on to the next town looking for better prices. However, the following accommodations are fully modern and quite pleasant.

Robertson's B&B, 41 Mackenzie Rd. (☎ 867/777-3111; fax 867/777-3112; e-mail robertbb@permafrost.com), has two guest rooms with shared bathroom. Rates, including full breakfast, are C$70 to C$80 (US$47 to US$53) double.

Right in Inuvik is **Happy Valley Campground,** operated by the territorial parks department, with showers and electrical hookups. Between Inuvik and the airport is **Chuk Campground,** with no hookups. The camping fee for both is C$13 (US$9).

○ **Finto Motor Inn.** 288 Mackenzie Rd. (P.O. Box 1925, Inuvik, NWT X0E 0T0). ☎ **800/661-0843** or 867/777-2647. Fax 867/777-3442. 40 units. A/C TV TEL. C$125 (US$83) double. Senior rates available. AE, ER, MC, V.

The newest and quietest place to stay in Inuvik is the Finto Motor Inn, a large wood-sided building on the southern edge of town. The guest rooms are good-sized and nicely furnished, all with computer jacks; some have kitchenettes. This is where most government people stay when they come up for business, because it's the most modern and comfortable hotel. The Peppermill Restaurant (☎ **867/777-2999**) offers gourmet renditions of local game and fishes, in addition to traditional steaks and other meats; main courses run C$18 to C$28 (US$12 to US$19). The Sunday brunch is a major social event in Inuvik. In summer, a dinner theater operates from the hotel.

Mackenzie Hotel. P.O. Box 1618, Inuvik, NWT X0E 0T0. ☎ **867/777-2861.** Fax 867/777-3317. www.inuvik.net/mack. E-mail mack@permafrost.com. 33 units. TV TEL. C$120 (US$80) double. AE, DC, MC, V.

In the town center, the Mackenzie is the oldest of Inuvik's hotels (which makes it only 30). The guest rooms are large and nicely furnished, each with a couch, a couple of chairs, a desk, and a full-sized closet. On weekends, ask for a room away from the bar entrance and parking area. The staff is friendly and welcoming. The Green Briar Dining Room, with main courses at C$13 to C$20 (US$9 to US$13), has a wide selection of northern game and mainstream dishes; it's probably the best restaurant in Inuvik. There's also a coffee shop.

BAFFIN ISLAND: ADVENTURE & INUIT ART

One of the most remote and uninhabited areas in North America, rugged and beautiful **Baffin Island** is an excellent destination for the traveler willing to spend some time and money for an adventure vacation; it's also a great place if your mission is to find high-quality Inuit arts and crafts.

It's easy to spend a day or two exploring the galleries and museums of Iqaluit, but if you've come this far, you definitely should continue on to yet more remote and traditional communities. Iqaluit is the population and governmental center of Baffin, but far more scenic and culturally significant destinations are just a short plane ride away. The coast of Baffin Island is heavily incised with fjords flanked by towering glacier-hung mountains. Life in the villages remains based on traditional hunting and fishing, though some of the smallest Baffin communities have developed worldwide reputations as producers of museum-quality carvings, prints, and weavings.

Though Baffin is the fifth-largest island in the world, it has a population of only 15,000. However, it's the largest population and cultural center—and capital—of the new territory of **Nunavut,** which split off from the rest of the Northwest Territories in 1999.

○ **NorthWinds,** P.O. Box 820, Iqaluit, NT X0A 0H0 (☎ **800/549-0551** or 867/979-0551; fax 867/979-0573; www.northwinds-arctic.com/northwinds.html; e-mail plandry@nunanet.com), is Baffin Island's leading adventure-tour operator. A specialty of NorthWinds is its dogsledding expeditions. The 7-day Arctic Odyssey tour (C$2,500/US$1,668) involves 5 days on the sea ice amid the amazing fjords of the Baffin coast; all members of the party get a chance to drive the dogs. NorthWinds also offers a 12-day tour to Lake Harbour at C$6,500 (US$4,336). In spring, North-Winds offers a wildlife viewing tour (C$3,750/US$2,501) at the floe edge off Bylot Island to view narwhals, polar bears, seals, and birds. In summer, it leads hiking expeditions—10 and 14 days, costing C$2,300 and C$3,300 (US$1,534 and US$2,201)—into Auyuittuq National Park and 8-day walking and rafting trips through Katannilik Park (C$2,150/US$1,434).

ESSENTIALS

VISITOR INFORMATION   For information about Baffin Island communities, contact **Nunavut Tourism,** P.O. Box 1450, Iqaluit, NT X0A 0H0 (☎ **800/491-7910** or 867/979-6551; fax 867/979-1261; www.nunatour.nt.ca; e-mail nunatour@ nunanet.com). Any serious traveler should get hold of *The Baffin Handbook,* an excellent government-sponsored guide available from local bookstores.

You might also look into the NWT Arctic Tourism homepage at **www.nwttravel. nt.ca**. Another useful Web site is an online version of the Nunavut Handbook at **www.arctic-travel.com**. It provides information on Nunavut's land, wildlife, history, people, culture, and practical tips for travelers.

GETTING THERE   Iqaluit, 2,266km (1,511 miles) from Yellowknife, is the major transport hub on Baffin and is linked to the rest of Canada by flights from Montréal, Ottawa, Winnipeg, and Yellowknife on **First Air** (☎ **800/267-1247**) and **Canadian North** (☎ **800/426-7000**). Flights are very expensive; full-coach tickets from Yellowknife are nearly C$2,800 (US$1,868). To make the airfare more affordable, consider using frequent-flier miles.

Because there are no roads linking communities here, travel between small villages is also by plane. First Air is the major local carrier, centering out of Iqaluit; a bevy of smaller providers fill in the gaps.

SPECIAL EVENTS   A festival of spring, **Toonik Tyme** is held the last week of April, featuring igloo building, ice sculpture, dogsled racing, and reputedly the toughest snowmobile race in the world. Cultural activities include Inuit dancing and singing, an arts fair, and traditional competitions like harpoon throwing and whip cracking.

On July 9, Nunavut celebrates its recent accession to territorial status with **Nunavut Day,** with festivities in every community. At this new celebration, traditional events might include bicycle races, running races, a tea-boiling contest, and other games of skill. The Elders play an important part in this celebration.

IQALUIT: GATEWAY TO BAFFIN ISLAND

On the southern end of the island, **Iqaluit** is the major town on Baffin and like most Inuit settlements is quite young; it grew up alongside a U.S. Air Force airstrip built here in 1942. The rambling village overlooking Frobisher Bay now boasts a population of more than 4,200 and is a hodgepodge of weather-proofed government and civic buildings (the futuristic grade school looks like an ice-cube tray lying on its side) and wind-beaten public housing.

For a small town, there's a lot of activity here, with children roaring down the steep, rocky hills on mountain bikes; planes roaring; and husky pups yelping for attention. As in all Arctic towns, at any given time in summer, the entire population seems to be strolling somewhere. Even though no roads link Iqaluit to anywhere else, everyone seems to have at least one vehicle to drive endlessly around the town's labyrinth of dusty paths. There are no street addresses, because there are few roads organized enough to bother calling streets.

What to See in Town

Begin at the **Unikkaarvik Visitor/Information Centre** (☎ 867/979-4636), overlooking the bay, with a friendly staff to answer questions and a series of displays on local native culture, natural history, and local art. There's even an igloo to explore. June 1 to Labour Day, the center is open daily 10am to 5pm; the rest of the year, it's open Monday to Friday the same hours.

Next door is the **Nunuuta Sunakkutaangit Museum** (☎ 867/979-5537), housed in an old Hudson's Bay Company building. The collection of Arctic arts and crafts here is excellent; this is a good place to observe the stylized beauty of native carvings. It's open Tuesday to Sunday 1 to 5pm. The **Government of Nunavut Building,** at Iqaluit's "four corners," also has a good display of Northern art in the lobby.

If you aren't planning to go any farther afield in Baffin, you may wish to catch a taxi out to **Sylvia Grinnel Park** and take a hike on the tundra. The park is only 5km (3.1 miles) from Iqaluit but is on the other side of the ridge from town; it's a relatively quiet and protected place to see wildflowers and walk along an Arctic river. Another good **hiking trail** runs from Iqaluit to the "suburb" of Apex, following the beach and headland above Frobisher Bay. The trail begins near the Iqaluit cemetery; watch for the "inuksuks" (manlike stone cairns) marking the trail.

Iqaluit is the primary center for **Baffin Island art.** Local galleries carry works from communities around the island; ask at the visitor center for a map of arts and crafts locations if you're interested in buying; prices here can be at least half of what they are down south.

Where to Stay

✪ **Discovery Lodge Hotel.** P.O. Box 387, Iqaluit, NT X0A 0H0. ☎ **867/979-4433.** Fax 867/979-6591. www.arctic-travel.com/DIS/covery.html. E-mail disclodge@nunanet. com. 53 units. TV TEL. C$140–C$185 (US$93–US$123) double; C$235 (US$157) suite. AE, DC, ER, MC, V.

About halfway between town and the airport, the Discovery Lodge is a newer hotel with nicely furnished, good-sized guest rooms and an inviting public sitting area. All rooms come with two beds (some are specially designed wedge-shaped beds meant to save space). No-smoking rooms (a rarity in the North) are in their own wing. The Discovery Lodge in general is better maintained than most Arctic hotels; for many travelers who've been to the North before, the fact that there's no public bar in the hotel will be a plus. The restaurant is good (you can have a drink with a meal); it's one of the more formal places to eat in Iqaluit.

✪ **Pearson's Arctic Home Stay.** P.O. Box 449, Iqaluit, NT X0A 0H0. ☎ **867/ 979-6408.** Fax 867/979-4888. 3 units (can sleep up to 8), none with bathroom. C$125 (US$83) per person. Rates include breakfast. V.

At Iqaluit's premier B&B, you get to stay with the town's former mayor in a lovely home filled with Inuit carving and artifacts. The rooms are simply decorated but comfortable; one has a foldout bed.

Regency Frobisher Inn. P.O. Box 610, Iqaluit, NT X0A 0H0. ☎ **867/979-2222.** Fax 867/979-0427. www.explorerhotel.nt.ca. E-mail frobinn@nunet.com. 49 units. TV TEL. C$185 (US$123) double. AE, ER, MC, V.

High above the town, the "Frobe," as it's known by regulars, is in the same complex of buildings that houses the regional government offices, a small shopping arcade, and the municipal pool. The guest rooms are well heated and pleasantly furnished and decorated, each with a desk, a dresser, and two chairs. The views on the bay side are quite panoramic. There's a very lively bar as well as an excellent restaurant, with a mix of French and Northern choices.

PANGNIRTUNG & AUYUITTUQ NATIONAL PARK

Called "Pang" by Territorians, **Pangnirtung** is at the heart of one of the most scenic areas in Nunavut. Located on a deep, mountain-flanked fjord, Pang is the jumping off point for 21,497km² (8,300-sq.-mile) Auyuittuq National Park, often referred to as "the Switzerland of the Arctic." Pang is served by daily flights from Iqaluit on First Air.

Pang itself is a lovely little village of 1,200 people, with a postcard view up the narrow fjord to the glaciered peaks of Auyuittuq. The local population is very friendly and outgoing, which isn't the case in some other Inuit villages. The **Angmarlik Visitor/Interpretive Centre** (☎ 867/473-8737) is definitely worth a stop, with well-presented displays on local Inuit history and culture. June 15 to Labour Day, it's open daily 10am to 5pm. Immediately across the street are print and weaving shops, where you can visit local artisans.

Most people go to Pang to reach **Auyuittuq National Park,** 31km (19 miles) farther up Pangnirtung Fjord. *Auyuittuq* means "the land that never melts" and refers to 5,698km² (2,200-sq.-mile) Penny Ice Cap, which covers the high plateaus of the park, and the glaciers that edge down into the lower valleys and cling to the towering granite peaks. The landscapes are extremely dramatic: Cliffs rise from the milky-green sea, terminating in hornlike glacier-draped peaks 2,333m (7,654 ft.) high; in fact, the world's longest uninterrupted cliff face (over 0.8km/0.5 mile of sheer rock) is in the park. Auyuittuq is largely the province of long-distance hikers and rock climbers; if you're looking for an adventurous walking holiday in magnificent scenery, this might be it. The best time to visit is July to mid-August, when the days are long and afternoons bring short-sleeve weather. You'll need to hire an outfitter with a boat to take you to the park trailhead; costs are C$85 to C$100 (US$57 to US$67). For details, contact the Auyuittuq Park Superintendent, P.O. Box 353, Pangnirtung, NT X0A 0R0 (☎ 867/473-8828; fax 867/473-8612; e-mail Nunavut_Info@pch.gc.ca).

ACCOMMODATIONS & DINING   The only year-round place to stay and eat in Pang is **Auyuittuq Lodge** (☎ 867/473-8955; fax 867/473-8611), more a hostel than a hotel. There are 25 clean, cheerful rooms, each with two twin beds; the bathroom is down the hall. Meals are served family-style in the pleasant guest lounge and at set times only. Simple lodging is C$135 (US$90) per person; for three meals, it's an extra C$65 (US$43). Nonguests are welcome for meals; reservations are requested. In summer there's a free campground on the edge of Pang.

OUTFITTERS   The best of the local outfitters is **Joavee Alivaktuk,** a personable Pang native with 25 years of experience as a professional guide. Joavee provides boat service to Auyuittuq for C$95 (US$63) and operates day trips to Kekerten Historic Park for C$150 (US$100), Arctic char–fishing trips, and whale-watching trips into Cumberland Sound. Contact **Alivaktuk Outfitting** at P.O. Box 3, Pangnirtung, NT X0A 0R0 (☎ and fax **867/473-8721**).

POND INLET

In many ways, the best reason to make the trip to **Pond Inlet** on Baffin's northern shore is simply to see the landscape. On a clear day, the flight from Iqaluit up to Pond is simply astounding: hundreds of miles of knife-edged mountains, massive ice caps (remnants of the ice fields that once covered all North America), glacier-choked valleys, and deep fjords flooded by the sea. It's an epic landscape—in all the country, perhaps only the Canadian Rockies can match the eastern coast of Baffin Island for sheer scenic drama.

Pond Inlet sits on **Eclipse Sound,** near the top of Baffin Island in the heart of this rugged beauty. Opposite the town is **Bylot Island,** a wildlife refuge and part of Sirmilik (North Baffin) National Park. Its craggy peaks rear 2,167m (7,109 ft.) straight up from the sea; from its central ice caps, two massive glaciers pour down into the sound directly across from town.

Considering the amazing scenery in the area, Pond Inlet is relatively untouristed. The peak tourist season is May and June, when local outfitters offer trips out to the edge of the ice floes, the point where the ice of the protected bays meets the open water of the Arctic Ocean. In spring this is where you find much of the Arctic's ✪ **wildlife:** seals, walruses, bird life, polar bears, narwhals, and other species converge here to feed, often on one another. A wildlife-viewing trip out to the floe edge (by snowmobile or dogsled) requires at least 3 days, with 5-day trips advised for maximum viewing opportunities. Other recreation opportunities open up in August, when the ice clears out of Eclipse Sound. Bird-watching boat trips out to Bylot Island are offered (the rare ivory gull nests here), as well as narwhal-watching trips in the fjords. Hill walking to glaciered peaks, sea kayaking in fjords, and superlative Arctic char fishing are also popular summer activities. It's best to allow several days in Pond Inlet if you're coming for summer trips; the weather is very changeable this far north.

ACCOMMODATIONS & DINING   The local co-op also operates the **Sauniq Hotel** (☎ **867/899-8928;** fax 867/899-8770), offering 12 rooms with TVs; rates are C$185 (US$123), including full board. First Air flies into Pond Inlet 5 days a week from Iqaluit.

OUTFITTERS   Two outfitters operate out of Pond Inlet. The local **Toonoonik Sahoonik Co-op,** General Delivery, Pond Inlet, NT X0A 0S0 (☎ **867/899-8812;** fax 867/899-8770), offers a variety of trips throughout the year. **Polar Sea Adventures,** P.O. Box 60, Pond Inlet, NT X0A 0C0 (☎ **867/899-8870;** fax 867/899-8817; www.polarseaadventures.com; e-mail info@polarseaadventures.com), is operated by Scottish-born John Henderson and offers naturalist-guided floe-edge trips and guided hiking and boat trips in summer; Polar Sea is the best contact for sea kayaking or narwhal-watching trips on Milne Ilet.

LAKE HARBOUR (KIMMIRUT): STONE CARVERS & KATANNILIK TERRITORIAL PARK

The center for Baffin Island's famed stone-carving industry, **Lake Harbour,** or **Kimmirut,** is located along a rocky harbor, directly south of Iqaluit on the southern shore of Baffin Island. While many people make the trip to this dynamic picturesque community to visit the workshops of world-renowned carvers, Katannilik Territorial Park is a preserve of Arctic wildlife and lush tundra vegetation and offers access to Soper River. The Soper, a Canadian Heritage River, is famed for its many waterfalls in side valleys and for its long-distance float and canoe trips.

Many people visit **Katannilik Territorial Park** for a less demanding version of rugged Auyuittuq National Park farther north. Wildlife viewing is good, and hiking trails wind through the park. Canoeing or kayaking the Soper River is a popular 3-day trip that's full of adventure but still suitable for a family. For more information on the park, contact the Katannilik Park Manager, Lake Harbour, NT X0A 0N0 (☎ **867/ 939-2084;** fax 867/939-2406). For information on canoe rentals and guided trips through Katannilik Park, contact NorthWinds (see above).

To watch local artists at work, visit the carving studio across from the tourist office. For a selection of local carvings, go to the co-op store.

ACCOMMODATIONS & DINING　Lodging is available in Lake Harbour at the **Kimik Co-op Hotel** (☎ **867/939-2093;** fax 867/939-2005), with eight rooms costing C$125 (US$83); full board is available for an extra C$60 (US$40).

OTHER ARCTIC DESTINATIONS

BATHURST INLET　One of the most notable Arctic lodges, **Bathurst Inlet Lodge** was founded in 1969 for naturalists and those interested in the Arctic's natural history and ecology. The lodge is at the mouth of the Burnside River, in a rugged landscape of tundra and rocky cliffs, housed in the historic buildings of a former Oblate mission and the old Hudson's Bay Company trading post.

The lodge provides custom quotes and can make arrangements to suit your individual needs, such as fly-ins, fishing, hiking, cross-country skiing, or dog-teaming; flightseeing, caribou-viewing, wildlife photography; use of a wilderness cabin in any season, including winter, with rentals by the day, week, month, or year. For more details, contact **Bathurst Inlet Lodge,** P.O. Box 820, Yellowknife, NT X1A 2N6 (☎ **867/873-2595;** fax 867/920-4263; www.virtualnorth.com/bathurst; e-mail bathurst@internorth.com).

QUTTINIRPAAQ (Ellesmere Island) National Park Reserve　A good part of the intrigue of **Ellesmere Island** is its absolute remoteness. A preserve of rugged glacier-choked mountains, ice fields, mountain lakes and fjords, and Arctic wildlife, Ellesmere Island National Park is the most northerly point in Canada. During the short summer, experienced hikers and mountaineers make their way to this wilderness area to explore some of the most isolated and inaccessible land in the world.

Getting to Ellesmere is neither easy nor cheap. From Resolute Bay (served by regularly scheduled flights on Air North and First Air), park visitors must charter a private airplane for the 960km (595-mile) flight farther north. There are no facilities or improvements in the park itself, so you must be prepared for extremes of weather and physical endurance. The most common activity is hiking from Lake Hazen at the center of the park to Tanquary Fjord in the southwest corner. This 129km (80-mile) trek crosses rugged tundra moorland, as well as several glaciers, and demands fords of major rivers. Needless to say, Ellesmere Island Park isn't for the uninitiated.

For more information and an up-to-date listing of outfitters who run trips into the park, contact **Parks Canada,** P.O. Box 353, Pangnirtung, NT X0A 0R0 (☎ **867/473-8828;** fax 867/473-8612; e-mail Nunavut_Info@pch.gc.ca). You can also visit the Web site devoted to Canada's territorial and national parks at **www.parcscanada.gc.ca.**

Appendix: Canada in Depth

by Bill McRae

Canada's sheer amount of elbow space can make you dizzy. At 3.8 million square miles (200,000 more than the United States), this colossal expanse contains only 29 million people—nearly 10 million fewer than the state of California alone. Most of the population is clustered in a relatively narrow southern belt that boasts all the nation's large cities and nearly all its industries. The silent Yukon, Northwest Territories, and Nunavut—where 55,000 people dot 1.5 million square miles—remain a frontier, stretching to the Arctic shores and embracing thousands of lakes no one has ever charted, counted, or named.

It's impossible to easily categorize this land or its people—just when you think you know Canada, you discover another place, another temperament, another hidden side.

1 History 101

THE FOUNDING OF NEW FRANCE

The Vikings landed in Canada more than 1,000 years ago, but the French were the first Europeans to get a toehold in the country. In 1608, Samuel de Champlain established a settlement on the cliffs overlooking the St. Lawrence River—today's Québec City. This was exactly a year after the Virginia Company founded Jamestown. Hundreds of miles of unexplored wilderness lay between the embryo colonies, but they were inexorably set on a collision course.

The early stages of the struggle for the new continent were explorations, and there the French outdid the English. Their fur traders, navigators, soldiers, and missionaries opened up not only Canada but also most of the United States. At least 35 of the 50 United States were either discovered, mapped, or settled by the French. Gradually, they staked out an immense colonial empire that, in patches and minus recognized borders, stretched from Hudson Bay in the Arctic to the Gulf of Mexico. Christened New France, it was run on an ancient seigniorial system, whereby settlers were granted land by the Crown in return for military service.

The military obligation was essential, for the colony knew hardly a moment of peace during its existence. New France blocked the path of western expansion by England's seaboard colonies with a string of forts that lined the Ohio-Mississippi Valley. The Anglo-Americans were determined to break through, and so the frontier clashes crackled and

Dateline

- **1608** Samuel de Champlain founds the settlement of Kebec—today's Québec City.
- **1642** The French colony of Ville-Marie established, later renamed Montréal.
- **1759** The British defeat the French at the Plains of Abraham. Québec City falls.
- **1763** All "New France" (Canada) ceded to the British.
- **1775** American Revolutionary forces capture Montréal but are repulsed at Québec City.
- **1813** Americans blow up Fort York (Toronto) in the War of 1812.
- **1841** The Act of Union creates the United Provinces of Canada.
- **1855** Ottawa becomes Canada's capital.
- **1869** The Hudson's Bay Company sells Rupert's Land to Canada. It becomes the Province of Alberta.
- **1873** The Northwest Mounted Police (the Mounties) are created.
- **1875** The West Coast community of Gastown is incorporated as the city of Vancouver. The Northwest Mounted Police build the log fort that will develop into the city of Calgary.
- **1885** Under Louis Riel, the Métis rebel in western Saskatchewan.
- **1887** The Transcontinental Railroad reaches Vancouver, connecting Canada from ocean to ocean.
- **1896** The Klondike gold rush brings 100,000 people swarming into the Yukon.
- **1914** Canada enters World War I alongside Britain. Some 60,000 Canadians die in combat.
- **1920** The Northwest Territories separate from the Yukon.

continues

flared, with the native tribes participating ferociously. These miniature wars were nightmares of savagery, waged with knives and tomahawks as much as with muskets and cannons, characterized by raids and counter-raids, burning villages, and massacred women and children.

The French retaliated in kind. They converted the Abenaki tribe to Christianity and encouraged them to raid deep into New England territory, where, in 1704, they totally destroyed the town of Deerfield, Massachusetts. The Americans answered with a punitive blitz expedition by the famous green-clad Roger's Rangers, who wiped out the main Abenaki village and slaughtered half its population.

By far the most dreaded of the tribes was the Iroquois, who played the same role in the Canadian east as the Sioux (another French label) played in the American West. Astute politicians, the Iroquois learned to play the English against the French and vice versa, lending their scalping knives first to one side, then to the other. It took more than a century before they finally succumbed to the whites' smallpox, firewater, and gunpowder—in that order.

THE FALL OF QUÉBEC

There were only about 65,000 French settlers in the colony, but they more than held their own against the million Anglo-Americans, first and foremost because they were natural forest fighters—one Canadian trapper could stalemate six redcoats in the woods. Mainly, however, it was because they made friends with the local tribes whenever possible. The majority of tribes sided with the French and made the English pay a terrible price for their blindness.

Even before French and English interests in the New World came to the point of armed struggle in the Seven Years' War, the British had largely taken control of Acadia, though its lush forests and farmlands were dotted with French settlements. The governors knew there would be war, so, suspicious of Acadia's French-speaking inhabitants, they decided on a bold and ruthless plan: All Acadians who wouldn't openly pledge allegiance to the British sovereign would be deported. The order came in 1755, and French-speaking families throughout the province were forcibly moved from their homes, many resettling in the French territory of Louisiana, where their Cajun language and culture are still alive today. To replace the

Acadians, shiploads of Scottish and Irish settlers arrived from the British Isles, and the province soon acquired the name Nova Scotia—New Scotland.

When the final round of fighting began in 1754, it opened with a series of shattering English debacles. The French had a brilliant commander, the Marquis de Montcalm, exactly the kind of unorthodox tactician needed for the fluid semiguerrilla warfare of the American wilderness. Britain's proud General Braddock rode into a French-Indian ambush that killed him and scattered his army. Montcalm led an expedition against Fort Oswego that wiped out the stronghold and turned Lake Ontario into a French waterway. The following summer he repeated the feat with Fort William Henry, at the head of Lake George, which fell amid ghastly scenes of massacre, later immortalized by James Fenimore Cooper in *The Last of the Mohicans*. Middle New York now lay wide open to raids, and England's hold on America seemed to be slipping.

Then, like a cornered boxer bouncing from the ropes, the British came back with a devastating right-left-right that not only saved their colonies but also won them the entire continent. The first punches were against Fort Duquesne, in Pennsylvania, and against the Fortress of Louisbourg, on Cape Breton, both of which they took after bloody sieges. Then, where least expected, came the ultimate haymaker, aimed straight at the enemy's solar plexus—Québec.

In June 1759, a British fleet nosed its way from the Atlantic down the St. Lawrence River. In charge of the troops on board was the youngest general in the army, 32-year-old James Wolfe, whose military record was remarkable and whose behavior was so eccentric he had the reputation of being "mad as a March hare." The struggle for Québec dragged on until September, when Wolfe, near desperation, played his final card. He couldn't storm those gallantly defended fortress walls, though the British guns had shelled the town to rubble. Wolfe therefore loaded 5,000 men into boats

- **1930** Depression and mass unemployment hit Canada.
- **1939** Canada enters World War II with Britain.
- **1947** Huge oil deposits are discovered at Leduc, southwest of Edmonton. The Alberta oil boom begins.
- **1959** The opening of the St. Lawrence Seaway turns Toronto into a major seaport.
- **1967** Montréal hosts the World Expo.
- **1968** The Parti Québecois is founded by René Lévesque. The separatist movement begins.
- **1970** Cabinet Minister Pierre Laporte is kidnapped and murdered. The War Measures Act is imposed on Québec Province.
- **1976** Montréal becomes the site of the Olympic Games.
- **1988** Calgary hosts the Winter Olympics.
- **1989** The Canada-U.S. Free Trade Agreement eliminates all tariffs on goods of national origin moving between the two countries.
- **1993** The Conservative party is swept out of power in elections.
- **1995** Québec votes narrowly to remain in Canada.
- **1997** Jean Chrétien is reelected prime minister.
- **1999** Nunavut severs itself from the rump Northwest Territories to become a self-governed territory and Inuit homeland.

A Confederation of Provinces

Canada has always been a loosely linked country, a confederation of provinces, not a union of states. Canadians are quick to tell you theirs is a "cultural mosaic" of people, not a "melting pot." These factors account in great part for two of Canada's most striking characteristics: its cultural vitality and its habits of mistrust and contention.

The First Scalpers

According to some historians, the English introduced scalping to North America by offering a cash bounty for each French scalp the native braves brought in.

and rowed upriver to a cove behind the city. Then they silently climbed the towering cliff face in the darkness, and when morning came Wolfe had his army squarely astride Montcalm's supply lines. Now the French had to come out of their stronghold and fight in the open.

The British formed their famous "thin red line" across the bush-studded Plains of Abraham, just west of the city. Montcalm advanced on them with five regiments, all in step, and in the next quarter of an hour the fate of Canada was decided. The redcoats stood like statues as the French drew closer—100 yards, 60 yards, 40 yards. Then a command rang out, and (in such perfect unison it sounded like a single thunderclap) the English muskets crashed. The redcoats advanced four measured paces, halted, fired, advanced another four paces with robot precision—halted, fired again. Then it was all over.

The plain was covered with the fallen French. Montcalm lay mortally wounded, and the rest of his troops fled helter-skelter. Among the British casualties was Wolfe himself. With two bullets through his body, he lived just long enough to hear that he'd won. Montcalm died a few hours after him. Today, overlooking the boardwalk of Québec, you'll find a unique memorial to these men—a statue commemorating both victor and vanquished of the same battle.

THE U.S. INVASION

The capture of Québec determined the war and left Britain ruler of all North America down to the Mexican border. Yet, oddly enough, this victory generated Britain's worst defeat. For if the French had held Canada, the British government would certainly have been more careful in its treatment of the American colonists. As it was, the British felt cocksure and decided to make the colonists themselves pay for the outrageous costs of the French and Indian Wars. The taxes slapped on all imports—especially tea—infuriated the colonists to the point of open rebellion against the Crown.

But if the British misjudged the temper of the colonists, the Americans were equally wrong about the mood of the Canadians. Washington felt sure the French in the north would join the American Revolution or at least not resist an invasion of American soldiers. He was terribly mistaken on both counts. The French had little love for either of the English-speaking antagonists. But they were staunch Royalists and devout Catholics, with no sympathy for the "godless" republicans from the south. Only a handful changed sides, and most French Canadians fought grimly shoulder to shoulder with their erstwhile enemies.

Thirty-eight years later, in the War of 1812, another U.S. army marched up the banks of the Richelieu River where it flows from Lake Champlain to the St. Lawrence. And once again the French Canadians stuck by the British and flung back the invaders. The war ended in a draw, but with surprisingly happy results. Britain and the young United States agreed to demilitarize the Great Lakes and to extend their mutual border along the 49th parallel to the Rockies.

LOYALISTS & IMMIGRANTS

One of the side effects of the American Revolution was an influx of English-speaking newcomers for Canada. About 50,000 Americans who had remained faithful to George III, the United Empire Loyalists, migrated to Canada because they were given rough treatment in the States. They settled mostly in Nova Scotia and began to populate the almost-empty shores of what's now New Brunswick.

After the Napoleonic Wars, a regular tide of immigrants came from England, which was going through the early and cruelest stages of the Industrial Revolution. They were fleeing from the hideously bleak factory towns, from workhouses, starvation wages, and impoverished Scottish farms. Even the unknown perils of the New World seemed preferable to these blessings of the Dickens era. By 1850, more than half a million immigrants had arrived, pushing Canada's population above 2 million. The population centers began to shift westward, away from the old seaboard colonies in the east, opening up the territories eventually called Ontario, Manitoba, and Saskatchewan.

With increased population came the demand for confederation, largely because the various colony borders hampered trade. Britain complied rather promptly. In 1867, Parliament passed an act creating a federal union out of the colonies of Upper and Lower Canada, Nova Scotia, and New Brunswick. British Columbia hesitated over whether to remain separate, join the United States, or merge with Canada, but finally voted itself in. Remote Newfoundland hesitated longest of all—it remained a distinct colony until 1949, when it became Canada's 10th province.

THE MÉTIS REBELLION

Geographically, Canada stretched from the Atlantic to the Pacific, but in reality most of the immense region in between lay beyond the rule of Ottawa, the nation's capital. The endless prairies and forest lands of the West and Northwest were inhabited by about 40,000 people, more than half of them nomadic tribes pushed there by the waves of white settlers. They lived by hunting, fishing, and trapping, depending largely on buffalo for food, clothing, and shelter. As the once-enormous herds began to dwindle, life grew increasingly hard for the nomads. Adding to their troubles were whiskey traders peddling poisonous rotgut for furs and packs of outlaws who took what they wanted at gunpoint.

Ordinary law officers were nearly useless. In 1873, the federal government created a quite extraordinary force: the Northwest Mounted Police, now called the Royal Canadian Mounted Police (and now rarely mounted). The scarlet-coated Mounties earned a legendary reputation for toughness, fairness, and the ability to hunt down wrongdoers. And unlike their American counterparts, they usually brought in prisoners alive.

But even the Mounties couldn't handle the desperate uprising that shook western Saskatchewan in 1885. As the railroad relentlessly pushed across the prairies and the buffalo vanished, the people known as the Métis felt they had to fight for their existence. The Métis, offspring of French trappers and native women, were superb hunters and trackers. The westward expansion had driven them from Manitoba to the banks of the Saskatchewan River, where some 6,000 of them now made their last stand against iron rails and wooden farmhouses. They had a charismatic leader in Louis Riel, a man educated enough to teach school and mad enough to think God wanted him to found a new religion.

With Riel's rebels rose their natural allies, the Plains tribes, under chiefs Pound-maker and Big Bear. Together, they were a formidable force. The Métis attacked the Mounted Police at Duck Lake, cut the telegraph wires, and proclaimed an independent republic. Their allies stormed the town of Battleford, then captured and burned Fort Pitt. The alarmed administration in Ottawa sent an army marching westward under General Middleton, equipped with artillery and Gatling machine guns. The Métis checked them briefly at Fish Creek but had to fall back on their main village of Batoche. There the last battle of the west took place—long lines of redcoats charging with fixed bayonets, the Métis fighting from house to house, from rifle pits and crude trenches, so short of ammunition they had to shoot lead buttons instead of bullets.

Batoche fell (you can still see the bullet marks on the houses there), and the rebellion was completely crushed shortly afterward. Louis Riel was tried for treason and murder. Though any court today probably would've found him insane, the Canadian authorities hanged him.

RAILROADS, WHEAT & WAR

The reason the army was able to crush Riel's rebellion so quickly was also the reason for its outbreak: the Canadian Pacific Railway. The railroad was more than a marvel of engineering—it formed a steel band holding the country together, enabling Canada to live up to its motto, *A Mari Usque ad Mare* ("From Sea to Sea").

Though the free-roaming prairie people hated the iron horse, railroads were vital to Canada's survival as a nation. They had to be pushed through, against all opposition, because the isolated provinces threatened to drift into the orbit of the United States. Without the western provinces, the Dominion would cease to exist. As one journalist of the time put it: "The whistle of a locomotive is the true cradle song and anthem of our country." As the country's transportation system developed, the central provinces emerged as one of the world's biggest breadbaskets. In a single decade, wheat production zoomed from 56 million bushels to more than 200 million, putting Canada on a par with the United States and Russia as a granary.

And despite the bitterness engendered by Riel's execution, in the following year Canada elected its first prime minister of French heritage. Sir Wilfrid Laurier had one foot in each ethnic camp and proved to be a superlative leader—according to some, the best his country ever produced. His term of office (1896 to 1911) was a period in which Canada flexed its muscles like a young giant and looked forward to unlimited growth and a century of peaceful prosperity—just like an equally optimistic American neighbor to the south.

With the onset of World War I, the Dominion went to war allied with Britain and likewise tried to fight it on a volunteer basis. It didn't work. The tall, healthy Canadians, together with the Australians, formed the shock troops of the British Empire and earned that honor with torrents of blood. The entire western front in France was littered with Canadian bones. The flow of volunteers became a trickle, and in 1917 the Dominion was forced to introduce conscription. The measure ran into violent opposition from the French-speaking minority, who saw conscription as a device to thin out their numbers.

The draft law went through, but it strained the nation's unity almost to the breaking point. The results were ghastly. More than 60,000 Canadians fell in battle, a terrible bloodletting for a country of 250,000. (In World War II, by contrast, Canada lost 40,000 from a population of 11.5 million.)

TOWARD WORLD POWER

Between the world wars, the fortunes of Canada more or less reflected those of the United States, except that Canada was never foolish enough to join the "noble experiment" of Prohibition. Some of its citizens, in fact, waxed rich on the lucrative bootlegging trade across the border.

But the Great Depression, coupled with disastrous droughts in the western provinces, hit all the harder in Canada. There was no equivalent of Roosevelt's New Deal in the Dominion. The country staggered along from one financial crisis to the next until the outbreak of World War II totally transformed the situation. The war provided the boost Canada needed to join the ranks of the major industrial nations. And the surge of postwar immigration provided the numbers required to work the new industries. From 1941 to 1974, Canada doubled in population and increased its gross national product nearly tenfold.

With the discovery of huge uranium deposits in Ontario and Saskatchewan, Canada was in the position to add nuclear energy to its power resources. And the opening of the St. Lawrence Seaway turned Toronto—more than 1,000 miles from the nearest ocean—into a major seaport. All these achievements propelled Canada into its present position: a powerhouse of manufacturing and trading, with a standard of living to match that of the United States. But, simultaneously, old ghosts were raising their heads again.

TROUBLE IN QUÉBEC

As an ethnic enclave, the French Canadians had won their battle for survival with flying colors. From their original 65,000 settlers, they had grown to more than 6 million, without receiving reinforcements from overseas. They had preserved and increased their presence by means of large families, rigid cultural cohesion, and the unifying influence of their Catholic faith. But they had fallen far behind the English-speaking majority economically and politically. Few of them held top positions in industry or finance, and they enjoyed relatively little say in national matters.

What rankled most with them was that Canada never recognized French as a second national language. In other words, the French were expected to be bilingual if they wanted good careers, but the English-speakers got along nicely with just their own tongue. On a general cultural basis too the country overwhelmingly reflected Anglo-Saxon attitudes rather than an Anglo-French mixture.

By the early 1960s, this discontent led to a dramatic radicalization of Québecois politics. A new separatist movement arose that regarded Québec not as simply 1 of 10 provinces but as *l'état du Québec,* a distinct state that might, if it chose, break away from the country. The most extreme faction, the Front de Liberation du Québec (FLQ), was frankly revolutionary and terrorist. It backed its demands with bombs, arson, and murder, culminating in the kidnap-killing of Cabinet Minister Pierre Laporte in October 1970.

The Ottawa government, under Prime Minister Pierre Trudeau, imposed the War Measures Act and moved 10,000 troops into the province. The police used their exceptional powers under the act to break up civil disorders, arrest hundreds of suspects, and catch the murderers of Laporte. And in the 1973 provincial elections, the separatists were badly defeated, winning only 6 seats from a total of 110.

The crisis eventually calmed down. In some ways, its effects were beneficial. The federal government redoubled its efforts to remove the worst grievances of the French Canadians. Federal funds flowed to French schools outside Québec (nearly half the schoolchildren of New Brunswick, for example, are French-speaking). French Canadians were appointed to senior positions. Most important, all provinces were asked to make French an official language, which entailed making signs, government forms, transportation schedules, and other printed matter bilingual. Civil servants had to bone up on French to pass their exams, and the business world began to stipulate bilingualism for men and women aiming at executive positions. All these measures were already afoot before the turmoil began, but there's no doubt that bloodshed helped to accelerate them.

UNION OR SEPARATION?

Ever since the violent crisis, Canadian politicians of all hues have been trying to patch up some sort of compromise that would enable their country to remain united. They appeared close to success when they formulated the so-called Meech Lake Accord in the 1980s. Québec's premier set up a commission to study ways to change the province's constitutional relationship with Ottawa's federal government. This aroused the ire of other provinces, which failed to see why Québec should be granted a "special" position in Canada. During this time, the separatist Parti Québecois rallied its forces and staged a political comeback. The Meech Lake agreement became too unwieldy to pass muster, and an alliance of French Canadians, native Canadian groups, western Canadian libertarians—and the province of New Brunswick—drove a stake through the heart of the accord. So the proposals, memorandums, and referendums go on and on; each one vetoed by the other camp and none coming closer to a solution.

The rift between Québec's French and English speakers—and between Québec and the other provinces—is today wider than ever. To make the situation even more complex, the only population segment in Québec that's growing is that of non-English- and non-French-speaking immigrants. Winning over the immigrant vote is suddenly big political business in Québec.

In October 1995, Québec again faced a referendum asking whether the French-speaking province should separate from the rest of Canada, and suddenly Canada teetered on the brink of splitting apart. The vote went in favor of the pro-unity camp by a razor-thin margin, but the issue was hardly resolved: In all likelihood, it lives to be reborn as another referendum. Meanwhile, as public officials debate separatism, Québec's younger generation is voting with its feet. Many of its brightest and best are heading west, particularly to more prosperous British Columbia and Alberta. However, these western provinces—no lovers of Ottawa—themselves dream of loosening the federal laws binding them to eastern Canada.

By now, most Canadians are heartily tired of the Québec debate, though nobody seems to have a clear idea how to end it. Some say secession is the only way out; others favor the Swiss formula of biculturalism and bilingualism. For Québec, the breakaway advocated by Francophone hotheads could spell economic disaster. Most of Canada's industrial and financial power is in the English-speaking provinces. An independent Québec would be a poor country. But all Canada would be poorer by losing the special flavor and rich cultural heritage imparted by the presence of La Belle Province.

ONWARD INTO THE MILLENNIUM:
THE CREATION OF NUNAVUT & MORE

Elements of the Canadian economy are still adapting to the landmark Free Trade Agreement concluded with the States in 1989. While free trade hasn't done much to revive the smokestack industries that once were the engines of eastern Canada, the agreement, combined with the weak dollar, has actually been good for much of Canada's huge agricultural heartland. However, the globalization of trade is transforming the Canadian economy in ways that produce confusion and hostility in the average citizen. Many Canadians are deeply ambivalent about being so closely linked to their powerful southern neighbor,

Canada has sought "unity through diversity" as a national ideal, and its people are even more diverse than its scenery. In the eastern province of Québec live 6 million French Canadians, whose motto, Je me souviens ("I remember"), has kept them "more French than France" through 2 centuries of Anglo domination. They've transformed Canada into a bilingual country where everything official—including parking tickets and airline passes—comes in two tongues.

The English-speaking majority of the populace is a mosaic rather than a block. Two massive waves of immigration—one before 1914, the other between 1945 and 1972—poured 6.5 million assorted Europeans and Americans into the country, providing muscles and skills, as well as a kaleidoscope of cultures. The 1990s saw another wave of immigration—largely from Asia and particularly from Hong Kong—that has transformed the economics and politics of British Columbia. Thus, Nova Scotia is as Scottish as haggis and kilts, Vancouver has the largest Chinese population outside Asia, the plains of Manitoba are sprinkled with the onion-shaped domes of Ukrainian churches, and Ontario offers Italian street markets and a theater festival featuring the works of Shakespeare at, yes, Stratford.

You can attend a native-Canadian tribal assembly, a Chinese New Year dragon parade, an Inuit spring celebration, a German Bierfest, a Highland gathering, or a Slavic folk dance. There are group settlements on the prairies where the working parlance is Danish, Czech, or Hungarian, and entire villages speak Icelandic.

and the trade agreement (and U.S. culture in general) often gets the blame for everything that's going wrong with Canada. At the same time, the reality of the joined Canadian and U.S. economies—85% of Canada's trade is with its southern neighbor—has started a dialogue in Jean Chrétien's center-left cabinet about linking the Canadian and U.S. dollars, a move many heralded as the beginning of the end of an independent Canada.

Public interest in protecting the environment runs high, as reflected in public policy. Recycling is commonplace, and communities across the country have made great strides in balancing economic interests with environmental goals. On Vancouver Island, for example, environmentalists and timber companies agreed in 1995 on forestry standards that satisfy both parties. When salmon fishing boats blockaded an Alaska ferry in Prince Rupert in 1997, the issue for the Canadians was perceived as overfishing by Americans. Salmon have been reduced to an endangered species in much of the Pacific Northwest, and the Canadians consequently don't think much of U.S. fisheries policies.

In 1999, the huge Northern Territories divided in two. The eastern half, which takes in Baffin Island, the land around Hudson's Bay, and most of the Arctic islands, is now called Nunavut and essentially functions as an Inuit homeland. The rump Northwest Territories officially retains the territory's old name, though many refer to the region as the Western Arctic.

The success of the Nunavut negotiations has emboldened other native groups to settle their own land claims with the Canadian government. While many of the claims in northern Canada can be settled by transferring government land and money to native groups, those in southern Canada are more complex. Some tribes assert a prior claim to land currently owned by non-Indians; in other areas, native groups refuse to abide by environmental laws that seek to protect endangered runs of salmon. The situation in a number of communities has moved beyond protests and threats to armed encounters and road barricades. The path seems set for more and increasingly hostile confrontations between official Canada and its native peoples.

Canada is challenged internally on many fronts, with social and economic forces working to fragment a cohesive sense of national identity. Whether the long-standing cultural and political institutions that have guided the country successfully for so many years will survive is a question that'll be answered in the very near future.

2 Wilderness & Wonder: Canada's National & Provincial Parks

THE NATIONAL PARKS

Canada is in the process of creating several new national parks in the Far North. Recently accorded agreements with the region's native peoples call for the development of parks on part of the land that was once administered by the government. Additionally, Parks Canada (**www.parkscanada.pch.gc.ca**) operates hundreds of Historic Parks that feature historic buildings or sites (often with summer programs and activities). But these exceptions aside, I've listed the national parks, offering a quick rundown on the defining characteristics of each.

Kejimkujik National Park (Nova Scotia): There are two parts to this park. The first is a wilderness of rolling hills and lakes in the heart of Nova Scotia; the other preserves a stretch of wild and undeveloped southern coastline flanked by steep cliffs. This section of the park protects the rare shorebird, the piping plover, and marine animals.

Cape Breton Highlands National Park (Nova Scotia): This far-flung coastal wilderness, similar in terrain and grandeur to the Scottish Highlands, appealed to hearty Scots who founded small settlements among the mountains. The Cabot Trail highway rings the park, with tremendous views down from pink granite coastal cliffs.

Fundy National Park (New Brunswick): Covered bridges, the world's highest tides, and plenty of hiking trails characterize this small coastal park on the southern New Brunswick coast.

Kouchibouguac National Park (New Brunswick): A small low-key park on the Acadian Coast, Kouchibouguac features beaches, bike paths, and hikes to salt marshes and offshore dunes. Swimmers will enjoy the park's pleasant lagoon waters, known as the warmest north of the Carolinas.

Prince Edward Island National Park (Prince Edward Island): This park combines a popular stretch of sandy beach on the Gulf of St. Lawrence and Green Gables house, a Victorian estate in Cavendish that served as the setting for the popular children's tale *Anne of Green Gables*.

Gros Morne National Park (Newfoundland): A spectacular preserve with glacier-carved mountains and fjords, Gros Morne stretches along the west coast of Newfoundland. Hiking trails lead to Western Brook Pond, which is in fact a freshwater fjord lined by cliffs towering 2,000 feet high.

Terra Nova National Park (Newfoundland): A scenic spot on the Labrador Sea, Terra Nova is covered with dense coniferous forests that provide backcountry adventure. Sea kayakers come here to probe the multitudes of tiny inlets and coves found along the headlands.

La Mauricie National Park (Québec): A maze of lakes, rivers, and deep forest, La Mauricie is popular with canoe-campers who paddle through the extensive natural water system much as did the early Indians and French trappers. In winter, 50 miles of cross-country ski trails are groomed, with warming huts every 3 miles.

Mingan Archipelago National Park (Québec): A string of 47 limestone islands along the northern shores of the Gulf of St. Lawrence, Mingan is uninhabited except by seabirds and marine mammals.

Forillon National Park (Québec): At the end of the Gaspé Peninsula, this park is famous for its 600-foot-high limestone cliffs that drop into the Gulf of St. Lawrence. Hiking trails lead to dizzying overlooks; watch for whales in summer.

St. Lawrence Islands National Park (Ontario): Canada's smallest national park, these 23 islands in the St. Lawrence River are part of the larger Thousand Islands area. The tiny flower-covered islands are mostly undeveloped and offer free campsites to those with boats.

Pukaskwa National Park (Ontario): Ontario's largest national park, Pukaskwa is in the boreal forests on the north shore of Lake Superior. Preserved as a wilderness, it can be accessed by boat only.

Bruce Peninsula National Park (Ontario): The rugged 50-mile Bruce Peninsula juts into Lake Huron and is popular with long-distance hikers on the Bruce Trail. From a point near the park's headquarters at Tobermory, ferries leave for Manitoulin Island.

Georgian Bay Islands National Park (Ontario): A collection of 50 islands in Lake Huron's Georgian Bay, this park is popular with boaters, who are able to access the more remote islands. Water taxis are available to Beausoleil Island, the park headquarters.

Point Pelee National Park (Ontario): Point Pelee is famous for its bird watching (this peninsula of sand in Lake Erie is at the junction of two migratory flyways) and for the fall gathering of monarch butterflies, which flock here before their annual migration.

Riding Mountain National Park (Manitoba): Manitoba's only national park, Riding Mountain is a habitat crossroads where prairie, boreal forest, and deciduous life zones intersect. Wolf, moose, bison, and elk are found here in great numbers. The park is popular with summertime campers, who fish and boat in the many lakes.

Grasslands National Park (Saskatchewan): The first national park to preserve the native prairie ecosystem, this park in southern Saskatchewan protects the only remaining black-tailed prairie-dog colony in Canada. Other wildlife includes coyotes, deer, pronghorn, and many bird species.

Prince Albert National Park (Saskatchewan): Located where the southern prairies give way to the lake country, this national park is the nesting ground for one of Canada's largest colonies of white pelicans; moose, wolf, caribou, and bison also live here. The early environmentalist/author Grey Owl lived here in the 1930s; his cabin still stands on Ajawaan Lake.

Waterton Lakes National Park (Alberta): Joined with Montana's Glacier National Park, this international peace park is famed for its beautiful lakes glimmering in glacial basins between finlike mountain ranges. The most popular activity is the boat ride from the Canadian to the U.S. side of the park.

Banff National Park (Alberta): The most popular destination in all Canada, Banff is extremely beautiful and often crowded. The views onto towering cliff-sided mountains are unforgettable; easy hiking trails to lakes and alpine meadows make this a popular park for families. Banff Town and Lake Louise Village provide world-class accommodations and boutiques.

Jasper National Park (Alberta): The largest park in the Canadian Rockies, Jasper sits astride the central crest of the continent. The Columbia Icefields, natural hot springs, shimmering glacial lakes, soaring mountain peaks, and superb long-distance hiking trails make this one of the gems of the Canadian Park system.

Yoho National Park (British Columbia): *Yoho* means "awe" in Cree, and the park's many lakes, towering peaks, and mighty waterfalls (Takakkawa Falls drops 1,200 ft.) certainly provoke it. The Kicking Horse River is one of the best white-water rivers in the Rockies, and glacier-fed Emerald and O'Hara lakes are famed beauty spots.

Glacier National Park (British Columbia): Heavy snowfalls maintain more than 400 glaciers and snowfields in this park located at the crest of the rugged Columbia Mountains; more than 14% of the park's landscape is covered in permanent ice.

Kootenay National Park (British Columbia): A collection of natural marvels on the western slopes of the Rockies' Main Range, Kootenay is noted for its rugged limestone canyons, Radium Hot Springs resort, and highly colored mineral springs.

Elk Island National Park (Alberta): A major preserve of the wildlife that once roamed the northern prairies, Elk Island is just east of Edmonton. Moose, two species of bison, a large number of elk, beaver, and other species are all easily viewed from hiking trails.

Wood Buffalo National Park (Alberta/Northwest Territory): The world's largest national park, Wood Buffalo protects many animal species, including the once-feared-extinct wood buffalo and the whooping crane. The park also preserves unique ecosystems, like the Peace-Athabasca river delta and a natural salt plain.

Pacific Rim National Park (British Columbia): The only national park on Vancouver Island, Pacific Rim is composed of three units: Long Beach; the Broken Group Islands, an archipelago of more than 100 islets in Barkley Sound; and the West Coast Trail, a long-distance trail skirting the rugged coastline.

Gwaii Haanas National Park (British Columbia): On the southern end of the Queen Charlotte Archipelago, Gwaii Haanas is jointly administered by Parks Canada and the Haida Nation. The 138-island park is filled with ancient village and totem sites sacred to the Haida.

Mount Revelstoke National Park (British Columbia): Roads lead to the top of Mount Revelstoke, a peak in the Selkirk Mountains. Hiking trails lead into inland rain forests and alpine meadows.

Kluane National Park (Yukon): Canada's highest peaks and largest nonpolar ice caps are in this rugged park on the Gulf of Alaska. Long-distance trails lead to enormous valley glaciers; the park's mighty rivers are popular with white-water rafters.

Nahanni National Park (Northwest Territories): Known throughout the world for its superlative rafting and canoeing, Nahanni is also famous for massive Virginia Falls, twice as high as Niagara.

Ivvavik National Park (Yukon): Fronting onto the Arctic Ocean and accessible only by small aircraft, Ivvavik was formed to protect the porcupine caribou herd. Approximately 10% of the world's caribou live here.

Vuntut National Park (Yukon): Just south of Ivvavik National Park, Vuntut is a habitat preserve for caribou, grizzly bear, and other Arctic animals. The park was the hunting grounds for the native Gwitchin, who called the area Old Crow Flats.

Aulavik National Park (Northwest Territories): Banks Island is home to the largest musk-oxen herds in the world, and this Arctic island park is designed to preserve their fragile tundra habitat.

Ellesmere Island National Park (Nunavut): The most northerly and second largest of Canada's national parks, this remote and rugged wilderness of tundra, glacier, and mountains is literally at the top of the world.

Auyuittuq National Park (Nunavut): *Auyuittuq* means "the land that never melts," and much of this precipitously rugged fjord-bit park on Baffin Island is covered with a permanent ice cap. A long-distance fjord-to-fjord hiking trail leads across the park, accessing some of the world's longest rock faces, popular with climbers.

THE BEST OF THE PROVINCIAL PARKS

Canada has hundreds of provincial parks (British Columbia alone has 330), many of them simply campgrounds or public beaches in popular recreation areas. Others contain sites of great scenic or historic interest and definitely deserve a detour. Below are some I consider outstanding.

Mont-Orford (Québec): Always popular with family camping groups, this mountainous park is ablaze with autumn color each year. The hiking paths through hardwood forest that are so popular in summer become cross-country ski trails when the snow falls.

Algonquin Provincial Park (Ontario): A wilderness of lakes and deep forest, Algonquin is perfect for extended canoe-camping trips, with nearly 1,000 miles of charted routes.

Dinosaur Provincial Park (Alberta): The Badlands of Alberta are filled with Cretaceous-era dinosaur-bone fossils, and this park protects one of the richest quarry areas. You can tour or join a dig and watch fossils being prepared at the visitor center.

Head-Smashed-In Buffalo Jump (Alberta): The Plains Indians once stampeded bison off cliffs as part of their yearly food-gathering cycle. This interpretive center preserves one of these cliffs and relates the area's natural and human history.

Mount Robson (British Columbia): The highest peak in the Canadian Rockies, Mount Robson towers above glacial lakes and roaring rivers just west of Jasper National Park.

Strathcona (British Columbia): Strathcona is the largest wilderness park on Vancouver Island, with lots of skiing and hiking. The high point, though, is the 2-day hiking trail into Dalla Falls; at more than 1,440 feet, they're the highest in North America.

Index

Index

Index

Index

FROMMER'S® NATIONAL PARK GUIDES

Family Vacations in the
  National Parks
Grand Canyon

National Parks of the
  American West
Rocky Mountain

Yellowstone & Grand Teton
Yosemite & Sequoia/
  Kings Canyon
Zion & Bryce Canyon

FROMMER'S® MEMORABLE WALKS

Chicago
London

New York
Paris

San Francisco
Washington D.C.

FROMMER'S® GREAT OUTDOOR GUIDES

New England
Northern California

Southern California & Baja
Southern New England

Washington & Oregon

FROMMER'S® BORN TO SHOP GUIDES

Born to Shop: China
Born to Shop: France

Born to Shop: Italy
Born to Shop: London

Born to Shop: New York
Born to Shop: Paris

FROMMER'S® IRREVERENT GUIDES

Amsterdam
Boston
Chicago
Las Vegas

London
Los Angeles
Manhattan
New Orleans

Paris
San Francisco
Seattle & Portland
Vancouver

Walt Disney World
Washington, D.C.

FROMMER'S® BEST-LOVED DRIVING TOURS

America
Britain
California

Florida
France
Germany

Ireland
Italy
New England

Scotland
Spain
Western Europe

THE UNOFFICIAL GUIDES®

Bed & Breakfasts in
  California
Bed & Breakfasts in
  New England
Bed & Breakfasts in
  the Northwest
Beyond Disney
Branson, Missouri
California with Kids
Chicago

Cruises
Disneyland
Florida with Kids
Golf Vacations in the
  Eastern U.S.
The Great Smoky &
  Blue Ridge
  Mountains
Inside Disney

Hawaii
Las Vegas
London
Miami & the Keys
Mini Las Vegas
Mini-Mickey
New Orleans
New York City
Paris

Safaris
San Francisco
Skiing in the West
Walt Disney World
Walt Disney World
  for Grown-ups
Walt Disney World
  for Kids
Washington, D.C.

SPECIAL-INTEREST TITLES

Frommer's Britain's Best Bed & Breakfasts and
  Country Inns
Frommer's Britain's Best Bike Rides
The Civil War Trust's Official Guide
  to the Civil War Discovery Trail
Frommer's Caribbean Hideaways
Frommer's Food Lover's Companion to France
Frommer's Food Lover's Companion to Italy
Frommer's Gay & Lesbian Europe
Frommer's Exploring America by RV
Hanging Out in Europe
Israel Past & Present

Mad Monks' Guide to California
Mad Monks' Guide to New York City
Frommer's The Moon
Frommer's New York City with Kids
The New York Times' Unforgettable
  Weekends
Places Rated Almanac
Retirement Places Rated
Frommer's Road Atlas Britain
Frommer's Road Atlas Europe
Frommer's Washington, D.C., with Kids
Frommer's What the Airlines Never Tell You

Next time, make your *own* hotel arrangements.

Yahoo! Travel